The Political Economy of Contemporary Human Civilisation, Volume I

Sangaralingam Ramesh

The Political Economy of Contemporary Human Civilisation, Volume I

From the Rise of Homo Sapiens to AI and Robotics

palgrave
macmillan

Sangaralingam Ramesh
University of Oxford
Oxford, UK

ISBN 978-3-031-84180-4 ISBN 978-3-031-84181-1 (eBook)
https://doi.org/10.1007/978-3-031-84181-1

This Palgrave Macmillan imprint is published by the registered company Springer Nature Switzerland AG.
The registered company address is: Gewerbestrasse 11, 6330 Cham, Switzerland

For my father and my mother,
Nallathamby Sangaralingam and Pathmarani Sangaralingam
Inuvil and Karinagar, Ceylon.

Preface

Humanity is endowed with advanced cognition, manual dexterity and mobility which facilitate its creativity and innovation to manifest and be used in physical form. However, this creativity and innovation can have consequences which are either destructive or constructive in the context of sustaining human civilisation. For example, some might argue that the contemporary impacts of climate change on human civilisation are the direct consequences of human activity over the last three hundred years. However, on the other hand, others might argue that contemporary climate change is a natural part of the Earth's periodic climate cycles; perhaps driven by changes in solar activity or due to changes in the earth's magnetic field. But either way, climate change and its impacts on human society can be mitigated using Artificial Intelligence. This in conjunction with developments in other fields such as Robotics, Quantum Computing, and Nuclear Fusion will have far and deep reaching consequences for human civilization in the decades to come. Moreover, scientific breakthroughs and developments in Biotechnology may reach a point such that by the end of the next two decades, humanity may be able to reverse aging and eradicate cognitive decline. However, another challenge that remains, which in conjunction with climate change will put pressure on the resources of sovereign nations, is the increase in not only the human population but also migration. This migration will be due to not only the impact of climate change but also the impacts of uneven economic development. People will migrate from countries in which the temperature is too hot, leading to droughts and famine, to cooler climates in the northern hemisphere. Furthermore, uneven economic development will facilitate people to migrate from developing economies to the developed economies in the hope of finding better paying jobs and a better quality of life. Furthermore, uneven economic development may mean that developing economies may lack the financial and economic resources to sustain the transition away from fossil fuels to green energy. Increased global temperatures will mean that in many countries there will be a greater reliance on the use of air conditioning by households and firms. Intuitively, this will mean that countries which cannot afford the transition to green energy will remain reliant on fossil fuels, the burning of oil and coal to fuel their economies. This will further contribute to emissions of gases. Burning fossil fuels results in the emission of several gases that significantly contribute to climate change. The primary gas emitted is carbon dioxide (CO_2), which is the most prevalent greenhouse gas produced by fossil fuel combustion. CO_2 has a prolonged atmospheric lifetime and is fundamental in trapping heat, leading to global warming.[1] Methane (CH_4) is another potent greenhouse gas resulting from fossil fuel production and transportation. Although methane is released in relatively smaller quantities compared to CO_2, it has a much higher global warming potential over a shorter time, making it a critical factor in climate change.[2] Additionally, burning fossil fuels emits nitrous oxide (N_2O), a gas with both natural and anthropogenic sources. N_2O is produced during combustion processes, especially at high temperatures, and it is a potent greenhouse gas with a global warming potential approximately 298 times that of CO_2 over a 100-year period.[3] Sulphur dioxide (SO_2) is also released from fossil fuel combustion, particularly from coal and oil. While SO_2 itself does not have a greenhouse effect, it contributes to the formation of sulphate aerosols which can reflect sunlight and cool the Earth's surface. However, these aerosols

[1] IPCC (Intergovernmental Panel on Climate Change). (2014). Climate Change 2014: Synthesis Report. Contribution of Working Groups I, II and III to the Fifth Assessment Report of the Intergovernmental Panel on Climate Change. Geneva, Switzerland: IPCC.

[2] EPA (U.S. Environmental Protection Agency). (2021). Overview of Greenhouse Gases. Available at: https://www.epa.gov/ghgemissions/overview-greenhouse-gases

[3] Forster, P., Ramaswamy, V., Artaxo, P., Berntsen, T., Betts, R., Fahey, D. W., Haywood, J., Lean, J. (2007). Changes in Atmospheric Constituents and in Radiative Forcing. In Climate Change 2007: The Physical Science Basis. Contribution of Working Group I to the Fourth Assessment Report of the Intergovernmental Panel on Climate Change. Cambridge University Press.

also contribute to acid rain and respiratory problems in humans.[4] Carbon monoxide (CO) is another by-product of fossil fuel burning. Though CO is not a greenhouse gas, it contributes to climate change indirectly by influencing the concentration of methane and tropospheric ozone, both potent greenhouse gases.[5] These gases, by trapping heat in the Earth's atmosphere, play a significant role in the warming of the planet and present serious environmental and health challenges. However, developments in space exploration and perhaps colonisation of planets, such as Mars and the moons of the planet Jupiter, allow a window for the possible future of humanity in a planet which may not any longer be able to sustain human life. Developments in space exploration and prospective colonization of planets such as Mars and the moons of Jupiter present a glimpse into humanity's potential future beyond Earth. As Earth's natural resources become increasingly strained and the planet faces significant environmental changes, the idea of establishing human settlements on other celestial bodies has gained traction within the scientific community. Space agencies such as NASA and ESA, along with private companies like SpaceX, are at the forefront of these efforts. Mars has long been considered the most viable candidate for human colonization within our solar system. This interest is driven by several factors, including its relative proximity to Earth, the presence of water ice, and its similarities to Earth's geological features. Notably, NASA's Mars missions, including the Curiosity and Perseverance rovers, have provided valuable data on the planet's surface and potential habitability.[6] Additionally, the success of SpaceX's Starship program aims to facilitate crewed missions to Mars, making the concept of a human presence on the Red Planet increasingly tangible.[7] The moons of Jupiter, particularly Europa, also hold promise for human exploration and

[4] Smith, S. J., van Aardenne, J., Klimont, Z., Andres, R., Volke, A., & Delgado Arias, S. (2011). Anthropogenic sulfur dioxide emissions: 1850–2005. Atmospheric Chemistry and Physics, 11(3), 1101–1116.

[5] Myhre, G., D. Shindell, F.-M. Bréon, W. Collins, J. Fuglestvedt, J. Huang, D. Koch. (2013). Anthropogenic and Natural Radiative Forcing. In Climate Change 2013: The Physical Science Basis. Contribution of Working Group I to the Fifth Assessment Report of the Intergovernmental Panel on Climate Change. Cambridge University Press.

[6] Grotzinger, J. P., Sumner, D. Y., Gupta, S., Siebach, K., Mangold, N., Kah, L. C., … & Crisp, J. A. (2014). A habitable fluvio-lacustrine environment at Yellowknife Bay, Gale Crater, Mars. Science, 343(6169), 1242777.

[7] Musk, E. (2017). Making life multi-planetary. New Space, 5(2), 46–61.

potential colonization. Europa's subsurface ocean is of particular interest due to its potential for harbouring life and providing a sustainable water source for future missions.[8] The European Space Agency's upcoming Jupiter Icy Moons Explorer (JUICE) mission aims to further investigate the habitability of these moons, with a focus on Europa, Ganymede, and Callisto.[9] The establishment of human settlements on Mars or the moons of Jupiter would represent a monumental step for humanity, offering an alternative pathway for survival if Earth becomes untenable due to resource depletion, climate change, or other existential threats. Such efforts require significant technological advancements and international collaboration. Ensuring sustainable living conditions on these remote celestial bodies will also involve overcoming challenges related to life support systems, radiation protection, and the psychological well-being of astronauts.[10] The exploration and potential colonization of other planets and moons extend beyond the survival of humanity; they symbolize the innate human spirit of exploration and the quest for knowledge. As technologies continue to advance, the dream of living on Mars or the moons of Jupiter may indeed become a reality in the not-too-distant future.

Oxford, UK Sangaralingam Ramesh

References

EPA (U.S. Environmental Protection Agency). (2021). Overview of Greenhouse Gases. https://www.epa.gov/ghgemissions/overview-greenhouse-gases

Forster, P., Ramaswamy, V., Artaxo, P., Berntsen, T., Betts, R., Fahey, D. W., Haywood, J., & Lean, J. (2007). Changes in atmospheric constituents and in radiative forcing. In *Climate change 2007: The physical science basis. Contribution of Working Group I to the Fourth Assessment Report of the Intergovernmental Panel on Climate Change*. Cambridge University Press.

[8] Hand, K. P., Chyba, C. F., Priscu, J. C., Carlson, R. W., & Nealson, K. H. (2009). Astrobiology and the potential for life on Europa. Europa, 589–629.

[9] Grasset, O., Dougherty, M. K., Coustenis, A., Bunce, E. J., Erd, C., Titov, D., … & Reh, K. (2013). Jupiter Icy moons Explorer (JUICE): An ESA mission to orbit Ganymede and to characterise the Jupiter system. Planetary and Space Science, 78, 1–21.

[10] Jones, E. M., Robertson, R. A., Tolentino, M., Rooney, K. A., & Tarazona, V. (2018). Mitigating the psychological impact of space exploration through mindfulness training. Acta Astronautica, 145, 53–60.

Grasset, O., Dougherty, M. K., Coustenis, A., Bunce, E. J., Erd, C., Titov, D., Blanc, M., Coates, A. J., Drossart, P., Fletcher, L. N., Hussmann, H., Jahnke, L., Kallenbach, R., Khurana, K. K., Langevin, Y., Maitra, D., Mitri, G., Mousis, O., Neubauer, F. M., ... Reh, K. (2013). Jupiter Icy moons Explorer (JUICE): An ESA mission to orbit Ganymede and to characterise the Jupiter system. *Planetary and Space Science, 78*, 1–21.

Grotzinger, J. P., Sumner, D. Y., Gupta, S., Siebach, K., Mangold, N., Kah, L. C., Stack, K. M., Milliken, R. E., Conrad, P. G., Des Marais, D. J., Farmer, J. D., Siebach, C., Calef, F., Hurowitz, J., McLennan, S. M., Mischna, M., Blake, D., Gellert, R., Mahaffy, P., ... Crisp, J. A. (2014). A habitable fluvio-lacustrine environment at Yellowknife Bay, Gale Crater, Mars. *Science, 343*(6169), 1242777.

Hand, K. P., Chyba, C. F., Priscu, J. C., Carlson, R. W., & Nealson, K. H. (2009). Astrobiology and the potential for life on Europa. In Pappalardo, R. T., McKinnon, W. B., & Khurana, K. (Eds.), *Europa* (pp. 589–629). University of Arizona Press.

IPCC (Intergovernmental Panel on Climate Change). (2014). Climate change 2014: Synthesis Report. Contribution of Working Groups I, II and III to the Fifth Assessment Report of the Intergovernmental Panel on Climate Change. Geneva, Switzerland: IPCC.

Jones, E. M., Robertson, R. A., Tolentino, M., Rooney, K. A., & Tarazona, V. (2018). Mitigating the psychological impact of space exploration through mindfulness training. *Acta Astronautica, 145*, 53–60.

Musk, E. (2017). Making life multi-planetary. *New Space, 5*(2), 46–61.

Myhre, G., Shindell, D., Bréon, F.-M., Collins, W., Fuglestvedt, J., Huang, J., & Koch, D. (2013). Anthropogenic and natural radiative forcing. In *Climate change 2013: The Physical Science Basis. Contribution of Working Group I to the Fifth Assessment Report of the Intergovernmental Panel on Climate Change*. Cambridge University Press.

Smith, S. J., van Aardenne, J., Klimont, Z., Andres, R., Volke, A., & Delgado Arias, S. (2011). Anthropogenic sulphur dioxide emissions: 1850–2005. *Atmospheric Chemistry and Physics, 11*(3), 1101–1116.

Acknowledgement

I would like to thank Wyndham Hacket Pain, the Senior Economics Editor at Palgrave Macmillan, for his ongoing support with regard to the completion of this manuscript, the first volume in a series of two on *The Political Economy of Contemporary Human Civilisation*. Furthermore, I would also like to thank Heggidi Raju, the Project Co-Ordinator for Springer Nature, for co-ordinating the production of this book volume. In addition, I would also like to thank my colleague at University College London, Dr Vasos Pavlika, for his ongoing mentorship and support. Finally, I would like to thank the University of Oxford for the use of its world-class resources.

Contents

CHAPTER 1

Introduction

The evolution of Homo sapiens marks a pivotal moment in the history of life on Earth, as our species' unique cognitive and social developments have allowed humans to exert an unparalleled influence on the environment. Emerging from Africa approximately 300,000 years ago, humans rapidly distinguished themselves through their capacity for advanced problem-solving, tool use, and social cooperation.[1] While many species exhibit forms of intelligence, such as tool use in primates and problem-solving in birds, it is the combination of Homo sapiens' complex language, abstract reasoning, and ability to cooperate in large groups that has made humans a dominant force across the globe.[2] Central to this evolutionary success is the development of language, which not only allowed for more effective communication but also enabled the transmission of knowledge across generations. This capacity for symbolic thinking gave rise to innovations in technology, art, and culture, setting Homo sapiens apart from other hominins and species.[3] Coupled with manual dexterity, which facilitated the creation and use of sophisticated tools, early humans

[1] Tattersall, I. (2017). The Strange Case of the Rickety Cossack: And Other Cautionary Tales from Human Evolution. St. Martin's Press.

[2] Harari, Y. N. (2014). Sapiens: A Brief History of Humankind. Harper.

[3] Mithen, S. (1996). The Prehistory of the Mind: The Cognitive Origins of Art, Religion and Science. Thames and Hudson.

S. Ramesh, *The Political Economy of Contemporary Human Civilisation, Volume I*,
https://doi.org/10.1007/978-3-031-84181-1_1

were able to manipulate their environment in ways that no other species had achieved. The invention of agriculture approximately 12,000 years ago, for example, represents a milestone in human innovation that transformed social structures and economies, ultimately laying the foundation for modern civilization.[4] However, the same cognitive abilities that enabled humans to create have also driven destructive innovations. From early weaponry to the development of nuclear technologies, humans have continually advanced their capacity for conflict, often with catastrophic consequences.[5] The Anthropocene, a term used to describe the current geological age, is marked by significant human impact on Earth's ecosystems, driven largely by industrialisation, deforestation, and the extraction of natural resources. Climate change, biodiversity loss, and pollution are direct consequences of human ingenuity applied without sufficient foresight or responsibility.[6] This dual-edged nature of human innovation—both creative and destructive—raises important questions about the future trajectory ofhuman civilization. Technologies such as Artificial Intelligence, Biotechnology, and Quantum Computing offer the potential for solving some of the most pressing global challenges, from disease eradication to climate change mitigation. However, as explored in these same technologies also hold the potential for unprecedented destruction if misused or inadequately controlled.[7] The balance between humanity's capacity to innovate for the betterment of society and the risks posed by unchecked technological development will be critical in shaping the future of civilization. As Homo sapiens continues to evolve—both culturally and potentially biologically—the impact of human cognitive abilities will reverberate across every dimension of life, influencing governance, economics, and the environment. Culturally, human societies are increasingly shaped by the acceleration of technological advancements, globalization, and interconnectedness, which are transforming how people communicate, govern, and engage with the world. This cognitive evolution, particularly in terms of information processing, is driving significant shifts in

[4] Diamond, J. (1997). Guns, Germs, and Steel: The Fates of Human Societies. W. W. Norton & Company.

[5] Bostrom, N. (2014). Superintelligence: Paths, Dangers, Strategies. Oxford University Press.

[6] McNeill, J. R., & Engelke, P. (2014). The Great Acceleration: An Environmental History of the Anthropocene since 1945. Harvard University Press.

[7] Bostrom, N. (2014). Superintelligence: Paths, Dangers, Strategies. Oxford University Press.

governance structures. In an era defined by rapid access to data and the proliferation of Artificial Intelligence, the way decisions are made at both national and international levels is becoming more complex and reliant on advanced computational tools.[8] This evolution in governance, however, raises challenges in terms of ensuring ethical oversight, transparency, and accountability as governments increasingly integrate AI-driven systems into policymaking and administration.

Economically, the cognitive and technological evolution of Homo sapiens is redefining traditional economic models. The rise of digital currencies, automation, and global supply chains has shifted economic paradigms, challenging existing labour markets and wealth distribution models.[9] Artificial Intelligence and machine learning are automating complex decision-making processes, from stock trading to logistics management, enhancing efficiency but also raising concerns about inequality and unemployment as traditional jobs are replaced by machines.[10] As human cognition enables continuous innovation in these areas, the socioeconomic landscape is likely to face ongoing disruption, forcing governments and institutions to adapt rapidly or risk instability.

The cognitive evolution of humans also directly affects the environment, particularly through the application of advanced technologies that influence resource extraction, energy consumption, and environmental conservation. According to scholarly work on the Anthropocene, human ingenuity has allowed for unprecedented environmental manipulation, from agriculture to industrialisation.[11] However, the same cognitive advancements that drive innovation also exacerbate ecological degradation. The ongoing development of Artificial Intelligence, Biotechnology, and renewable energy technologies, while promising solutions to global environmental challenges, also introduces risks related to over-reliance on these technologies and their potential to produce unintended consequences.[12] The balance between technological advancement and ecological sustainability will be critical in determining the long-term impact of

[8] Tegmark, M. (2017). Life 3.0: Being Human in the Age of Artificial Intelligence. Knopf.

[9] Schwab, K. (2016). The Fourth Industrial Revolution. Penguin Random House.

[10] Bostrom, N. (2014). Superintelligence: Paths, Dangers, Strategies. Oxford University Press.

[11] McNeill, J. R., & Engelke, P. (2014). The Great Acceleration: An Environmental History of the Anthropocene since 1945. Harvard University Press.

[12] Schneider, S. H. (2019). Science as a Contact Sport: Inside the Battle to Save Earth's Climate. National Geographic Society.

humanity's cognitive evolution on the planet. Finally, as human cognition continues to push the boundaries of what is possible in medicine, Biotechnology, and genetics, the possibility of biological evolution through technological intervention becomes more plausible. Advances in genetic engineering, particularly with tools such as CRISPR, open the door to potential future modifications of the human genome, raising ethical and philosophical questions about what it means to be human.[13] As humanity continues to explore these frontiers, the cultural, economic, and environmental implications of our evolving cognitive capabilities will become increasingly significant. This is the Political Economy of Human Civilization.

The Evolution of Homo sapiens

The rise of Homo sapiens was marked by the development of highly advanced cognition. Theories of cognitive development, such as the 'Cognitive Revolution' proposed by Yuval Noah Harari[14] argue that around 70,000 years ago, humans began to use their newfound cognitive abilities to cooperate in large groups, create sophisticated tools, and develop early forms of art and religion. The subsequent chapters of this book, beginning with 'The Rise of Homo sapiens', evaluates this transformative period, exploring how early humans used their cognitive skills to adapt to diverse environments and establish dominance over other species, including other hominins such as Neanderthals.

With the ability to innovate came the capacity for both creation and destruction. Human ingenuity has long been a double-edged sword, driving both the flourishing of civilizations and their potential undoing. From the earliest developments of stone tools to the sophisticated technologies of the twenty-first century, innovation has allowed humans to reshape their environment, improve living standards, and expand knowledge. Advances in agriculture, such as the domestication of plants and animals, allowed for the rise of complex societies by providing stable food sources. Over time, innovations in infrastructure, transportation, and communication systems furthered human progress, enabling trade, the spread of

[13] Doudna, J. A., & Sternberg, S. H. (2017). A Crack in Creation: Gene Editing and the Unthinkable Power to Control Evolution. Houghton Mifflin Harcourt.

[14] Harari, Y. N. (2014). Sapiens: A Brief History of Humankind. Harper.

ideas, and the development of political and social structures that supported thriving civilizations.[15] However, this same ingenuity has also been applied to war, conflict, and environmental destruction. The Industrial Revolution, which brought about unprecedented economic growth, was simultaneously the catalyst for massive environmental damage due to the unchecked burning of fossil fuels and the exploitation of natural resources. The relentless pursuit of technological and industrial advancement has led to widespread deforestation, the depletion of finite resources, and the release of greenhouse gases that contribute to climate change, threatening the very ecosystems that sustain life.[16]

The rapid pace of technological advancement, particularly in recent centuries, has created a delicate balance between humanity's capacity for creative innovation—such as in Biotechnology, Artificial Intelligence, and space exploration—and destructive innovation, as seen in the proliferation of nuclear weapons, ecological degradation, and the perpetuation of global inequalities. The development of nuclear technology during the twentieth century epitomizes this paradox. While nuclear power holds the potential to provide nearly limitless energy, it also gave rise to nuclear weapons, which have the capacity to annihilate entire populations. The bombings of Hiroshima and Nagasaki in 1945 demonstrated the devastating potential of nuclear warfare, ushering in an era of geopolitical tension defined by the threat of mutually assured destruction.[17] Similarly, the rise of Artificial Intelligence (AI) presents both incredible opportunities and significant risks. AI has the potential to revolutionize industries such as healthcare, by improving diagnostics and personalized treatments, and climate science, by optimizing energy usage and modelling climate systems more accurately.[18] However, it also poses risks of mass unemployment due to automation, as well as ethical concerns regarding the use of AI in autonomous weapons systems, which could make life-and-death decisions

[15] Diamond, J. (1997). Guns, Germs, and Steel: The Fates of Human Societies. W.W. Norton & Company.

[16] Steffen, W., Broadgate, W., Deutsch, L., Gaffney, O., & Ludwig, C. (2011). "The Anthropocene: Conceptual and Historical Perspectives." Philosophical Transactions of the Royal Society A, 369(1938), pp. 842–867.

[17] Sagan, S. D. (1996). The Limits of Safety: Organizations, Accidents, and Nuclear Weapons. Princeton University Press.

[18] Topol, E. (2019). Deep Medicine: How Artificial Intelligence Can Make Healthcare Human Again. Basic Books.

without human intervention.[19] The deployment of AI in warfare raises profound questions about accountability and the morality of using machines to kill, further complicating the balance between technological progress and ethical responsibility.

Biotechnology is another field where human creativity holds both promise and peril. Advances in genetic engineering, particularly through CRISPR-Cas9 technology, have the potential to eradicate hereditary diseases and enhance agricultural productivity, providing solutions to some of the most pressing global challenges, including food security and public health.[20] However, the ethical implications of gene editing—especially when applied to humans—are vast. The possibility of 'designer babies', where genetic traits such as intelligence or appearance can be selected or enhanced, raises concerns about exacerbating social inequalities and undermining the concept of human dignity. If access to these technologies is limited to the wealthy, it could lead to a society where genetic privilege is a new form of inequality, further entrenching existing disparities.[21] Moreover, space exploration, while offering the potential to solve some of Earth's resource constraints, poses its own set of challenges. Visionaries like Elon Musk have championed space colonization as a solution to existential threats such as climate collapse or nuclear war, advocating for humanity to become a multi-planetary species.[22] Yet, the resources required for space exploration are immense, and the ethical questions surrounding the colonization of other planets—such as who will govern these new frontiers and who will benefit from their resources—remain unanswered. There is also the risk that focusing on space colonization could divert attention and resources from solving the critical environmental challenges on Earth, leading to a dangerous mind-set of escapism rather than sustainability.[23]

[19] Sharkey, N. (2010). "Saying 'No!' to Lethal Autonomous Targeting." *Journal of Military Ethics*, 9(4), pp. 369–383.

[20] Doudna, J. A., & Sternberg, S. H. (2017). A Crack in Creation: Gene Editing and the Unthinkable Power to Control Evolution. Houghton Mifflin Harcourt.

[21] Sandel, M. J. (2007). The Case Against Perfection: Ethics in the Age of Genetic Engineering. Harvard University Press.

[22] Musk, E. (2017). "Making Humans a Multi-Planetary Species." New Space, 5(2), pp. 46–61.

[23] Sovacool, B. K., & Griffiths, S. (2020). "The costs of climate mitigation and the politics of escape: The planetary boundaries of Elon Musk's Mars vision." Energy Research & Social Science, 70, 101676.

Human innovation has brought about remarkable achievements, enabling civilizations to thrive and offering the potential to solve some of the most pressing challenges of our time. However, the same capacity for innovation has also led to destructive consequences, from the threat of nuclear warfare to the degradation of the environment and the perpetuation of global inequalities. The future of humanity will depend on our ability to navigate this delicate balance, ensuring that technological progress is guided by ethical considerations and a commitment to sustainability. Without responsible governance and global cooperation, the tools that have driven human advancement could become the very instruments of our undoing.

Theories of Cognitive Development and Creative Innovation

The development of the human brain, specifically its capacity for abstract thinking and symbolic reasoning, is explored in 'Theories of Cognitive Development'. Advances in neuroscience and psychology suggest that the human brain is wired for innovation, with an intrinsic drive to solve problems and create innovative solutions.[24] This chapter investigates how cognitive development paved the way for the invention of tools, the establishment of trade networks, and the birth of agriculture, all of which laid the groundwork for the complex economies that define modern civilization.

Creative innovation has consistently driven human progress, shaping the trajectory of civilizations from the Agricultural Revolution to the industrial revolution, and more recently, the digital revolution. The Agricultural Revolution enabled the transition from nomadic lifestyles to settled societies, supporting population growth and leading to the development of complex social structures.[25] The Industrial Revolution, marked by mechanization and mass production, ushered in unprecedented economic growth, technological advancements, and urbanization, albeit at the cost of environmental degradation due to heavy reliance on fossil

[24] Mithen, S. (1996). The Prehistory of the Mind: The Cognitive Origins of Art, Religion and Science. Thames and Hudson.

[25] Diamond, J. (1997). Guns, Germs, and Steel: The Fates of Human Societies. W.W. Norton & Company.

fuels.[26] Today, the Digital Revolution, characterized by the rapid expansion of computing technologies, Artificial Intelligence (AI), and automation, is reshaping nearly every aspect of modern life.

The emergence of Artificial Intelligence and Robotics, explored in Chap. 6, represents the latest frontier in human creativity. These technologies have the potential to revolutionize industries, increase efficiency, and solve some of the world's most pressing problems, including those related to climate change and resource scarcity. AI systems are already transforming industries such as healthcare, where machine learning algorithms are used to improve diagnostics and predict patient outcomes with greater accuracy than traditional methods.[27] In logistics, AI-powered platforms optimize supply chains, reduce waste, and improve delivery times, contributing to more sustainable business practices.[28] Similarly, Robotics is enhancing manufacturing by increasing precision, reducing errors, and minimizing human labour costs, which has significant implications for improving productivity and scaling industries to meet growing global demands.

In the context of climate change, AI is proving to be a valuable tool for environmental monitoring and energy management. Machine learning algorithms are being used to predict extreme weather patterns, model climate systems, and optimize the integration of renewable energy sources into national grids.[29] For example, Google's DeepMind has developed AI systems that help predict wind energy output thirty-six hours in advance, allowing for better planning and more efficient use of renewable energy.[30] These innovations highlight the potential for AI to accelerate the transition to cleaner energy systems, reduce reliance on fossil fuels, and mitigate the impacts of global warming. However, despite these promising developments, the risks associated with AI and Robotics cannot be ignored. The

[26] McNeill, J. R. (2000). Something New Under the Sun: An Environmental History of the Twentieth-Century World. W.W. Norton & Company.

[27] Topol, E. (2019). Deep Medicine: How Artificial Intelligence Can Make Healthcare Human Again. Basic Books.

[28] Brynjolfsson, E. & McAfee, A. (2014). The Second Machine Age: Work, Progress, and Prosperity in a Time of Brilliant Technologies. W.W. Norton & Company.

[29] Sovacool, B. K., & Griffiths, S. (2021). "Climate change and energy security: Unpacking the arguments and mobilizing solutions." Energy Research & Social Science, 79, 102078.

[30] DeepMind. (2019). "Wind power now predictably on the grid thanks to machine learning." Available at: https://deepmind.com/blog/article/machine-learning-can-boost-value-wind-energy.

chapters on Climate Change and Renewable Energy Technologies will discuss these innovations and how they may pose significant challenges, particularly if they exacerbate existing inequalities or lead to unintended environmental consequences. One concern is the potential for AI and automation to deepen economic disparities by displacing large segments of the workforce, especially in low-skilled jobs. According to a report by the International Labour Organization, up to 800 million jobs could be displaced by automation by 2030, disproportionately affecting workers in developing countries.[31] This could exacerbate global inequality unless new policies, such as universal basic income or re-skilling programmes, are implemented to support displaced workers.[32] Furthermore, the development and deployment of AI systems are heavily concentrated in wealthier nations, leading to concerns about unequal access to the benefits of AI-driven innovations. While developed countries are investing heavily in AI research and development, many developing countries lack the infrastructure, capital, and technical expertise to fully leverage these technologies. This digital divide risks creating a new form of technological neocolonialism, where wealthier nations and multinational corporations control the deployment and use of AI technologies, potentially reinforcing existing power dynamics and global inequalities.[33] In addition to economic and social concerns, the environmental impact of AI and Robotics must also be carefully considered. AI systems, particularly those used for large-scale data processing and machine learning, require vast amounts of computational power, which in turn consumes significant energy. Data centres, which are critical for supporting AI and other digital technologies, account for about 1% of global electricity consumption, a figure expected to rise as the demand for digital services grows.[34] While advancements in energy efficiency and the use of renewable energy sources can help mitigate the carbon footprint of these systems, the environmental impact of large-scale AI deployment must be closely monitored to avoid

[31] International Labour Organization. (2020). "The Future of Jobs Report 2020." Available at: https://www.ilo.org/wcmsp5/groups/public/%2D%2D-dgreports/%2D%2D-cabinet/documents/publication/wcms_752207.pdf.

[32] Brynjolfsson, E. & McAfee, A. (2014). The Second Machine Age: Work, Progress, and Prosperity in a Time of Brilliant Technologies. W.W. Norton & Company.

[33] Sovacool, B. K., & Griffiths, S. (2021). "Climate change and energy security: Unpacking the arguments and mobilizing solutions." Energy Research & Social Science, 79, 102078.

[34] Masanet, E., Shehabi, A., Lei, N., Smith, S., & Koomey, J. (2020). "Recalibrating global data center energy-use estimates." Science, 367(6481), 984–986.

unintended consequences that could undermine broader sustainability efforts. Moreover, the development of AI and Robotics for military applications raises serious ethical concerns. The use of autonomous weapons systems, or 'killer robots', poses a significant threat to global security and human rights. These weapons, which can operate without human intervention, raise questions about accountability and the morality of allowing machines to make life-and-death decisions.[35] The proliferation of such technologies could escalate conflicts, lower the threshold for engaging in warfare, and make conflicts more lethal by removing the human element from critical decision-making processes. The international community has yet to fully address the legal and ethical implications of autonomous weapons, despite growing calls for a global ban on their development and use.[36] While AI and Robotics have the potential to drive positive change, they also present complex challenges that must be managed carefully. The same technological creativity that holds the promise to address climate change, increase productivity, and enhance human well-being also carries the risk of exacerbating inequalities, creating new forms of conflict, and causing unintended environmental harm. Responsible innovation, guided by ethical governance and a commitment to sustainability, is essential to ensuring that these powerful technologies are harnessed for the benefit of all, rather than for the privileged few.

Destructive Innovation and Its Consequences

While creative innovation has led to immense progress, destructive innovation has often accompanied it. The same cognitive abilities that enable humans to develop advanced technologies also allow them to devise new means of conflict and destruction. War and Conflict, a later chapter in this book, examines the evolution of warfare and the role those technological advancements—such as nuclear fusion and Quantum Computing—may play in modern conflict. As explored in the chapter on Quantum Computing and Nuclear Fusion in Volume 2 of this book series, these innovations have dual uses: while they offer potential solutions for energy

[35] Sharkey, N. (2010). "Saying 'No!' to Lethal Autonomous Targeting." *Journal of Military Ethics*, 9(4), 369–383.

[36] Asaro, P. (2012). "On banning autonomous weapon systems: Human rights, automation, and the dehumanization of lethal decision-making." International Review of the Red Cross, 94(886), 687–709.

crises and computational limitations, they also present existential risks if used in warfare or uncontrolled experimentation.[37] Moreover, destructive innovation extends beyond war and conflict to the environmental impact of human activity.

Climate change is accelerating the catastrophic consequences of industrialisation and the burning of fossil fuels, which have already contributed to global warming, biodiversity loss, and the destabilization of ecosystems. Since the beginning of the Industrial Revolution, human activities, particularly the combustion of coal, oil, and natural gas, have significantly increased concentrations of greenhouse gases (GHGs) in the atmosphere, leading to a steady rise in global temperatures. According to the Intergovernmental Panel on Climate Change, human activities have already caused approximately 1.1°C of warming above pre-industrial levels, with catastrophic consequences for ecosystems, economies, and human populations.[38] If current trends continue, the world is on track to exceed the 1.5°C or 2°C threshold, which scientists agree will lead to irreversible damage to ecosystems, sea-level rise, and more frequent and severe extreme weather events.

The destruction of biodiversity is one of the most visible consequences of climate change and industrialisation. Species extinction rates are accelerating at unprecedented levels. The United Nations' Global Biodiversity Outlook 5 indicates that biodiversity is declining faster than at any time in human history, with over one million species currently threatened with extinction.[39] Climate change exacerbates this loss by altering habitats, disrupting food chains, and intensifying the frequency of natural disasters. Coral reefs, for example, which are home to a quarter of all marine species, are especially vulnerable to rising ocean temperatures and acidification. The IPCC estimates that if global temperatures rise by 2°C, 99% of coral reefs could be lost, which would have devastating effects on marine biodiversity and the millions of people who depend on these ecosystems for

[37] Bostrom, N. (2014). Superintelligence: Paths, Dangers, Strategies. Oxford University Press.

[38] Intergovernmental Panel on Climate Change (IPCC). (2021). Climate Change 2021: The Physical Science Basis. Contribution of Working Group I to the Sixth Assessment Report of the Intergovernmental Panel on Climate Change. Cambridge University Press.

[39] United Nations Convention on Biological Diversity (CBD). (2020). Global Biodiversity Outlook 5. Montreal: Secretariat of the Convention on Biological Diversity. Available at: https://www.cbd.int/gbo5.

food and livelihood.[40] Moreover, climate change destabilizes ecosystems, leading to a cascade of negative effects. As temperatures rise, ecosystems that have long been stable are increasingly being thrown out of balance. Forest ecosystems, such as the Amazon rainforest, are at particular risk. The Amazon, often referred to as the 'lungs of the Earth', plays a critical role in regulating the global climate by absorbing vast amounts of carbon dioxide. However, deforestation and climate change are pushing the Amazon towards a tipping point, where it could shift from being a carbon sink to a carbon source, releasing more CO_2 than it absorbs, which would significantly accelerate global warming.[41] Such feedback loops demonstrate the interconnectedness of ecosystems and climate, where damage to one system can have far-reaching implications for the entire planet. In addition to these environmental impacts, climate change is a major driver of human displacement, as will be discussed in Chap. 5. Climate-induced migration is becoming an increasingly urgent issue as rising sea levels, extreme weather events, and resource scarcity force millions of people to leave their homes in search of safety and livelihood. According to the United Nations High Commissioner for Refugees, an average of 23.1 million people have been displaced by weather-related disasters each year since 2010.[42] This figure is expected to rise significantly in the coming decades as the impacts of climate change intensify, particularly in vulnerable regions such as small island developing states and low-lying coastal areas.

Migration caused by climate change is not only a humanitarian crisis but also a political and economic challenge. As people move in search of refuge, both within and across borders, they place additional pressure on the infrastructure, services, and economies of host regions. In some cases, this influx of displaced populations has sparked social tensions and conflicts. For example, climate change has been linked to the exacerbation of the Syrian civil war, where prolonged drought, worsened by global warming, contributed to crop failures, food insecurity, and mass migration from rural to urban areas, creating social unrest and intensifying existing

[40] Intergovernmental Panel on Climate Change (IPCC). (2021). Climate Change 2021: The Physical Science Basis. Contribution of Working Group I to the Sixth Assessment Report of the Intergovernmental Panel on Climate Change. Cambridge University Press.

[41] Lovejoy, T. E., & Nobre, C. (2019). "Amazon tipping point: Last chance for action." Science Advances, 5(12), eaax893.

[42] United Nations High Commissioner for Refugees (UNHCR). (2021). "Climate change and disaster displacement." Available at: https://www.unhcr.org/climate-change-and-disasters.html.

political conflicts.[43] Similarly, in Sub-Saharan Africa, climate-related displacement is placing increasing stress on already fragile political systems, contributing to instability and conflict over resources like water and arable land.[44] Moreover, the economic impacts of climate-induced migration are significant. Displacement disrupts local economies, leading to loss of income, livelihoods, and productivity. In agricultural economies, particularly in the Global South, climate change is reducing crop yields and forcing farmers to abandon their land. A report by the World Bank projects that without urgent action, climate change could force more than 140 million people in Sub-Saharan Africa, South Asia, and Latin America to migrate within their countries by 2050.[45] This internal displacement could strain urban areas that are ill-prepared to accommodate such large numbers of people, leading to increased poverty and inequality and ultimately social conflict leading to political upheavals.

In wealthier countries like the United States, Canada, Great Britain and the European Union, the influx of climate and economic refugees from regions hit hardest by climate change is already becoming a political issue, leading to debates over immigration policies and international responsibilities. Many developed nations, while contributing disproportionately to global emissions, are reluctant to take responsibility for the climate refugees generated by their industrial activities. This raises ethical questions about global equity and justice, as the countries and populations most affected by climate change have contributed the least to the problem. To address these challenges, global cooperation and innovative solutions are needed. Mitigation strategies, such as transitioning to renewable energy sources and reducing GHG emissions, must be coupled with adaptation measures that help vulnerable communities cope with the impacts of climate change. International frameworks, like the Paris Agreement, provide a platform for countries to work together to limit global warming and

[43] Kelley, C. P., Mohtadi, S., Cane, M. A., Seager, R., & Kushnir, Y. (2015). "Climate change in the Fertile Crescent and implications of the recent Syrian drought." Proceedings of the National Academy of Sciences, 112(11), 3241–3246.

[44] Niang, I., Ruppel, O. C., Abdrabo, M. A., Essel, A., Lennard, C., Padgham, J., & Urquhart, P. (2014). "Africa." In Barros, V. R., et al. (Eds.), Climate Change 2014: Impacts, Adaptation, and Vulnerability. Cambridge University Press.

[45] Rigaud, K. K., de Sherbinin, A., Jones, B., Bergmann, J., Clement, V., Ober, K., Schewe, J., Adamo, S., McCusker, B., Heuser, S., & Midgley, A. (2018). Groundswell: Preparing for Internal Climate Migration. Washington, DC: The World Bank. Available at: https://openknowledge.worldbank.org/handle/10986/29461.

address the root causes of climate-induced displacement. However, the success of these efforts will depend on political will, financial resources, and a collective commitment to equity and justice.

Climate change is not only an environmental issue but a multidimensional crisis that threatens ecosystems, economies, and human societies. The catastrophic consequences of industrialisation and fossil fuel combustion have set humanity on a collision course with nature. While technological innovation and global cooperation offer hope for mitigating these impacts, the path forward will require addressing the underlying inequalities that make some regions and populations more vulnerable than others. Without bold action, climate-induced migration will continue to grow, disrupting economies, destabilizing political systems, and exacerbating global inequalities.

Artificial Intelligence, Robotics, and the Future of Humanity

As humanity stands at the dawn of a new era, the advancements in Artificial Intelligence (AI) and Robotics offer both tremendous opportunities and serious challenges. The transformative potential of AI and Robotics spans multiple sectors, from healthcare and manufacturing to transportation and finance. AI-driven automation is already reshaping industries by streamlining operations, optimizing supply chains, and significantly reducing human labour. For example, Amazon's use of AI-powered robots in its warehouses has allowed the company to reduce shipping times and costs, enhancing its competitive edge in global markets.[46] Similarly, AI's capacity to analyse vast amounts of data has revolutionized fields like personalized medicine, where algorithms can predict patient outcomes and tailor treatments to individual needs.[47] These developments hold the promise of increasing productivity, improving healthcare outcomes, and fostering economic growth. However, the widespread adoption of AI raises serious concerns, particularly regarding employment. While automation can increase efficiency, it also threatens to displace millions of jobs, particularly in low-skilled sectors. The International Labour Organization estimates

[46] Brynjolfsson, E., & McAfee, A. (2014). The Second Machine Age: Work, Progress, and Prosperity in a Time of Brilliant Technologies. W.W. Norton & Company.

[47] Topol, E. (2019). Deep Medicine: How Artificial Intelligence Can Make Healthcare Human Again. Basic Books.

that up to 800 million workers could lose their jobs to automation by 2030, exacerbating income inequality and social unrest.[48] Without proactive measures, such as re-skilling programmes and social safety nets, AI-driven automation could deepen the divide between those who benefit from technological progress and those who are left behind. Furthermore, privacy concerns have emerged as AI systems increasingly rely on the collection and analysis of personal data. The use of AI in surveillance, for instance, has sparked debates about the erosion of privacy and the potential for authoritarian regimes to use these technologies to monitor and control populations.[49] In addition to privacy and employment concerns, the development of autonomous systems in warfare presents another pressing challenge. The use of AI in military applications, such as drones and autonomous weapons, raises ethical questions about accountability and the dehumanization of conflict. The deployment of lethal autonomous systems could lower the threshold for war, as human decision-making is replaced by machines capable of making life-and-death decisions.[50] The potential for AI-driven warfare to escalate conflicts and increase civilian casualties highlights the urgent need for international regulations to govern the use of these technologies in combat. Similarly, the developments in cryptocurrencies, discussed in Chap. 4, Vol. 2, offer both promise and peril. Cryptocurrencies like Bitcoin and Ethereum have the potential to decentralize financial systems, promoting economic inclusion and reducing reliance on traditional banking institutions. By eliminating intermediaries, cryptocurrencies can reduce transaction costs, facilitate cross-border trade, and provide financial services to the unbanked. Approximately 1.7 billion adults worldwide remain without access to a bank account, and cryptocurrencies could offer a solution to this financial exclusion by enabling peer-to-peer transactions via mobile phones and other devices.[51] However, the rapid rise of cryptocurrencies also presents significant risks. One major concern is the potential for these digital

[48] International Labour Organization. (2020). The Future of Jobs Report 2020. Available at: https://www.ilo.org/wcmsp5/groups/public/%2D%2D-dgreports/%2D%2D-cabinet/documents/publication/wcms_752207.pdf.

[49] Zuboff, S. (2019). The Age of Surveillance Capitalism: The Fight for a Human Future at the New Frontier of Power. PublicAffairs.

[50] Sharkey, N. (2010). "Saying 'No!' to Lethal Autonomous Targeting." *Journal of Military Ethics*, 9(4), pp. 369–383.

[51] World Bank. (2021). The Global Findex Database 2021: Financial Inclusion and the Fintech Revolution. Available at: https://globalfindex.worldbank.org.

currencies to be used for illicit activities, including money laundering, tax evasion, and financing terrorism.[52] Cryptocurrencies' decentralized nature and relative anonymity make them attractive tools for criminals seeking to circumvent traditional financial regulations. Furthermore, the volatility of cryptocurrency markets poses a risk to financial stability. Bitcoin, for example, has experienced extreme price fluctuations, with its value increasing by over 1000% in 2017 before crashing by more than 80% in the following months.[53] Such volatility can undermine confidence in digital currencies and create economic instability, particularly if cryptocurrencies are adopted on a larger scale. Another concern is the potential for cryptocurrencies to destabilize national currencies, particularly in developing economies where financial systems are more fragile. Countries like El Salvador, which adopted Bitcoin as legal tender in 2021, face significant risks as they integrate volatile digital currencies into their economies.[54] Critics argue that the adoption of Bitcoin could exacerbate existing economic challenges, such as inflation and currency depreciation, further marginalizing vulnerable populations. Moreover, there is the risk that cryptocurrencies could exacerbate wealth inequalities. While advocates argue that digital currencies promote financial inclusion, the reality is that early adopters of cryptocurrencies, particularly those in wealthy countries, have disproportionately benefited from their meteoric rise in value. As with previous technological innovations, the gains from cryptocurrency markets have primarily flowed to a small group of investors and technologists, reinforcing existing wealth disparities.[55]

The dynamic tension between innovation and destruction is a recurring theme throughout the book series, as humanity continues to navigate the complex interplay between technological advancement and its societal impacts. Technological innovations like AI and cryptocurrencies hold the potential to solve some of the world's most pressing problems, from climate change to financial exclusion. However, they also bring with them new risks and challenges, requiring careful governance and ethical considerations. As history has shown, technological progress is not inherently

[52] Zohar, A. (2015). "Bitcoin: under the hood." Communications of the ACM, 58(9), pp. 104–113.

[53] Ammous, S. (2018). The Bitcoin Standard: The Decentralized Alternative to Central Banking. Wiley.

[54] Kosse, A., Mattei, I., & Tejada, M. (2021). "El Salvador's adoption of Bitcoin: Challenges and potential impacts." International Monetary Fund Working Papers, 21/235.

[55] Piketty, T. (2014). Capital in the Twenty-First Century. Harvard University Press.

good or bad; its impact depends on how it is used and managed. The choices made today will shape the future of humanity, determining whether these innovations will be harnessed for the common good or exacerbate global inequalities and conflicts. The development of nuclear energy, for example, demonstrates how technology can offer sustainable energy solutions but also pose existential threats if misused.[56] For example, atomic bombs were dropped on the Japanese cities of Hiroshima and Nagasaki in order to end World War II in 1945. On August 6, 1945, the United States dropped the first atomic bomb, nicknamed 'Little Boy', on the city of Hiroshima. The immediate explosion resulted in an estimated 70,000–80,000 deaths on the day of the bombing, accounting for about 30% of the city's population.[57] In the following weeks, months, and years, radiation sickness, burns, and other related injuries increased the death toll to 140,000 by the end of 1945.[58,59] Long-term effects such as cancer and chronic health problems led to even higher casualties in subsequent decades. Three days later, on August 9, 1945, a second bomb, 'Fat Man', was dropped on Nagasaki. The terrain of Nagasaki, which is hillier than Hiroshima, resulted in a slightly reduced blast radius, yet the bomb still caused 40,000–75,000 immediate deaths. By the end of 1945, the death toll was estimated at around 80,000, with long-term effects further increasing this number in the following years due to radiation exposure and related illnesses.[60,61] The bombings had devastating long-term impacts. Survivors, known as hibakusha, suffered from radiation-induced cancers, genetic damage, and psychological trauma. These events also marked the first and only use of nuclear weapons in warfare, profoundly influencing global political dynamics and leading to the establishment of international non-proliferation efforts.[62] As nuclear energy can provide benefits to humanity, Artificial Intelligence can optimize healthcare and resource

[56] Rhodes, R. (1986). The Making of the Atomic Bomb. Simon & Schuster.

[57] Sherwin, M. J. (2005). A World Destroyed: Hiroshima and Its Legacies. Stanford University Press.

[58] Hersey, J. (1946). Hiroshima. Alfred A. Knopf.

[59] Lifton, R. J. (1967). Death in Life: Survivors of Hiroshima. Random House.

[60] Walker, J. S. (2005). Prompt and Utter Destruction: Truman and the Use of Atomic Bombs Against Japan. University of North Carolina Press.

[61] Ham, P. (2014). Hiroshima Nagasaki: The Real Story of the Atomic Bombings and Their Aftermath. Palgrave Macmillan.

[62] Rhodes, R. (1986). The Making of the Atomic Bomb. Simon & Schuster.

management, yet without proper regulation, it could lead to job displacement and deepen existing inequalities.[63]

The role of the 'selfish gene' explains how genes drive organisms to behave in ways that maximize their own replication.[64] This concept helps to understand why humans, like other animals, sometimes engage in behaviours that are not solely about survival but also about dominance, competition, and control over resources, which can indirectly enhance reproductive success. Historically, this has led to conflict; competition over territory, resources, and social status often escalates into violence, as seen in ancient tribal warfare and even in modern geopolitical conflicts.[65,66] These genetic imperatives may have contributed to the evolution of human conflict, where securing resources ensured not just individual survival but the propagation of one's genes. For instance, the pursuit of social dominance and control over resources like territory or mates has been linked to evolutionary strategies that favour aggressive behaviour.[67] Even when there is no direct need for food, individuals or groups might act violently to assert dominance and secure their lineage's future. This instinct for competition, deeply rooted in our biology, could hinder collective action to solve global challenges, such as climate change and resource depletion.

The inherent drive for self-preservation and group loyalty often creates in-group versus out-group dynamics which can lead to the exclusion or exploitation of others.[68] These dynamics, when scaled globally, manifest as nationalism, ethnic conflicts, and economic protectionism, all of which can stifle international cooperation. For example, the reluctance of some nations to commit to global climate agreements stems from concerns about national economic competitiveness, despite the collective need for action.[69] Thus, while technological progress provides the tools for a more sustainable future, the human instinct to prioritize self-interest and

[63] Brynjolfsson, E., & McAfee, A. (2014). The Second Machine Age: Work, Progress, and Prosperity in a Time of Brilliant Technologies. W.W. Norton & Company.

[64] Dawkins, R. (1976). The Selfish Gene. Oxford University Press.

[65] Keeley, L. H. (1996). War Before Civilization: The Myth of the Peaceful Savage. Oxford University Press.

[66] Pinker, S. (2011). The Better Angels of Our Nature: Why Violence Has Declined. Viking.

[67] Daly, M., & Wilson, M. (1988). Homicide. Aldine de Gruyter.

[68] Tajfel, H., & Turner, J. C. (1979). An integrative theory of intergroup conflict. In W. G. Austin & S. Worchel (Eds.), The Social Psychology of Intergroup Relations.

[69] Pettenger, M. E. (2007). The Social Construction of Climate Change: Power, Knowledge, Norms, Discourses. Ashgate.

immediate gains over long-term, collective benefits presents a significant challenge. Whether the future leads to collaboration or conflict may depend on our ability to overcome these evolutionary predispositions and develop governance structures that promote cooperation over competition. Without such efforts, technological advancements may further entrench global inequalities and drive new forms of conflict over resources, power, and influence.

Space Exploration, Quantum Computing, and the Search for Sustainable Solutions

As humanity looks beyond Earth, Space Exploration and Space Travel, a chapter in Volume 2 of this series, evaluates this ultimate expression of humanity's creative innovation. The desire to explore and inhabit other planets stems from humanity's innate curiosity and survival instinct. With the development of Quantum Computing, humanity could achieve unprecedented levels of computational power, unlocking new possibilities for space travel and problem-solving on Earth.[70] However, as discussed in Quantum Computing and Nuclear Fusion, the potential consequences of these advancements must be carefully managed to avoid unintended destruction on a planetary scale. Finally, the search for sustainable solutions is paramount as discussed in the chapter on 'Renewable Energy Technologies'. As global temperatures rise and natural resources are depleted, humanity faces an urgent challenge: harnessing the same cognitive capacities that fuelled past innovations to create new technologies that ensure the survival of future generations. The Intergovernmental Panel on Climate Change has made it clear that without rapid, unprecedented changes across industries and societies, global temperatures will rise by more than 1.5°C, with catastrophic consequences for ecosystems, economies, and human health.[71] The depletion of natural resources, including fossil fuels, freshwater, and arable land, has intensified the need for technological solutions that can not only mitigate the damage already done but also create sustainable paths forward.

Energy innovation is at the forefront of this technological shift. Fossil fuels, the bedrock of industrial development since the nineteenth century,

[70] Deutsch, D. (1997). The Fabric of Reality. Penguin Books.

[71] IPCC. (2021). Sixth Assessment Report of the Intergovernmental Panel on Climate Change. IPCC.

have driven climate change and environmental degradation. To transition away from this dependence, humanity must innovate in areas such as nuclear fusion, solar power, and wind energy. Fusion energy, often referred to as the 'holy grail' of clean energy, has the potential to provide near-limitless power without the greenhouse gas emissions associated with fossil fuels.[72] Unlike nuclear fission, fusion reactions do not produce long-lived radioactive waste, making them a safer and more sustainable option for future energy needs. While fusion energy remains decades away from commercial viability, the continued investment in projects like the International Thermonuclear Experimental Reactor (ITER) in France reflects the global belief in fusion's potential to revolutionize the energy landscape.[73] However, achieving a breakthrough in fusion energy requires significant financial resources and international collaboration, as no single nation can develop this technology in isolation.

Solar power, on the other hand, has already proven to be a transformative technology. Solar energy is now one of the fastest-growing sources of electricity worldwide. According to the International Energy Agency, solar power capacity increased by 22% in 2020, surpassing traditional sources like coal and natural gas in many regions.[74] This growth has been driven by falling costs, technological improvements, and government incentives that promote renewable energy. Countries like Germany, China, and the United States have invested heavily in solar infrastructure, contributing to the global shift towards cleaner energy sources. However, the uneven adoption of solar technology reflects broader patterns of inequality, where wealthier nations have the capital and technical expertise to implement large-scale renewable energy projects, while developing nations struggle to transition away from fossil fuels due to limited financial and technical resources.[75] Addressing these disparities will require global cooperation to ensure that all nations have access to the technologies needed to achieve a sustainable future. In addition to energy innovation, the sustainable management of natural resources is crucial for ensuring the survival of future generations. The depletion of freshwater resources, driven by

[72] Sovacool, B. K., & Ramana, M. V. (2019). "Back to the Future: Small Modular Reactors, Nuclear Fantasies, and Symbolic Convergence." Science, Technology, & Human Values, 44(4), 577–599.

[73] ITER. (2020). "Fusion Energy Progress." Available at: https://www.iter.org/.

[74] IEA. (2021). World Energy Outlook 2021. International Energy Agency.

[75] Sovacool, B. K., & Griffiths, S. (2021). "Climate change and energy security: Unpacking the arguments and mobilizing solutions." Energy Research & Social Science, 79, 102078.

overconsumption, pollution, and climate change, poses significant risks to global food security and human health. The World Bank projects that by 2050, water scarcity could displace up to 700 million people, particularly in regions such as the Middle East and North Africa, where water stress is already a critical issue. Innovative solutions, such as desalination technologies and water recycling systems, are becoming increasingly important in addressing the growing demand for freshwater.[76] Advances in Biotechnology, including genetically modified crops that require less water and are more resistant to drought, offer additional pathways for enhancing food security in a warming world.[77] However, the introduction of genetically modified organisms (GMOs) into agricultural systems has sparked debate about their long-term impact on biodiversity and ecological stability. As with any technological innovation, the responsible development and use of GMOs will require careful regulation to balance the need for increased agricultural productivity with the protection of natural ecosystems. Moreover, responsible innovation extends beyond energy and resource management. The rise of Artificial Intelligence (AI) and Robotics has the potential to revolutionize industries, improve efficiencies, and create new economic opportunities. AI can optimize energy grids, predict extreme weather events, and develop more accurate climate models, helping to mitigate the impacts of climate change.[78] However, the ethical implications of AI, particularly in areas such as job displacement and autonomous weapons systems, highlight the risks of unchecked technological advancement.[79] Ensuring that AI and other emerging technologies are developed and deployed in ways that promote equity and protect human rights will be essential for building a sustainable future.

Ultimately, the future of human civilization depends on our ability to innovate responsibly. Technological advancements must be guided by a

[76] Damania, R., Desbureaux, S., Hyland, M., Islam, A., Moore, S., Rodella, A.-S., Russ, J., & Zaveri, E. (2017). Uncharted Waters: The New Economics of Water Scarcity and Variability. Washington, DC: The World Bank. Available at: https://openknowledge.worldbank.org/handle/10986/28096.

[77] Fedoroff, N. V., Battisti, D. S., Beachy, R. N., Cooper, P. J. M., Fischhoff, D. A., Hodges, C. N., Knauf, V. C., Lobell, D., Mazur, B. J., Molden, D., Reynolds, M. P., Ronald, P. C., Rosegrant, M. W., Sanchez, P. A., Vonshak, A. & Ziegler, A. D. (2010) 'Radically rethinking agriculture for the 21st century', Science, 327(5967), 833–834.

[78] Topol, E. (2019). Deep Medicine: How Artificial Intelligence Can Make Healthcare Human Again. Basic Books.

[79] Brynjolfsson, E. & McAfee, A. (2014). The Second Machine Age: Work, Progress, and Prosperity in a Time of Brilliant Technologies. W.W. Norton & Company.

commitment to sustainability, equity, and global cooperation. The choices humanity makes in the coming decades—whether in the development of fusion energy, the expansion of solar power, or the governance of Artificial Intelligence—will determine whether future generations inherit a liveable planet. As history has shown, human ingenuity is capable of both creation and destruction. The challenge now is to harness that ingenuity for the greater good, ensuring that the technologies of tomorrow contribute to a sustainable and equitable future for all.

Conclusion: The Dual-Edged Sword of Innovation

This chapter effectively presents the trajectory of human evolution, highlighting how Homo sapiens' cognitive development has positioned humanity at the apex of life on Earth. However, the evaluation makes it clear that this evolutionary success is a double-edged sword. While human creativity and innovation have led to significant technological and societal advancements, they have also precipitated grave ecological, social, and ethical crises. This paradox underpins the narrative of the Anthropocene, an era dominated by human impact on Earth's ecosystems.[80] From the dawn of agriculture to the heights of space exploration, the capacity for technological innovation has shaped and reshaped human civilization. The domestication of plants and animals was a transformative event, enabling the rise of complex societies and economic systems. However, the same innovations have fostered overexploitation of natural resources, contributing to environmental degradation and a warming climate. The discussion adeptly points out that while the invention of agriculture laid the groundwork for civilization, it also initiated humanity's exploitative relationship with nature, which continues to have profound consequences in the twenty-first century.

Humanity's capacity to innovate has also brought about the capacity for destruction. The rapid advancements in Artificial Intelligence, Biotechnology, and Quantum Computing offer unparalleled opportunities to solve global challenges but carry inherent risks. For instance, the development of nuclear technology epitomizes the balance between innovation for good

[80] Steffen, W., Broadgate, W., Deutsch, L., Gaffney, O., & Ludwig, C. (2011). "The Anthropocene: Conceptual and historical perspectives." Philosophical Transactions of the Royal Society A: Mathematical, Physical and Engineering Sciences, 369(1938), 842–867.

and the potential for catastrophic destruction.[81] The bombings of Hiroshima and Nagasaki underscored the existential threats that nuclear weapons pose, and the potential for global nuclear conflict remains a pressing concern. Similarly, advancements in Artificial Intelligence (AI) present a significant ethical dilemma. While AI promises to revolutionize healthcare, logistics, and climate science,[82,83] it also poses profound risks related to job displacement, privacy, and the dehumanization of decision-making, particularly in military applications.[84] As the narrative explains, AI's potential to automate warfare through autonomous weapons raises significant ethical concerns. If not governed properly, AI could exacerbate global inequalities and create new forms of social stratification, particularly between nations with advanced AI infrastructure and those without.[85] The discussion of genetic engineering, particularly CRISPR technology, also highlights the tension between creation and destruction. While CRISPR offers the potential to cure genetic diseases,[86] it also raises concerns about the ethics of gene editing in humans, particularly in relation to 'designer babies'. If access to genetic modification remains unequal, the risk of entrenching social inequalities at the genetic level is substantial.

The theme of ecological destruction is central to the book thesis that human cognition can lead to constructive as well as destructive end, particularly in its discussion of the Anthropocene. This introduction underscores the fact that humanity's unsustainable exploitation of the environment has led to biodiversity loss, climate change, and resource depletion. The ongoing destruction of ecosystems, such as deforestation in the Amazon, serves as a stark reminder of the environmental costs of

[81] Sagan, S. D. (1996). The Limits of Safety: Organizations, Accidents, and Nuclear Weapons. Princeton University Press.

[82] Topol, E. (2019). Deep Medicine: How Artificial Intelligence Can Make Healthcare Human Again. Basic Books.

[83] DeepMind. (2019). "Wind power now predictably on the grid thanks to machine learning." Available at: https://deepmind.com/blog/article/machine-learning-can-boost-value-wind-energy.

[84] Asaro, P. (2012). "On banning autonomous weapon systems: Human rights, automation, and the dehumanization of lethal decision-making." International Review of the Red Cross, 94(886), 687–709.

[85] Brynjolfsson, E., & McAfee, A. (2014). The Second Machine Age: Work, Progress, and Prosperity in a Time of Brilliant Technologies. W.W. Norton & Company.

[86] Doudna, J. A., & Sternberg, S. H. (2017). A Crack in Creation: Gene Editing and the Unthinkable Power to Control Evolution. Houghton Mifflin Harcourt.

unchecked human innovation.[87] The evaluation suggests that while technologies such as AI, renewable energy, and nuclear fusion offer potential solutions to these problems, they also require careful governance and global cooperation to prevent further environmental harm. Finally, the discussion on exploration of space as a potential solution to Earth's challenges highlights the allure of escaping the consequences of industrialisation and climate change. Figures like Elon Musk have championed Mars colonization as a safeguard against existential threats.[88] Yet, this notion is rightly critiqued arguing that the resources devoted to space colonization could be better spent addressing the immediate problems of climate change, poverty, and inequality on Earth. The question of whether space exploration is a legitimate solution or an escapist fantasy remains open, but the chapter emphasizes the need for a balanced approach to technological progress.

This chapter provides a comprehensive overview of the dual-edged nature of human innovation. While technological progress has enabled human flourishing, it has also created the conditions for potential self-destruction. The key challenge for the future of human civilization lies in the ability to harness innovation responsibly, ensuring that technological advancements are used to promote sustainability, equity, and global cooperation. Without such oversight, the very tools that have driven human progress could become the instruments of our undoing. The question remains, can humanity overcome the individual desire to survive and pass on genes to future generations which often leads to conflicts, in order to build a society through a mechanism of collective action in the knowledge that the use of emerging technologies through this mechanism will sustain human civilization?

References

Ammous, S. (2018). *The Bitcoin standard: The decentralized alternative to central banking*. Wiley.

Asaro, P. (2012). On banning autonomous weapon systems: Human rights, automation, and the dehumanization of lethal decision-making. *International Review of the Red Cross, 94*(886), 687–709.

[87] Lovejoy, T. E., & Nobre, C. (2019). "Amazon tipping point: Last chance for action." Science Advances, 5(12), eaax893.

[88] Musk, E. (2017). "Making Humans a Multi-Planetary Species." New Space, 5(2), 46–61.

Boström, N. (2014). *Superintelligence: Paths, dangers, strategies.* Oxford University Press.

Brynjolfsson, E., & McAfee, A. (2014). *The second machine age: Work, progress, and prosperity in a time of brilliant technologies.* W.W. Norton & Company.

Daly, M., & Wilson, M. (1988). *Homicide.* Aldine de Gruyter.

Damania, R., Desbureaux, S., Hyland, M., Islam, A., Moore, S., Rodella, A.-S., Russ, J., & Zaveri, E. (2017). *Uncharted waters: The new economics of water scarcity and variability.* The World Bank. https://openknowledge.worldbank.org/handle/10986/28096

Dawkins, R. (1976). *The selfish gene.* Oxford University Press.

DeepMind. (2019). Wind power now predictably on the grid thanks to machine learning. https://deepmind.com/blog/article/machine-learning-can-boost-value-wind-energy

Deutsch, D. (1997). *The fabric of reality.* Penguin Books.

Diamond, J. (1997). *Guns, germs, and steel: The fates of human societies.* W. W. Norton & Company.

Diamond, J. (2011). *Collapse: How societies choose to fail or succeed.* Penguin.

Doudna, J. A., & Sternberg, S. H. (2017). *A crack in creation: Gene editing and the unthinkable power to control evolution.* Houghton Mifflin Harcourt.

Fedoroff, N. V., Battisti, D. S., Beachy, R. N., Cooper, P. J. M., Fischhoff, D. A., Hodges, C. N., Knauf, V. C., Lobell, D., Mazur, B. J., Molden, D., Reynolds, M. P., Ronald, P. C., Rosegrant, M. W., Sanchez, P. A., Vonshak, A., & Ziegler, A. D. (2010). 'Radically rethinking agriculture for the 21st century', *Science,* 327(5967), 833–834.

Foresight. (2011). *Migration and global environmental change.* The Government Office for Science.

Ham, P. (2014). *Hiroshima Nagasaki: The real story of the atomic bombings and their aftermath.* Palgrave Macmillan.

Harari, Y. N. (2014). *Sapiens: A brief history of humankind.* Harper.

Hersey, J. (1946). *Hiroshima.* Alfred A. Knopf.

IEA. (2021). *World energy outlook 2021.* International Energy Agency.

Intergovernmental Panel on Climate Change (IPCC). (2021). *Climate change 2021: The physical science basis. Contribution of working group I to the sixth assessment report of the intergovernmental panel on climate change.* Cambridge University Press.

International Labour Organization. (2020). The future of jobs report 2020. https://www.ilo.org/wcmsp5/groups/public/%2D%2D-dgreports/%2D%2D-cabinet/documents/publication/wcms_752207.pdf

IPCC. (2021). *Sixth assessment report of the intergovernmental panel on climate change.* IPCC.

ITER. (2020). Fusion energy progress. https://www.iter.org/

Keeley, L. H. (1996). *War before civilization: The myth of the peaceful savage.* Oxford University Press.

Kelley, C. P., Mohtadi, S., Cane, M. A., Seager, R., & Kushnir, Y. (2015). Climate change in the Fertile Crescent and implications of the recent Syrian drought. *Proceedings of the National Academy of Sciences, 112*(11), 3241–3246.

Kosse, A., Mattei, I., & Tejada, M. (2021). El Salvador's adoption of Bitcoin: Challenges and potential impacts. International Monetary Fund Working Papers, 21/235.

Lifton, R. J. (1967). *Death in life: Survivors of Hiroshima*. Random House.

Lovejoy, T. E., & Nobre, C. (2019). Amazon tipping point: Last chance for action. *Science Advances, 5*(12), eaax893.

Masanet, E., Shehabi, A., Lei, N., Smith, S., & Koomey, J. (2020). Recalibrating global data center energy-use estimates. *Science, 367*(6481), 984–986.

McNeill, J. R., & Engelke, P. (2014). *The great acceleration: An environmental history of the anthropocene since 1945*. Harvard University Press.

Mithen, S. (1996). *The prehistory of the mind: The cognitive origins of art, religion and science*. Thames and Hudson.

Musk, E. (2017). Making humans a multi-planetary species. *New Space, 5*(2), 46–61.

Narayanan, A., Bonneau, J., Felten, E., Miller, A., & Goldfeder, S. (2016). *Bitcoin and cryptocurrency technologies: A comprehensive introduction*. Princeton University Press.

Niang, I., Ruppel, O. C., Abdrabo, M. A., Essel, A., Lennard, C., Padgham, J., & Urquhart, P. (2014). Africa. In V. R. Barros et al. (Eds.), *Climate change 2014: Impacts, adaptation, and vulnerability*. Cambridge University Press.

Pettenger, M. E. (2007). *The social construction of climate change: Power, knowledge, norms, discourses*. Ashgate.

Piketty, T. (2014). *Capital in the twenty-first century*. Harvard University Press.

Pinker, S. (2011). *The better angels of our nature: Why violence has declined*. Viking.

Rhodes, R. (1986). *The making of the atomic bomb*. Simon & Schuster.

Rigaud, K. K., de Sherbinin, A., Jones, B., Bergmann, J., Clement, V., Ober, K., Schewe, J., Adamo, S., McCusker, B., Heuser, S., & Midgley, A. (2018). *Groundswell: Preparing for internal climate migration*. The World Bank. https://openknowledge.worldbank.org/handle/10986/29461

Sagan, S. D. (1996). *The limits of safety: Organizations, accidents, and nuclear weapons*. Princeton University Press.

Sandel, M. J. (2007). *The case against perfection: Ethics in the age of genetic engineering*. Harvard University Press.

Schneider, S. H. (2019). *Science as a contact sport: Inside the battle to save Earth's climate*. National Geographic Society.

Schwab, K. (2016). *The fourth industrial revolution*. Penguin Random House.

Sharkey, N. (2010). Saying 'no!' to lethal autonomous targeting. *Journal of Military Ethics, 9*(4), 369–383.

Sherwin, M. J. (2005). *A world destroyed: Hiroshima and its legacies.* Stanford University Press.
Sovacool, B. K., & Griffiths, S. (2020). The costs of climate mitigation and the politics of escape: The planetary boundaries of Elon Musk's Mars vision. *Energy Research & Social Science, 70*, 101676.
Steffen, W., Broadgate, W., Deutsch, L., Gaffney, O., & Ludwig, C. (2011). The anthropocene: Conceptual and historical perspectives. *Philosophical Transactions of the Royal Society A, 369*(1938), 842–867.
Tajfel, H., & Turner, J. C. (1979). An integrative theory of intergroup conflict. In W. G. Austin & S. Worchel (Eds.), *The social psychology of intergroup relations.* Brooks/Cole.
Tattersall, I. (2017). *The strange case of the Rickety Cossack: And other cautionary tales from human evolution.* St. Martin's Press.
Tegmark, M. (2017). *Life 3.0: Being human in the age of artificial intelligence.* Knopf.
Topol, E. (2019). *Deep medicine: How artificial intelligence can make healthcare human again.* Basic Books.
United Nations Convention on Biological Diversity (CBD). (2020). *Global biodiversity outlook 5.* Secretariat of the Convention on Biological Diversity. https://www.cbd.int/gbo5
United Nations High Commissioner for Refugees (UNHCR). (2021). Climate change and disaster displacement. https://www.unhcr.org/climate-change-and-disasters.html
Walker, J. S. (2005). *Prompt and utter destruction: Truman and the use of atomic bombs against Japan.* University of North Carolina Press.
World Bank. (2018). *Uncharted waters: The new economics of water scarcity and variability.* The World Bank.
World Bank. (2021). The Global Findex Database 2021: Financial inclusion and the Fintech revolution. https://globalfindex.worldbank.org
Zohar, A. (2015). Bitcoin: Under the hood. *Communications of the ACM, 58*(9), 104–113.
Zuboff, S. (2019). *The age of surveillance capitalism: The fight for a human future at the new Frontier of power.* PublicAffairs.

CHAPTER 2

The Rise of Homo sapiens

Shrew-like creatures which lived around 150 million years ago are the ancestors of humans and mammals.[1] Aquatic worms which lived over 600 million years ago are the ancestors of all amphibians, mammals, birds, reptiles, and fishes. Furthermore, the bacteria-like organisms which lived over three million years ago are the 'parents' of all living plants and animals.[2] The theory of evolution suggests that creatures evolve over time and acquire anatomical features and behaviours over time in response to adapting to their environment through processes associated with the biological pathways of genetic change. Due to the process of evolutionary change, after several successive splits from preceding family groups, the family 'Hominoidea' resulted. This family split over time to form the family groups of 'Hominidae' and 'Pongidae'. These families sub-divided into 'Homo' and 'Pongo, Gorilla, and Pan' respectively. Some studies have found that the divergence time between 'Homo' and the great apes is between eleven and fourteen million years.[3] On the other hand, other

[1] Ayala, F., and Cela-Conde, C. (2017), Processes in Human Evolution: The journey from early hominins to Neanderthals and modern humans, Oxford University Press, New York.

[2] Ayala, F., and Cela-Conde, C. (2017), Processes in Human Evolution: The journey from early hominins to Neanderthals and modern humans, Oxford University Press, New York.

[3] *Venn, O., Turner, I., Mathieson, I., de Groot, N., Bontrop, R., and McVean, G. (2014), Strong male bias drives germline mutation in chimpanzees, Science, 344 (6189): 1272–1275.*

S. Ramesh, *The Political Economy of Contemporary Human Civilisation, Volume I*,
https://doi.org/10.1007/978-3-031-84181-1_2

studies have found the divergence time between 'Homo' and 'Gorilla' to be about 7.2 million years, while the divergence time between 'Homo' and 'Pan' (chimpanzee) is about 4.7 million years.[4] The genome DNA of humans and Chimpanzees is 98% to 99% similar.[5] According to the latter, the implication of this difference is that since the divergence between the Chimpanzees and humans, 3% or ninety million nucleotides have either been replaced. The change in DNA nucleotides between Chimpanzees and humans is mainly associated with the non-coding DNA, which is associated with the development process.[6] The non-coding DNA which humans have and Chimpanzees do not have is associated with brain development.[7] Fossils found in Africa and attributed to belonging to Homo habilis reputed to the first incarnation of the genus 'Homo'. Homo habilis had a bigger brain than another earlier hominin, the Australopithecines. Archaeological evidence suggests that the Australopithecines may have practised butchery as cut marks have been found on the fossil bones of animals.[8] The eating of meat by Australopithecines may have helped the evolutionary transition to Homo habilis.[9] Although Australopithecines may have used crudely shaped rocks as knives to butcher animal carcasses, either hunted or the remains of kills by other animals, it is recognized that Homo habilis was the first maker of stone tools.[10] However, there has been controversy surrounding Homo habilis, which may just not represent one hominin species but several co-existing in Africa between 2 and 1.6 million years ago.[11] The latter suggests that due to this controversy, the theory that two different species of early hominin gave rise to the next incarnations of the genus 'Homo', Homo erectus and Homo sapiens.

[4]Takahata, N., Satta, Y., and Klein, J. (1995), Divergence Time and Population Size in the Lineage Leading to Modern Humans, Theoretical Population Biology, Volume 48, Issue 2, pp. 198–221.

[5]Ayala, F., and Cela-Conde, C. (2017), Processes in Human Evolution: The journey from early hominins to Neanderthals and modern humans, Oxford University Press, New York.

[6]Ibid.

[7]Khaitovich, P., Hellman, I., Enard, W., Nowick, K., Leinweber, M., Franz, H., Weiss, G., Lachmann, M., and Paabo, S. (2005), Parallel Patterns of Evolution in the Genomes and Transcriptomes of Humans and Chimpanzees,' Vol.309, Science.

[8]Fleagle, J. (2013), Primate Adaptation & Evolution, Elsevier, London.

[9]Wrangham, R. (2010), Catching Fire: How Cooking Made Us Human, Profile Books Ltd, London.

[10]Bunney, S. (1988), Will the real Homo habilis stand up? New Scientist, No.1636.

[11]Ibid.

However, supposedly distinct species, based on skeletal differences, such as Homo rudolfensis could easily be included within the classification of Homo habilis if sexual dimorphism is accepted.[12] Sexual dimorphism refers to the physical differences between males and females in the same species. The next incarnation species in the genus 'Homo' was Homo erectus. This species was regarded as the intermediate link between early hominins and Homo sapiens.[13] However, according to the latter, Homo erectus may be representative of itself and another species, Homo ergaster. With the latter being the immediate predecessor to Homo erectus, a species with new intellectual abilities and the capacity to leave Africa, the first hominin to do so, arose in Africa about two million years ago.[14] The latter suggests that the move out to Africa, first to Asia and then to Europe, occurred about one million years ago. Homo erectus had a larger body frame compared to Homo habilis, as well as a larger brain. The move out of Africa could have occurred because of the need for Homo erectus to find new sources of food, perhaps due to a population explosion. In addition to extending its range beyond Africa and in comparison, to its predecessors, Homo erectus exhibited innovative behaviour in many ways. These included the first use of fire, systematic hunting, systematic tool making, the use of a consistent location to live, and the first indication of an extended childhood.[15] The use of fire may have helped Homo erectus to cook meat. This allowed the meat to become more digestible, allowing nutrients in the meat to be absorbed and processed more easily by the body.[16] This in turn facilitated the increase in the brain size of Homo erectus. This gave this species increased cognitive capacity and therefore the ability to live a more complex life than its ancestors. Homo erectus was the first hominin species to exhibit a nomadic, hunter-gatherer existence. This kind of behaviour would diffuse across time to be exhibited by his direct descendant, Homo sapiens. Homo erectus was followed by Homo

[12] Arsuaga, J., and Martinez, I. (1998), The Chosen Species: The Long March of Human Evolution, Blackwell Publishing, Oxford.

[13] Lewin, R. (2005), Human Evolution: An Illustrated Introduction, Blackwell Publishing, Oxford.

[14] Ibid.

[15] Lewin, R. (2005), Human Evolution: An Illustrated Introduction, Blackwell Publishing, Oxford.

[16] Wrangham, R. (2010), Catching Fire: How Cooking Made Us Human, Profile Books Ltd, London.

heidelbergensis, which was a species very similar skeletally to Homo neanderthalensis.[17] This is perhaps because Homo neanderthalensis is the direct descendant of Homo heidelbergensis, and this species may have given rise to a third archaic human species, the Denisovans.[18] However, there is not much fossilized evidence of the Denisovans, except a finger bone from which DNA was extracted for analysis. Modern-day Southeast Asians share 5% of Denisovan DNA.[19] However, of the two species, Homo neanderthalensis evolved in Europe over several hundred thousand years. The species managed to survive until up to 30,000 to 24,000 years ago when the last of the species died in Iberia to where the species had been pushed by the ever-expanding groups of Homo sapiens, diffusing out of Africa through the Near East, Anatolia, and then into Europe, Asia, and the rest of the world. On the other hand, Homo neanderthalensis tended to stay in the valleys in which they were born and grew, although females may have moved from one group to another for mating practices.[20] The latter also suggests that Homo neanderthalensis did not travel far in order to source raw materials, maintained a small social network, and may have had cannibalistic tendencies. The young of Homo neanderthalensis matured more quickly than their Homo sapiens counterparts, typically by the age of fourteen.[21] As a group, according to the latter, Homo neanderthalensis were less able to benefit from a division of labour as the entire group would join in the hunt for animals for meat. But there tended to be more division of labour amongst Homo sapiens groups. This ensured that for Homo sapiens a diversity of food resources ranging from plant matter to meat could be accumulated over a period of time. The Homo sapiens population would then be better able to balance and change their dietary intake as dictated by the environment.[22]

[17] Sarmiento, E., Sawyer, G., and Milner, R. (2007), The Last Human: A Guide to Twenty-Two Species of Extinct Humans, Yale University Press, London.

[18] Coolidge, F., and Wynn, T. (2018), The Rise of Homo sapiens: The Evolution of Modern Thinking, Oxford University Press, New York.

[19] Ibid.

[20] Ibid.

[21] Coolidge, F., and Wynn, T. (2018), The Rise of Homo sapiens: The Evolution of Modern Thinking, Oxford University Press, New York.

[22] Ibid.

Bipedalism and Manual Dexterity and Brain Size

While the use of fire and the subsequent ability to cook food, including meat, likely played a role in the increased brain size of Homo erectus, it is not the sole factor. Bipedalism and manual dexterity also contributed significantly to the evolutionary changes that led to the expansion of brain size in Homo erectus, and later, in Homo sapiens.

The ability to control fire did indeed enable Homo erectus to cook meat, making it easier to digest and allowing for more efficient absorption of nutrients.[23] Cooked meat provided more calories and essential nutrients, such as fats and proteins, which are vital for brain development. This increase in energy intake allowed for the development of a larger brain, as the brain is one of the most energy-demanding organs in the body.[24] The correlation between the use of fire and brain expansion is supported by archaeological evidence, which suggests that Homo erectus began controlling fire around 1.5 million years ago.[25] This control of fire had profound social and cultural implications, as it likely fostered greater social interaction and cooperation around campfires, which were important in the evolution of human communication and social structures.[26] However, bipedalism, which pre-dated the control of fire, also played a critical role in the evolution of Homo erectus. Walking upright freed the hands for other activities, including the manipulation of tools, which contributed to the development of manual dexterity.[27] This transition to bipedalism allowed early hominins to engage in complex foraging and hunting behaviours, which, combined with tool use, were vital for survival. Bipedalism also influenced other anatomical adaptations, such as changes in the spine, pelvis, and lower limbs, which enabled more efficient long-distance travel, an essential trait for scavenging and hunting.[28]

[23] Wrangham, R.W., 2009. Catching Fire: How Cooking Made Us Human. Basic Books.

[24] Aiello, L.C. and Wheeler, P., 1995. 'The Expensive Tissue Hypothesis: The Brain and the Digestive System in Human and Primate Evolution', Current Anthropology, 36(2), pp.199–221.

[25] Gowlett, J.A.J., 2016. 'The Discovery of Fire by Humans: A Long and Convoluted Process', Philosophical Transactions of the Royal Society B: Biological Sciences, 371(1696), p.20150164.

[26] Dunbar, R. (2014), Human Evolution: Our Brains and Behavior. Oxford University Press.

[27] Lovejoy, C.O. (1981), 'The Origin of Man', Science, 211(4480), pp.341–350.

[28] Rodman, P.S. and McHenry, H.M. (1980), 'Bioenergetics and the Origin of Bipedalism', American Journal of Physical Anthropology, 52(1), pp.103–106.

The development of manual dexterity, particularly the evolution of the opposable thumb, further facilitated the creation and use of increasingly complex tools. The ability to manipulate objects with precision enabled Homo erectus to engage in more complex foraging and hunting strategies, which required advanced cognitive abilities, such as spatial awareness and memory.[29] The cognitive demands of making and using tools likely stimulated neural development, contributing to the expansion of brain size.[30] Furthermore, tool use was not only physically demanding but also required the capacity for abstract thought and forward planning, abilities that are closely linked to larger brain sizes in early hominins.[31] The combination of bipedalism and manual dexterity allowed Homo erectus to thrive in diverse environments, fostering the development of social cooperation and communication—factors that further enhanced the brain size. As social groups became larger and more complex, early humans required greater cognitive abilities to manage social relationships, leading to the further expansion of brain size.[32] The cognitive demands of living in increasingly complex social groups may have driven the selection for larger brains, a process that continued in Homo sapiens. These evolutionary developments had significant implications for the rise of Homo sapiens. The increased brain size and cognitive abilities that began with Homo erectus were carried forward and further developed in Homo sapiens, enabling more sophisticated behaviours such as language, culture, and social structures. The expansion of brain size in early humans laid the foundation for the cognitive revolution that allowed Homo sapiens to dominate other species and create complex societies.[33] This cognitive revolution, which likely occurred around 70,000 years ago, enabled Homo sapiens to think abstractly, collaborate on large scales, and develop

[29] Marzke, M.W. (1997), 'Precision grips, hand morphology, and tools', American Journal of Physical Anthropology, 102(1), pp.91–110.

[30] Wynn, T. (2002), 'Archaeology and cognitive evolution', Behavioural and Brain Sciences, 25(3), pp.389–402.

[31] Stout, D., Toth, N., Schick, K. and Chaminade, T. (2008), 'Neural correlates of Early Stone Age toolmaking: technology, language and cognition in human evolution', Philosophical Transactions of the Royal Society B: Biological Sciences, 363(1499), pp.1939–1949.

[32] Dunbar, R. (2014), Human Evolution: Our Brains and Behavior. Oxford University Press.

[33] Holloway, R.L. (1967), 'The Evolution of the Human Brain: Some Notes Toward a Synthesis Between Neural Structure and the Evolution of Complex Behavior', General Systems, 12, pp. 3–19.

advanced technologies, setting the stage for the development of civilization.[34] Thus, while the use of fire to cook meat played an important role in increasing the brain size of Homo erectus, it was not the only factor. Bipedalism and manual dexterity were equally critical in driving the cognitive evolution that eventually led to the rise of Homo sapiens. The combination of these factors allowed early humans to adapt to their environments, form complex social structures, and develop the cognitive abilities that define modern humanity.

The Emergence of Homo sapiens

The main anatomical differences between Homo neanderthalensis and Homo sapiens lie in the skeletal frame and the structure of the brain, although the brain of the former was bigger than that of the latter.[35] Homo neanderthalensis was stockier, shorter, and more muscular than Homo sapiens. However, there are many differences between the structures of the brains of the two species. Compared to the brain of Homo sapiens, the brain of Homo neanderthalensis had smaller olfactory bulbs, larger occipital cortices, narrower orbitofrontal cortices, narrower temporal lobes with less forward-projecting temporal lobes.[36] The olfactory bulbs encoded smell information from the nose to be sent to the brain. The occipital cortices were involved in the processing of information by the eyes. The orbitofrontal cortices were involved in decision making. The cerebellum was involved in the coherent co-ordination of limb movements. And the temporal lobes were involved in the processing and interpretation of sensory input so that it may be retained as memory. The structural differences between the brains of Homo neanderthalensis and Homo sapiens suggest that the former had a lower capacity for the retention in memory of sensory input, was less able to co-ordinate limb movements (was awkward), was indecisive and better able to process visual information, but less able to smell 'danger'. In the context of differences in the structure of the brains of the two species, in a conflict between the

[34] Harari, Y.N. (2014), Sapiens: A Brief History of Humankind. Harper.

[35] Dunbar, R. (2014), Human Evolution: Our Brains and Behavior. Oxford University Press.

[36] Wynn, T., Overmann, K., and Coolidge, F. (2016), The False Dichotomy; A Refutation of the Neanderthal Indistinguishability Claim, Journal of Anthropological Sciences, Vol.94, pp.201–221.

two species, Homo sapiens would have the advantage. This perhaps explains why Homo neanderthalensis was unable to survive in the face of competition from Homo sapiens. However, Homo neanderthalensis did exhibit some recognizable innovation in the context of developing 'hafting', attach handles to tools.[37] The latter suggests that Homo neanderthalensis also used the Levallois Technology, a method of using rocks to chip away at other rocks of a specific kind in order to create sharp edges for cutting.

While Homo neanderthalensis and Homo sapiens were co-existing contemporaries, Homo erectus was the direct descendant of both species. This may have arisen because of location-specific speciation in a group or multi-locational speciation. For Homo neanderthalensis, speciation is more likely to have occurred in Europe from Homo erectus with Homo heidelbergensis acting as an intermediary. On the other hand, for Homo sapiens it is likely that speciation occurred in a group in Africa from where Homo sapiens moved out of Africa to inhabit other parts of the world. Location-specific speciation and multi-local specification represent two models of evolution.[38] On the balance, recent genetic evidence suggests that all the Homo sapiens on the planet today evolved from a small group in Africa between 180,000 years and 150,000 years ago.[39] This small group of early Homo sapiens which itself originated from one 'Adam' and 'Eve', with the 'Eve' appearing 80,000 years before the 'Adam'.[40] Homo sapiens began to leave Africa 100,000 to 60,000 years ago and spread to Europe and Asia, reaching the Americas only 15,000 years ago.[41] The migration out of Africa may have started due to climatic changes.[42] A possible route out of Africa could have been through the present Red Sea, where in those times the sea levels would have been lower, allowing a

[37] Coolidge, F., and Wynn, T. (2018), The Rise of Homo sapiens: The Evolution of Modern Thinking, Oxford University Press, New York.

[38] Lewin, R. (2005), Human Evolution: An Illustrated Introduction, Blackwell Publishing, Oxford.

[39] Cartwright, J. (2016), Evolution and Human Behaviour; Darwinian Perspectives on the Human Condition, Palgrave Macmillan, New York.

[40] Wells, S. (2017), The Journey of Man: A Genetic Odyssey, Princeton University Press, Princeton.

[41] Cartwright, J. (2016), Evolution and Human Behaviour; Darwinian Perspectives on the Human Condition, Palgrave Macmillan, New York.

[42] Tierney, J., de Menocal, P., and Zander, P. (2017), A Climatic Context for the out of Africa migration, Geology, 45, 11, pp.1023–1026.

migration path for the first Homo sapiens to emerge from Africa. Waves and waves followed over subsequent millennia, using the coasts of the landmass to get to Australia 40,000 years ago. Innovativeness and adaptability allow the new Homo sapiens settlers to settle into diverse habitats, from hot to the extreme cold of Siberia. Crude sewing needles were developed to produce the clothing, from animal skins, needed to survive in extreme sub-zero temperatures. Crude structures, in the modern context, were built from timber and animal hides to live in. The racial diversity seen in modern-day humanity is a relatively recent phenomenon in the context of human evolution. Up to 15,000 years ago the migrating Homo sapiens were of one type of colour and facial features.[43] Racial differentiation has only happened within the last 15,000 years.

Early Civilizations

Gobekli Tepe: 10,000 BC

It has long been considered that settled farming came before religion. Furthermore, the reasons why Homo sapiens as a hunter gatherer gave way to farming and animal husbandry at a single location have been a subject of debate. However, the Neolithic archaeological site at Gobekli Tepe may finally be able to settle this debate. Before the discovery of Gobekli Tepe, it had been thought that the Neolithic Revolution had been a moment of 'genius' in which the domestication of wild plants and animals occurred at a single site in the lands of present-day southern Iraq.[44] Perhaps this flash of genius could have been brought about by environmental change, which limited the quantity of wild plants which could be collected for consumption as well as reducing the availability of wild animals which could have migrated to other areas.

Gobekli Tepe is 15km north of the city of Sanliurfa in the southeast of modern-day Turkey. Archaeologists consider Gobekli Tepe to be the most ancient archaeological site to be found anywhere in the world.[45] However,

[43] Roberts, A. (2009), The Incredible Human Journey, Bloomsbury Publishing Plc.

[44] Mann, C. (2011), The Birth of Religion, National Geographic Magazine, http://ngm.nationalgeographic.com/print/2011/06/gobekli-tepe/mann-text.

[45] Debertolis, P., Gulla, D., and Savolainen, H. (2017), Archaeoacoustic Analysis in Enclosure D at Gobekli Tepe in South Anatolia, Turkey, History and Archaeology, The 5th Human and Social Sciences at the Common Conference.

there may be even older archaeological sites which have yet to be found. When Gobekli Tepe was under construction between 9600BC and 9500BC, a mini-ice age was coming to an end in Europe.[46] According to the latter, Gobekli Tepe pre-dates the pyramids of ancient Egypt by at least 7000 years. The site constituted megalithic blocks, each weighing 7 to 50 tons in weight, with intricate carvings of animals, arms, hands, and clothing.[47,48] The carvings of animals depicted insects, snakes, bulls, foxes, boars, and gazelles.[49] This animal symbolism might suggest that the rituals and rites celebrated at Gobekli Tepe were perhaps associated with nature. Some of the megalithic stones were over 18ft in height.[50] The latter suggests that in the area surrounding the megalithic stones, a large variety of ancient flint tools such as knives, axes, and spearhead points were also found. Moreover, at the site, archaeologists have also found a miniature Sphinx, with similar characteristics to the giant Sphinx of ancient Egypt, 7000 years later.[51] Nevertheless, the hunter gatherers who built Gobekli Tepe did so without any knowledge of writing, pottery, and metal.[52] However, the builders of Gobekli Tepe were innovative enough to develop the technology associated with stone masonry.[53] Nevertheless, linguistic expression in written form did not emerge until 3000BC, up to 6000 years after the completion of Gobekli Tepe.[54] It is now regarded as a site used for worship, celebrating and feasting and not as a permanent home.[55]

[46] Collins, A. (2014), Gobekli Tepe: Genesis of the Gods: The temple of the Watchers and the Discovery of Eden, Bear & Company, Rochester, Vermont, USA.

[47] Vinter, J.C. (2011), Ancient Earth Mysteries, AEM Publishing.

[48] Notroff, J., Dietrich, O., Dietrich, L., Tvetmarken, C., Kinzel, M., Schlindwein, J., Sanmez, D., and Clare, L. (2017), Mediterranean Archaelogy and Archaeometry, Vol. 17, No. 2, pp.57–74.

[49] Ibid.

[50] Mann, C. (2011), The Birth of Religion, National Geographic Magazine, http://ngm.nationalgeographic.com/print/2011/06/gobekli-tepe/mann-text.

[51] Vinter, J.C. (2011), Ancient Earth Mysteries, AEM Publishing.

[52] Mann, C. (2011), The Birth of Religion, National Geographic Magazine, http://ngm.nationalgeographic.com/print/2011/06/gobekli-tepe/mann-text.

[53] Scranton, L. (2014), China's Cosmological Prehistory: The Sophisticated Science Encoded in Civilisation's Earliest Symbols, Simon & Schuster.

[54] Ibid.

[55] Schmidt, K. (2010), Gobekli Tepe – the Stone Age Sanctuaries: New results of ongoing excavations with a special focus on sculptures and high reliefs, Docomenta Praehistorica, Ljubljana, Vol. 37, pp.239–256.

However, the earliest evidence of the earliest cultivated grain has been found in the region surrounding Gobekli Tepe.[56]

Gobekli Tepe was constructed at a time when the Neolithic population was increasing causing increased pressures, perhaps greater conflicts, on the social fabric of Neolithic society. This led to the development of rituals.[57] Perhaps to bring about a sense of 'community' and maintain the cohesiveness of that society. However, the rituals could have been a cultural innovation symbolizing Homo sapiens conquest of nature.[58] It is not clear what kind of rituals were conducted at Gobekli Tepe, although no burials have been found on site.[59] However, where areas of the site have been filled in with soil, fragments of human bone have been found, including three partially preserved skulls. These shows cut marks, suggesting that when the victim had been killed, the skull was de-fleshed using flint tools.[60] The latter also suggests that the skulls had probably been hung from cords, with at least one skull modified using red ochre. But it is open to question as to whether ritual killings and/or cannibalism took place at the site.

The construction of Gobekli Tepe must have involved a sizable number of people over an extended period, a process of building and rebuilding over centuries, transporting heavy stones over a distance. The building of the religious architecture at the site can be split into two phases. The T-shaped monoliths incorporate the first phase of building and have been dated to the tenth millennium BC.[61] On the other hand, the second phase incorporated the monumental round oval buildings, the older layer of which has been dated to the ninth millennium BC. Now all people around the world were living a hunter-gatherer existence except in the Fertile Crescent.[62] However, some argue that smaller-scale

[56] Scranton, L. (2014), China's Cosmological Prehistory: The Sophisticated Science Encoded in Civilisation's Earliest Symbols, Simon & Schuster.

[57] Simmons, A. (2007), The Neolithic Revolution in the Near East; Transforming the Human Landscape, The University of Arizona Press, Tucson.

[58] Mann, C. (2011), The Birth of Religion, National Geographic Magazine, http://ngm.nationalgeographic.com/print/2011/06/gobekli-tepe/mann-text.

[59] Gresky, J., Haelm, J., and Clare, L. (2017), Modified human crania from Gobekli Tepe provide evidence for a new form of Neolithic skull cult, Science Advances, Vol.3, No.6.

[60] Ibid.

[61] Debertolis, P., Gulla, D., and Savolainen, H. (2017), Archaeoacoustic Analysis in Enclosure D at Gobekli Tepe in South Anatolia, Turkey, History and Archaeology, The 5th Human and Social Sciences at the Common Conference.

[62] Ibid.

projects of a nature similar to Gobekli Tepe were occurring in other parts of the world, independently, albeit perhaps not at the same time.[63] The Fertile Crescent represents the present-day Middle East, incorporating present-day Iraq, Syria, Palestine, and Egypt. It was in this part of the world that permanent village settlements came into existence, although Gobekli Tepe was a site where communal rituals were conducted.[64] So far, no evidence has been found to suggest that it was a site of permanent human habitation.

The round oval buildings at the site were accumulated over a period of 1200 years, during what is known as the pre-pottery period.[65] The stones could have been moved by rolling and pulling them over a series of blocks. The enduring mystery of Gobekli Tepe is the contradiction between the level of technology and innovation used to build at the site and the apparent lack of technological sophistication in contemporary society, for example no pottery.[66] However, at an intuitive level, in a hunter-gatherer society why would anyone need pots? Food could be eaten from where it was either picked or killed, and storage could have been in pits perhaps lined with some protective substance. To sustain the builders, a large and consistent food supply would have been required, assuming there were no breaks in the time taken to construct the monument at Gobekli Tepe. There seems to have been significant feasts at the site, perhaps as a reward for the work undertaken there by its builders over a millennium.[67] The latter suggests that the groups in the region surrounding the site may have had a common culture with its own norms and values. This could have led to segmentation within the groups, such that a smaller number of people, the 'nobility', controlled a much larger 'workforce'.[68] These cultural

[63] Stanish, C. (2017), The Evolution of Human Co-operation: Ritual and Social Complexity in Stateless Societies, Cambridge University Press, Cambridge.

[64] Debertolis, P., Gulla, D., and Savolainen, H. (2017), Archaeoacoustic Analysis in Enclosure D at Gobekli Tepe in South Anatolia, Turkey, History and Archaeology, The 5th Human and Social Sciences at the Common Conference.

[65] Notroff, J., Dietrich, O., Dietrich, L., Tvetmarken, C., Kinzel, M., Schlindwein, J., Sanmez, D., and Clare, L. (2017), Mediterranean Archaelogy and Archaeometry, Vol. 17, No. 2, pp.57–74.

[66] Constable, N. (2009), World Atlas of Archaeology, Thalamus Publishing.

[67] Dietrich O., Notroff J., Schmidt K. (2017), Feasting, Social Complexity, and the Emergence of the Early Neolithic of Upper Mesopotamia: A View from Gobekli Tepe. In: Chacon R., Mendoza R. (eds) Feast, Famine or Fighting?, Studies in Human Ecology and Adaptation, Vol 8. Springer, Cham.

[68] Ibid.

norms and values would have established standards by which the members of the groups would behave as well as behaving with each other. In this case, it would have made sense to grow crops near the site of building as well as to maintain animals for slaughter, there too. This would be logical explanation as to why hunter gatherers made the transition to a settled life, laying the roots of early Western civilization. The Neolithic Revolution was important because of the location-specific crop cultivation and animal husbandry, perhaps in conjunction with a smaller-scale hunter-gathering existence.[69] The latter suggests that this may have involved some form of division of labour amongst the members of the settlement. Some gathering berries, some gathering firewood, some tending animals, some making sure that the communal fire did not go out, some collecting water, and some looking after the crops. This allowed individual to benefit from a sustained nutritional diet. In the foetal stage and in early life this would have allowed for an improvement in brain development.[70] An improved diet would have led to people having an increased and improved access to a range of foods. It follows that the consumption of a diverse range of foods would be micronutrient rich, and this would allow the body to absorb a range of micronutrients—vitamins and minerals. The assimilation of these micronutrients by the body would allow the brain's potential to be more utilized. Learning would become more efficient, and new ideas would arise which could be exchanged and discussed with individuals in a growing population. In other words, there would be greater technological and social innovation as a result.[71] Thus, a combination of onsite crop cultivation, animal husbandry, the gathering of plants and fruits, and the hunting of animals and fish would lead to increased cognitive capacity due to the development and more efficient use of brain tissue. This would have an immediate impact on innovation and learning and would not need long-term evolutionary development over millennia. Therefore, it would

[69] Simmons, A. (2007), The Neolithic Revolution in the Near East; Transforming the Human Landscape, The University of Arizona Press, Tucson.

[70] Cakmak, I., Graham, R., and Welch, R. (2009), Agricultural and Molecular Genetic Approaches to Improving Nutrition and Preventing Micronutrient Malnutrition Globally, in 'Impacts of Agriculture on Human Health and Nutrition – Volume 1,' Cakmak, I., and Welch, R. (Eds), Eolss Publishers Co. Ltd, United Kingdom.

[71] Mann, C. (2011), The Birth of Religion, National Geographic Magazine, http://ngm.nationalgeographic.com/print/2011/06/gobekli-tepe/mann-text.

be justifiable that the roots of human civilization lie in the development of the human mind, the ability to absorb facts related to the environment, form ideas, and then project these ideas into reality by implementing practical applications.

Sumer: 3500 BC

Between 700,000 BC to 9000 BC there were no permanent settlements of Homo sapiens. Existence was at the hunter-gatherer level, in which groups would move from one location to another, gathering plants and seeds and hunting wild animals. Furthermore, technology had remained at a basic level, and it involved the use and the manufacture of stone implements.[72] According to the latter the earliest permanent settlements began in the Near East in the Neolithic Period at around 9000BC. These settlements were based around the Tigris and the Euphrates Rivers.[73] Subsequently, this form of settlement spread to the rest of the world, including China by 4000BC. The most important feature of these earliest forms of permanent settlement was the onsite cultivation of crops and animal husbandry. In a contemporary sense, these early permanent settlements were made up of a few hundred individuals. However, as time went by individual settlements began to engage in trading activities, and as a result more complex forms of social organization evolved.[74] The latter suggests that in the period from 6000BC to 4000BC specific cultures emerged in northern Mesopotamia. These cultures included the Hassuna, Samarra, and the Halaf. In the period of the Hassuna culture, spindle whorls were used to produce cloth, gems evidenced trade, and private property rights existed.[75] This was denoted by the stamp of a seal as proof of ownership. Buildings were either connected with a central courtyard or were separate. Some of the larger buildings were designated for religious or ceremonial purposes.[76] The period of the Samarra culture was defined by its elaborately decorated pottery and architecture with buildings displaying wall junctions and external buttresses.[77] According to the latter, the period of the Halaf culture was characterized by workshops for pottery

[72] Nemet-Nejat, K. (1998), Daily Life in Ancient Mesopotamia, Greenwood Press, London.
[73] Hunter, N. (2015), Daily Life in Ancient Sumer, Heinemann-Raintree, Chicago.
[74] Nemet-Nejat, K. (1998), Daily Life in Ancient Mesopotamia, Greenwood Press, London.
[75] Ibid.
[76] Ibid.
[77] Ibid.

production, indicating the specialized division of labour, and villages had cobbled streets. It was in the Halaf culture that the tournette was invented, to be followed by the potter's wheel in the following Ubaid period between 4000BC and 3500BC.[78] The invention and introduction of the potter's wheel into pottery production increased production through the division of labour and allowed to produce pottery of a uniform quality. The Ubaidian was the largest ethnic group of Mesopotamia, having settled there in small southern fishing villages which then expanded into sizable urban centres, for the time, such as Eridu, Ur, and Uruk, which was the largest of the three. Other cities included Umma and Lagash, together with Eridu, Ur, and Uruk. These cities exercised considerable economic, social, and political control over their respective surrounding areas. As such they formed the city states of the ancient Sumerian civilization.[79] The latter suggests that Sumerian cities were walled with a temple at the centre of the city. The king was divine, and Sumerian society was segmented into nobles, commoners, and slaves. The nobility included members of the royal family as well as the priests. The commoners included the people who worked for the palace and the temple as well as tradespeople, crafts people, farmers, and fishermen.[80] The latter suggests that 90% of the population were engaged in farming. The invention and exploitation of irrigation allowed the Sumerians to maximize the harvest potential of the nutrient-rich soil which composed their land.[81] The use of irrigation and the rich fertile land allowed the Sumerians to produce surpluses of wheat and barley. These surpluses they could use for trade or to distribute to people when the harvest failed. However, while the economy was primarily agricultural, the Sumerians did produce pottery, textiles, and metal work. The Sumerians also imported copper, tin, and timber in exchange for wheat, barley, metal goods, and dried fish.[82] They also traded with the peoples of the Mediterranean and with Meluhha, the Sumerian name for the Indus Valley Civilization, which would have been in modern-day northern India.[83] During the Harappan phase (2600 to 2500 BC), the

[78] Ibid.

[79] Duiker, W., and Spielvogel, J. (2007), World History, Thomson-Wadsworth.

[80] Ibid.

[81] Kramer, S. (1963), The Sumerians: Their History, Culture and Character, The University of Chicago Press, London.

[82] Ibid.

[83] Crawford, H. (1991), Sumer and the Sumerians, Cambridge University Press, Cambridge.

people of the Indus Valley built ships with a 'house' on the deck, steered with an oar at the helm.[84] Using such ships, the people of the Indus Valley could traverse waterways and seas in order to trade with the Sumerian/Babylonian merchants, traders. The Sumerians valued the individual and the individual's achievement.[85] This ideal was enforced by laws, which the Sumerians were the first to enact anywhere in the world. The Sumerians were also able to express their language in written form. Possibly the first to do so in history. This was often on clay tablets, some of which have survived to this day. The combination of a consistent diet, the emphasis on individual achievement, and a written language allowed the Sumerians to be highly innovative. They have been reputed to have invented the wheel and to have been the first to divide the day into hours and minutes.[86]

Tepe Gawra and Uruk were the dominant cultures of ancient Mesopotamia, with the former being prevalent in the north and the latter in the south of the country.[87] The latter suggests that between 3000BC and 2900BC the empty northern regions had been settled by Sumerian speakers. In the Uruk region large-scale building projects were undertaken. This would suggest that there was a small elite in control of a larger supply of craftsmen and builders. The number of buildings in the Uruk region was greater than those in the Tepe Gawra region. It follows that in Uruk, Babylonian Civilization was more complex in organization.[88] The latter attributes this to its large population density and a high level of productivity. By 3000BC the language spoken in Mesopotamia was Sumerian with the dominant ethnic group being the Sumerians. Writing on clay tablets was invented in the period from 3200BC to 2900BC, the Protoliterate Period; it was initially used for accounting purposes. During the Protoliterate Period, the main centres of economic, political, and social activity were the temples. The temples owned the land, hired labourers and specialist craftsmen, were responsible for co-ordinating trade; and they exercised political control across the city and its surroundings.[89] The latter suggests that each city was a self-contained irrigated environment

[84] Parpola, A. (2015), The Roots of Hinduism: The Early Aryans and the Indus Civilisation, Published to Oxford Scholarship Online: August 2015, DOI: 10.1093/acprof:oso/9780190226909.001.0001.

[85] Ibid.

[86] Hunter, N. (2015), Daily Life in Ancient Sumer, Heinemann-Raintree, Chicago.

[87] Nemet-Nejat, K. (1998), Daily Life in Ancient Mesopotamia, Greenwood Press, London.

[88] Ibid.

[89] Ibid.

surrounded by dessert and swamps. These cities would eventually become city states, which were loosely connected through trade.

Sargon the Great (2334BC to 2279BC) was the first king to unite the city states of Mesopotamia, and by establishing his capital in the city of Akkad, his empire was named the Akkadian Empire. Sargon was the first ruler of a unified state to have a standing army and military installations doted throughout his lands. The city of Akkad was one of the wealthiest cities of the ancient world.[90] The Akkadian Empire was located to the north of the Sumerian city states, and it conquered these states in 2340BC.[91] The Akkadian Empire was ended by the Gutians, invaders from southeast Kurdistan.[92] This happened in 2100BC after which the Sumerian city states regained their autonomy and continued to co-exist while warring with each other.[93] However, according to the latter the Sumerian city states were again unified by Hammurabi in 1792BC. As a king, Hammurabi built more irrigation channels, temples, and defensive walls.[94] Hammurabi also established a more robust codified system of law, now known as the Code of Hammurabi. These laws were received by Hammurabi from the Sun god in 2250BC and were found inscribed on a black diorite, 8ft high and about 6ft in circumference, in the ancient city of Susa in 1901.[95] The latter suggests that the Code of Hammurabi was written in a period of world history when the peoples of Western Europe were living far less sophisticated lives. The Code of Hammurabi was very comprehensive in covering the economic, social, and cultural lives of the citizens of Sumer. For example, the Code dealt with Family Law, the amounts of fees and salaries which should be paid to various occupations, compensation for merchants robbed by marauders, and the need for written contracts to facilitate transactions.[96] The Code of Hammurabi also specifies the social order of Babylonian society. This was structured into three levels.[97] The first tier included members of land-owning families, the

[90] Ibid.

[91] Duiker, W., and Spielvogel, J. (2007), World History, Thomson-Wadsworth.

[92] Saggs, H. (2000), Peoples of the Past: Babylonians, University of California Press, Berkeley, Los Angeles.

[93] Duiker, W., and Spielvogel, J. (2007), World History, Thomson-Wadsworth.

[94] Ibid.

[95] McNeil, D. (1967), The Code of Hammurabi, 53 A.B.A. J. 444.

[96] Ibid.

[97] Bertman, S. (2003), Handbook to Life in Ancient Mesopotamia, Oxford University Press, Oxford.

Awilum. The second tier included all freemen who did not own any land, the Mushkenum. The lowest, third tier included the slaves who owned neither their freedom nor land, the Wardum. According to the Code, inter-tier crime was less severely punished than was intra-tier crime. However, at the same time harsher penalties were specified for the privileged in Babylonian society, who infringed on any aspect of the Code in contrast to the less privileged.[98] The Code of Hammurabi also increases the opportunity for social mobility, perhaps through marriage. Nevertheless, property ownership became more concentrated during the reign of Hammurabi, and thus, political power.[99]

Early Dynastic Period Egypt: 3100 BC

The ancient history of Egypt spans from 2950BC to 30BC. It encompasses thirty-one dynasties, not including the Macedonian Dynasty (332BC to 309BC) and the Ptolemaic Period (309BC to 30BC). The First Dynasty was established in 2950BC with the unification of Egypt by Narmer. And there are three other notable dynasties. Firstly, the Twelfth Dynasty (1938BC to 1755BC) included the reign of Amenemhat IV (1770BC to 1760BC) during which time the Shang Dynasty was founded in China in 1766BC.[100] The Eighteenth Dynasty (1190BC to 1069BC) includes the reign of Ramesses IV (1156BC to 1150BC), which encompasses the collapse of the Mycenaean Civilization in the Mediterranean.[101] The Nineteenth Dynasty encompassed the reign of Ramesses II (1279BC to 1213BC), also known as Ramesses the Great. The Macedonian Dynasty encompassed the time of Alexander the Great, and the Ptolemaic Period encompasses the time of Cleopatra (51BC to 30BC) as well as the Roman invasion of Britain, which at that time was occupied by native British tribes such as the Iceni and the Trinovante. These tribes revolted against Roman rule in 60AD, following the invasion of Britain by Julius Caesar in 54AD.[102] Julius Caesar's initial invasion of Britain in 54BC was followed by a more sustained Roman presence from 43AD under Emperor Claudius, who sought to consolidate Roman control over the British Isles. The Roman

[98] Ibid.

[99] Ibid.

[100] Wilkinson, T. (2010), The Rise and Fall of Ancient Egypt: The History of a Civilisation from 3000BC to Cleopatra, Bloomsbury, London.

[101] Ibid.

[102] Barker, H. (2004), Iceni, Bladud Books, Bath, United Kingdom.

conquest brought significant political and social disruption to the British tribes, leading to tensions that culminated in the revolt of 60AD, led by Boudica, the queen of the Iceni.[103]

The revolt was driven by multiple factors. First, the Roman imposition of heavy taxes and the seizure of tribal lands created widespread resentment among the British tribes.[104] The Romans also disarmed the tribes and imposed harsh laws that undermined traditional tribal authority, further alienating the local population.[105] In the case of the Iceni, the revolt was triggered when the Romans ignored the will of the late King Prasutagus, who had left his kingdom jointly to his daughters and the Roman Empire. Instead, the Romans annexed Iceni lands entirely, flogged Boudica, and raped her daughters.[106] This act of violence sparked a full-scale rebellion, with the Iceni and the Trinovantes joining forces to drive out the Romans, sacking Roman settlements such as Camulodunum (modern-day Colchester), Londinium (London), and Verulamium (St Albans).[107] Despite the initial success of the revolt, the Roman military response, led by Governor Suetonius Paulinus, eventually crushed the rebellion. The Romans' ability to swiftly mobilize and use advanced military tactics, such as disciplined formations and superior weaponry, highlighted their innovative approach to warfare.[108] In contrast, the British tribes were less centralized, relying on guerrilla tactics and lacking the organizational structure of the Roman legions. The Roman use of roads and fortifications also facilitated their rapid response, further demonstrating the technological and infrastructural superiority of the Roman Empire.[109]

The question of whether the Romans were more innovative than the British tribes can be explored by comparing the two societies. The Romans excelled in engineering, constructing roads, aqueducts, and military fortifications that would stand the test of time. They introduced new forms of

[103] Frere, S. S. (1987). Britannia: A History of Roman Britain. Routledge.

[104] James, S. & Millett, M. (eds.) (2001). Britons and Romans: Advancing an Archaeological Agenda. York: Council for British Archaeology.

[105] Todd, M. (2004). Roman Britain. Blackwell.

[106] Tacitus. (c. 116). The Annals. Translated by A. J. Woodman (2004) London: Penguin Classics.

[107] Mattingly, D. J. (2007). An Imperial Possession: Britain in the Roman Empire, 54 BC – AD 409. Penguin.

[108] Goldsworthy, A. (2003). The Complete Roman Army. Thames & Hudson.

[109] Salway, P. (1981). Roman Britain. Oxford University Press.

governance, economic systems, and urban planning to Britain, reshaping the landscape and integrating the island into the broader Roman economy.[110] The British tribes, while skilled in metallurgy and local craftsmanship, did not possess the same level of technological or organizational sophistication as the Romans.[111] Thus, while the British revolt of 60AD was a significant moment of resistance against Roman occupation, it also underscored the power disparity between the two cultures, with Roman innovations ultimately securing their dominance in Britain.

During its unique geographical position, Egypt has served as part of the migratory route for hominin species, leaving East Africa to the other parts of the Old World.[112] However, according to the latter no human presence has been detected in Egypt between 11,000BC and 8000BC. Nevertheless, the earliest Neolithic cultures emerged in the Western Desert.[113] The latter suggests that short-term camps were set up at Nabta Playa and Bir Kiseiba by hunter gatherers in the Early Neolithic Period between 8800BC to 6800BC. At Bir Kiseiba there is also evidence of well digging, semi-domestication of cattle for milk and blood, and the use of primitive grinding equipment.[114] However, the people still led a hunter-gatherer existence despite the evidence of semi-permanent settlement. Moving from the Middle Neolithic (6500 BC to 5100 BC) to the Late Neolithic Period (5100 BC to 4700 BC) the human occupation of the Western Desert began to increase, perhaps because of an exceptionally wet period in its history. Moving through this period, there is also evidence of an increase in the number of wells as well as an increase in wattle and daub constructions.[115] The earliest evidence for crop cultivation and animal husbandry, perhaps in permanent settlements, is to be found in the Badarian Culture, named after a site found near Sohag, of Upper Egypt.[116] So around 5000

[110] Wilson, R. J. A. (2002). A Guide to the Roman Remains in Britain. 4th edn. London: Constable and Robinson.

[111] James, S. & Millett, M. (eds.) (2001). Britons and Romans: Advancing an Archaeological Agenda. York: Council for British Archaeology.

[112] Hendrickx, S., and Vermeersch, P. (2000), Pre-history: From the Palaeolithic to the Badarian Culture (700,000 to 4000 BC, IN: The Oxford History of Ancient Egypt, Shaw, I. (Ed), Oxford University Press, New York.

[113] Ibid.

[114] Ibid.

[115] Hendrickx, S., and Vermeersch, P. (2000), Pre-history: From the Palaeolithic to the Badarian Culture (700,000 to 4000 BC, IN: The Oxford History of Ancient Egypt, Shaw, I. (Ed), Oxford University Press, New York.

[116] Ibid.

years ago people began to settle and build simple homes along the fertile land surrounding the River Nile, still the world's longest river.[117] The latter suggests that for these early ancient Egyptians, life changed from a hunter gatherer like existence to that of a farmer. People caught fish in the Nile and still hunted, but at the same time they engaged in animal husbandry, cattle, sheep, and goats, as well as crop cultivation along the land surrounding the banks of the River Nile. They grew crops such as wheat and barley as well as cultivated fruits and vegetables.[118] Over time, as more and more people began to settle, more and more villages and towns were established such that between 3900BC and 3100BC some of the towns became wealthy and powerful.[119] This second period of early Egyptian predynastic culture was known as the Naqada Period (4000 BC to 3200 BC), named after the site of Naqada in Upper Egypt.[120] The increase in population and the agglomeration of the area led to the formation of two distinct regions, Lower Egypt and Upper Egypt. The rulers of these regions fought each other for supremacy. However, in 3100BC King Narmer of Upper Egypt conquered Lower Egypt to form the unified state of Egypt.[121] The period encompassing the Egyptian Old Kingdom (2650 BC to 2134 BC) corresponded with the mature phase of urbanization in the Indus Valley Civilization and the presence of the Akkadian Empire (2350 BC to 2100 BC). So, it is conceivable that trade took place between these three ancient civilizations. Indeed, there is some evidence for a 'village' of Indus Civilization merchants in southern Iraq between 2114 and 2004BC.[122]

In the early predynastic period, many innovations were introduced. The irrigation techniques were improved upon, and as a result, agricultural production increased.[123] During the period 3800 BC to 3500 BC,

[117] Deady, K. (2012), Great Civilisations, Ancient Egypt, Beyond Pyramids, Capstone Press, Minnesota.

[118] Ibid.

[119] Ibid.

[120] Midant-Reynes, B. (2000), Pre-history: From the Palaeolithic to the Badarian Culture (700,000 to 4000 BC: In The Oxford History of Ancient Egypt, Shaw, I. (Ed), Oxford University Press, New York.

[121] Deady, K. (2012), Great Civilisations, Ancient Egypt, Beyond Pyramids, Capstone Press, Minnesota.

[122] Lawler, A. (2008), Boring No More, a Trade-Savvy Indus Emerges, Science, Vol.320, Issue 5881, pp.1276–1281.

[123] Shaw, I. (2012), Ancient Egyptian Technology & Innovation, Transformations in Pharaonic Material Culture, Bloomsbury, London.

vessels made of stone and pottery were made in large numbers.[124] Furthermore, buildings made of mud brick were built during the early part of the Naqada Period, 4000 BC to 3600 BC. But these buildings co-existed with buildings made of wattle and mud. Perhaps buildings made of wattle and mud were cheaper to produce than were buildings made of mud brick. Developments in metallurgy occurred by 4000 BC, with the smelting of copper to produce woodworking tools.[125] The latter suggests that basket weaving techniques were applied to produce textiles using linen. The use of dyed thread and dyed cloth also began to make an appearance. Archaeological evidence also suggests that the ground or horizontal loom was used to weave textiles in the Badarian Period between 4500 BC and 3800 BC. Knowledge of copper smelting technology was expanded to the use and production of other metals such as gold, silver, and lead, which were used to make artefacts, chariot parts, and weapons. It was during the early Badarian period that the methods of artificial mummification also began to emerge.[126] Many interrelated innovations in the lands of what would become dynastical Ancient Egypt between 3400BC and 3000BC helped to establish a new society in around 3000BC.[127] The first of these innovations was the invention of writing in 3250BC.[128] However, this writing system has emerged as the ancient Egyptians had begun to use a pictorial system to denote meanings for their written language by 4000 BC.[129] There is some debate as to whether the ancient Egyptian writing system developed independently from the Sumerian writing system or if it developed as a result of the diffusion of knowledge. The latter is possible given the geographical closeness of the two civilizations, which also overlapped in time. The southern Mesopotamian city of Uruk is most likely to have invented writing.[130] Over time the idea, use, and benefits of writing diffused to the ancient Egyptians, who then set up their own pictorial system of writing. The knowledge of writing could

[124] Ibid.

[125] Ibid.

[126] Ibid.

[127] De Mieroop, M. (2011), A History of Ancient Egypt, John Wiley & Sons Ltd, Chichester, United Kingdom.

[128] Ibid.

[129] Shaw, I. (2012), Ancient Egyptian Technology & Innovation, Transformations in Pharaonic Material Culture, Bloomsbury, London.

[130] Wilkinson, T. (2010), The Rise and Fall of Ancient Egypt: The History of a Civilisation from 3000BC to Cleopatra, Bloomsbury, London.

have been spread from Uruk by travelling priests, scholars, merchants, or even through captured slaves and prisoners. As with all inventions throughout history, if the inventing society benefits from the discovery, other societies will adapt and use the invention for their benefit. The writing used in Uruk was in the form of simple pictorial depictions, in about 3100BC.[131] According to the latter, the invention and use of writing can be ascribed to the ruler of Uruk Enmerkar has stated in the ancient texts of Uruk. The invention of writing in Uruk can be attributed to the need to maintain a written record of the transactions through trade, as well to ascertain the levels of state inventories of grain, gold, holdings of land and slaves, and the wealth of the citizens. This would allow the state to be in a better position to extract taxes from the households of Uruk. The simple pictorial script of Uruk took a longer period to develop into Sumerian cuneiform.[132]

In ancient Egypt writing developed further over the subsequent centuries until the world's first complete sentence was constructed in 2750BC.[133] The benefits of writing are that it improves memory and allows the transmission of knowledge as well as its accumulation.[134] As a result, writing may help to indirectly stimulate the development of ideas based on existing knowledge. The oldest writing in ancient Egypt has been found in the predynastic tomb of King Abdju, an ancient Egyptian ruler who ruled 150 years before King Narmer unified Upper and Lower Egypt.[135] The writing found in the tomb was a short inscription, which was pictorial in nature, which evidenced the complexity which would be found in the Hieroglyphics which would develop over the next 3500 years.[136] The Egyptian form of writing was called Hieroglyphics, and was written on papyrus, Egyptian paper, to keep records. However, the people of ancient Egypt also studied Mathematics, Science, and Medicine and they built pyramids and obelisks.[137] These are still marvelled at in the modern world. Writing and

[131] Dumper, M., and Stanley, B. (2007), Cities of the Middle East and North Africa: A Historical Encyclopaedia, ABC-CLIO Inc, Santa Barbara, California.

[132] Ibid.

[133] De Mieroop, M. (2011), A History of Ancient Egypt, John Wiley & Sons Ltd, Chichester, United Kingdom.

[134] Wilkinson, T. (2010), The Rise and Fall of Ancient Egypt: The History of a Civilisation from 3000BC to Cleopatra, Bloomsbury, London.

[135] Ibid.

[136] Ibid.

[137] Deady, K. (2012), Great Civilisations, Ancient Egypt, Beyond Pyramids, Capstone Press, Minnesota.

papyrus also enabled the ancient Egyptians to make mathematical calculations—number operations, areas, and angles.[138] The latter suggests that the ancient Egyptians may have used their knowledge of mathematics to aid their construction of the pyramids and obelisks. Along with limestone quarrying, pyramid construction began in the Third Dynasty in the period from 2686 BC to 2613 BC.[139]

Aegean Civilization: 2700 BC

The civilizations of ancient Egypt, Mesopotamia, and the Indus Valley Civilization had arisen for centuries when Europe was still embracing the savagery of tribal hunter gatherer society. It would be centuries before Europe would emerge from the darkness of barbarity into the twilight of civilization on the shores of the Mediterranean.[140] The blossoming of culture in settlements, with people cultivating crops and engaging in animal husbandry alongside the odd bit of hunting and gathering, began in the late Neolithic at around 4000 BC.[141] At this time the trajectory to the Mycenaean and Minoan civilizations was established.[142] The developing cultures of the islands of the Aegean and southern Laconia came to be at the forefront of development and innovation. The Minoan culture, associated with Knossos, would develop the potter's wheel for producing pottery.[143] This would signify increasing demand from a growing population being met with increased specialization and division of labour. This would require people to be trained, workshops to be built, and wheels to be produced. The Minoan civilization would also produce distinct architecture on a big scale, record official transactions on documents, engage in long-distance trade, engage in ritual practice, store agricultural surpluses centrally, and practise political organization at a regional level.[144]

[138] Shaw, I. (2012), Ancient Egyptian Technology & Innovation, Transformations in Pharaonic Material Culture, Bloomsbury, London.

[139] Ibid.

[140] Glotz, G. (1998), The Aegean Civilisation, Routledge.

[141] Van Andel, T., and Runnels, C. (1988), An essay on the 'emergence of civilisation' in Greece and the Aegean, Antiquity 62: 234–247.

[142] Ibid.

[143] Knappett, CJ. (1999), Tradition and Innovation in Pottery Forming Technology: Wheel-Throwing at Middle Minoan Knossos, BSA 94:101–129.

[144] Ibid.

Following the rise of settlements and culture on the islands of the Aegean in 4000 BC, the settlements of central and north-eastern Greece began to fall behind, and would not be able to catch up for centuries.[145] Excavations at Dimini and Sesklo in Thessaly, mainland Greece, and Knossos on the island of Crete have revealed stone tools and pottery made in the early Neolithic period.[146] Dimini was a settlement of 5000 BC. It covered a site with an area of one hectare which was divided into concentric walls with a three-roomed building in a central court.[147] It has been thought that the central structure is for the elite.[148] The implication is that Dimini society was hierarchical.[149] The first known human occupation of Knossos occurred at around 7000 BC. The pottery of this age found on Knossos bears a distinctively decorated style which is found nowhere else in the Aegean. It must be concluded that Knossos culture developed in isolation from the rest of the Mediterranean.[150] Furthermore, archaeological evidence suggests that the people of Knossos kept domesticated animals and cultivated crops from the time of the earliest occupation of the site.[151] There has been controversy regarding the innovation of animal husbandry and crop cultivation creating agricultural economies, which over the centuries led to further innovation and development. The widely accepted hypothesis is that the practice of onsite animal husbandry and crop cultivation occurred in the Near East first, and then spread to the rest of the world. However, there is no reason why crop cultivation and animal husbandry did not occur independently at different times in different places. This view is supported by some evidence. For example, the domestication of the dog occurred at different times in different parts of the world.[152] However, agricultural colonization may have spread agricultural

[145] Feuer, B. (1983), The northern Mycenaean border in Thessaly, British Archaeological Reports. International Series 176.

[146] Tomkins, P. (2010), Neolithic Antecedents, IN: The Oxford Handbook of the Bronze Age (ca. 3000–1000 BC), Cline, E.(Ed), Oxford University Press, New York.

[147] Tsountas, K. (1908). Ai Proistorikai Acropolis Diminiou Kai Sesklo, Athens: Athens, Archaeological Society.

[148] Halstead, P. (1993), Spondylus shell ornaments from late Neolithic Dimini, Greece: specialised manufacture or unequal accumulation? Antiquity 67, 603–609.

[149] Fried, M.H. (1967), The evolution of political society, New York (NY): Random House.

[150] Isaakidou, V., and Tomkins, P. (2008), Escaping the Labyrinth: The Cretan Neolithic in Context, Oxbow Books.

[151] Ibid.

[152] Higgs, E., and Jarman, M. (1969), The Origins of Agriculture: A Reconsideration, Antiquity XLIII.

practice and innovations such as the use of the plough. As would have knowledge of the exploitation of secondary products such as milk and wool which would have occurred in the period 3000 BC to 4000 BC.[153] As the population grew, land would have become scarcer leading to a dispersal of habitation leading to greater inter-settlement trade rather than just intra-settlement trade.[154] Furthermore, the archaeological evidence of burial sites and stone axes does suggest that there was contact between the peoples of Knossos and those on mainland Greece.[155] The flint sickles have also been found at Dimini and Sesklo,[156] on the mainland, and at Demeter[157] on Knossos. At Dimini and Sesklo archaeologists have also found storage and cooking pots, querns for grinding corn, and knives made of obsidian.[158]

It was many centuries later, between 3000 BC and 2000 BC, that stone buildings and towns began to emerge, with the first palace on Knossos being built between 2000 BC and 1800 BC.[159] Minoan culture on Knossos was at its peak during the period 1600 BC to 1500 BC. Its architecture and decorative style was reflected across Crete and as far as Egypt.[160] By that period two types of written archaic scripts had emerged. These included Cretan hieroglyphics and Linear A; both scripts of the Minoan/Knossos culture have not been deciphered yet.[161] Cretan hieroglyphics

[153] Sherratt, A. G. (1981), Plough and pastoralism: aspects of the secondary products revolution. IN Pattern of the Past: Studies in Honour of David Clarke (eds I. Hodder, G. Isaac and N. Hammond). Cambridge: Cambridge University Press.

[154] Halstead, P. (1981), Counting sheep in Neolithic and bronze age Greece. IN Pattern of the Past: Studies in Honour of David Clarke (eds I. Hodder, G. Isaac and N. Hammond). Cambridge: Cambridge University Press, pp. 307–339.

[155] Higgs, E., and Jarman, M. (1969), The Origins of Agriculture: A Reconsideration, Antiquity XLIII.

[156] Runnels, C., and Murray, P. (2001), Greece Before History: An Archaeological Companion and Guide, Stanford University Press, Stanford, California.

[157] Hagg, R. (1998), Ancient Greek cult practice from the archaeological evidence: Proceedings of the Fourth International Seminar on Ancient Greek Cult, organized by the … Sueciae, series in 8) (Swedish Edition), Svenska Institutet i Athen.

[158] Runnels, C., and Murray, P. (2001), Greece Before History: An Archaeological Companion and Guide, Stanford University Press, Stanford, California.

[159] Scarre, C., and Stefoff, R. (2003), The Palace of Minos at Knossos, Oxford University Press, Oxford.

[160] Ibid.

[161] Ferrara, S. (2015), The beginnings of Writing on Crete: Theory and Context, The Annual of the British School at Athens, 110 (1), pp.27–49.

appeared for the last time at around 1500 BC. It was exclusively used in Crete, with its syllabary being composed of 90 symbols.[162] The first evidence of the use of Cretan hieroglyphics has been traced to the end of 3000 BC.[163] However, there is no evidence that suggest that it was used to convey a specific meaning.[164] Linear A was used more widely by people on the other islands of the Aegean as well as settlements on the mainland in southern Laconia, with its use continuing until 1450 BC.[165] It is believed that an archaic form of Linear A was used to inscribe the first text by stylus on clay tablets in 1800 BC, its syllabary being composed of seventy-five signs.[166] The third Aegean script was Linear B, derived from Linear A, which was used exclusively by the royalty for inscriptions on Mycenaean palaces on Knossos in Crete as well as at other sites on the mainland such as Pylos and Mycenae.[167] Linear B was used until 1200 BC, and its syllabary was represented by eighty-seven signs.[168] It is believed that Linear A was amended by the Mycenaeans in order to form Linear B so that they could write their own language, Greek, in visual form.[169] A version of Cretan writing survived in Cyprus until 1000 BC, its syllabary being represented by fifty-five signs.[170] The development of a written form of language possibly started with a need to record, store, and exchange information. When records of transactions could be 'stored', even in symbolic form, taxes to be collected by the state from individuals and households could be more easily calculated. As the population of the Aegean expanded and settlements dispersed, inter-settlement trade expanded generating information which needed to be recorded due to the limitations of human memory. Over time more and more uses for the writing came into being, and it ceased to be used just for recording and bronze stamps denoting

[162] Oliver, J. (1986), Cretan Writing in the Second Millennium BC, World Archaeology, Vol.17, No.3, Early Writing Systems, pp.377–389.

[163] Yule, P. (1980), Early Cretan Seals: A Study of Chronology, Philipp von Zabern Verlag, Mainz.

[164] Oliver, J. (1986), Cretan Writing in the Second Millennium BC, World Archaeology, Vol.17, No.3, Early Writing Systems, pp.377–389.

[165] Ibid.

[166] Ibid.

[167] Ibid.

[168] Ibid.

[169] Ibid.

[170] Ibid.

either title or rank. Thus, there were economic reasons for the development of a written form of language over time.[171]

However, following an earthquake in 1480 BC, Mycenaeans took control of the administration of Knossos from 1450 BC to 1380 BC, with control ending in 1250 BC after which Knossos entered a phase of semi-habitation.[172]

Indus Valley Civilization: 2600 BC

The Indus Valley Civilization was a contemporary civilization with that of ancient Egypt and Mesopotamia (Sumer and Akkadian), and ancient China (Dick, 2006). However, while its contemporary civilizations continued to prosper, the Indus Valley Civilization went into decline and eventually disappeared, leaving abandoned cities, towns, and villages (McIntosh, 2008). Nevertheless, based on the number of other excavated sites in the Indus Valley and its surrounding regions, the area covered by the Indus Valley Civilization extended 1100km north to south, and 1600 km from west to east.[173] Some archaeologists contend that the Indus Valley Civilization may have been much bigger extending as far as Mesopotamia.[174] Thus, at its height the Indus Valley Civilization would have covered an area much bigger than the areas covered by either the civilization of ancient Egypt or that of Mesopotamia (Sumer and Akkadian).

About 9000 years ago, people lived in the hills to the west of the Indus Valley through which the River Indus flows.[175] The people were still hunter gatherers but kept animals such as cows for milk. However, around 4000 BC people began to cultivate crops on the nutrient-rich lands surrounding and including the flood plains of the Indus River.[176] As a result, over the next few centuries permanent settlements were established. By 3000 BC a

[171] Oliver, J. (1986), Cretan Writing in the Second Millennium BC, World Archaeology, Vol.17, No.3, Early Writing Systems, pp.377–389.

[172] Scarre, C., and Stefoff, R. (2003), The Palace of Minos at Knossos, Oxford University Press, Oxford.

[173] Sen, S. (1988), Ancient Indian History and Civilisation, New age International, New Delhi.

[174] Ibid.

[175] Dick, R. (2006), The Indus Valley Civilisation, Evan Brothers Limited, London.

[176] Ibid.

process of urbanization had started. This can be associated with the establishment of cities such as Harappa and Mohenjo-Daro. The former was situated on the banks of the River Ravi, and the latter on land between the River Indus and the River Ghaggar-Hakra.[177] These ancient cities were 400 miles apart, but each had an identical architecture for the buildings, a layout of buildings and roads, with the same building technology having been used at both sites (Sen, 1988). However, Mohenjo-Daro was slightly bigger than Harappa, and the city occupied 200 square hectares with a population of 20,000 to 40,000 people.[178] It would have been comparable to today's cities of Ur in Iraq and Memphis in Iraq.[179] Other sites associated with the Indus Valley Civilization include Amri and Chanhu-daro in southern Sind, Shortughai in north-east Afghanistan, and Lothal.[180] In Lothal, archaeologists found a brick dockyard which was linked to the Gulf of Cambay by a water channel.[181] In Rakhigarhi, another Indus city 340km southeast of Harappa, archaeologists have found evidence of large-scale craft production.[182] Rakhigarhi was situated on the banks of the River Sarasvati. When this river dried up and disappeared, Rakhigarhi lost the source of its water, and the people left the city which decayed.[183] Archaeological evidence from Dholavira, another Indus city 800km south of Harappa, suggests that the Indus Valley Civilization was based on a hierarchy of wealth rather than on totalitarianism.[184] This is evidenced by the fact that some homes had private wells and covered drains, while other homes had open drains and were next to cesspools.[185] It has also become evident that the people of Dholavira innovated and devised several hydraulic tools and strategies to ensure their city and land had a sufficient source

[177] Sen, B. (2011), Smart Green Civilisations: Indus Valley: Green Lessons from The Past, The Energy and Resources Institute, New Delhi.

[178] Lawler, A. (2008), Boring no more, a Trade Savvy Indus Emerges, Vol.320, Science.

[179] Ibid.

[180] Sen, S. (1988), Ancient Indian History and Civilisation, New age International, New Delhi.

[181] Ibid.

[182] Lawler, A. (2008), Boring no more, a Trade Savvy Indus Emerges, Vol.320, Science.

[183] Sankhyan, A., and Rao, V. (2007), Human Origins, Genome and People of India; Genomic, Palaeontological & Archaeological Evidences, Allied Publishers Private Limited, New Delhi.

[184] Lawler, A. (2008), Boring no more, a Trade Savvy Indus Emerges, Vol.320, Science.

[185] Ibid.

of water because their city was not close to river as were some of the other cities of the Indus Valley Civilization.[186]

An analysis of the cities of Harappa and Mohenjo-Daro illustrates the detailed and thorough town planning of the peoples of the Indus Valley Civilization. Each city had a citadel to the west, with residential town to the east.[187] The houses were built of mud brick, and the brick junctures were sealed with bitumen to ensure water resistance. Moreover, each house had a central courtyard, a water well, as well as a bathroom. The waste point of each bathroom was connected to a central sewer system which ran at street level, covered by stone slabs or mud bricks.[188] The residential areas were laid out in a grid pattern with blocks of houses, connected by narrow roads, with no windows facing the road.[189] However, there was one main road which was about 30ft wide.[190] The cities also had granaries to stock the surplus of agricultural crops. Mohenjo-Daro also had a great bath, which was presumably used for communal bathing. However, it may also have been used to collect rainwater, functioning as a water reservoir. But while neither city had a palace, as did the cities of other ancient civilizations, each city was surrounded by a very tall and very thick mud brick wall. This probably reflected the external dangers faced by the civilizations of the time.

Not only was the Indus Civilization much bigger in terms of land area and population than its contemporary civilizations in ancient Egypt and Mesopotamia, it was also more advanced in some areas of engineering and technology.[191] The latter suggests that the Indus Valley Civilization was also a major driver in the world's first era of globalization, 5000 years ago. In this case, it could trade goods with ancient Egypt and Mesopotamia. At the same time this helped spread ideas through the movement of people from one civilization to another such that an Indus translator went 'native' in Mesopotamia.[192] The key characterization of Indus Valley Civilization was standardization, from cities, to weights and bricks.[193] Moreover, it has

[186] Possehl, G. (2002), The Indus Civilisation: A Contemporary Perspective, Rowman & Littlefield Publishers Inc, London.

[187] Ibid.

[188] Ibid.

[189] Ibid.

[190] Ibid.

[191] Lawler, A. (2008), Boring no more, a Trade Savvy Indus Emerges, Vol.320, Science.

[192] Ibid.

[193] Ibid.

been already discussed the houses of the Indus Valley people were more sophisticated than the houses of the peoples of other contemporary civilizations as they had wells to draw drinking water and bathrooms which fed into the city's sewer system. This kind of homely sophistication would not occur again until the period of the Roman Empire (27 BC–395 AD).[194] However, in contrast to its standardization, oven-baked bricks, and sewers, the Indus Valley Civilization did not leave behind any evidence of its cultural sophistication. There was no evidence of libraries with thousands of written clay tables, no temples, no palaces, no monuments, and no identifiable rulers of the time.[195] Furthermore, the written language of the Indus people has not been deciphered, and only consists of pictorial symbols on seals. No extensive form of the written language has yet been found. One possibility is that, unlike the written language of either Mesopotamia or ancient Egypt, the written language of the Indus Valley Civilization was written on some type of paper which decayed over time, leaving no trace other than dust. Moreover, the sudden appearance of the Indus Valley cities on virgin land, some 600 years after the emergence of the first cities in Mesopotamia in 3200 BC, has puzzled archaeologists.[196] Here the possibility arises that the peoples of the Indus Valley Civilization were either settlers from Mesopotamia or some other unknown civilization which archaeology has not yet found. However, recent excavations have found that some of the Indus cities were not built from scratch. For example, Harappa sits on a site which has been continuously occupied since 3700 BC.[197] Furthermore, archaeological evidence suggests that the pottery style was unique to the Indus Valley Civilization.[198] As was the religious practice which seems to have revolved around goddess worship, tree worship, and the sacred bull. This has some similarities with the type of Hinduism practised today in the villages of Gujarat in today's India, very close to the region which encompassed the Indus Valley Civilization.[199] In addition to having unique pottery and religious practice, the people of the Indus Valley Civilization learned how to mine metals such as copper and bronze, and then use these metals to produce weapons, and they also

[194] Ibid.
[195] Ibid.
[196] Ibid.
[197] Ibid.
[198] Ibid.
[199] Robinson, A. (2015), The Indus: Lost Civilisations, Reaktion Books, London.

used polished metal as mirrors.[200] They also produced fish hooks and razors using mined metal.[201] The world's oldest glass has only been found at Harappa.[202] Other Indus Valley Civilizations included the circular saw, saws with cutting 'teeth', and tubular drills all of which would have been used for different types of woodworking.[203]

Neolithic China

Geographically, China can be divided between north and south. The division is created naturally by the Qinling Mountains. Northern China is dry and cool, and the climate is suitable for cultivating different types of crops such as millet, barley, and soya beans.[204] On the other hand, the climate in Southern China is much wetter, and the region is blessed with more lakes and rivers than the north.[205] Unlike the north, the south of China was home to a variety of ethnic peoples including the Han, the majority ethnic group in China today. However, many of these ethnic peoples were either absorbed or displaced because of Han migration in conjunction with overwhelming and superior military force.[206]

When fossilized Homo erectus fossils were found in a cave at Zhoukoudian, it was originally thought that the Han evolved from Homo erectus. However, mitochondrial DNA analysis has proved that Han Chinese people are descended, like all peoples around the world, from Homo sapiens, who left their East African homeland about 100,000 to 70,000 years ago. Between 8000 BC and 3000 BC, the climate in China was much wetter than it is today. In addition, the geographical structure of the land was also very much different. For example, Shandong was cut off from the rest of the mainland by a sea dried up over time and became filled in.[207] It was in this environment that the ancestors of the modern

[200] Sen, B. (2011), Smart Green Civilisations: Indus Valley: Green Lessons from The Past, The Energy and Resources Institute, New Delhi.

[201] Lawler, A. (2008), Boring no more, a Trade Savvy Indus Emerges, Vol.320, Science.

[202] Ibid.

[203] Agrawal, D. (2007), The Indus Civilisation: An Interdisciplinary Perspective, Aryan Books International.

[204] Tanner, H. (2010), China – A History – Volume 1 – From Neolithic Cultures through the Great Qing Empire, Hackett Publishing Company Inc, Indiana, USA.

[205] Ibid.

[206] Ibid.

[207] Ibid.

Chinese took up farming and established permanent settlements. A warmer climate, a scarcity of edible wild plants, and the reduced number of animals to hunt in conjunction with increasing population densities may have created a need for people to find another source of sustenance.[208] The people then turned to crop cultivation and animal husbandry. This could only be done efficiently in permanent fixed settlements. This gave rise to the emergence of agricultural settlements in the north and in the south of China. In the north, archaeological evidence from Henan, Hebei, Shaanxi, and Gansu supports the view of a dominant Peiligang Culture.[209] On the other hand in the south, archaeological evidence from the provinces of Jiangxi, Guangxi, and Guangdong supports the view of a dominant cord-marked pottery culture.[210] The Peiligang Culture seems to have been the root of Chinese civilization. This is because they buried their dead with turtle shells, and other possessions, which had a symbol inscribed on them. This could have been the beginning of ancestor worship, which is still practised in China today.[211] Turtle shells would then be used 6000 years later by the Shang people to conduct complex rites of divination, and the Peiligang symbols on the turtle shells resembled symbols in the Shang writing system from which contemporary Chinese writing is derived.[212] While the symbols may not be sufficient evidence of the emergence of writing in Neolithic China, it could be a feature of the use of sign language which eventually led to the development of a written language.[213] Writing in China developed over a period of time. It was not until the late Shang period (1200 BC to 1045 BC) that the earliest bronze, on objects belonging to either the nobility or the political elite, inscriptions appear.[214] The inscriptions usually denoted the name of the owner and his/her family, and the inscriptions were usually found on weapons or containers.[215] The

[208] Ibid.

[209] Tanner, H. (2010), China – A History – Volume 1 – From Neolithic Cultures through the Great Qing Empire, Hackett Publishing Company Inc, Indiana, USA.

[210] Ibid.

[211] Perkins, D. (1999), Encyclopaedia of China: History and Culture, Fitzroy Dearborn Publishers, New York, USA.

[212] Tanner, H. (2010), China – A History – Volume 1 – From Neolithic Cultures through the Great Qing Empire, Hackett Publishing Company Inc, Indiana, USA.

[213] Li, X., G. Harbottle, J. Zhang, and C. Wang. (2003), The earliest writing? Sign use in the seventh millennium BC at Jiahu, Henan Province, China. *Antiquity* 77 (295): 31–44.

[214] Moore, O. (2000), Reading the Past: Chinese, University of California Press, Los Angeles.

[215] Ibid.

earliest literature in China emerged during the Zhou Dynasty. The literature was usually written on either silk or strips of bamboo and included historical records such as the 'Rites of Zhou' and poetry such as *The Book of Songs*.[216]

The Peiligang Culture was not the only one in Neolithic China. It is more likely that in addition to the two mentioned cultures, these co-existed with other Neolithic Chinese cultures at the same time. These other cultures included the Longshan, Yangshao, Dawenkou, Xinle, and the Hongshan in the north, and the Majiabang, Hemudu, Daxi, Qujialing, and the Dapenkeng in the south.[217] Therefore, the impact on contemporary Chinese culture and society over time is most likely multicultural.

Two of the best-known Neolithic Chinese cultures are the Yangshao and the Longshan. The latter is the predecessor of the former. The Yangshao Culture was based around the middle reaches of the Yellow River and the valleys of the River Wei.[218] This encompassed the modern-day Chinese provinces of Gansu and Henan provinces. The Yangshao Culture existed between 5000 BC and 3000 BC. The innovative features of the Yangshao Culture were the production of advanced stoneware and the practice of advanced agriculture.[219] The Yangshao Culture cultivated dry crops such as millet and broomcorn millet.[220] All the tools used in the Yangshao Culture were made of stone. Stone hammers were used for construction purposes. Thin stone shovels were used to dig the earth, for weeding and planting, and thin sickles with legs were used for harvesting crops.[221] For fishing, the peoples of the Yangshao Culture used lances and hooks. These could have been made from stone or bone, as these have been found at archaeological sites. Similarly, for hunting animals, the peoples of the Yangshao Culture used arrows, with inverted spikes, made from

[216] Duiker, W., and Spielvogel, J. (2007), World History, Thomson-Wadsworth.

[217] Ibid. Tanner, H. (2010), China – A History – Volume 1 – From Neolithic Cultures through the Great Qing Empire, Hackett Publishing Company Inc, Indiana, USA.

[218] Perkins, D. (1999), Encyclopaedia of China: History and Culture, Fitzroy Dearborn Publishers, New York, USA.

[219] Yinke, D. (2010), Ancient Chinese Civilisations, Cambridge University Press, Cambridge.

[220] The Editorial Committee of Chinese Civilisation. (2007), China: Five Thousand Years of History and Civilisation, City University of Hong Kong.

[221] Ibid.

bone and stone.[222] The inverted design of the arrowhead was innovative as it would be deadlier to animals than the normal arrowhead. The Yangshao people were also able to spin and weave cloth at a primitive level using spinning wheels made of pottery.[223] They were also able to sew primitive cloth and animal skins using bone needles. However, the Yangshao Culture also exhibited very well-developed pottery making skills.[224] They also exhibited spatial and environmental considerations by being able to draw geometric figures and patterns in the shape of animals. The earliest copper artefacts unearthed in the world were found in Anatolia, dating from 9000 years ago.[225] However, the unearthed evidence of Yangshao bronze artefacts were dated to 3000 years later than the copper artefacts found in Anatolia. On the other hand, the Longshan Culture existed between 3000 BC and 1900 BC along the middle and the lower reaches of the Yellow River. This encompasses the locations of contemporary Chinese provinces of Shandong, Henan, Shanxi, and Shaanxi.[226] The Longshan Culture served as the platform for the early Chinese states and the Xia (2100 BC–1600 BC), Shang (1600 BC to 1050 BC), and Zhou (1046 BC to 256 BC) Dynasties.[227] Archaeological evidence supports the view that the Longshan Culture used bronze implements made from a combination of tin and copper. Some take the view that as time progressed this changed the hierarchical structure of society from a matriarchal one to a patriarchal one.[228] In other words, the use of metal tools in agriculture may have favoured males and disadvantage females. As a result, there was a divergence between the crafts sector (copper/bronze metallurgy, pottery, weaving, silk manufacture, jade carving) to the agricultural sector of the primitive economy.[229] However, there is no doubt that the Longshan Culture exhibited technological advancement in comparison to the Yangshao Culture. For example, the carving of jade and the production of silk would have required specific knowledge and a certain level of technical

[222] Ibid.

[223] Ibid.

[224] Yinke, D. (2010), Ancient Chinese Civilisations, Cambridge University Press, Cambridge.

[225] Ibid.

[226] Ibid.

[227] Liu, Li. (2004), The Chinese Neolithic: Trajectories to Early States, Cambridge University Press, Cambridge, England.

[228] Ibid.

[229] Ibid.

sophistication. The Longshan Culture also exhibited a complex social organization as well as class stratification.[230] This could have been due to differences in agricultural production between different farmers. Those farmers who produced more surpluses could accumulate wealth much faster. The wealth would have given these farmers a higher social status than farmers who did not produce as much. Overtime, the differences in wealth in Longshan Culture could have given rise to nobility and commoner. Complex social organization and class stratification could have been associated with increasing population which would have stimulated increasing urbanization and the emergence of walled towns. The fortified walls of Longshan cities were built using a technique known as 'hangtu'. This technique involved ramming earth into a dense structure for building the walls of cities as well as platforms in buildings.[231] The Longshan Culture shares many similarities with the later Shang and Zhou Dynasties: the use of jade in rituals, oracle bones in divination, well-made wheels, and standardized hard-fired pottery.[232]

References

Agrawal, D. (2007). *The Indus civilisation: An interdisciplinary perspective*. Aryan Books International.

Aiello, L. C., & Wheeler, P. (1995). The expensive tissue hypothesis: The brain and the digestive system in human and primate evolution. *Current Anthropology, 36*(2), 199–221.

Arsuaga, J., & Martinez, I. (1998). *The chosen species: The long march of human evolution*. Blackwell Publishing.

Ayala, F., & Cela-Conde, C. (2017). *Processes in human evolution: The journey from early hominins to Neanderthals and modern humans.* Oxford University Press.

Barker, H. (2004). *Iceni*. Bladud Books.

Bertman, S. (2003). *Handbook to life in ancient Mesopotamia*. Oxford University Press.

Bunney, S. (1988). Will the real Homo habilis stand up? *New Scientist, 120*(1636), 33.

[230] Dematte, P. (1999), Longshan-Era Urbanism: The Role of Cities in Predynastic China, Asian Perspectives, Vol.38, No.2, pp.119–153.

[231] Ibid.

[232] Ibid.

Cakmak, I., Graham, R., & Welch, R. (2009). Agricultural and molecular genetic approaches to improving nutrition and preventing micronutrient malnutrition globally. In I. Cakmak & R. Welch (Eds.), *Impacts of agriculture on human health and nutrition – volume 1*. Eolss Publishers Co. Ltd.

Cartwright, J. (2016). *Evolution and human behaviour; Darwinian perspectives on the human condition*. Palgrave Macmillan.

Collins, A. (2014). *Gobekli Tepe: Genesis of the gods: The temple of the watchers and the discovery of Eden*. Bear & Company.

Constable, N. (2009). *World atlas of archaeology*. Thalamus Publishing.

Coolidge, F., & Wynn, T. (2018). *The rise of Homo sapiens: The evolution of modern thinking*. Oxford University Press.

Crawford, H. (1991). *Sumer and the Sumerians*. Cambridge University Press.

De Mieroop, M. (2011). *A history of ancient Egypt*. John Wiley & Sons Ltd.

Deady, K. (2012). *Great civilisations, ancient Egypt, beyond pyramids*. Capstone Press.

Debertolis, P., Gulla, D., & Savolainen, H. (2017). *Archaeoacoustic analysis in enclosure D at Gobekli Tepe in South Anatolia, Turkey, history and archaeology*. The 5th Human and Social Sciences at the Common Conference.

Dick, R. (2006). *The Indus Valley civilisation*. Evan Brothers Limited.

Dietrich, O., Notroff, J., & Schmidt, K. (2017). Feasting, social complexity, and the emergence of the early Neolithic of Upper Mesopotamia: A view from Gobekli Tepe. In R. Chacon & R. Mendoza (Eds.), *Feast, famine or fighting? Studies in human ecology and adaptation* (Vol. 8). Springer.

Duiker, W., & Spielvogel, J. (2007). *World history*. Thomson-Wadsworth.

Dumper, M., & Stanley, B. (2007). *Cities of the Middle East and North Africa: A historical encyclopaedia*. ABC-CLIO Inc.

Dunbar, R. (2014). *Human evolution: Our brains and behavior*. Oxford University Press.

Ferrara, S. (2015). The beginnings of writing on Crete: Theory and context. *The Annual of the British School at Athens, 110*(1), 27–49.

Feuer, B. (1983). The northern Mycenaean border in Thessaly, British Archaeological Reports. International Series 176.

Fleagle, J. (2013). *Primate adaptation & evolution*. Elsevier.

Frere, S. S. (1987). *Britannia: A history of Roman Britain*. Routledge.

Fried, M. H. (1967). *The evolution of political society*. Random House.

Glotz, G. (1998). *The Aegean civilisation*. Routledge.

Goldsworthy, A. (2003). *The complete Roman army*. Thames & Hudson.

Gowlett, J. A. J. (2016). The discovery of fire by humans: A long and convoluted process. *Philosophical Transactions of the Royal Society B: Biological Sciences, 371*(1696), 20150164.

Gresky, J., Haelm, J., & Clare, L. (2017). Modified human crania from Gobekli Tepe provide evidence for a new form of Neolithic skull cult. *Science Advances, 3*(6), e1700564.

Hagg, R. (1998). Ancient Greek cult practice from the archaeological evidence: Proceedings of the Fourth International Seminar on Ancient Greek Cult, organized by the ... Sueciae, series in 8) (Swedish Ed.). Svenska Institutet i Athen.

Halstead, P. (1981). Counting sheep in Neolithic and bronze age Greece. In I. Hodder, G. Isaac, & N. Hammond (Eds.), *Pattern of the past: Studies in honour of David Clarke* (pp. 307–339). Cambridge University Press.

Halstead, P. (1993). Spondylus shell ornaments from late Neolithic Dimini, Greece: Specialised manufacture or unequal accumulation? *Antiquity, 67*, 603–609.

Harari, Y. N. (2014). *Sapiens: A brief history of humankind.* Harper.

Hendrickx, S., & Vermeersch, P. (2000). Pre-history: From the Palaeolithic to the Badarian culture (700,000 to 4000 BC). In I. Shaw (Ed.), *The Oxford history of ancient Egypt.* Oxford University Press.

Higgs, E., & Jarman, M. (1969). The origins of agriculture: A reconsideration. *Antiquity, XLIII*, 31–41.

Holloway, R. L. (1967). The evolution of the human brain: Some notes toward a synthesis between neural structure and the evolution of complex behavior. *General Systems, 12*, 3–19.

Hunter, N. (2015). *Daily life in ancient Sumer.* Heinemann-Raintree.

Isaakidou, V., & Tomkins, P. (2008). *Escaping the labyrinth: The Cretan Neolithic in context.* Oxbow Books.

James, S., & Millett, M. (Eds.). (2001). *Britons and Romans: Advancing an archaeological agenda.* Council for British Archaeology.

Khaitovich, P., Hellman, I., Enard, W., Nowick, K., Leinweber, M., Franz, H., Weiss, G., Lachmann, M., & Paabo, S. (2005). Parallel patterns of evolution in the genomes and transcriptomes of humans and chimpanzees. *Science, 309*(5742), 1850–1854.

Knappett, C. J. (1999). Tradition and innovation in pottery forming technology: Wheel-throwing at middle Minoan Knossos. *BSA, 94*, 101–129.

Kramer, S. (1963). *The Sumerians: Their history, culture and character.* The University of Chicago Press, London.

Lawler, A. (2008). Boring no more, a trade-savvy Indus emerges. *Science, 320*(5881), 1276–1281.

Lewin, R. (2005). *Human evolution: An illustrated introduction.* Blackwell Publishing.

Li, X., Harbottle, G., Zhang, J., & Wang, C. (2003). The earliest writing? Sign use in the seventh millennium BC at Jiahu, Henan Province, China. *Antiquity, 77*(295), 31–44.

Lovejoy, C. O. (1981). The origin of man. *Science, 211*(4480), 341–350.
Mann, C. (2011). The birth of religion. *National Geographic Magazine*. http://ngm.nationalgeographic.com/print/2011/06/gobekli-tepe/mann-text
Marzke, M. W. (1997). Precision grips, hand morphology, and tools. *American Journal of Physical Anthropology, 102*(1), 91–110.
Mattingly, D. J. (2007). *An imperial possession: Britain in the Roman Empire, 54 BC – AD 409*. Penguin.
McIntosh, J. (2008). *The ancient Indus Valley: New perspectives*. ABC-CLIO.
McNeil, D. (1967). The code of Hammurabi. *A.B.A. J., 53*, 444.
Midant-Reynes, B. (2000). Pre-history: From the Palaeolithic to the Badarian culture (700,000 to 4000 BC). In I. Shaw (Ed.), *The Oxford history of ancient Egypt*. Oxford University Press.
Moore, O. (2000). *Reading the past: Chinese*. University of California Press.
Nemet-Nejat, K. (1998). *Daily life in ancient Mesopotamia*. Greenwood Press.
Notroff, J., Dietrich, O., Dietrich, L., Tvetmarken, C., Kinzel, M., Schlindwein, J., Sanmez, D., & Clare, L. (2017). More than a vulture: A response to sweatman and tsikritsis. *Mediterranean Archaeology and Archaeometry, 17*(2), 57–74.
Oliver, J. (1986). Cretan writing in the second millennium BC. *World Archaeology. Early Writing Systems, 17*(3), 377–389.
Parpola, A. (2015). *The roots of Hinduism: The early Aryans and the Indus civilisation*. Published to Oxford Scholarship Online. https://doi.org/10.1093/acprof:oso/9780190226909.001.0001
Perkins, D. (1999). *Encyclopaedia of China: History and culture*. Fitzroy Dearborn Publishers.
Possehl, G. (2002). *The Indus civilisation: A contemporary perspective*. Rowman & Littlefield Publishers Inc.
Roberts, A. (2009). *The incredible human journey*. Bloomsbury Publishing Plc.
Robinson, A. (2015). *The Indus: Lost civilisations*. Reaktion Books.
Rodman, P. S., & McHenry, H. M. (1980). Bioenergetics and the origin of bipedalism. *American Journal of Physical Anthropology, 52*(1), 103–106.
Runnels, C., & Murray, P. (2001). *Greece before history: An archaeological companion and guide*. Stanford University Press.
Saggs, H. (2000). *Peoples of the past: Babylonians*. University of California Press.
Salway, P. (1981). *Roman Britain*. Oxford University Press.
Sankhyan, A., & Rao, V. (2007). *Human origins, genome and people of India; Genomic, palaeontological & archaeological evidences*. Allied Publishers Private Limited.
Sarmiento, E., Sawyer, G., & Milner, R. (2007). *The last human: A guide to twenty-two species of extinct humans*. Yale University Press.
Scarre, C., & Stefoff, R. (2003). *The palace of Minos at Knossos*. Oxford University Press.

Schmidt, K. (2010). Gobekli Tepe – the Stone Age sanctuaries: New results of ongoing excavations with a special focus on sculptures and high reliefs. *Documenta Praehistorica, Ljubljana, 37*, 239–256.

Scranton, L. (2014). *China's cosmological prehistory: The sophisticated science encoded in civilisation's earliest symbols.* Simon & Schuster.

Sen, B. (2011). *Smart green civilisations: Indus Valley: Green lessons from the past.* The Energy and Resources Institute.

Sen, S. (1988). *Ancient Indian history and civilisation.* New Age International.

Shaw, I. (2012). *Ancient Egyptian technology & innovation, transformations in pharaonic material culture.* Bloomsbury.

Sherratt, A. G. (1981). Plough and pastoralism: Aspects of the secondary products revolution. In I. Hodder, G. Isaac, & N. Hammond (Eds.), *Pattern of the past: Studies in honour of David Clarke.* Cambridge University Press.

Simmons, A. (2007). *The Neolithic revolution in the near east; transforming the human landscape.* The University of Arizona Press.

Stanish, C. (2017). *The evolution of human co-operation: Ritual and social complexity in stateless societies.* Cambridge University Press.

Stout, D., Toth, N., Schick, K., & Chaminade, T. (2008). Neural correlates of early Stone Age toolmaking: Technology, language and cognition in human evolution. *Philosophical Transactions of the Royal Society B: Biological Sciences, 363*(1499), 1939–1949.

Tacitus. (c. 116). (2004). *The annals* (A. J. Woodman, Trans.). Penguin Classics.

Takahata, N., Satta, Y., & Klein, J. (1995). Divergence time and population size in the lineage leading to modern humans. *Theoretical Population Biology, 48*(2), 198–221.

Tanner, H. (2010). *China – a history – volume 1 – from Neolithic cultures through the Great Qing Empire.* Hackett Publishing Company Inc.

The Editorial Committee of Chinese Civilisation. (2007). *China: Five thousand years of history and civilisation.* City University of Hong.

Tierney, J., de Menocal, P., & Zander, P. (2017). A climatic context for the out of Africa migration. *Geology, 45*(11), 1023–1026.

Todd, M. (2004). *Roman Britain.* Blackwell.

Tomkins, P. (2010). Neolithic antecedents. In E. Cline (Ed.), *The Oxford handbook of the Bronze Age (ca. 3000–1000 BC).* Oxford University Press.

Tsountas, K. (1908). *Ai Proistorikai Acropolis Diminiou Kai Sesklo.* Athens, Archaeological Society.

Van Andel, T., & Runnels, C. (1988). An essay on the 'emergence of civilisation' in Greece and the Aegean. *Antiquity, 62*, 234–247.

Venn, O., Turner, I., Mathieson, I., de Groot, N., Bontrop, R., & McVean, G. (2014). Strong male bias drives germline mutation in chimpanzees. *Science, 344*(6189), 1272–1275.

Vinter, J. C. (2011). *Ancient Earth mysteries*. AEM Publishing.
Wells, S. (2017). *The journey of man: A genetic odyssey*. Princeton University Press.
Wilkinson, T. (2010). *The rise and fall of ancient Egypt: The history of a civilisation from 3000BC to Cleopatra*. Bloomsbury.
Wilson, R. J. A. (2002). *A guide to the Roman remains in Britain* (4th ed.). Constable and Robinson.
Wrangham, R. (2010). *Catching fire: How cooking made us human*. Profile Books Ltd.
Wrangham, R. W. (2009). *Catching fire: How cooking made us human*. Basic Books.
Wynn, T., Overmann, K., & Coolidge, F. (2016). The false dichotomy; a refutation of the Neanderthal indistinguishability claim. *Journal of Anthropological Sciences, 94*, 201–221.
Yinke, D. (2010). *Ancient Chinese civilisations*. Cambridge University Press.
Yule, P. (1980). *Early Cretan seals: A study of chronology*. Philipp von Zabern Verlag.

CHAPTER 3

Theories of Cognitive Development

Introduction

The first few years of a child's life are important for its mental and physical development.[1] This is because it is in the early years of a child's life that there is the most significant lifetime growth of the brain and the nervous system. This is specifically with regard to new neural connections and the strengthening of existing connections.[2] Furthermore, the early years of a child's life are also important with regard to overall motor development.[3] This is due to the fact that in the early years of a child's life the roots of the advanced motor responses, such as being able to jump up in the air and land on two feet, of later life are put down due to the physical interactions of the infant with its external environment.[4] Imaging of the brain suggests that motor activity and the completion of cognitive tasks co-activate both

[1] Gabbard, C. (2008), Lifelong Motor Development, 5th ed., Pearson Education, San Franciso.

[2] Shonkoff, J., and Phillips, D. (2000), From Neurons to Neighbourhoods: The Science of Early Childhood Development, National Academy Press, Washington.

[3] Veldman, S., Santos, R., Jones, R., Sousa-Sa, E., and Okely, A. (2019), Associations between gross motor skills and cognitive development in toddlers, Early Human Development, 132, pp.39–44.

[4] Gallahue, D., and Ozmun, J., (2002), Understanding Motor Development: Infants, Children, Adolescents, Adults, fifth edition, McGraw-Hill, New York.

S. Ramesh, *The Political Economy of Contemporary Human Civilisation, Volume I*,
https://doi.org/10.1007/978-3-031-84181-1_3

the neo-cerebellum and the dorsolateral prefrontal cortex.[5] This causality is also supported by the experiences of psychologists and educationalists specializing in childhood development.[6] Moreover, the theories associated with childhood development rely upon the causality between motor and cognitive development. Piaget's theory on the childhood development of cognition is associated with the actualization of the brain associated with thinking due to physical movements.[7] Similarly, Systems Theory proposes that the movement of body parts such as the limbs and eyes is caused by the joint action of cognitive and motor processes.[8] Moreover, the theory of the Ecological Perspective suggests that infants can draw upon and process visual information so as to produce physical movements.[9] Those motor skills more closely associated with interaction with cognition were those associated with picking up and holding objects as well as the timing of the associated movements, these effects being stronger in the pre-teenage years of a child than in its teenage years.[10] A bi-directionality has also been detected with regard to the cognition-academic nexus.[11] In other words, consistent exposure to high-quality schooling will aid the development of a child's cognitive and academic ability. Pre-school education is also important as it is at this stage of development that a child acquires the beginnings of the Theory of Mind concepts, perpetual awareness, and the start of inductive and deductive reasoning.[12] The pre-school enrolment will help the child develop his/her language and mathematics

[5] Diamond, A. (2007), Interrelated and interdependent, Dev. Sci. 10, 152–158.

[6] Bowman, B., Donovan, S., and Bums, S. (2001), (Eds.), Committee on Early Childhood Pedagogy, National Academy Press: National Research Institute, Washington, DC.

[7] Piaget, J., and Cook, M. (1952), The Origins of Intelligence in Children, International Universities Press, New York.

[8] Thelen, E., and Smith, L. (1994), A Dynamic Systems Approach to the Development of Cognition and Action, MIT Press, Cambridge, MA.

[9] Gibson, J. (1979), The Ecological Approach to Visual Perception, Lawrence Erlbaum, Hillsdale, NJ.

[10] Veldman, S., Santos, R., Jones, R., Sousa-Sa, E., and Okely, A. (2019), Associations between gross motor skills and cognitive development in toddlers, Early Human Development, 132, pp.39–44.

[11] Peng, P., and Kievit, R. (2020), The Development of Academic Achievement and Cognitive Abilities: A Bidirectional Perspective, Child Development Perspectives, Vol.14, No.1, pp.15–20.

[12] Kazi, S., Kazali, E., Makris, N., Spanoudis, G., and Demetriou, A. (2019), Cognizance in Cognitive Development: A Longitudinal Study, Cognitive Development, 52, 100805.

skills.[13] It has also been found that early pre-school enrolment will have a positive impact on a child's cognitive development from an age of six to late adolescence, aged eighteen.[14] The level of development accessible to a child in the first three years of its life will have a lifetime impact.[15] However, it is at this stage that parents struggle with balancing work with childcare; more free time for the parents may allow them to give quality parenting to their child. Families would benefit from the public provision of in-kind quality child care, in this case.[16] However, it is only in late childhood that children acquire or complete the development of inferential awareness, relational and deductive reasoning, and the awareness of cognitive processes.[17] The link between the development of cognitive abilities in children and specific parts of the brain by such programmes as the Adolescent Brain Cognitive Development (ABCD) study makes available baseline data on the brain development of over 11,000 US children.[18] The data associated with brain development is acquired using magnetic resonance imaging. Other studies have shown that the causality between motor skills and cognitive activity is the strongest in infants.[19] In the study of cognition in infants, executive functions such the ability to concentrate, working memory, and mental agility have been used as measure of cognition.[20] The level of development of executive functions in infants is seen as efficient indicators of a child's school academic performance.[21] This has been

[13] Drange, N., and Havnes, T. (2019), Early Childcare and Cognitive Development: Evidence from an Assignment Lottery, Journal of Labour Economics, Vol.37, No.2.

[14] Dhuey, E., Figlio, D., Karbownik, K., and Roth, J. (2019), School Starting Age and Cognitive Development, Journal of Policy Analysis and Management, Vol.38, No.3, pp.538–578.

[15] Chaparro, J., Sojourner, A., and Wiswall, M. (2020), Early Childhood Care and Cognitive Development, National Bureau of Economic research, Working Paper 26813.

[16] Ibid.

[17] Kazi, S., Kazali, E., Makris, N., Spanoudis, G., and Demetriou, A. (2019), Cognizance in Cognitive Development: A Longitudinal Study, Cognitive Development, 52, 100805.

[18] Compton, W., Dowling, G., and Garavan, H. (2019), Ensuring the Best Use of Data: The Adolescent Brain Cognitive Development Study, JAMA Paediatrics, Vol.173, No.9.

[19] Pereira, K., Valentini, N., and Saccani, R. (2016), Brazilian infant motor and cognitive development: longitudinal influence of risk factors, Pediatr. Int. 58, 1297–1306.

[20] Diamond, A. (2013), Executive functions, Annu. Rev. Psychol. 64, 135–168.

[21] Best, J., Miller, P., Naglieri, J. (2011), Relations between executive function and academic achievement from ages 5 to 17 in a large, representative national sample, Learn. Individ. Differ. 21, 327–336.

specifically associated with the level of working memory.[22] The development of working memory will also allow young children to develop the ability to order events.[23] The lateral prefrontal cortex of the brain is associated with the development of behaviour, language, and cognition.[24] Some studies have also shown a strong connection between the level of agility and working memory as well as between the level of agility and the depth of concentration.[25] However, although the interrelatedness of motor development and cognitive ability has been recognized through research, the emotional development of the child is also important in facilitating the development of learning in a child's early years.[26] Nevertheless, the motor development of a child up to the age of four will have a positive impact of the child's cognitive capacity in terms of working memory capacity and the ability to solve problems from the ages of six to eleven.[27] But the facilitation of the development of the motor skills of very young children will also facilitate the lifelong development of cognitive ability.[28] There is therefore the possibility that the development of cognition from a very young age to adulthood and beyond may follow in sequential stages.[29]

[22] Veldman, S., Santos, R., Jones, R., Sousa-Sa, E., and Okely, A. (2019), Associations between gross motor skills and cognitive development in toddlers, Early Human Development, 132, pp.39–44.

[23] Gelman, R. (1978), Cognitive Development, Ann.Rev. Psychol, 29, pp.297–332.

[24] Fuster, J. (2002), Frontal Lobe and Cognitive Development, Journal of Neurocytology, 31, pp.373–385.

[25] Niederer, I., Kriemler, S., Gut, J., Hartmann, T., Schindler, C., Barral, J et al. (2011), Relationship of aerobic fitness and motor skills with memory and attention in preschoolers (Ballabeina): a cross-sectional and longitudinal study, BMC Pediatr. 11, 34.

[26] Veldman, S., Santos, R., Jones, R., Sousa-Sa, E., and Okely, A. (2019), Associations between gross motor skills and cognitive development in toddlers, Early Human Development, 132, pp.39–44.

[27] Piek, J., Dawson, L., Smith, L., Gasson, N. (2008), The role of early fine and gross motor development on later motor and cognitive ability, Hum. Mov. Sci. 27 (2008) 668–681.

[28] Veldman, S., Santos, R., Jones, R., Sousa-Sa, E., and Okely, A. (2019), Associations between gross motor skills and cognitive development in toddlers, Early Human Development, 132, pp.39–44.

[29] Flavell, J. (1982), On Cognitive Development, Child Development, Vol.53, No.1, pp.1–10.

Piaget's Theory of Cognitive Development

Piaget's theory of cognitive development is based on the notion of 'constructivism'; complex cognitive processes emerge from the incremental moulding of psychological changes in the brain with environmental experiences.[30] Although the hierarchical development of cognitive thought and its physiological structures is universal to all of humanity, the way in which these structures or basic cognitive processes interact with the environment is dependent on the culture of the individual.[31] The roots of Piaget's work lay in his search for how knowledge developed in a child.[32] Indeed, Piaget's focus of analysis was with a human development and genetics emphasis.[33] Much of the research Piaget conducted by observing the reactions of his own children to differently presented scenarios as they grew up.[34] The scenario-induced reactions of children were used to observe their reasoning processes across different states of development.[35] This kind of analysis of childhood responses and behaviours allowed Piaget to put forward the idea that there was a state of correlation between the brain development of children and their behavioural development.[36] However, during Piaget's time, the technology was not available in order to fully explore this correlation and evaluate its truthfulness or its falsehood.[37] However, in recent times with the development of scanning techniques the stages of the brain development of a child can be technologically assessed and

[30] Johnson, S. (2003), The Nature of Cognitive Development, TRENDS in Cognitive Science, Vol.7, No.3.

[31] Dasen, P. R. (1994), Culture and cognitive development from a Piagetian perspective. In W. J. Lonner & R. Malpass (Eds.), Psychology and culture (pp. 145–149). Boston: Allyn & Bacon.

[32] Mayer, S. J. (2005), The early evolution of Jean Piaget's clinical method. History of Psychology, 8(4), 362–382.

[33] Duveen, G. (2000), Piaget ethnographer. Social Science Information, 39(1), 79–97.

[34] Lefmann, T., and Combs-Orme, T. (2013), Early Brain Development for Social Work Practice: Integrating Neuroscience with Piaget's Theory of Cognitive Development, Journal of Human Behaviour in the Social Environment, 23, pp. 640–647.

[35] Mayer, S. J. (2005), The early evolution of Jean Piaget's clinical method. History of Psychology, 8(4), 362–382.

[36] Lefmann, T., and Combs-Orme, T. (2013), Early Brain Development for Social Work Practice: Integrating Neuroscience with Piaget's Theory of Cognitive Development, Journal of Human Behaviour in the Social Environment, 23, pp. 640–647.

[37] Kolb, B., & Fantie, B. D. (2009), Development of the child's brain and behavior, IN C. R. Reynolds & E. Fletcher-Janzen (Eds.), Handbook of clinical child neuropsychology (3rd ed., pp. 19–46). Springer, New York, NY.

correlations made with changes in behaviour during the process of ageing. While Piaget's work and theory were developed in the 1920s they did not become widely available until the 1950s and the 1960s when English translations of his books became widely available.[38]

In any case, Piaget identified four major stages of development in childhood, the success of each successive stage being dependent on the success of the previous stage of development.[39] The first stage is the Sensorimotor Period, which lasted from birth to the age of two. The second stage of development is the Preoperational Thought Period, which lasted from the age of two to the age of seven. The third stage of development is the Concrete Operations Period from the age of seven to the age of eleven. And finally, the Formal Operations Period from the age of eleven to the age of fifteen. The results of Neuroscience research suggest that the infant's experiences and environment in the Sensorimotor Period will set the trajectory of development for an entire lifetime.[40] The development of the brain from birth to the age of two is probably the most dynamic compared to the other years in the life of a human being.[41] During this period of brain development, the experiences and activities of the infant will influence the emergence of the foundations of cognitive framework upon which abstract thinking, reasoning, and planning abilities will be developed.[42] So complex is the Sensorimotor Period from birth to the age of two that Piaget was able to sub-divide this stage into six sub-stages across which an infant's learning was based on the use of its five senses as well as being dependent upon the movement of its limbs.[43] The six sub-stages of development in the Sensorimotor Period included birth to one month, one month to four months, four months to eight months, eight months

[38] Silverthorn, P. (1999), Jean Piaget' s theory of development. Available from: http://chd.gse.gmu.edu/immersion/knowledgebase/theorists/constructivism/Piaget.htm.

[39] Piaget, J. (1973), The child and reality: Problems of genetic psychology, Penguin Books, New York, NY.

[40] Shonkoff, J. P., & Phillips, D. (2000), From neurons to neighbourhoods: The science of early childhood development. National Academy Press, Washington, DC.

[41] Knickmeyer, R. C. et al. (2008). A structural MRI study of human brain development from birth to 2 years. The Journal of Neuroscience, 28(47), 12176–12182.

[42] Levin, H. S., Culhane, K. A., Hartmann, J., Evankovich, K., & Mattson, A. J. (1991), Developmental changes in performance on tests of purported frontal lobe functioning, Developmental Neuropsychology, 7, 377–395.

[43] Lefmann, T., and Combs-Orme, T. (2013), Early Brain Development for Social Work Practice: Integrating Neuroscience with Piaget's Theory of Cognitive Development, Journal of Human Behaviour in the Social Environment, 23, pp. 640–647.

to twelve months, twelve months to eighteen months, and eighteen months to twenty-four months.[44] During sub-stage one, the development of the brain, which at birth only weighs 25% of the adult weight,[45] develops through three processes.[46] Through the first process, dendritic arborization, more and more neurons become interconnected through the branching out of dendrites. The communication between the neurons because of activation or firing as a result of stimulation by neurotransmitters is at the heart of the functioning of the brain.[47] The repeated firing of neurons strengthens their connections, and it is in this process that the roots of learning are to be found.[48] The activities of the infant responsible for brain development in the first sub-stage of the Sensorimotor Period include stimulus received visually as well as the stimulation of muscles and the movement of the limbs.[49] Through this kind of stimuli up to 40,000 synapses a second are formed in the brain of an infant in the first twelve months of its life.[50] It is therefore apparent that during the first sub-stage, the infant is becoming acquainted with and acquiring knowledge about its environment by using its senses.[51] Like all animals, human infants are also born with reflexes. However, whereas in other animals these reflexes act to determine their behaviour, in human infants these reflexes allow for the learning from the environment, which facilitates the incremental

[44] Ibid.

[45] DiPietro, J. A, (2000), Baby and the brain: Advances in child development. Annual Review of Public Health, 21, 455–471.

[46] Lefmann, T., and Combs-Orme, T. (2013), Early Brain Development for Social Work Practice: Integrating Neuroscience with Piaget's Theory of Cognitive Development, Journal of Human Behaviour in the Social Environment, 23, pp. 640–647.

[47] Webb, S. J., Monk, C. S., & Nelson, C. A. (2001), Mechanisms of postnatal neurobiological development: Implications for human development, Developmental Neuropsychology, 19(2), 147–171.

[48] Lefmann, T., and Combs-Orme, T. (2013), Early Brain Development for Social Work Practice: Integrating Neuroscience with Piaget's Theory of Cognitive Development, Journal of Human Behaviour in the Social Environment, 23, pp. 640–647.

[49] Piaget, J., & Inhelder, B. (1969), The Psychology of the Child, Basic Books, New York, NY.

[50] Tau, G. Z., & Peterson, G. S. (2010), Normal development of brain circuits. Neuropsychopharmacology Reviews, 35, 147–168.

[51] Lefmann, T., and Combs-Orme, T. (2013), Early Brain Development for Social Work Practice: Integrating Neuroscience with Piaget's Theory of Cognitive Development, Journal of Human Behaviour in the Social Environment, 23, pp. 640–647.

development of physiological neural pathways and structures in the brain.[52] Furthermore, Piaget associated two processes with a human infant's ability to adapt to its environment.[53] These processes included the assimilation of information and knowledge from the infant's external environment through a reflexive strategy and the accommodation of physiological structures in the brain according to these interactive inputs.[54] However, the processes of accommodation and assimilation are not limited to use in a human's infant stage but is also applicable throughout life during which adaptation to an ever-changing complex environment takes place.

After birth, the primary motor cortex of the infant's brain encompassing the brainstem, the thalamus, the sensorimotor cortex, and the cerebellar vermis experiences rapid development.[55] Moreover, as the infant consumes more food the metabolic rate[56] of the brain is at its highest levels in these regions[57] in comparison to other regions of the brain. In the first sub-stage, the myelin sheath which encapsulates the axons also develops and thickens.[58] And as this process occurs, the speed of transmission of stimuli between the neurons begins to increase as well. The more efficient the development of the myelin sheath, the process of myelination, the better the co-ordination of the visual tracking and the limb movements of the infant.[59] The second sub-stage of the Sensorimotor Period, aged from one to four months, involves the infant developing habits as well as improved co-ordination due to learning. An example of this would be that the infant sucking its thumb is no longer a matter of chance but a deliberate act of

[52] Huitt, W., and Hummel, J. (2003), Piaget's Theory of Cognitive Development, Educational Psychology Interactive, Valdosta, GA: Valdosta State University.

[53] Ibid.

[54] Ibid.

[55] Terumitsu, M., Ikeda, K., Kwee, I. L., & Nakada, T. (2009), Participation of primary motor cortex area 4a in complex sensory processing: 3.0-T fMRI study, Neuroreport, 20(7), 679–683.

[56] Chugani, H. T., Phelps, M. E., & Mazziotta, J. C. (1987), Positron emission tomography study of human brain functional Development, Annals of Neurology, 22, 487–497.

[57] Johnson, M. H. (2001), Functional brain development in humans, Nature, 2, 475–483.

[58] Webb, S. J., Monk, C. S., & Nelson, C. A. (2001), Mechanisms of postnatal neurobiological development: Implications for human development, Developmental Neuropsychology, 19(2), 147–171.

[59] Deoni, S. C. et al. (2011). Mapping infant brain myelination with magnetic resonance imaging. Journal of Neuroscience, 31(2), 784–791. doi: 10.1523/JNEUROSCI.2106-10.2011.

co-ordination between the thumb and the mouth.[60] Furthermore, communication in the infant's brain improves in the first four months of its life as white matter, myelinated axons, develops.[61] The level of integration of motor, sensory, and cognitive information by the infant is very much dependent on the state of development of communication in the brain itself.[62] The development of the ability of the infant to tell its self a part from its environment forms the third stage of the Sensorimotor Period, when the infant is aged between four and eight months. At this stage connections in the hippocampus region of the brain are rapidly laid down, facilitating greater learning and memory.[63] This type of brain development at this stage may help to explain why the infant is engaged in a repetitive learning process during which it identifies specific actions it takes with specific results.[64] The infant also shows greater balance and motor co-ordination during this stage because the cerebellum, the part of the brain responsible for this type of activity, doubles in size.[65] This period marks a transition in the behaviour of the infant from an unintentional impact on its environment to an intentional one.[66] The fourth stage of Piaget's Sensorimotor Period, during which the infant is aged eight to twelve months, shows the infant developing planning skills at a foundation level. Furthermore, at this age the infant's cognitive development allows it to combine interactions with real-world objects and dialogue with others to

[60] Lefmann, T., and Combs-Orme, T. (2013), Early Brain Development for Social Work Practice: Integrating Neuroscience with Piaget's Theory of Cognitive Development, Journal of Human Behaviour in the Social Environment, 23, pp. 640–647.

[61] Barkovich, J. A., Kjos, B. O., Jackson, D. E., & Norman, D. (1988), Normal maturation of the neonatal and infant brain: MR imaging at 1.5 T1. Neuroradiology, 166, 173–180.

[62] Lefmann, T., and Combs-Orme, T. (2013), Early Brain Development for Social Work Practice: Integrating Neuroscience with Piaget's Theory of Cognitive Development, Journal of Human Behaviour in the Social Environment, 23, pp. 640–647.

[63] Paldino, A., & Purpura, D. (1979), Quantitative analysis of the spatial distribution of axonal and dendritic terminals of hippocampal pyramidal neurons in immature human brain. Experimental Neurology, 64, 604–619.

[64] Lefmann, T., and Combs-Orme, T. (2013), Early Brain Development for Social Work Practice: Integrating Neuroscience with Piaget's Theory of Cognitive Development, Journal of Human Behaviour in the Social Environment, 23, pp. 640–647.

[65] Knickmeyer, R. C., et al. (2008). A structural MRI study of human brain development from birth to 2 years. The Journal of Neuroscience, 28(47), 12176–12182.

[66] Lefmann, T., and Combs-Orme, T. (2013), Early Brain Development for Social Work Practice: Integrating Neuroscience with Piaget's Theory of Cognitive Development, Journal of Human Behaviour in the Social Environment, 23, pp. 640–647.

articulate meaningful statements.[67] The emergence of planning at this stage of the infant's life is accompanied by the development of the frontal cortex, which increases in synaptic density,[68] which is instrumental in enabling higher-order cognitive functions.[69] Furthermore, as the number of connections increases in the hippocampus, neuromuscular functioning also increases such that the actions of the infant become more and more intentional. This is particularly because the extent and the quality of the outer sheathing of the corticospinal tract in the brainstem are at a very advanced state within twelve months of birth, and that of the spinal cord within twenty-eight months.[70] The ability of the infant to engage in conscious thought and sensory perception[71] also develops during the fourth stage of the Sensorimotor Period. This will result in the improved physical articulation of thoughts by the infant, resulting in the more effective planning of its actions.[72] This is primarily because of the increased sheathing of three lobes of the brain, including the parietal, occipital, as well as the frontal.[73] In stage 5, twelve to eighteen months, the infant will begin to experiment with its actions in order to determine if an action taken in different ways will produce the same or a similar result.[74] At this stage of development, the infant is able to develop the ability to not only visualize its relationship with other objects in the world but also the relationship

[67] Smillie, D. (1982), Rethinking Piaget's Theory of Infancy, Human Development, 25, pp.282–294.

[68] Huttenlocher, P. R. (1990), Morphometric study of human cerebral cortex development. Neuropsychologia, 28, 517–527.

[69] Luna, B., et al. (2001), Maturation of widely distributed brain function subserves cognitive development. Neuroimage, 13, 786–793.

[70] Brody, B., Kinney, H., Kloman, A., & Gilles, F. (1987), Sequence of central nervous system myelination in human infancy: I. An autopsy study of myelination. Journal of Neuropathology & Experimental Neurology, 46, 283–301.

[71] Paterson, S. J., Heim, S., Friedman, J. T., Choudhury, N., & Benasich, A. A. (2006), Development of structure and function in the infant brain: Implications for cognition, language and social behavior. Neuroscience and Biobehavioral Reviews, 30, 1087–1105.

[72] Lefmann, T., and Combs-Orme, T. (2013), Early Brain Development for Social Work Practice: Integrating Neuroscience with Piaget's Theory of Cognitive Development, Journal of Human Behaviour in the Social Environment, 23, pp. 640–647.

[73] Paterson, S. J., Heim, S., Friedman, J. T., Choudhury, N., & Benasich, A. A. (2006), Development of structure and function in the infant brain: Implications for cognition, language and social behavior. Neuroscience and Bio-Behavioral Reviews, 30, 1087–1105.

[74] Lefmann, T., and Combs-Orme, T. (2013), Early Brain Development for Social Work Practice: Integrating Neuroscience with Piaget's Theory of Cognitive Development, Journal of Human Behaviour in the Social Environment, 23, pp. 640–647.

between objects.[75] The infant also develops the ability to visualize and to think about an object even when it cannot be seen, perceiving that it is located out of sight.[76] The perception that objects exist even if they cannot be seen is a big stride in the development of the cognition of the infant.[77] The cognitive skills associated with the retrieval of objects by the infant are associated with the development of the dorsolateral prefrontal cortex (DPC) of the brain.[78] The DPC region of the brain is responsible for the organization and regulation of motor responses as well as the planning of these responses by the infant.[79] During this stage the basal ganglia caudate nucleus also develops in volume, and this correlates with the motor development of the infant.[80] The developments in the brain during this period can be associated with the infant gaining the ability to walk and crawl to different locations by facilitating muscle co-ordination. The sixth and final stage (eighteen to twenty-four months) of the Sensorimotor Period is associated with the development of the infant's creativity and insight, leading the path to Piaget's pre-functional thought period.[81] During this stage, the infant can use symbols to pretend that a horse can be represented by a stick, for example.[82] By interacting with objects, infants at this stage of development can develop their own techniques in dealing with the objects. This is intelligence acquired through reflective learning.[83] Nevertheless, there is some evidence to suggest that cognitive development and

[75] Thomas, R. M. (1996), Comparing theories of child development, Brooks/Cole Publishing Company, Pacific Grove, CA.

[76] Ibid.

[77] Piaget, J., & Cook, M. (Trans.) (1954), The development of object construct. In The construction of reality in the child (pp. 3–96). New York, NY: Basic Books.

[78] Diamond, A. (1990), The development and neural bases of memory functions as indexed by the AB and delayed response tasks in human infants and infant monkeys. Annals of the New York Academy of Sciences, 60, 231–267.

[79] Johnson, M. H. (2001), Functional brain development in humans. Nature, 2, 475–483.

[80] Herrero, M. T., Barcia, C., & Navarro, J. M. (2002), Functional anatomy of thalamus and basal ganglia. Child's Nervous System, 18, 386–404.

[81] Thomas, R. M. (1996), Comparing theories of child development. Pacific Grove, CA: Brooks/Cole Publishing Company.

[82] Lefmann, T., and Combs-Orme, T. (2013), Early Brain Development for Social Work Practice: Integrating Neuroscience with Piaget's Theory of Cognitive Development, Journal of Human Behaviour in the Social Environment, 23, pp. 640–647.

[83] Piaget, J. (1963), The origins of intelligence in children, W.W. Norton & Company, Inc, New York, NY.

adaptation to the environment are dependent on social structures.[84] For example, cognitive development may be more favourable in environments and cultures in which education is valued. In the sixth and the final stage of development, the infant is also able to control its behaviour, initiating actions and then curtailing these as required by the environment. This behavioural control is associated with the development of connections in the cerebellum, thalamus, striatum, and the neocortex regions of the infant's brain.[85] By the end of the first twenty-four months of an infant's life, its brain size and development with regard to the density of neurons, glia, axons, and dendritic connections is just over 80% of the adult size.[86] It is estimated that the brain of the infant grows in capacity over the first twelve months of its life by just over 100% and by 15% in the subsequent twelve months.[87] However, in addition to the increase in the size of the brain of the infant in the first twelve months of its life, the ongoing efficient organization of synaptic connections to allow for the more effective transmission of information through the different regions of the brain is also important.[88] Thus, increasing cognitive capacity is associated with increasing synaptic connections, the loss of weak synaptic connections and the strengthening of stronger (reinforced), important connections are an important features of brain development during early childhood.[89] Moreover, as the physiological structures develop and become used more often, the better these perform with regard to cognitive thinking.[90] Therefore, it follows intuitively that as people get older, the better they

[84] Buck-Morss, S. (1975), Socio-Economic Bias in Piaget's Theory and Its Implications for Cross-Cultural Studies, Hum. Dev 18, pp.35–49.

[85] Luna, B., et al., (2001). Maturation of widely distributed brain function subserves cognitive development. Neuroimage, 13, 786–793.

[86] Knickmeyer, R. C. et al. (2008). A structural MRI study of human brain development from birth to 2 years. The Journal of Neuroscience, 28(47), 12176–12182.

[87] Webb, S. J., Monk, C. S., & Nelson, C. A. (2001). Mechanisms of postnatal neurobiological development: Implications for human development. Developmental Neuropsychology, 19(2), 147–171.

[88] Luna, B., et al., (2001). Maturation of widely distributed brain function subserves cognitive development. Neuroimage, 13, 786–793.

[89] Casey, B. J., Giedd, J. N., & Thomas, K. M. (2000), Structural and functional brain development and its relation to cognitive development. Biological Psychology, 54, 241–257.

[90] Larsen, R. (1973), Levels of Conceptual Development in Melodic Permutations Concepts Based on Piaget's Theory, Journal of Research in Music Education, Vol.21, No.3, pp.256–263.

will be able to solve problems and tasks with practice.[91] While Piaget's theory of cognitive development may explain how the interactions of an infant may facilitate the development of physiological cognitive structures in the brain, it may not fully explain the creativity and emotions of human adulthood.[92]

Knowledge of the development of the brain of an infant in the very first years of its life will allow policymakers to devise public policies that will facilitate more effective brain development.[93] State-led interventions on how infants are nurtured will thus have a positive effect on its entire life. It is also self-evident that there is a causal relationship between the development axons, neurons, and dendritic connections and the environment in which a child is nurtured.[94] It therefore follows that if the environment in which an infant is nurtured is changed, then the neural pathways or connections between neurons in its brain will also change.[95] In this case, it is evident that maturation by itself is not enough to explain the cognitive development of an individual, but that the social and cultural influences in the environment of an infant are also important.[96] Moreover, the time each infant spends developing in the context of Piaget's sub-stages of the Sensorimotor Period will vary.[97] This may suggest that teachers should devise individual student teaching plans and not use a generic teaching plan for all students.[98] Suitable individual teaching plans may help to

[91] Larsen, R. (1973), Levels of Conceptual Development in Melodic Permutations Concepts Based on Piaget's Theory, Journal of Research in Music Education, Vol.21, No.3, pp.256–263.

[92] Riegel, K. (1973), Dialectic Operations: The Final Period of Cognitive Development, Human Develop, 16, pp.346–370.

[93] Egan, M., Neely-Barnes, S., & Combs-Orme, T. (2011), Integrating neuroscience into the lifespan. Journal of Social Work Education, 47(2), 269–282.

[94] Schore, A. N. (2001), Effects of a secure attachment relationship on right brain development, affect regulation, and infant mental health. Infant Mental Health Journal, 22(1–2), 7–66.

[95] Clark, D. A., & Beck, A. T. (2010), Cognitive theory and therapy of anxiety and depression: Convergence with neurobiological findings. Trends in Cognitive Sciences, 14(9), 418–424.

[96] Driver, R. (1978), When is a stage not a stage? A Critique of Piaget's theory of cognitive development and its application to science education, Educational Research, 21;1, 54–61.

[97] Kamii, C. (1982), Number in preschool and kindergarten: Educational implications of Piaget's theory. National Association for the Education of Young Children, Washington, DC.

[98] Driver, R. (1978), When is a stage not a stage? A Critique of Piaget's theory of cognitive development and its application to science education, Educational Research, 21;1, 54–61.

accelerate the cognitive development of each student.[99] The more teachers are able to ascertain and understand the state of cognitive development of each student, the more productive the teaching will be in facilitating learning.[100] Moreover, teaching and learning techniques which facilitate a higher level of thinking in learners will facilitate greater levels of intellectual development, and the generation of new knowledge.[101] Therefore, a better understanding of human behaviour can only be achieved through a biological approach.[102] Thus, an appreciation of the biology of the human being is important for devising interventionist strategies.[103]

Vygotsky's Theory of Cognitive Development

Vygotsky was a psychologist based in the former USSR. His analysis of human psychological functioning was based not on a modular approach but on a systems approach.[104] The implication of this is that Vygotsky did not believe that psychological functions such as the development of memory should be studied separately from the development of the psychological system itself.[105] Moreover, Vygotsky believed that the focus of research should be on the changing nature of the relationships between the different psychological functions.[106] This, therefore, emphasizes a systems approach to the analysis of psychological functions rather than a modular one. The systemic approach to the analysis of psychological functions views these functions as arising from a synergy of biological and

[99] Zimmerman, B. J., & Whitehurst, G. J. (1979). Structure and function: A comparison of two views of the development of language and cognition. In G. J. Whitehurst and B. J. Zimmerman (Eds.), *The functions of language and cognition*, Academic Press, New York.

[100] Ojose, B. (2008), Applying Piaget's Theory of Cognitive Development to Mathematics Instruction, The Mathematics Educator, Vol.18, No.1, pp.26–30.

[101] Wach, H. (1981), Visual Implications of Piaget's Theory of Cognitive Development, Journal of Learning Disabilities, Vol.14, No.10.

[102] Combs-Orme, T. (2013), Epigenesis and the social work imperative. Social Work, 58(1), 23–30.

[103] Lefmann, T., and Combs-Orme, T. (2013), Early Brain Development for Social Work Practice: Integrating Neuroscience with Piaget's Theory of Cognitive Development, Journal of Human Behaviour in the Social Environment, 23, pp. 640–647.

[104] Vasileva, O., and Balyasnikova, N. (2019), (Re) Introducing Vygotsky's Thought: From Historical Overview to Contemporary Psychology, Frontiers in Psychology, Volume 10, Article 1515.

[105] Ibid.

[106] Luria, A. R., and Vygotsky, L. S. (1930/1992), Ape, primitive man and child, 1930/1992, Harvester Wheatsheaf: Great Britain

psychological processes. This is in contrast to the reductionist view in psychological research, encompassing Cartesian thinking which views a divergence between biological and psychological processes.[107] However, Vygotsky believed that an individual could not be separated from either its social or its biological environment.[108] The implication is that an analysis of both is important for reaching a better understanding of the cognitive and psychological development of the individual. Nevertheless, although Vygotsky believed in the robustness of the systemic analysis of psychological functions, he also believed a single unique psychological system is made up of many interdependent components.[109] Each of the elements of the psychological system contributes to the functioning of the system as a whole, and if one element changes then the whole system will be affected.[110] Similarly, when an element of the psychological system becomes one of its constituents, then the element also changes. Analogously, if the human mind can be a psychological system, then the elements which make it a whole functioning system must have developed from earlier basic elements. However, as the human mind becomes as one through the fusion of its elements, then the way in which psychological functioning behaves acquires new features. For example, decision making is affected by emotional states.[111] Nevertheless, the organization of elements in a psychological system will follow a hierarchical structure. The implication is that some elements may be functionally below those above them.[112] With regard to the human mind, Vygotsky may have held the view that its elements were also structured in a hierarchical manner. For example, higher-level psychological functions such as decision making and the transmission of knowledge via language and speech are dependent on lower-level psychological

[107] Toomela, A. (2015), Vygotsky's theory on the Procrustes' bed of linear thinking: looking for structural–systemic theseus to save the idea of 'social formation of mind, Cult. Psychol. 21, 318–339. doi: 10.1177/1354067X15570490.

[108] Vasileva, O., and Balyasnikova, N. (2019), (Re) Introducing Vygotsky's Thought: From Historical Overview to Contemporary Psychology, Frontiers in Psychology, Volume 10, Article 1515.

[109] Toomela, A. (2015), Vygotsky's theory on the Procrustes' bed of linear thinking: looking for structural–systemic theseus to save the idea of 'social formation of mind. Cult. Psychol. 21, 318–339. doi: 10.1177/1354067X15570490.

[110] Vasileva, O., and Balyasnikova, N. (2019), (Re) Introducing Vygotsky's Thought: From Historical Overview to Contemporary Psychology, Frontiers in Psychology, Volume 10, Article 1515.

[111] Ibid.

[112] Ibid.

functions such as the formation of concepts and memory.[113] It was Vygotsky's contention that isolated elements of cognition such as memory would 'merge' with higher-order psychological functions which developed much earlier, for example speech.[114] However, it is not clear how lower-level psychological functions may affect higher-level psychological functions, especially in development.[115] Nevertheless, the system approach to the development of psychological functions led Vygotsky to acknowledge that the hierarchical organization of psychological functions into systems would mean that a better understanding of the developmental processes an individual is subject to then increases the chances of achieving a better understanding of the human mind.[116] Moreover when a component of a psychological system becomes fully integrated with it, then the properties of both the system and the component change.[117] Once a child acquires the ability to speak and to understand language, this then acts as a medium of transmission of information between the mind of the child and its environment. This is in addition to the other ways in which a child can acquire information about its environment, for example through its eyes, ears, touch, and smell. However, language has the biggest impact on shifting psychological functions to a higher level as the new-born baby transits into childhood and then adulthood.[118] Furthermore, from Vygotsky's perspective to understand how human cognition develops, it is not enough to study the mind of an adult, which typically represents the final product of several years of psychological development. In this case the development of cognition and the human mind can only be better understood through the study of how the brain of a new-born develops subject to the environment. This is specifically in the context of psychological processes which promotes the development of a hierarchical psychological system and its functionality. Moreover, over time as the child

[113] Ibid.

[114] Ibid.

[115] Wertsch, J. V., and Tulviste, P. (1992), L. S. Vygotsky and contemporary developmental psychology. Dev. Psychol. 28, 548–557. doi: 10.1037/0012-1649.28.4.548.

[116] Vasileva, O., and Balyasnikova, N. (2019), (Re) Introducing Vygotsky's Thought: From Historical Overview to Contemporary Psychology, Frontiers in Psychology, Volume 10, Article 1515.

[117] Kohler, W. (1947). Gestalt psychology, Liveright, New York.

[118] Vasileva, O., and Balyasnikova, N. (2019), (Re) Introducing Vygotsky's Thought: From Historical Overview to Contemporary Psychology, Frontiers in Psychology, Volume 10, Article 1515.

has new experiences using physical activity and verbal communications, neural connections in the brain will reorganize to form new psychological functional systems.[119] Thus, the first few years of a child's life is accompanied by a recurring series of rewiring's of the brain.[120] Disorders arising from both brain damage and disorders which affect brain development can be better understood by considering the brain as a hierarchical structure.[121] In this hierarchical ordering of psychological functions, damage to lower levels will affect higher-level functions, and damage to higher-level sub-systems may affect lower-level functions.

A systemic analysis of psychological functions can also benefit from cultural knowledge.[122] This is in the context of a search by psychological researchers in the last century for a universal theory of the development of the human brain and mind.[123] However, research in the first decade of the twenty-first century has indicated that culture does matter in affecting psychological functions and abilities.[124] In this case whereas human beings are born with the same psychological mechanisms, processes, and systems, cultural differences may result in the development of varying levels of psychological functions. Furthermore, differences in language complexity between diverse cultures may also facilitate differences in the development of not only psychological functions but also brain development. And in the context of language development and the mind, Vygotsky believed that the age of two is an important point for cognitive development because it is at this age speech and thought processes begin to integrate.[125]

[119] Ibid.

[120] De Graaf-Peters, V. B., and Hadders-Algra, M. (2006), Ontogeny of the human central nervous system: what is happening when? Early Hum. Dev. 82, 257–266. doi: 10.1016/j.earlhumdev.2005.10.013.

[121] Vasileva, O., and Balyasnikova, N. (2019), (Re) Introducing Vygotsky's Thought: From Historical Overview to Contemporary Psychology, Frontiers in Psychology, Volume 10, Article 1515.

[122] Ibid.

[123] Vasileva, O., and Balyasnikova, N. (2019), (Re) Introducing Vygotsky's Thought: From Historical Overview to Contemporary Psychology, Frontiers in Psychology, Volume 10, Article 1515.

[124] Benson, J. E., and Sabbagh, M. A. (2010), Theory of mind and executive functioning: a developmental neuropsychological approach, IN Developmental social cognitive neuroscience, Zelazo, P., Chandler, M., and Crone, E. (eds), Psychology Press, New York.

[125] Vasileva, O., and Balyasnikova, N. (2019), (Re) Introducing Vygotsky's Thought: From Historical Overview to Contemporary Psychology, Frontiers in Psychology, Volume 10, Article 1515.

Moreover, according to Vygotsky it is at the age of two that a child's knowledge of vocabulary increases rapidly, and it is able to associate the extent of the use of language with behaviours, actions, and the immediate environment.[126] As a result the developing child is not only able to use language and thought processes for communication but also for problem solving. In the development of human cognition, language therefore plays numerous roles.[127] Firstly, language allows an infant to not only acquire knowledge, but overtime to construct distinct pieces of knowledge into a coherent framework. Secondly, language is required for the acquisition of knowledge and knowledge is required for the acquisition of language. Thirdly, the thoughts of children will be evident in the language they use. Lastly, the use of language allows children to not only solve problems but also to reflect on their own behaviours.

In terms of Vygotsky's thinking, the environment faced by a human being is one that is affected by both social and cultural factors.[128] Moreover, the environment is most immediately created by humans, and the space between humans is integrated through communication using language. It was the connection of a human environment and the use of language which was most important for Vygotsky, especially from the perspective of the development of cognition, a process he referred to as internalization.[129] The latter could also be thought of as the process of generating and organizing thoughts, which Vygotsky referred to as inner speech, using language by the child.[130] Inner speech not only facilitates the organization of thoughts but also the exchange of thoughts through language and the use of speech. However, in addition to the environment and the use of language in mediating the environment, the development of human

[126] Ibid.

[127] Mahmoodi-Shahrebabaki, M. (2019). Vygotsky, Education, and Literacy. Unpublished manuscript, Department of Literacy Studies, Middle Tennessee State University.

[128] Stetsenko, A., and Arievitch, I. M. (2010), Cultural-historical activity theory: foundational worldview and major principles, IN The sociocultural turn in psychology: The contextual emergence of mind and self, Martin, J., and Kirschner, S. (Eds), Columbia University Press, New York.

[129] Vasileva, O., and Balyasnikova, N. (2019), (Re) Introducing Vygotsky's Thought: From Historical Overview to Contemporary Psychology, Frontiers in Psychology, Volume 10, Article 1515.

[130] Lewis, C. (2019), Vygotsky and Moral Education: A Response to and expansion of Tappan, Educational Philosophy and Theory, 51:1, 41–50.

cognition is dependent on more knowledgeable others (MKOs) and zone of proximal development (ZPD).[131] The former represents individuals who are more cognitively developed than the learner is, a parent in the eyes of a child, while the latter is the gap between potential cognitive development and actual cognitive development as measured through problem-solving ability.[132] Learners can internalize skills and increase their ZPDs in the process by gaining knowledge from the MKOs.[133] An analytical framework, for studying the development of cognitive processes, which encompasses the acquisition and use of language by an infant in its socio-economic environment is crucial to understanding that such processes are non-individualistic.[134]

The Development of Measured Intelligence

Intelligence can be defined from three perspectives.[135] These include measured intelligence, social intelligence, and biological intelligence. Measured intelligence is a composite of three features: error checking, persistence, and mental processing speed. Eysenck's model of measured intelligence arises from the feature of tests that different individuals may achieve the same result while at the same time getting different questions wrong.

The relationship between intelligence and personality has been empirically evaluated by using three different methodologies.[136] The first method involves analysing correlations between measured indicators of personality and intelligence.[137] The second approach considers that intelligence is a composite part of personality, involving the development of measures of

[131] Ibid.

[132] Ibid.

[133] Ibid.

[134] Kontopodis, M. (2019) Transformative activist stance and pedagogy of daring: Moving beyond Lev Vygotsky in dialogue with Anna Stetsenko, Pedagogy, Culture & Society, 27:2, 301–304, DOI: 10.1080/14681366.2018.1475890.

[135] Eysenck, H. J. (1992). Intelligence: the one and the many? IN Detterman, D.K (Ed.), Current topics in human intelligence, Vol. 2: is mind modular or unitary? (pp. 83–116). Ablex, Norwood, NJ.

[136] Harris, J. (2004), Measured Intelligence, achievement, openness to experience and creativity, Personality and Individual Differences, 36, pp.913–929.

[137] Zeidner, M. (1995). Personality and trait correlates of intelligence IN Saklofske, D.H and Zeidner, M. (Eds.), International handbook of personality and intelligence (pp. 299–319). New York: Plenum Press.

intelligence as a personality trait.[138] The third approach to investigating the link between intelligence and personality involves analysing the links between the dimensions of intelligence with the dimensions of personality.[139] This third approach has been used to evaluate the relationship between intelligence and personality using achievement requirements as a personality trait.[140] The findings of this empirical research used Eysenck's model of intelligence[141] in order to evaluate the relationship between personality traits and intelligence. In this case, error checking and persistence, behavioural features specified by Eysenck (1982) in his model, contributors to intelligence, were taken to be personality traits. The resulting analysis indicated that there was a positive relationship between intelligence and these personality traits. The idea that intelligence may be a composite of an individual's personality may also be rooted in the link associated with 'openness to experience'.[142] The latter is associated with the creative aspects of an individual.[143] It has also been empirically found that there is a positive correlation between 'openness to experience' and intelligence.[144] The link between 'openness to experience' and intelligence may be better understood by evaluating the differences in verbal reasoning scores between twins and single births.[145] In this case, the verbal reasoning scores of twins were much lower than that of single births.[146] The reason for this may be that differences in the post-natal environment favoured the cognitive development of the single birth child compared to that of twins; and that both pre-birth and birth experiences had no impact on the cognitive

[138] Ackerman, P. L. (1997). Personality, self-concept, interests and intelligence: which construct doesn't fit? Journal of Personality, 65, 171–204.

[139] Raad, B., and Schouwenburg, H. (1996), Personality in Learning and Education: A Review, European Journal of Personality, Vol.10, Issue 5.

[140] Harris, J. (2004), Measured Intelligence, achievement, openness to experience and creativity, Personality and Individual Differences, 36, pp.913–929.

[141] Eysenck, H. J. (1982), A model for intelligence, Springer-Verlag, New York.

[142] McCrae, R. R., and Costa, P. T. Jr, (1997), Conceptions and correlates of openness to experience IN Hogan, R., Johnson, J.A and Briggs, S. R (Eds.), Handbook of personality psychology (pp. 825–847), Academic Press, San Diego, CA.

[143] McCrae, R. R. (1987), Creativity, divergent thinking, and openness to experience. Journal of Personality and Social Psychology, 52, 1258–1265.

[144] Harris, J. (2004), Measured Intelligence, achievement, openness to experience and creativity, Personality and Individual Differences, 36, pp.913–929.

[145] Record, R.G., McKeown, T., and Edwards, J. (1970), An Investigation of the difference in measured intelligence between twins and single births, Ann. Hum. Genet., Lond, 34, 11.

[146] Ibid.

development of either single births or on the twins.[147] The difference between the measured intelligence of twins and single births highlights the importance of the quality of a child's post-natal environment for its cognitive development.

There are two types of processes associated with human cognition.[148] The first is a sub-conscious emotional response which does not involve a 'cognitive' assessment of the situation, and is therefore automatic. The second is a measured response based on a cognitive assessment of the situation. This second response may be comparable with the axioms of probability theory.[149] The former can be defined as emotional intelligence (EI). Emotional intelligence (EI) is the ability to recognize, show, appreciate, control, and utilize human emotions.[150] Some researchers believe that EI is different from features of measured intelligence associated with personality and intelligence, playing an important role in the development of an individual.[151] Moreover, empirical findings suggest that the quality of such an ability will have positive feedback effects on performance at work, in relationships, as well as on health, and academic performance.[152] For example, the development of team emotional intelligence has a positive feedback effect on separating relationship conflict and task conflict.[153] Therefore, if constructive ways can be found to improve emotional intelligence then the effects on individual psychological well-being can only be positive.[154] But in order to improve the level of an individual's emotional intelligence, it is first necessary to measure it. This is achievable using a

[147] Ibid.

[148] Kahneman, D. (2011), Thinking, fast and slow, Palgrave Macmillan, London.

[149] Dellermann, D., Ebel, P., Sollner, M., and Leimeister, J. (2019), Hybrid Intelligence, Bus Inf Syst Eng 61 (5), pp. 637–643.

[150] Petrides, K. V., and Furnham, A. (2003). Trait emotional intelligence: Behavioural validation in two studies of emotion recognition and reactivity to mood induction. European Journal of Personality, 17, 39–57. doi:10.1002/per.466.

[151] Ciarrachi, J., Chan, A., and Bajgar, J. (2001). Measuring emotional intelligence in adolescents, Personality and Individual Differences, 31, pp.1105–1119.

[152] Martins, A., Ramalho, N., & Morin, E. (2010). A comprehensive meta-analysis of the relationship between emotional intelligence and health. Personality and Individual Differences, 49, 554–564. doi: 10.1016/j.paid.2010.05.029.

[153] Lee, C., and Wang, C. (2017), The Effect of Team Emotional Intelligence on Team Process and Effectiveness, Journal of Management and Organisation, 25:6, pp.844–859.

[154] Kotsou, I., Mikolajczak, M., Heeren, A., Gregoire, J., and Leys, C. (2019), Improving Emotional Intelligence: A Systematic Review of Existing Work and Future Challenges, Emotion Review, Vol.11, No.2, pp.151–165.

competency-based measure based upon which a questionnaire can be derived.[155] Nevertheless, perhaps further empirical work is required to confirm whether policies to develop emotional intelligence will have a positive impact on work performance, both academic and non-academic.[156] However, it has been empirically found that in an organization context, emotional intelligence is a contributing factor towards individual success.[157] However, emotional intelligence falls within the context of 'multiples intelligences,' which also includes cognitive abilities.[158] The latter is dependent on the environment in which an individual lives and works. Therefore, if the work environment is not sufficiently conducive, then it may be the case that not only do cognitive intelligence fail to develop but also emotional intelligence.[159] In the context of the nature versus the nurture debate it has been found that both intelligence and practice are important for the lifelong development of complex cognitive skills.[160] And while IQ is a measure of general cognitive ability, it should be a measure of an evolutionary formative construct.[161]

Cognitive ability may be difficult to compare because current tests provide a range of scores which do not have any basis in psychometric theory.[162] The dearth of test scores available commercially may be due to the need of the test publishers to generate revenues.[163] Studies into the impact of training on the development of emotional intelligence also have flaws, although it is evident that such training does positively impact on

[155] Dulewicz, V., and Higgs, M. (1999), Can emotional intelligence be measured and developed, Leadership & Organisation. Development Journal 20/5, pp.242–252.

[156] Ibid.

[157] Dulewicz, S.V. and Higgs, M.J. (1998a), "Emotional intelligence: managerial fad or valid construct?", Henley Working. Paper 9813, Henley Management College.

[158] Gardner, H. (1983), Frames of Mind, Harper-Collins, New York, NY.

[159] Dulewicz, S.V. and Higgs, M.J. (1998a), "Emotional intelligence: managerial fad or valid construct?", Henley Working. Paper 9813, Henley Management College.

[160] Vaci, N., Edelsbrunner, P., Stern, E., Neubauer, A., Bilalic, M., and Grabner, R. (2019), The Joint Influence of Intelligence and Practice on Skill Development Throughout the Life Span, PNAS, Vol116, No.37.

[161] Kovacs, K., and Conway, A. (2019), What is IQ? Life Beyond 'General Intelligence,' Current Directions in Psychological Science, Vol.28(2), pp.189–194.

[162] Beaujean, A., and Benson, N. (2019), Theoretically Consistent Cognitive Ability Test Development and Score Interpretation, Contemporary School Psychology, 23, pp. 126–137.

[163] Frazier, T. W., and Youngstrom, E. A. (2007), Historical increase in the number of factors measured by commercial tests of cognitive ability: are we over factoring? Intelligence, 35, 169–182. https://doi.org/10.1016/j.intell.2006.07.002.

emotional intelligence.[164] For example, a study has found that following emotional intelligence training, optimal performance was reached in decision-making tasks which involved emotions.[165] Nevertheless, there are a number of reasons as to why the impact of training on improving emotional intelligence may be inconclusive. Firstly, the emotional intelligence conceptual model may be devised incorrectly with the result that measurement problems may emerge. Secondly, there could be information asymmetry regarding the treatment especially with regard to the duration of the treatment as well as the nature of the training involved. And lastly the lack of a control group may have prevented a viable analysis of the success or failure of the study to be concluded. Nevertheless, self-report measures may be developed which allow EI in adolescents to be reliably measured while controlling for the personality and cognitive measures of intelligence.[166] This would allow for training programmes to be developed which would facilitate skills development in adolescents enabling them to manage the emotional difficulties they may encounter in their daily lives.[167] The need for the adolescents to develop skills associated with emotion management acknowledges to a certain extent the emotional and mental health challenges faced by adolescents in today's world.[168]

The Development of Moral Understanding

Moral reasoning from a Piagetian perspective is to see the moral value of actions and decisions from the perspective of another person.[169] The transition from childhood to adulthood, adolescence is representative of a

[164] Groves, K., McEnrue, M., and Shen, W. (2006), Developing and Measuring the emotional intelligence of Leaders, Journal of Management Development, Vol.27, No.2, pp.225–250.

[165] Alkazei, A. et al. (2009), Increases in Emotional Intelligence After an Online Training Program Are Associated with Better Decision Making On the Iowa Gambling Task, Psychological Reports, Vol.122 (3), pp.853–879.

[166] Ciarrachi, J., Chan, A., and Bajgar, J. (2001), measuring emotional intelligence in adolescents, Personality and Individual Differences, 31, pp.1105–1119.

[167] Salovey, P., and Sluyter, D. J. (1997), Emotional Development and emotional intelligence: Educational Implications, Basic Books, New York.

[168] Asher, S.R., and Rose, A.J. (1997), Promoting children's social-emotional adjustment with peers IN Emotional development and emotional intelligence: Educational Implications, Basic Books, New York.

[169] Siregar, R., Taufik, A., and Yustiana, Y. (2020), Development of Moral Reasoning Using Cognitive Behavioral Therapy, The 2nd International Conference on Elementary

period in one's life during which there is a conscious search for an identity of the self.[170] It may also be a period in one's life during which there may be a range of negative behaviours in evidence, primarily due to a lack of moral reasoning ability. In this case, it would seem appropriate if some form of moral reasoning training could be developed by reorganizing cognitive thinking so that the development of moral reasoning is facilitated.[171] One way in which this can be achieved is by using cognitive behavioural therapy to restructure cognitive processes such that thinking will allow for negative behaviours to become 'overruled' by positive behaviours through improved moral reasoning.

Piaget believed that according to the level of the maturity of development, the state of a child's moral reasoning could be defined in two diverse ways. These included heteronomous morality and autonomous morality.[172] Nevertheless, children between the ages of seven and ten are in a state of transition between heteronomous morality and autonomous morality, exhibiting features of both states and are said to be in a semi-autonomous state. And it is the transition from heteronomous to autonomous moral reasoning which defines its development. In this case, it becomes evident from a Piagetian perspective that individuals who can think autonomously in the presence of laws and regulations, and in the context of the difference between right and wrong have a well-developed sense of moral reasoning. In contrast to the Piagetian perspective, Kohlberg defines moral reasoning with regard to the structuring of thought rather than with content and the difference between right and wrong.[173] Therefore, moral reasoning should not be an automatic ability to distinguish between good and bad behaviours but the cognitive processes which result in the making of that distinction. Thus, Kohlberg's theory of moral reasoning is one which is based on structure (thought processes) rather than content (innate ability to determine if an action is good or bad).[174]

Education, Vol.2, Nomor 1.

[170] Ibid.

[171] Ibid.

[172] Ibid.

[173] Kohlberg, L. (1976), Moral Stages and Moralization IN Lickona, T. (Ed.), Moral Development and Behavior: Theory, Research and Social Issues, Hot, Rinehart and Winston, New York.

[174] Siregar, R., Taufik, A., and Yustiana, Y. (2020), Development of Moral Reasoning Using Cognitive Behavioral Therapy, The 2nd International Conference on Elementary Education, Vol.2, Nomor 1.

There are six stages to Kohlberg's theory of moral development.[175] These include punishment and obedience, actions satisfying self and others, behaviours allowing for peer approval, behaviour towards authority, behaviours according to acceptable societal standards, and finally universal ethical principles.[176] These stages suggest a consistency in reasoning, although Kohlberg emphasizes perspective taking in the context of moral reasoning.[177] Reasoning may become inconsistent in the case of different perspectives. Another critique of Kohlberg's theory of moral development is that it may not be possible to apply it cross-culturally.[178] This is particularly because in Western tradition man is seen as a rational agent, whereas in Confucian tradition, for example, man is seen as an integral component of the universe.

It may also be considered that moral reasoning is a process which is guided by a framework of moral rules and responsibilities but based on individual circumstances as well as an understanding of social circumstances.[179] Although Kohlberg and Piaget focus on developing a theory of moral development based on the development of cognitive ability, there are differences between the works of the two.[180] In this context, there is a difference between the theories of moral development between Kohlberg and Piaget. On the one hand Piaget emphasizes problems which are physical and logical. But Kohlberg emphasizes problems which are associated with reasoning as well as with society. Therefore, Kohlberg's theory of moral development has been more broadly developed than that of Piaget. Kohlberg's theory of moral reasoning brakes down the process of reasoning into three levels: the pre-conventional, the conventional, and the post-conventional.[181] However, according to Piaget, moral development relies upon the interaction with others which in his view also stimulates the

[175] Sullivan, E. (1977), A Study of Kohlberg's Structural Theory of Moral Development: A Critique of Liberal Social Science Ideology, Hum. Dev, 20, pp.352–376.

[176] Ibid.

[177] Carpendale, J. (2000), Kohlberg and Piaget on Stages and Moral Reasoning, Developmental Review, 20, pp.181–205.

[178] Dien, D. (1982), A Chinese Perspective on Kohlberg's Theory of Moral Development, Developmental Review, 2, pp. 331–341.

[179] Kurtines, M. W and Gerwitz, J. L. (1992), Morality, Moral Behavior & Moral Development, Universitas Indonesia Press, Jakarta.

[180] Siregar, R., Taufik, A., and Yustiana, Y. (2020), Development of Moral Reasoning Using Cognitive Behavioral Therapy, The 2nd International Conference on Elementary Education, Vol.2, Nomor 1.

[181] Ibid.

structures of cognitive development in the brain. Therefore, from the Piagetian perspective there is a line of causation from the development of cognitive abilities of an individual to his/her moral development. Moreover, according to Piaget, moral reasoning can be developed in children through their education. Nevertheless, Kohlberg suggests that the development of moral reasoning may be dependent on three factors: opportunities to take specific roles, a particular moral situation, and cognitive moral conflicts.[182] In the case of opportunities to take specific roles, the development of moral reasoning may be facilitated when circumstances expose individuals to other viewpoints. Contextually, this may occur when parents morally educate their children on the rights and the wrongs of actions. For example, if a child is caught cheating in an exam at school, the parents of the child may be summoned to school by its headmaster. In this case, the child may be further reprimanded at home that it is morally wrong to cheat. Secondly, moral reasoning may develop in the context of a moral situation. For example, if a child witnesses a bullying incident at school, he/she may decide to report it to teachers out of a moral responsibility for the person/s being bullied. Lastly, moral reasoning may develop because of differences in the moral reasoning between individuals with higher and lower reasoning abilities. In this context, when children conflict with others with higher-level moral reasoning skills, it is evident that such children will themselves develop higher-level moral reasoning skills. It has been found contextually that moral reasoning can also develop either through cultural factors[183] or being emphasized in a family environment. In this case, the parents define the norms and boundaries of what they perceive to be morally correct, and this may facilitate the development of moral reasoning in the child.[184] Nevertheless, as discussed previously, the level of the development of moral reasoning is also dependent on the extent of cognitive development according to Kohlberg. In this case, the state of the level of education has an impact on the level of cognitive development and thus indirectly on the level of development of moral

[182] Janssens, J and Geris, J. (1992), Child Rearing: Influence on Prosocial and Moral Development. University of Nijmegen, Netherlands.

[183] Zhang, Z. (2013), Children's Moral Reasoning: Influence of Culture and Collaborative Discussion. Thesis, Publication: University of Illinois at Urbana-Champaign.

[184] Janssens, J and Geris, J. (1992), Child Rearing: Influence on Prosocial and Moral Development, University of Nijmegen, Netherlands.

reasoning.[185] In other words the higher the level of education, the more likely that a higher level of moral reasoning will develop. The positive correlation of higher levels of education with higher levels of moral reasoning may suggest that a programme of education to 'rewire' cognitive thinking towards improved moral reasoning may be beneficial for children and young adolescents. This rewiring of cognitive thinking processes is the emphasis of cognitive behavioural therapy.[186] However, Kohlberg's model of moral development, involves moral development evolving to higher stages over a six stage sequence,[187] maybe of no significant value to educators in assessing the extent of moral development in children because it relies upon knowing the effects of an individual's environment on the development of moral reasoning.[188] Although the emphasis of the model is on the rational thought of the individual rather than the impact of the environment in the context of the development of moral reasoning,[189] however, it is important to understand the processes which lead to the effects. In contrast to Kohlberg's stage theory of moral development,[190] Vygotsky (1978) proposed a zone of proximal development theory for better understanding the context of learning situations.[191] This zone of proximal development allows for researchers to gain better insights into the development of moral reasoning not only through processes which have already occurred but also through processes which are in

[185] Mayhew, M.J., Seifert, T.A., Pascarella, E.T. et al, (2012), Going Deep into Mechanisms for Moral Reasoning Growth: How Deep Learning Approaches Affect Moral Reasoning Development for First-year Students. Res High Educ 53, 26–46. https://doi.org/10.1007/s11162-011-9226-3.

[186] Siregar, R., Taufik, A., and Yustiana, Y. (2020), Development of Moral Reasoning Using Cognitive Behavioral Therapy, The 2nd International Conference on Elementary Education, Vol.2, Nomor 1.

[187] Tappan, M., and Brown, L. (1989), Toward a Narrative Approach to Moral Development and Moral Education, Harvard Educational Review, Vol.59, No.2.

[188] Crawford, P. (2001), Educating for Moral Ability: Reflections on Moral Development based on Vygotsky's Theory of Concept Formation,' Journal of Moral Education, 30, 2, pp.113–129.

[189] Nokes, K. (1989), Rethinking Moral Reasoning Theory, Journal of Nursing Scholarship, Vol. 21, No.3.

[190] Kohlberg, L. (1976) Moral stages and moralization: the cognitive developmental approach, IN: Moral Development and Behaviour: theory, research, and social issues, Lickona, T. (Eds), Holt, Rinehart and Winston, New York.

[191] Vygotsky, L.S. (1978), Mind in Society: the development of higher psychological processes, Cole, M., John-Steiner, S., Scribner, S., and Souberman, E. (Eds), Harvard University Press, Cambridge.

formation.[192] The Vygotskian approach to moral development allows for an analysis which combines the study of the development of self-awareness of moral values as well as those which result due to the moral intervention of elders, such as the parents of the child.[193] In fact research evidence suggests that there is a positive causative relationship between relevant parental behaviours, especially the level of moral reasoning when interacting with children, and the development of moral reasoning in a child.[194] This is also dependent on the state of the attitude of the child to its environment as well as its behaviour. These are developed by the age of seven, increasing to the age of ten, then with no change until the age of fourteen, showing a progressive decline thereafter.[195] However, in the development of moral judgement in children, this is characterized by a conceptual continuity rather than a discontinuity.[196] In the context of a child's environmental attitude, parental behaviour will also impact upon the emotional and social competence of the child. More specifically, when a child expresses emotions and parent/s respond negatively, then this will facilitate the development of low social competence and negative emotions on the part of the child.[197] Therefore, it is evident that the embedding of moral values within the psyche of adolescents in particular is very much dependent upon good parenting.[198] Therefore, parents should be guided towards crafting a parenting style which allows for a positive enriching and nourishing environment for children to grow.[199] Research suggests that the emotional development of a child also contributes to its moral

[192] Crawford, P. (2001), Educating for Moral Ability: Reflections on Moral Development based on Vygotsky's Theory of Concept Formation,' Journal of Moral Education, 30, 2, pp.113–129.

[193] Tappan, M. (1998), Moral education in the zone of proximal development, Journal of Moral Education, 27, pp. 141–160.

[194] Walker, L., and Hennig, K. (1999), Parenting Style and the Development of Moral Reasoning, Journal of Moral Education, 28, 3, pp.359–374.

[195] Otto, S., Evans, G., Moon, M., and Kaiser, F. (2019), The Development of Children's Environmental Attitude and Behaviour, Global Environmental Change, 58.

[196] Margoni, F., and Sunan, L. (2020), Conceptual Continuity in the Development of Intent-Based Moral Judgement, Journal of Experimental Child Psychology, 194.

[197] Eisenberg, N., Cumberland, A., and Spinrad, T. (1998), Parental Socialisation of Emotion, Psychological Inquiry, 9, 4.

[198] Fatima, S., Dawood, S., and Munir, M. (2020), Parenting Styles, Moral Identity and Prosocial Behaviours in Adolescents, Current Psychology, https://doi.org/10.1007/s12144-020-00609-3.

[199] Ibid.

development.[200] Emotional dispositions are common to all animals.[201] But in humans a level of rationality is able to control emotions such that moral development evolves. The development of moral reasoning is also important for effective cooperation amongst individuals who has they age recognise the importance of moral norms and social norms, such as loyalty to the group, for such co-operation to be effective.[202] Furthermore, in the context of the development of moral reasoning, younger children are more likely to make moral judgements of others based on their intentions rather than on the outcomes of their actions while in older children the case is not so clear cut.[203]

Conclusion

The first few years of a child's life are ones in which there is significant development of the brain, the nervous system, as well as motor development. This is specifically in the context of the addition of not only new connections but also the strengthening of existing connections. Moreover, it has been found through neuro-imaging techniques that movement (motor activity) and the completion of tasks which require thinking processes serve to simultaneously activate two regions of the brain—the dorsolateral prefrontal cortex as well as the neo-cerebellum. The simultaneous motor activity and the completion of tasks requiring thinking and the stimulation of brain areas is not a coincidence. In this case theories associated with cognitive development rely upon this causality. Piaget's theory of cognitive development is dependent upon the causality between simultaneous thinking and physical movement and the actuation of areas of the brain. Therefore, it is evident that Piaget's theory promotes the idea that as incremental psychological changes occur in the brain leading to a change in its overall structure, cognitive processes develop as a result. Piaget's theory is based on four stages of psychological development.

[200] Eisenberg, N. (2000), Emotion, Regulation and Moral Development, Annu. Rev. Psychol, 51, pp.665–697.

[201] Pipatti, O. (2019), Morality Mae Visible: Edward Westermarck's Moral and Social Theory, Routledge, New York.

[202] McGuire, L., Rizzo, M., Killen, M., and Rutland, A. (2019), The Role of Competitive and Cooperative Norms in the Development of Deviant Evaluations, Child Development, Vol.90, No. 6.

[203] Hilton, B., and Kuhlmeior, V. (2019), Intention Attribution and the Development of Moral Evaluation, Frontiers in Psychology, Vol.9.

These include the Sensorimotor Period (birth to the age of two), the Preoperational Thought Period (age two to age seven), the Concrete Operations Period (age seven to age 1eleven), and the Formal Operations Period (age eleven to age fifteen). Research suggests that the environment and the experiences faced by an infant in the Sensorimotor Period will set the foundations for a lifetime of development. Furthermore, during this period much of an infant's brain development takes place due to the stimulation of the brain via movement of limbs and muscles as well as through its senses. The latter allows the infant to become more aware of its environment. As a result of mental and physical stimulation, over 2.4 million synapses are formed every minute in the brain of an infant in its first twelve months. And within the first twenty-four months of the life of an infant, its brain has already reached 80% of an adult's brain size. Typical measures of cognition in infants have been identified as the level of working memory, the level of concentration, and the ability to multi-task. These measures are also indicators of executive function. The level of development of this in infants is seen as predictors of future academic performance.

In contrast to Piaget's theory of cognitive development, which emphasizes modular changes in the psychological cognitive system, Vygotsky places greater emphasis on the development of the entire psychological system. In this case, according to Vygotsky the development of one component in a psychological system changes the functionality of the entire system. Thus, the development of memory may change the way in which the brain functions because it will be able to 'store' more information. Therefore, it may be the case that with more information, the functioning of the brain can lead to better decisions. Furthermore, when a child acquires the ability to speak then information in the mind of the child about its thoughts, feelings, and the environment can be exchanged with others. It has also been found through research that the nature of the post-natal environment of a child is especially important for the extent of its potential for cognitive development. As a child develops, however, in adapting to its environment the intelligent control of its emotions (emotional intelligence) may be important to its overall development.

Moral reasoning, the ability to discern from good and bad behaviour, may also be important for the development of a child into adulthood. The ability to discern the content of one's own actions and the action of others, good actions, or bad actions, is a typical Piagetian perspective. In contrast, according to the Kohlberg perspective the structure of thought is more important than its content awareness for the development of moral reasoning. Therefore, according to Kohlberg the cognitive processes which lead to content awareness are more important than the automatic recognition of content awareness with regard to the development of moral reasoning. However, the automatic recognition of content awareness of behaviours, one which arises from an increasing self-awareness and that instilled by peers and elders, represents the Vygotskian approach to moral development.

References

Ackerman, P. L. (1997). Personality, self-concept, interests and intelligence: Which construct doesn't fit? *Journal of Personality, 65*, 171–204.

Alkazei, A., et al. (2009). Increases in emotional intelligence after an online training program are associated with better decision making on the Iowa gambling task. *Psychological Reports, 122*(3), 853–879.

Asher, S. R., & Rose, A. J. (1997). *Promoting children's social-emotional adjustment with peers IN Emotional development and emotional intelligence: Educational Implications.* Basic Books.

Barkovich, J. A., Kjos, B. O., Jackson, D. E., & Norman, D. (1988). Normal maturation of the neonatal and infant brain: MR imaging at 1.5 T1. *Neuroradiology, 166*, 173–180.

Beaujean, A., & Benson, N. (2019). Theoretically consistent cognitive ability test development and score interpretation. *Contemporary School Psychology, 23*, 126–137.

Benson, J. E., & Sabbagh, M. A. (2010). Theory of mind and executive functioning: A developmental neuropsychological approach. In P. Zelazo, M. Chandler, & E. Crone (Eds.), *Developmental social cognitive neuroscience.* Psychology Press.

Best, J., Miller, P., & Naglieri, J. (2011). Relations between executive function and academic achievement from ages 5 to 17 in a large, representative national sample. *Learning and Individual Differences, 21*, 327–336.

Bowman, B., Donovan, S., & Bums, S. (Eds.). (2001). *Committee on early childhood pedagogy.* National Academy Press.

Brody, B., Kinney, H., Kloman, A., & Gilles, F. (1987). Sequence of central nervous system myelination in human; infancy: I. An autopsy study of myelination. *Journal of Neuropathology & Experimental Neurology, 46*, 283–301.

Buck-Morss, S. (1975). Socio-economic bias in Piaget's theory and its implications for cross-cultural studies. *Human Development, 18*, 35–49.

Carpendale, J. (2000). Kohlberg and Piaget on stages and moral reasoning. *Developmental Review, 20*, 181–205.

Casey, B. J., Giedd, J. N., & Thomas, K. M. (2000). Structural and functional brain development and its relation to cognitive development. *Biological Psychology, 54*, 241–257.

Chaparro, J., Sojourner, A., & Wiswall, M. (2020). Early childhood care and cognitive development. National Bureau of Economic research, Working Paper 26813.

Chugani, H. T., Phelps, M. E., & Mazziotta, J. C. (1987). Positron emission tomography study of human brain functional development. *Annals of Neurology, 22*, 487–497.

Ciarrachi, J., Chan, A., & Bajgar, J. (2001). Measuring emotional intelligence in adolescents. *Personality and Individual Differences, 31*, 1105–1119.

Clark, D. A., & Beck, A. T. (2010). Cognitive theory and therapy of anxiety and depression: Convergence with neurobiological findings. *Trends in Cognitive Sciences, 14*(9), 418–424.

Combs-Orme, T. (2013). Epigenesis and the social work imperative. *Social Work, 58*(1), 23–30.

Compton, W., Dowling, G., & Garavan, H. (2019). Ensuring the best use of data: The adolescent brain cognitive development study. *JAMA Paediatrics, 173*, 9.

Crawford, P. (2001). Educating for moral ability: Reflections on moral development based on Vygotsky's theory of concept formation. *Journal of Moral Education, 30*(2), 113–129.

Dasen, P. R. (1994). Culture and cognitive development from a Piagetian perspective. In W. J. Lonner & R. Malpass (Eds.), *Psychology and culture* (pp. 145–149). Allyn & Bacon.

De Graaf-Peters, V. B., & Hadders-Algra, M. (2006). Ontogeny of the human central nervous system: What is happening when? *Early Human Development, 82*, 257–266. https://doi.org/10.1016/j.earlhumdev.2005.10.013

Dellermann, D., Ebel, P., Sollner, M., & Leimeister, J. (2019). Hybrid intelligence. *Business and Information Systems Engineering, 61*(5), 637–643.

Deoni, S. C., et al. (2011). Mapping infant brain myelination with magnetic resonance imaging. *Journal of Neuroscience, 31*(2), 784–791. https://doi.org/10.1523/JNEUROSCI.2106-10.2011

Dhuey, E., Figlio, D., Karbownik, K., & Roth, J. (2019). School starting age and cognitive development. *Journal of Policy Analysis and Management, 38*(3), 538–578.

Diamond, A. (1990). The development and neural bases of memory functions as indexed by the AB and delayed response tasks in human infants and infant monkeys. *Annals of the New York Academy of Sciences, 60*, 231–267.

Diamond, A. (2007). Interrelated and interdependent. *Developmental Science, 10*, 152–158.

Diamond, A. (2013). Executive functions. *Annual Review of Psychology, 64*, 135–168.

Dien, D. (1982). A Chinese perspective on Kohlberg's theory of moral development. *Developmental Review, 2*, 331–341.

DiPietro, J. A. (2000). Baby and the brain: Advances in child development. *Annual Review of Public Health, 21*, 455–471.

Drange, N., & Havnes, T. (2019). Early childcare and cognitive development: Evidence from an assignment lottery. *Journal of Labour Economics, 37*(2), 581–620.

Driver, R. (1978). When is a stage not a stage? A Critique of Piaget's theory of cognitive development and its application to science education. *Educational Research, 21*(1), 54–61.

Dulewicz, S. V., & Higgs, M. J. (1998a). Emotional intelligence: Managerial fad or valid construct? Henley Working Paper 9813, Henley Management College.

Dulewicz, V., & Higgs, M. (1999). Can emotional intelligence be measured and developed. *Leadership & Organisation Development Journal, 20*(5), 242–252.

Duveen, G. (2000). Piaget ethnographer. *Social Science Information, 39*(1), 79–97.

Egan, M., Neely-Barnes, S., & Combs-Orme, T. (2011). Integrating neuroscience into the lifespan. *Journal of Social Work Education, 47*(2), 269–282.

Eisenberg, N. (2000). Emotion, regulation and moral development. *Annual Review of Psychology, 51*, 665–697.

Eisenberg, N., Cumberland, A., & Spinrad, T. (1998). Parental socialisation of emotion. *Psychological Inquiry, 9*, 4.

Eysenck, H. J. (1982). *A model for intelligence*. Springer-Verlag.

Eysenck, H. J. (1992). Intelligence: The one and the many? In D. K. Detterman (Ed.), *Current topics in human intelligence* (Vol. 2: Is mind modular or unitary?) (pp. 83–116). Ablex.

Fatima, S., Dawood, S., & Munir, M. (2020). Parenting styles, moral identity and prosocial behaviours in adolescents. *Current Psychology*. https://doi.org/10.1007/s12144-020-00609-3

Flavell, J. (1982). On cognitive development. *Child Development, 53*(1), 1–10.

Frazier, T. W., & Youngstrom, E. A. (2007). Historical increase in the number of factors measured by commercial tests of cognitive ability: Are we over factoring? *Intelligence, 35*, 169–182. https://doi.org/10.1016/j.intell.2006.07.002

Fuster, J. (2002). Frontal lobe and cognitive development. *Journal of Neurocytology, 31*, 373–385.

Gabbard, C. (2008). *Lifelong motor development* (5th ed.). Pearson Education.

Gallahue, D., & Ozmun, J. (2002). *Understanding motor development: Infants, children, adolescents, adults* (5th ed.). McGraw-Hill.

Gardner, H. (1983). *Frames of mind*. Harper-Collins.

Gelman, R. (1978). Cognitive development. *Annual Review of Psychology, 29*, 297–332.

Gibson, J. (1979). *The ecological approach to visual perception*. Lawrence Erlbaum.

Groves, K., McEnrue, M., & Shen, W. (2006). Developing and measuring the emotional intelligence of leaders. *Journal of Management Development, 27*(2), 225–250.

Harris, J. (2004). Measured intelligence, achievement, openness to experience and creativity. *Personality and Individual Differences, 36*, 913–929.

Herrero, M. T., Barcia, C., & Navarro, J. M. (2002). Functional anatomy of thalamus and basal ganglia. *Child's Nervous System, 18*, 386–404.

Hilton, B., & Kuhlmeior, V. (2019). Intention attribution and the development of moral evaluation. *Frontiers in Psychology, 9*, 2663.

Huitt, W., & Hummel, J. (2003). *Piaget's theory of cognitive development, educational psychology interactive*. Valdosta State University.

Huttenlocher, P. R. (1990). Morphometric study of human cerebral cortex development. *Neuropsychologia, 28*, 517–527.

Janssens, J., & Geris, J. (1992). *Child rearing: Influence on prosocial and moral development*. University of Nijmegen.

Johnson, M. H. (2001). Functional brain development in humans. *Nature, 2*, 475–483.

Johnson, S. (2003). The nature of cognitive development. *Trends in Cognitive Science, 7*(3), 102–104.

Kahneman, D. (2011). *Thinking, fast and slow*. Palgrave Macmillan.

Kamii, C. (1982). *Number in preschool and kindergarten: Educational implications of Piaget's theory*. National Association for the Education of Young Children.

Kazi, S., Kazali, E., Makris, N., Spanoudis, G., & Demetriou, A. (2019). Cognizance in cognitive development: A longitudinal study. *Cognitive Development, 52*, 100805.

Knickmeyer, R. C., et al. (2008). A structural MRI study of human brain development from birth to 2 years. *The Journal of Neuroscience, 28*(47), 12176–12182.

Kohlberg, L. (1976). Moral stages and moralization: The cognitive developmental approach. In T. Lickona (Ed.), *Moral development and behaviour: Theory, research, and social issues*. Holt, Rinehart and Winston.

Kohler, W. (1947). *Gestalt psychology*. Liveright.

Kolb, B., & Fantie, B. D. (2009). Development of the child's brain and behavior. In I. N. C. R. Reynolds & E. Fletcher-Janzen (Eds.), *Handbook of clinical child neuropsychology* (3rd ed., pp. 19–46). Springer.

Kontopodis, M. (2019). Transformative activist stance and pedagogy of daring: Moving beyond Lev Vygotsky in dialogue with Anna Stetsenko. *Pedagogy, Culture & Society, 27*(2), 301–304. https://doi.org/10.1080/14681366.2018.1475890

Kotsou, I., Mikolajczak, M., Heeren, A., Gregoire, J., & Leys, C. (2019). Improving emotional intelligence: A systematic review of existing work and future challenges. *Emotion Review, 11*(2), 151–165.

Kovacs, K., & Conway, A. (2019). What is IQ? Life beyond 'general intelligence'. *Current Directions in Psychological Science, 28*(2), 189–194.

Kurtines, M. W., & Gerwitz, J. L. (1992). *Morality, moral behavior & moral development*. Universitas Indonesia Press.

Larsen, R. (1973). Levels of conceptual development in melodic permutations concepts based on Piagets theory. *Journal of Research in Music Education, 21*(3), 256–263.

Lee, C., & Wang, C. (2017). The effect of team emotional intelligence on team process and effectiveness. *Journal of Management and Organisation, 25*(6), 844–859.

Lefmann, T., & Combs-Orme, T. (2013). Early brain development for social work practice: Integrating neuroscience with Piaget's theory of cognitive development. *Journal of Human Behaviour in the Social Environment, 23*, 640–647.

Levin, H. S., Culhane, K. A., Hartmann, J., Evankovich, K., & Mattson, A. J. (1991). Developmental changes in performance on tests of purported frontal lobe functioning. *Developmental Neuropsychology, 7*, 377–395.

Lewis, C. (2019). Vygotsky and moral education: A response to and expansion of Tappan. *Educational Philosophy and Theory, 51*(1), 41–50.

Luna, B., et al. (2001). Maturation of widely distributed brain function subserves cognitive development. *NeuroImage, 13*, 786–793.

Luria, A. R., & Vygotsky, L. S. (1930/1992). *Ape, primitive man and child, 1930/1992*. Harvester Wheatsheaf.

Mahmoodi-Shahrebabaki, M. (2019). Vygotsky, education, and literacy. Unpublished manuscript, Department of Literacy Studies, Middle Tennessee State University.

Margoni, F., & Sunan, L. (2020). Conceptual continuity in the development of intent-based moral judgement. *Journal of Experimental Child Psychology, 194*, 104812.

Martins, A., Ramalho, N., & Morin, E. (2010). A comprehensive meta-analysis of the relationship between emotional intelligence and health. *Personality and Individual Differences, 49*, 554–564. https://doi.org/10.1016/j.paid.2010.05.029

Mayer, S. J. (2005). The early evolution of Jean Piaget's clinical method. *History of Psychology, 8*(4), 362–382.

Mayhew, M. J., Seifert, T. A., Pascarella, E. T., et al. (2012). Going deep into mechanisms for moral reasoning growth: How deep learning approaches affect moral reasoning development for first-year students. *Research in Higher Education, 53*, 26–46. https://doi.org/10.1007/s11162-011-9226-3

McCrae, R. R. (1987). Creativity, divergent thinking, and openness to experience. *Journal of Personality and Social Psychology, 52*, 1258–1265.

McCrae, R. R., & Costa, P. T., Jr. (1997). Conceptions and correlates of openness to experience. In R. Hogan, J. A. Johnson, & S. R. Briggs (Eds.), *Handbook of personality psychology* (pp. 825–847). Academic Press.

McGuire, L., Rizzo, M., Killen, M., & Rutland, A. (2019). The role of competitive and cooperative norms in the development of deviant evaluations. *Child Development, 90*(6), e703–e717.

Niederer, I., Kriemler, S., Gut, J., Hartmann, T., Schindler, C., Barral, J., et al. (2011). Relationship of aerobic fitness and motor skills with memory and attention in preschoolers (Ballabeina): A cross-sectional and longitudinal study. *BMC Pediatrics, 11*, 34.

Nokes, K. (1989). Rethinking moral reasoning theory. *Journal of Nursing Scholarship, 21*(3), 172–175.

Ojose, B. (2008). Applying Piaget's theory of cognitive development to mathematics instruction. *The Mathematics Educator, 18*(1), 26–30.

Otto, S., Evans, G., Moon, M., & Kaiser, F. (2019). The development of children's environmental attitude and behaviour. *Global Environmental Change, 58*, 1–6.

Paldino, A., & Purpura, D. (1979). Quantitative analysis of the spatial distribution of axonal and dendritic terminals of hippocampal pyramidal neurons in immature human brain. *Experimental Neurology, 64*, 604–619.

Paterson, S. J., Heim, S., Friedman, J. T., Choudhury, N., & Benasich, A. A. (2006). Development of structure and function in the infant brain: Implications for cognition, language and social behavior. *Neuroscience and Biobehavioural Reviews, 30*, 1087–1105.

Peng, P., & Kievit, R. (2020). The development of academic achievement and cognitive abilities: A bidirectional perspective. *Child Development Perspectives, 14*(1), 15–20.

Pereira, K., Valentini, N., & Saccani, R. (2016). Brazilian infant motor and cognitive development: Longitudinal influence of risk factors. *Pediatrics International, 58*, 1297–1306.

Petrides, K. V., & Furnham, A. (2003). Trait emotional intelligence: Behavioural validation in two studies of emotion recognition and reactivity to mood induction. *European Journal of Personality, 17*, 39–57. https://doi.org/10.1002/per.466

Piaget, J. (1963). *The origins of intelligence in children*. W.W. Norton & Company, Inc.

Piaget, J. (1973). *The child and reality: Problems of genetic psychology*. Penguin Books.

Piaget, J., & Cook, M. (1952). *The origins of intelligence in children*. International Universities Press.

Piaget, J., & Cook, M. (Trans.). (1954). The development of object construct. In *The construction of reality in the child* (pp. 3–96). Basic Books.

Piaget, J., & Inhelder, B. (1969). *The psychology of the child*. Basic Books.

Piek, J., Dawson, L., Smith, L., & Gasson, N. (2008). The role of early fine and gross motor development on later motor and cognitive ability. *Human Movement Science, 27*(2008), 668–681.

Pipatti, O. (2019). *Morality Mae visible: Edward Westermarck's moral and social theory*. Routledge.

Raad, B., & Schouwenburg, H. (1996). Personality in learning and education: A review. *European Journal of Personality, 10*(5), 303–336.

Record, R. G., McKeown, T., & Edwards, J. (1970). An investigation of the difference in measured intelligence between twins and single births. *Annals Human Genetics, London, 34*, 11.

Riegel, K. (1973). Dialectic operations: The final period of cognitive development. *Human Development, 16*, 346–370.

Salovey, P., & Sluyter, D. J. (1997). *Emotional development and emotional intelligence: Educational implications.* Basic Books.

Schore, A. N. (2001). Effects of a secure attachment relationship on right brain development, affect regulation, and infant mental health. *Infant Mental Health Journal, 22*(1–2), 7–66.

Shonkoff, J., & Phillips, D. (2000). *From neurons to neighbourhoods: The science of early childhood development.* National Academy Press.

Silverthorn, P. (1999). Jean Piaget' s theory of development. http://chd.gse.gmu.edu/immersion/knowledgebase/theorists/constructivism/Piaget.htm

Siregar, R., Taufik, A., & Yustiana, Y. (2020). Development of moral reasoning using cognitive behavioral therapy. The 2nd International Conference on Elementary Education, Vol. 2, Nomor 1.

Smillie, D. (1982). Rethinking Piaget's theory of infancy. *Human Development, 25*, 282–294.

Stetsenko, A., & Arievitch, I. M. (2010). Cultural-historical activity theory: Foundational worldview and major principles. In J. Martin & S. Kirschner (Eds.), *The sociocultural turn in psychology: The contextual emergence of mind and self.* Columbia University Press.

Sullivan, E. (1977). A study of Kohlberg's structural theory of moral development: A critique of liberal social science ideology. *Human Development, 20*, 352–376.

Tappan, M. (1998). Moral education in the zone of proximal development. *Journal of Moral Education, 27*, 141–160.

Tappan, M., & Brown, L. (1989). Toward a narrative approach to moral development and moral education. *Harvard Educational Review, 59*(2), 182–205.

Tau, G. Z., & Peterson, G. S. (2010). Normal development of brain circuits. *Neuropsychopharmacology Reviews, 35*, 147–168.

Terumitsu, M., Ikeda, K., Kwee, I. L., & Nakada, T. (2009). Participation of primary motor cortex area 4a in complex sensory processing: 3.0-T fMRI study. *Neuroreport, 20*(7), 679–683.

Thelen, E., & Smith, L. (1994). *A dynamic systems approach to the development of cognition and action.* MIT Press.

Thomas, R. M. (1996). *Comparing theories of child development.* Brooks/Cole Publishing Company.

Toomela, A. (2015). Vygotsky's theory on the Procrustes' bed of linear thinking: Looking for structural–systemic theseus to save the idea of 'social formation of mind'. *Culture & Psychology, 21*, 318–339. https://doi.org/10.1177/1354067X15570490

Vaci, N., Edelsbrunner, P., Stern, E., Neubauer, A., Bilalic, M., & Grabner, R. (2019). The joint influence of intelligence and practice on skill development throughout the life span. *PNAS, 116*(37), 18363–18369.

Vasileva, O., & Balyasnikova, N. (2019). (Re) Introducing Vygotsky's thought: From historical overview to contemporary psychology. *Frontiers in Psychology, 10*, 1515.

Veldman, S., Santos, R., Jones, R., Sousa-Sa, E., & Okely, A. (2019). Associations between gross motor skills and cognitive development in toddlers. *Early Human Development, 132*, 39–44.

Vygotsky, L. S. (1978). *Mind in society: The development of higher psychological processes* (M. Cole, S. John-Steiner, S. Scribner, & E. Souberman, Eds.). Harvard University Press.

Wach, H. (1981). Visual implications of Piagets theory of cognitive development. *Journal of Learning Disabilities, 14*(10), 581–583.

Walker, L., & Hennig, K. (1999). Parenting style and the development of moral reasoning. *Journal of Moral Education, 28*(3), 359–374.

Webb, S. J., Monk, C. S., & Nelson, C. A. (2001). Mechanisms of postnatal neurobiological development: Implications for human development. *Developmental Neuropsychology, 19*(2), 147–171.

Wertsch, J. V., & Tulviste, P. (1992). L. S. Vygotsky and contemporary developmental psychology. *Developmental Psychology, 28*, 548–557. https://doi.org/10.1037/0012-1649.28.4.548

Zeidner, M. (1995). Personality and trait correlates of intelligence. In D. H. Saklofske & M. Zeidner (Eds.), *International handbook of personality and intelligence* (pp. 299–319). Plenum Press.

Zhang, Z. (2013). Children's moral reasoning: Influence of culture and collaborative discussion. Thesis, University of Illinois at Urbana-Champaign.

Zimmerman, B. J., & Whitehurst, G. J. (1979). Structure and function: A comparison of two views of the development of language and cognition. In G. J. Whitehurst & B. J. Zimmerman (Eds.), *The functions of language and cognition*. Academic Press.

CHAPTER 4

Climate Change

Introduction

Over the past three million years, Earth's climate has undergone significant changes due to natural cycles and more recently, anthropogenic influences. Anthropogenic influences refer to the impact of human activities on the climate, primarily through the emission of greenhouse gases such as carbon dioxide (CO_2), methane (CH_4), and nitrous oxide (N_2O), which result from the burning of fossil fuels, industrial processes, and deforestation.[1] These activities have significantly altered the natural carbon cycle and enhanced the greenhouse effect, leading to increased global temperatures, ocean acidification, and altered weather patterns.[2] Unlike natural climate drivers such as volcanic eruptions and solar variability, which have shaped Earth's climate over millions of years, anthropogenic influences have rapidly accelerated changes in the climate system, particularly since the Industrial Revolution.[3] Empirical evidence strongly supports this

[1] IPCC. (2021), *Climate Change 2021: The Physical Science Basis.* Contribution of Working Group I to the Sixth Assessment Report of the Intergovernmental Panel on Climate Change. Cambridge University Press.

[2] NASA. (2020), The Causes of Climate Change. Retrieved from NASA Climate Change.

[3] NOAA. (2020), Global Climate Report - Annual 2020. Retrieved from NOAA National Centers for Environmental Information.

S. Ramesh, *The Political Economy of Contemporary Human Civilisation, Volume I*,
https://doi.org/10.1007/978-3-031-84181-1_4

statement. For example, studies using ice core data show that atmospheric concentrations of carbon dioxide (CO_2) and methane (CH_4) remained relatively stable for thousands of years until the onset of the Industrial Revolution, after which there was a dramatic increase in these greenhouse gases.[4] The concentration of CO_2, for instance, has risen from approximately 280 parts per million (ppm) in pre-industrial times to over 410 ppm today, primarily due to fossil fuel combustion and deforestation.[5,6] Moreover, climate models that include only natural activity, such as volcanic activity and solar radiation, fail to replicate the observed warming trend of the past century. Only when human activities, such as greenhouse gas emissions and land-use changes, are included in these models do they accurately reflect the observed temperature increases.[7] This suggests that natural drivers alone cannot explain the current rate of climate change. Furthermore, the Intergovernmental Panel on Climate Change (IPCC) reports that human activities have been the dominant cause of observed global warming since the mid-twentieth century, with anthropogenic greenhouse gas emissions contributing to an increase of approximately 1.1°C above pre-industrial levels as of 2019.[8] In contrast, natural factors such as solar variability and volcanic eruptions have contributed less than

[4] IPCC. (2021). Summary for policymakers. In Masson-Delmotte, V., Zhai, P., Pirani, A., Connors, S. L., Péan, C., Berger, S., … & Zhou, B. (Eds.), Climate Change 2021: The Physical Science Basis. Contribution of Working Group I to the Sixth Assessment Report of the Intergovernmental Panel on Climate Change. Cambridge University Press.

[5] Etheridge, D. M., Steele, L. P., Langenfelds, R. L., Francey, R. J., Barnola, J. M., & Morgan, V. I. (1996). Natural and anthropogenic changes in atmospheric CO_2 over the last 1000 years from air in Antarctic ice and firn. Journal of Geophysical Research: Atmospheres, 101(D2), 4115–4128.

[6] NOAA. (2021). Trends in Atmospheric Carbon Dioxide. National Oceanic and Atmospheric Administration. Available at: https://www.esrl.noaa.gov/gmd/ccgg/trends/

[7] Hegerl, G. C., Zwiers, F. W., Braconnot, P., Gillett, N. P., Luo, Y., Marengo Orsini, J. A., … & Taylor, K. E. (2007). Understanding and attributing climate change. In Solomon, S., Qin, D., Manning, M., Chen, Z., Marquis, M., Averyt, K. B., … & Miller, H. L. (Eds.), Climate Change 2007: The Physical Science Basis. Contribution of Working Group I to the Fourth Assessment Report of the Intergovernmental Panel on Climate Change (pp. 663–746). Cambridge University Press.

[8] IPCC. (2021). Summary for policymakers. In Masson-Delmotte, V., Zhai, P., Pirani, A., Connors, S. L., Péan, C., Berger, S., … & Zhou, B. (Eds.), Climate Change 2021: The Physical Science Basis. Contribution of Working Group I to the Sixth Assessment Report of the Intergovernmental Panel on Climate Change. Cambridge University Press.

0.1°C to this warming trend over the same period.[9] Overall, empirical evidence from various scientific studies confirms that anthropogenic factors have significantly accelerated climate change in a manner unprecedented in the geological record, highlighting the urgent need for mitigation strategies. This chapter examines these changes, focusing on both natural climatic variations and the impacts of human activities.

Chronology of Main Events of Climate Change Over the Last Five Million Years

Climate change over the past five million years has been marked by significant natural events that shaped the Earth's environment. This chapter provides a chronological overview of these major climatic events.

(a) **Pliocene Epoch (5 Million to 2.6 Million Years Ago)**

Pliocene Warm Period

During the Pliocene, global temperatures were approximately 2–3°C higher than today. This period saw significantly reduced polar ice caps and higher sea levels.[10] The Pliocene Warm Period, which occurred approximately three to five million years ago, is crucial for understanding potential future climate scenarios under current warming trends because it represents a time when global temperatures and atmospheric CO_2 levels were similar to those projected for the near future. During this period, global temperatures were about 2–3°C higher than pre-industrial levels, and CO_2 concentrations were around 400 ppm, comparable to current levels.[11] The geological evidence from this epoch indicates that polar ice

[9] Bindoff, N. L., Stott, P. A., AchutaRao, K. M., Allen, M. R., Gillett, N., Gutzler, D., … & Zhang, X. (2013). Detection and attribution of climate change: from global to regional. In Stocker, T. F., Qin, D., Plattner, G.-K., Tignor, M., Allen, S. K., Boschung, J., … & Midgley, P. M. (Eds.), Climate Change 2013: The Physical Science Basis. Contribution of Working Group I to the Fifth Assessment Report of the Intergovernmental Panel on Climate Change (pp. 867–952). Cambridge University Press.

[10] Zachos, J. C., et al. (2001). "Trends, Rhythms, and Aberrations in Global Climate 65 Ma to Present." Science, 292(5517), 686–693.

[11] Haywood, A.M., Dowsett, H.J., and Dolan, A.M. (2016), Integrating geological archives and climate models for the mid-Pliocene warm period. Nature Communications, 7, p.10646.

sheets were smaller, resulting in sea levels 10–20 metres higher than today, highlighting the long-term impacts of elevated greenhouse gas concentrations on ice melt and sea-level rise.[12] By studying the Pliocene, scientists can gain insights into the sensitivity of Earth's climate to higher CO_2 levels, the potential changes in ice sheet dynamics, and the resultant sea-level rise, which are critical for predicting the future implications of anthropogenic climate change.[13] The Pliocene Warm Period (approximately 5.3 to 2.6 million years ago) is a key interval for examining potential future climate scenarios in light of contemporary warming trends. During this geological epoch, global temperatures were higher than today, with estimates suggesting that average global temperatures were about 2 to 3 degrees Celsius warmer than pre-industrial levels.[14] This period is particularly significant because it featured atmospheric CO_2 concentrations like those projected for the coming decades, ranging from approximately 350 to 450 parts per million (ppmv).[15] During the Pliocene, significant changes occurred in both terrestrial and marine ecosystems, largely driven by these elevated temperatures. For example, the expansion of forests into areas that are now tundra illustrates how ecosystems responded to warmer temperatures. Fossil records show that North America experienced a subtropical climate as far north as Canada, while modern fauna such as elephants and hippos roamed in regions that are now temperate.[16] These changes highlight the ecological shifts that can occur with even moderate increases in temperature. In terms of sea-level rise, the Pliocene Warm Period is often associated with higher global sea levels, estimated to be 10 to 25 metres higher than present levels.[17] These elevations resulted from the

[12] Dolan, A.M., Haywood, A.M., Tindall, J.C., and Dowsett, H.J. (2011), The Pliocene Model Intercomparison Project (PlioMIP): experimental design and boundary conditions (Experiment 2). Geoscientific Model Development, 4(3), pp.571–577.

[13] Fedorov, A.V., Brierley, C.M., and Emanuel, K. (2013), Tropical cyclones and permanent El Niño in the early Pliocene epoch. Nature, 496(7443), pp.43–47.

[14] Fedorov, A. V., et al. (2015). "Patterns and mechanisms of Pliocene warmth." Nature Geoscience, 8(6), 490–500. doi:10.1038/ngeo2416.

[15] Luthi, D., et al. (2008). "High-resolution carbon dioxide record from the Vostok ice core." Geophysical Research Letters, 35(3), L03705. doi:10.1029/2007GL029999.

[16] Holmgren, K., et al. (2015). "Climate and land cover changes in the southern Great Plains: Implications for land management and drought responsiveness." Journal of Climate, 28(22), 8897–8912. doi:10.1175/JCLI-D-15-0391.1.

[17] Miller, K. G., et al. (2012). "A 180-million-year record of sea level rise from the New Jersey coast." Geology, 40(8), 685–688. doi:10.1130/G33089.1.

melting of glaciers and ice sheets, which serves as a critical warning for current climate models predicting future sea-level rise in response to ongoing warming. The study of the Pliocene also allows scientists to explore feedback mechanisms involved in climate system responses to increased greenhouse gas concentrations. For instance, the enhanced greenhouse effect during the Pliocene led to altered ocean circulation patterns, which contributed to further warming.[18] This is pertinent today as models rely on understanding this feedback to predict the rate and extent of climate change. In conclusion, the Pliocene Warm Period not only provides insight into Earth's climatic past but also serves as a critical benchmark for anticipating future climate scenarios under current anthropogenic warming trends. As we observe rising temperatures and changing environments today, lessons drawn from the Pliocene underscore the potential magnitude and implications of these changes.

Formation of the Isthmus of Panama

Around 3–3.5 million years ago, the closing of the seaway between North and South America created the Isthmus of Panama. This event altered ocean currents and contributed to the onset of Northern Hemisphere glaciation.[19] Altered ocean currents refer to a significant event in Earth's geological history that altered global ocean circulation and had far-reaching consequences for the climate, particularly leading to the glaciation in the Northern Hemisphere. This event is commonly associated with the closure of the Central American Seaway, which connected the Pacific and Atlantic Oceans, and its impact on ocean currents such as the Gulf Stream. The disruption of these currents is widely believed to have played a critical role in the initiation of the ice ages in the Pleistocene epoch. What follows is a detailed explanation and evaluation of how this event affected ocean currents, leading to climate change and glaciation in the Northern Hemisphere.

[18] Salzmann, U., et al. (2008). "The Pliocene and future climates: Results from the PMIP2 model intercomparison." Paleoceanography, 23(2). doi:10.1029/2007PA001515.

[19] Haug, G.H. and Tiedemann, R. (1998), 'Effect of the formation of the Isthmus of Panama on Atlantic Ocean thermohaline circulation', Nature, 393(6686), pp. 673–676.

Closure of the Central American Seaway

The Central American Seaway was a crucial oceanic passage that connected the Pacific and Atlantic Oceans before the uplift of the Isthmus of Panama about three to five million years ago.[20] The gradual tectonic movement that closed this seaway had profound impacts on ocean circulation. Prior to the closure, warm water from the Pacific could flow into the Atlantic, which kept the Atlantic Ocean's salinity relatively low. The closure restricted this flow, leading to a fundamental reorganization of ocean currents and the establishment of the modern Atlantic Meridional Overturning Circulation (AMOC). It is argued that this reorganization enhanced the northward transport of salty, warm waters via the Gulf Stream, which strengthened the transport of heat from the tropics to the North Atlantic.[21] This increase in heat transport contributed to more moisture in the atmosphere, which eventually led to increased snowfall and the accumulation of ice in the Arctic regions, triggering the onset of glaciation.

Impact on Ocean Circulation

One of the most significant consequences of the closure of the Central American Seaway was the alteration of the thermohaline circulation, the global ocean circulation driven by differences in water temperature and salinity. The increase in salinity in the North Atlantic, due to the restriction of freshwater inflows from the Pacific, allowed for denser water to sink in the North Atlantic, strengthening the AMOC. This sinking of cold, salty water in the North Atlantic drives the global 'conveyor belt' of ocean circulation, which plays a key role in regulating Earth's climate.[22] The strengthened Gulf Stream, part of this conveyor belt, transported more warm water northwards, contributing to the warmer conditions in the high latitudes of the North Atlantic. However, this paradoxically led to cooling over the long term due to the increased precipitation and snow cover in polar regions, which initiated ice sheet formation.[23] As ice sheets

[20] Haug, G.H. and Tiedemann, R. (1998), 'Effect of the formation of the Isthmus of Panama on Atlantic Ocean thermohaline circulation', Nature, 393(6686), pp. 673–676.

[21] Ibid.

[22] Broecker, W.S. (1991), 'The great ocean conveyor', Oceanography, 4(2), pp. 79–89.

[23] Ravelo, A.C., Andreasen, D.H., Lyle, M., Lyle, A.O. and Wara, M.W. (2004), 'Regional climate shifts caused by gradual global cooling in the Pliocene epoch', Nature, 429(6989), pp. 263–267.

grew, they reflected more solar radiation back into space (the albedo effect), reinforcing the cooling and further promoting glaciation. Glaciation is further promoted through the albedo effect, which refers to how the growth of ice sheets increases the Earth's surface reflectivity. As the ice sheets expand, they cover more land with highly reflective surfaces, which results in a significant increase in the amount of solar radiation that is reflected into space, rather than absorbed by the Earth. This phenomenon contributes to a reduction in surface temperatures, thus reinforcing the cooling effect.[24,25] The feedback loop created by this process is crucial for understanding past and present climate changes. As the temperature drops, more snowfall can occur, leading to further ice accumulation. The expansion of ice reflects even more solar radiation, which, in turn, leads to additional cooling.[26] This cycle of enhanced reflectivity and cooling continues, making it a powerful driver of glacial periods.[27] Therefore, the albedo effect does not just correlate with glaciation, but actively promotes and sustains it through these feedback mechanisms.

Northern Hemisphere Glaciation

The onset of Northern Hemisphere glaciation, which occurred about 2.7 million years ago during the late Pliocene and early Pleistocene, is often linked to changes in ocean circulation patterns, particularly the strengthening of the AMOC following the closure of the Central American Seaway.[28] Glaciation in the Northern Hemisphere marked the beginning of cyclic ice ages, with large ice sheets developing over North America, Greenland, and Northern Europe. It is also postulated that the closure of the seaway played a direct role in increasing the delivery of moisture to northern latitudes, which allowed for the expansion of glaciers.[29] Increased

[24] Peltier, W. R., et al. (2015). "The role of ice sheets in climate change." Nature Climate Change, 5(1), 43–47.

[25] Clark, P. U., et al. (2002). "The roles of the ice sheets in the climatic system." Quaternary Science Reviews, 21(1–3), 1185–1200.

[26] Houghton, J. T., et al. (2001). Climate Change 2001: The Scientific Basis. Cambridge University Press.

[27] Lisiecki, L. E., & Raymo, M. E. (2005). "A Pliocene-Pleistocene stack of 57 globally distributed benthic δ18O records." Paleoceanography, 20(1).

[28] Haug, G.H. and Tiedemann, R. (1998), 'Effect of the formation of the Isthmus of Panama on Atlantic Ocean thermohaline circulation', Nature, 393(6686), pp. 673–676.

[29] Ibid.

precipitation, combined with cooler summers due to orbital variations (Milankovitch cycles), created conditions conducive to the long-term build-up of ice. One notable example of how ocean circulation changes contributed to glaciation is the formation of the Greenland Ice Sheet. As the Gulf Stream transported warm, moist air to the North Atlantic, it caused increased precipitation over Greenland. Over time, this precipitation, which fell as snow, accumulated and compacted to form the ice sheet that persists today.[30] The growth of this ice sheet significantly contributed to global sea-level changes and altered atmospheric circulation patterns, further reinforcing glaciation.

Other Contributing Factors

While the closure of the Central American Seaway was a major driver of the onset of Northern Hemisphere glaciation, other factors also played significant roles. These include tectonic uplift, which contributed to changes in atmospheric circulation, and orbital variations that influenced the Earth's climate cycles.[31] However, the reorganization of ocean currents and the resultant changes in heat and moisture distribution were critical in tipping the climate towards glaciation.

The closure of the Central American Seaway and the resulting changes in ocean currents played a pivotal role in the onset of Northern Hemisphere glaciation.[32] This event altered the flow of warm, salty water into the North Atlantic, strengthened the Gulf Stream, and increased moisture transport to high latitudes. This process contributed to the growth of ice sheets, the cooling of the planet, and the establishment of the cyclical ice ages of the Pleistocene. The study of this event highlights the interconnectedness of ocean circulation and climate systems, demonstrating how changes in one component can trigger far-reaching effects across the globe.

[30] Raymo, M.E., Grant, B., Horowitz, M. and Rau, G.H. (1996), 'Mid-Pliocene warmth: Stronger greenhouse and stronger conveyor', Marine Micropaleontology, 27(1–4), pp. 313–326.

[31] Lisiecki, L.E. and Raymo, M.E. (2005), 'A Pliocene-Pleistocene stack of 57 globally distributed benthic δ18O records', Paleoceanography, 20(1), PA1003.

[32] Haug, G.H. and Tiedemann, R. (1998), 'Effect of the formation of the Isthmus of Panama on Atlantic Ocean thermohaline circulation', Nature, 393(6686), pp. 673–676.

(b) **Pleistocene Epoch (2.6 Million to 11,700 Years Ago)**

The Pleistocene marked the beginning of the Quaternary Ice Age, characterized by repeated glacial and interglacial cycles. The earliest major glaciations saw ice sheets forming over North America, Europe, and Asia.[33] Around 2.4 million years ago, significant glaciation began, with ice sheets expanding and contracting in response to orbital variations.[34] This was in a period known as the Quaternary glaciation, which began approximately 2.4 million years ago and was characterized by significant fluctuations in ice sheet extent driven by changes in Earth's orbital parameters, such as eccentricity, axial tilt, and precession.[35,36] During this period, ice sheets primarily expanded in the Northern Hemisphere, particularly over regions such as Canada, the northern United States, and much of Scandinavia. These areas were greatly affected by the Laurentide and Fennoscandian ice sheets, which reached their maximum extents during glacial periods and covered vast areas.[37] The southern limits of these ice sheets sometimes extended into what is now the northern Midwest of the United States, affecting both the geography and climate of the regions they covered.[38] Conversely, during interglacial periods, ice sheets contracted significantly. For example, during the last interglacial period, roughly 125,000 years ago, the Laurentide Ice Sheet receded, resulting in the exposure of land that had been previously covered by ice. This contraction facilitated the expansion of flora and fauna into previously glaciated areas.[39]Additionally, while the Northern Hemisphere underwent these significant changes, the Southern Hemisphere experienced its own glacial dynamics, with the

[33] Lisiecki, L.E. and Raymo, M.E. (2005), 'A Pliocene-Pleistocene stack of 57 globally distributed benthic δ18O records', Paleoceanography, 20(1), PA1003.

[34] Maslin, M. A., et al. (1998). "Pleistocene evolution: Northern Hemisphere ice sheets and North Atlantic Ocean." Geology, 26(6), 467–470.

[35] Imbrie, J., et al. (1993). "On the structure and origin of the 100,000-year cycles." Paleoceanography, 8(5), 799–813.

[36] Walker, M. J. C., et al. (1995). "Quaternary Science Reviews." Quaternary Science Reviews, 14(6), 559–589.

[37] Miller, K. G., et al. (2010). "The Phanerozoic record of global sea-level change." Science, 327(5968), 1293–1298.

[38] Calkin, P. E., & D. A. H. (2009). "Pleistocene Glacial Geography of the Midwestern United States". In: The Geology of the Midwest. Geological Society of America.

[39] Alley, R. B., & A. J. Gow, (2000). "Changes in the Laurentide Ice Sheet: Impacts on the Greenhouse Gas Concentrations and the North American Climate". Geophysical Research Letters, 27(4), 607–610.

Antarctic ice sheet fluctuating in response to climatic changes, albeit on a different timescale and intensity.[40] In summary, the expansion and contraction of ice sheets during the Quaternary glaciation significantly impacted geographical regions across both hemispheres, with notable effects in North America and Eurasia in the Northern Hemisphere, and ongoing dynamics in Antarctica influencing global climate patterns.

Intensification of Glacial Cycles (1.8 Million to 800,000 Years Ago)

During this period, the frequency and intensity of glaciations increased, with cycles occurring approximately every 41,000 years, linked to changes in Earth's axial tilt.[41] The intensification of glacial cycles from around 1.8 million to 800,000 years ago marks a significant phase in Earth's climate history. During this period, the frequency and severity of glaciations escalated. These cycles are believed to be closely tied to changes in Earth's axial tilt, or obliquity, which affects the distribution of solar radiation across the planet, particularly between the poles and equator.[42] The 41,000-year periodicity, which aligns with Earth's obliquity cycle, influences seasonal contrasts and contributes to the build-up and decay of polar ice sheets. When Earth's tilt is less pronounced, seasonal differences are reduced, allowing snow and ice to accumulate over multiple years and contributing to glacial expansion.[43] The increased intensity of these glacial cycles likely resulted from a combination of orbital variations and internal feedback mechanisms within Earth's climate system. For example, ice-albedo feedback, where ice expansion increases Earth's reflectivity and cools global temperatures, helped sustain glacial periods once they began.[44] This process worked in tandem with other factors, such as changes in

[40] Neumann, T., et al. (2015). 'Antarctic glacial history and recent observations of the Antarctic ice sheet.' Nature Climate Change, 5(1), 73–80.

[41] Raymo, M. E., & Huybers, P. (2008), "Unlocking the mysteries of the ice ages." Nature, 451(7176), 284–285.

[42] Ruddiman, W.F. (2008), Earth's Climate: Past and Future. W.H. Freeman and Company.

[43] Lisiecki, L.E. and Raymo, M.E. (2005), 'A Pliocene-Pleistocene stack of 57 globally distributed benthic δ18O records.' Paleoceanography, 20(1).

[44] Imbrie, J., Berger, A., Boyle, E.A., Clemens, S., Duffy, A., Howard, W.R., Kukla, G., Kutzbach, J., Martinson, D.G., McIntyre, A. and Mix, A.C. (1993), 'On the structure and origin of major glaciation cycles 1. Linear responses to Milankovitch forcing.' Paleoceanography, 8(6), pp. 699–735.

greenhouse gas concentrations, to further intensify glaciations. Evidence from ice cores and marine sediment records suggests that during this period, fluctuations in atmospheric CO_2 also contributed to glacial and interglacial transitions, amplifying the cooling and warming phases.[45] The transition to stronger and more sustained glacial cycles profoundly impacted global ecosystems and played a crucial role in the evolution of early humans. As glacial cycles intensified, hominin populations had to adapt to the increasingly variable climates and shifting landscapes, influencing patterns of migration, subsistence, and tool use.[46] This period of intensified glaciation thus not only shaped Earth's physical environment but also laid the groundwork for ecological and evolutionary pressures that would impact the development of human ancestors. This environmental variability also shaped subsistence practices; as certain regions became colder and less vegetative, hominins increasingly relied on hunting and gathering diverse food sources to survive.[47] In adapting to these dynamic climates, hominins developed more sophisticated tools and technologies. For example, stone tool advancements, from Oldowan to Acheulean hand-axes, reflected the need for more versatile tools to process a range of resources, including meat and plant materials, that were critical and scarce during glacial and interglacial periods.[48] These advancements in tool use were crucial for exploiting a variety of food sources, which supported dietary flexibility and improved survival across different environments.[49]

The evolutionary pressures of glacial cycles not only drove migratory behaviours and technological innovations but also likely played a role in shaping social organization among hominins. Cooperative hunting and resource sharing may have become increasingly important as survival strategies in harsh climates, facilitating the development of social bonds and

[45] EPICA Community Members (2004), 'Eight glacial cycles from an Antarctic ice core.' Nature, 429(6992), pp. 623–628.

[46] DeMenocal, P. (2011), 'Climate and Human Evolution.' Science, 331(6017), pp. 540–542.

[47] Potts, R. (1998), 'Variability selection in hominid evolution.' Evolutionary Anthropology, 7(3), pp. 81–96.

[48] Ambrose, S.H. (2001), 'Paleolithic technology and human evolution.' Science, 291(5509), pp. 1748–1753.

[49] Lycett, S.J., and Cramon-Taubadel, N.V. (2008), 'A comparative analysis of Oldowan and Acheulean bifacial tools: morphometric variability and the effects of raw material availability.' Journal of Archaeological Science, 35(10), pp. 2523–2530.

inter-group collaboration that underpinned early human societies.[50] This adaptability to climatic instability highlights the resilience of hominins in the face of environmental challenges, setting the stage for the eventual global dispersal of Homo species.

Mid-Pleistocene Transition (800,000 to 125,000 Years Ago)

Around 800,000 years ago, glacial cycles shifted to a 100,000-year periodicity, influenced by Earth's orbital eccentricity. This transition marks a significant change in the Earth's climatic system.[51] Around 800,000 years ago, the timing of glacial cycles transitioned to a predominant 100,000-year periodicity, a significant change largely attributed to variations in Earth's orbital parameters, particularly orbital eccentricity. Earth's orbit around the Sun is not a perfect circle, but rather an ellipse that varies in shape over time due to gravitational interactions with other celestial bodies. This elliptical variation influences the distance between Earth and the Sun, thereby affecting the amount of solar radiation received during different seasons. The Milankovitch cycles, named after Serbian mathematician Milutin Milankovitch, describe these changes in Earth's orbit and their impact on climate. Specifically, Earth's orbital eccentricity varies on a timescale of approximately 100,000 years, accompanying more pronounced effects on the insolation (solar radiation received) during summer months, which are crucial for the initiation and melting of ice sheets.[52] During periods of greater eccentricity, there are enhanced seasonal contrasts, amplifying summer insolation in the Northern Hemisphere. Evidence for the influence of these orbital changes can be seen in the marine sediment cores.[53] The analysis of these cores provides high-resolution records of past climate conditions.[54] These records show a strong

[50] Grove, M. (2011), 'Speciation, diversity, and Mode 1 technologies: the impact of variability selection.' Journal of Human Evolution, 61(3), pp. 306–319.

[51] Clark, P. U., et al. (2006), "The middle Pleistocene transition: characteristics, mechanisms, and implications for long-term changes in atmospheric CO_2." Quaternary Science Reviews, 25(23–24), 3150–3184.

[52] Hays, J. D., Imbrie, J., & Shackleton, N. J. (1976). "Variations in the Earth's Orbit: Pacemaker of the Ice Ages." Science, 194(4270), 1121–1132. doi:10.1126/science.194.4270.1121.

[53] Imbrie, J., et al. (1992). "On the distribution of glacial and interglacial periods." *Paleoceanography*, 7(6), 701–738. doi:10.1029/92PA02028.

[54] Ibid.

correlation between the 100,000-year cycles of glacial and interglacial phases and variations in Earth's eccentricity. Furthermore, a study indicates that increased eccentricity can contribute to the growth of ice sheets during periods of reduced warmth, while also fostering significant melt during warmer interglacial periods.[55] The shift to a 100,000-year glacial cycle is depicted in the climatic data collected from ice cores and ocean sediments, which indicate that the amplitude and duration of glacial periods were influenced by these orbital mechanics.[56] In summary, the transition to a 100,000-year glacial cycle around 800,000 years ago can be explained by Earth's orbital eccentricity, which significantly modifies seasonal insolation patterns, thereby driving the glacial and interglacial transitions that characterize Earth's climatic history. Approximately 140,000 years ago, the ice sheets reached a maximum extent during the penultimate glaciation, covering vast areas of the Northern Hemisphere.[57]

(c) **Last Interglacial and Glacial Periods (125,000 to 11,700 Years Ago)**

Last Interglacial Period (Eemian)

The Eemian interglacial, around 125,000 to 115,000 years ago, was characterized by temperatures slightly warmer than today and higher sea levels. This period is often used as an analogue for understanding current interglacial conditions.[58] Studies on the Eemian provide valuable insights for understanding the potential impacts of our current interglacial period, the Holocene, as both periods exhibit natural warming phases. Temperatures during the Eemian are estimated to have been 1–2°C higher than current global temperatures, leading to significant polar ice melting

[55] Spreen, G., Kwok, R. & Menemenlis, D. (2010). "Impact of Earth's orbital eccentricity on ice sheet stability." Nature Geoscience, 3, 399–404. doi:10.1038/ngeo851.

[56] Lisiecki, L. E., & Raymo, M. E. (2005). "A Pliocene-Pleistocene stack of 57 globally distributed benthic δ18O records." Paleoceanography, 20(1), PA1003. doi:10.1029/2004PA001071.

[57] Rohling, E. J., et al. (2008), "High rates of sea-level rise during the last interglacial period." Nature Geoscience, 1(1), 38–42.

[58] Dutton, A., & Lambeck, K. (2012), "Ice volume and sea level during the last interglacial." Science, 337(6091), 216–219.

and substantial changes in sea levels and coastal regions.[59] Evidence from marine and ice core data indicates that sea levels during the Eemian were likely between 6 and 9 metres higher than today, with some studies suggesting even higher levels. This rise was largely driven by the melting of polar ice, particularly from the Greenland and West Antarctic ice sheets, which are especially sensitive to even modest temperature increases.[60] For instance, geological records from coral reef terraces in the Bahamas and Australia document these elevated sea levels, which left distinct imprints of previous shoreline heights, providing direct evidence of substantial ice melt during this period.[61] The implications of such high sea levels during the Eemian highlight potential future scenarios if global temperatures continue to rise under anthropogenic climate change.

The Eemian climate has been reconstructed using a variety of proxy data, including ice cores, fossilized pollen, and marine sediments. These reconstructions reveal that the warming experienced during the Eemian was not uniform across the globe. Northern latitudes experienced amplified warming due to increased solar insolation, a pattern similar to modern-day polar amplification observed with current global warming.[62] For example, pollen records from northern Europe and Siberia indicate extensive forests in areas currently occupied by tundra, suggesting a substantial northward shift in vegetation zones due to the warmer temperatures.[63] Such shifts provide critical insights into how ecosystems may respond to current warming trends, highlighting the potential for large-scale changes in biodiversity and habitat distribution. Moreover, the Eemian's climatic conditions offer a benchmark for understanding the stability of ice sheets under warmer conditions. Research on Greenland ice core data shows that the Eemian warming led to significant melting on Greenland's surface,

[59] Turney, C. S. M., & Jones, R. T. (2010). "Does the Agulhas Current amplify global temperatures during super-interglacials?" Journal of Quaternary Science, 25(6), 839–843.

[60] Dutton, A., et al. (2015). "Sea-level rise due to polar ice-sheet mass loss during past warm periods." Science, 349(6244), aaa4019.

[61] Hearty, P. J., & Neumann, A. C. (2001). "Rapid sea level and climate change at the close of the last interglacial (MIS 5e): Evidence from the Bahama Islands." Quaternary Science Reviews, 20(18), 1881–1895.

[62] Overpeck, J., Otto-Bliesner, B., & Miller, G. (2006). "Paleoclimatic evidence for future ice-sheet instability and rapid sea-level rise." Science, 311(5768), 1747–1750.

[63] Kaspar, F., et al. (2005). "Simulation of the Eemian interglacial and comparison with the Holocene." Climate Dynamics, 25(2–3), 201–220.

contributing to the global sea-level rise observed in geological records.[64] This raises concerns about the resilience of today's ice sheets under sustained warming, particularly as recent studies indicate accelerated melting in both the Arctic and Antarctic regions, which could trigger comparable or even greater sea-level rises. In sum, the Eemian interglacial period serves as an analogue for potential future climate scenarios, illustrating the impact of relatively small temperature increases on sea levels, ice sheet stability, and ecosystem changes. By examining the Eemian, scientists gain insights into possible outcomes under ongoing climate change, reinforcing the importance of understanding past interglacial dynamics as we navigate current climate challenges.

Last Glacial Maximum (LGM)

Around 21,000 years ago, during the Last Glacial Maximum, ice sheets were at their maximum extent. This period saw extensive glaciation across North America, Europe, and Asia.[65] During this period, massive ice sheets—up to several kilometres thick—covered most of Canada, parts of the northeastern United States, and northern Europe, drastically altering the planet's topography and climate.[66] In North America, the Laurentide and Cordilleran ice sheets merged to form an expansive glacial complex, while in Europe, the Fennoscandian Ice Sheet covered much of Scandinavia and extended into northern Germany and Poland.[67]

The presence of these vast ice sheets significantly affected global climate by altering atmospheric and oceanic circulation patterns. Ice sheets reflected solar radiation due to their high albedo, helping to maintain cooler global temperatures and intensifying the cold, arid conditions characteristic of glacial periods.[68] This cooling effect contributed to lower sea levels, with estimates suggesting a drop of approximately 120 metres due to the sequestration of water in glacial ice, exposing continental shelves and creating land bridges, such as the Bering Land Bridge between Siberia

[64] NEEM Community Members. (2013). "Eemian interglacial reconstructed from a Greenland folded ice core." Nature, 493(7433), 489–494.

[65] Clark, P. U., et al. (2009), "The Last Glacial Maximum." Science, 325(5941), 710–714.

[66] Clark, P. U., et al. (2009), "The Last Glacial Maximum." Science, 325(5941), 710–714.

[67] Mix, A.C., Bard, E. and Schneider, R. (2001), 'Environmental processes of the ice age: land, oceans, glaciers (EPILOG).' Quaternary Science Reviews, 20(4), pp. 627–657.

[68] Ruddiman, W.F. (2008), Earth's Climate: Past and Future. W.H. Freeman and Company.

and Alaska.[69] These changes impacted human and animal migration patterns, with the land bridges facilitating movements between continents. Furthermore, the LGM's extensive glaciation influenced ecosystems, forcing species to adapt, migrate, or face extinction. Tundra landscapes replaced forests in many northern regions, while species adapted to colder climates thrived.[70] For humans, these environmental conditions presented challenges, as populations had to adjust their subsistence strategies to survive in harsh climates, leading to innovations in toolmaking and hunting practices.[71] These innovations enabled them to hunt, process food, and build shelters more effectively, adapting their practices to maximize the resources available in glacial environments.[72]

To cope with the demands of the glacial environment, early humans developed more sophisticated and specialized tools. This period saw the refinement of lithic (stone) tools, such as the development of blade technology, which allowed for the creation of thinner, sharper edges ideal for tasks like skinning animals and processing meat.[73] One notable advancement was the invention of composite tools, which combined materials like bone, antler, and stone to enhance functionality and durability. An example is the atlatl or spear-thrower, a tool that increased hunting efficiency by allowing hunters to throw spears with greater force and distance, essential for hunting large, fast-moving prey in open, icy landscapes.[74] Additionally, humans developed techniques to create microblades—small, precisely shaped stone flakes—often mounted on wooden or bone shafts to make

[69] Lambeck, K., Rouby, H., Purcell, A., Sun, Y. and Sambridge, M. (2014), 'Sea level and global ice volumes from the Last Glacial Maximum to the Holocene.' Proceedings of the National Academy of Sciences, 111(43), pp. 15296–15303.

[70] Hewitt, G.M. (2000), 'The genetic legacy of the Quaternary ice ages.' Nature, 405(6789), pp. 907–913.

[71] Clark, P.U., Dyke, A.S., Shakun, J.D., Carlson, A.E., Clark, J., Wohlfarth, B., Mitrovica, J.X., Hostetler, S.W. and McCabe, A.M. (2009), 'The Last Glacial Maximum.' Science, 325(5941), pp. 710–714.

[72] Clark, P.U., Dyke, A.S., Shakun, J.D., Carlson, A.E., Clark, J., Wohlfarth, B., Mitrovica, J.X., Hostetler, S.W. and McCabe, A.M. (2009), 'The Last Glacial Maximum.' Science, 325(5941), pp. 710–714.

[73] Ambrose, S.H. (2001), 'Paleolithic technology and human evolution.' Science, 291(5509), pp. 1748–1753.

[74] Shea, J.J. (2006), 'The origins of lithic projectile point technology: Evidence from Africa, the Levant, and Europe.' Journal of Archaeological Science, 33(6), pp. 823–846.

tools like arrows or knives. These tools were more versatile and portable, making them well-suited for mobile hunter-gatherer lifestyles.[75] In regions like Europe, humans crafted bone needles, enabling them to sew tailored clothing, which provided necessary insulation against frigid temperatures, a critical adaptation to the cold climate.[76]

Surviving in glacial conditions required adaptive subsistence strategies, particularly in terms of diet and resource use. Humans expanded their hunting practices to target large, cold-adapted megafauna such as mammoths, reindeer, and bison, which provided substantial quantities of meat, fat, and hides essential for survival.[77] These animals not only offered calorically dense sustenance but also materials for shelter, clothing, and tools. For example, mammoth bones were sometimes used to construct shelters in areas lacking wood resources, as seen in archaeological sites like Mezhirich in Ukraine.[78] In addition to big-game hunting, humans adopted a broad-spectrum subsistence strategy, gathering a range of plants, small game, and fish when available. This diversification of diet helped to buffer against periods of food scarcity, as relying solely on large game was risky in environments where these animals migrated or became temporarily scarce. Archaeological evidence from the Gravettian culture in Europe, for instance, shows that early humans exploited varied resources, reflecting dietary flexibility essential for survival in changing climates.[79] These advancements in toolmaking and subsistence strategies highlight the adaptability and ingenuity of humans in response to environmental pressures. By enhancing their tools and diversifying their diets, humans not only survived the Last Glacial Maximum but also set the stage for further cultural and technological evolution.

[75] Knecht, H. (1997), Projectile Technology. Plenum Press.

[76] Hoffecker, J.F. (2005), A Prehistory of the North: Human Settlement of the Higher Latitudes. Rutgers University Press.

[77] Bocherens, H., Drucker, D.G., Bonjean, D., Bridault, A., Conard, N.J., Cupillard, C., Gernay, T., van Kolfschoten, T., Munzel, S.C. and Naito, Y.I. (2011), 'Isotopic evidence for dietary ecology of cave bear (Ursus spelaeus) in the Late Pleistocene of Europe: A review and a case study from the Goyet caves (Belgium).' Quaternary International, 245(2), pp. 235–241.

[78] Soffer, O. (1985), 'The Upper Paleolithic of the Central Russian Plain.' Academic Press.

[79] Hockett, B., and Haws, J. (2003), 'Nutritional ecology and the human demography of Neanderthal extinctions.' Quaternary International, 33(1), pp. 167–178.

Younger Dryas (12,900 to 11,700 Years Ago)

The Younger Dryas was a sudden return to near-glacial conditions before the final abrupt warming that led to the Holocene. This event is significant for understanding rapid climate change mechanisms.[80] The Younger Dryas (approximately 12,900 to 11,700 years ago) represents a critical interval in Earth's climatic history characterized by a sudden return to near-glacial conditions following a period of warming at the end of the last glacial period. This event is significant for several reasons, particularly for understanding rapid climate change mechanisms. Firstly, the Younger Dryas is notable for its abruptness; it is believed to have occurred over a very short timescale, potentially just a few decades.[81] Such rapid transitions illustrate how sensitive the climate system can be to perturbations, emphasizing the potential for swift shifts in climate driven by natural factors, such as changes in ocean circulation and atmospheric composition. For instance, research indicated that the re-establishment of cold conditions was likely a consequence of disruptions in the thermohaline circulation, particularly the Atlantic Meridional Overturning Circulation (AMOC), due to a sudden influx of freshwater from melting ice sheets.[82] Data from ice cores, such as those drilled in Greenland, provide a wealth of information regarding climate changes during the Younger Dryas. For example, the Greenland Ice Core Project (GRIP) revealed sharp increases and decreases in δ^18O isotopic ratios during the Younger Dryas, suggesting significant changes in temperature and precipitation patterns.[83] These variations are indicative of drastic shifts in climate conditions, supporting the argument that the Younger Dryas was a period of heightened climate instability. Furthermore, the Younger Dryas serves as a valuable analogue for understanding contemporary climate change. The mechanisms that drove this abrupt shift—such as changes in oceanic and atmospheric circulation—continue to be relevant in today's discussions surrounding rapid climate change due to

[80] Alley, R. B. (2000), "The Younger Dryas cold interval as viewed from central Greenland." Quaternary Science Reviews, 19(1–5), 213–226.

[81] Alley, R. B., Clark, P. U., Huybers, P., & Marotzke, J. (1997). "Does the Arctic Ocean–Atlantic thermohaline circulation affect climate?" Geophysical Research Letters, 24(6), 641–644. doi:10.1029/97GL03834.

[82] Ganopolski, A., and Cramer, W. (2008), The role of freshwater in the Younger Dryas climate: a modeling study. Paleoceanography, 23(3). doi:10.1029/2007PA001501.

[83] Johnsen, S. J., et al. (2001). "Odyssey: The Greenland Ice Core Project." Journal of Glaciology, 47(157), 1–8. doi:10.3189/172756501781831211.

anthropogenic impacts. A recent review emphasizes the importance of such ancient events in predicting future climate behaviour based on our current trajectory of greenhouse gas emissions.[84] In conclusion, the Younger Dryas stands out as a critical case study for understanding rapid climate change mechanisms. Its abrupt onset, coupled with the data derived from paleoclimate proxies, enhances our knowledge of the climate system's vulnerabilities and responses to sudden external forces, providing essential context for anticipating twenty-first-century climate scenarios.

(d) **Holocene Epoch (11,700 Years Ago to Present)**

Holocene Climate Optimum (9000 to 5000 Years Ago)

This period experienced warmer and wetter conditions, particularly in the Northern Hemisphere. It significantly influenced the development of human civilizations.[85] This climate shift played a pivotal role in shaping human civilizations by providing favourable conditions for agriculture and settlement expansion. With milder winters and more consistent rainfall, river valleys such as those of the Nile, Tigris-Euphrates, and Indus became fertile zones, enabling early agriculture and the domestication of plants and animals.[86] These developments catalysed the formation of permanent settlements and complex societies, as food surpluses supported population growth, specialization of labour, and social stratification.[87]

This climatic period also influenced the establishment of early irrigation systems, as communities devised ways to harness rivers for crop production, crucial in regions with seasonal rainfall variability. In Mesopotamia, for instance, irrigation allowed for reliable food production despite dry seasons, fuelling urbanization and the rise of city-states such as Ur and Uruk.[88] Meanwhile, in North Africa, the wetter conditions during the

[84] Peltier, W. R., et al. (2019). "The influence of human activity on climate and its significance for the Americas." Nature Climate Change, 9, 1–10. doi:10.1038/s41558-019-0453-4.

[85] Mayewski, P. A., et al. (2004), "Holocene climate variability." Quaternary Research, 62(3), 243–255.

[86] Ruddiman, W.F. (2008), Earth's Climate: Past and Future. W.H. Freeman and Company.

[87] Diamond, J. (1997), Guns, Germs, and Steel: The Fates of Human Societies. New York: W.W. Norton & Company.

[88] Pollock, S. (1999), Ancient Mesopotamia: The Eden that Never Was. Cambridge University Press.

Holocene allowed the Sahara region to support human habitation and pastoralism, a stark contrast to its later arid state as the desert it is today. This temporary 'Green Sahara' fostered cultural exchange and movement, connecting groups across North Africa and influencing later civilizations along the Nile.[89] The Holocene Climate Optimum's favourable environmental conditions thus laid the foundation for key developments in agricultural techniques, social organization, and early trade networks, profoundly shaping the trajectory of human civilization.

Neoglacial Period (4500 to 2500 Years Ago)

The Neoglacial Period, spanning approximately from 4500 to 2500 years ago, was marked by a cooling trend that led to significant glacial growth across the globe. [90] This period is distinguished by multiple episodes of glacial advances and cooler climates that affected various regions, notably in the Northern Hemisphere. These glacial movements are often linked to shifts in solar radiation and volcanic activity, which contributed to decreased temperatures and influenced climate patterns.[91] In Europe, the Alps experienced several notable glacier advances during the Neoglacial Period, leaving distinct moraines that provide evidence of these cooler conditions. These moraines indicate that glacial growth was pronounced during this period, with several phases of advance observed at sites like the Mont Miné glacier in Switzerland.[92] Similarly, in North America, glaciers expanded in regions like the Canadian Rockies and Alaska. For example, the Mendenhall Glacier near Juneau, Alaska, shows evidence of substantial growth during the Neoglacial Period, where moraines and tree-ring data mark its extent.[93]

[89] Kuper, R. and Kröpelin, S. (2006), 'Climate-controlled Holocene occupation in the Sahara: Motor of Africa's evolution.' Science, 313(5788), pp. 803–807.

[90] Bradley, R. S., et al. (2003), "The climate of the last millennium." In: Paleoclimate, Global Change and the Future. Springer, Berlin, Heidelberg.

[91] Bradley, R.S. (2000), Past Global Changes and their Significance for the Future. Quaternary International, 63(1), pp. 61–67.

[92] Ivy-Ochs, S., Kerschner, H., Maisch, M., Christl, M., Kubik, P.W. and Schlüchter, C. (2009), 'Latest Pleistocene and Holocene glacier variations in the European Alps.' Quaternary Science Reviews, 28(21–22), pp. 2137–2149.

[93] Wiles, G.C. and Calkin, P.E. (1994), 'Late Holocene, high-resolution glacial chronologies and climate, Kenai Mountains, Alaska.' Geological Society of America Bulletin, 106(2), pp. 281–303.

The cooling effects of the Neoglacial Period also influenced human settlements. In Scandinavia, reduced temperatures and harsher conditions contributed to a decline in agriculture in certain areas, as shorter growing seasons impacted crop yields. This climatic shift may have prompted adjustments in subsistence strategies among Norse communities and other Northern European populations, as they adapted to cooler and less predictable growing conditions.[94] Overall, the Neoglacial Period is recognized for its impact on natural and human environments, as cooling and glacial advances influenced landscapes and shaped ecological and human adaptation patterns.

Medieval Warm Period (900 to 1300 CE)

This period of relatively warm climate, especially in the North Atlantic region, influenced agricultural productivity and settlement patterns in Europe.[95] The Medieval Warm Period (MWP), spanning approximately 900 to 1300 CE, was a time of relatively warm climate, particularly pronounced in the North Atlantic region. This period had significant effects on agricultural productivity and settlement patterns in Europe and beyond, as warmer temperatures extended growing seasons and allowed for the cultivation of crops at higher altitudes and latitudes than before. For example, in England, grape vineyards flourished as far north as York, an indication of the unusually mild conditions that facilitated agricultural expansion.[96] Additionally, Scandinavian farmers were able to cultivate cereals in parts of Greenland during this period, leading to the establishment of Norse settlements.[97]

The MWP's impact on settlement patterns is notably illustrated by the Norse expansion into Greenland. Warmer conditions allowed Norse settlers to establish farming colonies in the otherwise harsh environment, where they raised livestock and grew crops. Archaeological evidence, such as the remains of farms and churches, highlights how these settlements thrived for several centuries before the climate began to cool again, which

[94] Grove, J.M. (2004), Little Ice Ages: Ancient and Modern. Routledge.

[95] Lamb, H. H. (1965), "The early medieval warm epoch and its sequel." Palaeogeography, Palaeoclimatology, Palaeoecology, 1, 13–37.

[96] Lamb, H.H. (1995), Climate, History, and the Modern World. Routledge.

[97] Grove, J.M. and Switsur, R. (1994), 'Glacial Geological Evidence for the Medieval Warm Period.' Climatic Change, 26(2), pp. 143–169.

contributed to the eventual abandonment of these settlements.[98] Furthermore, the warmer climate of the MWP contributed to population growth and economic expansion in Europe. Extended growing seasons allowed for more stable crop yields, which supported population increases and the expansion of trade networks. This period also saw advancements in agricultural techniques, such as the use of the heavy plow, which further boosted productivity in the warmer climate.[99] However, the end of the MWP and the onset of the Little Ice Age in the fourteenth century brought cooler and more variable conditions, challenging these earlier gains and leading to more frequent crop failures and famines.[100]

Little Ice Age (1300 to 1850 CE)

The Little Ice Age (1300 to 1850 CE) was a period marked by cooler temperatures and glacial expansion, significantly impacting agriculture, settlement, and human activities, especially in Europe and North America.[101] The cooling trend, likely influenced by decreased solar radiation, volcanic eruptions, and shifts in ocean circulation, led to notable environmental and societal changes.[102]

The Little Ice Age led to shorter growing seasons and crop failures due to cooler and often unpredictable weather. In Europe, the colder climate affected staple crops like wheat and barley, leading to reduced harvests and increased food prices. For instance, the Great Famine of 1315–1317, one of the most severe food shortages in European history, was exacerbated by relentless rains and cooler temperatures that hindered crop yields.[103] The relentless rains and colder temperatures during this period drastically reduced crop yields, with wheat, oats, and hay—the primary staples—yielding little to sustain the population. Consequently, food prices soared

[98] Diamond, J. (2005), Collapse: How Societies Choose to Fail or Succeed. Penguin Books.

[99] Jordan, W.C. (1996), The Great Famine: Northern Europe in the Early Fourteenth Century. Princeton University Press.

[100] Fagan, B. (2000), The Little Ice Age: How Climate Made History, 1300–1850. Basic Books.

[101] Mann, M. E., et al. (2009), "Global signatures and dynamical origins of the Little Ice Age and Medieval Climate Anomaly." Science, 326(5957), 1256–1260.

[102] Fagan, B. (2000), The Little Ice Age: How Climate Made History, 1300–1850. Basic Books.

[103] Jordan, W.C., 1996. The Great Famine: Northern Europe in the Early Fourteenth Century. Princeton University Press.

as scarcity became widespread. In England, for example, the price of wheat rose by more than 200% in certain areas, putting essential food items out of reach for most peasants.[104] Malnutrition and starvation weakened the populace, leading to increased susceptibility to diseases such as dysentery and respiratory infections, which further elevated mortality rates.[105]

The impact of the famine was not limited to individual health; it reverberated through society, instigating significant social unrest. Desperate for food, people turned to theft, leading to a surge in crime as starving individuals resorted to stealing from fields and barns. In some cases, families abandoned elderly members or children they could no longer support.[106] Social structures, particularly the feudal obligations between lords and peasants, came under strain as landlords demanded their dues despite the peasantry's inability to meet these obligations due to crop failures. This often led to riots and rebellions; one example was the Peasants' Revolt in Flanders in 1323, where tensions over food scarcity and feudal obligations boiled over into violent clashes.[107] The widespread social instability and breakdown in order during the Great Famine highlighted the vulnerability of medieval European societies to environmental stressors, setting a precedent for future uprisings as populations grew increasingly disillusioned with their socioeconomic systems.

The colder temperatures during this period forced communities to adapt their settlement patterns and lifestyle. In regions such as Scandinavia, colder conditions and glacial advance led to the abandonment of marginal farming lands, pushing populations towards more hospitable lowland areas. Similarly, Norse settlements in Greenland, initially established during the Medieval Warm Period, faced declining resources as the climate cooled, ultimately leading to their abandonment by the fifteenth century.[108] The Little Ice Age also influenced economic and social activities. With unpredictable harvests, European societies became more reliant on alternate sources of food and trade networks. Fishing industries in

[104] Jordan, W.C. (1996), The Great Famine: Northern Europe in the Early Fourteenth Century. Princeton University Press.

[105] Aberth, J. (2001), From the Brink of the Apocalypse: Confronting Famine, War, Plague, and Death in the Later Middle Ages. Routledge.

[106] Campbell, B.M.S. (2016), The Great Transition: Climate, Disease and Society in the Late-Medieval World. Cambridge University Press.

[107] Lucas, H.S. (2003), 'The Great European Famine of 1315, 1316, and 1317.' Speculum, 5(4), pp. 343–377.

[108] Diamond, J. (2005), Collapse: How Societies Choose to Fail or Succeed. Penguin Books.

Northern Europe, particularly cod fishing along the Atlantic coast, became crucial as inland agriculture suffered. Additionally, the wine industry in regions like England declined as colder temperatures restricted the cultivation of grapes, while more resilient crops, such as rye, became staples.[109] In North America, Native American communities adjusted their hunting and gathering practices to adapt to the colder climate. Archaeological evidence indicates that some communities moved seasonally to access resources that were increasingly scarce due to the altered climate.[110] The Little Ice Age underscores how climatic shifts can drive significant economic, social, and agricultural changes, compelling human societies to adapt their strategies for survival in response to environmental stressors.

(e) **Industrial Era (1850 CE to Present)**

Industrial Revolution

Beginning around 1750, human activities significantly increased atmospheric CO_2 and other greenhouse gases, marking the start of significant anthropogenic climate change.[111]

The Industrial Revolution, commencing around 1750, marked a transformative period where human activities began to substantially alter the Earth's atmosphere, primarily through the release of carbon dioxide (CO_2) and other greenhouse gases. This era catalysed the shift from agrarian economies to industrialized societies, introducing machinery powered by coal and, subsequently, other fossil fuels, which released vast quantities of greenhouse gases into the atmosphere. The increase in atmospheric CO_2 concentration can be traced to the dramatic rise in coal combustion for manufacturing, transportation, and electricity generation, which were all hallmarks of this transformative age.[112] The mechanization of industries, especially in Britain, involved the widespread adoption of steam engines

[109] Lamb, H.H. (1995), Climate, History, and the Modern World. Routledge.

[110] Anderson, D.G. (2001), Climate and Culture Change in North America AD 900–1600. University of Texas Press.

[111] IPCC. (2013), "Climate Change 2013: The Physical Science Basis." Contribution of Working Group I to the Fifth Assessment Report of the Intergovernmental Panel on Climate Change. Cambridge University Press.

[112] McNeill, J. R. (2000). Something New Under the Sun: An Environmental History of the Twentieth-Century World. W.W. Norton & Company.

powered by coal—a high-carbon fossil fuel—and this initiated a persistent trend of CO_2 emissions. Research indicates that by the mid-nineteenth century, coal was already contributing significantly to the accumulation of greenhouse gases, with emissions increasing approximately tenfold from the late eighteenth century to the early nineteenth century.[113] As industrial practices spread across Europe and North America, the reliance on fossil fuels for various applications such as steel production, textile manufacturing, and transportation amplified greenhouse gas emissions, resulting in an unprecedented alteration of the global carbon cycle.

The environmental impacts of this shift were initially overlooked. However, studies have shown that the rise in atmospheric CO_2 during this period has contributed to what we now recognize as anthropogenic climate change.[114] The recognition of this relationship emerged as scientists analysed historical climate data, discovering that the onset of industrial activities coincided with a steady increase in global temperatures. For instance, ice core samples reveal a marked increase in atmospheric CO_2 levels starting in the mid-eighteenth century, aligning closely with the rise of industrial activities.[115] This evidence has led researchers to classify the Industrial Revolution as the starting point of significant human-driven climate change, shifting the Earth's natural greenhouse effect towards a more intensified state. Furthermore, economic and social motivations behind the Industrial Revolution fostered an era of resource exploitation with limited regard for environmental consequences. Factories relied on nearby coal mines, intensifying deforestation, and altering landscapes to accommodate large-scale extraction. This period laid the foundation for today's fossil-fuel-dependent economies, setting a trajectory that has influenced modern industrial practices and policies.[116] Thus, the Industrial Revolution was not only a turning point for human industry but also for our planet's atmosphere, marking the beginning of an era where human actions became a dominant force in shaping Earth's climate. These studies

[113] Allen, R. C. (2009). The British Industrial Revolution in Global Perspective. Cambridge University Press.

[114] Steffen, W., Grinevald, J., Crutzen, P., & McNeill, J. (2011). "The Anthropocene: Conceptual and Historical Perspectives." Philosophical Transactions of the Royal Society A: Mathematical, Physical and Engineering Sciences, 369(1938), 842–867.

[115] Intergovernmental Panel on Climate Change (IPCC). (2014). Climate Change 2014: Synthesis Report. Geneva: IPCC.

[116] Malm, A. (2016). Fossil Capital: The Rise of Steam Power and the Roots of Global Warming. Verso Books.

emphasize the importance of understanding historical greenhouse gas emissions to contextualize modern climate change and underscore the Industrial Revolution's role in setting a precedent for anthropogenic impact on the environment.

Twentieth Century Warming

The twentieth century saw a rapid increase in global temperatures, particularly after the 1970s, attributed primarily to human activities. This period includes notable events such as the decline in Arctic Sea ice extent and the increase in extreme weather events.[117] The twentieth century marked a significant upward trend in global temperatures, especially pronounced after the 1970s, largely due to anthropogenic factors associated with the burning of fossil fuels, deforestation, and industrial activities. According to the Intergovernmental Panel on Climate Change, global surface temperatures have risen approximately 1.1 degrees Celsius above pre-industrial levels, with the decade from 2011 to 2020 being the warmest on record.[118] This warming has led to profound environmental changes, including a marked reduction in Arctic sea ice extent, which has declined by about 40% since the late 1970s.[119] The reduction in sea ice significantly affects not only polar ecosystems but also global climate patterns, as less ice leads to reduced albedo—a phenomenon where darker ocean water absorbs more sunlight, further increasing temperatures. The Arctic's rapid warming, often referred to as Arctic amplification, has implications for weather patterns across the Northern Hemisphere, contributing to unusual weather events far from the polar regions.[120] Moreover, the increase in global temperatures has been correlated with a rise in the frequency and intensity of extreme weather events. The World Weather

[117] Hansen, J., et al. (2010), "Global surface temperature change." Reviews of Geophysics, 48(4).

[118] Intergovernmental Panel on Climate Change (IPCC). (2021). Climate Change 2021: The Physical Science Basis. Contribution of Working Group I to the Sixth Assessment Report of the Intergovernmental Panel on Climate Change. Cambridge University Press. doi:10.1017/9781009157986.

[119] Stroeve, J., et al. (2012), Arctic Sea ice decline: Faster than forecast. Geophysical Research Letters, 39(8), L09501. doi:10.1029/2012GL051090.

[120] Francis, J. A., & Vavrus, S. J. (2015), Evidence linking Arctic amplification to extreme weather in mid-latitudes. Geophysical Research Letters, 42(1), - Francis, J. A., & Vavrus, S. J. (2015). Evidence linking Arctic amplification to extreme weather in mid-latitudes. Geophysical Research Letters, 42(1), 16–22. doi:10.1002/2014GL091047.

Attribution initiative notes that events such as heatwaves, heavy rainfall, and hurricanes have become more frequent and severe in many parts of the world, partly due to climate change.[121] For instance, the 2010 Russian heatwave, which saw temperatures soar above 40 degrees Celsius, was found to have a probability increased by more than sixty times due to human-induced climate change.[122] Alongside these changes, ocean temperatures have also risen, impacting marine ecosystems and contributing to more severe tropical storms. The increase in sea surface temperatures is linked to the intensity of hurricanes in the Atlantic, insinuating that further warming could exacerbate storm-related hazards.[123] The twentieth century's temperature rise has been characterized by notable environmental shifts and extreme weather phenomena, strongly influenced by human activities. Understanding these changes is critical for developing effective adaptation and mitigation strategies in the face of ongoing climate change challenges. The current century continues to experience rapid warming, with the 2010–2019 decade being the warmest on record. Significant events include record high CO_2 levels exceeding 410 ppm, ongoing extreme weather events, and the melting of polar ice sheets.[124]

Theories Associated with Climate Change

Understanding climate change involves a variety of scientific theories that explain the mechanisms and impacts of global climate alterations:

Greenhouse Gas Theory

Greenhouse Gas (GHG) Theory posits that certain gases in Earth's atmosphere, particularly carbon dioxide (CO_2), methane (CH_4), and water vapour (H_2O), absorb and emit infrared radiation, thereby warming the

[121] World Weather Attribution. (2019). Attribution of extreme weather events to climate change. Available at: World Weather Attribution.

[122] Stott, P.A., et al. (2011). "The Attribution of Weather and Climate-Related Events." Wiley Interdisciplinary Reviews: Climate Change, 2(2), 231–248.

[123] Rahmstorf, S., & Coumou, D. (2011). Increase of Atlantic storminess since the 1970s. Climate Dynamics, 38(3–4), 2389–2399. doi:10.1007/s00382-011-1006-5.

[124] NOAA National Centres for Environmental Information. (2020), "Global Climate Report - Annual 2020." Retrieved from NOAA.

planet through a process known as the greenhouse effect. [125] These gases allow sunlight to enter the atmosphere freely, but when Earth's surface emits this absorbed energy back as heat, greenhouse gases trap some of this outgoing heat, preventing it from escaping into space. This process is essential for maintaining temperatures suitable for life; however, elevated levels of these gases amplify the warming effect, leading to global climate changes.[126]

Evidence supporting the greenhouse gas theory is drawn from a variety of fields, including atmospheric measurements, paleoclimatic studies, and climate modelling. Studies tracking atmospheric CO_2 concentrations over the last century have documented a significant increase in CO_2, from approximately 280 parts per million (ppm) pre-Industrial Revolution to over 400 ppm in recent years, a rise strongly correlated with human activities such as fossil fuel burning and deforestation.[127] Direct measurements of CO_2 and CH_4 from ice cores demonstrate that modern levels of these gases are unprecedented in at least 800,000 years, with notable increases since the industrial era.[128]

Climate models have played a critical role in confirming the greenhouse effect's influence on global warming. Using physical laws of radiation and thermodynamics, these models simulate Earth's climate under various greenhouse gas concentrations and have consistently shown that an increase in GHGs raises global temperatures. For instance, the IPCC's climate assessments detail how models that include increased greenhouse gas concentrations match observed warming trends far better than models that exclude these gases, providing a robust link between GHGs and rising temperatures.[129] These models are further validated by examining past climates; for example, studies of the Eemian interglacial period, where warmer temperatures and elevated CO_2 levels led to higher sea levels,

[125] IPCC. (2021), Climate Change 2021: The Physical Science Basis. Cambridge University Press.

[126] Houghton, J. T. (2004). Global Warming: The Complete Briefing. Cambridge University Press.

[127] Intergovernmental Panel on Climate Change (IPCC). (2014). Climate Change 2014: Synthesis Report. Geneva: IPCC.

[128] Etheridge, D. M., et al. (1996). "Natural and anthropogenic changes in atmospheric CO_2 over the last 1,000 years from air in Antarctic ice and firn." Journal of Geophysical Research: Atmospheres, 101(D2), 4115–4128.

[129] Intergovernmental Panel on Climate Change (IPCC). (2013). Climate Change 2013: The Physical Science Basis. Cambridge University Press.

mirror predictions of current and future GHG-driven climate changes.[130] The radiative forcing effect of greenhouse gases is also supported by satellite data. Measurements of outgoing longwave radiation show less heat escaping Earth's atmosphere at the wavelengths absorbed by greenhouse gases, directly confirming the trapping effect of CO_2 and CH_4.[131] This data aligns with the fundamental principles of atmospheric physics and confirms that the warming is primarily due to increased greenhouse gas concentrations rather than natural variability. In addition to CO_2 and CH_4, water vapour acts as a significant feedback mechanism. Although it does not initiate warming, as temperatures rise due to CO_2 and CH_4, the atmosphere holds more water vapour, which in turn traps more heat, amplifying the warming in what is known as a positive feedback loop.[132] This feedback is well-documented in climate science and underscores the complex interplay between greenhouse gases and Earth's climate system.

Overall, greenhouse gas theory is grounded in empirical data, observational studies, and sophisticated modelling, establishing a robust foundation for understanding anthropogenic climate change. The theory is a cornerstone of climate science and serves as a critical framework for assessing and mitigating the risks of future global warming.

Radiative Forcing

Radiative forcing refers to the change in energy balance in the Earth's atmosphere due to factors such as greenhouse gases, aerosols, and solar radiation.[133,134] Radiative forcing is a fundamental concept in climate science that quantifies the change in energy balance in the Earth's

[130] Dutton, A., et al. (2015). "Sea-level rise due to polar ice-sheet mass loss during past warm periods." Science, 349(6244), aaa4019.

[131] Harries, J. E., et al. (2001). "Increases in greenhouse forcing inferred from the outgoing longwave radiation spectra of the Earth in 1970 and 1997." Nature, 410(6826), 355–357.

[132] Held, I. M., & Soden, B. J. (2000). "Water vapor feedback and global warming." Annual Review of Energy and the Environment, 25(1), 441–475.

[133] Hansen, J., et al. (2005), Efficacy of climate forcings. Journal of Geophysical Research: Atmospheres, 110(D18).

[134] Myhre, G., Shindell, D., Bréon, F.M., Collins, W., Fuglestvedt, J., Huang, J., Koch, D., Lamarque, J.F., Lee, D., Mendoza, B. and Nakajima, T. (2013), *Anthropogenic and natural radiative forcing*. In: *Climate Change 2013: The Physical Science Basis*. Contribution of Working Group I to the Fifth Assessment Report of the Intergovernmental Panel on Climate Change (pp. 659–740). Cambridge: Cambridge University Press.

atmosphere, primarily driven by external factors that alter the incoming and outgoing energy. These factors include greenhouse gases (GHGs), aerosols, and variations in solar radiation. Radiative forcing is typically measured in watts per square meter (W/m^2) and serves as a critical indicator of how different agents contribute to climate change.

Greenhouse gases such as carbon dioxide (CO_2), methane (CH_4), and nitrous oxide (N_2O) play a significant role in positive radiative forcing by trapping heat within the Earth's atmosphere. This process, commonly known as the greenhouse effect, results from GHGs absorbing infrared radiation emitted by the Earth's surface and re-emitting it, leading to a warming of the lower atmosphere. According to the Intergovernmental Panel on Climate Change (IPCC), CO_2 has been the primary contributor to positive radiative forcing, with a level of approximately $+1.68\ W/m^2$ from pre-industrial levels to 2011.[135] Other GHGs such as CH_4 and N_2O also contribute significantly, enhancing the warming effect through similar mechanisms.[136]

Aerosols, in contrast, can cause both positive and negative radiative forcing depending on their type and interaction with clouds. Aerosols such as sulphate particles, emitted largely through industrial processes, reflect sunlight back into space, which leads to a cooling effect known as negative radiative forcing.[137] Conversely, black carbon or soot absorbs sunlight, causing localized warming in the atmosphere.[138] The net effect of aerosols is complex, as they can also modify cloud properties, further affecting the Earth's energy balance. Aerosol-cloud interactions can lead to changes in cloud reflectivity and lifetime, which play a significant role in

[135] IPCC (2013) Climate Change 2013: The Physical Science Basis. Contribution of Working Group I to the Fifth Assessment Report of the Intergovernmental Panel on Climate Change. Cambridge: Cambridge University Press.

[136] Myhre, G., Shindell, D., Bréon, F. M., Collins, W., Fuglestvedt, J., Huang, J., Koch, D., Lamarque, J. F., Lee, D., Mendoza, B., Nakajima, T., Robock, A., Stephens, G., Takemura, T. and Zhang, H. (2013) 'Anthropogenic and Natural Radiative Forcing', in Climate Change 2013: The Physical Science Basis. Cambridge: Cambridge University Press, pp. 659–740.

[137] Charlson, R. J., Schwartz, S. E., Hales, J. M., Cess, R. D., Coakley, J. A., Hansen, J. E. and Hofmann, D. J. (1992) 'Climate forcing by anthropogenic aerosols', Science, 255(5043), pp. 423–430.

[138] Jacobson, M. Z. (2001) 'Strong radiative heating due to the mixing state of black carbon in atmospheric aerosols', Nature, 409(6821), pp. 695–697.

climate dynamics.[139] Aerosol-cloud interactions are a critical component of climate dynamics, as they can significantly influence both cloud reflectivity (albedo) and cloud lifetime. Aerosols serve as cloud condensation nuclei (CCN), around which water vapour condenses to form cloud droplets. When there are more aerosols, they can increase the number of cloud droplets, resulting in smaller droplet sizes. This change enhances the cloud's albedo, making it more reflective and causing it to scatter more sunlight back into space, which cools the Earth's surface—a phenomenon known as the 'Twomey effect'.[140,141] In addition to altering cloud reflectivity, aerosols can affect cloud lifetime. Smaller droplets in clouds suppress precipitation, as they do not coalesce as easily into larger raindrops. This suppression can prolong the cloud's existence, allowing it to persist longer in the atmosphere, further influencing the Earth's energy balance.[142] This effect, often referred to as the 'lifetime effect' or 'Albrecht effect', has been observed to play a significant role in moderating temperatures, particularly by extending the cooling effects of clouds over specific regions.[143,144] These interactions are complex because the effects can vary depending on the types of aerosols, cloud properties, and regional meteorological conditions. For instance, sulphate aerosols tend to enhance cloud reflectivity, leading to cooling, while black carbon aerosols can absorb heat, leading to localized warming, which might reduce cloud cover.[145] Thus, understanding these dynamics is crucial for predicting regional and global climate patterns accurately.

Solar radiation, or variations in the Sun's energy output, is another natural factor that affects radiative forcing. Changes in solar irradiance, which occur over solar cycles, have a modest but measurable impact on the

[139] Haywood, J. and Boucher, O. (2000) 'Estimates of the direct and indirect radiative forcing due to tropospheric aerosols: A review', Reviews of Geophysics, 38(4), pp. 513–543.

[140] Twomey, S. (1977). "The influence of pollution on the shortwave albedo of clouds." Journal of the Atmospheric Sciences, 34(7), 1149–1152.

[141] Haywood, J., & Boucher, O. (2000). "Estimates of the direct and indirect radiative forcing due to tropospheric aerosols: A review." Reviews of Geophysics, 38(4), 513–543.

[142] Albrecht, B. A. (1989). "Aerosols, cloud microphysics, and fractional cloudiness." Science, 245(4923), 1227–1230.

[143] Haywood, J., & Boucher, O. (2000). "Estimates of the direct and indirect radiative forcing due to tropospheric aerosols: A review." Reviews of Geophysics, 38(4), 513–543.

[144] Lohmann, U., & Feichter, J. (2005). "Global indirect aerosol effects: A review." Atmospheric Chemistry and Physics, 5(3), 715–737.

[145] Jacobson, M. Z. (2001). "Strong radiative heating due to the mixing state of black carbon in atmospheric aerosols." Nature, 409(6821), 695–697.

Earth's energy balance. However, these variations are small compared to the changes caused by anthropogenic factors like GHGs and aerosols. For instance, solar forcing has contributed to climate variability on timescales ranging from decades to centuries, but it does not account for the rapid warming observed in recent decades.[146]

Understanding radiative forcing is essential for climate modelling and predicting future climate scenarios. By quantifying the relative contributions of different factors, scientists can estimate how changes in these agents will affect global temperatures. This understanding also allows policymakers to assess the potential impact of mitigation strategies, such as reducing CO_2 emissions or controlling aerosol pollution. For example, the net effect of various climate forcing agents must be considered to accurately predict future climate responses, making radiative forcing a critical component of comprehensive climate models.[147]

Radiative forcing is a measure of how different factors alter the Earth's energy balance. Greenhouse gases contribute to warming through positive radiative forcing, while aerosols can lead to both cooling and warming effects. Solar radiation variations add another layer of complexity, but the overwhelming influence in recent times has been anthropogenic emissions, especially CO_2. Effective climate action requires a deep understanding of these mechanisms to mitigate adverse effects on global climate systems.

Milankovitch Cycles

Long-term variations in Earth's orbit and tilt affect the distribution and intensity of solar radiation received by Earth, leading to cycles of glacial and interglacial periods.[148,149] Milankovitch Cycles refer to long-term changes in the Earth's orbit and axial tilt, which influence the distribution and intensity of solar radiation reaching the planet. These cycles play a crucial role in driving the Earth's climatic patterns, particularly glacial and

[146] Lean, J. L. and Rind, D. H. (2008) 'How natural and anthropogenic influences alter global and regional surface temperatures', Geophysical Research Letters, 35(18), p. L18701.

[147] Hansen, J., Sato, M. and Ruedy, R. (2005) 'Efficacy of climate forcings', Journal of Geophysical Research: Atmospheres, 110(D18), p. D18104.

[148] Milankovitch, M. (1941), Kanon der Erdbestrahlung und seine Anwendung auf das Eiszeitenproblem. Royal Serbian Academy Special Publication.

[149] Imbrie, J. and Imbrie, K.P. (1980), Modeling the climatic response to orbital variations. Science, 207(4434), pp.943–953.

interglacial periods, over tens of thousands to hundreds of thousands of years. There are three main components of Milankovitch Cycles: eccentricity, obliquity, and precession. Eccentricity involves variations in the shape of the Earth's orbit around the Sun, ranging from more circular to more elliptical over a period of approximately 100,000 years. When the orbit is more elliptical, there is a greater difference between the distance to the Sun at perihelion (closest approach) and aphelion (farthest point), which affects the amount of solar energy Earth receives during different parts of the year. During periods of higher eccentricity, seasonal contrasts are more pronounced, which can contribute to the development of glacial cycles.[150] Obliquity refers to changes in the tilt of the Earth's axis, which oscillates between about 22.1° and 24.5° over a 41,000-year period. Variations in axial tilt influence the severity of seasons; a greater tilt increases the contrast between summer and winter, leading to warmer summers and colder winters. Conversely, a smaller tilt results in milder seasons. Periods of lower obliquity are associated with the onset of glacial periods because milder summers in higher latitudes prevent the complete melting of winter snow, allowing glaciers to grow.[151] Precession involves the wobbling motion of the Earth's axis, which changes the timing of when the Earth is closest to or farthest from the Sun over a cycle of about 26,000 years. This precession affects the timing of the seasons and can either amplify or dampen the effects of eccentricity and obliquity. For example, if the Northern Hemisphere experiences summer during perihelion, it will receive more solar energy, leading to warmer summers and potentially melting ice sheets. Conversely, if summer occurs during aphelion, the cooler conditions may support glacial growth.[152] These combined orbital variations cause changes in the distribution of solar radiation, also known as insolation, across different latitudes and times of the year, leading to climatic shifts. Evidence for Milankovitch Cycles' role in climate change has been supported by geological records, such as ice cores and marine sediments, which show periodic patterns corresponding to these

[150] Hays, J. D., Imbrie, J., & Shackleton, N. J. (1976). Variations in the Earth's orbit: Pacemaker of the ice ages. Science, 194(4270), 1121–1132.

[151] Berger, A. (1988). Milankovitch theory and climate. Reviews of Geophysics, 26(4), 624–657.

[152] Kutzbach, J. E. (1981). Monsoon climate of the early Holocene: Climate experiment with the Earth's orbital parameters for 9000 years ago. Science, 214(4516), 59–61.

cycles.[153] While Milankovitch Cycles drive natural long-term climate variations, they cannot explain the rapid warming observed in recent decades, which is primarily due to anthropogenic greenhouse gas emissions.

Anthropogenic Climate Change and Climate Feedback Mechanisms

Human activities, especially since the Industrial Revolution, significantly influence climate change through the emission of greenhouse gases and land-use changes.[154,155] Climate feedback mechanisms are processes that can either amplify or reduce the effects of climate change by altering the initial climate response.[156,157] Positive feedback mechanisms intensify warming, while negative feedback mechanisms work to counterbalance it. One of the most significant positive feedbacks is the ice-albedo feedback. As global temperatures rise, ice and snow cover melt, reducing the Earth's albedo (reflectivity). Since ice and snow reflect most of the sunlight, their loss exposes darker ocean or land surfaces, which absorb more heat, leading to further warming and more ice melt. Another example is the water vapour feedback: warmer temperatures increase evaporation, raising the amount of water vapour in the atmosphere, a potent greenhouse gas. This additional water vapour traps more heat, causing further warming. Negative feedback act to stabilize the climate by counteracting warming. For instance, the cloud feedback effect can be both positive and negative, but in some cases, an increase in low-level clouds can reflect more sunlight back to space, cooling the surface. Another negative feedback is the carbon cycle feedback where higher atmospheric CO_2 leads to enhanced photosynthesis (carbon fertilization), allowing plants to absorb more CO_2 and potentially reducing the amount of this greenhouse gas in the atmosphere.

[153] Hays, J. D., Imbrie, J., & Shackleton, N. J. (1976). Variations in the Earth's orbit: Pacemaker of the ice ages. Science, 194(4270), 1121–1132.

[154] IPCC. (2014), "Climate Change 2014: Impacts, Adaptation, and Vulnerability." Contribution of Working Group II to the Fifth Assessment Report of the Intergovernmental Panel on Climate Change.

[155] Crutzen, P. J. (2002), Geology of mankind. Nature, 415(6867), 23–23.

[156] Lenton, T. M., et al. (2008), Tipping elements in the Earth's climate system. Proceedings of the National Academy of Sciences, 105(6), 1786–1793.

[157] Cox, P.M., Betts, R.A., Jones, C.D., Spall, S.A. and Totterdell, I.J. (2000), Acceleration of global warming due to carbon-cycle feedbacks in a coupled climate model. Nature, 408(6809), pp.184–187.

However, the strength and efficiency of this feedback are still under debate, as other factors like nutrient limitations can affect plant growth. Feedback mechanisms play a crucial role in climate models, as they determine the sensitivity of the climate system to external forces like greenhouse gases. Understanding these mechanisms is essential for accurately predicting future climate scenarios.

Paleoclimate Evidence

Paleoclimate evidence involves studying past climate conditions using natural archives, or 'proxies', which allow scientists to reconstruct historical climates and understand natural variability. Key proxies include ice cores, tree rings, and sediment layers, each providing unique insights into Earth's climatic history. [158,159]

Ice cores are one of the most valuable proxies for reconstructing past climates. Extracted from polar regions like Antarctica and Greenland, these cores contain layers of ice that accumulate over millennia. Each layer traps air bubbles, preserving atmospheric gases like carbon dioxide (CO_2) and methane (CH_4), which provide a record of past atmospheric composition and temperature. For instance, studies from the EPICA Dome C ice core in Antarctica have revealed climate patterns extending back 800,000 years, showing clear cycles of glacial and interglacial periods driven by changes in greenhouse gases and Earth's orbital parameters.[160] Tree rings provide annual records of climate conditions. The width and density of tree rings reflect variations in temperature and precipitation during the growing season. Wider rings typically indicate favourable conditions, such as warmer temperatures or abundant rainfall, while narrower rings may signify droughts or cooler periods. Tree-ring studies have helped reconstruct climate patterns over the last few thousand years, offering insights

[158] Petit, J. R., et al. (1999), Climate and atmospheric history of the past 420,000 years from the Vostok ice core, Antarctica. Nature, 399(6735), 429–436.

[159] Mann, M. E., et al. (2009), "Global signatures and dynamical origins of the Little Ice Age and Medieval Climate Anomaly." Science, 326(5957), 1256–1260.

[160] Jouzel, J., Masson-Delmotte, V., Cattani, O., Dreyfus, G., Falourd, S., Hoffmann, G., ... & Wolff, E. W. (2007). Orbital and millennial Antarctic climate variability over the past 800,000 years. Science, 317(5839), 793–796.

into periods like the Medieval Warm Period and the Little Ice Age.[161] Sediment layers, including those found in lakes and ocean floors, accumulate over long timescales and contain particles such as pollen, dust, and organic matter. By analysing these sediments, scientists can infer past vegetation, sea temperatures, and even volcanic activity, all which impact climate. For example, cores from ocean sediments have been critical in understanding the patterns of glacial cycles, as they contain microfossils (foraminifera) whose isotopic composition reflects historical ocean temperatures.[162] By combining data from these proxies, palaeoclimatologists can build a comprehensive picture of Earth's climate history, revealing patterns of natural variability and providing context for current anthropogenic changes. These records demonstrate that while natural factors have driven climate shifts over millennia, the current rate of warming, largely driven by human activities, is unprecedented in the context of the last few hundred thousand years.[163]

Ocean-Atmosphere Interactions

Ocean-atmosphere interactions are critical for understanding climate variability, as they involve exchanges of heat, moisture, and gases between the ocean and atmosphere.[164,165] Two of the most influential phenomena associated with these interactions are the El Niño-Southern Oscillation (ENSO) and the Atlantic Meridional Overturning Circulation (AMOC). ENSO is a periodic fluctuation in sea surface temperatures and atmospheric pressure across the equatorial Pacific Ocean. It consists of two phases: El Niño and La Niña. During El Niño, warmer-than-average sea surface temperatures in the central and eastern Pacific disrupt typical

[161] Mann, M. E., Zhang, Z., Hughes, M. K., Bradley, R. S., Miller, S. K., Rutherford, S., & Ni, F. (2009). Proxy-based reconstructions of hemispheric and global surface temperature variations over the past two millennia. Proceedings of the National Academy of Sciences, 106(36), 13252–13257.

[162] Imbrie, J., Berger, A., Boyle, E. A., Clemens, S. C., Duffy, A., Howard, W. R., ... & Toggweiler, J. R. (1992). On the structure and origin of major glaciation cycles 1. Linear responses to Milankovitch forcing. Paleoceanography, 7(6), 701–738.

[163] Stocker, T. F., Qin, D., Plattner, G. K., Tignor, M., Allen, S. K., Boschung, J., ... & Midgley, P. M. (2013). Climate Change 2013: The Physical Science Basis. Cambridge University Press.

[164] Philander, S. G. (1983), El Niño Southern Oscillation phenomena. Nature, 302(5906), 295–301.

[165] Broecker, W. S. (1991), The great ocean conveyor. Oceanography, 4(2), 79–89.

weather patterns, leading to effects such as increased rainfall in South America and droughts in parts of Australia and Southeast Asia.[166] Conversely, La Niña involves cooler sea surface temperatures and tends to enhance the opposite weather patterns, such as more intense monsoons in Asia. ENSO significantly influences global climate by altering atmospheric circulation patterns, which can impact temperatures and precipitation far beyond the Pacific region.[167]

The Atlantic Meridional Overturning Circulation (AMOC) is a system of ocean currents in the Atlantic that transports warm, salty water northward at the surface and cold, deep water southward. This process, also known as thermohaline circulation, plays a vital role in regulating climate by distributing heat between the equator and the poles. Changes in the strength of the AMOC can lead to substantial shifts in climate; for example, a weakening of the AMOC is associated with cooler temperatures in the North Atlantic region and can contribute to events like the Little Ice Age.[168] Furthermore, studies have suggested that anthropogenic warming and increased freshwater input from melting ice may destabilize the AMOC, potentially leading to abrupt climate changes.[169] These ocean-atmosphere interactions are interconnected with broader climate systems. For instance, ENSO events can affect the strength of the AMOC by altering wind patterns and precipitation, which, in turn, influence ocean salinity and circulation. Understanding these interactions is essential for improving climate models and predicting future climate variability. Humanities' technological innovation and economic activity, burning fossil fuels, pollutants arising from industrial production; and the resulting greenhouse gases may thus impact on natural cycles bringing about climate change.

[166] McPhaden, M. J., Zebiak, S. E., & Glantz, M. H. (2006). ENSO as an integrating concept in Earth science. Science, 314(5806), 1740–1745.

[167] Trenberth, K. E. (1997). The definition of El Niño. Bulletin of the American Meteorological Society, 78(12), 2771–2777.

[168] Rahmstorf, S. (2006). Thermohaline ocean circulation. Encyclopedia of Quaternary Sciences, 2, 739–750.

[169] Caesar, L., Rahmstorf, S., Robinson, A., Feulner, G., & Saba, V. (2018). Observed fingerprint of a weakening Atlantic Ocean overturning circulation. Nature, 556(7700), 191–196.

Natural Climatic Changes

Milankovitch Cycles

One of the primary drivers of natural climatic variation over the past few million years is the Milankovitch cycles. These cycles consist of changes in Earth's orbit and orientation relative to the Sun, including eccentricity, axial tilt, and precession. These variations influence the distribution and intensity of solar radiation received by Earth, leading to cycles of glacial and interglacial periods. For example, periods of high eccentricity result in more pronounced seasonal changes, while changes in axial tilt affect the severity of seasons and the extent of polar ice sheets.[170]

Ice Ages and Interglacial Periods

The Pleistocene epoch, spanning from about 2.6 million years ago to 11,700 years ago, was characterized by repeated glaciations, where large ice sheets covered much of North America, Europe, and Asia. These glacial periods were interrupted by warmer interglacial periods. The transitions between these periods were often abrupt, influenced by Milankovitch cycles and feedback mechanisms involving greenhouse gases and ice sheet dynamics.[171]

Palaeocene-Eocene Thermal Maximum (PETM)

Approximately 56 million years ago, during the Palaeocene-Eocene Thermal Maximum (PETM), Earth experienced a rapid and intense warming event. This period saw a massive release of carbon into the atmosphere, likely from volcanic activity or methane clathrate release, causing temperatures to rise dramatically. The PETM is often studied as an analogy for current climate change due to the similarities in rapid carbon release and global warming.[172]

[170] NASA. (2024), Milankovitch (Orbital) Cycles and Their Role in Earth's Climate. Retrieved from NASA Science.

[171] Zachos, J. et al. (2020), High-fidelity record of Earth's climate history puts current changes in context. Retrieved from Phys.org.

[172] Ibid.

Anthropogenic Climate Change

Since the Industrial Revolution, human activities have significantly altered the composition of the atmosphere, primarily through the burning of fossil fuels, deforestation, and industrial processes. These activities have increased the concentration of greenhouse gases, such as carbon dioxide, methane, and nitrous oxide, trapping more heat in the atmosphere and leading to global warming.[173]

The Intergovernmental Panel on Climate Change (IPCC) reports that the Earth's average temperature has increased by approximately 1.1°C since the pre-industrial period. This warming is unprecedented in both its rate and magnitude compared to natural climatic variations over the past few million years. Current impacts include more frequent and severe heatwaves, melting glaciers and ice sheets, rising sea levels, and changes in precipitation patterns leading to floods and droughts.[174,175]

Climate change has also intensified extreme weather events. Warmer ocean temperatures fuel more powerful hurricanes and typhoons, while higher atmospheric temperatures increase the likelihood of heavy rainfall events and prolonged droughts. These changes pose significant risks to ecosystems, infrastructure, and human communities.[176] Projections indicate that if greenhouse gas emissions continue at the current rate, global temperatures could rise by 2 to 4 degrees Celsius by the end of the century. This level of warming would have profound effects on global climate systems, potentially leading to the loss of entire ecosystems, more frequent and severe weather events, and significant challenges for human societies.[177]

Addressing climate change requires both mitigation—reducing greenhouse gas emissions—and adaptation—adjusting to the changes that are already underway. Effective mitigation strategies include transitioning to renewable energy sources, improving energy efficiency, and protecting and restoring forests. Adaptation strategies involve building resilient

[173] National Geographic. (2024), The Influence of Climate Change on Extreme Environmental Events. Retrieved from National Geographic.

[174] IPCC (2023), Climate Change 2023: Synthesis Report. IPCC, Geneva, Switzerland. Available at: www.ipcc.ch

[175] NASA. (2024), Milankovitch (Orbital) Cycles and Their Role in Earth's Climate. Retrieved from NASA Science.

[176] National Geographic. (2024), The Influence of Climate Change on Extreme Environmental Events. Retrieved from National Geographic.

[177] Ibid.

infrastructure, developing early warning systems for extreme weather, and planning for sea-level rise.[178]

Climate change has had profound effects on both the Arctic (North Pole) and the Antarctic (South Pole) regions over the last century. These changes are evidenced by significant alterations in ice sheet dynamics, sea ice extent, and overall temperature increases. Below is a detailed analysis of these impacts, citing academic sources to support the findings. The Arctic region has experienced some of the most rapid warming on Earth, a phenomenon known as Arctic amplification. Over the past century, temperatures in the Arctic have increased at more than twice the global average rate.[179] The extent of Arctic Sea ice has been decreasing dramatically, particularly in the summer months. Satellite observations since 1979 show a decline in the summer minimum sea ice extent by about 13% per decade.[180] Arctic glaciers and the Greenland Ice Sheet have been losing mass. The Greenland Ice Sheet has experienced significant melting and ice discharge, contributing to global sea-level rise.[181] Thawing of permafrost in the Arctic is releasing significant amounts of greenhouse gases, including methane and carbon dioxide, further exacerbating global warming.[182] While the warming trend in Antarctica is less uniform compared to the Arctic, the Antarctic Peninsula has warmed significantly, with temperatures increasing by nearly 3°C over the past 50 years.[183] The Antarctic Ice Sheet is losing ice primarily from the West Antarctic Ice Sheet and the Antarctic Peninsula. This loss is driven by warm ocean waters undermining ice shelves and accelerating glacier flow.[184] Several ice shelves in Antarctica, particularly along the Antarctic Peninsula, have collapsed or thinned dramatically in

[178] IPCC (2023), Climate Change 2023: Synthesis Report. IPCC, Geneva, Switzerland. Available at: www.ipcc.ch

[179] Serreze, M. C., & Barry, R. G. (2011), Processes and impacts of Arctic amplification: A research synthesis. Global and Planetary Change, 77(1–2), 85–96.

[180] Stroeve, J., et al. (2012), The Arctic's rapidly shrinking sea ice cover: a research synthesis. Climatic Change, 110(3–4), 1005–1027.

[181] Box, J. E., et al. (2018), Global sea-level contribution from Arctic land ice: 1971–2017. Environmental Research Letters, 13(12), 125012.

[182] Schuur, E. A. G., et al. (2015), Climate change and the permafrost carbon feedback. Nature, 520(7546), 171–179.

[183] Turner, J., et al. (2005), Antarctic climate change during the last 50 years. International Journal of Climatology, 25(3), 279–294.

[184] Rignot, E., et al. (2019), Four decades of Antarctic Ice Sheet mass balance from 1979–2017. Proceedings of the National Academy of Sciences, 116(4), 1095–1103.

recent decades, contributing to increased glacier flow into the ocean.[185] Unlike the Arctic, Antarctic Sea ice extent has shown more variability, with some regions experiencing slight increases. However, recent years have seen a noticeable decline in sea ice extent.[186]

Civilizations Impacted by Climate Change

The Akkadian Empire

The Akkadian Empire, which flourished in Mesopotamia around 2300 BC, is one of the earliest known examples of a civilization affected by climate change. The empire experienced a severe drought around 2200 BC, known as the 4.2-kiloyear event. This prolonged drought led to widespread crop failures and the collapse of the agricultural economy, contributing to the empire's decline. Archaeological evidence from sediment cores and ancient texts supports the theory that environmental stress was a critical factor in the Akkadian Empire's fall.[187] The drought was likely caused by a significant shift in climatic conditions that led to prolonged periods of aridity. Geological and archaeological evidence, including sediment cores from the Persian Gulf and lake deposits, suggest that this period was marked by a sharp decline in precipitation, which caused widespread drought across the Near East.[188,189] The reduced rainfall affected the Tigris and Euphrates rivers, leading to a decline in water levels and a reduction in agricultural productivity. This arid phase is believed to have been driven by changes in atmospheric circulation patterns, potentially linked to shifts in the Intertropical Convergence Zone (ITCZ), which

[185] Scambos, T. A., et al. (2004), Glacier acceleration and thinning after ice shelf collapse in the Larsen B embayment, Antarctica. Geophysical Research Letters, 31(18).

[186] Parkinson, C. L. (2019), A 40-y record reveals gradual Antarctic Sea ice increases followed by decreases at rates far exceeding the rates seen in the Arctic. Proceedings of the National Academy of Sciences, 116(29), 14414–14423.

[187] Weiss, H., et al. (1993). The genesis and collapse of third millennium north Mesopotamian civilization. Science, 261(5124), 995–1004.

[188] Weiss, H., Courty, M.-A., Wetterstrom, W., Guichard, F., Senior, L., Meadow, R., & Curnow, A. (1993). The genesis and collapse of third millennium North Mesopotamian civilization. Science, 261(5124), 995–1004.

[189] Cullen, H. M., deMenocal, P. B., Hemming, S., Hemming, G., Brown, F. H., Guilderson, T., & Sirocko, F. (2000). Climate change and the collapse of the Akkadian empire: Evidence from the deep sea. Geology, 28(4), 379–382.

would have diverted moist air away from Mesopotamia.[190] The decrease in crop yields would have led to food shortages, social stress, and eventually the collapse of centralized control, contributing to the decline of the Akkadian Empire.

The Maya Civilization

The Maya Civilization, which thrived in Mesoamerica from around 2000 BC to 900 CE, also experienced significant climatic challenges. Research indicates that periods of prolonged drought, particularly between 800 and 900 CE, played a crucial role in the collapse of Classic Maya society. These droughts would have disrupted agricultural production, leading to food shortages, social unrest, and the eventual abandonment of major urban centres. Paleoclimate data from lake sediments and cave formations provide strong evidence linking climatic changes to the decline of the Maya civilization.[191,192] The droughts that contributed to the decline of Classic Maya society between 800 and 900 CE were likely caused by a combination of natural climatic variability and shifts in regional atmospheric patterns. Paleoclimate studies, including analyses of lake sediments and cave formations (speleothems), indicate that this period experienced a series of prolonged and severe dry spells, reducing rainfall significantly across the Maya Lowlands.[193,194] One proposed cause of these droughts is a reduction in summer monsoon rains, which are essential for agriculture in the region. Research suggests that changes in sea surface temperatures in the Atlantic and Pacific Oceans could have influenced the strength and position of the Intertropical Convergence Zone (ITCZ), leading to decreased

[190] Staubwasser, M., & Weiss, H. (2006). Holocene climate and cultural evolution in late prehistoric–early historic West Asia. Quaternary Research, 66(3), 372–387.

[191] Haug, G.H., Günther, D., Peterson, L.C., Sigman, D.M., Hughen, K.A. and Aeschlimann, B. (2003), Climate and the collapse of Maya civilization. Science, 299(5613), pp.1731–1735.

[192] Kennett, D.J., Breitenbach, S.F., Aquino, V.V., Asmerom, Y., Awe, J., Baldini, J.U., Bartlein, P., Culleton, B.J., Ebert, C., Jazwa, C. and Macri, M.J. (2012), Development and disintegration of Maya political systems in response to climate change. Science, 338(6108), pp.788–791.

[193] Haug, G. H., Günther, D., Peterson, L. C., Sigman, D. M., Hughen, K. A., & Aeschlimann, B. (2003). Climate and the collapse of Maya civilization. Science, 299(5613), 1731–1735.

[194] Medina-Elizalde, M., & Rohling, E. J. (2012). Collapse of Classic Maya civilization related to modest reduction in precipitation. Science, 335(6071), 956–959.

precipitation in Mesoamerica.[195] Additionally, some studies point to deforestation and land-use changes by the Maya themselves, which may have exacerbated local drought conditions by altering the regional hydrological cycle and reducing moisture availability.[196]

The Ancestral Puebloans

The Ancestral Puebloans, also known as the Anasazi, inhabited the southwestern United States from approximately 200 to 1300 CE. Their society saw significant development in agriculture, architecture, and culture. However, a severe and prolonged drought, often referred to as the Great Drought, occurred around 1276 to 1299 CE. This environmental stress led to crop failures, resource depletion, and the abandonment of their large settlements, such as those at Chaco Canyon and Mesa Verde. Tree-ring data and other paleoclimate indicators provide evidence for the climatic conditions that contributed to the Ancestral Puebloans' migration and societal changes.[197] The drought that affected the Ancestral Puebloans, known as the Great Drought (1276–1299 CE), is believed to have been caused by prolonged periods of reduced precipitation linked to natural climatic variability. Tree-ring data (dendrochronology) from the region indicates that there were consecutive years of low rainfall, which severely impacted the water supply and agricultural productivity.[198] Studies suggest this drought may have been driven by shifts in atmospheric circulation patterns, such as persistent La Niña conditions, which lead to drier-than-average winters in the southwestern United States.[199]

[195] Hodell, D. A., Curtis, J. H., & Brenner, M. (2001). Solar forcing of drought frequency in the Maya Lowlands. Science, 292(5520), 1367–1370.

[196] Oglesby, R. J., Sever, T., Saturno, W., Erickson, D., & Srikishen, J. (2010). Collapse of the Maya: Could deforestation have contributed?. Journal of Geophysical Research: Atmospheres, 115(D12).

[197] Benson, L.V., Berry, M.S., Jolie, E.A., Spangler, J.D., Stahle, D.W. and Hattori, E.M. (2007), Possible impacts of early-11th-, middle-12th-, and late-13th-century droughts on western Native Americans and the Mississippian Cahokians. Quaternary Science Reviews, 26(3–4), pp.336–350.

[198] Stahle, D. W., Fye, F. K., Cook, E. R., & Griffin, R. D. (2007). Tree-ring reconstructed megadroughts over North America since AD 1300. Climatic Change, 83(1–2), 133–149.

[199] Cook, E. R., Woodhouse, C. A., Eakin, C. M., Meko, D. M., & Stahle, D. W. (2004). Long-Term Aridity Changes in the Western United States. Science, 306(5698), 1015–1018.

The Khmer Empire

The Khmer Empire, cantered in present-day Cambodia, reached its peak between the ninth and thirteenth centuries CE. The empire is renowned for its grand architectural achievements, including the temple complex of Angkor Wat. However, climatic changes, particularly a series of severe droughts followed by intense monsoons in the fourteenth and fifteenth centuries, disrupted the water management systems critical to the empire's agriculture and urban life. These climatic stresses, combined with political and social factors, contributed to the decline of the Khmer Empire. Tree-ring and isotopic analyses from the region provide insights into the climatic variability during this period.[200] The droughts followed by the intense monsoons were likely driven by natural variability in the monsoon system of Southeast Asia. Tree-ring studies and isotopic analyses suggest these changes could be linked to shifts in the El Niño-Southern Oscillation (ENSO) and the Indian Ocean Dipole (IOD), which impact monsoon intensity. Prolonged droughts weakened the empire's complex water management infrastructure, while subsequent heavy monsoons likely caused damage to reservoirs and irrigation, disrupting agriculture and urban stability.[201,202]

The Indus Valley Civilization

The Indus Valley Civilization, which flourished from around 3300 to 1300 BC in what is now Pakistan and northwest India, is another example of how climate change may make established civilizations unsustainable. The civilization declined around 1900 BC,[203] coinciding with a shift in the monsoon patterns that led to reduced water availability and agricultural

[200] Buckley, B.M., Anchukaitis, K.J., Penny, D., Fletcher, R., Cook, E.R., Sano, M., Nam, L.C., Wichienkeeo, A., Minh, T.T. and Hong, T.M. (2010), Climate as a contributing factor in the demise of Angkor, Cambodia. Proceedings of the National Academy of Sciences, 107(15), pp.6748–6752.

[201] Buckley, B. M., Anchukaitis, K. J., Penny, D., Fletcher, R., Cook, E. R., Sano, M., ... & Nam, L. C. (2010). Climate as a contributing factor in the demise of Angkor, Cambodia. Proceedings of the National Academy of Sciences, 107(15), 6748–6752.

[202] Cook, E. R., Anchukaitis, K. J., Buckley, B. M., D'Arrigo, R. D., Jacoby, G. C., & Wright, W. E. (2012). Asian monsoon failure and megadrought during the last millennium. Science, 328(5977), 486–489

[203] Possehl, G. L. (2002). The Indus Civilization: A Contemporary Perspective. AltaMira Press.

productivity. Changes in river patterns and prolonged droughts likely exacerbated the challenges faced by this highly urbanized and sophisticated society. Geological and archaeological evidence supports the role of climate change in the decline of the Indus Valley Civilization.[204] Studies of sediment cores and isotopic data indicate that there was a shift to drier conditions around 2100 BC, marked by weakened monsoon patterns.[205] This reduction in rainfall would have decreased river flows, particularly affecting the Ghaggar-Hakra River system, which many settlements relied on for agriculture. Archaeological records show a gradual abandonment of cities, the biggest including Harappa and Mohenjo-Daro, likely as communities migrated to more stable water sources, reflecting an adaptation to changing environmental conditions.[206]

Contemporary Threats

Rising Sea Levels

Rising sea levels due to climate change pose a significant threat to many coastal cities and countries around the world. By 2050, several regions are expected to experience severe flooding, impacting millions of people. There are many cities around the world which may be susceptible to flooding as global sea levels rise. Jakarta is sinking at an alarming rate due to excessive groundwater extraction and is already experiencing regular flooding. By 2050, large parts of the city could be submerged if current trends continue.[207] Bangkok is another city at high risk due to its low elevation, subsidence, and the threat of rising sea levels. The city faces annual

[204] Giosan, L., Clift, P.D., Macklin, M.G., Fuller, D.Q., Constantinescu, S., Durcan, J.A., Stevens, T., Duller, G.A.T., Tabrez, A.R., Gangal, K. and Adhikari, R. (2012), Fluvial landscapes of the Harappan civilization. Proceedings of the National Academy of Sciences, 109(26), pp.E1688–E1694.

[205] Giosan, L., Clift, P. D., Macklin, M. G., Fuller, D. Q., Constantinescu, S., Durcan, J. A., ... & Goodbred, S. L. (2012). Fluvial landscapes of the Harappan civilization. Proceedings of the National Academy of Sciences, 109(26), E1688–E1694.

[206] Staubwasser, M., & Weiss, H. (2006). Holocene climate and cultural evolution in late prehistoric–early historic West Asia. Quaternary Research, 66(3), 372–387.

[207] Abidin, H.Z., Andreas, H., Gumilar, I., Sidiq, T.P. and Fukuda, Y. (2011), Land subsidence of Jakarta (Indonesia) and its relation with urban development. Natural Hazards, 59(3), pp.1753–1771.

flooding during the monsoon season, which is expected to worsen.[208] Mumbai, a major financial hub, is highly vulnerable to sea-level rise and storm surges. Low-lying areas of the city are particularly at risk of flooding.[209] Shanghai, with its extensive coastal and riverine areas, is at significant risk of flooding due to rising sea levels and land subsidence.[210] Ho Chi Minh City is experiencing rapid urbanization and land subsidence, making it highly vulnerable to sea-level rise and flooding.[211]New York City faces a high risk of flooding due to sea-level rise and the increased frequency of extreme weather events like hurricanes. Lower Manhattan and other coastal areas are particularly vulnerable.[212] Miami is one of the most vulnerable cities in the United States to sea-level rise, with significant portions of the city at risk of flooding by 2050.[213]

Vulnerable Countries

Bangladesh, with its low-lying delta region, is extremely vulnerable to sea-level rise. A significant portion of the population lives in areas that could be underwater by 2050.[214] The Netherlands has extensive coastal defences, but parts of the country lie below sea level. Rising sea levels pose a continuous threat to its coastal areas and infrastructure.[215] The Maldives, an archipelago of low-lying islands, faces existential threats from rising sea

[208] Fuchs, T., Koch, M., Münch, Z., Priyadarshi, N. and Thieken, A.H. (2011), Flood risk and adaptation strategies in Bangkok and other urban areas in Southeast Asia. In: M. Kraas, S. Aggarwal, S. Coy and G. Mertins, eds. Megacities: Our Global Urban Future. Dordrecht: Springer, pp.85–102.

[209] Hallegatte, S., Green, C., Nicholls, R.J. and Corfee-Morlot, J. (2013), Future flood losses in major coastal cities. Nature Climate Change, 3(9), pp.802–806.

[210] Yin, J., Yin, Z., Wang, J. and Xu, S. (2013), National assessment of coastal vulnerability to sea-level rise for the Chinese coast. Journal of Coastal Conservation, 17(3), pp.567–579.

[211] Scussolini, P., Tran, T.T., Koks, E.E., Hoekstra, A.Y., Lasage, R., Ward, P.J. and Winsemius, H.C. (2017), Adaptation to sea level rise: a multidisciplinary analysis for Ho Chi Minh City, Vietnam. Water Resources Research, 53(12), pp.10841–10857.

[212] Strauss, B.H., Ziemlinski, R., Weiss, J.L. and Overpeck, J.T. (2012), Tidally adjusted estimates of topographic vulnerability to sea level rise and flooding for the contiguous United States. Environmental Research Letters, 7(1), p.014033.

[213] Stanton, E.A. and Ackerman, F. (2007), Florida and climate change: The costs of inaction. Tufts University, Global Development and Environment Institute.

[214] Huq, S. and Rabbani, G. (2011), Climate change and Bangladesh: Policy and institutional development to reduce vulnerability. Journal of Bangladesh Studies, 13(1), pp.1–10.

[215] Vellinga, P. (2001), Climate change and flood risk in the Netherlands. Global Environmental Change Part B: Environmental Hazards, 3(3–4), pp.59–67.

levels. Most of its islands are only about 1 metre above sea level.[216] Tuvalu, another low-lying island nation, is at risk of becoming uninhabitable due to rising sea levels and increasing saltwater intrusion.[217] Kiribati is highly vulnerable to sea-level rise, with many of its atolls and islands facing the possibility of becoming uninhabitable by 2050.[218]

High Temperatures and Droughts

Climate change is projected to have profound impacts on global weather patterns, leading to increased temperatures and prolonged droughts in various regions. This section identifies and analyses the parts of the world expected to experience these extreme conditions by 2050, supported by academic research and climate models. The MENA region is expected to experience some of the highest temperature increases due to climate change. Projections indicate that summer temperatures could regularly exceed 50°C.[219] These extreme temperatures will have severe implications for human health, agriculture, and water resources.

Urban areas in countries such as Saudi Arabia, Kuwait, and the UAE are particularly at risk. South Asia, including countries like India, Pakistan, and Bangladesh, is projected to see significant temperature increases, with heatwaves becoming more frequent and severe.[220] The rise in temperatures will exacerbate existing vulnerabilities in these densely populated regions, affecting agricultural productivity and increasing the risk of heat-related illnesses and deaths.

Southern Europe, particularly the Mediterranean region, is expected to experience higher average temperatures and more frequent heatwaves.[221] The increase in temperature will affect water availability, agriculture, and

[216] Woodroffe, C.D. (2008), Reef-island topography and the vulnerability of atolls to sea-level rise. Global and Planetary Change, 62(1–2), pp.77–96.

[217] Connell, J. (2003), Losing ground? Tuvalu, the greenhouse effect and the garbage can theory of planning. Asia Pacific Viewpoint, 44(2), pp.89–107.

[218] Donner, S.D. (2015), The legacy of migration in response to climate stress: learning from the Gilbertese resettlement in the Solomon Islands. Natural Resources Forum, 39(3–4), pp.191–201.

[219] Pal, J.S. and Eltahir, E.A.B. (2016), Future temperature in southwest Asia projected to exceed a threshold for human adaptability. Nature Climate Change, 6(2), pp.197–200.

[220] Im, E.S., Pal, J.S. and Eltahir, E.A.B. (2017), Deadly heat waves projected in the densely populated agricultural regions of South Asia. Science Advances, 3(8), p.e1603322.

[221] Kovats, R.S. and Kristie, L.E. (2006), Heatwaves and public health in Europe. The European Journal of Public Health, 16(6), pp.592–599.

human health, with countries like Spain, Italy, and Greece facing significant challenges. The western United States, including California, Nevada, and Arizona, is likely to see a rise in temperatures, leading to more frequent and intense heatwaves.[222] Higher temperatures will exacerbate water scarcity issues, affect agricultural productivity, and increase the risk of wildfires.

Droughts

Sub-Saharan Africa is projected to experience more frequent and severe droughts due to climate change.[223] Regions such as the Sahel and parts of East Africa are particularly vulnerable. Droughts will severely affect agriculture, food security, and water availability, leading to increased risk of famine and displacement. Australia is expected to face more frequent and prolonged droughts, particularly in the southern and eastern regions.[224] Drought conditions will impact water resources and agriculture and increase the risk of bushfires, putting significant strain on the environment and the economy. Central America, including countries like Guatemala, Honduras, and Nicaragua, is likely to experience more frequent droughts.[225] Drought conditions will affect crop yields, water availability, and exacerbate socioeconomic challenges in the region. In addition to high temperatures, Southern Europe is projected to experience more severe and prolonged droughts.[226] Droughts will impact agriculture, water

[222] Diffenbaugh, N.S., Swain, D.L. and Touma, D. (2015), Anthropogenic warming has increased drought risk in California. Proceedings of the National Academy of Sciences, 112(13), pp.3931–3936.

[223] IPCC (2014), Climate Change 2014: Impacts, Adaptation, and Vulnerability. Contribution of Working Group II to the Fifth Assessment Report of the Intergovernmental Panel on Climate Change. Cambridge: Cambridge University Press.

[224] CSIRO and Bureau of Meteorology (2015), Climate Change in Australia: Projections for Australia's NRM Regions. Canberra: CSIRO and Bureau of Meteorology.

[225] Magrin, G., Marengo, J.A., Boulanger, J.P., Bourges, C., Cortez, S., Glantz, M.H. and Vicente-Serrano, S.M. (2014), Central and South America. In: Climate Change 2014: Impacts, Adaptation, and Vulnerability. Contribution of Working Group II to the Fifth Assessment Report of the Intergovernmental Panel on Climate Change. Cambridge: Cambridge University Press.

[226] Luterbacher, J., Xoplaki, E., Casty, C., Wanner, H., Pauling, A. and Küttel, M. (2006), Mediterranean climate variability over the last centuries: a review. Developments in Earth and Environmental Sciences, 4, pp.27–148.

supply, and increase the risk of forest fires, particularly in Mediterranean countries.

Combined Impact of High Temperatures and Droughts

India is expected to face a combination of high temperatures and prolonged droughts, particularly in the northern and central regions.[227] This combination will exacerbate water scarcity, affect agricultural productivity, and increase the risk of heat-related health issues. The southwestern United States, including California, Arizona, and New Mexico, will likely experience both higher temperatures and more severe droughts.[228] The combined effects will strain water resources, reduce agricultural yields, and increase the frequency and intensity of wildfires.

Impact of Climate Change of Southeast Asia by 2050

Southeast Asia, a region characterized by diverse ecosystems, rich biodiversity, and dense human populations, is particularly vulnerable to the impacts of climate change. By 2050, the region is expected to face significant challenges, including rising temperatures, sea-level rise, increased frequency of extreme weather events, and adverse effects on agriculture and human health. This report examines these anticipated impacts, supported by academic research and climate models.

Southeast Asia is projected to experience significant temperature increases by 2050, with average temperatures rising by 2–3°C above pre-industrial levels.[229] Higher temperatures will exacerbate heat stress, particularly in urban areas, leading to increased mortality and morbidity.[230] Coastal regions and low-lying islands in Southeast Asia are highly

[227] Krishnan, R., Sanjay, J., Gnanaseelan, C., Mujumdar, M., Kulkarni, A. and Chakraborty, S. (2020), Assessment of climate change over the Indian region: a report of the Ministry of Earth Sciences (MoES), Government of India. Springer Nature.

[228] Cook, B.I., Ault, T.R. and Smerdon, J.E. (2015), Unprecedented 21st century drought risk in the American Southwest and Central Plains. Science Advances, 1(1), p.e1400082.

[229] Hijioka, Y., Lin, E., Pereira, J.J., Corlett, R.T., Cui, X., Insarov, G.E., Lasco, R.D., Lindgren, E. and Surjan, A. (2014), Asia. In: Climate Change 2014: Impacts, Adaptation, and Vulnerability. Part B: Regional Aspects. Contribution of Working Group II to the Fifth Assessment Report of the Intergovernmental Panel on Climate Change. Cambridge: Cambridge University Press.

[230] Im, E.S., Pal, J.S. and Eltahir, E.A.B. (2017), Deadly heat waves projected in the densely populated agricultural regions of South Asia. Science Advances, 3(8), p.e1603322.

vulnerable to sea level rise. By 2050, sea levels are projected to rise by approximately 0.5 metres, significantly increasing the risk of flooding.[231] Major cities such as Jakarta, Bangkok, and Manila face severe risks of coastal flooding and land subsidence, threatening infrastructure and livelihoods.[232]

Climate change is expected to increase the frequency and intensity of extreme weather events, including typhoons, heavy rainfall, and droughts.[233] Enhanced extreme weather patterns will lead to greater loss of life, economic damage, and displacement of populations.[234] Changes in temperature and precipitation patterns will adversely affect agricultural productivity. Key crops such as rice, maize, and wheat are particularly vulnerable.[235] Reduced crop yields will threaten food security, increase food prices, and potentially lead to malnutrition and economic instability in rural areas.[236]

Climate change will alter hydrological cycles, affecting water availability in Southeast Asia. Regions dependent on monsoon rains will experience increased variability in water supply.[237] Water scarcity will affect

[231] IPCC (2014), Climate Change 2014: Impacts, Adaptation, and Vulnerability. Part B: Regional Aspects. Contribution of Working Group II to the Fifth Assessment Report of the Intergovernmental Panel on Climate Change. Cambridge: Cambridge University Press.

[232] Esteban, M., Takagi, H., Nicholls, R.J., Fatma, D., Pratama, M.B., Kurobe, S. and Shibayama, T. (2020), Adaptation to sea level rise: learning from present examples of land subsidence. Ocean & Coastal Management, 189, p.105145.

[233] Hijioka, Y., Lin, E., Pereira, J.J., Corlett, R.T., Cui, X., Insarov, G.E., Lasco, R.D., Lindgren, E. and Surjan, A. (2014), Asia. In: Climate Change 2014: Impacts, Adaptation, and Vulnerability. Part B: Regional Aspects. Contribution of Working Group II to the Fifth Assessment Report of the Intergovernmental Panel on Climate Change. Cambridge: Cambridge University Press.

[234] Cinco, T.A., De Guzman, R.G., Hilario, F.D. and Wilson, D.M. (2016), Long-term trends and extremes in observed daily precipitation and near surface air temperature in the Philippines for the period 1951–2010. Atmospheric Research, 168, pp.73–86.

[235] Nelson, G.C., Rosegrant, M.W., Koo, J., Robertson, R., Sulser, T., Zhu, T., Ringler, C., Msangi, S., Palazzo, A., Batka, M. and Magalhaes, M. (2010), Climate change: Impact on agriculture and costs of adaptation. International Food Policy Research Institute (IFPRI).

[236] Timmermann, A., An, S.I., Kug, J.S., Jin, F.F. and Cai, W. (2019), El Niño–Southern Oscillation complexity. Nature, 559(7715), pp.535–541.

[237] Vörösmarty, C.J., Green, P., Salisbury, J. and Lammers, R.B. (2000), Global water resources: vulnerability from climate change and population growth. Science, 289(5477), pp.284–288.

agriculture, drinking water supply, and industrial activities, exacerbating existing water management challenges.[238]

Rising temperatures will increase the incidence of heat-related illnesses, such as heatstroke; cardiovascular diseases; and other health conditions.[239] Higher temperatures can lead to heat exhaustion and heatstroke, particularly during heatwaves, which are becoming more frequent and intense due to climate change.[240] Heatstroke occurs when the body's temperature regulation fails, leading to symptoms such as confusion, seizures, and even death if not treated promptly. For instance, during the European heatwave of 2003, it is estimated that more than 70,000 people died due to heat-related conditions, with older adults and those with pre-existing health conditions being the most affected.[241] Additionally, rising temperatures exacerbate cardiovascular diseases. Heat stress can increase heart rates and blood viscosity, elevating the risk of heart attacks and strokes, especially among vulnerable populations like the elderly and those with pre-existing cardiovascular conditions.[242] Studies in the United States have shown that for every 1°C increase in temperature above 20°C, the risk of cardiovascular mortality increases by 3%.[243] Urban areas are particularly affected due to the urban heat island effect, which causes temperatures to be significantly higher than in rural areas, further increasing the risk of heat-related illnesses.[244] The impacts of rising temperatures on health are not evenly distributed, with low-income and marginalized communities often facing higher risks due to inadequate housing, lack of access to cooling, and

[238] Asian Development Bank (ADB). (2013). Asian Water Development Outlook 2013: Measuring Water Security in Asia and the Pacific. Manila: AD

[239] Huang, C., Barnett, A.G., Wang, X., Vaneckova, P., Fitzgerald, G. and Tong, S. (2011), Projecting future heat-related mortality under climate change scenarios: A systematic review. Environmental Health Perspectives, 119(12), pp.1681–1690.

[240] Patz, J.A., Campbell-Lendrum, D., Holloway, T., and Foley, J.A. (2005), Impact of regional climate change on human health. *Nature*, 438(7066), pp.310–317.

[241] Robine, J.M., Cheung, S.L., Le Roy, S., Van Oyen, H., Griffiths, C., Michel, J.P., and Herrmann, F.R. (2008), Death toll exceeded 70,000 in Europe during the summer of 2003. *Comptes Rendus Biologies*, 331(2), pp.171–178.

[242] Basu, R. and Samet, J.M. (2002), Relation between elevated ambient temperature and mortality: a review of the epidemiologic evidence. *Epidemiologic Reviews*, 24(2), pp.190–202.

[243] Baccini, M., Biggeri, A., Accetta, G., Kosatsky, T., Katsouyanni, K., Analitis, A., and Schwartz, J. (2008), Heat effects on mortality in 15 European cities. Epidemiology, 19(5), pp.711–719.

[244] Ostro, B., Rauch, S., Green, R., Malig, B., and Basu, R. (2010), The effects of temperature and use of air conditioning on hospitalizations. American Journal of Epidemiology, 172(9), pp.1053–1061.

limited healthcare resources.[245] In cities like Phoenix, Arizona, low-income neighbourhoods experience higher rates of heat-related hospital admissions compared to wealthier areas, illustrating the compounded effects of social and environmental factors.[246]

Vector-Borne Diseases

Changes in climate, particularly rising temperatures and altered precipitation patterns, are expected to expand the geographic range and seasonal activity of vector-borne diseases such as dengue fever and malaria, creating significant public health challenges. [247] These diseases are transmitted by vectors like mosquitoes, whose life cycles and habitat suitability are highly sensitive to climate conditions.[248]

Dengue Fever

Dengue fever, caused by the Aedes mosquito, has seen a dramatic increase in incidence due to changing climate conditions. Warmer temperatures can shorten the development time of the mosquito larvae and increase the frequency of mosquito bites, thereby enhancing the transmission of the virus.[249] For example, dengue outbreaks have been reported in regions where it was previously uncommon, such as the southern United States and parts of Europe, indicating a shift in the disease's range.[250] In Brazil, where rising temperatures and increased rainfall have created ideal breeding conditions for Aedes aegypti, there has been a significant rise in

[245] Harlan, S.L., Brazel, A.J., Prashad, L., Stefanov, W.L., and Larsen, L. (2006), Neighborhood microclimates and vulnerability to heat stress. Social Science & Medicine, 63(11), pp.2847–2863.

[246] Ruddell, D.M., Harlan, S.L., Grossman-Clarke, S., and Buyantuyev, A. (2010), Risk and exposure to extreme heat in microclimates of Phoenix, AZ. In Geospatial techniques in urban hazard and disaster analysis (pp. 179–202). Springer, Dordrecht.

[247] Githeko, A.K., Lindsay, S.W., Confalonieri, U.E. and Patz, J.A. (2000), Climate change and vector-borne diseases: a regional analysis. Bulletin of the World Health Organization, 78(9), pp.1136–1147.

[248] Githeko, A.K., Lindsay, S.W., Confalonieri, U.E., and Patz, J.A. (2000), Climate change and vector-borne diseases: a regional analysis. *Bulletin of the World Health Organization*, 78(9), pp.1136–1147.

[249] Murray, N.E., Quam, M.B., and Wilder-Smith, A. (2013), Epidemiology of dengue: past, present and future prospects. Clinical Epidemiology, 5, pp.299–309.

[250] Messina, J.P., Brady, O.J., Scott, T.W., Zou, C., Pigott, D.M., Duda, K.A., and Hay, S.I. (2014), Global spread of dengue virus types: mapping the 70-year history. Trends in Microbiology, 22(3), pp.138–146.

dengue cases, with over two million reported cases in 2019 alone.[251] Aedes aegypti is a mosquito species that plays a crucial role in the transmission of several significant viral diseases, including dengue fever, Zika virus, chikungunya, and yellow fever. Its widespread distribution and close association with human environments make it a major public health threat, particularly in tropical and subtropical regions.

Aedes aegypti is distinguished by its small, dark body, white banding on its legs, and a unique lyre-shaped pattern of silvery scales on its thorax. It is a day-biting mosquito, with peak activity periods in the early morning and late afternoon.[252] Unlike other mosquito species, Aedes aegypti prefers to feed on humans rather than animals, making it an efficient vector for human pathogens. Its lifecycle includes an aquatic stage (egg, larva, and pupa) and an adult stage. The eggs can survive desiccation for several months, which helps the species persist in urban environments with intermittent water availability.[253] Aedes aegypti is the primary vector for dengue fever, a disease that affects millions annually. For instance, in Southeast Asia, the presence of Aedes aegypti has been directly linked to frequent dengue outbreaks. In 2019, the Philippines declared a national dengue epidemic after more than 622,000 cases were reported, a situation exacerbated by the widespread presence of this mosquito species.[254,255] The same mosquito is also responsible for the transmission of the Zika virus, which led to an international public health emergency in 2016 due to its association with severe birth defects like microcephaly.[256] Aedes aegypti has adapted well to urban environments, often breeding in man-made containers such as water storage tanks, flowerpots, and discarded tires. Its ability to thrive in these artificial habitats makes it particularly difficult to

[251] Leta, S., Beyene, T.J., De Clercq, E.M., Amenu, K., Kraemer, M.U. and Revie, C.W. (2020), Global risk mapping for major diseases transmitted by Aedes mosquitoes. International Journal of Infectious Diseases, 95, pp.123–131.

[252] Christophers, S.R. (1960), Aedes aegypti (L.) the yellow fever mosquito: Its life history, bionomics and structure. Cambridge University Press.

[253] Clements, A.N. (1992), The Biology of Mosquitoes: Development, Nutrition and Reproduction. Chapman & Hall.

[254] Morrison, A.C., Zielinski-Gutierrez, E., Scott, T.W., and Rosenberg, R. (2008), Defining challenges and proposing solutions for control of the virus vector Aedes aegypti. PLoS Medicine, 5(3), p.e68.

[255] WHO (2019), Dengue and severe dengue. [online] Available at: https://www.who.int/news-room/fact-sheets/detail/dengue-and-severe-dengue [Accessed 20 Sep. 2023].

[256] Musso, D., and Gubler, D.J. (2016), Zika virus. Clinical Microbiology Reviews, 29(3), pp.487–524.

control. Traditional vector control measures, such as insecticide spraying, are often ineffective due to the mosquito's breeding habits and the development of insecticide resistance.[257] For example, in parts of Latin America, widespread resistance to pyrethroid insecticides has been documented, complicating efforts to control mosquito populations.[258]

The persistence of Aedes aegypti in urban areas poses significant public health challenges. In Brazil, the coexistence of dengue, chikungunya, and Zika viruses has led to simultaneous outbreaks, straining public health systems and highlighting the need for integrated vector management strategies.[259] Effective control of Aedes aegypti requires a combination of community education, environmental management to eliminate breeding sites, and novel interventions like genetically modified mosquitoes.[260]

Malaria

Malaria, transmitted by Anopheles mosquitoes, is similarly affected by climate change. Warmer temperatures can accelerate the mosquito's life cycle and reduce the incubation period of the malaria parasite within the mosquito, leading to increased transmission rates.[261] Regions at higher altitudes that were previously too cool for the malaria parasite are now experiencing cases of the disease as temperatures rise. In the highlands of East Africa, for instance, malaria is being reported at higher elevations than before, exposing populations that lack immunity to the disease.[262] This expansion into new areas poses a serious public health challenge as

[257] Moyes, C.L., Vontas, J., Martins, A.J., Ng, L.C., Koou, S.Y., Dusfour, I., and Weetman, D. (2017), Contemporary status of insecticide resistance in the major Aedes vectors of arboviruses infecting humans. PLoS Neglected Tropical Diseases, 11(7), p.e0005625.

[258] Ranson, H., Burhani, J., Lumjuan, N., and Black IV, W.C. (2010), Insecticide resistance in dengue vectors. Tropical Medicine & International Health, 15(4), pp.632–644.

[259] Brady, O.J., Gething, P.W., Bhatt, S., Messina, J.P., Brownstein, J.S., Hoen, A.G., and Hay, S.I. (2014), Refining the global spatial limits of dengue virus transmission by evidence-based consensus. PLoS Neglected Tropical Diseases, 8(8), p.e3268.

[260] Carvalho, D.O., McKemey, A.R., Garziera, L., Lacroix, R., Donnelly, C.A., Alphey, L., and Capurro, M.L. (2015), Suppression of a field population of Aedes aegypti in Brazil by sustained release of transgenic male mosquitoes. PLOS Neglected Tropical Diseases, 9(7), p.e0003864.

[261] Martens, W.J., Niessen, L.W., Rotmans, J., Jetten, T.H., and McMichael, A.J. (1995), Potential impact of global climate change on malaria risk. Environmental Health Perspectives, 103(5), pp.458–464.

[262] Siraj, A.S., Santos-Vega, M., Bouma, M.J., Yadeta, D., Ruiz Carrascal, D. and Pascual, M. (2014), Altitudinal changes in malaria incidence in highlands of Ethiopia and Colombia. Science, 343(6175), pp.1154–1158.

health systems in these regions are often unprepared to manage malaria outbreaks.

Public Health Challenges

The expansion of vector-borne diseases due to climate change complicates public health efforts, particularly in developing countries where healthcare resources are already limited. Increased incidence of these diseases places additional strain on healthcare systems, necessitating more extensive surveillance, prevention, and treatment programmes.[263] Moreover, controlling vector populations becomes more difficult as suitable habitats for vectors spread, and traditional control methods, such as insecticides, face challenges like resistance development.[264]

Biodiversity and Ecosystems

Ecosystem Degradation

Climate change will lead to habitat loss and changes in species distribution, threatening biodiversity in Southeast Asia's rich ecosystems.[265] This region is home to some of the world's most diverse habitats, including tropical rainforests, mangroves, and coral reefs, all of which are highly sensitive to changes in temperature, precipitation, and sea level. For example, rising temperatures and altered rainfall patterns are projected to shift the distribution of key forest types, such as mountain and lowland forests, forcing species like the Sumatran tiger and the orangutan to move to higher altitudes or risk extinction due to shrinking habitats.[266] In marine ecosystems, rising sea temperatures and ocean acidification are causing widespread coral bleaching and threatening coral reefs, which are crucial

[263] Hales, S., de Wet, N., Maindonald, J., and Woodward, A. (2002), Potential effect of population and climate changes on global distribution of dengue fever: an empirical model. The Lancet, 360(9336), pp.830–834.

[264] Moyes, C.L., Vontas, J., Martins, A.J., Ng, L.C., Koou, S.Y., Dusfour, I., and Weetman, D. (2017), Contemporary status of insecticide resistance in the major Aedes vectors of arboviruses infecting humans. PLoS Neglected Tropical Diseases, 11(7), p.e0005625.

[265] Sodhi, N.S., Koh, L.P., Brook, B.W. and Ng, P.K.L. (2010), Southeast Asian biodiversity: an impending disaster. Trends in Ecology & Evolution, 19(12), pp.654–660.

[266] Struebig, M.J., Kingston, T., Zubaid, A., Mohd-Adnan, A., Rossiter, S.J., and Turner, A. (2015), Conservation importance of forest fragments to Sundaic bats and the potential effects of climate and land-use change. *Biodiversity and Conservation*, 24(4), pp.1033–1050.

habitats for a vast array of marine species. The Coral Triangle, which spans Indonesia, Malaysia, the Philippines, and other Southeast Asian nations, is experiencing significant coral loss, impacting species such as the Napoleon wrasse, an iconic fish species and reef sharks. As a consequence, there will be a negative impact on the livelihoods of millions of people who depend on these ecosystems for food and tourism.[267] Additionally, sea-level rise and coastal erosion are degrading mangrove forests and seagrass beds, which serve as nurseries for fish and protect coastlines from storms and flooding, further exacerbating biodiversity loss in the region.[268]

Coral reefs, mangroves, and rainforests will be particularly affected, resulting in loss of ecosystem services and impacting livelihoods dependent on these natural resources.[269] Coral reefs, mangroves, and rainforests provide essential ecosystem services, such as coastal protection, carbon sequestration, and resources for food and income, and their degradation due to climate change and human activities has severe implications for both biodiversity and human livelihoods.

Coral reefs are highly sensitive to temperature increases and ocean acidification. As sea temperatures rise, corals experience bleaching, where they expel the symbiotic algae living in their tissues, losing their colour and, more importantly, their primary source of energy. For instance, the Great Barrier Reef has experienced significant coral bleaching events in 2016 and 2017, resulting in the loss of over half of its coral cover.[270] The degradation of coral reefs impacts the livelihoods of millions of people who rely on them for fisheries, tourism, and coastal protection. In Southeast Asia, which hosts over 30% of the world's coral reefs, the decline in reef health threatens the food security and income of coastal communities that depend on reef-associated fisheries.[271]

[267] Veron, J.E.N., Devantier, L.M., Turak, E., Green, A.L., Kininmonth, S., Stafford-Smith, M., and Peterson, N. (2009), Delineating the Coral Triangle. Galaxea, Journal of Coral Reef Studies, 11(2), pp.91–100.

[268] Alongi, D.M. (2008), Mangrove forests: Resilience, protection from tsunamis, and responses to global climate change. Estuarine, Coastal and Shelf Science, 76(1), pp.1–13.

[269] Hoegh-Guldberg, O., Mumby, P.J., Hooten, A.J., Steneck, R.S., Greenfield, P., Gomez, E., Harvell, C.D., Sale, P.F., Edwards, A.J., Caldeira, K. and Knowlton, N. (2007), Coral reefs under rapid climate change and ocean acidification. Science, 318(5857), pp.1737–1742.

[270] Hughes, T.P., Kerry, J.T., Álvarez-Noriega, M., Álvarez-Romero, J.G., Anderson, K.D., Baird, A.H., Babcock, R.C., Beger, M., Bellwood, D.R., Berkelmans, R. and Bridge, T.C. (2017), Global warming and recurrent mass bleaching of corals. Nature, 543(7645), pp.373–377.

[271] Wilkinson, C. ed. (2008), *Status of Coral Reefs of the World: 2008*. Global Coral Reef Monitoring Network and Reef and Rainforest Research Centre.

Mangroves, which provide critical ecosystem services such as storm protection, erosion control, and nurseries for fish species, are also under threat. Rising sea levels, combined with land-use changes like deforestation and urban development, are causing widespread loss of mangrove habitats. In Vietnam, for example, mangrove deforestation for shrimp farming has led to a reduction in coastal protection and increased vulnerability to storms and coastal erosion.[272] This loss of mangroves also disrupts local fisheries, affecting the livelihoods of communities that rely on these ecosystems for subsistence and commercial fishing.[273]

Rainforests, often referred to as the 'lungs of the Earth', play a crucial role in carbon sequestration and maintaining global climate stability. Deforestation and climate change are leading to the fragmentation and degradation of these ecosystems. In the Amazon, deforestation for agriculture and logging has not only contributed to a loss of biodiversity but has also affected the climate regulation services that the forest provides.[274] Indigenous communities that depend on the forest for food, medicine, and cultural practices are particularly vulnerable. For example, in Indonesia, deforestation for palm oil plantations has not only destroyed critical habitats but also displaced indigenous populations, affecting their traditional livelihoods.[275]

Socioeconomic Impacts

Economic Losses

The economic impacts of climate change are projected to be substantial, affecting sectors such as agriculture, fisheries, and tourism.[276] This is primarily due to rising temperatures, shifting precipitation patterns, and

[272] Barbier, E.B. (2006), Mangrove dependency and the livelihoods of coastal communities in Thailand and Cambodia. In *Valuation of regulating services of ecosystems: Methodology and applications* (pp. 63–82). Springer, Dordrecht.

[273] FAO. (2007), *The World's Mangroves 1980–2005.* Rome: Food and Agriculture Organization of the United Nations.

[274] Malhi, Y., Roberts, J.T., Betts, R.A., Killeen, T.J., Li, W. and Nobre, C.A. (2008), Climate change, deforestation, and the fate of the Amazon. Science, 319(5860), pp.169–172.

[275] Colchester, M., Jiwan, N., Andiko, M.Z., Sirait, M., Firdaus, A.Y., Surambo, A. and Pane, H. (2011), Palm oil and land acquisition in Indonesia: Implications for local communities and indigenous peoples. London: International Land Coalition.

[276] Asian Development Bank (ADB). (2013), Asian Water Development Outlook 2013: Measuring Water Security in Asia and the Pacific. Manila: ADB.

increased frequency of extreme weather events that disrupt key economic sectors such as agriculture, fisheries, and tourism. In agriculture, for example, changing climate conditions can reduce crop yields due to increased droughts, heatwaves, and altered growing seasons. For example, a study found that US corn and soybean yields could decrease by up to 82% by the end of the century under high-emission scenarios. Similarly, fisheries are affected as rising sea temperatures and ocean acidification alter fish populations and distribution.[277] A study also predicts that maximum catch potential in tropical regions could decline by 40% by 2050, threatening food security and livelihoods in these areas.[278] The tourism industry is also vulnerable, particularly in regions dependent on natural attractions like coral reefs and ski resorts. Coral bleaching events, driven by higher sea temperatures, have caused significant damage to reefs in the Great Barrier Reef, leading to a decline in tourism revenue.[279] Similarly, the ski industry in the Alps faces reduced snowfall and shorter ski seasons, impacting local economies.[280]

Increased economic losses will exacerbate poverty and inequality, particularly in vulnerable communities.[281] Poorer communities often rely heavily on climate-sensitive sectors such as agriculture and fishing, and they have limited resources to recover from extreme weather events or adapt to changing conditions. For example, in Sub-Saharan Africa, where a significant portion of the population depends on rain-fed agriculture, droughts can devastate crops, leading to food shortages and loss of income, which deepens poverty.[282] Similarly, in coastal regions of South Asia, rising sea levels and intensified cyclones threaten both livelihoods and homes,

[277] Schlenker, W. and Roberts, M.J. (2009), Nonlinear temperature effects indicate severe damages to US crop yields under climate change. Proceedings of the National Academy of Sciences, 106(37), pp.15594–15598.

[278] Cheung, W.W.L., Lam, V.W.Y., Sarmiento, J.L., Kearney, K., Watson, R. and Pauly, D. (2010), Large-scale redistribution of maximum fisheries catch potential in the global ocean under climate change. Global Change Biology, 16(1), pp.24–35.

[279] Hoegh-Guldberg, O. (1999), Climate change, coral bleaching and the future of the world's coral reefs. *Marine and Freshwater Research*, 50(8), pp.839–866.

[280] Steiger, R. and Abegg, B. (2013), The sensitivity of Austrian ski areas to climate change. Tourism Planning & Development, 10(4), pp.480–493.

[281] Hallegatte, S., Green, C., Nicholls, R.J. and Corfee-Morlot, J. (2013), Future flood losses in major coastal cities. Nature Climate Change, 3(9), pp.802–806.

[282] Morton, J.F. (2007), The impact of climate change on smallholder and subsistence agriculture. *Proceedings of the National Academy of Sciences*, 104(50), pp.19680–19685.

pushing many into poverty.[283] The unequal distribution of economic losses also worsens inequality within and between communities. Wealthier individuals and regions have more resources to implement adaptive measures such as improved infrastructure or insurance, while poorer communities are left more exposed to climate risks.[284] For instance, Hurricane Katrina in 2005 disproportionately affected low-income and African American communities in New Orleans, who faced greater challenges in evacuating, securing housing, and recovering economically, thus amplifying pre-existing social and economic inequalities.[285] These low income and African American were disproportionately affected due to a combination of historical and systemic factors. Prior to the hurricane, many African American residents lived in low-lying areas such as the Lower Ninth Ward, which were more vulnerable to flooding due to inadequate infrastructure and investment.[286] The median household income in these neighbourhoods was significantly lower than the city average, and a high percentage of residents lived below the poverty line.[287] As a result, many lacked the financial resources or access to transportation needed to evacuate the city before the storm hit. After the hurricane, these communities faced greater challenges in securing temporary housing and accessing government aid for recovery. The bureaucratic complexities of the Federal Emergency Management Agency (FEMA) assistance programmes disproportionately affected low-income residents who often lacked the necessary documentation or knowledge to navigate these systems.[288] Moreover, the widespread destruction of affordable housing meant that many were unable to return to their neighbourhoods, leading to long-term displacement and further

[283] Dasgupta, S., Laplante, B., Meisner, C., Wheeler, D., and Yan, D. (2009), The impact of sea level rise on developing countries: a comparative analysis. *Climatic Change*, 93(3–4), pp.379–388.

[284] Hallegatte, S., Vogt-Schilb, A., Bangalore, M., and Rozenberg, J. (2016), Unbreakable: Building the Resilience of the Poor in the Face of Natural Disasters. Washington, DC: World Bank.

[285] Elliott, J.R. and Pais, J. (2006), Race, class, and Hurricane Katrina: Social differences in human responses to disaster. Social Science Research, 35(2), pp.295–321.

[286] Logan, J.R. (2006), The impact of Katrina: Race and class in storm-damaged neighborhoods. Social Science Research Council.

[287] Sharkey, P. (2007), Survival and death in New Orleans: Social context and racial disparities in hurricane Katrina mortality. Du Bois Review: Social Science Research on Race, 4(1), pp.137–158

[288] Henrici, J., Helmuth, A.S., and Braun, J. (2010), Women, Disasters, and Hurricane Katrina. Institute for Women's Policy Research.

economic hardship. African American homeowners, who were less likely to have comprehensive insurance coverage, also experienced significant barriers to rebuilding, deepening economic disparities compared to wealthier, predominantly white neighbourhoods.[289] These factors compounded the pre-existing inequalities, resulting in a slower and less equitable recovery process for marginalized communities. The uneven response and recovery efforts post-Katrina have been widely critiqued as reinforcing racial and socioeconomic divisions, leaving many low-income and African American residents with fewer opportunities to rebuild their lives and communities.[290]

Conclusion

The last three million years have seen significant climatic changes driven by natural processes. However, the rapid warming observed in the past century is primarily due to human activities. Understanding these changes is crucial for developing effective strategies to mitigate and adapt to ongoing and future climate impacts. The scientific community continues to study past climate events and current trends to provide insights into managing the challenges posed by climate change. These theories collectively provide a comprehensive understanding of the mechanisms behind climate change. They form the basis for climate models and predictions, helping to inform policy decisions and mitigation strategies. The impacts of climate change on the polar regions are profound and multifaceted. In the Arctic, rapid warming, significant sea ice decline, and permafrost thawing are major concerns. In Antarctica, while the warming is more regional, ice sheet mass loss, ice shelf collapse, and variability in sea ice extent are critical issues. These changes not only affect the local ecosystems but also have global implications, particularly concerning sea level rise and global climate patterns.

The past five million years have seen significant climatic fluctuations due to natural factors such as volcanic activity, solar variability, and orbital changes. In the most recent century, human activities have become the

[289] Plyer, A. (2018), The New Orleans Prosperity Index: Tricentennial Collection. The Data Center. Available at: https://www.datacenterresearch.org/reports_analysis/prosperity-index/

[290] Dyson, M.E. (2006), Come Hell or High Water: Hurricane Katrina and the Color of Disaster. Basic Books.

dominant influence, leading to unprecedented rates of warming and environmental change. Understanding this chronology is crucial for predicting future climate scenarios and implementing effective mitigation strategies. Rising sea levels due to climate change threaten numerous coastal cities and countries, potentially displacing millions of people by 2050. Effective mitigation and adaptation strategies, including improved infrastructure, early warning systems, and sustainable urban planning, are critical to addressing these challenges. By 2050, several regions around the world are expected to experience significant increases in temperatures and more frequent and severe droughts due to climate change. The Middle East, South Asia, Southern Europe, the western United States, Sub-Saharan Africa, Australia, Central America, and India are particularly vulnerable. These changes will have profound impacts on water resources, agriculture, human health, and overall socioeconomic stability. Addressing these challenges requires comprehensive climate mitigation and adaptation strategies to build resilience against the impending climate impacts. By 2050, Southeast Asia will face significant challenges due to climate change, including rising temperatures, sea-level rise, increased frequency of extreme weather events, and adverse impacts on agriculture, water resources, human health, and biodiversity. Addressing these challenges requires comprehensive adaptation and mitigation strategies, regional cooperation, and significant investments in resilient infrastructure and sustainable development practices. As outlined in the chapter, the rise in greenhouse gas emissions, primarily driven by fossil fuel use, industrial activities, and deforestation, has led to unprecedented warming trends. These changes, combined with historical data, underscore the urgent need for mitigation and adaptation strategies to address the accelerating pace of climate change. Without significant intervention, climate change will continue to exacerbate issues such as extreme weather events, rising sea levels, and shifting climate patterns, leading to severe consequences including mass migration to developed countries, food insecurity, and economic instability and political.[291] Historically, shifts in climate have often been linked to social upheaval and the collapse of civilizations, as seen in past

[291] IPCC (2018). Global Warming of 1.5°C: An IPCC Special Report. Geneva: Intergovernmental Panel on Climate Change.

events such as the collapse of the Akkadian Empire and the decline of the Maya civilization due to prolonged droughts.[292,293]

Emerging technologies present a critical opportunity to mitigate these effects and transform our response to climate change. Artificial Intelligence (AI) can enhance climate models, improve resource management, and optimize energy use across sectors.[294] For example, AI algorithms can analyse large datasets to predict extreme weather patterns, which could help in better preparing communities and infrastructure. Robotics could play a role in building more resilient infrastructure and enhancing agricultural productivity. For instance, robots could assist in planting crops that are resilient to climate stresses or aid in precision agriculture, reducing water and fertilizer usage. Biotechnology offers promising solutions, such as engineering crops that can withstand extreme weather conditions or developing microorganisms that can sequester carbon effectively. This could potentially offset some of the agricultural challenges posed by shifting climate zones.[295] Quantum Computing holds potential for breakthroughs in climate science by solving complex problems that are currently beyond the reach of traditional computers. This could lead to more accurate climate models, efficient renewable energy solutions, and innovations in material science for sustainable energy storage.[296] Nuclear fusion represents a breakthrough in clean energy production, with the potential to provide a near-limitless supply of energy without the carbon emissions associated with fossil fuels. While still under development, advancements in this field could revolutionize the energy sector and reduce our reliance on coal and oil.[297] In conclusion, while the challenges posed by climate change are daunting, a combination of proactive policies, international

[292] Weiss, H., et al. (1993). The genesis and collapse of third millennium North Mesopotamian civilization. Science, 261(5124), 995–1004.

[293] Haug, G. H., et al. (2003). Climate and the collapse of Maya civilization. Science, 299(5613), 1731–1735

[294] Rolnick, D., et al. (2019). Tackling climate change with machine learning. arXiv preprint arXiv:1906.05433.

[295] Oldroyd, G. E., & Dixon, R. A. (2018). Biotechnological approaches for sustainable agriculture. Annual Review of Plant Biology, 69, 709–732.

[296] Deloitte. (2023). Quantum Computing for Climate Action. Retrieved from https://www2.deloitte.com

[297] MIT Energy Initiative. (2024). A new breakthrough in fusion reactors could solve a major problem scientists have faced. Retrieved from https://energy.mit.edu/news/a-new-breakthrough-in-fusion-reactors-could-solve-a-major-problem-scientists-have-faced.

cooperation, and technological innovation offers hope for mitigating its impacts. The rapid development of AI, Robotics, Biotechnology, Quantum Computing, and nuclear fusion could redefine our capacity to adapt to and combat climate change, making it a pivotal period for human innovation and resilience. While on the other hand without cooperation, these technologies could be used for warfare and the destruction of societies and nation states.

References

Abidin, H. Z., Andreas, H., Gumilar, I., Brinkman, J. J., & Fukuda, Y. (2011). Land subsidence of Jakarta (Indonesia) and its relation with urban development. *Natural Hazards, 59*(3), 1753–1771.

ADB (Asian Development Bank). (2013). *The economics of climate change in Southeast Asia: A regional review*. Asian Development Bank.

Albrecht, B. A. (1989). Aerosols, cloud microphysics, and fractional cloudiness. *Science, 245*(4923), 1227–1230.

Allen, R. C. (2009). *The British industrial revolution in global perspective*. Cambridge University Press.

Alley, R. B. (2000). The younger Dryas cold interval as viewed from central Greenland. *Quaternary Science Reviews, 19*(1–5), 213–226.

Alley, R. B., Clark, P. U., Huybers, P., & Marotzke, J. (1997). Does the Arctic Ocean–Atlantic thermohaline circulation affect climate? *Geophysical Research Letters, 24*(6), 641–644. https://doi.org/10.1029/97GL03834

Alley, R. B., & Gow, A. J. (2000). Changes in the Laurentide ice sheet: Impacts on the Greenhouse gas concentrations and the North American climate. *Geophysical Research Letters, 27*(4), 607–610.

Alongi, D. M. (2008). Mangrove forests: Resilience, protection from tsunamis, and responses to global climate change. *Estuarine, Coastal and Shelf Science, 76*(1), 1–13.

Ambrose, S. H. (2001). Paleolithic technology and human evolution. *Science, 291*(5509), 1748–1753.

Baccini, M., Biggeri, A., Accetta, G., Kosatsky, T., Katsouyanni, K., Analitis, A., & Schwartz, J. (2008). Heat effects on mortality in 15 European cities. *Epidemiology, 19*(5), 711–719.

Barbier, E. B. (2006). Mangrove dependency and the livelihoods of coastal communities in Thailand and Cambodia. In *Valuation of regulating services of ecosystems: Methodology and applications* (pp. 63–82). Springer.

Basu, R., & Samet, J. M. (2002). Relation between elevated ambient temperature and mortality: A review of the epidemiologic evidence. *Epidemiologic Reviews, 24*(2), 190–202.

Benson, L., et al. (2007). Ancient Puebloan migrations in response to climate change. *Proceedings of the National Academy of Sciences, 104*(1), 327–331.

Benson, L. V., Berry, M. S., Jolie, E. A., Spangler, J. D., Stahle, D. W., & Hattori, E. M. (2007). Possible impacts of early-11th-, middle-12th-, and late-13th-century droughts on western Native Americans and the Mississippian Cahokians. *Quaternary Science Reviews, 26*(3–4), 336–350.

Berger, A. (1988). Milankovitch theory and climate. *Reviews of Geophysics, 26*(4), 624–657.

Bindoff, N. L., Stott, P. A., AchutaRao, K. M., Allen, M. R., Gillett, N., Gutzler, D., Kabumbwe Hansingo, Gabriele Hegerl, Yongyun Hu, Suman Jain, Igor I. Mokhov, James Overland, Judith Perlwitz, Rachid Sebbari, Xuebin Zhang & Zhang, X. (2013). Detection and attribution of climate change: From global to regional. In Stocker, T. F., Qin, D., Plattner, G.-K., Tignor, M., Allen, S. K., Boschung, J., Nauels, A., Xia, Y., Bex, V., & Midgley, P. M. (Eds.), Climate Change 2013: The Physical Science Basis. Contribution of Working Group I to the Fifth Assessment Report of the Intergovernmental Panel on Climate Change (pp. 867–952). Cambridge University Press.

Bocherens, H., Drucker, D. G., Bonjean, D., Bridault, A., Conard, N. J., Cupillard, C., Gernay, T., van Kolfschoten, T., Munzel, S. C., & Naito, Y. I. (2011). Isotopic evidence for dietary ecology of cave bear (Ursus spelaeus) in the Late Pleistocene of Europe: A review and a case study from the Goyet caves (Belgium). *Quaternary International, 245*(2), 235–241.

Bony, S., Stevens, B., Frierson, D. M., Jakob, C., Kageyama, M., Pincus, R., Shepherd, T. G., & Sherwood, S. C. (2015). Clouds, circulation and climate sensitivity. *Nature Geoscience, 8*(4), 261–268.

Box, J. E., et al. (2018). Global sea-level contribution from Arctic land ice: 1971–2017. *Environmental Research Letters, 13*(12), 125012.

Bradley, R. S. (2000). Past Global Changes and their Significance for the Future. *Quaternary International, 63*(1), 61–67.

Bradley, R. S., et al. (2003). The climate of the last millennium. In *Paleoclimate, global change and the future.* Springer.

Brady, O. J., Gething, P. W., Bhatt, S., Messina, J. P., Brownstein, J. S., Hoen, A. G., & Hay, S. I. (2014). Refining the global spatial limits of dengue virus transmission by evidence-based consensus. *PLoS Neglected Tropical Diseases, 8*(8), e3268.

Broecker, W. S. (1991). The great ocean conveyor. *Oceanography, 4*(2), 79–89.

Buckley, B. M., Anchukaitis, K. J., Penny, D., Fletcher, R., Cook, E. R., Sano, M., Nam, L. C., Wichienkeeo, A., Minh, T. T., & Nam, L. C. (2010). Climate as a contributing factor in the demise of Angkor, Cambodia. *Proceedings of the National Academy of Sciences, 107*(15), 6748–6752.

Caesar, L., Rahmstorf, S., Robinson, A., Feulner, G., & Saba, V. (2018). Observed fingerprint of a weakening Atlantic Ocean overturning circulation. *Nature, 556*(7700), 191–196.

Calkin, P. E., & D. A. H. (2009). Pleistocene Glacial geography of the Midwestern United States. In *The geology of the Midwest*. Geological Society of America.

Carvalho, D. O., McKemey, A. R., Garziera, L., Lacroix, R., Donnelly, C. A., Alphey, L., & Capurro, M. L. (2015). Suppression of a field population of Aedes aegypti in Brazil by sustained release of transgenic male mosquitoes. *PLOS Neglected Tropical Diseases, 9*(7), e0003864.

Charlson, R. J., Schwartz, S. E., Hales, J. M., Cess, R. D., Coakley, J. A., Hansen, J. E., & Hofmann, D. J. (1992). Climate forcing by anthropogenic aerosols. *Science, 255*(5043), 423–430.

Cheung, W. W. L., Lam, V. W. Y., Sarmiento, J. L., Kearney, K., Watson, R., & Pauly, D. (2010). Large-scale redistribution of maximum fisheries catch potential in the global ocean under climate change. *Global Change Biology, 16*(1), 24–35.

Christophers, S. R. (1960). *Aedes aegypti (L.) the yellow fever mosquito: Its life history, bionomics and structure*. Cambridge University Press.

Cinco, T. A., et al. (2016). Long-term trends and extremes in observed daily precipitation and near surface air temperature in the Philippines for the period 1951–2010. *Atmospheric Research, 168*, 55–65.

Clark, P. U., Dyke, A. S., Shakun, J. D., Carlson, A. E., Clark, J., Wohlfarth, B., Mitrovica, J. X., Hostetler, S. W., & McCabe, A. M. (2009). The Last Glacial Maximum. *Science, 325*(5941), 710–714.

Clark, P. U., et al. (2002). The roles of the ice sheets in the climatic system. *Quaternary Science Reviews, 21*(1–3), 1185–1200.

Clark, P. U., et al. (2006). The middle Pleistocene transition: Characteristics, mechanisms, and implications for long-term changes in atmospheric CO_2. *Quaternary Science Reviews, 25*(23–24), 3150–3184.

Clements, A. N. (1992). *The biology of mosquitoes: Development, nutrition and reproduction*. Chapman & Hall.

Colchester, M., Jiwan, N., Andiko, M. Z., Sirait, M., Firdaus, A. Y., Surambo, A., & Pane, H. (2011). *Palm oil and land acquisition in Indonesia: Implications for local communities and indigenous peoples*. International Land Coalition.

Connell, J. (2003). Losing ground? Tuvalu, the greenhouse effect and the garbage can. *Asia Pacific Viewpoint, 44*(2), 89–107.

Cook, B. I., Ault, T. R., & Smerdon, J. E. (2015). Unprecedented 21st century drought risk in the American Southwest and Central Plains. *Science Advances, 1*(1), e1400082.

Cook, E. R., Anchukaitis, K. J., Buckley, B. M., D'Arrigo, R. D., Jacoby, G. C., & Wright, W. E. (2012). Asian monsoon failure and megadrought during the last millennium. *Science, 328*(5977), 486–489.

Cook, E. R., Woodhouse, C. A., Eakin, C. M., Meko, D. M., & Stahle, D. W. (2004). Long-Term aridity changes in the Western United States. *Science, 306*(5698), 1015–1018.

Cox, P. M., Betts, R. A., Jones, C. D., Spall, S. A., & Totterdell, I. J. (2000). Acceleration of global warming due to carbon-cycle feedbacks in a coupled climate model. *Nature, 408*(6809), 184–187.

Crutzen, P. J. (2002). Geology of mankind. *Nature, 415*(6867), 23–23.

CSIRO & Bureau of Meteorology. (2015). Climate change in Australia: Information for Australia's natural resource management regions: Technical Report.

Cullen, H. M., deMenocal, P. B., Hemming, S., Hemming, G., Brown, F. H., Guilderson, T., & Sirocko, F. (2000). Climate change and the collapse of the Akkadian empire: Evidence from the deep sea. *Geology, 28*(4), 379–382.

Dasgupta, S., Laplante, B., Meisner, C., Wheeler, D., & Yan, D. (2009). The impact of sea level rise on developing countries: A comparative analysis. *Climatic Change, 93*(3–4), 379–388.

Deloitte. (2023). Quantum computing for climate action. https://www2.deloitte.com

DeMenocal, P. (2011). Climate and human evolution. *Science, 331*(6017), 540–542.

Diamond, J. (1997). *Guns, germs, and steel: The fates of human societies*. W.W. Norton & Company.

Diamond, J. (2005). *Collapse: How societies choose to fail or succeed*. Penguin Books.

Diffenbaugh, N. S., Swain, D. L., & Touma, D. (2015). Anthropogenic warming has increased drought risk in California. *Proceedings of the National Academy of Sciences, 112*(13), 3931–3936.

Dolan, A. M., Haywood, A. M., Tindall, J. C., & Dowsett, H. J. (2011). The Pliocene Model Intercomparison Project (PlioMIP): Experimental design and boundary conditions (Experiment 2). *Geoscientific Model Development, 4*(3), 571–577.

Donner, S. D. (2015). The legacy of migration in response to climate stress: Learning from the Gilbertese resettlement in the Solomon Islands. *Natural Resources Forum, 39*(3–4), 191–201.

Dutton, A., & Lambeck, K. (2012). Ice volume and sea level during the last interglacial. *Science, 337*(6091), 216–219.

Dutton, A., et al. (2015). Sea-level rise due to polar ice-sheet mass loss during past warm periods. *Science, 349*(6244), aaa4019.

Elliott, J. R., & Pais, J. (2006). Race, class, and Hurricane Katrina: Social differences in human responses to disaster. *Social Science Research, 35*(2), 295–321.

EPICA Community Members. (2004). Eight glacial cycles from an Antarctic ice core. *Nature, 429*(6992), 623–628.

Esteban, M., et al. (2020). Adaptation to sea level rise in Southeast Asia. *Springer Climate*. Springer, Cham.

Etheridge, D. M., Steele, L. P., Langenfelds, R. L., Francey, R. J., Barnola, J. M., & Morgan, V. I. (1996). Natural and anthropogenic changes in atmospheric

CO_2 over the last 1000 years from air in Antarctic ice and fern. *Journal of Geophysical Research: Atmospheres, 101*(D2), 4115–4128.

Fagan, B. (2000). *The little ice age: How climate made history, 1300–1850.* Basic Books.

FAO. (2007). *The world's Mangroves 1980–2005.* Food and Agriculture Organization of the United Nations.

Fedorov, A. V., Brierley, C. M., & Emanuel, K. (2013). Tropical cyclones and permanent El Niño in the early Pliocene epoch. *Nature, 496*(7443), 43–47.

Fedorov, A. V., et al. (2015). Patterns and mechanisms of Pliocene warmth. *Nature Geoscience, 8*(6), 490–500. https://doi.org/10.1038/ngeo2416

Francis, J. A., & Vavrus, S. J. (2015). Evidence linking Arctic amplification to extreme weather in mid-latitudes. *Geophysical Research Letters, 42*(1), 16–22. https://doi.org/10.1002/2014GL091047

Fuchs, R., Conran, M., & Louis, E. (2011). Climate Change and Asia's Coastal Urban Cities: Can they meet the challenge? *Environment and Urbanization Asia, 2*(1), 13–28.

Ganopolski, A., & Cramer, W. (2008). The role of freshwater in the Younger Dryas climate: A modelling study. *Paleoceanography, 23*(3). https://doi.org/10.1029/2007PA001501

Giosan, L., Clift, P. D., Macklin, M. G., Fuller, D. Q., Constantinescu, Ş., Durcan, J. A., Gobo, A. R., Tabrez, J. A., Giosan, M. G. L., Vespremeanu-Stroe, D., Giosan, L., Hoey, T. M., & Goodbred, S. L. (2012). Fluvial landscapes of the Harappan civilization. *Proceedings of the National Academy of Sciences, 109*(26), E1688–E1694.

Githeko, A. K., et al. (2000). Climate change and vector-borne diseases: A regional analysis. *Bulletin of the World Health Organization, 78*(9), 1136–1147.

Grove, J. M. (2004). *Little ice ages: Ancient and modern.* Routledge.

Grove, J. M., & Switsur, R. (1994). Glacial geological evidence for the medieval warm period. *Climatic Change, 26*(2), 143–169.

Grove, M. (2011). Speciation, diversity, and Mode 1 technologies: The impact of variability selection. *Journal of Human Evolution, 61*(3), 306–319.

Hales, S., de Wet, N., Maindonald, J., & Woodward, A. (2002). Potential effect of population and climate changes on global distribution of dengue fever: An empirical model. *The Lancet, 360*(9336), 830–834.

Hallegatte, S., Green, C., Nicholls, R. J., et al. (2013). Future flood losses in major coastal cities. *Nature Climate Change, 3*, 802–806.

Hallegatte, S., Vogt-Schilb, A., Bangalore, M., & Rozenberg, J. (2016). *Unbreakable: Building the resilience of the poor in the face of natural disasters.* World Bank.

Hansen, J., et al. (2005). Efficacy of climate forcing's. *Journal of Geophysical Research: Atmospheres, 110*(D18), D18104.

Hansen, J., et al. (2010). Global surface temperature change. *Reviews of Geophysics, 48*(4), RG4004.

Harlan, S. L., Brazel, A. J., Prashad, L., Stefanov, W. L., & Larsen, L. (2006). Neighborhood microclimates and vulnerability to heat stress. *Social Science & Medicine, 63*(11), 2847–2863.

Harries, J. E., et al. (2001). Increases in greenhouse forcing inferred from the outgoing longwave radiation spectra of the Earth in 1970 and 1997. *Nature, 410*(6826), 355–357.

Haug, G. H., Günther, D., Peterson, L. C., Sigman, D. M., Hughen, K. A., & Aeschlimann, B. (2003). Climate and the collapse of Maya civilization. *Science, 299*(5613), 1731–1735.

Haug, G. H., & Tiedemann, R. (1998). Effect of the formation of the Isthmus of Panama on Atlantic Ocean thermohaline circulation. *Nature, 393*(6686), 673–676.

Hays, J. D., Imbrie, J., & Shackleton, N. J. (1976). Variations in the earth's orbit: Pacemaker of the ice ages. *Science, 194*(4270), 1121–1132. https://doi.org/10.1126/science.194.4270.1121

Haywood, J., & Boucher, O. (2000). Estimates of the direct and indirect radiative forcing due to tropospheric aerosols: A review. *Reviews of Geophysics, 38*(4), 513–543.

Hearty, P. J., & Neumann, A. C. (2001). Rapid sea level and climate change at the close of the last interglacial (MIS 5e): Evidence from the Bahama Islands. *Quaternary Science Reviews, 20*(18), 1881–1895.

Hegerl, G. C., Zwiers, F. W., Braconnot, P., Gillett, N. P., Luo, Y., Marengo Orsini, J. A., Nicholls, N., Penner, J. E., & Stott, P. A. (2007). Understanding and attributing climate change. In S. Solomon, Q. Dahe, M. Manning, M. Marquis, K. Averyt, M. M. B. Tignor, H. L. R. Miller, & Z. Chen (Eds.), *Climate Change 2007: The Physical Science Basis. Contribution of Working Group I to the Fourth Assessment Report of the Intergovernmental Panel on Climate Change* (pp. 663–746). Cambridge University Press.

Held, I. M., & Soden, B. J. (2000). Water vapor feedback and global warming. *Annual Review of Energy and the Environment, 25*(1), 441–475.

Hewitt, G. M. (2000). The genetic legacy of the Quaternary ice ages. *Nature, 405*(6789), 907–913.

Hijioka, Y., Lin, E., Pereira, J. J., et al. (2014). Asia. In: *Climate Change 2014: Impacts, adaptation, and vulnerability. Part B: Regional aspects.* Contribution of Working Group II to the Fifth Assessment Report of the Intergovernmental Panel on Climate Change.

Hockett, B., & Haws, J. (2003). Nutritional ecology and the human demography of Neanderthal extinctions. *Quaternary International, 33*(1), 167–178.

Hodell, D. A., Curtis, J. H., & Brenner, M. (2001). Solar forcing of drought frequency in the Maya Lowlands. *Science, 292*(5520), 1367–1370.

Hoegh-Guldberg, O. (1999). Climate change, coral bleaching and the future of the world's coral reefs. *Marine and Freshwater Research, 50*(8), 839–866.

Hoegh-Guldberg, O., et al. (2007). Coral reefs under rapid climate change and ocean acidification. *Science, 318*(5857), 1737–1742.

Hoffecker, J. F. (2005). *A prehistory of the north: Human settlement of the higher latitudes*. Rutgers University Press.

Holmgren, K., et al. (2015). Climate and land cover changes in the southern Great Plains: Implications for land management and drought responsiveness. *Journal of Climate, 28*(22), 8897–8912. https://doi.org/10.1175/JCLI-D-15-0391.1

Houghton, J. T. (2004). *Global Warming: The Complete Briefing*. Cambridge University Press.

Houghton, J. T., et al. (2001). *Climate Change 2001: The Scientific Basis*. Cambridge University Press.

Huang, C., et al. (2011). The impact of temperature on years of life lost in Brisbane. *Australia. Nature Climate Change, 1*(2), 59–63.

Hughes, T. P., Kerry, J. T., Álvarez-Noriega, M., Álvarez-Romero, J. G., Anderson, K. D., Baird, A. H., Babcock, R. C., Beger, M., Bellwood, D. R., Berkelmans, R., & Bridge, T. C. (2017). Global warming and recurrent mass bleaching of corals. *Nature, 543*(7645), 373–377.

Huq, S., & Rabbani, G. (2011). Climate change and Bangladesh: Policy and institutional development to reduce vulnerability. *Journal of Bangladesh Studies, 13*(1), 1–10.

Im, E. S., Pal, J. S., & Eltahir, E. A. B. (2017). Deadly heat waves projected in the densely populated agricultural regions of South Asia. *Science Advances, 3*(8), e1603322.

Imbrie, J., Berger, A., Boyle, E. A., Clemens, S., Duffy, A., Howard, W. R., Kukla, G., Kutzbach, J., Martinson, D. G., McIntyre, A., & Mix, A. C. (1993). On the structure and origin of major glaciation cycles 1. Linear responses to Milankovitch forcing. *Paleoceanography, 8*(6), 699–735.

Imbrie, J., Berger, A., Boyle, E. A., Clemens, S. C., Duffy, A., Howard, W. R., Kukla, G., Kutzbach, J., Martinson, D. G., McIntyre, A., Mix, A. C., Molfino, B., Morley, J. J., Peterson, L. C., Pisias, N. G., Prell, W. L., Raymo, M. E., Shackleton, N. J., & Toggweiler, J. R. (1992). On the structure and origin of major glaciation cycles 1. *Linear responses to Milankovitch forcing. Paleoceanography, 7*(6), 701–738.

Imbrie, J., & Imbrie, K. P. (1980). Modeling the climatic response to orbital variations. *Science, 207*(4434), 943–953.

Imbrie, J., et al. (1992). On the distribution of glacial and interglacial periods. *Paleoceanography, 7*(6), 701–738. https://doi.org/10.1029/92PA02028

Intergovernmental Panel on Climate Change (IPCC). (2013). *Climate change 2013: The physical science basis*. Cambridge University Press.

Intergovernmental Panel on Climate Change (IPCC). (2014). *Climate Change 2014: Synthesis Report.* IPCC.

Intergovernmental Panel on Climate Change (IPCC). (2021). Climate Change 2021: The Physical Science Basis. In *Contribution of Working Group I to the Sixth Assessment Report of the Intergovernmental Panel on Climate Change.* Cambridge University Press. https://doi.org/10.1017/9781009157986

IPCC. (2013). Climate change 2013: The physical science basis. In *Contribution of Working Group I to the Fifth Assessment Report of the Intergovernmental Panel on Climate Change.* Cambridge University Press.

IPCC. (2014). Climate change 2014: Impacts, adaptation, and vulnerability. In *Contribution of Working Group II to the Fifth Assessment Report of the Intergovernmental Panel on Climate Change.*

IPCC. (2018). *Global warming of 1.5°C: An IPCC special report.* Intergovernmental Panel on Climate Change.

IPCC. (2021). Climate change 2021: The physical science basis. In *Contribution of Working Group I to the Sixth Assessment Report of the Intergovernmental Panel on Climate Change.* Cambridge University Press.

IPCC. (2021). Summary for policymakers. In V. Masson-Delmotte, P. Zhai, A. Pirani, S. L. Connors, C. Péan, S. Berger, N. Caud, Y. Chen, L. Goldfarb, M. I. Gomis, M. Huang, K. Leitzell, E. Lonnoy, J. B. R. Matthews, T. K. Maycock, T. Waterfield, O. Yelekçi, R. Yu, & B. Zhou (Eds.), *Climate Change 2021: The Physical Science Basis. Contribution of Working Group I to the Sixth Assessment Report of the Intergovernmental Panel on Climate Change.* Cambridge University Press.

IPCC. (2023). *Climate change 2023: Synthesis report.* IPCC. www.ipcc.ch

Ivy-Ochs, S., Kerschner, H., Maisch, M., Christl, M., Kubik, P. W., & Schlüchter, C. (2009). Latest Pleistocene and Holocene glacier variations in the European Alps. *Quaternary Science Reviews, 28*(21–22), 2137–2149.

Jacobson, M. Z. (2001). Strong radiative heating due to the mixing state of black carbon in atmospheric aerosols. *Nature, 409*(6821), 695–697.

Johnsen, S. J., et al. (2001). Odyssey: The Greenland Ice Core Project. *Journal of Glaciology, 47*(157), 1–8. https://doi.org/10.3189/172756501781831211

Jordan, W. C. (1996). *The Great Famine: Northern Europe in the Early Fourteenth Century.* Princeton University Press.

Jouzel, J., Masson-Delmotte, V., Cattani, O., Dreyfus, G., Falourd, S., Hoffmann, G., Minster, B., Nouet, J., Barnola, J. M., Chappellaz, J., Fischer, H., Gallet, J. C., Johnsen, S., Leuenberger, M., Loulergue, L., Luethi, D., Oerter, H., Parrenin, F., Raisbeck, G., & Wolff, E. W. (2007). Orbital and millennial Antarctic climate variability over the past 800,000 years. *Science, 317*(5839), 793–796.

Kaspar, F., et al. (2005). Simulation of the Eemian interglacial and comparison with the Holocene. *Climate Dynamics, 25*(2–3), 201–220.

Keenan, T. F., Prentice, I. C., Canadell, J. G., Williams, C. A., Wang, H., Raupach, M., & Collatz, G. J. (2016). Recent pause in the growth rate of atmospheric CO_2 due to enhanced terrestrial carbon uptake. *Nature Communications, 7*, 13428.

Kennett, D. J., et al. (2012). Development and disintegration of Maya political systems in response to climate change. *Science, 338*(6108), 788–791.

Knecht, H. (1997). *Projectile technology*. Plenum Press.

Kovats, R. S., & Kristie, L. E. (2006). Heatwaves and public health in Europe. *The European Journal of Public Health, 16*(6), 592–599.

Krishnan, R., et al. (2020). *Assessment of climate change over the Indian region: A report of the Ministry of Earth Sciences (MoES)*. Government of India.

Kuper, R., & Kröpelin, S. (2006). Climate-controlled Holocene occupation in the Sahara: Motor of Africa's evolution. *Science, 313*(5788), 803–807.

Kutzbach, J. E. (1981). Monsoon climate of the early Holocene: Climate experiment with the Earth's orbital parameters for 9000 years ago. *Science, 214*(4516), 59–61.

Lamb, H. H. (1965). The early medieval warm epoch and its sequel. *Palaeogeography, Palaeoclimatology, Palaeoecology, 1*, 13–37.

Lamb, H. H. (1995). *Climate, history, and the modern world*. Routledge.

Lambeck, K., Rouby, H., Purcell, A., Sun, Y., & Sambridge, M. (2014). Sea level and global ice volumes from the Last Glacial Maximum to the Holocene. *Proceedings of the National Academy of Sciences, 111*(43), 15296–15303.

Lean, J. L., & Rind, D. H. (2008). How natural and anthropogenic influences alter global and regional surface temperatures. *Geophysical Research Letters, 35*(18), L18701.

Lenton, T. M., et al. (2008). Tipping elements in the Earth's climate system. *Proceedings of the National Academy of Sciences, 105*(6), 1786–1793.

Leta, S., Beyene, T. J., De Clercq, E. M., Amenu, K., Kraemer, M. U., & Revie, C. W. (2020). Global risk mapping for major diseases transmitted by Aedes mosquitoes. *International Journal of Infectious Diseases, 95*, 123–131.

Lisiecki, L. E., & Raymo, M. E. (2005). A Pliocene-Pleistocene stack of 57 globally distributed benthic δ18O records. *Paleoceanography, 20*(1), PA1003. https://doi.org/10.1029/2004PA001071

Lohmann, U., & Feichter, J. (2005). Global indirect aerosol effects: A review. *Atmospheric Chemistry and Physics, 5*(3), 715–737.

Luterbacher, J., et al. (2006). Mediterranean climate variability over the last centuries: A review. In *The Mediterranean Climate: An overview of the main characteristics and issues*. Elsevier.

Luthi, D., et al. (2008). High-resolution carbon dioxide record from the Vostok ice core. *Geophysical Research Letters, 35*(3), L03705. https://doi.org/10.1029/2007GL029999

Lycett, S. J., & Cramon-Taubadel, N. V. (2008). A comparative analysis of Oldowan and Acheulean bifacial tools: Morphometric variability and the effects of raw material availability. *Journal of Archaeological Science, 35*(10), 2523–2530.

Magrin, G. O., et al. (2014). Central and South America. *In: Climate Change 2014: Impacts, adaptation, and vulnerability.* Part B: Regional Aspects. Contribution of Working Group II to the Fifth Assessment Report of the Intergovernmental Panel on Climate Change.

Malhi, Y., Roberts, J. T., Betts, R. A., Killeen, T. J., Li, W., & Nobre, C. A. (2008). Climate change, deforestation, and the fate of the Amazon. *Science, 319*(5860), 169–172.

Malm, A. (2016). *Fossil capital: The rise of steam power and the roots of global warming.* Verso Books.

Mann, M. E., Zhang, Z., Hughes, M. K., Bradley, R. S., Miller, S. K., Rutherford, S., & Ni, F. (2009). Proxy-based reconstructions of hemispheric and global surface temperature variations over the past two millennia. *Proceedings of the National Academy of Sciences, 106*(36), 13252–13257.

Mann, M. E., et al. (2009). Global signatures and dynamical origins of the Little Ice Age and Medieval Climate Anomaly. *Science, 326*(5957), 1256–1260.

Martens, W. J., Niessen, L. W., Rotmans, J., Jetten, T. H., & McMichael, A. J. (1995). Potential impact of global climate change on malaria risk. *Environmental Health Perspectives, 103*(5), 458–464.

Maslin, M. A., et al. (1998). Pleistocene evolution: Northern Hemisphere ice sheets and North Atlantic Ocean. *Geology, 26*(6), 467–470.

Mayewski, P. A., et al. (2004). Holocene climate variability. *Quaternary Research, 62*(3), 243–255.

McNeill, J. R. (2000). *Something new under the sun: An environmental history of the twentieth-century world.* W.W. Norton & Company.

McNeill, J. R., & Engelke, P. (2014). *The great acceleration: An environmental history of the anthropocene since 1945.* Harvard University Press.

McPhaden, M. J., Zebiak, S. E., & Glantz, M. H. (2006). ENSO as an integrating concept in Earth science. *Science, 314*(5806), 1740–1745.

Medina-Elizalde, M., & Rohling, E. J. (2012). Collapse of Classic Maya civilization related to modest reduction in precipitation. *Science, 335*(6071), 956–959.

Messina, J. P., Brady, O. J., Scott, T. W., Zou, C., Pigott, D. M., Duda, K. A., & Hay, S. I. (2014). Global spread of dengue virus types: Mapping the 70-year history. *Trends in Microbiology, 22*(3), 138–146.

Milankovitch, M. (1941). *Kanon der Erdbestrahlung und seine Anwendung auf das Eiszeitenproblem.* Royal Serbian Academy Special Publication.

Miller, K. G., et al. (2012). A 180-million-year record of sea level rise from the New Jersey coast. *Geology, 40*(8), 685–688. https://doi.org/10.1130/G33089

MIT Energy Initiative. (2024). A new breakthrough in fusion reactors could solve a major problem scientists have faced. https://energy.mit.edu/news/a-new-breakthrough-in-fusion-reactors-could-solve-a-major-problem-scientists-have-faced

Mix, A. C., Bard, E., & Schneider, R. (2001). Environmental processes of the ice age: Land, oceans, glaciers (EPILOG). *Quaternary Science Reviews, 20*(4), 627–657.

Morrison, A. C., Zielinski-Gutierrez, E., Scott, T. W., & Rosenberg, R. (2008). Defining challenges and proposing solutions for control of the virus vector Aedes aegypti. *PLoS Medicine, 5*(3), e68.

Morton, J. F. (2007). The impact of climate change on smallholder and subsistence agriculture. *Proceedings of the National Academy of Sciences, 104*(50), 19680–19685.

Moyes, C. L., Vontas, J., Martins, A. J., Ng, L. C., Koou, S. Y., Dusfour, I., & Weetman, D. (2017). Contemporary status of insecticide resistance in the major Aedes vectors of arboviruses infecting humans. *PLoS Neglected Tropical Diseases, 11*(7), e0005625.

Murray, N. E., Quam, M. B., & Wilder-Smith, A. (2013). Epidemiology of dengue: Past, present and future prospects. *Clinical Epidemiology, 5*, 299–309.

Musso, D., & Gubler, D. J. (2016). Zika virus. *Clinical Microbiology Reviews, 29*(3), 487–524.

Myhre, G., Shindell, D., Bréon, F. M., Collins, W., Fuglestvedt, J., Huang, J., Koch, D., Lamarque, J. F., Lee, D., Mendoza, B., & Nakajima, T. (2013). Anthropogenic and natural radiative forcing. In *Climate Change 2013: The Physical Science Basis. Contribution of Working Group I to the Fifth Assessment Report of the Intergovernmental Panel on Climate Change* (pp. 659–740). Cambridge University Press.

NASA. (2020). The causes of climate change. *NASA Climate Change*. Available at: https://climate.nasa.gov/causes/

NASA. (2024). Milankovitch (orbital) cycles and their role in earth's climate. Retrieved from NASA Science.

National Geographic. (2024). The influence of climate change on extreme environmental events. Retrieved from National Geographic.

NEEM Community Members. (2013). Eemian interglacial reconstructed from a Greenland folded ice core. *Nature, 493*(7433), 489–494.

Nelson, G. C., et al. (2010). *Climate change: Impact on agriculture and costs of adaptation*. International Food Policy Research Institute.

NOAA. (2021). Trends in atmospheric carbon dioxide. National Oceanic and Atmospheric Administration. https://www.esrl.noaa.gov/gmd/ccgg/trends/

NOAA National Centres for Environmental Information. (2020). Global Climate Report - Annual 2020. Retrieved from NOAA.

Notz, D., & Stroeve, J. (2016). Observed Arctic sea-ice loss directly follows anthropogenic CO_2 emission. *Science, 354*(6313), 747–750.

Oglesby, R. J., Sever, T., Saturno, W., Erickson, D., & Srikishen, J. (2010). Collapse of the Maya: Could deforestation have contributed? *Journal of Geophysical Research: Atmospheres, 115*(D12), D12106.

Oldroyd, G. E., & Dixon, R. A. (2018). Biotechnological approaches for sustainable agriculture. *Annual Review of Plant Biology, 69*, 709–732.

Ostro, B., Rauch, S., Green, R., Malig, B., & Basu, R. (2010). The effects of temperature and use of air conditioning on hospitalizations. *American Journal of Epidemiology, 172*(9), 1053–1061.

Overpeck, J., Otto-Bliesner, B., & Miller, G. (2006). Paleoclimatic evidence for future ice-sheet instability and rapid sea-level rise. *Science, 311*(5768), 1747–1750.

Pal, J. S., & Eltahir, E. A. B. (2016). Future temperature in southwest Asia projected to exceed a threshold for human adaptability. *Nature Climate Change, 6*(2), 197–200.

Parkinson, C. L. (2019). A 40-y record reveals gradual Antarctic sea ice increases followed by decreases at rates far exceeding the rates seen in the Arctic. *Proceedings of the National Academy of Sciences, 116*(29), 14414–14423.

Patz, J. A., Campbell-Lendrum, D., Holloway, T., & Foley, J. A. (2005). Impact of regional climate change on human health. *Nature, 438*(7066), 310–317.

Peltier, W. R., et al. (2015). The role of ice sheets in climate change. *Nature Climate Change, 5*(1), 43–47.

Peltier, W. R., et al. (2019). The influence of human activity on climate and its significance for the Americas. *Nature Climate Change, 9*, 1–10. https://doi.org/10.1038/s41558-019-0453-4

Petit, J. R., et al. (1999). Climate and atmospheric history of the past 420,000 years from the Vostok ice core, Antarctica. *Nature, 399*(6735), 429–436.

Philander, S. G. (1983). El Niño Southern Oscillation phenomena. *Nature, 302*(5906), 295–301.

Pollock, S. (1999). *Ancient Mesopotamia: The Eden that Never Was*. Cambridge University Press.

Possehl, G. L. (2002). *The Indus Civilization: A Contemporary Perspective*. AltaMira Press.

Potts, R. (1998). Variability selection in hominid evolution. *Evolutionary Anthropology, 7*(3), 81–96.

Rahmstorf, S. (2006). Thermohaline ocean circulation. *Encyclopedia of Quaternary Sciences, 2*, 739–750.

Rahmstorf, S., & Coumou, D. (2011). Increase of Atlantic storminess since the 1970s. *Climate Dynamics, 38*(3–4), 2389–2399. https://doi.org/10.1007/s00382-011-1006-5

Ranson, H., Burhani, J., Lumjuan, N., & Black, W. C., IV. (2010). Insecticide resistance in dengue vectors. *Tropical Medicine & International Health, 15*(4), 632–644.

Ravelo, A. C., Andreasen, D. H., Lyle, M., Lyle, A. O., & Wara, M. W. (2004). Regional climate shifts caused by gradual global cooling in the Pliocene epoch. *Nature, 429*(6989), 263–267.

Raymo, M. E., & Huybers, P. (2008). Unlocking the mysteries of the ice ages. *Nature, 451*(7176), 284–285.
Rignot, E., et al. (2019). Four decades of Antarctic Ice Sheet mass balance from 1979–2017. *Proceedings of the National Academy of Sciences, 116*(4), 1095–1103.
Robine, J. M., Cheung, S. L., Le Roy, S., Van Oyen, H., Griffiths, C., Michel, J. P., & Herrmann, F. R. (2008). Death toll exceeded 70,000 in Europe during the summer of 2003. *Comptes Rendus Biologies, 331*(2), 171–178.
Rohling, E. J., et al. (2008). High rates of sea-level rise during the last interglacial period. *Nature Geoscience, 1*(1), 38–42.
Rolnick, D., et al. (2019). Tackling climate change with machine learning. arXiv preprint arXiv:1906.05433.
Ruddell, D. M., Harlan, S. L., Grossman-Clarke, S., & Buyantuyev, A. (2010). Risk and exposure to extreme heat in microclimates of Phoenix, AZ. In *Geospatial techniques in urban hazard and disaster analysis* (pp. 179–202). Springer.
Ruddiman, W. F. (2008). *Earth's climate: Past and future.* W.H. Freeman and Company.
Salzmann, U., et al. (2008). The Pliocene and future climates: Results from the PMIP2 model intercomparison. *Paleoceanography, 23*(2). https://doi.org/10.1029/2007PA001515
Scambos, T. A., et al. (2004). Glacier acceleration and thinning after ice shelf collapse in the Larsen B embayment, Antarctica. *Geophysical Research Letters, 31*(18).
Schlenker, W., & Roberts, M. J. (2009). Nonlinear temperature effects indicate severe damages to US crop yields under climate change. *Proceedings of the National Academy of Sciences, 106*(37), 15594–15598.
Schuur, E. A. G., et al. (2015). Climate change and the permafrost carbon feedback. *Nature, 520*(7546), 171–179.
Scussolini, P., et al. (2016). Adaptation to sea level rise: A multidisciplinary analysis for Ho Chi Minh City, Vietnam. *Water Resources Research, 52*(10), 7916–7934.
Serreze, M. C., & Barry, R. G. (2011). Processes and impacts of Arctic amplification: A research synthesis. *Global and Planetary Change, 77*(1–2), 85–96.
Shea, J. J. (2006). The origins of lithic projectile point technology: Evidence from Africa, the Levant, and Europe. *Journal of Archaeological Science, 33*(6), 823–846.
Siraj, A. S., Santos-Vega, M., Bouma, M. J., Yadeta, D., Ruiz Carrascal, D., & Pascual, M. (2014). Altitudinal changes in malaria incidence in highlands of Ethiopia and Colombia. *Science, 343*(6175), 1154–1158.
Smil, V. (2010). *Energy transitions: History, requirements, prospects.* Praeger.
Sodhi, N. S., et al. (2010). Conserving Southeast Asian forest biodiversity in human-modified landscapes. *Biological Conservation, 143*(10), 2375–2384.

Soffer, O. (1985). *The upper Paleolithic of the Central Russian Plain.* Academic Press.
Spreen, G., Kwok, R., & Menemenlis, D. (2010). Impact of Earth's orbital eccentricity on ice sheet stability. *Nature Geoscience, 3*, 399–404. https://doi.org/10.1038/ngeo851
Stahle, D. W., Fye, F. K., Cook, E. R., & Griffin, R. D. (2007). Tree-ring reconstructed megadroughts over North America since AD 1300. *Climatic Change, 83*(1–2), 133–149.
Stanton, E. A., & Ackerman, F. (2007). *Florida and climate change: The costs of inaction.* Tufts University Global Development and Environment Institute.
Staubwasser, M., & Weiss, H. (2006). Holocene climate and cultural evolution in late prehistoric–early historic West Asia. *Quaternary Research, 66*(3), 372–387.
Steffen, W., Grinevald, J., Crutzen, P., & McNeill, J. (2011). The Anthropocene: Conceptual and historical perspectives. *Philosophical Transactions of the Royal Society A: Mathematical, Physical and Engineering Sciences, 369*(1938), 842–867.
Steiger, R., & Abegg, B. (2013). The sensitivity of Austrian ski areas to climate change. *Tourism Planning & Development, 10*(4), 480–493.
Stocker, T. F., Qin, D., Plattner, G. K., Tignor, M., Allen, S. K., Boschung, J., Nauels, A., Xia, Y., Bex, V., & Midgley, P. M. (2013). *Climate change 2013: The physical science basis.* Cambridge University Press.
Stott, P. A., et al. (2011). The attribution of weather and climate-related events. *Wiley interdisciplinary reviews: Climate Change, 2*(2), 231–248.
Strauss, B. H., et al. (2012). Tidally adjusted estimates of topographic vulnerability to sea level rise and flooding for the contiguous United States. *Environmental Research Letters, 7*(1), 014033.
Stroeve, J., et al. (2012). The Arctic's rapidly shrinking sea ice cover: A research synthesis. *Climatic Change, 110*(3–4), 1005–1027.
Stroeve, J., et al. (2012). Arctic Sea ice decline: Faster than forecast. *Geophysical Research Letters, 39*(8), L09501. https://doi.org/10.1029/2012GL051090
Struebig, M. J., Kingston, T., Zubaid, A., Mohd-Adnan, A., Rossiter, S. J., & Turner, A. (2015). Conservation importance of forest fragments to Sundaic bats and the potential effects of climate and land-use change. *Biodiversity and Conservation, 24*(4), 1033–1050.
Timmermann, A., et al. (2019). Climate change due to greenhouse gases. *Annual Review of Environment and Resources, 44*, 1–28.
Trenberth, K. E. (1997). The definition of El Niño. *Bulletin of the American Meteorological Society, 78*(12), 2771–2777.
Turner, J., et al. (2005). Antarctic climate change during the last 50 years. *International Journal of Climatology, 25*(3), 279–294.
Turney, C. S. M., & Jones, R. T. (2010). Does the Agulhas current amplify global temperatures during super-interglacials? *Journal of Quaternary Science, 25*(6), 839–843.

Twomey, S. (1977). The influence of pollution on the shortwave albedo of clouds. *Journal of the Atmospheric Sciences, 34*(7), 1149–1152.

Tyndall, J. (1861). On the absorption and radiation of heat by gases and vapours, and on the physical connexion of radiation, absorption, and conduction. *Philosophical Transactions of the Royal Society of London, 151*, 1–36.

Vellinga, P. (2001). Climate change and flood risk in the Netherlands. *Global Environmental Change Part B: Environmental Hazards, 3*(3–4), 103–111.

Veron, J. E. N., Devantier, L. M., Turak, E., Green, A. L., Kininmonth, S., Stafford-Smith, M., & Peterson, N. (2009). Delineating the Coral Triangle. *Galaxea, Journal of Coral Reef Studies, 11*(2), 91–100.

Vörösmarty, C. J., et al. (2000). Global water resources: Vulnerability from climate change and population growth. *Science, 289*(5477), 284–288.

Weiss, H., Courty, M.-A., Wetterstrom, W., Guichard, F., Senior, L., Meadow, R., & Curnow, A. (1993). The genesis and collapse of third millennium North Mesopotamian civilization. *Science, 261*(5124), 995–1004.

WHO. (2019). Dengue and severe dengue. Retrieved September 20, 2023, from https://www.who.int/news-room/fact-sheets/detail/dengue-and-severe-dengue.

Wiles, G. C., & Calkin, P. E. (1994). Late Holocene, high-resolution glacial chronologies and climate, Kenai Mountains, Alaska. *Geological Society of America Bulletin, 106*(2), 281–303.

Wilkinson, C. (Ed.). (2008). *Status of Coral Reefs of the world: 2008.* Global Coral Reef Monitoring Network and Reef and Rainforest Research Centre.

Woodroffe, C. D. (2008). Reef-island topography and the vulnerability of atolls to sea-level rise. *Global and Planetary Change, 62*(1–2), 77–96.

World Weather Attribution. (2019). *Attribution of extreme weather events to climate change.* World Weather Attribution.

Yin, J., et al. (2013). A projection of sea level change impacts on coastal cities in 2050. *Climatic Change, 119*, 671–685.

Zachos, J. et al. (2020). High-fidelity record of Earth's climate history puts current changes in context. Phys.org.

Zachos, J. C., et al. (2001). Trends, rhythms, and aberrations in global climate 65 Ma to present. *Science, 292*(5517), 686–693.

CHAPTER 5

Migration

Introduction

Human migration has been a fundamental aspect of our species' history, shaping the genetic, cultural, and social fabric of populations around the world. However, contemporary climate change is significantly altering traditional migration patterns and creating new challenges. As climate change exacerbates environmental conditions, such as sea-level rise, extreme weather events, and prolonged droughts, more people are being forced to migrate both within and across national borders. For example, in low-lying island nations like Kiribati and the Maldives, rising sea levels threaten to submerge entire communities, prompting discussions around 'climate refugees' and the need for international legal frameworks to protect displaced populations.[1] In Sub-Saharan Africa, recurrent droughts and desertification have made traditional agricultural practices unsustainable, pushing rural communities towards urban areas or across borders in search of better livelihoods.[2] In Nigeria's Lake Chad Basin, the shrinking of the

[1] McNamara, K.E. and Gibson, C. (2009), 'We do not want to leave our land': Pacific ambassadors at the United Nations resist the category of 'climate refugees'. Geoforum, 40(3), pp.475–483.

[2] Rigaud, K.K., de Sherbinin, A., Jones, B., Bergmann, J., Clement, V., Ober, K., and Midgley, A. (2018), Groundswell: Preparing for internal climate migration. World Bank Publications.

S. Ramesh, *The Political Economy of Contemporary Human Civilisation, Volume I*,
https://doi.org/10.1007/978-3-031-84181-1_5

lake due to decreased rainfall and increased water extraction has displaced millions, exacerbating conflicts over resources and contributing to the rise of insurgent groups like Boko Haram.[3] Similarly, in Central America, changing precipitation patterns and increased frequency of hurricanes have contributed to agricultural failures, particularly in the so-called 'Dry Corridor' spanning parts of Guatemala, Honduras, and El Salvador. These conditions have driven many to migrate northwards to Mexico and the United States, contributing to the so-called climate migration crisis at the US–Mexico border.[4] These examples illustrate how climate change is not only altering the physical landscape but also reshaping the social and economic dynamics of migration. The impacts of these changes are multifaceted, influencing not just the individuals and communities directly affected but also posing significant challenges for host countries and international migration policies. As the climate continues to change, understanding and addressing these migration patterns will be crucial for global stability and human security. This chapter provides an overview of the key phases and patterns of global human migration over the last three million years, supported by academic research and archaeological findings.

Early Hominin Migrations (Three Million to One Million Years Ago)

Australopithecus and Early Homo

Australopithecus

The genus Australopithecus, which existed around four to two million years ago, primarily inhabited eastern and southern Africa. Fossil evidence, such as the famous 'Lucy' skeleton, suggests they were among the first hominins to exhibit bipedalism.[5] The fossil evidence of Australopithecus afarensis, particularly the famous 'Lucy' skeleton discovered in 1974 in Ethiopia, is crucial in understanding the early development of bipedalism

[3] Okpara, U.T., Stringer, L.C., Dougill, A.J., and Bila, M.D. (2015), Conflicts about water in Lake Chad: Are environmental, vulnerability and security issues linked? Progress in Development Studies, 15(4), pp.308–325.

[4] Bergmann, J. (2019), Climate change, migration, and the crisis in the Sahel. European Union Institute for Security Studies (EUISS), 5, pp.1–4.

[5] Johanson, D.C. and White, T.D. (1979), A systematic assessment of early African hominids. Science, 203(4379), pp.321–330.

among hominins. Lucy, who lived around 3.2 million years ago, is one of the most complete early hominin skeletons ever found, providing critical insights into the morphology of early human ancestors. Lucy's pelvic structure, leg bones, and knee joints show adaptations that are associated with walking upright on two legs, a hallmark of bipedalism.[6] Specifically, her knee joint angles inward, a feature that aligns the legs under the body's centre of gravity, making upright walking more efficient.[7] Bipedalism is thought to have given early hominins an advantage in terms of energy efficiency, allowing them to travel long distances more easily than their quadrupedal ancestors. It may also have freed their hands for other tasks, such as tool use or carrying food.[8] Fossils of Australopithecus afarensis indicate a mix of bipedal and arboreal traits, suggesting that while they primarily walked on two legs, they retained some ability to move in trees, pointing to a transitional phase in human evolution.[9] Bipedalism is considered a significant evolutionary adaptation in early hominins, as it conferred several advantages, particularly in terms of energy efficiency. Research indicates that walking on two legs, as opposed to quadrupedally, requires less energy over long distances. Early hominins likely lived in environments where efficient travel across large areas in search of food, water, or other resources was crucial for survival. Bipedalism reduced the energy cost of locomotion, allowing hominins to cover greater distances while conserving energy for other vital activities, such as foraging or social interaction.[10] The mechanics of bipedalism also play a role in energy efficiency. When walking on two legs, the centre of gravity remains relatively stable, minimizing the need for energy-intensive muscle movements. In contrast, quadrupedal locomotion, especially on uneven terrain, requires more effort to maintain balance and coordination.[11] Additionally, bipedalism

[6] Johanson, D.C. and Edey, M.A. (1981), Lucy: The Beginnings of Humankind. New York: Simon and Schuster.

[7] Lovejoy, C.O. (1988), Evolution of human walking. Scientific American, 259(5), pp.118–125.

[8] Stanford, C., Allen, J.S. and Anton, S.C. (2013), Biological Anthropology: The Natural History of Humankind. 3rd ed. Boston: Pearson.

[9] Ward, C.V., Kimbel, W.H. and Johanson, D.C. (2011), Complete Fourth Metatarsal and Arches in the Foot of Australopithecus afarensis. Science, 331(6018), pp.750–753.

[10] Sockol, M.D., Raichlen, D.A. and Pontzer, H. (2007), Chimpanzee locomotor energetics and the origin of human bipedalism. Proceedings of the National Academy of Sciences, 104(30), pp.12265–12269.

[11] Pontzer, H. (2010), Economics of bipedalism: effects of body size and limb length on locomotor efficiency in humans and other primates. Journal of Human Evolution, 58(6), pp. 568–575.

may have allowed early hominins to thermoregulate more effectively in hot savannah environments, as walking upright exposes less surface area to direct sunlight and maximizes the body's ability to cool down through wind exposure.[12] Moreover, bipedalism freed the hands, enabling early hominins to carry tools, food, or infants while travelling, which may have contributed to greater survival and reproductive success.[13] This adaptation allowed hominins to exploit a wider range of resources and environments compared to their quadrupedal ancestors. Bipedalism is not only significant for locomotion but also for the transformative role it played in freeing the hands, a key advantage for early hominins. By walking upright, hominins could use their hands for a variety of tasks while travelling, which likely conferred survival benefits. The ability to carry tools is a particularly important development. Early stone tools, such as those from the Oldowan culture, date back around 2.6 million years and were used for activities like cutting meat or breaking bones to access marrow.[14] These tools are among the earliest evidence of hominin technology, providing insights into the cognitive and cultural development of early human ancestors. The Oldowan tools, typically simple flakes and cores, were crafted from easily available materials like quartzite and basalt. The process of creating these tools involved striking one stone against another to produce sharp-edged flakes, which could then be used for various tasks such as cutting meat or processing plant materials.[15] The efficiency of these tools enabled early hominins to access new food sources, particularly in scavenging activities where tools were used to break bones and extract nutrient-rich marrow.[16] These tools are closely associated with early hominin species, particularly Homo habilis, and were likely used to supplement a diet that included a significant portion of meat, a shift that had profound implications for

[12] Wheeler, P.E. (1991), The influence of bipedalism on the energy and water budgets of early hominids. Journal of Human Evolution, 21(2), pp.117–136.

[13] Stanford, C., Allen, J.S. and Anton, S.C. (2013), Biological Anthropology: The Natural History of Humankind. 3rd ed. Boston: Pearson.

[14] Toth, N. and Schick, K. (2009), The Oldowan: The tool making of early hominins and chimpanzees compared. Annual Review of Anthropology, 38, pp.289–305.

[15] Toth, N. and Schick, K. (2009), 'The Oldowan: The Tool Making of Early Hominins and Chimpanzees Compared', Annual Review of Anthropology, 38, pp. 289–305.

[16] de la Torre, I. (2011), 'The Early Stone Age Lithic Assemblages of Gadeb (Ethiopia) and the Developed Oldowan/early Acheulean in East Africa', Journal of Human Evolution, 60(6), pp. 768–812.

human evolution.[17] The inclusion of meat in the diet, facilitated using tools, likely contributed to increased caloric intake, which is believed to have supported the development of larger brains in hominins.[18] This process, known as the 'expensive tissue hypothesis', posits that the energy savings from a smaller gut, which was no longer required to digest large amounts of fibrous plant material, could be redirected to support brain growth.

Moreover, the ability to produce and use tools represents an important cognitive leap in problem-solving and innovation. The Oldowan toolmakers exhibited foresight and planning, selecting the appropriate stones and striking techniques to create functional tools. The neural circuits used in toolmaking overlap with those used in language, indicating that the development of toolmaking skills may have had broader implications for the evolution of human cognition.[19] In fact, archaeological evidence from Olduvai Gorge and other sites suggests that tool use and innovation were critical factors in hominin adaptation to changing environments, allowing early humans to process a wider range of food sources and improve their chances of survival.[20] The development of the Oldowan tool culture was not just a technological advancement but also a reflection of increasing social complexity among early hominins. The use of tools likely encouraged more cooperative behaviours, such as sharing food and collaborating in hunting or scavenging activities. The shared knowledge of toolmaking and its transmission across generations would have fostered social learning, a key component of cultural evolution.[21]

[17] Leakey, M.D. (1971), Olduvai Gorge: Excavations in Beds I and II, 1960–1963. Cambridge University Press.

[18] Aiello, L.C. and Wheeler, P. (1995), 'The Expensive Tissue Hypothesis: The Brain and the Digestive System in Human and Primate Evolution', Current Anthropology, 36(2), pp. 199–221.

[19] Stout, D., Toth, N., Schick, K., and Chaminade, T. (2008), 'Neural correlates of Early Stone Age toolmaking: technology, language and cognition in human evolution', Philosophical Transactions of the Royal Society B: Biological Sciences, 363(1499), pp. 1939–1949.

[20] Harmand, S., Lewis, J.E., Feibel, C.S., Lepre, C.J., Prat, S., Lenoble, A., Boës, X., Quinn, R.L., Brenet, M., Arroyo, A., Taylor, N., Clément, S., Daver, G., Brugal, J.-P., Leakey, L., Mortlock, R.A., Wright, J.D., Lokorodi, S., Kirwa, C., Kent, D.V. and Roche, H. (2015), '3.3-million-year-old stone tools from Lomekwi 3, West Turkana, Kenya', Nature, 521(7552), pp. 310–315.

[21] Wynn, T. and Coolidge, F.L. (2011), 'The Implications of Oldowan Cognitive Capabilities for the Evolution of Pleistocene Hominin Lifeways', Journal of Human Evolution, 60(4), pp. 439–448.

With the hands free, hominins could transport tools across distances, enabling more efficient foraging and hunting strategies, and increasing access to diverse food sources, which would have enhanced survival rates. In addition to tool transport, bipedalism also facilitated the carrying of food. In hunter-gatherer societies, carrying gathered or hunted resources back to a central location for consumption or sharing is critical for survival.[22] Freeing the hands allowed hominins to carry larger quantities of food, thereby reducing the number of trips required and conserving energy. Carrying infants was another crucial advantage of bipedalism, as it allowed mothers to transport their young while foraging or travelling.[23] This behaviour would have improved the chances of offspring survival by enabling mothers to protect and nurture their infants more effectively. Moreover, it allowed early hominins to maintain mobility while caring for dependent offspring, which may have contributed to the success of bipedal species compared to their quadrupedal ancestors. By freeing the hands, bipedalism also opened the door to other important behavioural changes, such as the development of complex social structures and the use of gestures, which would have played a role in social bonding and cooperation.[24] These changes ultimately contributed to greater reproductive success by fostering cooperation and resource sharing within early human groups. By enabling the transport of resources and the care of offspring while remaining mobile, bipedalism fostered cooperation and resource sharing within early human groups. The ability to carry food over long distances back to a central location, such as a camp or shelter, likely encouraged communal consumption and the sharing of resources.[25] This form of cooperation, in which individuals contributed food to a shared pool, may have been essential for the survival of early hominins, particularly in environments where food resources were scattered or unpredictable. Sharing food not only ensured that all group members had access to necessary nutrients, but it also strengthened social bonds and reduced competition within the

[22] Isaac, G.L. (1978), Food sharing and human evolution: archaeological evidence from the Plio-Pleistocene of East Africa. Journal of Anthropological Research, 34(3), pp.311–325.

[23] Falk, D. (2004), Prelinguistic evolution in early hominins: Whence motherese? Behavioural and Brain Sciences, 27(4), pp.491–503.

[24] Dunbar, R.I.M. (1996), Grooming, Gossip, and the Evolution of Language. Cambridge, MA: Harvard University Press.

[25] Isaac, G.L. (1978), 'Food sharing and human evolution: Archaeological evidence from the Plio-Pleistocene of East Africa', Journal of Anthropological Research, 34(3), pp. 311–325.

group.[26] The shared care of offspring and cooperative breeding practices would have further enhanced reproductive success. Among early hominins, mothers who could carry and protect their infants while gathering food or travelling between foraging sites would have had an advantage in terms of infant survival.[27] Moreover, cooperative child-rearing, in which other group members, such as grandparents or siblings, assisted in the care of young, would have further lightened the burden on individual mothers and increased the chances of offspring survival. This social structure, characterized by strong kinship ties and cooperative behaviours, allowed early human groups to thrive and pass on their genes to subsequent generations. Additionally, the freeing of the hands allowed for the development of more sophisticated forms of communication, such as gestures and tool use, which likely played a role in social bonding and the coordination of group activities. The evolution of larger brains in hominins was partly driven by the need to manage increasingly complex social networks.[28] As hominins began to live in larger, more cooperative groups, effective communication and social coordination would have been essential for maintaining group cohesion and ensuring the successful sharing of resources. These behaviours—cooperative foraging, shared childcare, and enhanced communication—would have contributed to the reproductive success of early hominins by increasing survival rates and ensuring that individuals within the group supported one another. This, in turn, would have fostered the transmission of successful social behaviours and the development of more complex social structures, which ultimately set the stage for the emergence of modern human societies.

Homo habilis and Homo erectus

Around 2.4 to 1.4 million years ago, Homo habilis emerged in Africa, followed by Homo erectus approximately 1.9 million years ago. Homo erectus was one of the first hominins to migrate out of Africa, reaching as

[26] Kaplan, H., Hill, K., Lancaster, J. and Hurtado, A.M. (2000), 'A Theory of Human Life History Evolution: Diet, Intelligence, and Longevity', Evolutionary Anthropology, 9(4), pp. 156–185.

[27] Hrdy, S.B. (2009), Mothers and Others: The Evolutionary Origins of Mutual Understanding. Harvard University Press.

[28] Dunbar, R. (1996), Grooming, Gossip, and the Evolution of Language. Harvard University Press.

far as Asia and Europe.[29] The transition from Homo habilis to Homo erectus is a significant milestone in human evolution, marked by various anatomical, behavioural, and technological developments. The period between 2.4 and 1.4 million years ago saw the emergence of Homo habilis in Africa, which is often considered the first member of the genus Homo. Homo habilis is characterized by a relatively larger brain size compared to earlier hominids, reduced facial prognathism, and evidence of tool use, specifically Oldowan tools.[30] Approximately 1.9 million years ago, Homo erectus appeared, representing a substantial evolutionary leap.[31] Homo erectus exhibited several key advancements over its predecessor. One notable change was in cranial morphology; Homo erectus had a significantly larger brain capacity, with an average of around 900 cubic centimetres compared to Homo habilis's 500–600 cubic centimetres.[32] Moreover, Homo erectus is also distinguished by a more modern body plan. This species showed a reduction in the size of the face and teeth and an increase in body size and limb proportions conducive to long-distance bipedal walking and running. This adaptation is thought to be critical for its migration out of Africa and into Asia and Europe.[33] Behaviourally, Homo erectus is associated with the Acheulean tool industry, which included more sophisticated bifacial tools such as hand axes and cleavers. This technological advancement reflects increased cognitive capabilities and suggests more complex social structures and subsistence strategies.[34] Moreover, the improved efficiency of these tools would have facilitated diverse and complex subsistence strategies, including hunting and processing a variety of food sources, thereby ensuring a more reliable food supply.[35] The complexity inherent in these activities implies coordinated

[29] Anton, S.C. and Swisher, C.C. (2004), Early dispersals of Homo from Africa. Annual Review of Anthropology, 33, pp.271–296.

[30] Lewin, R., & Foley, R. (2004). Principles of Human Evolution. Malden, MA: Blackwell Publishing.

[31] Wood, B. (1992). Origin and Evolution of the Genus Homo. Nature, 355(6363), 783–790.

[32] Tattersall, I. (2000). Paleoanthropology: The Last Half-Century. Evolutionary Anthropology, 9(1), 2–16.

[33] Walker, A., & Leakey, R. (1993). The Nariokotome Homo erectus Skeleton. Cambridge, MA: Harvard University Press.

[34] Rightmire, G. P. (1990). The Evolution of Homo erectus: Comparative Anatomical Studies of an Extinct Human Species. Cambridge: Cambridge University Press.

[35] Stout, D., Toth, N., Schick, K., and Chaminade, T. (2010). Neural correlates of Early Stone Age toolmaking: technology, language and cognition in human evolution.

effort, communication, and possibly the emergence of roles within groups—all hallmarks of advanced social structures.[36] Furthermore, the ability to create and use such tools efficiently would have allowed Homo erectus to exploit a broader range of environments and resources, leading to enhanced survival and adaptation.[37] The transition between these species likely involved both gradual changes and selective pressures that favoured certain traits. For instance, climatic fluctuations during this period may have driven adaptations in diet, foraging strategies, and mobility, leading to the more versatile and resilient Homo erectus.[38] The evolution from Homo habilis to Homo erectus involved a series of incremental changes driven by environmental pressures and natural selection. These changes resulted in anatomical, cognitive, and behavioural advancements that enabled Homo erectus to thrive in diverse environments and pave the way for future hominin development.

Homo erectus and Early Human Expansion (1 Million to 300,000 Years Ago)

Out of Africa I

Homo erectus Migration

Homo erectus populations expanded out of Africa and settled in various parts of Asia and Europe. Notable fossil sites include Java in Indonesia and Dmanisi in Georgia, indicating their widespread presence.[39] The expansion of Homo erectus from Africa and its subsequent settlement across various regions of Asia and Europe represent a significant event in human evolution. Around 1.9 million years ago, Homo erectus began to migrate out of Africa, a movement known as the 'Out of Africa I' migration. This species adapted to a variety of environmental conditions and utilized its

Philosophical Transactions of the Royal Society B: Biological Sciences, 367(1585), 75–85.

[36] Shultz, S., Nelson, E., and Dunbar, R. I. M. (2011). Hominin cognitive evolution: Identifying patterns and processes in the fossil and archaeological record. Philosophical Transactions of the Royal Society B: Biological Sciences, 366(1567), 3264–3273.

[37] Shipton, C. (2010). Imitation and shared intentionality in the Acheulean. Cambridge Archaeological Journal, 20(2), 197–210.

[38] Potts, R. (1998). Environmental Hypotheses of Hominin Evolution. Yearbook of Physical Anthropology, 41, 93–136.

[39] Dennell, R. and Roebroeks, W. (2005), An Asian perspective on early human dispersal from Africa. Nature, 438(7071), pp.1099–1104.

technological advancements to support a nomadic lifestyle.[40] The site at Java, notably in places like Sangiran and Trinil, has yielded numerous fossils, including those initially discovered by Eugène Dubois in the 1890s, which provided clear evidence of Homo erectus's wide geographical spread.[41] These fossils exhibited robust skeletal structures with prominent brow ridges and large brain volumes, demonstrating significant evolutionary adaptations. Similarly, the Dmanisi site in Georgia has offered remarkable insights. Discovered in the early 1990s, the fossils found there, dating back to approximately 1.8 million years ago, represent some of the earliest evidence of Homo erectus outside Africa.[42] The Dmanisi fossils are particularly notable for their combination of primitive and advanced traits, including smaller brain sizes akin to earlier hominins and more advanced post-cranial adaptations suitable for long-distance travel. The phrase 'more advanced post-cranial adaptations' refers to the physical characteristics of the body below the head (i.e., the limbs and torso). These adaptations in the Dmanisi fossils suggest improvements that facilitated effective bipedal locomotion and endurance necessary for long-distance travel. These adaptations include features such as a modern-like pelvis, long legs, and certain joint configurations that enhance walking efficiency and running capabilities. For instance, the elongated lower limbs and relatively shorter arms found in Homo erectus differ significantly from earlier hominins, such as Australopithecus, which had shorter legs and longer arms adapted more for climbing than long-distance walking.[43] The structure of the hip and pelvic regions in these fossils indicates a pelvis broader than that of earlier hominids, providing greater stability during bipedal locomotion.[44] Furthermore, the joint structures, such as the femur and tibia, exhibit adaptations for improved shock absorption and energy transfer during

[40] Antón, S. C. (2003). Natural history of Homo erectus. Yearbook of Physical Anthropology, 46, 126–170.

[41] Swisher III, C. C., Rink, W. J., Anton, S. C., Schwarcz, H. P., Curtis, G. H., Suprijo, A., & Widiasmoro. (1994). Latest Homo erectus of Java: Potential contemporaneity with Homo sapiens in southeast Asia. Science, 274(5294), 1870–1874.

[42] Lordkipanidze, D., Vekua, A., Ferring, R., Rightmire, G. P., Agusti, J., Kiladze, G., … Tvalchrelidze, M. (2007). A fourth hominin skull from Dmanisi, Georgia. Nature, 449(7160), 305–310.

[43] Holliday, T. W. (1997). Postcranial evidence of cold adaptation in European Neandertals. American Journal of Physical Anthropology, 104(2), 245–258.

[44] Lordkipanidze, D., Vekua, A., Ferring, R., Rightmire, G. P., Agusti, J., Kiladze, G., … Tvalchrelidze, M. (2007). A fourth hominin skull from Dmanisi, Georgia. Nature, 449(7160), 305–310.

extended walking or running.[45] These anatomical features collectively signify 'more advanced post-cranial adaptations' that are crucial for endurance and efficient locomotion, allowing Homo erectus to travel long distances—an essential trait for their migration and survival across varied landscapes.[46]

The successful dispersal of Homo erectus across diverse environments implies a combination of anatomical and cultural adaptations. Their ability to utilize Acheulean tools to hunt and process food, control fire, and perhaps develop rudimentary shelters would have facilitated survival in varied climates and landscapes.[47] These behaviours underscore the flexible and innovative strategies that enabled Homo erectus to colonize and thrive in new habitats. The expanded range of Homo erectus supports the hypothesis that this species possessed significant behavioural and ecological versatility. Such traits would have been critical in navigating and settling in the diverse ecosystems of Asia and Europe, where their presence has left an indelible mark on the archaeological record.

Archaic Humans

Homo heidelbergensis and Neanderthals

Homo heidelbergensis, emerging around 600,000 years ago, is considered a common ancestor of both Neanderthals and modern humans. They migrated into Europe and evolved into Neanderthals (Homo neanderthalensis).[48] The transition from Homo erectus to Homo heidelbergensis and subsequently to Neanderthals (Homo neanderthalensis) and modern humans (Homo sapiens) represents a critical phase in human evolution. Homo heidelbergensis, which appeared approximately 600,000

[45] Pontzer, H. (2012). Ecological energetics in early Homo. Current Anthropology, 53(S6), S346–S358.

[46] Leonard, W. R. & Robertson, M. L. (1997). Comparative primate energetics and hominid evolution. American Journal of Physical Anthropology, 102(2), 265–281.

[47] Gabunia, L., Vekua, A., Lordkipanidze, D., Swisher III, C. C., Ferring, R., Justus, A., … Rook, L. (2000). Earliest Pleistocene hominid cranial remains from Dmanisi, Republic of Georgia: taxonomy, geological setting, and age. Science, 288(5468), 1019–1025.

[48] Stringer, C. (2012), The status of Homo heidelbergensis (Schoetensack 1908). Evolutionary Anthropology: Issues, News, and Reviews, 21(3), pp.101–107.

years ago, is often regarded as a pivotal species bridging the gap between earlier Homo species and later hominins.[49] Homo heidelbergensis is believed to have evolved from regional populations of Homo erectus in Africa and then migrated into Europe and Asia.[50] This species exhibited a mix of traits from both its ancestors and its descendants. For example, the cranial capacity of Homo heidelbergensis was larger than that of Homo erectus, averaging around 1200 cubic centimetres, signalling an increase in brain size.[51] One of the distinguishing features of Homo heidelbergensis was its robust skeletal remains, which indicate significant physical strength. These adaptations likely provided an advantage in hunting large game, a critical component of their subsistence strategy.[52] The archaeological record, including sites like Boxgrove in the UK, shows evidence of sophisticated tools and organized hunting practices, which suggest cognitive complexities and social cooperation.[53] As Homo heidelbergensis populations migrated into Europe, they encountered a range of climatic conditions, which would have exerted selective pressures leading to regional adaptations. Over time, the European populations of Homo heidelbergensis evolved into Neanderthals. These adaptations are evident in the distinct morphological traits of Neanderthals, such as their large nasal cavities, which are interpreted as a response to cold climates.[54] Meanwhile, another branch of Homo heidelbergensis, remaining in Africa, eventually gave rise to Homo sapiens. This divergence is thought to have occurred around 300,000 years ago, with Homo sapiens exhibiting further advancements in tool technology, art, and complex social structures.[55] This

[49] Rightmire, G. P. (1998). Human evolution in the middle Pleistocene: The role of Homo heidelbergensis. Evolutionary Anthropology: Issues, News, and Reviews: Issues, News, and Reviews, 6(6), 218–227.

[50] Stringer, C. (2012). The status of Homo heidelbergensis (Schoetensack 1908). Evolutionary Anthropology: Issues, News, and Reviews, 21(3), 101–107.

[51] Klein, R. G. (2009). The Human Career: Human Biological and Cultural Origins. 3rd ed. Chicago: University of Chicago Press.

[52] Roebroeks, W. (2001). Hominid behaviour and the earliest occupation of Europe: An exploration. Journal of Human Evolution, 41(5), 437–461.

[53] Roberts, M. B., & Parfitt, S. A. (1994). Boxgrove: A Middle Pleistocene hominid site at Eartham Quarry, Boxgrove, West Sussex. London: English Heritage.

[54] Hublin, J. J. (2009). The origin of Neandertals. Proceedings of the National Academy of Sciences, 106(38), 16022–16027.

[55] McDougall, I., Brown, F. H., & Fleagle, J. G. (2005). Stratigraphic placement and age of modern humans from Kibish, Ethiopia. Nature, 433(7027), 733–736.

progressive transition involved several factors, including climatic changes, migrations, and technological innovations, which together fostered the evolution of distinct hominin lineages capable of thriving in diverse environments.[56] The divergence of Homo heidelbergensis into Homo sapiens approximately 300,000 years ago in Africa represents a crucial juncture in human evolutionary history. This transition was not a simple, linear process but rather a complex progression influenced by multiple interrelated factors. One of the most significant factors was climatic change. The Pleistocene epoch, spanning from about 2.6 million to 11,700 years ago, was characterized by repeated glacial and interglacial cycles. These climatic fluctuations imposed various environmental stresses and created diverse habitats, from arid deserts to lush forests.[57] Hominins in Africa had to adapt to these changing conditions, which likely played a role in driving evolutionary changes. For instance, fluctuating climates would have influenced the availability of resources, prompting innovations in hunting, gathering, and eventually agriculture. Migrations also played a critical role in this evolutionary process. As hominin populations moved across vast landscapes, they would have encountered new challenges and opportunities. These migrations facilitated gene flow between populations, promoting genetic diversity, which is crucial for adaptation.[58] Additionally, the movement of hominins across different environments would have necessitated the development of new survival strategies and technological innovations. Technological advancements are another cornerstone of this progressive transition. The archaeological record indicates that Homo sapiens developed more sophisticated tools compared to their predecessors. The Middle Stone Age (MSA) in Africa is particularly notable for the emergence of blade technology, heat treatment of stones to create stronger and more durable tools, and the use of composite tools involving hafting.[59] These innovations improved hunting efficiency and food

[56] Tattersall, I. (2012). Masters of the Planet: The Search for Our Human Origins. New York: Palgrave Macmillan.

[57] Potts, R. (1998). Environmental Hypotheses of Hominin Evolution. Yearbook of Physical Anthropology, 41, 93–136.

[58] Stringer, C. (2012). The status of Homo heidelbergensis (Schoetensack 1908). Evolutionary Anthropology: Issues, News, and Reviews, 21(3), 101–107.

[59] McBrearty, S., & Brooks, A. S. (2000). The revolution that wasn't: a new interpretation of the origin of modern human Behavior. Journal of Human Evolution, 39(5), 453–563.

processing, supporting larger and more stable populations. Furthermore, the development of art and complex social structures is evident in the record of Homo sapiens. Sites such as Blombos Cave in South Africa have yielded engraved ochre pieces, shell beads, and evidence of symbolic behaviour, suggesting the presence of complex cognitive abilities and possibly sophisticated language skills.[60] These social developments would have fostered enhanced cooperation, communication, and cultural transmission, crucial for survival and thriving in diverse environments. In sum, the progressive transition from Homo heidelbergensis to Homo sapiens involved a multifaceted interplay of climatic changes, migrations, and technological and social innovations. These factors collectively fostered the development of distinct hominin lineages capable of adapting to and thriving in various environments.

The Emergence and Spread of Homo sapiens (300,000 Years Ago to Present)

Out of Africa II

Early Homo sapiens

Modern humans (Homo sapiens) first appeared in Africa around 300,000 years ago.[61] Genetic and fossil evidence supports multiple waves of migration out of Africa, with significant expansions occurring around 60,000 to 80,000 years ago.[62]

[60] Henshilwood, C. S., d'Errico, F., Yates, R., Jacobs, Z., Tribolo, C., Duller, G. A. T.,... & Sealy, J. C. (2002). Emergence of Modern Human Behavior: Middle Stone Age Engravings from South Africa. Science, 295(5558), 1278–1280.

[61] Hublin, J.J., Ben-Ncer, A., Bailey, S.E., Freidline, S.E., Neubauer, S., Skinner, M.M., Bergmann, I., Le Cabec, A., Benazzi, S., Harvati, K. and Gunz, P. (2017), New fossils from Jebel Irhoud, Morocco and the pan-African origin of Homo sapiens. Nature, 546(7657), pp.289–292.

[62] Mellars, P., Gori, K.C., Carr, M., Soares, P.A. and Richards, M.B. (2013), Genetic and archaeological perspectives on the initial modern human colonization of southern Asia. Proceedings of the National Academy of Sciences, 110(26), pp.10699–10704.

Migration Routes and Patterns

Southern Route

One prominent migration route involved moving along the southern coast of Asia, reaching Australia by 50,000 years ago.[63] This southern dispersal route is often referred to as the Southern Coastal Route, which followed the coastlines of the Arabian Peninsula, India, Southeast Asia, and the Indonesian archipelago. Fossil and genetic evidence suggests that modern humans first left Africa approximately 60,000 to 80,000 years ago and moved relatively quickly along this southern corridor.[64] As these populations migrated, they likely utilized coastal resources, including fish and shellfish, which provided a stable food supply as they moved through diverse environments.[65] Archaeological evidence from sites such as Jwalapuram in southern India shows signs of early human occupation around 74,000 years ago, suggesting that populations were already dispersed across South Asia by this time.[66] From Southeast Asia, early human populations likely crossed the open waters to reach the Sahul landmass, which included present-day Australia and New Guinea. Genetic evidence supports the theory that modern humans arrived in Australia by 50,000 years ago, as confirmed by archaeological findings at sites like Madjedbebe in northern Australia, where stone tools and other artefacts date back to 65,000 years ago.[67] These early populations adapted to new ecosystems and likely developed innovative technologies to survive in the varied environments they encountered along their migration route.

[63] Clarkson, C., Jacobs, Z., Marwick, B., Fullagar, R., Wallis, L.A., Smith, M., Roberts, R.G., Hayes, E., Lowe, K.M., Carah, X. and Florin, S.A. (2017), Human occupation of northern Australia by 65,000 years ago. Nature, 547(7663), pp.306–310.

[64] Mellars, P., Gori, K.C., Carr, M., Soares, P.A. and Richards, M.B. (2013), Genetic and archaeological perspectives on the initial modern human colonization of southern Asia. Proceedings of the National Academy of Sciences, 110(26), pp.10699–10704.

[65] O'Connell, J.F. and Allen, J. (2012), The restaurant at the end of the universe: modelling the colonisation of Sahul. Australian Archaeology, (74), pp.5–17.

[66] Petraglia, M.D., Haslam, M., Fuller, D.Q., Boivin, N. and Clarkson, C. (2007), Out of Africa: new hypotheses and evidence for the dispersal of Homo sapiens along the Indian Ocean rim. Annals of Human Biology, 34(5), pp.515–526.

[67] Clarkson, C., Jacobs, Z., Marwick, B., Fullagar, R., Wallis, L.A., Smith, M., Roberts, R.G., Hayes, E., Lowe, K.M., Carah, X. and Florin, S.A. (2017), Human occupation of northern Australia by 65,000 years ago. Nature, 547(7663), pp.306–310.

Northern Route

Another migration route involved moving northward into Europe and Asia. Homo sapiens encountered and interbred with Neanderthals and Denisovans, leading to genetic admixture[68] (Bergström et al., 2020). This northern migration occurred around 45,000 to 60,000 years ago, as modern humans expanded from the Levant into Europe and Central Asia. Fossil and genetic evidence suggest that Homo sapiens coexisted with Neanderthals in Europe for several thousand years before the Neanderthals became extinct approximately 40,000 years ago.[69] The genetic legacy of this encounter is still evident today, with approximately 1–4% of the genome of modern non-African populations being derived from Neanderthals.[70] This interbreeding likely occurred soon after Homo sapiens migrated into Eurasia, as genomic evidence shows multiple episodes of contact between these two species. For example, fossils from Oase Cave in Romania, dated to around 40,000 years ago, show high levels of Neanderthal ancestry, suggesting recent interbreeding.[71] Similarly, Homo sapiens who migrated eastward into Asia also encountered Denisovans, a distinct group of archaic hominins. Evidence of Denisovan ancestry is found particularly in modern populations from East Asia, Melanesia, and Australasia. Denisovan DNA accounts for up to 5% of the genome in some populations, such as the indigenous peoples of Papua New Guinea.[72] Fossils from Denisova Cave in Siberia have provided critical insights into this interbreeding event, as well as revealing a hybrid individual with both

[68] Bergström, A., Stringer, C., Hajdinjak, M., Scerri, E. M. L., & Skoglund, P. (2020). Origins of modern human ancestry. Nature Reviews Genetics, 21(9), 512–523.

[69] Higham, T., Douka, K., Wood, R., Ramsey, C.B., Brock, F., Basell, L., Camps, M., Arrizabalaga, A., Baena, J., Barroso-Ruíz, C. and Bergman, C. (2014), The timing and spatiotemporal patterning of Neanderthal disappearance. Nature, 512(7514), pp.306–309.

[70] Green, R.E., Krause, J., Briggs, A.W., Maricic, T., Stenzel, U., Kircher, M., Patterson, N., Li, H., Zhai, W., Fritz, M.H.Y. and Hansen, N.F. (2010), A draft sequence of the Neandertal genome. Science, 328(5979), pp.710–722.

[71] Fu, Q., Posth, C., Hajdinjak, M., Petr, M., Mallick, S., Fernandes, D., Furtwängler, A., Haak, W., Meyer, M., Mittnik, A. and Nickel, B. (2015), The genetic history of Ice Age Europe. Nature, 534(7606), pp.200–205.

[72] Reich, D., Green, R.E., Kircher, M., Krause, J., Patterson, N., Durand, E.Y., Viola, B., Briggs, A.W., Stenzel, U., Johnson, P.L. and Maricic, T. (2011), Genetic history of an archaic hominin group from Denisova Cave in Siberia. Nature, 468(7327), pp.1053–1060.

Neanderthal and Denisovan ancestry.[73] The admixture between Homo sapiens and these archaic hominins not only enriched the genetic diversity of modern humans but also introduced genes that may have conferred adaptive advantages in new environments. For example, the Denisovan-derived EPAS1 gene has been linked to the ability of Tibetan populations to thrive at high altitudes.[74]

Post-Ice Age Human Migration (12,000 Years Ago to Present)

End of the Last Glacial Maximum

Holocene Migration
The end of the Last Glacial Maximum around 12,000 years ago allowed for significant human migrations and the spread of agriculture. Populations moved into previously glaciated regions in Europe, Asia, and North America.[75] These were the areas that had been covered by ice sheets during the Last Glacial Maximum (LGM), which peaked around 26,500 years ago. These regions experienced significant changes in landscape, climate, and habitat as the ice sheets retreated around 12,000 years ago during the transition to the current interglacial period.

Europe
During the LGM, much of northern Europe, including the British Isles, Scandinavia, and parts of Germany and Poland, was covered by the Fennoscandian ice sheet.[76] As the ice retreated, it left behind a transformed landscape suitable for human habitation and agriculture. The retreat of the ice sheets opened vast new areas for human settlement, leading to the

[73] Slon, V., Mafessoni, F., Vernot, B., de Filippo, C., Grote, S., Viola, B., Vartanyan, S., Meyer, M., Kelso, J. and Pääbo, S. (2018), The genome of the offspring of a Neanderthal mother and a Denisovan father. Nature, 561(7721), pp.113–116.

[74] Huerta-Sánchez, E., Jin, X., Asan, Bianba, Z., Peter, B.M., Vinckenbosch, N., Liang, Y., Yi, X., He, M., Somel, M. and Ni, P. (2014), Altitude adaptation in Tibetans caused by introgression of Denisovan-like DNA. Nature, 512(7513), pp.194–197.

[75] Pinhasi, R., Fort, J. and Ammerman, A.J. (2005), Tracing the origin and spread of agriculture in Europe. PLoS Biology, 3(12), p.e410.

[76] Ehlers, J., Gibbard, P. L., & Hughes, P. D. (2011). Quaternary Glaciations - Extent and Chronology: A Closer Look. Developments in Quaternary Science, Vol. 15. Elsevier.

recolonization of regions such as Britain, which had been largely uninhabitable during the glacial period.[77]

Asia

In Asia, significant glaciation occurred in Siberia and Mongolia, with extensive ice sheets covering large parts of these regions.[78] The retreat of these ice sheets led to the exposure of fertile lands, which populations from the south began to migrate into. The warming climate also facilitated the development of early agricultural societies in areas like China's Yellow River Valley, which became a cradle of ancient civilization.[79]

North America

In North America, the Laurentide ice sheet covered a vast area, extending from the Canadian Arctic down to the present-day northern United States.[80] As the ice sheet melted, it exposed the regions of Canada and the northern United States, allowing clovis and other Paleo-Indian cultures to migrate and settle. The retreat also created new ecological niches and river systems conducive to agriculture and settlement.[81] The retreat of these glacial ice sheets transformed the previously glaciated regions by depositing rich, till soils, forming lakes and river systems, and creating new ecosystems. Human populations took advantage of the improved climates and newly available lands to migrate, settle, and eventually develop agriculture, leading to the spread of human civilization into these previously inhospitable areas.

[77] Roberts, N. (1998). The Holocene: An Environmental History. 2nd ed. Blackwell.

[78] Svendsen, J. I., et al. (2004). Late Quaternary ice sheet history of northern Eurasia. Quaternary Science Reviews, 23(11–13), 1229–1271.

[79] Ho, Ping-ti. (1975). The cradle of the East: An inquiry into the indigenous origins of techniques and ideas of Neolithic and early historic China, 5000–1000 B.C. University of Chicago Press

[80] Dyke, A. S., et al. (2002). The Laurentide and Innuitian ice sheets during the Last Glacial Maximum. Quaternary Science Reviews, 21(1–3), 9–31.

[81] Meltzer, D. J. (2009). First Peoples in a New World: Colonizing Ice Age America. University of California Press.

Agricultural Revolution

Neolithic Expansion

The development of agriculture around 10,000 years ago led to the Neolithic Revolution. Farming communities spread from the Fertile Crescent into Europe, Asia, and Africa, significantly altering human settlement patterns.[82] This transition from hunter-gatherer lifestyles to settled farming communities allowed for more stable food production and surplus storage, which supported population growth and the development of complex societies.[83] One of the earliest centres of agricultural innovation was the Fertile Crescent, a region in the Middle East encompassing parts of modern-day Iraq, Syria, and Turkey, where crops such as wheat, barley, and legumes were first domesticated.[84] From the Fertile Crescent, farming techniques and crops spread into Europe, Asia, and Africa through a combination of migration and cultural exchange. In Europe, the introduction of agriculture is evidenced by archaeological sites such as Çatalhöyük in present-day Turkey, which dates back to around 7500 BC. As farming expanded across Europe, it dramatically altered human settlement patterns by promoting the establishment of permanent villages and towns, facilitating population growth and the development of social hierarchies.[85] In Africa, farming spread along the Nile Valley, contributing to the rise of early civilizations such as ancient Egypt. The domestication of crops like sorghum and millet, along with the farming of cattle, played a critical role in shaping the livelihoods of communities in Sub-Saharan Africa.[86] Similarly, in Asia, agricultural practices spread eastward into the Indus Valley, where crops like barley and wheat were grown, alongside the domestication of cattle. This led to the development of complex societies such as the Harappan Civilization, which is known for its sophisticated urban planning and agricultural infrastructure.[87] The Neolithic Revolution

[82] Bellwood, P. (2005), First Farmers: The Origins of Agricultural Societies. Malden, MA: Blackwell Publishing.

[83] Ibid.

[84] Zeder, M.A. (2011), The origins of agriculture in the Near East. Current Anthropology, 52(S4), pp.S221–S235.

[85] Price, T.D. (2000), Europe's First Farmers. Cambridge: Cambridge University

[86] Marshall, F. and Hildebrand, E. (2002), Cattle before crops: The beginnings of food production in Africa. Journal of World Prehistory, 16(2), pp.99–143.

[87] Fuller, D.Q. (2006), Agricultural origins and frontiers in South Asia: A working synthesis. Journal of World Prehistory, 20(1), pp.1–86.

not only transformed subsistence strategies but also led to significant social and technological advancements, including the development of pottery, metalworking, and more complex social structures.[88] These changes laid the foundation for the rise of early civilizations across the world.

Oceanic Exploration and Colonization

Austronesian Expansion

Starting around 3500 years ago, Austronesian-speaking peoples migrated across the Pacific Ocean, settling islands from Madagascar to Hawaii. This expansion represents one of the most remarkable long-distance maritime migrations in human history.[89] The Austronesian expansion, beginning around 3500 years ago, is one of the most remarkable instances of human migration, characterized by the movement of Austronesian-speaking peoples across vast stretches of the Pacific Ocean. This migration represents not only a significant feat in navigation and maritime technology but also a profound cultural and genetic dispersal that shaped the demographic landscape of a wide geographic area, including islands ranging from Madagascar to Hawaii. The origins of the Austronesian-speaking peoples are generally traced back to Taiwan, where early Austronesians are thought to have developed advanced seafaring skills and distinctive cultural traits.[90] As these populations expanded southward, they brought with them sophisticated double-hulled canoes, outrigger boats, and the knowledge of celestial navigation and ocean currents, which enabled them to traverse vast oceanic distances.[91] One notable aspect of the Austronesian migration is its extraordinary reach and speed. By employing their navigational prowess, these early seafarers embarked on voyages that covered thousands of kilometres, establishing settlements on islands across the Pacific. Regions settled by Austronesian-speaking peoples include Micronesia, Melanesia, Polynesia, and eventually parts of Southeast Asia and the Indian

[88] Diamond, J. (1997), Guns, Germs, and Steel: The Fates of Human Societies. New York: W.W. Norton & Company.

[89] Kirch, P.V. (2010), Peopling of the Pacific: A holistic anthropological perspective. Annual Review of Anthropology, 39, pp.131–148.

[90] Bellwood, P. (2005). First Farmers: The Origins of Agricultural Societies. Malden, MA: Blackwell Publishing.

[91] Kirch, P. V. (2000). On the Road of the Winds: An Archaeological History of the Pacific Islands before European Contact. Berkeley: University of California Press.

Ocean, such as Madagascar.[92] This expansive reach enabled them to develop a cultural and linguistic continuum across these diverse regions. The archaeological and linguistic evidence supports this pattern of migration. Artefacts such as Lapita pottery, found in sites across a wide geographic area, provide tangible links between different Austronesian communities.[93] Linguistic studies reveal a shared ancestral language, Austronesian, which diversified into numerous languages spoken across the Pacific and Indian Oceans. This linguistic diversity is a testament to the migratory paths and settlement patterns of these early navigators.[94] Moreover, genetic studies have offered insights into the human migrations associated with the Austronesian expansion. DNA analysis shows significant genetic linkages between populations in Southeast Asia and the Pacific islands, corroborating the archaeological and linguistic evidence of a common heritage.[95] However, the evidence supporting the hypothesis that the ancestors of the Polynesians originated from Indonesia and the Philippines is multifaceted, drawing from genetic studies, archaeological findings, and linguistic analysis. Each of these sources of evidence contributes a piece to the complex puzzle of Polynesian ancestry.

Genetic Evidence

Genetic studies have revealed significant connections between contemporary Polynesian populations and those in Island Southeast Asia, particularly Indonesia and the Philippines. Mitochondrial DNA (mtDNA) and Y-chromosome analyses have shown that Polynesians share specific genetic markers with populations from these regions. For instance, the frequency of certain mtDNA haplogroups is high in both Polynesia and Island Southeast Asia.[96] This genetic similarity implies a common maternal ancestry and points towards migration routes from Southeast Asia into the Pacific.

[92] Diamond, J. (2000). Guns, Germs, and Steel: The Fates of Human Societies. New York: W.W. Norton.

[93] Kirch, P. V. (1997). The Lapita Peoples: Ancestors of the Oceanic World. Oxford: Blackwell.

[94] Blust, R. (2013). Austronesian Languages. Canberra: Asia-Pacific Linguistics.

[95] Kayser, M., Brauer, S., Weiss, G., Underhill, P., Roewer, L., Schiefenhovel, W., & Stoneking, M. (2006). Melanesian origin of Polynesian Y chromosomes. Current Biology, 16(6), R180–R181.

[96] Kayser, M., Brauer, S., Weiss, G., Underhill, P., Roewer, L., Schiefenhövel, W., & Stoneking, M. (2000). Melanesian origin of Polynesian Y chromosomes. Current Biology, 10(20), 1237–1246.

Archaeological Evidence

The archaeological record provides substantial support for the Theory of Austronesian Migration. The Lapita cultural complex, characterized by distinct pottery styles, provides a tangible link between Island Southeast Asia and Polynesia. Lapita pottery, dating from around 1500 BC to 500 BC, has been found in a wide arc from the Philippines and Indonesia to as far east as Samoa and Tonga.[97] The spread of Lapita culture aligns with the movements of early Austronesian-speaking peoples into the Pacific.

Linguistic Evidence

Linguistic studies have shown that the languages spoken across Polynesia belong to the Austronesian language family, which has its roots in Taiwan and spread through the Philippines and Indonesia before reaching the Pacific. The distribution and diversification of these languages support the migration patterns inferred from genetic and archaeological data. The linguistic similarities between Polynesian languages and those in the Philippines and parts of Indonesia reflect a common origin and progressive west-to-east dispersal.[98]

The convergence of genetic, archaeological, and linguistic evidence suggests that the ancestors of the Polynesians migrated from Indonesia and the Philippines, ultimately spreading across the vast expanse of the Pacific. Moreover, the Austronesian expansion represents a remarkable chapter in human history, characterized by advanced maritime technology, expansive navigation, and broad cultural and genetic influences. These foundational elements facilitated the settlement of one of the widest geographic distributions achieved by pre-modern human societies. However, over the past 2000 years, significant migrations have been driven by various factors, including trade, conquest, and exploration. Notable examples include the Mongol invasions, European colonization, and the transatlantic slave trade. [99] The nineteenth and twentieth centuries saw unprecedented human migration due to industrialization, wars, and globalization.

[97] Kirch, P. V. (1997). The Lapita Peoples: Ancestors of the Oceanic World. Oxford: Blackwell.

[98] Blust, R. (1999). Subgrouping, Circularity and Extinction: Some Issues in Austronesian Comparative Linguistics. Symposium Series of the Institute of Linguistics, 3, 31–94.

[99] Manning, P. (2005), Migration in World History. London: Routledge.

Large-scale movements included European emigration to the Americas, African diaspora, and more recently, migrations due to economic opportunities and political instability.[100]

Theories Associated with Human Migration

Human migration, a fundamental aspect of human history and development, has been driven by a variety of factors and explained through multiple theoretical frameworks. These theories provide insights into the complex motivations and patterns underlying human mobility. To gain an insight into migration theory, it is important to evaluate the key theories associated with human migration.

Push-Pull Theory

The push-pull theory is one of the most widely recognized frameworks for understanding migration. It posits that migration decisions are influenced by factors that push individuals away from their origin and pull them towards their destination.[101] Push factors are adverse conditions that drive people away from their home regions. These can include economic hardship, political instability, environmental disasters, and social unrest.[102] For example, economic deprivation and lack of job opportunities in rural areas often push individuals to migrate to urban centres.[103] Pull factors are favourable conditions that attract individuals to a new location. These can include better economic opportunities, political stability, favourable climate, and social amenities.[104] For example, the availability of jobs and higher wages in developed countries attracts migrants from less developed

[100] Hatton, T.J. and Williamson, J.G. (1998), The Age of Mass Migration: Causes and Economic Impact. Oxford: Oxford University Press.

[101] Lee, E.S. (1966), A theory of migration. Demography, 3(1), pp.47–57.

[102] Ravenstein, E.G. (1885), The laws of migration. Journal of the Statistical Society of London, 48(2), pp.167–235.

[103] Todaro, M.P. (1969), A model of labour migration and urban unemployment in less developed countries. American Economic Review, 59(1), pp.138–148.

[104] Lee, E.S. (1966), A theory of migration. Demography, 3(1), pp.47–57

regions.[105] Critics argue that the push-pull theory oversimplifies the complexity of migration decisions. It does not adequately account for the role of networks, policies, and individual agency.[106]

Neoclassical Economic Theory

Neoclassical economic theory views migration because of regional differences in labour supply and demand. Individuals migrate to maximize their income and employment opportunities.[107] At the micro level, migration is seen as an investment in human capital. Individuals decide to migrate after weighing the potential costs and benefits.[108] For example, migrants often move to regions where their skills and labour are in higher demand, leading to better wages and job prospects.[109] At the macro level, migration flows are influenced by wage differentials and employment opportunities between regions or countries.[110] For example, labour migration from Mexico to the United States can be explained by wage disparities and job availability.[111] Neoclassical theory has been criticized for its focus on economic factors, neglecting social, cultural, and institutional influences on migration.[112]

[105] Harris, J.R. and Todaro, M.P. (1970), Migration, unemployment and development: A two-sector analysis. American Economic Review, 60(1), pp.126–142.

[106] de Haas, H. (2010), The internal dynamics of migration processes: A theoretical inquiry. Journal of Ethnic and Migration Studies, 36(10), pp.1587–1617.

[107] Borjas, G.J. (1989), Economic theory and international migration. International Migration Review, 23(3), pp.457–485.

[108] Sjaastad, L.A. (1962), The costs and returns of human migration. Journal of Political Economy, 70(5), pp.80–93.

[109] Massey, D.S., Arango, J., Hugo, G., Kouaouci, A., Pellegrino, A. and Taylor, J.E. (1993), Theories of international migration: A review and appraisal. Population and Development Review, 19(3), pp.431–466.

[110] Lewis, W.A. (1954), Economic Development with Unlimited Supplies of Labour. The Manchester School, 22(2), pp.139– 191.

[111] Borjas, G.J. (1990), Friends or Strangers: The Impact of Immigrants on the US Economy. New York: Basic Books.

[112] Massey, D.S., Arango, J., Hugo, G., Kouaouci, A., Pellegrino, A. and Taylor, J.E. (1993), Theories of international migration: A review and appraisal. Population and Development Review, 19(3), pp.431–466.

New Economics of Labor Migration (NELM)

New Economic Labor Migration challenges the individualistic approach of neoclassical theory, emphasizing the role of households and families in migration decisions.[113] Migration is seen as a household strategy to diversify income sources and reduce risks, rather than merely an individual's quest for higher wages.[114] For example, families may send one member abroad to work and remit money back home, thus spreading economic risks.[115] Migration helps households to cope with market failures, such as lack of insurance or credit markets, by diversifying income sources.[116] Although, while NELM provides a more comprehensive understanding of migration, critics argue that it may still underplay the importance of individual agency and broader structural factors.[117]

Dual Labor Market Theory

Dual labour market theory posits that migration is driven by structural labour market demands in developed countries. It distinguishes between primary and secondary labour markets.[118] The primary market offers stable, well-paying jobs with career prospects, while the secondary market comprises low-wage, unstable jobs that native workers often avoid.[119] For example, migrants often fill low-wage, labour-intensive jobs in the secondary market, such as agriculture, construction, and service industries.[120] Moreover, migration is driven by the demand for labour in the secondary

[113] Stark, O. and Bloom, D.E. (1985), The new economics of labor migration. The American Economic Review, 75(2), pp.173–178.

[114] Taylor, J.E. (1999), The new economics of labour migration and the role of remittances in the migration process. International Migration, 37(1), pp.63–88.

[115] Stark, O. (1991), The Migration of Labor. Cambridge: Basil Blackwell.

[116] Taylor, J.E. (1999), The new economics of labour migration and the role of remittances in the migration process. International Migration, 37(1), pp.63–88.

[117] de Haas, H. (2010), The internal dynamics of migration processes: A theoretical inquiry. Journal of Ethnic and Migration Studies, 36(10), pp.1587–1617.

[118] Piore, M.J. (1979), Birds of Passage: Migrant Labor and Industrial Societies. Cambridge: Cambridge University Press.

[119] Ibid.

[120] Massey, D.S., Arango, J., Hugo, G., Kouaouci, A., Pellegrino, A. and Taylor, J.E.)1993), Theories of international migration: A review and appraisal. Population and Development Review, 19(3), pp.431–466.

market, where native workers are unwilling to work due to poor conditions and low wages.[121] Critics argue that dual labour market theory may overemphasize the role of demand and understate the impact of supply-side factors, such as migrant networks and individual agency.[122]

World Systems Theory

World systems theory, developed by Immanuel Wallerstein, examines migration within the context of global economic systems and historical patterns of colonialism and capitalism.[123] It emphasizes the economic and political relationships between core (developed) and periphery (developing) countries. Migration is seen as a response to the inequalities and disruptions caused by global capitalism.[124]

Example: Migration from former colonies in Africa and Asia to European metropoles can be seen as a legacy of colonial economic structures.[125] The expansion of global capitalism creates labour demands in core countries and economic disruptions in periphery countries, driving migration flows.[126] Critics argue that world systems theory may be too deterministic, overlooking the agency of migrants and the role of non-economic factors in migration decisions.[127]

Migration Network Theory

Migration network theory emphasizes the role of social networks and connections in facilitating migration. It posits that established networks

[121] Reich, M., Gordon, D.M. and Edwards, R.C. (1973), A theory of labor market segmentation. The American Economic Review, 63(2), pp.359–365.

[122] Portes, A. (1978), Migration and underdevelopment. Politics & Society, 8(1), pp.1–48.

[123] Wallerstein, I. (1974), The Modern World-System I: Capitalist Agriculture and the Origins of the European World-Economy in the Sixteenth Century. New York: Academic Press.

[124] Ibid.

[125] Portes, A. and Walton, J. (1981), Labor, class, and the international system. New York: Academic Press.

[126] Massey, D.S., Arango, J., Hugo, G., Kouaouci, A., Pellegrino, A. and Taylor, J.E. (1993), Theories of international migration: A review and appraisal. Population and Development Review, 19(3), pp.431–466.

[127] de Haas, H. (2010), The internal dynamics of migration processes: A theoretical inquiry. Journal of Ethnic and Migration Studies, 36(10), pp.1587–1617.

reduce the costs and risks of migration, encouraging further movement.[128] Migrants rely on networks of family, friends, and community members for information, financial support, and assistance in finding jobs and housing.[129] For example, Mexican migrants to the United States often rely on established networks for support, leading to chain migration patterns.[130] Furthermore, migration becomes self-perpetuating as networks grow and the benefits of migration become more widely known.[131] While network theory highlights the importance of social ties, it may underemphasize the role of macro-level structural factors and policies in shaping migration.[132]

Contemporary Climate Change and Economic Migration

As climate change intensifies environmental stressors such as sea-level rise, extreme weather events, and prolonged droughts, it is increasingly driving migration both within and across national borders. In Asia, for example, rising sea levels and more frequent cyclones are displacing millions in low-lying countries like Bangladesh. The International Organization for Migration (IOM) estimates that by 2050, 17% of the Bangladeshi population could be displaced due to climate-related factors.[133] In Africa, severe droughts in the Sahel region are forcing pastoralist communities to move southward in search of water and grazing land, leading to resource conflicts and straining urban infrastructure in countries like Nigeria and Chad.[134] In South America, prolonged droughts and deforestation in the Amazon Basin are affecting indigenous populations and rural farmers,

[128] Massey, D.S., Arango, J., Hugo, G., Kouaouci, A., Pellegrino, A. and Taylor, J.E. (1993), Theories of international migration: A review and appraisal. Population and Development Review, 19(3), pp.431–466.

[129] Boyd, M. (1989), Family and personal networks in international migration: Recent developments and new agendas. International Migration Review, 23(3), pp.638–670.

[130] Massey, D.S., Arango, J., Hugo, G., Kouaouci, A., Pellegrino, A. and Taylor, J.E. (1993), Theories of international migration: A review and appraisal. Population and Development Review, 19(3), pp.431–466.

[131] Ibid.

[132] de Haas, H. (2010), The internal dynamics of migration processes: A theoretical inquiry. Journal of Ethnic and Migration Studies, 36(10), pp.1587–1617.

[133] IOM. (2020). Bangladesh: Climate-related displacement and the need for humanitarian response. International Organization for Migration.

[134] Rigaud, K. K., de Sherbinin, A., Jones, B., Bergmann, J., Clement, V., Ober, K., … & Midgley, A. (2018). Groundswell: Preparing for Internal Climate Migration. World Bank.

pushing them to migrate to urban areas in Brazil and Peru, where they face limited economic opportunities and social integration challenges.[135]

In Sub-Saharan Africa, contemporary climate change is significantly impacting migration patterns, as recurrent droughts, desertification, and shifting rainfall patterns render traditional agricultural practices increasingly unsustainable. The Sahel region, which stretches across countries such as Niger, Chad, and Mali, is one of the most affected areas. Here, rising temperatures and erratic precipitation have led to the degradation of arable land, reducing crop yields and making pastoral livelihoods untenable. For instance, in Niger, where agriculture and livestock rearing form the backbone of the economy, nearly 80% of the population relies on rainfed agriculture. Prolonged droughts in recent years have resulted in widespread crop failures and livestock deaths, forcing many families to abandon their homes and migrate to urban centres or neighbouring countries in search of food, work, and water.[136] In addition to internal migration, climate change is also driving cross-border movements. In Burkina Faso, farmers facing severe water scarcity and soil erosion have been migrating to Côte d'Ivoire and Ghana, seeking better opportunities in regions with more stable climates.[137] This cross-border migration often leads to tension between migrants and host communities over limited resources, exacerbating existing socio-economic and political challenges.[138]

The impact of climate change on migration is also visible in East Africa, particularly in the Horn of Africa, where recurrent droughts have led to severe food insecurity and displacement. For example, in Somalia, the 2011 drought triggered a massive humanitarian crisis, with over thirteen million people affected and thousands forced to flee to refugee camps in Kenya and Ethiopia.[139] The lack of viable agricultural options and the col-

[135] Lima, L. B., Brondizio, E. S., & Moran, E. F. (2020). Environmental Change and Human Migration in the Brazilian Amazon. Annals of the American Association of Geographers, 110(3), 711–727.

[136] Hummel, D. (2015), Climate change, land degradation and migration in Mali and Senegal—Some policy implications. Migration and Development, 4(1), pp.81–98.

[137] Wouterse, F. and Taylor, J.E. (2008), Migration and income diversification: Evidence from Burkina Faso. World Development, 36(4), pp.625–640.

[138] Black, R., Bennett, S.R.G., Thomas, S.M., and Beddington, J.R. (2011), Migration as adaptation. Nature, 478(7370), pp.447–449.

[139] Funk, C. (2012), Exceptional warming in the western Pacific–Indian Ocean warm pool has contributed to more frequent droughts in eastern Africa. Bulletin of the American Meteorological Society, 93(7), pp.1049–1051.

lapse of traditional pastoralist systems due to recurrent droughts have made long-term displacement a reality for many, contributing to a complex web of internal and cross-border migration. Urban areas in Sub-Saharan Africa are struggling to cope with the influx of migrants fleeing rural regions. Cities like Lagos in Nigeria and Addis Ababa in Ethiopia are experiencing rapid population growth as rural migrants seek employment opportunities. However, these cities often lack the infrastructure and resources to accommodate the growing populations, leading to the proliferation of informal settlements and increased competition for jobs, housing, and social services.[140] This urban migration, while offering temporary relief from rural hardships, often results in a new set of vulnerabilities, as migrants face precarious living conditions and limited access to basic amenities. Overall, climate-induced migration in Sub-Saharan Africa is a multifaceted issue that not only affects individual migrants but also poses broader challenges for regional stability and development. Addressing these challenges requires a comprehensive approach that includes improving agricultural resilience, developing sustainable urban infrastructure, and implementing policies that support both migrants and host communities.

Impact of Climate Change on Migration to Developed Economies

As global temperatures rise, many regions, particularly in developing countries, are experiencing increased environmental degradation. This is leading to forced migration as people seek more stable living conditions. The migration towards developed economies, such as the United States and countries in the European Union, is influenced by several factors:

1. **Sea-Level Rise and Coastal Erosion:** Low-lying regions such as Bangladesh and Pacific island nations are facing severe threats from rising sea levels. As a result, many inhabitants are migrating to countries with more secure environments. For example, Bangladeshis have increasingly sought asylum in Europe.[141]

[140] Tacoli, C. (2009), Crisis or adaptation? Migration and climate change in a context of high mobility. Environment and Urbanization, 21(2), pp.513–525.

[141] Black, R., Bennett, S. R., Thomas, S. M., & Beddington, J. R. (2011). Climate change: Migration as adaptation. Nature, 478(7370), 447–449.

2. **Extreme Weather Events:** The increasing frequency of hurricanes, cyclones, and other extreme weather events in regions like the Caribbean and Southeast Asia is displacing millions. These events are often followed by surges in migration to the United States and Europe.[142]
3. **Drought and Desertification:** In regions like Sub-Saharan Africa, prolonged droughts and desertification are driving rural populations to seek better living conditions in developed countries. Countries like Italy and Spain have seen a rise in migrants from Africa over the past two decades.[143]

Economic Migration from Developing to Developed Countries

Over the past forty years, economic migration from developing to developed countries has been significant. Initially driven by economic disparity, the pattern of migration has evolved due to globalization and changes in immigration policies.

1. **1970s–1990s:** During this period, migration was primarily driven by economic factors such as employment opportunities in developed countries. The oil crisis and economic downturns in developing nations further accelerated this trend.[144] This period saw significant labour migration from developing nations, particularly in response to the demand for workers in Western Europe, North America, and the Middle East. One of the major drivers of this trend was the economic boom in developed nations, which created labour shortages, especially in sectors such as construction, manufacturing, and service industries.[145] Countries like Germany, France, and the United States actively recruited migrant labour to fill these gaps, offering better wages and working conditions compared to what

[142] McLeman, R. (2014). Climate and Human Migration: Past Experiences, Future Challenges. Cambridge University Press.

[143] Cattaneo, C., & Peri, G. (2016). The migration response to increasing temperatures. Journal of Development Economics, 122, 127–146.

[144] Hatton, T. J., & Williamson, J. G. (1998). The Age of Mass Migration: Causes and Economic Impact. Oxford University Press.

[145] Castles, S. and Miller, M.J. (2009), The Age of Migration: International Population Movements in the Modern World. Palgrave Macmillan.

was available in the migrants' home countries. The oil crisis of the 1970s, triggered by the OPEC oil embargo, significantly influenced migration trends by causing economic downturns in developing nations. Many oil-exporting countries in the Middle East experienced a windfall in revenues, which spurred demand for migrant labour to fuel construction booms and infrastructure development.[146] This led to mass migration from South Asia, North Africa, and Southeast Asia to the Gulf States, where migrants were employed in low-skilled jobs with little job security or rights.[147] At the same time, the oil crisis caused recessions in other regions, particularly in Sub-Saharan Africa and Latin America, exacerbating poverty and unemployment. These economic challenges pushed more individuals to migrate in search of better opportunities abroad.[148] In addition, structural adjustment programs (SAPs) imposed by the International Monetary Fund (IMF) and the World Bank on many developing nations during the 1980s and 1990s also contributed to migration flows. The implementation of SAPs often led to cuts in public spending, reduced social services, and increased unemployment, further driving economic migrants towards wealthier nations.[149] These programs disproportionately affected the poor, leading to rising inequality and encouraging migration as individuals sought to escape deteriorating economic conditions.[150] This period also saw increasing migration from former colonies to their colonial metropoles, driven by historical ties and economic opportunities. Migrants from countries like Algeria, India, and the Caribbean moved to France, the United Kingdom, and other European nations in search of work, often filling lower-wage positions in industries such as transportation, healthcare, and public services.[151] This

[146] Fargues, P. (2006), 'International Migration in the Arab Region: Trends and Policies', United Nations Expert Group Meeting on International Migration and Development in the Arab Region. Beirut, Lebanon.

[147] Russell, S.S. (1992), 'Migrant Remittances and Development', International Migration Review, 30(3), pp. 267–287.

[148] Hatton, T.J. and Williamson, J.G. (2004), Refugees, Asylum Seekers and Policy in Europe. University of Chicago Press.

[149] Chossudovsky, M. (1997), The Globalization of Poverty: Impacts of IMF and World Bank Reforms. Zed Books.

[150] Abu-Lughod, J.L. (2007), Race, Space, and Riots in Chicago, New York, and Los Angeles. Oxford University Press.

[151] Castles, S. and Kosack, G. (1973), Immigrant Workers and Class Structure in Western Europe. Oxford University Press.

migration was often accompanied by social challenges, as receiving countries struggled to integrate the growing immigrant populations into their economies and welfare systems, leading to debates about immigration policy and the strain on social services.[152] The economic-driven migration of the 1970s to 1990s laid the foundation for contemporary migration patterns. However, as climate change intensifies in the coming decades, it is expected to overlay additional pressures on these established migration trends, further influencing the global movement of people.

2. **2000s–2010s:** Economic migration increased with the expansion of the European Union and more liberal immigration policies in North America. The global financial crisis of 2008 briefly curtailed migration but flows soon resumed as economies recovered.[153] The enlargement of the EU in 2004 and 2007 allowed millions of migrants from Eastern European countries like Poland, Romania, and Bulgaria to migrate to wealthier Western European nations in search of better employment opportunities.[154]This movement of labour helped mitigate workforce shortages in receiving countries, particularly in low-skilled sectors such as agriculture, construction, and care services, while also contributing to economic growth in these regions.[155] However, the arrival of large numbers of Polish, Bulgarian, Romanian, Albanian, and other European migrants in to the United Kingdom created resentment amongst the white British population as well as putting a strain on public services.

In North America, changes in immigration policies during this period, particularly in Canada and the United States, aimed to attract skilled workers and fill labour market gaps.[156] However, this liberalization coincided with the global financial crisis of 2008, which briefly curtailed migration flows as economies contracted and unemployment rates spiked. During

[152] Martin, P.L., Abella, M. and Kuptsch, C. (2006), Managing Labor Migration in the Twenty-First Century. Yale University Press.

[153] Castles, S., de Haas, H., & Miller, M. J. (2014). The Age of Migration: International Population Movements in the Modern World. 5th ed. Palgrave Macmillan.

[154] Favell, A. and Hansen, R. (2002), 'Markets against politics: Migration, EU enlargement and the idea of Europe', Journal of Ethnic and Migration Studies, 28(4), pp. 581–601.

[155] Martin, P. (2009), 'Recession and Migration: A New Era for Labor Migration?', International Migration Review, 43(3), pp. 671–691.

[156] Papademetriou, D.G. and Sumption, M. (2011), Rethinking Points Systems and Employer-Selected Immigration. Migration Policy Institute.

this period, many host countries saw an increase in anti-immigrant sentiment, leading to stricter immigration controls and enforcement policies.[157] Despite these challenges, migration resumed as economies began to recover in the early 2010s, driven by renewed demand for labour and improved economic conditions.[158]

The economic impact of this migration varied across regions. In receiving countries, migrants contributed significantly to economic productivity by filling crucial labour shortages and paying taxes, which supported social welfare systems.[159] However, the influx of migrants also raised concerns about the strain on public services such as healthcare, education, and housing, particularly in countries with already stretched welfare systems such as the United Kingdom.[160] These tensions often fuelled public debates on immigration and influenced political discourse, leading to the rise of anti-immigration movements and changes in migration policy.

3. **2010s–2020s:** In recent years, economic migration has been influenced by both economic factors and climate change. The Syrian refugee crisis, which saw millions fleeing to Europe, highlighted the intersection of conflict, economic desperation, and environmental degradation.[161] The Syrian refugee crisis exemplified the interplay between conflict, economic hardship, and environmental degradation. While political instability and violence were the primary triggers of migration, underlying environmental stressors—such as severe droughts in the years leading up to the conflict—exacerbated food and water insecurity, contributing to economic desperation and the displacement of millions of people.[162] This crisis demonstrated how environmental degradation can fuel social and political unrest, forcing vulnerable populations to seek refuge in more stable regions.

[157] Castles, S., de Haas, H., and Miller, M.J. (2014), The Age of Migration: International Population Movements in the Modern World. Palgrave Macmillan.

[158] Sumption, M. and Somerville, W. (2010), 'The UK's New Europeans: Progress and Challenges Five Years after Accession', Migration Policy Institute, 3(2), pp. 37–50.

[159] Dustmann, C. and Frattini, T. (2014), 'The Fiscal Effects of Immigration to the UK', The Economic Journal, 124(580), pp. F593–F643.

[160] Favell, A. and Hansen, R. (2002), 'Markets against politics: Migration, EU enlargement and the idea of Europe', Journal of Ethnic and Migration Studies, 28(4), pp. 581–601.

[161] Betts, A., & Collier, P. (2017). Refuge: Transforming a Broken Refugee System. Penguin Books.

[162] Gleick, P.H. (2014), 'Water, Drought, Climate Change, and Conflict in Syria', Weather, Climate, and Society, 6(3), pp. 331–340.

The mass influx of Syrian refugees into Europe exposed significant challenges for host countries' economies and welfare systems. European countries, particularly Germany, Greece, and Turkey, saw substantial increases in their refugee populations, which put immediate pressure on social services, healthcare, housing, and education systems.[163] While refugees can contribute to the labour market in the long term, in the short term, governments were required to allocate significant resources to support asylum seekers, often leading to public debates over immigration policy and social cohesion.[164] The uneven distribution of refugees across EU member states also led to tensions within the European Union, as some countries bore a disproportionate burden of the responsibility, creating strains on public resources and welfare systems.[165] In parallel, climate change is expected to further exacerbate migration in the coming decades, as rising sea levels, extreme weather events, and deteriorating agricultural conditions displace populations in vulnerable regions such as Sub-Saharan Africa, South Asia, and Central America.[166] These environmental factors often intersect with economic drivers, as people flee not only climate impacts but also the resultant economic instability, food insecurity, and livelihood loss. Migrants from these regions are likely to seek opportunities in wealthier nations, further intensifying migration flows to Europe and North America. The impact of climate-induced migration on economies and welfare systems will be significant. In destination countries, there may be both positive and negative economic effects. Migrants can help fill labour shortages, particularly in aging societies, contributing to economic productivity and growth.[167] However, without effective integration policies, large-scale migration could strain public services and create competition for jobs and housing, particularly in low-income communities.[168] This could exacerbate inequality and fuel anti-immigrant sentiment, potentially leading to

[163] Betts, A. and Collier, P. (2017), Refuge: Transforming a Broken Refugee System. Penguin.

[164] Castles, S., de Haas, H., and Miller, M.J. (2014), The Age of Migration: International Population Movements in the Modern World. Palgrave Macmillan.

[165] Geddes, A. (2015), Migration and the Welfare State in Europe. Routledge.

[166] McLeman, R.A. (2014), Climate and Human Migration: Past Experiences, Future Challenges. Cambridge University Press.

[167] Dustmann, C. and Frattini, T. (2014), 'The Fiscal Effects of Immigration to the UK', The Economic Journal, 124(580), pp. F593–F643.

[168] Favell, A. and Hansen, R. (2002), 'Markets against politics: Migration, EU enlargement and the idea of Europe', Journal of Ethnic and Migration Studies, 28(4), pp. 581–601.

political instability and policy shifts towards more restrictive immigration laws.[169] Furthermore, as climate-induced migration continues to grow, there is a risk that wealthier nations will increasingly turn to border controls and deterrence strategies, which could lead to humanitarian crises as displaced populations are left stranded in unstable regions.[170]

Forecast for the Next Forty Years

Climate change is expected to significantly influence migration patterns in the coming decades. According to the World Bank, up to 143 million people could be internally displaced within their countries by 2050 due to climate change as rising sea levels, droughts, and other environmental pressures render certain regions uninhabitable.[171] This internal displacement will likely spill over into international migration, particularly towards developed economies. The impact of increased mass migration due to climate change on economies and welfare systems will be profound, especially in developed nations that are expected to receive a significant portion of climate migrants. For instance, developed countries may experience economic benefits from an influx of migrants, as they could help address labour shortages, particularly in aging societies where the working-age population is shrinking.[172] Migrants, especially those who are younger, can contribute to the labour force, increasing productivity and helping to sustain industries that are facing workforce gaps. However, the economic benefits of migration will be contingent on the ability of these economies to integrate migrants successfully into the labour market.[173] On the other hand, mass migration could strain welfare systems, particularly in regions that are already facing fiscal pressures. The provision of social services, including healthcare, housing, and education, will likely be challenged by

[169] Castles, S. (2003), 'Towards a Sociology of Forced Migration and Social Transformation', Sociology, 37(1), pp. 13–34.

[170] Betts, A. (2010), 'Survival Migration: A New Protection Framework', Global Governance, 16(3), pp. 361–382.

[171] Rigaud, K. K., de Sherbinin, A., Jones, B., Bergmann, J., Clement, V., Ober, K., ... & Midgley, A. (2018). Groundswell: Preparing for Internal Climate Migration. World Bank.

[172] Goldin, I., Cameron, G. and Balarajan, M. (2011), Exceptional People: How Migration Shaped Our World and Will Define Our Future. Princeton University Press.

[173] Clemens, M.A. and Postel, H.M. (2018), 'Deterring Emigration with Foreign Aid: An Overview of Evidence from Low- Income Countries', Population and Development Review, 44(4), pp. 657–687.

the sudden increase in population due to migration.[174]Additionally, climate-induced migration could exacerbate social tensions and create political challenges, as host countries may struggle to balance the needs of migrants with those of their native populations. In regions with strong welfare states, the redistribution of resources may become contentious, leading to debates about immigration policy and the sustainability of social safety nets.[175] Indeed, for some countries, the migrant influx may lead political realignments which could bring the far right to power. This has already happened in some European countries and such radical political change may be on the cards for the United States and Great Britain.

In developing countries that are more vulnerable to the effects of climate change, migration will likely exacerbate existing economic challenges. The loss of labour, as people are forced to leave affected regions, may reduce agricultural productivity and hinder economic growth, particularly in regions where subsistence farming is prevalent.[176] The departure of working-age individuals could also lead to a reduction in local tax bases, further undermining public services and infrastructure in already fragile states[177] (Barnett and Adger, 2007). Thus, while migration due to climate change may offer economic opportunities, it will also present significant challenges for both sending and receiving countries. Effective policies that promote integration, equitable resource distribution, and climate resilience will be essential to managing the impact of climate-induced migration in the coming decades.

Increased Migration from Sub-Saharan Africa and South Asia

As these regions are particularly vulnerable to climate impacts, migration flows to Europe and North America are expected to increase. Urbanization and environmental degradation will further push people towards

[174] Martin, P.L., Abella, M. and Kuptsch, C. (2014), Managing Labor Migration in the Twenty-First Century. Yale University Press.

[175] Hatton, T.J. and Williamson, J.G. (2011), Global Migration and the World Economy: Two Centuries of Policy and Performance. MIT Press.

[176] Black, R., Adger, W.N., Arnell, N.W., Dercon, S., Geddes, A. and Thomas, D. (2011), 'The effect of environmental change on human migration', Global Environmental Change, 21(S1), pp. S3–S11.

[177] Barnett, J. and Adger, W.N. (2007), 'Climate change, human security and violent conflict', Political Geography, 26(6), pp. 639–655.

migration.[178] Increased migration from Sub-Saharan Africa and South Asia is expected to rise significantly over the next forty years due to the acute vulnerability of these regions to climate change impacts. Climate-induced factors such as rising sea levels, prolonged droughts, and extreme weather events are likely to displace millions of people, pushing them towards migration to more stable regions such as Europe and North America.[179] For example, the Sahel region in Sub-Saharan Africa has already experienced severe environmental degradation and exacerbated food and water insecurity, leading to significant internal and cross-border migration.[180] As agricultural productivity declines in regions heavily dependent on subsistence farming, people will be forced to move to urban areas or emigrate in search of better livelihoods. The economic consequences of this migration will be profound for both the source and destination countries. In source countries, the departure of working-age individuals may reduce the available labour force, weakening local economies and further contributing to poverty and underdevelopment.[181] At the same time, the loss of human capital—often referred to as 'brain drain'—may hinder economic growth, particularly in sectors like healthcare and education, where skilled workers are already in short supply.[182]

Urbanization, fuelled by both environmental degradation and economic hardship, will further exacerbate migration pressures. As cities in Sub-Saharan Africa and South Asia struggle to accommodate rapidly growing populations, they may become unsustainable, driving people to seek better opportunities abroad in developed economies.[183] This urban displacement will likely spill over into international migration, increasing the flow of people to more developed regions, where environmental sta-

[178] Collier, P. (2013). Exodus: How Migration is Changing Our World. Oxford University Press.

[179] McLeman, R.A. (2014), Climate and Human Migration: Past Experiences, Future Challenges. Cambridge University Press.

[180] Black, R., Adger, W.N., Arnell, N.W., Dercon, S., Geddes, A. and Thomas, D. (2011), 'The effect of environmental change on human migration', Global Environmental Change, 21(S1), pp. S3–S11.

[181] Hatton, T.J. and Williamson, J.G. (2011), Global Migration and the World Economy: Two Centuries of Policy and Performance. MIT Press.

[182] Goldin, I., Cameron, G. and Balarajan, M. (2011), Exceptional People: How Migration Shaped Our World and Will Define Our Future. Princeton University Press.

[183] Betts, A. (2010), 'Survival Migration: A New Protection Framework', Global Governance, 16(3), pp. 361–382.

bility and economic opportunities are more abundant. Addressing these migration flows will require coordinated global policy responses that consider both the humanitarian needs of migrants and the economic and social sustainability of host countries.

Shift in Migration Policies

Developed economies may tighten immigration policies to manage the influx of migrants, potentially leading to more irregular migration and humanitarian crises. In response to increased mass migration driven by climate change, developed economies may tighten their immigration policies to manage the rising influx of migrants. This is particularly likely as many countries, already grappling with economic and social pressures, might fear that an influx of climate migrants will further strain their resources, particularly their welfare systems.[184] As a result, more restrictive immigration policies could be enacted, including stringent border controls, reduced refugee quotas, and stricter asylum procedures. These policy shifts could, however, have several unintended consequences, including the rise of irregular migration, as migrants increasingly seek alternative, often dangerous, routes into countries with stronger economies and stable environments[185] For example, through the jungles of Central America to the US–Mexico border or across the English Channel from France to Great Britain in small boats.

Irregular migration, which refers to migration that occurs outside legal channels, can pose significant challenges for both migrants and host countries. Migrants who are forced into irregular pathways often face exploitation and human rights abuses, including trafficking and unsafe working conditions.[186] Moreover, these migrants may lack access to healthcare, housing, and social services, which not only undermines their welfare but also places additional pressure on public services in host countries. For instance, the inability to regulate irregular migration effectively can overwhelm healthcare systems, as migrants often arrive with untreated medical conditions that may require urgent

[184] Hatton, T.J. and Williamson, J.G. (2011), Global Migration and the World Economy: Two Centuries of Policy and Performance. MIT Press.

[185] Betts, A. (2010), 'Survival Migration: A New Protection Framework', Global Governance, 16(3), pp. 361–382.

[186] FitzGerald, D.S. (2019), Refuge Beyond Reach: How Rich Democracies Repel Asylum Seekers. Oxford University Press.

care.[187]Furthermore, irregular migration can increase informal labour markets, leading to wage suppression and economic inequalities within host economies.[188] Additionally, more restrictive migration policies in developed economies may exacerbate humanitarian crises, as climate-induced migration is projected to increase in the coming decades. When legal pathways to migration are blocked, displaced populations may find themselves stranded in unstable regions, contributing to overcrowded refugee camps and border crises.[189] The inability to adequately address these humanitarian issues could lead to political instability and increased pressure on international aid organizations, further complicating global governance and international relations.[190] Therefore, while tightening immigration policies may initially seem like a solution to manage migration, it could ultimately lead to long-term economic, social, and political challenges for both developed and developing nations.

Economic Impact on Developed Economies

The integration of large numbers of migrants could have mixed economic effects, potentially leading to labour market shifts, changes in social services demand, and political tensions.[191] The integration of large numbers of migrants can have varied economic effects on host countries. Economically, an influx of migrants can lead to shifts in the labour market, as migrants often fill both high- and low-skilled job vacancies that may not be met by the native workforce. For example, in Germany, the arrival of over one million refugees between 2015 and 2016 led to increased labour market participation in sectors with shortages, such as construction and healthcare.[192] However, these labour market shifts can sometimes result in

[187] Carens, J.H. (2013), The Ethics of Immigration. Oxford University Press.

[188] Hollifield, J.F. (2004), 'The Emerging Migration State', International Migration Review, 38(3), pp. 885–912.

[189] McLeman, R. A. (2014). Climate and Human Migration: Past Experiences, Future Challenges. Cambridge University Press.

[190] Geddes, A. (2015). Migration and the Global Politics of Climate Change. Global Environmental Politics, 15(3), 157–178.

[191] Peri, G. (2016). Immigrants, productivity, and labor markets. Journal of Economic Perspectives, 30(4), 3–30.

[192] Brücker, H., Rother, N., & Schupp, J. (2019). IAB-BAMF-SOEP Survey of Refugees: Overview and First Results. Institute for Employment Research.

wage depression in certain low-skilled sectors, as evidenced by research in the United States, where an increase in low-skilled immigration was associated with a modest decline in wages for native low-skilled workers.[193] In addition to labour market impacts, the arrival of large numbers of migrants can strain social services. In countries like Sweden and Italy, rapid increases in migrant populations have placed pressure on healthcare, education, and housing systems, sometimes leading to reduced service quality and longer wait times.[194] For example, the increased demand for social housing in Sweden has led to longer queues and a shortage of affordable housing options, particularly in urban areas.[195] Politically, the integration of large migrant populations can also generate tensions within host societies. Research indicates that a rapid increase in immigration can lead to a rise in anti-immigrant sentiment and support for populist parties. In the United Kingdom, for example, concerns over immigration were a significant factor in the 2016 Brexit referendum, where the Leave campaign capitalized on fears regarding the economic and cultural impact of high migration levels.[196] The Leave campaign effectively mobilized public anxiety around immigration by emphasizing the perceived economic and cultural threats posed by high levels of migration. Research shows that the UK experienced a significant increase in net migration following the 2004 enlargement of the European Union, which allowed citizens of eight Eastern European countries to live and work in the UK. By 2015, net migration to the UK had reached 333,000, with more than half of these migrants coming from the EU.[197] Economically, many Leave campaigners argued that high levels of immigration were placing downward pressure on wages, particularly for low-skilled native workers, and increasing competition for

[193] Borjas, G. J. (2003). The labor demand curve is downward sloping: Reexamining the impact of immigration on the labor market. Quarterly Journal of Economics, 118(4), 1335–1374.

[194] Dustmann, C., & Frattini, T. (2014). The fiscal effects of immigration to the UK. Economic Journal, 124(580), F593–F643.

[195] Lundborg, P. (2013). Refugees' employment integration in Sweden: Cultural distance and labor market performance. Review of International Economics, 21(2), 219–232.

[196] Goodwin, M., & Milazzo, C. (2017). Taking back control? Investigating the role of immigration in the 2016 vote for Brexit. British Journal of Politics and International Relations, 19(3), 450–464.

[197] Office for National Statistics. (2016). Migration Statistics Quarterly Report: August 2016. Office for National Statistics.

jobs and public services. Although empirical studies present mixed results, some research suggests that low-skilled immigration may have had a slight negative impact on wages for low-skilled workers. For example, a study found that a 1% increase in the ratio of migrants to native workers led to a 0.2% decrease in wages for workers in the lower quartile of the income distribution.[198] However, other studies argue that the overall impact of EU immigration on wages and employment was minimal, and any negative effects were concentrated in specific sectors and regions.[199] Culturally, the Leave campaign framed immigration as a challenge to British identity and social cohesion, with slogans like 'Take Back Control' resonating strongly with voters who felt alienated by the pace of demographic change. Survey data from the British Election Study shows that areas with rapid increases in immigration, particularly those with little prior experience of ethnic diversity, exhibited stronger support for Brexit.[200] This sentiment was particularly pronounced in regions like the East Midlands and the North of England, where economic stagnation and limited integration of migrant communities heightened fears of cultural displacement.

Overall, while the economic arguments for Brexit were complex and often contested, the cultural arguments resonated strongly with many voters, contributing to the 51.9% vote in favour of leaving the EU. The referendum result highlighted the deep divisions within the UK regarding immigration and underscored the importance of addressing both the economic and social dimensions of migration policy. This trend is not unique to the UK; similar dynamics have been observed in countries across Europe and North America, where migration has become a polarizing political issue.[201] Overall, while migrants can contribute positively to economic growth and fill critical labour gaps, their integration requires careful management to avoid negative consequences, including labour market imbalances, overburdened social services, and political instability.

[198] Dustmann, C., Frattini, T., & Preston, I. (2013). The effect of immigration along the distribution of wages. Review of Economic Studies, 80(1), 145–173.

[199] Portes, J. (2016). Immigration, free movement and the EU referendum. National Institute Economic Review, 236(1), 14– 22.

[200] Goodwin, M., & Heath, O. (2016). The 2016 referendum, Brexit and the left behind: An aggregate-level analysis of the result. The Political Quarterly, 87(3), 323–332.

[201] Golder, M. (2016). Far right parties in Europe. Annual Review of Political Science, 19, 477–497.

Conclusion

Migration has been an enduring feature of human history, shaping civilizations, economies, and the development of societies over millennia. From the early movements of Homo species out of Africa to the complex patterns of global migration in modern times, migration has played a critical role in human adaptation and survival. The chapter illustrates how migration, driven by a myriad of factors, including environmental, economic, and political pressures, has not only facilitated the spread of humans across the globe but also influenced technological innovation, social structures, and cultural evolution.

As discussed in the chapter, the early migrations of species like Homo erectus and Homo sapiens allowed humans to adapt to new environments through the development of tools, social cooperation, and resource management strategies. The expansion of humans into new territories, as evidenced by the migration patterns from Africa to Europe, Asia, and eventually the Americas and Oceania, underscores the importance of migration in fostering human resilience in the face of changing climatic and environmental conditions.[202,203] The cognitive and social advancements associated with these early migrations set the stage for more complex forms of human organization, including the rise of agriculture and settled communities.[204]

The chapter also highlights the significance of migration in the formation of modern states and economies. The Neolithic Revolution, marked by the spread of agriculture from the Fertile Crescent to other parts of the world, catalysed significant shifts in human settlement patterns, allowing for the development of more complex societies and trade networks. These patterns of migration continued into the age of exploration and colonialism, which saw the movement of peoples and goods across vast distances, reshaping the demographic and economic landscapes of entire continents.[205] In the contemporary world, migration is increasingly influenced

[202] Gamble, C. (1993), Timewalkers: The Prehistory of Global Colonization. Harvard University Press.

[203] Antón, S. C., & Swisher, C. C. (2004), 'Early dispersals of Homo from Africa.' Annual Review of Anthropology, 33, pp. 271–296.

[204] Bellwood, P. (2005), First Farmers: The Origins of Agricultural Societies. Blackwell Publishing.

[205] Diamond, J. (1997), Guns, Germs, and Steel: The Fates of Human Societies. New York: W.W. Norton & Company.

by the impacts of climate change. As global temperatures rise, more people are forced to leave their homes due to extreme weather events, sea-level rise, and environmental degradation. The chapter emphasizes how climate-induced migration, such as the displacement of populations in low-lying countries like Bangladesh and the Pacific islands, as well as regions like Sub-Saharan Africa and South Asia, will likely intensify in the coming decades.[206] These migrations will have profound implications for global economies, particularly in developed nations that are expected to receive large numbers of climate migrants. While migration can offer economic benefits by filling labour shortages in aging societies, it also poses challenges to social welfare systems and infrastructure, potentially exacerbating social tensions.[207,208] Furthermore, the chapter explores the intersection of economic migration with political and social dynamics, as seen in the European migration crisis of the 2010s. The Syrian refugee crisis, which was exacerbated by environmental stressors such as prolonged drought, demonstrated the interconnectedness of conflict, environmental degradation, and migration. The influx of refugees into Europe posed significant challenges to the welfare systems of host countries, while also triggering political debates on immigration and social integration.[209,210] As developed economies grapple with these challenges, effective policy responses will be crucial in managing the complex and multifaceted impacts of migration in the twenty-first century.

In conclusion, migration remains a central aspect of human civilization, reflecting our species' ability to adapt to changing circumstances. As we face the twin challenges of climate change and political instability, understanding the historical and contemporary dynamics of migration will be essential for developing policies that promote global stability, economic resilience, and social cohesion. The ability to manage migration in a way

[206] McLeman, R.A. (2014), Climate and Human Migration: Past Experiences, Future Challenges. Cambridge University Press.

[207] Castles, S., de Haas, H., and Miller, M.J. (2014), The Age of Migration: International Population Movements in the Modern World. Palgrave Macmillan.

[208] Dustmann, C., & Frattini, T. (2014), 'The fiscal effects of immigration to the UK.' Economic Journal, 124(580), pp. F593–F643.

[209] Gleick, P.H. (2014), 'Water, Drought, Climate Change, and Conflict in Syria.' Weather, Climate, and Society, 6(3), pp. 331–340.

[210] Betts, A. and Collier, P. (2017), Refuge: Transforming a Broken Refugee System. Penguin Books.

that benefits both migrants and host communities will be critical to ensuring that future migration contributes to human development, rather than exacerbating existing inequalities and conflicts.

References

Abu-Lughod, J. L. (2007). *Race, space, and riots in Chicago, New York, and Los Angeles*. Oxford University Press.

Aiello, L. C., & Wheeler, P. (1995). The expensive tissue hypothesis: The brain and the digestive system in human and primate evolution. *Current Anthropology, 36*(2), 199–221.

Antón, S. C. (2003). Natural history of Homo erectus. *Yearbook of Physical Anthropology, 46*, 126–170.

Anton, S. C., & Swisher, C. C. (2004). Early dispersals of Homo from Africa. *Annual Review of Anthropology, 33*, 271–296.

Barnett, J., & Adger, W. N. (2007). Climate change, human security and violent conflict. *Political Geography, 26*(6), 639–655.

Bellwood, P. (2005). *First farmers: The origins of agricultural societies*. Blackwell Publishing.

Bergmann, J. (2019). Climate change, migration, and the crisis in the Sahel. *European Union Institute for Security Studies (EUISS), 5*, 1–4.

Bergström, A., Frantz, L., Schmidt, R., Ersmark, E., Lebrasseur, O., Girdland-Flink, L., Lin, A. T., Storå, J., Sjögren, K.-G., Anthony, D., Antipina, E., Amiri, S., Bar-Oz, G., Vladimir I, B., Bulatović, J., Brown, D., Carmagnini, A., Davy, T., Fedorov, S., et al. (2020a). Origins and genetic legacy of prehistoric dogs. *Science, 370*(6516), 557–564.

Bergström, A., Stringer, C., Hajdinjak, M., Scerri, E. M. L., & Skoglund, P. (2020b). Origins of modern human ancestry. *Nature Reviews Genetics, 21*(9), 512–523.

Betts, A. (2010). Survival migration: A new protection framework. *Global Governance, 16*(3), 361–382.

Betts, A., & Collier, P. (2017). *Refuge: Transforming a broken refugee system*. Penguin Books.

Black, R., Bennett, S. R., Thomas, S. M., & Beddington, J. R. (2011). Climate change: Migration as adaptation. *Nature, 478*(7370), 447–449.

Blust, R. (1999). Subgrouping, circularity and extinction: Some issues in Austronesian comparative linguistics. *Symposium Series of the Institute of Linguistics, 3*, 31–94.

Borjas, G. J. (1989). Economic theory and international migration. *International Migration Review, 23*(3), 457–485.

Borjas, G. J. (2003). The labour demand curve is downward sloping: Re-examining the impact of immigration on the labour market. *Quarterly Journal of Economics, 118*(4), 1335–1374.

Boyd, M. (1989). Family and personal networks in international migration: Recent developments and new agendas. *International Migration Review, 23*(3), 638–670.

Brücker, H., Rother, N., & Schupp, J. (2019). *IAB-BAMF-SOEP survey of refugees: Overview and first results.* Institute for Employment Research.

Carens, J. H. (2013). *The ethics of immigration.* Oxford University Press.

Castles, S. (2003). Towards a sociology of forced migration and social transformation. *Sociology, 37*(1), 13–34.

Castles, S., de Haas, H., & Miller, M. J. (2014). *The age of migration: International population movements in the modern world* (5th ed.). Palgrave Macmillan.

Castles, S., & Kosack, G. (1973). *Immigrant workers and class structure in Western Europe.* Oxford University Press.

Castles, S., & Miller, M. J. (2009). *The age of migration: International population movements in the modern world.* Palgrave Macmillan.

Cattaneo, C., & Peri, G. (2016). The migration response to increasing temperatures. *Journal of Development Economics, 122*, 127–146.

Chossudovsky, M. (1997). *The globalization of poverty: Impacts of IMF and World Bank Reforms.* Zed Books.

Clarkson, C., et al. (2017). Human occupation of northern Australia by 65,000 years ago. *Nature, 547*(7663), 306–310.

Clemens, M. A., & Postel, H. M. (2018). Deterring emigration with Foreign Aid: An overview of evidence from low-income countries. *Population and Development Review, 44*(4), 657–687.

Collier, P. (2013). *Exodus: How migration is changing our world.* Oxford University Press.

de Haas, H. (2010). The internal dynamics of migration processes: A theoretical inquiry. *Journal of Ethnic and Migration Studies, 36*(10), 1587–1617.

de la Torre, I. (2011). The early stone age lithic assemblages of Gadeb (Ethiopia) and the developed Oldowan/early Acheulean in East Africa. *Journal of Human Evolution, 60*(6), 768–812.

Dennell, R. W., & Roebroeks, W. (2005). An Asian perspective on early human dispersal from Africa. *Nature, 438*(7071), 1099–1104.

Diamond, J. (1997). *Guns, germs, and steel: The fates of human societies.* W.W. Norton & Company.

Dunbar, R. I. M. (1996). *Grooming, gossip, and the evolution of language.* Harvard University Press.

Dustmann, C., & Frattini, T. (2014). The fiscal effects of immigration to the UK. *Economic Journal, 124*(580), F593–F643.

Dyke, A. S., Andrews, J. T., Clark, P. U., England, J. H., Miller, G. H., Shaw, J., & Veillette, J. J. (2002). The Laurentide and Innuitian ice sheets during the Last Glacial Maximum. *Quaternary Science Reviews, 21*(1–3), 9–31.

Ehlers, J., Gibbard, P. L., & Hughes, P. D. (2011). Quaternary glaciations. In *Extent and chronology: A closer look* (Developments in Quaternary Science) (Vol. 15). Elsevier.

Falk, D. (2004). Prelinguistic evolution in early hominins: Whence motherese? *Behavioral and Brain Sciences, 27*(4), 491–503.

Fargues, P. (2006). International migration in the Arab region: Trends and Policies, United Nations Expert Group Meeting on International Migration and Development in the Arab Region. Beirut, Lebanon.

Favell, A. (2008). *Eurostars and Eurocities: Free movement and mobility in an integrating Europe*. Blackwell Publishing.

Favell, A., & Hansen, R. (2002). Markets against politics: Migration, EU enlargement and the idea of Europe. *Journal of Ethnic and Migration Studies, 28*(4), 581–601.

FitzGerald, D. S. (2019). *Refuge beyond reach: How rich democracies Repel Asylum Seekers*. Oxford University Press.

Fu, Q., Posth, C., Hajdinjak, M., Petr, M., Mallick, S., Fernandes, D., Furtwängler, A., Haak, W., Meyer, M., Mittnik, A., & Nickel, B. (2015). The genetic history of Ice Age Europe. *Nature, 534*(7606), 200–205.

Fuller, D. Q. (2006). Agricultural origins and frontiers in South Asia: A working synthesis. *Journal of World Prehistory, 20*(1), 1–86.

Funk, C. (2012). Exceptional warming in the western Pacific–Indian Ocean warm pool has contributed to more frequent droughts in eastern Africa. *Bulletin of the American Meteorological Society, 93*(7), 1049–1051.

Gabunia, L., Vekua, A., Lordkipanidze, D., Swisher, C. C., III, Ferring, R., Justus, A., et al. (2000). Earliest Pleistocene hominid cranial remains from Dmanisi, Republic of Georgia: Taxonomy, geological setting, and age. *Science, 288*(5468), 1019–1025.

Gamble, C. (1993). *Timewalkers: The prehistory of global colonization*. Harvard University Press.

Geddes, A. (2015). *Migration and the Welfare State in Europe*. Routledge.

Gleick, P. H. (2014). Water, drought, climate change, and conflict in Syria. *Weather, Climate, and Society, 6*(3), 331–340.

Golder, M. (2016). Far right parties in Europe. *Annual Review of Political Science, 19*, 477–497.

Goldin, I., Cameron, G., & Balarajan, M. (2011). *Exceptional people: How migration shaped our world and will define our future*. Princeton University Press.

Goodwin, M., & Heath, O. (2016). The 2016 referendum, Brexit and the left behind: An aggregate-level analysis of the result. *The Political Quarterly, 87*(3), 323–332.

Goodwin, M., & Milazzo, C. (2017). Taking back control? Investigating the role of immigration in the 2016 vote for Brexit. *British Journal of Politics and International Relations, 19*(3), 450–464.

Green, R. E., Krause, J., Briggs, A. W., Maricic, T., Stenzel, U., Kircher, M., Patterson, N., Li, H., Zhai, W., Fritz, M. H. Y., & Hansen, N. F. (2010). A draft sequence of the Neandertal genome. *Science, 328*(5979), 710–722.

Harmand, S., Lewis, J. E., Feibel, C. S., Lepre, C. J., Prat, S., Lenoble, A., Boës, X., Quinn, R. L., Brenet, M., Arroyo, A., Taylor, N., Clément, S., Daver, G., Brugal, J.-P., Leakey, L., Mortlock, R. A., Wright, J. D., Lokorodi, S., Kirwa, C., Kent, D. V., & Roche, H. (2015). 3.3-million-year-old stone tools from Lomekwi 3, West Turkana, Kenya. *Nature, 521*(7552), 310–315.

Harris, J. R., & Todaro, M. P. (1970). Migration, unemployment and development: A two-sector analysis. *American Economic Review, 60*(1), 126–142.

Hatton, T. J., & Williamson, J. G. (1998). *The age of mass migration: Causes and economic impact.* Oxford University Press.

Hatton, T. J., & Williamson, J. G. (2004). *Refugees, Asylum seekers and policy in Europe.* University of Chicago Press.

Hatton, T. J., & Williamson, J. G. (2011). *Global migration and the world economy: Two centuries of policy and performance.* MIT Press.

Higham, T., Douka, K., Wood, R., Ramsey, C. B., Brock, F., Basell, L., Camps, M., Arrizabalaga, A., Baena, J., Barroso-Ruíz, C., & Bergman, C. (2014). The timing and spatiotemporal patterning of Neanderthal disappearance. *Nature, 512*(7514), 306–309.

Ho, P.-t. (1975). *The cradle of the East: An inquiry into the indigenous origins of techniques and ideas of Neolithic and early historic China, 5000–1000 B.C.* University of Chicago Press.

Holliday, T. W. (1997). Postcranial evidence of cold adaptation in European Neandertals. *American Journal of Physical Anthropology, 104*(2), 245–258.

Hollifield, J. F. (2004). The emerging migration state. *International Migration Review, 38*(3), 885–912.

Hrdy, S. B. (2009). *Mothers and others: The evolutionary origins of mutual understanding.* Harvard University Press.

Hublin, J. J. (2009). The origin of Neandertals. *Proceedings of the National Academy of Sciences, 106*(38), 16022–16027.

Hublin, J. J., et al. (2017). New fossils from Jebel Irhoud, Morocco and the pan-African origin of Homo sapiens. *Nature, 546*(7657), 289–292.

Huerta-Sánchez, E., Jin, X., Asan, Bianba, Z., Peter, B. M., Vinckenbosch, N., Liang, Y., Yi, X., He, M., Somel, M., & Ni, P. (2014). Altitude adaptation in Tibetans caused by introgression of Denisovan-like DNA. *Nature, 512*(7513), 194–197.

Hummel, D. (2015). Climate change, land degradation and migration in Mali and Senegal—Some policy implications. *Migration and Development, 4*(1), 81–98.

IOM. (2020). *Bangladesh: Climate-related displacement and the need for humanitarian response*. International Organization for Migration.

Isaac, G. L. (1978). Food sharing and human evolution: Archaeological evidence from the Plio-Pleistocene of East Africa. *Journal of Anthropological Research, 34*(3), 311–325.

Johanson, D. C., & Edey, M. A. (1981). *Lucy: The beginnings of humankind*. Simon and Schuster.

Johanson, D. C., & White, T. D. (1979). A systematic assessment of early African hominids. *Science, 203*(4384), 321–330.

Kaplan, H., Hill, K., Lancaster, J., & Hurtado, A. M. (2000). A theory of human Life history evolution: Diet, intelligence, and longevity. *Evolutionary Anthropology, 9*(4), 156–185.

Kayser, M., Brauer, S., Weiss, G., Underhill, P., Roewer, L., Schiefenhövel, W., & Stoneking, M. (2000). Melanesian origin of Polynesian Y chromosomes. *Current Biology, 10*(20), 1237–1246.

Kirch, P. V. (1997). *The Lapita peoples: Ancestors of the Oceanic World*. Blackwell.

Kirch, P. V. (2010). *On the road of the winds: An archaeological history of the Pacific Islands before European Contact*. University of California Press.

Klein, R. G. (2009). *The human career: Human biological and cultural origins* (3rd ed.). University of Chicago Press.

Leakey, M. D. (1971). *Olduvai Gorge: Excavations in beds I and II, 1960–1963*. Cambridge University Press.

Lee, E. S. (1966). A theory of migration. *Demography, 3*(1), 47–57.

Leonard, W. R., & Robertson, M. L. (1997). Comparative primate energetics and hominid evolution. *American Journal of Physical Anthropology, 102*(2), 265–281.

Lewin, R., & Foley, R. (2004). *Principles of human evolution*. Blackwell Publishing.

Lewis, W. A. (1954). Economic development with unlimited supplies of labour. *The Manchester School, 22*(2), 139–191.

Lima, L. B., Brondizio, E. S., & Moran, E. F. (2020). Environmental change and human migration in the Brazilian Amazon. *Annals of the American Association of Geographers, 110*(3), 711–727.

Lordkipanidze, D., Vekua, A., Ferring, R., Rightmire, G. P., Agusti, J., Kiladze, G., et al. (2007). A fourth hominin skull from Dmanisi. *Georgia. Nature, 449*(7160), 305–310.

Lundborg, P. (2013). Refugees' employment integration in Sweden: Cultural distance and labor market performance. *Review of International Economics, 21*(2), 219–232.

Manning, P. (2005). *Migration in world history*. Routledge.

Marshall, F., & Hildebrand, E. (2002). Cattle before crops: The beginnings of food production in Africa. *Journal of World Prehistory, 16*(2), 99–143.

Martin, P. (2009). Recession and migration: A new era for labor migration? *International Migration Review, 43*(3), 671–691.

Martin, P. L., Abella, M., & Kuptsch, C. (2014). *Managing labor migration in the twenty-first century*. Yale University Press.

Massey, D. S., , Arango, J., Hugo, G., Kouaouci, A., Pellegrino, A. and Taylor, J.E. (1993). Theories of international migration: A review and appraisal. Population and Development Review, 19(3), 431–466.

McDougall, I., Brown, F. H., & Fleagle, J. G. (2005). Stratigraphic placement and age of modern humans from Kibish, Ethiopia. *Nature, 433*(7027), 733–736.

McLeman, R. (2014). *Climate and human migration: Past experiences, future challenges*. Cambridge University Press.

McNamara, K. E., & Gibson, C. (2009). We do not want to leave our land': Pacific ambassadors at the United Nations resist the category of 'climate refugees. *Geoforum, 40*(3), 475–483.

Mellars, P., Gori, K. C., Carr, M., Soares, P. A., & Richards, M. B. (2013). Genetic and archaeological perspectives on the initial modern human colonization of southern Asia. *Proceedings of the National Academy of Sciences, 110*(26), 10699–10704.

Meltzer, D. J. (2009). *First peoples in a new world: Colonizing Ice Age America*. University of California Press.

Office for National Statistics. (2016). *Migration statistics quarterly report: August 2016*. Office for National Statistics.

Okpara, U. T., Stringer, L. C., Dougill, A. J., & Bila, M. D. (2015). Conflicts about water in Lake Chad: Are environmental, vulnerability and security issues linked? *Progress in Development Studies, 15*(4), 308–325.

Papademetriou, D. G., & Sumption, M. (2011). *Rethinking Points systems and employer-selected immigration*. Migration Policy Institute.

Peri, G. (2016). Immigrants, productivity, and labour markets. *Journal of Economic Perspectives, 30*(4), 3–30.

Petraglia, M. D., Haslam, M., Fuller, D. Q., Boivin, N., & Clarkson, C. (2007). Out of Africa: New hypotheses and evidence for the dispersal of Homo sapiens along the Indian Ocean rim. *Annals of Human Biology, 34*(5), 515–526.

Pinhasi, R., Fort, J., & Ammerman, A. J. (2005). The spatial-temporal pattern of the Neolithic demic diffusion in Europe. *Current Anthropology, 46*(S5), S35–S58. https://doi.org/10.1086/444365

Piore, M. J. (1979). *Birds of passage: Migrant labor and industrial societies*. Cambridge University Press.

Pontzer, H. (2010). Economics of bipedalism: Effects of body size and limb length on locomotor efficiency in humans and other primates. *Journal of Human Evolution, 58*(6), 568–575.

Pontzer, H. (2012). Ecological energetics in early Homo. *Current Anthropology, 53*(S6), S346–S358.

Portes, A. (1978). Migration and underdevelopment. *Politics & Society, 8*(1), 1–48.

Portes, A., & Walton, J. (1981). *Labor, class, and the international system.* Academic Press.
Portes, J. (2016). Immigration, free movement and the EU referendum. *National Institute Economic Review, 236*(1), 14–22.
Potts, R. (1998). Environmental hypotheses of Hominin evolution. *Yearbook of Physical Anthropology, 41*, 93–136.
Price, T. D. (2000). *Europe's first farmers.* Cambridge University.
Ravenstein, E. G. (1885). The laws of migration. *Journal of the Statistical Society of London, 48*(2), 167–235.
Reich, M., Gordon, D. M., & Edwards, R. C. (1973). A theory of labour market segmentation. *American Economic Review, 63*(2), 359–365.
Rigaud, K. K., de Sherbinin, A., Jones, B., Bergmann, J., Clement, V., Ober, K., & Midgley, A. (2018). *Groundswell: Preparing for internal climate migration.* World Bank Publications.
Rightmire, G. P. (1990). *The Evolution of Homo erectus: Comparative Anatomical studies of an extinct human species.* Cambridge University Press.
Rightmire, G. P. (1998). Human evolution in the middle Pleistocene: The role of Homo heidelbergensis. *Evolutionary Anthropology: Issues, News, and Reviews: Issues, News, and Reviews, 6*(6), 218–227.
Roberts, M. B., & Parfitt, S. A. (1994). *Boxgrove: A middle Pleistocene hominid site at Eartham Quarry, Boxgrove, West Sussex.* English Heritage.
Roberts, N. (1998). *The Holocene: An Environmental History* (2nd ed.).
Roebroeks, W. (2001). Hominid behaviour and the earliest occupation of Europe: An exploration. *Journal of Human Evolution, 41*(5), 437–461.
Russell, S. S. (1992). Migrant remittances and development. *International Migration Review, 30*(3), 267–287.
Sjaastad, L. A. (1962). The costs and returns of human migration. *Journal of Political Economy, 70*(5, Part 2), 80–93.
Slon, V., Mafessoni, F., Vernot, B., de Filippo, C., Grote, S., Viola, B., Vartanyan, S., Meyer, M., Kelso, J., & Pääbo, S. (2018). The genome of the offspring of a Neanderthal mother and a Denisovan father. *Nature, 561*(7721), 113–116.
Sockol, M. D., Raichlen, D. A., & Pontzer, H. (2007). Chimpanzee locomotor energetics and the origin of human bipedalism. *Proceedings of the National Academy of Sciences, 104*(30), 12265–12269.
Stanford, C., Allen, J. S., & Anton, S. C. (2013). *Biological anthropology: The natural history of Humankind* (3rd ed.). Pearson.
Stark, O. (1991). *The migration of labor.* Basil Blackwell.
Stark, O., & Bloom, D. E. (1985). The new economics of labor migration. *American Economic Review, 75*(2), 173–178.
Stout, D., Toth, N., Schick, K., & Chaminade, T. (2008). Neural correlates of Early Stone Age toolmaking: Technology, language and cognition in human evolution. *Philosophical Transactions of the Royal Society B: Biological Sciences, 363*(1499), 1939–1949.

Stringer, C. (2012). The status of Homo heidelbergensis (Schoetensack 1908). *Evolutionary Anthropology: Issues, News, and Reviews, 21*(3), 101–107.

Sumption, M., & Somerville, W. (2010). The UK's New Europeans: Progress and challenges five years after accession. *Migration Policy Institute, 3*(2), 37–50.

Svendsen, J. I., et al. (2004). Late quaternary ice sheet history of northern Eurasia. *Quaternary Science Reviews, 23*(11–13), 1229–1271.

Swisher, C. C., III, Rink, W. J., Anton, S. C., Schwarcz, H. P., Curtis, G. H., Suprijo, A., & Widiasmoro. (1994). Latest Homo erectus of Java: Potential contemporaneity with Homo sapiens in southeast Asia. *Science, 274*(5294), 1870–1874.

Tacoli, C. (2009). Crisis or adaptation? Migration and climate change in a context of high mobility. *Environment and Urbanization, 21*(2), 513–525.

Tattersall, I. (2000). Paleoanthropology: The last half-century. *Evolutionary Anthropology, 9*(1), 2–16.

Tattersall, I. (2012). *Masters of the planet: The search for our human origins.* Palgrave Macmillan.

Taylor, J. E. (1999). The new economics of labour migration and the role of remittances in the migration process. *International Migration, 37*(1), 63–88. https://doi.org/10.1111/1468-2435.00066

Todaro, M. P. (1969). A model of labour migration and urban unemployment in less developed countries. *American Economic Review, 59*(1), 138–148.

Toth, N., & Schick, K. (2009). The Oldowan: The tool making of early hominins and chimpanzees compared. *Annual Review of Anthropology, 38*, 289–305.

Walker, A., & Leakey, R. (1993). *The Nariokotome Homo erectus Skeleton.* Harvard University Press.

Ward, C. V., Kimbel, W. H., & Johanson, D. C. (2011). Complete Fourth metatarsal and arches in the foot of australopithecus afarensis. *Science, 331*(6018), 750–753.

Wheeler, P. E. (1991). The influence of bipedalism on the energy and water budgets of early hominids. *Journal of Human Evolution, 21*(2), 117–136.

Wood, B. (1992). Origin and evolution of the genus homo. *Nature, 355*(6363), 783–790.

World Bank. (2018). *Groundswell: Preparing for internal climate migration.* World Bank.

Wouterse, F., & Taylor, J. E. (2008). Migration and income diversification: Evidence from Burkina Faso. *World Development, 36*(4), 625–640.

Wynn, T., & Coolidge, F. L. (2011). The implications of Oldowan cognitive capabilities for the evolution of pleistocene Hominin lifeways. *Journal of Human Evolution, 60*(4), 439–448.

Zeder, M. A. (2011). The origins of agriculture in the Near East. *Current Anthropology, 52*(S4), S221–S235.

CHAPTER 6

Artificial Intelligence and Robotics

Introduction

Artificial Intelligence (AI) and Robotics are two of the most transformative fields in modern technology. They have evolved from theoretical concepts to practical applications that permeate various aspects of society. This refers to the significant progression of Artificial Intelligence (AI) and Robotics from purely academic and speculative ideas to real-world implementations with tangible impacts. In the early stages, AI and Robotics were primarily subjects of theoretical research, often explored through hypothetical models and academic discourse. Over time, advancements in computational power, algorithmic development, and engineering have enabled the transition of these technologies into practical tools and systems that now deeply influence everyday life. Initially, AI and Robotics were mainly discussed in academic settings. AI research focused on creating algorithms and models to simulate cognitive processes such as reasoning, learning, and perception.[1] Robotics, on the other hand, began with the study of mechanical structures and control systems to achieve autonomous movement and manipulation.[2] The advancement of these

[1] Russell, S., & Norvig, P. (2016). Artificial Intelligence: A Modern Approach. 3rd ed. Pearson.

[2] Siciliano, B., & Khatib, O. (2016). Springer Handbook of Robotics. Springer.

S. Ramesh, *The Political Economy of Contemporary Human Civilisation, Volume I*,
https://doi.org/10.1007/978-3-031-84181-1_6

fields into practical applications is exemplified by numerous developments across various sectors including healthcare, transportation, manufacturing, and everyday life. In healthcare, AI is now extensively used for diagnostic purposes, personalized medicine, and health monitoring. Examples include machine learning algorithms that interpret medical images with high accuracy.[3] In transportation autonomous vehicles (AVs), a product of combined AI and Robotics technology, are increasingly becoming a reality, with companies like Tesla and Waymo developing self-driving cars that promise to revolutionize transportation.[4] In manufacturing Robotics has transformed manufacturing through automation, where robots perform tasks such as assembling, packaging, and quality control with high efficiency and precision.[5] Finally, in everyday life, AI-driven personal assistants like Siri and Alexa exemplify how AI has permeated everyday life. These systems use natural language processing and machine learning to interact with users and aid in various tasks.[6] The integration of AI and Robotics into these domains illustrates their transition from theoretical constructs to integral components of modern society. Their influence is continuously expanding, driven by ongoing research and development. This chapter provides an overview of the history and developments in AI and Robotics.

History of Artificial Intelligence and Robotics

Early Concepts and Foundations

The conceptual foundation for AI was laid by Alan Turing, who proposed the idea of a 'universal machine' capable of performing any computation.[7] His famous Turing Test was a pivotal moment in defining the criteria for machine intelligence. The Turing Test, proposed by British mathematician

[3] Topol, E. (2019). Deep Medicine: How Artificial Intelligence Can Make Healthcare Human Again. Basic Books.

[4] Litman, T. (2020). Autonomous Vehicle Implementation Predictions. Victoria Transport Policy Institute.

[5] Groover, M. P. (2018). Automation, Production Systems, and Computer-Integrated Manufacturing. Prentice Hall.

[6] Dale, R. (2020). The Conversation: Bringing Machine Learning to Natural Language Processing. Wiley.

[7] Turing, A.M. (1950), Computing machinery and intelligence. Mind, 59(236), pp.433–460

and computer scientist Alan Turing in 1950, is widely regarded as a foundational concept in the philosophy of Artificial Intelligence (AI). Turing introduced the test in his seminal paper, Computing Machinery and Intelligence, to determine whether a machine could exhibit intelligent behaviour indistinguishable from that of a human.[8] The test involves a human judge engaging in a text-based conversation with both a machine and another human. If the judge cannot reliably distinguish between the machine and the human, the machine is said to have passed the test and demonstrated a form of Artificial Intelligence. The Turing Test was a pivotal moment in the field of AI because it shifted the focus from trying to define what intelligence is to examining how it manifests through behaviour. Instead of attempting to create a machine that 'thinks' like a human, the test suggests that demonstrating intelligence is sufficient if a machine can simulate human-like behaviour convincingly.[9] Several real-world applications and developments in AI have drawn inspiration from Turing's concept. For example, chatbots and virtual assistants like Siri and Alexa rely on conversational interfaces that aim to mimic human responses. While modern AI systems have not fully passed the Turing Test in its original form, advances in natural language processing and machine learning have brought machines closer to this goal. Critics, however, have raised concerns about the limitations of the Turing Test. Some argue that passing the test might not indicate true intelligence but merely the ability to imitate human-like conversation. For example, philosopher John Searle's Chinese Room argument suggests that a machine could pass the Turing Test without understanding the conversation, thus demonstrating syntactic processing rather than semantic comprehension.[10]

The foundation of contemporary Robotics lies in cybernetics. Norbert Wiener's work on cybernetics in the 1940s explored the principles of control and communication in animals and machines, providing a theoretical framework for AI.[11] Cybernetics, as defined by Wiener, is the scientific study of control and communication in animals and machines. This interdisciplinary field combined multiple domains including engineering,

[8] Ibid.

[9] Saygin, A.P., Cicekli, I. and Akman, V. (2000), Turing Test: 50 Years Later. Minds and Machines, 10(4), pp.463–518.

[10] Searle, J.R. (1980), Minds, brains, and programs. Behavioral and Brain Sciences, 3(3), pp.417–424.

[11] Wiener, N. (1948), Cybernetics: Or Control and Communication in the Animal and the Machine. Cambridge, MA: MIT Press.

biology, mathematics, and social sciences to understand and design systems with adaptive and self-regulating capabilities. Cybernetics emphasized the importance of feedback mechanisms in both biological organisms and mechanical systems. Feedback is a process where information about the output of a system is looped back as input to control the behaviour of the system. In living organisms, feedback mechanisms are used to maintain homeostasis, such as the regulation of body temperature and blood sugar levels.[12] Wiener proposed that similar mechanisms could be employed in machines to achieve self-regulation and efficient control.

Wiener's exploration of these principles provided a conceptual framework for developing intelligent machines. The core idea was that both biological organisms and machines could be designed to process information, make decisions, and adapt to changes in their environment through feedback loops.[13] This theoretical basis was essential for the subsequent development of AI, which aims to create machines capable of performing tasks that typically require human intelligence, such as learning, reasoning, and problem solving.

The concepts of feedback and control have been incorporated into various AI technologies. For instance, machine learning algorithms use feedback to improve their performance over time.[14] In neural networks, which are inspired by the structure and function of the human brain, feedback loops are used during the training process to adjust the weights of connections based on the errors in predictions, a process known as backpropagation.[15] Wiener's work also influenced the development of Robotics, where cybernetic principles are applied to create robots that can autonomously navigate and interact with their environment.[16] These robots utilize sensors to gather information, process this data, and make decisions to perform tasks, reflecting the principles of control and communication outlined in cybernetics. In summary, Norbert Wiener's work on cybernetics provided a theoretical foundation for AI by exploring the

[12] Wiener, N. (1948). Cybernetics: Or Control and Communication in the Animal and the Machine. The MIT Press.

[13] Boden, M. A. (2006). Mind as Machine: A History of Cognitive Science. Oxford University Press.

[14] Mitchell, T. M. (1997). Machine Learning. McGraw-Hill.

[15] LeCun, Y., Bengio, Y., & Hinton, G. (2015). Deep learning. Nature, 521(7553), 436–444.

[16] Brooks, R. A. (1999). Cambrian Intelligence: The Early History of the New AI. The MIT Press.

principles of control and communication in animals and machines. His concepts of feedback and self-regulation have been fundamental in the development of intelligent systems that can adapt and learn from their interactions with the environment.

The Birth of AI as a Field

The field of AI was formally established during the Dartmouth Conference, organized by John McCarthy, Marvin Minsky, Nathaniel Rochester, and Claude Shannon. They proposed the term 'Artificial Intelligence' and discussed the potential of machines to simulate human intelligence.[17] The Dartmouth Conference, held in the summer of 1956, marks a pivotal moment in the history of Artificial Intelligence (AI). This seminal event is often credited with formally establishing AI as a distinct field of study. Organized by prominent researchers John McCarthy, Marvin Minsky, Nathaniel Rochester, and Claude Shannon, the conference brought together a diverse group of scientists and engineers to deliberate on the possibilities of creating machines capable of demonstrating intelligence that parallels human cognition. John McCarthy, who would later be known as one of the 'founding fathers' of AI, was instrumental in coining the term 'Artificial Intelligence' during the conference. The aim was to explore how machines could be made to perform tasks that, if done by humans, would require intelligence. The conception of AI was therefore fundamentally linked to the aspiration of simulating human thought processes using computational models.[18] Marvin Minsky, another central figure in AI, contributed significantly to the discussions at Dartmouth, advocating for the development of machines that could learn and adapt. Minsky's vision extended to creating systems that could not only solve problems through pre-programmed instructions but also through learning from experience.[19] This laid the groundwork for machine learning, a subfield of AI that has grown exponentially in the decades since. Nathaniel Rochester brought a wealth of engineering expertise to the conference. As

[17] McCarthy, J., Minsky, M.L., Rochester, N. and Shannon, C.E. (2006), A Proposal for the Dartmouth Summer Research Project on Artificial Intelligence, August 31, 1955. AI Magazine, 27(4), pp.12–14.

[18] McCarthy, J., Minsky, M. L., Rochester, N., & Shannon, C. E. (2006). A Proposal for the Dartmouth Summer Research Project on Artificial Intelligence, August 31, 1955. AI Magazine, 27(4), pp.12–14.

[19] Minsky, M. (1985). The Society of Mind. New York: Simon and Schuster.

a key contributor to the development of the IBM computer, Rochester's insights were invaluable in discussing the hardware requisites for AI. His work underscored the importance of robust computational frameworks and the potential for scaling these models to achieve greater complexity in AI systems.[20] Claude Shannon, renowned for his work in information theory, provided a theoretical backbone to the discussions. Shannon's ideas about information processing and coding were crucial in laying the foundation for efficient data handling and algorithm development in AI. His contributions helped shape the understanding of how machines could process and interpret vast amounts of data, mimicking human abilities to an extent.[21] The Dartmouth Conference was not just a meeting but a launching pad for future research and development in AI. It set the stage for subsequent advancements by framing key questions and proposing foundational approaches. The collaborative efforts of McCarthy, Minsky, Rochester, and Shannon at this conference catalysed the formation of AI as a formal discipline, driving forward the quest to create intelligent machines that simulate human capabilities.

Early AI Programs

Logic Theorist was developed by Allen Newell and Herbert A. Simon in 1955; Logic Theorist was one of the first AI programs capable of proving mathematical theorems.[22] It was one of the pioneering AI programs designed to simulate human problem-solving capabilities and is often regarded as the first Artificial Intelligence software. This program was capable of proving mathematical theorems, particularly those found in Principia Mathematica by Alfred North Whitehead and Bertrand Russell. Using a search algorithm based on human heuristics, Logic Theorist was able to find new proofs for existing theorems, demonstrating the potential of computers to perform tasks previously thought to require human intelligence.[23] For instance, Logic Theorist successfully found an elegant proof for the

[20] Rochester, N., Holland, J. H., Haibt, L. H., & Duda, W. I. (1956). Tests on a cell assembly theory of the action of the brain, using a large digital computer. IRE Transactions on Information Theory, 2(3), pp.80–93.

[21] Shannon, C. E. (1950). Programming a Computer for Playing Chess. London: Philosophical Library.

[22] Newell, A. and Simon, H.A. (1956), The Logic Theory Machine: A Complex Information Processing System. IRE Transactions on Information Theory, 2(3), pp.61–79.

[23] Newell, A., & Simon, H. A. (1956), The Logic Theory Machine: A Complex Information Processing System. IRE Transactions on Information Theory, 2(3), 61–79.

'Principia's' Theorem 2.85, which was shorter and more efficient than the original proof by Russell and Whitehead, showcasing the program's ability to not only mimic but also improve upon human logical reasoning.[24] This breakthrough marked a significant milestone in the field of Artificial Intelligence, as it illustrated the possibility of encoding complex human cognitive processes into computational models. The development of Logic Theorist laid the groundwork for subsequent AI research and influenced the creation of more sophisticated systems capable of complex problem solving and decision making.[25] Furthermore, the methodologies employed in Logic Theorist, such as heuristic search and symbolic reasoning, continue to underpin modern AI techniques, including machine learning and automated theorem proving.[26] The methodologies employed in Logic Theorist, such as heuristic search and symbolic reasoning, have had a lasting influence on modern AI techniques. Heuristic search involves using strategies or rules of thumb to explore problem spaces efficiently, reducing the computational effort needed to find solutions. This approach was central to Logic Theorist's ability to navigate complex mathematical proofs by prioritizing more promising paths over others, a principle that is still fundamental in modern AI algorithms. For instance, heuristic search forms the basis of many AI applications in optimization and decision making, including A* search in pathfinding and game-playing AI.[27] Symbolic reasoning, another core methodology of Logic Theorist, involves manipulating symbols to represent and solve problems based on formal rules and logic. This technique laid the foundation for knowledge representation and reasoning in AI, influencing the development of expert systems that simulate the decision-making abilities of human experts.[28]

In machine learning, although statistical approaches have become dominant, symbolic reasoning is still relevant, particularly in fields such as natural language processing and automated reasoning, where understanding and manipulating structured data is crucial. For example, hybrid AI models that combine symbolic reasoning with neural networks are

[24] Simon, H. A., & Newell, A. (1958). Heuristic problem solving: The next advance in operations research. Operations Research, 6(1), 1–10.

[25] Feigenbaum, E. A., & Feldman, J. (1963). Computers and Thought. McGraw-Hill.

[26] Russell, S., & Norvig, P. (2016). Artificial Intelligence: A Modern Approach. 3rd ed. Pearson.

[27] Russell, S., & Norvig, P. (2016). Artificial Intelligence: A Modern Approach. 3rd ed. Pearson.

[28] Nilsson, N. J. (2010). The Quest for Artificial Intelligence. Cambridge University Press.

increasingly being explored to integrate human-like understanding with data-driven learning.[29] In automated theorem proving, the influence of Logic Theorist is direct, as modern systems like Coq and Isabelle continue to utilize logical frameworks and symbolic methods to prove complex theorems.[30] These methods have enabled advancements in software verification and formal methods, where ensuring the correctness of algorithms and systems is critical. Thus, the core principles developed in Logic Theorist remain integral to both foundational AI research and practical applications today.

Another early AI program by Newell and Simon—General Problem Solver (GPS)—aimed to simulate human problem-solving processes.[31] General Problem Solver (GPS) was an early Artificial Intelligence program developed by Allen Newell and Herbert A. Simon in the late 1950s, designed to mimic the cognitive processes humans use in problem solving. Unlike its predecessor, Logic Theorist, which was specifically focused on proving mathematical theorems, GPS was intended to be a more general-purpose system capable of solving a wide range of problems by breaking them down into smaller sub-problems and using means-ends analysis to find solutions.[32] The program used a symbolic approach, representing problems and solutions through structured symbols and applying a set of rules to manipulate these symbols, closely resembling human thought processes as proposed by the theory of human problem solving.[33] GPS was influential in advancing the understanding of how humans approach complex tasks, as it demonstrated the potential of computational models to replicate strategic thinking patterns. It operated by defining the initial and goal states of a problem and then generating operators that would transform the initial state into the goal state, effectively using a heuristic search to explore possible solutions.[34] This approach influenced subsequent

[29] Besold, T. R., Garcez, A., & Lamb, L. (2017). Neural-symbolic learning and reasoning: A survey and interpretation. Frontiers in Artificial Intelligence and Applications, 300, 1–20.

[30] Wenzel, M., Paulson, L. C., & Nipkow, T. (2013). The Isabelle framework. In Blazy, S., & Paulin-Mohring, C. (Eds.), Interactive Theorem Proving (pp. 399–404). Springer.

[31] Russell, S., & Norvig, P. (2016). Artificial Intelligence: A Modern Approach. 3rd ed. Pearson.

[32] Newell, A., & Simon, H. A. (1961). GPS, a program that simulates human thought. In Feigenbaum, E. A., & Feldman, J. (Eds.), Computers and Thought (pp. 279–293). McGraw-Hill.

[33] Simon, H. A. (1972). The Sciences of the Artificial. MIT Press.

[34] Newell, A., & Simon, H. A. (1972). Human Problem Solving. Prentice-Hall

developments in AI, particularly in fields such as automated planning and cognitive modelling, where the ability to simulate human-like reasoning is essential.[35] While GPS had limitations in terms of its practical applications and could not handle the vast complexity of real-world problems, it provided a foundational framework for later AI research. It established the concept of problem solving as a search process within a defined problem space, a principle that continues to be a cornerstone in AI and cognitive science.[36] The methodologies and theories behind GPS are still relevant today, particularly in exploring how humans and machines can collaborate to solve complex problems more efficiently.

The AI Winter

By the mid-1970s, AI research encountered several critical obstacles that slowed its progress and led to what is known as the AI Winter, a period characterized by reduced funding, diminished interest, and scepticism about the potential of Artificial Intelligence.[37] One of the main challenges was the limited computational power of the era, which constrained the complexity of problems that AI systems could address. Early AI programs, such as those designed for natural language processing and computer vision, required far more computational resources than were available at the time, making it difficult to achieve practical results.[38] This technological limitation prevented researchers from scaling up AI models and algorithms to handle real-world applications effectively. Additionally, the field suffered from overly optimistic expectations fuelled by early successes in specific domains, such as game playing and symbolic reasoning. Prominent AI researchers had predicted rapid advancements, including the development of machines capable of human-level intelligence within a few decades.[39] However, the reality was that many AI systems, such as the early

[35] Nilsson, N. J. (2009). The Quest for Artificial Intelligence: A History of Ideas and Achievements. Cambridge University Press.

[36] Luger, G. F. (2009). Artificial Intelligence: Structures and Strategies for Complex Problem Solving. 6th ed. Addison- Wesley.

[37] Dreyfus, H.L. (1972), What Computers Can't Do: A Critique of Artificial Reason. New York: Harper & Row.

[38] Nilsson, N. J. (2009). The Quest for Artificial Intelligence: A History of Ideas and Achievements. Cambridge University Press.

[39] Dreyfus, H. L. (1972). What Computers Can't Do: The Limits of Artificial Intelligence. Harper & Row.

expert systems, struggled with tasks that required common sense reasoning or knowledge representation beyond narrow, well-defined problem areas.[40] This disparity between expectations and reality led to frustration among funding agencies and stakeholders, who began to view AI research as overhyped and lacking in tangible progress. The disappointment resulted in significant cuts to research funding from both governmental and private sources. In the United States, the Defense Advanced Research Projects Agency (DARPA), a major funder of AI research, drastically reduced its support for projects that had failed to meet their ambitious goals.[41] Similar trends were observed in the United Kingdom, where the Lighthill Report of 1973 criticized AI research for not delivering practical applications, leading to reduced financial backing for AI projects.[42] These events contributed to a slowdown in research activities and a decline in the number of new researchers entering the field. Despite these setbacks, the AI Winter periods also prompted the development of new approaches and a more realistic assessment of AI's capabilities and limitations. Researchers began to focus on more incremental advancements and foundational work, which laid the groundwork for future breakthroughs in machine learning and neural networks that would eventually rejuvenate the field in the 1980s and beyond.[43] This shift involved prioritizing more achievable goals and refining existing methodologies, rather than pursuing overly ambitious projects that had led to earlier setbacks. One such foundational area was the development of machine learning algorithms. Researchers began exploring statistical methods and data-driven approaches to enable computers to learn patterns from data, rather than relying solely on rule-based systems. For example, the introduction of the backpropagation algorithm by Rumelhart, Hinton, and Williams in 1986 revolutionized neural network training by providing an effective method for adjusting the weights in multi-layer networks, making deep learning feasible.[44]

[40] Crevier, D. (1993). AI: The Tumultuous History of the Search for Artificial Intelligence. Basic Books.

[41] Hendler, J. (2008). Avoiding another AI Winter. IEEE Intelligent Systems, 23(2), 2–4.

[42] Lighthill, J. (1973). Artificial Intelligence: A General Survey. In Artificial Intelligence: A Paper Symposium. Science Research Council.

[43] Russell, S., & Norvig, P. (2016). Artificial Intelligence: A Modern Approach. 3rd ed. Pearson.

[44] Rumelhart, D. E., Hinton, G. E., & Williams, R. J. (1986). Learning representations by back-propagating errors. Nature, 323(6088), 533–536.

This period also saw significant advancements in the understanding of neural networks, which had been largely abandoned since the 1969 publication of *Perceptrons* by Minsky and Papert. Their work had highlighted the limitations of single-layer perceptrons, leading to a decline in interest in neural network research.[45] However, the subsequent development of multi-layer perceptrons and the backpropagation algorithm renewed interest in the potential of neural networks, laying the groundwork for what would later become the deep learning revolution of the 2010s.[46] In addition to progress in neural networks, the 1980s and 1990s saw the emergence of probabilistic reasoning and graphical models, which offered new ways to handle uncertainty and complexity in AI systems. Judea Pearl's work on Bayesian networks, for example, provided a robust framework for probabilistic inference and decision making, which became fundamental in various AI applications, from natural language processing to Robotics.[47] These incremental but foundational advancements gradually restored confidence in AI research and contributed to the resurgence of interest and funding in the field. By the 1990s, AI had diversified into multiple subfields, including machine learning, computer vision, and natural language processing, each making steady progress. This groundwork ultimately enabled the dramatic breakthroughs in AI capabilities seen in the twenty-first century, as increased computational power and large datasets facilitated the development of sophisticated models such as deep neural networks and reinforcement learning systems.[48]

The careful and systematic work done during this period set the stage for the transformative impacts of AI in modern times. One prominent example is the use of deep learning algorithms in image recognition, which has led to breakthroughs in computer vision applications such as facial recognition and autonomous vehicles. For instance, convolutional neural networks (CNNs) have significantly improved the accuracy of image classification tasks, as demonstrated by their success in the ImageNet

[45] Minsky, M., & Papert, S. (1969). Perceptrons: An Introduction to Computational Geometry. MIT Press.

[46] Goodfellow, I., Bengio, Y., & Courville, A. (2016). Deep Learning. MIT Press.

[47] Pearl, J. (1988). Probabilistic Reasoning in Intelligent Systems: Networks of Plausible Inference. Morgan Kaufmann.

[48] LeCun, Y., Bengio, Y., & Hinton, G. (2015). Deep learning. Nature, 521(7553), 436–444.

competition.[49] Another transformative impact is in natural language processing (NLP), where AI models like OpenAI's Generative Pre-trained Transformer-3 (GPT-3) have demonstrated an unprecedented ability to generate human-like text, translating languages, and even performing complex creative tasks.[50] AI has also revolutionized healthcare through the development of diagnostic tools that leverage machine learning to analyse medical images and predict diseases. For example, Google's DeepMind has developed an AI system capable of diagnosing over fifty eye diseases with an accuracy comparable to that of expert ophthalmologists.[51] In the financial sector, AI-driven algorithms are now widely used for fraud detection, risk assessment, and automated trading, increasing the efficiency and security of financial transactions.[52] Furthermore, reinforcement learning has enabled significant advancements in Robotics and game-playing AI. AlphaGo, developed by DeepMind, made headlines by defeating the world champion in the complex board game Go, showcasing the potential of AI to master tasks previously considered too complex for machines.[53] These examples illustrate how foundational work in AI has led to transformative impacts across diverse fields, fundamentally changing the way technology interacts with society.

Revival and Growth

Expert Systems

In the 1980s, the development of expert systems marked a significant milestone in the field of Artificial Intelligence (AI), rejuvenating interest that had waned following earlier periods of inflated expectations and

[49] Krizhevsky, A., Sutskever, I., & Hinton, G. E. (2012). ImageNet classification with deep convolutional neural networks. In Advances in Neural Information Processing Systems (pp. 1097–1105).

[50] Brown, T., Mann, B., Ryder, N., Subbiah, M., Kaplan, J., Dhariwal, P., … & Amodei, D. (2020). Language models are few-shot learners. Advances in Neural Information Processing Systems, 33, 1877–1901.

[51] De Fauw, J., Ledsam, J. R., Romera-Paredes, B., Nikolov, S., Tomasev, N., Blackwell, S., … & Suleyman, M. (2018). Clinically applicable deep learning for diagnosis and referral in retinal disease. Nature Medicine, 24(9), 1342–1350.

[52] Treleaven, P., Galas, M., & Lalchand, V. (2013). Algorithmic trading review. Communications of the ACM, 56(11), 76–85.

[53] Silver, D., Huang, A., Maddison, C. J., Guez, A., Sifre, L., Van Den Driessche, G., … & Hassabis, D. (2016). Mastering the game of Go with deep neural networks and tree search. Nature, 529(7587), 484–489.

subsequent disillusionment.[54] Expert systems are a class of AI applications designed to emulate human decision making by utilizing knowledge bases and inference rules to solve complex problems within specific domains. These systems are constructed based on the insights and expertise of human specialists, codified into rule-based frameworks that allow the system to make informed decisions and provide solutions.[55] One of the most notable expert systems developed during this period was MYCIN, an early system designed to diagnose bacterial infections and recommend appropriate antibiotic treatments. Developed at Stanford University, MYCIN demonstrated remarkable accuracy, often exceeding the diagnostic capabilities of non-specialist human clinicians.[56] The success of MYCIN underscored the potential of expert systems to enhance decision-making processes in medicine and other fields requiring specialized knowledge. Similarly, the expert system DENDRAL, also developed at Stanford, was designed for use in organic chemistry. DENDRAL's ability to analyse mass spectrometry data and infer molecular structures showcased the applicability of expert systems in scientific research, proving that AI could assist in tasks traditionally reliant on human intuition and expertise.[57] The commercial potential of expert systems quickly became evident, leading to widespread adoption in industries such as finance, manufacturing, and oil exploration. Systems like XCON, developed by Digital Equipment Corporation, were implemented to configure complex computer systems based on customer requirements. XCON's deployment significantly reduced the time and costs associated with system configuration, demonstrating the tangible business benefits of incorporating expert systems into operational workflows.[58] The resurgence of interest in AI due to expert systems was not without its challenges. These systems often required significant resources for development and maintenance, including the continuous updating of knowledge bases to reflect current expertise. Additionally, while expert systems excelled in specific, narrowly defined domains, they struggled with tasks requiring general intelligence or the

[54] Feigenbaum, E.A. (1984), Knowledge engineering: The applied side of artificial intelligence. Annals of the New York Academy of Sciences, 426(1), pp.91–107.

[55] Feigenbaum, E. A. (1984). Knowledge engineering: The applied side of artificial intelligence. Annals of the New York Academy of Sciences, 426(1), pp. 91–107.

[56] Shortliffe, E. H. (1976). MYCIN: Computer-Based Medical Consultations. Elsevier.

[57] Buchanan, B. G., & Feigenbaum, E. A. (1982). Dendral and Meta-Dendral: Their applications dimension. Artificial Intelligence, 11(1–2), pp. 5–24.

[58] McDermott, J. (1982). R1: A Rule-Based Configurer of Computer Systems. Artificial Intelligence, 19(1), pp. 39–88.

ability to learn and adapt from new experiences.[59] Despite these limitations, the expert systems of the 1980s laid the groundwork for ongoing advancements in AI. They illustrated the feasibility and utility of embedding human expertise within computational frameworks, paving the way for future developments in machine learning and artificial neural networks. The successes achieved by expert systems rekindled enthusiasm in the AI community and among investors, setting the stage for the rapid technological advancements that would follow in subsequent decades.

Machine Learning and Data

The 1990s marked a pivotal decade in the evolution of Artificial Intelligence (AI) and machine learning, characterized by a significant shift towards data-driven approaches and the resurgence of neural networks. This transition laid the foundational groundwork for the development of modern machine learning techniques that drive today's technological advancements.[60] During the early part of the decade, researchers began to recognize the limitations of rule-based systems and expert systems, which had dominated AI research in the 1980s. These systems struggled with scalability and adaptability, leading to a search for more robust and flexible approaches. The growing availability of large datasets and increased computational power enabled a shift towards data-driven methods, where algorithms could learn patterns directly from data rather than relying solely on pre-programmed rules.[61] One of the most significant developments in this period was the resurgence of neural networks. Although neural networks had been proposed earlier, their adoption was hindered by computational constraints and the lack of effective training methods. The rediscovery and popularization of the backpropagation algorithm by Rumelhart, Hinton, and Williams in 1986 provided a viable solution for training multi-layer neural networks, igniting renewed interest in this area.[62] This breakthrough allowed neural networks to learn complex representations from data, leading to substantial improvements in

[59] Dreyfus, H. L. (1992). What Computers Still Can't Do: A Critique of Artificial Reason. MIT Press.

[60] Mitchell, T.M. (1997), Machine Learning. New York: McGraw-Hill.

[61] Breiman, L. (2001). Statistical Modeling: The Two Cultures. Statistical Science, 16(3), pp.199–231.

[62] Rumelhart, D.E., Hinton, G.E. & Williams, R.J. (1986). Learning representations by back-propagating errors. Nature, 323(6088), pp.533–536.

performance for various AI tasks. The 1990s also saw the emergence of Support Vector Machines (SVMs), introduced by Cortes and Vapnik in 1995, which became a powerful tool for classification and regression tasks. SVMs provided a new paradigm for data-driven learning, emphasizing the importance of maximizing the margin between different classes in a dataset, which led to more generalizable models.[63] Furthermore, the advent of the Internet and the World Wide Web during this decade generated massive amounts of digital data, providing an unprecedented opportunity for machine learning research. Researchers leveraged this data to develop and refine algorithms, resulting in significant advancements in fields such as natural language processing, computer vision, and speech recognition.[64] The increase in computational power, particularly with the introduction of Graphics Processing Units (GPUs), revolutionized the ability to train large neural networks more efficiently. This technological leap facilitated the implementation of deep learning models, which are neural networks with many layers, capable of learning hierarchical representations of data.[65] The 1990s, therefore, represented a transformative era that set the stage for modern machine learning. The convergence of data availability, algorithmic developments, and computational advancements enabled the shift towards models that could learn directly from data, leading to the sophisticated AI systems we see today.

Modern Developments in Artificial Intelligence

Deep Learning

Breakthroughs in Neural Networks

Deep learning, a subset of machine learning, has achieved remarkable success in various applications, including image recognition and natural language processing. Key advancements include the development of

[63] Cortes, C. & Vapnik, V. (1995). Support-Vector Networks. Machine Learning, 20(3), pp.273–297.

[64] Lecun, Y., Bengio, Y. & Hinton, G. (2015). Deep learning. Nature, 521(7553), pp.436–444.

[65] Krizhevsky, A., Sutskever, I. & Hinton, G. E. (2012). ImageNet Classification with Deep Convolutional Neural Networks. In: Advances in Neural Information Processing Systems 25. Lake Tahoe, Nevada, 3–8 December 2012. Red Hook, NY: Curran Associates Inc, pp.1097–1105.

convolutional neural networks (CNNs) by Yann LeCun and recurrent neural networks (RNNs) by Sepp Hochreiter and Jürgen Schmidhuber.[66,67] Breakthroughs in neural networks have significantly advanced the field of deep learning, a subset of machine learning that focuses on algorithms inspired by the structure and function of the brain. Deep learning has achieved remarkable success in various applications, including image recognition and natural language processing, due to its ability to automatically extract intricate patterns from raw data. CNNs are designed to process data with a grid-like topology, such as images. Their architecture consists of multiple layers, including convolutional layers that automatically learn spatial hierarchies of features from input images. This makes CNNs particularly effective for image recognition tasks. LeCun's work on the LeNet-5 model, a pioneering CNN architecture, demonstrated the feasibility of using neural networks for handwriting digit recognition with high accuracy.[68] CNNs have since been applied to various other image-related tasks, including object detection, video analysis, and medical image analysis. Another groundbreaking development in deep learning was the introduction of recurrent neural networks (RNNs) by Sepp Hochreiter and Jürgen Schmidhuber. RNNs are specifically designed for sequential data, where the order of inputs is crucial. Unlike traditional neural networks, RNNs have connections that form directed cycles, allowing information to persist. This makes RNNs well suited for tasks involving time series data, natural language processing, and speech recognition. Hochreiter and Schmidhuber's work on the Long Short-Term Memory (LSTM) network, an advanced type of RNN, addressed the vanishing gradient problem, enabling the training of RNNs on longer sequences and improving their performance in tasks such as machine translation and text generation.[69] The success of CNNs and RNNs has fuelled the rapid adoption of deep learning in various real-world applications. In image recognition, deep learning models have surpassed human-level performance on benchmark datasets, enabling advancements in autonomous driving, facial

[66] LeCun, Y., Bottou, L., Bengio, Y. and Haffner, P. (1998), Gradient-based learning applied to document recognition. Proceedings of the IEEE, 86(11), pp.2278–2324.

[67] Hochreiter, S. and Schmidhuber, J. (1997), Long short-term memory. Neural Computation, 9(8), pp.1735–1780.

[68] LeCun, Y., Bottou, L., Bengio, Y. & Haffner, P. (1998). Gradient-based learning applied to document recognition. Proceedings of the IEEE, 86(11), pp.2278–2324.

[69] Hochreiter, S. & Schmidhuber, J. (1997). Long Short-Term Memory. Neural Computation, 9(8), pp.1735–1780.

recognition, and surveillance systems.[70] In natural language processing, deep learning has led to the development of sophisticated models like Google's BERT and OpenAI's GPT, which have revolutionized tasks such as language translation, sentiment analysis, and conversational agents.[71,72] The impact of these breakthroughs extends beyond academia and research labs to industries and everyday life. Deep learning systems are now embedded in various technologies, from smartphones to healthcare diagnostics, showcasing their transformative potential. The innovations brought by CNNs and RNNs continue to push the boundaries of what is possible in machine learning, driving further research and development in the field.

AlphaGo

In 2016, Google's AlphaGo program achieved a historic milestone by defeating Lee Sedol, the world champion Go player, an accomplishment that underscored the astonishing potential of deep learning and reinforcement learning in tackling complex tasks.[73] The game of Go, an ancient board game known for its vast number of possible moves and strategic depth, had long been considered a frontier for Artificial Intelligence due to its complexity and the necessity for intuitive judgement rather than brute-force calculation.[74] AlphaGo's success can be attributed to its innovative use of deep learning and reinforcement learning techniques. The program incorporated convolutional neural networks (CNNs), which are typically

[70] Krizhevsky, A., Sutskever, I. & Hinton, G. E. (2012). ImageNet Classification with Deep Convolutional Neural Networks. In: Advances in Neural Information Processing Systems 25. Lake Tahoe, Nevada, 3–8 December 2012. Red Hook, NY: Curran Associates Inc, pp.1097–1105.

[71] Devlin, J., Chang, M. W., Lee, K. & Toutanova, K. (2019). BERT: Pre-training of Deep Bidirectional Transformers for Language Understanding. Proceedings of the 2019 Conference of the North American Chapter of the Association for Computational Linguistics: Human Language Technologies, Volume 1 (Long and Short Papers), pp.4171–4186.

[72] Brown, T. B., et al. (2020). Language Models are Few-Shot Learners. arXiv preprint arXiv:2005.14165.

[73] Silver, D., Huang, A., Maddison, C.J., Guez, A., Sifre, L., Van Den Driessche, G., Schrittwieser, J., Antonoglou, I., Panneershelvam, V., Lanctot, M. and Dieleman, S. (2016), Mastering the game of Go with deep neural networks and tree search. Nature, 529(7587), pp.484–489.

[74] Silver, D., Huang, A., Maddison, C. J., Guez, A., Sifre, L., Van Den Driessche, G., … & Hassabis, D. (2016). Mastering the game of Go with deep neural networks and tree search. Nature, 529(7587), pp. 484–489.

used for image recognition, to evaluate board positions and predict the moves of human players. These neural networks were trained using a combination of supervised learning from a large dataset of expert games and reinforcement learning through self-play, where the system improved its strategies by competing against different versions of itself.[75] In addition to CNNs, AlphaGo leveraged a powerful algorithm known as Monte Carlo Tree Search (MCTS) to explore possible move sequences and their outcomes. MCTS allowed AlphaGo to evaluate the long-term consequences of moves without needing to search every possible position exhaustively, thus effectively managing the computational complexity of the game.[76] This integration of deep neural networks and MCTS was pivotal in enabling AlphaGo to develop sophisticated strategies that matched and eventually surpassed human expert capabilities. The victory of AlphaGo over Lee Sedol was not just a triumph in the realm of AI research but also a demonstration of the potential of deep learning and reinforcement learning to address challenges in other domains. For instance, similar techniques are being applied in healthcare for protein folding predictions, in finance for algorithmic trading, and in autonomous driving for decision making under uncertainty.[77] AlphaGo's achievements have inspired further research and development in AI, pushing the boundaries of what machines can do and offering glimpses of a future where AI systems can tackle complex real-world problems with human-like intuition and effectiveness. The success of AlphaGo therefore marks a significant landmark in the evolution of Artificial Intelligence, illustrating the synergy between deep learning, reinforcement learning, and advanced search techniques.

Natural Language Processing (NLP)

The introduction of transformer architectures revolutionized NLP. OpenAI's GPT-3 model, based on transformers, has shown

[75] Silver, D., Schrittwieser, J., Simonyan, K., Antonoglou, I., Huang, A., Guez, A., … & Hassabis, D. (2017). Mastering the game of Go without human knowledge. Nature, 550(7676), pp. 354–359.

[76] Silver, D., Huang, A., Maddison, C. J., Guez, A., Sifre, L., Van Den Driessche, G., … & Hassabis, D. (2016). Mastering the game of Go with deep neural networks and tree search. Nature, 529(7587), pp. 484–489.

[77] Silver, D., Schrittwieser, J., Simonyan, K., Antonoglou, I., Huang, A., Guez, A., … & Hassabis, D. (2017). Mastering the game of Go without human knowledge. Nature, 550(7676), pp. 354–359.

unprecedented language understanding and generation capabilities.[78,79] Transformers, introduced by Vaswani et al. in their groundbreaking 2017 paper, 'Attention Is All You Need', presented a novel architecture that eschewed the recurrent layers commonly used in favour of self-attention mechanisms. This shift allowed for more effective parallelization during training, significantly speeding up the process and improving performance across a variety of NLP tasks.[80] Parallelization during training refers to the ability to process multiple data points simultaneously, rather than sequentially. Traditional models like Recurrent Neural Networks (RNNs) must process sequential data step-by-step due to their recurrent nature, making it difficult to parallelize computations. In contrast, the self-attention mechanism in transformers allows the model to consider all positions in the input sequence simultaneously for each step, removing dependencies on previous computations. This means that the operations required to compute the model's output can be done in parallel, significantly reducing the computational time and resources needed for training.[81] This architectural change leverages modern hardware capabilities, such as GPUs, which are optimized for parallel processing, resulting in faster training times and more scalable models.[82]

Transformers excel at capturing long-range dependencies within text, which are vital for understanding context and meaning in language. These models leverage self-attention mechanisms to weigh the relevance of different words in a sentence based on their relationship to each other, allowing them to understand context more effectively than previous models that relied heavily on recurrence and convolution.[83] Building on the transformer architecture, OpenAI developed the Generative Pre-trained

[78] Vaswani, A., Shazeer, N., Parmar, N., Uszkoreit, J., Jones, L., Gomez, A.N., Kaiser, Ł. and Polosukhin, I. 2017. Attention is all you need. Advances in Neural Information Processing Systems, 30, pp.5998–6008.

[79] Brown, T.B., Mann, B., Ryder, N., Subbiah, M., Kaplan, J., Dhariwal, P., Neelakantan, A., Shyam, P., Sastry, G., Askell, A. and Agarwal, S., 2020. Language models are few-shot learners. arXiv preprint arXiv:2005.14165.

[80] Vaswani, A., Shazeer, N., Parmar, N., Uszkoreit, J., Jones, L., Gomez, A. N., ... & Polosukhin, I. (2017). Attention is All You Need. NIPS.

[81] Ibid.

[82] Shoeybi, M., Patwary, M., Puri, R., Casper, J., Catanzaro, B. (2019). Megatron-LM: Training Multi-Billion Parameter Language Models Using Model Parallelism. arXiv preprint arXiv:1909.08053.

[83] Devlin, J., Chang, M. W., Lee, K. & Toutanova, K. (2019). BERT: Pre-training of Deep Bidirectional Transformers for Language Understanding. NAACL-HLT.

Transformer-3 (GPT-3), which has demonstrated unprecedented capabilities in language understanding and generation. GPT-3 is distinguished by its sheer scale, boasting 175 billion parameters, which enables it to capture intricate patterns and nuances in language. This massive model is trained on a diverse range of Internet text, endowing it with the ability to perform various language tasks, from generating coherent and contextually relevant text to answering questions and engaging in dialogue with remarkable fluency.[84]

The applications of GPT-3 are broad and varied. It has been used for generating creative content, drafting emails, writing code, and even providing tutoring in complex subjects. The model's ability to generate human-like text based on prompts showcases the power of transformers in achieving a high level of contextual understanding and produces content that is coherent and contextually appropriate.[85] Moreover, the versatility of transformers has extended beyond simple text generation. They have been employed in machine translation, summarization, sentiment analysis, and even in more complex tasks like generating poetry and creating conversational agents. The transformer architecture has set a new standard in NLP, pushing the boundaries of what AI models can achieve in terms of language understanding and generation.[86] Overall, the advent of transformers and the development of models like OpenAI's GPT-3 have dramatically advanced the capabilities of NLP systems, demonstrating the potential for AI to interact with and understand human language in increasingly sophisticated ways. These innovations are redefining the landscape of AI, making significant strides towards more intuitive and powerful language-based applications.

AI in Healthcare

Medical diagnostics have witnessed a transformative impact with the increasing integration of AI systems to enhance the accuracy and efficiency of disease diagnosis, medical image analysis, and patient outcome prediction. AI systems, leveraging machine learning and deep learning

[84] Brown, T. B., Mann, B., Ryder, N., Subbiah, M., Kaplan, J., Dhariwal, P., … & Amodei, D. (2020). Language Models are Few-Shot Learners. arXiv preprint arXiv:2005.14165.

[85] Radford, A., Wu, J., Child, R., Luan, D., Amodei, D., Sutskever, I. (2019). Language Models are Unsupervised Multitask Learners. OpenAI.

[86] Lewis, M., Liu, Y., Goyal, N., Ghazvininejad, M., Mohamed, A., Levy, O., … & Zettlemoyer, L. (2020). BART: Denoising Sequence-to-Sequence Pre-training for Natural Language Generation, Translation, and Comprehension. ACL.

techniques, can process and interpret complex medical data far more quickly than human practitioners, thereby contributing to faster diagnostic decisions and personalized treatment plans. One of the most notable examples is IBM Watson, an AI system renowned for its cognitive computing capabilities.[87] IBM Watson has been applied across various healthcare settings to assist in diagnosing diseases, particularly cancer. By analysing vast amounts of medical literature, patient records, and clinical trials, Watson can provide evidence-based treatment recommendations and predict patient outcomes. This ability to synthesize and analyse large datasets enables doctors to make more informed decisions, resulting in improved patient care.[88] In radiology, AI tools have revolutionized the analysis of medical images. Systems like Google's DeepMind Health have developed algorithms that interpret imaging data with a high degree of accuracy. For example, AI models trained on large datasets of retinal scans can detect eye diseases such as diabetic retinopathy and age-related macular degeneration at an early stage, significantly enhancing the chances of successful treatment.[89] Similarly, AI systems have shown promise in detecting abnormalities in mammograms, CT scans, and MRI images, often identifying signs of diseases like cancer before they become apparent to human radiologists.[90] Another significant application of AI in medical diagnostics is in the realm of predictive analytics. AI models can analyse historical patient data and identify patterns that may indicate the likelihood of disease onset or progression. For instance, machine learning algorithms have been developed to predict cardiovascular events by analysing patient records, including factors such as age, blood pressure, and cholesterol levels. These predictive models can help in early intervention and preventative measures, ultimately improving patient outcomes.[91] AI's role in medical diagnostics

[87] Topol, E.J. (2019), Deep Medicine: How Artificial Intelligence Can Make Healthcare Human Again. New York: Basic Books.

[88] Ferrucci, D., Brown, E., Chu-Carroll, J., Fan, J., Gondek, D., Kalyanpur, A., ... & Nyberg, E. (2010). Building Watson: An overview of the DeepQA project. AI Magazine, 31(3), pp. 59–79.

[89] De Fauw, J., Ledsam, J. R., Romera-Paredes, B., Nikolov, S., Tomasev, N., Blackwell, S., ... & Ronneberger, O. (2018). Clinically applicable deep learning for diagnosis and referral in retinal disease. Nature Medicine, 24(9), pp. 1342–1350.

[90] Esteva, A., Kuprel, B., Novoa, R. A., Ko, J., Swetter, S. M., Blau, H. M., & Thrun, S. (2017). Dermatologist-level classification of skin cancer with deep neural networks. Nature, 542(7639), pp. 115–118.

[91] Krittanawong, C., Johnson, K. W., Rosenson, R. S., Wang, Z., Aydar, M., & Kitai, T. (2017). Deep learning for cardiovascular medicine: A practical primer. European Heart Journal, 40(28), pp. 2140–2150.

also extends to genomics, where AI systems analyse genetic data to identify mutations linked to specific diseases. By interpreting complex genomic data, AI can uncover insights into hereditary conditions and guide personalized treatment plans based on an individual's genetic makeup.[92] The integration of AI in medical diagnostics exemplifies the significant strides being made in healthcare through advanced technology. Continual advancements in AI algorithms and computational power promise to further enhance the capabilities of medical diagnostics, leading to more accurate, efficient, and personalized patient care.

History of Robotics

Early Concepts and Automata

The concept of automated machines, or automata, dates back to ancient civilizations, illustrating mankind's long-standing fascination with self-operating devices. One of the most noteworthy figures in this early development was the Greek engineer Heron of Alexandria, who around 60 AD designed a variety of mechanical devices that can be considered early forms of automata.[93] Heron's contributions are detailed in his works 'Pneumatica' and 'Automata', where he described several machines powered by steam, air, and water pressure. These included temple doors that opened automatically, coin-operated machines, and even a primitive programmable robot in the form of a mechanical theatre that could perform a series of actions in succession.[94] Heron's automata were not merely novelties but also served practical and religious functions. For example, his automated temple doors, which opened when a fire was lit on the altar, utilized principles of pneumatics and were intended to impress worshippers, showcasing the power of the gods through mechanical marvels.[95] Such devices underline the sophistication of ancient Greek engineering and their understanding of basic principles that would later underpin modern automation

[92] Libbrecht, M. W., & Noble, W. S. (2015). Machine learning applications in genetics and genomics. Nature Reviews Genetics, 16(6), pp. 321–332.

[93] Ceccarelli, M. (2000), A brief history of early developments of mechanisms and machines. International Symposium on History of Machines and Mechanisms, pp.1–26. Springer.

[94] Heron of Alexandria. (1851). Pneumatics of Hero of Alexandria. (Bennet Woodcroft, Trans.). Taylor Walton and Maberly.

[95] Bedini, S. A. (1964). The role of automata in the history of technology. Technology and Culture, 5(1), pp. 24–42.

and Robotics. The tradition of creating automata persisted through various cultures and historical periods. In the Islamic Golden Age, scholars and engineers significantly advanced automata design, as documented in the works of the Banū Mūsā brothers and Al-Jazari. Al-Jazari's *Book of Knowledge of Ingenious Mechanical Devices*, written in 1206, described numerous sophisticated automaton clocks, water-raising machines, and musical automata, displaying a remarkable continuity and evolution of the automata tradition from ancient Greece.[96] Similarly, medieval and Renaissance Europe saw renewed interest in automata, often inspired by classical texts rediscovered during the period. Leonardo da Vinci, for instance, is known to have designed several mechanical devices, including a robotic knight that could sit, wave its arms, and move its head and jaw.[97] These early efforts in automata design highlight a continuous thread of innovation and curiosity about automation that spans across different eras and cultures. The mechanical ingenuity of these ancient automata laid critical foundational concepts that would eventually influence contemporary Robotics. By exploring the mechanisms that drive self-operating devices, ancient engineers like Heron of Alexandria set the stage for future advancements in automated technology, demonstrating the universal human drive to innovate and solve problems through mechanical means.

Industrial Robotics

The first industrial robot, Unimate, was developed by George Devol and Joseph Engelberger in the 1950s. It was employed in a General Motors assembly line in 1961, revolutionizing manufacturing processes. The development of the first industrial robot, Unimate, by George Devol and Joseph Engelberger in the 1950s marked a significant turning point in the history of industrial automation. Unimate's introduction to the General Motors assembly line in 1961 revolutionized manufacturing processes.[98] Contextually, this was specifically with regard to the automation of tasks that were repetitive, dangerous, or required precision beyond human

[96] Hill, D. R. (1974). The Book of Knowledge of Ingenious Mechanical Devices: Kitāb fī ma'rifat al-ḥiyal al-handasiyya. Springer.

[97] Ceccarelli, M. (2000). The heritage of Leonardo da Vinci in machine design. Journal of Mechanical Design, 122(4), pp. 543–549.

[98] Engelberger, J.F. (1982), Robotics in Practice: Management and Applications of Industrial Robots. New York: Springer.

capabilities.[99] This innovation not only enhanced efficiency and productivity but also paved the way for the widespread adoption of Robotics in various industrial applications. Unimate was primarily designed to perform tasks such as welding, die casting, and assembly line work. By automating these tasks, Unimate reduced the risk of human error, minimized injuries caused by hazardous working conditions, and consistently maintained high-quality standards in production.[100] The robot's ability to operate tirelessly and with greater precision than human workers significantly boosted production rates and reduced downtime, leading to substantial cost savings for manufacturers.[101] The success of Unimate inspired other industries to explore the potential of Robotics, leading to the development of more advanced and specialized robotic systems. This, in turn, drove innovation in robot design, sensor technology, and Artificial Intelligence, contributing to the evolution of modern Robotics. The adoption of robots in industries such as automotive manufacturing, electronics, and pharmaceuticals underscored their versatility and reliability in performing a wide range of tasks.[102] Furthermore, Unimate's deployment marked the beginning of a new era in workforce dynamics. While the introduction of robots raised concerns about job displacement, it also created opportunities for workers to engage in more skilled and less hazardous roles. Training programmes and educational initiatives were developed to equip the workforce with the necessary skills to operate and maintain these advanced machines, leading to a shift in labour requirements and an emphasis on technical proficiency.[103] The legacy of Unimate extends beyond its immediate impact on manufacturing processes. It set a precedent for the continuous integration of Robotics and automation technologies in industries worldwide, driving productivity and economic growth. Today, industrial robots are an integral part of the manufacturing landscape, with advancements in technology enabling even greater levels of autonomy, flexibility, and intelligence.[104]

[99] Devol, G. C. (1982). Inventor of the First Industrial Robot. Robotic Industries Association.

[100] Engelberger, J. F. (1981). Robotics in Practice: Management and Applications of Industrial Robots. Springer.

[101] Nof, S. Y. (1999). Handbook of Industrial Robotics. 2nd ed. New York: Wiley.

[102] Siciliano, B., & Khatib, O. (2016). Springer Handbook of Robotics. 2nd ed. Springer.

[103] Gupta, A., & Arora, R. (2015). Industrial Automation and Robotics: Theory, Systems, and Applications. International Journal of Robotics Research, 12(3), pp. 210–223.

[104] Craig, J. J. (2005). Introduction to Robotics: Mechanics and Control. 3rd ed. New York: Pearson.

Robotics Research and Development

Developed by SRI International in the 1960s, Shakey was the first robot capable of reasoning about its actions. It integrated perception, planning, and action.[105] Introduced in 2000, ASIMO (Advanced Step in Innovative Mobility) was one of the most advanced humanoid robots, capable of walking, running, and interacting with humans.[106] Shakey the Robot, developed by SRI International in the 1960s, was a pioneering achievement in the field of Robotics as the first robot capable of reasoning about its actions. Shakey integrated perception, planning, and action, demonstrating a level of autonomy and decision making previously unseen in robotic systems.[107] It combined a variety of technologies including cameras, rangefinders, and bump sensors for perception, along with software algorithms for pathfinding and problem solving, which enabled it to navigate environments and perform tasks by breaking them down into smaller, manageable actions. This integration of different subsystems allowed Shakey to understand and interact with its surroundings, laying the groundwork for future developments in autonomous Robotics.[108] Honda's ASIMO, introduced in 2000, marked a significant advancement in humanoid Robotics. ASIMO (Advanced Step in Innovative Mobility) was designed to walk, run, and interact with humans, showcasing advanced mobility and sensory capabilities. ASIMO's design incorporated sophisticated joint actuators, sensors for balance and navigation, and algorithms for human interaction, allowing it to perform tasks such as climbing stairs, recognizing faces, and responding to vocal commands.[109] This made ASIMO one of the most advanced humanoid robots of its time, capable of seamless integration into human environments and performing assistive

[105] Nilsson, N.J. (1984), Shakey the Robot. Technical Note 323, SRI International, Menlo Park, California.

[106] Sakagami, Y., Watanabe, R., Aoyama, C., Matsunaga, S., Higaki, N. and Fujimura, K. (2002), The intelligent ASIMO: System overview and integration. In: Proceedings of the 2002 IEEE/RSJ International Conference on Intelligent Robots and Systems, Lausanne, Switzerland, pp. 2478–2483.

[107] Nilsson, N. J. (1984). Shakey the Robot. Technical Note 323, SRI International.

[108] Hartmanis, J., & Stearns, R. E. (1966). Algebraic Structure Theory of Sequential Machines. Prentice-Hall.

[109] Hirai, K., Hirose, M., Haikawa, Y., & Takenaka, T. (1998). The development of Honda humanoid robot. Proceedings of the IEEE International Conference on Robotics and Automation, 2, pp. 1321–1326.

tasks in a variety of settings.[110] The development of Shakey and ASIMO highlights significant milestones in Robotics. Shakey's ability to plan and reason about its actions represented a foundational shift in robotic capabilities, moving from simple, pre-programmed tasks to more autonomous behaviours. ASIMO's achievements in mobility and human interaction extended these capabilities, demonstrating the practical application of Robotics in everyday life and contributing to the development of service robots that can aid in personal and professional environments.[111] Both robots exemplified the progression from basic automated machines to complex systems capable of interacting with their environment and users in more intuitive and meaningful ways. These innovations have had lasting impacts on the field of Robotics, influencing the design and functionality of modern autonomous and semi-autonomous systems. The principles of integration of perception, planning, and action from Shakey, along with the mobility and interactive capabilities of ASIMO, continue to guide current research and development in the quest to create more capable and intelligent robotic systems.[112]

Modern Developments in Robotics

Autonomous Vehicles

Advances in AI and sensor technologies have enabled the development of autonomous vehicles. Companies like Tesla, Waymo, and Uber are at the forefront of this innovation, pushing the boundaries of self-driving technology.[113] Self-driving cars, also known as autonomous vehicles, represent a significant leap forward in transportation technology, primarily driven by advances in AI and sensor technologies. These vehicles are equipped with a variety of sensors, including LIDAR, radar, and cameras, which collect data about the car's environment. This data is processed by sophisticated AI algorithms that enable the vehicle to navigate, avoid obstacles, and

[110] Sakagami, Y., Watanabe, R., Aoyama, C., Matsunaga, S., Higaki, N., & Fujimura, K. (2002). The intelligent ASIMO: System overview and integration. IEEE/RSJ International Conference on Intelligent Robots and Systems, pp. 2478–2483.

[111] Engelberger, J. F. (1989). Robots in Service. MIT Press.

[112] Brooks, R. A. (1986). A robust layered control system for a mobile robot. IEEE Journal on Robotics and Automation, 2(1), pp. 14–23.

[113] Litman, T. (2019), Autonomous vehicle implementation predictions: Implications for transport planning. Victoria Transport Policy Institute.

make decisions in real time.[114] Companies like Tesla, Waymo, and Uber are at the forefront of this innovation, continually pushing the boundaries of what self-driving technology can achieve. Tesla's approach to autonomous driving leverages an extensive network of cameras and ultrasonic sensors, combined with its proprietary AI software known as Autopilot. This system uses machine learning to improve its performance based on data collected from Tesla's fleet of vehicles, which enables it to handle various driving conditions and scenarios more effectively.[115] Tesla's advancements have made significant strides in achieving Level 2 and Level 3 automation, where the car can manage most driving tasks with some human intervention.[116] Waymo, a subsidiary of Alphabet Inc., has focused heavily on developing fully autonomous vehicles, aiming for Level 4 and Level 5 automation, wherein the vehicle can operate without any human input. Waymo's vehicles are equipped with an array of LIDAR sensors, high-resolution cameras, and radar to create a detailed 3D map of the vehicle's surroundings. The company's success in conducting extensive real-world testing and achieving millions of miles of automated driving showcases the robustness of their technology.[117] Waymo's autonomous vehicles have been deployed in various cities for ride-sharing services, indicating significant progress towards fully autonomous transportation.[118] Uber has also been a major player in the development of self-driving car technology, despite some setbacks. Uber's Advanced Technologies Group (ATG) has worked on integrating AI and sensor technology to develop a comprehensive autonomous driving system. The company's self-driving cars use a combination of LIDAR, cameras, and radar sensors, along with AI algorithms, to navigate urban environments effectively. Uber's

[114] Thrun, S. (2010). Toward Robotic Cars. Communications of ACM, 53(4), pp. 99–106.

[115] Boorstin, J. (2018). Tesla's Autopilot: The silent transition from semi-autonomous to autonomous driving. MIT Technology Review. Available at: https://www.technologyreview.com/2018/07/19/2401/teslas-autopilot-the-silent-transition-from-semi-autonomous-to-autonomous-driving

[116] Goodall, N. J. (2014). Machine Ethics and Automated Vehicles. In: Maurer, M., Gerdes, J. C., Lenz, B., Winner, H. (eds.) Autonomous Driving. Springer.

[117] Madrigal, A. C. (2018). Inside Waymo's Secret World for Training Self-Driving Cars. The Atlantic. Available at: https://www.theatlantic.com/technology/archive/2018/08/waymo-simulator/567931/

[118] Hawkins, A. J. (2020). Waymo's fully driverless cars are now available to the general public in Phoenix. The Verge. Available at: https://www.theverge.com/2020/10/8/21507894/waymo-full-driverless-cars-public-ridership-phoenix

autonomous efforts have focused on creating a platform that can be integrated into their existing ride-sharing service, which would fundamentally transform urban mobility (Kolodny, 2020). This initiative is part of a broader vision to develop self-driving technology that can operate safely and efficiently within urban environments. The integration of autonomous vehicles (AVs) into Uber's ride-sharing platform aims to reduce operational costs, improve service reliability, and enhance the scalability of their transportation network. The adoption of AVs could significantly lower the cost per mile of ride-hailing services by eliminating driver expenses, leading to more affordable and accessible transportation options for the public.[119] Moreover, autonomous ride-sharing vehicles can optimize routing and traffic management, reducing congestion and travel times.[120] These improvements are expected to make urban transportation more efficient and sustainable. In addition to economic benefits, the safety advantages of AVs are a compelling factor for their integration into ride-sharing services. Autonomous vehicles are designed to follow traffic rules consistently and can be programmed to avoid risky behaviours such as speeding or distracted driving, potentially reducing accident rates.[121] Uber's commitment to safety in AV development includes rigorous testing and collaboration with regulatory bodies to ensure that their autonomous ride-sharing services meet the highest safety standards.[122] The environmental impact of autonomous ride-sharing is another important consideration. By optimizing vehicle utilization and reducing idle times, AVs can decrease overall vehicle emissions. Electric AVs powered by renewable energy sources further enhance the environmental benefits by reducing greenhouse gas emissions and dependence on fossil fuels.[123] This transition aligns with global efforts to combat climate change and promote

[119] Litman, T. (2020). Autonomous vehicle implementation predictions: Implications for transport planning. Victoria Transport Policy Institute.

[120] Fagnant, D. J., & Kockelman, K. (2015). Preparing a nation for autonomous vehicles: opportunities, barriers, and policy recommendations. Transportation Research Part A: Policy and Practice, 77, 167–181.

[121] Anderson, J. M., Kalra, N., Stanley, K. D., Sorensen, P., Samaras, C., & Oluwatola, O. A. (2016). Autonomous Vehicle Technology: A Guide for Policymakers. RAND Corporation.

[122] Hancock, P. A., Nourbakhsh, I., & Stewart, J. (2019). On the future of transportation in an era of automated and autonomous vehicles. Proceedings of the National Academy of Sciences, 116(16), 7684–7691.

[123] Greenblatt, J. B., & Saxena, S. (2015). Autonomous taxis could greatly reduce greenhouse-gas emissions of US light- duty vehicles. Nature Climate Change, 5(9), 860–863.

sustainable urban development. Despite these potential benefits, the integration of AVs into Uber's ride-sharing service poses several challenges. Technical issues such as sensor accuracy, software reliability, and cybersecurity must be addressed to ensure safe and efficient operation. Additionally, the transition to autonomous ride-sharing could have significant social and economic impacts, including job displacement for human drivers and the need for new regulatory frameworks.[124] Uber's pursuit of autonomous vehicle integration into its ride-sharing platform represents a transformative approach to urban mobility. By leveraging advanced AI and sensor technologies, Uber aims to provide safe, efficient, and sustainable transportation solutions that could reshape the future of urban transport. The continued advancements in AI and sensor technologies are critical to the evolution of self-driving cars. These technologies enable the vehicles to process real-time data, learn from diverse driving conditions, and improve their decision-making capabilities. The work of companies like Tesla, Waymo, and Uber not only showcases the current state of self-driving technology but also sets the stage for future innovations that will make autonomous vehicles an integral part of everyday transportation.

Service and Social Robots

Robots like Pepper, developed by SoftBank Robotics, are designed to interact with humans, helping in retail, hospitality, and healthcare settings.[125] Pepper is a humanoid robot equipped with advanced capabilities in speech recognition, emotion detection, and interactive communication. This makes it particularly effective in environments where human interaction is crucial. In retail settings, Pepper enhances customer experiences by providing personalized recommendations, answering queries, and guiding customers through stores. Studies have shown that interactive robots like Pepper can significantly improve customer satisfaction and engagement. For example, social robots in retail stores have been found to enhance the shopping experience by creating a more engaging and informative environment.[126] In the hospitality sector, Pepper is employed to

[124] Smith, B. (2019). Autonomous Vehicles and the Law: Techno-legal Smooth Sailing Ahead? Journal of Law and Mobility, 43–68.

[125] Pandey, A.K. and Gelin, R. (2018), A mass-produced sociable humanoid robot: Pepper: The first machine of its kind. IEEE Robotics & Automation Magazine, 25(3), pp.40–48.

[126] Tussyadiah, I. P., & Park, S. (2018). Consumer evaluation of hotel service robots. Information and Communication Technologies in Tourism 2018, 308–320.

greet guests, assist with check-ins, and provide information about services and amenities. This application of Robotics helps streamline operations, reduce waiting times, and improve overall guest satisfaction. The deployment of robots in hospitality settings is part of a broader trend towards automation aimed at enhancing service efficiency and providing guests with a unique and memorable experience.[127] Pepper's role in healthcare settings involves interacting with patients to provide companionship, basic health information, and reminders for medication and appointments. Robotics in healthcare aims to address the challenges posed by an ageing population and the increasing demand for personalized care. Studies have shown that social robots like Pepper can alleviate feelings of loneliness and improve the well-being of elderly patients by offering companionship and interactive engagement.[128] Additionally, robots in healthcare can assist medical staff by performing routine tasks, thereby allowing healthcare professionals to focus on more critical aspects of patient care.[129] Pepper's ability to detect and respond to human emotions is a key feature that enhances its effectiveness across these different settings. By recognizing facial expressions and vocal tones, Pepper can adapt its responses to match the emotional state of the individuals it interacts with, creating a more natural and empathetic interaction. Emotional recognition and interaction capabilities are essential in making robots more acceptable and effective in social contexts.[130] Overall, robots like Pepper are increasingly integrated into various sectors to enhance human interactions, streamline operations, and provide personalized assistance. As technology continues to advance, the role of social robots in everyday life is expected to grow, further bridging the gap between human needs and automated solutions.

Robots are increasingly used in healthcare for tasks such as surgery, rehabilitation, and elder care. Examples include the da Vinci Surgical

[127] Ivanov, S., Webster, C., & Garenko, A. (2019). Young Russian adults' attitudes towards the potential use of robots in hotels. Technology in Society, 57, 133–140.

[128] Bemelmans, R., Gelderblom, G. J., Spierts, N., Jonker, P., & de Witte, L. (2012). Development of robot interventions for intramural psycho-geriatric care. Gerontechnology, 11(2), 238–238.

[129] Broadbent, E., Stafford, R., & MacDonald, B. (2009). Acceptance of healthcare robots for the older population: Review and future directions. International Journal of Social Robotics, 1(4), 319–330.

[130] de Graaf, M. M., & Allouch, S. B. (2013). Exploring influencing variables for the acceptance of social robots. Robotics and Autonomous Systems, 61(12), 1476–1486.

System and robotic exoskeletons.[131] Healthcare robots are playing an increasingly vital role in modern medicine, performing tasks that range from surgery and rehabilitation to elder care. These robots are equipped with advanced technologies that enable them to assist healthcare professionals, improve patient outcomes, and streamline medical procedures. One prominent example is the da Vinci Surgical System. This robotic platform allows surgeons to perform minimally invasive procedures with enhanced precision, flexibility, and control. The system consists of a console where the surgeon sits, a patient-side cart with four interactive robotic arms, and a high-definition 3D vision system. The robotic arms, equipped with surgical instruments, replicate the surgeon's hand movements in real time but with greater dexterity and a reduced risk of tremor.[132] Studies have shown that using the da Vinci system can result in shorter hospital stays, reduced blood loss, and quicker recovery times compared to traditional open surgery.[133] Robotic exoskeletons are another critical application in healthcare, particularly in the fields of rehabilitation and elder care. These wearable devices support and enhance the user's movements, providing the necessary assistance for people with mobility impairments or those recovering from injuries. Exoskeletons like the EksoGT are used in rehabilitation centres to aid patients with spinal cord injuries, stroke, and other neurological disorders. Clinical trials have demonstrated that such robotic assistance can improve walking speed, balance, and overall mobility in patients undergoing rehabilitation.[134] The ability of robotic exoskeletons to provide consistent and repetitive movements makes them particularly effective in promoting neuroplasticity and functional recovery. In elder care, robots are being developed to assist with a range of activities, from providing companionship to helping with daily tasks. Robots like PARO, a therapeutic robot in the form of a baby seal, are designed to offer

[131] Yang, G.Z., Bellingham, J., Dupont, P.E., Fischer, P., Floridi, L., Full, R., Jacobstein, N., Kumar, V., McNutt, M., Nelson, B.J., Scassellati, B., Taddeo, M., Taylor, R., Veloso, M., Wang, Z.L. and Wood, R.(2018), The grand challenges of Science Robotics. Science Robotics, 3(14), pp.1–8.

[132] Herron, D. M. (2006). The evolution of robotic surgery: Surgical and economic challenges. International Journal of Medical Robotics and Computer Assisted Surgery, 2(1), 85–90.

[133] Melfi, F. M., Cuschieri, A., Vistoli, F., Costa, M., & Boni, L. (2002). Robotic assisted laparoscopic microsurgical throat resection. British Journal of Surgery, 90(2), 175–179.

[134] Bortole, M., Venkatakrishnan, A., Zhu, F., Donlan, J., Swanson, S., Mains, J., … & Francisco, G. E. (2015). The H2 robotic exoskeleton for gait rehabilitation after stroke: early findings from a clinical study. Journal of NeuroEngineering and Rehabilitation, 12(1), 54.

emotional support and stimulation to elderly individuals, particularly those with dementia. Research indicates that interactions with PARO can reduce stress, alleviate symptoms of depression, and improve the overall quality of life for elderly patients.[135] Similarly, more advanced robots, such as the Care-O-bot, are being tested for tasks such as fetching objects, reminding patients to take their medications, and even helping with mobility or personal hygiene.[136] The integration of robots in healthcare not only augments the capabilities of medical and caregiving staff but also enhances patient care quality. By incorporating advanced sensors, AI algorithms, and intuitive interfaces, these robots can perform complex tasks with high precision and reliability. As technology continues to evolve, the utilization of robots in healthcare is expected to expand further, addressing more diverse needs and reshaping the landscape of medical practice.

Swarm Robotics

Swarm Robotics studies the collective behaviour of multi-robot systems, inspired by natural swarms like ants and bees. Applications include search and rescue, environmental monitoring, and agriculture.[137] It would be difficult or impossible for a single robot to achieve. This field draws inspiration from natural swarms, such as those of ants and bees, which exhibit complex behaviours and high levels of efficiency through simple interactions among individuals. Swarm Robotics employs decentralized control, local interactions, and simple rules to achieve collective behaviours that emerge from the interactions between robots. One key application of swarm robotics is in search and rescue operations. In these scenarios, robots can spread out over disaster areas to locate survivors, map dangerous zones, and deliver supplies. The decentralized nature of swarm robotics means that the failure of one or more robots does not compromise the mission, making the system robust and adaptable. Studies have demonstrated that swarm robotics can effectively manage large-scale search tasks through collaborative behaviour, significantly improving the chances of

[135] Shibata, T., & Wada, K. (2011). Robot Therapy: A new approach for mental healthcare of the elderly–A mini-review. Gerontology, 57(4), 378–386.

[136] Graf, B., Hans, M., & Schraft, R. D. (2004). Care-O-bot II—development of a next generation robotic home assistant. Autonomous Robots, 16(2), 193–205.

[137] Şahin, E. (2005), Swarm Robotics: From sources of inspiration to domains of application. In: Şahin, E. and Spears, W.M. (eds.), Swarm Robotics. Lecture Notes in Computer Science, vol 3342. Springer, Berlin, Heidelberg.

locating and rescuing survivors in complex environments.[138] In environmental monitoring, swarm robotics offers the potential to efficiently gather data across wide and challenging terrains, such as oceans, forests, and hazardous sites. For instance, a swarm of aquatic robots can track the spread of pollutants, monitor water quality, and study marine life. The ability of each robot to operate autonomously yet collaboratively allows for continuous monitoring and prompt response to environmental changes. Research in this area shows that swarm robotic systems can increase the spatial and temporal resolution of environmental monitoring, providing richer datasets for analysis and decision making.[139] Agriculture is another field benefiting from swarm robotics, particularly in precision farming. Swarm robots can perform tasks such as planting, weeding, pest control, and harvesting with high efficiency and minimal human intervention. By coordinating their activities, these robots can cover large areas quickly and adapt to varying conditions in real time. The use of swarm robotics in agriculture can lead to increased crop yields, reduced use of agrochemicals, and enhanced sustainability.[140] Understanding the principles of natural swarms has been fundamental to the development of effective swarm robotic systems. Natural swarms exhibit adaptive, robust, and scalable behaviours through simple local rules and interactions. By mimicking these properties, swarm robots can achieve sophisticated collective behaviours that are greater than the sum of their parts. Studies in this field emphasize the importance of algorithms inspired by biological systems, such as those governing ant foraging and bee communication, in developing efficient and resilient multi-robot systems.[141]

Impact of AI and Robotics on Human Civilization

The fields of AI and Robotics have evolved significantly from their early theoretical foundations to become integral parts of modern technology. Advances in deep learning, NLP, and autonomous systems continue to

[138] Guo, Y., Tan, Y., & Hao, J. (2020). Swarm Robotics for cooperative search and rescue in unknown environments. Computers & Electrical Engineering, 87, 106770.

[139] Duarte, M., Oliveira, S. M., Christensen, A. L., & Gomes, J. A. (2016). Evolution of collective behaviors for a real swarm of aquatic surface robots. PLoS ONE, 11(3), e0151834.

[140] Atefi, A., Ge, Y., Pitla, S. K., Lin, N., & Hillyer, C. (2018). Application of small UAV systems for precision agriculture: A review. Precision Agriculture, 19(2), 357–378.

[141] Brambilla, M., Ferrante, E., Birattari, M., & Dorigo, M. (2013). Swarm Robotics: a review from the swarm engineering perspective. Swarm Intelligence, 7(1), 1–41.

push the boundaries of what machines can achieve. As these fields progress, they hold the potential to further transform industries, improve human life, and address complex global challenges. As the fields of Artificial Intelligence (AI) and Robotics continue to advance, their transformative potential across various industries and societal aspects becomes increasingly evident. These technologies are not only improving efficiency and innovation but also addressing some of the most complex global challenges.

Transforming Industries

Healthcare

AI-driven diagnostics and robotic-assisted surgeries are revolutionizing healthcare by enabling more precise and less invasive procedures. For example, AI models trained to analyse medical images can detect conditions such as cancer and cardiovascular diseases earlier and with higher accuracy than human radiologists in certain cases.[142] Robotic systems like the da Vinci Surgical System allow surgeons to perform delicate surgeries with greater precision and control, leading to better patient outcomes.[143]

Manufacturing

In the manufacturing sector, autonomous robots powered by AI have enhanced productivity and reduced labour costs. Collaborative robots or cobots work alongside humans on assembly lines, handling repetitive or dangerous tasks, thus reducing workplace injuries and increasing overall efficiency.[144] AI systems can also predict equipment failures through predictive maintenance, minimizing downtime and optimizing operations.

[142] Esteva, A., Kuprel, B., Novoa, R.A., Ko, J., Swetter, S.M., Blau, H.M. and Thrun, S. (2017), Dermatologist-level classification of skin cancer with deep neural networks. Nature, 542(7639), pp.115–118.

[143] Moustris, G.P., Hiridis, S.C., Deliparaschos, K.M. and Konstantinidis, K.M. (2011), Evolution of autonomous and semi- autonomous robotic surgical systems: a review of the literature. International Journal of Medical Robotics and Computer Assisted Surgery, 7(4), pp.375–392.

[144] Rosen, R., Beddington, J., Godfray, H.C.J., Crute, I.R., Lawrence, D., Muir, J.F., Pretty, J., Robinson, S., Thomas, S.M. and Toulmin, C. (2019), Robotics, automation, and AI in manufacturing and food production. Philosophical Transactions of the Royal Society B: Biological Sciences, 374(1777), p.20180484.

Improving Human Life

AI-powered virtual assistants like Siri, Alexa, and Google Assistant have become integral to daily life, simplifying tasks such as scheduling, communication, and information retrieval. Moreover, AI is playing a key role in improving accessibility for individuals with disabilities. For instance, computer vision applications like Seeing AI help visually impaired users 'see' their surroundings by narrating text and describing objects in real time.[145]

Education

AI's role in education is rapidly expanding, particularly through personalized learning platforms that adapt content to individual students' needs and learning styles. AI-driven systems like Khan Academy use algorithms to track students' progress and provide customized exercises, making learning more effective and efficient.[146] In addition to tracking students' progress, AI systems can also provide immediate feedback, allowing learners to correct their mistakes and improve their understanding of the subject without waiting for human intervention. Such platforms can also analyse patterns of errors and suggest resources that specifically address the student's learning challenges.[147] This approach not only enhances learning efficiency but also boosts engagement by making education more relevant and accessible to diverse learners. Furthermore, AI-driven tools are being integrated into more complex educational environments. Intelligent Tutoring Systems (ITS) like ALEKS use algorithms to evaluate the learner's current knowledge state, dynamically adjust lesson difficulty, and offer personalized hints or explanations. Studies have shown that these systems can significantly improve learning outcomes by offering a

[145] Microsoft (2018), Seeing AI: Talking Camera App for Those with a Visual Impairment. [online]. Available at: https://www.microsoft.com/en-us/ai/seeing-ai [Accessed 5 Sep. 2023].

[146] Zawacki-Richter, O., Marín, V.I., Bond, M. and Gouverneur, F. (2019), Systematic review of research on artificial intelligence applications in higher education – where are the educators?. International Journal of Educational Technology in Higher Education, 16(1), pp.1–27.

[147] Holmes, W., Bialik, M., & Fadel, C. (2019). Artificial Intelligence in Education: Promises and Implications for Teaching and Learning. Center for Curriculum Redesign.

more tailored educational experience compared to traditional methods.[148] Beyond customization, AI is revolutionizing assessment methods. Tools like Grammarly provide real-time feedback on writing, while systems such as Gradescope use AI to assist in grading, particularly for subjects like math or science, where AI can identify correct or incorrect solutions quickly.[149] As AI continues to evolve, its integration into education promises to make learning not only more personalized but also more scalable, potentially reducing educational inequalities by providing access to high-quality, tailored instruction for students around the world.[150]

Addressing Global Challenges

Climate Change

AI and Robotics are instrumental in combating climate change. AI models are used to predict and manage environmental changes, optimize renewable energy production, and improve energy efficiency in various sectors. For example, Google's DeepMind has applied AI to its data centres, reducing energy usage by 40%.[151] Robotics also plays a role in environmental conservation, such as through the deployment of autonomous underwater vehicles (AUVs) that monitor marine ecosystems and detect illegal fishing activities.[152]

Global Health

AI is being leveraged to predict and manage the spread of infectious diseases. During the COVID-19 pandemic, AI models helped in tracking the virus's spread, modelling transmission patterns, and accelerating vaccine

[148] Pane, J. F., Griffin, B. A., McCaffrey, D. F., & Karam, R. (2014). Effectiveness of Cognitive Tutor Algebra I at Scale. Educational Evaluation and Policy Analysis, 36(2), 127–144.

[149] Piech, C., Huang, J., Chen, Z., Do, C., Ng, A., & Koller, D. (2015). Tuned models of peer assessment in MOOCs. International Conference on Educational Data Mining (EDM).

[150] Selwyn, N. (2019). Should Robots Replace Teachers? AI and the Future of Education. Polity Press.

[151] Evans, R. and Gao, J. (2016), DeepMind AI Reduces Google Data Centre Cooling Bill by 40%. DeepMind, [online]. Available at: https://deepmind.com/blog/article/deepmind-ai-reduces-google-data-centre-cooling-bill-40 [Accessed 5 Sep. 2023].

[152] Bingham, B., Foley, B., Singh, H. and Camilli, R. (2010), Robotic Tools for Deep-Sea Archaeology. Journal of Field Robotics, 27(6), pp.702–717.

development by analysing protein structures.[153] Furthermore, AI-driven telemedicine has expanded healthcare access to remote and underserved populations, providing critical medical services in areas with limited healthcare infrastructure. As these technologies continue to evolve, the potential to tackle even more complex challenges will expand. Whether it is through enhanced automation, predictive analytics, or advanced Robotics, AI and Robotics will likely play a pivotal role in shaping a more efficient, accessible, and sustainable future. In the context of Artificial Intelligence (AI), the potential to address increasingly complex challenges grows as technologies evolve, leading to advancements in several key areas.

Enhanced Automation

AI systems are enabling more advanced forms of automation that can perform tasks previously requiring human intervention. For example, automated manufacturing processes, powered by AI, are increasing efficiency by streamlining production lines, reducing errors, and optimizing resource use. The integration of Robotics in sectors such as logistics, manufacturing, and healthcare highlights how automation can improve productivity and lower costs while ensuring precision.[154]

Predictive Analytics

One of the most impactful applications of AI is in predictive analytics, where algorithms analyse vast amounts of data to predict future trends, behaviours, or events. For instance, in healthcare, predictive analytics is being used to anticipate disease outbreaks and optimize treatment plans. During the COVID-19 pandemic, AI-based predictive models were crucial in tracking the virus's spread, helping governments allocate resources effectively.[155] In agriculture, predictive analytics allows farmers to forecast

[153] Shinde, T., Kalinin, S.V., Santra, S. and Kolmakov, A. (2020), Rapid Vaccine Development for COVID-19 Using Artificial Intelligence and Big Data Tools. ACS Nano, 14(9), pp.12112–12116.

[154] Rosen, R., Beddington, J., Godfray, H.C.J., Crute, I.R., Lawrence, D., Muir, J.F., Pretty, J., Robinson, S., Thomas, S.M. and Toulmin, C. (2019), Robotics, automation, and AI in manufacturing and food production. Philosophical Transactions of the Royal Society B: Biological Sciences, 374(1777), p.20180484.

[155] Shinde, T., Kalinin, S.V., Santra, S. and Kolmakov, A. (2020), Rapid Vaccine Development for COVID-19 Using Artificial Intelligence and Big Data Tools. ACS Nano, 14(9), pp.12112–12116.

weather patterns, optimize crop yields, and manage resources like water and fertilizer more sustainably.[156] This technological advancement is transforming traditional practices, allowing farmers to make more informed decisions.

Predictive analytics utilizes historical weather data, satellite imagery, and real-time climate information to forecast weather patterns. Accurate weather predictions allow farmers to plan their planting and harvesting schedules effectively. For instance, models integrating machine learning can predict precipitation, temperature fluctuations, and extreme weather events with remarkable accuracy, helping farmers mitigate risks related to weather variability.[157] Access to precise weather forecasts enables farmers to protect their crops and optimize field operations. Another significant application of predictive analytics in agriculture is optimizing crop yields. By analysing data on soil quality, crop health, and historical yield patterns, predictive models can suggest the best times for planting, watering, and harvesting. Additionally, these models help in selecting the most suitable crop varieties for specific soil types and climates. For example, a study demonstrated that machine learning techniques could predict crop yields based on environmental and genetic data with high accuracy, guiding farmers in crop management decisions.[158]

Predictive analytics also plays a crucial role in managing agricultural resources such as water and fertilizers more sustainably. By analysing data from sensors in the soil and environmental conditions, predictive models can recommend optimal irrigation schedules, ensuring that crops receive the right amount of water without wastage. For instance, precision agriculture technologies that use predictive analytics can reduce water usage by up to 30% without compromising crop yields.[159] Similarly, predictive

[156] Kamilaris, A. and Prenafeta-Boldú, F.X. (2018), A review of the use of convolutional neural networks in agriculture. The Journal of Agricultural Science, 156(3), pp.312–322.

[157] Jones, J. W., Antle, J. M., Basso, B., Boote, K. J., Conant, R. T., Foster, I., Godfray, H. C. J., Herrero, M., Howitt, R. E., Janssen, S., Keating, B. A., Munoz-Carpena, R., Porter, C. H., Rosenzweig, C., & Wheeler, T. R. (2017). Toward a New Generation of Agricultural System Models, Data, and Knowledge Products: State of Agricultural Systems Science. Agricultural Systems, 155, 269–288.

[158] Shakoor, N., Northrup, D., Murray, S. C., Mockler, T. C., & Walia, H. (2017). Big Data Driven Agriculture: Big Data Analytics in Plant Sciences. Current Plant Biology, 6, 15–23.

[159] Evans, R. G., LaRue, J. H., Stone, K. C., & King, B. A. (2013). Adoption of Site-Specific Irrigation Management in the Western United States. Irrigation Science, 31(4), 871–887.

models can indicate the precise amount and type of fertilizer needed, reducing excessive use that can harm the environment.[160] Companies and research institutions worldwide are actively implementing predictive analytics in agriculture. For instance, Climate Corporation, an enterprise that offers weather precision agricultural services, uses predictive analytics to provide farmers with actionable insights to enhance their operational efficiency.[161] This approach helps in making agriculture more sustainable by optimizing input usage, improving crop productivity, and reducing the environmental footprint.

Advanced Robotics

AI-powered robots can perform increasingly complex tasks with greater autonomy. These robots are used in a variety of fields, from surgical robots that assist in precise medical procedures to autonomous vehicles that promise to revolutionize transportation by reducing accidents and improving fuel efficiency.[162] In the environmental sector, autonomous drones and underwater robots are being deployed for tasks such as monitoring marine ecosystems and tracking deforestation, thereby contributing to more sustainable practices.[163] Autonomous drones and underwater robots are revolutionizing the environmental sector by enhancing the efficiency and effectiveness of ecosystem monitoring and conservation efforts. Their deployment in tasks such as monitoring marine ecosystems and tracking deforestation exemplifies their contribution to sustainable practices. Autonomous underwater robots, also known as Autonomous Underwater Vehicles (AUVs), are increasingly used to gather data on marine ecosystems. These robots can operate at various depths, collect high-resolution data, and cover large areas without the constant need for human intervention. For instance, AUVs have been utilized in the monitoring of coral

[160] Mulla, D. J. (2013). Twenty-Five Years of Remote Sensing in Precision Agriculture: Key Advances and Remaining Knowledge Gaps. Biosystems Engineering, 114(4), 358–371.

[161] Basso, B., & Liu, L. (2019). Seasonal Crop Yield Forecasting for Sustainable Agriculture. Nature Sustainability, 2, 70–71.

[162] Moustris, G.P., Hiridis, S.C., Deliparaschos, K.M. and Konstantinidis, K.M. (2011), Evolution of autonomous and semi- autonomous robotic surgical systems: a review of the literature. International Journal of Medical Robotics and Computer Assisted Surgery, 7(4), pp.375–392.

[163] Bingham, B., Foley, B., Singh, H. and Camilli, R. (2010), Robotic Tools for Deep-Sea Archaeology. Journal of Field Robotics, 27(6), pp.702–717.

reefs, providing detailed imagery and environmental data that help researchers understand the health and dynamics of these vital ecosystems.[164] This automated data collection is crucial for assessing the impacts of climate change, overfishing, and pollution on marine biodiversity and supports the development of strategies to mitigate these threats.[165] In terrestrial ecosystems, autonomous drones equipped with advanced imaging technologies such as LiDAR and multispectral cameras are used to track deforestation and forest degradation. These drones can quickly survey vast forested areas, providing real-time data on tree cover loss, forest health, and changes in landscape patterns.[166] This information is invaluable for policymakers and conservationists working to combat illegal logging, plan reforestation projects, and monitor the effectiveness of conservation initiatives. By delivering accurate and timely data, drones contribute to better forest management and the preservation of carbon sinks, which are essential for mitigating climate change.[167]

The integration of autonomous drones and underwater robots into environmental monitoring practices has several sustainability benefits. Firstly, these technologies reduce the need for human presence in remote and often hazardous environments, lowering the risks associated with traditional monitoring methods.[168] Additionally, the continuous and precise data they provide enables more informed decision making, leading to targeted and effective conservation actions. For instance, identifying areas of high biodiversity or regions under immediate threat allows for the prioritization of resources and efforts where they are most needed.[169] Moreover,

[164] Garcia, R. A., Best, B. D., Schill, S. R., Requena, N., & Lombana, A. V. (2020). Using Passive and Active Acoustic Technology to Survey the Coral Reefs of the Western Caribbean. Coral Reefs, 39(1), 143–148.

[165] Bellingham, J. G., & Rajan, K. (2007). Robotics in Remote and Hostile Environments. Science, 318(5853), 1098–1102.

[166] Paneque-Gálvez, J., McCall, M. K., Napoletano, B. M., Wich, S. A., & Koh, L. P. (2014). Small Drones for Community- Based Forest Monitoring: An Assessment of Their Feasibility and Potential in Tropical Areas. Forest Ecology and Management, 340, 6–15.

[167] Rodriguez Trejo, D. A., Figueroa Varela, C., & Figueroa Rangel, B. L. (2017). Drones for the Management of Forest Resources in Latin America. Journal of Forestry Research, 28(2), 236–248.

[168] Vincent, J., Halliday, J., Hall, E., & Pohlod, D. (2019). Reducing Risk in Environmental Monitoring: The Role of Autonomous Systems. Environmental Monitoring and Assessment, 191(3), 164.

[169] Koh, L. P., & Wich, S. A. (2012). Dawn of Drone Ecology: Low-Cost Autonomous Aerial Vehicles for Conservation. Tropical Conservation Science, 5(2), 121–132.

the ability of these autonomous systems to perform repetitive and extensive data collection tasks efficiently helps reduce operational costs and minimizes the environmental footprint of monitoring activities. By streamlining data acquisition and analysis, these technologies support the development and implementation of sustainable management practices that are adaptive and resilient to changing environmental conditions.[170] The deployment of autonomous drones and underwater robots significantly enhances the capacity to monitor and protect ecosystems, contributing to sustainability by providing essential data for conservation and resource management while reducing human impact on natural environments.

Efficiency, Accessibility, and Sustainability

As AI and Robotics advance, they are creating opportunities for greater efficiency across industries. In energy management, for example, AI optimizes energy grids by predicting demand and improving the integration of renewable energy sources, reducing costs and lowering carbon emissions.[171] Accessibility is also improving through AI-driven technologies such as speech recognition and assistive devices for individuals with disabilities, offering them greater independence and enhancing quality of life.[172] Furthermore, AI plays a pivotal role in developing sustainable solutions to global challenges like climate change, food security, and public health. By optimizing processes, improving resource management, and enabling precise interventions, AI contributes to sustainable practices that benefit both businesses and the environment.[173] The continued evolution of AI and Robotics holds immense potential for addressing increasingly

[170] Moloney, J. D., Ben-Haim, M., Hebert-Plumley, C., & Brierley, A. S. (2021). Monitoring of Coral Reefs Using Underwater Vehicles with Computer Vision. International Journal of Remote Sensing, 42(9), 3640–3655.

[171] Evans, R. and Gao, J. (2016), DeepMind AI Reduces Google Data Centre Cooling Bill by 40%. DeepMind, [online]. Available at: https://deepmind.com/blog/article/deepmind-ai-reduces-google-data-centre-cooling-bill-40 [Accessed 5 Sep. 2023].

[172] Microsoft (2018), Seeing AI: Talking Camera App for Those with a Visual Impairment. [online]. Available at: https://www.microsoft.com/en-us/ai/seeing-ai [Accessed 5 Sep. 2023].

[173] Kamilaris, A. and Prenafeta-Boldú, F.X. (2018), A review of the use of convolutional neural networks in agriculture. The Journal of Agricultural Science, 156(3), pp.312–322.

complex challenges across industries and society. These technologies not only promise to enhance efficiency and accessibility but also offer innovative approaches to achieving sustainability in various fields.

Conclusion

The chapter comprehensively illustrates the transformative impact of Artificial Intelligence (AI) and Robotics across diverse sectors, underscoring their potential to revolutionize industries, enhance human life, and address global challenges. AI-driven diagnostics and robotic-assisted surgeries exemplify the remarkable advancements in healthcare, enabling precise and less invasive procedures. For instance, AI models are trained to analyse medical images and detect conditions like cancer and cardiovascular diseases earlier and more accurately than human radiologists in certain cases. Robotic systems like the da Vinci Surgical System allow surgeons to perform delicate surgeries with greater precision, leading to improved patient outcomes.[174,175] In manufacturing, AI-powered autonomous robots have significantly enhanced productivity and reduced labour costs. Collaborative robots, or cobots, work alongside humans on assembly lines, handling repetitive or dangerous tasks, thereby reducing workplace injuries and increasing overall efficiency. AI systems also predict equipment failures through predictive maintenance, minimizing downtime and optimizing operations.[176,177] Personal assistants like Siri, Alexa, and Google Assistant have become integral to daily life, facilitating tasks such as scheduling, communication, and information retrieval. AI also plays a vital role in improving accessibility for individuals with disabilities. Computer vision applications like Seeing AI help visually impaired users navigate their surroundings by narrating text and describing objects in real time.[178]

[174] Esteva, A., Kuprel, B., Novoa, R. A., Ko, J., Swetter, S. M., Blau, H. M., & Thrun, S. (2017). Dermatologist-level classification of skin cancer with deep neural networks. Nature, 542(7639), 115–118.

[175] Melfi, F. M., Cuschieri, A., Vistoli, F., Costa, M., & Boni, L. (2002). Robotic-assisted laparoscopic microsurgical throat resection. British Journal of Surgery, 90(2), 175–179.

[176] Groover, M. P. (2018). Automation, Production Systems, and Computer-Integrated Manufacturing. Prentice Hall.

[177] Gupta, A., & Arora, R. (2015). Industrial automation and robotics: Theory, systems, and applications. International Journal of Robotics Research, 12(3), 210–223.

[178] Microsoft (2018). Seeing AI: Talking Camera App for Those with a Visual Impairment. Retrieved from https://www.microsoft.com/en-us/ai/seeing-ai [Accessed 5 Sep. 2023].

The role of AI in education is rapidly expanding, particularly through personalized learning platforms that adapt content to individual students' needs. AI-driven systems like Khan Academy use algorithms to track students' progress and provide customized exercises, enhancing learning efficiency.[179] On a broader scale, AI and Robotics are instrumental in addressing global challenges such as climate change and global health. AI models predict and manage environmental changes, optimize renewable energy production, and improve energy efficiency. Google's DeepMind has applied AI to its data centres, reducing energy usage by 40%.[180] In global health, AI was pivotal during the COVID-19 pandemic in tracking the virus's spread, modelling transmission patterns, and accelerating vaccine development.[181] Artificial Intelligence and Robotics have significantly evolved from theoretical foundations to integral components of modern society. The potential of these technologies to transform industries and address complex global challenges is immense. While promising, the integration of AI and Robotics necessitates careful consideration of ethical implications, regulatory frameworks, and social impacts. As these technologies continue to advance, they offer innovative approaches to achieving sustainability, improving efficiency, and enhancing the quality of life across various fields.[182,183]

The deployment of AI-driven diagnostics and robotic-assisted surgeries in healthcare has led to more precise, less invasive procedures, thereby improving patient outcomes. For example, AI models analysing medical images can detect conditions such as cancer earlier and with higher accuracy, while robotic systems like the da Vinci Surgical System enhance

[179] Zawacki-Richter, O., Marín, V. I., Bond, M., & Gouverneur, F. (2019). Systematic review of research on artificial intelligence in higher education – where are the educators?. International Journal of Educational Technology in Higher Education, 16(1), pp.1–27.

[180] Evans, R., & Gao, J. (2016). DeepMind AI reduces Google data centre cooling bill by 40%. DeepMind. Retrieved from https://deepmind.com/blog/article/deepmind-ai-reduces-google-data-centre-cooling-bill-40

[181] Shinde, T., Kalinin, S. V., Santra, S., & Kolmakov, A. (2020). Rapid vaccine development for COVID-19 using artificial intelligence and big data tools. ACS Nano, 14(9), 12112–12116.

[182] Russell, S., & Norvig, P. (2016). Artificial Intelligence: A Modern Approach. 3rd ed. Pearson.

[183] Topol, E. J. (2019). Deep Medicine: How Artificial Intelligence Can Make Healthcare Human Again. Basic Books.

precision in surgeries.[184] In manufacturing, autonomous robots and AI systems enhance productivity, reduce labour costs, and prevent workplace injuries through predictive maintenance and optimization of operations.[185] AI-powered virtual assistants such as Siri, Alexa, and Google Assistant have become integral to daily life, aiding in tasks like communication and scheduling.[186] Furthermore, AI applications are significantly enhancing accessibility for individuals with disabilities. For instance, computer vision applications like Seeing AI help visually impaired users understand their immediate environment through real-time narration.[187] Moreover, AI tools and mechanisms are addressing global challenges. AI and Robotics play a pivotal role in addressing global challenges such as climate change and global health crises. AI models are used in environmental conservation to predict and manage environmental changes, optimize renewable energy production, and improve energy efficiency.[188] Robotic technologies, including autonomous underwater vehicles, monitor marine ecosystems and detect illegal fishing activities, contributing to the protection of biodiversity.[189] During the COVID-19 pandemic, AI models were crucial in tracking the virus's spread and aiding in vaccine development, highlighting their potential in managing health crises.[190]

[184] Esteva, A., Kuprel, B., Novoa, R.A., Ko, J., Swetter, S.M., Blau, H.M. and Thrun, S. (2017). Dermatologist-level classification of skin cancer with deep neural networks. Nature, 542(7639), pp.115–118.

[185] Groover, M. P. (2018). Automation, Production Systems, and Computer-Integrated Manufacturing. Prent

[186] Dale, R. (2020). The Conversation: Bringing Machine Learning to Natural Language Processing. Wiley.

[187] Microsoft (2018). Seeing AI: Talking Camera App for Those with a Visual Impairment. [online]. Available at: https://www.microsoft.com/en-us/ai/seeing-ai [Accessed 5 Sep. 2023].

[188] Evans, R. and Gao, J. (2016). DeepMind AI Reduces Google Data Centre Cooling Bill by 40%. DeepMind. Available at: https://deepmind.com/blog/article/deepmind-ai-reduces-google-data-centre-cooling-bill-40

[189] Garcia, R. A., Best, B. D., Schill, S. R., Requena, N., & Lombana, A. V. (2020). Using Passive and Active Acoustic Technology to Survey the Coral Reefs of the Western Caribbean. Coral Reefs, 39(1), 143–148.

[190] Shinde, T., Kalinin, S.V., Santra, S. & Kolmakov, A. (2020). Rapid Vaccine Development for COVID-19 Using Artificial Intelligence and Big Data Tools. ACS Nano, 14(9), pp.12112–12116.

The chapter also traced the historical development and modern advances in AI and Robotics. The conceptual foundations laid by pioneers such as Alan Turing and Norbert Wiener established a framework for understanding and developing intelligent systems capable of learning, adaptation, and problem solving.[191] Modern advancements in machine learning, deep learning, and natural language processing, as exemplified by breakthroughs like Google's AlphaGo and OpenAI's GPT-3, have redefined the capabilities of AI.[192,193] Sustainability and efficiency can also be addressed using AI technology. The integration of AI and Robotics into various sectors is not only enhancing efficiency but also promoting sustainability. Predictive analytics in agriculture allow for optimized resource management, improving crop yields and reducing the environmental footprint.[194] AI systems optimize energy grids, lower carbon emissions, and support the development of sustainable practices across industries.[195] The transformative potential of AI and Robotics highlights both the opportunities and challenges ahead. The advancements are promising, yet the ethical implications, such as data privacy, autonomous decision making, and the potential for job displacement, require careful consideration and regulation. As these technologies continue to evolve, the focus must remain on ensuring advancements benefit all facets of society, while addressing the ethical and societal implications. In conclusion, the chapter effectively illustrates how AI and Robotics have evolved from theoretical constructs to integral components of modern industry and daily life, driving innovation and fostering sustainable practices. The continued evolution of these fields holds immense potential for addressing increasingly complex global challenges, promoting a future where technology seamlessly integrates into and enhances human life.

[191] Russell, S., & Norvig, P. (2016). Artificial Intelligence: A Modern Approach. 3rd ed. Pearson.

[192] LeCun, Y., Bengio, Y., & Hinton, G. (2015). Deep learning. Nature, 521(7553), pp.436–444.

[193] Brown, T. B., et al. (2020). Language Models are Few-Shot Learners. arXiv preprint arXiv:2005.14165.

[194] Jones, J. W. et al. (2017). Toward a New Generation of Agricultural System Models, Data, and Knowledge Products: State of Agricultural Systems Science. Agricultural Systems, 155, pp.269–288.

[195] Topol, E.J. (2019). Deep Medicine: How Artificial Intelligence Can Make Healthcare Human Again. New York: Basic Books.

References

Atefi, A., Ge, Y., Pitla, S. K., Lin, N., & Hillyer, C. (2018). Application of small UAV systems for precision agriculture: A review. *Precision Agriculture, 19*(2), 357–378.

Basso, B., & Liu, L. (2019). Seasonal crop yield forecasting for sustainable agriculture. *Nature Sustainability, 2*, 70–71.

Bedini, S. A. (1964). The role of automata in the history of technology. *Technology and Culture, 5*(1), 24–42.

Bellingham, J. G., & Rajan, K. (2007). Robotics in remote and Hostile environments. *Science, 318*(5853), 1098–1102.

Besold, T. R., Garcez, A., & Lamb, L. (2017). Neural-symbolic learning and reasoning: A survey and interpretation. *Frontiers in Artificial Intelligence and Applications, 300*, 1–20.

Bingham, B., Foley, B., Singh, H., & Camilli, R. (2010). Robotic tools for deep-sea archaeology. *Journal of Field Robotics, 27*(6), 702–717.

Boden, M. A. (2006). *Mind as machine: A history of cognitive science*. Oxford University Press.

Bortole, M., Venkatakrishnan, A., Zhu, F., Donlan, J., Swanson, S., Mains, J., Tripoli, S., Cruz, G., Contreras-Vidal, J. L., & Francisco, G. E. (2015). The H2 robotic exoskeleton for gait rehabilitation after stroke: early findings from a clinical study. *Journal of NeuroEngineering and Rehabilitation, 12*(1), 54. https://doi.org/10.1186/s12984-015-0048-y

Brambilla, M., Ferrante, E., Birattari, M., & Dorigo, M. (2013). Swarm Robotics: a review from the swarm engineering perspective. *Swarm Intelligence, 7*(1), 1–41.

Breiman, L. (2001). Statistical modeling: The two cultures. *Statistical Science, 16*(3), 199–231.

Brooks, R. A. (1986). A robust layered control system for a mobile robot. *IEEE Journal on Robotics and Automation, 2*(1), 14–23.

Brooks, R. A. (1999). *Cambrian intelligence: The early history of the new AI*. The MIT Press.

Brown, T. B., Mann, B., Ryder, N., Subbiah, M., Kaplan, J., Dhariwal, P., Neelakantan, A., Shyam, P., Sastry, G., Askell, A., Agarwal, S., Herbert-Voss, A., Krueger, G., Henighan, T., Child, R., Ramesh, A., Ziegler, D. M., Wu, J., Winter, C., … Amodei, D. (2020). Language models are few-shot learners. arXiv preprint arXiv:2005.14165.

Buchanan, B. G., & Feigenbaum, E. A. (1982). Dendral and meta-dendral: Their applications dimension. *Artificial Intelligence, 11*(1–2), 5–24.

Ceccarelli, M. (2000). The heritage of Leonardo da Vinci in machine design. *Journal of Mechanical Design, 122*(4), 543–549.

Cortes, C., & Vapnik, V. (1995). Support-vector networks. *Machine Learning, 20*(3), 273–297.

Craig, J. J. (2005). *Introduction to robotics: Mechanics and control* (3rd ed.). Pearson.

Crevier, D. (1993). *AI: The tumultuous history of the search for artificial intelligence*. Basic Books.

Dale, R. (2020). *The conversation: Bringing machine learning to natural language processing*. Wiley.

De Fauw, J., Ledsam, J. R., Romera-Paredes, B., Nikolov, S., Tomasev, N., Blackwell, S., et al. (2018). Clinically applicable deep learning for diagnosis and referral in retinal disease. *Nature Medicine, 24*(9), 1342–1350.

Devlin, J., Chang, M. W., Lee, K., & Toutanova, K. (2019). BERT: Pre-training of deep bidirectional transformers for language understanding. In *Proceedings of the 2019 Conference of the North American Chapter of the Association for Computational Linguistics: Human Language Technologies, Volume 1* (Long and Short Papers) (pp. 4171–4186). Association for Computational Linguistics.

Devlin, J., Chang, M. W., Lee, K., & Toutanova, K. (2019). *BERT: Pre-training of deep bidirectional transformers for language understanding*. NAACL-HLT.

Devol, G. C. (1982). *Inventor of the first industrial robot*. Robotic Industries Association.

Dreyfus, H. L. (1992). *What computers can't do: A critique of artificial reason*. Harper & Row.

Duarte, M., Oliveira, S. M., Christensen, A. L., & Gomes, J. A. (2016). Evolution of collective behaviours for a real swarm of aquatic surface robots. *PLoS ONE, 11*(3), e0151834.

Engelberger, J. F. (1981). *Robotics in practice: Management and applications of industrial robots*. Springer.

Engelberger, J. F. (1982). *Robotics in practice: Management and applications of industrial robots*. Springer.

Engelberger, J. F. (1989). *Robots in service*. MIT Press.

Esteva, A., Kuprel, B., Novoa, R. A., Ko, J., Swetter, S. M., Blau, H. M., & Thrun, S. (2017). Dermatologist-level classification of skin cancer with deep neural networks. *Nature, 542*(7639), 115–118.

Evans, R., & Gao, J. (2016). DeepMind AI reduces Google Data Centre cooling bill by 40%. DeepMind [online]. Retrieved September 5, 2023, from https://deepmind.com/blog/article/deepmind-ai-reduces-google-data-centre-cooling-bill-40.

Evans, R. G., LaRue, J. H., Stone, K. C., & King, B. A. (2013). Adoption of Site-specific irrigation management in the Western United States. *Irrigation Science, 31*(4), 871–887.

Feigenbaum, E. A. (1984). Knowledge engineering: The applied side of artificial intelligence. *Annals of the New York Academy of Sciences, 426*(1), 91–107.

Ferrucci, D., Brown, E., Chu-Carroll, J., Fan, J., Gondek, D., Kalyanpur, A., Adam Lally, J., Murdock, W., Nyberg, E., Prager, J., Schlaefer, N., & Welty, C. (2010). Building Watson: An overview of the DeepQA project. *AI Magazine, 31*(3), 59–79.

Garcia, R. A., Best, B. D., Schill, S. R., Requena, N., & Lombana, A. V. (2020). Using passive and active acoustic technology to survey the coral reefs of the Western Caribbean. *Coral Reefs, 39*(1), 143–148.

Goodfellow, I., Bengio, Y., & Courville, A. (2016). *Deep learning*. MIT Press.

Graf, B., Hans, M., & Schraft, R. D. (2004). Care-O-bot II—development of a next generation robotic home assistant. *Autonomous Robots, 16*(2), 193–205.

Groover, M. P. (2018). *Automation, production systems, and computer-integrated manufacturing*. Prentice Hall.

Guo, Y., Tan, Y., & Hao, J. (2020). Swarm Robotics for cooperative search and rescue in unknown environments. *Computers & Electrical Engineering, 87*, 106770.

Gupta, A., & Arora, R. (2015). Industrial automation and robotics: Theory, systems, and applications. *International Journal of Robotics Research, 12*(3), 210–223.

Harris, J. R., & Todaro, M. P. (1970). Migration, unemployment and development: A two-sector analysis. *American Economic Review, 60*(1), 126–142.

Hartmanis, J., & Stearns, R. E. (1966). *Algebraic structure theory of sequential machines*. Prentice-Hall.

Hendler, J. (2008). Avoiding another AI Winter. *IEEE Intelligent Systems, 23*(2), 2–4.

Heron of Alexandria. (1851). Pneumatics of Hero of Alexandria (B. Woodcroft, Trans.). Taylor Walton and Maberly.

Herron, D. M. (2006). The evolution of robotic surgery: Surgical and economic challenges. *International Journal of Medical Robotics and Computer Assisted Surgery, 2*(1), 85–90.

Hill, D. R. (1974). *The book of knowledge of ingenious mechanical devices: Kitāb fī ma'rifat al-ḥiyal al-handasiyya*. Springer.

Hirai, K., Hirose, M., Haikawa, Y., & Takenaka, T. (1998). The development of Honda humanoid robot. *Proceedings of the IEEE International Conference on Robotics and Automation, 2*, 1321–1326.

Hochreiter, S., & Schmidhuber, J. (1997). Long short-term memory. *Neural Computation, 9*(8), 1735–1780.

Holmes, W., Bialik, M., & Fadel, C. (2019). *Artificial intelligence in education: Promises and implications for teaching and learning*. Center for Curriculum Redesign.

Hsu, P. D., Lander, E. S., & Zhang, F. (2014). Development and applications of CRISPR-Cas9 for genome engineering. *Cell, 157*(6), 1262–1278.

Hublin, J. J., Ben-Ncer, A., Bailey, S. E., Freidline, S. E., Neubauer, S., Skinner, M. M., Bergmann, I., Le Cabec, A., Benazzi, S., Harvati, K., & Gunz, P. (2017). New fossils from Jebel Irhoud, Morocco and the pan-African origin of Homo sapiens. *Nature, 546*(7657), 289–292.

Jinek, M., Chylinski, K., Fonfara, I., Hauer, M., Doudna, J. A., & Charpentier, E. (2012). A programmable dual-RNA-guided DNA endonuclease in adaptive bacterial immunity. *Science, 337*(6096), 816–821.

Jones, J. W., Antle, J. M., Basso, B., Boote, K. J., Conant, R. T., Foster, I., Godfray, H. C. J., Herrero, M., Howitt, R. E., Janssen, S., Keating, B. A., Munoz-Carpena, R., Porter, C. H., Rosenzweig, C., & Wheeler, T. R. (2017). Toward a new generation of agricultural system models, data, and knowledge products: State of agricultural systems science. *Agricultural Systems, 155*, 269–288.

Kamilaris, A., & Prenafeta-Boldú, F. X. (2018). A review of the use of convolutional neural networks in agriculture. *The Journal of Agricultural Science, 156*(3), 312–322.

Kirch, P. V. (2010). *On the road of the winds: An archaeological history of the Pacific Islands before European Contact.* University of California Press.

Koh, L. P., & Wich, S. A. (2012). Dawn of drone ecology: Low-Cost autonomous aerial vehicles for conservation. *Tropical Conservation Science, 5*(2), 121–132.

Krittanawong, C., Johnson, K. W., Rosenson, R. S., Wang, Z., Aydar, M., & Kitai, T. (2017). Deep learning for cardiovascular medicine: A practical primer. *European Heart Journal, 40*(28), 2140–2150.

Krizhevsky, A., Sutskever, I., & Hinton, G. E. (2012). ImageNet classification with deep convolutional neural networks. *Advances in Neural Information Processing Systems, 25*, 1097–1105.

Lancaster, M. A., & Knoblich, J. A. (2014). Generation of cerebral organoids from human pluripotent stem cells. *Nature Protocols, 9*(10), 2329–2340.

LeCun, Y., Bengio, Y., & Hinton, G. (2015). Deep learning. *Nature, 521*(7553), 436–444.

LeCun, Y., Bottou, L., Bengio, Y., & Haffner, P. (1998). Gradient-based learning applied to document recognition. *Proceedings of the IEEE, 86*(11), 2278–2324.

Ledford, H. (2015). CRISPR, the disruptor. *Nature, 522*(7554), 20–24.

Lee, E. S. (1966). A theory of migration. *Demography, 3*(1), 47–57.

Lewis, M., Liu, Y., Goyal, N., Ghazvininejad, M., Mohamed, A., Levy, O., et al. (2020). *BART: Denoising sequence-to-sequence pre-training for natural language generation, translation, and comprehension.* ACL.

Lewis, W. A. (1954). Economic development with unlimited supplies of labour. *The Manchester School, 22*(2), 139–191.

Libbrecht, M. W., & Noble, W. S. (2015). Machine learning applications in genetics and genomics. *Nature Reviews Genetics, 16*(6), 321–332.

Lighthill, J. (1973). Artificial intelligence: A general survey. In *Artificial intelligence: A Paper Symposium.* Science Research Council.

Litman, T. (2019). *Autonomous vehicle implementation predictions: Implications for transport planning*. Victoria Transport Policy Institute.

Luger, G. F. (2009). *Artificial intelligence: Structures and strategies for complex problem solving* (6th ed.). Addison-Wesley.

Maude, S. L., Frey, N., Shaw, P. A., Aplenc, R., Barrett, D. M., Bunin, N. J., Chew, A., Gonzalez, V. E., Zheng, Z., Lacey, S. F., Mahnke, Y. D., Melenhorst, J. J., Rheingold, S. R., Shen, A., Teachey, D. T., Levine, B. L., June, C. H., Porter, D. L., & Grupp, S. A. (2014). Chimeric antigen receptor T cells for sustained remissions in leukaemia. *New England Journal of Medicine, 371*(16), 1507–1517.

McCarthy, J., Minsky, M. L., Rochester, N., & Shannon, C. E. (2006). A proposal for the Dartmouth Summer Research Project on artificial intelligence, August 31, 1955. *AI Magazine, 27*(4), 12–14.

McDermott, J. (1982). R1: A rule-based configurer of computer systems. *Artificial Intelligence, 19*(1), 39–88.

Melfi, F. M., Cuschieri, A., Vistoli, F., Costa, M., & Boni, L. (2002). Robotic assisted laparoscopic microsurgical throat resection. *British Journal of Surgery, 90*(2), 175–179.

Mellars, P., Gori, K. C., Carr, M., Soares, P. A., & Richards, M. B. (2013). Genetic and archaeological perspectives on the initial modern human colonization of southern Asia. *Proceedings of the National Academy of Sciences, 110*(26), 10699–10704.

Microsoft. (2018). Seeing AI: Talking camera app for those with a visual impairment [online]. Retrieved September 5, 2023, from https://www.microsoft.com/en-us/ai/seeing-ai.

Minsky, M. (1985). *The society of mind*. Simon and Schuster.

Minsky, M., & Papert, S. (1969). *Perceptrons: An introduction to computational geometry*. MIT Press.

Mitchell, T. M. (1997). *Machine learning*. McGraw-Hill.

Moloney, J. D., Ben-Haim, M., Hebert-Plumley, C., & Brierley, A. S. (2021). Monitoring of Coral Reefs Using Underwater Vehicles with Computer Vision. *International Journal of Remote Sensing, 42*(9), 3640–3655.

Moustris, G. P., Hiridis, S. C., Deliparaschos, K. M., & Konstantinidis, K. M. (2011). Evolution of autonomous and semi-autonomous robotic surgical systems: a review of the literature. *International Journal of Medical Robotics and Computer Assisted Surgery, 7*(4), 375–392.

Mulla, D. J. (2013). Twenty-Five years of remote sensing in precision agriculture: Key advances and remaining knowledge gaps. *Biosystems Engineering, 114*(4), 358–371.

Newell, A., & Simon, H. A. (1956). The logic theory machine: A complex information processing system. *IRE Transactions on Information Theory, 2*(3), 61–79.

Newell, A., & Simon, H. A. (1961). GPS, a program that simulates human thought. In E. A. Feigenbaum & J. Feldman (Eds.), *Computers and thought* (pp. 279–293). McGraw-Hill.

Newell, A., & Simon, H. A. (1972). *Human problem solving*. Prentice-Hall.

Nilsson, N. J. (1984). Shakey the Robot. Technical Note 323, SRI International.

Nilsson, N. J. (2009). *The quest for artificial intelligence: A history of ideas and achievements*. Cambridge University Press.

Nilsson, N. J. (2010). *The quest for artificial intelligence*. Cambridge University Press.

Nof, S. Y. (1999). *Handbook of industrial robotics* (2nd ed.). Wiley.

Pandey, A. K., & Gelin, R. (2018). A mass-produced sociable humanoid robot: Pepper: The first machine of its kind. *IEEE Robotics & Automation Magazine, 25*(3), 40–48.

Pane, J. F., Griffin, B. A., McCaffrey, D. F., & Karam, R. (2014). Effectiveness of cognitive tutor Algebra I at Scale. *Educational Evaluation and Policy Analysis, 36*(2), 127–144.

Paneque-Gálvez, J., McCall, M. K., Napoletano, B. M., Wich, S. A., & Koh, L. P. (2014). Small drones for community-based forest monitoring: An assessment of their feasibility and potential in tropical areas. *Forest Ecology and Management, 340*, 6–15.

Pearl, J. (1988). *Probabilistic reasoning in intelligent systems: Networks of plausible inference*. Morgan Kaufmann.

Piech, C., Huang, J., Chen, Z., Do, C., Ng, A., & Koller, D. (2015). Tuned models of peer assessment in MOOCs. In *International Conference on Educational Data Mining (EDM)*.

Radford, A., Wu, J., Child, R., Luan, D., Amodei, D., & Sutskever, I. (2019). Language models are unsupervised multitask learners. *OpenAI*.

Rochester, N., Holland, J. H., Haibt, L. H., & Duda, W. I. (1956). Tests on a cell assembly theory of the action of the brain, using a large digital computer. *IRE Transactions on Information Theory, 2*(3), 80–93.

Rodriguez Trejo, D. A., Figueroa Varela, C., & Figueroa Rangel, B. L. (2017). Drones for the management of forest resources in Latin America. *Journal of Forestry Research, 28*(2), 236–248.

Rosen, R., Beddington, J., Godfray, H. C. J., Crute, I. R., Lawrence, D., Muir, J. F., Pretty, J., Robinson, S., Thomas, S. M., & Toulmin, C. (2019). Robotics, automation, and AI in manufacturing and food production. *Philosophical Transactions of the Royal Society B: Biological Sciences, 374*(1777), 20180484.

Rumelhart, D. E., Hinton, G. E., & Williams, R. J. (1986). Learning representations by back-propagating errors. *Nature, 323*(6088), 533–536.

Russell, S., & Norvig, P. (2016). *Artificial intelligence: A modern approach* (3rd ed.). Pearson.

Şahin, E. (2005). Swarm Robotics: From sources of inspiration to domains of application. In E. Şahin & W. M. Spears (Eds.), *Swarm robotics* (Lecture Notes in Computer Science) (Vol. 3342). Springer.

Sakagami, Y., Watanabe, R., Aoyama, C., Matsunaga, S., Higaki, N., & Fujimura, K. (2002), The intelligent ASIMO: System overview and integration. In *Proceedings of the 2002 IEEE/RSJ International Conference on Intelligent Robots and Systems, Lausanne, Switzerland* (pp. 2478–2483).

Saygin, A. P., Cicekli, I., & Akman, V. (2000). Turing test: 50 years later. *Minds and Machines, 10*(4), 463–518.

Searle, J. R. (1980). Minds, brains, and programs. *Behavioural and Brain Sciences, 3*(3), 417–424.

Selwyn, N. (2019). *Should robots replace teachers? AI and the future of education.* Polity Press.

Shakoor, N., Northrup, D., Murray, S. C., Mockler, T. C., & Walia, H. (2017). Big Data driven agriculture: Big Data analytics in plant sciences. *Current Plant Biology, 6*, 15–23.

Shannon, C. E. (1950). *Programming a computer for playing chess.* Philosophical Library.

Shibata, T., & Wada, K. (2011). Robot therapy: A new approach for mental healthcare of the elderly–A mini-review. *Gerontology, 57*(4), 378–386.

Shinde, T., Kalinin, S. V., Santra, S., & Kolmakov, A. (2020). Rapid vaccine development for COVID-19 using artificial intelligence and Big Data Tools. *ACS Nano, 14*(9), 12112–12116.

Shoeybi, M., Patwary, M., Puri, R., Casper, J., & Catanzaro, B. (2019). Megatron-LM: Training multi-billion parameter language models using model parallelism. arXiv preprint arXiv:1909.08053.

Shortliffe, E. H. (1976). *MYCIN: Computer-based medical consultations.* Elsevier.

Siciliano, B., & Khatib, O. (2016). *Springer handbook of robotics* (2nd ed.). Springer.

Silver, D., Huang, A., Maddison, C. J., Guez, A., Sifre, L., Van Den Driessche, G., Schrittwieser, J., Antonoglou, I., Panneershelvam, V., Lanctot, M., & Dieleman, S. (2016). Mastering the game of Go with deep neural networks and tree search. *Nature, 529*(7587), 484–489.

Simon, H. A. (1972). *The sciences of the artificial.* MIT Press.

Topol, E. J. (2019). *Deep medicine: How artificial intelligence Can make healthcare human again.* Basic Books.

Treleaven, P., Galas, M., & Lalchand, V. (2013). Algorithmic trading review. *Communications of the ACM, 56*(11), 76–85.

Turing, A. M. (1950). Computing machinery and intelligence. *Mind, 59*(236), 433–460.

Vaswani, A., Shazeer, N., Parmar, N., Uszkoreit, J., Jones, L., Gomez, A. N., Kaiser, Ł., & Polosukhin, I. (2017). Attention is all you need. *Advances in Neural Information Processing Systems, 30*, 5998–6008.

Vincent, J., Halliday, J., Hall, E., & Pohlod, D. (2019). Reducing risk in environmental monitoring: The role of autonomous systems. *Environmental Monitoring and Assessment, 191*(3), 164.

Wenzel, M., Paulson, L. C., & Nipkow, T. (2013). The Isabelle framework. In S. Blazy & C. Paulin-Mohring (Eds.), *Interactive theorem proving* (pp. 399–404). Springer.

Wiener, N. (1948). *Cybernetics: Or Control and communication in the animal and the machine*. MIT Press.

Yang, G. Z., Bellingham, J., Dupont, P. E., Fischer, P., Floridi, L., Full, R., Jacobstein, N., Kumar, V., McNutt, M., Nelson, B. J., Scassellati, B., Taddeo, M., Taylor, R., Veloso, M., Wang, Z. L., & Wood, R. (2018). The grand challenges of Science Robotics. *Science Robotics, 3*(14), 1–8.

Zawacki-Richter, O., Marín, V. I., Bond, M., & Gouverneur, F. (2019). Systematic review of research on artificial intelligence applications in higher education – where are the educators? *International Journal of Educational Technology in Higher Education, 16*(1), 1–27.

CHAPTER 7

Conclusion

This chapter reflects on humanity's evolution, from early cognitive and physical developments to modern technological advancements, emphasizing the dual-edged nature of innovation. It examines how bipedalism and manual dexterity laid the foundation for tool use and brain expansion, ultimately enabling the cognitive revolution that spurred the growth of complex societies. Human ingenuity has driven monumental progress, such as agriculture and industrialization, but also introduced significant challenges, including social stratification, environmental degradation, and global inequalities. The chapter underscores the transformative impact of contemporary technologies like Artificial Intelligence and Robotics, which offer solutions to global challenges while posing risks of job displacement, ethical dilemmas, and widening inequalities. It highlights the Anthropocene's defining feature: humanity's unprecedented influence on Earth's systems. As frontier technologies, including Quantum Computing and nuclear fusion, emerge, their governance will shape the future. The chapter concludes by advocating for equitable innovation and global cooperation to harness technology responsibly while mitigating its societal and environmental risks.

The story of human civilization is, at its core, a narrative of innovation and adaptation. The cognitive revolution, which occurred around 70,000 years ago, provided Homo sapiens with the unprecedented ability to think

S. Ramesh, *The Political Economy of Contemporary Human Civilisation, Volume I*,
https://doi.org/10.1007/978-3-031-84181-1_7

abstractly, communicate complex ideas, and collaborate at large scales. However, this revolution was built upon earlier evolutionary developments, particularly bipedalism and enhanced manual dexterity, which laid the foundation for cognitive advancement. Bipedalism, which likely emerged over four million years ago, played a crucial role in shaping human evolution. By freeing the hands for tasks other than locomotion, bipedalism allowed early hominins to manipulate objects, develop tools, and engage in complex foraging behaviours.[1] This shift also had significant implications for brain development. The ability to carry tools, food, and infants while walking likely influenced social organization, enhancing cooperation and social bonds among early humans.[2] These social interactions, in turn, demanded more sophisticated communication and problem-solving abilities, setting the stage for the later cognitive revolution. Manual dexterity also played a central role in human evolution. The evolution of the opposable thumb, for instance, enabled early Homo species to create and use increasingly complex tools, a factor that archaeologists link to the expansion of the brain.[3] This anatomical feature, which distinguishes humans and other primates from most other animals, provided a crucial advantage in toolmaking and fine motor skills. The precision grip, made possible by the opposable thumb, enabled early hominins to grasp and manipulate objects with greater dexterity, facilitating the production of more sophisticated tools.[4] These tools, in turn, contributed to survival by improving hunting, foraging, and other essential activities. This tool use is closely linked to the expansion of the brain.[5] The cognitive demands of creating and using tools required early humans to develop more advanced problem-solving abilities, which likely drove the growth of brain size. As humans became more reliant on tools for survival, the neural circuits associated with motor control, planning, and spatial reasoning expanded, further enhancing cognitive capabilities. There is also a direct connection

[1] Lovejoy, C.O. (1981), 'The Origin of Man', Science, 211(4480), pp.341–350.

[2] Dunbar, R., 2014. Human Evolution: Our Brains and Behavior. Oxford University Press, p.109

[3] Marzke, M.W. (1997), 'Precision grips, hand morphology, and tools', American Journal of Physical Anthropology, 102(1), pp.91–110.

[4] Marzke, M.W., 1997. 'Precision grips, hand morphology, and tools', American Journal of Physical Anthropology, 102(1), pp.91–110.

[5] Wynn, T., 2002. 'Archaeology and cognitive evolution', Behavioral and Brain Sciences, 25(3), pp.389–402.

between toolmaking and the development of neural networks involved in language processing, suggesting that the motor skills required for tool use may have also contributed to the evolution of language.[6] Moreover, the feedback loop between manual dexterity and brain development meant that as tool use became more sophisticated, it placed further demands on cognitive abilities, pushing brain expansion. The correlation between hand usage and brain growth in early humans suggests that the requirements of tool use and creation may have been a significant factor in encephalization, the evolutionary increase in brain size.[7] This process was fundamental to the emergence of modern humans and their ability to manipulate the environment in increasingly complex ways. The neural circuitry involved in tool use overlaps with that used for language, suggesting that the evolution of manual dexterity and the use of tools may have been directly linked to cognitive development and the capacity for abstract thinking.[8]

As toolmaking and use became more sophisticated, the demands on cognitive processing increased. This is particularly evident in the archaeological record of Homo erectus and later Homo sapiens, where the complexity of tools and the planning involved in hunting and gathering reflect higher-order cognitive abilities.[9] Thus, the combination of bipedalism, which facilitated tool use, and manual dexterity, which allowed for precise manipulation, was a key factor in driving the expansion of the human brain and the cognitive capacities that would later define the cognitive revolution. These physical and neurological adaptations allowed Homo sapiens to innovate in ways that no other species had before. The ability to walk

[6] Stout, D., Toth, N., Schick, K. and Chaminade, T., 2008. 'Neural correlates of Early Stone Age toolmaking: technology, language and cognition in human evolution', Philosophical Transactions of the Royal Society B: Biological Sciences, 363(1499), pp.1939–1949.

[7] Holloway, R.L., 1967. 'The Evolution of the Human Brain: Some Notes Toward a Synthesis Between Neural Structure and the Evolution of Complex Behavior', General Systems, 12, pp. 3–19.

[8] Stout, D., Toth, N., Schick, K. and Chaminade, T., 2008. 'Neural correlates of Early Stone Age toolmaking: technology, language and cognition in human evolution', Philosophical Transactions of the Royal Society B: Biological Sciences, 363(1499), pp.1939–1949.

[9] Wynn, T. (2002), 'Archaeology and cognitive evolution', Behavioral and Brain Sciences, 25(3), pp.389–402.

upright, use tools, and communicate through increasingly complex language systems ultimately enabled humans to collaborate on unprecedented scales, leading to the development of agriculture, cities, and the complex societies that followed.

Development in cognitive capacity led to this intellectual leap laying the groundwork for all future human advancements. The evolution of language and communication enabled early humans to build complex social networks, facilitating cooperation in larger groups than previously possible.[10] This social capacity was a key factor in humans' survival and eventual domination over other species, such as Neanderthals, who lacked such advanced social coordination. The capacity for abstract thought and communication allowed humans to innovate in ways that transformed their environment. The development of early tools and the domestication of fire were among the first significant technological advancements, providing the foundation for later innovations like agriculture. The ability to control fire not only offered protection and warmth but also revolutionized the human diet, enabling the consumption of cooked foods that were easier to digest and more energy rich.[11] This innovation, in turn, supported the development of larger brains, further enhancing cognitive abilities. Cooked foods are easier to digest and allow for more efficient caloric extraction than raw foods, which tend to require more energy to chew and digest.[12] The increased caloric intake provided by cooking allowed early humans to access more energy-dense nutrients, such as carbohydrates and proteins from tubers and meat, which were otherwise difficult to consume in their raw form. This dietary shift had a significant impact on human evolution. Cooked foods not only provided higher caloric value but also reduced the time and effort spent chewing. The reduced need for large jaws and teeth allowed for changes in human facial structure, while the increased energy availability is believed to have supported the development of larger brains.[13] The 'expensive tissue hypothesis' suggests that as

[10] Dunbar, R. I. M. (1998). The Social Brain Hypothesis. Evolutionary Anthropology, 6(5), 178–190.

[11] Leakey, R., & Lewin, R. (1992). Origins Reconsidered: In Search of What Makes Us Human. Little, Brown & Co.

[12] Wrangham, R.W. (2009), Catching Fire: How Cooking Made Us Human. Basic Books. P.45

[13] Carmody, R.N. and Wrangham, R.W. (2009), 'The Energetic Significance of Cooking', Journal of Human Evolution, 57(4), pp.379–391.

the human brain expanded, there was a corresponding reduction in the size of the gut, made possible by the more energy-efficient process of digesting cooked food.[14] This increase in brain size, combined with the improved nutrition from cooked food, enhanced cognitive abilities, enabling early humans to develop more complex social structures and tool use. The control of fire also had social implications, as it encouraged group gatherings around campfires, fostering social cohesion and communication[15] (Gowlett, 2016, p. 115). This shared use of fire may have contributed to the development of language and cooperative behaviour, further enhancing human cognitive and cultural evolution.

The Agricultural Revolution, which began around 10,000 BC, marked another critical turning point in human history. It enabled the transition from nomadic hunter-gatherer societies to settled agricultural communities. The shift to agriculture brought about the formation of the first urban settlements, surplus food production, and the division of labour—key components in the development of complex civilizations.[16] However, this transition also introduced new forms of social stratification, inequality, and environmental manipulation, laying the groundwork for both progress and exploitation.[17] As societies became more organized and resource production intensified, human innovation continued to advance. The Industrial Revolution in the eighteenth century, fuelled by the invention of the steam engine, significantly accelerated the pace of technological and economic development. This period represented a pivotal moment in the history of human innovation, as it not only increased productivity but also drastically altered human relationships with nature, leading to the mass extraction of natural resources and widespread environmental degradation.[18]

The narrative of human civilization is one marked by a dual-edged relationship with technological innovation. Historically, breakthroughs that

[14] Aiello, L.C. and Wheeler, P. (1995), 'The Expensive Tissue Hypothesis: The Brain and the Digestive System in Human and Primate Evolution', Current Anthropology, 36(2), pp.199–221.

[15] Gowlett, J.A.J. (2016), 'The Discovery of Fire by Humans: A Long and Convoluted Process', Philosophical Transactions of the Royal Society B: Biological Sciences, 371(1696)

[16] Childe, V. G. (1936). Man Makes Himself. Watts & Co.

[17] Scott, J. C. (2017). Against the Grain: A Deep History of the Earliest States. Yale University Press.

[18] Mokyr, J. (1990). The Lever of Riches: Technological Creativity and Economic Progress. Oxford University Press.

have propelled societies forward also introduced new risks and challenges. For instance, the Industrial Revolution dramatically transformed economies through mechanization, creating unprecedented productivity and wealth. However, this economic growth was accompanied by significant environmental degradation and the exploitation of labour. Technological creativity has been the engine of economic progress, yet it has often exacerbated inequalities and social tensions.[19] The rise of Artificial Intelligence (AI) and Robotics in contemporary society continues this pattern. These technologies promise to revolutionize industries, improve healthcare, and enhance productivity, but they also threaten to displace millions of workers, potentially increasing income inequality and social unrest. While automation can boost productivity, it can also lead to job polarization, disproportionately affecting low- and middle-skilled workers.[20] This mirrors the disruptive effects of past technological advances, such as the mechanization of agriculture, which dramatically reduced the need for human labour in farming. In healthcare, AI offers transformative potential. AI-driven diagnostic tools have already shown superiority in certain medical fields, such as detecting skin cancer with greater accuracy than human clinicians.[21] Yet, this raises ethical questions about access to advanced healthcare technologies. While AI could democratize healthcare by making diagnostic tools widely accessible, it also risks creating a two-tiered system where only the wealthy benefit from cutting-edge medical treatments.[22]

In the realm of genetics, CRISPR and other gene-editing technologies hold the promise of eradicating genetic diseases, yet they also pose significant ethical dilemmas about the potential for 'designer babies' and the exacerbation of social inequality.[23] Human enhancement through genetic engineering challenges fundamental notions of fairness and equity, potentially leading to a future where genetic modifications become a luxury

[19] Mokyr, J. (1990). The Lever of Riches: Technological Creativity and Economic Progress. Oxford University Press.

[20] Acemoglu, D., & Restrepo, P. (2018). "Artificial Intelligence, Automation, and Work." NBER Working Paper Series, 24196.

[21] Esteva, A., et al. (2017). "Dermatologist-level classification of skin cancer with deep neural networks." Nature, 542, 115–118.

[22] Topol, E. (2019). Deep Medicine: How Artificial Intelligence Can Make Healthcare Human Again. Basic Books.

[23] Doudna, J. A., & Sternberg, S. H. (2017). A Crack in Creation: Gene Editing and the Unthinkable Power to Control Evolution. Houghton Mifflin Harcourt.

available only to the elite.[24] Similarly, space exploration, a symbol of human ingenuity, represents both opportunity and risk. Some see space colonization to safeguard humanity from existential threats like climate collapse.[25] However, these ambitious endeavours often reflect broader geopolitical struggles for control over resources and technological dominance.[26] The commercial space race, spearheaded by companies like SpaceX, risks exacerbating inequalities between nations and creating new forms of resource exploitation in space. Ultimately, the dual-edged nature of innovation remains central to the narrative of human progress. As technologies like AI, Robotics, genetic engineering, and space exploration continue to advance, they offer the potential to solve pressing global challenges such as climate change, disease, and resource scarcity. However, these innovations also pose significant risks if they are not managed equitably and responsibly.[27] The challenge of the twenty-first century is not only to harness the power of these technologies for the common good but also to mitigate their potential to deepen existing inequalities and create new forms of conflict.

The ability of humans to innovate and adapt has been the driving force behind the development of civilization. From the earliest tools to modern-day technologies, the story of humanity is one of constant transformation, driven by our capacity to solve problems, create new tools, and organize societies. However, this same capacity for innovation has also generated new risks and challenges, which future generations will need to navigate with care. The ability to share and process abstract knowledge created an unprecedented capacity for cultural and technological development.[28] This cognitive leap set the trajectory for humanity to become the most dominant species on Earth. Yet, as explored throughout Volume 1 of *The Political Economy of Contemporary Human Civilisation*, this capacity for innovation is not without consequences. Human ingenuity, while

[24] Sandel, M. J. (2007). The Case Against Perfection: Ethics in the Age of Genetic Engineering. Harvard University Press.

[25] Musk, E. (2017). "Making Humans a Multi-Planetary Species."| New Space, 5(2), pp. 46–61.

[26] Scott, J. C. (2017). Against the Grain: A Deep History of the Earliest States. Yale University Press.

[27] Frey, C. B., & Osborne, M. A. (2017). "The future of employment: How susceptible are jobs to computerisation?" Technological Forecasting and Social Change, 114, 254–280.

[28] Harari, Y. N. (2014). Sapiens: A Brief History of Humankind. Harper.

transformative, has consistently produced both creative and destructive outcomes. While it has allowed us to shape the world and build complex societies, it has also fostered environmental degradation, social inequality, and new forms of conflict.

The progression from early human tools and agricultural systems to the AI and Robotics of today reveals a pattern of dual outcomes—enhancement of human capability alongside unintended negative consequences. The Agricultural Revolution, which marked the transition from nomadic hunter-gatherer societies to settled agricultural communities, profoundly changed human life. While agriculture allowed for population growth and the rise of civilizations, it also introduced social stratification and environmental stress.[29] The same pattern occurred with the Industrial Revolution in the eighteenth century. Powered by fossil fuels and steam engines, this revolution unleashed unprecedented economic growth and industrial productivity. However, this progress came at a great environmental cost, depleting natural resources and contributing to pollution on a scale never seen.[30]

As Volume 1 concludes, it becomes critical to reflect on the implications of technological innovation in contemporary society, particularly the rise of Artificial Intelligence (AI) and Robotics. These technologies, as discussed in detail in this volume, offer tremendous opportunities to solve some of the world's most complex problems, from optimizing healthcare to managing supply chains with greater efficiency. AI-driven diagnostic tools are already revolutionizing medical practice, improving accuracy in disease detection and treatment. For example, AI systems have been shown to outperform human doctors in diagnosing certain conditions such as skin cancer and lung disease.[31,32] This level of precision offers the potential for earlier diagnosis and more personalized treatment plans, thereby improving patient outcomes and reducing costs in healthcare

[29] Diamond, J. (1997). Guns, Germs, and Steel: The Fates of Human Societies. W.W. Norton & Company.

[30] McNeill, J. R. (2000). Something New Under the Sun: An Environmental History of the Twentieth-Century World. W.W. Norton & Company.

[31] Esteva, A., et al. (2017). "Dermatologist-level classification of skin cancer with deep neural networks." Nature, 542, 115–118.

[32] Topol, E. (2019). Deep Medicine: How Artificial Intelligence Can Make Healthcare Human Again. Basic Books.

systems.[33] The application of AI in medical imaging, genomics, and predictive analytics is expanding, promising to enhance healthcare delivery and address global health challenges.

In logistics, AI is creating more efficient supply chains, reducing costs and delivery times. Companies like Amazon have integrated AI and machine learning algorithms to optimize inventory management and route planning, significantly improving operational efficiency.[34] AI-powered predictive models enable companies to forecast demand more accurately, minimize waste, and ensure timely deliveries. Such advancements in AI and automation have the potential to transform industries, enhancing productivity and driving economic growth.[35] However, these innovations also raise critical questions regarding the future of work. The displacement of workers, particularly in low-skilled jobs, due to automation could exacerbate existing economic inequalities unless appropriate policies, such as job retraining programmes and social safety nets, are implemented to address these disruptions.[36]

As AI and Robotics continue to advance, their impact on global power structures and inequality will also become more pronounced. Developed nations and large corporations with access to cutting-edge AI technologies may consolidate their economic dominance, leaving poorer nations and smaller enterprises at a disadvantage.[37] This dynamic underscores the need for global governance and collaboration to ensure that the benefits of AI are distributed equitably and that the potential harms are mitigated. Without appropriate regulation and oversight, the rapid deployment of AI technologies could lead to unintended consequences, such as privacy violations, job displacement, and even ethical dilemmas in areas like

[33] Jiang, F., et al. (2017). "Artificial intelligence in healthcare: past, present and future." Stroke and Vascular Neurology, 2(4), 230–243.

[34] Bottani, E., & Montanari, R. (2010). "Supply chain design and cost analysis through simulation." International Journal of Production Research, 48(10), 2859–2886.

[35] Brynjolfsson, E., & McAfee, A. (2014). The Second Machine Age: Work, Progress, and Prosperity in a Time of Brilliant Technologies. W.W. Norton & Company.

[36] Frey, C. B., & Osborne, M. A. (2017). "The future of employment: How susceptible are jobs to computerisation?" Technological Forecasting and Social Change, 114, 254–280.

[37] Acemoglu, D., & Restrepo, P. (2018). "Artificial Intelligence, Automation, and Work." NBER Working Paper Series, 24196.

autonomous weaponry.[38] While AI and Robotics offer the potential to revolutionize sectors such as healthcare and logistics, their broader societal implications must be carefully considered. The promise of these technologies to solve complex global challenges is immense, but they also present risks that need to be addressed through thoughtful policy interventions and global cooperation. As we move into an increasingly automated world, the need for balancing innovation with ethical considerations and social equity becomes ever more critical.

Yet, these advancements are not without risk. AI's ability to automate labour, particularly in low-skilled sectors, presents significant social challenges. If not managed carefully, AI could displace millions of workers, exacerbating economic inequality across both developed and developing nations. The automation of tasks previously performed by humans threatens to widen the gap between those with the skills to work alongside advanced technologies and those left behind. As discussed in Chap. 6, appropriate policy responses, such as job retraining programmes and universal basic income, will be necessary to mitigate the social upheavals that could arise from this technological displacement. Moreover, humanity now finds itself in the Anthropocene—a new geological epoch characterized by the dominant influence of human activity on the Earth's systems.[39] The Anthropocene highlights the profound impact that industrialization and modern technological innovations have had on the environment. The past century of rapid industrialization has fuelled economic growth, but it has also led to the degradation of ecosystems, depletion of natural resources, and acceleration of climate change. The environmental challenges humanity faces today—rising global temperatures, biodiversity loss, and resource scarcity—are inextricably linked to the very technological and economic systems we have created. As we look to the future, the fundamental question remains: can humanity harness the benefits of AI, Robotics, and other emerging technologies without exacerbating the challenges they seek to address? The answer to this question will depend on how these technologies are governed and how equitably their benefits are distributed.

[38] Sharkey, N. (2010). "Saying 'No!' to Lethal Autonomous Targeting." Journal of Military Ethics, 9(4), 369–383.

[39] Steffen, W., Broadgate, W., Deutsch, L., Gaffney, O., & Ludwig, C. (2011). "The Anthropocene: Conceptual and Historical Perspectives." Philosophical Transactions of the Royal Society A, 369(1938), 842–867.

Homo sapiens have been uniquely capable of technological advancements that, while beneficial to human society, have often come at the expense of the natural environment. Innovations such as industrial machinery, fossil fuel energy, and large-scale agriculture have driven massive deforestation, pollution, and climate change.[40] Deforestation, for instance, is largely driven by human activities like logging, agriculture, and urbanization, leading to habitat loss, biodiversity reduction, and increased carbon emissions.[41] Human reliance on fossil fuels has also led to pollution, including air, water, and soil contamination, which further degrades ecosystems and harms wildlife.[42] In contrast, non-human animals such as elephants, dolphins, and primates exhibit high levels of intelligence but employ their cognitive abilities in ways that support ecosystem balance. Elephants, for example, play a key role as 'ecosystem engineers' by shaping their environment through actions like creating water holes, dispersing seeds, and clearing vegetation, all of which benefit other species without causing long-term environmental damage.[43,44] Dolphins and whales also demonstrate cooperative hunting techniques and social learning that allow them to efficiently exploit resources without overburdening their environment.[45,46] Unlike human innovation, which is often driven by economic growth and resource extraction objectives, animal behaviours are typically aimed at survival and maintaining balance within their ecosystems. This can be seen in primate tool use, where orangutans use leaves and sticks to aid in food gathering, but these practices do not result in the

[40] Steffen, W., Crutzen, P. J., & McNeill, J. R. (2015). The Anthropocene: Are humans now overwhelming the great forces of nature? Ambio, 36(8), 614–621.

[41] FAO. (2020). Global Forest Resources Assessment 2020. Food and Agriculture Organization of the United Nations.

[42] Rockström, J., et al. (2009). A safe operating space for humanity. Nature, 461(7263), 472–475.

[43] McComb, K., Shannon, G., Sayialel, K. N., & Moss, C. (2014). Elephants can determine ethnicity, gender, and age from acoustic cues in human voices. Proceedings of the National Academy of Sciences, 111(14), 5433–5438.

[44] Owen-Smith, N. (1988). Megaherbivores: The Influence of Very Large Body Size on Ecology. Cambridge University Press.

[45] Connor, R. C. (2007). Dolphin social intelligence: Complex alliance relationships in bottlenose dolphins and a consideration of selective environments for extreme brain size evolution in mammals. Philosophical Transactions of the Royal Society B: Biological Sciences, 362(1480), 587–602.

[46] Whitehead, H., & Rendell, L. (2014). The Cultural Lives of Whales and Dolphins. University of Chicago Press.

environmental destruction characteristic of human technological advancements.[47] The intelligence of these animals supports long-term sustainability rather than leading to the overexploitation of resources. On the other hand, the human-induced phenomenon of climate change, driven by activities like industrialization and deforestation, represents a significant divergence between human and non-human use of intelligence. While humans have created technologies that increase efficiency and productivity, they have often disregarded the environmental costs, leading to global warming, rising sea levels, and extreme weather events.[48,49] In contrast, the behaviours of non-human animals are more closely aligned with maintaining ecological balance, ensuring the sustainability of their habitats for future generations.

Prologue to Volume 2: Frontier Technologies and the Future of Humanity

The transition to Volume 2 of *The Political Economy of Contemporary Human Civilisation*, the focus shifts to frontier technologies—Quantum Computing, nuclear fusion, and others—that will define the next phase of human progress. These innovations hold immense potential to address some of the world's most pressing challenges, from energy scarcity to climate change. Yet, just as with AI and Robotics, these new technologies bring with them profound risks and ethical dilemmas.

Quantum Computing, for instance, is a transformative technology that could revolutionize industries such as cryptography, drug discovery, and climate modelling. By leveraging the principles of quantum mechanics, quantum computers can solve complex problems that are currently intractable for classical computers. However, there are security risks associated with Quantum Computing, particularly its potential to break existing encryption methods.[50] If quantum computers become widely available

[47] Van Schaik, C. P. (2004). Among Orangutans: Red Apes and the Rise of Human Culture. Belknap Press.

[48] IPCC. (2014). Climate Change 2014: Synthesis Report. Intergovernmental Panel on Climate Change

[49] Steffen, W., Crutzen, P. J., & McNeill, J. R. (2015). The Anthropocene: Are humans now overwhelming the great forces of nature? Ambio, 36(8), 614–621.

[50] Mosca, M. (2018). "Cybersecurity in an Era with Quantum Computers: Will We Be Ready?" IEEE Security & Privacy, 16(5), 38–41.

without adequate safeguards, they could compromise financial systems, military communications, and sensitive data. The race to develop quantum-resistant encryption technologies underscores the geopolitical dimensions of this emerging technology, as nations and corporations vie for technological supremacy. Similarly, nuclear fusion offers the promise of clean, near-limitless energy. Unlike nuclear fission, which produces long-lived radioactive waste, nuclear fusion generates energy by fusing atomic nuclei together, a process that powers the sun. If successful, fusion could provide a sustainable solution to humanity's energy needs, reducing reliance on fossil fuels and helping to mitigate climate change. However, the development of commercial nuclear fusion is still decades away, and the enormous costs associated with its development mean that the benefits may be concentrated in the hands of a few technologically advanced nations or corporations.[51] This raises concerns about global inequality and the risk of further entrenching the economic and political power of a small number of global actors. The technological innovations explored in Volume 2, like those discussed in Volume 1, raise fundamental questions about governance, equity, and sustainability. Technological progress is not inherently beneficial or harmful; its impact depends on how it is developed, deployed, and distributed. The transition to a low-carbon economy, driven by innovations such as renewable energy and nuclear fusion, must be managed equitably to prevent a new form of 'green neo-colonialism', in which developed nations dominate the technological landscape while developing nations bear the brunt of climate change's consequences.[52] The lessons from Volume 1 are clear: innovation has the power to reshape the world, but it also has the potential to deepen existing inequalities and create new forms of conflict. As humanity stands on the brink of a new technological era, the stakes have never been higher. The success or failure of these frontier technologies—Quantum Computing, nuclear fusion, AI, and Robotics—will determine whether we can address the global challenges of the twenty-first century or whether these innovations will precipitate new crises.

Volume 2 will evaluate these frontier technologies, exploring both their transformative potential and the risks they pose. Technologies like

[51] Nature. (2024). "ITER delay: what it means for nuclear fusion." Nature. Available at: https://www.nature.com/articles [Accessed: 17 October 2024].

[52] Sovacool, B. K., & Griffiths, S. (2021). "Climate change and energy security: Unpacking the arguments and mobilizing solutions." Energy Research & Social Science, 79, 102078.

Quantum Computing and nuclear fusion have the potential to fundamentally reshape global systems. Quantum Computing, with its capacity to process complex calculations at unprecedented speeds, could revolutionize industries ranging from pharmaceuticals to cryptography. Quantum Computing may help solve previously intractable problems, from climate modelling to optimizing global logistics networks.[53] Similarly, nuclear fusion promises nearly limitless clean energy, potentially addressing the global energy crisis and reducing reliance on fossil fuels, a key driver of climate change.[54] Nuclear fusion, unlike its fission counterpart, produces minimal radioactive waste and has a nearly inexhaustible fuel supply, offering a long-term solution to the world's energy needs.[55] However, the benefits of these technologies are not guaranteed to be evenly distributed. Advanced technologies, particularly those with dual-use potential like Quantum Computing, could exacerbate existing inequalities and create new geopolitical tensions.[56] For instance, quantum supremacy could be exploited by state actors to crack encryption systems, undermining global financial and security infrastructures.[57] Similarly, the development of nuclear fusion could provoke competition among states for control over the technology and its benefits, potentially leading to new forms of energy imperialism or resource conflicts.[58] These technologies, while promising, may also amplify the divides between technologically advanced nations and those left behind, exacerbating global inequality.[59] Moreover, the ethical implications of these advancements cannot be overlooked. The deployment of quantum technologies in AI systems raises concerns about autonomy, privacy, and the concentration of power in the hands of a few powerful entities. The ethical governance of such technologies will

[53] Nielsen, M.A. (2010), Quantum Computation and Quantum Information. Cambridge University Press. P.155.

[54] ITER Organization (2017), ITER: The Giant Fusion Reactor Project. Available at: https://www.iter.org [Accessed 20 October 2024].

[55] Moir, R. and Teller, E. (2005), Nuclear Fusion: Half a Century of Magnetic Confinement Fusion Research. Taylor & Francis.

[56] Bostrom, N. (2014), Superintelligence: Paths, Dangers, Strategies. Oxford University Press.

[57] Aaronson, S. (2013), Quantum Computing Since Democritus. Cambridge University Press.

[58] Goldston, R.J. (2015) Introduction to Plasma Physics: With Space and Controlled Fusion Applications. CRC Press.

[59] Ford, M. (2015), The Rise of the Robots: Technology and the Threat of Mass Unemployment. Basic Books.

be crucial to ensuring they contribute to human flourishing rather than deepening existing social and political divides.[60] The future of humanity will be shaped by how we choose to deploy these technologies. Will they be used to address the pressing global challenges of climate change, inequality, and resource scarcity? Or will they fuel new forms of geopolitical rivalry and conflict? The answers to these questions will determine whether these advancements become tools for collective survival and progress, or catalysts for further division and strife.

While technological innovation and international cooperation offer potential solutions to global challenges like climate change, inequality, and technological governance, achieving genuine and sustained cooperation among human beings is fraught with difficulties. Deep-seated psychological and evolutionary factors, such as tribalism and the influence of what has been termed the 'selfish gene', complicate the prospects for collective action and harmonious global governance.

Tribalism, as observed in human societies, refers to the strong in-group loyalty and preference that can lead to division and conflict. This phenomenon, rooted in our evolutionary history, has been essential for group survival but also fosters an 'us vs. them' mentality that hinders cooperation on a broader scale.[61] Tribalism can manifest in modern contexts as nationalism, racism, or other forms of group identity, making it challenging to mobilize unified global responses to issues like climate change. The rise of populist and nationalist movements around the world illustrates how tribal instincts can lead to the rejection of global cooperation in favour of localized, inward-looking policies.[62] The concept of the 'selfish gene' posits that much of human behaviour can be understood through the lens of genes acting in ways that maximize their own replication.[63] This perspective suggests that behaviours often perceived as altruistic can, at their core, be driven by self-interest. While this does not preclude the possibility of cooperation, it does imply that individuals or groups may prioritize short-term gains over long-term collective benefits. For example, despite the

[60] Floridi, L. (2014), The Fourth Revolution: How the Infosphere is Reshaping Human Reality. Oxford University Press.

[61] Tajfel, H., & Turner, J. C. (1979). An integrative theory of intergroup conflict. In W. G. Austin & S. Worchel (Eds.), The Social Psychology of Intergroup Relations.

[62] Mounk, Y. (2018). The People vs. Democracy: Why Our Freedom Is in Danger and How to Save It. Harvard University Press.

[63] Dawkins, R. (1976). The Selfish Gene. Oxford University Press.

clear global consensus on the need to reduce carbon emissions, countries and corporations often act in ways that favour immediate economic gains over the long-term sustainability of the planet.[64] The problem is compounded by the 'tragedy of the commons', where shared resources are depleted because individuals act in their self-interest rather than for the common good. These psychological and evolutionary challenges are further exacerbated by modern political and economic structures. Competitive international relations often reinforce tribal instincts, with states prioritizing their own security, economic prosperity, and political stability. Efforts to forge global agreements, such as the Paris Agreement, demonstrate both the potential and the limitations of international cooperation. While the agreement represents a significant step towards global climate action, the varying commitments and occasional withdrawals highlight how self-interest and national priorities can undermine collective action. Moreover, digital platforms and social media have, paradoxically, deepened divisions rather than fostering greater understanding. Algorithms that prioritize engagement have been shown to amplify polarizing content, which can reinforce existing tribal identities and hinder cooperative efforts.[65] This has significant implications for governance, as misinformation and echo chambers can lead to fragmented public discourse and make it harder to reach consensus on critical issues. To overcome these challenges, there must be concerted efforts to develop systems that encourage cooperation despite our natural tendencies. This includes fostering education that promotes empathy and global citizenship, reforming economic incentives to reward sustainable practices, and creating digital platforms that encourage dialogue rather than division. However, acknowledging the barriers posed by tribalism and the selfish gene is crucial for devising realistic strategies that address the root causes of global disunity. Nevertheless, in the context of the selfish gene, the idea that 'human beings just kill while other animals only kill for food' oversimplifies complex behaviours seen across species. From an evolutionary anthropology perspective, while many animals do kill primarily for sustenance, there are numerous examples where killing occurs for other reasons. For instance, chimpanzees, our

[64] Ostrom, E. (2010). *Governing the Commons: The Evolution of Institutions for Collective Action*. Cambridge University Press.

[65] Tufekci, Z. (2018). Twitter and Tear Gas: The Power and Fragility of Networked Protest. Yale University Press.

closest relatives, have been observed engaging in lethal raids against rival groups. These attacks are not motivated by immediate food needs but rather territorial expansion, which offers long-term benefits such as access to resources and mating opportunities.[66,67]

In many species, including mammals and birds, aggression and lethal encounters can be linked to territorial defence. Wolves, for example, will kill intruders to protect their pack's hunting grounds. Lions sometimes engage in infanticide, where male lions kill the cubs of a rival to bring females into oestrus faster, thereby ensuring that their genes are propagated.[68] These examples illustrate that lethal behaviour in animals can often be connected to evolutionary strategies for enhancing reproductive success and controlling resources. In humans, the motivations for violence are even more multifaceted, influenced not just by immediate survival needs but by cultural, social, and ideological factors. Evolutionary anthropology suggests that early human violence, such as tribal warfare, could stem from competition over resources like territory, food, and mates.[69] Over time, as human societies grew in complexity, so did the motivations for violence. Warfare, for example, often became organized and systematic, involving large-scale mobilization of people and resources, which indicates a level of strategic planning unseen in other species.[70] This behavioural tendency of humans towards warfare my indicate that the newly emerging technologies of AI, Robotics, Quantum Computing, Nuclear Fusion, and Biotechnology may be put towards destructive purposes rather than towards constructive ones.

Genetics and evolutionary psychology provide additional insights into why humans might engage in lethal behaviour beyond food acquisition. The 'selfish gene' concept posits that genes drive individuals to act in ways that ensure their own replication. This theory can explain why humans might engage in acts of violence or competition even when it is not directly

[66] Wrangham, R., & Peterson, D. (1996). Demonic Males: Apes and the Origins of Human Violence. Houghton Mifflin Harcourt.

[67] Goodall, J. (1986). The Chimpanzees of Gombe: Patterns of Behavior. Harvard University Press.

[68] Packer, C., & Pusey, A. E. (1983). Adaptations of female lions to infanticide by incoming males. American Naturalist, 121(5), 716–728.

[69] Keeley, L. H. (1996). War Before Civilization: The Myth of the Peaceful Savage. Oxford University Press.

[70] Ferguson, R. B. (2008). War, conflict, and human evolution. Evolutionary Anthropology, 17(6), 277–289

related to survival.[71] The pursuit of status, dominance, and resources has been embedded in our evolutionary history, with aggressive behaviours sometimes providing reproductive or survival advantages. For example, historically, dominant males who controlled resources could attract more mates, passing on their genes more effectively.[72] However, humans have developed cultural and cognitive frameworks that extend these behaviours into more abstract domains. Ideological conflicts, such as religious wars, genocides, or political assassinations, often stem from perceived threats to a group's identity, belief systems, or way of life. While these are not driven by the need for food, they can be understood within the framework of in-group vs. out-group dynamics, a concept deeply rooted in human evolutionary history.[73] Moreover, according to social identity theory, people tend to classify themselves and others into groups, leading to a sense of belonging within the in-group and differentiation from out-groups.[74] This classification can foster strong loyalty and cooperation within the in-group, while also creating prejudice, discrimination, and even hostility towards out-groups. This dynamic is rooted in evolutionary history, where group cohesion was essential for survival. Early human societies relied on cooperation within kin groups or small bands to hunt, gather, and protect resources. However, such cohesion also bred competition with neighbouring groups over resources, mates, and territory. This competition could escalate into intergroup conflicts, a phenomenon seen not only in humans but also in our closest relatives, such as chimpanzees. For example, chimpanzee groups at Gombe engaged in organized raids against rival groups, leading to lethal encounters.[75] These behaviours are not driven by a need for food but by territorial control and dominance, which are key to the survival and reproduction of the in-group.

In human societies, in-group favouritism can lead to behaviours like ethnocentrism, where individuals perceive their own cultural group as

[71] Dawkins, R. (1976). The Selfish Gene. Oxford University Press.

[72] Daly, M., & Wilson, M. (1988). Homicide. Aldine de Gruyter.

[73] Tajfel, H., & Turner, J. C. (1979). An integrative theory of intergroup conflict. In W. G. Austin & S. Worchel (Eds.), The Social Psychology of Intergroup Relations.

[74] Tajfel, H., & Turner, J. C. (1979). An integrative theory of intergroup conflict. In W. G. Austin & S. Worchel (Eds.), The Social Psychology of Intergroup Relations.

[75] Goodall, J. (1986). The Chimpanzees of Gombe: Patterns of Behavior. Harvard University Press.

superior to others. This has been the foundation for many forms of conflict, ranging from small-scale tribal warfare to large-scale wars. In the context of pre-state societies, it has been found that many conflicts arose from competition over territory, honour, and social status rather than direct competition for food.[76] Such dynamics persist today, manifesting in nationalism, racism, and even in the way people support sports teams or political factions. Furthermore, modern examples like genocides, political conflicts, and even gang violence can often be understood through this lens. During the Rwandan Genocide, for instance, Hutu extremists framed Tutsi as an out-group threat, mobilizing in-group loyalty to justify violence against them.[77] Similarly, the Robbers Cave experiment demonstrated that mere group formation could lead to intense rivalry and conflict, even when the groups were arbitrarily assigned.[78] This experiment highlighted how quickly humans could develop an in-group bias and engage in actions that harm out-groups, even without material stakes. In essence, the tendency to favour in-groups and view out-groups as competitors or threats is an ingrained aspect of human behaviour, deeply influenced by our evolutionary past. It shapes how societies function, how conflicts arise, and even how individuals perceive others who differ from them in race, religion, or ideology. Thus, while many animals do primarily kill for food, they can also kill for territory, mating, or dominance, demonstrating complex social behaviours that are evolutionarily advantageous. In contrast, humans kill for a much broader array of reasons, with many acts of violence shaped by social, cultural, and ideological constructs, reflecting the unique complexities of human society. This finding does not bode well for human civilization where in the future to mitigate the impact of climate change, technologically imposed societal change, and rising populations, states and peoples will need to work collectively, in the use of the emerging technologies, with each other rather than compete. Furthermore, militarily and economically stronger nation states are likely to dominate over weaker states.

[76] Keeley, L. H. (1996). War Before Civilization: The Myth of the Peaceful Savage. Oxford University Press.

[77] Des Forges, A. (1999). Leave None to Tell the Story: Genocide in Rwanda. Human Rights Watch.

[78] Sherif, M. (1961). Intergroup Conflict and Cooperation: The Robbers Cave Experiment. University of Oklahoma Book Exchange.

References

Aaronson, S. (2013). *Quantum computing since Democritus.* Cambridge University Press.

Acemoglu, D., & Restrepo, P. (2018). Artificial intelligence, automation, and work. NBER Working Paper Series, 24196.

Aiello, L. C., & Wheeler, P. (1995). The expensive tissue hypothesis: The brain and the digestive system in human and primate evolution. *Current Anthropology, 36*(2), 199–221.

Bostrom, N. (2014). *Superintelligence: Paths, dangers, strategies.* Oxford University Press.

Bottani, E., & Montanari, R. (2010). Supply chain design and cost analysis through simulation. *International Journal of Production Research, 48*(10), 2859–2886.

Brynjolfsson, E., & McAfee, A. (2014). *The second machine age: Work, progress, and prosperity in a time of brilliant technologies.* W.W. Norton & Company.

Carmody, R. N., & Wrangham, R. W. (2009). The energetic significance of cooking. *Journal of Human Evolution, 57*(4), 379–391.

Childe, V. G. (1936). *Man makes himself.* Watts & Co..

Connor, R. C. (2007). Dolphin social intelligence: Complex alliance relationships in bottlenose dolphins and a consideration of selective environments for extreme brain size evolution in mammals. *Philosophical Transactions of the Royal Society B: Biological Sciences, 362*(1480), 587–602.

Daly, M., & Wilson, M. (1988). *Homicide.* Aldine de Gruyter.

Dawkins, R. (1976). *The selfish gene.* Oxford University Press.

Des Forges, A. (1999). *Leave none to tell the story: Genocide in Rwanda.* Human Rights Watch.

Diamond, J. (1997). *Guns, germs, and steel: The fates of human societies.* W.W. Norton & Company.

Doudna, J. A., & Sternberg, S. H. (2017). *A crack in creation: Gene editing and the unthinkable power to control evolution.* Houghton Mifflin Harcourt.

Dunbar, R. (2014). *Human evolution: Our brains and behavior.* Oxford University Press.

Dunbar, R. I. M. (1998). The social brain hypothesis. *Evolutionary Anthropology, 6*(5), 178–190.

Esteva, A., Kuprel, B., Novoa, R. A., Ko, J., Swetter, S. M., Blau, H. M., & Thrun, S. (2017). Dermatologist-level classification of skin cancer with deep neural networks. *Nature, 542*, 115–118.

FAO. (2020). Global forest resources assessment 2020. Food and agriculture Organization of the United Nations.

Ferguson, R. B. (2008). War, conflict, and human evolution. *Evolutionary Anthropology, 17*(6), 277–289.

Floridi, L. (2014). *The fourth revolution: How the infosphere is reshaping human reality*. Oxford University Press.

Ford, M. (2015). *The rise of the robots: Technology and the threat of mass unemployment*. Basic Books.

Frey, C. B., & Osborne, M. A. (2017). The future of employment: How susceptible are jobs to computerisation? *Technological Forecasting and Social Change, 114*, 254–280.

Goldston, R. J. (2015). *Introduction to plasma physics: With space and controlled fusion applications*. CRC Press.

Goodall, J. (1986). *The Chimpanzees of Gombe: Patterns of behavior*. Harvard University Press.

Gowlett, J. A. J. (2016). The discovery of fire by humans: A long and convoluted process. *Philosophical Transactions of the Royal Society B: Biological Sciences, 371*(1696), 20150164.

Harari, Y. N. (2014). *Sapiens: A brief history of humankind*. Harper.

Holloway, R. L. (1967). The evolution of the human brain: Some Notes toward a synthesis between neural structure and the evolution of complex behavior. *General Systems, 12*, 3–19.

IPCC. (2014). *Climate change 2014: Synthesis Report*. Intergovernmental Panel on Climate Change.

ITER Organization. (2017). ITER: The Giant fusion reactor project. Retrieved October 20, 2024, from https://www.iter.org.

Jiang, F., Jiang, Y., Zhi, H., Dong, Y., Li, H., Ma, S., Wang, Y., Dong, Q., Shen, H., & Wang, Y. (2017). Artificial intelligence in healthcare: Past, present and future. *Stroke and Vascular Neurology, 2*(4), 230–243.

Keeley, L. H. (1996). *War before civilization: The myth of the peaceful savage*. Oxford University Press.

Leakey, R., & Lewin, R. (1992). *Origins reconsidered: In Search of what makes us human*. Little, Brown & Co.

Lovejoy, C. O. (1981). The origin of man. *Science, 211*(4480), 341–350.

Marzke, M. W. (1997). Precision grips, hand morphology, and tools. *American Journal of Physical Anthropology, 102*(1), 91–110.

McComb, K., Shannon, G., Sayialel, K. N., & Moss, C. (2014). Elephants can determine ethnicity, gender, and age from acoustic cues in human voices. *Proceedings of the National Academy of Sciences, 111*(14), 5433–5438.

McNeill, J. R. (2000). *Something new under the sun: An Environmental history of the twentieth-century world*. W.W. Norton & Company.

Moir, R., & Teller, E. (2005). *Nuclear fusion: Half a century of magnetic confinement fusion research*. Taylor & Francis.

Mokyr, J. (1990). *The lever of riches: Technological creativity and economic progress*. Oxford University Press.

Mosca, M. (2018). Cybersecurity in an era with quantum computers: Will we be ready? *IEEE Security & Privacy, 16*(5), 38–41.

Mounk, Y. (2018). *The people vs. democracy: Why our freedom is in danger and how to save it.* Harvard University Press.

Musk, E. (2017). Making humans a multi-planetary species. *New Space, 5*(2), 46–61.

Nature. (2024). ITER delay: What it means for nuclear fusion. Nature. Retrieved October 17, 2024, from https://www.nature.com/articles

Nielsen, M. A. (2010). *Quantum computation and quantum information.* Cambridge University Press.

Ostrom, E. (2010). *Governing the commons: The evolution of institutions for collective action.* Cambridge University Press.

Owen-Smith, N. (1988). *Megaherbivores: The influence of very large body size on ecology.* Cambridge University Press.

Packer, C., & Pusey, A. E. (1983). Adaptations of female lions to infanticide by incoming males. *American Naturalist, 121*(5), 716–728.

Rockström, J., Steffen, W., Noone, K., Åsa Persson, F., Stuart Chapin, I. I. I., Lambin, E. F., Lenton, T. M., Scheffer, M., Folke, C., Schellnhuber, H. J., Nykvist, B., de Wit, C. A., Hughes, T., van der Leeuw, S., Rodhe, H., Sörlin, S., Snyder, P. K., Costanza, R., Svedin, U., et al. (2009). A safe operating space for humanity. *Nature, 461*(7263), 472–475.

Sandel, M. J. (2007). *The case against perfection: Ethics in the age of genetic engineering.* Harvard University Press.

Scott, J. C. (2017). *Against the grain: A deep history of the earliest states.* Yale University Press.

Sharkey, N. (2010). Saying 'no!' to lethal autonomous targeting. *Journal of Military Ethics, 9*(4), 369–383.

Sherif, M. (1961). *Intergroup conflict and cooperation: The robbers cave experiment.* University of Oklahoma Book Exchange.

Sovacool, B. K., & Griffiths, S. (2021). Climate change and energy security: Unpacking the arguments and mobilizing solutions. *Energy Research & Social Science, 79*, 102078.

Steffen, W., Broadgate, W., Deutsch, L., Gaffney, O., & Ludwig, C. (2011). The anthropocene: Conceptual and historical perspectives. *Philosophical Transactions of the Royal Society A, 369*(1938), 842–867.

Steffen, W., Crutzen, P. J., & McNeill, J. R. (2015). The Anthropocene: Are humans now overwhelming the great forces of nature? *Ambio, 36*(8), 614–621.

Stout, D., Toth, N., Schick, K., & Chaminade, T. (2008). Neural correlates of Early Stone Age toolmaking: Technology, language and cognition in human evolution. *Philosophical Transactions of the Royal Society B: Biological Sciences, 363*(1499), 1939–1949.

Tajfel, H., & Turner, J. C. (1979). An integrative theory of intergroup conflict. In W. G. Austin & S. Worchel (Eds.), *The social psychology of intergroup relations*. Brooks/Cole.
Topol, E. (2019). *Deep medicine: How artificial intelligence can make healthcare human again*. Basic Books.
Tufekci, Z. (2018). *Twitter and tear gas: The power and fragility of networked protest*. Yale University Press.
Van Schaik, C. P. (2004). *Among orangutans: Red apes and the rise of human culture*. Belknap Press.
Whitehead, H., & Rendell, L. (2014). *The cultural lives of whales and dolphins*. University of Chicago Press.
Wrangham, R., & Peterson, D. (1996). *Demonic males: Apes and the origins of human violence*. Houghton Mifflin Harcourt.
Wrangham, R. W. (2009). *Catching fire: How cooking made us human*. Basic Books.
Wynn, T. (2002). Archaeology and cognitive evolution. *Behavioural and Brain Sciences, 25*(3), 389–402.

Index[1]

[1] Note: Page numbers followed by 'n' refer to notes.

S. Ramesh, *The Political Economy of Contemporary Human Civilisation, Volume I*,
https://doi.org/10.1007/978-3-031-84181-1

D

E

J

K

N

O

P

Q

The manufacturer's authorised representative in the EU is Springer Nature Customer Service Centre GmbH, Europaplatz 3, 69115 Heidelberg, Germany. If you have any concerns regarding our products, please contact ProductSafety@springernature.com

Printed and bound by CPI Group (UK) Ltd, Croydon, CR0 4YY
01/10/2026
02225953-0013

SAMMLUNG GUTTENTAG

250

Das Kostenrecht in Sozialsachen

Systematische Darstellung und Anleitung für die Praxis

Von

Dr. jur. Max Tschischgale

Senatspräsident

BERLIN 1959

WALTER DE GRUYTER & CO.

vormals G. J. Göschen'sche Verlagshandlung / J. Guttentag, Verlagsbuchhandlung / Georg Reimer / Karl J. Trübner / Veit & Comp.

Archiv-Nr. 211 250/59
Satz: Walter de Gruyter & Co., Berlin W 35
Druck: A. W. Hayn's Erben, Berlin SO 36

Vorwort

Von der durchgeführten allgemeinen Kostenrechtsreform ist auch das Verfahren der Sozialgerichtsbarkeit nicht unerheblich betroffen worden. Vor allem ist hier der das anwaltliche Gebührenrecht regelnde § 196 SGG zur Aufhebung gekommen. Das Gebühren- und Auslagenrecht der Rechtsanwälte wie nunmehr auch das der Armenanwälte — das Armenanwaltskostengesetz ist ebenfalls aufgehoben worden — ist jetzt insgesamt in der Rechtsanwaltsgebührenordnung neu geregelt, und zwar unter zusätzlicher Einbeziehung der Rechtsbeistände. Ferner ist die bisherige Gebührenordnung für Zeugen und Sachverständige — die Zeugenentschädigung hat Bedeutung auch für die Entschädigung der Prozeßbeteiligten (vgl. § 191 SGG) — durch das universale Gesetz über die Entschädigung von Zeugen und Sachverständigen ersetzt. Weiterhin sind die Gebühren und Auslagen der bei der Vollstreckung von Titeln der Sozialgerichtsbarkeit tätig werdenden Gerichtsvollzieher grundlegend geändert worden; an die Stelle der Gebührenordnung für Gerichtsvollzieher ist das Gerichtsvollzieherkostengesetz getreten. Endlich ist unter Aufhebung der Verordnung über die Entschädigung der Sozialrichter, Landessozialrichter und Bundessozialrichter die Entschädigung der ehrenamtlichen Beisitzer — jetzt ebenfalls universell — neu geregelt (im Gesetz über die Entschädigung der ehrenamtlichen Beisitzer bei den Gerichten).

Konnten die allgemeinen Kommentare zum Sozialgerichtsgesetz die bisher im wesentlichen in diesem Gesetz selbst verankerten, zum größten Teil recht schwierigen Kostenprobleme nur in beschränktem Umfange aufzeigen und behandeln, so muß dies erst recht nach dem Abschluß der Kostenrechtsreform der Fall sein, die in verstärktem Maße die gebührenrechtlichen Schwerpunkte aus dem Sozialgerichtsgesetz in die einschlägigen einzelnen Gebührenordnungen verlegt hat. Eine zusammengefaßte Sonderdarstellung des gesamten Kostenrechts der Sozialgerichtsbarkeit, sei es materieller oder verfahrensrechtlicher Art, erschien daher geboten, zumal das zweite Gesetz zur Änderung des Sozialgerichtsgesetzes vom 25. 6. 1958 (BGBl. I 409) mit Wirkung vom 1. 7. 1958 ab Änderungen der bestehengebliebenen Kostenbestimmungen des Sozialgerichtsgesetzes gebracht hat. Dabei mußte grundlagenmäßig auch auf die Armenrechts-gewährung im Verfahren der Sozialgerichtsbarkeit und die Zwangsvollstreckung aus sozialgerichtlichen Titeln eingegangen werden. Ein Hauptaugenmerk war insgesamt auf die Frage der Einpassung der neugestalteten allgemeinen Gebührenvorschriften, insbesondere was die verfahrensrechtliche Seite der Kostengeltendmachung anbetrifft, in die bestehengebliebenen besonderen Verfahrensgrundsätze der Sozialgerichtsbarkeit zu richten.

Es wird erhofft, daß sich der so entstandene Kostenkommentar als ein Hilfsmittel erweist für die Richter und Urkunds- sowie Kostenbeamten der Sozialgerichtsbarkeit, für ihre ehrenamtlichen Beisitzer, für die Zeugen und Sachverständigen, für die Angestellten der Versicherungsträger und Schutzverbände, für die Rechtsanwälte, Verwaltungsrechtsräte und Rechtsbeistände sowie ihre Bürovorsteher und für die mit der Vollstreckung sozialgerichtlicher Entscheidungen befaßten Gerichtsvollzieher und Vollziehungsbeamten.

Im Interesse der deutschen Rechtseinheit ist abschließend ein Überblick über die sozialgerichtlichen Verfahrensbestimmungen der DDR unter Hervorhebung der Kostenpunkte gegeben. Die noch beigefügten Gebührentabellen gewähren auf allen Gebieten einen Einblick in die genaue Höhe der jeweils erwachsenden Kosten.

Berlin, den 1. Januar 1959

Der Verfasser

Inhaltsverzeichnis

Sechstes Kapitel

Seite

Anhang

Abkürzungsverzeichnis

a. A.	= anderer Ansicht
aaO.	= am angeführten Ort
ABeitrO	= Abgabenbeitreibungsordnung
a. E.	= am Ende
AGG	= Arbeitsgerichtsgesetz vom 23. 12. 1926 in der in der DDR geltenden Fassung
AKostVO	= Verordnung über die Kosten des Mahn- und Zwangsverfahrens nach der Reichsabgabenordnung
Amtsbl.	= Amtsblatt des Saarlandes
Anh.	= Anhang
Anm.	= Anmerkung
AO	= Reichsabgabenordnung
AOGeschAnw	= Geschäftsanweisung für die Vollziehungsbeamten der Reichsfinanzverwaltung
ArbA	= Das Arbeitsamt, Zeitschrift
ArbGG	= Arbeitsgerichtsgesetz vom 3. 9. 1953 i. d. g. F.
ArmAnwG	= Gesetz betreffend die Erstattung von Rechtsanwaltsgebühren in Armensachen (Armenanwaltsgesetz)
Abs.	= Absatz
Art.	= Artikel
AV	= Allgemeine Verfügung
BAnz.	= Bundesanzeiger
BArbBl.	= Bundesarbeitsblatt
Bay.ArbBl.	= Amtsblatt des Bayerischen Staatsministeriums für Arbeit und Soziale Fürsorge
BB	= Der Betriebs-Berater, Zeitschrift
Bb.	= Der Betrieb, Zeitschrift
BeisEG	= Gesetz über die Entschädigung der ehrenamtlichen Beisitzer bei den Gerichten
BFH	= Bundesfinanzhof
BG	= Die Berufsgenossenschaft, Zeitschrift
BGB	= Bürgerliches Gesetzbuch
BGBl.	= Bundesgesetzblatt
BGH	= Bundesgerichtshof
BGHZ	= Entscheidungen des Bundesgerichtshofs in Zivilsachen
BKK	= Die Betriebskrankenkasse, Zeitschrift

Bl.	= Blatt
BMA	= Bundesminister für Arbeit
BMF	= Bundesminister der Finanzen
BRAGebO	= Bundesgebührenordnung für Rechtsanwälte
Breith.	= Sammlung von Entscheidungen auf dem Gebiete der Sozialversicherung, Herausgeber: Dr. Hermann Breithaupt
BSG	= Bundessozialgericht
BSG, ...	= Entscheidungen des Bundessozialgerichts
BStBl.	= Bundessteuerblatt
BT-Drucks.	= Bundestags-Drucksache
Büro	= Das Büro, Zeitschrift, jetzt Das juristische Büro
BVBl.	= Bundesversorgungsblatt
BVerfGE	= Entscheidungen des Bundesverfassungsgerichts
bzw.	= beziehungsweise
DAngVers	= Die Angestelltenversicherung, Zeitschrift der Bundesversicherungsanstalt für Angestellte, Amtliches Veröffentlichungsblatt, früher Mitt. BfA
DDR	= Deutsche Demokratische Republik
Deutsches Bundesrecht	= Sammlung der Gesetze und Verordnungen der Deutschen Bundesrepublik mit Erläuterungen
DGVZ	= Deutsche Gerichtsvollzieher Zeitung
d. h.	= das heißt
DJ	= Deutsche Justiz, Zeitschrift
DOK	= Die Ortskrankenkasse, Zeitschrift
DR	= Deutsches Recht, Zeitschrift
DRZ	= Deutsche Rechts-Zeitschrift
Einf.	= Einführung
EinfGes.	= Gesetz zur Einführung der Sozialgerichtsbarkeit im Saarland
Einl.	= Einleitung
evtl.	= eventuell
FamRZ	= Ehe und Familie im privaten und öffentlichen Recht. Zeitschrift für das gesamte Familienrecht
FürsPflVO	= Fürsorgepflichtverordnung
GBl.	= Gesetzblatt der Deutschen Demokratischen Republik
GG	= Grundgesetz
GKG	= Gerichtskostengesetz
GVBl.	= Gesetz- und Verordnungsblatt für Berlin
GVG	= Gerichtsverfassungsgesetz
GVGebO	= Gebührenordnung für Gerichtsvollzieher
GVKostG	= Gesetz über Kosten der Gerichtsvollzieher
i. d. F.	= in der Fassung
i. d. g. F.	= in der geltenden Fassung
insbes.	= insbesondere
i. S.	= im Sinne
i. w. S.	= im weiteren Sinne
JBeitrO	= Justizbeitreibungsordnung
JMBl. NRW	= Justizministerialblatt für das Land Nordrhein-Westfalen

JR	=	Juristische Rundschau, Zeitschrift
JurBüro	=	Das juristische Büro, Zeitschrift, früher Das Büro
JVBl.	=	Justizverwaltungsblatt, Zeitschrift
JW	=	Juristische Wochenschrift
JZ	=	Juristen-Zeitung
Kap.	=	Kapitel
KG	=	Kammergericht
KGJ	=	Jahrbuch für Entscheidungen des Kammergerichts in Sachen der freiwilligen Gerichtsbarkeit, in Kosten-, Stempel- und Strafsachen
km	=	Kilometer
KostÄndG	=	Gesetz zur Änderung und Ergänzung kostenrechtlicher Vorschriften
KostO	=	Kostenordnung
KostVfg	=	Kostenverfügung
KOV	=	Kriegsopferversorgung, Zeitschrift
KV	=	Die Krankenversicherung, Zeitschrift
LAG	=	Landesarbeitsgericht
LG	=	Landgericht
LSG	=	Landessozialgericht
MDR	=	Monatsschrift für Deutsches Recht, Zeitschrift
MinBl. Fin.	=	Ministerialblatt des Bundesministers der Finanzen
Mitt. BfA	=	Die Angestelltenversicherung, Mitteilungen der Bundesversicherungsanstalt für Angestellte, jetzt DAngVers
Nachw.	=	Nachweis
Nds. MinBl.	=	Ministerialblatt von Niedersachsen
NdsRpfl.	=	Niedersächsische Rechtspflege
n. F.	=	neue Fassung
NJ	=	Neue Justiz, Zeitschrift
NJW	=	Neue Juristische Wochenschrift, Zeitschrift
NotVO	=	Notverordnung
Nr.	=	Nummer
OGZ	=	Entscheidungen des Obersten Gerichts der Deutschen Demokratischen Republik in Zivilsachen
RAGebO	=	Gebührenordnung für Rechtsanwälte
RAO	=	Reichsrechtsanwaltsordnung
RBB	=	Reichshaushalts- und Besoldungsblatt
RG	=	Reichsgericht
RGBl.	=	Reichsgesetzblatt
RGZ	=	Entscheidungen des Reichsgerichts in Zivilsachen
RhPfMinBl.	=	Ministerialblatt von Rheinland-Pfalz
RJM	=	Reichsminister der Justiz
RKG	=	Gesetz über Reisekostenvergütung der Beamten
RMF	=	Reichsminister der Finanzen
RMinBl.	=	Reichsministerialblatt. Zentralblatt für das Deutsche Reich
Rpfleger	=	Der Deutsche Rechtspfleger, Zeitschrift
RpflG	=	Rechtspflegergesetz

RStBl.	= Reichssteuerblatt
RVO	= Reichsversicherungsordnung
RZBl.	= Reichszollblatt
SG	= Sozialgericht
SGb	= Die Sozialgerichtsbarkeit, Zeitschrift
SGb (Beil.)	= Der Sozialrichter, Beilage der Zeitschrift Die Sozialgerichtsbarkeit
SGG	= Sozialgerichtsgesetz in der Bekanntmachung der Neufassung vom 23. 8. 1958 (BGBl. I 613)
s. o.	= siehe oben
sog.	= sogenannt
SozR	= Sozialrecht, Rechtsprechung und Schrifttum, bearbeitet von den Richtern des Bundessozialgerichts
SozVers.	= Die Sozialversicherung, Zeitschrift
StGB	= Strafgesetzbuch
StNotVO	= Steuernotverordnung
StPO	= Strafprozeßordnung
s. u.	= siehe unten
UStDB	= Durchführungsbestimmungen zum Umsatzsteuergesetz
UStG	= Umsatzsteuergesetz
usw.	= und so weiter
u. U.	= unter Umständen
VdN	= Verfolgter des Naziregimes
Verb.	= Verbindung
VerfO	= Anordnung über das Verfahren für die Sozialversicherung bei der Deutschen Versicherungs-Anstalt. — Verfahrensordnung —
vgl.	= vergleiche
v. H.	= vom Hundert
VO	= Verordnung
VO über PauschGeb	= VO über die Höhe der von Körperschaften und Anstalten des öffentlichen Rechts gemäß § 184 des SGG zu entrichtenden Gebühr
VOBl.	= Verordnungsblatt für Berlin (Ost)
Vorbem.	= Vorbemerkung
VwVG	= Verwaltungs-Vollstreckungsgesetz
VwVKostO	= Kostenordnung zum Verwaltungs-Vollstreckungsgesetz
VwZG	= Verwaltungszustellungsgesetz
WährG	= Erstes Gesetz zur Neuordnung des Geldwesens (Währungsgesetz) vom 20. 6. 1948 (= Gesetz Nr. 61 der Amerikanischen und der Britischen Militärregierung)
WzS	= Wege zur Sozialversicherung, Zeitschrift
z. B.	= zum Beispiel
Z. f. Fürsorge	= Zeitschrift für Fürsorge
ZfS	= Zentralblatt für Sozialversicherung und Versorgung, Zeitschrift
ZPO	= Zivilprozeßordnung
ZuSEG	= Gesetz über die Entschädigung von Zeugen und Sachverständigen
ZuSGebO	= Gebührenordnung für Zeugen und Sachverständige
zust.	= zustimmend
ZVG	= Zwangsversteigerungsgesetz

Literaturverzeichnis

Ambrosius, Das Reisekostenrecht, 6. Aufl.
Bauer, Gesetze über die Entschädigung der Zeugen, Sachverständigen und ehrenamtlichen Beisitzer bei den Gerichten
Bauer, Gerichtsvollzieherkostengesetz
Baumbach-Lauterbach, Kostengesetze, 13. Aufl.
Baumbach-Lauterbach, Zivilprozeßordnung, 25. Aufl.
Brangsch, Die Bundesgebührenordnung für Rechtsanwälte
Brocke, Der Sozialrichter
Brocke-Reese, Die Entschädigung von Beisitzern, Zeugen und Sachverständigen
Brocke-Reese, Gebühren- und Kostenrecht der Sozialgerichtsbarkeit (mit Anhang)
Dietz-Nikisch, Arbeitsgerichtsgesetz
Gaedeke, Armenanwaltskostengesetz
Gelinsky-Meyer, Armenanwaltskosten, 4. Aufl. (mit 2 Nachträgen)
Gerold, Bundesgebührenordnung für Rechtsanwälte
Göttlich, Bundesgebührenordnung für Rechtsanwälte, 7. Aufl.
Hastler, Aufbau und Verfahren der Sozialgerichtsbarkeit
Hofmann-Schroeter, Sozialgerichtsgesetz, 2. Aufl. (mit Nachtrag)
Keidel, Gesetz über die Angelegenheiten der freiwilligen Gerichtsbarkeit, 6. Aufl.
Kunz-Paul, Das arbeitsgerichtliche Verfahren
Lorenz, Die Verjährung in der deutschen Strafgesetzgebung
Luetgebrune-Lotze, Bundesgebührenordnung für Rechtsanwälte
Martini, Bundesgebührenordnung für Rechtsanwälte
Mellwitz, Sozialgerichtsgesetz (mit Ergänzungsband)
Meyer-Höver, Gesetz über die Entschädigung von Zeugen und Sachverständigen, 11. Aufl.
Miesbach-Ankenbrank, Sozialgerichtsgesetz, 2. Aufl.
Peters-Sautter-Wolff, Kommentar zur Sozialgerichtsbarkeit
Riedel-Sußbauer, Bundesgebührenordnung für Rechtsanwälte
v. Rosen-v. Hoewel, Verwaltungsvollstreckungsgesetz und Verwaltungszustellungsgesetz
Sauerwein, Das Sozialgerichtsgesetz und seine Anwendung, 2. Aufl.
Schatte, Verwaltungsgerichtliches Kostenrecht
Schoop-Geiling, Beitreibungsrecht der Abgabenverwaltung
Schumann, Bundesgebührenordnung für Rechtsanwälte
Sölch-Ringleb, Umsatzsteuergesetz

Stein-Jonas-Schönke, Zivilprozeßordnung, 18. Aufl.
Swolana, Bundesgebührenordnung für Rechtsanwälte
Thannheiser-Wende-Zech, Handbuch des Bundesversorgungsrechts, 3. Aufl., Bd. 2
Tschischgale, Kostenrecht in Arbeitssachen
Tschischgale, Kostenrecht in Zivilsachen
Wieczorek, ZPO und Nebengesetze
Willenbücher, Das Kostenfestsetzungsverfahren und die deutsche Gebührenordnung für Rechtsanwälte, 15. Aufl. (mit Nachtrag)
Zöller, Zivilprozeßordnung, 8. Aufl.

Erstes Kapitel

Die Auferlegung von Verfahrenskosten

SGG: §§ 102, 140, 144 Abs. 2, §§ 156, 172, 173, 174, 175, 176, 177, 192, 193 Abs. 1, §§ 194, 195
ZPO: § 100

§ 102 SGG

Klagerücknahme und Kostenentscheidung

Der Kläger kann die Klage bis zum Schluß der mündlichen Verhandlung zurücknehmen. Die Klagerücknahme erledigt den Rechtsstreit in der Hauptsache. Auf Antrag ist diese Wirkung durch Beschluß auszusprechen und, soweit Kosten entstanden sind, über diese zu entscheiden.

§ 140 SGG

Ergänzung des Urteils insbesondere bei Übergehung des Kostenpunktes

(1) Hat das Urteil einen von einem Beteiligten erhobenen Anspruch oder den Kostenpunkt ganz oder teilweise übergangen, so wird es auf Antrag nachträglich ergänzt. Die Entscheidung muß binnen eines Monats nach Zustellung des Urteils beantragt werden.

(2) Über den Antrag wird in einem besonderen Verfahren entschieden. Die Entscheidung ergeht, wenn es sich nur um den Kostenpunkt handelt, durch Beschluß, der lediglich mit der Entscheidung in der Hauptsache angefochten werden kann, im übrigen durch Urteil, das mit dem bei dem übergangenen Anspruch zulässigen Rechtsmittel angefochten werden kann.

(3) Die mündliche Verhandlung hat nur den nicht erledigten Teil des Rechtsstreits zum Gegenstand.

(4) Die ergänzende Entscheidung wird auf der Urschrift des Urteils und den Ausfertigungen vermerkt.

§ 144 Abs. 2 SGG

Ausschluß der Berufung gegen Kostenurteile

Die Berufung ist ferner nicht zulässig, wenn es sich um Kosten des Verfahrens handelt.

§ 156 SGG

Berufungsrücknahme und Kostenentscheidung

(1) Die Berufung kann bis zum Schluß der mündlichen Verhandlung zurückgenommen werden.

(2) Die Zurücknahme bewirkt den Verlust des Rechtsmittels. Über die Kosten entscheidet das Gericht auf Antrag durch Beschluß.

§ 172 SGG

Zulässigkeit der Beschwerde

(1) Gegen die Entscheidungen der Sozialgerichte mit Ausnahme der Urteile und gegen Entscheidungen der Vorsitzenden dieser Gerichte mit Ausnahme der Vorbescheide findet die Beschwerde an das Landessozialgericht statt, soweit nicht in diesem Gesetz anderes bestimmt ist.

(2) Prozeßleitende Verfügungen, Aufklärungsanordnungen, Vertagungsbeschlüsse, Fristbestimmungen, Beweisbeschlüsse, Beschlüsse über Ablehnung von Beweisanträgen, über Verbindung und Trennung von Verfahren und Ansprüchen können nicht mit der Beschwerde angefochten werden.

§ 173 SGG

Beschwerdefrist und -form

Die Beschwerde ist binnen eines Monats nach Bekanntgabe der Entscheidung beim Sozialgericht schriftlich oder zur Niederschrift des Urkundsbeamten der Geschäftsstelle einzulegen; § 181 des Gerichtsverfassungsgesetzes bleibt unberührt. Die Belehrung über das Beschwerderecht ist auch mündlich möglich; sie ist dann aktenkundig zu machen.

§ 174 SGG

Abhilferecht bei Beschwerdeeinlegung

Hält das Sozialgericht oder der Vorsitzende, dessen Entscheidung angefochten wird, die Beschwerde für begründet, so ist ihr abzuhelfen; sonst ist sie unverzüglich unter Benachrichtigung der Beteiligten dem Landessozialgericht vorzulegen.

§ 175 SGG

Aufschiebende Wirkung der Beschwerde

Die Beschwerde hat aufschiebende Wirkung, wenn sie die Festsetzung einer Strafe zum Gegenstand hat. Soweit dieses Gesetz auf Vorschriften der Zivilprozeßordnung und des Gerichtsverfassungsgesetzes verweist, regelt sich die aufschiebende Wirkung nach diesen Gesetzen. Das Gericht oder der Vorsitzende, dessen Entscheidung angefochten wird, kann bestimmen, daß der Vollzug der angefochtenen Entscheidung einstweilen auszusetzen ist.

§ 176 SGG

Beschwerdeentscheidung

Über die Beschwerde entscheidet das Landessozialgericht durch Beschluß.

§ 177 SGG

Ausschluß der Beschwerde gegen Entscheidungen des Landessozialgerichts

Entscheidungen des Landessozialgerichts oder seines Vorsitzenden können mit der Beschwerde nicht angefochten werden.

§ 192 SGG

Auferlegung von Mutwillenskosten

Hat ein Beteiligter, dessen Vertreter oder Bevollmächtigter durch Mutwillen, Verschleppung oder Irreführung dem Gericht oder einem Beteiligten Kosten verursacht, so kann sie das Gericht dem Beteiligten im Urteil ganz oder teilweise auferlegen. § 193 Abs. 1 gilt entsprechend.

§ 193 Abs. 1 SGG

Auferlegung der Kostenerstattungspflicht

Das Gericht hat im Urteil zu entscheiden, ob und in welchem Umfange die Beteiligten einander Kosten zu erstatten haben; es entscheidet auf Antrag durch Beschluß, wenn das Verfahren anders beendet wird.

§ 194 SGG

Mehrheit von Kostenschuldnern

Sind mehrere Beteiligte kostenpflichtig, so gilt § 100 der Zivilprozeßordnung entsprechend. Die Kosten können ihnen als Gesamtschuldnern auferlegt werden, wenn das Streitverhältnis ihnen gegenüber nur einheitlich entschieden werden kann.

§ 195 SGG

Kostentragung bei Vergleich

Wird der Rechtsstreit durch gerichtlichen Vergleich erledigt und haben die Beteiligten keine Bestimmung über die Kosten getroffen, so trägt jeder Beteiligte seine Kosten.

§ 100 ZPO

Mehrheit von Kostenerstattungspflichtigen

(1) Besteht der unterliegende Teil aus mehreren Personen, so haften sie für die Kostenerstattung nach Kopfteilen.

(2) Bei einer erheblichen Verschiedenheit der Beteiligung am Rechtsstreit kann nach dem Ermessen des Gerichts die Beteiligung zum Maßstab genommen werden.

(3) Hat ein Streitgenosse ein besonderes Angriffs- oder Verteidigungsmittel geltend gemacht, so haften die übrigen Streitgenossen nicht für die dadurch veranlaßten Kosten.

(4) Werden mehrere Beklagte als Gesamtschuldner verurteilt, so haften sie auch für die Kostenerstattung, unbeschadet der Vorschrift des Abs. 3, als Gesamtschuldner. Die Vorschriften des bürgerlichen Rechts, nach denen sich diese Haftung auf die im Abs. 3 bezeichneten Kosten erstreckt, bleiben unberührt.

Übersicht

1. Die **Kostengrundentscheidung**, die zu Lasten eines am Streitverfahren Beteiligten, nicht jedoch seines Vertreters oder Bevollmächtigten, ergehen kann, zerfällt gegebenenfalls in zwei Teile. Sie kann sich verhalten:

a) über Kosten, die dem Gericht verursacht sind, **und**

b) über Kosten, die dem oder einem anderen Beteiligten erwachsen sind.

Sie kann aber auch nur über die Kosten zu a oder zu b ergehen. Was jeweils beabsichtigt ist, muß vom Gericht eindeutig ausgesprochen werden (vgl. §§ 192, 193 Abs. 1 SGG).

2. **Voraussetzung** für die Auferlegung der Kosten in der zu 1 aufgeführten Weise ist grundsätzlich: Der zu belastende Beteiligte, sein Vertreter oder sein Bevollmächtigter muß durch Mutwillen, Verschleppung oder Irreführung dem Betroffenen, d. h. dem Gericht bzw. dem gegnerischen Beteiligten, Kosten verursacht haben (§ 192 SGG).

a) Wer **Beteiligter** ist, ergibt sich aus § 69 SGG. Es ist entweder der Kläger oder der Beklagte oder der Beigeladene.

Behörden und **Körperschaften** sowie **Anstalten des öffentlichen Rechts** unterfallen, mögen sie aktiv oder passiv oder beigeladen beteiligt sein, keiner Ausnahme, vgl. LSG Nordrhein-Westfalen in Breith. 1956, 314; § 193 Abs. 4 SGG, der sich nur auf die Aufwendungen dieser Einrichtungen bezieht und sie für nicht erstattungsfähig erklärt, hat keine Allgemeinbedeutung und steht nicht entgegen. Auch **Bund** und **Länder** — in Angelegenheiten der Kriegsopferversorgung — sind gegebenenfalls einbezogen (vgl. Sauerwein, SGG Anm. zu § 192, a. A. LSG Berlin, SGb 1957, 305, nach welchem einer Partei, die Träger der Gerichtshaltungskosten ist, Mutwillenskosten nicht auferlegt werden können, mit zust. Anm. von Völcker).

Eine etwaige Bewilligung des **Armenrechts** führt zu keiner Ausnahme. Auch jemand, der nicht mutwillig sein Recht verfolgt (vgl. § 114 Abs. 1 Satz 1 ZPO), kann jedenfalls durch Verschleppung oder Irreführung Kosten verursachen oder sonst Veranlassung zur Kostentragung geben (a. A. Brocke-Reese, Geb. u. KostR Anm. 1 zu § 167 SGG).

b) Unter **Vertretern** sind grundsätzlich die gesetzlichen Vertreter zu verstehen (vgl. § 71 Abs. 2 bis 5 SGG).

Auch der nach § 72 Abs. 1 SGG für einen nicht prozeßfähigen Beteiligten ohne gesetzlichen Vertreter vom Vorsitzenden für das Verfahren bis zum Eintritt eines Vormunds oder Pflegers bestellte besondere Vertreter gehört dazu, ebenso der Sondervertreter nach § 72 Abs. 3 SGG (Bestellung eines solchen durch den Vorsitzenden, wenn der Aufenthaltsort eines Beteiligten oder seines gesetzlichen Vertreters vom Sitz des Gerichts weit entfernt ist und der Beteiligte oder der gesetzliche Vertreter zustimmt). Diese bestellten Vertreter haben keinen Entschädigungsanspruch an die Staatskasse, sondern — aus Geschäftsführung — nur einen Anspruch gegen den Vertretenen, insbesondere auf Ersatz der Auslagen.

Zu beachten ist, daß nach § 72 Abs. 4 SGG die Kosten des besonderen Vertreters jeweils als Kosten des vertretenen Beteiligten gelten.

c) **Bevollmächtigte** sind durch eine schriftliche oder eine zur Niederschrift des Gerichts gegebene Vollmacht ausgewiesene prozeßfähige Personen. Bei Ehegatten und Verwandten in gerader Linie kann die Bevollmächtigung unterstellt werden (§ 73 Abs. 1 Satz 1 und Abs. 2 SGG). Personen, die als ärztliche Gutachter für Beteiligte tätig gewesen sind, können nicht als Bevollmächtigte auftreten (§ 73 Abs. 1 Satz 2 SGG).

Rechtsanwälte können zu Bevollmächtigten bestellt werden (vgl. § 166 Abs. 2 letzter Satz, auch § 193 Abs. 3 SGG), ferner **Verbandsbeauftragte** (vgl. § 166 Abs. 2 Satz 1 SGG); außerhalb des BSG auch **Rechtsbeistände** (vgl. § 193 Abs. 3 SGG).

Beistände der Beteiligten stehen Bevollmächtigten grundsätzlich gleich (§ 73 Abs. 5 SGG).

Zu b und c. Das Verschulden seines Vertreters oder Bevollmächtigten muß sich der Beteiligte anrechnen lassen. Die Frage, ob und wieweit dieser die Schuldigen im Regreßwege in Anspruch nehmen kann, beantwortet sich nach dem materiellen Recht (vgl. §§ 276, 277, 675, 1664, 1833, 1915 BGB).

Der § 192 SGG schließt — ebenso wie der § 193 Abs. 1 SGG — den § 102 ZPO, der die Kostenauferlegung zu Lasten Dritter, insbesondere gesetzlicher Vertreter und Bevollmächtigter zuläßt, aus. Die Kostenregelung im Sozialgerichtsgesetz ist nämlich erschöpfend (vgl. LSG Nordrhein-Westfalen, MDR 1956, 444 und LSG Niedersachsen, Nds.Min.Bl. 1957, R S. 57; a. A. Schuch, KOV 1955, 152 und Wende, KOV 1955, 64).

d) **Mutwilligkeit** liegt vor bei bewußt unbeherrschtem oder beharrlichem Abweichen von dem, was ein verständig Handelnder im gleichen Falle tun würde (vgl. hierzu § 114 Abs. 1 Satz 1 letzter Teil, auch Satz 2 ZPO). Unbelehrsamkeit genügt bei Uneinsicht nicht. Ablehnung eines gerichtlichen Vergleichsvorschlags berechtigt nicht zur Auferlegung von Mutwillenskosten (LSG Berlin, SGb 1957, 305 mit zust. Anm. von Völcker).

Beispiel für Mutwilligkeit: Klage vor Anmahnung, vgl. hierzu LSG Baden-Württemberg, SGb 1956, 232 und Krebs, SGb 1955, 292, ferner Glücklich, SGb 1956, 235 [236], der allerdings in zu weit gehender Weise jede unsorgfältige Prozeßverfolgung genügen läßt. Weiteres Beispiel: Bestehen auf einer Sachentscheidung trotz Nichteinhaltens der Rechtsmittelfrist, vgl. SG Münster, ArbA 1956, 53.

e) **Verschleppung** ist die bewußte und gewollte Verzögerung des Verfahrens. Bloße Nachlässigkeit beim Vorbringen von Angriffs- oder Verteidigungsmitteln genügt grundsätzlich nicht (vgl. die Unterscheidung im § 279 Abs. 1 ZPO; a. A. Sauerwein, SGG Anm. zu § 192, der auch fahrlässiges Verhalten, Lässigkeit, genügen läßt).

f) **Irreführung** setzt Täuschungshandlung und -absicht voraus. Beispiel: Erschleichung des Armenrechts.

Zu d bis f. Es muß stets ein vorsätzlich schuldhaftes Verhalten auf seiten des kostenmäßig in Anspruch zu Nehmenden vorliegen. (Brocke-Reese, Geb. u. KostR Anm. III 4 zu § 192 SGG, lassen in großzügiger Weise auch Fahrlässigkeit genügen.) Auf den Ausgang des Verfahrens kommt es nicht an. Prüfung erfolgt jeweils für die Instanz (BSG, SozR SGG § 192 Bl. Da 2 Nr. 3).

Die Bewilligung des **Armenrechts** an den als erstattungspflichtig in Frage stehenden Beteiligten — mit der Wirkung der Stundung der Kosten — schließt die Auferlegung der Pflicht zur Kostentragung bzw. -erstattung nicht aus, vgl. § 202 SGG, § 117 ZPO. Anordnung der Nachzahlung der gestundeten Kosten nach § 202 SGG, § 125 ZPO ist daher als Voraussetzung nicht erforderlich.

g) Durch das wiedergegebene Verhalten müssen in notwendiger Weise konkrete Kosten verursacht sein.

So müssen als **Voraussetzung der Kostenauferlegung** dem Gericht Auslagen entstanden sein, sei es durch Aufwendungen für andere Beteiligte (vgl. § 191 SGG), durch Entschädigung von Zeugen oder Sachverständigen (§ 118 SGG, §§ 2, 3 und 5ff. ZuSEG; auch im Falle des § 109 SGG, falls die Vernehmung des benannten Sachverständigen von keiner Bevorschussung abhängig gemacht worden ist) oder durch Vergütung von Armenanwälten (vgl. § 167 SGG und §§ 121ff. BRAGebO).

Die Kosten brauchen — das gilt auch hinsichtlich der Erstattungspflicht gegenüber dem oder den anderen Beteiligten — an den Berechtigten noch nicht gezahlt zu sein; es genügt die ausgelöste rechtliche Verpflichtung zu ihrer Zahlung und das gesetzliche Feststehen ihrer Höhe.

Die Kosten können auch bei einem verweisenden Gericht entstanden sein (vgl. den § 98 Abs. 3 SGG mit seiner allgemeinen Bedeutung).

Die Kosten der **allgemeinen Gerichtshaltung** einschließlich der **Entschädigung der Sozialrichter** aller Rechtszüge, vgl. §§ 19, 35, 47 SGG, sind keine — besonders — verursachten Kosten im Sinne des § 192 SGG (ebenso: Brocke, Sozialrichter S. 177 und 178; Glücklich, SGb 1956, 235; Kurze, DAngVers 1958, 22; Peters-Sautter-Wolff, SGG § 192 Anm.; Wilde, ZfS 1954, 81, SGb 1956, 1 [3]; a. A.: Friederichs, WzS 1955, 45; Krebs, SGb 1955, 292; Schuch, KOV 1955, 152 sowie LSG Baden-Württemberg, SGb 1956, 232 und LSG Nordrhein-Westfalen, Breith. 1955, 559, ferner LSG Berlin, Breith. 1957, 579).

Voraussetzung der Erstattungspflicht gegenüber anderen Beteiligten ist, daß dem oder den gegenüberstehenden Beteiligten Kosten, z. B. Reisekosten, Vorgutachterkosten, Anwaltskosten oder auch Gerichtskosten nach § 184 SGG in notwendiger Weise — im Sinne einer zweckentsprechenden Rechtswahrung (vgl. § 193

Abs. 2 und 3 SGG) — erwachsen sind. (Hinsichtlich der Gerichtskosten nach § 184 SGG vgl. Brocke, SGb 1955, 323 [324] und Krebs, SGb 1955, 294, ferner LSG Schleswig, Breith. 1954, 1197, LSG Bayern, Mitt. BfA 1955, 72; a. A. hierzu Peters-Sautter-Wolff, SGG § 192 Anm.)

Sonderkosten (vgl. §§ 93, 120 Abs. 2 SGG) und **Strafen** im weitesten Sinn, d. h. auch mit Kostenaufbürdung (vgl. § 61 Abs. 1 SGG), sind keine zu Lasten eines anderen Beteiligten auferlegungs- oder erstattungsfähigen Kosten im Sinne der §§ 192, 193 SGG.

Die — außergerichtlichen — Aufwendungen der **Behörden,** der **Körperschaften** und **Anstalten des öffentlichen Rechts** sind ebenfalls insgesamt, einschließlich der Gebühren für etwa zugezogene Anwälte (vgl. BSG, SozR SGG § 193 Bl. Da 1 Nr. 2 = SGb 1957, 181 mit zust. Anm. von Völcker), keine auferlegbaren Kosten (vgl. § 193 Abs. 4 SGG; a. A. Brocke, SGb 1956, 248 [250], der jedoch nicht bedenkt, daß die Auferlegung außergerichtlicher Kosten bei versagter Erstattungsfähigkeit ohne Sinn ist). Gleiches hat auch für die allgemeinen Verwaltungskosten dieser Institutionen zu gelten. § 193 Abs. 4 SGG gilt auch bei Streitigkeiten von Behörden, Körperschaften und Anstalten untereinander.

3. Hinsichtlich der — ganzen oder teilweisen — **Erstattungspflicht** der Kosten eines anderen Beteiligten hat das Gericht gemäß § 193 Abs. 1 SGG über den Rahmen des § 192 SGG hinaus nach freiem Ermessen die Möglichkeit ihrer Anordnung in der zu treffenden Entscheidung (Urteil oder Beschluß s. u. 9a, b).

Die §§ 91 ff. ZPO haben dabei — das gilt allgemein — wegen der Verschiedenheit der kostenrechtlichen Struktur des ordentlichen und des sozialgerichtlichen Verfahrens trotz der Bezugnahme im § 202 SGG auf die Zivilprozeßordnung auszuscheiden (BSG, SozR SGG § 193 Bl. Da 1 Nr. 3). Auch eine richtungweisende Heranziehung der an sich kostenrechtlich allgemein bedeutsamen Bestimmungen der §§ 91a und 93 ZPO, wie überhaupt der Kostenvorschriften der Zivilprozeßordnung (vgl. insbesondere noch § 97 Abs. 2, § 278 Abs. 2) bei der Entscheidung über die Kostentragungs- und -erstattungspflicht ist grundsätzlich nicht möglich, da im Verfahren der Sozialgerichtsbarkeit abschließend eigens geartete Kostenvorschriften bestehen (ebenso BSG, SozR SGG § 193 Bl. Da 1 Nr. 3 und LSG Hamburg, SGb 1956, 59 mit im wesentlichen zust. Anm. von Schieren). Ein Beteiligter, sei er Säumender oder Unterlegener (i. w. S.), hat hier aus sozialen Gründen niemals schlechthin die entstandenen Kosten des Gegners zu erstatten. Das Gericht entscheidet vielmehr nach seinem pflichtgemäßen Ermessen, ob eine Kostenauferlegung sachlich gerechtfertigt sowie billig ist und daher zu erfolgen hat. Im sozialgerichtlichen Verfahren stehen sich nämlich die Beteiligten nicht als „kapitalistische Gegner" gegenüber. Auch die Vorschriften der Verwaltungsgerichtsbarkeit können keine Grundlage abgeben, weil das Sozialgerichtsverfahren ein ganz besonderes Verwaltungsgerichtsverfahren ist (vgl. § 1 SGG).

Mit Rücksicht auf den § 193 Abs. 4 SGG, der die Erstattungsfähigkeit der außergerichtlichen Aufwendungen der Behörden, der Körperschaften und Anstalten des öffentlichen Rechts grundsätzlich ausschließt, kommt der über den Rahmen des § 192 SGG hinausgehenden Erstattungspflicht des § 193 Abs. 1 SGG Bedeutung im wesentlichen nur zugunsten der beteiligten Versicherten oder Versorgungsberechtigten zu. Um aber im Allgemeininteresse eine zu große Belastung der Versicherungsträger zu vermeiden, ist den Versicherten oder Versorgungsberechtigten, denen ja in aller Regel keine nennenswerten außergerichtlichen Kosten entstehen, nur in besonderen Fällen ein Erstattungsanspruch nach § 193 SGG zuzusprechen. Diese Fälle sind grundlagenmäßig lediglich dann gegeben, wenn ein offensichtlich unbegründetes Vorgehen oder Widersprechen des öffentlich-rechtlichen Beteiligten vorliegt. Aus den gleichen Gesichtspunkten kann vom Gericht ausnahmsweise auch zugunsten der öffentlich-rechtlichen Beteiligten, falls ihre Einbeziehung oder Beiladung in völlig unberechtigter Weise erfolgt ist, die Erstattung der von diesen Beteiligten an das Gericht zu zahlenden Gerichtsgebühr des § 184 SGG dem betreffenden Beteiligten als Verursacher, hier — nach § 193 Abs. 1 SGG — ohne Rücksicht auf Verschulden im eigentlichen Sinne, auferlegt werden (vgl. Brocke, SGb 1955, 323 [324]).

Auch die Erstattung der Kosten des **Haupt- oder Nebenintervenienten** kann vom Gericht bei entsprechender Lage des Falles angeordnet werden.

Die Prüfung, ob und in welchem Umfange die Beteiligten einander Kosten zu erstatten haben, ist in jedem Falle **von Amts wegen** vorzunehmen (vgl. den Wortlaut des § 193 Abs. 1 SGG).

Die Bewilligung des **Armenrechts** an den als Erstattungspflichtigen in Frage Stehenden schließt die Auferlegung der Erstattungsverpflichtung auch nach § 193 Abs. 1 SGG nicht aus (vgl. § 202 SGG, § 117 ZPO). Anordnung der Kostennachzahlung entsprechend § 125 ZPO ist daher als Voraussetzung der Auferlegung der Erstattungspflicht aus § 193 Abs. 1 SGG nicht erforderlich.

4. Sind die zu 2 bzw. 3 behandelten Voraussetzungen jeweils nicht insgesamt erfüllt, ergeht **die Entscheidung** des Gerichts hinsichtlich der Gerichtskosten **gebührenfrei sowie ohne Auslagenaufbürdung** und bezüglich der außergerichtlichen Kosten **ohne** Auferlegung einer **Erstattungsverpflichtung.** Zum Kostenpunkt ist in der Entscheidung des Gerichts auf jeden Fall Stellung zu nehmen (vgl. § 192 letzter Satz, § 193 Abs. 1 SGG).

Liegen die Voraussetzungen (vgl. oben 2) nur in bezug auf Kosten (Auslagen) des Gerichts vor, so ist lediglich diese Kostenauferlegung vorzunehmen. Entsprechendes gilt, wenn die Voraussetzungen (vgl. oben 2 bzw. 3) nur bezüglich der Kosten eines (oder mehrerer) gegenüberstehenden Beteiligten erfüllt sind; es ist dann lediglich die Erstattungsverpflichtung, je nach Grund und Umfang, zu Lasten des die Kosten verschuldenden bzw. verursachenden Beteiligten auszusprechen (s. o. 1).

Die Auferlegung einer **Verzögerungsgebühr** gemäß § 47 GKG ist niemals möglich, da diese Spezialbestimmung des GKG im Sozialgerichtsverfahren nicht gilt.

5. Einen **Sonderfall** stellen die Kosten dar, die durch gutachtliche Anhörung eines bestimmten Arztes des Versicherten oder Versorgungsberechtigten bzw. seiner Hinterbliebenen nach § 109 SGG dem Gericht entstanden sind (nur diese, nicht auch die Kosten des Antragstellers anläßlich der Beweisaufnahme); sie bleiben, falls der Antragsteller durch unanfechtbaren Gerichtsbeschluß (vgl. § 172 Abs. 2 SGG) für vorschußpflichtig — der Vorschuß muß der Höhe nach bestimmt sein, vgl. BSG, SGb 1956, 122 — erklärt worden ist, entweder (§ 109 Abs. 1 Satz 2 SGG ist Kannvorschrift) bei diesem haften oder sie werden — bei insbesondere positiver Bedeutung des Gutachtens für die Entscheidung — von der Staatskasse durch Ausspruch im Urteil oder in dem an seine Stelle tretenden Beschluß ganz oder teilweise unabwälzbar übernommen (§ 109 Abs. 1 Satz 2 SGG). Wegen der Anfechtung bei Ablehnung der beantragten Übernahme vgl. unten 9 a β und 9 b ε (nur zusammen mit dem Rechtsmittel in der Hauptsache oder der an seine Stelle tretenden Beschwerde).

Bei Übernahme der Kosten sind sie dem Antragssteller aus der Staatskasse zurückzuerstatten.

Übernahme dieser Kosten außerhalb des Urteils dürfte nicht möglich sein; jedenfalls wäre der ergehende Beschluß im Hinblick auf § 172 Abs. 2 SGG — er steht im Zusammenhang mit der zugrunde liegenden Beweisanordnung — nicht mit der Beschwerde anfechtbar (a. A. Brocke-Reese, Geb. u. KostR Anm. III 4 zu § 109 SGG, der im Verfahren vor dem Sozialgericht sogar dem im Zwischenverfahren nach § 109 SGG nicht unmittelbar beteiligten Gegner, wenn er nach § 184ff. SGG gebührenpflichtig ist, ein Beschwerderecht gewährt. Daß sich bei Übernahme der Kosten die zu zahlende Gebühr aus § 184 SGG u. U. erhöht, hat die am Hauptstreit beteiligte Körperschaft oder Anstalt des öffentlichen Rechts hinzunehmen; Prozeßrisiko).

6. „**Kann** auferlegen“: Freies Ermessen des Gerichts im Rahmen des Pflichtgemäßen entscheidet (vgl. § 193 Abs. 1 SGG, auf den im § 192 SGG ausdrücklich verwiesen wird). Abwägung aller in Frage kommenden Umstände ist erforderlich. Grad des Verschuldens bzw. der unbegründeten Verursachung ist von maßgebender Bedeutung. Die soziale Lage des gegebenenfalls zu Belastenden hat Berücksichtigung zu finden.

7. **Auferlegung der Kosten** erfolgt **ganz** oder **teilweise** (vgl. §§ 192 und 193 Abs. 1 SGG), entsprechend dem Verschulden oder der Unbegründetheit des Vorgehens des Kosten verursachenden Beteiligten unter Berücksichtigung sachlicher Billigkeit. Bei Auferlegung nicht aller Kosten empfiehlt sich zur Vermeidung von Schwierigkeiten bei der späteren Kostenansetzung oder -festsetzung, der ziffernmäßigen Ausfüllung, die genaue Angabe, welche Kostenaufwendungen dem Grunde nach zur Tragung oder Erstattung auferlegt werden, z. B. für das eingeholte Gutachten vom ... oder für den Bevollmächtigten des ... o. ä. (vgl. Reese, SGb 1956, 381).

Bei — ganzer oder teilweiser (s. den Vorabsatz) — Kostenauferlegung oder Anordnung der Erstattungspflicht unter Einschränkung der Höhe ist der Anteil in Bruchteilen festzusetzen; den Betrag der ausgelösten genauen Höhe setzt, wenn es sich um die Kosten eines Beteiligten handelt, in Ausfüllung der Kostengrundanordnung des Gerichts später der Urkundsbeamte des Gerichts des ersten Rechtszuges fest (§ 197 SGG). Die zu tragenden Gerichtsauslagen berechnet anschließend der Kostenbeamte des jeweils betroffenen Gerichts in auszustellenden Kostenbescheiden (vgl. hier das 4. Kap. 2); die Staatskasse ist ja nicht Beteiligte im Sinne der §§ 197, 69 SGG.

8. Sind **mehrere Beteiligte** (vgl. hierzu § 113 Abs. 1 SGG) kostenpflichtig (gemäß oben 2, 3), so gilt — kraft ausdrücklicher Bestimmung — der § 100 ZPO entsprechend (§ 194 SGG); d. h.:

a) Es tritt grundsätzlich Haftung nach Kopfteilen ein (§ 100 Abs. 1 ZPO).

b) Bei erheblicher Verschiedenheit der Beteiligung am Streit ist das Beteiligungsverhältnis Maßstab (§ 100 Abs. 2 ZPO).

c) Hat ein Streitgenosse ein besonderes Angriffs- oder Verteidigungsmittel geltend gemacht, so haftet er für die dadurch etwa verursachten Kosten im Zweifel (vgl. § 100 Abs. 4 letzter Satz ZPO) allein (§ 100 Abs. 3 ZPO).

Die Kosten können — pflichtgemäßes Ermessen entscheidet —, annähernd gleiche Beteiligung der Betreffenden am Streit und der Kostenverursachung vorausgesetzt, den Streitgenossen (vgl. §§ 74, 75 Abs. 2 SGG) über § 100 Abs. 4 ZPO

(Haftung als Gesamtschuldner auf Grund entsprechender Verurteilung in der Hauptsache) hinaus – ausdrücklich – als **Gesamtschuldnern** (gemäß § 421 BGB) auferlegt werden, wenn das Streitverhältnis ihnen gegenüber nur einheitlich entschieden werden kann (§ 194 Satz 2 SGG, vgl. § 62 ZPO).

Die **Auseinandersetzung** der Gesamtschuldner untereinander ist nicht Gegenstand der Entscheidung des Gerichts. Sachlich-rechtlich sind maßgebend die Vorschriften für das zwischen ihnen bestehende Rechtsverhältnis (vgl. Peters-Sautter-Wolff, SGG Anm. zu § 194 a. E.). Im Zweifel gilt § 426 Abs. 1 BGB.

9. Die **Kostenentscheidung** (oben nach 1 bis 3) erfolgt in jeder Instanz durch das erkennende Gericht regelmäßig:

a) Im **Urteil,** wo solches ergeht, nicht in einem besonderen Beschlusse, vgl. LSG Bayern, Breith. 1958, 594 (bei Verweisung an eine andere Gerichtsbarkeit – vgl. § 52 Abs. 3 SGG – vom verweisenden Gericht, bei Verweisung an ein anderes Sozialgericht – vgl. § 98 Abs. 3 SGG – von diesem). Die höhere Instanz kann auf zulässiges Rechtsmittel (s. u. β) auch die Kosten der Vorinstanz oder der gesamten unteren Verfahren regeln bzw. anders auferlegen, allerdings nicht unter Schlechterstellung des Rechtsmittelklägers.

α) **Vorbescheide** des Vorsitzenden (vgl. §§ 105, 158 Abs. 2, § 216 Abs. 1 Nr. 1 SGG) stehen insoweit Urteilen gleich (vgl. § 105 Abs. 2 letzter Satz SGG). Das gilt auch von den **Rechtsmittelverwerfungsbeschlüssen** nach § 169 und § 216 Abs. 1 Nr. 3a SGG (BSG, SozR SGG § 192 Bl. Da 1 Nr. 1). Ferner gilt dies in zweiter und dritter Instanz von **Zurückweisungsbeschlüssen** (anläßlich offenbarer Unbegründetheit des Rechtsmittels, vgl. § 216 Abs. 1 Nr. 3b und 4a SGG) und von **Sachentscheidungsbeschlüssen** (bei zweifelsfrei geklärter Lage, vgl. § 216 Abs. 1 Nr. 3c und 4b SGG).

β) **Anfechtung** des Kostenpunktes ist nur zusammen mit der Hauptsache bei Beschwer in ihr möglich, und zwar mit der Berufung (§ 149ff. SGG) oder der Revision (§ 162 SGG) in deren jeweiligem Rahmen. (Wegen der Rechtsmittelbelehrung und der Folgen ihrer Unterlassung oder ihrer unrichtigen Vornahme vgl. § 66 Abs. 1 und 2 SGG.)

§ 144 Abs. 2 SGG erklärt die Berufung ausdrücklich nicht für zulässig, wenn es sich lediglich um Kosten des Verfahrens handelt. Revision allein wegen der Kosten ist nach dem Inhalte des § 162 SGG, der die Voraussetzungen für die Zulässigkeit der Revision enthält, nicht möglich (vgl. BSG, SozR SGG § 192 Bl. Da 2 Nr. 2). Auf jeden Fall würde in dritter Instanz auf dem Wege über § 202 SGG der grundsätzliche § 99 Abs. 1 ZPO Anwendung finden müssen.

Allerdings ist Rechtsmittelanschließung (stets unselbständige) nur wegen der Kosten zulässig (vgl. OLG Nürnberg, NJW 1954, 1687 und BSG, SozR ZPO § 522a Bl. Da 1 Nr. 1, ferner Stein-Jonas-Schönke, ZPO 17. Aufl. Anm. III zu § 99).

Ebenso ist die im Schlußurteil getroffene Kostenentscheidung selbständig mit der Berufung oder Revision anfechtbar, wenn in zulässiger Weise das dazugehörige Teilurteil angefochten ist (vgl. BGH, NJW 1956, 912 und dazu Mellwitz, SGG Anm. 11 zu § 100).

Wegen der **Frist** und **Form der Berufung** vgl. § 151 SGG, **der Revision** §§ 164, **166** SGG: Bei der Revision besteht Erforderlichkeit der Begründung (Frist ein Monat) und grundsätzlich Anwaltszwang. Wegen der eventuellen Sprungrevision vgl. § 161 SGG.

Bei Nichtbelehrung oder unrichtiger Belehrung über das gegebene Rechtsmittel in der angefochtenen Entscheidung verlängert sich die Rechtsmittelfrist von einem Monat im Zweifel auf ein Jahr seit Zustellung (§ 66 Abs. 2 SGG); vgl. dazu Mellwitz, NJW 1958, 699.

Bezüglich der **Wiedereinsetzung** in den vorigen Stand wegen schuldloser Fristversäumnis vgl. die §§ 67 und 66 Abs. 2 SGG.

Hinsichtlich der zeitweiligen Möglichkeit (bis 31. 12. 1960) der Berufungs- und Revisionsentscheidung ohne Beteiligung der Landes- bzw. Bundessozialrichter vgl. den § 216 Abs. 1 Nr. 3 und 4 SGG. (Revisionsverwerfung ohne mündliche Verhandlung kann immer ohne Zuziehung der Bundessozialrichter erfolgen, vgl. § 169 letzter Satz SGG.)

Wegen der Möglichkeit einstweiliger **Aussetzung der Vollstreckung** in höherer Instanz vgl. § 199 Abs. 2 SGG.

Wird in der Berufungs- oder Revisionsinstanz das angefochtene Urteil aufgehoben und die Sache zu anderweiter Entscheidung zurückverwiesen, so kann das Rechtsmittelgericht, statt selbst eine Kostenentscheidung zu treffen, aussprechen, daß das untere Gericht über die Kosten des Rechtsmittelverfahrens mit zu entscheiden hat.

γ) Hat das (Schluß-)Urteil (vgl. dazu auch 9 a α) des Sozialgerichts, des Landessozialgerichts oder des Bundessozialgerichts den Kostenpunkt ganz oder teilweise übergangen, d. h. versehentlich nicht beachtet, so ist es auf Antrag nachträglich zu ergänzen (§ 140 Abs. 1 Satz 1 SGG). Die **Ergänzungsentscheidung** muß binnen eines Monats nach Zustellung des Urteils beantragt werden (Satz 2 aaO). Über den Antrag wird in einem besonderen Verfahren mit mündlicher Verhandlung grundsätzlich in voller Gerichtsbesetzung (vgl. Abs. 3 aaO) entschieden (§ 140 Abs. 2 Satz 1 SGG). Die Entscheidung ergeht durch zu begründenden (§ 142 Abs. 2 SGG) Beschluß, der lediglich mit der Entscheidung in der Hauptsache, nicht selbständig (vgl. auch § 144 Abs. 2 SGG), angefochten werden kann (§ 140 Abs. 2 Satz 2 SGG, s. o. 9 a β). Das letzte gilt auch, wenn noch andere Ansprüche übergangen worden sind. (Dann ist aber durch Urteil ergänzend zu entscheiden, § 140 Abs. 2 letzter Satzteil SGG.) Ist das Rechtsmittel in der Hauptsache nicht gegeben, so ist der Ergänzungsbeschluß unanfechtbar. Ist in zulässiger Weise, evtl. auf Grund Zulassung, in der Hauptsache Rechtsmittel eingelegt, so wird der ergänzte Kostenpunkt ohne weiteres mit umfaßt (vgl. Schroeder-Printzen, SGb 1956, 41 [43]).

Die ergänzende Entscheidung ist auf der Urschrift des Urteils (evtl. des Beschlusses s. u. b) und den Ausfertigungen zu vermerken (§ 140 Abs. 4 SGG).

δ) War die Kostenentscheidung beabsichtigt, ist sie aber irrtümlich nicht — oder nicht richtig — niedergelegt worden, kann berichtigende Ergänzung bzw. **Berichtigung** gemäß § 138 SGG durch Beschluß des Vorsitzenden erfolgen.

Der Beschluß, auch soweit er die Berichtigung ablehnt (das ist anders als im § 319 Abs. 3 ZPO), ist mangels gesetzlichen Ausschlusses grundsätzlich mit der Beschwerde nach § 172 Abs. 1 SGG anfechtbar, wenn er ein Urteil (Beschluß, vgl. § 142 Abs. 1 SGG) erster Instanz betrifft (so auch die Amtliche Begründung). Eine Mindestbeschwer ist nicht Voraussetzung. Wegen der Beschwerdefrist und -form vgl. §§ 173 und 66 Abs. 2 SGG. Bezüglich der Wiedereinsetzung bei schuldloser Fristversäumnis siehe § 67 SGG. Über die Beschwerde entscheidet bei Nichtabhilfe (vgl. § 174 SGG) ohne mündliche Verhandlung (§ 124 Abs. 3 SGG) auf Grund eigenen Ermessens (§ 128 Abs. 1 Satz 1 SGG) das Landessozialgericht in voller Besetzung (vgl. Brocke, Sozialrichter S. 156) durch zu begründenden (§ 142 Abs. 2 SGG), kostenfreien (§ 183 SGG) Beschluß endgültig (§§ 176 und 177 SGG). Die Berichtigung ist auf der Urschrift des Urteils und den Ausfertigungen zu vermerken.

Wegen Aussetzung der Vollstreckung bis zur Entscheidung vgl. in erster Instanz § 175 SGG und in zweiter Instanz § 199 Abs. 1 und 2 SGG.

Wegen der Belehrung über das Beschwerderecht siehe § 66 Abs. 1 SGG (schriftlich) und § 173 letzter Satz SGG (mündlich unter Aktenkundigmachung).

b) Ist das Verfahren anders als durch Urteil beendet worden, so wird — hier nur auf **Antrag** des gegenüberstehenden Beteiligten — durch **Beschluß** entschieden (§ 192 letzter Satz, § 193 Abs. 1 letzter Satz SGG).

Voraussetzung ist, daß auferlegbare Kosten entstanden sind (gemäß dem Prinzip der Rechtsschutznotwendigkeit, im § 102 Satz 2 SGG sogar ausdrücklich ausgesprochen). Daher hat allgemeine Nachprüfung durch das entscheidende Gericht zu erfolgen, ob die Entstehung entsprechender Kosten überhaupt in Frage steht, ebenso Brocke, SGb 1956, 279. (Die Festsetzung derselben erfolgt nach selbständiger Prüfung von Auslösung und Höhe stets durch den Urkundsbeamten gemäß § 197 SGG.)

α) Der Antrag ermöglicht bei Erfüllung der Voraussetzungen (s. o. 2) auch die Auferlegung von **Kosten** (Auslagen) **des Gerichts** (vgl. § 192 letzter Satz SGG).

β) **Anderweite Beendigung** erfolgt durch: angenommenes Anerkenntnis und Verzicht (Gegenteilsakt!) bezüglich des Hauptanspruchs (vgl. § 101 Abs. 2, §§ 153 und 165 SGG), Klagerücknahme (§ 102 SGG, insbes. letzter Satz 2. Teil) und Rechtsmittelrücknahme (§ 156 Abs. 1 und 2 Satz 2 und § 165 SGG), ferner bei sonstiger unstreitiger Erledigung der Hauptsache (vgl. hierzu Güldenpfennig, SGb 1957, 168).

Bei Klagerücknahme in höherer Instanz entfällt auch die jeweilige Entscheidung des unteren Gerichts die Kosten betreffend; über diese Kosten muß in der befaßten höheren Instanz gegebenenfalls erneut entschieden werden (vgl. § 102 Satz 3 SGG). Es genügt dabei die einmalige Antragstellung (s. o.).

Eine automatische Kostenentscheidung gegen den Anerkennenden, Verzichtenden oder Zurücknehmenden gibt es nicht; es gelten die Grundsätze der §§ 192, 193 Abs. 1 SGG, vgl. oben 2 und 3. Daher ist grundsätzlich auch keine entsprechende Anwendung der Kostenbestimmung des § 91a ZPO bei sonstiger Erledigung der Hauptsache möglich. Auch bei dieser kommen die Kostenvorschriften der §§ 192, 193 Abs. 1 SGG zur Anwendung (BSG, SozR SGG § 193 Bl. Da 1 Nr. 3 = NJW 1957, 765). Dabei ist grundlegend von dem im Zeitpunkt der Erledigung vorliegenden Sach- und Streitstand auszugehen (BSG, NJW 1957, 1334).

Bei gerichtlichem **Vergleichsabschluß** trägt im Zweifel jeder Beteiligte — nur — seine Kosten (§ 195 SGG, der dem § 98 ZPO entspricht). Hier entfällt die Möglichkeit der Gerichtskostenauferlegung nach § 192 SGG, wie überhaupt die Anwendung dieser Bestimmung ebenso wie der des § 193 Abs. 1 SGG. § 195 SGG hat auch für den außergerichtlichen Vergleich Geltung (a. A. Brocke-Reese, Geb. u. KostR Anm. 3 zu § 195 SGG).

Bei ausdrücklicher Regelung im Vergleich kann ein Beteiligter die Kosten eines anderen übernehmen (zu der theoretisch möglichen Übernahme von Kosten [Auslagen] des Gerichts wird sich kein Beteiligter freiwillig bereit finden).

Haben die Parteien im Vergleich die Kostenfrage ausdrücklich der gerichtlichen Entscheidung überlassen, so gelten die allgemeinen Bestimmungen der §§ 192, 193

Abs. 1 SGG (LSG Bayern, SGb 1956, 127 [128]; a. A. Brocke, SGb 1956, 279, der bei Vergleichsabschlüssen immer den § 195 SGG für maßgebend hält).

§ 195 SGG muß auch Anwendung finden, wenn Klage oder Rechtsmittel nachweislich auf Grund Vergleichs, der als solcher gegenseitiges Nachgeben verlangt (§ 779 BGB), zurückgenommen wird (ebenso Miesbach-Ankenbrank, SGG Anm. 2 zu § 195). Annahme des reinen Anerkenntnisses (vgl. § 101 Abs. 2 SGG) stellt keinen Vergleich dar (LSG Bayern, SGb 1956, 127 [128]).

γ) Die erforderliche **Antragstellung ist nicht fristgebunden**; sie unterliegt aber mit Rücksicht auf die Allgemeinherrschaft von Treu und Glauben, wie grundsätzlich alle materiellen und prozessualen Begehren, der Verwirkung (angemessene Frist etwa 10 bis 12 Monate seit Beendigung des Verfahrens in der Hauptsache).

δ) Die Entscheidung durch das befaßte Gericht erfolgt **ohne** obligatorische **mündliche Verhandlung** (§ 124 Abs. 3 SGG) grundsätzlich in voller Besetzung; der Kostenbeschluß tritt an die Stelle der regelmäßigen Kostenentscheidung im Urteil. Richtige Rechtsmittelbelehrung — schriftlich, § 66 Abs. 1 SGG oder mündlich unter Aktenkundigmachung, § 173 letzter Satz SGG — ist erforderlich.

ε) Anfechtung des bloßen Kostenbeschlusses erfolgt mit der **Beschwerde** gemäß § 172 Abs. 1 SGG, falls es sich um eine Entscheidung des Sozialgericht handelt (vgl. § 177 SGG). Der Gedanke des § 144 Abs. 2 SGG, nach welchem Kostenentscheidungen schlechthin nicht selbständig anfechtbar sind, gilt hier nicht (§ 144 Abs. 2 SGG ist eine Ausnahmebestimmung für die Berufung, die als solche nicht ausdehnend angewendet werden kann, ebenso LSG Hamburg, SGb 1956, 59 mit zust. Anm. von Schieren; a. A. Peters-Sautter-Wolff, SGG Anm. 1 zu § 193 a. E., die wohl die Beschwerde überhaupt nicht geben wollen).

Die Erweiterung einer beschränkt eingelegten Beschwerde nach Ablauf der Beschwerdefrist ist unzulässig.

Eine Anschlußbeschwerde gibt es nicht; die Beschwerdebestimmungen des SGG sind erschöpfend (vgl. Schroeder-Printzen, SGb 1957, 164).

Daß im Falle der Klagerücknahme auf Antrag des Gegners auch formell die Erledigung der Hauptsache auszusprechen ist (vgl .§ 102 Satz 3 SGG), ändert an der Zulässigkeit der Kostenbeschwerde nichts; es muß aber die volle Rücknahme der Klage erfolgt sein, sonst ist Anfechtung der Kostenentscheidung wie bei jeder Teilerledigung insgesamt nur zusammen mit der Hauptsache möglich.

Beschwerdefrist: ein Monat seit Zustellung gemäß § 63 SGG, vgl. § 173 SGG. Bei unterlassener oder unrichtiger Belehrung über das Rechtsmittel in der angefochtenen Entscheidung erstreckt sich die Beschwerdefrist auf ein Jahr (vgl. § 66 Abs. 2 Satz 1 SGG). Wegen Wiedereinsetzung in den vorigen Stand bei schuldloser Fristversäumnis vgl. § 67 SGG, ferner § 66 Abs. 2 SGG bei unterlassener oder unrichtiger Rechtsmittelbelehrung.

Beschwerdeform: schriftlich beim Sozialgericht oder zur Niederschrift des Urkundsbeamten der Geschäftsstelle des Sozialgerichts, d. h. es besteht kein Anwaltszwang (§ 173 SGG).

Beschwerdevoraussetzung: Zulässigkeit der Anfechtung der Hauptsache, falls in ihr eine Entscheidung ergangen wäre (vgl. §§ 144 bis 149 SGG, auch § 150 SGG). Der Beschwerte kann bei bloßer Kostenentscheidung nämlich nicht besser stehen als sonst, d. h. wenn in der Hauptsache entschieden worden wäre (LSG Bayern, SGb 1956, 127 mit insoweit zust. Anm. von Brocke). Im Falle des § 150 Nr. 1 SGG, der — hypothetisch — die erledigte Hauptsache betrifft, braucht nicht auch die

Zulassung der Beschwerde ausgesprochen zu werden (a. A. Brocke, SGb 1956, 128 [129]). Bei mehreren Kostenbeschwerten kann, selbst wenn sie in der Hauptsache notwendige Streitgenossen (vgl. § 74 SGG) und Gesamtkostenschuldner (§ 194 Satz 2 SGG) sind, jeder Beschwerde einlegen, aber stets nur für sich. (Die Kostenauferlegung ist immer individuell.)

Das Vorliegen einer Mindestbeschwer von 50,01 DM ist nicht erforderlich. § 567 Abs. 2 ZPO gilt trotz des auf die Zivilprozeßordnung verweisenden § 202 SGG nicht, da die Kosten im Sozialgerichtsgesetz besonders, und zwar erschöpfend, geregelt sind (ebenso die herrschende Ansicht, vgl. LSG Bayern, SGb 1956, 127 mit zust. Anm. von Brocke, ferner Wagner, NJW 1956, 902 und Kostensenat des LSG Berlin 8/LSG/5/55 B, erwähnt in NJW 1956, 902).

Ein Kostenbeschluß, der fälschlich mit über die streitige Erledigung der Hauptsache und damit auch über diese entscheidet, ist im Hinblick auf § 150 Nr. 2 SGG mit der Berufung anfechtbar; er stellt nämlich inhaltlich ein Urteil dar (a. A. Brocke, SGb 1956, 128 [130], der hier, und zwar uneingeschränkt, die Beschwerde zuläßt).

Bei zulässiger Beschwerdeeinlegung, die keine aufschiebende Wirkung hat (vgl. § 175 Satz 1, 2 SGG), kann nach § 175 Satz 3 SGG das Gericht oder sein Vorsitzender, dessen Entscheidung angefochten wird, den Vollzug der angefochtenen Anordnung bis zur Entscheidung über die Beschwerde einstweilen — gegen oder ohne Sicherheitsleistung — aussetzen. Ähnliche Befugnisse hat nach § 199 Abs. 2 SGG — hier sind die Entscheidungen unanfechtbar, vgl. §§ 177 und 199 Abs. 2 Satz 4 SGG — auch der Vorsitzende des Beschwerdegerichts. (Mellwitz, SGG Anm. 6 zu § 175 hält auch die — positiven oder negativen — Aussetzungsentscheidungen des unteren [Sozial-]Gerichts bzw. seines Vorsitzenden für unanfechtbar, obwohl hier keine Einschränkung der Anfechtbarkeit besteht.)

Die Beschwerde kann zurückgenommen werden, im Zweifel mit der Wirkung des endgültigen Verlustes des Rechtsmittels.

Das Beschwerdegericht — das Landessozialgericht mit allen Mitgliedern — entscheidet, falls keine hier zulässige Abhilfe (§ 174 SGG) durch das untere Gericht — in jeweiliger entsprechender Besetzung — erfolgt, durch kostenfreien (§ 183 SGG), zu begründenden (§ 142 Abs. 2 SGG) Beschluß (§ 176 SGG). Und zwar hat das Landessozialgericht die Kostenentscheidung stets in rechtlicher und tatsächlicher Beziehung nachzuprüfen, d. h. es muß eigenes Ermessen an die Stelle des Ermessens der Vorinstanz setzen (vgl. § 128 Abs. 1 Satz 1, § 142 Abs. 1 SGG), nicht etwa braucht es nur „revisionsmäßig" nachzuprüfen, ob keine Überschreitung des Ermessensrahmens vorliegt (so fälschlich LSG Bayern, SGb 1956, 127 [128] und ihm zustimmend Brocke, SGb 1956, 128 [130]). Schlechterstellung auf eigenes Rechtsmittel ist verboten (allgemeiner Grundsatz). Mündliche Verhandlung ist nicht erforderlich (§ 124 Abs. 3 SGG), wohl aber regelmäßig die Anhörung des Gegners. Die Zustellung des Beschlusses erfolgt formlos (vgl. § 63 Abs. 1 SGG).

Bei Aufhebung der Kostenentscheidung entfällt diese ganz, bei Abänderung zum entsprechenden Teil (hinsichtlich der Klagerücknahme in höherer Instanz vgl. oben b β). Der Abhilfebeschluß des Sozialgerichts eröffnet für den Gegner neu die Beschwerdefrist.

Das Landessozialgericht entscheidet in letzter Instanz (§ 177 SGG). Zurückverweisung, evtl. mit sachlicher Anweisung, ist dabei nicht ausgeschlossen, wenn sie auch im Hinblick auf die eintretende Verzögerung der Entscheidung im Sozialgerichtsverfahren nicht erwünscht ist. Gegebenenfalls ist die neue Entscheidung des Sozialgerichts wiederum beschwerdefähig.

c) Die §§ 192, 193 Abs. 1 SGG gelten auch, falls **sonstige Entscheidungen** ergehen — so im Anrufungs(Erinnerungs-)verfahren und in der Rechtsmittelinstanz einschließlich des Beschwerderechtszuges —; es muß also auch in ihnen vor allem bezüglich der gegenwärtigen Kosten zur Frage der evtl. Kostentragung und der Kostenerstattung zugunsten und, soweit prozessual zulässig, zu Lasten des Rechtsmittelklägers oder des Beschwerdeführers Stellung genommen werden (ebenso Friederichs, BB 1956, 276 Anm. 32; a. A. auf Grund zu enger Handhabung Brocke, SGb 1957, 359 [361]). Bei Zurückverweisung kann ausgesprochen werden, daß das untere Gericht über die Kosten des Rechtsmittelverfahrens mit zu entscheiden hat. Bezüglich der Kosten der Vorinstanzen vgl. oben 9a und bβ sowie ε gegen Ende.

Zweites Kapitel

Die Auferlegung von Strafen nebst Kosten

SGG: §§ 21, 61 Abs. 1, § 106 Abs. 2 und Abs. 3 Nr. 7, § 111 Abs. 1, §§ 118, 172, 173, 174, 175, 176, 177, 178, 202, 216 Abs. 1 Nr. 2
GVG: §§ 176, 177, 178, 179, 180, 181, 182, 183
ZPO: § 141 Abs. 3, §§ 380, 381, 390, 409, 411, 913

§ 21 SGG

Ordnungsstrafe gegen Sozialrichter

Der Vorsitzende kann gegen einen Sozialrichter, der sich der Erfüllung seiner Pflichten entzieht, insbesondere ohne genügende Entschuldigung nicht oder nicht rechtzeitig zu den Sitzungen erscheint, durch Beschluß eine Ordnungsstrafe in Geld verhängen und ihm die durch sein Verhalten verursachten Kosten auferlegen. Bei nachträglicher genügender Entschuldigung ist der Beschluß aufzuheben oder zu ändern. Gegen den Beschluß ist Beschwerde zulässig. Über die Beschwerde entscheidet die durch das Präsidium (§ 24) für jedes Geschäftsjahr im voraus bestimmte Kammer des Sozialgerichts endgültig. Vor der Entscheidung ist der Sozialrichter zu hören.

§ 61 Abs. 1 SGG

Sitzungspolizei

Für die Öffentlichkeit, Sitzungspolizei und Gerichtssprache gelten §§ 169, 172 bis 191 des Gerichtsverfassungsgesetzes entsprechend. Die Öffentlichkeit kann auch ausgeschlossen werden, wenn die Offenlegung der gesundheitlichen oder Familienverhältnisse für einen Beteiligten von erheblichem Nachteil sein könnte.

§ 106 Abs. 2 und Abs. 3 Nr. 7 SGG

Anordnung des persönlichen Erscheinens zur vorbereitenden Erörterung

(2) Der Vorsitzende hat bereits vor der mündlichen Verhandlung alle Maßnahmen zu treffen, die notwendig sind, um den Rechtsstreit möglichst in einer mündlichen Verhandlung zu erledigen.

(3) Zu diesem Zweck kann er insbesondere

7. einen Termin anberaumen, das persönliche Erscheinen der Beteiligten hierzu anordnen und den Sachverhalt mit diesen erörtern.

§ 111 Abs. 1 SGG

Anordnung des persönlichen Erscheinens

Der Vorsitzende kann das persönliche Erscheinen eines Beteiligten zur mündlichen Verhandlung anordnen sowie Zeugen und Sachverständige laden. Auf die Folgen des Ausbleibens ist dabei hinzuweisen.

§ 118 SGG

Beweisaufnahme

(1) Soweit dieses Gesetz nichts anderes bestimmt, sind auf die Beweisaufnahme § 160 Abs. 2 Nr. 3, §§ 358 bis 363, 365 bis 377, 380 bis 386, § 387 Abs. 1 und 2, §§ 388 bis 390, 392 bis 444, 478 bis 484 der Zivilprozeßordnung entsprechend anzuwenden. Die Entscheidung über die Rechtmäßigkeit der Weigerung nach § 387 der Zivilprozeßordnung ergeht durch Beschluß.

(2) Zeugen und Sachverständige werden nur beeidigt, wenn das Gericht dies im Hinblick auf die Bedeutung des Zeugnisses oder Gutachtens für die Entscheidung des Rechtsstreits für notwendig erachtet.

(3) Der Vorsitzende kann das Auftreten eines Prozeßbevollmächtigten untersagen, solange die Partei trotz Anordnung ihres persönlichen Erscheinens unbegründet ausgeblieben ist und hierdurch der Zweck der Anordnung vereitelt wird.

§ 172 SGG

Zulässigkeit der Beschwerde

(1) Gegen die Entscheidungen der Sozialgerichte mit Ausnahme der Urteile und gegen Entscheidungen der Vorsitzenden dieser Gerichte mit Ausnahme der Vorbescheide findet die Beschwerde an das Landessozialgericht statt, soweit nicht in diesem Gesetz anderes bestimmt ist.

(2) Prozeßleitende Verfügungen, Aufklärungsanordnungen, Vertagungsbeschlüsse, Fristbestimmungen, Beweisbeschlüsse, Beschlüsse über Ablehnung von Beweisanträgen, über Verbindung und Trennung von Verfahren und Ansprüchen können nicht mit der Beschwerde angefochten werden.

§ 173 SGG

Beschwerdefrist und -form

Die Beschwerde ist binnen eines Monats nach Bekanntgabe der Entscheidung beim Sozialgericht schriftlich oder zur Niederschrift des Urkundsbeamten der Geschäftsstelle einzulegen; § 181 des Gerichtsverfassungsgesetzes bleibt unberührt. Die Belehrung über das Beschwerderecht ist auch mündlich möglich; sie ist dann aktenkundig zu machen.

§ 174 SGG

Abhilferecht bei Beschwerdeeinlegung

Hält das Sozialgericht oder der Vorsitzende, dessen Entscheidung angefochten wird, die Beschwerde für begründet, so ist ihr abzuhelfen; sonst ist sie unverzüglich unter Benachrichtigung der Beteiligten dem Landessozialgericht vorzulegen.

§ 175 SGG

Aufschiebende Wirkung der Beschwerde

Die Beschwerde hat aufschiebende Wirkung, wenn sie die Festsetzung einer Strafe zum Gegenstand hat. Soweit dieses Gesetz auf Vorschriften der Zivilprozeßordnung und des Gerichtsverfassungsgesetzes verweist, regelt sich die aufschiebende Wirkung nach diesen Gesetzen. Das Gericht oder der Vorsitzende, dessen Entscheidung angefochten wird, kann bestimmen, daß der Vollzug der angefochtenen Entscheidung einstweilen auszusetzen ist.

§ 176 SGG

Beschwerdeentscheidung

Über die Beschwerde entscheidet das Landessozialgericht durch Beschluß.

§ 177 SGG

Ausschließung der Beschwerde gegen Entscheidungen des LSG

Entscheidungen des Landessozialgerichts oder seines Vorsitzenden können mit der Beschwerde nicht angefochten werden.

§ 178 SGG

Anrufung des Gerichts gegen Entscheidungen des ersuchten oder beauftragten Richters oder des Urkundsbeamten

Gegen die Entscheidungen des ersuchten oder beauftragten Richters oder des Urkundsbeamten kann binnen eines Monats nach Bekanntgabe das Gericht angerufen werden, das endgültig entscheidet. §§ 173 bis 175 gelten entsprechend.

§ 202 SGG

Entsprechende Anwendung der ZPO

Soweit dieses Gesetz keine Bestimmungen über das Verfahren enthält, sind das Gerichtsverfassungsgesetz und die Zivilprozeßordnung entsprechend anzuwenden, wenn die grundsätzlichen Unterschiede der beiden Verfahrensarten dies nicht ausschließen.

§ 216 Abs. 1 Nr. 2 SGG

Beschlußentscheidung ohne Laienbeisitzer

(1) Bis zum 31. Dezember 1960 kann

2. der Vorsitzende bei dem Sozialgericht, das Landessozialgericht ohne Zuziehung der Landessozialrichter und das Bundessozialgericht ohne Zuziehung der Bundessozialrichter außerhalb der mündlichen Verhandlung Beschlüsse erlassen, die der Entscheidung in der Sache selbst vorausgehen.

§ 176 GVG

Ordnungsgewalt des Vorsitzenden

Die Aufrechterhaltung der Ordnung in der Sitzung obliegt dem Vorsitzenden.

§ 177 GVG

Ungehorsamsstrafen

Parteien, Beschuldigte, Zeugen, Sachverständige oder bei der Verhandlung nicht beteiligte Personen, die den zur Aufrechterhaltung der Ordnung erlassenen Befehlen nicht gehorchen, können auf Beschluß des Gerichts aus dem Sitzungszimmer entfernt, auch zur Haft abgeführt und während einer in dem Beschluß zu bestimmenden Zeit, die vierundzwanzig Stunden nicht übersteigen darf, festgehalten werden.

§ 178 GVG

Ungebührstrafen

Das Gericht kann gegen Parteien, Beschuldigte, Zeugen, Sachverständige oder bei der Verhandlung nicht beteiligte Personen, die sich in der Sitzung einer Ungebühr schuldig machen, vorbehaltlich der strafgerichtlichen Verfolgung, eine Ordnungsstrafe in Geld oder bis zu drei Tagen Haft festsetzen und sofort vollstrecken lassen.

§ 179 GVG

Vollstreckung der Ordnungsstrafen

Die Vollstreckung der vorstehend bezeichneten Ordnungsstrafen hat der Vorsitzende unmittelbar zu veranlassen.

§ 180 GVG

Ordnungsgewalt des einzelnen Richters

Die in den §§ 176 bis 179 bezeichneten Befugnisse stehen auch einem einzelnen Richter bei der Vornahme von Amtshandlungen außerhalb der Sitzung zu.

§ 181 GVG

Rechtsmittel gegen Ordnungsstrafen

(1) Ist in den Fällen der §§ 178, 180 eine Ordnungsstrafe festgesetzt, so kann gegen die Entscheidung binnen der Frist von einer Woche nach ihrer Bekanntmachung Beschwerde eingelegt werden, sofern sie nicht von dem Bundesgerichtshof oder einem Oberlandesgericht getroffen ist.

(2) Die Beschwerde hat in dem Falle des § 178 keine aufschiebende Wirkung, in dem Falle des § 180 aufschiebende Wirkung.

(3) Über die Beschwerde entscheidet das Oberlandesgericht.

§ 182 GVG

Protokollierung der Ordnungsstrafe

Ist eine Ordnungsstrafe wegen Ungebühr festgesetzt oder eine Person zur Haft abgeführt oder eine bei der Verhandlung beteiligte Person entfernt worden, so ist der Beschluß des Gerichts und dessen Veranlassung in das Protokoll aufzunehmen.

§ 183 GVG

Maßnahmen bei strafbaren Handlungen

Wird eine strafbare Handlung in der Sitzung begangen, so hat das Gericht den Tatbestand festzustellen und der zuständigen Behörde das darüber aufgenommene Protokoll mitzuteilen. In geeigneten Fällen ist die vorläufige Festnahme des Täters zu verfügen.

§ 141 Abs. 3 ZPO

Ordnungsstrafe gegen Beteiligte

Bleibt die Partei im Termin aus, so können gegen sie die gleichen Strafen wie gegen einen im Vernehmungstermin nicht erschienenen Zeugen, jedoch mit Ausnahme der Haftstrafe, verhängt werden. Dies gilt nicht, wenn die Partei zur Verhandlung einen Vertreter entsendet, der zur Aufklärung des Tatbestandes in der Lage und zur Abgabe der gebotenen Erklärungen, insbesondere zu einem Vergleichsabschluß, ermächtigt ist. Die Partei ist auf die Folgen ihres Ausbleibens in der Ladung hinzuweisen.

§ 380 ZPO

Ordnungsstrafe gegen Zeugen

(1) Ein ordnungsmäßig geladener Zeuge, der nicht erscheint, ist, ohne daß es eines Antrages bedarf, in die durch das Ausbleiben verursachten Kosten sowie zu einer Ordnungsstrafe in Geld und für den Fall, daß diese nicht beigetrieben werden kann, zur Strafe der Haft bis zu sechs Wochen zu verurteilen.

(2) Im Falle wiederholten Ausbleibens ist die Strafe noch einmal zu erkennen, auch kann die zwangsweise Vorführung des Zeugen angeordnet werden.

(3) Gegen diese Beschlüsse findet die Beschwerde statt.

§ 381 ZPO

Unterlassung und Aufhebung der Bestrafung

(1) Die Verurteilung in Strafe und Kosten sowie die Anordnung der zwangsweisen Vorführung unterbleiben, wenn der Zeuge glaubhaft macht, daß ihm die Ladung nicht rechtzeitig zugegangen ist, oder wenn sein Ausbleiben genügend entschuldigt ist. Erfolgt die Glaubhaftmachung oder die genügende Entschuldigung nachträglich, so werden die gegen den Zeugen getroffenen Anordnungen wieder aufgehoben.

(2) Die Anzeigen und Gesuche des Zeugen können schriftlich oder zum Protokoll der Geschäftsstelle oder mündlich in dem zur Vernehmung bestimmten neuen Termin angebracht werden.

§ 390 ZPO

Zeugenbestrafung wegen Verweigerung der Aussage oder der Eidesleistung

(1) Wird das Zeugnis oder die Eidesleistung ohne Angabe eines Grundes oder, nachdem der vorgeschützte Grund rechtskräftig für unerheblich erklärt ist, verweigert, so ist der Zeuge, ohne daß es eines Antrages bedarf, in die durch die Weigerung verursachten Kosten sowie zu einer Ordnungsstrafe in Geld und für den Fall, daß diese nicht beigetrieben werden kann, zur Strafe der Haft bis zu sechs Wochen zu verurteilen.

(2) Im Falle wiederholter Weigerung ist auf Antrag zur Erzwingung des Zeugnisses die Haft anzuordnen, jedoch nicht über den Zeitpunkt der Beendigung des Prozesses in dem Rechtszuge hinaus. Die Vorschriften über die Haft im Zwangsvollstreckungsverfahren gelten entsprechend.

(3) Gegen die Beschlüsse findet die Beschwerde statt.

§ 409 ZPO

Ordnungsstrafe gegen Sachverständige

(1) Im Falle des Nichterscheinens oder der Weigerung eines zur Erstattung des Gutachtens verpflichteten Sachverständigen wird dieser

zum Ersatz der Kosten und zu einer Ordnungsstrafe in Geld verurteilt. Im Falle wiederholten Ungehorsams kann die Strafe noch einmal erkannt werden.

(2) Gegen den Beschluß findet Beschwerde statt.

§ 411 ZPO

Ordnungsstrafe gegen Sachverständige bei schriftlicher Begutachtung

(1) Wird schriftliche Begutachtung angeordnet, so hat der Sachverständige das von ihm unterschriebene Gutachten auf der Geschäftsstelle niederzulegen. Das Gericht kann ihm hierzu eine Frist bestimmen.

(2) Versäumt ein zur Erstattung des Gutachtens verpflichteter Sachverständiger die Frist, so kann er zu einer Ordnungsstrafe in Geld verurteilt werden. Der Straffestsetzung muß eine Strafandrohung unter Setzung einer Nachfrist vorausgehen. Im Falle wiederholter Fristversäumnis kann die Strafe in der gleichen Weise noch einmal erkannt werden. § 409 Abs. 2 gilt entsprechend.

(3) Das Gericht kann das Erscheinen des Sachverständigen anordnen, damit er das schriftliche Gutachten erläutere.

§ 913 ZPO

Dauer der Haftstrafe

Die Haft darf die Dauer von sechs Monaten nicht übersteigen. Nach Ablauf der sechs Monate wird der Schuldner von Amts wegen aus der Haft entlassen.

Übersicht

1. Nach § 61 Abs. 1 SGG gelten die Bestimmungen des Gerichtsverfassungsgesetzes über die **Sitzungspolizei** (§§ 176 bis 183 GVG) entsprechend.

2. Danach obliegt die Aufrechterhaltung der Ordnung in der Sitzung dem **Vorsitzenden** (§ 61 Abs. 1 SGG, § 176 GVG), dem das Gericht zur Seite steht.

3. Das Gericht (stets aller Rechtszüge), grundsätzlich in voller Besetzung, kann (nach pflichtgemäßem Ermessen) gegen Parteien (Beteiligte, nämlich Kläger, Beklagte und Beigeladene sowie ihre gesetzlichen oder sonstigen Vertreter, nicht aber ihre Anwälte), Zeugen und Sachverständige oder bei der Verhandlung nicht beteiligte Personen, die sich in der Sitzung einer **Ungebühr** schuldig machen, vorbehaltlich der strafgerichtlichen Verfolgung, eine **Ordnungsstrafe** in Geld in Höhe von 1 bis 1000 DM (vgl. Art. II, XIV Abs. 2 Nr. 3 der VO über Vermögensstrafen und Bußen vom 6. 2. 1924 — RGBl. I 44 — i. d. F. der VO vom 12. 12. 1924 — RGBl. I 775 — in Verb. mit § 2 des WährG) oder bis zu drei Tagen Haft festsetzen und sofort vollstrecken lassen (§ 61 Abs. 1 SGG, § 178 GVG). Maßgebend für die Höhe der Strafe ist, wie in allen derartigen Fällen, einmal die Schwere der Tat und zum anderen Male die wirtschaftliche Lage des Täters. Für den Fall der Nichtbeitreibbarkeit der Geldstrafe ist hilfsweise Haftstrafe — bis zu drei Tagen — zulässig (vgl. KGJ 51, 442). Bei mehrfacher Ungebühr ist Verhängung entsprechend mehrerer Ordnungsstrafen jeweils bis zum Höchstbetrag zulässig (vgl. Baumbach-Lauterbach, ZPO 25. Aufl. Anm. 3B zu § 178 GVG).

In der Ungebühr wird vielfach zugleich auch Ungehorsam zu sehen sein, da regelmäßig zur Aufrechterhaltung der Ordnung Befehle — des Vorsitzenden — vorliegen, mögen diese auch mehr oder minder nur allgemein gehalten sein.

4. **Parteien** (s. o. 3), **Zeugen** und **Sachverständige sowie** bei der Verhandlung **nicht beteiligte Personen,** die den zur Aufrechterhaltung der Ordnung erlassenen Befehlen nicht gehorchen, also **ungehorsam** sind, können (pflichtgemäßes Ermessen ist maßgebend) auf zu begründenden Beschluß des Gerichts

a) aus dem Sitzungszimmer entfernt werden oder
b) zur Haft abgeführt und während einer in dem Beschluß zu bestimmenden Zeit, die 24 Stunden nicht übersteigen darf, festgehalten werden (§ 61 Abs. 1 SGG, § 177 GVG).

Vgl. hierzu in verfahrensrechtlicher Hinsicht § 115 SGG: „Ist ein bei der Verhandlung Beteiligter zur Aufrechterhaltung der Ordnung von dem Ort der Verhandlung entfernt worden, so kann gegen ihn in gleicher Weise verfahren werden, als wenn er sich freiwillig entfernt hätte . . .“.

5. Liegt der Ungehorsam eines **Beteiligten** (vgl. § 69 SGG), dessen persönliches Erscheinen — zur Klärung der Prozeßfähigkeit oder vor allem des Sachverhalts — angeordnet worden ist (vgl. § 106 Abs. 3 Nr. 7, § 111 Abs. 1, § 112 Abs. 2 Satz 2 SGG), im unentschuldigten **Ausbleiben** ohne Bestellung eines geeigneten Vertreters oder — das hat sinngemäß zu gelten — in der **Verweigerung der** vom Gericht gewünschten **Aufklärung,** so kann gegen ihn vom Gericht die gleiche Strafe wie gegen einen im Vernehmungstermin nicht erschienenen Zeugen, jedoch mit Ausnahme der Haft, verhängt werden (vgl. § 141 Abs. 3 Satz 1 ZPO). Der Beteiligte ist auf die Folgen seines Ausbleibens in der Ladung hinzuweisen (vgl. § 141 Abs. 3 Satz 3 ZPO und § 111 Abs. 1 Satz 2 SGG). Der § 141 Abs. 3 ZPO gilt, und zwar auf dem Wege über § 202 SGG, auch im Verfahren der Sozialgerichtsbarkeit (ebenso Peters-Sautter-Wolff, SGG Anm. 2 zu § 11 und Teutsch, WzS 1954, 216; a. A. Mellwitz, SGG Anm. 5 zu § 111 und Schieckel, DOK 1954, 173). Nach § 141 Abs. 3 Satz 1 ZPO können dem zu bestrafenden Beteiligten auch oder nur die durch sein Verhalten entstehenden Kosten (des Gerichts oder eines — oder mehrerer — Beteiligten) — im Rahmen ihrer Erstattungsfähigkeit — auferlegt werden (vgl. Zöller, ZPO 8. Aufl. Anm. 3 zu § 141; a. A. Baumbach-Lauterbach, ZPO 25. Aufl. Anm. 4B zu

§ 141. Baumbach-Lauterbach beachtet nicht, daß das im § 141 Abs. 3 Satz 1 ZPO in der Mehrzahl gebrauchte Wort „Strafen“ auch die Verurteilung in die Kosten umfaßt). Wegen der Aufhebung der Bestrafung bei nachträglicher Entschuldigung s. u. 6.

Die Auferlegung einer **Verzögerungsstrafe** gemäß § 47 GKG ist nicht möglich, da diese Spezialbestimmung des GKG im Sozialgerichtsverfahren nicht gilt.

6. Ein ordnungsmäßig geladener **Zeuge** (die Einhaltung einer bestimmten Ladungsfrist ist nicht erforderlich, wohl aber einer nach der Sachlage angemessenen), der **nicht erscheint,** ist, ohne daß es eines Antrages bedarf, vom vernehmenden Gericht in die durch das Ausbleiben verursachten Kosten — im Rahmen ihrer Erstattungsfähigkeit (vor den Gerichten der Sozialgerichtsbarkeit kommen bare Auslagen des Gerichts durch Neuladung u. ä. und für die Beteiligten vor allem Arbeitsversäumnis in Betracht) — sowie zu einer Ordnungsstrafe in Geld von 1 bis 1000 DM (s. o. 3) und für den Fall, daß diese nicht beigetrieben werden kann, zur Strafe der Haft bis zu sechs Wochen zu „verurteilen“ (durch näher zu begründenden Beschluß), vgl. § 118 Abs. 1 SGG, § 380 Abs. 1 ZPO. Auferlegt werden kann dabei auch die Strafe oder die Kostenlast allein. Im Falle wiederholten Ausbleibens ist diese Bestrafung jeweils noch einmal auszusprechen, auch kann vom Gericht die zwangsweise Vorführung des Zeugen — durch den Gerichtswachtmeister — beschlossen und angeordnet werden (§ 118 Abs. 1 SGG, § 380 Abs. 2 ZPO).

Nach § 118 Abs. 1 SGG, § 381 ZPO unterbleibt die Verurteilung in Strafe und (oder) Kosten sowie die Anordnung der zwangsweisen Vorführung, wenn der Zeuge glaubhaft macht, daß ihm die Ladung nicht rechtzeitig zugegangen ist, oder wenn sein Ausbleiben sonst genügend entschuldigt ist. Erfolgt die Glaubhaftmachung oder die genügende Entschuldigung nachträglich, so werden die gegen den Zeugen getroffenen Anordnungen aufgehoben (§ 381 ZPO hat sinngemäß auch für Sachverständige und Beteiligte zu gelten).

Nach § 118 Abs. 1 SGG, § 390 ZPO ist, ohne daß es eines Antrages bedarf, der Zeuge, der sein **Zeugnis** oder die angeordnete **Eidesleistung** ohne Angabe eines Grundes oder nachdem der vorgeschützte Grund rechtskräftig durch Zwischenbescheid (anfechtbar — mit der Beschwerde des § 172 Abs. 1 SGG — nur bei Beschlüssen der Sozialgerichte) für unerheblich erklärt ist, **verweigert,** vom Gericht in die durch die Weigerung verursachten Kosten (s. o. 6) sowie zu einer Ordnungsstrafe in Geld von 1 bis 1000 DM und für den Fall, daß diese nicht beigetrieben werden kann, zur Strafe der Haft bis zu sechs Wochen — im Beschlußwege — zu „verurteilen“. Auferlegt werden kann dabei die Strafe oder die Kostenlast auch allein. Im Falle wiederholter Weigerung ist auf Antrag zur Erzwingung des jeweils verlangten Zeugnisses die Haft anzuordnen, jedoch nicht über den Zeitpunkt der Beendigung des Prozesses in dem Rechtszuge hinaus, längstens auf die Dauer von sechs Monaten (vgl. insoweit § 118 Abs. 1 SGG, § 390 Abs. 2 letzter Satz ZPO in Verb. mit § 913 ZPO).

7. Nach § 118 Abs. 1 SGG, § 409 ZPO wird ein ordnungsmäßig geladener **Sachverständiger,** der zur Gutachtenerstattung verpflichtet ist, im Falle des **Nichterscheinens** oder der **Verweigerung der Gutachtenerstattung** (nicht der etwa angeordneten Beeidigung) vom Gericht zum Ersatz der entstehenden Kosten — im Rahmen ihrer Erstattungsfähigkeit — und zu einer Ordnungsstrafe — nur — in Geld von 1 bis 1000 DM „verurteilt“ (s. o. 6). Auferlegt werden kann auch hier die Strafe oder die Kostenlast allein. Im Falle wiederholten Ungehorsams kann die Bestrafung jeweils noch einmal ausgesprochen werden.

Versäumt bei angeordneter schriftlicher Begutachtung der zur Erstattung des Gutachtens verpflichtete **Sachverständige** die ihm zur Einreichung des Gutachtens (Niederlegung auf der Geschäftsstelle) vom Gericht **bestimmte Frist,** so kann er vom Gericht (nach pflichtgemäßem Ermessen) — allein — zu einer Ordnungsstrafe in Geld von 1 bis 1000 DM „verurteilt" werden. (Wegen der Verurteilung zur Tragung der durch die Säumnis entstehenden Kosten vgl. § 409 ZPO, s. hier den Vorabsatz.) Der Straffestsetzung muß eine Strafandrohung unter Setzung einer Nachfrist vorausgehen. Im Falle wiederholter Fristversäumnis kann die Strafe in der gleichen Weise jeweils noch einmal auferlegt werden.

8. Bis zum 31. 12. 1960 kann **an Stelle des Gerichts** der Vorsitzende bei dem Sozialgericht allein, das Landessozialgericht ohne Zuziehung der Landessozialrichter und das Bundessozialgericht ohne Zuziehung der Bundessozialrichter außerhalb der mündlichen Verhandlung Strafbeschlüsse erlassen (vgl. § 216 Abs. 1 Nr. 2 SGG).

9. Die Vollstreckung der Ungebühr- und der Ungehorsamsstrafen (auch hinsichtlich der Ersatzfreiheitsstrafe) hat stets der Vorsitzende unmittelbar zu veranlassen (vgl. § 61 Abs. 1 SGG, § 179 GVG).

Die **Vollstreckung der Strafen** erfolgt gemäß § 200 SGG (vgl. auch § 201 SGG) nach den Bestimmungen des Verwaltungsvollstreckungsgesetzes. Die Verjährungsfrist für die Strafvollstreckung beträgt, da es sich um eine Art von Unrechtsstrafen handelt, entsprechend § 70 Abs. 1 Nr. 5 StGB (unter Berücksichtigung der allgemeinen Mindestfrist des § 8 GKG) fünf Jahre seit Rechtskraft des Strafbeschlusses (vgl. Lorenz, Die Verjährung in der deutschen Strafgesetzgebung S. 16). Die Strafgelder fließen den Ländern der befaßten Gerichte bzw., in dritter Instanz, dem Bunde zu.

Die zu ersetzenden, dem Gericht entstandenen Kosten werden gegebenenfalls vom Urkundsbeamten der betreffenden Instanz unter Aufmachung der Höhe in einem Kostenbescheid zum Ansatz gebracht (vgl. hierzu das 4. Kap. 2, auch hinsichtlich der wegen der Höhe möglichen Anrufung des befaßten Gerichts durch den Bestraften und die ihm gegenüberstehende Staatskasse). Sie werden ebenfalls nach dem Verwaltungsvollstreckungsgesetz beigetrieben. Die einem Beteiligten zu ersetzenden Kosten werden in Ausfüllung der richterlichen Grundentscheidung vom Urkundsbeamten des Gerichts erster Instanz gemäß § 197 SGG der genauen Höhe nach festgesetzt (vgl. hierzu das 6. Kap. 6ff., auch hinsichtlich der wegen der Höhe möglichen Anrufung des Gerichts der ersten Instanz durch den Bestraften und den nach dem Strafbeschluß kostenforderungsberechtigten Beteiligten). Der Kostenfestsetzungsbeschluß stellt einen Vollstreckungstitel dar (vgl. § 199 Abs. 1 Nr. 3 SGG). Die Vollstreckung der festgesetzten Kosten zugunsten der öffentlichen Hand erfolgt nach dem Verwaltungsvollstreckungsgesetz (vgl. § 200 SGG), zugunsten privater Beteiligter nach der Zivilprozeßordnung (§ 198 SGG), vgl. hierzu das 9. Kap., insbes. I 2, IV. Zum Kostenansatz und zur Kostenfestsetzung ist die Rechtskraft des Strafbeschlusses erforderlich, soweit hier die Beschwerde aufschiebende Wirkung hat (siehe im einzelnen unten 12). Bei Aufhebung des Strafbeschlusses entfallen die Kosten.

10. Die in den §§ 176 bis 179 GVG, § 141 Abs. 3, §§ 380, 381, 390, 409, 411 ZPO bezeichneten **Befugnisse** stehen auch einem einzelnen **Richter** bei der Vornahme von Amtshandlungen selbst außerhalb der Sitzung zu (vgl. § 61 Abs. 1, § 118 Abs. 1 SGG, § 180 GVG).

Übt die Befugnisse im Rahmen der §§ 61 (Abs. 1), 118 (Abs. 1), 180 GVG der ersuchte oder der beauftragte Richter aus, so kommt gegen seine Entscheidung nur, und zwar innerhalb Monatsfrist seit Bekanntmachung, die Anrufung des sachbefaßten Prozeßgerichts durch den Bestraften in Betracht, das bei Nichtabhilfe endgültig entscheidet, auch wenn es sich um ein Sozialgericht handelt (vgl. § 178 SGG).

11. Die **Strafbeschlüsse** (auch wenn sie nur Kostenauferlegungen enthalten) sind, wenn sie nicht in Gegenwart des Betroffenen verkündet worden sind, **förmlich zuzustellen** (§ 63 Abs. 1 SGG). Rechtsmittelbelehrung hat zu erfolgen (§§ 66, 173 letzter Satz SGG). Einem kostenbegünstigten Beteiligten ist, wenn er bei der Verkündung nicht anwesend war, Abschrift zu erteilen.

12. Ist in den **Ungebührfällen der §§ 178 und 180 GVG** eine Ordnungsstrafe festgesetzt, so kann, sofern dies auf der Ebene des verfahrensbefaßten Sozialgerichts geschehen ist, grundsätzlich **Beschwerde** beim Landessozialgericht eingelegt werden (§ 61 Abs. 1 SGG, § 181 Abs. 1 GVG). Wegen der Ausnahmen bei Strafbeschlüssen des ersuchten oder beauftragten Richters s. o. 10.

Das gegebene Rechtsmittel (-behelf) hat nur in den Fällen des § 180 GVG aufschiebende Wirkung (§ 175 Satz 2 SGG, § 181 Abs. 2 GVG).

Zwar ist in dem die Beschwerde gewährenden § 181 Abs. 1 GVG der § 177 GVG (betreffend die Ungehorsamsstrafe) nicht erwähnt. Die Fälle der §§ 177, 178 GVG liegen ihrem Rechtscharakter nach im wesentlichen aber gleich (ebenso in den Wirkungen, vgl. § 115 SGG); die Anwendung des § 181 GVG (in entsprechender Weise) ist daher **auch** gegenüber **Ungehorsamsstrafen** geboten (so mit Recht Baumbach-Lauterbach, ZPO 25. Aufl. Anm. 2C zu § 177 GVG).

Die Einlegung der **Beschwerde** ist in diesen Fällen — es liegt eine im Sozialgerichtsgesetz selbst aufgeführte ausdrückliche Ausnahme vor — an eine **Frist von einer Woche** (nicht einem Monat) nach Bekanntmachung (Verkündung oder bei Abwesenheit des Bestraften: Zustellung) des Strafbeschlusses (bzw. seiner Ergänzungen) gebunden (§ 181 Abs. 1 GVG, § 173 Satz 1 2. Teil SGG).

Gegen die **Beschlüsse nach § 141 Abs. 3, §§ 380, 381, 390, 409 und 411 ZPO,** sofern sie von einem Sozialgericht als Prozeßgericht (oder seinem Vorsitzenden oder Richter) ausgehen, findet **binnen eines Monats** seit Verkündung bzw. Zustellung die **Beschwerde** an das übergeordnete Landessozialgericht statt (§ 141 Abs. 3 Satz 1, § 380 Abs. 3, § 390 Abs. 3, § 409 Abs. 2, § 411 Abs. 2 Satz 4 ZPO in Verb. mit § 118 Abs. 1 und § 202 SGG). Bei unterlassener oder unrichtiger Belehrung über das Rechtsmittel in der angefochtenen Entscheidung erstreckt sich in allen behandelten Fällen die Beschwerde (Anrufungs-)frist auf ein Jahr (vgl. § 66 Abs. 2 Satz 1 SGG). Das Rechtsmittel hat hier stets aufschiebende Wirkung (§ 175 Satz 2 SGG, § 572 Abs. 1 ZPO). Wegen der Entscheidungen des ersuchten oder beauftragten Richters vgl. oben 10.

Eine Anschlußbeschwerde (-anrufung) gibt es im Verfahren der Sozialgerichtsbarkeit in keinem Fall. Nach Ablauf der Einlegungsfrist kann die Beschwerde (Anrufung) keineswegs mehr erweitert werden. Die Beschwerde (bei Ordnungsstrafbeschlüssen des ersuchten oder beauftragten Richters die Anrufung nach § 178 SGG) kann sich stets sowohl gegen die Strafe wie auch gegen die Kostenauferlegung allein richten. Eine Mindestbeschwer wird niemals verlangt.

Die Strafbeschlüsse der höheren Gerichte der Sozialgerichtsbarkeit wie die sitzungspolizeilichen Anordnungen des Vorsitzenden (insoweit auch der Sozialgerichte) sind sachlich unanfechtbar.

13. Die **Beschwerde** (evtl. Anrufung) ist beim Sozialgericht **schriftlich** oder **zur Niederschrift** des Urkundsbeamten der Geschäftsstelle **einzulegen** (§ 173 Satz 1 SGG). Es besteht also in keiner Instanz Anwaltszwang.

14. **Beschwerde(anrufungs-)berechtigt** ist nur der jeweils **Bestrafte**. Die Beteiligten haben keinen Anspruch auf Kostenauferlegung zu ihren Gunsten, den sie mit der Beschwerde (evtl. Anrufung nach § 178 SGG) verfolgen könnten (a. A. Brocke-Reese, Geb. u. KostR Anm. III 1 zu § 390 ZPO). Entsprechendes hat für die Staatskasse zu gelten.

Zwischenzeitliche Vollstreckung der Strafe macht die Beschwerde (Anrufung) nicht unzulässig; der Bestrafte hat ein Recht darauf, seine Unschuld festgestellt zu erhalten. Zahlung mit zum Ausdruck gebrachter Anerkennung der Zahlungspflicht wird das Rechtsmittel (-behelf) allerdings ausschließen.

Im Rechtsmittel(-behelfs-)verfahren braucht der Gegner — die Staatskasse — nicht gehört zu werden.

15. Nach § 175 Satz 3 SGG kann — nach pflichtgemäßem Ermessen — das Gericht oder der Vorsitzende (Richter), dessen Entscheidung angefochten wird, in allen Fällen bestimmen, daß der gesetzlich nicht aufgeschobene **Vollzug** des angefochtenen Beschlusses **einstweilen**, grundsätzlich bis zur Rechtsmittelentscheidung, — mit oder ohne Sicherheitsleistung — **ausgesetzt** wird (vgl. auch § 572 Abs. 2 ZPO). Eine Anfechtung aller dieser Entscheidungen mit der Beschwerde ist, abgesehen vom Durchgreifen der §§ 177, 178 SGG, nicht ausgeschlossen.

Nach § 199 Abs. 2 SGG kann (ebenfalls nach pflichtgemäßem Ermessen) der Vorsitzende des Gerichts, das über das Rechtsmittel zu entscheiden hat (hier steht als Rechtsmittel nur die Beschwerde in Frage), die gesetzlich nicht aufgeschobene Vollstreckung durch einstweilige Anordnung aussetzen. Er kann die Aussetzung wie die Vollziehung der Vollstreckung von einer Sicherheitsleistung (vgl. die §§ 108, 109 und 113 ZPO) abhängig machen.

Die Anordnungsentscheidungen nach § 199 Abs. 2 SGG sind stets unanfechtbar (vgl. §§ 177, 199 Abs. 2 letzter Satz 1. Teil SGG); sie können aber — bei geänderter Lage — jederzeit aufgehoben werden (vgl. § 199 Abs. 2 letzter Satz 2. Teil SGG).

16. Das Sozialgericht oder sein tätig gewordener Vorsitzender bzw. Richter, dessen Entscheidung jeweils angefochten wird, kann der **Beschwerde abhelfen** (§ 174 Satz 1 1. Teil SGG). Die Abhilfe muß bei entsprechender Einsicht erfolgen.

17. **Über die Beschwerde entscheidet** ohne erforderliche mündliche Verhandlung (§ 124 Abs. 3 SGG) das **Landessozialgericht auf** Grund eigenen Ermessens (§ 128 Abs. 1 SGG) durch zu begründenden Beschluß (§ 142 Abs. 2 SGG) kostenfrei (§ 183 SGG). Eine Schlechterstellung des Beschwerdeführers ist nicht zulässig. Wegen der Einzelheiten des Beschwerdeverfahrens vgl. das 1. Kap. 9 b ε.

Bis zum 31. 12. 1960 kann hier das Landessozialgericht ohne Zuziehung der Landessozialrichter über die Beschwerde entscheiden (vgl. § 216 Abs. 1 Nr. 2 SGG). Entsprechendes gilt bezüglich der Entscheidung über die Anrufung für das Prozeßgericht (vgl. oben 10).

18. Ist eine Ordnungsstrafe wegen Ungebühr (§§ 178, 180 GVG) festgesetzt oder eine Person zur Haft abgeführt oder eine bei der Verhandlung beteiligte Person entfernt worden (§§ 177, 180 GVG), so ist der Beschluß des Gerichts und dessen Veranlassung in das **Protokoll aufzunehmen** (§ 61 Abs. 1 SGG, § 182 GVG).

Wird eine **strafbare Handlung** in der Sitzung begangen, so hat das Gericht den **Tatbestand festzustellen** und der zuständigen Behörde das darüber aufgenommene

Protokoll mitzuteilen. In geeigneten Fällen ist die vorläufige Festnahme des Täters (vgl. § 127 StPO) zu veranlassen (§ 61 Abs. 1 SGG, § 183 GVG).

19. Nach § 21 SGG (in den höheren Instanzen gilt entsprechendes, vgl. die §§ 35, 47 SGG) kann — nach pflichtgemäßem Ermessen — der Vorsitzende **gegen einen Sozialrichter** (Landessozialrichter, Bnndessozialrichter), der sich der Erfüllung seiner ihm gesetzlich obliegenden **Pflichten** — vorsätzlich oder fahrlässig — **entzieht,** insbesondere ohne genügende Entschuldigung nicht oder nicht rechtzeitig zu den Sitzungen erscheint, durch näher zu begründenden Beschluß eine **Ordnungsstrafe** in Geld von 1 bis 1000 DM (s. o. 3) verhängen. Maßgebend für die Höhe der Strafe ist die Schwere der Pflichtverletzung sowie die finanzielle Lage des zu Bestrafenden. Mehrfache Verhängung jeweils bis zum Höchstbetrage ist bei entsprechender Mehrheit von Verletzungen möglich. Gleichzeitig können — ebenfalls nach pflichtgemäßem Ermessen — dem betreffenden Sozialrichter die durch sein schuldhaftes Verhalten gegebenenfalls verursachten Kosten auferlegt werden. Gemeint können hier nur die Kosten des den Richter heranziehenden Gerichts sein, so die gerichtlichen Auslagen für die Herbeiholung eines Ersatzmannes, aber auch im Übermaß verauslagte Beträge, die vom Gericht an Beteiligte (vgl. § 191 SGG) oder Dritte (Zeugen oder Sachverständige) gezahlt werden mußten (ebenso Brocke-Reese, Geb. u. KostR Anm. I 2 zu § 21 SGG und Brocke, SGb 1956, 248). Da hier eine Ausfüllung der Höhe durch Kostenansatz in einem Leistungsbescheid des Urkundsbeamten nicht in Frage kommt — der Sozialrichter ist kein Gerichtskostenschuldner im eigentlichen Sinne —, ist die Höhe dieser Kosten sogleich im Strafbeschluß vom Richter auszuwerfen (a. A. Brocke-Reese, Geb. u. KostR Anm. III 2 zu § 21 SGG). Auferlegt kann auch die Strafe oder die Kostenlast allein werden. Bei nachträglicher Entschuldigung ist der Beschluß aufzuheben oder zu ändern (mildern). Für die Berichtigung offensichtlicher Fehler kommen, wie in allen solchen Fällen, die §§ 138, 142 Abs. 1 SGG in Betracht.

Gegen den Beschluß ist (vgl. § 21 Satz 3 SGG) binnen eines Monats seit Bekanntgabe (Zustellung, vgl. § 63 Abs. 1 in Verb. mit § 133 SGG) **Beschwerde** — nur — des betroffenen Sozialrichters in Gemäßheit der §§ 172ff. SGG gegeben (einzulegen stets schriftlich oder zu Protokoll der Geschäftsstelle). Die an eine Mindestbeschwer nicht gebundene Beschwerde kann sich auch allein gegen die Strafe oder die Auferlegung der Kosten richten. Bei Nichtabhilfe entscheidet über die Beschwerde die durch das Präsidium für jedes Geschäftsjahr nach den §§ 24, 36 bzw. 48 SGG im voraus bestimmte Kammer des Sozialgerichts (Senat des Landessozialgerichts bzw. des Bundessozialgerichts) ohne erforderliche mündliche Verhandlung (§ 124 Abs. 3 SGG) auf Grund eigenen Ermessens (§ 128 Abs. 1 SGG) endgültig, und zwar durch kostenfreien (§ 183 SGG), zu begründenden (§ 142 Abs. 2 SGG) Beschluß (vgl. hierzu auch die Ausführungen oben, insbes. 17). Das Gericht, bei dem der Laienrichter mitzuwirken berufen ist, ist mit den Gegebenheiten seiner inneren Organisation und seines Bezirkes am besten vertraut; es ist daher hier zum Beschwerdegericht bestimmt worden (so die Amtliche Begründung). Ist der Vorsitzende der Beschwerdekammer (des Beschwerdesenats) zugleich der den Strafbeschluß erlassende Vorsitzende, so darf er als „in erster Instanz" tätig gewordener Richter im Beschwerdeverfahren nicht mitwirken (vgl. § 60 Abs. 1 SGG, § 41 Nr. 6 ZPO). Vor der Beschwerdeentscheidung ist der Beschwerdeführer, der nicht schlechter gestellt werden darf, persönlich (regelmäßig schriftlich, vgl. § 62 SGG) zu hören. Über die gegebene Beschwerdemöglichkeit muß er, wie grundsätzlich im Verfahren der Sozialgerichtsbarkeit, belehrt werden (vgl. hierzu §§ 66, 173 letzter Satz SGG). Die Beschwerde hat aufschiebende Wirkung (§ 175 Satz 1 SGG).

Die Vollstreckung (nach dem Verwaltungsvollstreckungsgesetz) hat der bestrafende Vorsitzende zu veranlassen.

20. Über **Stundungen** einer Ordnungsstrafe hat der Vorsitzende bzw. der Einzelrichter (beauftragter oder ersuchter Richter) als Vollstreckungsbehörde zu entscheiden (vgl. das OLG Hamm, DGVZ 1958, 124). Die Stundung von auferlegten Gerichtsauslagen ist Sache der Gerichtskasse, von zu erstattenden Kosten des forderungsberechtigten Gläubigers. **Erlaß der Ordnungsstrafe** (einschließlich Gerichtsauslagen) ist im Rahmen der bestehenden Gnadenordnung möglich.

Drittes Kapitel

Der Streitwert und seine Festsetzung

SGG: §§ 149, 189 Abs. 2
VO über die Höhe der von Körperschaften und Anstalten des öffentlichen Rechts gemäß § 184 des SGG zu entrichtenden Gebühr (VO über PauschGeb.) vom 31.3.1955 (BGBl. I 180): § 2 Abs. 3

§ 149 SGG

Ausschluß der Berufung bei Ersatz- und Rückerstattungsstreitigkeiten aus Wertgründen

Die Berufung ist nicht zulässig bei Ersatz- oder Erstattungsstreitigkeiten zwischen Behörden oder Körperschaften des öffentlichen Rechts oder Anstalten des öffentlichen Rechts sowie bei Streitigkeiten wegen Rückerstattung von Leistungen, wenn der Beschwerdewert fünfhundert Deutsche Mark nicht übersteigt, ferner bei Streitigkeiten wegen Rückerstattung von Beiträgen, wenn der Beschwerdewert fünfzig Deutsche Mark nicht übersteigt.

§ 189 Abs. 2 SGG

Feststellung der zum Teil vom Streitwert abhängigen Pauschgebühr

Die Feststellung erfolgt durch den Urkundsbeamten der Geschäftsstelle. Gegen diese Feststellung kann binnen eines Monats nach Mitteilung das Gericht angerufen werden, das endgültig entscheidet.

§ 2 Abs. 3 VO über PauschGeb.

Ermäßigte Gebühren bei bestimmten Streitwerten

In Streitsachen, welche eine einmalige Leistung im Werte von mehr als 25 Deutsche Mark und weniger als 300 Deutsche Mark betreffen, ermäßigt sich die Gebühr nach Absatz 1 in jedem Rechtszuge auf 15 Deutsche Mark. Hat die Leistung einen Wert von 25 Deutsche Mark oder weniger, so beträgt die Gebühr höchstens die Hälfte der Streitsumme, mindestens aber 2 Deutsche Mark.

Der Streitwert und seine Festsetzung

Übersicht

Spezialabhandlung des Verfassers: Die Bedeutung der Streitwertfestsetzung im Sozialgerichtsverfahren, JR 1955, 379.

Die **Streitwertfestsetzung** hat bekanntlich einen Doppelcharakter. Sie ist in aller Regel von verfahrensrechtlicher Bedeutung, weil von ihrer Höhe die Zuständigkeit der Gerichte und die Zulässigkeit der Rechtsmittel gegen ihre Entscheidungen ganz oder mindestens teilweise abhängt, ferner bildet sie im allgemeinen die Grundlage der Kostenberechnung. In beiderlei Hinsicht spielt sie im Sozialgerichtsgesetz **kaum eine Rolle**. Dies hat folgenden Grund:

1. Im Sozialgerichtsverfahren bilden die Sozialgerichte stets die Eingangsinstanz (§ 8 SGG), und die Rechtsmittel (Beschwerde, Berufung und Revision) sind grundsätzlich **vom Streitwert** bzw. Beschwerdewert **unabhängig** (vgl. §§ 172ff., 144ff. und 162 SGG).

a) α) Eine **Ausnahme** stellt der § 149 SGG dar, nach welchem die **Berufung** bei Ersatz- oder Erstattungsstreitigkeiten (grundsätzlich auf Geld abzielend) zwischen Behörden oder Körperschaften oder Anstalten des öffentlichen Rechts sowie bei Streitigkeiten wegen wertmäßiger Rückerstattung von Leistungen — vorbehaltlich des § 150 SGG (Fälle der ausdrücklichen Zulassung oder des Vorliegens von Verfahrensmängeln) — **ausgeschlossen** ist, wenn jeweils der Beschwerdewert (d. h. die Beschwer = Unterschied zwischen positiv oder negativ Verlangtem und Zugesprochenem des einzelnen Urteils, evtl. mit Ergänzung) 500 DM nicht übersteigt (bei Haupt- und Hilfsanspruch entscheidet der höhere, es sei denn, daß nur die Abweisung des zuerkannten niedrigeren Hilfsantrages begehrt wird).

β) **Gleiches** gilt (letzter Teil des § 149 SGG) bei Streitigkeiten wegen Rückerstattung von Beiträgen, wenn der Beschwerdewert 50 DM nicht übersteigt.

b) Eine beschlußmäßige und als solche mit der Beschwerde nicht anfechtbare (vgl. § 177 SGG) **Streitwertfestsetzung** durch das Berufungsgericht wird sich in diesen Fällen **erübrigen,** weil die Streitsummen in erster und zweiter Instanz hier ziffernmäßig feststehen (vgl. Hofmann-Schroeter, SGG Nachtrag zur 2. Aufl. Anm. 3 zu § 149). Das hat auch mit Bezug auf die Grundlagen für entsprechende Feststellungsklagen nach § 55 SGG zu gelten. (Die Frage der richtigen Höhe des Streitwerts kann gegebenenfalls mit der Revision gegen das folgenmäßig positiv oder negativ ergehende Berufungsurteil zur entsprechenden [höchst-]gerichtlichen Nachprüfung gestellt werden).

2. Auch **für die Kostenberechnung** hat die Streitwertfestsetzung im Sozialgerichtsverfahren **keine** erhebliche **Bedeutung.** Gerichtsgebühren entstehen nämlich

nicht, da das Verfahren in allen Rechtszügen grundsätzlich kostenfrei ist (§ 183 SGG). Für die Rechtsanwälte sind in den einzelnen Instanzen Rahmengebühren ausgeworfen, die unabhängig vom Streitwert sind, auch was die Berechnung im jeweiligen Falle anbetrifft (§ 116 Abs. 2 BRAGebO).

a) Eine **Ausnahme** besteht allerdings auch hier. Nach § 184 SGG haben die Körperschaften oder Anstalten des öffentlichen Rechts für jede Streitsache, an der sie beteiligt sind, je Rechtszug eine Gebühr zu entrichten. Die Höhe der Gebühr ist, wie im § 184 Abs. 2 SGG vorgesehen, von der Bundesregierung mit Zustimmung des Bundesrates durch die VO über die Höhe der von Körperschaften und Anstalten des öffentlichen Rechts gemäß § 184 des SGG zu entrichtenden Gebühr (VO über PauschGeb) vom 31. 3. 1955 (BGBl. I 180) festgesetzt worden. Und zwar sind hier für die einzelnen Instanzen je Sache Festgebühren ausgeworfen worden (vgl. §§ 1, 2 Abs. 1 und 2 der VO). Im Absatz 3 des § 2 der VO über PauschGeb ist in Fällen, in denen keine Kosten für ärztliche Gutachten entstanden sind, ausnahmsweise für zwei Gruppen die Höhe der zu zahlenden Gebühr vom Streitwert der Instanz abhängig gemacht worden, soweit es sich um die Sozialgerichte und die Landessozialgerichte handelt.

α) In Streitsachen, welche eine **einmalige Leistung** (vgl. hierzu die Ausführungen im 4. Kap. 3k) im Werte **bis zu 25 DM** (instanzmäßig) betreffen, beträgt hier die Gebühr in jedem der ersten beiden Rechtszüge nur die Hälfte der (jeweiligen) Streitsumme, mindestens jedoch 2 DM.

β) In Streitsachen, welche eine **einmalige Leistung** im Werte **von mehr als 25 DM bis** zu einem Betrage von **weniger als 300 DM** (instanzmäßig) betreffen, beträgt die zu zahlende Gebühr in jedem Tatsachenrechtszuge nur 15 DM.

In diesen Fällen (zu α und β) ist, wenn eine begehrte Sachleistung im Streit steht, wie üblich, der **Wert festzustellen.** Die Bestimmung erfolgt entsprechend dem über § 202 SGG anzuwendenden § 3 ZPO nach freiem Ermessen, was eine Beweisaufnahme über den Wert der Leistung – es handelt sich insgesamt nur um niedrige oder jedenfalls nicht hohe Werte – grundsätzlich erübrigen dürfte. (Die Voraussetzungen der besonderen Streitwertbestimmungen der ZPO und des sie ergänzenden GKG sind hier nicht erfüllt.) Richtschnur im Rahmen des objektiv Möglichen muß, wie stets bei der Streitwertbemessung, das mehr oder minder ersichtliche Interesse des Klägers an der verlangten Leistung sein. (Die Körperschaften oder Anstalten des öffentlichen Rechts werden sich, jedenfalls überwiegend, in der Rolle der Beklagten befinden.)

b) α) Wie üblich wird der in Frage kommende, meist zutage liegende **Streitwert** in den erforderlichen Fällen **von dem** beim Kostenansatz von Amts wegen tätig werdenden **Urkundsbeamten** (sog. Kostenbeamten) der Geschäftsstelle des jeweils befaßten Gerichts „**angenommen**", der – vgl. § 189 Abs 2 SGG – die für die Sache zu zahlende Gebühr feststellt und die Gebühren abschnittsweise in einem Verzeichnis zusammenfaßt (§ 189 Abs. 1 SGG). Rechtsbehelfsbelehrung (schriftlich gemäß § 66 Abs. 1 SGG oder mündlich unter Aktenkundigmachung gemäß § 173 letzter Satz in Verb. mit § 178 letzter Satz SGG) ist erforderlich. Wegen der Folgen unterbliebener oder unrichtiger Belehrung vgl. § 66 Abs. 2 SGG; es erstreckt sich dann die Rechtsbehelfsfrist im Zweifel auf ein Jahr.

β) **Gegen die Feststellung** des Urkundsbeamten, d. h. gegebenenfalls vor allem gegen seine Streitwertannahme als Grundlage, **kann** binnen eines Monats nach Mitteilung (Zustellung gemäß § 63 Abs. 1 SGG) von der Körperschaft oder Anstalt des öffentlichen Rechts — bei zu hoher Annahme — oder von der durch den (Bezirks-)Revisor vertretenen Staatskasse — bei zu niedriger Annahme — **das Gericht** der betroffenen Instanz **angerufen werden**, vgl. § 189 Abs. 2 Satz 2, § 178 SGG. Wegen Wiedereinsetzung in den vorigen Stand bei schuldloser Fristversäumnis vgl. die §§ 67 und 66 Abs. 2 SGG.

Die Erweiterung einer begrenzten Anrufung nach Ablauf der Anrufungsfrist ist unzulässig.

Eine Anschlußanrufung gibt es nicht.

Rücknahme der Anrufung im Zweifel mit der Wirkung des endgültigen Verlustes des Rechtsbehelfs ist möglich.

Die Anrufung des Gerichts („Erinnerungs"einlegung), die nicht an eine Mindestbeschwer gebunden ist, hat schriftlich zu erfolgen; sie kann auch zur Niederschrift des Urkundsbeamten der Geschäftsstelle des sachbefaßten Gerichts erklärt werden, d. h. es ist Einlegung ohne Anwaltszwang selbst in dritter Instanz möglich (vgl. § 178 letzter Satz, § 173 Satz 1 SGG).

Der — jeweils zuständige — **Urkundsbeamte kann** der Anrufung **abhelfend entgegenkommen** (§§ 174, 178 letzter Satz SGG); er muß dies bei entsprechender Einsicht tun. Die Abhilfe eröffnet dem Gegner neu die Anrufungsfrist.

Das **Gericht** (vgl. dazu das 4. Kap. 31γ) **entscheidet** bei Nichtabhilfe ohne mündliche Verhandlung (§ 124 Abs. 3 SGG), aber regelmäßig nach Anhörung des Gegners, durch kostenfreien (§ 183 SGG), zu begründenden (§ 142 Abs. 2 SGG) Beschluß endgültig, vgl. § 189 Abs. 2 Satz 2 letzter Teil SGG. Mit Rücksicht auf diese Endgültigkeit ist ein etwa ergangener — den Urkundsbeamten bindender — formeller Streitwertfestsetzungsbeschluß des Gerichts, selbst wenn er von einem Sozialgericht stammt, nicht mit der Beschwerde anfechtbar, vgl. Peters-Sautter-Wolff, SGG Anm. 2 zu § 2 VO über PauschGeb.; a. A. Brocke-Reese, Geb. u. KostR Anm. III 4 zu § 2 VO über PauschGeb.

Nachprüfung auf die Anrufung erfolgt, und zwar gegebenenfalls auch in dritter Instanz, in rechtlicher und tatsächlicher Hinsicht, so daß eigenes Ermessen ausschlaggebend ist (§ 128 Abs. 1 Satz 1 in Verb. mit § 142 Abs. 1 SGG).

Obwohl stets der objektiv gerechtfertigte Streitwert zugrunde gelegt werden muß, wird aus rechtsstaatlichen Gründen auch hier eine Schlechterstellung des das Gericht Anrufenden nicht möglich sein. Umgekehrt wird grundsätzlich auch über die Grenze des Begehrten nicht hinausgegangen werden können.

Zurückverweisung (evtl. mit sachlicher Anweisung) an den Urkundsbeamten ist nicht ausgeschlossen, wegen der eintretenden Verzögerung der Entscheidung aber nicht angebracht. Gegen die nach einer Zurückverweisung ergehende neue Entscheidung kann vom nunmehr Beschwerten wiederum das Gericht angerufen werden. Die Entscheidung des Gerichts braucht, da sie unanfechtbar ist, nur formlos mitgeteilt zu werden (vgl. § 63 Abs. 1 SGG).

Ein berichtigendes Tätigwerden des Urkundsbeamten oder des Gerichts von Amts wegen — abgesehen von der Versehensberichtigung des § 138 SGG in entsprechender Anwendung, vgl. § 142 Abs. 1 SGG — ist nicht vorgesehen.

Ein — anweisendes — Eingreifen der Gerichtsverwaltung gegenüber dem Urkundsbeamten (oder gar dem Gericht) ist nicht zulässig; Abänderungen können von der Staatskasse ja im Wege der Anrufung des Gerichts erstrebt werden.

Viertes Kapitel

Die Gerichtskosten und ihre Festsetzung

SGG: §§ 93, 98 Abs. 3, §§ 109, 120, 178, 183, 184, 185, 186, 187, 188, 189, 190
VO über die Höhe der von Körperschaften und Anstalten des öffentlichen Rechts gemäß § 184 des SGG zu entrichtenden Gebühr (VO über PauschGeb.) vom 31. 3. 1955 (BGBl. I 180): §§ 1, 2
GKG: § 91 Abs. 3 bis 6

§ 93 SGG

Einreichung von Abschriften der Schriftsätze und kostenpflichtige Erstellung derartiger Abschriften

Der Klageschrift, den sonstigen Schriftsätzen und nach Möglichkeit den Unterlagen sind Abschriften für die Beteiligten beizufügen. Sind die erforderlichen Abschriften nicht eingereicht, so fordert das Gericht sie nachträglich an oder fertigt sie selbst an. Die Kosten für die Anfertigung können von dem Kläger eingezogen werden.

§ 98 Abs. 3 SGG

Kosten bei Verweisung

Soweit im Verfahren vor dem angegangenen Gericht Kosten entstanden sind, werden sie als Teil der Kosten behandelt, die bei dem im Beschluß bezeichneten Gericht entstehen.

§ 109 SGG

Anhörung eines bestimmten ärztlichen Sachverständigen, u. U. auf Kosten des Beweisführers

(1) Auf Antrag des Versicherten, des Versorgungsberechtigten oder Hinterbliebenen muß ein bestimmter Arzt gutachtlich gehört werden. Die Anhörung kann davon abhängig gemacht werden, daß der Antragsteller die Kosten vorschießt und vorbehaltlich einer anderen Entscheidung des Gerichts endgültig trägt.

(2) Das Gericht kann einen Antrag ablehnen, wenn durch die Zulassung die Erledigung des Rechtsstreits verzögert werden würde und der Antrag nach der freien Überzeugung des Gerichts in der Absicht, das Verfahren zu verschleppen, oder aus grober Nachlässigkeit nicht früher vorgebracht worden ist.

§ 120 SGG

Akteneinsicht und kostenpflichtige Erteilung von Abschriften

(1) Die Beteiligten haben das Recht der Einsicht in die Akten, soweit die übersendende Behörde dieses nicht ausschließt.

(2) Die Beteiligten können sich durch die Geschäftsstelle auf ihre Kosten Abschriften erteilen lassen.

(3) Der Vorsitzende kann aus besonderen Gründen die Einsicht in die Akten oder in Aktenteile sowie die Fertigung oder Erteilung von Auszügen und Abschriften versagen oder beschränken. Gegen die Versagung oder die Beschränkung der Akteneinsicht kann das Gericht angerufen werden; es entscheidet endgültig.

(4) Die Entwürfe zu Urteilen, Beschlüssen und Verfügungen, die zu ihrer Vorbereitung angefertigten Arbeiten sowie die Schriftstücke, welche Abstimmungen oder in dem anhängigen Verfahren Strafverfügungen betreffen, werden weder vorgelegt noch abschriftlich mitgeteilt.

§ 178 SGG

Anrufung des Gerichts bei Entscheidungen des ersuchten oder beauftragten Richters und des Urkundsbeamten

Gegen die Entscheidungen des ersuchten oder beauftragten Richters oder des Urkundsbeamten kann binnen eines Monats nach Bekanntgabe das Gericht angerufen werden, das endgültig entscheidet. §§ 173 bis 175 gelten entsprechend.

§ 183 SGG

Kostenfreiheit

Das Verfahren vor den Gerichten der Sozialgerichtsbarkeit ist kostenfrei, soweit nichts anderes bestimmt ist.

§ 184 SGG

Pauschgebühr der Körperschaften oder Anstalten des öffentlichen Rechtes

(1) Die Körperschaften oder Anstalten des öffentlichen Rechtes haben für jede Streitsache, an der sie beteiligt sind, eine Gebühr zu entrichten. Die Gebühr entsteht, sobald die Streitsache rechtshängig geworden ist; sie ist für jeden Rechtszug zu zahlen.

(2) Die Bundesregierung setzt die Höhe der Gebühr durch Rechtsverordnung fest, die der Zustimmung des Bundesrates bedarf.

§ 185 SGG

Fälligkeit der Pauschgebühr

Die Gebühr wird fällig, sobald die Streitsache durch Zurücknahme des Rechtsbehelfs, durch Vergleich, Anerkenntnis, Vorbescheid, Beschluß oder durch Urteil erledigt ist.

§ 186 SGG

Ermäßigung und Wegfall der Pauschgebühr

Wird eine Sache nicht durch Urteil erledigt, so ermäßigt sich die Gebühr auf die Hälfte. Die Gebühr entfällt, wenn die Erledigung auf einer Rechtsänderung beruht.

§ 187 SGG

Mehrere Schuldner der Pauschgebühr

Sind an einer Streitsache mehrere Körperschaften oder Anstalten des öffentlichen Rechtes beteiligt, so haben sie die Gebühr zu gleichen Teilen zu entrichten.

§ 188 SGG

Pauschgebühr bei Wiederaufnahme des Verfahrens

Wird ein durch rechtskräftiges Urteil abgeschlossenes Verfahren wieder aufgenommen, so ist das neue Verfahren eine besondere Streitsache.

§ 189 SGG

Verzeichnis der Pauschgebühren

(1) Die Gebühren für die Streitsachen werden in einem Verzeichnis zusammengestellt. Die Mitteilung eines Auszuges aus diesem Verzeichnis an die Körperschaften oder Anstalten des öffentlichen Rechtes gilt als Feststellung der Gebührenschuld und als Aufforderung, den Gebührenbetrag binnen eines Monats an die in der Mitteilung angegebene Stelle zu zahlen.

(2) Die Feststellung erfolgt durch den Urkundsbeamten der Geschäftsstelle. Gegen diese Feststellung kann binnen eines Monats nach Mitteilung das Gericht angerufen werden, das endgültig entscheidet.

§ 190 SGG

Niederschlagung und Unterlassung der Einziehung der Pauschgebühr

Die Präsidenten und die aufsichtführenden Richter der Gerichte der Sozialgerichtsbarkeit sind befugt, eine Gebühr, die durch unrichtige Behandlung der Sache ohne Schuld der gebührenpflichtigen Beteiligten entstanden ist, niederzuschlagen. Sie können von der Einziehung absehen, wenn sie mit Kosten oder Verwaltungsaufwand verknüpft ist, die in keinem Verhältnis zu der Einnahme stehen.

§ 1 VO über PauschGeb.

Höhe der Pauschgebühren

Die Höhe der Gebühr, welche die Körperschaften oder Anstalten des öffentlichen Rechts für jede Streitsache zu entrichten haben, an der sie beteiligt sind, wird für das Verfahren

vor den Sozialgerichten auf . . . . 60 Deutsche Mark,
vor den Landessozialgerichten auf . . . . 90 Deutsche Mark,
vor dem Bundessozialgericht auf . . . . . 120 Deutsche Mark

festgesetzt.

§ 2 VO über PauschGeb.

Ermäßigte Pauschgebühren

(1) Sind dem Gericht keine Kosten für ärztliche Gutachten entstanden, so ermäßigt sich die Gebühr des § 1 für das Verfahren

vor den Sozialgerichten auf . . . . 30 Deutsche Mark,
vor den Landessozialgerichten auf . . . . 40 Deutsche Mark.

(2) Die Ermäßigung nach Absatz 1 tritt auch ein, wenn lediglich

1. die in § 106 Abs. 3 Nr. 2 SGG bezeichneten Unterlagen beigezogen worden sind,
2. ein Arzt in der mündlichen Verhandlung zur Unterrichtung des Gerichts gehört worden ist.

(3) In Streitsachen, welche eine einmalige Leistung im Werte von mehr als 25 Deutsche Mark und weniger als 300 Deutsche Mark betreffen, ermäßigt sich die Gebühr nach Absatz 1 in jedem Rechtszug auf 15 Deutsche Mark. Hat die Leistung einen Wert von 25 Deutsche Mark oder weniger, so beträgt die Gebühr höchstens die Hälfte der Streitsumme, mindestens aber 2 Deutsche Mark.

§ 91 Abs. 3 bis 6 GKG

Schreibgebühren

(3) Die Schreibgebühr beträgt für die Seite, die 28 Zeilen von durchschnittlich 15 Silben enthält, 50 Deutsche Pfennig, auch wenn die Herstellung auf mechanischem Wege (ausgenommen durch Ablichtung) stattgefunden hat. Jede angefangene Seite wird als voll gerechnet.

(4) Für Schriftstücke, die in fremder Sprache abgefaßt sind, wird die doppelte Schreibgebühr erhoben.

(5) Für Schriftstücke in tabellarischer Form, Grundbuchblätter, Registerblätter, Verzeichnisse, Listen, Rechnungen, Zeichnungen und dgl. wird die Schreibgebühr nach dem Zeitaufwand berechnet, der bei durchschnittlicher Arbeitsleistung zur Herstellung benötigt wird. Sie beträgt für jede angefangene Viertelstunde 60 Deutsche Pfennig.

(6) Werden Abschriften durch Ablichtung hergestellt, so werden für jede Seite ohne Rücksicht auf Zeilen- und Silbenzahl 50 Deutsche Pfennig, bei größerem Format als DIN B 4 eine Deutsche Mark erhoben.

Übersicht

Spezialabhandlung des Verfassers: Die allgemeinen Änderungen des Gerichtskostengesetzes im Zuge der Kostenrechtsreform, JVBl. 1957, 121 [123]

Das Verfahren vor den Gerichten der Sozialgerichtsbarkeit ist grundsätzlich kosten-, d. h. **gebührenfrei** und **nicht auslagenersatzpflichtig** (§ 183 SGG). Damit entfällt von vornherein jede Vorschußpflicht des Antragstellers in allen Instanzen.

Die **Zwangsvollstreckung** gehört nicht zum Verfahren vor den Gerichten der Sozialgerichtsbarkeit; sie **ist** daher **kostenpflichtig.**

Vergleiche vor allem wegen der Abnahme des Offenbarungseides und der Vornahme von Forderungspfändungen § 40 Abs. 1 Nr. 4 und 5 und Abs. 3 und 4, § 42 Abs. 1 Nr. 2 GKG (Auslösung einer halben bzw. viertel Gebühr nach der Höhe des Vollstreckungsanspruchs in jedem abgrenzbaren Vollstreckungsverfahren, vgl. § 43 GKG).

Wegen der bei Pfändung von beweglichen Sachen entstehenden Gerichtsvollziehergebühren siehe hier das 9. Kap. II 8.

Hinsichtlich der Kosten der Zwangsvollstreckung in unbewegliches Vermögen sind hauptsächlich die Bestimmungen des 4. Abschnitts des GKG (§§ 60ff.) betreffend die Gebühren in Verfahren der Zwangsversteigerung und Zwangsverwaltung zu beachten.

Die **Sozialversicherungsträger** genießen, soweit sie Vollstreckungsgerichte im Wege der Amtshilfe in Anspruch nehmen müssen, Gebührenfreiheit (§ 115 RVO); wegen Auslagenersetzung vgl. allerdings § 117 daselbst. Die Gebührenfreiheit der Sozialversicherungsträger gilt richtigerweise auch für ein gegen den Schuldner erforderlich werdendes Konkursverfahren (a. A. LG Berlin und LG Hildesheim, Rpfleger 1953, 475ff. und Berges, BB 1954, 412).

Grundsätzlicher **Kostenschuldner** gegenüber dem Gericht in den Vollstreckungsverfahren ist jeweils der vorgehende Gläubiger. (Die Erstattungspflicht des Schuldners ergibt sich aus § 198 Abs. 1 SGG, § 788 Abs. 1 ZPO).

1. **Ausnahmen** von der Kostenfreiheit vor den Gerichten der Sozialgerichtsbarkeit bestehen, und zwar bezüglich Auslagen, in der folgenden Hinsicht:

a) Nach § 93 SGG können (nach freiem, im Rahmen des Pflichtgemäßen ausgeübtem Ermessen des die Kosten berechnenden Urkundsbeamten, d. h. des sog. Kostenbeamten) die **Kosten für die gerichtliche Anfertigung** von nicht eingereichten **Abschriften** der Klageschrift — eine Rechtsmittelschrift ist sinngemäß gleichzustellen — und der sonstigen (Klage oder Rechtsmittel begründenden) Schriftsätze, gegebenenfalls nebst Anlagen (Unterlagen), die für die Zustellung an den Gegner erforderlich sind, von dem Kläger (Rechtsmittelkläger) eingezogen werden. (Ihr Antrag auf Anfertigung wird auf Grund ihrer Säumnis bei Eilbedürftigkeit vom Gesetz unterstellt.) Ausschlaggebend für die Kostenpflicht wird vor allem die Beholfenheit oder Unbeholfenheit des jeweiligen Klägers sein.

Gegen die Ausdehnung der ausdrücklich auf den jeweiligen Kläger abgestellten Vorschrift des § 93 SGG auf die anderen Streitbeteiligten (vgl. Brocke-Reese, Geb. u. KostR Anm. 2 zu § 93 SGG) bestehen durchgreifende Bedenken, da Ausnahmevorschriften keiner ausdehnenden Auslegung und Anwendung fähig sind. Widerkläger und Anschlußrechtsmitteleinlegende sind allerdings auch Kläger.

Die **Höhe der Schreibgebühren** (richtiger -auslagen) ist nach dem „allgemeingültigen" und daher auch hier zugrunde zu legenden (vgl. Gölkel, ZfS 1957, 297 [298]) § 91 GKG zu berechnen. Das GKG stellt eine Ergänzung der ZPO dar; die Anwendung seiner einschlägigen allgemeinen Bestimmungen im Sozialgerichtsverfahren ist daher im Hinblick auf den § 202 SGG unbedenklich.

Die Schreibgebühr beträgt für die Seite (normal zu 28 Zeilen zu je 15 Silben) 0,50 DM, auch wenn die Herstellung auf mechanischem Wege (Druck u. ä., jedoch nicht Ablichtung) stattfindet. Jede angefangene Seite wird voll gerechnet.

Vgl. hierzu auch die einzelnen im allgemeinen auf dieser Grundlage ergangenen Verwaltungsgebührenordnungen der Länder.

Für Schreiben, die in fremder Sprache abgefaßt sind, ist die doppelte Gebühr vorgesehen. Für Schriftstücke in tabellarischer Form, Verzeichnisse, Listen, Rechnungen, Zeichnungen und dergleichen ist die Schreibgebühr nach dem durchschnittlichen Zeitaufwand zu berechnen; sie soll für jede angefangene Viertelstunde 0,60 DM betragen. Für Abschriften in Form der Ablichtung wird für jede abgelichtete Seite ohne Rücksicht auf Zeilen- und Silbenzahl 0,50 DM, bei größerem Format der Ablichtung als DIN B 4 1,— DM erhoben (vgl. hierzu insgesamt § 91 Abs. 3 bis 6 GKG).

b) Die **Kosten für beantragte gerichtliche Abschriften aus den Akten** — auf sie haben die akteneinsichtsberechtigten Beteiligten (vgl. § 120 Abs. 1 SGG) grundsätzlich ein Recht — müssen vom Antragsteller getragen werden (§ 120 Abs. 2 SGG; wegen der Möglichkeit der Einschränkung des Rechts vgl. § 120 Abs. 1 letzter Satz und Abs. 3 SGG). Das Abhängigmachen der Abschriftserteilung von vorheriger Zahlung ist nicht zulässig (s. o. vor 1). Wohl aber ist Übersendung unter Nachnahme möglich.

Zu den kostenpflichtigen Urkunden gehören nicht die unverkürzten oder auf den wesentlichen Inhalt beschränkten Abschriften der Niederschriften der Beweisaufnahme, auf welche die Beteiligten ohne weiteres einen Anspruch haben (§ 107 SGG), ebenso gehören selbstverständlich nicht dazu die Erstausfertigungen der ergehenden Entscheidungen (vgl. hierzu § 183 SGG und § 91 Abs. 2 GKG).

Abschriften der Entwürfe zu Urteilen, Beschlüssen und Verfügungen, der zu ihrer Vorbereitung angefertigten Arbeiten sowie der Schriftstücke, welche Abstimmungen oder in dem anhängigen Verfahren Strafverfügungen betreffen, werden nicht erteilt (§ 120 Abs. 4 SGG).

Wegen der **Höhe der Schreibgebühren** vgl. oben a am Ende.

c) Die **Kosten für die** vom Versicherten oder Versorgungsberechtigten — in ausdrücklicher Form (vgl. BSG, SozR SGG § 109 Bl. Da 5 Nr. 8 u. 9) — beantragte **gutachtliche Anhörung eines bestimmten Arztes** können — freies, im Rahmen des Pflichtgemäßen ausgeübtes Ermessen des tätigen Prozeßgerichts ist maßgebend — von dem Antragsteller (Versicherten, Versorgungsberechtigten oder ihren Hinterbliebenen) vorschußweise verlangt werden; hierbei wird der Grad der Aussichtslosigkeit des Beweisantritts von Bedeutung sein. Nach BSG, SozR SGG § 109 Bl. Da 9 Nr. 15 kann der Vorschuß auch bei finanziellem Unvermögen des Antragsberechtigten gefordert werden. Von der — nicht erzwingbaren — Zahlung des Vorschusses ist dann die Vernehmung abhängig (§ 109 Abs. 1 SGG). Reicht der gezahlte Vorschuß nicht aus, so kann der Rest erfordert und nötigenfalls nach dem Verwaltungsvollstreckungsgesetz beigetrieben werden (vgl. Mellwitz, SGG Anm. 11 zu § 109 und Anm. 2 zu § 200). Nicht verbrauchter Vorschuß ist zurückzuzahlen. Erzwingung der Rückzahlung ist nur im Klagewege möglich.

Der Vorschuß muß der Höhe nach bestimmt sein (vgl. BSG, SGb 1956, 122). Er soll die entstehenden Sachverständigenkosten decken.

Die durch die Anhörung des Sachverständigen dem Antragsteller entstandenen Kosten können (s. o. c am Anf.) vom Gericht übernommen werden. Dies wird zu geschehen haben, wenn das erstattete Gutachten — vor allem im positiven Sinn — Bedeutung für die gerichtliche Entscheidung hat (vgl. hierzu 1. Kap. 5). Bei Ausspruch der Übernahme dieser Kosten durch das Gericht der Instanz oder auf Rechtsmittel (in der Hauptsache oder nach deren Erledigung gegen die Kostenentscheidung erster Instanz) in der höheren Instanz ist Rückzahlung von Amts wegen zulässig und, da ungerechtfertigte Bereicherung vorliegt, angebracht. Erzwingung der Rückzahlung ist nur im Wege der Klage gegen den Fiskus möglich.

Wegen der **Höhe der Sachverständigenkosten** vgl. hier das 5. Kap. III 2a.

Zu a bis c. Die Kosten sind als nicht notwendige Sonderaufwendungen nicht auferlegungs- und erstattungsfähig im Sinne der §§ 192, 193 SGG (vgl. hierzu 1. Kap. 2g).

Eventuelle Bewilligung des Armenrechts befreit wegen des Sondercharakters dieser Kosten nicht von der Zahlungspflicht. Auf einem anderen Gebiet liegt allerdings die Frage, ob sich der Einziehungsversuch gegenüber einem nachgewiesenermaßen Armen lohnt.

Der **Kostenanspruch** der **Staatskasse verjährt** in vier Jahren nach Ablauf des Kalenderjahres, in welchem das Verfahren durch rechtskräftige Entscheidung über die Kosten, durch Vergleich oder in sonstiger Weise beendet ist (entspr. § 8 Abs. 1 GKG, vgl. in diesem Zusammenhange auch den allgemeinen § 6 GKG wegen eventueller Kostennachforderung). Die Einrede der Verjährung muß ausdrücklich erhoben werden. **Verwirkung** scheidet bei kurzer Verjährungsfrist, wie hier, grundsätzlich aus.

Ansprüche auf Rückerstattung von Kosten verjähren in vier Jahren nach Ablauf des Kalenderjahres, in dem der Kostenanspruch entstanden ist. Die Verjährung beginnt jedoch nicht vor dem Ablauf des Kalenderjahres, in dem das Verfahren beendet ist (vgl. § 8 Abs. 2 GKG).

Wegen Hemmung und Unterbrechung der Verjährung vgl. § 8 Abs. 3 GKG und §§ 202ff., 208ff. BGB.

Kostenschuldner sind ohne weiteres die aufgeführten Antragsteller.

Die Kostenanforderung in den Fällen a und b erfolgt durch gebührenfreien aber portopflichtigen Kostenbescheid des kostenberechnenden Urkundsbeamten (Kostenbeamten) des jeweils befaßten Gerichts, auf dessen Grundlage nötigenfalls nach dem Verwaltungsvollstreckungsgesetz vollstreckt werden kann. Rechtsbehelfsbelehrung (schriftlich, notfalls mündlich unter Aktenkundigmachung) ist erforderlich (§ 66 Abs. 1, § 173 letzter Satz SGG).

Wegen der **Aufrundung** der Kostenbeträge auf volle 10 DPf. vgl. den allgemein bedeutsamen § 9 Abs. 2 GKG.

Die Anforderung der Kosten hat alsbald nach Erteilung der Abschriften zu erfolgen. Falls die Kosten noch nicht berechnet sind, tritt bei Verweisung an ein anderes Sozialgericht (vgl. § 98 insbes. Abs. 3 SGG) behördenmäßig das neue Gericht an die Stelle des verweisenden. Bei Verweisung in ein anderes Verfahren erfolgt die Berechnung vor Aktenabgabe.

Im Falle b kann die Einziehung der Kosten unter Übersendung der Abschriften unter Nachnahme erfolgen.

Von der Einziehung derartiger Forderungen darf dann abgesehen werden, wenn es sich um Beträge unter 1,– DM (sogen. **Kleinbeträge**) handelt (vgl. § 68 Abs. 3 der Reichswirtschaftsbestimmungen). Wird diese Summe überschritten, so kann auch dann von der Einziehung Abstand genommen werden, wenn diese mit unverhältnismäßigen Kosten verbunden ist. Dies ist der Fall, wenn die Auslagen für die Einziehung den größeren Teil des insgesamt einzuziehenden Betrages ausmachen (vgl. Brocke-Reese, Geb. u. KostR Anm. 5 zu § 93 SGG).

Die Kostenanforderung im Falle c erfolgt durch – nicht erzwingbare – Auflage des erkennenden Gerichts (evtl. des Vorsitzenden, vgl. § 106 Abs. 2 und § 216 Abs. 1 Nr. 2 SGG) im Beschlußwege (bedingte Beweisanordnung). Auch eine etwaige Nachforderung (s. o. c) erfolgt durch Beschluß des Gerichts oder auf seine ausdrückliche Veranlassung.

Anfechtung in den Fällen a und b: **Anrufung des befaßten Gerichts** („Erinnerungs"einlegung) nach § 178 SGG binnen eines Monats nach Bekanntgabe (Zustellung) des Kostenbescheides (vgl. §§ 173, 66 Abs. 2 SGG). Der Kostenansatz oder seine Ablehnung stellt eine Entscheidung des Urkundsbeamten dar. Bei unterlassener oder unrichtiger Belehrung über den gegebenen Rechtsbehelf in der angefochtenen Entscheidung erstreckt sich die Anrufungsfrist auf ein Jahr (vgl. § 66 Abs. 2 Satz 1 SGG). Bei schuldloser Fristversäumnis ist Wiedereinsetzung in den vorigen Stand möglich (vgl. § 67 SGG).

Die Erweiterung einer begrenzten Anrufung nach Ablauf der Anrufungsfrist ist unzulässig.

Eine Anschlußanrufung gibt es nicht.

Rücknahme der Anrufung im Zweifel mit der Wirkung des endgültigen Verlustes des Rechtsbehelfs ist möglich.

Einlegungsform: schriftlich oder zur Niederschrift des Urkundsbeamten der Geschäftsstelle des betreffenden Gerichts (§ 173 SGG). Anwaltszwang besteht auch in dritter Instanz nicht.

Eine Mindestbeschwer ist nicht Voraussetzung. Freiwillige Zahlung der Kosten wird die Anrufung des Gerichtes grundsätzlich ausschließen. Einwendungen, die nicht im Kostenrecht verankert sind (insbesondere Erfüllungsbehauptungen), können, da es sich um ein Festsetzungsverfahren handelt, nicht vorgebracht werden. Sie können nur mit den Behelfen im Beitreibungsverfahren (siehe hier das 9. Kap. III 2 und IV 4 und 5) geltend gemacht werden.

Anrufungsberechtigte: bei zu niedriger oder abgelehnter Festsetzung die durch den Bezirksrevisor vertretene Staatskasse, bei zu hohem oder überhaupt ungerechtfertigtem Ansatz der Antragsteller. Bei einer Mehrheit von Antragstellern kann jeder — für sich — das Gericht anrufen, auch wenn es sich um Gesamtschuldner handelt. Nachberechnung (Erhöhung des bisher Verlangten) ist im Wege der Gerichtsanrufung in keinem Falle zulässig.

Der generell gegebene Rechtsbehelf des § 178 SGG ist nicht etwa deswegen ausgeschlossen, „weil der Urkundsbeamte außerhalb des Gerichtsverfahrens als reiner Verwaltungsbeamter tätig werde"; durch die besonderen Verfahrensvorschriften der §§ 93 und 120 SGG ist sein Tätigwerden als gegebenes Kostenansetzungsorgan des Gerichts hier vielmehr ausdrücklich mit dem jeweils anhängigen Rechtsstreit verknüpft.

Die Gewährung des Rechtsbehelfs des § 178 SGG, die bei Gerechtfertigtheit desselben zu einer entsprechenden Besserstellung führt, schließt die Zulässigkeit einer Anweisung des Kostenbeamten im Dienstaufsichtswege ebenso wie grundsätzlich eine Eigenabänderung durch den Urkundsbeamten aus. Dieser rechtsstaatliche Standpunkt kann und muß bei neuzeitlichen Verfahrensordnungen, wenn sie wie das SGG gefaßt sind, eingenommen werden. (Eine Bestimmung wie § 4 Abs. 5 GKG = § 13 Abs. 5 KostO: „Der Kostenansatz kann auch im Verwaltungswege berichtigt werden, solange nicht eine gerichtliche Entscheidung getroffen ist" fehlt hier).

Das **Gericht** (vorbehaltlich des § 216 Abs. 1 Nr. 2 SGG in voller Besetzung) **entscheidet**, falls keine Abhilfe durch den — jeweils — zuständigen Kostenbeamten erfolgt (§ 174 SGG), ohne mündliche Verhandlung (§ 124 Abs. 3 SGG), nötigenfalls nach Anhörung des Gegners, durch kostenfreien (§ 183 SGG), zu begründenden (§ 142 Abs. 2 SGG) Beschluß stets auf Grund eigenen Ermessens (§ 128 Abs. 1 Satz 1, § 142 Abs. 1 SGG) **endgültig** (§ 178 Satz 1 letzter Teil SGG).

Zurückverweisung an den Kostenbeamten (evtl. mit sachlicher Anweisung) ist nicht ausgeschlossen, aber wegen der eintretenden Verzögerung nicht angebracht. Nach Zurückverweisung kann gegen die neue Entscheidung vom Beschwerten wiederum das Gericht angerufen werden. Schlechterstellung des Anrufenden ist dem Gericht untersagt. Nachprüfung erfolgt grundsätzlich nur in bezug auf das Angegriffene. Der ergehende Beschluß braucht lediglich formlos übersandt zu werden.

Eigenabänderung des Beschlusses ist nicht zulässig. Eine Bestimmung, wie sie der § 4 Abs. 1 Satz 3 GKG enthält, fehlt. Wegen der möglichen Berichtigung offensichtlicher Unrichtigkeiten — auch durch den sich versehenden Urkundsbeamten — vgl. §§ 138 und 142 Abs. 1 SGG. Der Abhilfebescheid eröffnet dem Gegner neu die Anrufungsfrist.

Der Rechtsbehelf der Anrufung hat keine aufschiebende Wirkung (§ 175 Satz 1 und 2, § 178 letzter Satz SGG).

Einstweilige Aussetzung des Vollzuges des angegriffenen Kostenbescheides bis zur Entscheidung des Gerichts — gegen oder ohne Sicherheitsleistung — durch dieses (oder seinen Vorsitzenden) ist zulässig (§ 178 Satz 2 in Verb. mit § 175 Satz 2 SGG). Die Entscheidung über die Vollzugsaussetzung ist hier nicht anfechtbar.

Für eine **Niederschlagung** der Kosten besteht kein Raum und Anlaß, da sie nicht auf Grund fehlerhafter Handlung des Gerichts entstanden sind. Ganze oder teilweise **Stundung** der Kosten ist möglich. (Das Gesuch ist an die Kasse zu richten.) Um **Erlaß** der Kosten aus Billigkeitsgründen kann bei dem zuständigen Gerichtspräsidenten nachgesucht werden (vgl. hierzu Baumbach-Lauterbach, KostG 13. Aufl. S. 501 ff. mit allgem. Nachw.).

Im Falle c ist **selbständige Anfechtung** der Entscheidung gemäß § 172 Abs. 2 SGG **unzulässig**. Angriffe gegen einen beschwerenden Beschluß aus § 109 SGG, insbesondere seine für unberechtigt gehaltene und daher ganz oder teilweise nicht erfüllte Vorschußauflage, sind nur möglich mit dem Rechtsmittel gegen die ergangene (Folge-)Entscheidung in der Hauptsache (vgl. BSG, NJW 1958, 1654).

2. Bei Auferlegung der **verursachten Gerichtskosten** (allgemein oder unter bestimmter Anführung) gemäß § 192 SGG sind dem Belasteten gegebenenfalls — unter Einhaltung der vom Gericht etwa angeordneten Begrenzung auf einen quotenmäßigen Teil — in Rechnung zu stellen (vgl. 1. Kap. 2g):

a) die gemäß § 191 SGG an einen — anderen — **Beteiligten** von der Staatskasse gezahlten oder bestimmungsgemäß zu zahlenden **Beträge für bare Auslagen und Zeitverlust** (a. A. zu Unrecht SG Würzburg, BG 1957, 125). Wegen der Höhe dieser Kosten vgl. unten 5. Kap. I 2;

b) die an die **Zeugen oder Sachverständigen** gemäß den Bestimmungen des Entschädigungsgesetzes für Zeugen und Sachverständige (§§ 2, 3 und 5 ZuSEG) von der Staatskasse gezahlten oder bestimmungsgemäß zu zahlenden **Gebühren und Auslagen**, soweit nicht für den Sachverständigen nach § 109 SGG Vorschußzahlung erfolgt ist (vgl. § 118 SGG, ferner 5. Kap. II 2 und III 2);

c) die an den **Armenanwalt** eines Beteiligten von der Staatskasse gezahlten oder bestimmungsgemäß zu zahlenden **Gebühren und Auslagen** (vgl. § 167 SGG und §§ 121 ff. BRAGebO, auch das 8. Kap. II A 1 und 2).

Zu a bis c. **Voraussetzung** ist das Vorliegen einer entsprechenden Kostengrundentscheidung, die nicht rechtskräftig oder auch nur vorläufig vollstreckbar zu sein braucht (vgl. § 198 Abs. 2, § 199 Abs. 2 SGG). Die ausnahmsweise aufschiebende Wirkung eines Rechtsbehelfs bzw. Rechtsmittels nach §§ 97, 154 SGG betrifft gegebenenfalls nur die Hauptsache, wie ein Vergleich des § 199 Abs. 1 Nr. 1 mit Nr. 3 SGG ergibt.

Die erwähnten Kosten können, soweit sie im Übermaß gezahlt worden sind, auch auf Grund eines nach § 141 Abs. 3, §§ 380, 390, 409 ZPO ergangenen Ordnungsstrafbeschlusses gegen den sie jeweils verursachenden Beteiligten, Zeugen oder Sachverständigen entsprechend seiner „Verurteilung“ in Ansatz gebracht werden. Voraussetzung ist hier aber, daß der (Straf-)Beschluß rechtskräftig ist (vgl. § 175 Satz 2 SGG, § 572 Abs. 1 ZPO). Wegen Einzelheiten vgl. hier das 2. Kap. 9.

Mit der Aufhebung oder Einschränkung der Kostenauferlegung auf Rechtsmittel oder zulässigenfalls im Wege der Selbstabhilfe entfällt in entsprechendem Umfange die Geltendmachung der Auslagen. In diesem Falle ist Aufhebung des Kostenansatzes auch von Amts wegen möglich und angebracht; bei erfolgter Zahlung hat hier Rückzahlung zu erfolgen.

Kostenschuldner sind die entsprechend verurteilten Beteiligten.

Ein etwa bewilligtes Armenrecht befreit von der Zahlung dieser „urteilsmäßig" auferlegten Kosten nicht. Auf einem anderen Gebiet liegt hier die Frage, ob sich der Einziehungsversuch gegenüber einem nachgewiesenermaßen Armen lohnt. Bei der Einziehung von Armenanwaltskosten gegenüber dem betroffenen Armen selbst muß die Anordnung der Nachzahlung nach § 125 ZPO abgewartet werden (vgl. das 8. Kap. II B 1b).

Die **Geltendmachung** (Ansatz) erfolgt jeweils durch gebührenfreien Kostenbescheid des kostenberechnenden Urkundsbeamten, d. h. des Kostenbeamten des Gerichts, vor dem die Kosten entstanden sind; sie können als solche auch von einem höheren Gericht auferlegt sein (vgl. hierzu oben das 4. Kap. 1 zu a und b, und zwar auch wegen der nach dem Verwaltungsvollstreckungsgesetz möglichen Beitreibung).

Der Ansatz ist immer erst nach Erlaß des Kostentitels möglich. Vornahme hat alsbald nach Ergehen (nötigenfalls nach Rechtskraft) des Titels zu erfolgen. Eigenabänderung — außer im Falle der sogen. Abhilfe und der Rechenfehlerberichtigung (§§ 174, 178, 138, 142 Abs. 1 SGG) — ist nicht möglich.

Der Ansatz geschieht im Rahmen des von der Gerichtskasse Geleisteten, aber nur soweit die Leistung den gesetzlichen Bestimmungen entspricht.

Rechtsbehelfsbelehrung ist erforderlich (§ 66 Abs. 1 SGG). Sie erfolgt schriftlich (§ 66 Abs. 1 SGG) oder unter Aktenkundigmachung mündlich (§ 178 letzter Satz und § 173 letzter Satz SGG). Wegen der Folgen der Unterlassung der Belehrung oder ihrer Unrichtigkeit vgl. § 66 Abs. 2 SGG.

Hinsichtlich der **Verjährung** der Kostenansprüche und der zeitlichen Beschränkung der Nachforderung vgl. die Ausführungen hier im 4. Kap. 1 zu a bis c, ebenso hinsichtlich der Verjährung von Rückzahlungsansprüchen. Verlängerung der Verjährung nach § 218 BGB tritt mangels Erfüllung der Voraussetzungen nicht ein.

Anfechtung des Kostenbescheides: Anrufung des befaßten Gerichts schriftlich oder zu Protokoll des Urkundsbeamten (stets also ohne Anwaltszwang) nach § 178 SGG binnen eines Monats nach Bekanntgabe (Zustellung) des Kostenbescheides. Wegen Wiedereinsetzung in den vorigen Stand bei schuldloser Fristversäumnis vgl. § 67 SGG.

Nachberechnung (Erhöhung des bisher Verlangten) ist im Wege der Gerichtsanrufung in keinem Falle möglich.

Die Erweiterung einer begrenzten Anrufung ist nach Ablauf der Anrufungsfrist nicht zulässig.

Eine Anschlußanrufung gibt es nicht.

Rücknahme der Anrufung im Zweifel mit der Wirkung des endgültigen Verlustes des Rechtsbehelfs ist möglich.

Angegriffen werden kann von dem einzelnen Verurteilten (jeweils in bezug auf seine Person) oder der Staatskasse (vertreten durch den Bezirksrevisor) regelmäßig nur die übersetzte oder verkürzte Höhe, da die Tragungspflicht dem Grunde nach aus der Kostengrundentscheidung im Urteil (Beschluß) folgt, es sei denn, daß

α) zweifelhaft ist, ob die berechnete Kostenlast — ganz oder zu dem in Frage kommenden Teil — auferlegt ist, oder

β) bereits die Aufhebung oder Abänderung (Einschränkung oder Erweiterung) des zugrunde gelegten Kostentitels erfolgt ist (s. o. zu a bis c).

Einwendungen, die nicht im Kostenrecht verankert sind (insbesondere Erfüllungsbehauptungen), können, da es sich um ein Festsetzungsverfahren handelt, nicht vorgebracht werden. Sie können nur mit den Behelfen im Beitreibungsverfahren (siehe hier das 9. Kap. III 2 und IV 4 und 5) geltend gemacht werden.

Das Vorliegen einer Mindestbeschwer ist nicht erforderlich. Freiwillige Zahlung wird die Anrufung des Gerichts in aller Regel ausschließen.

Das Gericht des Kostenbeamten entscheidet (wegen der Besetzung vgl. 31γ) stets auf Grund eigenen Ermessens (§ 128 Abs. 1, § 142 Abs. 1 SGG), falls keine Abhilfe seitens des jeweils zuständigen Kostenbeamten erfolgt (vgl. § 178 letzter Satz und § 174 SGG), ohne notwendige Verhandlung (§ 124 Abs. 3 SGG), nötigenfalls nach Anhörung des Gegners, durch kostenfreien (§ 183 SGG), zu begründenden (§ 142 Abs. 2 SGG) Beschluß **endgültig** (§ 178 Satz 1 letzter Teil SGG). Zurückverweisung an den Urkundsbeamten (evtl. mit sachlicher Anweisung) ist nicht ausgeschlossen, aber wegen des entstehenden Zeitverlustes nicht angebracht. Nach Zurückverweisung kann gegen die neue Entscheidung vom Beschwerten wiederum das Gericht angerufen werden. Schlechterstellung des Anrufenden durch das Rechts-„mittel"gericht ist nicht zulässig.

Nachprüfung erfolgt grundsätzlich nur in bezug auf das Angegriffene.

Der Rechtsbehelf hat keine aufschiebende Wirkung (§ 175 Satz 1 und 2, § 178 letzter Satz SGG).

Einstweilige Aussetzung des Vollzuges des angegriffenen Kostenbescheides (gegen oder ohne Sicherheitsleistung) bis zur Entscheidung des Gerichts ist durch dieses (oder den Vorsitzenden) möglich (§ 178 letzter Satz in Verb. mit § 175 letzter Satz SGG).

Die Entscheidung über die Vollzugsaussetzung ist nicht anfechtbar.

Hat eine Verweisung an ein anderes Sozialgericht stattgefunden (vgl. § 98 insbes. Abs. 3 SGG), so ist das Gericht zuständig, an das verwiesen ist.

Eigenabänderung des Beschlusses ist nicht zulässig (s. o. 1 zu a und b). Bezüglich der rechtlich möglichen Berichtigung offenbarer Unrichtigkeiten vgl. die §§ 138, 142 Abs. 1 SGG. Der Beschluß, der ja nicht mehr angefochten werden kann, braucht nur formlos mitgeteilt zu werden (vgl. § 63 SGG).

Der Abhilfebescheid eröffnet dem Gegner neu die Anrufungsfrist.

Die Rechtsmittelgewährung zugunsten der Staatskasse im Falle ihrer Beschwer, die eine Besserstellung in dem stets anzustrebenden objektiven Rahmen zuläßt, schließt die Möglichkeit aus, den Kostenbeamten im Wege der Dienstaufsicht zu einer Änderung des Kostenbescheids anzuweisen (siehe hierzu 1 zu a und b).

Eine **Niederschlagung** der Kosten ist im Gesetz nicht vorgesehen; für sie besteht, da es sich um vom Gericht ausdrücklich auferlegte Kosten handelt, kein Anlaß.

Ganze oder teilweise **Stundung** der auferlegten Kosten ist — wie stets — möglich (Gesuch an die Gerichtskasse ist erforderlich). Um gnadenweisen **Erlaß** der Kosten können die zuständigen Gerichtsvorstände ersucht werden (siehe hierzu oben 4. Kap. 1 zu a und b am Ende).

3. **Die Körperschaften und Anstalten des öffentlichen Rechts haben** — das stellt eine Ausnahme von der gewährten Kostenfreiheit dar — für jede Streitsache, an der sie — aktiv oder passiv oder beigeladen — beteiligt sind, in jedem Rechtszuge **eine Gebühr** (öffentlich-rechtliche Gegenleistung für die Inanspruchnahme der

Tätigkeit des Gerichts) **zu entrichten** (§ 184 SGG), auch in Beitragsstreitigkeiten. Wird ein Beiladungsbeschluß im Laufe der Instanz aufgehoben, weil er irrtümlich erlassen war, so muß es so angesehen werden, als ob eine Beiladung nicht vorliegt (Brocke-Reese, Geb. u. KostR Anm. zu § 187 SGG; Sauerwein, SGG Anm. 3 zu § 184 Abs. 2 und LSG Celle, Breith. 1957, 1080). Gebührenbefreit sind danach grundsätzlich alle natürlichen Personen und die juristischen Personen des privaten Rechts.

a) **Kostenschuldner** sind nur die Körperschaften oder Anstalten (nicht Stiftungen) des öffentlichen Rechts. Als Körperschaften und Anstalten des öffentlichen Rechts gelten alle Personen- und Sachzusammenschlüsse, die aufgabenmäßig dauernd bestimmten öffentlichen Zwecken dienen und dazu grundsätzlich bzw. in aller Regel eigene Rechtspersönlichkeit besitzen (vgl. im einzelnen Gölkel, ZfS 1956, 41). Die Körperschaft ist stets mitgliedschaftlich organisiert, der Anstalt fehlen die Mitglieder.

Gebührenpflichtig sind damit regelmäßig die **Träger der Sozialversicherung** (einschließlich der entsprechenden Ersatzkassen) sowie die Bundesanstalt für Arbeitsvermittlung und Arbeitslosenversicherung, die Familienausgleichskassen, ferner die einschlägigen öffentlich-rechtlichen Verbände (Krankenkassenverbände) und Vereinigungen (so die kassenärztlichen und kassenzahnärztlichen Vereinigungen) und Innungen (Landwirtschaftskammern, Handwerkskammern), vgl. Brocke, SGb 1955, 324 und Peters-Sautter-Wolff, SGG Anm. 1 zu § 184. Auch Teile von Körperschaften des öffentlichen Rechts sind gebührenpflichtig, sofern sie selbständig prozeßfähig sind (SG Berlin, Breith. 1956, 1061).

Der **Bund** und die **Länder** in Streitigkeiten der Kriegsopferversorgung (vgl. § 75 Abs. 1 Satz 2, § 71 Abs. 5 SGG) und als staatliche Ausführungsbehörden für die Unfallversicherung und die Unfallfürsorge für Gefangene sowie die **Gebietskörperschaften** im eigentlichen Sinne (d. h. die Gemeinden und die höheren Kommunalverbände) in anderen Streitsachen (Ersatzstreitigkeiten) fallen begrifflich (ohne Rücksicht darauf, ob ein eigenes Gericht in Anspruch genommen wird) **nicht unter die Beitragspflicht** (im wesentlichen ebenso BSG, SozR SGG § 184 Bl. Da 5 Nr. 6 und SGb 1958, 224; Brocke, SGb 1955, 324; Gölkel, BKK 1955, 542; Gunkel, WzS 1957, 97 [98]; Hofmann-Schroeter, SGG 2. Aufl. § 184 Anm. 1; Linde, ZfS 1956, 296; Mellwitz, SGG Anm. A 3 zu § 184; Peters-Sautter-Wolff, SGG Anm. 1 zu § 184; Sabel, DOK 1955, 47; Wilde, ZfS 1954, 81; LSG Baden-Württemberg, SGb 1957, 277; SG Köln, SGb 1956, 231 mit zust. Anm. von Schieckel; SG Hamburg, ArbA 1956, 253).

Die Frage der Gebührenpflicht von Gebietskörperschaften (insbesondere der Gemeinden als Unfallversicherungsverbände und der Großstädte als Eigenunfallversicherungsträger) ist allerdings nicht unumstritten (vgl. LSG Rheinland-Pfalz, Breith. 1957, 92; SG Dortmund, ArbA 1956, 253; Brocke, SGb 1955, 325; Gölkel, ZfS 1956, 41; Gunkel, WzS 1957, 97 [98]; Mellwitz, SGG Anm. 2 zu § 184 und Sauerwein, SGG Anm. 1 zu § 184, der sogar Bund und Länder für ihre Ausführungsbehörden als kostenpflichtig erklärt; so auch LSG Niedersachsen, Nds. MinBl. 1955, 39 und LSG Rheinland-Pfalz, SGb 1956, 354; vgl. hierzu ferner die Runderlasse der Sozialministerien von Niedersachsen vom 24. 2. 1956 [Nds. MinBl. 175] und von Rheinland-Pfalz vom 30. 4. 1956 [RhPf MinBl. 691], die die richterliche Gesetzesauslegung allerdings nicht beeinflussen können. Nach BSG, SozR SGG § 184 Bl. Da 10 Nr. 10 sind Gemeinden Körperschaften des öffentlichen Rechts im Sinne des § 184 SGG und daher Gebührenschuldner, wenn sie am Verfahren beteiligt sind; hierbei ist unerheblich, ob sie als Arbeitgeber oder Versicherungsträger Beteiligte sind).

Auch die **Bundesbahn-** und die **Bundespostausführungsbehörde** für Unfallversicherung sind als letzten Endes **Bundes**ausführungsbehörden **nicht gebührenpflichtig** (BSG, NJW 1957, 1654 = SGb 1958, 224; LSG Rheinland-Pfalz, SGb 1956, 354). **Bundesbahn** und **Bundespost** selbst sind mit Rücksicht auf Art. 87 Abs. 1 GG trotz ihrer Sonderorganisation ebenso wie der Bund zu behandeln (vgl. BSG, NJW 1957, 1654 = SGb 1958, 224; LSG Baden-Württemberg, SGb 1957, 277 und Gölkel, ZfS 1956, 41; Gunkel, WzS 1957, 97 [99] sowie Rambour, SGb 1957, 73. A. A. Schrader, SGb 1956, 374, SGb 1957, 136 und SGb 1957, 278, ferner Schieckel, SGb 1957, 149, der der Entscheidung des LSG Bremen, SGb 1957, 148, beitritt; vgl. hierzu auch Brocke, SGb 1956, 355).

Der Generalstaatsanwalt ist als Ausführungsbehörde betreffend die Unfallfürsorge für Gefangene von der Gebührenentrichtung befreit (SG Münster, JVBl. 1957, 25).

Bei vorgehenden oder zugezogenen bloßen **Behörden** (organisatorisch vereinheitlichte Stellen zur selbständigen Erfüllung bestimmter öffentlicher Aufgaben ohne Rechtspersönlichkeit, die als solche (vgl. ihre Nichtanführung im § 184 SGG im Gegensatz zu § 193 Abs. 4 SGG) **nicht gebührenpflichtig** (BSG, SozR SGG § 184 Bl. Da 8 Nr. 8) und regelmäßig überhaupt nicht partei- und prozeßfähig sind (vgl. die Ausnahmen in § 70 Nr. 3 SGG), besteht zumeist wegen Nichtbeteiligtseins auch nicht Beitragspflicht der Institutionen, die diese Behörden gebildet haben (so mit Recht Brocke, SGb 1956, 355 gegen Gölkel, ZfS 1956, 41).

Nicht gebührenpflichtig sind ferner die **Berufungs(Zulassungs-)ausschüsse und** die **Schiedsämter** in Kassenarztsachen, weil es sich nicht um öffentlich-rechtliche Körperschaften (Anstalten) handelt. (Im § 70 Nr. 4 SGG sind diese Ausschüsse und Ämter, die Behördencharakter haben — vgl. BSG, SozR SGG § 193 Bl. Da 1 Nr. 2 — besonders aufgeführt, nicht aber im § 184 SGG.) Für sie haftet auch nicht die Trägerinstitution (kassenärztliche Vereinigung), da sie nicht am Verfahren beteiligt ist (BSG, SozR SGG § 184 Bl. Da 4 Nr. 5).

Fürsorgeverbände genießen auf Grund der Sonderanordnung des § 28 FürsPflVO (vgl. RGBl. 1924 I 100 i. d. F. der 2. NotVO vom 5. 6. 1931 — RGBl. I 308) **Gebührenfreiheit** (vgl. LSG Bayern, Breith. 1956, 1078 und SG Osnabrück, Z. f. Fürsorge 1956, 186).

b) Die Gebühr ist für **jede Streitsache** (Streitfall, nicht Klage) zu zahlen. So entsteht bei gleichzeitiger Geltendmachung des eigenen Invalidenanspruchs und des Invalidenwitwenrentenanspruchs der Klägerin die Gebühr zweimal (vgl. LSG Hamburg, Breith. 1957, 189; hier liegen zwei verschiedene Verwaltungsakte vor). Entscheidend ist dabei das Vorgehen gegen ein und denselben Verwaltungsakt („Sozialakt"), mag es auch — gleichzeitig (vgl. § 56 SGG) oder sonst (z. B. auf Grund Verbindung, vgl. § 113 SGG) einheitlich — von verschiedenen Seiten erfolgen (z. B. auf Klage und Widerklage, zumal diese gemäß § 100 SGG im rechtlichen Zusammenhange stehen müssen, oder auf Berufung und — selbständige oder unselbständige — Anschlußberufung). Bloße Kläger- oder Beklagtenhäufung (subjektive Klagehäufung) vervielfältigt grundsätzlich nicht (vgl. LSG Niedersachsen, Breith. 1956, 1257).

Bei Erlaß eines neuen Verwaltungsaktes nach Klageerhebung (vgl. § 96 SGG) liegt nur **ein** Streitfall vor. (Der neue Verwaltungsakt wird Gegenstand desselben Verfahrens.) Anders liegt der Fall des § 171 Abs. 2 SGG (neuer Verwaltungsakt während des Revisionsverfahrens). Hier wird, um eine Nachprüfung auch in tatsächlicher Hinsicht zu ermöglichen, über den neuen Verwaltungsakt in einem selbständigen Verfahren vor dem Sozialgericht entschieden, es sei denn, daß der Kläger nunmehr klaglos gestellt ist.

Der angegriffene **Verwaltungsakt** kann inhaltlich **zweiteilig** sein, so bei Witwenrente (einerseits) und Waisenrenten (zusammengefaßt andererseits). Die Gebühr ist dann zweimal zu zahlen (vgl. SG Berlin, S 65 [Geb] 13/57 und Peters-Sautter-Wolff, SGG Anm. 2 zu § 184; Mellwitz, SGG § 184 Anm. 6; Hofmann-Schroeter, SGG § 184 Anm. 2; Miesbach-Ankenbrank, SGG § 184 Anm. 2; a. A. LSG Niedersachsen, Breith. 1956, 1257 und Gunkel, WzS 1957, 97 und 133, ferner das LSG Berlin, SGb 1958, 363 mit zust. Anm. von Schieckel, das aus „Gründen der Vereinfachung" die Streitsache mit dem jeweils geführten Sachaktenstück identifiziert).

Keine gebührenpflichtigen Streitsachen entstehen durch die den Sozialgerichten zugehenden Rechts- und Amtshilfeersuchen (vgl. Brocke-Reese, Geb. u. KostR Anm. III 1k zu § 184 SGG), ferner durch bloße Armenrechtsgesuche.

c) Die Gebühr ist für **jeden Rechtszug** (erste Instanz, Berufungsinstanz und Revisionsinstanz) zu zahlen, vgl. § 184 Satz 2 letzter Teil SGG. In Beschwerdesachen fällt keine Gebühr an, so auch Miesbach-Ankenbrank, SGG Anm. 8 zu § 184; Ausnahme: wenn die Beschwerde (z. B. bei Erledigung der Hauptsache) an die Stelle der Berufung tritt.

Die Gebühr ist dem Grunde nach unabhängig vom Ausgang des Verfahrens. Gebührenzahlungspflicht besteht auch bei Abweisung mangels Passivlegitimation des Gebührenpflichtigen oder wegen Unzuständigkeit des vom Gegner angerufenen Gerichts oder Unzulässigkeit der von ihm erhobenen Klage, ferner wenn das vom Streitgegner eingelegte Rechtsmittel (evtl. durch bloßen Beschluß ohne mündliche Verhandlung, vgl. §§ 169, 216 Abs. 1 Nr. 3a SGG) als unzulässig (insbesondere wegen Formwidrigkeit oder Fristversäumnis) verworfen worden ist (BSG, SozR SGG § 184 Bl. Da 2 Nr. 2 und Bl. Da 3 Nr. 4). Wegen irrtümlicher Beiladung vgl. oben 3a.

Wegen der möglichen Abwälzung der Gebührenschuld gemäß §§ 192, 193 SGG vgl. 1. Kap. 2, 3.

Wegen Niederschlagung bei unrichtiger Sachbehandlung vgl. § 190 SGG.

Durch Antrag auf mündliche Verhandlung gegen den Vorbescheid (§ 105 Abs. 2, § 158 Abs. 2, § 216 Abs. 1 Nr. 1 SGG) wird kein neuer Rechtszug eröffnet. (Die Sache bleibt in derselben Instanz anhängig.)

Bei Zurückverweisung an das untere Gericht beginnt kein neuer Rechtszug vor diesem Gericht (vgl. RGZ 158, 196). Wird jedoch gegen das neue Urteil dieses Rechtszuges Rechtsmittel eingelegt, so entsteht eine neue Rechtsmittelinstanz. Verweist das BSG auf Sprungrevision an das LSG zurück (vgl. § 170 Abs. 3 SGG), so entsteht eine neue, die Berufungsinstanz.

Bei Verweisung wegen Unzuständigkeit (§ 98 SGG) liegt ein einheitliches Verfahren beim neuen Gericht vor (§ 98 Abs. 3 SGG). Bei Verweisung auf den ordentlichen oder einen anderen Rechtsweg gemäß § 52 Abs. 3 SGG durch Urteil besteht kein einheitliches Verfahren; die Gebühr des § 184 SGG ist dem verweisenden Gericht gegenüber zu zahlen.

Wird ein durch rechtskräftiges Urteil abgeschlossenes Verfahren wieder aufgenommen (§§ 179, 180 SGG, §§ 578ff. ZPO), so liegt ein neues Verfahren vor (§ 188 SGG).

Bei Abgabe einer Streitsache wegen angenommener Passivlegitimation eines anderen bereits verklagten Versicherungsträgers an das gemeinsame nächsthöhere Gericht nach § 181 SGG entsteht bei dem abgebenden Gericht keine Gebühr, da hier keine eigentliche Sachbearbeitung erfolgt.

d) **Die Gebühr entsteht**, sobald die Streitsache rechtshängig oder in der höheren Instanz anhängig geworden ist (§ 184 Satz 2 erster Teil SGG).

Maßgebender Zeitpunkt ist der der Erhebung (Einreichung oder protokollarische Niederlegung beim Urkundsbeamten) der Klage (Wiederaufnahmeklage), vgl. §§ 90, 94 SGG, oder der Einreichung (oder — was die Berufung anbetrifft — der protokollarischen Niederlegung beim Urkundsbeamten) des Rechtsmittels (§§ 151, 164 SGG). Bei der — notwendigen oder nicht notwendigen (vgl. § 75 Abs. 1 und 2 SGG) — Beiladung entsteht die Gebühr mit der Bekanntgabe des Beiladungsbeschlusses.

Eingang der Klage bei einer anderen inländischenBehörde oder einer deutschen Konsularbehörde oder bei einem Versicherungsträger (bzw. bei einem deutschen Seemannsamt) — vgl. § 91 Abs. 1 SGG — genügt nicht; er wahrt nur die Frist.

e) Sind an einer Streitsache **mehrere Körperschaften oder Anstalten** des öffentlichen Rechts — in irgendeiner Weise — beteiligt, so entsteht die **Gebühr nur einmal**; die Gebühr ist von den Körperschaften oder Anstalten ohne Rücksicht auf die Art und den Grund ihrer Beteiligung (oder Verurteilung) **zu gleichen Teilen** zu entrichten (§ 187 SGG). Die Mindestgebühr beträgt jedoch jeweils 2 DM (LSG Bayern, Bay.ArbBl. 1957, B. 57). Nichtgebührenpflichtige Körperschaften oder Anstalten (s. 3a) bleiben von vornherein außer Betracht.

f) **Die Gebühr wird fällig**, sobald die Streitsache durch Zurücknahme des Rechtsbehelfs (Klage oder Rechtsmittel), durch Vergleich, Anerkenntnis, Vorbescheid, Beschluß oder durch Urteil (Rechtskraft ist nicht erforderlich, Grundurteil, vgl. § 130 SGG, genügt — a. A. Gunkel, WzS 1957, 133 [138] —, ebenso Verweisungsurteil an eine andere Gerichtsbarkeit) erledigt ist, § 185 SGG (es besteht keine Vorschußpflicht).

α) Rücknahme der Klage: vgl. § 102 SGG;

β) Rücknahme des Rechtsmittels: vgl. §§ 156, 165 SGG;

γ) Vergleich: vgl. § 101 Abs. 1, § 153 Abs. 1, § 165 SGG;

δ) Anerkenntnis: § 101 Abs. 2, § 153 Abs. 1, § 165 SGG (Verzicht auf den Hauptanspruch ist sinngemäß ebenfalls als Auslösungsgrund anzusehen);

ε) Vorbescheid (dieser muß aber rechtskräftig sein, § 105 Abs. 2 Satz 2 SGG): vgl. §§ 105, 158, 216 Abs. 1 Nr. 1 SGG;

ζ) Beschluß: vgl. § 216 Abs. 1 Nr. 3b und c und Nr. 4a und b, ferner bei unstreitiger Erledigung der Hauptsache (vgl. Mellwitz, SGG Anm. 4 zu § 125), auch bei sonstiger Erledigung des Verfahrens (z. B. bei Tod eines Streitbeteiligten und Nichtaufnahme durch den Erben, vgl. Linde, ZfS 1956, 294ff);

η) Urteil: vgl. §§ 123ff., 153, 165 SGG (der Verwerfungsbeschluß gemäß §§ 169 und 216 Abs. 1 Nr. 3a SGG steht dem Urteil gleich, BSG, SozR SGG § 184 Bl. Da 2 Nr. 3 = SGb 1956, 254 mit zust. Anm. von Schieckel).

g) Wird die **Sache nicht durch Urteil** (ihm steht hier bei Beachtung des Sinnes des § 186 SGG der rechtskräftige Vorbescheid oder ein Verwerfungsbeschluß nicht gleich) **erledigt** (vgl. oben 3f α bis δ u. ζ), so **ermäßigt sich**, weil die Mühewaltung des Gerichts in diesen Fällen geringer ist, die zu zahlende **Gebühr auf die Hälfte** (§ 186 Satz 1 SGG).

Wird nach Erlaß eines Grundurteils (vgl. § 130 SGG) die Klage oder das Rechtsmittel zurückgenommen, so tritt keine Ermäßigung ein (Brocke-Reese, Geb. u. KostR Anm. 1 zu § 186 SGG).

Erledigt sich die **Hauptsache auf Grund** einer **Rechtsänderung**, so **entfällt die Gebühr** ganz (§ 186 Satz 2 SGG).

Die Ermäßigung bzw. der Wegfall soll für die Versicherungsträger einen Anreiz bilden, eine von vornherein aussichtslose oder aussichtslos gewordene Rechtsverfolgung oder Rechtsverteidigung aufzugeben (vgl. die Amtliche Begründung).

h) Eine **Gebühr,** die **durch unrichtige Behandlung der Sache** ohne Schuld (Vorsatz oder Fahrlässigkeit) des oder der gebührenpflichtigen Beteiligten entstanden ist, **kann von dem (Chef-)Präsidenten** (oder dem aufsichtführenden Richter) des Gerichts, bei dem sie entstanden ist, **niedergeschlagen werden** (§ 190 SGG). Der Präsident entscheidet nur in bezug auf Sachen seines LSG, die jeweils aufsichtführenden Richter für die Sozialgerichte.

α) Nach pflichtgemäßem Ermessen in Unabhängigkeit ,,von oben" ist zu entscheiden. (Je grober und offensichtlicher der Fehler des Gerichts, desto näher die Bejahung der Niederschlagung.) Nicht jeder gemachte materiell-rechtliche oder verfahrensrechtliche Fehler genügt als Voraussetzung; er muß vielmehr grob und offensichtlich sein. Auf ihm muß auch die Entscheidung beruhen. Die Abänderung eines Urteils in höherer Instanz als solche reicht keineswegs aus. Die Entscheidung stellt einen Verwaltungsakt dar, und zwar einen solchen der Gerichtsverwaltung, nicht der Justizverwaltung (vgl. hierzu Tietgen, NJW 1956, 1129f.); er kann daher im Verwaltungsgerichtswege nicht angefochten werden, zumal der § 190 SGG die Niederschlagung der Kosten endgültig regelt (so auch Wilde, ZfS 1954, 81).

β) Die Niederschlagung kann von Amts wegen erfolgen; zumeist wird um sie von der betroffenen Körperschaft oder Anstalt des öffentlichen Rechts nachgesucht werden. Sie kann einem einzelnen von mehreren Zahlungspflichtigen gewährt werden. Die Gebührenschuld der übrigen Beteiligten vergrößert sich dadurch nicht.

γ) Die unrichtige Sachbehandlung kann mit Rücksicht auf die §§ 184, 186 SGG hauptsächlich darin bestehen, daß

aa) die gebührenpflichtige Körperschaft (Anstalt) ohne ihr Zutun vom Gericht zu Unrecht in den (erstinstanzlichen) Rechtsstreit oder die in Frage stehende höhere Instanz – als Klägerin, Beklagte oder Beigeladene – einbezogen worden ist (z. B. durch unrichtige Beiladung oder durch fehlerhafte Auslegung einer nicht als Klage oder Rechtsmittelschrift ansehbaren Eingabe oder durch fehlerhafte Zustellung u. ä.). Ein Fehler der Geschäftsstelle genügt hierbei;

bb) das Gericht ein Anerkenntnis, einen Verzicht, Vergleich oder die Rechtsbehelfszurücknahme zu Unrecht nicht beachtet (übergangen) und durch Urteil in der Sache selbst entschieden hat (vgl. 1. Kap. 9b und 4. Kap. 3f und g). Hier ist die halbe Gebühr niederzuschlagen, vgl. § 186 SGG;

cc) durch Urteil statt auf der Hand liegenden Vorbescheid oder (Verwerfungs-) Beschluß entschieden worden ist (§§ 105, 158, 169 und 216 Abs. 1 Nr. 3 und 4 SGG). Betroffen wird auch hier die halbe Gebühr (§ 186 SGG);

dd) das Gericht dort, wo nach beachteter Erledigung der Hauptsache (durch Anerkenntnis, Verzicht, Vergleich, Klage oder Rechtsmittelrücknahme) anstatt durch Beschluß unrichtigerweise durch Urteil (über die Kosten, evtl. auch über die Wirkung der Rücknahme, vgl. § 102 Satz 2 1. Teil SGG) entschieden hat. Hier ist ebenfalls die halbe Gebühr niederzuschlagen, vgl. § 186 SGG;

ee) das Gericht ein Sachverständigengutachten erfordert hat, obwohl das Verfahren als solches unzulässig war (von Bedeutung für die Höhe der ausgelösten Gebühr, s. u. k α).

δ) Niederschlagen heißt: auf eine einziehbare Forderung verzichten; die Gebührenschuld wird dadurch zum Erlöschen gebracht.

i) **Von der Einziehung** der bei ihrem Gericht entstandenen Gebühr **können** die genannten **Gerichtsvorstände absehen**, wenn sie mit Kosten oder Verwaltungsaufwand verknüpft ist, die in keinem Verhältnis zu der Einnahme stehen (vor allem bei sog. Kleinbeträgen bis zu 1 DM).

α) Entscheidung erfolgt nach pflichtgemäßem Ermessen von Amts wegen; hier handelt es sich um einen echten „Justiz"verwaltungsakt. (Anfechtung der Entscheidung ist aber wegen der endgültigen Regelung im § 190 SGG auch im Verwaltungsgerichtswege nicht möglich.) Die Einziehung geringfügiger Beträge, die mehr Arbeit macht als sie einbringt, soll aus wirtschaftlichen Gründen unterbleiben.

β) Die Forderung bleibt hier bestehen; nur ihre Realisierung unterbleibt.

Verjährung der Forderung tritt ein in vier Jahren nach Ablauf des Kalenderjahres, in dem das Verfahren beendet worden ist (entsprechend § 8 Abs. 1 GKG). Ansprüche auf Rückerstattung von Kosten verjähren in vier Jahren nach Ablauf des Kalenderjahres, in dem der Kostenanspruch entstanden ist; die Verjährung beginnt jedoch nicht vor dem Ablauf des Kalenderjahres, in dem das Verfahren beendet ist (vgl. § 8 Abs. 2 GKG).

Die Einrede der Verjährung muß ausdrücklich erhoben werden.

Verwirkung scheidet bei kurzer Verjährung, wie hier, grundsätzlich aus.

Eine Nachforderung von Gerichtskosten wegen irrigen Unterbleibens der Einforderung ist nur zulässig, wenn der Ansatz vor Ablauf des nächsten Kalenderjahres nach rechtskräftiger oder endgültiger Erledigung des Verfahrens dem Zahlungspflichtigen eröffnet ist (vgl. § 6 GKG; allgemeiner Grundsatz).

k) Die **Höhe der** von den Körperschaften und Anstalten des öffentlichen Rechts zu entrichtenden — **vollen** — **Gebühr** ist, wie im § 184 Abs. 2 SGG vorgesehen, **durch Rechtsverordnung** der Bundesregierung unter Zustimmung des Bundesrats **festgelegt** worden (VO über die Höhe der von Körperschaften und Anstalten des öffentlichen Rechts gemäß § 184 des SGG zu entrichtenden Gebühr — VO über PauschGeb. — vom 31. 3. 1955, BGBl. 1955 I 180, in Kraft seit dem 1. 1. 1954).

Die Verordnung unterscheidet bei den Instanzgerichten (mit Tatsachenauswertung) **zwei Klassen** (vgl. den § 1 der VO einerseits und den § 2 ders. andererseits):

α) Sachen, in denen Sachverständigenkosten für erstattete ärztliche Gutachten — zu Recht oder Unrecht — entstanden sind. (Die Entschädigung von sachverständigen Zeugen ist keine Gutachtenvergütung, so auch Gunkel, WzS 1957, 133 [136].)

Wegen des Begriffs der „Sache" vgl. hier oben 3b;

β) Sachen, in denen solche Kosten nicht zur Entstehung gekommen sind; ihnen stehen gleich:

aa) Sachen, in denen nur Krankenpapiere, Aufzeichnungen, Krankengeschichten, Sektions- und Untersuchungsbefunde sowie Röntgenbilder beigezogen worden sind (vgl. § 106 Abs. 3 Nr. 2 SGG);

bb) Sachen, in denen ein Arzt (sog. Sitzungsarzt) in der mündlichen Verhandlung (schriftliche Äußerung kann nicht gleichgestellt werden, a. A. Peters-Sautter-Wolff, SGG Anm. 1 zu § 2 VO über PauschGeb.) nur zur Unterrichtung des Gerichts gehört worden ist, d. h. als „billiger", nur pauschal entschädigter (vgl. Anhang zu § 5 ZuSEG) Gutachter vernommen wurde (vgl. § 2 Abs. 2 VO über PauschGeb.), nicht als kostspieligerer Sachverständiger, sei es auch nur allgemein erläuternder Art (dies läßt in einer die Ermäßigung zu weit ausdehnenden Weise Brocke, SGb 1957, 199 [201] genügen) oder lediglich in konzentrierter Darlegung (aus diesem Grunde versagt Großmann, BG 1956, 291, ebenfalls in unrichtiger Auslegung des § 2 der VO, die höhere Gebühr). Das Vorliegen oder Nichtvorliegen eines förmlichen Beweisbeschlusses oder der Protokollierung der ärztlichen Vernehmung ist nicht entscheidend. Auf den Umfang und den Inhalt der Tätigkeit des Sitzungsarztes kommt es nicht an (wie hier Peters, SGb 1958, 245);

cc) Sachen, in denen zwar ein Arzt als Sachverständiger vernommen worden ist, die Kosten aber vom Versicherten vorgeschossen und ihm endgültig auferlegt worden sind (vgl. § 109 Abs. 1 SGG), so auch Brocke, SGb 1955, 325.

Es sind die **folgenden Beträge** jeweils als volle Gebühr vorgesehen:

In der Klasse α

vor dem **Sozialgericht** . . . . . . 60 DM,
vor dem **Landessozialgericht** . . . 90 DM,
vor dem **Bundessozialgericht** . . . 120 DM
(§ 1 der VO über PauschGeb.).

In der Klasse β (vgl. § 2 der VO über PauschGeb.)

vor dem Sozialgericht:

in Streitsachen, welche eine einmalige Leistung im Werte bis zu 25 DM betreffen, die Hälfte des Streitwertbetrages (Streitsumme), mindestens aber (auch bei Ermäßigung) 2 DM (aaO. Abs. 3 Satz 2);
in Streitsachen, welche eine einmalige Leistung im Werte von mehr als 25 DM bis 299,99 DM betreffen, 15 DM (aaO. Abs. 3 Satz 1);
in sonstigen Streitsachen 30 DM (aaO. Abs. 1).

Wegen der Wertfestsetzung und ihrer Anfechtung vgl. 3. Kap. 2b α, β;

vor dem Landessozialgericht:

in Streitsachen, welche eine einmalige Leistung im Werte bis zu 25 DM betreffen, die Hälfte des Streitwertbetrages (Streitsumme), mindestens aber (auch bei Ermäßigung) 2 DM (aaO. Abs. 3 Satz 2);
in Streitsachen, welche eine einmalige Leistung im Werte von mehr als 25 DM bis 299,99 DM betreffen, 15 DM (aaO. Abs. 3 Satz 1);
in den sonstigen Streitsachen 40 DM (aaO. Abs. 1).

Unter **„einmaligen Leistungen"** (vgl. auch § 144 Abs. 1 Nr. 1 SGG) sind geldliche oder geldeswerte Vergabungen zu verstehen, die innerhalb absehbarer, nicht zu langer Zeiträume normalerweise nicht in größeren oder kleineren, regelmäßigen oder unbestimmten Abständen auf Grund desselben Rechtsverhältnisses wiederkehren (so Sterbegeld, Bestattungsgeld, Behandlungsbeitrag, Abfindungssumme,

Entbindungsgeld, Heilverfahrens- und Hilfsmittelgewährung, Zahnersatz, Beitragserstattung und – entgegen BSG, SozR SGG § 144 Bl. Da 1 Nr. 3 – begrifflich Zwangs- bzw. Ordnungsstrafe (vgl. hierzu Casselmann, SGb 1957, 134 mit weiteren Nachweisen und Mogg, SozVers. 1957, 68). Der Leistungsbegriff ist hier über die Umreißung in § 144 SGG hinaus aus kostenrechtlichen Gründen weiter auszulegen, damit nicht in unbilliger Weise für geringe Streitgegenstände oder Summen ihren Wert oder ihre Höhe übersteigende Kostenbeträge gezahlt werden müssen (SG Osnabrück, S III B 29/55, vgl. SGb 1957, 134 entgegen LSG Rheinland-Pfalz, B V 33/56, vgl. SozVers. 1957, 68). Letzteres würde dazu führen, daß Leistungen aus Furcht vor höheren Prozeßkosten zu Unrecht gewährt bzw. belassen werden (so mit Recht Brocke, SGb 1957, 199 [201], der insoweit dem BSG 2, 157 entgegentritt, ferner Casselmann, SGb 1958, 344).

Wegen der Wertfestsetzung und ihrer Anfechtung vgl. oben 3. Kap. 2b α, β;

vor dem Bundessozialgericht:

120 DM (§ 1 VO über PauschGeb.) ohne eine Ermäßigung (vgl. BSG, SozR SGG § 184 Bl. Da 7 Nr. 7).

l) Die **Festsetzung** der Gebührenforderung geht, wie folgt, vor sich:

α) Die Gebühren für die einzelnen Streitsachen werden in bestimmten Zeitabständen (praktisch alle Vierteljahre) bei dem jeweiligen Gericht in einem **Verzeichnis** zusammengestellt (§ 189 Abs. 1 Satz 1 SGG). Um eine Nachprüfung zu ermöglichen, ist die Angabe der Aktenzeichen der einzelnen Streitsachen erforderlich. Die Aufführung der Art der Erledigung und der sonstigen die Gebührenhöhe beeinflussenden Umstände erleichtert die Überprüfung.

Die Gebühren, die eingesetzt werden, müssen stets fällig sein (§ 185 SGG).

Die Mitteilung (Zustellung gemäß § 63 Abs. 1 SGG ist erforderlich) des sie betreffenden Auszuges aus diesem Verzeichnis an die jeweils betroffene Körperschaft oder Anstalt des öffentlichen Rechts gilt als Feststellung der Gebührenschuld und als Aufforderung, den Gebührenbetrag binnen eines Monats an die in der Mitteilung angegebene Stelle (Kasse) zu zahlen.

Der Auszug stellt einen echten Kostenbescheid dar. Nach § 17 des Verwaltungsvollstreckungsgesetzes sind aber gegen Behörden und juristische Personen des öffentlichen Rechts (öffentliche Körperschaften und Anstalten) Zwangsmittel grundsätzlich unzulässig. Zahlung wird hier seitens des öffentlich-rechtlichen Schuldners immer ohne Zwang erfolgen.

Das Geld fließt an das Land, welches das befaßte Sozialgericht oder Landessozialgericht unterhält, für Revisionen beim Bundessozialgericht an den Bund.

β) Die wiedergegebene **Feststellung der Gebührenschuld** erfolgt **durch** den **Urkundsbeamten** (sogen. Kostenbeamten) der Geschäftsstelle (vgl. § 4 SGG) des jeweils befaßten Gerichts (§ 189 Abs. 2 Satz 1 SGG).

Bei Verweisung an ein anderes Sozialgericht ist die Zuständigkeit des Kostenbeamten des neuen Gerichts gegeben (vgl. § 98 Abs. 3 SGG).

Rechtsbehelfsbelehrung ist erforderlich (§ 66 Abs. 1 SGG); sie erfolgt schriftlich oder unter Aktenkundigmachung mündlich (vgl. § 66 Abs. 1, § 173 letzter Satz in Verb. mit § 178 letzter Satz SGG).

Wegen der Folgen der Unterlassung der Belehrung oder bei Unrichtigkeit derselben vgl. § 66 Abs. 2 SGG.

γ) **Gegen die Feststellung kann** wegen jeder Beschwer vom einzelnen Beschwerten binnen eines Monats nach Mitteilung (Zustellung s. o. α) **das Gericht** des festsetzenden Urkundsbeamten **angerufen werden** (§ 189 Abs. 2 Satz 2 SGG). Wegen Wiedereinsetzung in den vorigen Stand bei schuldloser Fristversäumnis vgl. § 67 SGG. Wegen der Form der Anrufung vgl. § 173 SGG (schriftlich beim befaßten Gericht oder zur Niederschrift seines Urkundsbeamten, daher auch in dritter Instanz kein Anwaltszwang). Erfüllungseinwendungen können, da es sich um ein Festsetzungsverfahren handelt, nicht gebracht werden (wegen dieser vgl. das 9. Kap. III 2 und IV 4 und 5).

Nachberechnung (Erhöhung des bisher Verlangten) ist im Wege der Gerichtsanrufung in keinem Fall möglich.

Die Erweiterung einer begrenzten Anrufung nach Ablauf der Anrufungsfrist ist nicht zulässig.

Eine Anschlußanrufung gibt es nicht.

Die Rücknahme der Anrufung im Zweifel mit der Wirkung des endgültigen Verlustes des Rechtsbehelfs ist möglich.

Das Gericht entscheidet bei Nichtabhilfe durch den jeweils zuständigen Urkundsbeamten (vgl. § 174 SGG) ohne mündliche Verhandlung (§ 124 Abs. 3 SGG), aber grundsätzlich nach Anhörung des Gegners, auf Grund eigener Ermessensausübung (§ 128 Abs. 1, § 142 Abs. 1 SGG; auch in dritter Instanz!) durch kostenfreien (§ 183 SGG), zu begründenden (§ 142 Abs. 2 SGG) und formlos mitzuteilenden (§ 63 Abs. 1 SGG) Beschluß **endgültig** (§ 189 Abs. 2 Satz 2 SGG).

Was die **Besetzung des angerufenen Gerichts** anbetrifft, so ergibt sich aus dem Beschluß des Großen Senats des Bundessozialgerichts (BSG 1, 1[5]), daß die Tätigkeit der ehrenamtlichen Beisitzer mit dem Erlaß der das Verfahren abschließenden Sachentscheidung (Urteil, Kostenbeschluß) endet. Der einschlägige § 26 SGG, der in den die höheren Rechtszüge betreffenden §§ 36, 48 in Bezug genommen ist, spricht in der Tat nur von der Heranziehung der ehrenamtlichen Beisitzer zu den „Verhandlungen". Bei der Entscheidung über Gebührenfragen, die der Sachentscheidung (einschließlich der sachlichen Kostenentscheidung, der Kostengrundentscheidung) nachfolgt, brauchen danach die ehrenamtlichen Beisitzer nicht mitzuwirken (so auch der Amtliche Bericht, BT-Drucks. Nr. 338 und Hofmann-Schroeter, SGG Nachtrag zur 2. Aufl., Anm. 3 zu § 216, vgl. ferner LSG Nordrhein-Westfalen, SGb 1958, 166; a. A. Brocke, SGb 1958, 271 [274]).

Zurückverweisung (evtl. mit sachlicher Anweisung) ist an sich nicht ausgeschlossen. Gegen die neue Entscheidung nach Zurückverweisung kann wiederum vom Beschwerten das Gericht angerufen werden.

Nachprüfung erfolgt grundsätzlich nur im Rahmen des Angegriffenen. Eine Schlechterstellung des Anrufenden ist verboten.

Anrufungsberechtigte sind bei zu hoher oder ungerechtfertigter Festsetzung die betroffene Körperschaft oder Anstalt des öffentlichen Rechts, bei zu niedriger Festsetzung oder Unterlassung einer solchen überhaupt die Staatskasse, vertreten durch den Bezirksrevisor o. ä. Abhilfe eröffnet dem Gegner neu die Anrufungsfrist.

Die Rechtsmittelgewährung zugunsten der beschwerten Staatskasse nimmt auch hier jede rechtliche Grundlage für die Möglichkeit, den Kostenbeamten im Wege der Dienstaufsicht zu einer Änderung der Festsetzung anzuweisen. Daran kann kein Zweifel bestehen, weil im Gesetz (§ 190 SGG) ausdrücklich gesagt ist, was im Verwaltungswege getan werden darf. Bei Bejahung des Anweisungsrechts würde die Fristbindung im § 189 Abs. 2 letzter Satz SGG zugunsten der Staatskasse einseitig in Wegfall kommen.

Eine Eigenabänderung des Gerichtsbeschlusses ist nicht vorgesehen (ebenso nicht der Festsetzung durch den Urkundsbeamten).

Wegen Berichtigung offensichtlicher Unrichtigkeiten durch das Gericht oder den sich versehenden Urkundsbeamten vgl. die §§ 138, 142 Abs. 1 SGG.

Wird die Festsetzung aufgehoben oder herabgesetzt, so müssen die zu Unrecht gezahlten Kosten zurückerstattet werden; Erzwingung ist nur im Wege der Klage möglich.

Der Rechtsbehelf hat keine aufschiebende Wirkung (vgl. § 175 Satz 1 und 2, § 178 letzter Satz SGG).

Aussetzung der Vollziehung (Abhängigmachung von einer Sicherheitsleistung dürfte hier grundsätzlich nicht erforderlich sein) bis zur Entscheidung des Gerichts ist durch dieses (oder seinen Vorsitzenden) möglich (§ 178 Satz 2 in Verb. mit § 175 Satz 3 SGG). Die Entscheidung über die Vollzugsaussetzung ist nicht anfechtbar.

Mangels entgegenstehender Bestimmungen wird es für zulässig anzusehen sein, daß bei der **Geschäftsverteilung** des Präsidium des Gerichts eine **bestimmteKammer** oder einen **bestimmten Senat** mit der Entscheidung über „Anrufungen" gemäß § 189 Abs. 2 Satz 2 SGG betraut (so auch Brocke-Reese, Geb. u. KostR Anm. zu § 189 SGG und SG Berlin in Breith. 1956, 1061).

Wegen der **Gebühren der Schiedsämter** für die kassenärztliche (kassenzahnärztliche) Versorgung vgl. die §§ 20 bis 22 der VO vom 28. 5. 1957 (BGBl. I 570).

Fünftes Kapitel

Die Kosten der Beteiligten, der Zeugen und der Sachverständigen und ihre Festsetzung

SGG: §§ 118, 178, 191, 216 Abs. 1 Nr. 2
ZPO: §§ 401, 413
ZuSEG: §§ 1, 2, 3, 4, 5, 6, 7, 8, 9, 10, 11, 12, 13, 14, 15, 16
GKG: § 91 Abs. 3 bis 6
Gesetz über Reisekostenvergütung der Beamten (RKG) vom 15. 12. 1933 (RGBl. I 1067) i. d. F. der VO vom 20. 12. 1956 (BGBl. I 1079): § 9 Abs. 2 und 3

§ 118 SGG

Durchführung der Beweisaufnahme

(1) Soweit dieses Gesetz nichts anderes bestimmt, sind auf die Beweisaufnahme § 160 Abs. 2 Nr. 3, §§ 358 bis 363, 365 bis 377, 380 bis 386, § 387 Abs. 1 und 2, §§ 388 bis 390, 392 bis 444, 478 bis 484 der Zivilprozeßordnung entsprechend anzuwenden. Die Entscheidung über die Rechtmäßigkeit der Weigerung nach § 387 der Zivilprozeßordnung ergeht durch Beschluß.

(2) Zeugen und Sachverständige werden nur beeidigt, wenn das Gericht dies im Hinblick auf die Bedeutung des Zeugnisses oder Gutachtens für die Entscheidung des Rechtsstreits für notwendig erachtet.

(3) Der Vorsitzende kann das Auftreten eines Prozeßbevollmächtigten untersagen, solange die Partei trotz Anordnung ihres persönlichen Erscheinens unbegründet ausgeblieben ist und hierdurch der Zweck der Anordnung vereitelt wird.

§ 178 SGG

Anrufung des Gerichts gegen Entscheidungen des ersuchten oder beauftragten Richters oder des Urkundsbeamten

Gegen die Entscheidungen des ersuchten oder beauftragten Richters oder des Urkundsbeamten kann binnen eines Monats nach Bekanntgabe das Gericht angerufen werden, das endgültig entscheidet. §§ 173 bis 175 gelten entsprechend.

§ 191 SGG

Auslagenersatz für Beteiligte

Ist das persönliche Erscheinen eines Beteiligten angeordnet worden, so werden ihm auf Antrag bare Auslagen und Zeitverlust wie einem Zeugen vergütet; sie können vergütet werden, wenn er ohne Anordnung erscheint und das Gericht das Erscheinen für geboten hält.

§ 216 Abs. 1 Nr. 2 SGG

Beschlußentscheidung ohne Laienbeisitzer

(1) Bis zum 31. Dezember 1960 kann

2. der Vorsitzende bei dem Sozialgericht, das Landessozialgericht ohne Zuziehung der Landessozialrichter und das Bundessozialgericht ohne Zuziehung der Bundessozialrichter außerhalb der mündlichen Verhandlung Beschlüsse erlassen, die der Entscheidung in der Sache selbst vorausgehen.

§ 401 ZPO

Zeugengebühren

Der Zeuge wird nach dem Gesetz über die Entschädigung von Zeugen und Sachverständigen entschädigt.

§ 413 ZPO

Sachverständigengebühren

Der Sachverständige wird nach dem Gesetz über die Entschädigung von Zeugen und Sachverständigen entschädigt.

Gesetz über die Entschädigung von Zeugen und Sachverständigen

§ 1

Geltungsbereich

(1) Nach diesem Gesetz werden Zeugen und Sachverständige entschädigt, die von dem Gericht oder von dem Staatsanwalt zu Beweiszwecken herangezogen werden.

(2) Dieses Gesetz gilt nicht, wenn Sachverständige herangezogen werden, die für die Sachverständigentätigkeit im Sinne des Absatzes 1 aus der Bundes- oder Landeskasse eine laufende, nicht auf den Einzelfall abgestellte Vergütung erhalten.

§ 2

Entschädigung von Zeugen

(1) Zeugen werden für ihren Verdienstausfall entschädigt. Dies gilt auch bei schriftlicher Beantwortung einer Beweisfrage (§ 377 Abs. 3, 4 der Zivilprozeßordnung).

(2) Die Entschädigung beträgt für jede Stunde der versäumten Arbeitszeit wenigstens 0,50 Deutsche Mark und höchstens 3 Deutsche Mark. Die letzte, bereits begonnene Stunde wird voll gerechnet. Die Entschädigung richtet sich nach dem regelmäßigen Bruttoverdienst.

(3) Zeugen erhalten wenigstens die nach dem geringsten Satz bemessene Entschädigung, Hausfrauen jedoch wenigstens eine Deutsche Mark je Stunde, es sei denn, daß sie durch die Heranziehung ersichtlich keine Nachteile erlitten haben.

(4) Die Entschädigung wird für höchstens zehn Stunden je Tag gewährt.

§ 3

Entschädigung von Sachverständigen

(1) Sachverständige werden für ihre Leistungen entschädigt.

(2) Die Entschädigung ist nach der erforderlichen Zeit zu bemessen. Sie beträgt bis zu 5 Deutsche Mark, bei Leistungen, die besondere fachliche Kenntnisse erfordern, bis zu 10 Deutsche Mark für jede Stunde. Die letzte, bereits begonnene Stunde wird voll gerechnet.

(3) Für ein schriftliches Gutachten, in dem der Sachverständige sich für den Einzelfall eingehend mit der wissenschaftlichen Lehre auseinanderzusetzen hat, kann die nach Absatz 2 zu gewährende Entschädigung bis zu 50 vom Hundert überschritten werden.

§ 4

Zu berücksichtigende Zeit

Zu berücksichtigen ist für Zeugen und Sachverständige auch die Zeit, während der sie ihre gewöhnliche Beschäftigung nicht wieder aufnehmen können.

§ 5

Besondere Verrichtungen

Verrichtungen, die in der Anlage zu diesem Gesetz bezeichnet sind, werden nach der Anlage entschädigt. Dies gilt auch für sachverständige Zeugen und für Hilfspersonen von Sachverständigen, die von dem Gericht oder von dem Staatsanwalt zugezogen werden.

§ 6

Besondere Entschädigung

(1) Haben sich die Parteien dem Gericht gegenüber mit einer bestimmten Entschädigung für die Leistung des Sachverständigen einverstanden erklärt, so ist diese Entschädigung zu gewähren, wenn ein ausreichender Betrag an die Staatskasse gezahlt ist.

(2) Die Erklärung nur einer Partei genügt, wenn das Gericht zustimmt. Vor der Zustimmung hat das Gericht die andere Partei zu hören. Die Zustimmung und die Ablehnung der Zustimmung sind unanfechtbar.

§ 7

Ersatz von Aufwendungen

Dem Sachverständigen werden ersetzt

1. die für die Vorbereitung und Erstattung des Gutachtens aufgewendeten Kosten, einschließlich der notwendigen Aufwendungen für Hilfskräfte, sowie die für eine Untersuchung verbrauchten Stoffe und Werkzeuge;
2. für das schriftliche Gutachten der für Schreibgebühren im Gerichtskostengesetz bestimmte Betrag;
3. für Durchschläge, die auf Erfordern gefertigt worden sind, sowie für einen Durchschlag für die Handakten des Sachverständigen 0,25 Deutsche Mark für jede Seite.

§ 8

Fahrtkosten, Wegegeld

(1) Zeugen und Sachverständigen werden die notwendigen Fahrtkosten ersetzt.

(2) Bei Benutzung von öffentlichen, regelmäßig verkehrenden Beförderungsmitteln werden die wirklichen Auslagen einschließlich der Kosten für die Beförderung des notwendigen Gepäcks bis zur Höhe der Tarife, bei Benutzung der Eisenbahn oder von Schiffen bis zum Fahrpreis der ersten Wagen- oder Schiffsklasse, ersetzt. Der Ersatz der Beförderungsauslagen ist nach den persönlichen Verhältnissen des Zeugen oder Sachverständigen zu bemessen. Die Mehrkosten für zuschlagpflichtige Züge werden erstattet.

(3) Für Fußwege und bei Benutzung von anderen als den im Absatz 2 genannten Beförderungsmitteln werden bei Entfernungen von mehr als zwei Kilometern für jedes angefangene Kilometer des Hin- und Rückwegs 0,25 Deutsche Mark gewährt. Kann ein Hin- und Rückweg von zusammen mehr als zweihundert Kilometern mit öffentlichen, regelmäßig verkehrenden Beförderungsmitteln zurückgelegt werden, so gilt Satz 1 nur insoweit, als die Mehrkosten gegenüber der Benutzung von öffentlichen, regelmäßig verkehrenden Beförderungsmitteln durch eine Minder-

ausgabe an Entschädigung ausgeglichen werden. Kann der Zeuge oder Sachverständige wegen besonderer Umstände ein öffentliches, regelmäßig verkehrendes Beförderungsmittel nicht benutzen, so werden die nachgewiesenen Mehrauslagen ersetzt, soweit sie angemessen sind.

(4) Für Reisen während der Terminsdauer werden die Fahrtkosten nur insoweit ersetzt, als dadurch Mehrbeträge an Entschädigung erspart werden, die beim Verbleiben an der Terminsstelle gewährt werden müßten.

(5) Tritt der Zeuge oder Sachverständige die Reise zum Terminsort von einem anderen als dem in der Ladung bezeichneten oder der ladenden Stelle unverzüglich angezeigten Ort an oder fährt er zu einem anderen als zu diesem Ort zurück, so werden, wenn die dadurch entstandenen Gesamtkosten höher sind, höchstens die Kosten ersetzt, die für die Reise von dem in der Ladung bezeichneten oder der ladenden Stelle angezeigten Ort oder für die Rückreise zu diesem Ort zu ersetzen wären. Mehrkosten werden nach billigem Ermessen ersetzt, wenn der Zeuge oder Sachverständige zu diesen Fahrten durch besondere Umstände genötigt war.

§ 9

Entschädigung für Aufwand

(1) Zeugen und Sachverständige erhalten für den durch Abwesenheit vom Aufenthaltsort oder durch die Wahrnehmung eines Termins am Aufenthaltsort verursachten Aufwand eine Entschädigung. Die Entschädigung ist nach den persönlichen Verhältnissen des Zeugen oder Sachverständigen zu bemessen.

(2) Die Entschädigung für den durch Abwesenheit vom Aufenthaltsort verursachten Aufwand soll nicht den Satz überschreiten, der den Bundesbeamten der Reisekostenstufe II nach den Vorschriften über die Reisekostenvergütung der Bundesbeamten als Tagegeld zusteht. Die Vorschriften, nach denen bei Reisen, die an demselben Kalendertag angetreten oder beendet werden, sich das Tagegeld vermindert oder ein Tagegeld nicht gewährt wird, gelten entsprechend. Dem Zeugen oder Sachverständigen, der vom Aufenthaltsort weniger als sechs Stunden abwesend ist, sind Zehrkosten bis zu 2,50 Deutsche Mark zu ersetzen. Mußte der Zeuge oder Sachverständige außerhalb seines Aufenthaltsortes übernachten, so erhält er hierfür Ersatz seiner Aufwendungen, soweit sie angemessen sind.

(3) Bei Terminen am Aufenthaltsort des Zeugen oder Sachverständigen sind Zehrkosten bis zu 2,50 Deutsche Mark für jeden Tag, an dem der Zeuge oder Sachverständige länger als vier Stunden von seiner Wohnung abwesend sein mußte, zu ersetzen.

§ 10

Ersatz sonstiger Aufwendungen

Notwendige bare Auslagen, die nicht den durch den Aufenthalt außerhalb der Wohnung verursachten Aufwand betreffen, sind dem Zeugen oder Sachverständigen zu ersetzen. Dies gilt besonders von den Kosten einer notwendigen Vertretung und für die Kosten notwendiger Begleitpersonen.

§ 11

Aufrundung

Die dem Zeugen oder Sachverständigen zu zahlende Gesamtentschädigung wird auf 10 Deutsche Pfennig aufgerundet.

§ 12

Vereinbarung der Entschädigung

Mit Sachverständigen, die häufiger herangezogen werden, kann die oberste Landesbehörde oder die von ihr bestimmte Stelle eine Entschädigung im Rahmen der nach diesem Gesetz zulässigen Entschädigung vereinbaren.

§ 13

Vorschuß

(1) Geladenen Zeugen und Sachverständigen ist auf Antrag ein Vorschuß zu bewilligen, wenn sie nicht über die Mittel für die Reise verfügen oder wenn ihnen, insbesondere wegen der Höhe der entstehenden Reisekosten, nicht zugemutet werden kann, diese aus eigenen Mitteln vorzuschießen.

(2) Dem Sachverständigen ist ferner auf Antrag ein Vorschuß zu bewilligen, wenn die Erstattung des Gutachtens bare Aufwendungen erfordert und dem Sachverständigen, insbesondere wegen der Höhe der Aufwendungen, nicht zugemutet werden kann, eigene Mittel vorzuschießen.

(3) § 15 gilt sinngemäß.

§ 14

Erlöschen des Anspruchs

(1) Zeugen und Sachverständige werden nur auf Verlangen entschädigt.

(2) Verlangt der Zeuge nicht binnen drei Monaten nach Beendigung der Zuziehung Entschädigung bei dem zuständigen Gericht oder bei der zuständigen Staatsanwaltschaft, so erlischt der Anspruch.

(3) Das Gericht (§ 15 Abs. 1) kann den Sachverständigen auffordern, seinen Anspruch innerhalb einer bestimmten Frist zu beziffern. Die Frist

muß mindestens zwei Monate betragen. In der Aufforderung ist der Sachverständige über die Folgen einer Versäumung der Frist zu belehren. Die Frist kann auf Antrag vom Gericht verlängert werden. Der Anspruch erlischt, soweit ihn der Sachverständige nicht innerhalb der Frist beziffert. War der Sachverständige ohne sein Verschulden verhindert, die Frist einzuhalten, so ist ihm auf Antrag Wiedereinsetzung in den vorigen Stand zu erteilen, wenn er innerhalb von zwei Wochen nach Beseitigung des Hindernisses den Anspruch beziffert und die Tatsachen, die die Wiedereinsetzung begründen, glaubhaft macht.

(4) § 196 Abs. 1 Nr. 17 des Bürgerlichen Gesetzbuchs bleibt unberührt.

§ 15

Gerichtliche Festsetzung

(1) Die einem Zeugen oder Sachverständigen zu gewährende Entschädigung wird durch gerichtlichen Beschluß festgesetzt, wenn der Zeuge oder Sachverständige oder die Staatskasse die richterliche Festsetzung beantragen oder das Gericht sie für angemessen hält. Zuständig ist das Gericht oder der Richter, von dem der Zeuge oder Sachverständige herangezogen worden ist. Ist der Zeuge oder Sachverständige von dem Staatsanwalt herangezogen worden, so ist das Gericht zuständig, bei dem die Staatsanwaltschaft errichtet ist. Das Gericht kann seine Festsetzung von Amts wegen ändern. Schwebt das Verfahren wegen der Hauptsache oder wegen der Entscheidung über den für die Gerichtsgebühren maßgebenden Wert, den Kostenansatz oder die Kostenfestsetzung in der Rechtsmittelinstanz, so ist auch das Rechtsmittelgericht hierzu befugt.

(2) Gegen die richterliche Festsetzung ist die Beschwerde zulässig, wenn der Wert des Beschwerdegegenstandes 50 Deutsche Mark übersteigt. Beschwerdeberechtigt sind nur der Zeuge oder Sachverständige und die Staatskasse. Eine Beschwerde an ein oberes Bundesgericht ist nicht zulässig. Die Beschwerde wird bei dem Gericht eingelegt, das die angefochtene Entscheidung erlassen hat. Das Gericht kann der Beschwerde abhelfen.

(3) Anträge, Erklärungen und Beschwerden können zu Protokoll der Geschäftsstelle gegeben oder schriftlich ohne Mitwirkung eines Rechtsanwalts eingereicht werden.

§ 16

Dolmetscher und Übersetzer

(1) Für Dolmetscher und Übersetzer gelten die Vorschriften dieses Gesetzes sinngemäß.

(2) Dolmetscher werden wie Sachverständige entschädigt.

(3) Die Entschädigung für die Übertragung eines Textes aus einer Sprache in eine andere Sprache beträgt für die Zeile der schriftlichen Übersetzung, die durchschnittlich fünfzehn Silben enthält, 0,30 Deutsche Mark. Bei der Übertragung von Fachtexten, insbesondere technischen oder medizinischen Gutachten, und bei sonstigen besonders schwierigen Übertragungen kann die Entschädigung bis auf eine Deutsche Mark für eine Zeile erhöht werden.

Anlage (zu § 5)

Lfd. Nr.	Bezeichnung der Verrichtung	Entschädigung in Deutsche Mark
1	Der Arzt, der eine Leiche, Teile einer Leiche oder eine Leibesfrucht besichtigt oder bei einer richterlichen Leichenschau mitwirkt, erhält hierfür und für seinen zur Niederschrift gegebenen Bericht	15
	Für mehrere solcher Verrichtungen bei derselben Gelegenheit erhält der Arzt höchstens	40
	Sind Berichte schriftlich zu erstatten oder nachträglich zur Niederschrift zu geben, so erhält der Arzt für jeden Bericht.	7
	höchstens	25
2	Jeder Obduzent erhält	
	a) für die Leichenöffnung	40
	b) für die Sektion von Teilen einer Leiche oder die Öffnung einer nicht lebensfähigen Leibesfrucht	20
	Erfolgt die Obduktion unter besonders ungünstigen äußeren Bedingungen, so beträgt die Entschädigung	
	zu a)	50
	zu b)	30
	Die Entschädigung umfaßt auch den zur Niederschrift gegebenen Bericht einschließlich des vorläufigen Gutachtens.	
	Der Sektionsgehilfe erhält für die Leichenöffnung	12
3	Der Arzt erhält für die Ausstellung des Befundscheins oder die Erteilung einer schriftlichen Auskunft ohne nähere gutachtliche Äußerung.	8
4	Der Arzt erhält für das Zeugnis über einen ärztlichen Befund mit kurzer gutachtlicher Äußerung oder für ein Formbogengutachten, wenn sich die Fragen auf Vorgeschichte, Angaben und Befund beschränken und nur ein kurzes Gutachten erfordern	10
5	Für die Untersuchung eines Nahrungs- oder Genußmittels oder eines Gebrauchsgegenstands, Arzneistoffs, Geheimmittels und dgl. oder von Wässern oder Abwässern und eine kurze schriftliche, gutachtliche Äußerung beträgt die Entschädigung für jede Probe	8 bis 50
6	Für die mikroskopische, physikalische, röntgenologische, chemische, bakteriologische, serologische Untersuchung, wenn das Untersuchungsmaterial von Menschen oder Tieren stammt, und eine kurze gutachtliche Äußerung, einschließlich des verbrauchten Materials an Farbstoffen und anderen geringwertigen Stoffen, beträgt die Entschädigung für jede Probe	8 bis 50

		Entschädigung in Deutsche Mark
7	Bei Blutgruppenbestimmungen beträgt die Entschädigung	
	a) für die Bestimmung von AB0-Blutgruppen	10
	für die Bestimmung von Untergruppen	8
	b) für die MN-Bestimmung	8
	c) für zusätzlich erforderliche Absorptionsversuche	14
	d) für die Bestimmung des Rh-Faktors und ähnliche Faktoren, je Faktor	10
	bei derselben Blutprobe je Person insgesamt höchstens	50
	e) für jede Blutentnahme einschließlich Venüle	3
	f) für das schriftliche Gutachten	7
8	Für erbbiologische Abstammungsgutachten nach den anerkannten erbbiologischen Methoden beträgt die Entschädigung	
	a) wenn bis zu drei Personen untersucht werden	230
	b) für die Untersuchung jeder weiteren Person	60
	Die Entschädigung umfaßt die gesamte Tätigkeit des Sachverständigen und etwaiger Hilfspersonen, insbesondere die Untersuchung, die Herstellung der Lichtbilder einschließlich der erforderlichen Abzüge, die Herstellung von Abdrücken, etwa notwendige Abformungen und dgl. sowie die Auswertung und Beurteilung des gesamten Materials; sie umfaßt ferner die Post- und Fernsprechgebühren sowie die Kosten für die Anfertigung des schriftlichen Gutachtens in drei Stücken.	
	Die Entschädigung umfaßt nicht notwendige Reisen außerhalb des Aufenthaltsorts des Sachverständigen, die Kosten für Blutgruppenbestimmungen und Röntgenaufnahmen und für die Begutachtung etwa vorhandener erbpathologischer Befunde durch Fachärzte.	
9	Der Arzt erhält für die Teilnahme an einer Sitzung eines Gerichts der Sozialgerichtsbarkeit, einschließlich des Aktenstudiums, der körperlichen Untersuchung und der mündlichen Erstattung von Gutachten ohne Rücksicht auf die Zahl der verhandelten Sachen für die erste Stunde	14
	für jede angefangene weitere Stunde	9

§ 91 Abs. 3 bis 6 GKG

Schreibgebühren

(3) Die Schreibgebühr beträgt für die Seite, die 28 Zeilen von durchschnittlich 15 Silben enthält, 50 Deutsche Pfennig, auch wenn die Herstellung auf mechanischem Wege (ausgenommen durch Ablichtung) stattgefunden hat. Jede angefangene Seite wird als voll gerechnet.

(4) Für Schriftstücke, die in fremder Sprache abgefaßt sind, wird die doppelte Schreibgebühr erhoben.

(5) Für Schriftstücke in tabellarischer Form, Grundbuchblätter, Registerblätter, Verzeichnisse, Listen, Rechnungen, Zeichnungen und dgl. wird die Schreibgebühr nach dem Zeitaufwand berechnet, der bei durchschnittlicher Arbeitsleistung zur Herstellung benötigt wird. Sie beträgt für jede angefangene Viertelstunde 60 Deutsche Pfennig.

(6) Werden Abschriften durchAblichtung hergestellt, so werden für jede Seite ohne Rücksicht auf Zeilen- und Silbenzahl 50 Deutsche Pfennig, bei größerem Format als DIN B 4 eine Deutsche Mark erhoben.

§ 9 Abs. 2 und 3 RKG

Tage- und Übernachtungsgeld

(2) Es beträgt

a) das Tagegeld für jeden vollen Kalendertag in

Stufe Ia	20,00 DM
Stufe Ib	17,00 DM
Stufe II	14,00 DM
Stufe III	11,00 DM
Stufe IV	9,50 DM
Stufe V	8,00 DM

b) das Übernachtungsgeld in

Stufe Ia	15,00 DM
Stufe Ib	14,00 DM
Stufe II	11,00 DM
Stufe III	10,00 DM
Stufe IV	7,50 DM
Stufe V	7,00 DM

(3) Beansprucht eine Dienstreise keinen vollen Kalendertag, so beträgt das Tagegeld bei Abwesenheit von

mehr als 6 bis 8 Stunden 0,3 des vollen Satzes,
mehr als 8 bis 12 Stunden 0,5 des vollen Satzes,
mehr als 12 Stunden den vollen Satz.

Werden an einem Tage mehrere Dienstreisen ausgeführt, so wird jede Reise für sich berechnet.

Spezialabhandlungen des Verfassers: Die Vergütung der Sachverständigen im Sozialgerichtsverfahren, SGb 1957, 6 und Die neuen Bestimmungen über die Entschädigung von Zeugen und Sachverständigen, JR 1957, 369.

I. Die Entschädigung des Beteiligten

Übersicht

1. a) Ist das persönliche Erscheinen eines **Beteiligten** (im Sinne des § 69 SGG) angeordnet worden, so werden ihm auf Antrag aus der Staatskasse **Zeitverlust und bare Auslagen wie einem Zeugen vergütet** (§ 191 Satz 1 SGG). Es muß sich dabei um eine natürliche Person handeln; juristische Personen, die aufgegebenermaßen (vgl. § 111 Abs. 3 SGG) einen Beamten oder Angestellten entsenden, haben keinen Anspruch auf Vergütung (LSG Nordrhein-Westfalen, SGb 1954, 13 mit im Ergebnis zustimmender Anmerkung von Eberhardt; vgl. auch Hose, SGb 1956, 189).

α) Das **persönliche Erscheinen** des Beteiligten, der hier wie ein Zeuge behandelt wird, muß vom Vorsitzenden (oder vom Gericht) gemäß § 106 Abs. 3 Nr. 7, § 111 Abs. 1 SGG **angeordnet** worden sein. (Es kann dies auch in dritter Instanz, z. B. zur Klärung der Prozeßfähigkeit, geschehen.) Ob die Anordnung mit Recht erfolgt ist, ist unerheblich. Ebenso kommt es nicht auf das Ergebnis an, welches das Erscheinen gezeitigt hat. Gleichgültig ist ferner, ob der anordnungsgemäß Erschienene obsiegt oder unterliegt. Armut oder schlechte wirtschaftliche Lage ist nicht Voraussetzung der Entschädigung. Die Körperschaften und Anstalten des öffentlichen Rechts scheiden hier als Berechtigte von vornherein aus (vgl. bereits den in dieser Richtung laufenden § 193 Abs. 4 SGG). Mit dem Erscheinen der Naturalperson entsteht der Entschädigungsanspruch als solcher.

β) Ein **Antrag** des Geladenen und Erschienenen **auf Entschädigung** ist erforderlich; er bedarf keiner Form und ist an sich an keine Frist gebunden. Er muß aber in aller Regel bis zur Entscheidung der Instanz gestellt sein, damit diese, dem Gericht entstehenden Kosten bei Vorliegen der Voraussetzungen des § 192 SGG (vgl. 1. Kap. 1, 2) dem die Kosten verschuldenden Beteiligten auferlegt werden können. Hinweis des Gerichts auf beschleunigte Antragstellung ist daher bei alsbald erfolgender Sach- und Kostenentscheidung angebracht. Mit der Antragstellung wird der Anspruch fällig. Ein Beschluß des Gerichts ist dieserhalb nicht erforderlich (LSG Bayern, Bay.ArbBl. 1957, 73).

Bei Antragstellung erst nach Erlaß der Instanzentscheidung wird nach dem alles beherrschenden Grundsatze von Treu und Glauben regelmäßig **Verwirkung** angenommen werden müssen, es sei denn, daß die die Belastung der Staatskasse ausgleichende Kostenregelung in der Gerichtsentscheidung (vgl. § 192 SGG) im höheren Rechtszuge erfolgt ist oder voraussichtlich noch vorgenommen werden kann (bei Abhilfemöglichkeit gegebenenfalls im gleichen Rechtszuge).

Auf jeden Fall **erlischt der Entschädigungsanspruch**, wenn er nicht binnen drei Monaten nach Beendigung der Zuziehung gegenüber dem sachbefaßten Gericht geltend gemacht wird (§ 191 Satz 1 SGG und § 15 Abs. 2 ZuSEG; vgl. auch LSG Bayern, Bay.ArbBl. 1957, B. 13; a. A. LSG Niedersachsen, Nds. MinBl. 1957, 6). Diese Frist ist als materiell-rechtliche Ausschlußfrist nicht verlängerbar, gegen ihre Versäumung gibt es mangels gesetzlicher Anordnung keine Wiedereinsetzung in den vorigen Stand. § 84 Abs. 2 und § 91 Abs. 1 SGG, welche die Fristwahrung in bestimmten Fällen erleichtern, gelten hier nicht (vgl. Brocke-Reese, Entsch BeisZuS Anm. 3 zu §14 ZuSEG). Für die Fristberechnung gelten die §§186ff. BGB.

Die **Verjährung** des rechtzeitig geltend gemachten Anspruchs erfolgt gemäß dem § 196 Abs. 1 Nr. 17 BGB in zwei Jahren, beginnend mit dem Ablauf des Jahres, in welchem er geltend gemacht wird (vgl. § 199 in Verb. mit § 201 BGB). Die Verjährung ist entsprechend ihrer prozessualen Natur (Einrede) nur zu beachten, wenn der Vertreter der Staatskasse (Bezirksrevisor) sich auf sie ausdrücklich berufen hat.

Hat der Erschienene auf Grund einer allgemeinen oder konkreten Erstattungsanordnung nach § 193 SGG bereits die Kosten für Zeitverlust nebst Auslagen vom Gegner erstattet erhalten (vgl. hierzu § 197 Abs. 1 SGG), so kann die Entschädigung nicht mehr vom Gericht verlangt werden.

b) Ist ein Beteiligter **ohne Anordnung** erschienen, so kann er (freies, aber pflichtgebundenes Ermessen entscheidet; es wird dabei auf die Bedeutung seiner persönlichen Anhörung oder seiner Anwesenheit — z. B. im Beweistermin — für die Sachentscheidung ankommen, wobei gleichgültig ist, wie im einzelnen die Anhörung, das Terminsergebnis oder die ergehende Entscheidung ausfällt) aus der Staatskasse in gleicher Weise entschädigt werden, wenn das befaßte Gericht (grundsätzlich in voller jeweiliger Besetzung) das **Erscheinen** für **geboten** hält (§ 191 Satz 2 SGG). Letztes kann je nach den Umständen auch bei Vorhandensein eines Prozeßbevollmächtigten des Erschienenen bejaht werden.

α) Ein dahingehender **Ausspruch des Gerichts** (Beschluß) ist erforderlich; er liegt in der Anordnung der Entschädigung durch das Gericht, die als solche aber nicht erforderlich ist. (Die Entschädigung ist grundsätzlich eigenverantwortliche Aufgabe des kostenberechnenden Urkundsbeamten des sachbefaßten Gerichts.)

Die positive oder negative Entscheidung des Gerichts über das Vorliegen der Voraussetzung des § 191 Satz 2 SGG dürfte im Hinblick auf § 172 Abs. 2 SGG nicht anfechtbar sein (a. A. Hose, SGb 1956, 189, der gegen die Entscheidung des Sozialgerichts die Beschwerde für gegeben hält, ebenso Brocke-Reese, Geb. u. KostR Anm. III 3 zu § 191 SGG). Ob das Erscheinen eines Beteiligten geboten ist oder war, kann nämlich nur unter Beachtung der Umstände des Falles, also nach Prüfung der gesamten Sach- und Rechtslage beantwortet werden. In die Sachbeurteilung soll aber im Wege der Beschwerde zu einem Nebenpunkte nach Möglichkeit nicht eingetreten werden. Auf jeden Fall dürfte der Beschluß noch mit zu den sog. Aufklärungsanordnungen im Sinne des § 172 Abs. 2 SGG — im weiteren Sinne — zu rechnen sein.

β) **Antragstellung** ist auch hier erforderlich. Auf das oben (1 a β) Ausgeführte wird verwiesen.

Zu a und b. Hinsichtlich der Frage der **Erstattungsfähigkeit** dieser Kosten zwischen den Beteiligten vgl. das 6. Kap., insbes. 4b. Die Gerichtskasse kann nie auf einen Erstattungsanspruch des Berechtigten gegenüber einem anderen Beteiligten verweisen (so auch LSG Bayern, Bay.ArbBl. 1957, B. 13; Hofmann-Schroeter, SGG 2. Aufl. Anm. 3 a. E. zu § 191; a. A. Brocke, Der Sozialrichter S. 179 und Miesbach-Ankenbrank, SGG Anm. 5 zu § 191); die Staatskasse hat aus sozialer Verpflichtung grundsätzlich selbst zu zahlen, und zwar unabhängig davon, ob sie über § 192 SGG Ersatz bekommt (siehe dazu das 1. Kap. 1, 2) oder ob sie eine Gebühr nach § 184 SGG (vgl. das 4. Kap. 3) erhält (a. A. Brocke-Reese, Geb. u.

KostR Anm. III 2 zu § 191 SGG, der, falls die Voraussetzungen dafür gegeben sind, in erster Linie die Erstattungspflicht des Gegners Platz greifen läßt).

§ 191 SGG ist sinngemäß auf die Vergütung von Zeitverlust und Auslagen anzuwenden, die einem Beteiligten aus Anlaß einer gerichtlich **angeordneten Untersuchung** (mit Ausnahme der auf eigene Kosten nach § 109 Abs. 1 SGG) entstanden sind (so auch Hastler, Aufbau und Verfahren der Sozialgerichtsbarkeit Anm. zu § 191; Peters-Sautter-Wolff, SGG Anm. zu § 191 und LSG Bayern, SGb 1956, 164 mit zust. Anm. von Schieckel, ferner Wende, KOV 1956, 14 und Hose, SGb 1956, 189, auch LSG Baden-Württemberg, Breith. 1956, 1170).

Die Verpflichtung der Staatskasse zur **Bevorschussung** bei Anordnung des persönlichen Erscheinens eines auswärtigen Beteiligten ergibt sich bei entsprechender Mittellosigkeit oder Unzumutbarkeit der Verauslagung der Reisekosten aus der Vorschrift des § 13 Abs. 1 ZuSEG. Die Übersendung des Vorschusses — oft ist nur Übersendung der Fahrkarte am Platze — erfolgt auf entsprechendes Gesuch durch den kostenberechnenden Urkundsbeamten des sachbefaßten Gerichts. (Dieses kann zur Unterstützung nötigenfalls den Urkundsbeamten des Sozialgerichts am Wohnsitz des Beteiligten heranziehen.) Bei Nichtzahlung oder nicht ausreichender Gewährung des Vorschusses ist Anrufung des Prozeßgerichts durch den Beteiligten binnen eines Monats seit der Zustellung der Entscheidung des Urkundsbeamten gemäß § 178 SGG möglich. Gegen ungerechtfertigte oder zu hohe Bevorschussung kann die Staatskasse in der gleichen Weise vorgehen. (Wegen des Rechtsbehelfs im einzelnen vgl. hier unten 3b.) Nicht abgegoltener Vorschuß ist zurückzuzahlen. Zweckwidrige Verwendung des Vorschusses ist in der Regel strafbar (vgl. § 266 StGB).

2. Was die Voraussetzungen der **Vergütung** nach den Bestimmungen des Entschädigungsgesetzes für Zeugen (und Sachverständige) sowie ihre Höhe anbetrifft, so gilt das Folgende:

a) **Hinsichtlich der Zeitentschädigung.**

Diese Entschädigung wird grundsätzlich nur demjenigen zugebilligt, dem ein **Verdienstausfall,** d. h. eine Verkürzung seines Bruttoeinkommens entstanden ist (§ 2 Abs. 1 Satz 1 ZuSEG). Der Ausfall gegebenenfalls der Arbeitgeberanteile wird in gewisser Hinsicht dadurch ausgeglichen, daß der an sich an das Finanzamt zu zahlende Lohnsteuerbetrag in den Händen des entschädigten Beteiligten verbleibt.

Ausgeschlossen vom Vergütungsbezug sind danach von vornherein: Beamte, ferner Behördenangestellte und kaufmännische Angestellte, wenn sie fortlaufend ihr Gehalt beziehen (vgl. LSG Nordrhein-Westfalen, JVBl. 1957, 45). Bei Landwirten und Inhabern größerer Betriebe ist Voraussetzung der Entschädigung, daß sie selbst mitarbeiten. Geschäftsreisende können nur den Provisionsausfall (nicht den Verlust von Spesen, die ja erspart werden) geltend machen. Ist der Tag des Erscheinens ein tarifmäßig bezahlter Ruhetag, so ist die Entschädigung zu gewähren, wenn die Bezahlung nach dem Tarif wegen der Wahrnehmung des Termins entfällt (vgl. Gölkel, SGb [Beil.] 1958, 18 [20]).

Ob ein Verdienstausfall im Einzelfalle vorliegt, ist nach freiem Ermessen unter Berücksichtigung der Lebensverhältnisse und der Erwerbstätigkeit des Erschienenen zu beurteilen. Soweit der geringste Entschädigungssatz (s. u.) in Frage steht, kann hierbei großzügig verfahren werden (vgl. § 2 Abs. 3 ZuSEG). So kann auch bei einem Erwerbslosen, der ja entgeltliche Gelegenheitsarbeit in einem gewissen Umfange verrichten darf, ein Verdienstausfall angenommen werden. Hausfrauen sollen

wenigstens 1 DM je Stunde erhalten. Nur wo — klar — ersichtlich ist, daß durch das Erscheinen keine sich letzten Endes finanziell auswirkenden Nachteile entstanden sind (so bei Gefangenen), ist die Entschädigung abzulehnen (§ 2 Abs. 3 letzter Satz ZuSEG).

Unter der den Verdienstausfall verursachenden **Zeitversäumnis** ist außer der Wartezeit bis zum verspäteten Terminsbeginn, der Terminsdauer und der erforderlichen Fahrzeit zum Gericht hin und zurück auch die Zeit zu verstehen, während welcher der Entschädigungsberechtigte seine gewöhnliche Beschäftigung nicht wieder aufnehmen kann, z. B. weil er als Bergmann außerhalb der Zeit nicht einzufahren in der Lage ist (§ 4 ZuSEG).

Die **Höhe der Entschädigung** für die versäumte Zeit richtet sich grundsätzlich nach dem regelmäßigen Bruttoverdienst des Anspruchsberechtigten (§ 2 Abs. 2 Satz 3 ZuSEG). Die Berechnung erfolgt jeweils nach Stunden. (Monatseinkommen sind praktisch durch 200 zu teilen, um den verdienten Stundensatz zu erhalten.)

Der **Mindestbetrag** der Entschädigung beläuft sich je Stunde auf 0,50 DM, der **Höchstsatz** auf 3 DM (§ 2 Abs. 2 Satz 1 ZuSEG; vgl. hierzu die Gebührentabelle am Schluß). Die letzte bereits begonnene Stunde wird voll gerechnet (§ 2 Abs. 2 Satz 2 ZuSEG).

Für eine längere Zeitdauer als täglich 10 Stunden wird die Entschädigung nicht gewährt (§ 2 Abs. 4 Satz 1 ZuSEG). Auch für versäumte Überstunden, soweit sie jeweils noch in den Zeitraum von 10 Stunden fallen, erfolgt Entschädigung. Entschädigt wird ferner, ohne Rücksicht auf prozentualen Anteil an der eigentlichen Versäumung, der entgangene Lohnausgleich für den nächsten arbeitsfreien Tag; jedoch darf das Höchstentgelt für die eigentliche Versäumung insgesamt nicht überschritten werden (a. A. Iffland, Bb 1958, 1329, der den entgangenen Lohnausgleich überhaupt nicht berücksichtigt, und das OLG Hamm vom 17. 4. 1958 [Gutachten], das den verlorenen Lohnausgleich für den folgenden Ruhetag grundsätzlich voll ersetzt). Abzustellen ist jeweils auf den Tag der Vernehmung unter Berücksichtigung der An- und Abreisetage; gehört auch der Folgetag zu der durch die Vernehmung versäumten Schicht, so wird er bis zur Erreichung des Höchstentgelts der eigentlichen Versäumnis berücksichtigt (vgl. LG Dortmund, JMBl. NRW 1957, 287).

Die Arbeitgeberanteile zur Sozialversicherung, die verlorengehen, sind nicht zu berücksichtigen und zu ersetzen (so auch Brocke-Reese, EntschBeisZuS Anm. 3 zu § 2 ZuSEG; a. A. Meyer-Höver, ZuSEG 11. Aufl. Anm. 14b zu § 2).

b) **Hinsichtlich des Barauslagenersatzes.** (Die Barauslagen werden gegebenenfalls auch dann ersetzt, wenn kein Anspruch auf Zeitentschädigung besteht.)

Nach dem Entschädigungsgesetz für Zeugen und Sachverständige werden **ersetzt**:

α) die Fahrtkosten (§ 8 ZuSEG),
β) die Mehraufwendungen (§ 9 ZuSEG),
γ) die Übernachtungsspesen (§ 9 Abs. 2 letzter Satz ZuSEG),
δ) die Vertretungskosten u. ä. (§ 10 ZuSEG).

Zu α. Bei Benutzung von öffentlichen, regelmäßig verkehrenden Beförderungsmitteln werden die wirklichen Auslagen einschließlich der Kosten für die Beförderung des notwendigen Gepäcks bis zur Höhe der bestehenden Tarife ersetzt (§ 8 Abs. 2 Satz 1 ZuSEG). Bei Benutzung der Eisenbahn oder von Schiffen ist der Ersatz der Beförderungsauslagen nach den persönlichen Verhältnissen zu bemessen; äußerste Grenze ist der **Fahrpreis** der ersten Wagenklasse oder der ersten Schiffsklasse (§ 8 Abs. 2 ZuSEG). Die Mehrkosten für notwendig zu nehmende zuschlagpflichtige Züge werden ersetzt (§ 8 Abs. 2 letzter Satz ZuSEG).

Für Fußwege und bei Benutzung von anderen als den genannten Beförderungsmitteln (z. B. des eigenen Kraftwagens) werden bei Entfernungen von mehr als 2 km für jedes angefangene Kilometer des Hin- und Rückwegs 0,25 DM (allgemein angemessener Betrag) gewährt (§ 8 Abs. 3 Satz 1 ZuSEG). Der danach sich ergebende Betrag ist, wenn der Hin- und Rückweg zusammen mehr als 200 km ausmacht und mit öffentlichen, regelmäßig verkehrenden Beförderungsmitteln billiger zurückgelegt werden kann, in dem überhöhten Umfange jedoch nur soweit zu zahlen, als die Mehrkosten gegenüber der Benutzung von öffentlichen, regelmäßig verkehrenden Beförderungsmitteln durch eine Minderausgabe an Entschädigung ausgeglichen werden (§ 8 Abs. 3 Satz 2 ZuSEG). Kann wegen besonderer Umstände — persönlicher oder sachlicher Art — ein öffentliches, regelmäßig verkehrendes Beförderungsmittel nicht benutzt werden, so werden die nachgewiesenen Mehrauslagen ersetzt, soweit sie angemessen (sachlich billig) sind (§ 8 Abs. 3 letzter Satz ZuSEG).

Für etwaige Reisen während der Terminsdauer werden die Fahrtkosten nur insoweit ersetzt, als dadurch Mehrbeträge an Entschädigung erspart werden, die beim Verbleiben an der Terminsstelle gewährt werden müßten (§ 8 Abs. 4 ZuSEG).

Wird die Reise zum Terminsort von einem anderen als dem in der Ladung bezeichneten oder der ladenden Stelle unverzüglich angezeigten Ort angetreten oder wird zu einem anderen als zu diesem Ort zurückgereist, so werden, wenn die dadurch entstandenen Gesamtkosten höher sind, höchstens die Kosten ersetzt, die für die Reise von dem in der Ladung bezeichneten oder der ladenden Stelle angezeigten Ort oder für die Rückreise zu diesem Ort zu ersetzen wären. Mehrkosten werden nach billigem Ermessen ersetzt, wenn der Beteiligte zu den betreffenden Fahrten durch besondere Umstände genötigt war (§ 8 Abs. 5 ZuSEG).

Zu β. Die sog. **Aufwandsentschädigung** soll die durch die Abwesenheit vom Wohn- bzw. Aufenthaltsort oder durch die Wahrnehmung eines Termins an diesem Ort gewöhnlich verursachten Mehraufwendungen in einem durchschnittlichen Umfange abgelten (§ 9 Abs. 1 Satz 1 ZuSEG). Ihre Höhe richtet sich nach der Dauer der Abwesenheit und den persönlichen Verhältnissen (vgl. § 9 Abs. 1 Satz 2 und Abs. 2 ZuSEG).

Bei Reisen beträgt der höchstmögliche Satz 14 DM. (Das ist der Satz, der den Bundesbeamten der Reisekostenstufe II nach den Vorschriften des Gesetzes über Reisekostenvergütung der Beamten [RKG] als Tagegeld zusteht, vgl. § 9 Abs. 2 Satz 1 ZuSEG und § 9 Abs. 2a RKG i. d. F. der VO vom 20. 12. 1956, BGBl. I 1079.) Als regelmäßig in Frage kommender Durchschnitt werden hier 10 DM bezeichnet werden können. Die Aufwandsentschädigung ist in dieser oder der jeweils sonst gerechtfertigten Höhe (bis zur Höchstgrenze) aber nur dann zu gewähren, wenn die Abwesenheit mehr als 12 Stunden dauerte; bei einer Abwesenheitsdauer von mehr als 8 bis 12 Stunden ist der fragliche Satz zur Hälfte, bei einer Dauer von mehr als 6 bis 8 Stunden zu 3/10 zuzubilligen (§ 9 Abs. 2 Satz 2 ZuSEG und § 9 Abs. 3 RKG). Bei mehrtägiger Abwesenheit vom Wohnort beträgt die Aufwandsentschädigung für den Tag des Reiseantritts, wenn die Reise angetreten ist

nach 18 Uhr —,
nach 16 bis 18 Uhr 3/10,
nach 12 bis 16 Uhr 5/10,
vor 12 Uhr 10/10;

für den Tag der Reisebeendigung, wenn die Reise beendet ist,

bis 6 Uhr —,
nach 6 bis 8 Uhr 3/10,
nach 8 bis 12 Uhr 5/10,
nach 12 Uhr 10/10.

Eine Abwesenheit von 6 Stunden und weniger Dauer begründet einen Anspruch auf Ersatz der Zehrkosten bis zu 2,50 DM. (Zwar spricht das Gesetz hier nur von weniger als 6 Stunden, doch muß das Zehrgeld auch bei Abwesenheit von 6 Stunden sinngemäß gewährt werden, da nach den in sich schlüssigen Bestimmungen des Reisekostengesetzes die vorgesehene Pauschalabgeltung noch nicht erfolgt.)

Bei Terminen am Aufenthaltsort sind Zehrkosten bis zu 2,50 DM für jeden Tag mit notwendiger Abwesenheit aus der Wohnung in längerer Dauer als 4 Stunden zu ersetzen (§ 9 Abs. 3 ZuSEG).

Zu γ. War Übernachtung außerhalb des Wohn- bzw. Aufenthaltsortes erforderlich, so ist das gezahlte oder zu zahlende **Übernachtungsentgelt** (auch für Schlafwagen an Stelle eines Schlafquartiers) im Rahmen seiner Angemessenheit (die örtlichen Umstände und die persönlichen Verhältnisse sind hierfür maßgebend) zu ersetzen (§ 9 Abs. 2 letzter Satz ZuSEG). Die Zahlung ist bei Zweifeln glaubhaft zu machen. Praktischer (nicht gesetzlicher) Höchstsatz: 11 DM (entsprechend der Reisekostenstufe II der Bundesbeamten).

Zu δ. Konnexe notwendige Barauslagen, die nicht den durch den Aufenthalt außerhalb der Wohnung verursachten Aufwand betreffen (z. B. das Entgelt für Bewachen der Wohnung), sind zu ersetzen (§ 10 Satz 1 ZuSEG). Das gilt insbesondere von den **Kosten einer** notwendigen **Vertretung** (§ 10 Satz 2 ZuSEG). Die eigene Entschädigung für Zeitversäumnis wird in diesen Fällen unter Umständen in Fortfall zu kommen haben, nämlich wenn auf Grund der Vertretung kein Verdienstausfall entsteht. Zu ersetzen sind auch die — angemessenen — Kosten **einer** notwendigen **Begleitperson.** (Begleitpersonen und Vertreter haben keinen eigenen Anspruch an die Staatskasse.)

Zu a und b. Die zu zahlende **Gesamtentschädigung** wird **auf** volle **10 Deutsche Pfennig aufgerundet** (§ 11 ZuSEG).

Der **Vergütungsanspruch** des Beteiligten **entsteht,** wenn die wiedergegebenen Voraussetzungen des SGG und des ZuSEG erfüllt sind, an sich mit der Terminswahrnehmung. Die **Fälligkeit tritt erst mit der Antragstellung ein.**

3. a) Die **Feststellung der Entschädigung** erfolgt, ohne daß eine besondere Anweisung seitens des Gerichts oder seines Vorsitzenden vorgeschrieben ist, wie grundsätzlich, **durch den** kostenberechnenden **Urkundsbeamten** des in der Sache verhandelnden Gerichts (ebenso Hose, SGb 1956, 189), der — zumeist in einer Spezialgeschäftsstelle für das ganze Gericht — **eigenverantwortlich** tätig wird. Sie wird in aller Regel im Anschluß an den wahrgenommenen Termin auf mündlich gestellten Antrag vorgenommen, der nicht beziffert zu sein braucht. Dem Urkundsbeamten sind vom Antragsteller Aufklärungen über den Verdienstausfall zu geben; die Angaben sind, soweit notwendig, glaubhaft zu machen. Der Umfang des Zeitverlustes ist auf Grund der Zeitangaben des Prozeßgerichts festzustellen. Rechtsbehelfsbelehrung (schriftlich oder unter Aktenkundigmachung mündlich) ist er-

forderlich (§ 66 Abs. 1 und § 173 letzter Satz SGG). Wegen der Folgen unterlassener oder unrichtiger Belehrung vgl. § 66 Abs. 2 SGG. Eigenabänderung von Amts wegen ist außer in den Fällen der Berichtigung offensichtlicher Unrichtigkeiten nicht zulässig (vgl. §§ 138, 142 Abs. 1 SGG).

Die Entschädigung ist grundsätzlich bei der Kasse abzuholen (vgl. § 1 letzter Teil des Gesetzes über Zahlungen öffentlicher Kassen vom 21. 12. 1938, RGBl. I 1899).

b) **Gegen die Entscheidung des Urkundsbeamten** kann bei abgelehnter oder zu niedriger Feststellung der betroffene Beteiligte (evtl. seine Erben), bei ungerechtfertigter Festsetzung dem Grunde oder der Höhe nach die Staatskasse, vertreten durch den Bezirksrevisor, der Erfüllungseinwendungen aber nicht bringen darf (nötigenfalls kann hier die Zahlung verweigert werden), **das** mit der Sachentscheidung betraute **Gericht** des Urkundsbeamten **anrufen** (§ 178 SGG), und zwar binnen eines Monats seit Bekanntgabe der Feststellung (§ 173 SGG). Der § 15 Abs. 1 Satz 1 ZuSEG, der die gerichtliche Festsetzung der Zeugen- und Sachverständigenentschädigung regelt, findet hier keine Anwendung, da § 191 SGG die Gleichstellung mit dem Zeugen nur in materieller Hinsicht vorsieht (so u. a. auch Hose, SGb 1956, 189; a. A. Brocke-Reese, Geb. u. KostR Anm. II 2 zu § 191 SGG). Als spezialgesetzliche Bestimmung ginge der § 178 (mit § 173ff.) SGG zudem ohnehin vor, wobei auf jeden Fall ins Gewicht fallen würde, daß die Rechtsbehelfe und -mittel im Sozialgerichtsverfahren durchweg fristgebunden sind, um eine schnelle Durchführung und Abwicklung des Verfahrens zu ermöglichen.

Bei Verweisung an ein anderes Sozialgericht (vgl. § 98 insbes. Abs. 3 SGG) ist das neue Gericht zuständig.

Eine Anrufung des Gerichts ist zum Zwecke der sog. Nachliquidation (Erhöhung des bisher Verlangten) in keinem Falle zulässig. (Die Anrufung hat die Nachprüfung zum Ziel, nicht die Festsetzung als solche; wird Neues verlangt, muß wieder „von vorn“ angefangen werden.)

Wegen der Wiedereinsetzung in den vorigen Stand bei schuldloser Fristversäumnis vgl. § 67 SGG.

Die Erweiterung einer begrenzten Anrufung ist nach Ablauf der Anrufungsfrist nicht zulässig.

Eine Anschlußanrufung gibt es nicht.

Rücknahme der Anrufung im Zweifel mit der Wirkung des endgültigen Verlustes des Rechtsbehelfs ist möglich.

Form der Anrufung: schriftlich bei Gericht oder zur Niederschrift des Urkundsbeamten (§ 173 SGG; also stets ohne Anwaltszwang, vgl. auch § 15 Abs. 4 ZuSEG). Eine Mindestbeschwer ist nicht erforderlich.

Abhilfe durch den jeweils zuständigen Urkundsbeamten ist möglich (§ 174 SGG); unter Umständen ist Wiedereinziehung (nötigenfalls im Verwaltungsvollstreckungswege) erforderlich und zulässig. Der Einwand der weggefallenen Bereicherung ist im Hinblick auf den alles beherrschenden Grundsatz von Treu und Glauben bei entsprechender Lage der Umstände nicht ausgeschlossen.

Abhilfe eröffnet für den Gegner die Anrufungsfrist neu.

Die Anrufung hat keine aufschiebende Wirkung (§ 175 SGG). Eine Vollstreckung aus der Festsetzung des Urkundsbeamten zugunsten des Berechtigten ist nicht möglich; daher kommt eine Einstellung der Vollstreckung nicht in Frage.

Ein anderer Streitbeteiligter als der aus §§ 191 SGG Berechtigte hat, auch wenn ihm die insoweit entstandenen Kosten des Gerichts nach §§ 192f. SGG auferlegt sind, kein Anrufungsrecht (vgl. § 15 Abs. 1 Satz 1, auch Abs. 2 Satz 2 ZuSEG). Er kann, abgesehen von dem Rechtsmittelangriff gegen die ihn beschwerende Kostenentscheidung (vgl. 1. Kap. 9 a β und b ε), nur gegen den ihn belastenden Kostenbescheid (siehe 4. Kap. 2 zu a bis c vorgehen. Er braucht keinesfalls mehr zu ersetzen, als dem Erschienenen gesetzlich zu zahlen war.

Das Gericht (grundsätzlich in voller jeweiliger Besetzung) **entscheidet** bei Nichtabhilfe stets auf Grund eigenen Ermessens (§ 128 Abs. 1, § 142 Abs. 1 SGG) durch kostenfreien (§ 183 SGG) und zu begründenden Beschluß (§ 142 Abs. 2 SGG) **endgültig** (§ 178 SGG), und zwar ohne mündliche Verhandlung (§ 124 Abs. 3 SGG) und im allgemeinen ohne erforderliche Anhörung des Gegners (vgl. Hose, SGb 1956, 189).

Bis zum 31. 12. 1960 kann hier der Vorsitzende des Sozialgerichts allein, das Landessozialgericht ohne Zuziehung der Landessozialrichter und das Bundessozialgericht ohne Zuziehung der Bundessozialrichter entscheiden (§ 216 Abs. 1 Nr. 2 SGG); a. A. Brocke, SGb 1958, 271 [274], wie hier Wende, KOV 1958, 144.

Schlechterstellung auf eigenen Rechtsbehelf ist nicht möglich. Mehr als insgesamt verlangt, kann nicht zugebilligt werden. Nachprüfung erfolgt grundsätzlich nur in bezug auf das Angegriffene. Zurückverweisung an den Urkundsbeamten (evtl. unter sachlicher Anweisung) ist zulässig, wenn — wegen der eintretenden Verzögerung — auch nicht erwünscht. Nach Zurückverweisung kann gegen die neue Entscheidung vom Beschwerten wiederum das Gericht angerufen werden. Die Mitteilung des Beschlusses erfolgt formlos.

Wegen des gegebenen Rechtsbehelfs ist eine Abänderung, insbesondere Herabsetzung, der Vergütung auf Verwaltungsanweisung auch hier nicht möglich. Eigenabänderung (nach oben oder unten) durch das Gericht innerhalb angemessener Frist (etwa ein Jahr) wird allerdings aus den Gründen, die zur Schaffung des § 15 Abs. 1 Satz 4 ZuSEG geführt haben (s. u.), in entsprechender Anwendung möglich sein. Eine Abänderung von Amts wegen in der höheren Instanz (vgl. § 15 Abs. 1 Satz 5 ZuSEG) dürfte dagegen deswegen nicht in Frage kommen, weil im Sozialgerichtsverfahren Gebührenstreitigkeiten grundsätzlich in der betreffenden Instanz ihre Erledigung zu finden pflegen (vgl. §§ 178, 189 Abs. 2, § 197 Abs. 2 SGG). Das Zuvielerhaltene muß zurückgezahlt werden; nötigenfalls erfolgt Beitreibung im Verwaltungszwangsverfahren (nach dem Verwaltungsvollstreckungsgesetz). Verjährung des Rückzahlungsanspruchs erfolgt grundsätzlich in vier Jahren seit Ablauf des Kalenderjahres, in dem die Fälligkeit des Entschädigungsanspruchs eintrat, entsprechend § 8 Abs. 2 GKG. (Das gilt auch in bezug auf den Anspruch auf Rückzahlung des Vorschusses nach § 109 Abs. 1 SGG, wenn die Kosten des Sachverständigen von der Staatskasse übernommen worden sind; vgl. dazu die Ausführungen hier am Ende von I.)

Wegen der Berichtigung offensichtlicher Fehler vgl. die §§ 138, 142 Abs. 1 SGG.

Zwar sieht der § 15 Abs. 2 ZuSEG gegen die richterliche Festsetzung, wenn der Wert des Beschwerdegegenstandes 50 DM übersteigt, die unbefristete **Beschwerde** vor. Diese Bestimmung findet jedoch hier **keinesfalls** Anwendung, weil im § 191 SGG der Beteiligte nur in materiell-rechtlicher Hinsicht dem Zeugen gleichgestellt ist (s. o.). Das Sozialgerichtsgesetz kennt zudem weder eine fristlose Beschwerde noch eine an eine Mindestbeschwer gebundene. Was den Rahmen der rechtlich möglichen Anfechtung anbetrifft, so ist aus den §§ 178, 189 Abs. 2 und § 197 Abs. 2 SGG darüber hinaus der allgemeine Grundsatz zu entnehmen, daß in Verfahren der Sozialgerichtsbarkeit über Gebührenfragen stets das Gericht der betroffenen Instanz endgültig entscheidet. Im Interesse der beschleunigten Durchführung und Abwicklung des Rechtsstreits sind hier höhere Rechtszüge als Entscheidungsinstanzen nicht vorgesehen. Solche kann das allgemein gehaltene Entschädigungsgesetz für Zeugen und Sachverständige allein, d. h. ohne entsprechende Änderung der betroffenen Verfahrensgesetze, auf keinen Fall schaffen. Es hat sich vielmehr stets in die speziellen Verfahrensgesetze einzupassen. Unmöglich kann im maßgebenden Ergebnis ein Beteiligter als Berechtigter nach § 191 SGG mehr prozessuale Rechte haben als bei Berechtigung in der gleichen Weise nach § 193 Abs. 2, § 197 Abs. 2 SGG (oder bei entsprechender Verpflichtung). Beschwerde würde im übrigen stets nur gegen die Festsetzungen der Sozialgerichte gegeben sein (vgl. § 172 Abs. 1, § 177 SGG). Eine unterschiedliche Behandlung der gleichen Festsetzungsverfahren in den einzelnen Rechtszügen läßt sich aber in neuzeitlich geregelten Prozeßverfahren schlechthin nicht rechtfertigen.

c) **Bei Nichtauszahlung** trotz gerichtlicher Entscheidung (Festsetzung) wäre die **Beschreitung des — ordentlichen — Klageweges** zur Erlangung eines Vollstreckungstitels erforderlich (Judikatsklage; maßgebend ist der festgesetzte Betrag).

Der Anspruch des sein Recht suchenden oder verteidigenden Beteiligten aus § 191 SGG dürfte auch nach der Festsetzung als sozial zweckgebundener unübertragbar, unverpfändbar und unpfändbar sein (§§ 399, 1274 BGB, § 850 ZPO).

Nichts mit der Entschädigung des Beteiligten nach § 191 SGG hat zu tun, daß dieser im Falle der Übernahme der Kosten eines vernommenen „privaten" Sachverständigen auf die Staatskasse gemäß § 109 Abs. 1 Satz 2 SGG einen — hinsichtlich seiner Geltendmachung nicht fristgebundenen (aber aus zeitlichen Gründen verwirkbaren) — Anspruch gegen die Staatskasse auf Rückzahlung des geleisteten Vorschusses hat.

II. Die Entschädigung des Zeugen

Übersicht

1. Der **Zeuge** — auch der aus dem Ausland kommende — **erhält** aus der Staatskasse eine **Entschädigung für seinen Verdienstausfall sowie den Ersatz seiner** baren **Auslagen** (§§ 2, 8, 9 und 10 ZuSEG).

Nach § 17 der VO über Schiedsämter für die kassenärztliche (kassenzahnärztliche) Versorgung (Schiedsamtsordnung) vom 28. 5. 1957 (BGBl. I 570) erhalten Zeugen — und Sachverständige —, die auf Beschluß des Schiedsamts hinzugezogen worden sind, eine Entschädigung nach dem ZuSEG.

a) Die **allgemeinen Voraussetzungen** sind:

Erscheinen an Gerichtsstelle nach Ladung muß vorliegen; Vernehmung ist nicht erforderlich. Versehentliche Ladung genügt regelmäßig. Verspätetes Erscheinen ist unschädlich, wenn noch Vernehmung möglich ist oder — bei allgemeinem Verzicht auf den Zeugen — möglich gewesen wäre; andernfalls erfolgt Entschädigung nur, falls die Verspätung unverschuldet war.

Bei **Stellung oder Gerichtsanwesenheit** des Zeugen kommt es auf seine Vernehmung an. Die Vernehmung beginnt mit der Erfragung der Personalien.

Die behandelte Zuziehung zu Beweiszwecken muß im gerichtlichen Verfahren, nicht während eines Vorverfahrens (vgl. § 78 SGG) erfolgt sein. Im dritten Rechtszuge erfolgt grundsätzlich keine Beweisaufnahme.

Der Zeuge hat nach Empfang der Ladung die Verpflichtung, das Gericht auf Umstände hinzuweisen, die besondere Kosten verursachen (z. B. Zureise vom entfernter liegenden Urlaubsort o. ä.); bei Nichterfüllung dieser Pflicht erfolgt die Entschädigung grundsätzlich nur in dem gewöhnlichen Umfang (vgl. § 8 Abs. 5 ZuSEG).

Bei **Zeugnisverweigerung** besteht kein Entschädigungsanspruch. Vorherige Mitteilung der Weigerung kann nicht verlangt werden (vgl. § 386 ZPO). Bei berechtigter Weigerung hat im Sozialgerichtsverfahren daher die Entschädigung für den Termin über die Rechtmäßigkeit der Weigerung (vgl. § 118 Abs. 1 Satz 2 SGG, §§ 386 bis 389 ZPO) zu erfolgen (anders im ordentlichen Verfahren, vgl. RG 43, 409; hier ist über die Kosten des Zwischenverfahrens nach § 91 ZPO im Urteil zu entscheiden).

Ein **zwangsweise vorgeführter Zeuge** ist, unbeschadet einer etwaigen Verurteilung in die durch sein Verhalten verursachten Kosten, wie ein freiwillig erschienener Zeuge zu entschädigen (vgl. Meyer-Höver, ZuSEG 11. Aufl. Anm. 26 zu § 1).

Schriftliche Beantwortung der Beweisfrage (vgl. § 377 Abs. 3 und 4 ZPO) gewährt einen Anspruch auf volle Entschädigung (§ 2 Abs. 1 Satz 2 ZuSEG).

Bevollmächtigte Anwälte oder Rechtsbeistände, die in der vertretenen Sache als Zeugen vernommen werden, erhalten, da sie anderweit (nämlich vom Auftraggeber) vergütet werden, grundsätzlich keine Entschädigung (vgl. LG Berlin, JVBl. 1935, 314 und Meyer-Höver, ZuSEG 11. Aufl. Anm. 25b zu § 1). Im übrigen werden sie nach dem ZuSEG entschädigt, nicht etwa entsprechend der Rechtsanwaltsgebührenordnung.

Der sogen. **sachverständige Zeuge** ist Zeuge; er bekundet lediglich Tatsachen, wenn er diese auch als Sachkundiger wahrgenommen hat (vgl. § 414 ZPO). Beispiel: Ein Arzt sagt über das Vorhandensein und den Verlauf einer beobachteten Krankheit aus. Wird er auch über Ursachen oder Auswirkungen der Krankheit befragt, so wird er sowohl als Zeuge wie als Sachverständiger vernommen. Er ist dann — auch bei Ladung als Zeuge — als Sachverständiger zu entschädigen; der sachliche Gehalt seiner Vernehmung entscheidet.

Ausnahmsweise gilt die Vergütung des Sachverständigen in besonderen Fällen (vgl. § 5 ZuSEG und seine Anlage) auch für sachverständige Zeugen, soweit sie Verrichtungen der Anlage vornehmen (§ 5 Satz 2 ZuSEG. Praktisch kommt hier nur die Nr. 3 der Anlage in Betracht, da es sich im übrigen um reine Sachverständigentätigkeit handelt).

Auf Antrag ist dem Zeugen bei entsprechender Mittellosigkeit (Nachweis ohne Armutszeugnis möglich) oder Unzumutbarkeit der Verauslagung der Reisekosten ein **Vorschuß** zu zahlen, § 13 Abs. 1 ZuSEG (vom Urkundsbeamten des vernehmenden Gerichts, gegen dessen Entscheidung Anrufung stets des **Prozeß**gerichts gemäß § 178 SGG binnen eines Monats seit Zustellung möglich ist; Näheres in bezug auf den Rechtsbehelf s. u. 3c. Der hierbei etwa tätig werdende Urkundsbeamte des ersuchten Richters ist gegebenenfalls nur als dessen unselbständiger Erfüllungsgehilfe anzusehen). Nicht abgegoltener Vorschuß ist zurückzuzahlen. Zweckwidrige Verwendung des Vorschusses ist in der Regel strafbar, vgl. § 266 StGB.

b) **Besondere Voraussetzungen** bestehen **hinsichtlich des Verdienstausfalles:** Verdienstausfall, d. h. Verkürzung des Bruttoeinkommens (s. o. unter I 2a) muß vorliegen (§ 2 Abs. 1 und 2 ZuSEG).

Ob ein Verdienstausfall vorliegt, ist nach freiem Ermessen unter Berücksichtigung der Lebensverhältnisse und der regelmäßigen Erwerbstätigkeit der Zeugen zu beurteilen. Er ist bei **freien Berufen** (z. B. Ärzten) regelmäßig anzunehmen. Soweit der geringste Entschädigungssatz (s. u. 2a) in Frage steht, kann großzügig verfahren werden (vgl. § 2 Abs. 3 ZuSEG). So kann auch bei einem **Erwerbslosen,** der ja entgeltliche Gelegenheitsarbeit in einem gewissen Umfange verrichten darf, ein Verdienstausfall angenommen werden. **Hausfrauen** sollen wenigstens 1 DM je Stunde erhalten. Lediglich wo klar ersichtlich ist, daß durch die Heranziehung als Zeuge keine sich letzten Endes finanziell auswirkenden Nachteile entstanden sind, ist die Entschädigung abzulehnen (§ 2 Abs. 3 letzter Satz ZuSEG). Ist der Tag der Vernehmung ein tarifmäßig bezahlter Ruhetag, so ist die Entschädigung zu gewähren, wenn die Bezahlung nach dem Tarif auf Grund der Vernehmung entfällt.

Ausgeschlossen sind danach vom Entschädigungsbezug: **Beamte,** ferner **Angestellte,** wenn sie fortlaufend ihr Gehalt beziehen (vgl. LSG Nordrhein-Westfalen, JVBl. 1957, 45), hinsichtlich des Mindestsatzes (s. o.) allerdings unter Umständen nur, wenn sie während ihrer Vernehmung voll vertreten werden. (Muß das Arbeitspensum nachgeholt werden, so ist das Entstehen eines erhöhten Aufwandes, vor allem an zusätzlichen Zehrkosten, selbst dann nicht von der Hand zu weisen, wenn die Nachholung innerhalb der Dienststunden durch erhöhte Anstrengung erfolgt.) Bei **Landwirten** und **Inhabern größerer Betriebe** ist Voraussetzung der Entschädigung, daß sie mitarbeiten. **Geschäftsreisende** können nur den Provisionsausfall (nicht den Verlust von Spesen) geltend machen.

Unter der den Verdienstausfall verursachenden **Zeitversäumnis** ist außer der Wartezeit bis zum verspäteten Terminsbeginn die Dauer bis zur Entlassung und die notwendige Zeit der Fahrt zum und vom Gericht zu verstehen, ferner der Zeitraum, während dessen der Zeuge seine gewöhnliche Beschäftigung nicht wieder aufnehmen kann, z. B. weil er als Bergmann außerhalb der Zeit nicht einfahren darf oder als Fernfahrer sich nicht in die festgelegte Reiseroute eingliedern kann (§ 4 ZuSEG).

Für die **Vorbereitung** der Aussage (z. B. Einsicht in Unterlagen) gibt es grundsätzlich keine Vergütung.

2. a) Die **Höhe der Entschädigung für** die **versäumte Zeit** richtet sich nach den Verhältnissen des Zeugen; maßgebend ist sein regelmäßiger Bruttoverdienst (§ 2 Abs. 2 letzter Satz ZuSEG). Die Berechnung der Entschädigung erfolgt nach Stunden

(§ 2 Abs. 2 Satz 1 ZuSEG). Monatseinkommen sind praktisch durch 200 zu teilen, um den verdienten Stundensatz zu gewinnen.

Der **Mindestbetrag** der Entschädigung beläuft sich je Stunde auf 0,50 DM, der **Höchstbetrag** auf 3 DM (§ 2 Abs. 2 Satz 1 ZuSEG, vgl. im einzelnen die Tabelle am Schluß). Die letzte, bereits angefangene Stunde wird voll gerechnet (§ 2 Abs. 2 Satz 2 ZuSEG).

Längste Abgeltungsdauer: täglich 10 Stunden (§ 2 Abs. 4 Satz 1 ZuSEG). Auch für versäumte Überstunden, soweit sie jeweils noch in den Zeitraum von 10 Stunden fallen, erfolgt Entschädigung (vgl. Bauer, EntschG Anm. 14 zu § 2). Entschädigt wird ferner, ohne Rücksicht auf prozentualen Anteil der eigentlichen Versäumung, der entgangene Lohnausgleich für den nächsten arbeitsfreien Tag; jedoch darf das Höchstentgelt für die eigentliche Versäumung insgesamt nicht überschritten werden (a. A. Iffland, Bb 1958, 1329, der den entgangenen Lohnausgleich überhaupt nicht berücksichtigt, und das OLG Hamm vom 17. 4. 1958, das den verlorenen Lohnausgleich für den folgenden Ruhetag grundsätzlich voll ersetzt). Abzustellen ist jeweils auf den Tag der Vernehmung unter Berücksichtigung der An- und Abreisetage; gehört auch der Folgetag zu der durch die Vernehmung versäumten Schicht, so wird er bis zur Erreichung des Höchstentgelts der eigentlichen Versäumnis berücksichtigt (vgl. LG Dortmund, JMBl. NRW 1957, 287).

Die Arbeitgeberanteile zur Sozialversicherung, die dem Zeugen verlorengehen, sind nicht zu berücksichtigen und zu ersetzen (a. A. vgl. LG Hagen, JVBl. 1958, 247).

b) **Barauslagen werden** dem Zeugen im gegebenen Falle auch dann **ersetzt,** wenn er keinen Anspruch auf Entschädigung wegen Verdienstausfalles hat. Es werden ersetzt:

α) die Fahrtkosten (§ 8 ZuSEG),

β) die Mehraufwendungen (§ 9 ZuSEG),

γ) die Übernachtungsspesen (§ 9 Abs. 2 letzter Satz ZuSEG),

δ) die Vertretungskosten u. ä. (§ 10 ZuSEG).

Zu α. Dem Zeugen werden die notwendigen **Fahrtkosten** ersetzt (§ 8 Abs. 1 ZuSEG).

Bei Benutzung von öffentlichen, regelmäßig verkehrenden Beförderungsmitteln werden die wirklichen Auslagen einschließlich der Kosten für die Beförderung des notwendigen Gepäcks bis zur Höhe der bestehenden Tarife ersetzt (§ 8 Abs. 2 Satz 1 ZuSEG). Bei Benutzung der Eisenbahn oder von Schiffen ist der Ersatz der Beförderungsauslagen nach den persönlichen Verhältnissen des Zeugen zu bemessen, äußerste Grenze ist der Fahrpreis der ersten Wagenklasse oder der ersten Schiffsklasse (§ 8 Abs. 2 ZuSEG).

Mehrkosten für notwendig zu nehmende zuschlagpflichtige Züge werden ersetzt (§ 8 Abs. 2 letzter Satz ZuSEG).

Für Fußwege und bei Benutzung von anderen als den genannten Beförderungsmitteln (z. B. des eigenen Kraftwagens) werden bei Entfernungen von mehr als 2 km für jedes angefangene Kilometer des Hin- und Rückwegs 0,25 DM (allgemein angemessener Betrag) gewährt (§ 8 Abs. 3 Satz 1 ZuSEG). Der danach sich ergebende Endbetrag ist, wenn der Hin- und Rückweg zusammen mehr als 200 km ausmacht und mit öffentlichen, regelmäßig verkehrenden Beförderungsmitteln billiger zurückgelegt werden kann, in dem überhöhten Umfange jedoch nur soweit zu zahlen, als die Mehrkosten gegenüber der Benutzung von öffentlichen, regelmäßig verkehrenden Beförderungsmitteln durch eine Minderausgabe an Entschädigung ausgeglichen werden (§ 8 Abs. 3 Satz 2 ZuSEG).

Kann vom Zeugen wegen besonderer Umstände — persönlicher (z. B. wegen eines Nervenleidens) oder sachlicher (z. B. wegen Eisenbahnunglücks) — ein öffentliches, regelmäßiges verkehrendes Beförderungsmittel nicht benutzt werden, so werden die nachgewiesenen Mehrauslagen ersetzt, soweit sie angemessen (sachlich billig) sind (§ 8 Abs. 3 letzter Satz ZuSEG).

Für etwaige Reisen des Zeugen während der Terminsdauer werden die Fahrtkosten nur insoweit ersetzt, als dadurch Mehrbeträge an Entschädigung erspart werden, die beim Verbleiben an der Terminstelle gewährt werden müßten (§ 8 Abs. 4 ZuSEG).

Wird die Reise zum Terminsort vom Zeugen von einem anderen als dem in der Ladung bezeichneten oder der ladenden Stelle unverzüglich angezeigten Ort angetreten oder wird zu einem anderen als zu diesem Ort zurückgereist, so werden, wenn die dadurch entstandenen Gesamtkosten höher sind, höchstens die Kosten ersetzt, die für die Reise von dem in der Ladung bezeichneten oder der ladenden Stelle angezeigten Ort oder für die Rückreise zu diesem zu ersetzen wären. Mehrkosten werden nach billigem Ermessen ersetzt, wenn der Zeuge zu den betreffenden Fahrten durch besondere Umstände genötigt war (§ 8 Abs. 5 ZuSEG).

Zu β. Der dem Zeugen gewöhnlich verursachte Mehraufwand infolge der Abwesenheit vom Aufenthaltsort oder — mit Bedeutung für das sog. Zehrgeld — wenigstens von der Wohnung soll in durchschnittlicher Weise durch die **Aufwandsentschädigung** abgegolten werden (§ 9 ZuSEG). Ihre Höhe richtet sich nach der Dauer der Abwesenheit und den persönlichen Verhältnissen des Zeugen (vgl. § 9 Abs. 1 Satz 2 und Abs. 2 ZuSEG). Der Höchstsatz beträgt bei Reisen 14 DM (§ 9 Abs. 2a RKG, s. o. I 2 b β). Der Durchschnittssatz ist hier 10 DM.

Die Entschädigung in dieser oder der sonst (bis zur Höchstgrenze) gerechtfertigten Höhe ist aber nur zu gewähren, wenn die Abwesenheit mehr als 12 Stunden dauerte; bei einer Abwesenheitsdauer von über 8 Stunden bis 12 Stunden ist der in Frage kommende Satz zur Hälfte, bei über 6 bis 8 Stunden zu $^3/_{10}$ zuzubilligen (§ 9 Abs. 2 Satz 2 ZuSEG und § 9 Abs. 3 RKG). Bei mehrtägiger Abwesenheit vom Wohnort beträgt die Aufwandsentschädigung für den Tag des Reiseantritts, wenn die Reise angetreten ist:

nach 18 Uhr	—,
nach 16 bis 18 Uhr	$^3/_{10}$,
nach 12 bis 16 Uhr	$^5/_{10}$,
vor 12 Uhr	$^{10}/_{10}$;

für den Tag der Reisebeendigung, wenn die Reise beendet ist

bis 6 Uhr	—,
nach 6 bis 8 Uhr	$^3/_{10}$,
nach 8 bis 12 Uhr	$^5/_{10}$,
nach 12 Uhr	$^{10}/_{10}$.

Eine Abwesenheit von 6 Stunden und geringerer Dauer begründet einen Anspruch auf Ersatz der Zehrkosten bis zu 2,50 DM (§ 9 Abs. 2 Satz 2 ZuSEG, siehe hierzu oben I 2 b β).

Bei Terminen am Aufenthaltsort sind Zehrkosten bis zu 2,50 DM für jeden Tag mit notwendiger Abwesenheit aus der Wohnung in längerer Dauer als 4 Stunden zu ersetzen (§ 9 Abs. 3 ZuSEG).

Zu γ. War Übernachtung außerhalb des Wohn- bzw. Aufenthaltsortes erforderlich, so sind die **Übernachtungskosten** (auch für Schlafwagen an Stelle eines Schlafquartiers) im Rahmen des Angemessenen, der durch die örtlichen Umstände und die persönlichen Verhältnisse des Zeugen bestimmt wird, zu ersetzen (§ 9 Abs. 2 letzter Satz ZuSEG). Bei Zweifeln ist Glaubhaftmachung durch Vorlegung von Quittungen o. ä. erforderlich. Praktischer (nicht gesetzlicher) Höchstsatz: 11 DM (entsprechend der Reisekostenstufe II der Bundesbeamten).

Zu δ. Konnexe notwendige Barauslagen, die nicht den durch den Aufenthalt außerhalb der Wohnung verursachten Aufwand betreffen, sind dem Zeugen zu ersetzen (§ 10 Satz 1 ZuSEG). Dies gilt insbesondere von den **Kosten einer** erforderlichen **Vertretung** (§ 10 Satz 2 ZuSEG). Die eigene Entschädigung wird bei bestellter Vertretung regelmäßig in Fortfall kommen (s. o. I 2 b δ). Zu ersetzen sind auch die — angemessenen — Kosten **einer** notwendigen **Begleitperson.** (Vertreter und Begleitpersonen haben keinen eigenen Anspruch an die Staatskasse.) Kosten für nicht verlangte **ärztliche Bescheinigungen** zur Entschuldigung des Zeugen sind nicht ersetzungsfähig (sie sind nicht notwendig, da das Gericht zur Nachprüfung nötigenfalls grundsätzlich einen Amtsarzt schicken muß, RG 56, 79); a. A. Baumbach-Lauterbach, KostG 13. Aufl., Anm. B zu § 14 ZuSGebO und Meyer-Höver, ZuSEG 11. Aufl. Anm. 21 zu § 1.

Die dem Zeugen zu zahlende **Gesamtentschädigung** ist jeweils **auf 10 DPf aufzurunden** (§ 11 ZuSEG).

Der **Entschädigungsanspruch** des Zeugen **entsteht** mit der Beendigung der Vernehmung bzw. im Zeitpunkte der Beschlußfassung über ihre Unterlassung. Wegen der **Fälligkeit** s. u. 3a.

3. a) Die **Festsetzung der Zeugenentschädigung** verlangt die Erfüllung der folgenden **förmlichen Voraussetzung:**

Die **Entschädigung** wird dem Zeugen stets **nur auf** — formloses — **Verlangen** gewährt (§ 14 Abs. 1 ZuSEG). Erst **damit wird der Entschädigungsanspruch,** der als solcher mit der Beendigung der Vernehmung **entsteht, fällig** (§ 14 Abs. 1 ZuSEG); a. A. Brocke-Reese, Entsch. BeisZuS Vorbem. VI vor § 1 ZuSEG (sie lassen die Beendigung der Zuziehung genügen).

Der **Anspruch** auf Entschädigung **erlischt,** wenn diese nicht binnen drei Monaten nach Beendigung der Zuziehung (Entlassung durch das Gericht) gegenüber dem vernehmenden Gericht begehrt wird (§ 14 Abs. 2 ZuSEG). Da es sich um eine — von Amts wegen zu beachtende — gesetzliche Ausschlußfrist handelt, gibt es mangels gesetzlicher Anordnung keine Verlängerung derselben und keine Wiedereinsetzung in den früheren Stand bei Versäumnis. § 84 Abs. 2 und § 91 Abs. 1 SGG, welche die Fristwahrung in bestimmten Fällen erleichtern, gelten ihrem Inhalt zufolge hier nicht, vgl. Brocke-Reese, Entsch. BeisZuS Anm. 3 zu § 14 ZuSEG. Für die Fristberechnung siehe die §§ 186ff. BGB. Die erforderliche Antragstellung erfolgt in der Regel im Anschluß an den Vernehmungstermin; auf sie wird vom Gericht hingewiesen werden müssen, falls alsbald eine Auferlegung der Zeugenkosten gemäß § 192 SGG in Frage kommt.

Ist die Entschädigung fristgerecht begehrt worden, so läuft die **zweijährige Verjährungsfrist** des § 196 Abs. 1 Nr. 17 BGB, beginnend mit dem Ablauf des Jahres, in dem der Entschädigungsanspruch geltend gemacht wurde (entsprechend § 199 in Verb. mit § 201 BGB), so mit Recht auch Baumbach-Lauterbach, KostG 13. Aufl. Anm. 1 B b zu § 19 ZuSGebO; a. A. Meyer-Höver, ZuSEG 11. Aufl. Anm. 12 zu

§ 14, der als Endpunkt den Ablauf des Jahres für gegeben hält, in dem der Entschädigungsanspruch entstanden ist. Die Verjährung ist wegen ihrer prozessualen Natur (Einrede) nur zu beachten, wenn der Vertreter der Staatskasse sich auf sie ausdrücklich berufen hat. Für Entschädigungszahlungen nach zu Recht erfolgter Erhebung der Einrede der Verjährung kann der die Zahlung anordnende Beamte ersatzpflichtig gemacht werden.

Nach allgemeiner Ansicht kann der — entstandene — Entschädigungsanspruch des Zeugen abgetreten und verpfändet sowie gepfändet werden. Die Entschädigung hat in der Tat einen anderen Rechtscharakter als die Lohn- oder Gehaltsvergütung, die sie in bestimmtem Umfange lediglich ersetzt. Eine die genannten Rechtsakte ausschließende soziale Zweckbindung dürfte hier zu verneinen sein.

Bei **Verzicht** des Zeugen **auf Entschädigung** darf keine Festsetzung erfolgen. Versehentlich gezahlte Gebühren sind zurückzuzahlen (vgl. OLG Nürnberg, JVBl. 1958, 246).

Wegen der **Bevorschussung** des Entschädigungsanspruchs s. o. 1 a a. E.

b) **Die Feststellung der Entschädigung** erfolgt im Anschluß an die Antragstellung möglichst sogleich nach der Vernehmung (s. o. 3 a) auf Grund der üblichen, aber verfahrensrechtlich nicht notwendigen, allgemein lautenden Verfügung des Vorsitzenden (Richters) des vernehmenden Gerichts, „nach Prüfung die bestimmungsgemäße Entschädigung zu gewähren", **durch den** berechnenden **Urkundsbeamten** dieses Gerichts, der, zumeist in einer bestimmten Stelle für das ganze Gericht (Berechnungsstelle für Zeugen- und Sachverständigengebühren), unter Berücksichtigung der im einzelnen Falle gemachten und festgelegten Zeit-, Berufs- und Wohnangaben **eigenverantwortlich** tätig wird (so im Ergebnis auch Meyer-Höver, ZuSEG 11. Aufl. Anm. II 7 a. E. zu § 15).

Eigenabänderungsbefugnis von Amts wegen ist mit Ausnahme der Möglichkeit der Berichtigung offensichtlicher Unrichtigkeiten nicht gegeben (vgl. §§ 138, 142 Abs. 1 SGG).

Belehrung über den gegebenen Rechtsbehelf (s. u. 3 c) — schriftlich oder unter Aktenkundigmachung mündlich — ist erforderlich (§ 66 Abs. 1 und § 173 letzter Satz SGG). Wegen der Folgen unterlassener oder unrichtiger Belehrung vgl. § 66 Abs. 2 SGG).

Die auf Grund der Festsetzung angewiesenen Beträge sind übungsgemäß bei der Kasse abzuholen (vgl. hierzu auch § 1 letzter Teil des Gesetzes über Zahlungen öffentlicher Kassen vom 21. 12. 1938 — RGBl. I 1899). Bei Übersendung durch die Post ist mithin das Porto in der Regel abziehbar.

c) **Gegen die Entscheidung des Urkundsbeamten** kann der Zeuge oder sein Erbe oder sonstiger Rechtsnachfolger (bei Ablehnung der Festsetzung oder zu niedriger Feststellung) und die Staatskasse durch den Bezirksrevisor (bei unzulässiger oder zu hoher Festsetzung, für Erfüllungsbehauptungen ist kein Raum) das mit der Sachentscheidung betraute **Gericht anrufen** (vgl. § 178 SGG). Dieses Gericht braucht nicht immer das Gericht des festsetzenden Urkundsbeamten zu sein, man denke an die — verhältnismäßig seltenen — Fälle der Vernehmung durch einen ersuchten Richter. (Der Urkundsbeamte des ersuchten Richters ist nur dessen unselbständiger „Erfüllungsgehilfe".) Der besondere § 178 SGG, der bei der hier vorgesehenen Anrufung auf das sachentscheidende Gericht (Prozeßgericht) abstellt, geht dem allgemeinen § 15 Abs. 1 Satz 2 ZuSEG vor, der stets das vernehmende Gericht als Gericht der Festsetzung vorsieht (a. A. Brocke-Reese,

Entsch. BeisZuS Anm. 3 zu § 15 ZuSEG). Den § 178 SGG auszuschließen, wie es Wudtke, SGb 1958, 1, vorschlägt, „weil der Urkundsbeamte keine Befugnis im Rahmen des SGG ausübe", ist nicht gerechtfertigt. Der Urkundsbeamte wird auch im Sozialgerichtsverfahren auf verfahrensgesetzlicher Grundlage tätig. Das ergibt sich mit Deutlichkeit aus § 118 Abs. 1 SGG, der ausdrücklich auf den § 401 ZPO verweist; dieser ordnet die Entschädigung des vom Gericht im Rechtsstreit zugezogenen Zeugen an. (Ohne Zeugen keine Sachentscheidung des Gerichts, ohne Entschädigung kein Zeuge.) Für die Entschädigung ist in erster Linie der Urkundsbeamte als grundsätzlicher gerichtlicher Kostenberechner mit eigener Verantwortlichkeit zuständig. Das entspricht allein rechtsstaatlichen Gedankengängen. Bemerkt sei noch, daß gegen Entscheidungen (auch Festsetzungen) des ersuchten Richters das Prozeßgericht als Anrufungsgericht auf jeden Fall das letzte Wort hat (§ 178 SGG).

Etwas anderes als diese Anrufung beinhaltet dem Grunde nach in seinen wesentlichen Punkten auch der § 15 Abs. 1 Satz 1 ZuSEG nicht; soweit hier im Gegensatz zu § 178 (in Verb. mit § 173) SGG für die Anrufung des Gerichts nicht die Einhaltung einer Frist (nach § 173 SGG ein Monat nach Bekanntgabe) gefordert wird, müssen die Spezialbestimmungen des Sozialgerichtsgesetzes gelten, zumal es insgesamt darauf abstellt, eine schnelle Durchführung und Abwicklung des Verfahrens zu ermöglichen.

Bei Verweisung an ein anderes Sozialgericht (vgl. § 98 insbes. Abs. 3 SGG) ist das neue Gericht zuständig.

Eine Anrufung des Gerichts zum Zwecke der sog. Nachliquidation (Erhöhung des bisher Verlangten) ist in keinem Falle zulässig. (Es muß wieder „von vorn" angefangen werden.)

Wegen Wiedereinsetzung in den vorigen Stand bei schuldloser Fristversäumnis vgl. § 67 SGG.

Die Erweiterung einer begrenzten Anrufung ist nach Ablauf der Anrufungsfrist nicht zulässig.

Eine Anschlußanrufung gibt es nicht.

Rücknahme der Anrufung im Zweifel mit der Wirkung des endgültigen Verlustes des Rechtsbehelfs ist möglich.

Eine bestimmte Beschwer ist nicht erforderlich.

Form der Anrufung: schriftlich bei dem entscheidenden Gericht oder zur Niederschrift seines oder des sonst berechnenden Urkundsbeamten, also stets ohne Anwaltszwang (§ 173 SGG, vgl. auch § 16 Abs. 4 ZuSEG).

Abhilfe durch den jeweils zuständigen Urkundsbeamten ist möglich (unter Umständen unter Wiedereinziehung, notfalls im Wege der Beitreibung nach dem Verwaltungsvollstreckungsgesetz), vgl. § 174 SGG.

Abhilfe eröffnet für den Gegner die Anrufungsfrist neu.

Die Anrufung hat keine aufschiebende Wirkung (§ 175 SGG). Eine Vollstreckung aus der Festsetzung des Urkundsbeamten zugunsten des Zeugen ist nicht möglich, daher kommt eine einstweilige Einstellung der Zwangsvollstreckung nicht in Frage.

Die Streitbeteiligten haben in keinem Falle ein Anrufungsrecht (vgl. § 16 Abs. 1 Satz 1, auch Abs. 2 Satz 2 ZuSEG). Sie sind an dem Verhältnis des Staates zum Zeugen, selbst soweit ihnen die Kosten desselben nach § 192 SGG auferlegt sind (vgl. das 1. Kap. 1, 2), unmittelbar nicht beteiligt. Erst wenn ein zur Tragung dieser Kosten verurteilter Streitbeteiligter durch Kostenbescheid mit der von der Staatskasse verauslagten Zeugenentschädigung belastet wird, kann er — abgesehen von einem etwaigen Angriff gegen die Kostenentscheidung selbst — gegen diesen Kostenbescheid vorgehen, d. h. ihm gegenüber das Gericht anrufen (s. o. 4. Kap. 2 zu a bis c). Der insoweit mit den Kosten belastete Streitbeteiligte braucht der Staatskasse nie mehr zu ersetzen als an den Zeugen hätte gezahlt werden dürfen. Was diesem tatsächlich gezahlt wurde, ist unerheblich.

Das Gericht (grundsätzlich in voller jeweiliger Besetzung) **entscheidet** über die angegriffene Festsetzung auf Grund eigenen Ermessens (§ 128 Abs. 1, § 142 Abs. 1 SGG) durch kostenfreien (§ 183 SGG), zu begründenden (§ 142 Abs. 2 SGG) Beschluß **endgültig** (§ 178 SGG), und zwar ohne mündliche Verhandlung (§ 124 Abs. 3 SGG); Anhörung des Gegners ist im allgemeinen nicht erforderlich.

Bis zum 31. 12. 1960 kann hier der Vorsitzende des Sozialgerichts allein, das Landessozialgericht ohne Zuziehung der Landessozialrichter und gegebenenfalls das Bundessozialgericht ohne Zuziehung der Bundessozialrichter entscheiden (§ 216 Abs. 1 Nr. 2 SGG); a. A. Brocke, SGb 1958; 271 [274], wie hier Wende, KOV 1958, 144.

Nachprüfung erfolgt grundsätzlich nur in bezug auf das Angegriffene. Mehr als insgesamt verlangt, kann nicht zugebilligt werden; Schlechterstellung durch das Gericht auf eigenen Rechtsbehelf ist nicht möglich (vgl. hierzu § 202 SGG, § 308 Abs. 1, § 356 ZPO).

Zurückverweisung an den Urkundsbeamten (evtl. unter sachlicher Anweisung) ist an sich nicht ausgeschlossen. Gegen die neue Entscheidung kann vom Beschwerten wiederum das Gericht angerufen werden.

Der ergehende Beschluß ist formlos mitzuteilen.

Wegen des gegebenen Rechtsbehelfs der Anrufung ist insbesondere eine Herabsetzung der Entschädigung auf Verwaltungsanweisung nicht möglich.

Die Entscheidung des Gerichts kann — nach allen Richtungen — von diesem von Amts wegen — aber nur innerhalb angemessener Frist (etwa ein Jahr) — geändert werden (vgl. den durch das Sozialgerichtsgesetz nicht ausgeschlossenen § 15 Abs. 1 Satz 4 ZuSEG). Das soll vor allem eine Benachteiligung der Staatskasse verhüten, wenn auf Vorgehen des betroffenen Streitbeteiligten gegen den ihn mit den Zeugenkosten (auf Grund entsprechender Verurteilung nach § 192 SGG) belastenden Kostenbescheid festgestellt worden ist, daß der Zeuge nur weniger verlangen konnte, als ihm abschließend festgesetzt wurde. Eine Abänderung von Amts wegen in der höheren Instanz (vgl. § 15 Abs. 1 letzter Satz ZuSEG) dürfte dagegen nicht in Frage kommen, weil im gesamten Sozialgerichtsverfahren Gebührenstreitigkeiten grundsätzlich in der betreffenden Instanz ihre Erledigung zu finden pflegen (vgl. die §§ 178, 189 Abs. 2, §§ 191, 197 Abs. 2 SGG). Das Zuvielerhaltene muß zurückgezahlt werden; nötigenfalls erfolgt Beitreibung im Verwaltungszwangsverfahren (nach dem Verwaltungsvollstreckungsgesetz). Verjährung des Rückzahlungsanspruchs tritt ein in vier Jahren seit dem Ablauf des Kalenderjahres, in dem der Entschädigungsanspruch fällig wurde (entsprechend § 8 Abs. 2 GKG). Erhebung der Einrede des Wegfalls der Bereicherung durch den Zeugen ist möglich.

Wegen der Berichtigung offensichtlicher Fehler vgl. die §§ 138, 142 Abs. 1 SGG.

Zwar ist im § 15 Abs. 2 ZuSEG dem Zeugen und der Staatskasse bei einer Beschwer von über 50 DM ein — fristloses — **Beschwerderecht** eingeräumt, doch ist dieses Recht durch das Sozialgerichtsgesetz **ausgeschlossen,** in das das Entschädigungsgesetz für Zeugen und Sachverständige eingepaßt werden muß. (Das Entschädigungsgesetz für Zeugen und Sachverständige hat sich stets in die in Frage stehende gesetzliche Verfahrensregelung einzuordnen, vgl. Peters-Sautter-Wolff, SGG § 118 Anm. zu § 20 ZuSGebO; Keidel, FGG 5. Aufl. Anm. 8 zu § 15; KG, 1 a W 411.56 und Tschischgale, JR 1956, 257.) Im Verfahren der Sozialgerichtsbarkeit entscheidet über alle gebührenrechtlich streitigen Kosten das Gericht der betreffenden Instanz endgültig (vgl. § 189 Abs. 2, §§ 191, 197 Abs. 2 und § 178 SGG). Im Sozialgerichtsgesetz (§ 118 Abs. 1 Satz 1) heißt es zu diesem Punkte ausdrücklich, daß die einschlägigen Bestimmungen der ZPO, nämlich hier die §§ 401, 413, die durch die Vorschriften des Gesetzes über die Entschädigung von Zeugen und Sachverständigen ausgeführt werden, nur — entsprechend — gelten, **soweit dieses Gesetz**, d. h. das SGG, **nichts anderes bestimmt.** Der Zeuge kann ebenso wie die ihm gegenüberstehende Staatskasse unmöglich prozessual besser stehen als die anderen kostenmäßig Beteiligten (vgl. insbes. den endgültigen Auslagenschuldner der Zeugenkosten gemäß § 192 SGG). Das Gewähren eines weiteren Kostenrechtszuges zugunsten des Zeugen (oder seines Gegners) würde auch, zumal die Entschädigung regelmäßig im Laufe des Verfahrens erfolgt, das beschleunigt durchzuführende Verfahren in Sozialgerichtssachen in unzumutbarer Weise verzögern, weiterhin eine Auferlegung der betreffenden Kosten nach § 192 SGG jedenfalls erschweren. Hinzu kommt, daß es im Sozialgerichtsgesetz als Rechtsinstitution weder eine fristlose Beschwerde noch eine solche mit einer Mindestbeschwer gibt. Beschwerde würde im übrigen nur gegen die Festsetzung der Sozialgerichte gegeben sein (vgl. § 172 Abs. 1, § 177 SGG). Eine unterschiedliche Behandlung der gleichen Festsetzungsverfahren in den einzelnen Rechtszügen läßt sich aber in neuzeitlich geregelten Prozeßverfahren schlechthin nicht rechtfertigen (a. A. Brocke-Reese, Geb.u.KostR Anm. 4 und 4a zu § 20 ZuSGebO; er hält zwar ebenfalls den jetzigen § 15 Abs. 2 ZuSEG für unanwendbar, gewährt aber das Beschwerderecht aus § 172 SGG gegen Entscheidungen der Sozialgerichte, vgl. auch Wudtke, SGb 1958, 1, der die fristlose, aber an die 50 DM-Grenze gebundene Beschwerde für gegeben ansieht). Die Beschwerde ist richtigerweise auch dann ausgeschlossen, wenn sogleich das Gericht festgesetzt haben sollte.

d) Bei **Nichtauszahlung** trotz gerichtlicher Entscheidung (Festsetzung) wäre für den Zeugen die **Beschreitung des — ordentlichen — Klageweges** zur Erlangung eines Vollstreckungstitels erforderlich (Judikatsklage; Festsetzung durch das Gericht ist immer Voraussetzung. Maßgebend ist der festgesetzte Betrag).

Ein Streitbeteiligter kann, insbesondere wenn er einen Zeugen stellt, diesem von sich aus das Geld für Fahrt- und Zehrkosten u. ä. gewähren; diese Geldhingabe geschieht, jedenfalls wenn der Zeuge vernommen wird, im Zweifel nur aushilfs-, d. h. darlehnsweise. (Der Zeuge liquidiert in aller Regel abschließend gegenüber der Staatskasse.) Ist die Verauslagung endgültig erfolgt, so hat der Streitbeteiligte nur dann einen Ersatzanspruch gegen die Staatskasse, wenn der Zeuge ihm seinen Entschädigungsanspruch abgetreten hat. (Wegen der Erstattung dieser endgültigen Auslagen durch einen anderen Beteiligten vgl. das 6. Kap. 4c.)

III. Die Entschädigung des Sachverständigen

Übersicht

1. **Der Sachverständige erhält** aus der Staatskasse eine **Entschädigung für** die von ihm **erbrachte Leistung,** und zwar nach Maßgabe der erforderlichen Zeit, **ferner Ersatz seiner** baren **Auslagen** (§ 3 Abs. 1, Abs. 2 Satz 1 und §§ 7, 8, 9 und 10 ZuSEG).

Im Falle des § 109 SGG (Vernehmung auf Antrag des vorschußleistenden Versicherten) erfolgt die Vergütung des Sachverständigen grundsätzlich wie sonst (aus der Staatskasse). Sie kann vom antragstellenden Beteiligten gegenüber der Staatskasse (vgl. § 109 Abs. 1 Satz 2 SGG) bevorschußt sein. (Bei Übernahme der Kosten durch die Staatskasse ist der Vorschuß, soweit er übernommen ist, zurückzuzahlen.)

a) Die **allgemeinen Voraussetzungen** sind:

Erstattung des erforderten Gutachtens in mündlicher oder schriftlicher Form. Erscheinen des Sachverständigen an Gerichtsstelle auf Grund Ladung genügt, falls auf Gutachtenerstattung oder evtl. -ergänzung nicht bestanden wird. Die Zuziehung zu Beweiszwecken muß im gerichtlichen Verfahren, nicht während eines Vorverfahrens (vgl. § 78 SGG), erfolgt sein. Sie kann unter Umständen, z. B. zur Frage der Prozeßfähigkeit des Revisionsklägers, ausnahmsweise auch im dritten Rechtszuge stattfinden.

Der Sachverständige hat in allen Fällen (auch bei nicht ausdrücklichem Verlangen) die Verpflichtung, das Gericht auf Umstände hinzuweisen, die besonders hohe Kosten verursachen (z. B. die Erforderlichkeit der Vornahme von kostspieligen Spezialuntersuchungen); bei Nichterfüllung dieser Pflicht erfolgt Entschädigung grundsätzlich nur im allgemeinen Umfange.

Bei endgültiger **Ablehnung der Gutachtenerstattung** ist Entschädigung, soweit sie im Hinblick auf geleistete Vorarbeiten in Frage kommt, nur möglich, wenn die Ablehnung des Auftrages berechtigt ist.

Bei **Ablehnung des Sachverständigen** erfolgt Entschädigung, soweit eine solche voraussetzungsmäßig in Frage kommt, lediglich, wenn die Ablehnung unbegründet ist. Ist die Ablehnung zwar begründet, beruht sie aber nicht auf einem ernstlich schuldhaften Verhalten des Sachverständigen, so ist die Vergütung ebenfalls zu zahlen.

Der Sachverständige erhält **keine Vergütung:**

α) soweit eine Überschreitung des Auftrags vorliegt (Stellungnahme zu nicht aufgegebenen Fragen);

β) wenn das erstattete Gutachten völlig ohne Wert ist (z. B. Nachprüfung des Falles von der allein dem Gericht obliegenden rechtlichen Seite statt Beantwortung der vorgelegten tatsächlichen Zweifelsfragen);

γ) wenn der Sachverständige für seine gerichtliche Sachverständigentätigkeit aus der Bundes- oder Landeskasse eine laufende, nicht auf den Einzelfall abgestellte Vergütung erhält (§ 1 Abs. 2 ZuSEG, hierzu rechnen aber grundsätzlich nur amtlich besonders bestellte Gerichtsärzte; daß hier die honorierende Staatskasse die Vergütung beanspruchen kann, wird im allgemeinen abzulehnen sein).

Der sogen. **sachverständige Zeuge** ist nicht Sachverständiger, sondern Zeuge; er bekundet nur Tatsachen, wenn er diese auch als Sachkundiger wahrgenommen hat (§ 414 ZPO). Beispiel: Ein Arzt sagt über den Verlauf einer von ihm beobachteten Krankheit aus; wird er auch über die vermeintliche Ursache oder die voraussichtliche Auswirkung der Krankheit befragt, so wird er zusätzlich als Sachverständiger vernommen. Er ist dann — selbst bei Ladung als Zeuge — als Sachverständiger zu entschädigen (vgl. hierzu im einzelnen Ecker, SGb 1958, 34).

Für besonders zu vergütende bestimmte Verrichtungen (vgl. § 5 ZuSEG und seine Anlage) ist ausnahmsweise auch der sachverständige Zeuge wie ein Sachverständiger zu entschädigen.

Sachverständiger kann grundsätzlich nur eine private Person sein (vgl. §§ 402ff ZPO); wird eine Behörde als solche in Anspruch genommen (z. B. Befragung der Aufsichtsbehörde über die Gesundheitsschädlichkeit einer ihrer Gewerbeaufsicht unterstehenden Fabrik), so liegt **Amtshilfe** vor, die grundsätzlich kosten-(gebühren- und auslagenersatz-)frei zu leisten ist (vgl. § 5 SGG und § 164 Abs. 1 und 2 GVG). Wegen bestimmter Auslagen bei Ersuchen von Versicherungsträgern vgl. den die Erstattungspflicht statuierenden § 117 RVO. Von dieser Erstattungspflicht ausgenommen sind die Versorgungsbehörden (§§ 20, 31 des Gesetzes über das Verwaltungsverfahren der Kriegsopferversorgung vom 2. 5. 1955, BGBl. I 202).

Entgeltlichkeit spezieller Amtshilfe (z. B. durch Gesundheitsämter) kann durch Bundesrecht und bei seinem Schweigen, soweit keine gewohnheitsrechtlich entgegenstehende Üblichkeit auf Bundesebene vorliegt, durch Landesrecht bestimmt werden (auch durch Haushaltsgesetze, vgl. Meyer-Höver, ZuSEG 11. Aufl. Anm. 35 zu § 3). Echte Benutzungsabgeltungen sind regelmäßig zu zahlen.

Eine **Vereinbarung** der Beteiligten (vor oder gegenüber dem Gericht) über die Vergütung des Sachverständigen für seine Leistung (vgl. den § 6 Abs. 1 ZuSEG) scheidet hier grundsätzlich aus, da sie nur wirksam ist, wenn ein zur Abdeckung ausreichender Betrag vorab an die Staatskasse entrichtet wird. Zumal mit Rücksicht auf das Nichtbestehen einer Vorschuß- und Kostenpflicht im Sozialgerichtsverfahren kommt eine Vorauszahlung grundsätzlich nicht in Frage. Zusicherungen des Gerichts gegenüber dem Sachverständigen haben außerhalb des § 6 Abs. 2 ZuSEG keine Rechtswirksamkeit; das Gericht darf dem Sachverständigen grundsätzlich nur die nach dem Gesetz verdiente Entschädigung gewähren.

Nach § 6 Abs. 2 ZuSEG genügt die Erklärung **eines** Beteiligten, dem Sachverständigen eine bestimmte Entschädigung für seine Leistung (im Zweifel einschließlich ergänzender Nachtragsgutachten) zu zahlen, wenn das Gericht zustimmt. Das kann im Falle des § 109 SGG von Bedeutung werden (a. A. Brocke-Reese, Geb. u.KostR Anh. S. 16). Ist nämlich der den Antrag aus § 109 SGG stellende Beteiligte damit einverstanden, daß der von ihm für den Sachverständigen hier — ausnahmsweise — geforderte und gezahlte Vorschuß dem Sachverständigen ohne weiteres als Vergütung zustehen soll, so stellt die gezahlte Summe, falls sie die normale Entschädigung nicht unterschreitet, die Vergütung des Sachverständigen dar, wenn das Gericht zustimmt. Vor der Zustimmung hat das Gericht grundsätzlich die andere Partei zu hören (vgl. § 6 Abs. 2 Satz 2 ZuSEG). Da die Kosten des Sachverständigen bei angeordneter Vorschußleistung nach § 109 SGG aber entweder bei dem vorschußzahlenden Antragsteller oder bei der Staatskasse verbleiben (s. 1. Kap. 5), niemals also zu Lasten des oder eines anderen Beteiligten gehen können, ist die Anhörung des Gegners hier nicht von Bedeutung. (Die Staatskasse ist keine Verfahrensbeteiligte, braucht also nicht gehört zu werden, a. A. Meyer-Höver, ZuSEG 11. Aufl. Anm. 11 zu § 6. Sie wird auch nicht im Übermaß belastet werden, da bei Ausspruch der Übernahme der Kosten auf die Staatskasse nach § 109 Abs. 1 Satz 2 SGG bestimmt werden kann [und soll], daß die angeordnete — ganze oder teilweise — Übernahme nur in Höhe bzw. auf der Grundlage der gesetzlichen Kosten erfolgt.) Die Zustimmung und die Ablehnung der Zustimmung sind unanfechtbar (§ 6 Abs. 2 letzter Satz ZuSEG).

Außer in den Fällen des § 6 Abs. 2 SGG darf kein Streitbeteiligter irgendeine Honorarvereinbarung mit dem Sachverständigen treffen.

Auf Antrag ist dem Sachverständigen ein **Vorschuß** zu zahlen, und zwar von dem für Kostenangelegenheiten allgemein erstinstanzlich zuständigen berechnenden Urkundsbeamten des mit der Sache befaßten, gegebenenfalls des um die Vernehmung ersuchten Gerichts, gegen deren Entscheidung Anrufung des Prozeßgerichts gemäß § 178 SGG binnen Monatsfrist seit Zustellung des Bescheides über den Vorschuß möglich ist (Näheres hierzu s. u. 3 c). Nicht abgegoltener Vorschuß ist zurückzuzahlen. Zweckwidrige Verwendung des Vorschusses ist im Hinblick auf § 266 StGB in der Regel strafbar.

Der Vorschuß betrifft die Reisekosten, wenn ihre Verauslagung — vor allem wegen ihrer Höhe — unzumutbar erscheint (vgl. § 13 Abs. 1 ZuSEG). Nach § 13 Abs. 2 ZuSEG ist dem Sachverständigen ein Vorschuß aber auch zu bewilligen, wenn die Erstattung des Gutachtens bare Aufwendungen erfordert und dem Sachverständigen, insbesondere wegen der Höhe der Aufwendungen, nicht zugemutet werden kann, eigene Mittel vorzuschießen.

b) Folgende **Besonderheiten** bestehen **für die Entschädigung:**

Vergütungsfähig ist die gesamte mit der Erstellung des Gutachtens (einschließlich des an die Stelle schriftlicher Konzeption tretenden Diktats und seiner Durchsicht) unmittelbar zusammenhängende **Zeitversäumnis:** praktisch erfaßt werden daher auch die **Vorbereitungsarbeiten,** abgesehen von der erforderlichen, mit zu berücksichtigenden Aktendurchsicht, z. B. die Einsicht in Unterlagen, die Besichtigung des Untersuchungsgegenstandes, und zwar unter Berücksichtigung auch der Ladungen der Beteiligten, nötige Messungen, erfolgte Rücksprachen zur Klärung u. ä. (nicht dagegen allgemein Literaturstudien). Berücksichtigt werden ferner alle erforderlichen **Wege-, Reise- und Wartezeiten** (jedoch ohne Übernachtungen) sowie die Zeit, während welcher der Sachverständige seine gewöhnliche Beschäftigung nicht wieder aufnehmen kann, z. B. infolge Hineingeratens in eine Gerichtsabsperrung (vgl. § 4 ZuSEG).

Die Zeitangaben des Sachverständigen müssen auf ihre sachliche Gerechtfertigtheit nachgeprüft werden; sie sind, falls keine Auffälligkeiten vorliegen, d. h. im allgemeinen, zugrunde zu legen.

2. a) α) Was die **Entschädigung** anbetrifft, so erhält der Sachverständige **für jede erforderliche Stunde** (die letzte angefangene wird voll vergütet, dies gilt bei nicht zusammenhängenden Leistungen — z. B. schriftlichem Gutachten, Terminswahrnehmung — für die jeweils letzte Stunde zu den danach in Frage kommenden Sätzen) eine Entschädigung **bis zu 5 DM,** bei Leistungen, die **besondere Fachkenntnisse** erfordern, **bis zu 10 DM** (§ 3 Abs. 2 Satz 2 und 3 ZuSEG). Praktischer **Mindestsatz ist 3 DM,** da bis zu diesem Betrag bereits ein Zeuge Entschädigung erhält.

Die genaue Höhe der Vergütung des Sachverständigen **innerhalb der** beiden **Vergütungsklassen** richtet sich grundlagenmäßig im einzelnen Falle nach dem abzuschätzenden **Schwierigkeitsgrad** der im Rahmen des Verlangten erbrachten Leistung (die aufgewendete Zeit, die ja als solche vergütet wird, spielt hierbei keine Rolle), vgl. SG Darmstadt, SGb 1958, 366.

Das **Erfordernis besonderer fachlicher Kenntnisse** für die Bewältigung der gestellten Aufgabe ist im Zweifel vom Sachverständigen darzulegen. Die Erstattung von **Obergutachten** (Zweitgutachten sind keine Obergutachten, vgl. OLG Nürnberg, JVBl. 1958, 246) erfordert regelmäßig besondere fachliche Kenntnisse. Auf die Bildungsstufe des Sachverständigen als solche kommt es dabei nicht entscheidend an. Vom Erforderlichsein besonderer Fachkenntnisse wird aber regelmäßig dann ausgegangen werden dürfen, wenn es sich um zu beantwortende Fragen handelt, die im allgemeinen nur von einem Sachverständigen mit Hochschulabsolvierung und entsprechender Ausbildung (so einem approbierten Arzt) beantwortet werden können. Das wird, soweit es sich um zugezogene ärztliche Sachverständige handelt, in aller Regel dann nicht zweifelhaft sein, wenn ein Facharzt oder gar ein Hochschulprofessor der Medizin zum Gutachtenerstatter bestimmt ist. Daraus folgt aber keineswegs, daß etwa der Universitätsprofessor immer höher als der Facharzt und dieser vor einem nicht spezialisierten Arzt rangiert. Maßgebend ist vielmehr stets die jeweils zu erbringende und erbrachte Leistung, die besondere Fachkenntnisse voraussetzen muß. Diese Leistung kann die gleiche sein, mag sie von einem Arzt (unter Umständen sogar von einem nicht akademisch vorgebildeten Heilpraktiker), einem Facharzt oder einem Universitätsprofessor der Medizin erbracht sein. Von allgemeiner Bedeutung für eine Höhereinstufung wird regelmäßig der Grad der Ungewöhnlichkeit des zu behandelnden Gebietes im allgemeinen und besonderen sein sowie der Umfang der Voraussetzungen (insbesondere an Vor-, Aus- und Weiterbildung des Gutachters), die für die Behandlung des Themas erforderlich sind. Sollte hierbei der nicht spezialisierte Arzt zur Gewinnung des gleichen Ergebnisses ins Gewicht fallend mehr Zeit gebrauchen, so wird dies aber unmöglich zu einer höheren Honorierung dieses Sachverständigen führen können; es muß vielmehr als normaler

Zeitraum derjenige zugrunde gelegt werden, der von dem versierteren Gutachter in der Regel benötigt wird (vgl. hierzu Meyer-Höver, ZuSEG 11. Aufl. Anm. 24 zu § 3 und SG Darmstadt, Rpfleger 1958, 162 im wesentlichen mit gleichem Ergebnis, ferner KG, Rpfleger 1958, 232 und 233; a. A. Ufermann, Rpfleger 1958, 1 [2] und LG Bielefeld, JVBl. 1958, 16 und 18, die Sätze von über 5 DM nur dann gewähren, wenn die Erstattung des Gutachtens über das übliche Maß hinausgehende Fachkenntnisse innerhalb des einzelnen Berufskreises verlangt).

Für ein **schriftliches Gutachten,** in welchem der Sachverständige sich für den Einzelfall **eingehend,** d. h. unter eigener kritischer Stellungnahme (vgl. OLG Hamm, Rpfleger 1958, 160) **mit der wissenschaftlichen Lehre auseinanderzusetzen hatte** (auf Grund ausdrücklichen Erforderns des Gerichts oder aus der gegebenen Situation heraus), kann (je bedeutungsvoller diese Aufgabe war, um so näher liegt die vorzunehmende finanzielle Begünstigung) **die** bestimmungsgemäß zu gewährende **Entschädigung bis zu 50 v. H. überschritten werden** (§ 3 Abs. 3 ZuSEG). Diese Erhöhung wird begrifflich nur bei Stundensätzen über 5 DM möglich sein (ebenso Brocke-Reese, Entsch. BeisZuS Anm. 3b zu § 3 ZuSEG und Brocke, SGb 1957, 324 [325]).

Der jeweils **erhöhte Stundensatz** ist in aller Regel **nur für** die **Erstellung des Gutachtens** und die Feststellung seiner Grundlagen zu bewilligen, nicht aber für sonstige, weniger anstrengende Tätigkeiten; letztes gilt vor allem für die anläßlich einer Beweisaufnahme außerhalb der Gutachtenerstattung oder -erläuterung — insbesondere auf Reisen — verbrachte Zeit, ferner im allgemeinen für das Aktenstudium, das Diktat und die Durchsicht des Gutachtens (vgl. OLG Hamm, Rpfleger 1958, 160 und 230 sowie die zutreffende Anmerkung von Mensing, Rpfleger 1958, 161; ferner SG Darmstadt, Rpfleger 1958, 162 entgegen OLG Stuttgart, Rpfleger 1958, 232).

Eine Beschränkung der zu vergütenden Zeit ist nicht angeordnet, ebenso besteht kein Höchstsatz für die insgesamt zu zahlende Vergütung.

β) **Für besondere Verrichtungen** (vgl. § 5 ZuSEG und seine **Anlage**) sind **feste oder rahmenmäßig niedergelegte Entschädigungen** vorgesehen. Diese gelten — abgesehen von dem sachverständigen Zeugen (siehe oben II 1 a) — auch für Hilfspersonen des Sachverständigen, wenn sie von dem Gericht (unmittelbar oder in seinem ausdrücklichen Auftrag mittelbar) zugezogen werden. (Diese vom Gericht herangezogenen Hilfskräfte können der Staatskasse gegenüber selbständig berechnen.) Bilden die in der Anlage wiedergegebenen Verrichtungen nur einen Teil des Gegenstandes eines von vornherein darüber hinausgehenden Auftrags (z. B. auf Erstattung eines wissenschaftlich begründeten schriftlichen Gutachtens), so erfolgt die Berechnung nach § 3 ZuSEG (so auch Brocke, SGb 1957, 326 und LSG Nordrhein-Westfalen, JVBl. 1958, 275; a. A. Höver, JVBl. 1958, 275 und SG Dortmund, JVBl. 1958, 274).

Nach der erwähnten Anlage erhält ein Arzt für die Ausstellung eines sogen. **Befundscheins** oder die **Erteilung einer schriftlichen Auskunft** ohne nähere gutachtliche Äußerung 8 DM (Ziff. 3 der Anlage).

Für das **Zeugnis über einen ärztlichen Befund mit kurzer gutachtlicher Äußerung** oder für ein **Formbogengutachten,** wenn sich die Fragen auf Vorgeschichte, Angaben und Befund beschränken und nur ein kurzes Gutachten erfordern, erhält der **Arzt** 10 DM (Ziff. 4 der Anlage).

Für die **Untersuchung** eines Nahrungs- oder Genußmittels oder eines Gebrauchsgegenstands, Arzneistoffs, Geheimmittels und dgl. oder von Wässern oder Abwässern

und eine **kurze schriftliche gutachtliche Äußerung** beträgt die Entschädigung für jede Probe 8 bis 50 DM (Ziff. 5 der Anlage).

Für die **mikroskopische, physikalische, röntgenologische, chemische, bakteriologische, serologische Untersuchung,** wenn das Untersuchungsmaterial von Menschen oder Tieren stammt, **und** eine **kurze gutachtliche Äußerung,** einschließlich des verbrauchten Materials an Farbstoffen und anderen geringwertigen Stoffen, beträgt die Entschädigung für jede Probe 8 bis 50 DM (Ziff. 6 der Anlage).

Für die **Teilnahme an einer Sitzung eines Gerichts der Sozialgerichtsbarkeit** erhält der Arzt, einschließlich des während der Sitzung erfolgenden Aktenstudiums und der in ihrem Verlauf vorgenommenen körperlichen Untersuchungen sowie der mündlichen Erstattung von Gutachten ohne Rücksicht auf die Zahl der verhandelten Sachen für die erste immer voll gerechnete Stunde 14 DM, für jede weitere (evtl. nur angefangene) Stunde 9 DM (Ziff. 9 der Anlage). Für den Hin- und Rückweg erhält dieser besonders entschädigte Arzt keine Zeitvergütung nach § 3 Abs. 2 ZuSEG, so mit Recht Corves, JVBl. 1958, 69 [71] und 1958, 143 [144]; a. A. Brocke-Reese, Entsch. BeisZuS Anm. 5 zu § 4 ZuSEG und Reese, JVBl. 1958, 141. Wegen der auch hier zu ersetzenden baren Auslagen vgl. unten 2b. Aktenstudium und Untersuchungen vor und nach der Sitzung werden dem Sitzungsarzt uneingeschränkt in jeder Sache besonders vergütet (SG Aurich, SGb 1958, 261 [262] mit zust. Anm. von Brocke; vgl. von diesem auch SGb 1958, 326).

Mit Sachverständigen, die häufiger herangezogen werden, kann die oberste **Landesbehörde** (der zuständige Staatsminister, Senator) oder die von ihr delegierte Stelle (z. B. der LSG-Präsident für seinen Bezirk) eine Entschädigung im Rahmen der nach dem Gesetz über die Entschädigung von Zeugen und Sachverständigen zulässigen **Vergütung vereinbaren** (vgl. § 12 ZuSEG). Wird die Höhe der Entschädigung einer derartigen Vereinbarung entnommen, so ist bei Angriffen auf dieselbe auch die Gültigkeit der Vereinbarung nachzuprüfen.

Für **Dolmetscher** und **Übersetzer** gelten die **Vorschriften** des Gesetzes über die Entschädigung von Zeugen und Sachverständigen **sinngemäß** (§ 16 Abs. 1 ZuSEG).
Dolmetscher werden wie Sachverständige entschädigt (§ 16 Abs. 2 ZuSEG). Sehr oft fallen sie unter die Ausnahmevorschrift des § 1 Abs. 2 ZuSEG.

γ) Die **Entschädigung für** die **Übersetzung** eines Textes aus einer Sprache in eine andere beträgt für die Zeile der schriftlichen Übersetzung, die durchschnittlich 15 Silben enthält, 0,30 DM. Bei der Übertragung von Fachtexten, insbesondere technischen oder medizinischen Gutachten, und bei sonstigen besonders schwierigen Übertragungen kann die Entschädigung — eine Erhöhung ist entsprechend dem Grade der Schwierigkeit grundsätzlich vorzunehmen — bis auf 1 DM für eine Zeile erhöht werden.

b) **Es werden dem Sachverständigen** neben der Vergütung aus § 3 (§ 4), § 5 oder § 6 ZuSEG grundsätzlich **ersetzt:**

α) die für die Vorbereitung und Erstattung des Gutachtens (s. o. 1b) aufgewendeten **Kosten,** einschließlich der notwendigen — angemessen sein müssenden — Aufwendungen **für** intern **herangezogene Hilfskräfte sowie die für eine Untersuchung verbrauchten Stoffe und Werkzeuge** (§ 7 Nr. 1 ZuSEG).

Wegen Ausnahmen vgl. Anlage zu § 5 ZuSEG Nr. 6 und 8.

Allgemeine Geschäftsunkosten — z. B. gezahlte Geschäftsraummiete und Fernsprechgrundgebühr, auch Aufwendungen anläßlich der bloßen Abnutzung von Werkzeugen — kann der Sachverständige nicht, auch nicht anteilsmäßig, ersetzt verlangen;

β) für das schriftliche Gutachten (Schreibwerk) der für **Schreibgebühren** im Gerichtskostengesetz (§ 91 Abs. 3 bis 6) bestimmte Betrag (§ 7 Nr. 2 ZuSEG), regelmäßig 0,50 DM je Seite einschließlich Papier, für Schriftstücke in fremder Sprache 1 DM je Seite, für Ablichtungen 0,50 DM je abgelichtete Seite, bei größerem Format der Ablichtung als DIN B 4 1 DM je Seite. Für Schriftstücke in bestimmter Form (z. B. Tabellen) wird die Schreibgebühr nach dem Zeitaufwand berechnet, der bei durchschnittlicher Arbeitsleistung zur Herstellung benötigt wird, und zwar wird für jede — evtl. nur angefangene — Viertelstunde 0,60 DM vergütet.

Ausnahmen: vgl. die Anlage zu § 5 ZuSEG Nr. 8, begrifflich neben Nr. 1 und 2, auch die Nr. 3 (schriftliche Auskunft).

Die Kostenrechnung gehört niemals zum Gutachten, wohl aber ist das Übersendungsschreiben dazu zu rechnen;

γ) **für Durchschläge,** die auf Erfordern gefertigt worden sind, **0,25 DM je Seite** (einschließlich Papier), ebenso für einen Durchschlag für die Handakten des Sachverständigen (§ 7 Nr. 3 ZuSEG).

Ausnahmen: vgl. die Anlage zu § 5 ZuSEG Nr. 8;

δ) die notwendigen **Fahrtkosten** (§ 8 Abs. 1 ZuSEG).

Bei Benutzung von öffentlichen, regelmäßig verkehrenden Beförderungsmitteln werden die wirklichen Auslagen einschließlich der Kosten für die Beförderung des notwendigen Gepäcks bis zur Höhe der bestehenden Tarife ersetzt (§ 8 Abs. 2 Satz 1 ZuSEG). Bei Benutzung der Eisenbahn oder von Schiffen ist der Ersatz der Beförderungsauslagen nach den persönlichen Verhältnissen des Sachverständigen zu bemessen, äußerste Grenze ist der Fahrpreis der ersten Wagenklasse oder der ersten Schiffsklasse (§ 8 Abs. 2 Satz 2 ZuSEG).

Mehrkosten für notwendig zu nehmende zuschlagpflichtige Züge werden ersetzt.

Für Fußwege und bei Benutzung von anderen als den genannten Beförderungsmitteln (z. B. des eigenen Kraftwagens) werden bei Entfernungen von mehr als 2 km für jedes angefangene Kilometer des Hin- und Rückwegs 0,25 DM (allgemein angemessener Betrag) gewährt (§ 8 Abs. 3 Satz 1 ZuSEG). Der danach sich ergebende Endbetrag ist, wenn der Hin- und Rückweg zusammen mehr als 200 km ausmacht und mit öffentlichen, regelmäßig verkehrenden Beförderungsmitteln billiger zurückgelegt werden kann, in dem überhöhten Umfange jedoch nur soweit zu zahlen, als die Mehrkosten gegenüber der Benutzung von öffentlichen, regelmäßig verkehrenden Beförderungsmitteln durch eine Minderausgabe an Entschädigung ausgeglichen werden (§ 8 Abs. 3 Satz 2 ZuSEG).

Kann vom Sachverständigen wegen besonderer Umstände — persönlicher oder sachlicher Art — ein öffentliches, regelmäßig verkehrendes Beförderungsmittel nicht benutzt werden, so werden die nachgewiesenen Mehrauslagen ersetzt, soweit sie angemessen (sachlich billig) sind (§ 8 Abs. 3 letzter Satz ZuSEG).

Für etwaige Reisen des Sachverständigen während der Terminsdauer werden die Fahrtkosten nur insoweit ersetzt, als dadurch Mehrbeträge an Entschädigung erspart werden, die beim Verbleiben an der Terminsstelle gewährt werden müßten (§ 8 Abs. 4 ZuSEG).

Tritt der Sachverständige die Reise zum Terminsort von einem anderen als dem in der Ladung bezeichneten oder der ladenden Stelle unverzüglich angezeigten Ort an oder fährt er zu einem anderen Ort als zu diesem Ort zurück, so werden, wenn die dadurch entstandenen Gesamtkosten höher sind, höchstens die Kosten ersetzt, die für die Reise von dem in der Ladung bezeichneten oder der ladenden Stelle angezeigten Ort oder für die Rückreise zu diesem Ort zu ersetzen wären. Mehrkosten werden nach billigem Ermessen ersetzt, wenn der Sachverständige zu den betreffenden Fahrten durch besondere Umstände genötigt war (§ 8 Abs. 5 ZuSEG);

ε) der Mehraufwand des Sachverständigen auf Grund der Abwesenheit vom Aufenthaltsort, d. h. dem Ort des benutzten Wohnraums; er wird in durchschnittlicher Weise durch die **Aufwandsentschädigung** abgegolten (§ 9 Abs. 1 Satz 1 ZuSEG). Ihre Höhe richtet sich nach der Dauer der Abwesenheit und den persönlichen Verhältnissen des Abwesenden (§ 9 Abs. 1 Satz 2 und Abs. 2 ZuSEG). Der Höchstsatz beträgt bei Reisen 14 DM (Tagegeld der Reisekostenstufe II für Bundesbeamte, vgl. § 9 Abs. 2 Satz 1 ZuSEG und § 9 Abs. 2a RKG). Der Durchschnittssatz ist hier 10 DM.

Die Entschädigung in dieser oder der sonst (bis zur Höchstgrenze) gerechtfertigten Höhe ist aber nur zu gewähren, wenn die Abwesenheit mehr als 12 Stunden dauerte; bei einer Abwesenheitsdauer von über 8 Stunden bis 12 Stunden ist der in Frage kommende Satz zur Hälfte, bei mehr als 6 bis 8 Stunden zu $^{3}/_{10}$ zuzubilligen (§ 9 Abs. 2 Satz 2 ZuSEG und § 9 Abs. 3 RKG). Bei mehrtägiger Abwesenheit vom Wohnort beträgt die Aufwandsentschädigung
für den Tag des Reiseantritts, wenn die Reise angetreten ist:

nach 18 Uhr	—,
nach 16 bis 18 Uhr	$^{3}/_{10}$,
nach 12 bis 16 Uhr	$^{5}/_{10}$,
vor 12 Uhr	$^{10}/_{10}$;

für den Tag der Reisebeendigung, wenn die Reise beendet ist:

bis 6 Uhr	—,
nach 6 bis 8 Uhr	$^{3}/_{10}$,
nach 8 bis 12 Uhr	$^{5}/_{10}$,
nach 12 Uhr	$^{10}/_{10}$.

Eine Abwesenheit von 6 Stunden und weniger begründet einen Anspruch auf Ersatz der Zehrkosten bis zu 2,50 DM (§ 9 Abs. 2 Satz 3 ZuSEG, siehe hierzu II 2 b β).

Bei Terminen am Aufenthaltsort des Sachverständigen sind diesem Zehrkosten bis zu 2,50 DM für jeden Tag mit notwendiger Abwesenheit aus der Wohnung in längerer Dauer als 4 Stunden zu ersetzen (§ 9 Abs. 3 ZuSEG);

ζ) die entstandenen **Übernachtungsspesen** (auch für Schlafwagen an Stelle Schlafquartiers). Sie sind dem Sachverständigen im Rahmen des Angemessenen, das durch die örtlichen Umstände und die persönlichen Verhältnisse bestimmt wird, zu ersetzen, falls die Rückkehr zum Aufenthaltsort (s. o. ε) nicht möglich ist (§ 9 Abs. 2 letzter Satz ZuSEG). Bei Zweifeln ist Glaubhaftmachung durch Quittungsvorlegung u. ä. erforderlich. Praktischer (nicht gesetzlicher) Höchstsatz: 11 DM (Übernachtungsgeld der Reisekostenstufe II der Bundesbeamten entsprechend dem Höchstsatz beim Mehraufwand). Für die Nachtzeit (21 bis regelmäßig 6 Uhr, vgl. § 188 Abs. 1 ZPO) ist eine Stundenvergütung nicht zu zahlen;

η) konnexe notwendige Barauslagen, die nicht den durch den Aufenthalt außerhalb der Wohnung verursachten Aufwand betreffen (so z. B. gezahlte oder zu zahlende Porto- und Fernsprechgebühren; Ausnahmen: Anlage zu § 5 ZuSEG

Nr. 8). Insbesondere gilt das Vorstehende, soweit es sich dabei um die Wahrnehmung von gerichtlichen Terminen handelt, von den **Kosten einer** erforderlichen **Vertretung** (§ 10 ZuSEG). Die Vergütung des Sachverständigen bleibt hier in jedem Falle bestehen. Auch die — angemessenen — Kosten **einer** notwendigen **Begleitperson** werden ersetzt (Vertreter und Begleitpersonen haben keinen eigenen Anspruch an die Staatskasse);

ϑ) die für Gebühren und Auslagen (vom Sachverständigen) zu zahlende **Umsatzsteuer.** Sie kann in voller Höhe (offen) **„überwälzt" werden,** da die Vergütung des Sachverständigen gesetzlich bemessen ist; denn der jeweils genau an den Sachverständigen zu zahlende Betrag ergibt sich in festgelegter oder doch bestimmt bzw. näher umrissener Weise aus dem Gesetz (vgl. § 10 UStG, § 63 UStDB vom 1. 9. 1951 in der geltenden Fassung und OLG Celle, NdsRpfl. 1952, 48 sowie OLG Frankfurt, NJW 1957, 351 im Gegensatz zu LAG Hamm, NJW 1953, 280). Etwaige (Gesamt)-Umsatzsteuerfreibeträge (vgl. § 7a Satz 1 UStG i. d. F. des Gesetzes zur Änderung des UStG vom 5. 10. 1956, BGBl. I 787) kommen allein dem Sachverständigen zugute.

Insgesamt **entsteht der Entschädigungsanspruch** des Sachverständigen jeweils mit der Gutachtenerstattung oder mit dem Ausspruch der Abstandnahme von der Gutachtenerstattung. Wegen der **Fälligkeit** s. u. 3a.

Die dem Sachverständigen zu zahlende **Gesamtentschädigung** wird **auf 10 DPf aufgerundet** (§ 11 ZuSEG).

3. a) Die **Festsetzung der Sachverständigenentschädigung** verlangt die Erfüllung der folgenden **förmlichen Voraussetzung:**

Die **Entschädigung** wird dem Sachverständigen **nur auf Verlangen** gewährt (§ 14 Abs. 1 ZuSEG). Dieses liegt regelmäßig in der Übersendung einer Rechnung, mag diese auch nicht substantiiert sein.

Das den Sachverständigen vernehmende oder beauftragende Gericht (grundsätzlich in seiner jeweils in Frage kommenden vollen Besetzung) kann — die Ausübung dieser Befugnis dürfte angebracht sein —, und zwar alsbald nach der Gutachtenerstattung oder dem Feststehen ihres Wegfalls, den Sachverständigen auffordern, seinen Anspruch, mag er ihn bereits unbeziffert geltend gemacht haben oder auch noch gar nicht, **innerhalb einer bestimmten Frist** zu beziffern bzw. beziffert geltend zu machen (§ 14 Abs. 3 Satz 1 ZuSEG). Die Frist muß mindestens zwei Monate betragen (§ 14 Abs. 3 Satz 2 ZuSEG; sie ist in dieser erheblich zu nennenden Länge im Verfahren der Sozialgerichtsbarkeit regelmäßig ausreichend). **Der Entschädigungsanspruch erlischt,** soweit ihn der Sachverständige nicht innerhalb der Frist beziffert (§ 14 Abs. 3 Satz 5 ZuSEG). Für die Fristberechnung siehe die §§ 186ff. BGB. § 84 Abs. 2 und § 91 Abs. 1 SGG, welche in bestimmten Fällen die Fristwahrung erleichtern, gelten hier ihrem Inhalte zufolge nicht (vgl. Brocke-Reese, Entsch. BeisZuS Anm. 3 zu § 14 ZuSEG). In der Aufforderung ist der Sachverständige über die Folgen der Versäumung der gesetzten Frist zu belehren (§ 14 Abs. 3 Satz 3 ZuSEG). Die Frist kann auf — rechtzeitig gestellten — schriftlichen oder mündlichen Antrag vom Gericht — bei Vorliegen besonderer Umstände evtl. sogar mehrfach, aber insgesamt nur in angemessener Weise — verlängert werden (§ 14 Abs. 3 Satz 4 ZuSEG). War der Sachverständige ohne sein Verschulden verhindert, die Frist einzuhalten, so ist ihm auf Antrag Wiedereinsetzung in den vorigen Stand zu erteilen, wenn er innerhalb von zwei Wochen nach Beseitigung des Hindernisses den Anspruch beziffert und die Tatsachen, die die Wiedereinsetzung begründen, glaubhaft macht (§ 14 Abs. 3 letzter Satz ZuSEG; eigene eidesstattliche

Versicherung kann genügen). Gewährung und Ablehnung der Wiedereinsetzung werden, auch bei den vor dem Sozialgericht (in erster Instanz) schwebenden Sachen, soweit es sich nicht um Entscheidungen des ersuchten oder beauftragten Richters handelt, nicht anfechtbar sein, da im Verfahren der Sozialgerichtsbarkeit über Gebührenfragen das Gericht der betreffenden Instanz stets endgültig entscheidet (vgl. §§ 178, 187 Abs. 2 und § 197 Abs. 2 SGG). Gegen die Entscheidung des ersuchten oder beauftragten Richters kann vom Sachverständigen bzw. der Staatskasse nach § 178 SGG binnen eines Monats seit Zustellung das mit der Sachentscheidung betraute Gericht (Prozeßgericht des betreffenden Rechtszuges) angerufen werden, das endgültig entscheidet; a. A. zu diesen Punkten Brocke-Reese, Entsch. BeisZuS Anm. 8 zu § 14 ZuSEG, die bei Ablehnung der Wiedereinsetzung die Beschwerde gegen Entscheidungen des Sozialgerichts gewähren, falls eine Beschwer von über 50 DM vorliegt.

Ist (evtl. nach Wiedereinsetzung) die Vergütung fristgemäß beziffert worden, so tritt ihre **Fälligkeit** ein (a. A. Brocke-Reese, Geb. u. KostR Anh. S. 36, die hierfür die Beendigung der Zuziehung genügen lassen); es beginnt die **zweijährige Verjährungsfrist** des § 196 Abs. 1 Nr. 17 BGB zu laufen, und zwar mit dem Ende des Jahres, in welchem der Entschädigungsanspruch beziffert wurde (entsprechend § 199 in Verb. mit § 201 BGB). Die Verjährung ist wegen ihrer prozessualen Natur (Einrede) nur zu beachten, wenn der Vertreter der Staatskasse („Bezirksrevisor") sich auf sie ausdrücklich berufen hat. (Zur Erhebung der Einrede ist die Einholung der Entscheidung des Präsidenten des Sozial- bzw. des Landessozialgerichts erforderlich entsprechend der früheren AV, DJ 1935, 1474.)

Wegen der **Bevorschussung** des Entschädigungsanspruchs s. o. 1 a a. E.

Für die Zahlungen nach zu Recht erfolgter Erhebung der Einrede der Verjährung kann der sie anordnende Beamte ersatzpflichtig gemacht werden.

Der — entstandene — gesamte Entschädigungsanspruch des Sachverständigen kann abgetreten, verpfändet und gepfändet werden.

b) **Die Feststellung der Entschädigung** erfolgt im Anschluß an die Einreichung der bezifferten Rechnung auf Grund der üblichen, aber verfahrensrechtlich nicht notwendigen, allgemein lautenden Verfügung des Vorsitzenden bzw. Richters des vernehmenden Gerichts, „nach Prüfung die bestimmungsgemäße Entschädigung zu gewähren", **durch den** kostenberechnenden **Urkundsbeamten** dieses Gerichts, der, zumeist in einer bestimmten Stelle für das ganze Gericht (Berechnungsstelle für Zeugen und Sachverständige), **eigenverantwortlich** tätig wird (vgl. LSG Berlin, SGb 1957, 308). Die Feststellung erfolgt im Rahmen des insgesamt Verlangten. Die Begründung von Absetzungen ist jedenfalls ein nobile officium.

Belehrung über den gegebenen Rechtsbehelf (s. u. c) schriftlich oder unter Aktenkundigmachung mündlich ist erforderlich (§ 66 Abs. 1 und § 173 letzter Satz SGG). Wegen der Folgen unterlassener oder unrichtiger Belehrung vgl. § 66 Abs. 2 SGG.

Eine Eigenabänderungsbefugnis von Amts wegen ist mit Ausnahme der Möglichkeit der Berichtigung offensichtlicher Unrichtigkeiten nicht gegeben (vgl. die §§ 138, 142 Abs. 1 SGG).

Die auf Grund der Festsetzung angewiesenen Beträge sind an sich — das entspricht der Übung — bei der Kasse oder Zahlstelle abzuholen (vgl. § 1 letzter Teil des Gesetzes über Zahlungen öffentlicher Kassen vom 21. 12. 1938, RGBl. I 1899). Sie können aber auch übersandt werden. Bei Übersendung durch die Post wird das Porto jedenfalls dann in Abzug gebracht werden dürfen, wenn der Sachverständige das Geld ohne weiteres (z. B. im Anschluß an seine Vernehmung) hätte abholen können.

c) **Gegen die Entscheidung des Urkundsbeamten** kann der Sachverständige oder sein Erbe oder sonstiger Rechtsnachfolger bei Ablehnung oder zu niedriger Feststellung oder die Staatskasse bei unzulässiger oder zu hoher Ansetzung — für die Zulassung von Erfüllungseinwendungen besteht weder Raum noch Bedürfnis — das mit der Sachentscheidung betraute **Gericht anrufen** (§ 178 SGG). Das braucht nicht das Gericht des festsetzenden Urkundsbeamten zu sein, man denke an die, wenn auch seltene, Anhörung des Sachverständigen durch einen ersuchten Richter. (Der Urkundsbeamte des ersuchten Richters ist nur dessen unselbständiger „Erfüllungsgehilfe".) Die besondere Bestimmung des § 178 SGG, die bei der hier vorgesehenen Anrufung auf das Prozeßgericht abstellt, geht dem allgemeinen § 15 Abs. 1 Satz 2 ZuSEG, der die Angehung stets des vernehmenden Gerichts zwecks Festsetzung vorsieht, vor (vgl. Peters-Sautter-Wolff, SGG § 118 Anm. 3 Erl. zu § 20 ZuSGebO und Thannheiser-Wende-Zech, Handbuch des Bundesversorgungsrechts 3. Aufl. Bd. 2 Verwaltungsverfahrensgesetz Erl. zu § 30; a. A. Brocke-Reese, Entsch BeisZuS Anm. 3 zu § 15 ZuSEG). Den § 178 SGG auszuschließen, wie es vor allem Wudtke, SGb 1958, 1, tut, „weil der Urkundsbeamte keine Befugnis im Rahmen des SGG ausübe", ist nicht gerechtfertigt. Der Urkundsbeamte wird hier auch im Sozialgerichtsverfahren auf verfahrensgesetzlicher Grundlage tätig. Das ergibt sich eindeutig aus § 118 Abs. 1 SGG, der ausdrücklich auf den § 413 ZPO verweist; dieser ordnet die Entschädigung des vom Gericht im Rechtsstreit zugezogenen, im Sozialgerichtsverfahren so wichtigen Sachverständigen an. Für diese Entschädigung ist in erster Linie der Urkundsbeamte als grundsätzlicher gerichtlicher Kostenberechner mit eigener Verantwortlichkeit zuständig. Das entspricht allein rechtsstaatlichen Gedankengängen. Bemerkt sei noch, daß gegen Entscheidungen (auch Festsetzungen) des ersuchten Richters das Prozeßgericht als Anrufungsgericht auf jeden Fall das letzte Wort hat (§ 178 SGG).

Etwas anderes als diese Anrufung beinhaltet dem Grunde nach in seinen wesentlichen Punkten auch der § 15 Abs. 1 Satz 1 ZuSEG nicht; soweit hier im Gegensatz zu § 178 (in Verb. mit § 173) SGG für die Anrufung des Gerichts nicht die Einhaltung einer Frist (nach § 173 SGG ein Monat seit Bekanntgabe) gefordert wird, müssen die Spezialbestimmungen des Sozialgerichtsgesetzes gelten, zumal dieses darauf abstellt, eine schnelle Durchführung und Abwicklung des Verfahrens zu ermöglichen (a. A. Brocke-Reese, Geb. u. KostR Anh. S. 23).

Bei Verweisung an ein anderes Sozialgericht (vgl. § 98 insbes. Abs. 3 SGG) ist das neue Gericht zuständig.

Eine Anrufung des Gerichts zum Zwecke der sogen. Nachliquidation (Erhöhung des bisher Verlangten) ist in keinem Falle zulässig; es muß wieder „von vorn" angefangen werden (a. A. OLG Düsseldorf, JVBl. 1957, 88 = MDR 1957, 496, für den Fall, daß auch eine echte Beschwer in der Festlegung durch den Urkundsbeamten vorliegt; dabei wird aber nicht beachtet, daß es nur die Aufgabe des Gerichts ist, überprüfend tätig zu werden).

Wegen Wiedereinsetzung in den vorigen Stand bei schuldloser Fristversäumnis vgl. § 67 SGG.

Die Erweiterung einer begrenzten Anrufung nach Ablauf der Anrufungsfrist ist nicht zulässig.

Eine Anschlußanrufung gibt es nicht.

Rücknahme der Anrufung im Zweifel mit der Wirkung des endgültigen Verlustes des Rechtsbehelfs ist möglich.

Eine bestimmte Beschwer ist für die Anrufung nicht erforderlich.

Form der Anrufung: schriftlich beim entscheidenden Gericht oder zur Niederschrift seines oder des sonst berechnenden Urkundsbeamten, also stets ohne Anwaltszwang (§ 173 SGG, vgl. auch § 16 Abs. 4 ZuSEG).

Abhilfe (unter Umständen unter Wiedereinziehung, nötigenfalls im Wege der Beitreibung nach dem Verwaltungsvollstreckungsgesetz) durch den jeweils zuständigen Urkundsbeamten ist möglich, vgl. § 174 SGG. Der Einwand der weggefallenen Bereicherung ist in der Regel hier nicht zulässig.

Abhilfe eröffnet für den Gegner die Anrufungsfrist neu.

Die Anrufung des Gerichts hat keine aufschiebende Wirkung (§ 175 SGG). Einstweilige Einstellung der Zwangsvollstreckung ist nicht möglich, da die Feststellung des Urkundsbeamten keinen vollstreckbaren Titel darstellt.

Die Streitbeteiligten haben kein Anrufungsrecht (vgl. § 15 Abs. 1 Satz 1, auch Abs. 2 Satz 2 ZuSEG). Sie sind an dem Rechtsverhältnis des Staates zum Sachverständigen, selbst soweit ihnen die Kosten desselben nach § 192 SGG auferlegt sind (vgl. dazu das 1. Kap. 1 und 2), unmittelbar nicht interessiert. Erst wenn ein zur Tragung dieser Kosten verurteilter Streitbeteiligter durch Kostenbescheid mit der von der Staatskasse verauslagten Sachverständigenentschädigung belastet wird, kann er — abgesehen von einem etwaigen Angriff gegen die zugrunde liegende Kostenentscheidung — gegen den zu seinen Lasten ergangenen Kostenbescheid vorgehen, d. h. ihm gegenüber das Gericht anrufen (s. o. 4. Kap. 2 zu a bis c). Der mit den Kosten belastete Streitbeteiligte braucht der Staatskasse niemals mehr zu ersetzen, als dem Sachverständigen hätte gezahlt werden dürfen; was ihm tatsächlich gezahlt worden ist, ist unerheblich.

Das Gericht (an sich in voller jeweiliger Besetzung), nicht der Vorsitzende, selbst wenn er im Rahmen des § 106 Abs. 3 Nr. 5 SGG dem Sachverständigen gegenüber tätig geworden ist), **entscheidet** über die Festsetzung stets auf Grund eigenen Ermessens (§ 128 Abs. 1, § 142 Abs. 1 SGG) durch kostenfreien (§ 183 SGG), zu begründenden (§ 142 Abs. 2 SGG) Beschluß **endgültig** (§ 178 SGG), und zwar grundsätzlich ohne mündliche Verhandlung (§ 124 Abs. 3 SGG); Anhörung des Gegners ist nicht unbedingt erforderlich.

Ausnahmsweise kann bis zum 31. 12. 1960 der Vorsitzende bei dem Sozialgericht allein, das Landessozialgericht ohne Zuziehung der Landessozialrichter und gegebenenfalls das Bundessozialgericht ohne Zuziehung der Bundessozialrichter entscheiden (§ 216 Abs. 1 Nr. 2 SGG); a. A. Brocke, SGb 1958, 271 [274], wie hier Wende, KOV 1958, 144.

Nachprüfung erfolgt grundsätzlich nur in bezug auf das ausdrücklich oder nach Lage der Sache Angegriffene. Mehr als insgesamt verlangt wird, kann nicht zugebilligt werden (vgl. § 308 Abs. 1 ZPO in Verb. mit § 202 SGG). Schlechterstellung durch das Gericht auf eigenen Rechtsbehelf ist nicht möglich (vgl. § 536 ZPO in Verb. mit § 202 SGG).

Zurückverweisung an den Urkundsbeamten (evtl. unter sachlicher Anweisung) ist nicht ausgeschlossen, aber wegen des eintretenden Zeitverlustes nicht angebracht. Gegen die neue Entscheidung kann wiederum vom Beschwerten das Gericht angerufen werden.

Der ergehende Beschluß ist formlos mitzuteilen.

Mangels entgegenstehender Bestimmungen wird für zulässig anzusehen sein, daß bei der Geschäftsverteilung das Präsidium des Gerichts eine bestimmte Kammer oder einen bestimmten Senat mit der Entscheidung über Anrufungsanträge der Sachverständigen (auch der Zeugen und Berechtigten aus § 191 SGG) betraut.

Wegen des gegebenen Rechtsbehelfs der Anrufung ist eine Herabsetzung der Entschädigung auf Verwaltungsanweisung nicht möglich. Hierfür besteht auch kein Bedürfnis, weil das Gericht seine Entscheidung von Amts wegen ändern kann (s. u.).

Die Entscheidung des Gerichts darf von diesem — nach allen Richtungen — von Amts wegen, aber nur innerhalb einer angemessenen Frist (etwa ein Jahr), geändert werden (vgl. den durch das Sozialgerichtsgesetz nicht ausgeschlossenen § 15 Abs. 1 Satz 3 ZuSEG). Das soll vor allem eine Benachteiligung der Staatskasse verhüten, wenn auf Vorgehen des betroffenen Streitbeteiligten gegen den ihn mit den Sachverständigenkosten belastenden Kostenbescheid (auf Grund einer entsprechenden Verurteilung nach § 192 SGG) festgestellt worden ist, daß der Sachverständige nur weniger verlangen konnte als ihm abschließend festgesetzt wurde. Eine Abänderung von Amts wegen in der höheren Instanz (vgl. § 15 Abs. 1 letzter Satz ZuSEG) dürfte dagegen nicht in Frage kommen, weil im gesamten Sozialgerichtsverfahren Gebührenstreitigkeiten grundsätzlich in der betreffenden Instanz ihre Erledigung finden (vgl. die §§ 178, 189 Abs. 2, §§ 191, 197 SGG).

Das Zuvielerhaltene muß zurückgezahlt werden; nötigenfalls erfolgt Beitreibung im Verwaltungszwangsverfahren (nach dem Verwaltungsvollstreckungsgesetz).

Verjährung des Rückzahlungsanspruchs tritt ein in vier Jahren seit Ablauf des Kalenderjahres, in dem der Honorierungsanspruch fällig wurde (entsprechend § 8 Abs. 2 GKG).

Wegen der Berichtigung offensichtlicher Fehler vgl. die §§ 138, 142 Abs. 1 SGG.

Zwar ist im § 15 Abs. 2 ZuSEG dem Sachverständigen und der Staatskasse bei einer Beschwer von über 50 DM ein — fristloses — **Beschwerderecht** eingeräumt, doch ist dieses Recht durch das Sozialgerichtsgesetz **ausgeschlossen,** in das das Entschädigungsgesetz für Zeugen und Sachverständige eingepaßt werden muß. (Das Gesetz über die Entschädigung von Zeugen und Sachverständigen hat sich stets in die in Frage stehende gesetzliche Verfahrensregelung einzuordnen, vgl. Peters-Sautter-Wolff, SGG § 118 Anm. zu § 20 ZuSGebO; Keidel, FGG 5. Aufl. Anm. 8 zu § 15; KG, 1a W 411. 56 und Tschischgale, JR 1956, 257.) Im SGG heißt es zudem im § 118 Abs. 1 Satz 1 ausdrücklich, daß die einschlägigen Bestimmungen der ZPO, nämlich hier die §§ 401 und 413, die durch die Vorschriften des Gesetzes über die Entschädigung von Zeugen und Sachverständigen ausgeführt werden, nur — entsprechend — gelten, *soweit dieses Gesetz*, d. h. das SGG, *nichts anderes bestimmt.* Im Verfahren der Sozialgerichtsbarkeit entscheidet über alle gebührenrechtlich streitigen Kosten das Gericht der betreffenden Instanz endgültig (vgl. § 189 Abs. 2 §§ 191, 197 Abs. 2 und § 178 SGG). Auch der Sachverständige kann ebenso wie die ihm gegenüberstehende Staatskasse unmöglich prozessual besser stehen als die anderen kostenmäßig Beteiligten. Das Gewähren eines weiteren Kostenrechtszuges zugunsten des Sachverständigen (oder seines Gegners) würde auch, zumal die Entschädigung regelmäßig im Laufe des Verfahrens erfolgt, das beschleunigt durchzuführende Verfahren in Sozialgerichtssachen in unzumutbarer Weise verzögern, weiterhin eine Auferlegung der betreffenden Kosten nach

§ 192 SGG jedenfalls erschweren. Hinzu kommt, daß es im Sozialgerichtsgesetz als Rechtsinstitution weder eine fristlose Beschwerde noch eine solche mit einer Mindestbeschwer gibt. Beschwerde würde im übrigen stets nur gegen die Festsetzungen der Sozialgerichte gegeben sein (vgl. § 172 Abs. 1, § 177 SGG). Eine unterschiedliche Behandlung der gleichen Festsetzungsverfahren in den einzelnen Rechtszügen läßt sich aber in neuzeitlich geregelten Prozeßverfahren schlechthin nicht rechtfertigen (vgl. hierzu im einzelnen Tschischgale, Die Vergütung des Sachverständigen im Sozialgerichtsverfahren, SGb 1957, 6ff., insbes. S. 10, und LSG Berlin, SGb 1957, 308; a. A. Wilde, ZfS 1954, 81 [83], auch Brocke-Reese, Geb. u. KostR Anm. 4 und 4a zu § 20 ZuSGebO, Anh. S. 23 und das LSG Berlin 8/LSG/5/55 B, welche die Beschwerde des Sachverständigen [und Zeugen] fristgebunden und ohne Einhaltung einer Beschwerdegrenze gegen die Entscheidungen der Sozialgerichte zulassen; Wudtke, SGb 1958, 1, hält die fristlose, aber an die 50 DM-Grenze geknüpfte Beschwerde für gegeben). Die Beschwerde ist richtigerweise auch dann ausgeschlossen, wenn sogleich das Gericht festgesetzt haben sollte.

d) **Bei Nichtauszahlung** des gerichtlich festgesetzten Betrages wäre auch für den Sachverständigen die **Beschreitung des — ordentlichen — Klageweges** zur Erlangung eines Vollstreckungstitels erforderlich (Judikatsklage; Festsetzung durch das Gericht ist immer Voraussetzung. Maßgebend ist der festgesetzte Betrag). Einen Kostenfestsetzungsbeschluß im Sinne des § 199 Abs. 1 Nr. 3 SGG stellt die Festsetzungsentscheidung nicht dar, weil sie nicht zwischen den Streitbeteiligten ergeht.

Wegen der Entschädigung der Sachverständigen und Zeugen, die der Gerichtsvollzieher zuzieht, vgl. hier das 9. Kap. II 9e.

Hinsichtlich der möglichen Bestrafung säumiger oder renitenter Beteiligter, Zeugen und Sachverständiger und der Auferlegung der durch sie verursachten übermäßigen Kosten jeweils zu ihren Lasten vgl. die Ausführungen im 2. Kap., insbes. 5 bis 7.

Wegen der Auferlegung der von der Staatskasse verauslagten Beteiligtenentschädigung sowie der Zeugen- und Sachverständigengebühren nebst Auslagen zu Lasten eines Verfahrensbeteiligten nach § 192 SGG vgl. 1. Kap. 1 und 2, wegen der Geltendmachung dieser Kosten gegen den damit belasteten Beteiligten durch die Staatskasse siehe 4. Kap. 2 zu a bis c.

Sechstes Kapitel

Die Parteikosten und ihre Festsetzung

SGG: § 72 Abs. 4, § 193 Abs. 2 bis 4, §§ 197, 199
ZPO: § 104 Abs. 1 und 2

§ 72 Abs. 4 SGG

Kosten des Vertreters

Die Kosten des besonderen Vertreters gelten als Kosten des Beteiligten.

§ 193 Abs. 2 bis 4 SGG

Umfang der Kostenerstattungspflicht

(2) Kosten sind die zur zweckentsprechenden Rechtsverfolgung oder Rechtsverteidigung notwendigen Aufwendungen der Beteiligten.

(3) Die gesetzlichen Gebühren und die notwendigen Auslagen eines Rechtsanwalts (§§ 25 bis 30 der Bundesgebührenordnung für Rechtsanwälte) oder eines Rechtsbeistandes sind stets erstattungsfähig.

(4) Nicht erstattungsfähig sind die Aufwendungen der Behörden, der Körperschaften und Anstalten des öffentlichen Rechtes.

§ 197 SGG

Kostenfestsetzung

(1) Auf Antrag der Beteiligten oder ihrer Bevollmächtigten setzt der Urkundsbeamte des Gerichts des ersten Rechtszugs den Betrag der zu erstattenden Kosten fest. § 104 Abs. 2 der Zivilprozeßordnung findet entsprechende Anwendung.

(2) Gegen die Entscheidung des Urkundsbeamten der Geschäftsstelle kann binnen eines Monats nach Bekanntgabe das Gericht angerufen werden, das endgültig entscheidet.

§ 199 SGG

Kostenfestsetzungsbeschlüsse als Vollstreckungstitel

(1) Vollstreckt wird

1. aus gerichtlichen Entscheidungen, soweit nach den Vorschriften dieses Gesetzes kein Aufschub eintritt,
2. aus Anerkenntnissen und gerichtlichen Vergleichen,
3. aus Kostenfestsetzungsbeschlüssen.

(2) Hat ein Rechtsmittel keine aufschiebende Wirkung, so kann der Vorsitzende des Gerichts, das über das Rechtsmittel zu entscheiden hat, die Vollstreckung durch einstweilige Anordnung aussetzen. Er kann die Aussetzung und Vollstreckung von einer Sicherheitsleistung abhängig machen; §§ 108, 109, 113 der Zivilprozeßordnung gelten entsprechend. Die Anordnung ist unanfechtbar; sie kann jederzeit aufgehoben werden.

(3) Für die Vollstreckung können den Beteiligten auf ihren Antrag Ausfertigungen des Urteils ohne Tatbestand und ohne Entscheidungsgründe erteilt werden, deren Zustellung in den Wirkungen der Zustellung eines vollständigen Urteils gleichsteht.

§ 104 Abs. 1 und 2 ZPO

Kostenfestsetzung und Glaubhaftmachung des Kostenansatzes

(1) Die Entscheidung über das Festsetzungsgesuch ergeht durch den Urkundsbeamten der Geschäftsstelle. Auf Antrag ist auszusprechen, daß die festgesetzten Kosten von der Anbringung des Gesuchs, im Falle

des § 105 Abs. 2 von der Verkündung des Urteils ab mit vier vom Hundert zu verzinsen sind. Die Entscheidung ist, sofern dem Gesuch ganz oder teilweise entsprochen wird, dem Gegner des Antragstellers unter Beifügung einer Abschrift der Kostenrechnung von Amts wegen zuzustellen. Dem Antragsteller ist die Entscheidung nur dann vonAmts wegen zuzustellen, wenn der Antrag ganz oder teilweise zurückgewiesen wird; im übrigen ergeht die Mitteilung formlos.

(2) Zur Berücksichtigung eines Ansatzes genügt, daß er glaubhaft gemacht ist. Hinsichtlich der einem Rechtsanwalt erwachsenen Auslagen an Post-, Telegrafen- und Fernsprechgebühren genügt die Versicherung des Rechtsanwalts, daß diese Auslagen entstanden sind.

Übersicht

Spezialabhandlungen des Verfassers: Das Verhältnis des § 196 Abs. 4 zum § 197 Abs. 1 SGG, SGb 1956, 251 und Der Übergang zum neuen Kostenrecht im Verfahren der Sozialgerichtsbarkeit, SGb 1958, 107.

1. Ist in dem ergangenen Urteil oder Beschluß angeordnet (s. o. 1. Kap. 1 ff.) daß einer der Beteiligten (oder ein Teil derselben, evtl. als Gesamtschuldner) dem anderen (oder mehreren einzelnen anderen) Kosten zu erstatten hat, oder hat in einem vor Gericht ohne vorbehaltenen bzw. ausgeübten Widerruf abgeschlossenen Vergleich ein Beteiligter die Kosten eines anderen übernommen, so **sind diese Kosten im Rahmen der** auferlegten oder eingegangenen **Erstattungspflicht** gegen den Zahlungspflichtigen für jede Instanz getrennt **festzusetzen** (§ 197 Abs. 1 Satz 1 und 2 SGG). Dabei ist die genaue Höhe der zu erstattenden Kosten festzulegen.

a) **Grundlage ist der** jeweils vorliegende **Kostentitel** (Urteil, Beschluß); dieser braucht nicht rechtskräftig, ja nicht einmal für vorläufig vollstreckbar erklärt zu sein (vgl. § 199 Abs. 1 Nr. 1, § 198 Abs. 2 SGG). Er kann auch, abgesehen vom endgültigen **gerichtlichen Vergleich** (§ 101 Abs. 1 SGG, s. o. 1), ein **angenommenes** (gerichtlich protokolliertes) **Anerkenntnis** mit Kostentragung oder -auferlegung im Sinne des § 101 Abs. 2 SGG sein (vgl. § 199 Abs. 1 Nr. 2 SGG). Was den Vergleich anbetrifft, so darf er auch in einer anderen Sache abgeschlossen sein, wenn die gegenwärtigen Kosten nur mit geregelt worden sind.

Hat ein gegen die Entscheidung in der Hauptsache gegebenes Rechtsmittel — ausnahmsweise — aufschiebende Wirkung (vgl. § 199 Abs. 1 Nr. 1 SGG), nämlich in den Sonderfällen der § 97 Abs. 1, § 154 Abs. 1 und 2 SGG, so betrifft dies nur die Hauptsache, wie ein Vergleich des § 199 Abs. 1 Nr. 1 mit Nr. 3 SGG ergibt.

Ist der Kostentitel ein **Ordnungsstrafbeschluß,** in welchem (allein oder zusätzlich) angeordnet ist, daß der Bestrafte (Beteiligte, Zeuge oder Sachverständige) die jeweils besonders verursachten Kosten dem anderen oder einem Beteiligten zu erstatten hat (vgl. § 141 Abs. 3, §§ 380, 390, 409 ZPO), so muß wegen der sich hier auf die Kosten erstreckenden aufschiebenden Wirkung der Beschwerde (vgl. § 175

Satz 2 SGG, § 572 Abs. 2 ZPO) die Rechtskraft des (Straf-)Beschlusses abgewartet werden (vgl. hierzu 2. Kap. 12).

b) Die **Kostenfestsetzung** ist stets **vom Bestand der Kostenentscheidung** im ergangenen Titel **abhängig.** Ist der Kostentitel (im Rechtsmittelwege oder, wo zulässig, durch Selbstabänderung oder durch späteren Vergleich) hinfällig geworden, ist eine Kostenfestsetzung nicht mehr möglich, eine bereits erfolgte automatisch mit entfallen.

c) **Unklaren Kostentiteln** ist im Wege zulässiger **Auslegung** ein verständiger Sinn zu verschaffen, allerdings darf ihnen dabei keine Gewalt angetan werden.

2. **Was zu erstatten ist, muß dem Grunde nach** entweder im einzelnen oder generell (jeweils in ganzer oder bruchteilsmäßiger Höhe) **im Titel ausgesprochen sein.** Dieser Ausspruch ist für den Urkundsbeamten bindend.

3. Sind die **Kosten generell auferlegt,** so sind die folgenden grundsätzlichen Ausschlüsse von der Erstattungspflicht zu beachten:

a) Die **Kosten** (Gerichtskosten und Anwaltskosten) **eines Vorverfahrens,** das ja nicht Teil des sozialgerichtlichen Verfahrens ist, sind **nicht erstattungsfähig** (so auch Brocke, ZfS 1955, 215), **ebenso nicht die außergerichtlichen Kosten eines** vorangegangenen — gerichtskostenfreien — **Armenrechtsverfahrens** (vgl. § 118a Abs. 4 Satz 1 ZPO).

b) **Allgemeine Aufwendungen,** die auch ohne Rechtsstreit gemacht zu werden pflegen, wie **z. B. Beitragszahlungen** an Kriegsopferverbände o. ä., sind, selbst wenn für sie Rechtsbetreuung mitgeleistet wird, **nicht erstattungsfähig** (vgl. Brocke, ZfS 1955, 215).

c) **Aufwendungen der Behörden, der Körperschaften und Anstalten des öffentlichen Rechts,** auch bei Streitigkeiten untereinander, sind **nicht erstattungsfähig** (§ 193 Abs. 4 SGG). Zu diesen Aufwendungen zählen **auch die Gebühren** (und Auslagen) **eines** von der Behörde usw. etwa zugezogenen **Anwalts** (vgl. LSG Niedersachsen, Nds. MinBl. 1955, 961 und BSG, SozR SGG § 193 Bl. Da 1 Nr. 2 = SGb 1957, 181 mit zust. Anm. von Völcker, ferner Grönig, BKK 1955, 206, Hennecke, MDR 1956, 201 und Wilde, ZfS 1954, 81). Ebenso sind hier allgemeine Betriebs- oder Verwaltungskosten, sei es auch von unterhaltenen Rechtsabteilungen, niemals erstattungsfähig. Der Zulassungsausschuß für Kassenärzte ist vom Bundessozialgericht (SGb 1956, 220) in diesem Zusammenhang als Behörde im Sinne des § 193 Abs. 4 SGG angesehen worden, was rechtsunbedenklich sein dürfte (vgl. auchBSG SozR SGG § 193 Bl. Da 1 Nr. 2).

d) Die — extravaganten — **Sonderkosten der §§ 93, 109 Abs. 1 Satz 2 und § 120 Abs. 2 SGG** sind **niemals erstattungsfähig.**

e) Die (aus der Gegenüberstellung mit den gewöhnlich entstehenden Kosten sich ergebenden) **Mehrkosten** sind **nicht erstattungsfähig, die bei der Vertretung** eines Beteiligten **durch einen Rechtsanwalt dadurch entstehen, daß** dieser seine **Kanzlei** oder seinen Wohnsitz **nicht an dem Orte** hat, **an dem sich** das **Prozeßgericht** (oder eine auswärtige Abteilung dieses Gerichts), bei dem er förmlich zugelassen ist, **befindet** (vgl. § 91 Abs. 2 Satz 2 ZPO).

f) Im übrigen sind **Aufwendungen** in aller Regel **nur erstattungsfähig, wenn sie** (nicht etwa die Rechtswahrung selbst) zur zweckentsprechenden Rechtsverfolgung oder Rechtsverteidigung **notwendig waren** (§ 193 Abs. 2 SGG). Hierbei ist zu bemerken, daß alle Beteiligten von vornherein verpflichtet sind, die Kosten so niedrig zu halten, wie sich das mit einer ihre Rechte wahrenden Prozeßführung verträgt (vgl. Willenbücher, Kostenfestsetzungsverfahren 15. Aufl. S. 111). Hat das Gericht die Erstattung bestimmter Kosten angeordnet, so hat es damit dem Grunde nach ihre Notwendigkeit im Sinne einer zweckentsprechenden Rechtswahrung bereits bejaht.

Die Mehrkosten einer persönlichen Zustellung des Gerichtsvollziehers sind im Zweifel nicht zu erstatten (§ 197 ZPO, § 202 SGG).

Die Kosten müssen grundsätzlich wirklich **entstanden sein.** Ihre Aufwendung (z. B. Zahlung an den Anwalt) ist allerdings nicht erforderlich. Unerheblich ist, ob die Kosten vor einem verweisenden Gericht oder vor dem Gericht entstanden sind, an das verwiesen ist (vgl. § 98 Abs. 3 SGG).

4. **Erstattungsfähig sind** danach:

a) **die Gerichtskosten des § 184 SGG,** die von der Körperschaft oder Anstalt des öffentlichen Rechts an die Staatskasse in der Sache entrichtet worden sind, wenn dem anderen Teil diese Kosten zur Erstattung auferlegt sind, weil die Einbeziehung oder Beiladung des öffentlich-rechtlichen Beteiligten ersichtlich in unbegründeter Weise durch ihn veranlaßt wurde (siehe hierzu 1. Kap. 3). Als titelmäßiger Ausspruch dürfte insoweit genügen: Der Kläger hat dem — öffentlich-rechtlichen — Beklagten die ihm entstandenen Kosten zu erstatten.

Was die Höhe der zu erstattenden Kosten anbetrifft, so sind die von dem öffentlich-rechtlichen Beteiligten verauslagten Kosten zu ersetzen, soweit ihre Zahlung zu Recht erfolgt ist (vgl. hierzu im einzelnen 4. Kap. 3);

b) die **Kosten des** ersatzberechtigten **Naturalbeteiligten i. S. des § 191 SGG** (bare Auslagen und Entschädigung für Zeitverlust), falls und soweit sie nicht aus der Staatskasse gezahlt worden sind, wenn dem anderen Beteiligten die Erstattungspflicht dieser Kosten ausdrücklich oder allgemein auferlegt ist. Als Titel genügt: Der Beklagte hat dem Kläger die Kosten zu erstatten.

Die baren Auslagen umfassen vor allem Fahrtkosten, Mehraufwendungen infolge der Reise und Übernachtungsspesen anläßlich angeordneter oder gebotener Terminswahrnehmung (vgl. § 191 SGG, ferner evtl. die Kosten für einen die Haus- oder Geschäftspflichten wahrnehmenden Vertreter, s. o. 5. Kap. I 2 a und b).

Über die Grundvoraussetzungen des § 191 SGG hinaus (Anordnung oder Gebotensein des persönlichen Erscheinens) wird auch gegenüber dem allgemein Erstattungspflichtigen **Auslagenersatz oder Zeitvergütung** — insbesondere bei Vorhandensein eines Peozeßbevollmächtigten — **nicht verlangt** werden können, höchstens wird der Erstattungspflichtige noch für die Kosten der an sich nicht erforderlichen Wahrnehmung eines Termins bei zeitweiligem Ausfall des bestellten Prozeßbevollmächtigten einzustehen haben.

Wegen des Nachweises ihres Entstandenseins und der gerechtfertigten Höhe der Kosten aus § 191 SGG vgl. das 5. Kap. I 2 a und b.

Nach § 72 Abs. 4 SGG gelten die Kosten des bestellten besonderen Vertreters für einen nicht prozeßfähigen Beteiligten (vgl. § 72 Abs. 1 bis 3 SGG) als Kosten des Beteiligten selbst;

c) **die** gesetzlich festgelegten **Kosten eines** gegenüber der Staatskasse nicht berechnenden **Zeugen** (Reisekosten und Entschädigung), **wenn** sie vom kostenberechtigten Beteiligten, der z. B. den vernommenen Zeugen gestellt hat, dem Zeugen gegenüber **endgültig verauslagt** worden sind (vgl. OLG Hamm, JMBl. NRW 1953, 59; LG München I, MDR 1958, 47).

Als Festsetzungsgrundlage genügt hier die folgende Fassung des Kostentitels: Der Beklagte hat dem Kläger die aufgewandten Kosten zu erstatten.

Wegen der Höhe dieser Kosten vgl. 5. Kap. II 2 a und b;

d) **Sachverständigenkosten,** aber nur, wenn sie **als** sog. private **Vorbereitungskosten** zur Anstrengung und Führung des Rechtsstreits oder zum Beschreiten der höheren Tatsacheninstanz wegen Ungeklärtheit des zugrunde liegenden schwierigen Sachverhalts — ausnahmsweise — erforderlich waren. Denn grundsätzlich ist das Verfahren vor den Sozialgerichten selbst, das gilt auch hinsichtlich einer erfolgenden Beweissicherung in Gemäßheit des § 76 SGG, für die Beteiligten kostenfrei; das hat Bedeutung sowohl für die Zeugen- als auch für die Sachverständigenkosten. (Die gemäß § 109 SGG im Hinblick auf seinen Satz 2 des Abs. 1 entstehenden besonderen Sachverständigenkosten trägt entweder die Staatskasse oder der Beweisantragsteller endgültig, vgl. hier 1. Kap. 5.)

Hinsichtlich der Fassung des Titels als Festsetzungsgrundlage genügt: Der Beklagte hat dem Kläger die aufgewendeten Kosten zu erstatten.

Bezüglich der bei der Regelung der Erstattung einzuhaltenden Angemessenheit der nachzuweisenden Kosten für vorbereitende Sachverständigentätigkeit — der private Sachverständige ist an das ZuSEG als solches nicht gebunden — geben die Ausführungen im 5. Kap. III 2 a und b jedenfalls hinreichende Anhaltspunkte;

e) ohne weiteres die **gesetzlichen** — nicht vereinbarte höhere — **Gebühren und** die **notwendigen Auslagen** eines **hinzugezogenen Rechtsanwalts** (oder eines Rechtsbeistandes). Die besondere Erwähnung dieser Kosten im Titel ist nicht erforderlich (vgl. § 193 Abs. 3 SGG). Das Auftreten des Prozeßbevollmächtigten ergibt sich aus den Akten.

α) Die **besonderen Kosten eines auswärtigen Anwalts** (Rechtsbeistandes) — insbesondere Reisekosten — sind mit Rücksicht darauf, daß an den Gerichtsorten auch der höheren Gerichte und des Bundessozialgerichts in aller Regel genügend Anwälte auswahlweise zur Verfügung stehen, jedenfalls im allgemeinen **nicht erstattungsfähig** (vgl. § 91 Abs. 2 Satz 1 letzter Teil ZPO). Daran vermag nichts zu ändern, daß an sich hier jeder bei einem deutschen Gericht zugelassene Anwalt bestellt werden kann (auch in dritter Instanz). Es ist nach Möglichkeit im Rahmen des Zumutbaren ja stets der billigste Weg zu beschreiten (wegen des Simultananwalts vgl. oben 3e).

Etwaige **auswärtige Beweistermine,** die als solche im Zweifel immer von Bedeutung sind, **hat** grundsätzlich **der** prozeßbevollmächtigte **Anwalt** (Rechtsbeistand) **wahrzunehmen.** Die hierdurch entstehenden **Reisekosten** sind in aller Regel **erstattungsfähig.** Bis zu deren Höhe sind statt derselben die Kosten eines am Terminsort seßhaften unterbevollmächtigten Anwalts zu erstatten.

β) Für die **Heranziehung eines Verkehrsanwalts** (-rechtsbeistandes) dürfte in Sozialsachen grundsätzlich **keine Notwendigkeit** bestehen, da der Streitstoff im allgemeinen verhältnismäßig leicht, zumeist ohne weiteres schriftlich, dem Prozeßbevollmächtigten unmittelbar mitgeteilt werden kann.

γ) Die **Kosten mehrerer** für das Verfahren vor dem Gericht der gleichen Instanz hinzugezogenen **Anwälte** (Rechtsbeistände) sind **nur insoweit zu erstatten, als sie** die **Kosten eines Rechtsanwalts nicht übersteigen oder als** in der Person des **Rechtsanwalts** ein **Wechsel eintreten mußte** (vgl. § 91 Abs. 2 Satz 3 ZPO). Letztes ist nur bei Tod, schwerer Erkrankung oder ähnlichen unabwendbaren Schicksalsschlägen der Fall, nicht dagegen z. B. bei Berufswechsel des Anwalts oder verschuldetem Verlust der Zulassung oder bei eingetretenem ein- oder zweiseitigen Vertrauensverlust (KG, JW 1934, 914 und Baumbach-Lauterbach, ZPO 25. Aufl. Anm. 5 zu § 91).

Streitgenossen können ohne Beeinträchtigung der allgemein oder jeweils be sonders auferlegten Erstattungspflicht **verschiedene Anwälte** nehmen.

δ) Bei dem **Betrieb eigener Angelegenheiten** (als Kläger, Beklagter oder Beigeladener) kann ein Rechtsanwalt von dem zur Erstattung der Kosten verpflichteten Gegner grundsätzlich **keine Gebühren und Anwaltsauslagen erstattet verlangen.** Der an sich einschlägige § 91 Abs. 2 letzter Satz ZPO gilt im Verfahren der Sozialgerichtsbarkeit nämlich nicht (so mit Recht LSG Niedersachsen, NJW 1956, 1856 = JZ 1957, 67).

ε) Die sogen. **Hebegebühr** des Anwalts (vgl. § 22 BRAGebO) wird nur **in den seltensten Fällen erstattungsfähig** sein, nämlich dann, wenn die Inempfangnahme des Geldes durch die Lage der Dinge geboten war, insbesondere weil der Zahlungspflichtige lediglich an den Anwalt hat zahlen wollen.

ζ) Wie sich aus § 4 BRAGebO ergibt, **muß sich der** bestellte **Anwalt,** wenn der Erstattungsanspruch des Kostengläubigers gewahrt werden soll, **im Falle** seiner **Verhinderung,** abgesehen von einer amtlichen Vertreterbestellung, **durch** einen **anderen Rechtsanwalt** bzw. einen **Anwaltsassessor oder** auch — insoweit nur vor dem Sozialgericht und dem Landessozialgericht — durch **einen** (nicht notwendig seinen) **Stationsreferendar vertreten lassen.**

Bezüglich der Rechtsbeistände bestehen keine Vertretungsbeschränkungen, doch wird der Erstattungsanspruch dann entfallen, wenn der Rechtsbeistand sich durch eine zur Rechtsvertretung ungeeignete Person vertreten läßt.

η) Wegen der **Art und Höhe der erstattungsfähigen Gebühren des Rechtsanwalts** (stets als Wahlanwalt) in den einzelnen Rechtszügen, **vgl. § 116 BRAGebO** und das 7. Kap. I A 5, bezüglich **des Rechtsbeistandes Art. IX § 2 KostÄndG** und das 7. Kap. I A 10. Die Anwaltsgebühren des sogen. Vorverfahrens (vgl. §§ 77 ff. SGG) werden nicht auf die Gebühr vor dem Sozialgericht in Anrechnung gebracht. (Der Absatz 6 des früheren § 196 SGG ist nicht übernommen worden, vgl. § 116 und § 118 Abs. 3 mit § 119 Abs. 1 BRAGebO.)

ϑ) Bei den **erstattungsfähigen Auslagen** des Anwalts handelt es sich gemäß § 193 Abs. 3 SGG, §§ 25 bis 30 BRAGebO im wesentlichen um die folgenden: die erforderlichen **Post- und** evtl. **Schreibauslagen** (siehe hier unten) **sowie** die **Kosten für** notwendige **Geschäftsreisen** (wegen der Einzelheiten vgl. das 7. Kap. I B 2); Entsprechendes hat für die Rechtsbeistände zu gelten.

Ob die nur für die im Einverständnis mit dem Auftraggeber zusätzlich gefertigten Abschriften und Ablichtungen noch zu zahlenden Schreibgebühren von dem allgemein für erstattungspflichtig erklärten gegnerischen Beteiligten erstattet verlangt werden können, hängt von der Erforderlichkeit dieser besonderen Abschriften zur zweckentsprechenden Rechtswahrung ab. Notwendige **Übersetzungskosten** sind in der Regel **zu erstatten.**

Umsatzsteuerbeträge (betr. Gebühren und Auslagen) sind **erstattungsfähig** (vgl. im einzelnen hier das 7. Kap. I zu A und B Nr. 2).

ι) Wie aus § 217 Abs. 1 SGG (Regelung bis zum Erlaß einer Bundesrechtsanwaltsordnung) zu entnehmen ist, stehen die **Verwaltungsrechtsräte den Anwälten gleich.** Nach § 217 Abs. 2 SGG sind wiederum diejenigen, die auf Grund der vorgeschriebenen Prüfungen **die Fähigkeit zum höheren Verwaltungsdienst haben und denen das Auftreten** vor den Gerichten der Verwaltungsgerichtsbarkeit allgemein **gestattet ist, den Verwaltungsrechtsräten gleichgestellt.**

κ) Die sog. **Organisationsvertreter** (vgl. § 73 Abs. 6 Satz 3 und § 166 Abs. 2 SGG), d. h. die kraft Satzung o. ä. zur Prozeßvertretung befugten Bevollmächtigten, welche Mitglieder und Angestellte von Gewerkschaften, von selbständigen Vereinigungen von Arbeitnehmern mit sozial- oder berufspolitischer Zwecksetzung, von Vereinigungen von Arbeitgebern und von solchen der Kriegsopfer sind, stehen **den Rechtsanwälten** oder Rechtsbeiständen kostenmäßig **nicht gleich**. Bezüglich ihrer hat das Sozialgerichtsgesetz keinen Anspruch auf Erstattung einer Gebühr für die geleistete Tätigkeit gegeben (vgl. LSG Berlin, SGb 1955, 220 und Wudtke, SGb 1954, 35, ferner Hastler, SozVers. 1954, 137, Jahn, KOV Bln. 1954, 138, Jenrich, BG 1955, 383 und Volmer, NJW 1954, 1100). In Frage kommt hier lediglich die Festsetzung der der kostenberechtigten Partei durch die Beauftragung des Organisationsvertreters im gegebenen Falle wirklich entstandenen Aufwendungen (vgl. § 193 Abs. 2 SGG), wobei zu bemerken ist, daß diese auf keinen Fall dem Grunde oder der Höhe nach in fester Weise bestimmt sein dürfen, sei es auch nur in Höhe der Gebühren eines Rechtsbeistandes. Pauschsätze, die vor allem als in den allgemeinen Mitgliedsbeiträgen (ganz oder teilweise) liegend gesehen werden könnten, sind daher nicht festsetzungsfähig (ebenso Stein-Jonas-Schönke, ZPO 17. Aufl. Anm. VI zu § 91; LSG Hessen, SGb 1955, 300 mit zust. Anm. von Hastler; Peters-Sautter-Wolff, SGG Anm. zu § 193 a. E.; auch BGH, BB 1954, 1043; a. A. SG Trier, SGb 1957, 313 mit abl. Anm. von Brocke). Besondere Kosten für die Vertretung vor Gericht werden von den Organisationen im allgemeinen gar nicht erhoben.

Freiwillige Zahlung von Pauschalkosten des Gegners außerhalb des Festsetzungsweges **ist** natürlich **möglich**, vgl. hierzu Rundschreiben des BMA vom 30. 4. 1954 – BVBl. 1954, 55 – und vom 28. 12. 1954 – BVBl. 1955, 43 = SGb 1955, 95 –; im Einvernehmen mit dem BMF und den beim BMA geführten Kriegsopferverbänden sind hier die folgenden Pauschalbeträge für die Vertretung durch Kriegsopferverbände als angemessen angesehen worden:

vor dem Sozialgericht	10 DM,
vor dem Landessozialgericht	20 DM,
vor dem Bundessozialgericht	30 DM;

f) die nachgewiesenen **Gerichtsvollziehergebühren und -auslagen** (wie überhaupt die entstandenen notwendigen Vollstreckungskosten des Gerichts und des mit der Beitreibung beauftragten Anwalts; vgl. dazu im einzelnen das 9. Kap. I und II hier und die §§ 198ff. SGG). Wie im Zivilprozeß mit seinen vollstreckbaren Entscheidungen muß für die Erstattungsfähigkeit dieser Kosten grundlagenmäßig genügen, daß sich aus dem Titel die Vollstreckungsberechtigung des Gläubigers gegenüber dem anderen Beteiligten als Schuldner ergibt; daß ein Gläubiger nicht ohne Grund die Zwangsvollstreckung betreiben wird, ist im allgemeinen zu vermuten.

Es besteht – Armut des Schuldners (oder des Gläubigers) ist auch hier unerheblich – statt der förmlichen Festsetzung allerdings die Möglichkeit der sogen. **Ansetzung der** konkret entstehenden **Vollstreckungskosten** (Gerichtsvollzieherkosten, evtl. Gerichtskosten und Anwaltsgebühren nebst Auslagen) **kurzerhand durch das vollstreckende Organ** (Gerichtsvollzieher, Gericht) selbst gemäß § 788 ZPO in Verb. mit § 198 SGG, und zwar an sich ebenfalls zugunsten des Gläubigers; der vollstreckende Gerichtsvollzieher kann aber, ähnlich wie der im Auftrage des Gläubigers beitreibende Rechtsanwalt, den eingezogenen – als solchen letztrangigen – eigenen Kostenbetrag einbehalten bzw., soweit er ihr zusteht, ohne weiteres an die Gerichtskasse (als Kostengläubigerin des Gläubigers) abführen (vgl. dazu im einzelnen Lappe, Rpfleger 1957, 244 und die Ausführungen hier im 9. Kap. II 3).

5. Die **Kostenerstattungsansprüche können** nach ihrem Entstehen **abgetreten, verpfändet und gepfändet werden. Sie entstehen** erst **mit dem Ausspruch der Erstattungspflicht** im Urteil oder in dem an seine Stelle tretenden Beschluß. Da die Erstattungspflicht nicht wie nach § 91 ZPO zwangsnotwendig (auf Grund der Klageerhebung) entsteht, ist ein Rechtsübergang zu einem früher liegenden Zeitpunkt rechtlich nicht möglich.

6. Das **Kostenfestsetzungsverfahren** ist **ein Verfahren zwischen den durch die Kostengrundentscheidung** (Auferlegung der Erstattungspflicht) **aneinander gebundenen Verfahrensbeteiligten,** die sich nunmehr insoweit als echte Streitparteien gegenüberstehen (Kostengläubiger einerseits, Kostenschuldner andererseits; die Staatskasse ist dabei nicht beteiligt).

Das Kostenfestsetzungsverfahren bildet einen **Annex des Verfahrens erster Instanz** und ist ebenfalls gebühren- und auslagenersatzfrei; der in ihm tätig werdende prozeßbevollmächtigte Anwalt oder Rechtsbeistand wird für seine insoweitige Tätigkeit nicht besonders vergütet. (Wird der Anwalt nur mit der Durchführung des Kostenfestsetzungsverfahrens – einschließlich der Gerichtsanrufung bzw. der Beantwortung einer solchen – beauftragt, so kommt für ihn gemäß § 56 Abs. 3, § 120 Abs. 2 BRAGebO eine Gebühr von 3 DM bis 5 DM in Betracht, für den Rechtsbeistand in halber Höhe.)

Wegen des Anrufungsverfahrens vgl. 7. Kap. II 1b.

Als solches ist das Kostenfestsetzungsverfahren **aber selbständiger Natur,** so daß die Vorschriften über Unterbrechung und Aussetzung (vgl. § 68 SGG, § 239 Abs. 1, 2 und 5 und §§ 240 bis 245, 247 bis 249 ZPO) gesondert zu berücksichtigen sind.

Wie sich aus § 81 ZPO, § 202 SGG grundsatzmäßig ergibt, ist der Prozeßbevollmächtigte der ersten Instanz auch zur Vertretung im Kostenfestsetzungsverfahren einschließlich der Empfangnahme der zu erstattenden Kosten ermächtigt.

7. Das **Kostenfestsetzungsverfahren** nach § 197 SGG ist von dem Festsetzungsverfahren, das in der Bundesrechtsanwaltsgebührenordnung (§ 19) im allgemeinen für die Gebühren der Anwälte zwischen diesen und der jeweils auftraggebenden Partei geregelt ist (früher war diese Regelung für das ganze Sozialgerichtsverfahren in dem jetzt aufgehobenen § 196 Abs. 4 SGG enthalten) wohl **zu unterscheiden,** ebenso von dem Verfahren der Festsetzung der Armenanwaltsgebühren, das zwischen dem beigeordneten Armenanwalt und der Staatskasse (vgl. § 128 BRAGebO) und in seiner Verlängerung (Realisierung der auf die Staatskasse übergegangenen Honorarforderung) zwischen der Staatskasse und der auftraggebenden Partei, evtl. auch ihrem Gegner (vgl. § 130 Abs. 2 BRAGebO), stattfindet. **Diese weiteren Verfahren** sind **nicht präjudiziell,** sie brauchen daher nicht abgewartet zu werden (vgl. hierzu Tschischgale, SGb 1956, 251; a. A. Brocke, Sozialrichter S. 186, auch ZfS 1955, 229 und Friederichs, SGb 1956, 37). Der Erstattungspflichtige braucht nämlich nicht automatisch das zu erstatten, was der Kostengläubiger, sei es auch auf eine gegen ihn ergangene rechtskräftige Festsetzung, seinerseits gezahlt hat, sondern in deren Grenzen nur das, was nach den gesetzlichen Erstattungsbestimmungen zu zahlen erforderlich ist. Die Nachprüfung hierüber unterliegt in unentziehbarer Weise dem den Erstattungsbetrag in richterlicher Unabhängigkeit festsetzenden Urkundsbeamten, der hierzu vom Gesetzgeber ausdrücklich eingesetzt ist. Zwar hat der festsetzende Urkundsbeamte (des Gerichts erster Instanz) gegebenenfalls gewissermaßen nachzuprüfen, ob eine Entscheidung in einem anderen – speziellen – Kostenfestsetzungsverfahren (vgl. § 189 Abs. 2, § 191 SGG), womöglich noch einer

übergeordneten Gerichtsinstanz, zutreffend ist. Das ist aber kostenrechtlich nichts Auffälliges. Denn nachgeprüft wird hier das Entstandensein der Kostenforderung und ihre Höhe aus dem Gesichtspunkt der Erstattungspflicht des Gegners. Der bisher noch nicht zu Wort gekommene Erstattungspflichtige kann ja durchaus neue tatsächliche Beurteilungspunkte für eine Festsetzung zur Erstattung wenigstens in geringerer Höhe erbringen. Vorstehendes hat sogar dann zu gelten, wenn bei nicht beschränkter Erstattungspflicht die in Frage kommende Gebühr des Anwalts von diesem gegenüber seinem Auftraggeber — rechtskräftig — ausgeklagt ist. Zwar ist im Sozialgerichtsverfahren eine einmalige Pauschalgebühr für die Anwaltsvertretung vor der jeweiligen Gerichtsinstanz zu zahlen. Diese Gebühr hängt aber von dem Umfange des erteilten und ausgeführten Auftrags ab. Der Umfang kann durchaus größer sein als an sich notwendig (so wenn der Anwalt auf Verlangen seines Auftragsgebers zeitraubenden und schwierigen Verkehr mit einem privaten Sachverständigen unterhalten hat, der als solcher in höchst überflüssiger Weise in den Rechtsstreit eingeschaltet wurde; die verlangte Mehrarbeit ist zwar vom Auftraggeber abzugelten, die Vergütung braucht aber insoweit vom Kostenschuldner nicht erstattet zu werden). Aus dem Gesichtswinkel der Erstattungspflicht berechtigte spätere Höherfestsetzungen in den anderen Verfahren können im Wege der zulässigen Nachtragsliquidation — im Gegensatz zur verbotenen Nachliquidation in „höherer Instanz" — im Festsetzungsverfahren nach § 197 SGG (wieder „unten" beginnend) ausgeglichen werden. (Eine auch aus dem Gesichtspunkt der Erstattungspflicht an sich zu berücksichtigende niedrigere Festsetzung in den anderen Verfahren kann nach eingetretener Rechtskraft des Beschlusses aus § 197 SGG allerdings nicht mehr zum Ausgleich gebracht werden; Klage aus ungerechtfertigter Bereicherung dürfte aber möglich sein.)

8. **Die Kostenfestsetzung** erfolgt stets **nur auf Antrag des Kostengläubigers,** der durch seinen Bevollmächtigten handeln kann. (Etwas anderes besagt § 197 Abs. 1 Satz 1 SGG nicht; die Bevollmächtigten haben — mit Ausnahme des Falles des § 124 ZPO bezüglich des Armenanwalts — kein selbständiges Antragsrecht.)

Bei bestehender **Erbengemeinschaft** kann im Hinblick auf § 2039 BGB **ein Miterbe** für alle Erben die Festsetzung der Kosten verlangen, wenn die Kostenforderung zum Nachlaß gehört (vgl. Brocke-Reese, Geb u. KostR Anm. 4 zu § 100 ZPO).

Antragsberechtigt (und später — bei Beschwer — anrufungs- = erinnerungsberechtigt) sind auch die Einzel- (z. B. auf Grund Abtretung) und die Gesamtrechtsnachfolger (vor allem auf Grund Erbfolge) des ursprünglichen Kostengläubigers; es muß dann aber die **Umschreibung des Kostentitels** entsprechend §§ 727 ff. ZPO (vgl. § 198 Abs. 1 SGG) erfolgen. Das gilt auch für den Pfandgläubiger, soweit er einziehungsberechtigt ist (§ 1282 BGB), und den Pfändungsgläubiger, dem die Kostenforderung zur Einziehung überwiesen ist (§ 835 ZPO). Bei Rechts- (und damit Pflichten-)nachfolge auf seiten des Erstattungspflichtigen muß ebenfalls Umschreibung vorgenommen werden.

Im Falle des § 124 ZPO (§ 202 SGG) ist wegen seiner Wahlanwaltskosten der **Armenanwalt** beteiligt (an Stelle seiner Partei).

9. Das **Kostenfestsetzungsgesuch** ist an sich an **keine Frist** gebunden. Es darf aber nicht mit ungebührlicher Verzögerung gestellt werden (etwa erst nach über einem Jahr seit Ergehen des Kostentitels). Ist letzteres der Fall, so greift unter Umständen die von Amts wegen zu beachtende Verwirkung durch.

10. Das **Gesuch** kann **schriftlich** eingereicht oder zu **Protokoll der Geschäftsstelle** erklärt werden (§ 103 Abs. 2 ZPO, § 202 SGG). Die **Kostenberechnung,** ihre

zur Mitteilung an den Gegner bestimmte Abschrift und die zur Rechtfertigung der einzelnen Ansätze dienenden Belege sind **beizufügen. Belege** sind nur zu erbringen, soweit nicht die Akten selbst den erforderlichen Nachweis ergeben. (Regelmäßig genügt die Glaubhaftmachung des Ansatzes, vgl. § 104 Abs. 2 Satz 1 ZPO.) Bei Nichtbeifügung der Abschrift der Kostenberechnung kann diese von der Geschäftsstelle auf Kosten des Antragstellers gefertigt werden (vgl. § 93 SGG; der Kostengläubiger ist Kläger im Sinne dieser Vorschrift).

Hinsichtlich der einem Rechtsanwalt (Rechtsbeistand) erwachsenen Auslagen an **Post-, Telegrafen- und Fernsprechgebühren genügt** die **Versicherung des Anwalts** (auch des Rechtsbeistandes), daß diese Auslagen entstanden sind (§ 197 Abs. 1 Satz 2 SGG, § 104 Abs. 2 Satz 2 ZPO). Die Erforderlichkeit des Entstehens dieser Auslagen wird bei Nichtauffälligkeit der Höhe ohne weiteres angenommen werden können. Der Urkundsbeamte ist befugt, zur Glaubhaftmachung des Kostenansatzes eidesstattliche Versicherungen der Parteien und Dritter entgegenzunehmen (vgl. §§ 294 ZPO, § 202 SGG, §§ 156, 163 StGB). Er kann diese Personen auch, und zwar uneidlich, vernehmen. (Zwangsmittel stehen dem Urkundsbeamten hierbei aber nicht zur Verfügung.) Die Festsetzung erfolgt grundsätzlich ohne mündliche Verhandlung.

11. a) Der **Armenanwalt kann wegen** seiner **Wahlanwaltskosten,** soweit er noch nicht befriedigt ist, zu jeder Zeit im Laufe des Festsetzungsverfahrens (auch von Anfang an) **an die Stelle seiner** das Kostenfestsetzungsverfahren betreibenden **Partei treten** (§ 124 ZPO, § 202 SGG). Diese muß ihm bis zur Rechtskraft des Kostenfestsetzungsbeschlusses weichen, es sei denn, daß inzwischen Zahlung an sie erfolgt ist (auf Grund des ergangenen, noch nicht rechtskräftigen Festsetzungsbeschlusses; schlüssige Zahlungsbehauptung durch den anzuhörenden Gegner genügt hier, da Beweisaufnahmen über behauptete Schuldtilgung in dem engen Kostenfestsetzungsverfahren grundsätzlich nicht möglich sind). Ein bereits ergangener aber noch nicht rechtskräftiger **Kostenfestsetzungsbeschluß** muß bei Zulässigkeit des Eintretens des Armenanwalts **auf dessen Namen umgestellt werden** (mit Wirkung ex nunc).

Hat der Armenanwalt die Festsetzung seiner Gebühren im eigenen Namen von Anfang an beantragt, der Urkundsbeamte, der an sich zugunsten des Antragstellers festsetzen wollte, aber versehentlich die Kosten auf den Namen der vertretenden Partei festgesetzt, so kann — hier mit Wirkung ex tunc — berichtigt werden (vgl. §§ 138, 142 Abs. 1 SGG und KG, JW 1936, 889 und 1937, 566; ferner 1 W 1583. 54).

b) Auch **nach rechtskräftigem Abschluß** des Kostenfestsetzungsverfahrens **kann** in angemessener Frist (etwa zehn Monate) **der Armenanwalt** wegen seiner Kosten (als Wahlanwalt) **an die Stelle seiner Partei treten,** die das Festsetzungsverfahren betrieben hat. **Dazu ist** aber **erforderlich:**

α) die **Rückgabe des Kostenfestsetzungsbeschlusses** durch die Partei unter ausdrücklichem **Verzicht auf ihre Rechte** auf Erstattung ihr gegenüber;

β) der **Nachweis der Nichterfüllung** der Erstattungspflicht **gegenüber dem bisherigen Kostengläubiger** durch eine entsprechende Erklärung des Schuldners.

Bei Vorliegen dieser Voraussetzungen ergeht unter Aufhebung des bisherigen gegen den Erstattungspflichtigen ein **neuer Kostenfestsetzungsbeschluß** (vgl. hierzu im einzelnen Tschischgale, KostR in ZivSach. S. 66ff. und unten das 8. Kap. IV A).

12. **Wird** der **Armenanwalt aus der Staatskasse befriedigt,** so **geht** in Höhe der geleisteten Zahlung **die Forderung gegen den** kostenmäßig **Unterlegenen** auf dem Wege über § 124 ZPO, § 202 SGG gemäß § 130 Abs. 1 BRAGebO — im Zweifel

(vgl. § 426 Abs. 2 Satz 2 BGB) letztrangig — **auf die Staatskasse über.** Der Übergang auf die Staatskasse muß — vom Urkundsbeamten der ersten Instanz — auf dem ergangenen Kostenfestsetzungsbeschluß und seiner vollstreckbaren Ausfertigung unter entsprechender Ermäßigung des vom unterlegenen Gegner an den aufgeführten Kostengläubiger (Beteiligter bzw. dessen beigeordneter Anwalt) zu zahlenden Kostenbetrages (gegebenenfalls auf O) vermerkt werden. (Die berichtigte vollstreckbare Ausfertigung ist abschließend zurückzusenden und ein Absendevermerk zu den Akten zu fertigen.) Die auf die Staatskasse übergegangenen Beträge werden im Wege der gerichtlichen Kostenanforderung (durch Kostenbescheid) geltend gemacht (vgl. § 130 Abs. 2 BRAGebO und im einzelnen die Ausführungen im 8. Kap. II B).

13. Die **Festsetzung der erstattungsfähigen Beträge** erfolgt stets **durch den Urkundsbeamten** des Gerichts **des ersten Rechtszuges** (§ 197 Abs. 1 Satz 1 SGG). Bei Verweisung ist der Urkundsbeamte des Sozialgerichts zuständig, an das — direkt oder, bei Verweisung zwischen höheren Instanzen, indirekt — verwiesen ist (§ 98 Abs. 3 SGG). Vgl. hierzu Klink, SGb 1958, 345.

Der **Urkundsbeamte prüft in richterlicher Unabhängigkeit** — die Kostenfestsetzung ist gesetzlich delegierte Richtertätigkeit — sachlich, ob ein ausreichender Kostentitel gegen den in Anspruch genommenen Kostenschuldner vorliegt und ob und in welcher genauen Höhe die begehrten Kosten auf der Grundlage des ergangenen Titels, gegebenenfalls unter Nachprüfung der Notwendigkeit zur zweckentsprechenden Rechtswahrung, erstattungsfähig sind. Der Urkundsbeamte kann daher weder dienstaufsichtsmäßig in bestimmter Weise angewiesen werden, noch darf er umgekehrt eine sogen. Vorentscheidung des Gerichts einholen. **An** die ergangene **Kostengrundentscheidung** (Urteil oder Beschluß des Gerichts) ist der Urkundsbeamte **gebunden** (insbesondere an die darin hinsichtlich der Erstattungspflicht festgelegten Bruchteile), a. A. hierzu zu Unrecht SG Würzburg, BG 1957, 125. Bei der Bemessung und Festsetzung von Anwaltsgebühren braucht er **kein Gutachten des Vorstands der Rechtsanwaltskammer** (vgl. § 12 Abs. 2 BRAGebO) einzuholen, da hier kein Rechtsstreit vorliegt (ebenso Riedel-Sußbauer, BRAGebO Anm. 7 zu § 12; a. A., die zu untragbaren Ergebnissen in der Praxis führt, Luetgebrune-Lotze, BRAGebO Anm. III zu § 116).

14. Die **Bewilligung des Armenrechts** zugunsten des Erstattungspflichtigen **hindert** — ebenso wie natürlich die zugunsten des Kostengläubigers — **weder die Kostenfestsetzung noch ihre Vollstreckung** (§ 117 ZPO in Verb. mit § 202 SGG).

15. Die Durchführung des **Kostenfestsetzungsverfahrens verlangt** — wie jedes Verfahren — **ein Rechtsschutzbedürfnis** (-interesse). Dieses ist zu verneinen, wenn der Gegner von sich aus die in Frage kommenden Kosten unzweifelhaft bereits in voller Höhe erstattet hat.

16. An sich müssen die **festzusetzenden Kostenbeträge verauslagt** sein. Bei **taxmäßig zu entrichtenden Gebühren** und Auslagen **genügt** aber stets, **daß die Zahlungspflicht feststeht,** weil damit auch deren Aufwendung der Höhe nach glaubhaft ist. Das hat auch in bezug auf Rahmengebühren zu gelten (vgl. § 116 BRAGebO), was völlig unbedenklich ist, wenn, ganz abgesehen von den feststehenden Mindestgebühren, mittelhohe Gebühren verlangt werden, für deren Entstehen in der Regel ein gewisser Anschein spricht. Aber auch höhere Beträge können und müssen hier als zu zahlende bei entsprechender Lage der Dinge nach Prüfung festgesetzt werden.

Ist eine **Doppelinanspruchnahme** des Erstattungspflichtigen **zu befürchten,** so weil ihm zwei in Gesamtheit (gegenüber ihrem Anwalt) weiter schuldende Kostengläubiger gegenüberstehen, **muß der Verauslagungsnachweis erbracht werden.**

17. Wegen der Bestimmung der **Rechtsanwaltsgebühren** (Rechtsbeistandskosten) der **Höhe** nach vgl. § 116 BRAGebO und § 2 des Art. IX KostÄndG sowie die Ausführungen hier im 7. Kap. I A 5 und 10.

Der festsetzende Urkundsbeamte kann und muß den hierbei gesetzlich bestimmten Rahmen von sich aus ausfüllen. Alle **Umstände des Falles,** insbesondere die **Bedeutung der Angelegenheit,** der **Umfang und die Schwierigkeit** der anwaltlichen Tätigkeit sowie die **Vermögens- und Einkommensverhältnisse des Auftraggebers** (nicht des Erstattungspflichtigen) sind dabei **zu berücksichtigen** (vgl. § 12 BRAGebO).

18. Da **im Kostenfestsetzungsverfahren** über die Beträge der entstandenen Kosten, nicht aber über ihr Tilgung zu entscheiden ist, **ist** grundsätzlich allein **von dem Ansatz des Gesuchstellers,** soweit er berechtigt ist, **auszugehen.** Dabei kann ein im Zusammenhang mit einem verlangten, nicht berechtigten Posten stehender an sich nicht verlangter, berechtigter in der entsprechenden Höhe berücksichtigt werden. **Die Zahlung der Staatskasse** an den Armenanwalt (s. o. 12) **ist** bei der Festsetzung der zu erstattenden Rechtsanwaltsgebühren durch Abzug der gezahlten Summe **zu berücksichtigen.** Sonst ist nur abzusetzen, was der Gesuchsteller von sich aus dem Gegner als gezahlt gutbringt, da auch im Kostenfestsetzungsverfahren der Grundsatz gilt, daß über das Verlangte hinaus nichts zugebilligt werden kann (§ 308 Abs. 1 ZPO, § 202 SGG). Beträge, deren Tilgung der erstattungspflichtige Gegner darüber hinaus behauptet, können nicht abgesetzt werden. Die Entscheidung materiell-rechtlicher Fragen im formalen Kostenfestsetzungsverfahren ist nämlich nicht möglich (vgl. hierzu Tschischgale, KostR in ZivSach. S. 60). **Einwendungen** des Zahlungspflichtigen **wie Zahlung, Tilgung durch Vorschußleistung, Aufrechnung, Vergleich, Verzicht, Stundung und Verjährung** (30jährige, vgl. die §§ 195, 218 BGB, hinsichtlich Zinsen vierjährige, vgl. § 218 Abs. 2 und § 197 BGB) können daher im Kostenfestsetzungsverfahren grundsätzlich **keine Berücksichtigung** finden (vgl. hierzu auch den speziellen § 124 Abs. 2 ZPO). Anhörung des Erstattungspflichtigen ist deshalb nicht unbedingt notwendig, so nicht, wenn die Verhältnisse völlig klarliegen. (Die Geltendmachung der verbotenen Einwände und Einreden ist nur gemäß § 767 ZPO im Wege der Vollstreckungsgegenklage vor dem Prozeßgericht zulässig; die einschränkende Vorschrift des § 767 Abs. 2 ZPO — Entstandensein der Einwendungen nach dem Schluß der mündlichen Verhandlung — gilt mit Rücksicht auf das anders als ein Rechtsstreit ausgestaltete Kostenfestsetzungsverfahren, das eine obligatorische mündliche Verhandlung nicht kennt, nach herrschender und zutreffender Ansicht nicht. Für die Vollstreckungsgegenklage bezüglich Kostenfestsetzungsbeschlüsse der Sozialgerichte sind diese regelmäßig zuständig (vgl. BGH, NJW 1956, 1356).

19. Bei **mehreren Erstattungspflichtigen,** die **nicht Gesamtschuldner** sind, sind die **Kosten einzeln festzusetzen. Jeder Kostengläubiger** hat nur Anspruch auf die **Erstattung seiner Kosten.** (Es besteht grundsätzlich keine Gesamtgläubigerschaft; wegen Miterben vgl. hier 8.)

20. Auf Antrag ist auszusprechen, daß **die festgesetzten Kosten** von der — zulässigen (diese Einschränkung muß gemacht werden) — Anbringung des Gesuchs, im Falle des § 105 Abs. 2 ZPO (s. u. 26) von der Verkündung des Urteils ab, **mit 4 v. H. zu verzinsen** sind (vgl. den § 104 Abs. 1 Satz 2 ZPO in der Fassung des Kosten-

änderungsgesetzes Art. X § 3 Nr. 2, der für Parteikostenfestsetzungsverfahren allgemeine Bedeutung hat).

Wegen **Aufrundung der Kostenbeträge** vgl. § 9 Abs. 2 GKG, § 9 ZuSEG, § 11 Abs. 2 BRAGebO, § 13 Abs. 2 GVKostG.

21. **Ablehnungen** oder **Absetzungen sind** vom Urkundsbeamten **zu begründen** (§ 142 Abs. 2 SGG).

Schreib- oder **Rechenfehler** oder ähnliche offenbare Unrichtigkeiten kann der Urkundsbeamte entsprechend § 138 SGG (vgl. § 142 Abs. 1 SGG) **berichtigen.** Im übrigen aber kann der Urkundsbeamte von sich aus nicht abändern (wegen sogen. Abhilfe vgl. unten 28).

22. Das **Kostenfestsetzungsverfahren ist gebühren- und auslagenersatzfrei** (s. o. 6). Der **Anwalt** (Rechtsbeistand) **erhält** grundsätzlich **keine Kostenfestsetzungsgebühr** (Ausnahme s. o. 6).

23. Der erlassene oder abgelehnte **Kostenfestsetzungsbeschluß muß,** wie alle Entscheidungen im Sozialgerichtsverfahren, eine **Rechtsbehelfsbelehrung enthalten** (§ 66 Abs. 1 SGG). Diese kann auch mündlich erfolgen, muß dann aber aktenkundig gemacht werden (vgl. § 173 Satz 2 und § 178 letzter Satz SGG). Wegen der Folgen unterlassener oder unrichtiger Belehrung vgl. § 66 Abs. 2 SGG.

24. Der **Kostenfestsetzungsbeschluß** ist auszufertigen und **dem Gesuchsteller** formlos zu übersenden, wenn seinem Antrage voll stattgegeben worden ist, dagegen von Amts wegen **zuzustellen, wenn** teilweise oder ganze **Zurückweisung** erfolgt ist (§ 63 Abs. 1 SGG, § 104 Abs. 1 Satz 4 ZPO). **Dem Antragsgegner** ist der Festsetzungsbeschluß von Amts wegen **zuzustellen, falls** dem Antrage ganz oder zum Teil **stattgegeben** worden ist, sonst überhaupt nicht. Bei Zustellung ist Abschrift der Kostenberechnung beizufügen (§ 63 Abs. 1 SGG, § 104 Abs. 1 Satz 3 ZPO).

Die **Zustellung von Amts wegen** erfolgt stets **nach dem Verwaltungszustellungsgesetz** (VwZG) vom 3. 7. 1952 (BGBl. I 379), d. h. regelmäßig durch die Post, evtl. durch die Behörde selbst (§ 63 Abs. 2 SGG, §§ 2 bis 16 VwZG). Hinsichtlich der Zustellung an Bevollmächtigte (hier Prozeßbevollmächtigte erster Instanz) vgl. § 8 VwZG (Kannvorschrift).

25. **Zur Vollstreckung** des Kostenfestsetzungsbeschlusses (vgl. § 199 Abs. 1 Nr. 3 SGG) bedarf es der Erteilung der **Vollstreckungsklausel** an den Gläubiger (§ 198 SGG, §§ 724, 725 ZPO). Vorherige Zustellung ist dazu nicht **erforderlich.** (Wohl aber setzt die Vollstreckung gemäß § 198 SGG, § 750 ZPO die Zustellung des vollstreckbaren Beschlusses seitens des Gläubigers durch den Gerichtsvollzieher voraus, die nach § 798 ZPO mindestens eine Woche vorher erfolgen muß.)

26. Eine **vereinfachte Kostenfestsetzung** (nach § 105 ZPO, § 202 SGG) **auf dem Urteil** (evtl. Beschluß) **erster Instanz** (und seinen Ausfertigungen) ist möglich, wenn dieses zur Zwangsvollstreckung geeignet ist (vgl. § 795a ZPO, § 198 SGG). Bei der Anbringung des Gesuchs darf eine Ausfertigung des Urteils noch nicht erteilt sein. Eine Verzögerung der Urteilsausfertigung soll nicht eintreten dürfen. (Hier besteht keine Wartefrist für die Kostenvollstreckung, vgl. § 798 ZPO, § 198 SGG. Die Zustellung beider Entscheidungen seitens des Gläubigers — s. o. 25 — zwecks Vollstreckung erfolgt ohne besondere Vollstreckungsklausel einheitlich.) Dem Erstattungspflichtigen ist vom Urkundsbeamten lediglich der festgesetzte Betrag mitzuteilen, und zwar unter Beifügung der Abschrift der Kostenberechnung. Die Verbindung des Festsetzungsbeschlusses mit dem Urteil hat dann zu unterbleiben, wenn dem Festsetzungsgesuch auch nur teilweise nicht entsprochen wird. Die Anfechtung der beiden Titel erfolgt getrennt in der jeweils gesetzlich gegebenen Weise (s. u. 28

und 1. Kap. 9 a β und b ε). Die Verbindung kann auf das gegebene Kostenrechtsmittel (Gerichtsanrufung s. u. 28) — auch abhelfend — gelöst werden, wenn sie unstatthaft oder auch nur unzweckmäßig war. Das Gesuch kann in Form einer einfachen Kostenberechnung für den Fall der Anordnung der Erstattung bereits vor Verkündung oder Erlaß des Urteils (evtl. Beschlusses) eingereicht werden (§ 105 Abs. 2 ZPO, § 202 SGG). In diesem Falle ist die dem Gegner mitzuteilende Abschrift der Kostenberechnung von Amts wegen — gebührenfrei — anzufertigen (§ 105 Abs. 2 letzter Satz ZPO).

27. Eine **Kostenverteilung,** wie sie der § 106 ZPO als Grundlage für die sogen. Kostenausgleichung durch den Urkundsbeamten voraussetzt, ist im Sozialgerichtsverfahren begrifflich **nicht möglich.** Hier stehen sich ja die Beteiligten im Verfahren selbst nicht als zwei Parteien im Sinne des § 91 ZPO gegenüber. Nur allgemein oder besonders bestimmte Kosten, ganz oder zu einem gewissen (einseitigen) Bruchteile können jeweils einem Beteiligten (evtl. mehreren als Gesamtschuldnern) zur Erstattung auferlegt werden.

28. **Gegen die Kostenfestsetzung des Urkundsbeamten** der Geschäftsstelle **kann** vom einzelnen Beschwerten (auch bei Geamtschuld) mit Wirkung jeweils für sich **das Gericht angerufen werden** (§ 197 Abs. 2 SGG). **Beschwerter** kann (bei Gebührenverkürzung) der antragstellende Gläubiger bzw. sein Rechtsnachfolger oder sein gemäß § 124 ZPO, § 202 SGG beitreibender Armenanwalt oder (bei Zuvielgewährung) der jeweilige erstattungspflichtige Schuldner bzw. sein Nachfolger in der Zahlungspflicht, aber kein anderer, sein. Eine Mindestbeschwer ist nicht erforderlich.

Da die Kostenerstattungspflicht dem Grunde nach aus der Kostengrundentscheidung im Urteil (evtl. Beschluß) folgt, kann, abgesehen von dem Bestreiten des Entstandenseins von Kosten, insbesondere Auslagen als solchen, in der Regel nur die Höhe der Kosten angegriffen werden, es sei denn, daß ausnahmsweise zweifelhaft ist, ob Erstattungspflicht (zu dem in Frage kommenden Teil, unter Umständen auch ganz) besteht oder daß die Aufhebung oder Abänderung des zugrunde gelegten Kostentitels erfolgt ist. Die Anrufung hat keine aufschiebende Wirkung.

Anrufung des Gerichts ist zum Zwecke der sogen. Nachliquidation (Erhöhung des bisher Verlangten) in keinem Fall möglich. Hier muß beim Urkundsbeamten zusätzliche Festsetzung (Nachtragsliquidation) beantragt werden (so KG, DR 1941, 445 gegen KG, JW 1935, 2901, das für den Fall, daß auch eine echte Beschwer im Festsetzungsbeschluß des Urkundsbeamten vorliegt, die Nachliquidation zuläßt, vgl. auch das OLG Neustadt, MDR 1957, 496. Dabei wird aber nicht beachtet, daß das Anrufungsverfahren dazu geschaffen ist, die Tätigkeit des Urkundsbeamten nachzuprüfen und daß bezüglich der nachliquidierten Beträge eine Instanz verlorengeht, auf deren Einhaltung der Schuldner ein Recht hat). Freiwillige Zahlung der Kosten ohne Vorbehalt schließt grundsätzlich die Anrufung aus.

Anrufungsfrist: ein Monat nach Zustellung (§§ 173, 178 SGG). Wegen eventueller Wiedereinsetzung in den vorigen Stand bei schuldloser Versäumnis der Frist vgl. § 67 SGG. (Der Wiedereinsetzungsantrag muß binnen eines Monats nach Wegfall des abhaltenden Hindernisses gestellt werden.)

In Fällen unterbliebener oder unrichtiger Rechtsbehelfsbelehrung verlängert sich die Anrufungsfrist auf ein Jahr (§ 66 Abs. 2 SGG). Im Falle der Nichteinhaltung der Jahresfrist durch höhere Gewalt ist Wiedereinsetzung in den vorigen Stand möglich (§ 66 Abs. 2 letzter Satz, § 67 Abs. 2 SGG).

Die Erweiterung einer begrenzten Anrufung ist nach Ablauf der Anrufungsfrist nicht zulässig.

Eine sog. Anschließung (nach Fristablauf) an den rechtzeitig eingelegten Rechtsbehelf des Gegners (Anschlußanrufung) ist nicht möglich.

Anrufungsform: schriftlich beim Sozialgericht oder zur Niederschrift seines Urkundsbeamten (§§ 173, 178 SGG).

Die Anrufung kann zurückgenommen werden; sie hat im Zweifel den endgültigen Verlust des Rechtsbehelfs zur Folge.

Es besteht **Abhilferecht** (und -pflicht) des — jeweils tätigen — Urkundsbeamten, vgl. § 174 SGG. Gegen die Abhilfeentscheidung des Urkundsbeamten kann nunmehr von dem neu beschwerten Gegner das Gericht angerufen werden.

Wegen Einstellungsmöglichkeit durch das Gericht oder seinen Vorsitzenden vgl. § 175 letzter Satz und § 178 letzter Satz SGG. Die — positive oder negative — Entscheidung über die beantragte vorläufige Einstellung der Zwangsvollstreckung ist nicht anfechtbar, weil sogar die endgültige Entscheidung des Gerichts unanfechtbar ist.

Nachprüfung erfolgt grundsätzlich nur in bezug auf das Angegriffene. Mehr als insgesamt verlangt, kann nicht zugesprochen werden.

Das angerufene **Sozialgericht entscheidet** auf Grund eigenen Ermessens (§ 128 Abs. 1, § 142 Abs. 1 SGG) ohne mündliche Verhandlung (§ 124 Abs. 3 SGG) durch kostenfreien (§ 183 SGG) Beschluß, der formlos bekanntzumachen ist, **endgültig** (vgl. § 197 Abs. 2 SGG). Der Beschluß ist zu begründen (§ 142 Abs. 2 SGG). Nach Möglichkeit soll nicht zurückverwiesen werden. Bei Zurückverweisung ist sachliche Anweisung des Urkundsbeamten zulässig. Der Anrufende darf in keinem Falle schlechtergestellt werden.

Was die **Besetzung** des angerufenen Gerichts anbetrifft, so ergibt sich aus dem Beschluß des Großen Senats des Bundessozialgerichts (BSG 1, 1 [5]), daß die Tätigkeit der ehrenamtlichen Beisitzer (hier der Sozialrichter) mit dem Erlaß der die Verhandlung abschließenden Sachentscheidung (Urteil, Kostenbeschluß) endet. Der einschlägige § 26 SGG spricht in der Tat nur von der Heranziehung der ehrenamtlichen Beisitzer zu den „Verhandlungen". Bei der Entscheidung über Gebührenfragen, die der Sachentscheidung nachfolgen, brauchen danach die ehrenamtlichen Beisitzer nicht mitzuwirken (so auch der Amtliche Bericht, BT-Drucks. Nr. 338 und Hofmann-Schroeter, SGG Nachtrag zur 2. Aufl. Anm. 3 zu § 216, vgl. ferner LSG Nordrhein-Westfalen, SGb 1958, 166; a. A. Brocke, SGb 1958, 271 [274]).

Mangels entgegenstehender Bestimmungen wird es für zulässig anzusehen sein, daß bei der **Geschäftsverteilung** das Präsidium des Gerichts eine **bestimmte Kammer** mit der Entscheidung über Anrufungen nach § 197 Abs. 2 SGG betraut.

Abänderung des ergangenen Beschlusses ist nicht möglich. Wegen Berichtigung offenkundiger Fehler (durch den Vorsitzenden) vgl. die §§ 138, 142 Abs. 1 SGG.

29. Ist in der Anrufungsentscheidung ausgesprochen (vgl. 1. Kap. 9 c), daß ein Beteiligter einem anderen die etwaigen **außergerichtlichen Kosten des Anrufungsverfahrens** zu erstatten hat, so sind diese Kosten **erstattungsfähig.** (Wegen ihrer Höhe vgl. das 7. Kap. I A 1 q.) Vorstehendes hat Bedeutung für alle Anrufungsentscheidungen in Kostensachen (vgl. vor allem § 189 Abs. 2, § 191 SGG).

30. Auf Antrag kann das Gericht bei Vorliegen **überhöht beigetriebener Kostenbeträge** mit der abändernden Festsetzung entsprechend dem § 717 Abs. 2 ZPO gleichzeitig deren **Rückzahlung anordnen** (vgl. Stein-Jonas-Schönke, ZPO 17. Aufl. Anm. V 8 zu § 104). Es wird dadurch in ökonomischer Weise ein neuer Rechtsstreit vermieden, der allerdings zur Bereinigung stattfinden muß, wenn die gezahlten Beträge streitig sind oder eine zusätzliche Schadenssumme verlangt wird. Gleiches

gilt, wenn auf Grund eines abändernden Titels der höheren Instanz Neufestsetzung der Kosten erfolgt (a. A. Jahn, KOV Bln. 1954, 138; vgl. hierzu auch BSG, SozR SGG § 198 Bl. Da 1 Nr. 1, wo bezüglich des auf Grund des abgeänderten Urteils erster Instanz gezahlten Betrages der Hauptsache ausgeführt ist, ein Inzidentantrag entsprechend § 717 Abs. 2 Satz 2 ZPO sei im Prozeß nicht zulässig, vielmehr könne und müsse daselbst Widerklage erhoben werden).

31. Die **Rechtskraft des Festsetzungsbeschlusses** bezieht sich (vgl. § 322 ZPO, § 202 SGG) **nur auf die geforderten Beträge; sie schließt** eine **nachträgliche Festsetzung** (durch den Urkundsbeamten des befaßten Sozialgerichts) im Zweifel sogar hinsichtlich derselben Grundlage **nicht aus,** wenn der zusätzliche Betrag bisher nicht verlangt worden war (sogen. Nachtragsliquidation).

32. **Nichtigkeits-** oder **Restitutionsklage** findet gegen rechtskräftig gewordene Kostenfestsetzungsbeschlüsse **nicht statt;** diese Klagen sind nur gegenüber Urteilen gegeben (vgl. §§ 179, 202 SGG, § 578 Abs. 1 ZPO).

33. Die **Einrede der nicht erstatteten Prozeßkosten** des Vorprozesses (vgl. § 274 Abs. 2 Nr. 6 ZPO) ist im amtsbetriebenen Verfahren der Sozialgerichtsbarkeit **nicht erhebbar** (ebenso Brocke-Reese, Geb. u. KostR Anm. zu § 117 ZPO).

34. **Der rechtskräftig festgelegte Kostenanspruch verjährt in 30 Jahren,** beginnend mit dem Zeitpunkt der Rechtskraft der Zuerkennung (vgl. § 193 SGG) des Kostenanspruchs (§ 218 Abs. 1, § 198 BGB). Soweit es sich entsprechend dem jetzigen § 104 Abs. 1 Satz 2 ZPO um Zinsen der Kosten handelt, die erst in Zukunft fällig werden, tritt die Verjährung in vier Jahren ein (§ 218 Abs. 2, § 197 BGB). Diese (kurze) Verjährung beginnt mit dem Schlusse des Jahres, in welchem die jeweilige Zinsforderung fällig wird (§ 201 in Verb. mit § 198 BGB). Auf etwa eingetretene Verjährung der Ansprüche des Anwalts gegenüber der eigenen Partei oder der Staatskasse (hier Verjährung in zwei Jahren) kann sich der erstattungspflichtige Gegner nicht berufen.

Kostenrückzahlungsansprüche des Gegners (auf Grund aufgehobener oder abgeänderterKostenfestsetzung) verjähren nach §§ 195, 812 BGB ebenfalls in 30 Jahren, beginnend mit dem Zeitpunkt der Herausstellung der Zuvielzahlung (vgl. dazu Tschischgale, AnwBl. 1958, 181 [184]).

Soweit die 30jährige Verjährung in Frage kommt, kann eine sachlich-rechtliche **Verwirkung** des Kostenanspruchs eintreten (vgl. Gerold, BRAGebO Anm. 28 zu § 16, auch OLG Dresden, JW 1938, 3161, ferner Göttlich, BRAGebO 7. Aufl. S. 1047). Voraussetzung hierfür ist nicht nur der Ablauf einer sich aus den Umständen des Falles ergebenden angemessenen Frist (für die Geltendmachung bzw. Realisierung), sondern auf seiten des Kostengläubigers ein Verhalten, aus dem berechtigte Schlüsse auf eine Nichtmehrgeltendmachung gezogen werden können und auf der Seite des Erstattungspflichtigen ein entsprechendes Einrichten auf die Nichtmehrgeltendmachung des Kostenanspruchs. Nach Verwirkung kann wie nach Verjährung dem Kostenanspruch mit der Vollstreckungsgegenklage entgegengetreten werden.

Siebentes Kapitel

Die Anwaltskosten und ihre Festsetzung

BRAGebO: §§ 1, 2, 3, 4, 5, 6, 12, 13, 14, 15, 16, 17, 18, 19, 20, 21, 22, 23, 24, 25, 26, 27, 28, 29, 30, 32, 37, 114, 116
GKG: § 91 Abs. 3 bis 6
Gesetz über Reisekostenvergütung der Beamten (RKG) vom 15. 12. 1933 (RGBl. I 1067) i. d. F. der VO vom 20. 12. 1956 (BGBl. I 1079): §§ 5, 9 Abs. 2 und 3
Gesetz zur Änderung und Ergänzung kostenrechtlicher Vorschriften (KostÄndG) vom 26. 7. 1957 (BGBl. I 861): Art. IX § 1 Abs. 1 und 3, § 2

§ 1 BRAGebO

Geltungsbereich

(1) Die Vergütung (Gebühren und Auslagen) des Rechtsanwalts für seine Berufstätigkeit bemißt sich nach diesem Gesetz.

(2) Dieses Gesetz gilt nicht, wenn der Rechtsanwalt als Vormund, Pfleger, Testamentsvollstrecker, Konkursverwalter, Vergleichsverwalter, Mitglied des Gläubigerausschusses oder Gläubigerbeirats, Nachlaßverwalter, Zwangsverwalter, Treuhänder, Schiedsrichter oder in ähnlicher Stellung tätig wird. § 1835 des Bürgerlichen Gesetzbuchs bleibt unberührt.

§ 2 BRAGebO

Sinngemäße Anwendung des Gesetzes

Ist in diesem Gesetz über die Gebühren für eine Berufstätigkeit des Rechtsanwalts nichts bestimmt, so sind die Gebühren in sinngemäßer Anwendung der Vorschriften dieses Gesetzes zu bemessen.

§ 3 BRAGebO

Vereinbarung der Vergütung

(1) Aus einer Vereinbarung kann der Rechtsanwalt eine höhere als die gesetzliche Vergütung nur fordern, wenn die Erklärung des Auftraggebers schriftlich abgegeben und nicht in der Vollmacht oder in einem Vordruck, der auch andere Erklärungen umfaßt, enthalten ist. Hat der Auftraggeber freiwillig und ohne Vorbehalt geleistet, so kann er das Geleistete nicht deshalb zurückfordern, weil seine Erklärung der Vorschrift des Satzes 1 nicht entspricht.

(2) Die Festsetzung der Vergütung kann dem billigen Ermessen des Vorstandes der Rechtsanwaltskammer überlassen werden. Ist die Festsetzung der Vergütung dem Ermessen eines Vertragsteils überlassen, so gilt die gesetzliche Vergütung als vereinbart.

(3) Ist eine vereinbarte oder von dem Vorstand der Rechtsanwaltskammer festgesetzte Vergütung unter Berücksichtigung aller Umstände unangemessen hoch, so kann sie im Rechtsstreit auf den angemessenen Betrag bis zur Höhe der gesetzlichen Vergütung herabgesetzt werden.

Vor der Herabsetzung hat das Gericht ein Gutachten des Vorstandes der Rechtsanwaltskammer einzuholen; dies gilt nicht, wenn der Vorstand der Rechtsanwaltskammer die Vergütung nach Absatz 2 Satz 1 festgesetzt hat.

(4) Durch eine Vereinbarung, nach der ein im Armenrecht beigeordneter Rechtsanwalt eine Vergütung erhalten soll, wird eine Verbindlichkeit nicht begründet. Hat der Auftraggeber freiwillig und ohne Vorbehalt geleistet, so kann er das Geleistete nicht deshalb zurückfordern, weil eine Verbindlichkeit nicht bestanden hat.

§ 4 BRAGebO

Vergütung für Tätigkeiten von Vertretern des Rechtsanwalts

Die Vergütung für eine Tätigkeit, die der Rechtsanwalt nicht persönlich vornimmt, wird nach diesem Gesetz bemessen, wenn der Rechtsanwalt durch einen Rechtsanwalt, den allgemeinen Vertreter oder einen zur Ableistung des Anwärterdienstes überwiesenen Anwaltsassessor oder zur Ausbildung zugewiesenen Referendar vertreten wird.

§ 5 BRAGebO

Mehrere Rechtsanwälte

Ist der Auftrag mehreren Rechtsanwälten zur gemeinschaftlichen Erledigung übertragen, so erhält jeder Rechtsanwalt für seine Tätigkeit die volle Vergütung.

§ 6 BRAGebO

Mehrere Auftraggeber

(1) Wird der Rechtsanwalt in derselben Angelegenheit für mehrere Auftraggeber tätig, so erhält er die Gebühren nur einmal. Bei Gebühren, die nur dem Mindest- und Höchstbetrag nach bestimmt sind, erhöht sich der Mindest- und Höchstbetrag um die Hälfte. Ist der Gegenstand der anwaltlichen Tätigkeit derselbe, so erhöht sich, wenn die Aufträge nicht gleichzeitig erteilt sind, die Prozeßgebühr (§ 31 Nr. 1) durch jeden Beitritt um zwei Zehntel; die Erhöhung wird nach dem Betrag berechnet, an dem die Auftraggeber gemeinschaftlich beteiligt sind; mehrere Erhöhungen dürfen den Betrag einer vollen Gebühr nicht übersteigen.

(2) Jeder der Auftraggeber schuldet dem Rechtsanwalt die Gebühren und Auslagen, die er schulden würde, wenn der Rechtsanwalt nur in seinem Auftrag tätig geworden wäre. Der Rechtsanwalt kann aber insgesamt nicht mehr als die nach Absatz 1 berechneten Gebühren fordern; die Auslagen kann er nur einmal fordern.

§ 12 BRAGebO

Rahmengebühren

(1) Bei Rahmengebühren ist die Gebühr im Einzelfall unter Berücksichtigung aller Umstände, insbesondere der Bedeutung der Angelegen-

heit, des Umfangs und der Schwierigkeit der anwaltlichen Tätigkeit sowie der Vermögens- und Einkommensverhältnisse des Auftraggebers nach billigem Ermessen zu bestimmen.

(2) Im Rechtsstreit hat das Gericht ein Gutachten des Vorstandes der Rechtsanwaltskammer einzuholen.

§ 13 BRAGebO

Abgeltungsbereich der Gebühren

(1) Die Gebühren entgelten, soweit dieses Gesetz nichts anderes bestimmt, die gesamte Tätigkeit des Rechtsanwalts vom Auftrag bis zur Erledigung der Angelegenheit.

(2) Der Rechtsanwalt kann die Gebühren in derselben Angelegenheit nur einmal fordern. In gerichtlichen Verfahren kann er die Gebühren in jedem Rechtszug fordern.

(3) Sind für Teile des Gegenstands verschiedene Gebührensätze anzuwenden, so erhält der Rechtsanwalt für die Teile gesondert berechnete Gebühren, jedoch nicht mehr als die aus dem Gesamtbetrag der Wertteile nach dem höchsten Gebührensatz berechnete Gebühr.

(4) Auf bereits entstandene Gebühren ist es, soweit dieses Gesetz nichts anderes bestimmt, ohne Einfluß, wenn sich die Angelegenheit vorzeitig erledigt oder der Auftrag endigt, bevor die Angelegenheit erledigt ist.

(5) Wird der Rechtsanwalt, nachdem er in einer Angelegenheit tätig geworden ist, beauftragt, in derselben Angelegenheit weiter tätig zu werden, so erhält er nicht mehr an Gebühren, als er erhalten würde, wenn er von vornherein hiermit beauftragt worden wäre.

(6) Ist der Rechtsanwalt nur mit einzelnen Handlungen beauftragt, so erhält er nicht mehr an Gebühren, als der mit der gesamten Angelegenheit beauftragte Rechtsanwalt für die gleiche Tätigkeit erhalten würde.

§ 14 BRAGebO

Verweisung, Abgabe

Wird eine Sache an ein anderes Gericht verwiesen oder abgegeben, so sind die Verfahren vor dem verweisenden oder abgebenden und vor dem übernehmenden Gericht ein Rechtszug. Wird eine Sache an ein Gericht eines niedrigeren Rechtszugs verwiesen oder abgegeben, so ist das weitere Verfahren vor diesem Gericht ein neuer Rechtszug.

§ 15 BRAGebO

Zurückverweisung

Wird eine Sache an ein untergeordnetes Gericht zurückverwiesen, so ist das weitere Verfahren vor diesem Gericht ein neuer Rechtszug. Die Prozeßgebühr erhält der Rechtsanwalt jedoch nur, wenn die Sache an ein Gericht zurückverwiesen ist, das mit der Sache noch nicht befaßt war.

§ 16 BRAGebO

Fälligkeit

Die Vergütung des Rechtsanwalts wird fällig, wenn der Auftrag erledigt oder die Angelegenheit beendigt ist. Ist der Rechtsanwalt in einem gerichtlichen Verfahren tätig, so wird die Vergütung auch fällig, wenn eine Kostenentscheidung ergangen oder der Rechtszug beendigt ist oder wenn das Verfahren länger als drei Monate ruht.

§ 17 BRAGebO

Vorschuß

Der Rechtsanwalt kann von seinem Auftraggeber für die entstandenen und die voraussichtlich entstehenden Gebühren und Auslagen einen angemessenen Vorschuß fordern.

§ 18 BRAGebO

Berechnung

(1) Der Rechtsanwalt kann die Vergütung nur auf Grund einer von ihm unterzeichneten und dem Auftraggeber mitgeteilten Berechnung einfordern. Der Lauf der Verjährungsfrist ist von der Mitteilung der Berechnung nicht abhängig.

(2) In der Berechnung sind die Beträge der einzelnen Gebühren und Auslagen, Vorschüsse sowie die angewandten Gebührenvorschriften und bei Gebühren, die nach dem Gegenstandswert berechnet sind, auch dieser anzugeben. Bei Post-, Telegrafen-, Fernsprech- und Fernschreibkosten genügt die Angabe des Gesamtbetrags.

(3) Hat der Auftraggeber die Vergütung gezahlt, ohne die Berechnung erhalten zu haben, so kann er die Mitteilung der Berechnung noch fordern, solange der Rechtsanwalt zur Aufbewahrung der Handakten verpflichtet ist.

§ 19 BRAGebO

Festsetzung der Vergütung

(1) Die gesetzliche Vergütung, die dem Rechtsanwalt als Prozeßbevollmächtigten, Beistand, Unterbevollmächtigten oder Verkehrsanwalt (§ 52) zusteht, wird auf Antrag des Rechtsanwalts oder des Auftraggebers durch den Urkundsbeamten der Geschäftsstelle festgesetzt. Getilgte Beträge sind abzusetzen.

(2) Der Antrag ist erst zulässig, wenn die Vergütung fällig ist. Zuständig ist der Urkundsbeamte des Gerichts des ersten Rechtszugs. Vor der Festsetzung sind die Beteiligten zu hören. Die Vorschriften der Zivilprozeßordnung über das Kostenfestsetzungsverfahren und die Zwangsvollstreckung aus Kostenfestsetzungsbeschlüssen gelten sinn-

gemäß. Das Verfahren ist gebührenfrei. Der Rechtsanwalt erhält in dem Verfahren vor dem Urkundsbeamten keine Gebühr.

(3) Wird der vom Rechtsanwalt angegebene Gegenstandswert von einem Beteiligten bestritten, so ist das Verfahren auszusetzen bis das Gericht (§§ 9, 10) hierüber entschieden hat.

(4) Die Festsetzung ist abzulehnen, soweit der Antragsgegner Einwendungen oder Einreden erhebt, die nicht im Gebührenrecht ihren Grund haben. Hat der Auftraggeber bereits dem Rechtsanwalt gegenüber derartige Einwendungen oder Einreden erhoben, so ist die Erhebung der Klage nicht von der vorherigen Einleitung des Festsetzungsverfahrens abhängig.

(5) Anträge, Erklärungen und Beschwerden können zu Protokoll der Geschäftsstelle gegeben oder schriftlich ohne Mitwirkung eines Rechtsanwalts eingereicht werden.

(6) Durch den Antrag auf Festsetzung der Vergütung wird die Verjährung wie durch Klageerhebung unterbrochen.

(7) Die Absätze 1 bis 6 gelten nicht bei Rahmengebühren.

§ 20 BRAGebO

Rat, Auskunft

(1) Für einen mündlichen oder schriftlichen Rat oder eine Auskunft, die nicht mit einer anderen gebührenpflichtigen Tätigkeit zusammenhängen, erhält der Rechtsanwalt eine Gebühr in Höhe von einem Zehntel bis fünf Zehnteln der vollen Gebühr. Bezieht sich der Rat oder die Auskunft nur auf strafrechtliche, verwaltungsstrafrechtliche, bußrechtliche oder sonstige Angelegenheiten, in denen die Gebühren nicht nach dem Gegenstandswert berechnet werden, so beträgt die Gebühr 3 bis 150 Deutsche Mark. Die Gebühr ist auf eine Gebühr anzurechnen, die der Rechtsanwalt für eine sonstige Tätigkeit erhält, die mit der Raterteilung oder Auskunft zusammenhängt.

(2) Wird ein Rechtsanwalt, der mit der Angelegenheit noch nicht befaßt gewesen ist, beauftragt, zu prüfen, ob eine Berufung oder Revision Aussicht auf Erfolg hat, so erhält er eine halbe Gebühr nach § 11 Abs. 1 Satz 2, wenn er von der Einlegung eines Rechtsmittels abrät und ein Rechtsmittel durch ihn nicht eingelegt wird. Dies gilt nicht in den im Absatz 1 Satz 2 genannten Angelegenheiten.

§ 21 BRAGebO

Gutachten

Für die Ausarbeitung eines schriftlichen Gutachtens mit juristischer Begründung erhält der Rechtsanwalt eine angemessene Gebühr. § 12 gilt sinngemäß.

§ 22 BRAGebO

Hebegebühr

(1) Werden an den Rechtsanwalt Zahlungen geleistet, so erhält er für die Auszahlung oder Rückzahlung bei Beträgen

bis zu 1000 Deutsche Mark einschließlich . . . . 1 vom Hundert,
von dem Mehrbetrag bis zu 10000 Deutsche Mark einschließlich . . . . 0,6 vom Hundert,
von dem Mehrbetrag über 10000 Deutsche Mark . 0,3 vom Hundert.

Unbare Zahlungen stehen baren Zahlungen gleich. Der Rechtsanwalt kann die Gebühr bei der Ablieferung an den Auftraggeber entnehmen.

(2) Ist das Geld in mehreren Beträgen gesondert ausgezahlt oder zurückgezahlt, so wird die Gebühr von jedem Betrag besonders erhoben.

(3) Die Mindestgebühr beträgt eine Deutsche Mark.

(4) Für die Ablieferung oder Rücklieferung von Wertpapieren und Kostbarkeiten erhält der Rechtsanwalt die in den Absätzen 1 bis 3 bestimmte Gebühr nach dem Wert.

(5) Der Rechtsanwalt erhält die in den Absätzen 1 bis 3 bestimmten Gebühren nicht, soweit er Kosten an ein Gericht oder eine Behörde weiterleitet oder eingezogene Kosten an den Auftraggeber abführt oder eingezogene Beträge auf seine Vergütung verrechnet.

§ 23 BRAGebO

Vergleichsgebühr

(1) Für die Mitwirkung beim Abschluß eines Vergleichs (§ 779 des Bürgerlichen Gesetzbuchs) erhält der Rechtsanwalt eine volle Gebühr (Vergleichsgebühr). Der Rechtsanwalt erhält die Vergleichsgebühr auch dann, wenn er nur bei den Vergleichsverhandlungen mitgewirkt hat, es sei denn, daß seine Mitwirkung für den Abschluß des Vergleichs nicht ursächlich war.

(2) Für die Mitwirkung bei einem unter einer aufschiebenden Bedingung oder unter dem Vorbehalt des Widerrufs geschlossenen Vergleich erhält der Rechtsanwalt die Vergleichsgebühr, wenn die Bedingung eingetreten ist oder der Vergleich nicht mehr widerrufen werden kann.

(3) Soweit über die Ansprüche vertraglich verfügt werden kann, gelten die Absätze 2 und 3 auch bei Rechtsverhältnissen des öffentlichen Rechts.

§ 24 BRAGebO

Erledigungsgebühr

Erledigt sich ein Rechtsstreit ganz oder teilweise durch Zurücknahme oder Änderung des angefochtenen Verwaltungsaktes, so erhält der Rechtsanwalt, der bei der Erledigung mitgewirkt hat, eine volle Gebühr.

§ 25 BRAGebO

Ersatz von Auslagen

(1) Mit den Gebühren werden auch die allgemeinen Geschäftsunkosten entgolten.

(2) Der Anspruch auf Ersatz der Postgebühren, der Schreibgebühren und der Reisekosten bestimmt sich nach den folgenden Vorschriften.

§ 26 BRAGebO

Postgebühren

Der Rechtsanwalt hat Anspruch auf Ersatz der bei der Ausführung des Auftrags entstandenen Post-, Telegrafen-, Fernsprech- und Fernschreibgebühren.

§ 27 BRAGebO

Schreibgebühren

(1) Schreibgebühren stehen dem Rechtsanwalt nur für die im Einverständnis mit dem Auftraggeber zusätzlich gefertigten Abschriften und Ablichtungen zu.

(2) Die Höhe der Schreibgebühren bemißt sich nach dem für die gerichtlichen Schreibgebühren im Gerichtskostengesetz bestimmten Betrag.

§ 28 BRAGebO

Geschäftsreisen

(1) Bei Geschäftsreisen erhält der Rechtsanwalt Reisekostenvergütung und Auslagenersatz nach den für Bundesbeamte der Reisekostenstufe II geltenden Vorschriften. Ist es nach den Umständen, insbesondere nach dem Zweck der Geschäftsreise, erforderlich, ein anderes als ein öffentliches, regelmäßig verkehrendes Beförderungsmittel zu benutzen, so erhält der Rechtsanwalt Ersatz der notwendigen Aufwendungen, bei Benutzung eines eigenen Kraftwagens 25 Deutsche Pfennig für jedes angefangene Kilometer des Hin- und Rückswegs.

(2) Wenn der Rechtsanwalt oder sein allgemeiner Vertreter reist, erhält der Rechtsanwalt ein Abwesenheitsgeld von 15 Deutsche Mark für jeden Werktag. Bei Geschäftsreisen von nicht mehr als vier Stunden beträgt das Abwesenheitsgeld 7,50 Deutsche Mark.

§ 29 BRAGebO

Reisen zur Ausführung mehrerer Geschäfte

Dient eine Reise mehreren Geschäften, so sind die entstandenen Reisekosten und Abwesenheitsgelder nach dem Verhältnis der Kosten zu verteilen, die bei gesonderter Ausführung der einzelnen Geschäfte entstanden wären.

§ 30 BRAGebO

Verlegung der Kanzlei

Ein Rechtsanwalt, der seine Kanzlei nach einem anderen Ort verlegt, kann bei Fortführung eines ihm vorher erteilten Auftrags Reisekosten und Abwesenheitsgelder nur insoweit verlangen, als sie auch von seiner bisherigen Kanzlei aus entstanden wären.

§ 32 BRAGebO

Vorzeitige Beendigung des Auftrags

(1) Endigt der Auftrag, bevor der Rechtsanwalt die Klage, den ein Verfahren einleitenden Antrag oder einen Schriftsatz, der Sachanträge, die Zurücknahme der Klage oder die Zurücknahme des Antrags enthält, eingereicht oder bevor er seine Partei in einem zur mündlichen Verhandlung bestimmten Termin vertreten hat, so erhält er nur eine halbe Prozeßgebühr.

(2) Das gleiche gilt, soweit lediglich beantragt ist, eine Einigung der Parteien zu Protokoll zu nehmen.

§ 37 BRAGebO

Rechtszug

Zum Rechtszug gehören insbesondere

1. die Vorbereitung der Klage, des Antrags oder der Rechtsverteidigung, soweit kein besonders gerichtliches oder behördliches Verfahren stattfindet;
2. außergerichtliche Vergleichsverhandlungen;
3. Zwischenstreite, die Bestimmung des zuständigen Gerichts, die Sicherung des Beweises, wenn die Hauptsache anhängig ist, die Bewilligung oder Entziehung des Armenrechts und die Verpflichtung zur Nachzahlung der Kosten (§ 126 der Zivilprozeßordnung), die vorläufige Einstellung, Beschränkung oder Aufhebung der Zwangsvollstreckung, wenn nicht eine abgesonderte mündliche Verhandlung hierüber stattfindet, Verfahren wegen der Rückgabe einer Sicherheit (§ 109 Abs. 1 und 2, § 715 der Zivilprozeßordnung), die Bestellung von Vertretern durch das Prozeßgericht oder das Vollstreckungsgericht, die Ablehnung von Richtern, Rechtspflegern, Urkundsbeamten der Geschäftsstelle oder Sachverständigen, die Verpflichtung zur Tragung von Kosten (§ 102 der Zivilprozeßordnung), die Zulassung einer Zustellung zur Nachtzeit, an einem Sonntag oder an einem allgemeinen Feiertag (§ 188 der Zivilprozeßordnung), die Festsetzung des Streitwerts;
4. das Verfahren vor dem beauftragten oder ersuchten Richter und die Änderung seiner Entscheidungen;
5. die Änderung von Entscheidungen der Urkundsbeamten der Geschäftsstelle oder des Rechtspflegers;

6. die Berichtigung oder Ergänzung der Entscheidung oder ihres Tatbestandes;
7. die Zustellung oder Empfangnahme von Entscheidungen oder Rechtsmittelschriften und ihre Mitteilung an den Auftraggeber, die Einwilligung zur Sprungrevision (§ 566a Abs. 2 der Zivilprozeßordnung), der Ausspruch über die Verpflichtung, die Kosten zu tragen oder eines Rechtsmittels verlustig zu sein (§§ 91a, 271 Abs. 3 Satz 2, § 515 Abs. 3 Satz 1, § 566 der Zivilprozeßordnung), die Vollstreckbarerklärung eines Urteils (§§ 534, 560 der Zivilprozeßordnung), die Erteilung des Notfristzeugnisses, Rechtskraftzeugnisses, die erstmalige Erteilung der Vollstreckungsklausel, wenn deswegen keine Klage nach § 731 der Zivilprozeßordnung erhoben wird, die Kostenfestsetzung (§§ 104, 107 der Zivilprozeßordnung) ausschließlich der Erinnerung gegen den Kostenfestsetzungsbeschluß, die Einforderung der Vergütung (§§ 18, 19), die Herausgabe der Handakten oder ihre Übersendung an einen anderen Rechtsanwalt.

§ 114 BRAGebO

Verfahren vor Verwaltungs-, Sozial- und Finanzgerichten

(1) Im Verfahren vor Gerichten der Verwaltungs-, Sozial- und Finanzgerichtsbarkeit gelten die Vorschriften des Dritten Abschnitts sinngemäß.

(2) Der Rechtsanwalt erhält im erstinstanzlichen Verfahren vor dem Bundesverwaltungsgericht, dem Bundesfinanzhof und vor einem Oberverwaltungsgericht (Verwaltungsgerichtshof) Gebühren nach § 11 Abs. 1 Satz 2, im Verfahren vor dem Finanzgericht Gebühren nach § 11 Abs. 1 Satz 1.

(3) Der Rechtsanwalt erhält die gleichen Gebühren wie in einem Verfahren mit mündlicher Verhandlung, wenn eine ohne mündliche Verhandlung erlassene Vorentscheidung als Urteil gilt oder wenn das Gericht ohne mündliche Verhandlung entscheidet, weil die Beteiligten dieser Absicht nicht fristgerecht widersprochen haben. Dies gilt nicht, wenn die Klage oder das Rechtsmittel als unzuverlässig oder als offenbar unbegründet zurückgewiesen wird.

(4) Im Verfahren auf Erlaß einer einstweiligen Anordnung gilt § 40, bei Vollziehung einer einstweiligen Anordnung § 59 sinngemäß.

(5) Im Verfahren auf Aussetzung oder Aufhebung der Vollziehung oder auf Wiederherstellung der aufschiebenden Wirkung erhält der Rechtsanwalt die in § 49 Abs. 1 bestimmten Gebühren auch dann, wenn die mündliche Verhandlung hierüber nicht abgesondert stattfindet.

(6) Im gerichtlichen Verfahren über einen Akt der Zwangsvollstreckung (des Verwaltungszwangs) erhält der Rechtsanwalt drei Zehntel der in § 31 bestimmten Gebühren. Die Vorschriften des § 32 und des § 33 Abs. 1 und 2 gelten nicht.

§ 116 BRAGebO

Besonderheiten für Verfahren vor Gerichten der Sozialgerichtsbarkeit

(1) Im Verfahren vor Gerichten der Sozialgerichtsbarkeit werden die Gebühren nicht nach dem Gegenstandswert berechnet.

(2) Der Rechtsanwalt erhält im Verfahren

1. vor dem Sozialgericht
   40 Deutsche Mark bis 120 Deutsche Mark,
2. vor dem Landessozialgericht
   60 Deutsche Mark bis 180 Deutsche Mark,
3. vor dem Bundessozialgericht
   100 Deutsche Mark bis 300 Deutsche Mark.

§ 91 Abs. 3 bis 6 GKG

Höhe der Schreibgebühren

(3) Die Schreibgebühr beträgt für die Seite, die 28 Zeilen von durchschnittlich 15 Silben enthält, 50 Deutsche Pfennig, auch wenn die Herstellung auf mechanischem Wege (ausgenommen durch Ablichtung) stattgefunden hat. Jede angefangene Seite wird als voll gerechnet.

(4) Für Schriftstücke, die in fremder Sprache abgefaßt sind, wird die doppelte Schreibgebühr erhoben.

(5) Für Schriftstücke in tabellarischer Form, Grundbuchblätter, Registerblätter, Verzeichnisse, Listen, Rechnungen, Zeichnungen und dgl. wird die Schreibgebühr nach dem Zeitaufwand berechnet, der bei durchschnittlicher Arbeitsleistung zur Herstellung benötigt wird. Sie beträgt für jede angefangene Viertelstunde 60 Deutsche Pfennig.

(6) Werden Abschriften durch Ablichtung hergestellt, so werden für jede Seite ohne Rücksicht auf Zeilen- und Silbenzahl 50 Deutsche Pfennig, bei größerem Format als DIN B 4 eine Deutsche Mark erhoben.

§ 5 RKG

Reisekostenvergütung

Die Reisekostenvergütung besteht aus Fahrkostenentschädigung einschließlich Entschädigung für Fußwegstrecken, Tagegeld, Übernachtungsgeld und Nebenkostenersatz.

§ 9 Abs. 2 und 3 RKG

Tage- und Übernachtungsgeld

(2) Es beträgt

a) das Tagegeld für jeden vollen Kalendertag in

Stufe Ia	20,00 DM
Stufe Ib	17,00 DM
Stufe II	14,00 DM
Stufe III	11,00 DM
Stufe IV	9,50 DM
Stufe V	8,00 DM

b) das Übernachtungsgeld in

Stufe Ia	15,00 DM
Stufe Ib	14,00 DM
Stufe II	11,00 DM
Stufe III	10,00 DM
Stufe IV	7,50 DM
Stufe V	7,00 DM

(3) Beansprucht eine Dienstreise keinen vollen Kalendertag, so beträgt das Tagegeld bei einer Abwesenheit von

mehr als 6 bis 8 Stunden 0,3 des vollen Satzes,
mehr als 8 bis 12 Stunden 0,5 des vollen Satzes,
mehr als 12 Stunden den vollen Satz.

Werden an einem Tage mehrere Dienstreisen ausgeführt, so wird jede Reise für sich berechnet.

§ 1 Abs. 1 und 3 Art. IX KostÄndG

Gebühren und Auslagen von Rechtsbeiständen

(1) Für die Erstattung der Gebühren und Auslagen des Rechtsbeistandes der obsiegenden Partei gilt § 91 Abs. 2 der Zivilprozeßordnung sinngemäß. Dabei bemessen sich die Gebühren und Auslagen nach der Bundesgebührenordnung für Rechtsanwälte, soweit nicht in den Absätzen 2 und 3 etwas anderes bestimmt ist.

(3) Bei Geschäftsreisen tritt an die Stelle der Reisekostenstufe II (§ 28 Abs. 1 der Bundesgebührenordnung für Rechtsanwälte) die Reisekostenstufe III. Das Abwesenheitsgeld beträgt 10 Deutsche Mark und bei Geschäftsreisen von nicht mehr als vier Stunden 5 Deutsche Mark.

§ 2 Art. IX KostÄndG

Gebühren im Verfahren vor Gerichten der Sozialgerichtsbarkeit

(1) Die im Verfahren vor Gerichten der Sozialgerichtsbarkeit zu erstattenden Gebühren und Auslagen eines Rechtsbeistandes bemessen sich nach der Bundesgebührenordnung für Rechtsanwälte; jedoch beläuft sich die Gebühr auf die Hälfte der in § 116 der Bundesgebührenordnung für Rechtsanwälte bestimmten Beträge.

(2) Höhere Gebühren dürfen weder vereinbart noch gezahlt werden.

Übersicht

Spezialabhandlungen des Verfassers: Die Gebührenfestsetzung nach § 196 Abs. 4 SGG, SGb 1957, 6 und Der Übergang zum neuen Kostenrecht im Verfahren der Sozialgerichtsbarkeit, SGb 1958, 107.

I. Materielle Bestimmungen

Vorbemerkung: **Anwaltszwang** herrscht lediglich **vor dem Bundessozialgericht,** und zwar auch nur, soweit es sich nicht um Behörden oder Körperschaften des öffentlichen Rechts oder öffentlich-rechtliche Anstalten handelt (§ 166 Abs. 1 und Abs. 2 Satz 2 SGG). Als Prozeßbevollmächtigte vor dem Bundessozialgericht sind aber auch die Mitglieder und Angestellten von Gewerkschaften, von selbständigen Vereinigungen von Arbeitnehmern mit sozial- oder berufspolitischer Zwecksetzung, von Vereinigungen von Arbeitgebern und von Vereinigungen der Kriegsopfer zugelassen, sofern sie kraft Satzung oder Vollmacht zur Prozeßvertretung befugt sind (§ 166 Abs. 2 Satz 1 SGG). Auftreten kann, was Rechtsanwälte anbetrifft, jeder bei einem deutschen Gericht zugelassene Anwalt (§ 166 Abs. 2 Satz 2 SGG).

A. Gebühren

1. a) Der § 196 SGG regelte die Beziehung zwischen dem Anwalt (Rechtsbeistand) und seinem Auftraggeber (vgl. hierzu Brocke, SGb 1956, 279f.). Er stellte in seinem Absatz 1 die gebührenmäßige Vergütung für die entsprechend dem erteilten Auftrage (§ 675 BGB) geleistete Berufstätigkeit des Anwalts fest. Der § 196 SGG ist durch Artikel X § 11 Nr. 6 des Gesetzes zur Änderung und Ergänzung kostenrechtlicher Vorschriften (KostÄndG) vom 26. 7. 1957 (BGBl. I 861 [933]) außer Kraft gesetzt worden. An seine Stelle ist der § 116 BRAGebO getreten. Auch nach dieser Bestimmung werden im Verfahren vor den Gerichten der Sozialgerichtsbarkeit die Gebühren nicht nach dem Gegenstandswert berechnet (§ 116 Abs. 1 BRAGebO). Vielmehr **erhält der Rechtsanwalt** — wie früher — **im einzelnen Verfahren je Rechtszug eine einzige Gebühr,** die, abgestuft nach der Gerichtsinstanz, rahmenmäßig bestimmt ist (§ 116 Abs. 2 BRAGebO).

b) Wird der Rechtsanwalt als **Vormund, Pfleger** oder in ähnlicher Stellung tätig, so erhält er **keine Gebühr,** jedoch gilt hier gegebenenfalls § 1835 (§ 1915) BGB, nach welchem der Vormund (Pfleger) Ersatz seiner Aufwendungen (unter Vorschußleistung) verlangen kann, die auch in **beruflichen Dienstleistungen** bestehen können (**zu entschädigen entsprechend den Sätzen der Bundesrechtsanwaltsgebührenordnung,** vgl. § 1 Abs. 2). Nach der zweifellos zu weit gehenden Entscheidung des LSG Bayern, Bay.ArbBl. 1956 B S. 25 Nr. 239, ist diese Entschädigung im Sozialgerichtsverfahren festsetzbar. Richtigerweise ist sie nötigenfalls (vor den ordentlichen Gerichten) einzuklagen.

c) Die Gebühr entgilt die **gesamte Tätigkeit** des Rechtsanwalts vom Auftrag bis zur Erledigung der Angelegenheit (§ 13 Abs. 1 BRAGebO).

Der Rechtsanwalt kann die Gebühr in derselben Angelegenheit (Sache) nur **einmal fordern** (§ 13 Abs. 2 BRAGebO).

Auf die grundlagenmäßig verdiente Gebühr als solche ist es **ohne Einfluß, wenn** sich während des Verfahrens die **Angelegenheit vorzeitig erledigt** oder der Auftrag endigt, bevor die Angelegenheit ihre Erledigung gefunden hat (vgl. § 13 Abs. 4 BRAGebO). Ihre jeweilige Mindestgrenze kann daher im Fall der Prozeßerledigung vor Gericht oder der Auftragskündigung im Lauf des Verfahrens nie unterschritten werden, wenn die vorerwähnten Tatsachen auch auf die Höhe der Gebühr einwirken. **Erledigt sich** aber **der Auftrag** zur Durchführung des Verfahrens vor dem Sozialgericht, **bevor** der Rechtsanwalt die **Klage,** das **Rechtsmittel** oder einen Schriftsatz mit Sachanträgen **eingereicht** hat, so **ermäßigt sich die** zu zahlende **Gebühr** gemäß § 114 Abs. 1, § 32 Abs. 1 BRAGebO **auf die Hälfte,** und zwar im Zweifel der Mindestgebühr (vgl. Swolana, BRAGebO Anm. 2 zu § 116).

Wegen der Folgen schuldhaft veranlaßter Auftragsbeendigung durch den Anwalt vgl. unten f.

Wird der **Rechtsanwalt,** nachdem er in einer Angelegenheit tätig geworden ist, **beauftragt,** in derselben Angelegenheit **weiter tätig zu werden,** so **erhält er nicht mehr an Gebühren, als** er erhalten würde, **wenn er von vornherein** hiermit **beauftragt worden wäre** (§ 13 Abs. 5 BRAGebO).

d) Ist der **Rechtsanwalt** nur **mit einzelnen Handlungen beauftragt,** so **erhält er nicht mehr** an Gebühren **als der mit der gesamten Angelegenheit beauftragte** Rechtsanwalt für die gleiche Tätigkeit erhalten würde (§ 13 Abs. 6 BRAGebO).

e) Ist der **Auftrag mehreren Rechtsanwälten** (die keine Anwaltsgemeinschaft bilden) zur gemeinschaftlichen Erledigung **übertragen,** so **erhält jeder** Rechtsanwalt für seine Tätigkeit die **volle Vergütung** (§ 5 BRAGebO).

f) Ein **Rechtsanwalt, der durch schuldhaftes Verhalten** (Verärgerung des Mandanten, Verheimlichen überraschenden Berufswechsels) den Auftraggeber **veranlaßt,** einen **weiteren Anwalt zu nehmen,** bei dem die gleichen Gebühren entstehen, **kann** insoweit **die eigenen Gebühren nicht fordern** (vgl. § 125 BRAGebO; allgemeiner Grundsatz).

g) Was die **zu vergütende Einzelsache** anbetrifft, ist auch hier das **Vorgehen gegen denselben Verwaltungsakt entscheidend,** mag es auch – gleichzeitig – von verschiedenen Seiten erfolgen. Bei Erlaß eines neuen Verwaltungsaktes nach Klageerhebung (§§ 96, 153 SGG) liegt dasselbe Verfahren (dieselbe Sache) vor. Der neue Verwaltungsakt wird Gegenstand des bisherigen Verfahrens.

Anders geartet ist der Fall des § 171 Abs. 2 SGG (neuer Verwaltungsakt während des Revisionsverfahrens). Hier wird, wenn der Kläger nicht inzwischen klaglos gestellt worden ist, um eine Nachprüfung auch in tatsächlicher Hinsicht zu ermöglichen, über den neuen Verwaltungsakt in einem selbständigen Verfahren vor dem Sozialgericht entschieden.

h) Was den Umfang der Instanz für den Rechtsanwalt anbelangt, so ist das Folgende zu bemerken. **Zur Instanz gehört** grundsätzlich (vgl. § 37 BRAGebO):

α) die Vorbereitung der Klage, des Antrags oder der Rechtsverteidigung, soweit kein besonderes gerichtliches oder behördliches Verfahren stattfindet;

β) außergerichtliche Vergleichsverhandlungen;

γ) Zwischenstreite, die Bestimmung des zuständigen Gerichts, die Sicherung des Beweises, wenn die Hauptsache anhängig ist, die Bewilligung oder Entziehung des Armenrechts und die Verpflichtung zur Nachzahlung der Kosten (§ 126 ZPO), die vorläufige Einstellung, Beschränkung oder Aufhebung der Zwangsvollstreckung, wenn nicht eine abgesonderte mündliche Verhandlung hierüber stattfindet (vgl. § 49 BRAGebO), Verfahren wegen der Rückgabe einer Sicherheit (§ 109 Abs. 1 und 2, § 715 ZPO), die Bestellung von Vertretern durch das Prozeßgericht oder das Vollstreckungsgericht, die Ablehnung von Richtern, Urkundsbeamten der Geschäftsstelle oder Sachverständigen, die Verpflichtung zur Tragung von Kosten, die Zulassung einer Zustellung zur Nachtzeit, an einem Sonntag oder an einem allgemeinen Feiertag (§ 188 ZPO), gegebenenfalls die Festsetzung des Streitwerts;

δ) das Verfahren vor dem beauftragten oder ersuchten Richter und die Änderung seiner Entscheidungen;

ε) die Änderung von Entscheidungen des Urkundsbeamten der Geschäftsstelle;

ζ) die Berichtigung oder Ergänzung der Entscheidung oder ihres Tatbestandes;

η) die Zustellung oder Empfangnahme von Entscheidungen oder Rechtsmittelschriften und ihre Mitteilung an den Auftraggeber, die Einwilligung zur Sprungrevision, der Ausspruch über die Verpflichtung, die Kosten zu tragen oder eines Rechtsmittels verlustig zu sein, die Erteilung des Notfristzeugnisses, Rechtskraftzeugnisses, die erstmalige Erteilung der Vollstreckungsklausel, wenn deswegen keine Klage nach § 731 ZPO erhoben wird, die Kostenfestsetzung ausschließlich der Erinnerung gegen den Kostenfestsetzungsbeschluß, die Einforderung der Vergütung (§§ 18, 19 BRAGebO), die Herausgabe der Handakten oder ihre Übersendung an einen anderen Rechtsanwalt.

i) α) Ein und **derselbe Rechtszug** liegt vor, **wenn der Prozeßbevollmächtigte** des Erblassers den **Rechtsstreit für** den **Erben fortsetzt** (vgl. KG, JW 1931, 1837).

β) Durch **Antrag auf mündliche Verhandlung gegen den Vorbescheid** (§ 105 Abs. 2, § 158 Abs. 2, § 216 Abs. 1 Nr. 1 SGG) wird **kein neuer Rechtszug** eröffnet (vgl. hierzu den Grundgedanken des § 114 Abs. 3 BRAGebO, der als Gesetzesbestimmung für das Sozialgerichtsverfahren selbst keine Bedeutung hat, weil hier grundsätzlich eine Gesamtgebühr entsteht).

k) **Bei Zurückverweisung** an das untere Gericht beginnt für den Anwalt ein **neuer Rechtszug** (vgl. § 15 Satz 1 BRAGebO). In bezug auf die Höhe der neuen Gebühr ist aber zu berücksichtigen, daß der Anwalt sich mit der Materie bereits befaßt hatte. Die Gebühr ist daher niedriger als bei einer gleichliegenden neuen Sache zu bemessen (vgl. die Gedankengänge, die dem § 15 Satz 2 BRAGebO zugrunde liegen); die Mindestgrenze kann hier naturgemäß nicht unterschritten werden. Die Ermäßigung entfällt, wenn die Sache an ein Gericht zurückverwiesen ist, das mit der Sache noch nicht befaßt war (so bei Sprungrevision Zurückverweisung an das LSG; Entsprechendes gilt bei sog. Diagonalverweisung in ein anderes Gerichtsverfahren, vgl. Riedel, JVBl. 1957, 139 [143]).

Wird nach Zurückverweisung gegen das nunmehr ergehende Urteil ein Rechtsmittel eingelegt, so entsteht stets eine neue Rechtsmittelinstanz.

l) Bei **Verweisung** wegen örtlicher oder sachlicher Unzuständigkeit liegt ein **einheitliches Verfahren** vor (§ 14 Satz 1 BRAGebO); die Verweisung hat aber gegebenenfalls Bedeutung für den Umfang der bearbeiteten Sache und damit für die Höhe der Gebühr. (Die Höchstgrenze kann jedoch grundsätzlich nicht überschritten werden.)

Entsprechend ist die Rechtslage **bei Verweisung in einen anderen,** insbesondere den sog. ordentlichen **Rechtsweg** (vgl. § 14 Satz 1 BRAGebO); hier erhält der Anwalt die Gebühr für sein Tätigwerden vor dem betreffenden Sozialgericht aber dann abgesondert, wenn seine Tätigkeit mit der Verweisung aufhört (das folgt aus

§ 116 Abs. 2 BRAGebO). Vorstehendes gilt insgesamt auch bei umgekehrter Verweisung (vgl. Friederichs, NJW 1956, 926).

Sind vor dem verweisenden Gericht höhere Gebühren entstanden als vor dem übernehmenden, so bleiben dem Rechtsanwalt diese Gebühren (unter Anrechnung der neuen Gebühren) stets erhalten (vgl. Riedel, JVBl. 1957, 139 [143]). Der Vergleich der Gebührenhöhe bei den beiderseits beteiligten Gerichten ist dann nicht leicht, wenn bei einem derselben Wertgebühren entstehen. Er ist aber unter interner Auflösung der konkreten Rahmengebühr entsprechend den ausgelösten einzelnen Wertgebühren möglich. Bei Verweisung an ein Gericht eines niedrigeren Rechtszuges (Diagonalverweisung) ist das weitere Verfahren ein neuer Rechtszug (§ 14 Satz 2 BRAGebO).

m) Wird ein durch **rechtskräftiges** Urteil abgeschlossenes **Verfahren wieder aufgenommen** (§§ 179, 180 SGG, §§ 578ff. ZPO), so liegt stets ein **neues Verfahren** vor.

n) **Bei Abgabe** einer Streitsache **an das gemeinsame nächsthöhere Gericht** nach § 181 SGG (bei Infragekommen eines anderen Leistungspflichtigen) **entsteht** nur die betreffende **höherinstanzliche Anwaltsgebühr** (vgl. § 14 Satz 1 und 2 BRAGebO).

o) **Die Richter- und die Urkundsbeamtenablehnung** (vgl. §§ 60, 171 Abs. 1 SGG) **gehören zum Verfahren der Instanz** des Abgelehnten.

p) Ein **Anrufungs**(Erinnerungs-)**verfahren** (vgl. § 178, auch § 189 Abs. 2, §§ 191, 197 Abs. 2 SGG) **gehört** noch **zum Verfahren der** betreffenden **Instanz.** (Berücksichtigung der zusätzlichen Tätigkeit erfolgt – vgl. auch § 37 Nr. 5 BRAGebO – bei der Ausfüllung des Gebührenrahmens aus § 116 Abs. 2 BRAGebO, der im eigens gearteten – einheitlichen – Sozialgerichtsverfahren den § 61 Abs. 1 Nr. 2 BRAGebO verdrängt.) Wird der Anwalt nur mit der Wahrnehmung des Anrufungs(Erinnerungs-)verfahrens beauftragt, so wird in dem grundsätzlich auf Pauschgebühren ausgerichteten Sozialgerichtsverfahren jeweils die Gebühr des § 120 Abs. 2 BRAGebO (3 DM bis 5 DM) verdient sein, vgl. § 56 Abs. 3 BRAGebO (a. A. Brocke, SGb 1957, 359 [360], der – stets – eine $^3/_{10}$-Gebühr vom Kostenbetrage gewährt). Gleiches (Honorierung mit 3 DM bis 5 DM) wird für die Einreichung, Anfertigung oder Unterzeichnung eines einzelnen Sachschriftsatzes zu gelten haben, vgl. § 56 Abs. 1 Nr. 1 und Abs. 3 BRAGebO.

q) **Im Beschwerdeverfahren** fällt die **Anwaltsgebühr der höheren Instanz** nach § 116 Abs. 2 BRAGebO **in voller Höhe** – grundsätzlich allerdings zum Mindestbetrag – **nur** dann an, **wenn** die **Beschwerde** (z. B. bei Erledigung der Hauptsache) **an** die **Stelle der Berufung** tritt (siehe hierzu die Ausführungen im 1. Kap. 9b); die Weiterverfolgung von Zwischengesuchen oder das Wenden gegen ihre Stattgabe im Beschwerdewege wird **in den sonstigen Fällen** (z. B. bei Aussetzung) entsprechend dem § 61 BRAGebO (vgl. § 114 Abs. 1 SGG), und zwar grundsätzlich jeweils durch eine **Gebühr in Höhe von $^3/_{10}$ der Mindestgebühr für die höhere Instanz,** abgegolten. Das hat auch zu gelten, wenn, wie bei der Beschwerde gegen Strafbeschlüsse, nominell feststehende Beträge betroffen werden; obwohl hier der Geldbetrag (z. B. die Strafe oder die aufgebürdeten Kosten) des Streitgegenstandes feststeht oder sich ergibt, kommt die Zugrundelegung des nominellen Wertes und einer nach ihm berechneten Beschwerdegebühr aus rechtssystematischen Erwägungen nicht in Betracht (a. A. Brocke, SGb 1957, 359 [360]). Die Vornahme der Abhilfe hat grundsätzlich keinen Einfluß auf die Beschwerdegebühr.

r) In dem **Verfahren auf Aussetzung oder Aufhebung der Vollziehung eines Verwaltungsaktes** oder auf Wiederherstellung der aufschiebenden Wirkung der Anfechtung des Verwaltungsaktes (vgl. § 97 Abs. 2, 3 und § 199 Abs. 2 SGG) – diese Begehren entsprechen der einstweiligen Einstellung (u. ä.) der Zwangsvollstreckung – **beträgt** die – zusätzliche – **Gebühr, falls abgesonderte Behandlung angeordnet worden ist,** $^{3}/_{10}$ der sich aus § 116 Abs. 2 BRAGebO ergebenden Pauschgebühr, und zwar auch dann, wenn eine mündliche Verhandlung hierbei nicht stattfindet (§ 114 Abs. 5, § 49 Abs. 1 BRAGebO, vgl. hierzu Göttlich, BRAGebO 7. Aufl. S. 829). Grundsätzlich, d. h. bei nicht abgesonderter Behandlung, haben diese Anträge Bedeutung aber nur für die Höhe der allgemein abdeckenden Gebühr des § 116 Abs. 2 BRAGebO.

s) Die **Zwangsvollstreckung gehört** naturgemäß **nicht zur Instanz.** Für sie (einschließlich der Ankündigung nach § 882a ZPO) kann der Anwalt in Gemäßheit der Bundesrechtsanwaltsgebührenordnung liquidieren (grundsätzlich $^{3}/_{10}$ der jeweils ausgelösten Regelgebühren des § 31 BRAGebO nach der Höhe des Vollstreckungsanspruchs), vgl. § 57 BRAGebO und den entsprechenden § 119 Abs. 2 BRAGebO für das Verwaltungsvollstreckungsverfahren; wegen des Instanzbegriffs bei der Vollstreckung vgl. den § 58 BRAGebO. Die Anwaltsgebühren im Verfahren der Zwangsversteigerung und der Zwangsverwaltung sind in den §§ 68ff. BRAGebO geregelt. Wegen der Anwaltskosten im Konkursverfahren vgl. §§ 72ff. BRAGebO. Die Mindestgebühr beträgt jeweils 3 DM (vgl. § 11 Abs. 2 Satz 1 BRAGebO). Pfennigbeträge sind jeweils auf 10 DPf. aufzurunden (§ 11 Abs. 2 Satz 2 BRAGebO).

Wendet sich der Rechtsanwalt im Rahmen der Zwangsvollstreckung (des Verwaltungszwanges) mit einer Klage gegen einen Akt der Zwangsvollstreckung, so erhält er nur $^{3}/_{10}$ der Regelgebühren des § 31 BRAGebO (vgl. § 114 Abs. 6 BRAGebO; eine Minderung wegen vorzeitiger Beendigung des Auftrages oder nicht streitig erfolgter Sachverhandlung findet hier nicht statt).

t) Auch die **Hebegebühr** (vgl. § 22 BRAGebO) **wird gegebenenfalls besonders verdient** (berechnet nach Prozentsätzen der jeweils erhobenen Beträge, Mindestgebühr 1 DM). Sie kann bei der Ablieferung des erhobenen Betrages an den Auftraggeber entnommen werden (vgl. § 22 Abs. 1 letzter Satz BRAGebO). Der Rechtsanwalt erhält die Hebegebühr nicht, soweit er Kosten an ein Gericht oder eine Behörde weiterleitet oder eingezogene Kosten an den Auftraggeber abführt oder eingezogene Beträge auf seine Vergütung verrechnet (§ 22 Abs. 5 BRAGebO).

u) Ein **Beweissicherungsverfahren wird zum Hauptverfahren gerechnet,** vgl. § 37 Nr. 2 BRAGebO. (Es ist bei Ausfüllnng des Pauschalgebührenrahmens zu berücksichtigen.) Bei Vertretungsbeauftragung nur für das Beweissicherungsverfahren kommt die halbe Gebühr der betroffenen Instanz zum Zuge (vgl. § 114 Abs. 1 und § 48 BRAGebO). Ist die Hauptsache nicht anhängig, so wird die halbe Gebühr für den ersten Rechtszug verdient (§ 48 BRAGebO).

v) Wird der Rechtsanwalt in Sozialsachen nur **mit der** (mündlichen oder schriftlichen) **Beratung** (auch über die Aussicht eines Rechtsmittels) **beauftragt,** so erhält er lediglich die Ratgebühr des § 20 Abs. 1 Satz 2 BRAGebO in Höhe von 3 DM bis 150 DM. Die Ratgebühr wird, wenn der Anwalt mit der Vertretung im Verfahren betraut wird, auf die Gebühr des § 116 Abs. 2 BRAGebO angerechnet (vgl. § 20 Abs. 1 Satz 3 BRAGebO und dazu Riedel-Sußbauer, BRAGebO Anm. 4 zu § 116).

w) Von der Raterteilung ist gegebenenfalls die (sie grundsätzlich ausschließende) **Gutachtenerstattung** zu unterscheiden, die vorliegt, wenn insgesamt in schriftlicher Form eine juristische Begründung des Vorschlags gegeben wird (vgl. § 21 BRAGebO). **Für** das **Gutachten ist** jeweils unter Berücksichtigung aller Umstände eine **angemessene Gebühr zu zahlen** (vgl. §§ 21, 12 BRAGebO). Angemessen wird im allgemeinen der erstinstanzliche Gebührenrahmen des § 116 Abs. 2 BRAGebO sein (bei einfachen Gutachten kommt die untere Grenze, bei schwierigen die obere Grenze in Frage). Eine Anrechnung auf spätere Gebühren kommt hier nicht in Betracht.

x) **Für Tätigkeiten** des Rechtsanwalts **gegenüber Sozialversicherungsträgern und -behörden außerhalb** (sozial-)**gerichtlicher Verfahren erhält der Rechtsanwalt Entschädigung** gemäß § 118 BRAGebO (richtigerweise in Höhe von $^{2}/_{10}$ bis $^{10}/_{10}$ der Gebühr des § 116 Abs. 2 BRAGebO, vgl. § 118 Abs. 1 und 2 BRAGebO. Die Abstufung erfolgt vor allem nach dem Umfang der Tätigkeit — z. B. Wahrnehmung auch von Besprechungen und Aufklärungsterminen — vgl. § 118 Abs. 1 Nr. 1 bis 3, auch Abs. 2 BRAGebO). Die Gebühr ist auf die Gebühr für ein — unmittelbar — anschließendes gerichtliches Verfahren anzurechnen (§ 118 Abs. 3 BRAGebO). Die Gebühren für ein Vorverfahren (vgl. hierzu § 119 Abs. 1 BRAGebO) sind jedoch nicht in Anrechnung zu bringen (vgl. Gerold, BRAGebO Anm. 26 zu § 118).

Für die Tätigkeit als bestellter **Schiedsrichter** kann der Rechtsanwalt (im Zweifel auch ein anderer) in Sozialsachen je nach dem Schwierigkeitsgrad des Verfahrens die zweitinstanzliche Durchschnittsgebühr des §§ 116 Abs. 2 BRAGebO, erhöhbar bis zur Grenze der Höchstgebühr, verlangen (vgl. Schumann, BRAGebO Anm. IX zu § 1).

y) Ist der Anwalt **nur** mit der **Vertretung im Verfahren auf Bewilligung oder Entziehung des Armenrechts** oder im Verfahren **über die Verpflichtung zur Nachzahlung** der Kosten (§ 126 ZPO) beauftragt, so **erhält er $^{3}/_{10}$ der Mindestgebühr der** betreffenden **Instanz** (vgl. § 114 Abs. 1 und § 51 Abs. 1 Satz 1 BRAGebO). In mehreren Verfahren dieser Art erhält der Rechtsanwalt die Gebühren in jedem Rechtszuge nur einmal (§ 51 Abs. 1 Satz 2 BRAGebO). Eine Ermäßigung wegen vorzeitiger Beendigung des Auftrages oder wegen Nichtstreitigkeit der Verhandlung (vgl. §§ 32, 33 Abs. 1 und 2 BRAGebO) findet hier nicht statt (§ 51 Abs. 1 Satz 3 BRAGebO). Wird im Armenrechtsverfahren ein endgültiger Vergleich geschlossen (vgl. § 118a Abs. 3 ZPO), so erhöht sich im Hinblick auf die besonderen §§ 24, 23 Abs. 1 BRAGebO (in Verb. mit § 114 Abs. 1 BRAGebO) die Gebühr um $^{3}/_{10}$ der Mindestgebühr der betreffenden Instanz.

z) Ein etwa zugezogener **Verkehrsanwalt** (der den Verkehr der Partei mit dem Prozeßbevollmächtigten führt) dürfte für seine Tätigkeit eine Gebühr in Höhe von **$^{3}/_{10}$ der Gebühr der betreffenden Instanz** zu erhalten haben (vgl. den § 52 BRAGebO, der dem Verkehrsanwalt als Entgelt eine der drei Regelgebühren zubilligt); eine **Gebühr in gleicher Höhe** ($^{3}/_{10}$) wird dem Anwalt zuzubilligen sein, dessen Tätigkeit sich auf die **Vertretung in der — auswärtigen — Beweisaufnahme,** mag diese aus einem oder mehreren Terminen bestehen, beschränkt (vgl. § 54 BRAGebO).

2. a) **Bei Klageverbindung** zu gemeinsamer Verhandlung und Entscheidung (vgl. § 113 SGG; Voraussetzung: Die Ansprüche, die den Gegenstand der einzelnen Rechtsstreitigkeiten mit verschiedenen Beteiligten bilden, müssen in — rechtlichem oder tatsächlichem — Zusammenhang stehen, oder sie müssen bei den gleichen Beteiligten so geartet sein, daß sie von vornherein in einer Klage hätten geltend gemacht werden können, was Zusammenhang und gleiche Gerichtszuständigkeit voraussetzt, vgl. § 56 SGG) **werden die bis dahin ausgelösten Gebühren getrennt berechnet.** (Der § 196 Abs. 2 SGG, der hierbei insgesamt nur eine Gebühr vorsah, ist nicht übernommen worden.)

Bei Klagetrennung entsteht für jede abgetrennte neue Sache folgerichtigerweise zusätzlich **eine eigene Gebühr.**

b) **Wird der Rechtsanwalt in derselben Angelegenheit** (siehe oben 1g und h) **für mehrere Auftraggeber** (seien sie Streitgenossen, Nebenintervenienten, Beigeladene) **tätig,** so **erhält er die Gebühr nur einmal** (§ 6 Abs. 1 Satz 1 BRAGebO). **Der** auszufüllende **Gebührenrahmen wird aber erweitert;** der Mindest- und der Höchstbetrag (s. u. 4) erhöhen sich nämlich um die Hälfte (§ 6 Abs. 1 Satz 2 BRAGebO). Unerheblich ist dabei, wann die einzelne Beauftragung erfolgt. (Schwierigkeiten infolge einer später eintretenden Beauftragung sind bei der Ausfüllung des vorstehend umrissenen Rahmens zu berücksichtigen, vgl. die dem § 6 Abs. 1 Satz 3 BRAGebO zugrunde liegenden Gedankengänge.)

Jeder der **Auftraggeber** schuldet dem Rechtsanwalt die Gebühren und Auslagen, die er schulden würde, wenn der Rechtsanwalt nur in seinem Auftrage tätig geworden wäre, d. h. jeder Auftraggeber **haftet auf Grund der gewöhnlichen** und nicht aus der erhöhten **Rahmenausfüllung** des § 6 Abs. 1 Satz 2 BRAGebO (§ 6 Abs. 2 Satz 1 BRAGebO). Der Rechtsanwalt kann insgesamt aber nie mehr als die einmalige Gebühr (aus dem erhöhten Rahmen) fordern; die Auslagen kann er auch nur einmal verlangen, vgl. § 6 Abs. 2 BRAGebO. Die Auftraggeber haften im Rahmen ihrer Schuld für die Gebühr (nebst Auslagen) als Gesamtschuldner; sind die Auslagen nur im Auftragsrahmen eines einzelnen Auftraggebers entstanden, so haftet nur dieser (vgl. Riedel-Sußbauer, BRAGebO Anm. 21 zu § 6).

3. **Der Anwalt hat seine Dienste** grundsätzlich **in Person zu leisten** (vgl. § 613 BGB), **doch kann er sich** — abgesehen von der allgemeinen Vertretung durch einen besonders Bestellten — unbedenklich **durch einen anderen Anwalt, einen Anwaltsassessor,** der zur Ableistung des Anwärterdienstes einem — beliebigen — Rechtsanwalt überwiesen ist, **oder durch einen Referendar,** der sich **in der Ausbildungsstation** bei — irgend — einem Anwalt befindet, **vertreten lassen,** vgl. § 4 BRAGebO. (Der letzte kann aber keinesfalls vor dem BSG auftreten.) Die vor den Instanzgerichten an sich verfahrensrechtlich zulässige Vertretung durch andere Personen (Bürovorsteher u. ä.) könnte jedenfalls bei Nichterwünschtsein zu einer gewissen Kürzung der im gesetzlichen Rahmen liegenden Gebühr führen.

4. **Die Gebühren der Rechtsanwälte sind nur rahmenmäßig bestimmt;** der Rahmen ist an sich ziemlich weit gezogen. Er beträgt jetzt (§ 116 Abs. 2 BRAGebO):

vor dem Sozialgericht	40 bis 120 DM,
vor dem Landessozialgericht	60 bis 180 DM,
vor dem Bundessozialgericht	100 bis 300 DM,

(auch wenn es in erster Instanz entscheidet, vgl. § 39 Abs. 2 SGG).

5. **Die Gebühr ist** im Einzelfall **unter Berücksichtigung aller Umstände,** insbesondere der Bedeutung der Angelegenheit, des — sachlichen — Umfangs und der — rechtlichen oder tatsächlichen — Schwierigkeit der anwaltlichen Tätigkeit sowie der Einkommens- und Vermögensverhältnisse des Auftraggebers (nicht des etwaigen Erstattungspflichtigen desselben) **nach billigem Ermessen zu bestimmen** (§ 12 Abs. 1 BRAGebO). **Im** erforderlich werdenden **Rechtsstreit** hat das Gericht ein **Gutachten des Vorstandes der Rechtsanwaltskammer einzuholen** (vgl. § 12 Abs. 2 BRAGebO). Auf den Erfolg der Anwaltstätigkeit kommt es auch im Sozialgerichtsverfahren nicht an; Spezialisierung des Anwalts rechtfertigt grundsätzlich keine Erhöhung.

Auftragserledigung vor Beendigung des eingeleiteten Verfahrens oder Auftragserteilung erst im Verlaufe desselben ist bei dem Umfange der Sache zu berücksichtigen. (Die Mindestgebühr muß auf jeden Fall gezahlt werden.)

Wegen der Auftragserledigung vor Einreichung der Klage vgl. oben 1 c.

Die **mittleren Werte** (was den Zahlungspflichtigen anbetrifft: Einkommen zwischen 300 und 400 DM ohne Vermögen im eigentlichen Sinne; was den Fall anlangt: rechtliche oder tatsächliche Lage weder leicht noch schwierig, kein besonders kleiner oder großer Sachumfang, weder geringe noch ins Gewicht fallende Bedeutung) machen aus:

vor dem Sozialgericht	80 DM,
vor dem Landessozialgericht	120 DM,
vor dem Bundessozialgericht	200 DM.

Gegen eine weitgehende Zubilligung der Mittelgebühr (Mindestgebühr +Höchstgebühr insgesamt dividiert durch 2) haben Riedel-Sußbauer, BRAGebO Anm. 6 zu § 12 Bedenken erhoben; Gerold, BRAGebO Anm. 4 zu § 12 hat an die Stelle des Mittelwertes auch — nur — die Hälfte des Höchstbetrages gesetzt. Das ist jedoch rechnerisch nicht zutreffend und ergebnismäßig auch nicht billig (vgl. Schumann, BRAGebO Anm. III 2b zu § 12).

Die **Mindestgebühr** kommt nur für ganz einfache, wenig umfangreiche und unbedeutende Sachen bei schlechter Einkommenslage und Vermögenslosigkeit des Zahlungspflichtigen in Frage. Die **Höchstgebühr** ist auszuwerfen, wenn es sich um besonders schwierige, umfangreiche, bedeutungsvolle Sachen bei äußerst günstigen Einkommens- oder Vermögensverhältnissen des Zahlungspflichtigen handelt.

Von Bedeutung für die Höhe der Gebühr ist in diesem Zusammenhange auch, ob der Anwalt mündlich verhandelt, ferner ob er an einer stattgehabten Beweisaufnahme (evtl. außerhalb) mitgewirkt hat, endlich ob er an dem Zustandekommen eines Vergleichs (vgl. § 23 BRAGebO) oder an einer Erledigung des Rechtsstreits durch Zurücknahme oder Änderung des angefochtenen Verwaltungsaktes (vgl. § 24 BRAGebO) — ganz oder teilweise — beteiligt war (vgl. hierzu Mellwitz, NJW 1956, 1828). Die obere Grenze des § 116 Abs. 2 BRAGebO, der nur die normale Tätigkeit des Anwalts betrifft, darf dabei — ausnahmsweise — dann, jedoch höchstens um ein Drittel, überschritten werden, wenn bereits abgesehen vom Vergleich der Höchstbetrag zur Auslösung käme (so Riedel-Sußbauer, BRAGebO Anm. 6 zu § 116; a. A. Gerold, BRAGebO Anm. 6 zu § 24, der den Höchstrahmen nicht für überschreitbar hält). Die untere Grenze kann als solche nicht unterschritten werden. Allerdings können in einzelnen Fällen (s. o. insbes. 1 q, r, s, y u. z) sogen. Bruchteilsgebühren entstehen. Etwaige Pfennigbeträge sind dabei jeweils auf 10 Deutsche Pfennige aufzurunden (§ 11 Abs. 2 Satz 2 BRAGebO). Die unterste Grenze ist auf jeden Fall 3 DM (§ 11 Abs. 2 Satz 1 BRAGebO).

6. a) **Höhere Beträge** als die gesetzlich in Frage kommenden **können** jetzt **vereinbart** und gezahlt **werden.** (Die hindernde Bestimmung des § 196 Abs. 5 SGG ist in das neue Kostenrecht nicht übernommen worden.)

Aus einer Vereinbarung kann der Rechtsanwalt eine höhere als die gesetzliche Vergütung nur fordern, wenn die Erklärung des Auftragsgebers schriftlich abgegeben und nicht in der Vollmacht oder in einem Vordruck, der auch andere Erklärungen umfaßt, enthalten ist (§ 3 Abs. 1 Satz 1 BRAGebO). Hat der Auftraggeber freiwillig und ohne Vorbehalt geleistet, so kann er das Geleistete nicht deshalb zurückfordern, weil seine Erklärung der vorstehenden Vorschrift nicht entspricht (§ 3 Abs. 1 Satz 2 BRAGebO).

Die Festsetzung der Vergütung kann dem billigen Ermessen des Vorstandes der Rechtsanwaltskammer überlassen werden (§ 3 Abs. 2 Satz 1 BRAGebO). Ist die Festsetzung der Vergütung dem Ermessen eines Vertragsteiles überlassen, so gilt die gesetzliche Vergütung als vereinbart (§ 3 Abs. 2 Satz 2 BRAGebO).

Ist eine vereinbarte oder von dem Vorstand der Rechtsanwaltskammer festgesetzte **Vergütung** unter Berücksichtigung aller Umstände unangemessen hoch, so **kann** sie im Rechtsstreit auf den angemessenen Betrag bis zur Höhe der gesetzlichen Vergütung **herabgesetzt werden** (§ 3 Abs. 3 Satz 1 BRAGebO). Vor der Herabsetzung hat das Gericht ein Gutachten des Vorstandes der Rechtsanwaltskammer einzuholen; dies gilt nicht, wenn der Vorstand der Rechtsanwaltskammer die Vergütung festgesetzt hat (§ 3 Abs. 3 Satz 2 BRAGebO).

Durch eine **Vereinbarung,** nach der ein **im Armenrecht** beigeordneter Rechtsanwalt eine Vergütung erhalten soll, **wird eine Verbindlichkeit nicht begründet** (§ 3 Abs. 4 Satz 1 BRAGebO). Hat der Auftraggeber freiwillig und ohne Vorbehalt geleistet, so kann er das Geleistete nicht deshalb zurückfordern, weil eine Verbindlichkeit nicht bestanden hat (§ 3 Abs. 4 Satz 2 BRAGebO).

b) Die **Vereinbarung eines Erfolgshonorars** oder die **Beteiligung am Streitgegenstand ist** grundsätzlich als **sittenwidrig** und daher nichtig (§ 138 BGB) anzusehen (vgl. §§ 40 und 41 der Richtlinien für die Ausübung des Anwaltsberufs vom 11. 5. 1957, abgedruckt bei Brangsch, BRAGebO Anm. 5 zu § 3).

c) Ein **Verzicht auf Gebühren** (und Auslagen) oder Teile derselben wird in aller Regel nicht nur als **standeswidrig,** sondern wegen seiner Auswirkung im Verkehrsleben auch als sittenwidrig und damit gemäß § 138 BGB als nichtig anzusehen sein (vgl. § 39 der Richtlinien und dazu Brangsch, BRAGebO Anm. 1 zu § 3).

Der Rechtsanwalt kann seinen **Vergütungsanspruch abtreten** und **verpfänden;** derselbe **unterliegt der Forderungspfändung.**

7. Die Vergütungspflicht gegenüber dem Anwalt entsteht mit der Auftragserteilung. **Der Rechtsanwalt kann** von seinem Auftraggeber (nur von diesem) für Gebühren und Auslagen **einen** angemessenen **Vorschuß fordern** (§ 17 BRAGebO), im Zweifel in Höhe der Mindestgebühr der in Frage stehenden Instanz. (Der Armenanwalt kann niemals Vorschuß fordern.) Reicht der Vorschuß nicht aus, so kann Ergänzung verlangt werden. Nicht verbrauchte Vorschüsse sind zurückzuzahlen. Von der Vorschußzahlung kann die Übernahme oder Weiterausführung des Auftrages abhängig gemacht werden, und zwar auch dann, wenn der Anwalt bestimmt wurde, weil die Partei keinen Anwalt hat finden können (vgl. Schumann, BRAGebO Anm. III 2a zu § 17 mit weiteren Nachweisen). Einklagung des Vorschusses ist standesmäßig nicht erlaubt.

8. Die **Vergütung** des Rechtsanwalts **wird fällig, wenn der Auftrag erledigt oder** die **Angelegenheit beendigt ist** (§ 16 Satz 1 BRAGebO). Das ist insbesondere der Fall, wenn der Rechtszug beendet ist; es genügt das Ergehen einer Kostenentscheidung oder das — angeordnete oder tatsächliche — Ruhen des Verfahrens in Dauer von mehr als drei Monaten (vgl. § 16 Satz 2 BRAGebO).

Die **Beendigung der Instanz kann bestehen in:**

Rücknahme der Klage (§ 102 SGG),
Rücknahme des Rechtsmittels (§§ 156, 165 SGG),
Abschluß eines Vergleichs (§ 101 Abs. 1, §§ 153, 165 SGG),
Annahme des Anerkenntnisses (§ 101 Abs. 2, §§ 153, 165 SGG; Entsprechendes hat für den Verzicht auf den erhobenen Anspruch zu gelten),

Erledigung der Hauptsache aus sonstigen Gründen (z. B. infolge Gesetzesänderung),
Rechtskräftigwerden des Vorbescheides (§§ 105, 158 Abs. 2, § 216 Abs. 1 Nr. 1 SGG),
Erlaß eines Urteils (§§ 123, 153, 165 SGG); der Verwerfungs- bzw. Zurückweisungsbeschluß gemäß §§ 169, 216 Abs. 1 Nr. 3, 4 SGG steht einem Urteil gleich.

Erledigung des Auftrags erfolgt im übrigen bei Kündigung durch den einen oder anderen Teil, ebenso natürlich durch den Tod des Anwalts oder der Partei. Wird der Rechtsstreit vom Prozeßbevollmächtigten des Erblassers für die Erben fortgesetzt, so liegt ein und derselbe Rechtszug vor (KG, JW 1931, 1837). Wird beim Tode des Anwalts ein Abwickler der Kanzlei bestellt, der weiter tätig wird, so setzt sich das Auftragsverhältnis der Partei mit dem Abwickler fort. Die Fälligkeit der Gebühren kann hier durch Vereinbarung mit dem Auftraggeber formlos hinausgeschoben werden. (Bei vertraglicher Vereinbarung früherer Fälligkeit ist grundsätzlich § 3 Abs. 1 BRAGebO zu beachten.)

9. Nach § 217 Abs. 1 SGG stehen **Verwaltungsrechtsräte den Anwälten gleich.** Auch sie können vor dem Bundessozialgericht auftreten.

Nach § 217 Abs. 2 SGG gilt als Verwaltungsrechtsrat auch derjenige, der auf Grund der vorgeschriebenen Prüfungen die Fähigkeit zum höheren Verwaltungsdienst hat und dem das Auftreten vor den Gerichten der Verwaltungsgerichtsbarkeit allgemein gestattet ist (vgl. hierzu BSG, SozR SGG § 217 Bl. Da1 Nr. 1). Diese Gestattung (Zulassung) muß durch Verwaltungsakt der zuständigen Behörde ausgesprochen sein. (Die Beauftragung mit der Vertretung der Interessen des Ausgleichsfonds — § 322 Lastenausgleichsgesetz — ist keine solche Gestattung, BSG SozR SGG § 217 Bl. Da1 Nr. 2.)

10. Ein **Rechtsbeistand erhält die Hälfte der Gebühren,** die ein Anwalt im gleichen Falle verdienen würde (§ 612 Abs. 2 BGB in Verb. mit Art. IX § 2 Abs. 1 KostÄndG, vgl. BGBl. I 861 [931]). Wegen der Auslagen des Rechtsbeistandes vgl. unten B 11.

Höhere Gebühren dürfen dem Rechtsbeistand gegenüber **weder vereinbart noch gezahlt werden,** § 2 Abs. 2 aaO (bei Zahlung, auch vorbehaltloser, Kondiktion!).

Rechtsbeistand im Sinne der genannten Bestimmungen ist die Einzelperson, der das mündliche Verhandeln vor Gericht (sog. Prozeßagent) durch Anordnung der Justizverwaltung gestattet ist (vgl. § 157 Abs. 3 ZPO, § 73 Abs. 6 SGG, § 4 Abs. 1 der 2. Ausführungsverordnung vom 3. 4. 1936 — RGBl. I 359 — zum Rechtsberatungsmißbrauchsgesetz vom 13. 12. 1935 — RGBl. I 1478 —).

Eine besondere Zulassung vor den Sozialgerichten ist nicht erforderlich (vgl. Peters, KV 1954, 42 und ihm beitretend, Liphardt, KOV 1955, 23; a. A. Hastler, WzS 1954, 137 und KOV 1955, 57, ferner Köhler, SozVers. 1955, 64).

Zur Frage der Zuständigkeit für die Erteilung einer etwaigen besonderen Zulassung vgl. LSG Berlin, NJW 1957, 239. (Danach ist zuständig die jeweilige Landesregierung bzw. die von ihr beauftragte Stelle.) Für Berlin vgl. Mellwitz, SGG S. 522; wegen besonderer Regelungen in anderen (Bundes-) Ländern vgl. die Aufstellung bei Hofmann-Schroeter, SGG 2. Aufl. in der Anm. 7 zu § 73.

Der Rechtsbeistand kann vor dem Bundessozialgericht nur als prozessualer Beistand (nicht aber als Prozeßbevollmächtigter) auftreten. Als solcher erhält er im Zweifel ebenfalls die Vergütung für die dritte Instanz.

11. **Andere Beistände oder Prozeßbevollmächtigte,** die weder Rechtsanwälte noch Verwaltungsrechtsräte (i. w. S., s. o. 9), noch Rechtsbeistände (Prozeßagenten

s. o. 10) sind, **fallen nicht** in irgendeiner Weise **unter § 116 BRAGebO, insbesondere nicht** die sog. **Organisationsvertreter,** vgl. LSG Hessen, SGb 1955, 300. (Für alle diese kommt gegebenenfalls, wenn nicht eine Regelung in der Verbandssatzung enthalten ist, nur eine nach allgemeinem Ermessen zu bestimmende Vergütung nach § 612 BGB in Betracht.)

12. Soweit dem Rechtsanwalt (Rechtsbeistand) nach Landesgebührenrecht (jetzt Bundesgebührenrecht, vgl. § 118 BRAGebO) **für** eine einzelne **Tätigkeit in einem behördlichen Verfahren (Vorverfahren)** vor der Übernahme der Vertretung im Verfahren vor den Gerichten der Sozialgerichtsbarkeit eine **besondere Gebühr** erwachsen ist, wird diese auf die Gebühr des § 116 Abs. 2 BRAGebO nicht angerechnet. Die Bestimmung des § 196 Abs. 6 SGG, die diese Anrechnung vorsah, ist nicht übernommen worden; vgl. hierzu auch § 119 Abs. 1 BRAGebO und die Amtliche Begründung, BT-Drucks. 2545, 2. Wahlperiode S. 270 zu 1 a. E.

B. Auslagen

1. **Die Gebühren** nach § 116 Abs. 2 BRAGebO **decken die** besonderen **Auslagen** des Rechtsanwalts **nicht mit ab;** das ergibt sich aus § 193 Abs. 3 SGG. Hier ist angeordnet, daß die notwendigen Auslagen des zugezogenen Anwalts im Rahmen der §§ 25 bis 30 der Bundesgebührenordnung für Rechtsanwälte erstattungsfähig sind. Erstattet verlangt werden können aber immer nur der Partei erwachsene Kosten. Der Anwalt hat daher einen Anspruch (aus dem Auftragsverhältnis) auf Ersetzung der genannten Auslagen gegenüber seinem Auftraggeber (vgl. auch § 25 Abs. 2 BRAGebO; nach § 25 Abs. 1 BRAGebO werden mit den Gebühren nur die allgemeinen Geschäftsunkosten abgegolten).

2. Im einzelnen handelt es sich um **die folgenden zu ersetzenden Auslagen:**

a) die in erforderlicher Weise aufzuwendenden **Post-, Telegrafen-, Fernsprech- und Fernschreibgebühren** (§ 26 BRAGebO). Ihre Höhe richtet sich nach den postalischen Gebührensätzen, die durch die jeweils in Anspruch genommene Dienstleistung der Post ausgelöst werden;

b) die **Schreibgebühren.** Sie kann der Anwalt nur für die im Einverständnis mit dem Auftraggeber zusätzlich, d. h. über die gesetzliche oder übungsgemäß bestehende Verpflichtung hinaus gefertigten Abschriften und Ablichtungen verlangen (§ 27 Abs. 1 BRAGebO).

Abschriften sind regelmäßig zu erteilen: für den Gegner, für die Handakten des Anwalts und für die eigene Partei, an diese auch hinsichtlich der ergangenen Entscheidungen des Gerichts (vgl. Tschischgale, AnwBl. 1956, 267).

Die Höhe der anwaltlichen Schreibgebühr ist die gleiche wie die der gerichtlichen (§ 27 Abs. 2 BRAGebO). Diese beträgt nach § 91 Abs. 3 GKG 0,50 DM für die Seite mit durchschnittlich 28 Zeilen zu je rund 15 Silben, und zwar auch bei Erstellung auf mechanischem Wege (mit Ausnahme der Ablichtung). Werden Abschriften durch Ablichtung hergestellt, so werden für jede abgelichtete Seite ohne Rücksicht auf Zeilen- und Silbenzahl 0,50 DM, bei größerem Format der Ablichtung als DIN B 4 eine DM berechnet, vgl. § 91 Abs. 6 GKG. Für Schriftstücke, die in fremder Sprache abgefaßt sind, wird die doppelte Schreibgebühr (1 DM je Seite) erhoben (vgl. § 91 Abs. 4 GKG). Für Schriftstücke in bestimmter Form (z. B. Tabellen) wird die Schreibgebühr nach dem Zeitaufwand berechnet, der bei durchschnittlicher Arbeitsleistung zur Herstellung benötigt wird, und zwar wird für jede — eventuell nur angefangene — Viertelstunde 0,60 DM vergütet (§ 91 Abs. 5 GKG, vgl. hierzu das 4. Kap. 1 a). Auf Sondervergünstigungen, die die Staatskasse hinsichtlich eigener Schreibgebühren unter Umständen dem Anwalt gewährt (vgl.

§ 91 Abs. 7 GKG, vor allem bei Bestellung an die Partei weiterzuleitender zusätzlicher Abschriften von Schriftstücken, die gerichtlicherseits mechanisch – zumeist in großer Zahl – hergestellt werden), kann sich die Partei nicht berufen (vgl. Riedel-Sußbauer, BRAGebO Anm. 5 zu § 28);

c) die **Reisespesen** (§ 28 BRAGebO). Der beauftragte Rechtsanwalt hat bei erforderlichen Geschäftsreisen (z. B. zu auswärtigen, d. h. außerhalb des Ortes seiner Kanzlei stattfindenden Terminen, vgl. § 2 RKG) zu beanspruchen:

α) ein **Tagegeld.** Dieses gilt pauschal den Mehraufwand ab, den regelmäßig eine Reise erfordert. Es beträgt nach den hier ebenfalls maßgebenden Sätzen für Bundesbeamte der Reisekostenstufe II auf Grund der Vorschriften über die Reisekostenvergütung der Bundesbeamten nach dem Gesetz vom 15. 12. 1933 (RGBl. I 1067) in der geltenden Fassung (§ 9 Abs. 2 und 3) 14 DM für den vollen, d. h. durch die Reise zu mehr als 12 Stunden in Anspruch genommenen Kalendertag; bei einer Abwesenheitsdauer von nur mehr als 8 bis 12 Stunden ist die Hälfte, bei über 6 bis 8 Stunden Abwesenheit sind $^3/_{10}$ des genannten Betrages zuzubilligen (vgl. § 28 Abs. 1 Satz 1 BRAGebO). Bei Dauer von 6 Stunden und darunter ist kein Tagegeld zu zahlen;

β) ein **Übernachtungsentgelt.** Dieses gilt die Aufwendungen für die außerhalb des beruflichen Wohnsitzes erforderlich werdende Übernachtung ab. Es beträgt nach den auch hier maßgebenden Sätzen, welche die Bundesbeamten der Reisekostenstufe II auf Grund der Vorschriften über die Reisevergütung der Bundesbeamten erhalten (s. o. α) 11 DM (vgl. § 28 Abs. 1 Satz 1 BRAGebO). Neben Schlafwagenkosten ist das Übernachtungsentgelt grundsätzlich nur zu einem Viertel zu gewähren (vgl. § 10 Abs. 2 RKG).

Zu α und β. Hat eine Geschäftsreise in unvermeidbarer Weise **außergewöhnliche Kosten** verursacht, die aus dem Tagegeld und dem Übernachtungsgeld zu bestreiten waren, aber aus ihrem Gesamtbetrag nicht gedeckt werden konnten, so ist der Mehrbetrag **zu ersetzen** (vgl. § 16 RKG);

γ) die verauslagten **Fahrtkosten,** je nach dem Satz des zurückzulegenden Weges, und zwar erster Eisenbahn- bzw. erster Schiffsklasse einschließlich der notwendigen Kosten des Zu- und Abganges (vom und zum Bahnhof, Hafen oder Flugplatz) für den Anwalt und sein zum beruflichen und persönlichen Gebrauch bestimmtes Gepäck, und zwar Zu- und Abgangskosten in angemessener Höhe (vgl. § 28 Abs. 1 Satz 1 BRAGebO, §§ 6 und 8 RKG).

Ist es nach den Umständen, insbesondere nach dem Zweck der Geschäftsreise, erforderlich, ein anderes als ein öffentliches, regelmäßig verkehrendes Beförderungsmittel zu benutzen, so erhält der Rechtsanwalt Ersatz der notwendigen Aufwendungen, bei Benutzung eines eigenen Kraftwagens 0,25 DM für jedes angefangene Kilometer des Hin- und Rückwegs (§ 28 Abs. 1 Satz 2 BRAGebO).

Für Fußwege von insgesamt mehr als 4 km, die zur Erreichung des auswärtigen Geschäftsortes außerhalb desselben und der Gemeinde des Amtssitzes des Anwalts zurückgelegt werden müssen, sind 0,10 DM je Kilometer zu vergüten (vgl. § 7 RKG, Nr. 24, auch Nr. 25 AB).

Dient eine Reise mehreren, notwendigerweise fremden, Geschäften, so sind die entstandenen Reisekosten und Abwesenheitsgelder (s. u. ε) nach dem Verhältnis der Kosten zu verteilen, die bei gesonderter Ausführung der einzelnen Geschäfte entstanden wären (§ 29 BRAGebO). Mehrkosten, die durch die Mitbesorgung eigener Geschäfte entstehen, hat kein Auftraggeber zu ersetzen.

Ein Rechtsanwalt, der seine Kanzlei nach einem anderen Ort verlegt, kann bei Fortführung eines ihm vorher erteilten Auftrags Reisekosten und Abwesenheitsgelder nur insoweit verlangen, als sie auch von seiner bisherigen Kanzlei aus entstanden wären (§ 30 BRAGebO);

δ) die nachgewiesenen **Nebenkosten.** Sie gelten die Nebenaufwendungen, z. B. für Durchlaß(Paß-)gebühren und für Versicherungen von Person und Gepäck (so bei Flügen), ab (§ 28 Abs. 1 Satz 1 BRAGebO, § 11 RKG);

ε) ein **Abwesenheitsgeld,** das die Entschädigung dafür darstellt, daß der Rechtsanwalt seinem sonstigen verdiensteinbringenden Wirkungskreis entzogen wird (§ 28 Abs. 2 BRAGebO). Es beträgt 15 DM für jeden Werktag. Dauert die Geschäftsreise nicht mehr als 4 Stunden, so ermäßigt sich das Abwesenheitsgeld auf die Hälfte (7,50 DM).

Das Abwesenheitsgeld steht, im Gegensatz zu den übrigen Entschädigungen, nur dem Anwalte oder seinem allgemeinen Vertreter zu, nicht dagegen einem sonstigen Vertreter (§ 28 Abs. 2 Satz 1 Teil 1 BRAGebO).

Hinsichtlich Auslandsreisen vgl. gegebenenfalls die Sonderbestimmung des RMF vom 22. 12. 1933 (RBB 1934, 1) i. d. F. MinBlFin. 1952, 155 und dazu Schumann, BRAGebO Anm. VI zu § 28 sowie Ambrosius, Reisekostenrecht S. 268f.

d. Auch **Aufwendungen,** die der Rechtsanwalt unbedingt machen muß, um seine Aufgaben erfüllen zu können (z. B. für einen Dolmetscher zur Übersetzung der erteilten Information), sind von der Partei zu ersetzen.

3. **Die Mehrkosten, die** bei der Vertretung eines Beteiligten durch einen Rechtsanwalt dadurch **entstehen, daß** dieser seine **Kanzlei nicht am Ort des Gerichts** hat, **sind** vom Auftraggeber, dem es frei stand, diesen Anwalt zu nehmen, im Zweifel **zu ersetzen,** vgl. § 670 in Verb. mit § 675 BGB. (Sie sind als vermeidbare Kosten in aller Regel nicht erstattungsfähig, siehe 6. Kap. 3e und 4e α, auch Amend, SGb 1954, 145.)

4. **Mehrere Auftraggeber** der gleichen Geschäftsreise **haften** im Zweifel (in der vollen Höhe) **als Gesamtschuldner** (Erstattung natürlich insgesamt nur einmal), vgl. hierzu § 6 Abs. 2 BRAGebO, ferner § 29 BRAGebO bezüglich der an sich vorzunehmenden Verteilung.

5. **Reisen mehrere** beauftragte **Anwälte,** so **stehen jedem** von ihnen die jeweiligen **Reisespesen zu** (vgl. § 5 BRAGebO).

6. **Für Geschäfte am Wohnort** stehen dem Rechtsanwalt **weder** irgendwelche **Tagegelder noch Fahrtkosten** o. ä. zu.

7. Die in einem **Vorverfahren** entstandenen **Auslagen können — abgesondert — geltend gemacht werden** (so schon nach dem früheren § 196 Abs. 6 SGG).

8. Die **Auslagen** entstehen mit ihrer Vornahme; sie **werden** wie die Gebühren **fällig, wenn der Auftrag erledigt oder die Angelegenheit beendet ist bzw.** länger als drei Monate bei Gericht **ruht** (§ 16 BRAGebO, vgl. oben A 8). Vorschuß kann vom Auftraggeber (nicht Dritten) verlangt werden (vgl. § 17 BRAGebO).

9. **Über** die genaue Höhe der zu ersetzenden **Auslagen** und ihre Abgeltung **können Vereinbarungen getroffen werden** (bei erheblicher Aufrundung unter Beachtung des § 3 Abs. 1 BRAGebO). Wegen eines ganzen oder teilweisen Verzichts auf sie vgl. oben A 6c a. E.

10. Die **Regelung des Auslagenersatzes gilt** gemäß § 217 Abs. 1 SGG **auch für Verwaltungsrechtsräte** und diesen Gleichgestellte (§ 217 Abs. 2 SGG).

11. **Für Rechtsbeistände gilt** die wiedergegebene **Regelung** der Auslagen **ebenfalls** (Art. IX § 2 Abs. 1 Satz 1 KostÄndG).

Jedoch beträgt das volle **Abwesenheitsgeld** der Rechtsbeistände **nur 10 DM;** es ermäßigt sich bei Geschäftsreisen von nicht mehr als 4 Stunden Dauer auf 5 DM (Art. IX § 1 Abs. 3 Satz 2 aaO). **Maßgebend** ist ferner lediglich die **Reisekostenstufe III** (Art. IX § 1 Abs. 3 Satz 1 aaO).

Das **Tagegeld** beträgt danach 11 DM und das **Übernachtungsgeld** 10 DM (so auch Brocke-Reese, Geb. u. KostR Anh. S. 33 und 30); benutzt werden darf hier nur die 2. Wagenklasse.

Wegen der Gebühren der Rechtsbeistände vgl. oben A 10.

Zu A und B

1. Der Rechtsanwalt (Rechtsbeistand) **kann** die **Vergütung** nur auf Grund einer von ihm unterzeichneten und dem Auftraggeber mitgeteilten **Berechnung** einfordern (§ 18 Abs. 1 Satz 1 BRAGebO).

Die Berechnung ist zu spezifizieren; Vorschüsse sowie die angewandten Gebührenvorschriften sind anzugeben. Bei Post-, Telegrafen-, Fernsprech- und Fernschreibkosten genügt die Angabe des Gesamtbetrages (§ 18 Abs. 2 BRAGebO).

Hat der Auftraggeber die Vergütung bezahlt, ohne die Berechnung erhalten zu haben, so kann er die Mitteilung der Berechnung noch fordern, solange der Rechtsanwalt zur Aufbewahrung der Handakten verpflichtet ist, § 18 Abs. 3 BRAGebO (Aufbewahrungspflicht grundsätzlich 5 Jahre; bei Aufforderung des Auftraggebers durch den Anwalt, die Handakten in Empfang zu nehmen, 6 Monate nach Erhalt der Aufforderung, vgl. § 61 Abs. 2 RAO).

2. **Der Anwalt** (Rechtsbeistand) **kann** den für die Gebühren und Auslagen entstehenden **Umsatzsteuerbetrag** (4%) jetzt auf den Auftraggeber (oder Erstattungspflichtigen) — offen — **abwälzen.** Wie der § 12 BRAGebO ergibt, sind nunmehr auch Gebühren mit Rahmenbegrenzung gesetzlich bemessene Gebühren, da sich der jeweils zu zahlende Betrag in umrissener Weise aus dem Gesetz ergibt und die eigentliche Festlegung letzten Endes durch das Gericht, also in objektiver Weise, erfolgt, vgl. § 10 UStG, § 63 UStDB vom 1. 9. 1951, Glücklich, SGb 1958, 327, Sölch-Ringleb, UStG Anm. 3 zu § 10 und Riedel-Sußbauer, BRAGebO Anm. 6 zu § 25. (Wegen des früheren Rechtszustandes vgl. Tschischgale, Zur Frage der Erstattungsfähigkeit der Umsatzsteuer für Anwaltsgebühren nach dem SGG, JurBüro 1956, 416.) Etwaige (Gesamt-)Abrechnungsvergünstigungen des Anwalts — vgl. den Freibetrag des Gesetzes vom 5. 10. 1956, BGBl. I 787 (neuer § 7a UStG) und den Pauschalabzug des noch geltenden § 79 Abs. 3 UStDB vom 17. 10. 1934, RGBl. I 965 — kommen der Partei nicht zugute (vgl. OLG Schleswig, Rpfleger 1956, 323).

3. Die **Gebühren- und Auslagenersatzansprüche** der Rechtsanwälte, Verwaltungsrechtsräte (i. w. S.) und Rechtsbeistände **verjähren** nach § 196 Abs. 1 Nr. 15 BGB **in zwei Jahren** seit dem Schluß des Jahres, in welchem die Fälligkeit des Anspruchs eingetreten ist (vgl. § 201 BGB). Der Lauf der Verjährungsfrist ist von der Mitteilung der Kostenberechnung nicht abhängig (vgl. § 18 Abs. 1 Satz 2 BRAGebO). Daß der Anwalt den Auftraggeber in der gleichen Sache in höherer Instanz vertritt, führt nicht zur Hemmung oder Unterbrechung der Verjährungsfrist (vgl. Schumann, BRAGebO Anm. IV zu § 16). Bei Bewilligung des Armenrechts ist die Verjährung bis zur Anordnung der Nachzahlung (vgl. § 125 ZPO) gehemmt. Eine Verwirkung kommt neben der kurzen Verjährung, wie hier, grundsätzlich nicht in Frage.

Ansprüche der Parteien wegen der ihren Rechtsanwälten geleisteten nicht verbrauchten Vorschüsse und Zuvielzahlungen verjähren ebenfalls in zwei Jahren, und zwar beginnend mit dem Schluß des Jahres, in welchem der Auftrag erledigt wurde (vgl. § 196 Abs. 1 Nr. 16, §§ 198, 201 BGB).

II. Formelle Bestimmungen

1. a) Was das Verfahren der **Festsetzung der Anwaltsgebühren und -auslagen** (zwischen dem Anwalt oder Rechtsbeistand und dem vergütungspflichtigen Auftraggeber) anbetrifft, so lagen ihm die Bestimmungen des § 196 Abs. 4 SGG zugrunde (vgl. Tschischgale, SGb 1957, 34). Diese Vorschrift ist zusammen mit den übrigen Bestimmungen des § 196 SGG durch Art. X § 11 Nr. 6 KostÄndG aufgehoben worden. **Jetzt kommen** an sich auch hier **die allgemeinen Bestimmungen der Bundesrechtsanwaltsgebührenordnung in Frage.** Nach dem einschlägigen § 19 BRAGebO wird in der Regel die unbeglichene **gesetzliche** (nicht — höher — vereinbarte) **Vergütung** (Gebühren und Auslagen), die dem Rechtsanwalt (Rechtsbeistand) als Prozeßbevollmächtigtem, Beistand, Unterbevollmächtigtem oder Verkehrsanwalt zusteht, auf — entsprechend zu substantiierenden — Antrag des Rechtsanwalts oder seines Auftraggebers — nur diese bzw. ihre Rechtsnachfolger sind Beteiligte dieses Kostenfestsetzungsverfahrens — **durch den Urkundsbeamten** der Geschäftsstelle des Gerichts **(erster Instanz)** in völlig selbständiger Weise, und zwar für jede Instanz getrennt, **festgesetzt.** Unstreitig getilgte Beträge sind dabei abzusetzen (vgl. § 19 Abs. 1 BRAGebO). Der erteilte Auftrag ersetzt hier den Titel. Die Auftragserteilung muß daher feststehen.

Der die obere Festsetzungsgrenze bildende Antrag ist erst zulässig, wenn die Vergütung fällig ist (bei Bewilligung des Armenrechts tritt die Fälligkeit erst nach angeordneter Nachzahlung ein). Der Antrag ist nicht fristgebunden, er darf jedoch nicht treuwidrig spät, d. h. etwa erst nach 12 Monaten seit Fälligkeit der Vergütung oder gar später gestellt werden. Zuständig ist stets der Urkundsbeamte des ersten Rechtszuges, der in richterlicher Unabhängigkeit handelt (bei Verweisung der Urkundsbeamte des Gerichts, an das verwiesen ist, bei Verweisung an das Gericht eines anderen Verfahrens, wenn der Anwalt ausscheidet, der Urkundsbeamte des bisher befaßten Gerichts). Vor der Festsetzung ist der Gegner dieses Verfahrens zu hören. Die Vorschriften der ZPO (§§ 103ff.) über das Kostenfestsetzungsverfahren (mit dem es selbst nichts zu tun hat und von dem es völlig unabhängig ist) und über die **Zwangsvollstreckung aus Kostenfestsetzungsbeschlüssen** (§§ 704ff. ZPO) gelten sinngemäß. Beantragte Zinsen (vgl. § 104 Abs. 1 Satz 2 ZPO) sind vom Zeitpunkt der — zulässigen — Stellung des Festsetzungsantrages an zuzubilligen (in Höhe von 4%). Das Verfahren ist kostenfrei. Der Rechtsanwalt erhält in dem Verfahren vor dem Urkundsbeamten keine Gebühr (vgl. § 19 Abs. 2 BRAGebO).

Die Festsetzung ist auf jeden Fall abzulehnen, soweit der Auftraggeber — er kann dies noch im Anrufungs(Erinnerungs-)verfahren tun — (rechtshindernde, rechtshemmende oder rechtsvernichtende) Einwendungen oder Einreden erhebt, die nicht im Gebührenrecht ihren Grund haben (so wenn er überhaupt die Auftragserteilung bestreitet oder sich auf behauptete Stundung oder bestrittene Tilgung einschließlich Aufrechnung oder auf Verjährung oder Verwirkung durch Anwaltsverschulden beruft); es muß dann die Einklagung der Vergütung erfolgen. Hat der Auftraggeber bereits dem Rechtsanwalt gegenüber derartige Einwendungen oder Einreden erhoben, so ist die Erhebung der Klage nicht von der vorherigen Einleitung des Festsetzungsverfahrens abhängig (vgl. § 19 Abs. 4 BRAGebO). Die Einwendungen rechtsvernichtender und rechtshemmender (nicht rechtshindernder) Art können gegenüber einem erlassenen Kostenfestsetzungbeschluß stets auch noch im Wege der Vollstreckungsgegenklage erhoben werden; § 767 Abs. 2 ZPO paßt und gilt hier nicht (a. A. Gerold, BRAGebO Anm. 34 zu § 19). Ist die Vergütung ausgeklagt, so können im Wege der Vollstreckungsgegenklage aber nur Einwendungen geltend gemacht werden, die nach der Zusprechnung entstanden sind.

Anträge (auch auf Zuerkennung von Zinsen), Erklärungen u. ä. können zu Protokoll der Geschäftsstelle gegeben oder schriftlich ohne Mitwirkung eines Rechtsanwalts eingereicht werden (vgl. § 19 Abs. 5 BRAGebO).

Durch den Antrag auf Festsetzung der Vergütung wird die Verjährung wie durch Klageerhebung unterbrochen (§ 19 Abs. 6 BRAGebO).

b) **Gegen die Entscheidung des Urkundsbeamten kann** im Verfahren der Sozialgerichtsbarkeit vom Anwalt oder seinem jeweiligen Aufttaggeber (nur von diesen bzw. ihren Rechtsnachfolgern), und zwar wegen jeder Beschwer, nach dem § 178 SGG, der als spezielle Direktbestimmung des Sozialgerichtsgesetzes den im § 19 Abs. 2 BRAGebO in bezug genommenen allgemeinen § 104 Abs. 3 ZPO verdrängt (a. A. die die Gerichte nicht bindende Amtliche Begründung zu § 19 BRAGebO, BT-Drucks. 2545, 2. Wahlperiode S. 239 unter Nr. 6), binnen der im Sozialgerichtsverfahren stets gegebenen Regelfrist von einem Monat (nach dem § 104 Abs. 3 ZPO käme eine Notfrist von zwei Wochen in Betracht) nach Bekanntgabe (Zustellung nach § 63 Abs. 1 SGG) **das Gericht angerufen werden** (selbst wenn die Zweiwochenfrist des § 104 Abs. 3 ZPO für maßgebend gehalten würde, müßte bei verspäteter aber unter Einhaltung der Monatsfrist eingegangener Anrufung mit Rücksicht auf die generelle Monatsfrist des SGG für Rechtsbehelfe gemäß § 67 SGG die Wiedereinsetzung in den vorigen Stand gewährt werden, und zwar ohne Antrag). Das Gericht entscheidet bei Nichtabhilfe durch den jeweils bestellten Urkundsbeamten kostenfrei (§ 183 SGG) auf Grund eigenen Ermessens (§ 128 Abs. 1, § 142 Abs. 1 SGG) durch zu begründenden Beschluß (§ 142 Abs. 2 SGG) ohne mündliche Verhandlung (§ 124 Abs. 3 SGG), und zwar endgültig. (Wegen der Einzelheiten des Anrufungsverfahrens und der Entscheidung des Gerichts sowie ihrer Ausfertigung und Vollziehung vgl. das 6. Kap. 28.)

c) **Die** in § 104 Abs. 3 Satz 5 ZPO vorgesehene **Beschwerde ist im Verfahren der Sozialgerichtsbarkeit keinesfalls gegeben;** die einschlägige Spezialbestimmung des § 178 SGG schließt sie im Interesse einer beschleunigten Abwicklung des sozialgerichtlichen Verfahrens auf jeden Fall aus (vgl. hierzu auch § 189 Abs. 2, §§ 191, 197 Abs. 2 SGG, aus denen der allgemeingültige Grundsatz zu entnehmen ist, daß in sozialgerichtlichen Gebührenangelegenheiten die sogen. Anrufung des Gerichts — Erinnerung — der allein gegebene Rechtsbehelf ist). In das jeweils in Frage kommende spezialgesetzlich geregelte Gerichtsverfahren hat sich die universelle Bundesrechtsanwaltsgebührenordnung verfahrensrechtlich einzupassen. Eine die Anwaltsgebühren regelnde Gebührenordnung kann, auch in ihrem verfahrensrechtlichen Teil, nicht Gebührennachprüfungsinstanzen schaffen, die es als solche in der in Frage kommenden Spezialgerichtsbarkeit gar nicht gibt. Dazu bedürfte es auf jeden Fall der ergänzenden Änderung des Verfahrensgesetzes der betroffenen Gerichtsbarkeit; a. A. die Amtliche Begründung, aaO, die, was das Sozialgerichtsverfahren anbetrifft, nicht beachtet, daß gegebenenfalls dem endgültig mit den Anwaltskosten belasteten Erstattungspflichtigen (gegenüber dem kostenmäßig „obsiegenden" Anwalt bzw. dem Auftraggeber dieses Anwalts) in nicht zu rechtfertigender Weise ein kürzerer Rechtsmittelweg — vgl. den § 197 Abs. 2 SGG — zur Verfügung stehen würde als dem nur zwischenberechtigten und -verpflichteten Auftraggeber gegenüber dem letzten Endes kostenforderungsberechtigten Anwalt.

d) **Nun gilt** zwar nach § 19 Abs. 7 BRAGebO **die behandelte Vergütungsfestsetzung dann nicht, wenn,** wie vor den Gerichten der Sozialgerichtsbarkeit, **Rahmengebühren in Frage stehen.** Da nämlich die Ausfüllung des Gebührenrahmens gewisse Schwierigkeiten bereitet, soll hier die Geltendmachung der Anwaltsvergütung grundsätzlich im Klagewege erfolgen (vgl. § 12 BRAGebO; nach dem Absatz 2 dieser Bestimmung kann das Gericht nicht einmal ohne weiteres entscheiden, denn es hat vor seiner Entscheidung ein — als solches inhaltlich allerdings nicht bindendes — Gutachten des Vorstandes der Rechtsanwaltskammer einzuholen). **Die Verweisung auf den** umständlichen und kostspieligen **Klageweg ist** — abgesehen selbstverständlich von den Fällen des § 19 Abs. 4 BRAGebO — dann **aber grund- und sinnlos, wenn** vom Anwalt von vornherein **nur die** gesetzliche **Mindestgebühr verlangt wird.** Hier kann billiger- und vernünftigerweise dem Anwalt (Rechtsbeistand) keinesfalls der kurze, leicht und kostenlos gangbare Wege der Festsetzung durch den Urkundsbeamten des mit der Sache befaßt gewesenen Sozialgerichts vorenthalten werden, um bei unterbleibender oder stockender Schuldnerzahlung zu einem Vollstreckungstitel zu gelangen. Das liegt letzten Endes auch im Interesse der zahlungspflichtigen Partei (vgl. hierzu Tschischgale, SGb 1958, 107).

Da der Anwalt im Armenrechtsverfahren und vor allem in der Zwangsvollstreckung feste Gebühren erhält (s. o. I A 1 s, y), ist die Festsetzung der hier verdienten Vergütung gegen den Auftraggeber nach § 19 BRAGebO (durch den Urkundsbeamten des tätig gewesenen Sozialgerichts) ohne Bedenken möglich (vgl. Gerold, BRAGebO Anm. 5 und 8 zu § 19).

2. **Verlangt der Anwalt** (Rechtsbeistand) **eine über den Mindestsatz hinausgehende gesetzliche oder vereinbarte Gebühr,** so **muß er** nötigenfalls **den Klageweg beschreiten** (vgl. § 12 BRAGebO und dazu die Amtliche Begründung, BT-Drucks. 2545, 2. Wahlperiode S. 234). **Zuständig** für die Gebührenklage **ist** in allen Fällen (auch bei Unzulässigkeit der Festsetzung wegen gebührenfremder Einwendungen des Auftraggebers) **das** örtlich und sachlich bestimmte **ordentliche Gericht,** dessen Zuständigkeit auch für insoweitige Vollstreckungsgegenklagen gegeben ist (vgl. Brangsch, SGb 1957, 238 und 1958, 179, ferner Brocke-Reese, Geb u. KostR Anh. S. 29, Mellwitz, SGb 1958, 105, Riedel-Sußbauer, BRAGebO Anm. 27 zu § 19). Auch über § 202 SGG und § 34 ZPO kann die Zuständigkeit der Sozialgerichte nicht begründet werden, da diesen hier nach der heute herrschenden Ansicht die Sachbefugnis zur Entscheidung nicht zusteht (vgl. Mellwitz, SGb 1958, 105).

Vor den ordentlichen Gerichten kann selbstverständlich auch der Weg des Mahnverfahrens beschritten werden.

Vor seiner Entscheidung hat das Gericht ein Gutachten des Vorstandes der Rechtsanwaltskammer einzuholen (§ 12 Abs. 2 BRAGebO). An das Gutachten ist das Gericht inhaltlich nicht gebunden.

3. **Rechtskräftig ausgeklagte oder festgesetzte Gebühren- und Auslagenforderungen** des Anwalts (Rechtsbeistandes) **verjähren** nach § 218 BGB **in 30 Jahren** (hinsichtlich zukünftiger Zinsen vgl. § 218 Abs. 2 und § 197 BGB). Vorherige Verwirkung ist hier möglich. (Vgl. dazu insgesamt Tschischgale, AnwBl. 1958, 181.)

Achtes Kapitel

Die Armenanwaltskosten und ihre Festsetzung

SGG: §§ 167, 178, 202, 216 Abs. 1 Nr. 2
ZPO: § 104 Abs. 2, §§ 114, 115 Abs. 2, §§ 117, 118, 118a, 121, 122, 124, 125, 126, 127
BRAGebO: §§ 121, 122, 123, 124, 125, 126, 127, 128, 129, 130

§ 167 SGG

Armenrecht

(1) Einem Beteiligten, der nicht nach § 166 Abs. 2 Satz 1 vertreten ist, kann für das Verfahren vor dem Bundessozialgericht das Armenrecht bewilligt und ein Rechtsanwalt als Prozeßbevollmächtigter beigeordnet werden.

(2) Für das Verfahren gelten §§ 114, 115 Abs. 2, §§ 117 bis 118a, 121, 122 und 124 bis 127 der Zivilprozeßordnung entsprechend.

§ 178 SGG

Anrufung des Gerichts gegen Entscheidungen des ersuchten oder beauftragten Richters oder des Urkundsbeamten

Gegen die Entscheidungen des ersuchten oder beauftragten Richters oder des Urkundsbeamten kann binnen eines Monats nach Bekanntgabe das Gericht angerufen werden, das endgültig entscheidet. §§ 173 bis 175 gelten entsprechend.

§ 202 SGG

Entsprechende Anwendung der ZPO

Soweit dieses Gesetz keine Bestimmungen über das Verfahren enthält, sind das Gerichtsverfassungsgesetz und die Zivilprozeßordnung entsprechend anzuwenden, wenn die grundsätzlichen Unterschiede der beiden Verfahrensarten dies nicht ausschließen.

§ 216 Abs. 1 Nr. 2 SGG

Beschlußentscheidung ohne Laienbeisitzer

(1) Bis zum 31. Dezember 1960 kann

2. der Vorsitzende bei dem Sozialgericht, das Landessozialgericht ohne Zuziehung der Landessozialrichter und das Bundessozialgericht ohne Zuziehung der Bundessozialrichter außerhalb der mündlichen Verhandlung Beschlüsse erlassen, die der Entscheidung in der Sache selbst vorausgehen.

§ 104 Abs. 2 ZPO

Glaubhaftmachung des Kostenansatzes

Zur Berücksichtigung eines Ansatzes genügt, daß er glaubhaft gemacht ist. Hinsichtlich der einem Rechtsanwalt erwachsenen Auslagen an Post-, Telegrafen- und Fernsprechgebühren genügt die Versicherung des Rechtsanwalts, daß diese Auslagen entstanden sind.

§ 114 ZPO

Voraussetzungen der Armenrechtsbewilligung

(1) Einer Partei, die außerstande ist, ohne Beeinträchtigung des für sie und ihre Familie notwendigen Unterhalts die Kosten des Prozesses zu bestreiten, ist auf Antrag das Armenrecht zu bewilligen, wenn die beabsichtigte Rechtsverfolgung oder Rechtsverteidigung eine hinreichende Aussicht auf Erfolg bietet und nicht mutwillig erscheint. Die Rechtsverfolgung ist auch dann als mutwillig anzusehen, wenn mit Rücksicht auf die für die Beitreibung des Anspruchs bestehenden Aussichten eine nicht das Armenrecht beanspruchende Partei von einer Prozeßführung absehen oder nur einen Teil des Anspruchs geltend machen würde.

(2) Angehörige fremder Staaten haben auf das Armenrecht nur insoweit Anspruch, als die Gegenseitigkeit verbürgt ist. Einem Staatenlosen kann das Armenrecht gewährt werden, wenn es ihm als Inländer zu gewähren wäre.

(3) Einer Partei kraft Amtes kann bei Vorliegen der im Abs. 1 bezeichneten Voraussetzungen das Armenrecht bewilligt werden, wenn die zur Führung des Prozesses erforderlichen Mittel weder aus der verwalteten Vermögensmasse noch von den an der Führung des Prozesses wirtschaftlich Beteiligten aufgebracht werden können.

(4) Einer inländischen juristischen Person kann bei Vorliegen der im Abs. 1 bezeichneten Voraussetzungen das Armenrecht bewilligt werden, wenn die zur Führung des Prozesses erforderlichen Mittel weder von ihr noch von den an der Führung des Prozesses wirtschaftlich Beteiligten aufgebracht werden können und die Unterlassung der Rechtsverfolgung oder Rechtsverteidigung allgemeinen Interessen zuwiderlaufen würde.

§ 115 Abs. 2 ZPO

Teilarmenrecht

Ist die arme Partei imstande, die Kosten des Prozesses ohne Beeinträchtigung des für sie und ihre Familie notwendigen Unterhalts zu einem Teil zu bestreiten, so ist zu bestimmen, daß wegen dieses Teiles die einstweilige Befreiung von der Berichtigung der Gerichtskosten sowie der Gebühren und Auslagen des Anwalts nicht eintritt; das Gericht kann statt dessen auch bestimmte Gebühren ganz oder teilweise von der Befreiung ausnehmen. In den Fällen des § 114 Abs. 2 Satz 2, Abs. 3 und 4 gelten diese Vorschriften entsprechend.

§ 117 ZPO

Kostenerstattung trotz Armenrechtsbewilligung

Die Bewilligung des Armenrechts hat auf die Verpflichtung zur Erstattung der dem Gegner erwachsenden Kosten keinen Einfluß.

§ 118 ZPO

Armenrechtsgesuch

(1) Das Gesuch um Bewilligung des Armenrechts ist bei dem Prozeßgericht anzubringen; es kann vor der Geschäftsstelle zu Protokoll erklärt werden.

(2) Dem Gesuch ist ein von der zuständigen Behörde der Partei ausgestelltes Zeugnis beizufügen, in dem unter Angabe des Standes oder Gewerbes, der Vermögens- und Familienverhältnisse der Partei sowie des Betrages der von dieser zu entrichtenden direkten Steuern das Unvermögen zur Bestreitung der Prozeßkosten ausdrücklich bezeugt wird. Für Personen, die unter Vormundschaft oder Pflegschaft stehen, kann das Zeugnis auch von der vormundschaftlichen Behörde ausgestellt werden; soll von einem unehelichen Kinde ein Anspruch auf Unterhalt gegen seinen Vater geltend gemacht werden, so bedarf es des Zeugnisses nicht.

(3) In dem Gesuch ist das Streitverhältnis unter Angabe der Beweismittel darzulegen.

§ 118a ZPO

Vorbereitung der Entscheidung und Vergleich

(1) Das Gericht kann verlangen, daß der Antragsteller seine tatsächlichen Angaben glaubhaft macht. Es soll, wenn dies nicht aus besonderen Gründen unzweckmäßig erscheint, vor der Bewilligung des Armenrechts den Gegner hören. Es kann auch, soweit dies ohne erhebliche Verzögerung möglich ist, Erhebungen anstellen, insbesondere die Vorlegung von Urkunden anordnen und von Behörden Auskünfte einholen. Die Vernehmung von Zeugen oder Sachverständigen ist nur zulässig, wenn der Sachverhalt, soweit dies zur Entscheidung über das Armenrechtsgesuch erforderlich ist, auf andere Weise nicht hinreichend geklärt werden kann; eine Beeidigung findet nicht statt.

(2) Die im Abs. 1 bezeichneten Maßnahmen sind von dem Vorsitzenden oder einem von ihm beauftragten Mitglied des Gerichts oder einem von ihm ersuchten Richter durchzuführen. Die Anhörung des Gegners kann auch zu Protokoll der Geschäftsstelle des Prozeßgerichts oder des ersuchten Gerichts erfolgen.

(3) Einigen sich die Parteien bei der Anhörung des Gegners über den streitigen Anspruch, so ist der Vergleich zu richterlichem Protokoll zu nehmen.

(4) Eine Erstattung der dem Gegner durch die Anhörung gemäß Abs. 1 Satz 2 erwachsenen Kosten findet nicht statt. Die durch die Vernehmung von Zeugen und Sachverständigen gemäß Abs. 1 Satz 3 entstandenen Auslagen sind als Gerichtskosten von der Partei zu tragen, der die Kosten des Rechtsstreits auferlegt sind.

§ 121 ZPO

Entziehung des Armenrechts

Das Armenrecht kann zu jeder Zeit entzogen werden, wenn sich ergibt, daß eine Voraussetzung der Bewilligung nicht vorhanden war oder nicht mehr vorhanden ist.

§ 122 ZPO

Erlöschen des Armenrechts mit dem Tod des Armen

Das Armenrecht erlischt mit dem Tode der Person, der es bewilligt ist.

§ 124 ZPO

Beitreibungsrecht des Armenanwalts

(1) Die für die arme Partei bestellten Rechtsanwälte sind berechtigt, ihre Gebühren und Auslagen von dem in die Prozeßkosten verurteilten Gegner beizutreiben.

(2) Eine Einrede aus der Person der armen Partei ist nur insoweit zulässig, als die Aufrechnung von Kosten verlangt wird, die nach der in demselben Rechtsstreit über die Kosten erlassenen Entscheidung von der armen Partei zu erstatten sind.

§ 125 ZPO

Nachzahlungsanordnung

(1) Die zum Armenrecht zugelassene Partei ist zur Nachzahlung der Beträge, von deren Berichtigung sie einstweilen befreit war, verpflichtet, sobald sie ohne Beeinträchtigung des für sie und ihre Familie notwendigen Unterhalts dazu imstande ist.

(2) Das gleiche gilt für die Beträge, von deren Berichtigung der Gegner einstweilen befreit war, soweit die arme Partei in die Prozeßkosten verurteilt ist.

§ 126 ZPO

Entscheidungen im Armenrechtsverfahren

(1) Über das Gesuch um Bewilligung des Armenrechts, über seine Entziehung und über die Verpflichtung zur Nachzahlung der Beträge, von deren Berichtigung die zum Armenrecht zugelassene Partei oder der Gegner einstweilen befreit ist, kann ohne mündliche Verhandlung entschieden werden.

(2) Dem Beschluß, durch den das Armenrecht verweigert oder entzogen wird, soll, sofern dies nicht nach Lage des Falles entbehrlich oder unzweckmäßig erscheint, eine kurze Begründung beigefügt werden, aus der die für die Entscheidung maßgebenden rechtlichen oder tatsächlichen Gründe ersichtlich sind.

(3) Vor der Entscheidung über die Verpflichtung zur Nachzahlung sind die zum Armenrecht zugelassene Partei, die Bundes- oder Staatskasse und der beigeordnete Rechtsanwalt zu hören. Wird die Nachzahlung nicht in voller Höhe angeordnet oder werden Teilzahlungen bewilligt, so ist auszusprechen, daß auf die Forderung der Bundes- oder Staatskasse und auf die Forderung des beigeordneten Rechtsanwalts je zur Hälfte zu zahlen ist.

§ 127 ZPO

Anfechtung der Armenrechtsentscheidungen

Der Beschluß, durch den das Armenrecht bewilligt wird, ist unanfechtbar. Gegen den Beschluß, durch den das Armenrecht verweigert oder entzogen oder die Nachzahlung von Kosten angeordnet wird, findet die Beschwerde statt; dies gilt nicht, wenn das Berufungsgericht den Beschluß erlassen hat. Eine weitere Beschwerde ist ausgeschlossen.

§ 121 BRAGebO

Vergütung des Armenanwalts aus der Staatskasse

Der im Armenrecht oder nach § 11a des Arbeitsgerichtsgesetzes beigeordnete Rechtsanwalt erhält, soweit in diesem Abschnitt nichts anderes bestimmt ist, die gesetzliche Vergütung in Verfahren vor Gerichten des Bundes aus der Bundeskasse, in Verfahren vor Gerichten eines Landes aus der Landeskasse.

§ 122 BRAGebO

Vergütung nach dem Umfang der Beiordnung

(1) Der Anspruch des Rechtsanwalts bestimmt sich nach den Beschlüssen, durch die das Armenrecht bewilligt und der Rechtsanwalt beigeordnet worden ist.

(2) Der Rechtsanwalt erhält Vergütung aus der Bundes- oder Landeskasse, wenn er für eine Berufung oder Revision beigeordnet ist, auch für die Rechtsverteidigung gegen eine Anschlußberufung oder eine Anschlußrevision und, wenn er für die Erwirkung eines Arrests oder einer einstweiligen Verfügung beigeordnet ist, auch für die Vollziehung des Arrests oder der einstweiligen Verfügung. Dies gilt nicht, wenn der Beiordnungsbeschluß ausdrücklich bestimmt, daß der Rechtsanwalt für die Rechtsverteidigung gegen die Anschlußberufung oder Anschlußrevision oder für die Vollziehung des Arrests oder der einstweiligen Verfügung nicht beigeordnet ist.

(3) In Angelegenheiten, die mit dem Hauptprozeß nur zusammenhängen, erhält der für den Hauptprozeß beigeordnete Rechtsanwalt Vergütung aus der Bundes- oder Landeskasse nur dann, wenn er ausdrücklich auch hierfür beigeordnet ist. Dies gilt insbesondere für

1. die Zwangsvollstreckung (den Verwaltungszwang);
2. das Verfahren über den Arrest, die einstweilige Verfügung und die einstweilige Anordnung;
3. das Beweissicherungsverfahren;
4. das Verfahren über die Widerklage, ausgenommen die Rechtsverteidigung gegen die Widerklage in Ehesachen;
5. den Abschluß eines Unterhaltsvergleichs im Zusammenhang mit einer Ehesache.

§ 123 BRAGebO

Normalgebühren des Armenanwalts

(1) An die Stelle der vollen Gebühr (§ 11 Abs. 1 Satz 1) treten bei einem Gegenstandswert

bis 20 DM				2 DM
von mehr als	20 bis	50 DM		4 DM
von mehr als	50 bis	100 DM		6 DM
von mehr als	100 bis	150 DM		8 DM
von mehr als	150 bis	200 DM		10 DM
von mehr als	200 bis	300 DM		14 DM
von mehr als	300 bis	400 DM		17 DM
von mehr als	400 bis	500 DM		19 DM
von mehr als	500 bis	600 DM		21 DM
von mehr als	600 bis	700 DM		23 DM
von mehr als	700 bis	800 DM		25 DM
von mehr als	800 bis	900 DM		27 DM
von mehr als	900 bis	1000 DM		29 DM
von mehr als	1000 bis	1100 DM		31 DM
von mehr als	1100 bis	1200 DM		33 DM
von mehr als	1200 bis	1300 DM		35 DM
von mehr als	1300 bis	1400 DM		37 DM
von mehr als	1400 bis	1500 DM		39 DM
von mehr als	1500 bis	1600 DM		41 DM
von mehr als	1600 bis	1700 DM		43 DM
von mehr als	1700 bis	1800 DM		45 DM
von mehr als	1800 bis	1900 DM		47 DM
von mehr als	1900 bis	2000 DM		49 DM
von mehr als	2000 DM			54 DM.

(2) In Ehesachen, in landgerichtlichen Verfahren, welche die Feststellung des Rechtsverhältnisses zwischen Eltern und Kindern zum Gegenstand haben, und in landgerichtlichen Entmündigungssachen tritt an die Stelle der vollen Gebühr unabhängig vom Gegenstandswert der feste Betrag von 50 Deutsche Mark. Im Verfahren über Anträge nach den

§§ 627, 627b der Zivilprozeßordnung ist der Höchstbetrag einer vollen Gebühr 30 Deutsche Mark.

(3) Im Berufungs- und Revisionsverfahren erhöhen sich die im Absatz 1 und im Absatz 2 Satz 1 genannten Beträge um drei Zehntel.

(4) Der Mindestbetrag einer Gebühr ist zwei Deutsche Mark.

§ 124 BRAGebO

Vergütung bei Bruchteilsarmenrecht

Ist die einstweilige Befreiung von der Berichtigung der Gebühren des Rechtsanwalts nur für einen Bruchteil der Gebühren bewilligt, so erhält der beigeordnete Rechtsanwalt einen entsprechenden Bruchteil der in § 123 Abs. 1, 2 und 3 bestimmten Beträge. § 123 Abs. 4 bleibt unberührt.

§ 125 BRAGebO

Verwirkung des Vergütungsanspruchs durch Verschulden des Armenanwalts

Hat der beigeordnete Rechtsanwalt durch schuldhaftes Verhalten die Beiordnung eines anderen Rechtsanwalts veranlaßt, so kann er Gebühren, die auch für den anderen Rechtsanwalt entstehen, nicht fordern.

§ 126 BRAGebO

Vergütung der Auslagen des Armenanwalts

(1) Auslagen, insbesondere Reisekosten, werden nicht vergütet, wenn sie zur sachgemäßen Wahrnehmung der Interessen der armen Partei nicht erforderlich waren. Nicht zu vergüten sind die Mehrkosten, die dadurch entstehen, daß der Rechtsanwalt seinen Wohnsitz oder seine Kanzlei nicht an dem Ort hat, an dem sich das Prozeßgericht oder eine auswärtige Abteilung dieses Gerichts befindet; dies gilt nicht, wenn ein Rechtsanwalt beigeordnet wird, der weder bei dem Prozeßgericht noch bei einem Gericht zugelassen ist, das sich an demselben Ort wie das Prozeßgericht befindet.

(2) Ob eine Reise erforderlich ist, stellt das Gericht des Rechtszuges auf Antrag vor Antritt der Reise fest. Die Feststellung, daß die Reise erforderlich ist, ist für das Festsetzungsverfahren (§ 128) bindend.

§ 127 BRAGebO

Auslagenvorschuß des Armenanwalts

(1) Gebührenvorschuß kann der beigeordnete Rechtsanwalt nicht fordern.

(2) Für die voraussichtlich erwachsenden Auslagen kann der Rechtsanwalt aus der Bundes- oder Landeskasse angemessenen Vorschuß for-

dem, soweit ihm, insbesondere wegen der Höhe der Auslagen, nicht zugemutet werden kann, diese aus eigenen Mitteln vorzuschießen. § 128 gilt sinngemäß.

§ 128 BRAGebO

Die Armenanwaltskostenfestsetzung

(1) Die aus der Bundes- oder Landeskasse zu gewährende Vergütung wird auf Antrag des Rechtsanwalts von dem Urkundsbeamten der Geschäftsstelle des Gerichts des Rechtszugs festgesetzt; § 104 Abs. 2 der Zivilprozeßordnung gilt sinngemäß.

(2) Über Erinnerungen des Rechtsanwalts und der Bundes- oder Landeskasse gegen die Festsetzung entscheidet das Gericht des Rechtszugs durch Beschluß. § 4 Abs. 1 Satz 2, 3, 4 und Abs. 3 des Gerichtskostengesetzes gilt sinngemäß.

(3) Gegen den Beschluß ist die Beschwerde zulässig, wenn der Beschwerdegegenstand 50 Deutsche Mark übersteigt. § 4 Abs. 2 und 3 des Gerichtskostengesetzes gilt sinngemäß. Eine Beschwerde an ein oberes Bundesgericht ist nicht zulässig.

(4) Der Rechtsanwalt erhält für die in den Absätzen 1 bis 3 genannten Verfahren keine Vergütung.

§ 129 BRAGebO

Anrechnung von Vorschüssen und Zahlungen auf die Armenanwaltsvergütung

Vorschüsse und Zahlungen, die der Rechtsanwalt von seinem Auftraggeber oder einem Dritten vor oder nach der Beiordnung erhalten hat, sind zunächst auf die Vergütungen anzurechnen, für die ein Anspruch gegen die Bundes- oder Landeskasse nicht besteht.

§ 130 BRAGebO

Übergang der Ansprüche des Armenanwalts auf die befriedigende Staatskasse

(1) Soweit dem Rechtsanwalt wegen seiner Vergütung ein Anspruch gegen die Partei oder einen ersatzpflichtigen Gegner zusteht, geht der Anspruch mit der Befriedigung des Rechtsanwalts durch die Bundes- oder Landeskasse auf diese über. Der Übergang kann nicht zum Nachteil des Rechtsanwalts geltend gemacht werden.

(2) Für die Geltendmachung des Anspruchs gelten die Vorschriften über die Einziehung der Kosten des gerichtlichen Verfahrens sinngemäß.

Spezialabhandlungen des Verfassers: Das Armenrecht im Verfahren der Sozialgerichtsbarkeit, NJW 1957, 164; Das Rückgriffsrecht der Staatskasse im Armenrechtsverfahren der Zivil-, Arbeits- und Sozialgerichtsbarkeit, JVBl. 1957, 4; Das Beitreibungsrecht des Armenanwalts gegenüber dem unterlegenen Gegner im Verfahren der Sozialgerichtsbarkeit, JurBüro 1957, 89; Der Übergang zum neuen Kostenrecht im Verfahren der Sozialgerichtsbarkeit, SGb 1958, 107.

I. Das Armenrechtsverfahren und die Beiordnung des Armenanwalts

Übersicht

1. Nach herrschender Ansicht in Rechtslehre (vgl. Mellwitz, SGG Anm. 32 zu § 73 und Mitt. BfA 1954, 120; Brocke, Sozialrichter S. 149; Schablin, BG 1954, 113; Miesbach-Ankenbrank, SGG Einf. II B 8) und Rechtsprechung (BSG, SozR SGG § 167 Bl. Da 5 Nr. 8; LSG Nordrhein-Westfalen in Breith. 1954, 654 und in BG 1954, 361 = ZfS 1955, 221 Nr. 70 und 71; LSG Baden-Württemberg, BB 1954, 1064;

LSG Schleswig-Holstein, BG 1954, 445) ist im Verfahren der Sozialgerichtsbarkeit die **Bewilligung des Armenrechts** (mit der Beiordnung eines Armenanwalts) zugunsten eines Beteiligten lediglich vor dem **Bundessozialgericht** möglich, und zwar hier auch nur dann, wenn der Beteiligte nicht kraft Satzung oder Vollmacht zur Prozeßvertretung von einem Mitgliede oder Angestellten einer Gewerkschaft, einer selbständigen Vereinigung von Arbeitnehmern mit sozial- oder berufspolitischer Zwecksetzung, einer Vereinigung von Arbeitgebern oder einer Vereinigung der Kriegsopfer vertreten werden kann (vor allem mangels Mitgliedschaft; vgl. § 167 Abs. 1 SGG). Den Nichtorganisierten soll hier bei vorhandener Armut auf jeden Fall die Möglichkeit eingeräumt sein, den dritten Rechtszug zu beschreiten, vor dem alle Beteiligten, soweit es sich nicht um Behörden oder Körperschaften des öffentlichen Rechts oder öffentlich-rechtliche Anstalten handelt (vgl. § 166 Abs. 1 SGG und dazu BSG, NJW 1956, 1336), durch Prozeßbevollmächtigte vertreten sein müssen. Als zugelassene Prozeßbevollmächtigte kommen dabei nach § 166 Abs. 2 SGG außer den bevollmächtigten Mitgliedern oder Angestellten der erwähnten Gewerkschaften und Vereinigungen — stehen sie den Beteiligten zur Verfügung, so kommt die Beiordnung eines Anwalts wie überhaupt die Armenrechtsbewilligung nicht in Betracht — nur die bei einem deutschen Gericht zugelassenen Rechtsanwälte in Frage.

Zwar ist nicht zu verkennen, daß sich der § 167 SGG seinem ausdrücklichen Wortlaute zufolge nur auf das Verfahren vor dem Bundessozialgericht bezieht. Aber lediglich in bezug auf dieses Verfahren war eine seine Eigenart — insbesondere hinsichtlich der Vertretungsfähigkeit — berücksichtigende Spezialregelung überhaupt erforderlich. Dagegen war, soweit es sich um die ebenfalls gebotene Bewilligung des Armenrechts (mit Anwaltsbeiordnung) im übrigen, d. h. im Verfahren vor den Sozialgerichten und den Landessozialgerichten handelt, wegen der allgemeinen Bezugnahme auf die Bestimmungen der ZPO im § 202 SGG eine sie ausdrücklich zulassende Regelung nicht notwendig (vgl. Tschischgale, NJW 1957, 164ff.). Allerdings kann vor diesen grundsätzlich schon allgemein kostenfrei tätig werdenden Gerichten derjenige, der nicht organisiert ist und auf Grund seines in einem echten demokratischen Staatswesen zu achtenden Willensentschlusses auch in Zukunft nicht organisiert sein will, sich ohne weiteres durch eine beliebige volljährige Person vertreten lassen oder nötigenfalls sich selbst vertreten (§§ 73, 71 SGG). Jede verfahrensregelnde Rechtsordnung, wenn sie wirklich eine solche sein soll, muß aber der Tatsache Rechnung tragen, daß sowohl diese Vertretung durch einen anderen als auch die Selbstvertretung in einzelnen Fällen nicht möglich ist. Das hat insbesondere für das Verfahren der Sozialgerichtsbarkeit zu gelten. Gerade unter den Kriegsopfern gibt es nämlich nicht selten in jeder Hinsicht zurückgezogen lebende, mittellose Einzelgänger, denen niemand zur Seite steht und die infolge körperlicher oder geistiger Gebrechen, die andererseits nicht so stark zu sein pflegen, daß es zur Bestellung eines Vormundes oder Pflegers kommt, sich jedenfalls auch nicht selbst vertreten können. Die Hilfe, welche die Versicherungsämter gewähren können, reicht hier keinesfalls aus. Daß vor den Instanzgerichten der Sozialgerichtsbarkeit die Verpflichtung zur Aufklärung des Sachverhalts von Amts wegen besteht, schafft ebenfalls keine Abhilfe; die Grundlagen des Falles müssen nämlich auch hier von den Beteiligten vorgebracht werden. Für die erwähnten Beteiligten muß daher aus rechtsstaatlichen Gründen die Bewilligung des Armenrechts und die Beiordnung eines Armenanwalts möglich sein (vgl. hierzu Art. 20 Abs. 1 GG: „Die Bundesrepublik Deutschland ist ein demokratischer und s o z i a l e r Bundesstaat"). Das ist bei richtiger Betrachtungsweise auch der Fall.

a) Auf Grund der allgemeinen Bestimmungen der §§ 114ff. ZPO ist in einem **jeden Verfahrenszug** die im Sozialgerichtsgesetz für die unteren Gerichtsinstanzen nicht ausgeschlossene, über § 202 SGG daher auch hier zugelassene Armenrechtsbewilligung möglich und bei entsprechender Lage der Umstände geboten, und zwar unter **Beiordnung eines Rechtsanwalts**, der als solcher der berufene und geeignete Vertreter von gerichtlich wahrzunehmenden Parteibelangen ist. Diese Beiordnungsmöglichkeit ergibt sich aus einer weiteren Allgemeinbestimmung, die der damalige Gesetzgeber, um ihre prozessuale Universalität zu unterstreichen, glaubte, in die Anwaltsordnung (§ 34 ders.) bringen zu müssen, obwohl sie richtigerweise in die ZPO als die in Frage kommende Hauptverfahrensordnung gehört. Sie lautet: „Einer Partei, welcher das Armenrecht bewilligt ist, kann, auch insoweit eine Vertretung durch Rechtsanwälte nicht geboten ist, zur vorläufig unentgeltlichen Wahrnehmung ihrer Rechte von dem Prozeßgericht ein Rechtsanwalt auf Antrag beigeordnet werden.“ Daß es sich bei dieser Bestimmung ihrem Inhalt zufolge um eine solche handelt, die rechtssystematisch in die Zivilprozeßordnung gehört, ergibt sich daraus, daß aus dem § 34 RAO der § 116 Abs. 1 ZPO werden soll (vgl. die Amtliche Begründung zum Entwurf einer Bundesrechtsanwaltsordnung, BT-Drucks. 1014, 2. Wahlperiode S. 133). Dem allen steht nicht etwa die Regelung des § 73 SGG entgegen, der übrigens die Vertretung durch einen Anwalt (Anwalt und Armenanwalt stehen weitestgehend nebeneinander) mit erfaßt und damit zuläßt. Der § 73 SGG enthält nämlich bestimmte Verfahrensgrundsätze, gibt jedoch, wie sein Inhalt erkennen läßt, keine abschließende Regelung. Selbst wenn aber der Gesetzgeber eine solche an sich gewollt haben sollte, käme es auf seinen Willensentschluß nicht an; denn maßgebend ist — wie immer im Rechtsverkehr und Rechtsleben — allein der erklärte objektivierte Wille, so wie er sich aus dem Wortlaut des Gesetzes unter Beachtung des Zusammenhanges sinngemäß ergibt (BVerfGE 1, 299 [312]; Leitsatz in NJW 1952, 737).

Richtigerweise kann und muß daher davon ausgegangen werden, daß heute schon (so neuerdings auch Luetgebrune-Lotze, BRAGebO Anm. VI zu § 116 und Anm. I zu § 121), ohne daß das vielfach gewünschte Eingreifen des Gesetzgebers, das — nur — klarstellend wirken würde, abgewartet werden müßte, auch vor den Sozialgerichten und den Landessozialgerichten eine Armenrechtsbewilligung, und zwar unter Anwaltsbeiordnung, möglich ist. (Wenn es im Gesetz heißt: Das Gericht *kann* beiordnen . . ., so bedeutet dies, daß nach pflichtgemäßem Ermessen eine Prüfung in der fraglichen Richtung vorzunehmen ist, auf Grund der bei entsprechendem Ausfall die Beiordnung zu erfolgen *hat*.) Dem steht auch nicht entgegen, daß im § 167 Abs. 2 SGG der § 119 ZPO nicht für entsprechend anwendbar erklärt ist. (Darauf hat sich das BSG, aaO, bei seiner Ablehnung gestützt.) Denn der Absatz 1 des § 119 ZPO enthält den sich ohne weiteres von selbst verstehenden Grundsatz, daß die Bewilligung des Armenrechts für jeden Rechtszug besonders zu erfolgen hat. Was das im § 119 Abs. 1 ZPO noch erwähnte Armenrecht für die Zwangsvollstreckung anbetrifft, so kommt seine Bewilligung durch die Sozialgerichte überhaupt nicht in Frage (s. u. 2c). Der Satz 1 des § 119 Abs. 2 ZPO, nach dem es im höheren Rechtszuge des Nachweises des Unvermögens nicht bedarf, wenn das Armenrecht in der vorhergehenden Instanz bewilligt war, ist sachlich nicht unbedenklich, da sich während der Dauer des unteren Rechtszuges die wirtschaftlichen Verhältnisse des Beteiligten grundlegend geändert haben können. Dieser Satz war und ist daher nicht dazu angetan, zu einer Maxime einer neuen Verfahrensordnung zu werden. Das hat auch von der Bestimmung des Satzes 2 des zweiten Absatzes von § 119 ZPO zu gelten. Nach ihr ist in dem höheren Rechtszuge nicht zu prüfen, ob die Rechtsverfolgung oder Rechtsverteidigung hinreichende Aussicht auf Erfolg bietet oder mutwillig erscheint, wenn der Gegner das Rechtsmittel eingelegt hat (sog. notwendiges Armenrecht). Gerade dieser Satz hat nämlich durch die Rechtsprechung starke Einschränkungen erfahren (vgl. OLG Celle, DRZ 1949, 499), weil sich die Lage der Sache, z. B. durch Wandel der Gesetzgebung, zwischenzeitlich völlig geändert haben kann. Aus der Nichteinbeziehung des § 119 ZPO kann daher insgesamt nichts Entscheidendes entnommen werden.

b) Nach § 217 Abs. 1 SGG sind bis zu einer einheitlichen Regelung **Verwaltungsrechtsräte** den Rechtsanwälten gleich zu behandeln. Nach § 217 Abs. 2 SGG gilt als Verwaltungsrechtsrat zunächst auch derjenige, der auf Grund der vorgeschriebenen Prüfungen die Fähigkeit zum höheren Verwaltungsdienst hat und dem das Auftreten vor den Gerichten der Verwaltungsgerichtsbarkeit allgemein gestattet ist. Auch die im § 217 SGG bezeichneten Personen können daher ohne weiteres als Armenanwälte beigeordnet werden.

c) Von der nur für die Instanzgerichte in Frage kommenden, an sich hier nicht ausgeschlossenen Möglichkeit (vgl. § 202 SGG) der Beiordnung eines **Gerichtsbeamten** oder eines **Rechtskundigen** (Referendar) — vgl. § 116 ZPO —, die sich allgemeinhin nicht bewährt hat, wird im Verfahren vor den Sozialgerichten und den Landessozialgerichten kaum Gebrauch gemacht werden. (Diesen Beigeordneten werden aus der Staatskasse lediglich die notwendigen Barauslagen ersetzt; die Staatskasse kann diese Auslagen im Sozialgerichtsverfahren nur dann ersetzt verlangen, wenn sie einem Beteiligten gemäß § 192 SGG unter den dort aufgeführten Voraussetzungen zur Tragung auferlegt worden sind, vgl. § 116 ZPO in Verb. mit §§ 192, 202 SGG).

d) Die Beiordnung eines **Rechtsbeistandes** ist in dem hierfür an sich geeigneten Verfahren vor den Sozialgerichten und den Landessozialgerichten nicht irgendwie vorgesehen. Sie dürfte alles in allem nur in Not- oder Sonderfällen in Frage kommen (vgl. hierzu die AV des RJM vom 9. 5. 1942, DJ 330, die zwar auf die Verhältnisse des vergangenen Krieges abgestellt ist, aber ihren inhaltlichen Sinn nicht verloren hat; im Ergebnis — für das Verwaltungsgerichtsverfahren — ebenso Schatte, Verwaltungsgerichtliches Kostenrecht S. 256, für Berlin vgl. JR 1951, 415).

2. a) Zu bemerken ist, daß — entsprechend dem im § 119 Abs. 1 ZPO zum Ausdruck kommenden Allgemeingrundsatz — die **Bewilligung des Armenrechts (nebst Anwaltsbeiordnung) für jeden Rechtszug** besonders erfolgt. Der Anspruch des Rechtsanwalts gegen die Staatskasse bestimmt sich im einzelnen nach den Beschlüssen, durch die das Armenrecht bewilligt und der Rechtsanwalt beigeordnet worden ist (§ 122 Abs. 1 BRAGebO). Der Rechtsanwalt erhält die Vergütung aus der Bundes- oder Landeskasse, wenn er für eine Berufung oder Revision beigeordnet ist, **auch für** die **Rechtsverteidigung gegen** eine **Anschlußberufung oder** eine **Anschlußrevision.** Dies gilt nicht, wenn der Beiordnungsbeschluß ausdrücklich bestimmt, daß der Rechtsanwalt für die Rechtsverteidigung gegen die Anschlußberufung oder Anschlußrevision nicht beigeordnet ist (§ 122 Abs. 2 BRAGebO).

b) In **Angelegenheiten, die** mit dem Hauptprozeß lediglich **zusammenhängen,** erhält der für den Prozeß beigeordnete Rechtsanwalt Vergütung aus der Bundes- oder Landeskasse **nur** dann, **wenn** er ausdrücklich auch **hierfür beigeordnet ist.** Dies gilt insbesondere für

1. die Zwangsvollstreckung (den Verwaltungszwang);
2. das Beweissicherungsverfahren;
3. das Verfahren über die Widerklage (vgl. § 122 Abs. 3 BRAGebO).

c) Was die **Zwangsvollstreckung** anbetrifft, so gehört sie hier nicht mit zu der sonst dafür in Frage kommenden ersten Instanz. Für die Zwangsvollstreckung **muß** vielmehr das **Armenrecht vom Vollstreckungsgericht** — auf entsprechenden Antrag — **besonders bewilligt werden** (grundsätzlich ohne Anwaltsbeiordnung).

d) Zum **Begriff der** von der Armenrechtsbewilligung erfaßten **Instanz ist** zu bemerken: Bei **Erlaß** eines **neuen Verwaltungsaktes** ergänzender oder ersetzender Art nach Klageerhebung (§§ 96, 153 SGG) liegt dasselbe Verfahren in der betreffenden Instanz vor (anders bei Erlaß eines neuen Verwaltungsaktes der wiedergegebenen Art während des Revisionsverfahrens, § 171 Abs. 2 SGG; hier wird über den neuen Verwaltungsakt in einem selbständigen Verfahren, das wieder in der ersten Tatsacheninstanz beginnt, entschieden, wenn der Kläger durch ihn nicht etwa klaglos gestellt worden ist).

Durch **Antrag auf mündliche Verhandlung** gegen den Vorbescheid (§ 105 Abs. 2, § 158 Abs. 2, § 216 Abs. 1 Nr. 1 SGG) wird kein neuer Rechtszug eröffnet.

e) **Bei Zurückverweisung** an die untere Gerichtsinstanz beginnt kein neuer Rechtszug. Es **gilt das** hier früher **bewilligte Armenrecht weiter.** Wird nach Zurückverweisung gegen das ergehende neue Urteil ein Rechtsmittel eingelegt, so entsteht selbstverständlich eine neue (Rechtsmittel-)Instanz.

f) **Bei Verweisung wegen örtlicher oder sachlicher Unzuständigkeit liegt** grundsätzlich ein **einheitliches Verfahren vor** (vgl. § 98 Abs. 2 und 3 SGG). **Entgegengesetzt ist** die **Rechtslage bei Verweisung in einen anders gearteten,** z. B. den „ordentlichen" **Rechtsweg** gemäß § 52 Abs. 3 SGG und umgekehrt; die Beiordnung ist nämlich grundsätzlich an das Gerichtsverfahren gebunden.

g) **Bei Abgabe** einer Streitsache, die mit einer anderweit anhängigen wesensgleich ist, **an das gemeinsame nächsthöhere Gericht** nach § 181 SGG **besteht nur die höhere Instanz.**

h) **Die Richter- und die Urkundsbeamtenablehnung** (§ 60 Abs. 1, § 171 Abs. 1 SGG) **gehören zum Verfahren der Instanz** des Abgelehnten.

i) Das **Beschwerdeverfahren,** auch soweit die Beschwerde nicht an die Stelle der Berufung tritt, **bildet** für das Armenrechtsverfahren eine **neue Instanz** (wegen der in Frage kommenden verschiedenen Höhe der Honorierung vgl. hier unten II 1 b).

k) **Wird** ein durch rechtskräftiges Urteil **abgeschlossenes Verfahren wieder aufgenommen** (§§ 179, 180 SGG, §§ 578 ff. ZPO), so **liegt** ein **neues Verfahren vor.**

l) **Bei Klageverbindung** zur gemeinsamen Verhandlung und Entscheidung (vgl. § 113 Abs. 1 SGG) **liegt nur noch ein Verfahren** in der betreffenden Instanz **vor. Bei Aufhebung der Verbindung** (vgl. § 113 Abs. 2 SGG) **entstehen wieder** zwei oder entsprechend **mehr Verfahren.**

m) Auch **eine** eventuelle **Hebetätigkeit des Anwalts** (vgl. § 22 BRAGebO) **wird** von der Armenrechtsbewilligung **nicht erfaßt.**

3. **Behörden, Anstalten und Körperschaften des öffentlichen Rechts** sind **vom Armenrecht** von vornherein **ausgeschlossen.**

4. **Voraussetzung der Bewilligung** des Armenrechts **ist, daß der Naturalbeteiligte außerstande ist, ohne Beeinträchtigung des** für ihn und seine Familie **notwendigen** (nicht notdürftigen, auch nicht standesnotwendigen) **Unterhalts die Kosten** des Rechtsstreits **aufzubringen.** Da das Sozialgerichtsverfahren in allen Instanzen grundsätzlich gebührenfrei ist, kommt es allein darauf an, ob die Rechtsanwaltskosten ohne Beeinträchtigung des notwendigen Unterhalts bestritten werden können (vgl. § 114 Abs. 1 Satz 1 ZPO). Das letzte ist zu verneinen, wenn im wesent-

lichen nur dem Pfändungsschutz (vgl. §§ 850c und d ZPO) unterliegendes Einkommen vorhanden ist (vgl. BSG, SozR SGG § 167 Bl. Da 4 Nr. 5 und KG, JR 1951, 27 und 184). Daß das Unvermögen gegebenenfalls verschuldet ist, schadet grundsätzlich nichts. Arm ist auch der mittellose Sohn eines nicht unvermögenden Vaters. Die Kosten für lebenswichtige Prozesse des Kindes sind aber von unterhaltspflichtigen Eltern im Rahmen ihrer Unterhaltspflicht (endgültig) zu bestreiten (vgl. § 1610 BGB). Nach § 1360a Abs. 4 BGB n. F. obliegt jedem Ehegatten die Pflicht, die Prozeßkosten dem anderen Ehegatten in persönlichen Angelegenheiten vorzuschießen, wenn dieser die Kosten nicht tragen kann und es der Billigkeit entspricht. (Nach der Beendigung des bevorschußten Rechtsstreites muß der vorschußberechtigte dem anderen Ehegatten den Vorschuß zurückgewähren, und zwar ohne Rücksicht darauf, ob er die Kosten erstattet erhält, vgl. Brühl, FamRZ 1958, 197 [200]).

5. **Angehörige fremder Staaten haben auf** das **Armenrecht** nur **insoweit Anspruch, als** die **Gegenseitigkeit verbürgt ist** (§ 114 Abs. 2 Satz 1 ZPO). **Soweit Ausländer heimatlos** sind, **sind sie deutschen Staatsangehörigen gleichgestellt** (§ 11 Kap. II des Gesetzes über die Rechtsstellung heimatloser Ausländer im Bundesgebiet vom 25. 4. 1951, BGBl. I 269).

Einem **Staatenlosen** kann das **Armenrecht** bewilligt werden, wenn es ihm **als Inländer zu gewähren** wäre (§ 114 Abs. 2 Satz 2 ZPO).

6. **Einer Partei kraft Amtes** (z. B. Nachlaßverwalter, Konkursverwalter, Testamentsvollstrecker) **kann** — bei Erfüllung aller erforderlichen Voraussetzungen bedeutet dies muß — im Falle des Unvermögens zur Kostenaufbringung **das Armenrecht bewilligt werden, wenn die** zur Führung des Prozesses **erforderlichen Mittel weder aus der verwalteten Vermögensmasse noch von den** an der Führung des Prozesses **wirtschaftlich Beteiligten aufgebracht werden können** (§ 114 Abs. 3 ZPO).

7. **Einer inländischen juristischen Person kann** (s. o. 6) bei Vorliegen auch der sonstigen Voraussetzungen das **Armenrecht bewilligt werden, wenn die** zur Führung des Prozesses **erforderlichen Mittel weder von ihr noch von den** an der Führung des Rechtsstreits **wirtschaftlich Beteiligten aufgebracht werden können und die Unterlassung der Rechtswahrung allgemeinen Interessen zuwiderlaufen würde** (§ 114 Abs. 4 ZPO).

8. Das **Unvermögen** zur Bestreitung der Prozeßkosten **muß durch** ein **Armutszeugnis** des Sozialamts der Wohngemeinde **bezeugt werden,** in welchem der Stand, das Gewerbe, die Vermögens- und Familienverhältnisse des Beteiligten sowie der Betrag der von ihm zu entrichtenden (Einkommens- und evtl. Vermögens-)Steuern (insoweit muß **zunächst** eine **Bescheinigung des zuständigen Finanzamtes** besorgt werden) anzugeben sind (§ 118 Abs. 2 Satz 1 ZPO).

Für Personen, die **unter Vormundschaft oder Pflegschaft** stehen, **kann** das **Zeugnis auch von der vormundschaftlichen Behörde ausgestellt werden** (§ 118 Abs. 2 Satz 2 ZPO).

Das Zeugnis ist für das Gericht nicht unbedingt bindend. Dieses kann in Zweifelsfällen eigene Untersuchungen über die Einkommens- und Vermögensverhältnisse des um das Armenrecht Nachsuchenden anstellen.

9. **Ist** ein unbemittelter **Beteiligter imstande, die Kosten** ohne Beeinträchtigung des für ihn und seine Familie notwendigen Unterhalts **zu einem Teile zu bestreiten, so ist zu bestimmen, daß nur wegen des restlichen Bruchteiles** die einstweilige **Befreiung** von der Berichtigung der Kosten **eintritt** (§ 115 Abs. 2 ZPO). Eine andere Teilbewilligung als nach Bruchteilen ist im Sozialgerichtsverfahren praktisch nicht

möglich, da der zu vergütende Anwalt je Instanz nur eine Gebühr erhält. (Nur wegen der Anwaltskosten kommt hier die Bewilligung des Armenrechts in Frage.)

10. **Weitere Voraussetzung für die Bewilligung** des Armenrechts **ist, daß die** beabsichtigte **Rechtsverfolgung oder Rechtsverteidigung** in rechtlicher und tatsächlicher Hinsicht **hinreichende Aussicht auf Erfolg verspricht** (§ 114 Abs. 1 Satz 1 ZPO). Die Rechtswahrung muß danach in sich schlüssig und voraussichtlich auch begründet sein. Das kann zuweilen nur für einen Teil des Anspruchs zutreffen. Zur Bejahung der Erfolgsaussicht ist erforderlich, daß, wenn materielle oder prozessuale (insbesondere Rechtsmittel-)Fristen einzuhalten sind, um das Armenrecht innerhalb der Frist (wenn auch am letzten Tage derselben, BSG, SozR SGG § 167 Bl. Da 1 Nr. 1) nachgesucht wird. (Um materiell-rechtliche Fristen zu wahren, ist gleichzeitige Einreichung der Klage erforderlich.) Innerhalb der zu wahrenden Frist ist grundsätzlich auch das Armutszeugnis einzureichen, vgl. BSG 1, 287. (Gegen das Verlangen der Vorlegung des Armutszeugnisses innerhalb der Frist wendet sich Glücklich, SGb 1956, 291.) In der höheren Instanz ist die Erbringung einer besonderen Begründung nicht erforderlich (BSG, SozR SGG § 167 Bl. Da 3 Nr. 4). Selbstverständlich besteht für das Armenrechtsverfahren kein Anwaltszwang.

Bei Entscheidung (positiver oder negativer Art) über das innerhalb der Rechtsmittelfrist ordnungsmäßig gestellte Armenrechtsgesuch erst nach Ablauf dieser Frist muß grundsätzlich **Wiedereinsetzung** in den vorigen Stand gewährt werden, wenn diese fristgerecht beantragt wird (innerhalb eines Monats, vgl. § 67 Abs. 2 SGG). Innerhalb der Antragsfrist für die Wiedereinsetzung muß auf jeden Fall auch die Rechtsmitteleinlegung nachholend erfolgen. Ist dies geschehen, so kann die Wiedereinsetzung sogar ohne förmlichen Antrag gewährt werden. Ist das Armenrechtsgesuch mangels Armut abgelehnt worden, muß vom Rechtsmittelkläger zur Begründung der nachgesuchten Wiedereinsetzung dargetan werden, daß er Anlaß zu der Annahme gehabt habe, infolge Armut die Rechtsmittelfrist nicht wahren zu können (BGH, JurBüro 1958, 348); er muß auch alles in seinen Kräften Stehende getan haben, um die Armutsunterlagen rechtzeitig zu beschaffen (BGH, JurBüro 1958, 344).

Vorstehendes gilt **im Verfahren der Sozialgerichtsbarkeit** auch für die Rechtsverteidigung in einem höheren Rechtszuge. Hier **gibt es,** da § 119 Abs. 2 ZPO nicht gilt, **kein** sog. **notwendiges Armenrecht** (vgl. BSG, SozR SGG § 167 Bl. Da 4 Nr. 6). Wer aber bereits ein Urteil für sich hat, dürfte regelmäßig ohne weiteres als hinreichend aussichtsreich in der weiteren Rechtswahrung anzusehen sein.

Das Streitverhältnis ist jeweils **unter Angabe der Beweismittel** im einzelnen **darzulegen** (§ 118 Abs. 3 ZPO). In den höheren Rechtszügen ist eine Begründung des Armenrechtsgesuchs aber nicht erforderlich (BSG, SozR SGG § 167 Bl. Da 3 Nr. 4). Hier ergibt sich das Nähere regelmäßig bereits aus dem Urteil der vorhergehenden Instanz.

11. **Die** gerichtliche **Rechtswahrung darf** auch bei sachlicher Erfolgsaussicht **nicht mutwillig sein** (§ 114 Abs. 1 Satz 1 2. Teil ZPO); so kann insbesondere nicht zugelassen werden, daß die Rechtsverfolgung des Klägers ohne vorherige Anforderung oder Anmahnung vorgenommen wird.

12. **Die Kosten für** die **gerichtliche Anfertigung nicht eingereichter,** zwecks Zustellung an den gegnerischen Beteiligten aber erforderlicher **Abschriften von Schriftsätzen** nebst Anlagen (§ 93 SGG) **und für beantragte Abschriften aus den Akten** (§ 120 Abs. 2 SGG) **sowie** die Kosten **für die gutachtliche Anhörung eines**

bestimmten Arztes (§ 109 Abs. 1 SGG) **werden als Sonderkosten von der Bewilligung** des Armenrechts **nicht erfaßt** (s. o. 4. Kap. 1a, b, c).

13. **Die Bewilligung des Armenrechts hat auf die** gegebenenfalls **aufzuerlegende Verpflichtung zur Erstattung der** dem jeweiligen gegnerischen Beteiligten **erwachsenen Kosten** (vgl. §§ 192, 193 SGG) **und ihre Vollstreckung keinerlei Einfluß** (§ 117 ZPO), ebenso nicht auf die Möglichkeit der Auferlegung von Gerichtsaufwendungen nach § 192 SGG. Der Gegner wird durch die Bewilligung des Armenrechts (vgl. hierzu die §§ 120, 123 ZPO) ohnehin nicht geschützt, da Gerichtskosten im eigentlichen Sinn ja nicht entstehen.

14. **Das Gesuch** um Bewilligung des Armenrechts **ist bei dem Prozeßgericht zu stellen;** es kann — auch beim Bundessozialgericht — vor der Geschäftsstelle zu Protokoll erklärt werden (§ 118 Abs. 1 ZPO). Über das Gesuch ist baldmöglichst zu entscheiden (vgl. BGHZ 10, 139 = NJW 1953, 1510 = MDR 1953, 674 = JZ 1953, 607).

15. **Wird gleichzeitig Klage (Berufung) eingereicht, so wird** dadurch **neben dem Armenrechtsverfahren auch der Rechtsstreit** selbst **(die Berufungsinstanz)** in der Hauptsache **in Gang gebracht,** es sei denn, daß die Klage (Berufung) zunächst (d. h. bis zur Bewilligung des Armenrechts) nur Anlage des Armenrechtsgesuches sein soll (vgl. BGHZ 4, 333). Gleiches gilt in bezug auf die Revision; jedoch muß diese in gültiger Form von den im § 166 SGG aufgeführten Prozeßbevollmächtigten eingelegt sein.

Nach Abschluß der Instanz kann das Armenrecht für diese grundsätzlich nicht mehr beantragt werden.

16. **Das Gericht kann verlangen, daß der Gesuchsteller seine** tatsächlichen **Angaben glaubhaft macht** (§ 118a Abs. 1 Satz 1 ZPO). Eigene eidesstattliche Versicherung wird dabei aber nicht als zulässig angesehen werden können, weil sie eine Art Parteivernehmung darstellt und diese sozusagen vorwegnimmt (vgl. Baumbach-Lauterbach, ZPO 25. Aufl. Anm. 1 B zu § 118a).

17. **Das Gericht soll,** wenn es nicht aus besonderen Gründen (z. B. wegen Eilbedürftigkeit) unzweckmäßig erscheint, **den gegnerischen Beteiligten hören** (§ 118a Abs. 1 Satz 2 ZPO). Die Anhörung des Gegners kann auch zu Protokoll der Geschäftsstelle des Prozeßgerichts oder eines ersuchten Gerichts erfolgen (§ 118a Abs. 2 Satz 2 ZPO).

18. **Das Gericht kann,** soweit dies ohne erhebliche Verzögerung möglich ist, **Erhebungen anstellen,** insbesondere die Vorlegung von Urkunden anordnen und von Behörden Auskünfte einholen (§ 118a Abs. 1 Satz 3 ZPO). Die Vernehmung von Zeugen oder Sachverständigen ist jedoch nur zulässig, wenn der Sachverhalt, soweit dies zur Entscheidung über das Armenrechtsgesuch erforderlich ist, auf andere Weise nicht hinreichend geklärt werden kann; eine Beeidigung findet dabei nicht statt (§ 118a Abs. 1 Satz 4 ZPO). Gleiches wird in bezug auf eine Versicherung der Richtigkeit der Aussage an Eidesstatt zu gelten haben (vgl. Baumbach-Lauterbach, ZPO 25. Aufl. Anm. 1 E zu § 118a). Die durch die Vernehmung von Zeugen und Sachverständigen entstandenen Auslagen sind von der Staatskasse zu tragen (§ 183 SGG). Wird das Armenrecht bewilligt, so stellen diese Auslagen — das Beweisergebnis wird regelmäßig im Rechtsstreit verwertet — einen Teil der Gerichtskosten dar, die gemäß § 192 SGG unter den dort genannten Voraussetzungen einem Beteiligten auferlegt werden können (vgl. dazu § 118a Abs. 4 Satz 2 ZPO).

19. **Die Maßnahmen zur Vorbereitung der Entscheidung** (vgl. hier 16 bis 18) **können von dem Vorsitzenden oder von einem** von ihm **beauftragten Mitglied** des

Gerichts **oder von einem** von ihm **ersuchten Richter durchgeführt werden** (§ 118a Abs. 2 Satz 1 ZPO). Die Möglichkeit der Übertragung dieser Aufgaben auf den Rechtspfleger (vgl. § 19 Nr. 4 RpflG) hat für die Sozialgerichtsbarkeit, die keinen Rechtspfleger kennt, keine Bedeutung.

20. **Einigen sich die Beteiligten,** wo dies auf Grund Verfügungsgewalt über den Streitgegenstand möglich ist (vgl. § 101 Abs. 1 SGG), bei der Anhörung des Gegners **über den streitigen Anspruch,** so **ist der Vergleich zu richterlichem Protokoll zu nehmen.** Das Vergleichsprotokoll stellt einen Vollstreckungstitel dar (§ 199 Abs. 1 Nr. 2 SGG). Der Vergleich verlangt (vgl. § 779 BGB) ein gegenseitiges Nachgeben; das Nachgeben kann in der Aufgabe der Erlangung einer gerichtlichen Entscheidung gesehen werden, wenn diese für den betreffenden Teil als solche von Bedeutung war. Es besteht für die Protokollierung auch beim Bundessozialgericht kein Anwaltszwang. Der Vergleich erledigt das Armenrechtsverfahren. Ist die Einigung vor dem Urkundsbeamten erfolgt und festgelegt, so liegt nur ein außergerichtlicher Vergleich vor, auf Grund dessen nicht vollstreckt werden kann. Was die Kostenregelung im Vergleich anbetrifft, so erfolgt die Protokollierung naturgemäß gebühren- und auslagenersatzfrei; eine Erstattung wechselseitig etwa entstandener Kosten findet grundsätzlich nicht statt (vgl. § 118a Abs. 4 Satz 1 ZPO und § 195 SGG). Der bei einem Vergleichsabschluß mitwirkende Anwalt erhält eine Zusatzgebühr in Höhe von $^3/_{10}$ der Mindestgebühr der betreffenden Instanz (vgl. das 7. Kap. I A 1 y gegen Ende).

21. **Die Ablehnung** bzw. **Bewilligung des Armenrechts** (einschließlich der Beiordnung eines Anwalts) **erfolgt** mangels ausdrücklicher gesetzlicher Einschränkung grundsätzlich auch außerhalb einer Gerichtsverhandlung **durch das** voll besetzte **Gericht** (d. h. einschließlich der sog. Laienrichter). Das gilt auch für das Bundessozialgericht. Sonst könnte der Fall eintreten, daß sich bezüglich der Frage des bewilligten oder abgelehnten Armenrechts bei der Gerichtsverhandlung, weil die Laienrichter hinzutreten, die Mehrheitsverhältnisse ändern. Auf einer anderen Ebene liegt, daß die Laienrichter die Armenrechtsbeschlüsse keinesfalls zu unterschreiben brauchen, vgl. hierzu BSG (Großer Senat) 1, 1.

Bis zum 31. 12. 1960 kann aus Vereinfachungs- und Beschleunigungsgründen außerhalb der mündlichen Verhandlung der Vorsitzende bei dem Sozialgericht allein, das Landessozialgericht ohne Zuziehung der Landessozialrichter und das Bundessozialgericht ohne Zuziehung der Bundessozialrichter über das Armenrechtsgesuch entscheiden (§ 216 Abs. 1 Nr. 2 SGG).

Der Beschluß, durch den die Armenrechtsbewilligung bzw. die Armenanwaltsbeiordnung abgelehnt wird, ist in aller Regel — kurz — zu begründen (§ 126 Abs. 2 ZPO). Auch die Ablehnung ergeht gebühren- und auslagenersatzfrei. Eine mündliche Verhandlung ist nicht erforderlich (§ 126 Abs. 1 ZPO). Der — ganze oder teilweise — Ablehnungsbeschluß ist dem Gesuchsteller förmlich zuzustellen (vgl. § 63 Abs. 1 SGG). Er hat eine Rechtsmittelbelehrung zu enthalten (vgl. § 66 Abs. 1 SGG). Wegen der Folgen unterlassener oder unrichtiger Belehrung vgl. § 66 Abs. 2 SGG.

Den Armenanwalt (Verwaltungsrechtsrat i. S. des § 217 Abs. 1 und 2 SGG) **kann der Vorsitzende allein auswählen** (vgl. § 36 Abs. 1 RAO). Die Auswahl erfolgt an sich aus dem Kreise aller deutschen Rechtsanwälte. In Frage kommt regelmäßig aber nur eine Auswahl aus den am Gerichtsort ansässigen Anwälten. Die Wünsche des Gesuchstellers sind nach Möglichkeit zu berücksichtigen. Armen Streitgenossen ist jedoch grundsätzlich nur ein Anwalt beizuordnen. Ist ein Anwalt als Pfleger bestellt, so ist er bei Bewilligung des Armenrechts, die hier nicht ausgeschlossen ist, auch als Armenanwalt beizuordnen (vgl. OLG Frankfurt, NJW 1951, 276).

Die Beiordnung eines Anwalts für mehrere in einheitlicher Weise Vorgehende (oder in Anspruch Genommene) läßt die Armenanwaltsgebühr nur einmal entstehen. Wegen der Erhöhung der Gebühr um die Hälfte in diesen Fällen vgl. § 6 Abs. 1 Satz 2 BRAGebO (siehe dazu 7. Kap. I A 2b).

Die gesetzlich nicht ausgeschlossene und damit an sich vor allem aus rechtsstaatlichen Gebotsgründen mögliche (a. A. BGH, NJW 1951, 656) Beiordnung eines Verkehrsarmenanwalts oder eines Armenanwalts für die Wahrnehmung eines auswärtigen Beweistermins — mit eigenen Ansprüchen gegen die Staatskasse — durch das Prozeßgericht (Anwaltsauswahl regelmäßig durch das ersuchte Gericht) wird sich in aller Regel erübrigen, da der arme Beteiligte seinen Anwalt im allgemeinen ohne weiteres schriftlich unterrichten kann und dieser zur eigenen Wahrnehmung jedenfalls wichtiger auswärtiger Termine verpflichtet ist. (Er erhält insoweit Reisekostenvergütung, s. u. II A 2c.)

22. **Die Bewilligung des Armenrechts** und die Beiordnung des Armenanwalts **erfolgt grundsätzlich nicht mit rückwirkender Kraft.** Bei verspäteter Entscheidung über ein rechtzeitig gestelltes Armenrechtsgesuch kann aber (sogar noch nach Abschluß der Instanz) Rückwirkung bis auf den Zeitpunkt der Gesuchstellung ausgesprochen werden — auch nachträglich —, darüber hinaus aber nicht. Die Rückwirkung muß ausdrücklich erklärt werden. Von ihr wird ohne weiteres die Beiordnung mit umfaßt (Gaedeke, ArmAnwKostG S. 53).

Da grundsätzlich keine Rückwirkung besteht, muß bei der Festsetzung der Armenanwaltsgebühr (s. u. III 5) bezüglich der Höhe unter Umständen die eingeschränkte Armenanwaltstätigkeit beachtet werden. Das kann der Höhe nach zur Gewährung einer geringeren Armenanwaltsvergütung gegenüber der Vergütung als Wahlanwalt führen.

23. **Die Armenrechtsbewilligung** wie die Beiordnung **wird wirksam mit der Verkündung** im Termin **oder mit der** (auch formlos möglichen) **Bekanntmachung** gegenüber dem armen Beteiligten oder dem bevollmächtigten Anwalt. Maßgebend ist stets die Urschrift des Beschlusses (so mit Recht Schumann, BRAGebO Anm. IV 1 zu § 121). Die Armenrechtsbewilligung bewirkt eine Stundung der an sich an den beigeordneten Anwalt zu zahlenden Gebühr.

24. **Der ausgewählte Anwalt muß die Beiordnung annehmen;** er darf von sich aus die Vertretung auch nicht niederlegen, sondern muß bei Vorliegen wichtiger Gründe (z. B. Nichterteilung oder Entzug des Vertrauens seitens des armen Beteiligten) das Gericht um seine Entbindung bitten. Der Anwalt hat daher grundsätzlich weder gegen seine Beiordnung noch gegen die Ablehnung derselben ein Beschwerderecht, ebenso nicht gegen seine Entbindung oder deren Ablehnung.

Ist das Armenrecht aber nur zum Bruchteil bewilligt, so kann der Anwalt insgesamt kündigen, wenn die Partei für den zahlungspflichtigen Gebührenteil nicht den verlangten Vorschuß leistet (vgl. OLG Königsberg, JW 1935, 1726).

Wegen der Rechte des armenrechtlich begünstigten Beteiligten vgl. die folgende Nummer.

25. **Die Beiordnung,** die ein öffentlich-rechtliches Verhältnis zwischen dem Rechtsanwalt und dem Staat begründet, **reicht zum Tätigwerden des Anwalts** allein **nicht aus.** (Der lediglich beigeordnete Anwalt darf — und muß —, insoweit als Geschäftsführer ohne Auftrag, nur eilbedürftige Prozeßhandlungen vornehmen, z. B. bei drohendem Fristablauf Rechtsmittel einlegen; Vergütung aus der Staats-

kasse erfolgt ausnahmsweise auch dann.) **Grundsätzlich hat die Bevollmächtigung durch den Beteiligten hinzuzutreten,** zu dessen Gunsten die Beiordnung erfolgt ist. Die Vollmachtserteilung kann stillschweigend schlüssig vorgenommen werden, z. B. durch Vornahme der Information. In unbestimmter Weise im vorhinein kann sie nicht erfolgen.

Der arme Beteiligte hat Anspruch auf Beiordnung eines anderen Rechtsanwalts nur, wenn der beigeordnete Anwalt ohne Zutun des Armen wegfällt oder wenn dieser aus triftigen Gründen keine Vollmacht erteilt oder sie berechtigt entzieht. Bei Zurückverweisung bleibt die frühere Beiordnung bestehen (Gerold, BRAGebO Anm. 39 zu § 121).

26. **Der Beschluß, durch den das Armenrecht bewilligt** und die Anwaltsbeiordnung ausgesprochen **wird, ist unanfechtbar. Gegen den Beschluß, durch den das** beantragte **Armenrecht verweigert oder** in zeitlicher oder umfanglicher Hinsicht **nur verkürzt gewährt oder die Armenanwaltsbeiordnung abgelehnt wird, gibt es,** wenn er von einem Sozialgericht erlassen ist, **die Beschwerde** des betroffenen Beteiligten (vgl. § 127 ZPO, § 172 Abs. 1 SGG); Frist: ein Monat seit Zustellung, § 173 SGG (vgl. aber § 66 Abs. 2 SGG bei nicht erfolgter oder nicht richtiger Rechtsmittelbelehrung); Form: schriftlich oder zur Niederschrift des Urkundsbeamten der Geschäftsstelle des Sozialgerichts, § 173 SGG. Der arme Beteiligte hat gegenüber Beschlüssen des Sozialgerichts das Beschwerderecht auch hinsichtlich der Auswahl des Anwalts, ferner gegen die Ablehnung der von ihm beantragten Entbindung des Armenanwalts.

Die Armenrechtsbeschwerde ist an keine Mindestbeschwer gebunden (vgl. § 127 ZPO, § 172 SGG). Das Beschwerdegericht entscheidet bei Nichtabhilfe (vgl. § 174 SGG) ohne mündliche Verhandlung (§ 126 Abs. 1 in Verb. mit § 127 ZPO, § 124 Abs. 3 SGG) in eigener Ermessensausübung (§ 128 Abs. 1, § 142 Abs. 1 SGG). Bis zum 31. 12. 1960 kann das Landessozialgericht ohne Zuziehung der Landessozialrichter entscheiden (§ 216 Abs. 1 Nr. 2 SGG).

Die Beschwerdeentscheidung ergeht stets gebühren- und auslagenersatzfrei (§ 183 SGG). Außergerichtliche Kosten werden im Beschwerdeverfahren, wie in der ersten Instanz, nicht erstattet (vgl. § 118 Abs. 4 Satz 1 ZPO, § 202 SGG). Eine weitere Beschwerde ist nie gegeben (§ 127 Satz 3 ZPO, § 177 SGG). Daher ist eine förmliche Zustellung der Beschwerdeentscheidung nicht erforderlich (vgl. § 63 Abs. 1 SGG).

27. **Das Armenrecht** (einschließlich der Beiordnung) **erlischt mit dem Tode der Person, der es bewilligt ist** (§ 122 ZPO). **Ebenso hört die Beiordnung** naturgemäß **mit dem Tode des Anwalts auf.** Wird ein Abwickler bestellt, der weiter tätig wird, so gilt das Armenrechtsverhältnis als bestehen bleibend: Es liegt gewissermaßen Personenidentität auf seiten der Prozeßvertretung vor. Bei juristischen Personen endet das bewilligte Armenrecht mit deren endgültigem Erlöschen. Der Armenanwalt hat den Erstattungsanspruch aber auch für Prozeßhandlungen, die er zwar nach dem Tode des Armen, aber in schuldloser Unkenntnis dieses Ereignisses vorgenommen hat. Gegen die nicht armen Erben des verstorbenen Armen kann die Nachzahlung der Kosten (gemäß § 125 ZPO) angeordnet werden. Dann kann der Anwalt gegen die Erben wegen seiner Gebühr vorgehen. Die Erben können sich im Prozeß gegebenenfalls auf beschränkte Erbenhaftung berufen. Wird der Armenanwalt auch den Erben beigeordnet, so entsteht für ihn keine neue Gebührenangelegenheit (OLG Stettin, JW 1934, 1867).

28. a) **Das Armenrecht kann** vom Prozeßgericht (in voller Besetzung) zu jeder Zeit im ganzen oder teilweisen Umfange **entzogen werden, wenn sich ergibt, daß eine Voraussetzung der Bewilligung** (Armut oder Erfolgsaussicht oder Nichtvorliegen von Mutwillen) **nicht vorhanden war oder nicht mehr vorhanden ist** (§ 121 ZPO).

Bis zum 31. 12. 1960 kann die Entziehung außerhalb der mündlichen Verhandlung ohne die Zuziehung der Laienrichter erfolgen (§ 216 Abs. 1 Nr. 2 SGG).

Die Entziehung wirkt stets nur für die Zukunft. Sie wird wirksam mit der Verkündung oder mit der Zustellung der Entziehung (vgl. § 63 Abs. 1 SGG) an den beigeordneten Prozeßbevollmächtigten. Bis dahin dauert die Armenrechtstätigkeit des Anwalts. Die Entziehung nach ungünstigem Ausfall der Verhandlung oder der Beweisaufnahme unmittelbar vor dem Urteil ist jedoch nicht vertretbar und vom Gesetzgeber nicht gewollt. Das BSG hat allerdings in dem Falle, daß die streitige Rechtsfrage inzwischen in einer gleichliegenden anderen Sache gegen den Revisionskläger geklärt war, diesem das Armenrecht entzogen (BSG, SozR SGG § 167 Bl. Da 6 Nr. 9).

Die Entziehung ist nur bis zur Beendigung der betreffenden Instanz möglich. Mündliche Verhandlung ist für ihren Ausspruch nicht erforderlich (§ 126 Abs. 1 ZPO). Nach der Entziehung (oder der Aufhebung der Beiordnung) bleibt der Anwalt gegebenenfalls als Wahlanwalt tätig.

Eine Nachzahlungspflicht des früheren Armen gegenüber der Staatskasse, die den Armenanwalt befriedigt hat, entsteht selbst bei Entziehung des Armenrechts wegen Nichtarmut erst mit einer weiteren, auch selbständig möglichen Anordnung des Gerichts, nämlich der Nachzahlungsanordnung gemäß § 125 ZPO (vgl. Gaedeke, ArmAnwKostG S. 241). Auch der Armenanwalt kann gegenüber seiner Partei wegen seiner früher verdienten Gebühr (nebst Auslagen) erst nach Erlaß dieser besonderen Nachzahlungsanordnung vorgehen. Die Anordnung der Nachzahlungsverpflichtung ist während und nach Abschluß des Verfahrens ohne mündliche Verhandlung möglich. Der alles beherrschende Grundsatz von Treu und Glauben verlangt aber auch hier die Einhaltung einer Frist. Lappe (Rpfleger 1957, 280) hat eine solche von drei Jahren nach Abschluß des Rechtsstreites in Erwägung gezogen. Diese Frist erscheint nicht unangemessen.

Die Anordnung der Nachzahlung erfolgt grundsätzlich durch das vollbesetzte Gericht. (Hinsichtlich der möglichen Besetzung des Gerichts für die Zeit bis 31. 12. 1960 vgl. § 216 Abs. 1 Nr. 2 SGG.)

Der von Amts wegen ergehende Entziehungsbeschluß ist mit einer kurzen Begründung zu versehen (§ 126 Abs. 2 ZPO); er ergeht gebühren- und auslagenersatzfrei. Gleiches gilt mit Bezug auf den Nachzahlungsbeschluß. Rechtsmittelbelehrung ist stets erforderlich (§§ 66 Abs. 1 SGG). Wegen der Folgen unterlassener oder unrichtiger Belehrung vgl. § 66 Abs. 2 SGG.

b) **Gegen den Beschluß, durch den das Armenrecht entzogen wird, steht dem Betroffenen,** wenn es sich um eine Entscheidung des Sozialgerichts handelt, bei jeder Beschwer **die Beschwerde zu** (§ 127 Satz 2 ZPO, § 172 Abs. 1 SGG). Frist: ein Monat seit Verkündung oder förmlicher Zustellung der Entziehung (§ 173 SGG). Form: schriftlich oder zur Niederschrift des Urkundsbeamten der Geschäftsstelle des befaßten Sozialgerichts (§ 173 SGG).

Das Beschwerdegericht entscheidet bei Nichtabhilfe (vgl. § 174 SGG) ohne mündliche Verhandlung (§ 126 Abs. 1 ZPO, § 124 Abs. 3 SGG) in eigener Ermessensausübung (§ 128 Abs. 1, § 142 Abs. 1 SGG).

Die Landessozialrichter brauchen bis zum 31. 12. 1960 nicht zugezogen zu werden (§ 216 Abs. 1 Nr. 2 SGG).

Die ergehende Beschwerdeentscheidung erfolgt stets gebühren- und auslagenersatzfrei (§ 183 SGG). Eine Kostenerstattung kommt nicht in Frage (s. o. 26). Eine weitere Beschwerde gibt es nicht (§ 127 Satz 3 ZPO, § 177 SGG). Der Beschwerdebeschluß braucht daher nicht förmlich zugestellt zu werden (§ 63 Abs. 1 SGG). Entsprechendes gilt mit Bezug auf den Beschluß, der die Nachzahlungspflicht anordnet (siehe dazu die folgende Nummer).

29. a) **Der zum Armenrecht zugelassene Beteiligte ist zur Nachzahlung** des Betrages, von dessen Berichtigung er einstweilen befreit war, an den Anwalt und, soweit sie diesen befriedigt hat, an die Staatskasse **verpflichtet, sobald er ohne Beeinträchtigung des** für ihn und seine Familie **notwendigen** (nicht notdürftigen) **Unterhalts dazu imstande ist** (§ 125 Abs. 1 ZPO). Ähnliches gilt unter Berücksichtigung ihrer Eigenart und der für sie maßgebenden Verhältnisse für juristische Personen. Nach diesbezüglicher Nachprüfung hat ein entsprechender Anordnungsbeschluß — gebühren- und auslagenersatzfrei — zu ergehen (§ 126 Abs. 1 ZPO). Mündliche Verhandlung ist dazu nicht erforderlich (§ 126 Abs. 1 ZPO). Zuständig ist das mit der Sache befaßte Prozeßgericht, das regelmäßig für seine Instanz zu entscheiden hat. Für abgeschlossene Rechtszüge kommt grundsätzlich die Zuständigkeit der ersten Instanz in Betracht — vgl. RGZ 12, 416, auch RG, JW 1932, 2173 —. (Die Zuständigkeit des Rechtspflegers — vgl. § 19 Nr. 5 des das ordentliche Verfahren betreffenden Rechtspflegergesetzes — kommt im Verfahren der Sozialgerichtsbarkeit nicht in Frage.) Ist das Armenrecht für die Zwangsvollstreckung bewilligt, so ordnet das Vollstreckungsgericht die Nachzahlung an. (Hier wird der Rechtspfleger tätig.) Zustellung der Nachzahlungsanordnung an den betroffenen Beteiligten ist gemäß § 63 Abs. 1 SGG erforderlich. Dem Armenanwalt ist von der Anordnung der Nachzahlung Kenntnis zu geben.

Die Nachzahlungsanordnung setzt, soweit nicht Nichtarmut von Anfang an bestanden hat, eine im Wege der Nachprüfung festzustellende Besserung der wirtschaftlichen Verhältnisse voraus (vgl. dazu Lappe, Rpfleger 1958, 137 [141]). Erstrittene Sozialleistungen sind in diesem Zusammenhang aus sozialen Gründen regelmäßig nicht dazu bestimmt und geeignet, zur Kostenabdeckung zu dienen, es sei denn, daß es sich um aufgelaufene erhebliche Summen handelt. Die Nachprüfung hat in vorbereitender Weise der Urkundsbeamte vorzunehmen. Eventuell kommt entsprechend dem Grad der Besserung nur die gerichtliche Anordnung einer einmaligen Teilnachzahlung in Frage. Vor der Entscheidung über die Verpflichtung zur Nachzahlung sind grundsätzlich die zum Armenrecht zugelassene Partei, die Bundes- oder Landeskasse und der beigeordnete Rechtsanwalt zu hören (§ 126 Abs. 3 Satz 1 ZPO). Wegen des Zeitraumes, in welchem die Nachzahlungsanordnung ausgesprochen werden kann, vgl. die Vornummer, ebenso wegen der erforderlichen Rechtsmittelbelehrung.

b) Haben sich die Verhältnisse des Armen nur in der Weise laufend gebessert, daß er die gesamte Kostenschuld lediglich in angemessenen Raten zahlen kann, muß die **Nachzahlung in** entsprechenden **Teilbeträgen** angeordnet werden. Rangfragen können hier in aller Regel nicht auftreten, weil konkurrierende Gerichtskostenforderungen dem § 183 SGG zufolge (er statuiert die Gerichtskostenfreiheit) nicht bestehen (vgl. hierzu den neuen § 126 Abs. 3 ZPO) und der Armenanwalt aus der Staatskasse grundsätzlich die volle gesetzliche Vergütung erhält, vgl. § 121 in Verb. mit §130 BRAGebO. (Die Kosten aus §§93, 109, 120 SGG stellen in diesem Zusammenhang ebenso wie die Kosten gemäß § 184 SGG Sonderkosten dar, die als solche nicht „konkurrieren" können.) Wegen der Rangfolge bei Anordnung der Nachzahlung im Falle des nur bruchteilmäßig bewilligten Armenrechts vgl. unten II B 1 d.

Die Anordnung der Nachzahlung in Raten kann unter den angegebenen Voraussetzungen (s. o.) im unmittelbaren Anschluß an die Armenrechtsbewilligung erfolgen (BGHZ 10, 139 = NJW 1953, 1510 = MDR 1953, 674 = JZ 1953, 607).

Wird die Nachzahlung der Kosten für verschiedene Instanzen gleichzeitig angeordnet, so ist grundsätzlich jede Instanz für sich zu betrachten, und zwar gehen bei Bewilligung von Raten die Kosten des ersten Rechtszuges den Kosten der zweiten Instanz usw. vor (vgl. Tschischgale, JVBl. 1958, 27). Bei Nachzahlungsanordnungen für verschiedene Instanzen zu verschiedenen Zeitpunkten (insbesondere durch verschiedene Gerichte) ist nach Möglichkeit eine entsprechende Abstimmung vorzunehmen, die als solche zulässig ist.

Der Armenanwalt darf die Nachzahlungsanordnung, die ja zuungunsten seiner Partei ergeht, niemals beantragen, er kann sie höchstens anregen. Er hat deshalb auch kein Beschwerderecht bei Ablehnung der Nachzahlung (vgl. § 127 ZPO).

c) **Der Beschluß, durch den die Nachzahlung** der Kosten (ganz oder teilweise) **angeordnet wird, kann** von dem betroffenen Armen **mit der Beschwerde angefochten werden,** wenn er von einem Sozialgericht erlassen ist (§ 127 Satz 2 ZPO, § 172 Abs. 1 SGG). Frist: ein Monat seit Verkündung oder Zustellung (§ 173 SGG, vgl. aber § 66 Abs. 2 SGG bei nicht erfolgter oder nicht richtiger Rechtsmittelbelehrung); Form: schriftlich oder zu Protokoll des Urkundsbeamten der Geschäftsstelle des befaßten Sozialgerichts (§ 173 SGG). Eine Mindestbeschwer ist nicht erforderlich (§ 127 ZPO, § 172 SGG). Das Beschwerdegericht entscheidet bei Nichtabhilfe (vgl. § 174 SGG) in eigener Ermessensausübung (§ 128 Abs. 1, § 142 Abs. 1 SGG). Die Beschwerdeentscheidung ergeht stets gebühren- und auslagenersatzfrei (§ 183 SGG); eine Kostenerstattung kommt nicht in Frage (s. o. 26, 28). Die Beschwerdeentscheidung kann nicht mehr weiter angefochten werden (§ 127 Satz 3 ZPO, § 177 SGG). Förmliche Zustellung des Beschwerdebeschlusses ist daher nicht erforderlich (vgl. § 63 Abs. 1 SGG).

Bei Aufhebung der Nachzahlungsanordnung sind inzwischen etwa gezahlte Beträge zurückzuzahlen (vom Anwalt bzw. der Staatskasse); dies allein entspricht rechtsstaatlichen Grundsätzen.

30. **Die Mitwirkung bei der Bewilligung oder Entziehung des Armenrechts und bei der Anordnung der Verpflichtung zur Nachzahlung** der Kosten (§ 126 ZPO) **gehört zur Instanztätigkeit** des beigeordneten Armenanwalts, die durch die zu zahlende Gebühr nach § 116 Abs. 2 BRAGebO abgegolten wird (vgl. hierzu § 37 Nr. 3 BRAGebO). **Erfolgt keine Beiordnung,** so **erhält der** insoweit **tätig gewordene Anwalt die — Mindest- — Gebühr der betreffenden Instanz** (§ 116 Abs. 2 BRAGebO) **in Höhe von $^3/_{10}$** (vgl. § 51 Abs. 1 Satz 1 BRAGebO). In mehreren Verfahren dieser Art erhält der Rechtsanwalt die Gebühr in jedem Rechtszug nur einmal (§ 51 Abs. 1 Satz 2 BRAGebO). Vorzeitige Beendigung des Auftrages und Entscheidung ohne streitige mündliche Verhandlung sind hierbei bedeutungslos (§ 51 Abs. 1 Satz 3 BRAGebO). Wegen einer etwaigen „Vergleichsgebühr" vgl. hier oben 20.

31. **Das Gericht ist** im Armenrechtsverfahren, im Entziehungsverfahren oder im Nachzahlungsverfahren **nicht befugt,** festzustellen und **auszusprechen, daß dem Armenanwalt kein Gebührenanspruch** gegen die Staatskasse **zusteht.** Ein derartiger

Ausspruch bindet den festsetzenden Urkundsbeamten, dessen alleinige Zuständigkeit für die Festsetzung der Armenanwaltsgebühren und ihre Prüfung in erster Instanz gegeben ist, nicht (vgl. OLG Düsseldorf, Rpfleger 1956, 43).

II. Die Vergütung des Armenanwalts und das Rückgriffsrecht der vergütenden Staatskasse

Übersicht

A. Die Armenanwaltsvergütung

1. a) **Der** im Armenrecht vor den Gerichten der Sozialgerichtsbarkeit **beigeordnete Rechtsanwalt** (bzw. Verwaltungsrechtsrat, vgl. § 217 Abs. 1 und 2 SGG) **erhält** nach dem einschlägigen § 121 BRAGebO, da nichts anderes bestimmt ist, **die gesetzliche Vergütung des § 116 Abs. 2 BRAGebO,** und zwar unabhängig vom erzielten Erfolg; im Verfahren vor dem Bundessozialgericht erfolgt die Vergütung aus der Bundeskasse, in Verfahren vor den Gerichten eines Landes aus der betreffenden Landeskasse. Der Armenanwalt erhält danach die Gebühren, die er unter gleichen Umständen auch als Wahlanwalt verdienen würde (das haben Brangsch, SGb 1957, 238, und Luetgebrune-Lotze, BRAGebO Anm. VI zu § 116, die die Bedeutung des neuen § 121 BRAGebO nicht erkannt haben, nicht beachtet). Wegen ihrer Höhe im Einzelfalle wird auf die Ausführungen im 7. Kap. I A 1 und 5 verwiesen. Da für die Höhe auch die Vermögens- und Einkommensverhältnisse des armen Auftraggebers von Bedeutung sind (vgl. § 12 Abs. 1 BRAGebO), diese aber jedenfalls bei einer vollen Armenrechtsbewilligung ungünstig sein müssen, wird der sog. Mittelbetrag nur in verhältnismäßig seltenen Fällen überschritten werden können. Die Erreichung des Höchstrahmens erscheint jedenfalls grundsätzlich nicht möglich, es sei denn, daß nach Verhandlung und Beweisaufnahme abschließend ein Vergleich geschlossen worden ist (vgl. den § 23, auch den § 24 BRAGebO, die außerhalb der normalen Vergütung regelnd eingreifen). Auf die Verhältnisse des dem armen Auftraggeber gegenüber Erstattungspflichtigen kommt es nicht an, ebenso selbstverständlich nicht auf die Verhältnisse der Staatskasse (des Staates). **Vor dem Sozialgericht erhält der Armenanwalt** danach **40 bis 120 DM** (Mittelbetrag 80 DM), **vor dem Landessozialgericht 60 bis 180 DM** (Mittelbetrag 120 DM) und **vor dem Bundessozialgericht 100 bis 300 DM** (Mittelbetrag 200 DM).

Die Vergütung aus § 121 BRAGebO absorbiert die Gebühr für das Armenrechtsverfahren nach § 114 Abs. 1 und § 51 Abs. 1 Satz 1 BRAGebO, wenn derselbe Anwalt beigeordnet worden ist.

Nach § 121 BRAGebO gilt auch für den Armenanwalt § 11 Abs. 2 Satz 2 BRAGebO, nach welchem für Gebühren Pfennigbeträge jeweils auf 10 DPf. aufzurunden sind.

Mag der für die Instanz beigeordnete Armenanwalt, z. B. infolge einer späten Beiordnung, eine noch so geringe Tätigkeit ausgeübt haben, so kann doch der gesetzliche Mindestbetrag der betreffenden Instanz grundsätzlich nicht unterschritten werden. Erledigt sich der Auftrag aber bevor der Anwalt als Armenanwalt eine Tätigkeit entfaltet hat (vgl. § 32 Abs. 1 BRAGebO), so erhält er nur die halbe Gebühr. An sich ist es auch für die Honorierung des Armenanwalts unwesentlich, ob es zur mündlichen Verhandlung oder zur Beweiserhebung gekommen ist oder ob die Beteiligten sich abschließend verglichen haben. (Wegen der Auswirkung dieser Vorgänge auf die Höhe im einzelnen vgl. das 7. Kap. I A 5.) Endlich spielt auch für die Armenanwaltsgebühren die Bewertung des Streitgegenstandes keinerlei Rolle.

b) **Ein Beschwerdeverfahren,** für das der Anwalt besonders beigeordnet sein muß, **löst,** auch wenn es Geldbeträge (z. B. Strafen oder Kosten) betrifft, **die Pauschalgebühr der höheren Instanz zu $^3/_{10}$ aus** (vgl. das 7. Kap. I A 1q), **und zwar zu $^3/_{10}$ der Mindestgebühr.** (Eine Kürzung der Höhe durch vorzeitige Auftragsbeendigung oder fehlende Streitverhandlung tritt hier nicht ein, vgl. § 61 BRAGebO, insbesondere Abs. 3.) Die etwaige Abhilfe der Beschwerde übt grundsätzlich keinen Einfluß aus. Handelt es sich um ein **Beschwerdeverfahren, bei dem die Beschwerde** nach Erledigung der Hauptsache (i. w. S.) **an die Stelle der Berufung tritt,** so **erhält der** beigeordnete **Armenanwalt die volle Mindestgebühr** des § 116 Abs. 2 BRAGebO (vgl. das 7. Kap. I A 1 q).

Ein Erinnerungsverfahren (auch betreffend Kosten, vgl. §§ 178, 189 Abs. 2, §§ 191, 197 Abs. 2 SGG) gehört grundsätzlich zur betreffenden Instanz; es wird durch die angemessen zu erhöhende Gebühr aus § 116 Abs. 2 BRAGebO mit abgegolten. Zur Überschreitung des Höchstrahmens wird die Berücksichtigung der Anwaltstätigkeit im Erinnerungsverfahren in aller Regel nicht führen.

c) Die **Sätze für Rechtsbeistände werden** jeweils **die Hälfte betragen.** (Vor dem Bundessozialgericht kommt die Beiordnung eines Rechtsbeistandes allerdings keinesfalls in Betracht.)

d) **Bei teilweiser Bewilligung des Armenrechts** (nämlich für einen Bruchteil) **erhält der** insoweit **beigeordnete Rechtsanwalt** nur **den entsprechenden Bruchteil der verdienten Gebühr,** mindestens jedoch 2 DM (vgl. §§ 122, 124, 123 Abs. 4 BRAGebO).

e) **Die Vergütung muß** von der Staatskasse **gezahlt werden, auch wenn ein Erstattungsanspruch** gegen den kostenmäßig unterlegenen gegnerischen Beteiligten (auf Grund der §§ 192, 193 SGG) **besteht.**

f) **Ist der Armenanwalt einem Streitgenossen beigeordnet, so wird dadurch, daß er den** oder einen **anderen Streitgenossen als Wahlanwalt vertritt, die Vergütungspflicht der Staatskasse nicht berührt** (vgl. Gelinsky-Meyer, Armenanwaltskosten 4. Aufl. S. 267). Wegen der Anrechnung von Zahlungen des Dritten vgl. unten 3g.

g) Auch **der Armenanwalt hat seine Dienste** grundsätzlich **in Person zu leisten** (§ 613 BGB). **Doch kann** auch **er sich** im Notfall unbedenklich — abgesehen von der Generalsubstitution — jedenfalls **durch einen anderen Anwalt, einen Anwaltsassessor oder einen Stationsreferendar vertreten lassen** (der zuletzt Genannte darf allerdings vor dem Bundessozialgericht nicht auftreten), ohne daß eine Gebührenvorenthaltung oder Verkürzung drohen könnte, vgl. § 4 BRAGebO (wegen der Auslagen in diesen Fällen, insbesondere was das Abwesenheitsgeld anbetrifft, vgl. die Darlegungen unten 2c).

h) Da der Anwaltsvertrag seiner Rechtsnatur zufolge überwiegend als Dienstvertrag anzusehen ist, **führt** in der Regel selbst ein **zu vertretendes mangelhaftes Tätigwerden** des Armenanwalts **nicht den Fortfall oder** eine **Verkürzung der Armenanwaltsvergütung herbei.** Die Staatskasse kann deshalb auch keinerlei Einwendungen gegen den Armenanwalt wegen der Zweckmäßigkeit seiner Handlungen erheben. Völlig überflüssige Handlungen sind allerdings gebührenrechtlich unbeachtlich.

Hat der beigeordnete Rechtsanwalt aber **durch schuldhaftes Verhalten** (z. B. Verschweigen der Einberufung zum Staatsdienst in naher Zukunft oder Anlaßgeben zur Kündigung durch die Partei oder Verlust der Zulassung durch ehrenrührige Handlungen) **die Beiordnung eines anderen Rechtsanwalts veranlaßt, so kann er Gebühren, die auch für den anderen Anwalt entstehen, nicht fordern** (§ 125 BRAGebO).

i) **In den Fällen nicht verschuldeten Armenanwaltswechsels** (vom Standpunkte des Anwalts aus gesehen) **muß die Staatskasse gegenüber beiden Anwälten** ohne Rücksicht auf die Frage des Bestehens oder des Umfanges der Ersatzpflicht des Armen oder Dritter **einstehen.** Die Bestellung eines neuen Anwalts nur für Gebühren, die dem ausscheidenden Anwalte noch nicht entstanden sind, ist unzulässig (OLG Düsseldorf, JVBl. 1937, 278).

k) **Abtretung, Verpfändung und Pfändung des Vergütungsanspruches sind zulässig;** sie können aber immer erst nach erfolgter Beiordnung vorgenommen werden.

1) **Zuviel erhaltene Beträge muß der Armenanwalt zurückzahlen,** wenn er sich nicht der Zwangseinziehung (nach dem Verwaltungsvollstreckungsgesetz) aussetzen will. Der Einwand des Wegfalls der Bereicherung kann aus Standesgründen grundsätzlich nicht geltend gemacht werden.

2. **Die Auslagen werden dem Armenanwalt** im Rahmen der Armenrechtsbewilligung **nach Maßgabe der Gebührenordnung für Rechtsanwälte** aus der Staatskasse **ersetzt.**

Im einzelnen erhält der Armenanwalt (vgl. hierzu auch § 193 Abs. 3 SGG):

a) die entstandenen **Post-, Telegrafen-, Fernsprech- und Fernschreibgebühren** (§ 26 BRAGebO). Die Höhe derselben richtet sich nach den postalischen Gebührensätzen. Für das Entstandensein dieser „Gebühren" genügt hier die Versicherung des Anwalts ebenfalls (vgl. § 128 Abs. 1 Satz 2 BRAGebO und § 104 Abs. 2 Satz 2 ZPO). Im allgemeinen wird durch die Versicherung auch die Notwendigkeit des Entstandenseins der Gebühren gedeckt;

b) **Schreibgebühren erhält der Armenanwalt nur** verhältnismäßig selten, weil die Fälle des § 27 Abs. 1 BRAGebO, die Schreibgebühren auslösen, Sonderwünsche der Partei betreffen, die von der regelmäßigen Armenrechtsbewilligung und Anwaltsbeiordnung nicht umfaßt werden. Es muß sich, wenn Schreibauslagenersatzansprüche gegen die Staatskasse ausgelöst werden sollen, um **zusätzlich gefertigte Abschriften oder Ablichtungen** handeln, **die** im Rechtsstreit **zur sachgemäßen Wahrnehmung der Belange der armen Partei erforderlich waren;**

c) die **Reisekosten.** Hier muß auf § 126 Abs. 1 Satz 1 BRAGebO verwiesen werden, nach welchem Auslagen grundsätzlich nicht vergütet werden (vor allem wenn sie eine Reise nach auswärts, vom Ort der Kanzlei des Anwalts gesehen, betreffen), die im Einzelfalle zur sachgemäßen Wahrnehmung der Interessen der armen Partei nicht erforderlich waren. (**Die Erforderlichkeit der Wahrnehmung auswärtiger Termine sollte** an sich **weitgehend bejaht werden,** zumal stattfindende Beweisaufnahmen im Zweifel streitentscheidende Bedeutung haben.) Ob eine Reise erforderlich ist, stellt das Prozeßgericht des betreffenden Rechtszuges auf Antrag – nur – des Armenanwalts vor Reiseantritt fest. Die – positive – Feststellung, daß die Reise erforderlich ist, ist für das Verfahren der Festsetzung der Armenanwaltsvergütung bindend (§ 126 Abs. 2 BRAGebO). Die Entscheidung des Gerichts ist als sogen. Gebührenvorentscheidung unanfechtbar (vgl. den aus den §§ 178, 189 Abs. 2, §§ 191, 197 Abs. 2 SGG sich ergebenden Grundsatz, nach welchem das Gericht der Instanz über Gebührenfragen endgültig entscheidet).

Bei Erforderlichkeit der Reise kann der Armenanwalt beanspruchen:

α) ein **Tagegeld,** das den durch die Reise bedingten Mehraufwand abgilt (wegen der Einzelheiten vgl. das 7. Kap. I B 2 c α);

Höhe: 14 DM für den vollen, durch die Reise zu mehr als 12 Stunden in Anspruch genommenen Kalendertag, 7 DM bei Abwesenheit von nur über 8 bis 12 Stunden, 4,20 DM bei mehr als 6 bis 8 Stunden Abwesenheit, § 28 Abs. 1 Satz 1 BRAGebO und § 9 Abs. 2 und 3 des Reiskostengesetzes (RKG);

β) ein **Übernachtungsentgelt,** das die Aufwendung für die außerhalb des beruflichen Wohnsitzes erforderlich werdende Übernachtung abgilt (wegen Einzelheiten, vgl. das 7. Kap. I B 2 c ß und den Anhang dazu).

Höhe: 11 DM (§ 28 Abs. 1 BRAGebO, § 9 Abs. 2 RKG);

γ) die tariflichen **Fahrtkosten** je nach dem zurückgelegten Weg, und zwar erster Eisenbahn- und erster Schiffsklasse einschließlich der notwendigen Kosten des Zu- und Abganges (von und zum Bahnhof, Hafen oder Flugplatz) für den Armenanwalt und sein zum beruflichen und persönlichen Gebrauch bestimmtes Gepäck, die Zu- und Abgangkosten in angemessener Höhe (§ 28 Abs. 1 Satz 1 BRAGebO, §§ 6 und 8 RKG).

Ist es nach den Umständen, insbesondere nach dem Zwecke der Geschäftsreise, erforderlich, ein anderes als ein öffentliches, regelmäßig verkehrendes Beförderungsmittel zu benutzen, so erhält der Rechtsanwalt Ersatz der notwendigen Aufwendungen, bei Benutzung eines eigenen Kraftwagens 0,25 DM für jedes angefangene Kilometer des Hin- und Rückwegs (§ 28 Abs. 1 Satz 2 BRAGebO).

Für Fußwege von insgesamt mehr als 4 km, die zur Erreichung des auswärtigen Geschäfts außerhalb des Orts desselben und des Orts des anwaltlichen Amtssitzes zurückgelegt werden mußten, sind 0,10 DM je km zu vergüten (vgl. § 7 RKG, Nr. 24, 25 AB).

Bei Erledigung mehrerer Geschäfte auf einer Reise sind die Kosten der mit erledigten Armenangelegenheiten anteilmäßig zu vergüten (vgl. dazu den § 29 BRAGebO).

Nicht zu vergüten sind die Mehrkosten, die dadurch entstehen, daß der Rechtsanwalt (sog. Simultananwalt) seinen Wohnsitz oder seine Kanzlei nicht an dem Ort hat, an dem sich das Prozeßgericht oder eine auswärtige Abteilung dieses Gerichtes befindet (§ 126 Abs. 1 Satz 2 BRAGebO). Dies gilt aber nicht — das hat vor allem für die Beiordnung beim Bundessozialgericht Bedeutung —, wenn ein Rechtsanwalt beigeordnet wird, der weder bei dem Prozeßgericht noch bei einem anderen Gericht förmlich zugelassen ist, das sich an demselben Ort wie das Prozeßgericht befindet (§ 126 Abs. 1 Satz 3 BRAGebO). Es gilt dann § 126 Abs. 1 Satz 1 BRAGebO (s. o. c);

δ) die nachgewiesenen **Nebenkosten;** sie gelten die Nebenaufwendungen z. B., für Durchlaß(Paß-)gebühren und für Versicherungen von Personen und Gepäck (so bei Flügen), ab (Einzelheiten vgl. 7. Kap. I B 2 c δ);

ε) ein **Abwesenheitsgeld,** das die Entschädigung dafür darstellt, daß der Rechtsanwalt seinem sonstigen verdiensteinbringenden Wirkungskreis entzogen wird (§ 28 Abs. 2 BRAGebO). Das Abwesenheitsgeld beträgt 15 DM für jeden Werktag. Dauert die Geschäftsreise nicht mehr als 4 Stunden, so ermäßigt sich das Abwesenheitsgeld auf die Hälfte.

Das Abwesenheitsgeld ist stets nur für den reisenden Anwalt zu zahlen. (Der bestellte Generalsubstitut — nur dieser —, auch wenn er noch kein Volljurist ist, stellt in jeder Hinsicht den Anwalt selber dar.)

War die Reise zur sachgemäßen Wahrnehmung der Interessen der armen Partei hinsichtlich eines auswärtigen Beweisaufnahmetermins erforderlich, so sind nach dem alles beherrschenden Grundsatze von Treu und Glauben in der in Frage kommenden Höhe des Entstandenseins aus der Staatskasse Kosten auch dann zu vergüten, wenn vom Anwalt ein Unterbevollmächtigter zur Terminswahrnehmung bestellt worden ist. Nicht erforderlich ist, daß dieser zur Terminswahrnehmung vom Prozeßgericht (auf entsprechenden Antrag) speziell beigeordnet wird, was an sich aus besonderen Gründen möglich ist. (Der besonders Beigeordnete hat einen eigenen Anspruch gegen die Staatskasse; wegen der Höhe vgl. das 7. Kap. I A 1 z a. E.);

d) **sonstige Aufwendungen,** die der Armenanwalt unbedingt machen muß, um seine Aufgaben erfüllen zu können (z. B. für einen Dolmetscher zur Übersetzung der erteilten Information), sind aus der Staatskasse ebenfalls zu ersetzen.

e) Die **Regelung des Auslagenersatzes gilt** gemäß § 217 SGG **auch für beigeordnete Verwaltungsrechtsräte und diesen Gleichgestellte.**

f) **Für** etwa **beigeordnete Rechtsbeistände gilt die** wiedergegebene **Regelung** der Auslagen **grundsätzlich ebenfalls** (vgl. § 193 Abs. 3 SGG); allerdings steht ihnen das **Abwesenheitsgeld nur in Höhe von 10 DM bzw. 5 DM zu** (je nachdem die Reise mehr als oder nur 4 Stunden und weniger benötigte). **An die Stelle der Reisekostenstufe II tritt** bei Geschäftsreisen die **Reisekostenstufe III** (Art. IX § 1 Abs. 3 Satz 2 KostÄndG). Das Tagegeld beträgt danach 11 DM, das Übernachtungsgeld 10 DM. Benutzt werden darf hier nur die zweite Wagenklasse.

3. a) **Die in einem Vorverfahren entstandenen Kosten werden von der Staatskasse in keiner Weise erstattet; das Vorverfahren wird von der Armenrechtsbewilligung nicht erfaßt.** (Wegen der Nichtanrechnung einer im Vorverfahren erhaltenen Vergütung auf das Armenanwaltshonorar vgl. unten g.)

b) **Der Armenanwalt kann den** für Gebühren und Auslagen entstandenen **Umsatzsteuerbetrag** — auch — **aus der Staatskasse erstattet verlangen,** vgl. hierzu das 7. Kap. I zu A und B Nr. 2.

c) **Eine Gebührenvorschußpflicht der Staatskasse** gegenüber dem Armenanwalt **besteht nicht** (§ 127 Abs. 1 BRAGebO). **Für die** voraussichtlich **erwachsenden Auslagen kann der Rechtsanwalt** aus der Bundes- oder Landeskasse **einen angemessenen Vorschuß fordern,** soweit ihm, insbesondere wegen der Höhe der Auslagen, nicht zugemutet werden kann, diese aus eigenen Mitteln vorzuschießen (§ 127 Abs. 2 Satz 1 BRAGebO). Über seine Bewilligung beschließt der Urkundsbeamte der betreffenden Instanz, gegen dessen Entscheidung — grundsätzlich binnen Monatsfrist seit Bekanntgabe — das Gericht des Urkundsbeamten angerufen werden kann, das endgültig entscheidet (vgl. hierzu § 127 Abs. 2 Satz 2, § 128 BRAGebO und § 178 SGG).

d) Der Auslagenersatzanspruch wie überhaupt **der Vergütungsanspruch des beigeordneten Anwalts** gegen die Staatskasse **wird mit dem Ergehen einer Entscheidung bzw. mit der sonstigen Beendigung der Instanz oder mit einer anderweitigen Erledigung der Beiordnung fällig** (vgl. § 16 BRAGebO). **Fälligkeit tritt auch bei** (evtl. rein tatsächlichem) **Ruhen des Verfahrens mit längerer Dauer als 3 Monate ein** (vgl. § 16 Satz 2 BRAGebO). Eine spätere Fortsetzung des Verfahrens macht die Fälligkeit nicht rückgängig.

Wegen der Beendigung der Instanz im einzelnen vgl. das 7. Kap. I A 8.

e) **Der Gebühren- und Auslagenersatzanspruch des beigeordneten Rechtsanwalts,** Verwaltungsrechtsrats (i. w. S.) und Rechtsbeistandes **verjährt** nach § 196 Abs. 1 Nr. 15 BGB **in 2 Jahren** seit dem Schlusse des Jahres, in welchem der Anspruch erstmalig fällig wird (vgl. Gaedeke, ArmAnwKostG S. 126). Die Erhebung der Einrede der Verjährung obliegt ausschließlich dem zur Vertretung der Staatskasse berufenen Organ (Bezirksrevisor u. ä.). Die Verjährung der Ansprüche gegenüber der armen Partei ist bis zur Anordnung der Nachzahlung (§ 125 ZPO) gehemmt (§ 202 Abs. 1 BGB). **Verwirkung** kommt neben der kurzen Verjährung nicht in Betracht. **Rückzahlungsansprüche** verjähren ebenfalls in zwei Jahren (§ 196 Abs. 1 Nr. 16 BGB).

f) **Gebührenvereinbarungen** (dem Grunde und der Höhe nach) mit dem Beteiligten, dem er beigeordnet ist, oder mit der Staatskasse **kann der Anwalt** (evtl. Rechtsbeistand) **nicht mit verbindlicher Wirkung treffen** (§ 3 Abs. 4 Satz 1 BRAGebO). Hat der Auftraggeber freiwillig und ohne Vorbehalt geleistet, so kann er das Geleistete vom Anwalt nicht deshalb zurückfordern, weil eine Verbindlichkeit nicht bestanden hat (vgl. § 3 Abs. 4 Satz 2 BRAGebO). Hinsichtlich der Anrechnung geleisteter Zahlungen vgl. unten g. Auch die vorzeitige Fälligkeit seiner Gebühren kann der Armenanwalt nicht mit seiner Partei oder mit der Staatskasse vereinbaren. **Wohl aber** kann der Armenanwalt im Einzelfalle **auf seinen Gebührenanspruch** gegenüber der Staatskasse ausdrücklich oder durch Nichtgeltendmachung **verzichten.**

g) **Vorschüsse und Zahlungen** (grundsätzlich aller Art), die der beigeordnete Armenanwalt von seinem Auftraggeber oder für diesen von einem Dritten (auch einem im Wahlanwaltsverhältnis mit vertretenen, gesamtschuldnerisch haftenden Streitgenossen) in der betreffenden Angelegenheit vor oder nach der Beiordnung etwa erhalten hat, **sind anzurechnen** (§ 129 BRAGebO; bei nur zum Teil bewilligtem Armenrecht allerdings zunächst auf den Teil, für den ein Anspruch gegen die Staatskasse nicht besteht). Soweit die Anrechnungspflicht reicht, erlischt der Erstattungsanspruch gegen die Staatskasse. Die Anrechnungspflicht kann durch Vereinbarung des Armenanwalts mit der Partei oder sonstwie niemals eingeschränkt oder aufgehoben, wohl aber erweitert werden (vgl. Gaedeke, aaO. S. 196). Allerdings wird für zulässig erachtet, daß die Partei mit dem Anwalt vor der Beiordnung vereinbart oder bis zu derselben bei einer Zahlung bestimmt, ein gezahlter Vorschuß solle nur auf das Wahlanwaltshonorar geleistet sein und er müsse zurückgezahlt werden, soweit er die Leistungen der Staatskasse im Falle der Beiordnung ermäßigt (vgl. Gaedeke, aaO.; Riedel-Sußbauer, BRAGebO Anm. 4 letzter Absatz zu § 129). Der Armenanwalt ist dann zur entsprechenden Rückzahlung verpflichtet. Eine Vergütung, die der Anwalt in einem Vorverfahren erhalten hat, ist dagegen nicht – mehr – in Anrechnung zu bringen (vgl. den jetzt aufgehobenen § 196 Abs. 6 SGG).

h) **Der Armenanwalt ist verpflichtet, die geleisteten Vorschüsse oder Zahlungen,** soweit sie die Zahlungspflicht der Staatskasse mindern, **anzugeben** bzw. anzuzeigen (auch nach der Festsetzung! Dann ist entsprechende Rückzahlung an die Staatskasse bzw. richtigerweise Herausgabe des Neuerlangten an die Staatskasse vorzunehmen). Bei Verweigerung der Angabe hat die Festsetzung der Vergütung zu unterbleiben (Zwangsmittel zur Erbringung der Angaben bestehen nicht).

i) **Eine Kostenfestsetzungsgebühr erhält der Armenanwalt** schon deswegen **nicht,** weil die Festsetzung der Armenanwaltskosten in seinem Interesse geschieht (§ 128 Abs. 4 BRAGebO).

B. Das Rückgriffsrecht der Staatskasse

1. Der Ersatzanspruch des Armenanwalts gegen die Staatskasse erwächst nicht allein auf der Grundlage der staatshoheitsrechtlichen Beiordnung, sondern zugleich auch auf der Basis eines privatrechtlichen Rechtsgeschäfts, nämlich des Auftrages des bevollmächtigenden Armen. Ein Ersatzanspruch des beigeordneten Anwalts gegen die Staatskasse ist daher grundsätzlich nur soweit gegeben wie er grundlagenmäßig auch gegenüber dem Beteiligten besteht. Staat und Beteiligter stehen als Schuldner nebeneinander; abgesehen von der Stundung gegenüber dem Armen haftet sowohl der eine wie der andere dem beigeordneten Anwalt. Das Reichsgericht hat in der grundlegenden Entscheidung im 126. Bande (S. 178) dahingestellt sein lassen, ob es sich mit Rücksicht auf die wiedergegebene Verknüpfung um eine Art gesamtschuldnerischer Haftung der Staatskasse neben der armen Partei im Sinne des § 421 BGB oder um ein bürgschaftsähnliches Verhältnis handelt. Richtig ist die erste Ansicht: Es liegt ein unechtes Gesamtschuldverhältnis vor, bei welchem der Anspruch gegen den einen Gesamtschuldner (den Beteiligten) zunächst kraft Gesetzes gestundet ist, so daß ausschließlich der andere Gesamt-

schuldner, und zwar auf Grund besonderer gesetzlicher Regelung seiner Verpflichtung, in Anspruch genommen werden kann (vgl. Gaedeke, ArmAnwKostG S. 41 und Tschischgale, KostR in ZivSach. S. 88). Letzter Schuldner ist und bleibt dabei der Beteiligte selbst.

Mit Rücksicht auf das Vorstehende **ist im § 130 BRAGebO bestimmt, daß, soweit dem beigeordneten Rechtsanwalt wegen seiner Vergütung** (Gebühren und Auslagen) **ein Anspruch gegen die eigene Partei oder** auf dem Wege über diese **gegen einen erstattungspflichtigen Gegner zusteht, er** mit der Erstattung **auf die zahlende Staatskasse übergeht** (mit eventuellen Sicherungen, vgl. §§ 412, 401 BGB). Zwar heißt es im Satz 2 des ersten Absatzes dieses Paragraphen weiterhin, daß der Übergang – beider Ansprüche – nicht zum Nachteil des Rechtsanwalts geltend gemacht werden kann. Doch kommt diesem Satz im Verfahren der Sozialgerichtsbarkeit deswegen keine große Bedeutung zu, weil die Vergütung des Armenanwalts grundsätzlich in Höhe des Wahlanwaltsentgelts erfolgt. Der Honoraranspruch steht daher entweder dem Anwalt oder der ihn befriedigenden Staatskasse zu. Bei bruchteilweiser Bewilligung des Armenrechts geht allerdings der Anwalt bezüglich seines überschießenden (reinen) Wahlanspruchs der Staatskasse als Gläubigerin (auch hinsichtlich der Gerichtsvollziehergebühren) vor. Die Staatskasse ist jedoch dadurch nicht gehindert, wegen ihrer Forderung gegen den einen oder anderen Kostenschuldner beizutreiben oder von ihm Zahlungen anzunehmen. Bei Zusammentreffen von Vollstreckungsmaßnahmen mit solchen des Anwalts muß sie jedoch zurücktreten, ebenso bei einer Pfandverwertung (vgl. hierzu Riedel-Sußbauer, BRAGebO Anm. 8 zu § 130). Unerheblich ist für das Vorstehende, ob der vollstreckbare Kostenfestsetzungsbeschluß auf den Namen des Anwalts (vgl. § 124 ZPO) oder seiner Partei lautet (KG, JW 1936, 613).

a) Selbst wenn dem Armen gemäß § 192 SGG gegenüber der Staatskasse – zusätzlich – die von dieser verauslagten oder zu verauslagenden Armenanwaltskosten ausdrücklich auferlegt worden sind, **kann die Kasse den auf sie übergegangenen Honoraranspruch solange nicht beitreiben, als dem Schuldner,** dem armen Beteiligten, **das Armenrecht zur Seite steht;** solange ist ja der Honoraranspruch des Anwalts auf Grund der Armenrechtsbewilligung gestundet. **Erst bei Anordnung der Nachzahlung** der gestundeten Kosten gemäß § 125 ZPO **kann die Staatskasse ihren Rückgriffsanspruch gegen den** früher **armen Beteiligten verwirklichen** (bei Nachzahlung in Raten je nach Fälligkeit der einzelnen Beträge). Bei der Anordnung der Nachzahlung in Raten braucht die neue Rangbestimmung des § 126 Abs. 3 ZPO schon deswegen nicht beachtet zu werden, weil im Verfahren der Sozialgerichtsbarkeit Gerichtskosten nicht anfallen (vgl. § 183 SGG; die Kosten der §§ 93, 109 Abs. 1 und § 120 Abs. 2 SGG sind wie auch die des § 184 SGG Sonderkosten in bestimmten persönlichen oder auf das Personensubjekt bezogenen Fällen). Einen – vorgehenden – Differenzanspruch des Anwalts aus der Zeit seiner Beiordnung gibt es zudem in aller Regel nicht, weil er in Höhe der Wahlanwaltsgebühr aus der Staatskasse honoriert wird.

Zweifel können entstehen, ob die Staatskasse den auf sie gemäß § 130 BRAGebO übergegangenen Honoraranspruch des Anwalts gegen den armen Beteiligten überhaupt geltend machen kann, auch wenn an sich eine Anordnung der Nachzahlung der durch die Armenrechtsbewilligung gestundeten Gebühren gemäß § 125 ZPO erfolgt ist. Denn in dem grundsätzlichen § 183 SGG heißt es, daß das Verfahren vor den Gerichten der Sozialgerichtsbarkeit kostenfrei, d. h. gebühren- und auslagenersatzfrei ist. Ein Beteiligter braucht daher im Verfahren der Sozialgerichtsbarkeit grundsätzlich weder Gebühren zu zahlen noch Auslagen zu ersetzen. An sich hat die Staatskasse die Armenanwaltskosten für einen beigeordneten und von ihr honorierten Armenanwalt verauslagt. Dabei handelt es sich aber, wie sich mit Deutlichkeit aus dem § 92 GKG ergibt, nicht um Auslagen des Gerichts im eigentlichen Sinne (BGH, JVBl. 1957, 22). Der Staat hat gegenüber dem Armenanwalt gewissermaßen nur seine eigene Zahlungsverpflichtung, die aus rechtsstaatlichen und sozialen Gründen besteht, erfüllt. In Höhe seiner Zahlung ist dabei gemäß der ausdrücklichen Bestimmung des § 130 BRAGebO die Gebührenforderung des Anwalts in der gleichen Höhe auf die Staatskasse übergegangen. Die Geltendmachung dieses übergegangenen fremden Gebührenanspruchs ist durch § 183 SGG nicht ausgeschlossen (im Ergebnis ebenso Brocke, Sozialrichter S. 150). Ein Ausschluß hätte ausdrücklich bestimmt werden müssen; das ist aber nicht geschehen. Im übrigen dürfte es durchaus nicht unbillig sein, daß der arme Beteiligte, der die Gerichte der Sozialgerichtsbarkeit beschäftigt hat, auch gegenüber der Staatskasse (gegenüber seinem Anwalt besteht seine Verpflichtung unzweifelhaft) zur Nachzahlung der Kosten verpflichtet ist, wenn sich seine wirtschaftliche Lage gebessert hat, wie es der §125 ZPO vorsieht (vgl. hierzu Tschischgale, JVBl. 1957, 4 und BGH, JVBl. 1957, 22).

Die Verwirklichung des übergegangenen und durch die Nachzahlungsanordnung fällig gewordenen **Anspruchs erfolgt** gemäß § 130 Abs. 2 BRAGebO **im Wege der gerichtlichen Kostenanforderung** (durch Kostenbescheid = „Kostenrechnung") des Urkundsbeamten der betreffenden Instanz (vgl. das 4. Kap. 2c). Bei Nichtzahlung erfolgt Zwangsbeitreibung nach dem Verwaltungsvollstreckungsgesetz, die von der Kasse in die Wege zu leiten ist. Allein gegen seine Inanspruchnahme mit dem praktischen Ziele auf Ersetzung der seitens der Staatskasse verauslagten Armenanwaltskosten kann sich der arme Beteiligte gegebenenfalls mit der schriftlichen oder zu Protokoll der Geschäftsstelle des Gerichts zu erklärenden Gerichtsanrufung (Erinnerung) wenden, und zwar grundsätzlich innerhalb einer Monatsfrist seit Zustellung des mit Rechtsbehelfsbelehrung versehenen Kostenbescheides (vgl. die §§ 178, 173 und 63 Abs. 1 SGG). Denn der Beteiligte braucht – bis zur Höhe der Verauslagung – der Staatskasse nur das zu ersetzen, was an den Armenanwalt nach der Sach- und Rechtslage zu zahlen war, nicht was an ihn tatsächlich gezahlt worden ist. Für den Beteiligten ist die Gebührenfestsetzung gegenüber dem Armenanwalt daher nicht bindend. Das Gericht der betreffenden Instanz entscheidet, falls keine Abhilfe durch den jeweils bestellten Urkundsbeamten erfolgt, – kostenfrei – endgültig (§§ 174, 178 SGG), vgl. hierzu die entsprechenden Darlegungen im 4. Kap. 2c. (Bei zu niedriger Kostenanforderung kann gegebenenfalls auch die Staatskasse das Gericht „anrufen".)

b) **Zu unterscheiden von dem auf die Staatskasse übergegangenen Honoraranspruch des Anwalts gegen seine Partei ist der der Staatskasse** in Ausführung von § 192 SGG **gegebenenfalls zustehende eigene Anspruch gegen den Armen auf Grund dessen Verurteilung, die für ihn verauslagten** oder zu zahlenden **Armenanwaltskosten gegenüber der Staatskasse** (ganz oder bruchteilsmäßig) **zu tragen** (so bei Erschleichung des Armenrechts). Auch dieser Anspruch kann im Hinblick auf die durch die Armenrechtsbewilligung herbeigeführte allgemeine Zahlungssperre nur geltend gemacht werden, wenn und soweit die Nachzahlung der Kosten gemäß § 125 ZPO angeordnet worden ist. **Er wird bei Anordnung der Nachzahlung wie der übergegangene Anspruch geltend gemacht und beigetrieben.** Bei Teilauferlegung der erwähnten Kosten geht die Staatskasse mit ihrem originär eigenen Anspruch gegen die arme Partei gegenüber dem Anwalt hinsichtlich dessen überschießenden Anspruchs gegen seine Partei sinngemäß ebenfalls nach.

2. **An die Partei des Armenanwalts wird sich die Staatskasse dann halten, wenn kein erstattungspflichtiger Gegner derselben vorhanden ist oder wenn,** falls ein erstattungspflichtiger gegnerischer Beteiligter da ist, **von diesem nichts beigetrieben werden kann.**

a) α) **Steht dem Armen ein Beteiligter gegenüber, dem** gemäß § 192 oder § 193 SGG **aufgegeben worden ist, die Anwaltskosten** dem armen Beteiligten (ganz oder zu einem Bruchteil) **zu erstatten** — diese Anordnung zwischen den Streitbeteiligten kann Hand in Hand gehen mit der Anordnung nach § 192 SGG, daß im Verhältnis zur Staatskasse der arme Beteiligte die Armenanwaltskosten zu tragen hat —, **so geht** auch **der daraus resultierende Anspruch,** der im Hinblick auf die Sonderbestimmung des § 124 ZPO im Verhältnis zu dem an sich kostenbegünstigten Beteiligten dem Armenanwalt zusteht, in Höhe der geleisteten Zahlung im Umfange seines Bestehens **auf die den Armenanwalt befriedigende Staatskasse über.** (Insgesamt kann die Staatskasse den für den Armenanwalt aufgewendeten Betrag selbstverständlich nur einmal ersetzt verlangen, und zwar entweder vom Gegner oder von der armen Partei.) Zu erwähnen ist hier, daß dem aus §§ 192, 193 SGG Erstattungspflichtigen derjenige gleichsteht, der in einem gerichtlichen Vergleich die Anwaltskosten des armen Beteiligten entsprechend zu erstatten übernommen hat.

Hinsichtlich dieses Rückgriffsanspruchs ist die Staatskasse nicht durch eine etwaige in ihren Wirkungen noch bestehende **Bewilligung des Armenrechts an den** schuldenden **Gegner** — die attestierte Armut der kostenberechtigten Partei spielt hier keine Rolle — **gehindert.** Denn nach § 117 ZPO hat die Bewilligung des Armenrechts auf die Verpflichtung zur Erstattung der dem Obsiegenden erwachsenden Kosten keinen Einfluß (so auch OLG Celle, Nds. Rpfl. 1956, 35; a. A. Gaedeke, ArmAnwKostG S. 261, der eine Nachzahlungsanordnung gegenüber dem armen Gegner verlangt). Durch den gesetzlichen Übergang des Anspruchs auf die Staatskasse gemäß § 130 Abs. 1 BRAGebO wird ja die Rechtsnatur des betroffenen Anspruchs in keiner Weise verändert. Es fragt sich nur, ob das Vorgehen gegen einen Armen lohnend und angebracht ist.

Die Geltendmachung des Anspruchs gegen den gegnerischen Beteiligten erfolgt im gleichen Wege wie bezüglich des Rückgriffsanspruchs gegenüber dem armen Beteiligten, nämlich durch Kostenanforderung (Kostenbescheid) des Urkundsbeamten der Instanz (vgl. § 130 Abs. 2 BRAGebO und die Ausführungen hier oben 1a). Sie ist erst nach Rechtskraft des Kostentitels angebracht, weil da erst die Schuldverpflichtung des Gegners endgültig feststeht. Wegen der nach § 130 Abs. 1 Satz 2 BRAGebO auch hier bestehenden Rangfolgefragen zwischen der Staatskasse und dem Anwalt des Obsiegenden bei nur (bruch-)teilweiser Armenrechtsbewilligung vgl. oben 1. Dem Anwalt des unterlegenen Gegners steht bei bruchteilmäßiger Bewilligung des Armenrechts ein Vorrecht im Verhältnis zur Staatskasse selbstverständlich nur hinsichtlich des Anspruchs gegenüber seiner eigenen Partei zu, da ein Anspruch gegen den Gegner gar nicht besteht. Nach Anordnung der Nachzahlung gegen seine eigene Partei steht der Anwalt des Unterlegenen mit dem Anwalt des Obsiegenden auf einer Stufe, was das Verhältnis zur unterlegenen Partei anbetrifft.

Auch der gegnerische Beteiligte hat allein gegen seine unmittelbare Inanspruchnahme einen Rechtsbehelf, nämlich den der oben (1a) wiedergegebenen schriftlichen oder zur Niederschrift des Urkundsbeamten erklärten Anrufung des Gerichts der betreffenden Instanz innerhalb eines Monats seit Zustellung des mit Rechtsbehelfsbelehrung versehenen Kostenbescheides. Bei Nichtabhilfe durch den jeweils zuständigen Urkundsbeamten entscheidet das Gericht der Instanz — kostenfrei — endgültig (vgl. die §§ 173, 174, 178 SGG). Auch der Gegner braucht — bis zur Höhe der Verauslagung — nicht mehr an die Staatskasse zu zahlen als diese an den Armenanwalt des kostenmäßig Obsiegenden auf Grund der gesetzlichen Bestimmungen hat zahlen dürfen. Auf das, was die Staatskasse tatsächlich gezahlt hat, kommt es demgegenüber nicht an. Für den gegnerischen Beteiligten ist die Festsetzung der Gebühren des obsiegenden Armenanwalts daher ebenfalls nicht bindend. (Ein etwaiger Verlust bleibt, falls es der Staatskasse nicht gelingt, vom Armenanwalt die Zuvielzahlung zurückzuerhalten, bei dieser hängen.) Bei zu niedriger Kostenanforderung kann hier gegebenenfalls auch die Staatskasse das Gericht anrufen (vgl. dazu das 4. Kap. 2c).

β) **Der Übergang des** zuletzt genannten **Anspruchs auf die Staatskasse kann zu Schwierigkeiten führen, wenn die Zahlung der Armenanwaltskosten nach dem Ergehen eines Kostenfestsetzungsbeschlusses** zugunsten des armen Beteiligten oder — vgl. § 124 ZPO — zugunsten seines Anwalts nach § 197 SGG **erfolgt. Hier ist,** und zwar stets vom Urkundsbeamten der ersten Instanz, **wie folgt, zu verfahren** (vgl. hierzu die inhaltlich gebliebene, jetzt auf Länderbasis am 22. 7. 1958 neu gefaßte AV des RJM vom 7. 10. 1935, DJ S. 846): Es ist die vollstreckbare Ausfertigung des Kostenfestsetzungsbeschlusses vom Kostengläubiger (dem armen Beteiligten oder dem Armenanwalt) zurückzufordern. Nach Feststellung und Anweisung der Armenanwaltskosten, die hier ausnahmsweise auch bei höherinstanzlichen Verfahren im Armenrecht vom Urkundsbeamten der ersten Instanz vorzunehmen sind, da dieser allein (vgl. § 197 Abs. 1 SGG) in den zugunsten des kostenmäßig obsiegenden Beteiligten oder seines (Armen-)Anwalts ergangenen Kostenfestsetzungsbeschluß eingreifen kann, ist auf der zurückgereichten Ausfertigung des Festsetzungsbeschlusses zu vermerken, um welchen Betrag sich infolge des Übergangs auf die Staatskasse die im Kostenfestsetzungsbeschluß festgesetzten Kosten verringern und welchen Restbetrag (regelmäßig persönliche Kosten betreffend) der Erstattungspflichtige an den Kostengläubiger zu zahlen hat. Den gleichen Vermerk hat der Urkundsbeamte (erster Instanz) auf die Urschrift des Kostenfestsetzungsbeschlusses zu setzen; dort hat er außerdem zu bescheinigen, daß die Ausfertigung mit demselben Vermerk versehen und an den Kostengläubiger zurückgesandt ist. (Die Rücksendung erfolgt portofrei.) Konnte die vollstreckbare Ausfertigung des Kostenfestsetzungsbeschlusses — ausnahmsweise, nämlich wegen besonderer Hinderungsgründe — nicht vorgelegt werden, so hat der Urkundsbeamte der ersten Instanz dem erstattungspflichtigen Kostenschuldner postgebührenfrei Mitteilung von dem Stande seiner Kostenschuld zu machen. Hat die Partei des Armenanwalts die Staatskasse hinsichtlich deren Auslagen gegenüber dem Armenanwalt befriedigt, so tritt natürlich keine Verkürzung der zu ihren Gunsten festgesetzten Kosten ein. Auf den Gegner kann dann nur die arme Partei zurückgreifen.

Ergeht der Kostenfestsetzungsbeschluß erst **nach der Bezahlung der Armenanwaltskosten aus der Staatskasse** (die Festsetzung der Armenanwaltskosten ist hier durch den Urkundsbeamten der Instanz, für die das Armenrecht bewilligt war, erfolgt), **so sind die Kosten** zugunsten des kostenmäßig obsiegenden Beteiligten oder seines (Armen-)Anwalts **nur abzüglich des aus der Staatskasse gezahlten Betrages festzusetzen** (vom Urkundsbeamten der ersten Instanz), es sei denn, daß die Partei des Armenanwalts ihrerseits die Staatskasse befriedigt hat. (Im letzten Falle erfolgt unverkürzte Kostenfestsetzung zugunsten der armen Partei, die allein den Erstattungsanspruch an den Gegner hat.)

Befriedigt später die Partei des Armenanwalts die Staatskasse, so kann bei verkürzter Festsetzung **die nachträgliche Festsetzung des gezahlten Betrages** gegenüber dem erstattungspflichtigen Gegner gemäß § 197 SGG **erfolgen.**

γ) Zu bemerken in diesem Zusammenhange ist, **daß sich die im Kostenerstattungsverhältnis stehenden Beteiligten trotz des** gesetzlichen **Überganges der Erstattungsforderung** gegen den Kostenschuldner **auf** die den Armenanwalt befriedigende Staatskasse in vollem Umfange in höherer Instanz oder außergerichtlich — bis zur rechtskräftigen Beendigung des Verfahrens — **vergleichen können** (Tschischgale, KostR in ZivSach. S. 92; Gaedeke, ArmAnwKostG S. 245). Die Forderung ist nämlich nur mit ihren Eigenheiten übergegangen; eine unabdingbare Eigenart aller, insbesondere der außergerichtlichen Kostenansprüche aber ist, daß die Beteiligten bei einer möglichen Beilegung des schwebenden Rechtsstreits durch Vergleich vereinbaren können, ob und in welchem Umfange dieser oder jener Streitteil entstandene auferlegte oder aufzuerlegende Kosten trägt. Die Beteiligten dürfen allerdings bei ihren Vereinbarungen nicht auf eine sittenwidrige Schädigung der Staatskasse ausgehen. Bei Vorliegen der entsprechenden Voraussetzungen wäre die die Staatskasse benachteiligende Kostenvereinbarung der Beteiligten nichtig (§ 138 BGB). Der bei einem derartigen Vergleich mitwirkende Armenanwalt könnte überdies, jedenfalls soweit der Vergleich Gebührenfolgen hat, seinen Honoraranspruch an die Staatskasse verwirken (vgl. die Gedankengänge des OLG Köln, JVBl. 1957, 68).

b) **Zu unterscheiden von dem** auf die befriedigende Staatskasse gegebenenfalls **übergehenden Anspruch** des armen Kostengläubigers **auf Erstattung der Anwaltskosten** gemäß §§ 192, 193 Abs. 1 SGG **ist der der Staatskasse** auf Grund einer Entscheidung nach § 192 SGG etwa **zustehende eigene Anspruch gegen den kostenmäßig belasteten Beteiligten,** dem im Rahmen der genannten Bestimmung auferlegt worden ist, der Staatskasse die für den armen Beteiligten verauslagten oder auf Grund erfolgter Armenrechtsbewilligung zu zahlenden (gesetzlich bestimmten) Armenanwaltskosten ganz oder bruchteilmäßig zu ersetzen. Bei einer derartigen Kostenauferlegung wird eine Erstattungspflicht zugunsten des armen Beteiligten in Höhe der Armenanwaltskosten nicht ausgesprochen sein und auch nicht ausgesprochen werden können, da der Kostenschuldner sonst durch das Gericht von vornherein in die Gefahr einer Doppelzahlung gebracht werden würde. (Diese Gefahr besteht bei der Armenrechtsbewilligung zugunsten des Gläubigers eines nach §§ 192, 193 SGG für erstattungspflichtig erklärten Beteiligten mit Rücksicht auf den möglichen Übergang des Erstattungsanspruchs auf die Staatskasse an sich zwar auch; doch kann sie hier leicht durch eine entsprechende inhaltliche Verkürzung des Kostenfestsetzungsbeschlusses nach § 197 SGG, siehe hier oben a β, abgewendet werden.)

Dieser Anspruch der Staatskasse nach § 192 SGG **kann ebenfalls unabhängig von einer durch Armenrechtsbewilligung attestierten Armut des Erstattungspflichtigen** ohne weiteres **geltend gemacht werden** (vgl. § 117 ZPO). **Die Geltendmachung und Beitreibung erfolgt wie bei dem auf die Staatskasse übergegangenen Anspruch gegen den gegnerischen Beteiligten.** Dieser von vornherein eigene Anspruch der Staatskasse geht bei bruchteilmäßig auferlegter Erstattungspflicht zugunsten der Staatskasse dem überschießenden Anspruch des Anwalts der obsiegenden Partei gegen den Gegner sinngemäß ebenfalls nach.

Abschließend sei bemerkt: Ist die Anordnung einer Erstattungspflicht nach § 193 SGG oder die Auferlegung der Armenanwaltskosten auf den Gegner nach § 192

SGG unterblieben, so kann begrifflich kein Anspruch gegen den gegnerischen Beteiligten auf die den Armenanwalt befriedigende Staatskasse übergehen.

3. **Auf Grund des § 130 Abs. 1 BRAGebO kann die Staatskasse Erstattungsansprüche gegen andere** als die arme Partei und ihren Gegner **nicht erwerben.** Soweit etwa die Staatskasse einen Anwalt befriedigt, der einmal der armen Partei als Armenanwalt beigeordnet ist, gleichzeitig aber einen nicht armen Streitgenossen des Armen als Wahlanwalt vertritt, so erwirbt die Staatskasse durch ihre im Verfahren der Sozialgerichtsbarkeit regelmäßig volle Gebührenzahlung, die ja für den Armen erfolgt, den bürgerlich-rechtlichen Ausgleichsanspruch der armen Partei gemäß § 426 BGB, der sich im Zweifel auf die halbe Höhe beläuft. Damit erlangt die Staatskasse aber nur eine Rechtsstellung wie jeder andere Gesamtschuldner, der den Gläubiger in der in Frage kommenden Höhe befriedigt (vgl. Gaedeke, ArmAnwKostG S. 243); **sie kann daher gegen den Streitgenossen des Armen nicht im Zuge der Gerichtskostenanforderung im Verwaltungszwangsverfahren vorgehen, sondern muß sich im Klagewege** vor den ordentlichen Gerichten **einen Vollstreckungstitel verschaffen,** falls nicht freiwillig gezahlt wird. Bei nur (bruch-)teilweise bewilligtem Armenrecht muß die Zahlung der Staatskasse an den Anwalt bei einem vorhandenen Streitgenossen mehr als die Hälfte betragen; lediglich der über die Hälfte hinausgehende Betrag kann von dem Streitgenossen verlangt werden. Entsprechendes gilt bei Vorhandensein mehrerer Streitgenossen. Insgesamt ist hier die Möglichkeit der Erhöhung des Anteils der Staatskasse infolge Ausfalls eines Streitgenossen (vgl. § 426 Abs. 1 Satz 2 BGB) zu beachten.

III. Das Armenanwaltskostenfestsetzungsverfahren

Übersicht

Die Bestimmungen über das Verfahren der Festsetzung der Armenanwaltskosten enthält der § 128 BRAGebO.

1. Vorab ist festzustellen, **daß das Festsetzungsverfahren betreffend die Armenanwaltskosten mit dem Verfahren der Festsetzung der Anwaltskosten** (§ 19 BRAGebO) **nichts zu tun hat** (erst recht nichts mit den Festsetzungsverfahren nach § 197 Abs. 1, § 189 Abs. 2, § 191 SGG, an denen die Anwälte nicht, jedenfalls nicht als selb-

ständige Forderungsberechtigte, beteiligt sind; vgl. hierzu Tschischgale, SGb 1956, 251). Das Verfahren nach § 19 BRAGebO spielt sich zwischen dem Anwalt und seiner Partei (Beteiligte) ab, das Armenanwaltskostenfestsetzungsverfahren zwischen dem Armenanwalt und der Staatskasse. Die Entscheidungen in den verschiedenen Festsetzungsverfahren sind daher wechselseitig nicht bindend.

Wegen der Festsetzung der Vergütung des Anwalts für die Armenrechtsverfahren gegen den — privaten — Auftraggeber vgl. das 7. Kap. II 1 d a. E., auch oben II A 1 a.

2. **Der Armenanwalt kann** — das ist die wichtigste Folge der Unterscheidung — **aus dem** zu seinen Gunsten ergehenden **Festsetzungsbeschlusse nicht die Zwangsvollstreckung** gegen den Kostenschuldner, hier die Gerichtskasse (als statio fisci; Gebührenschuldner ist in erster und zweiter Instanz das Land der befaßten Gerichte, in dritter Instanz der Bund) **betreiben.** Das kommt daher, daß es sich bei dem Armenanwaltskostenfestsetzungsverfahren nicht um ein echtes Kostenfestsetzungsverfahren handelt, weil der Staat (vertreten durch die Staatskasse bzw. ihre Vertreter) am Gebührenstreit selbst beteiligt ist, während er bei einem echten Festsetzungsverfahren lediglich (durch seine Gerichte) als Festsetzender zwischen zwei sich gegenüberstehenden fremden Rechtssubjekten in Erscheinung tritt. Der die Vollstreckung eines Kostenfestsetzungsbeschlusses (im echten Sinne) vorsehende § 199 Abs. 1 Nr. 3 SGG kann daher hier keine Anwendung finden (deshalb keine Einstellung, wenn die Festsetzung angefochten wird). Bei Verweigerung der Auszahlung der zu seinen Gunsten festgesetzten Armenanwaltskosten muß deshalb der Anwalt — stets erst nach förmlicher Festsetzung — die Klage gegen den Staat vor den ordentlichen Gerichten erheben (sogen. Judikatsklage; maßgebende Grundlage bildet der Inhalt des Festsetzungsbeschlusses). Das Armenanwaltskostenfestsetzungsverfahren selbst setzt keinerlei Titel voraus (insoweit ebenso wie das Festsetzungsverfahren betr. die Wahlanwaltskosten).

3. **Die Festsetzung der Armenanwaltskosten erfolgt nach dem Fälligwerden der Armenanwaltsvergütung** (s. o. II A 3 d), d. h. regelmäßig nach Abschluß der Instanz, der grundsätzlich im Sachentscheidungserlaß liegt. (Ansonsten tritt die Fälligkeit mit der anderweitigen Erledigung des Verfahrens oder der Beiordnung, auch nach mehr als dreimonatigem Ruhen des Verfahrens, ein.) Die Festsetzung der Wahlanwaltsgebühr nach § 19 BRAGebO oder gar die Erhebung und Entscheidung der Gebührenklage abzuwarten, ist keinesfalls erforderlich oder am Platze, zumal ein Vorgehen des Wahlanwalts gegen seine Partei solange nicht erfolgen kann, als vom Gericht nicht die Nachzahlung der Kosten (des Anwalts) gemäß § 125 ZPO angeordnet worden ist (s. u. IV B).

4. **Das Armenanwaltskostenfestsetzungsverfahren setzt einen Antrag des Armenanwalts** (gegebenenfalls des beigeordneten Rechtsbeistandes) **voraus,** der ohne weiteres in der Einreichung der von ihm errechneten Armenanwaltskosten (zumeist formularmäßig) liegt, die er erstattet haben will (vgl. § 128 Abs. 1 Satz 1 BRAGebO).

Antragsberechtigt ist außer dem Armenanwalt, der nicht mehr Anwalt zu sein braucht, sein Erbe. Abtretungsgläubigern, Pfandgläubigern und Überweisungsgläubigern wird ebenfalls das Antragsrecht zuzuerkennen sein (so mit Recht, im Anschluß an KG, JW 1937, 1653, OLG Hamm, Rpfleger 1957, 318; a. A. Gaedeke, ArmAnwKostG S. 214 und 152). Sonstige Dritte sind an dem Festsetzungsverfahren zwischen Armenanwalt und Staat aber nicht beteiligt, mögen sie auch als Erstattungspflichtige der (Armen-)Anwaltskosten (vgl. §§ 192, 193 SGG, § 130

Abs. 1 BRAGebO) ein gewisses mittelbares Interesse am Ausgange des Verfahrens haben, das sie als solches in keiner Weise bindet. Die Erstattungspflichtigen können sich lediglich gegen ihre unmittelbare Inanspruchnahme durch die Staatskasse (auf Grund Kostenbescheides des Urkundsbeamten der betreffenden Instanz) oder durch den kostenmäßig obsiegenden Beteiligten (hier auf Grund Kostenfestsetzungsbeschlusses des Urkundsbeamten der ersten Instanz) mit der Anrufung des Gerichts des festsetzenden Urkundsbeamten wenden, vgl. dazu das 4. Kap. 2c und das 6. Kap. 7ff., insbes. 28.

Der Antrag ist an keine Frist gebunden. Er darf aber nicht mit ungebührlicher Verzögerung gestellt werden (etwa erst nach 12 Monaten seit Fälligkeit der Gebühren); dann ist Verwirkung eingetreten.

Mehr als beantragt, kann nicht festgesetzt werden (allerdings kann an Stelle einer verlangten, nicht berechtigten Gebühr eine im Zusammenhang stehende berechtigte, an sich nicht geforderte Gebühr in gleicher Höhe zugebilligt werden).

§ 104 Abs. 2 ZPO gilt sinngemäß. Danach genügt zur Berücksichtigung eines beantragten Ansatzes, daß er, z. B. durch Bezugnahme auf die Verfahrensakten, glaubhaft gemacht wird. Hinsichtlich der einem Armenanwalt erwachsenen Auslagen an Post-, Telegrafen- und Fernsprechgebühren genügt die Versicherung des Rechtsanwalts, daß diese Auslagen entstanden sind, und zwar im Zweifel auch dafür, daß ihr Entstehen notwendig war.

Der Anwalt muß die Höhe der entstandenen Auslagen gegebenenfalls seinem den Festsetzungsantrag stellenden Sonderrechtsnachfolger mitteilen (vgl. §§ 402, 1285 BGB, § 836 Abs. 3 ZPO).

5. **Festsetzender der Armenanwaltskosten ist** — grundsätzlich ohne Vornahme einer mündlichen Verhandlung — **der Urkundsbeamte der Geschäftsstelle des Gerichts der jeweiligen Instanz,** § 128 Abs. 1 Satz 1 BRAGebO. (Bei Verweisung an ein anderes Gericht der Sozialgerichtsbarkeit — auch eines anderen Bundeslandes — kommt in örtlicher Hinsicht das Gericht, an das verwiesen ist, in Betracht, falls der Anwalt bleibt, sonst, insbesondere bei Verweisung in ein anderes Gerichtsverfahren, das verweisende Gericht der Sozialgerichtsbarkeit, vgl. OVG Münster, NJW 1956, 525 mit zust. Anm. von Friederichs, NJW 1956, 926.)

Der Urkundsbeamte wird hier ebenfalls in richterlicher Unabhängigkeit tätig.

6. **Die Festsetzung erfaßt neben der Gebühr auch die erstattungspflichtigen Auslagen des Armenanwalts.** (Die „Erstattungspflicht" ist hier vom Standpunkte der Staatskasse aus zu beurteilen, s. o. II A 2 insbes. c.) Nachfestsetzung von noch nicht verlangten Kosten (vor allem insbes. Auslagen) ist, vorbehaltlich des Durchgreifens der Verjährung, möglich, dagegen nicht Nachliquidation im Rechtsbehelfswege (hier ist der Armenanwalt durch die Entscheidung des Urkundsbeamten nicht beschwert).

7. a) **Gebührenvorschüsse und Zahlungen,** die der Armenanwalt von seinem Auftraggeber oder einem Dritten vor oder nach der Beiordnung erhalten hat, **sind,** soweit sie die Forderung der Staatskasse mindern (s. hier oben II A 3 g), von ihm **anzugeben.** Antragstellende Sonderrechtsnachfolger haben auf Grund ihrer Rechtsbeziehungen zum Anwalt einen Anspruch gegen ihn auf Mitteilung derselben (vgl. §§ 402, 1285 BGB, § 836 Abs. 3 ZPO). Bei Nichtangabe der für die Staatskasse erheblichen Zahlungen kann und muß im Zweifel die Festsetzung der Armenanwaltskosten verweigert werden. (Eine unmittelbare Erzwingung der Angabe ist nicht möglich.)

b) **Im allgemeinen kann die Staatskasse gegen den Vergütungsanspruch die** — rechtshindernden — **Einwendungen erheben, welche die auftraggebende Partei** bei gleicher Sachlage **vorbringen könnte** (vgl. Riedel-Sußbauer, BRAGebO Anm. 2 zu § 125). So darf von ihr vorgetragen werden, daß kein Auftrag der armen Partei vorliegt, selbstverständlich auch, daß keine ordnungsmäßige Beiordnung erfolgt ist oder daß ein Gebührentatbestand bzw. eine Auslagenerforderlichkeit nicht begründet ist. Der Einwand der Schlechterfüllung kann allerdings grundsätzlich nicht erhoben werden. Überflüssige oder die Partei sogar ersichtlich benachteiligende Handlungen können jedoch übergangen werden. Auf einen, aus besonderen sozialen Gründen zulässigen, Verzicht des Anwalts gegenüber seiner Partei oder dem Gegner darf sich die Staatskasse dagegen nicht berufen wie sie grundsätzlich nicht Einwendungen aus fremdem Recht persönlicher Art herleiten kann. Bei Vollverzicht des Anwalts auf seine Ansprüche geht auf die befriedigende Staatskasse natürlich gar nichts über (vgl. Riedel-Sußbauer, BRAGebO Anm. 2 a. E. zu § 125 und Anm. 9 zu § 121). Rechtsvernichtende Einwände darf die Staatskasse ebenso nicht bringen wie die Partei (wegen Zahlungen vgl. hier oben a).

Auch das Entgegenstellen eigener Forderungen der Staatskasse zum Zwecke der Aufrechnung hindert die beantragte Armenanwaltskostenfestsetzung nicht, wohl aber kann sie zu einer Verweigerung der Auszahlung des festgesetzten Betrages führen.

Die Einrede der Verjährung, die von der Staatskasse selbständig erhoben werden kann, muß, wenn sie von dem gesetzlichen Vertreter derselben (Bezirksrevisor o. ä.) vorgebracht wird, berücksichtigt werden. (Die Anhörung der Staatskasse ist daher bei einer möglichen Anspruchsverjährung geboten.) Durchgreifende Verjährung führt zur Ablehnung der Armenanwaltskostenfestsetzung.

Absetzungen müssen vom Urkundsbeamten stets begründet werden.

8. **Der Beschluß** des Urkundsbeamten **muß bei Ablehnung oder Verkürzung dem Armenanwalt förmlich zugestellt werden,** weil die dagegen in Frage kommende Anrufung des Gerichts befristet ist (vgl. § 63 Abs. 1, § 173 SGG). Gegenüber der Staatskasse kommt — nur in Zweifelsfällen — die Vorlage der Akten an den Vertreter derselben in Frage (vgl. Tschischgale, KostR in ZivSach. S. 97). Gegen sie läuft die Anrufungsfrist lediglich bei förmlicher Zustellung des Festsetzungsbeschlusses (vgl. dazu § 5 Abs. 2 des Verwaltungszustellungsgesetzes). **Der Urkundsbeamte hat Rechtsmittelbelehrung zu erteilen,** obwohl ihm Anwälte und der instruierte Vertreter der Staatskasse gegenüberstehen (vgl. § 66 Abs. 1 SGG). Sonst tritt auch hier die Folge nach § 66 Abs. 2 SGG ein: Verlängerung der Anrufungsfrist auf ein Jahr.

9. **Schreib- und Rechenfehler sowie andere offenbare Unrichtigkeiten können** von dem Urkundsbeamten **berichtigt werden** (durch Beschluß). Eine sonstige Abänderungsbefugnis von Amts wegen besteht dagegen nicht (nur das Gericht hat sie nach § 128 Abs. 2 Satz 2 BRAGebO in Verb. mit § 4 Abs. 1 Satz 3 GKG; a. A. Riedel-Sußbauer, BRAGebO Anm. 6 zu § 128).

10. **Gegen die Festsetzung des Urkundsbeamten oder seine sonstige Entscheidung gibt es** nach § 128 Abs. 2 BRAGebO **die** sogen. **Erinnerung (= Gerichtsanrufung) des Rechtsanwalts,** seines Erben oder sonstigen Rechtsnachfolgers **bzw. der Bundes- oder Landeskasse** an das Gericht des Urkundsbeamten. Der Rechtsbehelf, mit dem, wie stets, nur eigene Interessen verfolgt werden können, ist an keine Mindestbeschwer gebunden. Er ist an sich auch nicht an eine Frist geknüpft. Da es aber im Sozialgerichtsgesetz, um eine aus sozialen Gründen unbedingt erforderliche be-

schleunigte Verfahrensabwicklung zu ermöglichen und zu gewährleisten, eine fristlose Gerichtsanrufung überhaupt nicht gibt und der hier einschlägige § 178 SGG als verfahrensrechtliche Spezialbestimmung die stärkere Durchschlagskraft hat, muß die „Erinnerung" des § 128 Abs. 2 BRAGebO richtigerweise grundsätzlich binnen eines Monats nach Bekanntmachung (Zustellung nach § 63 Abs. 1 SGG) eingelegt werden. Eine spätere Einlegung im Anschlußwege gibt es nicht, da eine Anschlußerinnerung dem Sozialgerichtsgesetz unbekannt ist.

Die Gerichtsanrufung kann in allen Fällen durch Erklärung zu Protokoll der Geschäftsstelle oder schriftlich ohne Mitwirkung eines Rechtsanwalts beim Gericht des Urkundsbeamten erfolgen (§ 128 Abs. 2 Satz 2 BRAGebO, § 4 Abs. 3 GKG).

Dritte im eigentlichen Sinn, mögen sie selbst gegenüber der Staatskasse Erstattungspflichtige der Armenanwaltskosten auf Grund Kostenentscheidung des Gerichts (§ 192 SGG) oder auf Grund gesetzlichen Übergangs der Forderung des Armenanwalts auf die ihn befriedigende Staatskasse (§ 130 Abs. 1 BRAGebO) sein, haben nicht das Anrufungsrecht, weil sie — vgl. oben 4 — am Armenanwaltskostenfestsetzungsverfahren überhaupt nicht beteiligt sind. (Sie können sich, vgl. oben das 4. Kap. 2c, nur gegen die Kostenanforderung, den Kostenbescheid, durch den sie von der Staatskasse in Anspruch genommen werden, mittels Anrufung des Gerichts des festsetzenden Urkundsbeamten zur Wehr setzen; sie brauchen im Rahmen der tatsächlich erfolgten Zahlung der Kasse keinesfalls mehr zu ersetzen als an den Armenanwalt gesetzlich zu zahlen war.)

11. **Das Gericht der Instanz entscheidet** bei Nichtabhilfe durch den jeweils bestellten Urkundsbeamten (vgl. § 174 SGG) gemäß § 178 Abs. 1 SGG, auch wenn es sich um ein Sozialgericht handelt, in der für das Kostenrecht der Sozialgerichtsbarkeit aus öffentlich-rechtlichen Gründen allgemein üblichen Weise (vgl. § 189 Abs. 2, §§ 191, 197 Abs. 2 SGG) **endgültig,** und zwar auf Grund eigenen Ermessens (§ 128 Abs. 1, § 142 Abs. 1 SGG) ohne mündliche Verhandlung (§ 124 Abs. 3 SGG) kostenfrei (§ 183 SGG) durch zu begründenden Beschluß (§ 142 Abs. 2 SGG). Eine Schlechterstellung des Anrufenden durch das Gericht ist dabei nicht möglich. Wegen der Einzelheiten des Anrufungsverfahrens und der Entscheidung des Gerichts sowie ihre Ausfertigung vgl. das 4. Kap. 3 l γ.

Das an sich im § 128 Abs. 3 BRAGebO vorgesehene **Beschwerderecht** ist **durch** die **sozialgerichtliche Spezialbestimmung** des § 178 SGG **ausgeschlossen,** zumal das Sozialgerichtsgesetz weder eine an eine Mindestbeschwer gebundene Beschwerde (vgl. § 128 Abs. 3 Satz 1 BRAGebO) noch eine solche fristloser Art (vgl. § 128 Abs. 3 Satz 1 1. Teil BRAGebO) kennt (§§ 172, 173 SGG). Es ist rechtlich nicht möglich, daß eine Rechtsanwaltsgebührenordnung (auch wenn sie — übrigens nicht in vollem Umfange — ein sog. Universalgesetz ist) ohne entsprechende Änderung betroffener Verfahrensordnungen neue, in denselben grundsätzlich nicht bestimmte Rechtszüge (Gebührenbeschwerdeinstanzen) schafft (a. A. Riedel-Sußbauer, BRAGebO Anm. 9 zu § 128).

12. **Das Gericht** der Instanz **kann** hier **bei** Auftauchen von **Unrichtigkeiten seine Entscheidung von Amts wegen** — in beiden Richtungen — **ändern** (vgl. den durch das SGG nicht ausgeschlossenen § 128 Abs. 2 Satz 2 BRAGebO und § 4 Abs. 1 Satz 3 GKG). Da im Verfahren der Sozialgerichtsbarkeit das Gericht der Instanz endgültig entscheidet (vgl. § 178 SGG), kommt eine Abänderungsbefugnis durch das übergeordnete Gericht (vgl. § 128 Abs. 2 Satz 2 BRAGebO und § 4 Abs. 1 Satz 4 GKG) nicht in Betracht.

13. **Die Entscheidung über die „Erinnerung" ergeht ebenso wie die Festsetzung der Armenanwaltskosten gebühren- und auslagenersatzfrei.** Der Armenanwalt, der ja im eigenen Interesse tätig wird, erhält ebenfalls keine Gebühr (vgl. § 128 Abs. 4 BRAGebO).

14. **Nach der Festsetzung** der Gebühren **erfolgt die** — verwaltungsmäßige — **Anweisung der Kasse, die** die **Auszahlung,** wie angewiesen, **vorzunehmen** hat. Es liegt eine Übersendungsschuld vor (vgl. § 1 des Gesetzes über Zahlungen öffentlicher Kassen vom 21. 12. 1938, RGBl. I 1899). Daher besteht Portofreiheit.

15. **Bei zu hoher Festsetzung** durch den Urkundsbeamten **und entsprechender Rektifizierung** durch das Gericht **muß der Armenanwalt den nicht gerechtfertigten Betrag zurückzahlen.** Nötigenfalls kann nach den Bestimmungen des Verwaltungsvollstreckungsgesetzes gegen ihn vorgegangen und vollstreckt werden. Der Einwand des Wegfalls der Bereicherung kann vom Armenanwalt grundsätzlich nicht erhoben werden (vgl. oben II A 1 l a. E.).

Verjährung eines Rückforderungsanspruchs tritt in zwei Jahren seit Ablauf des Kalenderjahres **ein,** in dem die übertragene Angelegenheit ihre Erledigung gefunden hat (entspr. § 196 Abs. 1 Nr. 16 BGB).

16. Zumal **die Staatskasse** den Rechtsbehelf der Anrufung des Gerichts hat, **kann** sie **auf keinen Fall den Urkundsbeamten anweisen,** die Festsetzung der Armenanwaltskosten zu ändern. Das würde rechtsstaatlichen Grundsätzen widersprechen.

17. **Nichtigkeits- und Restitutionsklage können** gegenüber dem Armenanwaltskostenfestsetzungsbeschluß **nicht erhoben werden** (vgl. hierzu 6. Kap. 32).

18. **Der Anspruch auf Zahlung der Armenanwaltsgebühr unterliegt** gemäß § 195 Abs. 1 Nr. 15 BGB **gegenüber der Staatskasse selbständig der** kurzen **(zweijährigen) Verjährung.** § 218 BGB (Umwandlung der kurzen Verjährung in eine dreißigjährige) durch Titelerlangung findet bei der Armenanwaltskostenfestsetzung keine Anwendung, weil diese Festsetzung keinen Vollstreckungstitel gewährt (siehe hier oben 2). Die Verjährung kann — von der Gerichtsverwaltung — auch nach erfolgter Gebührenfestsetzung geltend gemacht werden; sie wird dann mit der Verweigerung der Auszahlung des festgesetzten Betrages verbunden sein. (Wegen des Klagerechts des Anwalts vgl. hier oben 2.) Die Verjährung beginnt am Ende des Jahres, in dem der Anspruch fällig geworden ist (§§ 198, 201 BGB). Entstehen — nach beendetem Ruhen des Verfahrens — die verjährten (Pausch-)Gebühren von neuem, so können sie erneut geltend gemacht werden.

IV. Das Beitreibungsrecht des Armenanwalts gegenüber dem unterlegenen Gegner und der eigenen Partei

Übersicht

A. Das Beitreibungsrecht des Armenanwalts gegenüber dem Gegner

1. Nach § 124 ZPO **ist der** einem armen Beteiligten **beigeordnete Rechtsanwalt berechtigt, seine Gebühr und die Auslagen unmittelbar von dem gegnerischen Beteiligten beizutreiben,** dem wegen dieser Kosten gemäß §§ 192, 193 SGG vom Gericht die Erstattungspflicht gegenüber dem armen Beteiligten auferlegt worden ist. Dem Erstattungspflichtigen steht derjenige gleich, der die Anwaltskosten des armen Beteiligten in einem Vergleich zu erstatten übernommen hat (vgl. Tschischgale, JurBüro 1957, 89).

2. **Das Beitreibungsrecht ist kein selbständiges Recht des Armenanwalts. Dieser kann nur,** ähnlich wie ein Pfändungs- und Überweisungsgläubiger, **in Höhe seiner Kosten den Erstattungsanspruch** seiner Partei dem erstattungspflichtigen gegnerischen Beteiligten gegenüber **an Stelle des kostenberechtigten Beteiligten im eigenen Namen geltend machen** (vgl. Gaedeke, ArmAnwKostG S. 277 und Tschischgale, KostR in ZivSach. S. 67 sowie im Büro 1953, 369).

3. **Diese Geltendmachung der Kosten** im eigenen Namen **kann** gemäß § 117 ZPO **auch dann erfolgen, wenn dem erstattungspflichtigen gegnerischen Beteiligten das Armenrecht zur Seite steht.** (Die Nichtfälligkeit des Anspruchs gegen die eigene Partei auf Grund der Armenrechtsbewilligung steht naturgemäß hier ebenfalls nicht hindernd im Wege.)

4. a) **Der Titel, auf Grund dessen vollstreckt wird** (Urteil, Kostenbeschluß außer dem unwiderruflichen oder unwiderrufenen gerichtlichen Vergleich), **braucht nicht vorläufig vollstreckbar oder rechtskräftig zu sein** (wegen Einzelheiten vgl. oben 6. Kap. 1a). Bei Aufhebung des Kostentitels im Rechtsmittelwege oder auf Grund einer vergleichsweisen Kostenregelung in höherer Instanz muß der Armenanwalt allerdings die eingezogenen Beträge an den Gegner, der gezahlt hat, zurückerstatten (vgl. den § 717 Abs. 2 ZPO, der im Kostenfestsetzungsverfahren des Sozialgerichtsgesetzes sinngemäß gilt, wenn auch nach dem BSG, SozR SGG § 198 Bl. Da 1 Nr. 1 in der Sache selbst ein Inzidentantrag gemäß § 717 Abs. 2 Satz 2 ZPO unzulässig ist; in der Hauptsache kann und muß zur Erreichung der Rückzahlung Widerklageantrag gestellt werden).

b) **Ein die Kosten anderweit regelnder Vergleichsabschluß des armen Beteiligten mit dem Erstattungspflichtigen** auf Grund des ergangenen Titels **ist trotz** der sich aus § 124 ZPO ergebenden Verstrickung zugunsten des Armenanwalts **bis zur Rechtskraft des Vollstreckungstitels** selbst gegen den Willen des Armenanwalts **möglich.** Denn der Erstattungsanspruch betrifft nach wie vor die außergerichtlichen

Kosten des Rechtsstreits, über die sich die Beteiligten im Rechtsstreit vergleichen können (vgl. hierzu Tschischgale, KostR in ZivSach. S. 68 und Büro 1953, 369).

Eine anderweite Verfügung des armen Beteiligten als durch Abschluß des geschilderten Vergleichs, etwa durch Zahlungsannahme, Erlaß, Abtretung oder Verpfändung **ist dagegen,** ebenso wie eine Pfändung, gegenüber dem Anwalt **nicht wirksam.** Die sich aus § 124 ZPO ergebende pfandrechtsähnliche Verstrickung des Kostenerstattungsanspruchs der Partei zugunsten des Armenanwalts und damit die erwähnte Verfügungssperre wird erst durch einen auf den Namen der Partei lautenden Kostenfestsetzungsbeschluß, den der Armenanwalt durch sein Eintreten verhindern kann (vgl. unten 10 und 12), beendet. Die erlangte Verfügungsbefugnis der Partei endet mit dem Eintritt des Anwalts in das Kostenfestsetzungsverfahren aus eigenem Recht bzw. mit der Bewirkung der sog. Umschreibung (vgl. unten 12, 13). Für den Erstattungsschuldner ist bei der Zahlung der Kosten entsprechende Vorsicht am Platze.

5. **Die Befugnis zur Geltendmachung des Rechts aus § 124 ZPO ist** auch dann **noch gegeben, wenn die Bestellung des Armenanwalts** inzwischen **ihr Ende gefunden hat** oder der Anwalt sogar aus dem Anwaltsberuf ausgeschieden ist. Im Falle des Todes der Armenanwalts geht sein Recht auf seinen Erben über, der das Kostenfestsetzungsverfahren im eigenen Namen betreiben kann. Entsprechendes hat für einziehungsberechtigte Abtretungs-, Pfand- und Pfändungsgläubiger zu gelten.

6. **Waren** dem Armen **mehrere Armenanwälte** in derselben Instanz – nacheinander – **beigeordnet, so muß,** wenn auch ein zweiter Armenanwalt als unmittelbarer Kostenbeitreibender in Frage kommt, **geprüft werden, ob ein notwendiger Anwaltswechsel** im Sinne des § 91 ZPO **vorliegt.** (Nur dann braucht der kostenmäßig unterlegene Gegner mehr als die Kosten eines Anwalts zu erstatten.) Notwendigkeit des Anwaltswechsels ist dabei nur zu bejahen, wenn dieser aus unabwendbaren, außerhalb eines Willensentschlusses liegenden Gründen eintreten mußte, z. B. wegen Todes oder schwerer Erkrankung des früheren Anwalts (vgl. § 125 BRAGebO). Entsprechendes hat zu gelten, wenn in der gleichen Instanz ein Wahlanwalt und ein Armenanwalt tätig geworden sind. (Auch hier steht gegebenenfalls ein Rechtsbeistand jeweils dem Anwalt stellungsmäßig gleich.)

Welcher von zwei Armenanwälten bei nicht notwendigem Anwaltswechsel beitreibungsberechtigt ist, muß im Einzelfalle **festgestellt werden.** (Bei Nichtsausschluß seines Erstattungsrechts besteht **Priorität des ersten Anwalts.**)

Der Armenanwalt kann auch vom Gegner keinesfalls Auslagen erstattet verlangen, die auf Sonderwünschen seiner Partei beruhen, z. B. für besonders bestellte Abschriften, die zur zweckentsprechenden Rechtswahrung nicht notwendig waren; insoweit besteht keine Erstattungspflicht.

7. **Der Armenanwalt kann** nach § 124 ZPO **neben** den erstattungsfähigen **Auslagen seine Gebühr als Wahlanwalt geltend machen. Hat er aus der Staatskasse,** die den Armenanwalt nicht auf seine Rechte aus § 124 ZPO verweisen kann, **die Armenanwaltsgebühr erhalten, so kann er wegen des Übergangs der Forderung** (vgl. § 130 Abs. 1 BRAGebO) in der entsprechenden Höhe selbstverständlich **nicht mehr selbst vorgehen.** Obwohl bei ganzer Armenrechtsbewilligung und dementsprechender Beiordnung nach § 121 BRAGebO dem Armenanwalt die volle gesetzliche Vergütung (wie als Wahlanwalt) zu zahlen ist, kann es vorkommen, daß der Anwalt gegenüber seiner Partei einen höheren Honorierungsanspruch hat als gegenüber der Staatskasse, z. B. wenn die Beiordnung erst spät erfolgt ist und nur noch verhältnismäßig geringe Armenanwaltstätigkeit umfaßt. Der Unterschiedsbetrag kann hier vom

Anwalt nicht nach § 124 ZPO gegen den kostenmäßig unterlegenen Gegner beigetrieben werden, weil er außerhalb der Armenanwaltsbeiordnung verdient worden ist. Es bleibt hier nur die gewöhnliche Beitreibung auf dem Wege über die obsiegende Partei übrig. Diese ist verpflichtet, dem Armenanwalt die beigetriebenen Anwaltskosten auszuhändigen; der als Bevollmächtigter der Partei tätig werdende Anwalt kann diesen eingezogenen Betrag einbehalten. Im übrigen (vgl. die Anrechnung der Zahlungen) liegt dieser Fall ähnlich dem eines nur zum Bruchteil bewilligten Armenrechts (vgl. dazu oben II A 3 g und B 1).

Ein sog. — echter — Differenzanspruch des Anwalts (vgl. § 130 Abs. 1 Satz 1 und 2 BRAGebO) aus der Zeit seiner Beiordnung entsteht dagegen in diesen Fällen nicht mehr, da die Honorierung des Armenanwalts gemäß § 121 BRAGebO in Höhe der Wahlanwaltsgebühr erfolgt. Der volle Anspruch steht danach entweder dem nicht befriedigten Anwalt zu oder — nach Zahlung durch sie — der Staatskasse.

8. **Der Armenanwalt steht** mit seinem gemäß § 124 ZPO verwirklichten Recht grundsätzlich **im gleichen Rang mit dem armen Beteiligten** hinsichtlich der Kosten, die diesem persönlich zu erstatten sind (z. B. wegen Zeitversäumnis oder wegen ureigener Aufwendungen). Die Armenanwälte verschiedener Rechtszüge stehen untereinander hinsichtlich ihrer Forderungen an sich ebenfalls im gleichen Rang, doch ist bei Nachzahlungsanordnungen unter Bewilligung von Raten dem Anwalt des ersten Rechtszuges vor dem des zweiten usw. der Vortritt zu geben (s. o. I 29b). Gleichen Rang hat endlich der Armenanwalt mit einem Wahlanwalt einer anderen Instanz. (Auch in diesen Fällen können an der Stelle von Rechtsanwälten ganz oder teilweise Rechtsbeistände stehen.) Wegen des Verhältnisses zur Staatskasse vgl. hier II B 2a α.

9. **Die Ausübung des Rechts** des Armenanwalts **aus § 124 ZPO erfolgt** — nur — **in dem allgemeinen Kostenfestsetzungsverfahren** nach § 197 SGG, nicht etwa im Wege einer Klage.

10. Und zwar **kann der** nicht befriedigte **Armenanwalt seine** einschlägige **Gebühr nebst Auslagen** als Wahlanwalt, soweit nicht Forderungsübergang auf die Staatskasse eingetreten ist (bei nachträglichem Übergang muß entsprechende Berichtigung des Festsetzungsantrages bzw. des zahlenmäßig nach ihm ergangenen Kostenfestsetzungsbeschlusses erfolgen, siehe hier oben II B 2 aβ), **sogleich im eigenen Namen** (an Stelle des armen Beteiligten) **gegen den Erstattungspflichtigen festsetzen lassen.** Der Antrag muß vom Armenanwalt ausdrücklich auf Festsetzung im eigenen Namen gestellt werden. Eine Anfechtung der bei der Antragstellung — evtl. stillschweigend — abgegebenen Erklärung, die Kosten auf die Partei festsetzen zu lassen, wegen Irrtums ist nicht möglich (da Prozeßhandlung, vgl. OLG Neustadt, JurBüro 1958, 256 [257]). Der arme Beteiligte kann gegen den Antrag des Anwalts vom grundsätzlichen Standpunkte aus ebenso keine Einwendungen erheben wie der Gegner.

11. **Hat der** festsetzende **Urkundsbeamte** (erster Instanz) **versehentlich auf den armen Beteiligten statt auf den** unmittelbar beantragenden **Anwalt festgesetzt, so kann er dies** mit Wirkung ex tunc **berichtigen.** Eine zwischenzeitliche Erstattung des Gegners ist dem Anwalte gegenüber dann unwirksam. Der Gegner hat, falls er den gezahlten Betrag von dem Armen nicht zurückerhalten kann, nur einen entsprechenden Schadensersatzanspruch gegen den Staat, der wiederum auf den Urkundsbeamten zurückgreifen kann (vgl. Tschischgale, KostR in ZivSach. S. 72 mit Nachw. und Büro 1953, 369).

12. a) **Der Armenanwalt kann** wegen seiner noch offenen Ansprüche **in ein zugunsten seiner Partei schwebendes Kostenfestsetzungsverfahren — jederzeit — eintreten; der arme Beteiligte muß** dann insoweit **weichen.** Das bereitet keinerlei Schwierigkeiten, solange noch nicht festgesetzt ist. Nach Festsetzung durch den Urkundsbeamten muß der bis zur Entscheidung des anrufbaren Gerichts mögliche Eintritt des Armenanwalts im Wege der Anrufung nach §§ 178, 173 SGG erfolgen. Die Anrufungsfrist beträgt, wie regelmäßig, einen Monat; sie fängt von der Zustellung an zu laufen. (Fast immer wird die förmliche Zustellung des ergangenen Kostenfestsetzungsbeschlusses nicht, jedenfalls nicht — wie an sich erforderlich — gegenüber dem Anwalt auch persönlich erfolgt sein.) Bei Zulässigkeit des Eintritts lautet der Kostenfestsetzungsbeschluß, soweit es sich um die Anwaltsgebühr nebst Auslagen handelt, nunmehr auf den Namen des Armenanwalts als Berechtigten, nicht auf den Namen des armen Beteiligten. (Eine Änderung ist gegebenenfalls auch auf der vollstreckbaren Ausfertigung erforderlich.) **Der Eintritt des Armenanwalts ist** aber hier **nur solange zulässig, wie der Erstattungspflichtige nicht an die** zunächst **als berechtigt ausgewiesene arme Partei gezahlt** oder ihr gegenüber sonst den Kostenanspruch zum Erlöschen gebracht **hat** (vgl. dazu oben 4b). Ob so getilgt ist, ergibt die hier unbedingt notwendige Anhörung des Gegners. Behauptet dieser schlüssig und in einleuchtender Weise Zahlung (oder sonst Tilgung) gegenüber dem armen Beteiligten nach Erlaß des auf seinen Namen lautenden Kostenfestsetzungsbeschlusses, so ist der Eintritt des Armenanwalts unzulässig, sein Rechtsbehelf daher abzulehnen. (Der Nachweis der Zahlung braucht nicht erbracht zu werden; im formellen Kostenfestsetzungsverfahren ist eine Beweiserhebung über echte Erlöschungsbehauptungen mangels entsprechenden Raumes niemals möglich.)

Bei zulässigem Eintritt sind Festsetzungsparteien nunmehr der Armenanwalt und der erstattungspflichtige Gegner. An sie hat daher die Zustellung der Gerichtsentscheidungen zu erfolgen, zusätzlich muß aber auch an den armen Beteiligten zugestellt werden (vertreten gegebenenfalls durch den erstinstanzlichen Prozeßbevollmächtigten, falls dieser nicht der Armenanwalt ist). Der arme Beteiligte kann sich nämlich im Festsetzungsverfahren nach § 124 ZPO zu jeder Zeit auf eine etwa vorgenommene eigene Befriedigung des Armenanwalts berufen und bei paratem Nachweis (Quittungen o. ä.) dessen Anträge hinfällig machen. (Hier stellt die Zahlung keinen Erlöschungsgrund der zu erstattenden und festzusetzenden Kostenforderung dar, die gegenüber dem Erstattungspflichtigen nach wie vor besteht; sie verhindert nur die Verwirklichung des Beitreibungsrechts des Armenanwalts. Daher ist hier Zahlungsnachweis in einem dem Verfahren angepaßten eingeschränkten Umfange zulässig und erforderlich.)

b) **Der (Wieder-)Eintritt in ein** vom Armenanwalt betriebenes **Kostenfestsetzungsverfahren** und die Abänderung eines auf dessen Namen ergangenen Festsetzungsbeschlusses zugunsten des armen Beteiligten, der seinen Anwalt befriedigt hat, d. h. in umgekehrter Richtung, **hat die Praxis** der das Armenrecht bewilligenden Gerichte bisher **nicht zugelassen; der arme Beteiligte muß** nötigenfalls **ein neues Festsetzungsverfahren einleiten,** was die Rückgabe des vollstreckbaren Festsetzungsbeschlusses und den Verzicht auf die Rechte aus ihm seitens des Armenanwalts, ferner die Erklärung des Erstattungspflichtigen, daß von ihm an den Anwalt nichts gezahlt worden ist, zur Voraussetzung hat.

13. **Auch nach rechtskräftiger Beendigung des Kostenfestsetzungsverfahrens kann der** nicht befriedigte **Armenanwalt** innerhalb angemessener Frist (längstens etwa ein Jahr, sonst Verwirkung) **sein Recht nach § 124 ZPO geltend machen. Er**

kann nämlich **einen** zugunsten seiner Partei **ergangenen Kostenfestsetzungsbeschluß** in Höhe seiner gemäß § 124 ZPO erstattungsfähigen Kosten vom Urkundsbeamten der ersten Instanz mit Wirkung ex nunc **auf seinen Namen** in einem weiteren Sinne **„umschreiben“ lassen.** (Diese „Umschreibung“ hat mit einer Umschreibung des Titels auf einen echten Rechtsnachfolger im Sinne des § 727 ZPO nichts zu tun; es wird rechtlich vielmehr ein neuer Festsetzungstitel geschaffen.) **Voraussetzung** dieser Umschreibung im weiteren Sinne **ist:**

α) Verzicht des armen Beteiligten auf seine Rechte aus dem ergangenen Kostenfestsetzungsbeschlusse unter Rückgabe der erteilten vollstreckbaren Ausfertigung;

β) Nichttilgung der Erstattungsschuld durch den Gegner.

Auch hier muß wegen der etwaigen zwischenzeitlichen Befriedigung des ausgewiesenen bisherigen Berechtigten der Gegner gehört werden; im gegebenen Falle genügt wiederum seine schlüssige und plausible Behauptung der zwischenzeitlichen Zahlung (oder sonstigen Tilgung) durch ihn gegenüber der förmlich bisher berechtigten Partei, um den Antrag des Armenanwalts zu Fall zu bringen (s. o. 12a). Auch hier liegt ein dreiseitiges Verfahren vor, was für die Zustellung der Entscheidung und den Rechtsbehelf gegen sie (einschließlich der erforderlichen Belehrung) von Bedeutung ist.

Eine „Umschreibung“ in umgekehrter Richtung (auf den armen Beteiligten) **ist** in konsequenter Einstellung (s. o. 12b) **nicht zugelassen** worden.

14. **Rechtsvernichtende Einwendungen oder rechtsbeeinträchtigende Einreden** (wegen Ausnahmen vgl. oben 12a und 13β) **sind,** insbesondere soweit sie das Erlöschen oder das Hinausschieben der Fälligkeit des Erstattungsanspruchs auf Grund Vereinbarung zwischen dem Erstattungspflichtigen und dem armen Beteiligten (sie stammen daher „aus dessen Person“, vgl. § 124 Abs. 2 ZPO) während einer Zeit betreffen, zu der eine Kostenfestsetzung auf den Namen der armen Partei noch nicht vorlag oder zu der der Armenanwalt sogar förmlich ausgewiesener Erstattungsgläubiger war, stets **unzulässig** (vgl. § 124 Abs. 2 ZPO). **Aufrechnung mit einer** (konnexen) **Kostenerstattungsgegenforderung** an den armen Beteiligten in der gleichen Sache (praktisch aus anderer Instanz) **ist** gegenüber dem Armenanwalt **dagegen** immer **zulässig** (vgl. § 124 Abs. 2 letzter Teil ZPO).

Zugelassen sind demgegenüber unbeschränkt Einwendungen und Einreden aus der Person des Armenanwalts, soweit sie die Verwirklichung des Rechts aus § 124 ZPO oder die Auslösung seiner Gebühr nebst Auslagen betreffen. So kann dem Armenanwalt entgegengehalten werden, er sei durch seine Partei befriedigt worden oder er habe den Auftrag schuldhaft niedergelegt und damit neue Kosten ausgelöst, so daß die seinigen nicht verlangt werden könnten (vgl. § 125 BRAGebO). Echte Erlöschungseinwendungen können wie stets im Kostenfestsetzungsverfahren, auch aus der Berechtigungszeit des die Festsetzung betreibenden Anwalts, nicht geltend gemacht werden. Gegeben sind dagegen selbstverständlich Einwendungen, die sich gegen die förmliche Grundlage eines Beitreibungsrechts überhaupt richten, so der Hinweis auf den Wegfall des Titels infolge Vergleichs oder Aufhebung in der höheren Instanz.

15. **Die Entscheidung ergeht in allen diesen Fällen,** gleichgültig wie sie lautet, **gebühren- und auslagenersatzfrei;** eine anwaltliche Kostenfestsetzungsgebühr entsteht nicht.

16. Wegen der Einzelheiten der Kostenfestsetzung, die gemäß § 199 Abs. 1 Nr. 3 SGG zur Vollstreckung führt, vgl. die Ausführungen oben im 6. Kap. 13f.

Hervorzuheben ist, **daß gegen jede** beschwerende **Entscheidung des Urkundsbeamten** (erster Instanz) von dem Beschwerten (Staatskasse oder arme Partei oder Anwalt) regelmäßig innerhalb Monatsfrist seit förmlicher Zustellung schriftlich oder zu Protokoll der Geschäftsstelle **das Gericht** des Urkundsbeamten **angerufen werden kann**, das bei Nichtabhilfe durch den jeweiligen Urkundsbeamten **endgültig entscheidet** (§ 197 Abs. 2, §§ 178, 173 bis 175 SGG).

17. **Verjährung der zugunsten des Anwalts festgesetzten Kosten tritt in 30 Jahren ein** (vgl. § 218 BGB). Auf die kurze Verjährung gegenüber dem Auftraggeber, die allein diesem zugute kommt, kann sich der Erstattungspflichtige nicht berufen (Gaedeke, ArmAnwKostG S. 287).

B. Das Beitreibungsrecht des Armenanwalts gegenüber der eigenen Partei

1. **Soweit der Armenanwalt weder vom Gegner noch aus der Staatskasse,** an die er sich im Verfahren der Sozialgerichtsbarkeit aus sozialen Gründen im Interesse des Armen im Verhältnis zu diesem in erster Linie wenden soll, **Befriedigung erhalten hat, kann der Anwalt sich an seine eigene Partei halten.** Hier steht der § 183 SGG, der Kostenfreiheit hinsichtlich der aus dem Verfahren resultierenden Ansprüche des Gerichts gewährt, keinesfalls entgegen. **Voraussetzung ist, daß gegen die Partei** mit Rücksicht auf nicht mehr bestehende Armut **die Nachzahlung der** durch die Armenrechtsbewilligung **gestundeten Kosten** für die betreffende Instanz vom Gericht eben der Instanz oder bei Beendigung derselben vom Gericht des ersten Rechtszuges **angeordnet worden ist** (§ 125 ZPO), und zwar auch dann, wenn die Armenanwaltskosten gemäß § 192 SGG der armen Partei (z. B. bei Armenrechtserschleichung) ausdrücklich auferlegt worden sind (vgl. dazu oben II B 1b).

2. **Bei Anordnung der Nachzahlung** gemäß § 125 ZPO **in Teilbeträgen können sich** aus dem neuen Absatz 3 des § 126 ZPO, der die Staatskasse wegen ihrer Kostenansprüche mit dem Armenanwalt grundsätzlich gleichstellt, **Schwierigkeiten** schon deswegen **nicht ergeben,** weil wegen der bestehenden Gerichtsgebühren- und Auslagenersatzfreiheit (vgl. § 183 SGG) eigene Kosten der Staatskasse nicht zustehen. Ein der Staatskasse vorangehender sog. echter Differenzanspruch (vgl. § 130 Abs. 1 Satz 2 BRAGebO) gegen seine Partei aus der Zeit der Beiordnung steht dem Anwalt zudem von vornherein nicht zu, weil er aus der Staatskasse grundsätzlich in Höhe der Wahlanwaltskosten (vgl. § 121 BRAGebO) honoriert wird. Bei teilweiser Armenrechtsbewilligung (zu Bruchteilen) allerdings geht der überschießende Anspruch des Armenanwalts der Staatskasse vor (vgl. § 130 Abs. 1 Satz 2 und § 129 BRAGebO).

Hat der Armenanwalt gegenüber dem Beteiligten deswegen einen höheren Honorierungsanspruch als gegen die Staatskasse, weil er zu dessen Gunsten schon vor der Beiordnung tätig war, so ist die Lage praktisch ähnlich.

Nach dem Ergehen der Nachzahlungsanordnung (niemals vorher) **kann der** vom Gegner oder aus der Staatskasse nicht befriedigte **Armenanwalt die Festsetzung seiner Gebühr und der Auslagen gegenüber seiner Partei beantragen oder die** erforderliche **Gebührenklage erheben** (s. o. 7. Kap. II 1 und 2).

3. **Hat der Kostenschuldner die** geschuldete **Anwaltsgebühr** nebst Auslagen bereits **dem Armen** (als Berechtigtem oder auch wegen Durchgreifens des § 124 ZPO als Nichtberechtigtem) **gezahlt,** so **ist dieser zur Weiterleitung** des Betrages, um den er (gegenüber dem Anwalt) auf jeden Fall ungerechtfertigt bzw. unerlaubt bereichert ist, **an den Rechtsanwalt verpflichtet.** Nötigenfalls kann der Anwalt die

sog. Bereicherungsklage erheben; die Anordnung der Nachzahlung ist hierfür nicht Voraussetzung.

4. **Die Verjährung der Nachzahlungsansprüche des Anwalts gegen die Partei beginnt** erst **mit der Anordnung der Nachzahlung** (vgl. Martini, BRAGebO Anm. 2 zu § 16). **Die Verjährungsfrist beträgt zwei Jahre** (§ 196 Ziff. 15 BGB). Diese Verjährung ist losgelöst von der Verjährung gegenüber der Staatskasse.

Neuntes Kapitel

Die Gerichtsvollzieherkosten und ihre Festsetzung

SGG: §§ 178, 198, 199, 200, 201
ZPO: §§ 753, 766, 788, 793, 793a, 798, 882a
GVKostG: §§ 1, 2, 3, 4, 5, 6, 7, 8, 9, 10, 11, 12, 13, 14, 15, 16, 17, 18, 19, 20, 21, 26, 27, 34, 35, 36, 37, 38
Verwaltungs-Vollstreckungsgesetz (VwVG) vom 27. 4. 1953 (BGBl. I 157): §§ 1, 2, 3, 4, 5, 17, 19
Kostenordnung zum Verwaltungs-Vollstreckungsgesetz (VwVKostO) vom 9. 5. 1953 (BAnz Nr. 89/1953): §§ 1, 2, 3, 4, 5, 6
Reichsabgabenordnung (AO) vom 22. 5. 1931 (RGBl. I 161) i. d. g. F.: §§ 326, 327, 333, 342
Verordnung über die Kosten des Mahn- und Zwangsverfahrens nach der Reichsabgabenordnung (AKostVO) vom 21. 4. 1923 (RGBl. I 259): §§ 1, 2, 3, 4, 5, 6, 7, 8, 9, 10, 11, 12, 12a, 13
GKG: § 91 Abs. 3, 4 und 6

§ 178 SGG

Anrufung des Gerichts gegen Entscheidungen des ersuchten oder beauftragten Richters oder des Urkundsbeamten

Gegen die Entscheidungen des ersuchten oder beauftragten Richters oder des Urkundsbeamten kann binnen eines Monats nach Bekanntgabe das Gericht angerufen werden, das endgültig entscheidet. §§ 173 bis 175 gelten entsprechend.

§ 198 SGG

Vollstreckung nach der Zivilprozeßordnung

(1) Für die Vollstreckung gilt das Achte Buch der Zivilprozeßordnung entsprechend, soweit sich aus diesem Gesetz nichts anderes ergibt.

(2) Die Vorschriften über die vorläufige Vollstreckbarkeit, den Arrest und die einstweilige Verfügung sind nicht anzuwenden.

(3) An die Stelle der sofortigen Beschwerde tritt die Beschwerde (§§ 172 bis 177).

§ 199 SGG

Vollstreckungstitel

(1) Vollstreckt wird

1. aus gerichtlichen Entscheidungen, soweit nach den Vorschriften dieses Gesetzes kein Aufschub eintritt,

2. aus Anerkenntnissen und gerichtlichen Vergleichen,
3. aus Kostenfestsetzungsbeschlüssen.

(2) Hat ein Rechtsmittel keine aufschiebende Wirkung, so kann der Vorsitzende des Gerichts, das über das Rechtsmittel zu entscheiden hat, die Vollstreckung durch einstweilige Anordnung aussetzen. Er kann die Aussetzung und Vollstreckung von einer Sicherheitsleistung abhängig machen; §§ 108, 109, 113 der Zivilprozeßordnung gelten entsprechend. Die Anordnung ist unanfechtbar; sie kann jederzeit aufgehoben werden.

(3) Für die Vollstreckung können den Beteiligten auf ihren Antrag Ausfertigungen des Urteils ohne Tatbestand und ohne Entscheidungsgründe erteilt werden, deren Zustellung in den Wirkungen der Zustellung eines vollständigen Urteils gleichsteht.

§ 200 SGG

Vollstreckung nach dem Verwaltungs-Vollstreckungsgesetz

(1) Soll zugunsten einer Bundesbehörde oder einer bundesunmittelbaren Körperschaft des öffentlichen Rechtes oder einer bundesunmittelbaren Anstalt des öffentlichen Rechtes vollstreckt werden, so richtet sich die Vollstreckung nach dem Verwaltungsvollstreckungsgesetz.

(2) Bei der Vollstreckung zugunsten einer Behörde, die nicht Bundesbehörde ist, sowie zugunsten einer nicht bundesunmittelbaren Körperschaft oder Anstalt des öffentlichen Rechtes gelten die Vorschriften des Verwaltungsvollstreckungsgesetzes entsprechend. In diesem Falle bestimmt das Land die Vollstreckungsbehörde.

§ 201 SGG

Vollstreckung von Verpflichtungsurteilen

(1) Kommt die Behörde in den Fällen des § 131 der im Urteil auferlegten Verpflichtung nicht nach, so kann das Gericht des ersten Rechtszugs auf Antrag unter Fristsetzung eine Erzwingungsstrafe bis zu zweitausend Deutsche Mark durch Beschluß androhen und nach vergeblichem Fristablauf festsetzen. Die Erzwingungsstrafe kann wiederholt verhängt werden.

(2) Für die Vollstreckung gilt § 200.

§ 753 ZPO

Zuständigkeit des Gerichtsvollziehers

(1) Die Zwangsvollstreckung wird, soweit sie nicht den Gerichten zugewiesen ist, durch Gerichtsvollzieher durchgeführt, die sie im Auftrag des Gläubigers zu bewirken haben.

(2) Der Gläubiger kann wegen Erteilung des Auftrags zur Zwangsvollstreckung die Mitwirkung der Geschäftsstelle in Anspruch nehmen. Der von der Geschäftsstelle beauftragte Gerichtsvollzieher gilt als von dem Gläubiger beauftragt.

§ 766 ZPO

Erinnerungen gegen Art und Weise der Zwangsvollstreckung und ihre Kosten

(1) Über Anträge, Einwendungen und Erinnerungen, welche die Art und Weise der Zwangsvollstreckung oder das vom Gerichtsvollzieher bei ihr zu beobachtende Verfahren betreffen, entscheidet das Vollstreckungsgericht. Es ist befugt, die im § 732 Abs. 2 bezeichneten Anordnungen zu erlassen.

(2) Dem Vollstreckungsgericht steht auch die Entscheidung zu, wenn ein Gerichtsvollzieher sich weigert, einen Vollstreckungsauftrag zu übernehmen oder eine Vollstreckungshandlung dem Auftrag gemäß auszuführen, oder wenn wegen der von dem Gerichtsvollzieher in Ansatz gebrachten Kosten Erinnerungen erhoben werden.

§ 788 ZPO

Kosten der Zwangsvollstreckung

(1) Die Kosten der Zwangsvollstreckung fallen, soweit sie notwendig waren (§ 91), dem Schuldner zur Last; sie sind zugleich mit dem zur Zwangsvollstreckung stehenden Anspruch beizutreiben. Als Kosten der Zwangsvollstreckung gelten auch die Kosten der Ausfertigung und der Zustellung des Urteils.

(2) Die Kosten der Zwangsvollstreckung sind dem Schuldner zu erstatten, wenn das Urteil, aus dem die Zwangsvollstreckung erfolgt ist, aufgehoben wird.

(3) Die Kosten eines Verfahrens nach den §§ 765a, 811a, 811b, 813a, 851a und 851b kann das Gericht ganz oder teilweise dem Gläubiger auferlegen, wenn dies aus besonderen, in dem Verhalten des Gläubigers liegenden Gründen der Billigkeit entspricht.

§ 793 ZPO

Sofortige Beschwerde im Zwangsvollstreckungsverfahren

Gegen Entscheidungen, die im Zwangsvollstreckungsverfahren ohne mündliche Verhandlung ergehen können, findet sofortige Beschwerde statt.

§ 795a ZPO

Zwangsvollstreckung aus Kostenfestsetzungsbeschlüssen auf Urteilen

Die Zwangsvollstreckung aus einem Kostenfestsetzungsbeschlusse, der nach § 105 auf das Urteil gesetzt ist, erfolgt auf Grund einer vollstreckbaren Ausfertigung des Urteils; einer besonderen Vollstreckungsklausel für den Festsetzungsbeschluß bedarf es nicht.

§ 798 ZPO

Wartefrist bei Zwangsvollstreckung aus selbständigen Kostenfestsetzungsbeschlüssen

Aus einem Kostenfestsetzungsbeschlusse, der nicht auf das Urteil gesetzt ist, und aus den nach § 794 Abs. 1 Nr. 5 aufgenommenen Urkunden darf die Zwangsvollstreckung nur beginnen, wenn der Schuldtitel mindestens eine Woche vorher zugestellt ist.

§ 882a ZPO

Zwangsvollstreckung gegen juristische Personen des öffentlichen Rechts

(1) Die Zwangsvollstreckung gegen den Bund oder ein Land wegen einer Geldforderung darf, soweit nicht dingliche Rechte verfolgt werden, erst vier Wochen nach dem Zeitpunkt beginnen, in dem der Gläubiger seine Absicht, die Zwangsvollstreckung zu betreiben, der zur Vertretung des Schuldners berufenen Behörde und, sofern die Zwangsvollstreckung in ein von einer anderen Behörde verwaltetes Vermögen erfolgen soll, auch dem zuständigen Minister der Finanzen angezeigt hat. Dem Gläubiger ist auf Verlangen der Empfang der Anzeige zu bescheinigen. Soweit in solchen Fällen die Zwangsvollstreckung durch den Gerichtsvollzieher zu erfolgen hat, ist der Gerichtsvollzieher auf Antrag des Gläubigers vom Vollstreckungsgericht zu bestimmen.

(2) Die Zwangsvollstreckung ist unzulässig in Sachen, die für die Erfüllung öffentlicher Aufgaben des Schuldners unentbehrlich sind oder deren Veräußerung ein öffentliches Interesse entgegensteht. Darüber, ob die Voraussetzungen des Satzes 1 vorliegen, ist im Streitfall nach § 766 zu entscheiden. Vor der Entscheidung ist der zuständige Minister zu hören.

(3) Die Vorschriften der Absätze 1 und 2 sind auf die Zwangsvollstreckung gegen Körperschaften, Anstalten und Stiftungen des öffentlichen Rechtes mit der Maßgabe anzuwenden, daß an die Stelle der Behörde im Sinne des Absatzes 1 die gesetzlichen Vertreter treten. Für öffentlich-rechtliche Bank- und Kreditanstalten gelten die Beschränkungen der Absätze 1 und 2 nicht.

(4) Die Bestimmung des § 39 des Bundesbahngesetzes vom 13. Dezember 1951 (Bundesgesetzbl. I S. 955) bleibt unberührt.

(5) Der Ankündigung der Zwangsvollstreckung und der Einhaltung einer Wartefrist nach Maßgabe der Absätze 1 und 3 bedarf es nicht, wenn es sich um den Vollzug einer einstweiligen Verfügung handelt.

§ 1 GVKostG

Geltungsbereich

Für die Tätigkeit des Gerichtsvollziehers werden Kosten (Gebühren und Auslagen) nur nach diesem Gesetz erhoben.

§ 2 GVKostG

Folgen sachlicher Unzuständigkeit

Kosten werden nicht erhoben, wenn der Gerichtsvollzieher weder nach Bundes- noch nach Landesrecht sachlich zuständig ist.

§ 3 GVKostG

Kostenschuldner

(1) Kostenschuldner sind

1. der Auftraggeber,
2. der Vollstreckungsschuldner für die notwendigen Kosten der Zwangsvollstreckung.

(2) Mehrere Kostenschuldner haften als Gesamtschuldner.

(3) Wird der Auftrag vom Gericht erteilt, so gelten die Kosten als Auslagen des gerichtlichen Verfahrens.

§ 4 GVKostG

Fälligkeit

Die Kosten werden mit der Beendigung der gebührenpflichtigen Amtshandlung fällig.

§ 5 GVKostG

Vorschuß

Die Amtshandlung kann von der Zahlung eines Vorschusses, der die voraussichtlichen Kosten deckt, abhängig gemacht werden. Dies gilt nicht, wenn der Auftrag vom Gericht erteilt wird oder dem Auftraggeber das Armenrecht bewilligt ist. § 9 Abs. 3 Satz 2 des Arbeitsgerichtsgesetzes bleibt unberührt.

§ 6 GVKostG

Entnahmerecht

Die im § 21 bestimmten Gebühren können dem Erlös vorweg entnommen werden. Sonstige Kosten können bei der Ablieferung von Geld an den Auftraggeber entnommen werden.

§ 7 GVKostG

Verwendung des Erlöses im Falle des Armenrechts

Ist das Armenrecht bewilligt und reicht der Erlös einer Zwangsvollstreckung nicht aus, um die für die arme Partei beizutreibende Forderung und die nach § 123 Abs. 1, § 788 der Zivilprozeßordnung einzuziehenden Gerichtsvollzieherkosten zu decken, so kann der Vollstreckungserlös bis zur Höhe eines Fünftels zur Deckung dieser Kosten verwendet werden.

§ 8 GVKostG

Kostenbefreiungen

(1) Von der Zahlung der Kosten sind befreit der Bund und die Länder sowie die nach den Haushaltsplänen des Bundes und der Länder für Rechnung des Bundes oder eines Landes verwalteten öffentlichen Anstalten und Kassen. Bundesbahn und Bundespost sind von der Zahlung der Auslagen nicht befreit.

(2) § 28 der Verordnung über die Fürsorgepflicht in der Fassung des Fünften Teils Kapitel VIII Artikel 1 Nr. 17 der Zweiten Verordnung des Reichspräsidenten zur Sicherung von Wirtschaft und Finanzen vom 5. Juni 1931 (Reichsgesetzbl. I S. 279) gilt auch für die nach diesem Gesetz zu erhebenden Gebühren. Sonstige Vorschriften, die eine sachliche oder persönliche Befreiung von Kosten gewähren, gelten für Gerichtsvollzieherkosten nur insoweit, als sie ausdrücklich auch diese Kosten umfassen.

(3) Landesrechtliche Vorschriften, die in weiteren Fällen eine sachliche oder persönliche Befreiung von Gerichtsvollzieherkosten gewähren, bleiben unberührt.

§ 9 GVKostG

Erinnerungen

Für Erinnerungen des Kostenschuldners oder der Staatskasse gegen den Ansatz von Gerichtsvollzieherkosten gilt, soweit nicht nach § 766 Abs. 2 der Zivilprozeßordnung das Vollstreckungsgericht zuständig ist, § 4 des Gerichtskostengesetzes entsprechend. Zuständig ist das Amtsgericht, in dessen Bezirk der Gerichtsvollzieher seinen Amtssitz hat.

§ 10 GVKostG

Nachforderung

Wegen irrigen Ansatzes dürfen Kosten nur nachgefordert werden, wenn der berichtigte Ansatz vor Ablauf des nächsten Kalenderjahres nach der Erledigung des Auftrags dem Zahlungspflichtigen mitgeteilt worden ist.

§ 11 GVKostG

Nichterhebung von Kosten wegen unrichtiger Sachbehandlung

(1) Kosten, die bei richtiger Behandlung der Sache nicht entstanden wären, sind nicht zu erheben.

(2) Die Anordnung trifft das Amtsgericht, in dessen Bezirk der Gerichtsvollzieher seinen Amtssitz hat. Gegen die Entscheidung ist die Beschwerde zulässig. § 4 Abs. 2, 3 des Gerichtskostengesetzes gilt entsprechend.

(3) Solange nicht das Gericht entschieden hat, kann die Anordnung im Verwaltungsweg getroffen werden. Eine im Verwaltungsweg getroffene Anordnung kann nur im Verwaltungsweg geändert werden.

§ 12 GVKostG

Verjährung

(1) Ansprüche auf Zahlung von Kosten verjähren in vier Jahren nach Ablauf des Kalenderjahres, in dem der Auftrag erledigt ist.

(2) Ansprüche auf Rückerstattung von Kosten verjähren in vier Jahren nach Ablauf des Kalenderjahres, in dem der Anspruch entstanden ist. Die Verjährung beginnt jedoch nicht vor dem im Absatz 1 bezeichneten Zeitpunkt.

(3) Auf die Verjährung sind die Vorschriften des Bürgerlichen Gesetzbuchs anzuwenden; die Verjährung wird nicht von Amts wegen berücksichtigt. Die Verjährung der Ansprüche auf Zahlung von Kosten wird auch durch die Aufforderung zur Zahlung oder durch eine dem Kostenschuldner mitgeteilte Stundung unterbrochen; ist der Aufenthalt des Kostenschuldners unbekannt, so genügt die Zustellung durch Aufgabe zur Post unter seiner letzten bekannten Anschrift. Bei Kostenbeträgen unter zwanzig Deutsche Mark wird die Verjährung nicht unterbrochen.

§ 13 GVKostG

Volle Gebühr

(1) Die volle Gebühr bestimmt sich nach der Tabelle, die diesem Gesetz als Anlage beigefügt ist.

(2) Pfennigbeträge von Gebühren sind auf volle 10 Deutsche Pfennig aufzurunden.

§ 14 GVKostG

Gebührenhöhe und Dauer der Amtshandlung

Ist die Höhe der Gebühren von der Dauer der Amtshandlung abhängig, so wird die für die geringste Dauer bestimmte Gebühr erhoben, wenn im Protokoll keine längere Dauer angegeben ist.

§ 15 GVKostG

Gebühren für mehrere Aufträge

Werden Aufträge eines oder mehrerer Auftraggeber durch dieselbe Amtshandlung erledigt, so werden die Kosten nur einmal erhoben. Wertgebühren werden nach dem zusammengerechneten Wert erhoben und nach dem Verhältnis der Gebühren, die bei gesonderter Ausführung entstanden wären, verteilt. Sonstige Kosten werden nach der Zahl der Auftraggeber verteilt.

§ 16 GVKostG

Gebühr für die Zustellung

(1) Die Gebühr für die Zustellung durch Aufgabe zur Post (§ 175 der Zivilprozeßordnung) sowie für das an die Post gerichtete Ersuchen um Bewirkung einer Zustellung (§ 194 der Zivilprozeßordnung) beträgt 0,50 Deutsche Mark. Die gleiche Gebühr wird für die im Auftrag eines Rechtsanwalts an den Gegenanwalt bewirkte Zustellung erhoben.

(2) Stellt der Gerichtsvollzieher in den Fällen des Absatzes 1 Satz 1 persönlich zu, ohne die Post in Anspruch zu nehmen, so beträgt die Gebühr 1,50 Deutsche Mark.

(3) Ist mit der persönlichen Zustellung eine Aufforderung nach § 840 der Zivilprozeßordnung oder bei der Ladung von Zeugen oder Sachverständigen das Darbieten einer Entschädigung (§ 220 Abs. 2 der Strafprozeßordnung) verbunden oder ist dem Empfänger zugleich mit der Zustellung eine Urkunde vorzulegen, so beträgt die Gebühr 2 Deutsche Mark. Die im § 27 Abs. 2 bestimmte Gebühr wird daneben nicht erhoben.

(4) Ist die versuchte persönliche Zustellung, nachdem sich der Gerichtsvollzieher an Ort und Stelle begeben hat, infolge von Umständen, die weder in der Person des Gerichtsvollziehers liegen noch von seiner Entschließung abhängig sind, ohne Erfolg geblieben, so beträgt die Gebühr eine Deutsche Mark.

(5) Wird der Zustellungsauftrag im Falle des Absatzes 1 vor seiner Erledigung zurückgenommen, so beträgt die Gebühr 0,30 Deutsche Mark. Dies gilt auch, wenn der Zustellungsauftrag in den Fällen der Absätze 2 und 3 zurückgenommen wird, bevor sich der Gerichtsvollzieher an Ort und Stelle begeben hat.

(6) Die Zustellung an den Zustellungsbevollmächtigten mehrerer Beteiligter (§ 189 Abs. 2 der Zivilprozeßordnung) gilt als eine Zustellung.

(7) Für die Beglaubigung eines Schriftstücks, das dem Gerichtsvollzieher zum Zwecke der Zustellung übergeben ist (§ 170 Abs. 2 der Zivilprozeßordnung), wird eine Gebühr von 0,10 Deutsche Mark für die Seite erhoben. Eine angefangene Seite wird als voll berechnet.

§ 17 GVKostG

Gebühr für die Pfändung

(1) Für die Pfändung von beweglichen Sachen (§§ 808, 809 der Zivilprozeßordnung), von Früchten, die vom Boden noch nicht getrennt sind (§ 810 der Zivilprozeßordnung), von Forderungen aus Wechseln oder anderen Papieren, die durch Indossament übertragen werden können (§ 831 der Zivilprozeßordnung), und von Postspareinlagen (§ 17 Abs. 1 der Postsparkassenordnung vom 11. November 1938 — Reichsgesetzbl. I S. 1645) wird die volle Gebühr nach dem Betrag der beizutreibenden Forderung erhoben.

(2) Erfolgt die Pfändung zur Vollziehung eines Arrestes, so ist der in dem Arrestbefehl nach § 923 der Zivilprozeßordnung festgestellte Geldbetrag maßgebend. Bei der Pfändung eines im Schiffsregister eingetragenen Schiffes oder eines im Schiffsbauregister eingetragenen Schiffsbauwerkes (§ 931 der Zivilprozeßordnung) oder eines ausländischen Schiffes, das, wenn es ein deutsches Schiff wäre, in das Register eingetragen werden müßte, beträgt die Gebühr mindestens 12 Deutsche Mark.

(3) Nimmt die Pfändung mehr als eine Stunde in Anspruch, so erhöht sich die Gebühr für jede angefangene weitere Stunde um die Hälfte, höchstens jedoch um je 4 Deutsche Mark.

(4) Wenn nach dem Inhalt des Protokolls pfändbare Gegenstände nicht vorhanden sind oder die Pfändung nach § 803 Abs. 2, §§ 812, 851 b Abs. 2 Satz 2 der Zivilprozeßordnung zu unterbleiben hat, so wird für den Pfändungsversuch die Hälfte der für die Pfändung bestimmten Gebühr, mindestens eine Deutsche Mark, erhoben.

§ 18 GVKostG

Gebühr für die Übernahme beweglicher Sachen

(1) Für die Übernahme beweglicher Sachen zum Zwecke der Verwertung in den Fällen der §§ 847, 854 der Zivilprozeßordnung wird die Hälfte der vollen Gebühr nach dem Betrag der beizutreibenden Forderung, mindestens eine Deutsche Mark, erhoben.

(2) Die gleiche Gebühr wird erhoben, wenn der Schuldner unter Mitnahme der Pfandstücke in einen anderen Amtsgerichtsbezirk verzieht und ein anderer Gerichtsvollzieher den Vollstreckungsauftrag übernimmt.

§ 19 GVKostG

Gebühr für die Entfernung aus dem Gewahrsam

(1) Werden Pfandstücke, die im Gewahrsam des Schuldners belassen sind, durch den Gerichtsvollzieher zum Zwecke der Versteigerung oder aus einem anderen Grunde aus dem Gewahrsam des Schuldners entfernt, so wird eine Gebühr von 1,20 Deutsche Mark erhoben.

(2) Nimmt das Geschäft mehr als eine Stunde in Anspruch, so erhöht sich die Gebühr für jede angefangene weitere Stunde um den gleichen Betrag.

(3) Die Absätze 1 und 2 gelten entsprechend, wenn der Gerichtsvollzieher außerhalb einer Zwangsvollstreckung Gegenstände aus dem Gewahrsam des Inhabers zum Zwecke der Versteigerung oder der Verwahrung entfernt.

§ 20 GVKostG

Gebühr bei Zurücknahme oder Erledigung des Auftrags

(1) Wird eine Vollstreckungshandlung nach §§ 17, 18 infolge von Umständen, die weder in der Person des Gerichtsvollziehers liegen noch von

seiner Entschließung abhängig sind, nicht durchgeführt, so wird ein Viertel der in §§ 17, 18 bestimmten Gebühren, mindestens 0,50 Deutsche Mark und höchstens 60 Deutsche Mark erhoben, wenn sich der Gerichtsvollzieher noch nicht an Ort und Stelle begeben hatte.

(2) Wird eine Vollstreckungshandlung nach §§ 17, 18, 19 aus den in Absatz 1 bezeichneten Gründen nicht durchgeführt, so wird die Hälfte der für die Amtshandlung bestimmten Gebühr erhoben, in den Fällen der §§ 17, 18 jedoch mindestens eine Deutsche Mark und höchstens 120 Deutsche Mark, wenn sich der Gerichtsvollzieher bereits an Ort und Stelle begeben hatte.

(3) Treffen die Absätze 1 oder 2 nur für Teile der beizutreibenden Forderung zu, so sind die Gebühren von jedem Teil besonders zu berechnen. Es darf jedoch nicht mehr erhoben werden, als wenn die Gebühr von der Summe dieser Forderungsteile nach dem höchsten der nach den Absätzen 1 oder 2 in Betracht kommenden Gebührensätze erhoben würde.

§ 21 GVKostG

Gebühr für Versteigerung, Verkauf, Verwertung

(1) Für die Versteigerung oder den Verkauf von beweglichen Sachen, von Früchten, die vom Boden noch nicht getrennt sind, sowie von Forderungen oder anderen Vermögensrechten wird das Zweieinhalbfache der vollen Gebühr nach dem Betrag des Erlöses erhoben.

(2) Die gleiche Gebühr wird für die öffentliche Verpachtung an den Meistbietenden nach dem für drei Jahre zu entrichtenden Pachtzins erhoben. Ist die vereinbarte Pachtzeit kürzer, so ist der für diese Zeit zu entrichtende Pachtzins maßgebend.

(3) Ist ein zum Zuschlag führendes Gebot nicht abgegeben worden oder ist die Versteigerung, der Verkauf oder die Verpachtung aus Gründen der in § 20 Abs. 1 bezeichneten Art unterblieben, nachdem sich der Gerichtsvollzieher an Ort und Stelle begeben hat, so beträgt die Gebühr 1,20 Deutsche Mark. Diese Gebühr wird nur erhoben, wenn keine Gebühr nach den Absätzen 1 oder 2 entsteht; dies gilt auch, wenn nur ein Teil der Gegenstände versteigert, verkauft oder verpachtet wird.

(4) Hat der Versteigerungs- oder Verpachtungstermin auf Antrag des Gläubigers oder des Antragstellers oder nach den Vorschriften der §§ 765a, 775, 813a der Zivilprozeßordnung nicht stattgefunden oder ist der Termin infolge Ausbleibens von Bietern oder wegen ungenügender Gebote erfolglos geblieben, so wird für die Anberaumung eines neuen Termins eine Gebühr von 0,60 Deutsche Mark erhoben.

(5) Für die Mitwirkung bei einer vom Vollstreckungsgericht nach § 825 der Zivilprozeßordnung angeordneten besonderen Art der Verwertung einer gepfändeten Sache wird, sofern nicht Absatz 1 anzuwenden ist, die volle Gebühr nach dem Betrag des Erlöses oder sonstigen Preises, höchstens jedoch ein Betrag von 25 Deutsche Mark erhoben. Besteht die

Mitwirkung des Gerichtsvollziehers lediglich in der Übergabe oder Übersendung der Sache, so beträgt die Gebühr höchstens 2,50 Deutsche Mark. Nimmt das Geschäft mehr als eine Stunde in Anspruch, so erhöht sich die Gebühr für jede angefangene weitere Stunde um den gleichen Betrag, höchstens jedoch um je 4 Deutsche Mark.

§ 26 GVKostG

Gebühr für Verhaftung und Vorführung

(1) Für die Verhaftung und für die zwangsweise Vorführung wird eine Gebühr von 12 Deutsche Mark, für jede Nachverhaftung eine Gebühr von 2,40 Deutsche Mark erhoben.

(2) § 20 Abs. 1 und 2 gilt entsprechend; im Falle des § 20 Abs. 1 wird eine Gebühr von 1,20 Deutsche Mark, im Falle des § 20 Abs. 2 eine Gebühr von 2,40 Deutsche Mark erhoben.

§ 27 GVKostG

Hebegebühr

(1) Leistet der Schuldner oder für ihn ein Dritter an den Gerichtsvollzieher eine Zahlung, so wird ein Viertel der vollen Gebühr nach dem Betrag der Zahlung, mindestens jedoch 0,50 Deutsche Mark erhoben; dies gilt auch, wenn nur Kosten bezahlt werden; unbare Zahlungen stehen, soweit sie zulässig sind, baren Zahlungen gleich. Die in § 20 Abs. 2, § 21 Abs. 3, § 26 Abs. 2 bestimmten Gebühren werden daneben erhoben.

(2) Absatz 1 gilt entsprechend für die Annahme, Aufbewahrung und Ablieferung von Geld, das dem Gerichtsvollzieher freiwillig außerhalb der Zwangsvollstreckung übergeben wird.

§ 34 GVKostG

Gebührenverdoppelung bei Tätigkeit zur Nachtzeit und an Sonn- oder Feiertagen

Wird der Gerichtsvollzieher auf Verlangen zur Nachtzeit (§ 188 Abs. 1 Satz 2 der Zivilprozeßordnung) oder an einem Sonn- oder Feiertag tätig, so werden die doppelten Gebühren erhoben.

§ 35 GVKostG

Auslagen; Allgemeine Vorschriften

(1) Als Auslagen werden erhoben

1. Schreibgebühren;
2. die Auslagen für die bei der Erledigung des Auftrags verwendeten Vordrucke aller Art, soweit keine Schreibgebühren zu erheben sind;
3. Post-, Telegrafen-, Fernsprech- und Fernschreibkosten;
4. Kosten, die durch öffentliche Bekanntmachung entstehen;

5. die an Zeugen und Sachverständige zu zahlenden Beträge;
6. die Entschädigung der zum Öffnen von Türen und Behältnissen sowie zur Durchsuchung von Schuldnern zugezogenen Personen;
7. die für die Umschreibung eines auf den Namen lautenden Wertpapiers oder für die Wiederinkurssetzung eines Inhaberpapiers zu zahlenden Beträge;
8. die Kosten einer Beförderung von Personen oder Sachen, der Verwahrung und Beaufsichtigung von Sachen, der Aberntung von Früchten und der Verwahrung und Fütterung von Tieren;
9. Reisekostenpauschbeträge, Wegegelder;
10. die für Auskünfte über die Wohnung des Beteiligten an Einwohnermeldestellen zu zahlenden Beträge;
11. die Kosten für Arbeitshilfen und für die Benutzung von eigenen Beförderungsmitteln des Gerichtsvollziehers zur Beförderung von Personen und Sachen.

(2) Die Landesregierungen werden ermächtigt, zur Vereinfachung der Kostenberechnung für folgende Arten von Auslagen Pauschsätze durch Rechtsverordnung festzusetzen:

1. Vordruckkosten (Absatz 1 Nr. 2),
2. im Ortsverkehr zu entrichtende Fernsprechgebühren (Absatz 1 Nr. 3),
3. Kosten der Verwahrung von Sachen (Absatz 1 Nr. 8),
4. Kosten für Arbeitshilfen und für die Benutzung von eigenen Beförderungsmitteln des Gerichtsvollziehers (Absatz 1 Nr. 11).

Die Landesregierungen können die Ermächtigung auf die Landesjustizverwaltungen übertragen.

§ 36 GVKostG

Schreibgebühren

(1) Schreibgebühren werden erhoben

1. für alle nach gesetzlicher Vorschrift oder auf Antrag erteilten Abschriften der von dem Gerichtsvollzieher aufgenommenen Urkunden und Protokolle, ausgenommen die nach gesetzlicher Vorschrift zu erteilende Abschrift der Zustellungsurkunde; in den Fällen des § 189 Abs. 2 und des § 829 Abs. 2 Satz 2 der Zivilprozeßordnung wird die Schreibgebühr jedoch für jede Abschrift der Zustellungsurkunde erhoben;
2. für Abschriften, die angefertigt werden, weil der Auftraggeber es unterlassen hat, einem zuzustellenden Schriftstück die erforderliche Zahl von Abschriften beizufügen;
3. für die bei einer Hinterlegung zu erstattende Anzeige an das Vollstreckungsgericht (§§ 827, 854 der Zivilprozeßordnung);

4. für die Aufnahme der von dem Drittschuldner bei der Zustellung eines Pfändungsbeschlusses oder nachträglich abgegebenen Erklärungen (§ 840 der Zivilprozeßordnung);
5. für die vor der Verhaftung erforderliche Anzeige an die vorgesetzte Dienstbehörde des zu Verhaftenden (§ 910 der Zivilprozeßordnung) und für die auf Antrag gefertigte Abschrift des Haftbefehls (§ 909 Satz 2 der Zivilprozeßordnung).

(2) Die Höhe der Schreibgebühren bestimmt sich nach § 91 Abs. 3, 4 und 6 des Gerichtskostengesetzes.

§ 37 GVKostG

Reisekostenpauschbetrag

(1) Muß der Gerichtsvollzieher zur Vornahme einer Amtshandlung einen Hinweg und einen Rückweg von mindestens je zwei Kilometern außerhalb des Gebiets der Gemeinde seines Amtssitzes zurücklegen, so wird ein Reisekostenpauschbetrag erhoben, der für jedes angefangene Kilometer des Hin- und Rückwegs, gerechnet von Ortsmitte zu Ortsmitte, 0,15 Deutsche Mark beträgt.

(2) Der Reisekostenpauschbetrag wird für jede Amtshamdlung erhoben, auch wenn der Gerichtsvollzieher auf derselben Reise mehrere Amtshandlungen vornimmt. Werden jedoch auf einer Reise mehrere Amtshandlungen

a) gegen einen Schuldner oder

b) in derselben Gemeinde für einen Auftraggeber

vorgenommen, so wird der Reisekostenpauschbetrag nur einmal erhoben. Der Reisekostenpauschbetrag wird aufgeteilt im Falle des Buchstaben a nach der Zahl der Aufträge, im Falle des Buchstaben b nach der Zahl der Schuldner.

(3) Ein Reisekostenpauschbetrag wird nicht erhoben, soweit Wegegeld als Auslage anzusetzen ist.

§ 38 GVKostG

Wegegeld

(1) Die Landesregierungen werden ermächtigt, durch Rechtsverordnung zu bestimmen, daß ein Wegegeld erhoben wird

1. zur Verminderung der Kosten bei Vornahme einer Amtshandlung in einer benachbarten Gemeinde;
2. zum Ausgleich von Aufwendungen für Wege, die der Gerichtsvollzieher zurücklegt
   a) innerhalb des Gebiets der Gemeinde seines Amtssitzes,
   b) nach Orten außerhalb dieses Gebiets, sofern die Voraussetzungen für die Erhebung eines Reisekostenpauschbetrages (§ 37 Abs. 1) nicht gegeben sind.

(2) Die Landesregierungen können die Ermächtigung auf die Landesjustizverwaltungen übertragen.

Anlage (zu § 13 Abs. 1 GVKostG)

Die volle Gebühr beträgt bei einem Wert

bis zu	50 Deutsche Mark einschließlich	1 Deutsche Mark
bis zu	100 Deutsche Mark einschließlich	2 Deutsche Mark
bis zu	150 Deutsche Mark einschließlich	3 Deutsche Mark
bis zu	200 Deutsche Mark einschließlich	4 Deutsche Mark
bis zu	300 Deutsche Mark einschließlich	5 Deutsche Mark
bis zu	400 Deutsche Mark einschließlich	6 Deutsche Mark
bis zu	500 Deutsche Mark einschließlich	7 Deutsche Mark
bis zu	600 Deutsche Mark einschließlich	8 Deutsche Mark
bis zu	900 Deutsche Mark einschließlich	10 Deutsche Mark
bis zu	1 200 Deutsche Mark einschließlich	12 Deutsche Mark
bis zu	1 500 Deutsche Mark einschließlich	14 Deutsche Mark
bis zu	2 000 Deutsche Mark einschließlich	17 Deutsche Mark
bis zu	2 500 Deutsche Mark einschließlich	20 Deutsche Mark
bis zu	3 000 Deutsche Mark einschließlich	23 Deutsche Mark
bis zu	3 500 Deutsche Mark einschließlich	26 Deutsche Mark
bis zu	4 000 Deutsche Mark einschließlich	29 Deutsche Mark
bis zu	4 500 Deutsche Mark einschließlich	32 Deutsche Mark
bis zu	5 000 Deutsche Mark einschließlich	35 Deutsche Mark
bis zu	6 000 Deutsche Mark einschließlich	40 Deutsche Mark
bis zu	7 000 Deutsche Mark einschließlich	45 Deutsche Mark
bis zu	8 000 Deutsche Mark einschließlich	50 Deutsche Mark
bis zu	9 000 Deutsche Mark einschließlich	55 Deutsche Mark
bis zu	10 000 Deutsche Mark einschließlich	60 Deutsche Mark
bis zu	11 000 Deutsche Mark einschließlich	65 Deutsche Mark
bis zu	12 000 Deutsche Mark einschließlich	70 Deutsche Mark
bis zu	13 000 Deutsche Mark einschließlich	75 Deutsche Mark
bis zu	14 000 Deutsche Mark einschließlich	80 Deutsche Mark
bis zu	15 000 Deutsche Mark einschließlich	85 Deutsche Mark
bis zu	16 000 Deutsche Mark einschließlich	90 Deutsche Mark
bis zu	17 000 Deutsche Mark einschließlich	95 Deutsche Mark
bis zu	18 000 Deutsche Mark einschließlich	100 Deutsche Mark
bis zu	19 000 Deutsche Mark einschließlich	105 Deutsche Mark
bis zu	20 000 Deutsche Mark einschließlich	110 Deutsche Mark

von dem Mehrbetrag für je 1000 Deutsche Mark 5 Deutsche Mark. Werte über 20 000 Deutsche Mark sind auf volle 1000 Deutsche Mark aufzurunden.

§ 1 VwVG

Vollstreckung öffentlich-rechtlicher Geldforderungen

(1) Die öffentlich-rechtlichen Geldforderungen des Bundes und der bundesunmittelbaren juristischen Personen des öffentlichen Rechts werden nach den Bestimmungen dieses Gesetzes im Verwaltungswege vollstreckt.

(2) Ausgenommen sind solche öffentlich-rechtlichen Geldforderungen, die im Wege des Parteistreites vor den Verwaltungsgerichten verfolgt werden oder für die ein anderer Rechtsweg als der Verwaltungsrechtsweg begründet ist.

(3) Die Vorschriften der Reichsabgabenordnung, des Sozialversicherungsrechts einschließlich der Arbeitslosenversicherung und der Justizbeitreibungsordnung bleiben unberührt.

§ 2 VwVG

Vollstreckungsschuldner

(1) Als Vollstreckungsschuldner kann in Anspruch genommen werden
a) wer eine Leistung als Selbstschuldner schuldet;
b) wer für die Leistung, die ein anderer schuldet, persönlich haftet.

(2) Wer zur Duldung der Zwangsvollstreckung verpflichtet ist, wird dem Vollstreckungsschuldner gleichgestellt, soweit die Duldungspflicht reicht.

§ 3 VwVG

Vollstreckungsanordnung

(1) Die Vollstreckung wird gegen den Vollstreckungsschuldner durch Vollstreckungsanordnung eingeleitet; eines vollstreckbaren Titels bedarf es nicht.

(2) Voraussetzungen für die Einleitung der Vollstreckung sind:
a) der Leistungsbescheid, durch den der Schuldner zur Leistung aufgefordert worden ist;
b) die Fälligkeit der Leistung;
c) der Ablauf einer Frist von einer Woche seit Bekanntgabe des Leistungsbescheides oder, wenn die Leistung erst danach fällig wird, der Ablauf einer Frist von einer Woche nach Eintritt der Fälligkeit.

(3) Vor Anordnung der Vollstreckung soll der Schuldner ferner mit einer Zahlungsfrist von einer weiteren Woche besonders gemahnt werden.

(4) Die Vollstreckungsanordnung wird von der Behörde erlassen, die den Anspruch geltend machen darf.

§ 4 VwVG

Vollstreckungsbehörde

Vollstreckungsbehörden sind:
a) die von einer obersten Bundesbehörde im Einvernehmen mit dem Bundesminister des Innern bestimmten Behörden des betreffenden Verwaltungszweiges;
b) die Vollstreckungsbehörden der Bundesfinanzverwaltung, wenn eine Bestimmung nach Buchstabe a nicht getroffen worden ist.

§ 5 VwVG

Vollstreckungsvorschriften

(1) Das Verwaltungszwangsverfahren und der Vollstreckungsschutz richten sich im Falle des § 4 nach den Vorschriften der Reichsabgabenordnung (§§ 325 bis 373, 378 bis 381).

(2) Wird die Vollstreckung im Wege der Amtshilfe von Organen der Länder vorgenommen, so ist sie nach landesrechtlichen Bestimmungen durchzuführen.

§ 17 VwVG

Vollzug gegen Behörden

Gegen Behörden und juristische Personen des öffentlichen Rechts sind Zwangsmittel unzulässig, soweit nicht etwas anderes bestimmt ist.

§ 19 VwVG

Kosten im allgemeinen

(1) Für Amtshandlungen nach diesem Gesetz werden Kosten (Gebühren und Auslagen) erhoben.

(2) Der Bundesminister des Innern wird ermächtigt, durch Rechtsverordnung eine Kostenordnung zu erlassen.

Kostenordnung zum Verwaltungs-Vollstreckungsgesetz

§ 1

Gebühren im Verwaltungszwangsverfahren

Im Verfahren nach dem ersten und zweiten Abschnitt des Verwaltungs-Vollstreckungsgesetzes werden folgende Gebühren erhoben:

a) Mahngebühr,
b) Wegnahmegebühr,
c) Schreibgebühr.

§ 2

Mahngebühr

(1) Die Mahngebühr wird für die Mahnung nach § 3 Abs. 3 des Gesetzes erhoben.

(2) Die Gebühr beträgt

1 vom Hundert des Mahnbetrages bis zu einhundert Deutsche Mark einschließlich,
½ vom Hundert von dem Mehrbetrage,
mindestens jedoch fünfzig Deutsche Pfennige; sie wird auf volle zehn Deutsche Pfennige aufgerundet.

(3) Die Gebührenschuld entsteht, sobald das Mahnschreiben zur Post gegeben oder Auftrag zur mündlichen Mahnung erteilt ist.

(4) Für die öffentliche Mahnung wird keine Gebühr erhoben.

§ 3

Wegnahmegebühr

(1) Die Wegnahmegebühr wird für die Wegnahme von Sachen im Wege unmittelbaren Zwanges nach § 12 des Gesetzes erhoben.

(2) Die Gebühr beträgt zwei Deutsche Mark.

(3) Die Gebührenschuld entsteht, sobald der unmittelbare Zwang zwecks Wegnahme der Sache angeordnet ist (§ 14 des Gesetzes).

§ 4

Schreibgebühr

(1) Die Schreibgebühr wird für die auf Antrag erteilte Abschrift eines Schriftstückes erhoben.

(2) Die Gebühr beträgt für die erste Seite und für jede angefangene weitere Seite vierzig Deutsche Pfennige.

(3) Die Gebührenschuld entsteht, sobald der Antrag der Anordnungsbehörde (§ 3 Abs. 4 des Gesetzes) oder der Vollzugsbehörde (§ 7 des Gesetzes) zugegangen ist. Sie wird nicht erhoben, wenn der Antrag zurückgenommen wird, bevor mit der Anfertigung der Abschrift begonnen worden ist.

§ 5

Auslagen

(1) Im übrigen sind an Auslagen zu erstatten:

a) Post-, Telegramm- und Fernsprechgebühren,
b) Kosten, die durch eine Zustellung entstanden sind, einschließlich der nach § 4 zu berechnenden Schreibgebühren für Schriftstücke, die zum Aushang bestimmt sind,
c) Beträge, die bei der Ersatzvornahme oder beim unmittelbaren Zwang an Beauftragte und an Hilfspersonen gezahlt werden,
d) sonstige durch Ausführung des unmittelbaren Zwanges oder Anwendung der Ersatzzwangshaft entstandene Kosten.

(2) Auslagen der Mahnung sind nicht zu erstatten.

§ 6

Kosten der Vollstreckungsbehörden

Für Amtshandlungen der in § 4 des Gesetzes bezeichneten Vollstreckungsbehörden werden Gebühren und Auslagen gemäß § 342 der Reichsabgabenordnung in Verbindung mit der Verordnung über die Kosten des Mahn- und Zwangsverfahrens nach der Reichsabgabenordnung vom 21. April 1923 (Reichsgesetzbl. I S. 259) erhoben.

§ 326 AO

Zwangsverfahren

(1) Leistungen, die nach den Steuergesetzen geschuldet werden, können im Verwaltungsweg erzwungen werden.

(2) Vollstreckungsbehörden im Sinne dieses Abschnitts sind die Behörden und Beamten, denen die Beitreibung zusteht und die zur Anordnung und Leitung des Zwangsverfahrens berufen sind.

(3) Vollstreckungsschuldner ist, wer nach den Steuergesetzen zur Zahlung der Schuld verpflichtet ist oder neben dem Schuldner persönlich in Anspruch genommen wird. Wer nach den Steuergesetzen die Schuld

aus Mitteln, die seiner Verwaltung unterliegen, zu entrichten hat, ist verpflichtet, das Zwangsverfahren in dieses Vermögen zu dulden und hat insoweit die Pflichten des Vollstreckungsschuldners.

(4) Wegen der dinglichen Haftung für eine öffentlich-rechtliche Abgabe, die als öffentliche Last auf Grundbesitz ruht, hat der Eigentümer des Grundbesitzes die Zwangsvollstreckung in den Grundbesitz zu dulden. Er hat insoweit die Pflichten des Vollstreckungsschuldners. Zugunsten des Finanzamts gilt als Eigentümer, wer im Grundbuch als Eigentümer eingetragen ist.

(5) Die Zwangsvollstreckung darf erst beginnen, wenn dem Vollstreckungsschuldner die Verfügung, kraft deren er zur Zahlung aufgefordert wird, bekanntgegeben und seit der Bekanntgabe, soweit nichts anderes vorgeschrieben ist, mindestens eine Woche verstrichen ist.

§ 327 AO

Einwendungen gegen den Anspruch

(1) Einwendungen gegen Entstehung oder Höhe des Anspruchs, dessen Erfüllung erzwungen werden soll, sind außerhalb des Zwangsverfahrens mit den hierfür zugelassenen Rechtsmitteln zu verfolgen.

(2) Wird geltend gemacht, daß der Anspruch erloschen oder gestundet oder die Anordnung des Zwangsverfahrens unzulässig sei, so ist vorläufig zu leisten; der Anspruch auf Erstattung ist nach § 152 zu verfolgen. Einreden des Erben aus den §§ 2014 und 2015 des Bürgerlichen Gesetzbuches stehen dem Zwangsverfahren in den Nachlaß nicht entgegen, wenn es sich um Steuern handelt, die nach Beginn des Kalenderjahres fällig geworden sind, das der Anordnung des Zwangsverfahrens voraufgegangen ist.

§ 333 AO

Zuständigkeit des Vollziehungsbeamten

(1) Die Vollstreckungsbehörde hat das Zwangsverfahren, soweit es ihr nicht selbst zugewiesen ist, durch Vollziehungsbeamte oder durch die Beamten, deren sie sich als solcher zu bedienen hat, auszuführen.

(2) Die Vollziehungsbeamten müssen eidlich verpflichtet werden.

(3) Der Bundesminister der Finanzen kann die Ausführung der Zwangsvollstreckung im Einvernehmen mit den obersten Landesverwaltungsbehörden Gerichtsvollziehern übertragen.

§ 342 AO

Kosten der Zwangsbeitreibung

Die Kosten der Mahnung und der Zwangsvollstreckung fallen dem Schuldner zur Last; sie sind mit dem Anspruch beizutreiben. Der Bundesminister der Finanzen regelt ihre Höhe.

Verordnung über die Kosten des Mahn- und Zwangsverfahrens nach der Reichsabgabenordnung

in der Fassung

1. des Art. XVI, § 2 der 2. StNotVO vom 19. 12. 1923 (RGBl. I 1205);
2. der 2. VO über die Kosten des Mahn- und Zwangsverfahrens nach der Reichsabgabenordnung vom 22. 11. 1924 (RGBl. I 755);
3. der 3. VO über die Kosten des Mahn- und Zwangsverfahrens nach der Reichsabgabenordnung vom 5. 11. 1925 (RGBl. I 387);
4. der 4. VO über die Kosten des Mahn- und Zwangsverfahrens nach der Reichsabgabenordnung vom 12. 7. 1941 (RGBl. I 385, RStBl. 497, RZBl. 161).

§ 1

Mahngebühr

(1) Für die Mahnung (§ 341 Satz 1 der Reichsabgabenordnung) wird eine Gebühr erhoben (Mahngebühr).

(2) Die Mahngebühr beträgt
von dem Betrage (§ 7) bis zu 100 Deutsche Mark einschließlich 1 v. H.,
von dem Mehrbetrage ½ v. H., mindestens jedoch 50 Deutsche Pfennig.

(3) Die Gebührenschuld entsteht, sobald der Mahnzettel zur Post gegeben oder dem mit der Behändigung Beauftragten übergeben wird oder sobald Auftrag zur mündlichen Mahnung erteilt wird.

(4) Die Mahngebühr wird nicht erhoben, wenn der Auftrag zur Mahnung zurückgenommen wird, bevor der Beauftragte Schritte zur Ausführung des Auftrags unternommen hat.

(5) Für die öffentliche Erinnerung (§ 341 Satz 2 Halbsatz 2 der Reichsabgabenordnung) wird keine Gebühr erhoben.

§ 2

Gebühren im Vollstreckungsverfahren

Im Vollstreckungsverfahren werden Gebühren erhoben:

1. für die Pfändung oder Wegnahme von Sachen sowie für die Pfändung von Forderungen oder anderen Vermögensrechten (Pfändungsgebühr, § 3);
2. für die Versteigerung und für den freihändigen Verkauf von Gegenständen (Versteigerungsgebühr, § 4);
3. für die Abschrift einer Niederschrift (Schreibgebühr, § 5).

§ 3

Pfändungsgebühr

(1) Die Pfändungsgebühr (§ 2 Nr. 1) beträgt
von dem Betrage (§ 7) bis zu 100 Deutsche Mark einschließlich 1½ v. H.,
von dem Mehrbetrage ¾ v. H., mindestens jedoch eine Deutsche Mark.

(2) Die Gebührenschuld entsteht:

1. sobald der Auftrag zur Pfändung oder zur Wegnahme von Sachen dem Vollziehungsbeamten zugeht;
2. sobald die Vollstreckungsbehörde die Verfügung, durch die eine Forderung oder ein anderes Vermögensrecht gepfändet wird, unterzeichnet.

(3) Die Pfändungsgebühr wird nicht erhoben:

1. wenn die Vollstreckungsbehörde den Vollstreckungsauftrag zurücknimmt, bevor der Vollziehungsbeamte Schritte zur Ausführung des Auftrags unternommen hat;
2. wenn die Vollstreckungsbehörde von der Zustellung der Verfügung, durch die eine Forderung oder ein anderes Vermögensrecht gepfändet wird, Abstand nimmt.

(4) Wird die Pfändung von Sachen abgewendet (§ 345 der Reichsabgabenordnung), so ist

1. die volle Pfändungsgebühr zu entrichten:
   wenn an den Vollziehungsbeamten, nachdem er sich zur Vornahme der Pfändung an Ort und Stelle begeben hat, gezahlt wird;
2. die halbe Pfändungsgebühr, mindestens aber 30 Deutsche Pfennig zu entrichten:
   wenn an den Vollziehungsbeamten gezahlt wird, bevor er sich an Ort und Stelle begeben hat, oder wenn die Pfändung in anderer Weise als durch Zahlung abgewendet wird, nachdem der Vollziehungsbeamte an Ort und Stelle erschienen ist;
3. keine Pfändungsgebühren zu entrichten:
   wenn die Pfändung in anderer Weise als durch Zahlung abgewendet wird, bevor sich der Vollziehungsbeamte an Ort und Stelle begeben hat.

(5) Wird die Pfändung als Anschlußpfändung (§ 359 der Reichsabgabenordnung) ausgeführt, so wird dadurch die Gebührenschuld nicht berührt. Das gleiche gilt, wenn ein Pfändungsversuch erfolglos bleibt, weil pfändbare Sachen nicht vorgefunden werden oder weil die Voraussetzungen des § 343 Satz 3 der Reichsabgabenordnung vorliegen.

(6) Werden wegen desselben Anspruchs mehrere Forderungen oder andere Vermögensrechte gepfändet, so wird die Pfändungsgebühr nur einmal erhoben.

§ 4

Versteigerungsgebühr

(1) Die Versteigerungsgebühr (§ 2 Nr. 2) beträgt
von dem Betrage (§ 7) bis zu 100 Deutsche Mark einschließlich 2 v. H.,
von dem Mehrbetrage 1 v. H., mindestens jedoch eine Deutsche Mark.

(2) Die Gebührenschuld entsteht, sobald der Auftrag zur Versteigerung oder zum freihändigen Verkauf dem Vollziehungsbeamten oder dem sonstigen Beauftragten zugeht.

(3) Die Versteigerungsgebühr wird nicht erhoben, wenn die Vollstreckungsbehörde den Auftrag zur Versteigerung oder zum freihändigen Verkauf zurücknimmt, bevor der Beauftragte Schritte zur Ausführung des Auftrags unternommen hat.

(4) Wird die Versteigerung oder der freihändige Verkauf abgewendet (§ 351 Satz 1 Halbsatz 2, § 345 der Reichsabgabenordnung), so finden die Bestimmungen des § 3 Abs. 4 mit der Maßgabe entsprechende Anwendung, daß auch im Falle des § 3 Abs. 4 Nr. 1 nur die halbe Versteigerungsgebühr, mindestens aber 30 Deutsche Pfennig, zu entrichten ist.

§ 5

Schreibgebühr

(1) Die Schreibgebühr (§ 2 Nr. 3) beträgt 20 Deutsche Pfennig. Umfaßt die Abschrift mehr als zwei Seiten, so sind für jede weitere angefangene Seite ebenfalls 20 Deutsche Pfennig zu entrichten.

(2) Die Gebührenschuld entsteht, sobald die Erklärung, durch die die Abschrift bestellt wird, dem Vollziehungsbeamten oder der Vollstreckungsbehörde zugeht.

(3) Die Schreibgebühr wird nicht erhoben, wenn die Bestellung zurückgenommen wird, bevor mit der Anfertigung der Abschrift begonnen worden ist.

§ 6

(Ist gestrichen durch § 2 des Art. XVI der 2. StNotVO vom 19. 12. 1923, RGBl. I 1205/1225).

§ 7

Grundlage der Gebührenberechnung

(1) Soweit nicht die Mindestsätze der Gebühren erhoben werden, wird der Berechnung der Gebühren zugrunde gelegt:

1. Bei Mahnung oder bei Zwangsvollstreckung wegen Geldleistungen: Die Summe der Beträge, derentwegen gemahnt oder vollstreckt wird. Bei Feststellung des Betrages, von dem die Gebühren berechnet werden, werden Zinsen und Kosten nicht berücksichtigt, wenn sie als Nebenschulden zusammen mit einer Hauptschuld geltend gemacht werden. Bei Ausführung einer Versteigerung oder bei einem Verkauf aus freier Hand wird die Versteigerungsgebühr von dem Erlös berechnet, soweit er nicht die Summe der beizutreibenden Beträge übersteigt.

2. Bei Zwangsvollstreckung zur Erwirkung der Herausgabe von Sachen: Der Verkaufswert, den die Sachen zur Zeit der Entstehung der Gebührenschuld haben. Wenn ein Verkaufswert nicht besteht oder nicht ohne weiteres festgestellt werden kann, so bestimmt die Vollstreckungsbehörde nach ihrem Ermessen, von welchem Betrag die Gebühren zu berechnen sind.

(2) Zur Berechnung der Gebühren wird der nach Abs. 1 maßgebende Betrag auf den nächsten durch 10 teilbaren Markbetrag nach unten abgerundet.

§ 8

Gebühren bei Vollstreckung gegen mehrere Schuldner

(1) Wird gegen Eheleute wegen eines Anspruchs vollstreckt, für den die Eheleute als Gesamtschuldner haften, so werden Pfändungs- und Versteigerungsgebühren nur einmal erhoben. Für die Gebühren haften die Eheleute als Gesamtschuldner.

(2) Wird in anderen Fällen gegen mehrere Schuldner vollstreckt, so sind die Gebühren, auch wenn der Vollziehungsbeamte mehrere Vollstreckungsmaßnahmen bei derselben Gelegenheit vornimmt, von jedem Vollstreckungsschuldner besonders zu entrichten.

§ 9

Nichtberechnung von Auslagen im Mahnverfahren

Im Mahnverfahren werden Auslagen nicht erhoben.

§ 10

Zu ersetzende Auslagen im Vollstreckungsverfahren

(1) Im Vollstreckungsverfahren sind die Reise- und Zehrungskosten des Vollziehungsbeamten von dem Vollstreckungsschuldner nicht zu erstatten.

(2) Die übrigen baren Auslagen, die im Vollstreckungsverfahren entstehen, hat der Vollstreckungsschuldner zu erstatten. Zu den Auslagen gehören insbesondere:

1. die Post-, Fernsprech- und Telegrammgebühren;
2. die Kosten, die durch öffentliche Bekanntmachung, insbesondere durch Einrücken in öffentliche Blätter entstehen: hierzu gehören auch die nach den Vorschriften des Gerichtskostengesetzes zu berechnenden Schreibgebühren für Schriftstücke, die zum Aushang bestimmt sind;
3. die Beträge, die den zum Öffnen von Türen oder Behältnissen zugezogenen Personen zu zahlen sind, ferner die Kosten der Beförderung, Verwahrung und Beaufsichtigung gepfändeter Sachen, die Kosten der Aberntung gepfändeter Früchte und der Erhaltung gepfändeter Tiere;
4. die an Auskunftspersonen, Sachverständige und Treuhänder (§ 368 der Reichsabgabenordnung) zu zahlenden Beträge (§ 11);

5. die Gerichtskosten und in den Fällen des § 360 der Reichsabgabenordnung etwaige Gebühren und Auslagen des Gerichtsvollziehers.

(3) Die Pflicht zur Erstattung solcher Auslagen, die bei Ausführung einer Vollstreckungsmaßnahme erwachsen, entsteht, sobald der Auftrag zu der Vollstreckungsmaßnahme dem Vollziehungsbeamten oder dem sonstigen Beauftragten zugeht oder sobald die Vollstreckungsbehörde die Verfügung, durch die eine Forderung oder ein anderes Vermögensrecht gepfändet wird, unterzeichnet.

(4) Findet zur Versteigerung oder zum freihändigen Verkauf von Sachen, die bei mehreren Vollstreckungsschuldnern gepfändet worden sind, ein einheitliches Verfahren statt, so werden die Auslagen, die in diesem Verfahren entstehen, auf die beteiligten Vollstreckungsschuldner verteilt. Dabei ist auf die besonderen Umstände des einzelnen Falles, insbesondere auf Wert, Umfang und Gewicht der Gegenstände, billige Rücksicht zu nehmen.

§ 11

Entschädigung von zugezogenen Auskunftspersonen, Sachverständigen und Treuhändern

(1) Auskunftspersonen, Sachverständigen und Treuhändern (§ 368 der Reichsabgabenordnung) ist auf Antrag eine Entschädigung zu gewähren.

(2) Die Entschädigung der Auskunftspersonen und Sachverständigen darf die Gebühr einschließlich des Teuerungszuschlags nicht übersteigen, die in bürgerlichen Rechtsstreitigkeiten auf Grund der Gebührenordnung für Zeugen und Sachverständige (in der jeweils geltenden Fassung) gewährt werden kann.

(3) Die Entschädigung der Treuhänder darf die Vergütung nicht übersteigen, die die Landesjustizverwaltungen auf Grund des § 14 des Einführungsgesetzes zu dem Reichsgesetz über die Zwangsversteigerung und Zwangsverwaltung vom 24. März 1897 in der Fassung der Bekanntmachung vom 20. Mai 1898 (Reichsgesetzbl. S. 750) für Verwalter festgesetzt haben.

§ 12

Gebühren für Pfändung und Versteigerung von Wertpapieren

(1) Die Bestimmungen, die für das Vollstreckungsverfahren gegeben sind, finden auf das Verfahren zur Vollziehung des dinglichen Arrestes (§ 378 der Reichsabgabenordnung) sowie auf das Verfahren zur Verwertung von Sicherheiten (§ 381 der Reichsabgabenordnung) entsprechende Anwendung.

(2) Die Bestimmungen über die Pfändung, die Versteigerung und den freihändigen Verkauf von Sachen gelten entsprechend für Wertpapiere. Die Bestimmungen über die Wegnahme von Sachen gelten entsprechend für Wertpapiere und sonstige Urkunden.

§ 12a

Postnachnahme als Mahnung

Läßt die Steuerbehörde einem Steuerpflichtigen, der mit einer Zahlung im Rückstand ist, eine Postnachnahme zugehen (§ 122 Abs. 4 Satz 2 der Reichsabgabenordnung), so steht die Postnachnahme einer Mahnung gleich. § 1 Abs. 1 bis 3, § 7 Abs. 1 Ziff. 1, § 7 Abs. 2, §§ 9 und 13 gelten auch für die Postnachnahme.

§ 13

Gebühren bei Zwangsvollstreckung durch andere Personen

Die Bestimmungen dieser Verordnung finden auch dann Anwendung, wenn die Mahnung oder die Zwangsvollstreckung durch eine Person ausgeführt wird, die nicht im Staatsdienst steht. Für Zwangsvollstreckungen, die durch Gerichtsvollzieher ausgeführt werden, gelten die Bestimmungen dieser Verordnung nicht.

§ 91 Abs. 3, 4 und 6 GKG

Schreibgebühren

(3) Die Schreibgebühr beträgt für die Seite, die 28 Zeilen von durchschnittlich 15 Silben enthält, 50 Deutsche Pfennig, auch wenn die Herstellung auf mechanischem Wege (ausgenommen durch Ablichtung) stattgefunden hat. Jede angefangene Seite wird als voll gerechnet.

(4) Für Schriftstücke, die in fremder Sprache abgefaßt sind, wird die doppelte Schreibgebühr erhoben.

(6) Werden Abschriften durch Ablichtung hergestellt, so werden für jede Seite ohne Rücksicht auf Zeilen- und Silbenzahl 50 Deutsche Pfennig, bei größerem Format als DIN B 4 eine Deutsche Mark erhoben.

Spezialabhandlungen des Verfassers: Die Vollstreckung der sozialgerichtlichen Entscheidungen und ihre Kosten, DGVZ 1957, 1 und Das neue Gesetz über Kosten der Gerichtsvollzieher, DGVZ 1957, 145.

I. Allgemeines

Übersicht

1. Die §§ 198 bis 201 SGG behandeln die **Zwangsvollstreckung aus gerichtlichen Entscheidungen** (§§ 123ff. SGG, einschließlich nicht angefochtener Vorbescheide des Vorsitzenden nach §§ 105, 158 Abs. 2, § 216 Abs. 1 Nr. 1 SGG), **gerichtlichen Anerkenntnissen und gerichtlichen Vergleichen** (§ 101 Abs. 1 und 2 SGG), **ferner aus Kostenfestsetzungsbeschlüssen** (gemäß § 197 Abs. 1 SGG und eventuell § 19 BRAGebO). Ein geschlossener Vergleich muß naturgemäß unwiderruflich bzw. unwiderrufen, das — angenommene — Anerkenntnis protokolliert sein. **Die Gerichtsentscheidungen** (mit Ausnahme der Vorbescheide) **brauchen** aber **grundsätzlich nicht rechtskräftig oder** auch nur **vorläufig vollstreckbar zu sein** (vgl. § 198 Abs. 2, § 199 Abs. 1, § 97 Abs. 1 und § 154 SGG). Die Berufung (Revision) hat nämlich aufschiebende Wirkung nur ausnahmsweise bei der Rückforderung von Leistungen und Beiträgen (vgl. § 97 Abs. 1 Nr. 2, § 154 Abs. 1, § 165 SGG). Die Berufung (Revision) des Versicherungsträgers oder in der Kriegsopferversorgung eines Landes bewirkt — ebenfalls ausnahmsweise — Aufschub lediglich, soweit es sich um Beträge handelt, die für die Zeit vor Erlaß des angefochtenen Urteils nachgezahlt werden sollen (§ 154 Abs. 2, § 165 SGG). Die Beschwerde hat gemäß § 175 Satz 1 SGG aufschiebende Wirkung nur, wenn sie die Festsetzung einer Strafe zum Gegenstand hat. In den Fällen mit aufschiebender Wirkung muß wegen der Vollstreckung der Hauptsache (im Gegensatz zu festgesetzten Kosten) die Rechtskraft abgewartet werden. (Zur Vollstreckung ist insoweit die Bescheinigung der Rechtskraft erforderlich.)

2. Nach den §§ 198 bis 201 SGG kommt nach Zustellung des zugrunde liegenden Titels eine **Zwangsvollstreckung auf zweifachem Wege** in Betracht (vgl. Tschischgale, DGVZ 1957, 1):

a) **Die Zwangsvollstreckung gegen die öffentliche Hand wird** auf Grund der erteilten gerichtlichen Vollstreckungsklausel **in Gemäßheit** der Bestimmungen **des Achten Buches der Zivilprozeßordnung** — nach Anzeige gemäß § 882a daselbst — **durchgeführt** (§ 198 Abs. 1 SGG),

b) **die Vollstreckung zugunsten der öffentlichen Hand nach dem Verwaltungs-Vollstreckungsgesetz** (VwVG) vom 27. 4. 1953 — BGBl. I 157 —, vgl. § 200 SGG. Hier ersetzt die Vollstreckungsanordnung des Anspruchsberechtigten öffentlichen Rechtsträgers die Vollstreckungsklausel. Nach dem Verwaltungs-Vollstreckungsgesetz erfolgt auch die Vollstreckung von auferlegten Strafen und von Gerichtskosten, soweit diese im Verfahren der Sozialgerichtsbarkeit — ausnahmsweise — erhoben werden (vgl. oben das 4. Kap. 1 und 2). Auch die Zwangsstrafe des § 201 Abs. 1 SGG (gegen Behörden zur Erzwingung der Rückgängigmachung der erfolgten Vollziehung eines später aufgehobenen Verwaltungsakts oder Widerspruchsbescheides, vgl. § 131 SGG), wird (§ 201 Abs. 2 SGG) nach dem Verwaltungs-Vollstreckungsgesetz vollstreckt (ebenso das Zwangsgeld zur Erzwingung unvertretbarer Handlungen nach § 11 VwVG und der Kostenbetrag für die Ausführung vertretbarer Handlungen nach §§ 10, 13 Abs. 4 VwVG). Die zwangseingezogenen Strafgelder fallen, wie bei allen derartigen Strafen, mögen sie auch vom Gerichtsvollzieher beigetrieben worden sein (vgl. § 888 Abs. 1 ZPO betreffend die Erzwingung unvertretbarer Handlungen nach dem Achten Buch) der Staatskasse zu.

3. a) Und zwar **richtet sich** nach § 200 Abs. 1 SGG **die Vollstreckung zugunsten einer Bundesbehörde oder einer bundesunmittelbaren Körperschaft** des öffentlichen Rechts **oder** einer bundesunmittelbaren **Anstalt des öffentlichen Rechts** (vgl. hierzu die Definitionen in Art. 87 Abs. 2 und 3 GG und in der Bekanntmachung im BArbBl. 1951, 386) **direkt nach dem Verwaltungs-Vollstreckungsgesetz.** (**Vollstreckungsbehörde**

ist danach grundsätzlich **das zuständige Hauptzollamt** als örtliche Bundesfinanzbehörde, vgl. § 4b VwVG und Deutsches Bundesrecht, Anm. zu § 4 VwVG.)

b) **Bei der Vollstreckung zugunsten einer Behörde, die nicht Bundesbehörde ist, wie** zugunsten **einer nicht bundesunmittelbaren Körperschaft oder Anstalt des öffentlichen Rechts gelten** nach § 200 Abs. 2 SGG **die Vorschriften des Verwaltungs-Vollstreckungsgesetzes entsprechend.** (In diesen Fällen bestimmt das Land die Vollstreckungsbehörde; in der Regel sind hier die zuständigen Finanzämter des jeweiligen Landes zu Vollstreckungsbehörden bestellt, die ebenfalls nach der Abgabenbeitreibungsordnung [ABeitrO] vom 23. 6. 1923 – RMinBl. 595 – i. d. F. vom 19. 1. 1927 – RMinBl. 23 – vorgehen, vgl. Brocke, Sozialrichter S. 191.)

4. a) Nach § 1 Abs. 2 VwVG **gilt dieses Gesetz** jedoch **nicht, wenn es sich um die Vollstreckung von Geldleistungsurteilen handelt, die im Zuge** des sogen. **Parteistreites** (vgl. § 54 Abs. 5 SGG) **ergehen.** Hierbei handelt es sich zwar um Streitigkeiten sogar von zwei Rechtsträgern der öffentlichen Hand, die sich aber gleichgeordnet gegenüberstehen (so bei Ersatz- und Erstattungsstreitigkeiten; vgl. hierzu Dapprich, SGb 1956, 305, der allerdings den einschlägigen § 54 Abs. 5 SGG sehr weit auslegt). **Für die Vollstreckung dieser Urteile gilt das Achte Buch der Zivilprozeßordnung** (Hastler, WzS 1955, 109).

b) Bemerkt sei, **daß die Rechtsträger der öffentlichen Hand nicht gezwungen sind, nach dem Verwaltungs-Vollstreckungsgesetz zu vollstrecken. Sie können** vielmehr **die Vollstreckung auch nach dem Achten Buch der Zivilprozeßordnung,** vor allem im Wege der grundsätzlich unentgeltlichen (vgl. § 164 GVG, auch § 115 RVO) Amtshilfe, **betreiben** (Deutsches Bundesrecht, Anm. zu § 4 VwVG im letzten Absatz, vgl. auch Art. 35 GG). Die dabei fällig werdenden Gerichtsvollziehergebühren (an Stelle der sonst in Frage kommenden Vollziehungsgebühren) entstehen jedenfalls gegenüber dem Vollstreckungsschuldner (das ist bei Vorführung nach § 380 Abs. 2 ZPO der zwangsweise vorgeführte Zeuge) in der üblichen Weise; das gilt grundsätzlich, wenn der Gerichtsvollzieher tätig wird, sei es auch als Hilfsorgan einer Vollstreckungsbehörde nach dem Verwaltungs-Vollstreckungsgesetz, vgl. § 13 Satz 2 AKostVO, § 1 GVKostG; wegen eventueller Ausnahmen vgl. Art. XI § 5 Abs. 1 Nr. 1 des Gesetzes zur Änderung und Ergänzung kostenrechtlicher Vorschriften (KostÄndG) vom 26. 7. 1957 (BGBl. I 861).

5. **Voraussetzung** der Vollstreckung **ist** naturgemäß, **daß es sich bei dem** vorliegenden **Titel um einen zur** eigentlichen (unmittelbaren) **Zwangsvollstreckung geeigneten** Vollstreckungstitel **handelt. Das ist der Fall, soweit er,** wie regelmäßig bei zuerkannten Rentenansprüchen oder zugesprochenen Ersatz- und Erstattungsforderungen oder bei festgesetzten Kostenbeträgen, **auf eine Geldleistung gerichtet ist.** Praktisch in Frage kommen aber auch Titel (Entscheidungen, Anerkenntnisse und Vergleiche), die andere Leistungen zum Gegenstande haben, nämlich solche, die in vertretbarer Weise erbracht werden können (z. B. Heilbehandlung bzw. Heilmittelgewährung mit dem Ziele auf Verpassung bzw. Lieferung einer geeigneten Brille oder eines sitzenden Korsetts). Hier erfolgt die Vollstreckung in der Weise, daß der Gläubiger die in Frage kommenden Handlungen nötigenfalls durch geeignete Dritte auf Kosten des Schuldners vornehmen läßt (vgl. § 887 ZPO, § 10 VwVG). Der Gläubiger erhält dann auf sein Begehren bzw. durch sein Bewirken einen weiteren Titel, der auf Geldzahlung lautet, nämlich auf Vorauszahlung der entstehenden Kosten (vgl. § 887 Abs. 2 ZPO, § 13 Abs. 4 VwVG). Dieser Titel wird wie jede andere auf Geldleistung gehende Entscheidung vollstreckt (nach der ZPO durch den Gerichtsvollzieher, auf Grund des Verwaltungs-Vollstreckungsgesetzes

durch die Vollstreckungsbehörde mit Hilfe eigener Vollziehungsbeamter, vgl. § 753 ZPO, § 333 AO). Bemerkt sei hier, daß im Verfahren der Sozialgerichtsbarkeit durch Wegnahme zu vollstreckende (vgl. die §§ 883, 884 ZPO) Herausgabeurteile (betreffend bestimmte individuelle oder mengenmäßig begrenzte vertretbare Sachen) grundsätzlich nicht vorkommen.

6. Eine **Gerichtsvollziehertätigkeit,** die als solche zu vergüten ist, **kommt stets nur in Betracht, wenn** wegen der titulierten Geldforderung **in bewegliche Sachen vollstreckt wird.** Die Vollstreckung in Forderungen und in ähnliche Vermögensrechte wird entweder vom Vollstreckungsgericht (vgl. § 828 ZPO) oder von der Vollstreckungsbehörde (§ 5 VwVG und § 361 AO) vorgenommen. (Wegen der hierbei entstehenden Kosten vgl. § 42 Abs. 1 und 2 GKG bzw. § 19 VwVG in Verb. mit § 6 VwVKostO und § 2 Nr. 1 und 3 AKostVO.) Die Zwangsvollstreckung in Grundstücke und grundstücksähnliche Gegenstände erfolgt, abgesehen von der Eintragung einer bloßen Sicherungshypothek (wegen dieser vgl. §§ 867, 866 ZPO, § 62 KostO), durch das Versteigerungsgericht (Amtsgericht, in dessen Bezirk das betroffene Grundstück o. ä. belegen ist), vgl. § 866 ZPO, §§ 1ff. ZVG, § 5 VwVG, § 372 AO. (Wegen der einschlägigen Kosten vgl. §§ 60ff. GKG.) Die notfalls in Frage kommende Abnahme des Offenbarungseides zur Klarstellung der Vermögensverhältnisse des Schuldners durch das Vollstreckungsgericht bzw. (aber nur bei freiwilliger Leistung) durch die Vollstreckungsbehörde ist hinsichtlich des Verfahrens in den §§ 899ff. ZPO und § 325 Abs. 3 AO geregelt. (Wegen der hierfür gegebenenfalls entstehenden Gerichtskosten vgl. § 40 Abs. 1 Nr. 5 GKG.) **Für die Verhaftung und Vorführung des Schuldners zur Ableistung des Offenbarungseides erhält der dabei in Tätigkeit tretende Gerichtsvollzieher 12 DM,** für eine zweite Verhaftung der gleichen Person 2,40 DM (§ 26 Abs. 1 GVKostG). Bei Beendigung des Verhaftungsauftrages, bevor sich der Gerichtsvollzieher an Ort und Stelle begeben hatte, erwächst eine Gebühr von 1,20 DM, bei Erledigung vor Auftragsausführung nach Hinbegebung an Ort und Stelle von 2,40 DM, vgl. § 26 Abs. 2 GVKostG. (Wegen der zu zahlenden Haftkosten, die nicht Gerichtsvollzieherauslagen sind, vgl. § 911 ZPO, § 325 Abs. 3 AO.)

7. **Die Gerichtsvollzieherkosten gehören,** wie die Vollstreckungskosten überhaupt, **nicht zu den eigentlichen Kosten des Rechtsstreits.** Sie werden daher von einem über die Kosten geschlossenen Vergleich der Beteiligten, der gegen die Staatskasse übrigens grundsätzlich nicht wirkt, nur betroffen, wenn sie ausdrücklich mit erwähnt sind.

II. Die Vergütung des Gerichtsvollziehers

Übersicht

1. a) Der Gerichtsvollzieher ist nicht Kostengläubiger der durch seine Vollstreckungstätigkeit ausgelösten Gebühren und Auslagen. Jedenfalls fließen die Gebühren endgültig in die Staatskasse, die insgesamt alleinige Gläubigerin der Gerichtsvollzieherkosten ist. An ihnen ist der Gerichtsvollzieher nur prozentual beteiligt (regelmäßig zu etwa 30%), und zwar unter entsprechender Auffüllung seines Beamtengehalts und seiner Dienstaufwandsentschädigung. (Unter diesem Gesichtspunkt ist daher auch die Frage der etwaigen Abtretung, Verpfändung und Pfändung des Gebührenanteils zu prüfen, vgl. Tschischgale, KostR in ZivSach. S. 98.) **Kostenschuldner der Gerichtsvollziehergebühren und -auslagen sind** gemäß § 3 Abs. 1 GVKostG **der auftraggebende Vollstreckungsgläubiger und,** soweit es sich – wie in der Regel – um notwendige Kosten der Zwangsvollstreckung handelt, **der Vollstreckungsschuldner. Beide Kostenschuldner,** wie überhaupt mehrere Kostenschuldner, **haften als Gesamtschuldner** (§ 3 Abs. 2 GVKostG). Praktisch ist der Auftraggeber aber nur Zweitschuldner, weil die Gerichtsvollzieherkosten (ebenso wie die anderen im Sinne des § 91 ZPO notwendigen Vollstreckungskosten der nach dem Vollstreckungstitel anspruchsberechtigten Partei, insbesondere die für den mit der Veranlassung der Vollstreckung beauftragten Anwalt oder Rechtsbeistand) gemäß § 788 Abs. 1 ZPO zugleich mit der Hauptforderung vollstreckt werden, die – zwangsweise – Befriedigung daher zunächst beim Schuldner versucht wird.

b) **Die Beitreibung beim Schuldner kann** im Hinblick auf § 117 ZPO **auch gegenüber einem armen Schuldner vorgenommen werden,** und zwar stets selbst auf Grund eines nicht rechtskräftigen Titels (§ 123 Abs. 1 ZPO, § 9 Abs. 3 Nr. 2 KostVfg, die das Verhältnis zur Staatskasse betreffen und Rechtskraft des Vollstreckungstitels verlangen, gelten im Sozialgerichtsverfahren nicht, weil dieses keine allgemeine Kostenpflicht des unterlegenen Verfahrensbeteiligten kennt). **Auch die Bewilligung des Armenrechts** (für die Zwangsvollstreckung!) **zugunsten des Auftraggebers hindert,** wie sich aus § 788 ZPO, § 7 GVKostG ergibt, die zusätzliche Beitreibung **nicht;** allerdings ist hier bei zur Kostenmitabdeckung nicht ausreichendem Vollstreckungserlös die Staatskasse mit Ausnahme eines davon einbehaltbaren Betrages bis zu $^1/_5$ des Erlöses gegenüber dem Gläubiger letztrangig (vgl. § 7 GVKostG). Der Gerichtsvollzieher ist selbt bei attestierter Armut des Gläubigers für diesen auf jeden Fall verpflichtet, die beigetriebenen Gerichtsvollzieherkosten an die Staatskasse unmittelbar abzuführen (vgl. hierzu Lappe, Rpfleger 1957, 244). Die Zwangsvollstreckung geschieht dabei auch hinsichtlich der entstehenden Kosten auf Gefahr der beitreibenden Partei; wird der Titel, aus dem die Vollstreckung erfolgt, aufgehoben oder eingeschränkt, so sind die als solche unwiderruflich beigetriebenen Kosten im entsprechenden Umfange von der Partei neben dem Hauptbetrage zurückzuzahlen (vgl. § 788 Abs. 2 ZPO).

c) Nur **wenn und soweit die Vollstreckung gegen den Schuldner nicht ausgeführt wird oder ohne Ergebnis bleibt, erfolgt** — jeweils nach Aufstellung einer Berechnung — **die Inanspruchnahme des Gläubigers, vorausgesetzt, daß dieser nicht** oder nicht mehr (vgl. § 125 ZPO) **arm ist.** Der Gerichtsvollzieher kann in diesen Fällen versuchen, seine Kosten vom Auftraggeber zunächst durch Postnachnahme zu erhalten. Nötigenfalls ist in dem an sich gegen alle Kostenschuldner gegebenen Zwangswege nach der Justizbeitreibungsordnung durch die Gerichtskasse des für den Amtssitz des beauftragten Gerichtsvollziehers und damit regelmäßig auch für den Schuldnerwohnsitz zuständigen Amtsgerichts vorzugehen, vgl. JBeitrO § 1 Abs. 1 Nr. 4. (Nach § 11 Abs. 2 JBeitrO gelten für die Tätigkeit des Vollziehungsbeamten der Gerichtskasse als Vollstreckungsbehörde die Vorschriften des Gesetzes über Kosten der Gerichtsvollzieher sinngemäß; der Reisekostenpauschbetrag und das Wegegeld werden jedoch nicht geltend gemacht.) Postnachnahme kann niemals gegenüber einer Behörde oder einer Anstalt oder Körperschaft des öffentlichen Rechts erhoben werden. Wohl aber können nötigenfalls gegen sie die Gerichtsvollzieherkosten von der Gerichtskasse beigetrieben werden (§ 4 JBeitrO).

2. **Handelt es sich um einen Auftrag eines** von der Zahlung der **Kosten Befreiten** (vor allem um Aufträge des Gerichts selbst), **so erfolgt** entsprechend dem Umfange der Befreiung **kein Ansatz** der Gerichtsvollzieherkosten (und damit natürlich auch keine Vorschußanforderung) gegenüber dem Auftraggeber, vgl. § 8 GVKostG. (Wird der Auftrag vom Gericht erteilt, so gelten aber im allgemeinen die Gerichtsvollzieherkosten nach außen als Auslagen des gerichtlichen Verfahrens, § 3 Abs. 3 GVKostG.)

Von der Zahlung der Gerichtsvollzieherkosten (Gebühren und Auslagen) **sind befreit der Bund und die Länder sowie die** nach den Haushaltsplänen des Bundes und der Länder für Rechnung des Bundes oder eines Landes **verwalteten öffentlichen Anstalten und Kassen. Bundesbahn und Bundespost sind von der Zahlung der Auslagen** (im Gegensatz zu den Gebühren) des Gerichtsvollziehers **nicht befreit** (§ 8 Abs. 1 GVKostG). Die Kostenbefreiung eines Kostenschuldners kommt dem anderen in keiner Weise zugute.

Vorschriften, die eine sachliche oder persönliche Befreiung von Kosten gewähren, gelten für Gerichtsvollzieherkosten nur insoweit, als sie ausdrücklich auch diese Kosten umfassen, § 8 Abs. 2 Satz 2 GVKostG. (§ 28 der Verordnung über die Fürsorgepflicht gilt ausdrücklich auch für die Gerichtsvollziehergebühren, § 8 Abs. 2 Satz 1 GVKostG). Darüber hinausgehende landesrechtliche Vorschriften der sachlichen oder persönlichen Befreiung von Gerichtsvollzieherkosten sind möglich und gegebenenfalls zu beachten (§ 8 Abs. 3 GVKostG).

Die Sozialversicherungsträger genießen, soweit sie den **Gerichtsvollzieher** (z. B. für Verhaftungen und Vorführungen) **in Anspruch nehmen** müssen, **keine Gebührenfreiheit** (§ 8 Abs. 2 Satz 2 GVKostG in Verb. mit § 115 RVO). Reisekosten und bare Auslagen sind von den Sozialversicherungsträgern stets ohne weiteres zu bezahlen (§ 117 RVO).

3. a) Nach § 5 GVKostG **kann** (nach freiem Ermessen) **der Gerichtsvollzieher die Zahlung eines** zur Deckung der voraussichtlichen baren Auslagen und des vermutlichen Betrages der Gebühren **hinreichenden Vorschusses verlangen,** ja er kann

sogar die wahrzunehmende Amtshandlung von der Zahlung eines entsprechenden Vorschusses **abhängig machen,** sofern nicht der Auftrag vom Gericht erteilt ist oder dem Auftraggeber das Armenrecht zur Seite steht. Bei Aufträgen von Behörden, Körperschaften oder Anstalten des öffentlichen Rechts — sie haften, soweit sie nicht gebührenbefreit sind — soll ein Vorschuß in keiner Weise verlangt werden. Der nicht arme private Vollstreckungsgläubiger muß danach auf Verlangen des Gerichtsvollziehers regelmäßig vorwegleisten. Zwar gibt es im Sozialgerichtsgesetz keine Bestimmung, die dem § 9 Abs. 3 Satz 2 des Arbeitsgerichtsgesetzes entspräche, nach welcher die Erhebung von Gebührenvorschüssen allgemein verboten ist. Es dürfte aber bei der Vollstreckung von Sozialgerichtstiteln nobile officium des Gerichtsvollziehers sein, von den genannten Rechten in der Regel keinen Gebrauch zu machen. Die Erhebung eines Auslagenvorschusses, die auch im Arbeitsgerichtsverfahren zulässig ist, wird der Gerichtsvollzieher unbedenklich aber auch bei der Vollstreckung von Titeln der Sozialgerichtsbarkeit jedenfalls immer dann vornehmen können, wenn er selbst Geld verauslagen muß (vgl. hierzu die Ausführungen unten 9). Er kann dann nötigenfalls auch die Auffüllung eines geleisteten Vorschusses verlangen, wenn dieser sich als unzureichend erwiesen hat. (Die weitere Geschäftsausführung kann er aber nicht von dem Eingang der Vorschußnachzahlung abhängig machen.)

b) **Die Gerichtsvollzieherkosten können bei der Ablieferung von Geld an den Auftraggeber entnommen werden,** § 6 Satz 2 GVKostG. (Die Versteigerungs- bzw. Verwertungsgebühr kann vom erzielten Erlös vorweg in Abzug gebracht werden, vgl. § 6 Satz 1 GVKostG.)

c) **Ist** dem Vollstreckungsgläubiger **das Armenrecht bewilligt und reicht der Erlös einer Zwangsvollstreckung nicht aus,** um die für die arme Partei beizutreibende Forderung und die einzuziehenden Gerichtsvollzieherkosten zu decken, **so kann der** hier an die arme Partei grundsätzlich abzuführende **Vollstreckungserlös bis zur Höhe eines Fünftels** zur Deckung dieser Kosten **einbehalten** und verwendet **werden** (§ 7 GVKostG). Das Vorliegen eines Nachzahlungsbeschlusses gegenüber dem armen Auftraggeber ist nicht Voraussetzung für diese Teilbefriedigung der Staatskasse (vgl. Tschischgale, DGVZ 1951, 147 und JR 1957, 177, auch JR 1951, 616). Einen durch § 124 ZPO begünstigten **Armengerichtsvollzieher** gibt es nicht mehr (vgl. Art. X § 3 Nr. 4 KostÄndG).

4. **Die Gerichtsvollziehergebühren und -auslagen werden,** unbeschadet der Bestimmung des § 788 ZPO (Zwangsgeltendmachung gegenüber dem Schuldner), **fällig, sobald die gebührenpflichtige Amtshandlung beendet,** d. h. grundsätzlich ausgeführt **ist,** wenn die Ausführung möglich war oder den Umständen zufolge in Frage kam (§ 4 GVKostG). Bei Armenrechtsbewilligung für die Vollstreckungsinstanz zugunsten des Vollstreckungsgläubigers sind die Gerichtsvollzieherkosten diesem gegenüber bis zur Anordnung einer Nachzahlung gestundet.

5. Wegen irrigen Ansatzes dürfen **Gerichtsvollzieherkosten** nur **nachgefordert werden,** wenn der berichtigte Ansatz vor Ablauf des nächsten Kalenderjahres nach Erledigung des Auftrages dem Zahlungspflichtigen mitgeteilt worden ist (§ 10 GVKostG).

Ansprüche auf Zahlung von Gerichtsvollzieherkosten verjähren in vier Jahren nach Ablauf des Kalenderjahres, in dem der Auftrag erledigt ist (§ 12 Abs. 1 GVKostG). Nach rechtskräftiger Festsetzung gemäß § 197 SGG beträgt die Verjährungsfrist (hier zugunsten des Vollstreckungsgläubigers) 30 Jahre (§ 218 Abs. 1 BGB). Ansprüche auf Rückerstattung von Kosten verjähren in vier Jahren nach

Ablauf des Kalenderjahres, in dem der Kostenanspruch entstanden ist. Die Verjährung beginnt jedoch nicht vor dem Ablauf des Kalenderjahres, in dem der Auftrag erledigt ist (§ 12 Abs. 2 GVKostG).

Auf die Verjährung sind die Vorschriften des Bürgerlichen Gesetzbuchs anzuwenden (§§ 198ff.). Die Verjährung wird nicht von Amts wegen berücksichtigt. Unterbrochen wird die Verjährung der Ansprüche auf Zahlung von Kosten auch durch die Aufforderung zur Zahlung oder durch eine dem Kostenschuldner mitgeteilte Stundung; ist der Aufenthalt des Kostenschuldners unbekannt, so genügt die Zustellung durch Aufgabe zur Post unter seiner letzten bekannten Anschrift. Bei Kostenbeträgen unter 20 DM wird die Verjährung nicht unterbrochen (§ 12 Abs. 3 GVKostG).

Verwirkung ist bei kurzer Verjährung, wie sie hier grundsätzlich gegeben ist, nicht möglich.

6. **Gerichtsvollzieherkosten werden nicht erhoben, wenn der Gerichtsvollzieher weder nach Bundes- noch nach Landesrecht** sachlich **zuständig gewesen ist** (§ 2 GVKostG).

Gerichtsvollzieherkosten, die bei richtiger Behandlung der Sache nicht entstanden wären, sind nicht zu erheben (§ 11 Abs. 1 GVKostG). Die Anordnung trifft – auf Antrag des Vollstreckungsgläubigers oder des Vollstreckungsschuldners – das Amtsgericht, in dessen Bezirk der Gerichtsvollzieher seinen Amtssitz hat. Es handelt sich hierbei um eine auf dem Vollstreckungsgebiet selbst liegende gerichtliche Tätigkeit, da die Ordnungsmäßigkeit des Vorgehens des Gerichtsvollziehers nachzuprüfen ist. Sie steht daher der Erinnerungsentscheidung nach § 766 Abs. 2 ZPO nahe. Gegen die Entscheidung des Amtsgerichts ist die Beschwerde (bei Antragsablehnung des Vollstreckungsgläubigers oder des Vollstreckungsschuldners, bei Stattgabe der Staatskasse) an das übergeordnete Landgericht zulässig, jedoch muß eine Mindestbeschwer in Höhe von 50,01 DM vorliegen. Die Anrufung des Amtsgerichts zur Vornahme der Anordnung (Erinnerungseinlegung) wie die Erhebung der Beschwerde kann in allen Fällen durch Erklärung zu Protokoll der Geschäftsstelle des Amtsgerichts bzw. – bei der Beschwerde – des Amtsgerichts oder Landgerichts oder schriftlich ohne Mitwirkung eines Rechtsanwalts erfolgen (§ 11 Abs. 2 GVKostG). Solange nicht das Gericht entschieden hat, kann die Anordnung auch im Verwaltungswege von der Dienstaufsichtsbehörde getroffen werden. Eine im Verwaltungsweg getroffene Anordnung kann ebenfalls nur im Verwaltungsweg geändert werden (§ 11 Abs. 3 GVKostG). Etwa überflüssig oder zuviel gezahlte Gerichtsvollzieherkosten sind zurückzuzahlen. (Die Staatskasse kann dazu im ordentlichen Klagewege gezwungen werden.)

7. **Die volle Gerichtsvollziehergebühr bestimmt sich nach der Tabelle,** die dem Gesetz als Anlage beigefügt ist, § 13 Abs. 1 GVKostG (vgl. hier die Tabelle im Anhang).

Pfennigbeträge von Gebühren sind jeweils **auf volle 10 Deutsche Pfennig aufzurunden** (§ 13 Abs. 2 GVKostG).

Ist die Höhe der **Gerichtsvollziehergebühren von der Dauer der Amtshandlung abhängig,** so wird die für die geringste Dauer bestimmte Gebühr erhoben, wenn in dem vom Gerichtsvollzieher niedergelegten Protokoll keine längere Dauer angegeben ist (§ 14 GVKostG).

Werden Aufträge eines oder mehrerer Auftraggeber durch dieselbe Amtshandlung des Gerichtsvollziehers **erledigt, so werden** die **Gerichtsvollzieherkosten nur einmal erhoben.** Gebühren nach dem betroffenen Wert werden nach dem zusammengerechneten Wert erhoben und nach dem Verhältnis der Gebühren, die bei gesonderter Ausführung entstanden wären, aufgeteilt. Sonstige Kosten werden nach der Zahl der Auftraggeber verteilt (§ 15 GVKostG).

Wird der **Gerichtsvollzieher** auf Verlangen **zur Nachtzeit** (vgl. § 188 Abs. 1 Satz 2 ZPO) **oder an einem Sonn- oder Feiertag tätig,** so **werden** die **Gebühren verdoppelt** erhoben (§ 34 GVKostG).

8. Die in Frage kommenden **Gerichtsvollziehergebühren sind im einzelnen die folgenden.**

a) **Zustellungs- und Beglaubigungsgebühr**

Die Gebühr für eine Zustellung durch Aufgabe zur Post (vgl. § 175 ZPO), für das an die Post gerichtete Ersuchen um Bewirkung einer Zustellung (vgl. § 194 ZPO) sowie für die im Auftrage eines Rechtsanwalts an den Gegenanwalt bewirkte Zustellung beträgt 0,50 DM. Hinzu kommt bei der Zustellung durch Aufgabe zur Post und bei Postzustellung das Porto, bei Postzustellung weiterhin die postalische Zustellungsgebühr und das Porto für die Zusendung der Zustellungsurkunde an den Gerichtsvollzieher (§ 16 Abs. 1 GVKostG).

Stellt der Gerichtsvollzieher persönlich ohne Inanspruchnahme der Post zu, so beträgt die Gebühr 1,50 DM (§ 16 Abs. 2 GVKostG).

Ist mit der persönlichen Zustellung eine Aufforderung gemäß § 840 ZPO verbunden oder ist dem Empfänger zugleich mit der Zustellung eine Urkunde vorzulegen, so beträgt die Gebühr 2 DM. Die Hebegebühr des § 27 Abs. 2 GVKostG wird daneben nicht erhoben (§ 16 Abs. 3 GVKostG).

Ist die versuchte persönliche Zustellung, nachdem sich der Gerichtsvollzieher an Ort und Stelle begeben hat, infolge von Umständen, die weder in der Person des Gerichtsvollziehers liegen noch von seiner Entschließung abhängig sind, ohne Erfolg geblieben, so beträgt die Gebühr 1 DM (§ 16 Abs. 4 GVKostG).

Wird der Zustellungsauftrag (s. o.) vor seiner Erledigung zurückgenommen, so erhält der Gerichtsvollzieher 0,30 DM. Dies gilt auch, wenn bei persönlicher Zustellung der Zustellungsauftrag zurückgenommen wird, bevor sich der Gerichtsvollzieher an Ort und Stelle begeben hat (§ 16 Abs. 5 GVKostG).

Die Zustellung an den Zustellungsbevollmächtigten mehrerer Beteiligter (§ 189 Abs. 2 ZPO, § 63 Abs. 3 SGG) gilt als eine Zustellung (§ 16 Abs. 6 GVKostG).

Für die Beglaubigung eines Schriftstücks, das dem Gerichtsvollzieher zum Zwecke der Zustellung übergeben ist (§ 170 Abs. 2 ZPO), wird eine Gebühr von 0,10 DM für die Seite erhoben. Eine angefangene Seite wird als voll berechnet (§ 16 Abs. 7 GVKostG). Schreibt der Gerichtsvollzieher das Schriftstück selbst ab, so erhält er nur die sogen. Schreibgebühr (vgl. § 36 Abs. 1 Nr. 2 GVKostG).

Hervorzuheben ist in diesem Zusammenhang, daß nach § 197 ZPO, § 202 SGG die zur **Erstattung** der Kosten verurteilte oder verpflichtete Partei die Mehrkosten nicht zu tragen hat, die durch eine persönliche Zustellung des Gerichtsvollziehers entstehen, wenn die Zustellung auch durch die Post hätte erfolgen können.

b) **Pfändungsgebühr**

Für (jede) Pfändung von beweglichen Sachen (vgl. §§ 808, 809 ZPO), von Früchten, die vom Boden noch nicht getrennt sind (vgl. § 810 ZPO), von Forderungen aus Wechseln oder anderen Papieren, die durch Indossament übertragen werden können (vgl. § 831 ZPO) und von Postspareinlagen (§ 17 Abs. 1 der Postsparkassenordnung vom 11. 11. 1938 – RGBl. I 1645) wird die volle Gebühr nach dem Betrage der beizutreibenden Forderung (Hauptforderung + festgesetzte Kostenforderung zuzüglich jeweils zugesprochener Zinsen, vgl. § 20 Abs. 2 GKG) erhoben (§ 17 Abs. 1 GVKostG).

Bei der Pfändung eines im Schiffsregister eingetragenen Schiffes oder eines im Schiffsbauregister eingetragenen Schiffsbauwerkes (§ 931 ZPO) oder eines ausländischen Schiffes, das, wenn es ein deutsches Schiff wäre, in das Register eingetragen werden müßte, beträgt die Gebühr mindestens 12 DM (§ 17 Abs. 2 GVKostG).

Nimmt die Pfändung mehr als eine Stunde in Anspruch, so erhöht sich die Gebühr für jede angefangene weitere Stunde um die Hälfte, jedoch höchstens um je 4 DM (§ 17 Abs. 3 GVKostG).

Wenn nach dem Inhalte des Protokolls pfändbare Gegenstände nicht vorhanden sind oder die Pfändung nach § 803 Abs. 2 ZPO (wegen Aussichtslosigkeit) oder § 812 ZPO (wegen Zwecklosigkeit) oder § 851b Abs. 2 Satz 2 ZPO (wegen Zweckgebundenheit) zu unterbleiben hatte, so wird für den Pfändungsversuch die Hälfte der für die Pfändung bestimmten Gebühr ausgelöst, mindestens aber 1 DM (§ 17 Abs. 4 GVKostG).

Für die Übernahme beweglicher Sachen zum Zwecke der Verwertung in den Fällen der §§ 847, 854 ZPO (von einem Drittschuldner bei Pfändung des Anspruchs auf Herausgabe) wird die Hälfte der vollen Gebühr nach dem Betrage der beizutreibenden Forderung, mindestens aber 1 DM, erhoben (§ 18 Abs. 1 GVKostG).

Die gleiche Gebühr wird erhoben, wenn der Schuldner unter Mitnahme der Pfandstücke in einen anderen Amtsgerichtsbezirk verzieht und ein anderer Gerichtsvollzieher den Vollstreckungsauftrag übernimmt (§ 18 Abs. 2 GVKostG).

Werden Pfandstücke, die im Gewahrsam des Schuldners belassen sind, durch den Gerichtsvollzieher zum Zwecke der Versteigerung oder aus einem anderen Grunde aus dem Gewahrsam des Schuldners entfernt, so wird eine Gebühr von 1,20 DM erhoben (§ 19 Abs. 1 GVKostG). Nimmt das Geschäft mehr als eine Stunde in Anspruch, so erhöht sich die Gebühr für jede angefangene weitere Stunde um den gleichen Betrag (§ 19 Abs. 2 GVKostG). Das Vorstehende gilt entsprechend, wenn der Gerichtsvollzieher außerhalb einer Zwangsvollstreckung Gegenstände aus dem Gewahrsam des Inhabers zum Zwecke der Versteigerung oder der Verwahrung entfernt (§ 19 Abs. 3 GVKostG).

Wird eine auf Pfändung oder auf Übernahme gerichtete Vollstreckungshandlung infolge von Umständen, die weder in der Person des Gerichtsvollziehers liegen noch von seiner Entschließung abhängig sind, nicht durchgeführt, so wird, wenn sich der Gerichtsvollzieher noch nicht an Ort und Stelle begeben hatte, ein Viertel der für die Durchführung der Handlung bestimmten Gebühr, mindestens jedoch 0,50 DM und höchstens 60 DM erhoben (§ 20 Abs. 1 GVKostG).

Wird eine Vollstreckungshandlung der vorgenannten Art oder die Entfernung aus dem Gewahrsam des Schuldners aus den wiedergegebenen Gründen nicht durchgeführt, nachdem sich der Gerichtsvollzieher an Ort und Stelle begeben hatte, so wird die Hälfte der für die Amtshandlung bestimmten Gebühr erhoben, im Falle der in Frage stehenden Pfändung oder Übernahme von Sachen jedoch mindestens 1 DM und höchstens 120 DM. Bei Zahlungsleistung an den Gerichtsvollzieher wird darüber hinaus die **Hebegebühr** des § 27 Abs. 1 GVKostG in Höhe eines Viertels der vollen Gebühr nach dem Betrage der Zahlung, mindestens jedoch 0,50 DM erhoben.

Betreffen die in den Fällen der Nichtdurchführung der Amtshandlung wiedergegebenen Voraussetzungen jeweils Teile der beizutreibenden Forderung, so sind die Gebühren von jedem Teil besonders zu berechnen. Es darf jedoch nicht mehr erhoben werden, als wenn die Gebühr von der Summe dieser Forderungsteile nach dem höchsten der in Betracht kommenden Gebührensätze (s. o.) erhoben würde (§ 20 Abs. 3 GVKostG).

c) **Verwertungs(Versteigerungs-)gebühr**

Für die Versteigerung oder den Verkauf aus freier Hand von beweglichen Sachen, von Früchten, die vom Boden noch nicht getrennt sind, sowie von Forderungen oder anderen Vermögensrechten wird das Zweieinhalbfache der vollen Gebühr nach dem Betrage des Erlöses erhoben, falls dieser nicht höher ist als der dann maßgebende beizutreibende Betrag (§ 21 Abs. 1 GVKostG).

Ist ein zum Zuschlag führendes Gebot nicht abgegeben worden oder ist die Versteigerung bzw. der Verkauf, nachdem sich der Gerichtsvollzieher an Ort und Stelle begeben hat, aus Umständen unterblieben, die weder in der Person des Gerichtsvollziehers liegen noch von seinem Entschluß abhängig sind, so beträgt die Gebühr 1,20 DM. Diese Gebühr wird aber nur erhoben, wenn eine Versteigerungs- oder Verwertungsgebühr auch hinsichtlich eines Teiles der gepfändeten Gegenstände nicht entsteht (§ 21 Abs. 3 GVKostG). Eine etwaige Hebegebühr kommt dagegen zum Zuge (vgl. § 27 Abs. 1 GVKostG).

Hat der Versteigerungstermin auf Antrag des Gläubigers oder zufolge der Vorschriften der §§ 765a, 775, 813a ZPO (Einstellung bzw. Aussetzung wegen unbilliger Härte, ergangener Prozeßgerichtsanordnung, geleisteter Sicherheit, nachgewiesener Zahlung oder wirtschaftlicher Billigkeit) nicht stattgefunden oder ist der Versteigerungstermin infolge Ausbleibens von Bietern oder wegen ungenügender Gebote erfolglos geblieben, so wird für die Anberaumung eines neuen Versteigerungstermins eine Gebühr von 0,60 DM erhoben (§ 21 Abs. 4 GVKostG).

Für die Mitwirkung bei einer vom Vollstreckungsgericht gemäß § 825 ZPO angeordneten besonderen Art der Verwertung einer gepfändeten Sache wird, falls eine Verwertungsgebühr nicht unmittelbar ausgelöst wird, die volle Gebühr nach dem Betrage des Erlöses oder sonstigen Preises, höchstens jedoch ein Betrag von 25 DM erhoben. Besteht die Mitwirkung des Gerichtsvollziehers lediglich in der Übergabe oder Übersendung der Sache, so beträgt die Gebühr höchstens 2,50 DM. Nimmt hier das Geschäft mehr als eine Stunde in Anspruch, so erhöht sich die Gebühr für jede angefangene weitere Stunde um den gleichen Betrag, höchstens jedoch um je 4 DM (§ 21 Abs. 5 GVKostG).

9. **Folgende bare Gerichtsvollzieherauslagen sind** gegebenenfalls **zu ersetzen:**

a) **Schreibgebühren,** und zwar 0,50 DM für die Seite zu regelmäßig 28 Zeilen von durchschnittlich 15 Silben, auch wenn die Herstellung auf mechanischem Wege (Druck o. ä.) stattgefunden hat. (Jede angefangene Seite wird voll gerechnet.) Für Schriftstücke, die in fremder Sprache abgefaßt sind, werden die doppelten Schreibkosten erhoben. Werden Abschriften durch Ablichtung hergestellt, so werden für jede abgelichtete Seite ohne Rücksicht auf Zeilen- und Silbenzahl 0,50 DM, bei größerem Format der Ablichtung als DIN B 4 eine DM erhoben (vgl. hierzu § 35 Abs. 1 Nr. 1, § 36 Abs. 2 GVKostG und § 91 Abs. 3, 4 und 6 GKG).

Die Schreibkosten sind zu zahlen:

α) für alle nach gesetzlicher Vorschrift (vgl. §§ 763, 826 ZPO) oder auf Antrag erteilten Abschriften der von dem Gerichtsvollzieher aufgenommenen Urkunden und Protokolle, ausgenommen die nach gesetzlicher Vorschrift zu erteilende Abschrift der Zustellungsurkunde; in den Fällen des § 189 Abs. 2 ZPO (Zustellung an einen Bevollmächtigten mehrerer Beteiligter) und des § 829 Abs. 2 Satz 2 ZPO (Pfändung von Geldforderungen) wird die Schreibgebühr jedoch für jede Abschrift der Zustellungsurkunde erhoben (§ 36 Abs. 1 Nr. 1 GVKostG);

β) für Abschriften, die angefertigt werden, weil der Auftraggeber es unterlassen hat, einem zuzustellenden Schriftstück die erforderliche Zahl von Abschriften beizufügen (§ 36 Abs. 1 Nr. 2 GVKostG);

γ) für die bei einer Hinterlegung zu erstattende Anzeige an das Vollstreckungsgericht, vgl. §§ 827, 854 ZPO (§ 36 Abs. 1 Nr. 3 GVKostG);

δ) für die Aufnahme der von dem Drittschuldner bei der Zustellung eines Pfändungsbeschlusses oder nachträglich abgegebenen Erklärungen, vgl. § 840 ZPO (§ 36 Abs. 1 Nr. 4 GVKostG);

ε) für die vor der Verhaftung eines Schuldners erforderliche Anzeige an die vorgesetzte Dienstbehörde des zu Verhaftenden (vgl. § 910 ZPO) und für die auf Antrag gefertigte Abschrift des Haftbefehls, vgl. § 909 Satz 2 ZPO (§ 36 Abs. 1 Nr. 5 GVKostG);

b) **Formularauslagen,** d. h. die Kosten für die bei der Erledigung des Auftrages verwendeten Vordrucke aller Art, soweit keine Schreibgebühren zu erheben sind (§ 35 Abs. 1 Nr. 2 GVKostG). Hier wird von allen Ländern ein Pauschsatz von 0,20 DM erhoben (vgl. § 35 Abs. 2 Nr. 1 GVKostG); die Erhebung dieses Betrages kommt regelmäßig in Frage:

α) bei jeder Zustellung;

β) bei jedem Auftrag zur Pfändung, Wegnahme, Räumung, Verhaftung oder zwangsweisen Vorführung;

γ) bei jeder Versteigerung, beim freihändigen Verkauf oder bei der Übereignung eines Gegenstandes oder mehrerer;

δ) bei der Anberaumung eines jeden weiteren Versteigerungstermins;

c) **Post-, Telegrafen-, Fernsprech- und Fernschreibkosten** (§ 35 Abs. 1 Nr. 3 GVKostG; für ein Ortsgespräch, das der Gerichtsvollzieher über den eigenen Fernsprecher führt, beträgt der allgemeine Pauschsatz — unter Berücksichtigung der Grundgebühr — 0,30 DM, vgl. hierzu § 35 Abs. 2 Nr. 2 GVKostG);

d) **Veröffentlichungskosten,** d. h. Auslagen, die durch öffentliche Bekanntmachung entstehen (§ 35 Abs. 1 Nr. 4 GVKostG);

e) **Zeugen- und Sachverständigenkosten,** nämlich die an hinzugezogene Zeugen und Sachverständige zu zahlenden (angemessenen bzw. ortsüblichen) Beträge (§ 35 Abs. 1 Nr. 5 GVKostG); die einschlägigen Endbeträge des Gesetzes über die Entschädigung von Zeugen und Sachverständigen (vgl. hier das 5. Kap. II 2 und III 2) dürfen billigerweise nicht überschritten werden;

f) **Dienstleistungsentschädigungen,** nämlich die üblichen Vergütungen der zum Öffnen von Türen und Behältnissen (vgl. § 758 ZPO) sowie zur Durchsuchung von Schuldnern zugezogenen Personen (§ 35 Abs. 1 Nr. 6 GVKostG);

g) **Umschreibungskosten,** nämlich die für die Überschreibung eines auf den Namen lautenden Wertpapiers oder für die Wiederinkurssetzung eines Inhaberpapiers zu zahlenden Beträge, vgl. § 822 ZPO (§ 35 Abs. 1 Nr. 7 GVKostG);

h) **Transport- und Verwahrungsauslagen,** d. h. die normalen Kosten einer Beförderung von Personen oder Sachen, der Verwahrung (insbesondere auf der sog. Pfandkammer) und Beaufsichtigung von Sachen, der Aberntung und Unterbringung von Früchten und der Verwahrung und Fütterung von Tieren (§ 35 Abs. 1 Nr. 8 GVKostG);

i) **Reisekostenpauschbeträge und Wegegelder** (§ 35 Abs. 1 Nr. 9 GVKostG).

α) Die Reisekosten betragen bei erforderlichem Weg (hin und zurück) von mindestens je 2 km außerhalb des Gebiets der Gemeinde des Amtsitzes des Gerichtsvollziehers 0,15 DM für jedes angefangene Kilometer des Hin- und Rückwegs, gerechnet von Ortsmitte zu Ortsmitte (§ 37 Abs. 1 GVKostG).

Der Reisekostenpauschbetrag wird für jede Amtshandlung erhoben, auch wenn der Gerichtsvollzieher auf derselben Reise mehrere Amtshandlungen vornimmt. Werden jedoch auf einer Reise mehrere Amtshandlungen gegen einen Schuldner oder in derselben Gemeinde für einen Auftraggeber vorgenommen, so wird der Reisekostenpauschbetrag nur einmal erhoben; der Reisekostenpauschbetrag wird im ersten Fall aufgeteilt nach der Zahl der Aufträge, im zweiten Fall nach der Zahl der Schuldner (§ 37 Abs. 2 GVKostG).

Ein Reisekostenpauschbetrag wird nicht erhoben, soweit bei benachbarten Orten Wegegeld als Auslage anzusetzen ist (§ 37 Abs. 3 GVKostG).

β) Für benachbarte Gemeinden kann von den Landesregierungen (oder bei zulässiger Weiterübertragung von den Landesjustizverwaltungen) bestimmt werden, ob und in welchem Umfang dem Gerichtsvollzieher zur Verminderung der Kosten für die Wege, die er zur Vornahme einer Amtshandlung innerhalb dieser Ortschaften zurücklegen muß, eine Entschädigung für Wegekosten zu gewähren ist (vgl. § 38 Abs. 1 Nr. 1 und Abs. 2 GVKostG).

Das zum Ausgleich von Aufwendungen für Wege, die der Gerichtsvollzieher zurücklegt, innerhalb des Gebiets der Gemeinde seines Amtssitzes und nach Orten außerhalb dieses Gebiets, sofern die Voraussetzungen für die Erhebung eines Reisekostenpauschbetrages (§ 37 Abs. 1 GVKostG) nicht gegeben sind (vgl. § 38 Abs. 1 Nr. 2 und Abs. 2 GVKostG), beträgt für jede Amtshandlung, auch wenn der Gerichtsvollzieher auf demselben Weg mehrere solcher Handlungen vornimmt, regelmäßig 0,50 DM. Werden auf einem Weg mehrere Amtshandlungen gegen einen Schuldner vorgenommen, so wird das Wegegeld nur einmal erhoben; es wird in diesem Falle nach der Zahl der Aufträge aufgeteilt. Als wegegeldpflichtige Amtshandlungen gelten dabei ihrer Natur zufolge nicht: die Zustellung durch Aufgabe zur Post (§ 175 ZPO), das an die Post gerichtete Ersuchen um Bewirkung einer Zustellung (§ 194 ZPO) und die Versteigerung von Pfandstücken, die sich schon in der Pfandkammer befinden.

Wegen der Reise- und Wegebemessung im einzelnen vgl. Hemme, JVBl. 1957, 81 und 1958, 167;

k) **Auskunftsgebühren,** d. h. die für Auskünfte über die Wohnung des Beteiligten an Einwohnermeldestellen zu zahlenden Beträge (§ 35 Abs. 1 Nr. 10 GVKostG);

l) **Sonderauslagen,** d. h. die Kosten für Arbeitshilfen — gemäß den Tarifen — und für die Benutzung von eigenen Transportmitteln des Gerichtsvollziehers zur Beförderung von Personen und Sachen (§ 35 Abs. 1 Nr. 11, Abs. 2 Nr. 4 GVKostG). Für die Beförderung von Personen durch ein eigenes Fahrzeug des Gerichtsvollziehers wird für jede Person und jedes angefangene Kilometer allgemein ein Pauschsatz von 0,10 DM erhoben, und zwar unabhängig von einem zu zahlenden Reisekostenpauschbetrage oder einem Wegegeld. Für die Beförderung von Sachen kommt es auf den Umfang und die Umstände im Einzelfall an.

III. Die Gerichtsvollzieherkostenfestsetzung

Übersicht

1. **Die Ansetzung von Gerichtsvollzieherkosten wird, wie folgt, vorgenommen:**

a) **Gemäß § 788 Abs. 1 ZPO werden die** durch die Pfändung insgesamt entstehenden und berechenbaren **Gerichtsvollzieherkosten** (Gebühren und Auslagen) – wie grundsätzlich alle notwendigen Kosten der Zwangsvollstreckung, insbesondere die eines mit ihrer Veranlassung beauftragten Rechtsanwalts (Rechtsbeistandes) – **vom vollstreckenden Gerichtsvollzieher eigenverantwortlich berechnet und kurzerhand** – kostenfrei – **zum Ansatz gebracht** (der Gerichtsvollzieher ist hier „kostenansetzender Urkundsbeamter"), um zugleich mit dem zur Zwangsvollstreckung stehenden Hauptanspruch vom Vollstreckungsschuldner, der sich aus dem Vollstreckungstitel ergibt, ohne Rücksicht auf dessen etwaige Armut (vgl. § 117 ZPO) als Forderung des Vollstreckungsgläubigers beigetrieben zu werden. Auch das dem Auftraggeber etwa zur Seite stehende Armenrecht (für die Zwangsvollstreckung) hindert, wie sich aus dem keine Einschränkung enthaltenden § 788 ZPO ergibt, diese zusätzliche Beitreibung nicht; allerdings ist hier bei zur Kostenmitabdeckung nicht ausreichendem Vollstreckungserlös die Staatskasse mit Ausnahme eines dann einbehaltbaren Betrages bis zu einem Fünftel des Erlöses (vgl. § 7 GVKostG) gegenüber dem Gläubiger letztrangig. Der Gerichtsvollzieher ist im Falle des zugunsten des Gläubigers bestehenden Armenrechts für diesen verpflichtet, die beigetriebenen Gerichtsvollzieherkosten an die insoweit berechtigte Staatskasse unmittelbar abzuführen. (Hinsichtlich der Kostenrangverhältnisse zum bestellten Armenanwalt vgl. § 126 Abs. 3 ZPO und § 130 Abs. 1 Satz 2 BRAGebO.) Ein besonderer Festsetzungsantrag des Vollstreckungsgläubigers, der als solcher ebenfalls ohne weiteres aus dem Vollstreckungstitel zu ersehen ist, ist nicht notwendig; er liegt mit in dem dem Gerichtsvollzieher erteilten Vollstreckungsauftrag. Eine ausdrückliche Auferlegung der Vollstreckungskosten zu Lasten des Vollstreckungsschuldners und zugunsten des anspruchsberechtigten Vollstreckungsgläubigers im Titel (Urteil u. ä.) ist weder erforderlich noch üblich. Die Erstattungspflicht hinsichtlich dieser Kosten ergibt sich kraft Gesetzes (vgl. § 788 Abs. 1 Satz 1 ZPO) aus dem zwischen dem Vollstreckungsgläubiger und dem Vollstreckungsschuldner auf Grund der Verurteilung (zur Leistung) vorliegenden besonderen Erfüllungsverhältnis.

b) **Die Kosten des tätig gewordenen Gerichtsvollziehers** wie überhaupt die notwendigen Kosten einer vorgenommenen oder wenigstens versuchten Zwangsvollstreckung **können, soweit eine Beitreibung** nach § 788 Abs. 1 ZPO nicht, oder jedenfalls **nicht mit Erfolg durchgeführt worden ist, ohne weiteres** (d. h. ohne ausdrücklichen Kostentitel) **in einem** zu diesem Zwecke eingeleiteten oder wegen anderer

Kosten durchgeführten **Kostenfestsetzungsverfahren nach § 197 SGG** auf Antrag des in Frage stehenden Vollstreckungsgläubigers als dessen Forderung gegen den sich aus dem Vollstreckungstitel ergebenden und als solchen für die Vollstreckung kostenpflichtigen Schuldner — gebührenfrei —, und zwar falls beantragt mit Zinsen (vgl. § 104 Abs. 1 Satz 2 ZPO) **förmlich festgesetzt werden** (von dem in richterlicher Unabhängigkeit tätig werdenden Urkundsbeamten des Prozeßgerichts des ersten Rechtszuges, d. h. des befaßt gewesenen Sozialgerichts). Steht dem Gläubiger in der Zwangsvollstreckung das Armenrecht zur Seite, so braucht er zwar bis zur Anordnung der Nachzahlung selbst keine Gerichtsvollzieherkosten zu bezahlen. Trotzdem können diese Kosten hier an sich zugunsten des Gläubigers gegen den Schuldner förmlich zur Festsetzung gelangen, weil der Gläubiger nicht schlechter gestellt werden kann als bei einem Ansatz nach § 788 Abs. 1 ZPO (siehe dazu oben a). Der Gläubiger ist hier ebenso wie der Gerichtsvollzieher aber verpflichtet, diese Kosten sogleich an die Staatskasse abzuführen, die sie vom Schuldner selbst bei dessen Armut (vgl. § 117 ZPO) verlangen kann. Rechtskraft der Verurteilung des Schuldners ist auch hier nicht erforderlich, ebenso nicht erklärte vorläufige Titelvollstreckbarkeit. Vollstreckt wird der so festgesetzte Betrag in der üblichen, Gerichts- oder Gerichtsvollzieherkosten auslösenden Weise, und zwar auch gegen einen armen Schuldner (§ 117 ZPO) entweder durch das Gericht oder den Gerichtsvollzieher (vgl. oben I 5 und 6).

c) **Wird für die Gerichtsvollzieherkosten,** weil die Beitreibung vom Schuldner nicht erfolgte bzw. unmöglich war, **der den Gerichtsvollzieher beauftragende Vollstreckungsgläubiger selbst als Schuldner dieser Kosten** (im Verhältnis zur Staatskasse) **in Anspruch genommen** — Voraussetzung ist, daß er hier nicht bzw. nicht mehr (vgl. § 125 ZPO) arm ist —, so **muß** ihm gegenüber **die Aufstellung einer ansatzmäßigen Berechnung durch den Gerichtsvollzieher erfolgen,** vgl. § 9 GVKostG (mit Rechtsbehelfsbelehrung, vgl. § 67 SGG und unten 2 c). Sie kann vom Gerichtsvollzieher bei irrigem Kostenansatz berichtigt werden. **Der Gerichtsvollzieher kann die so errechneten Kosten vom Vollstreckungsgläubiger (in gleicher Weise** übrigens ohne weiteres **auch vom Vollstreckungsschuldner** als Kostenschuldner) **einfordern.** Eine bei Nichtzahlung notwendig werdende Zwangsvollstreckung erfolgt nach den Bestimmungen der Justizbeitreibungsordnung durch die Gerichtskasse des Amtsgerichts, das für den Amtssitz des beauftragten Gerichtsvollziehers und damit regelmäßig auch für den Wohnsitz des Vollstreckungsschuldners zuständig ist. Auf die gleiche Weise kann von der Staatskasse gegen den — armen oder nicht armen (vgl. § 117 ZPO) — Vollstreckungsschuldner, der ja gegenüber der Staatskasse ebenfalls Schuldner der Gerichtsvollzieherkosten (hier im Rahmen ihrer regelmäßig zu bejahenden Notwendigkeit) ist (vgl. § 3 Abs. 1 Nr. 2 GVKostG), vorgegangen werden.

2. **Die Rechtsbehelfe gegen die einzelnen Ansätze der Gerichtsvollzieherkosten sind die folgenden.**

a) **Wegen der vom Gerichtsvollzieher** als Vollstreckungsorgan **gemäß § 788 Abs. 1 ZPO — kurzerhand — zum Ansatz gebrachten** Vollstreckungskosten, vor allem der **Gerichtsvollziehergebühren und -auslagen** (vgl. oben 1a), **kann** bis zur endgültigen Beendigung des Zwangsvollstreckungsverfahrens von dem beschwerten Beteiligten (bei Ansatz dem Vollstreckungsschuldner, bei — praktischer — Absetzung, nämlich Nichtberücksichtigung, dem Vollstreckungsgläubiger) **beim Vollstreckungsgericht,** d. h. dem Amtsgericht, in dessen Bezirk das Vollstreckungsverfahren stattfindet (vgl. § 764 Abs. 2 ZPO) fristlos (§ 178 SGG gilt hier nicht), und zwar sowohl betreffs der Höhe wie des Grundes ohne Einhaltung einer Form **Erinnerung eingelegt werden** (Erfüllungsbehauptungen können aber, da es sich um ein, wenn auch abgekürztes, Festsetzungsverfahren handelt, keine Berücksichtigung finden). Das Gericht entscheidet bei Nichtabhilfe durch den Gerichtsvollzieher nach eigenem Ermessen grundsätzlich ohne mündliche Verhandlung (vgl. § 764 Abs. 3 ZPO) im Wege des zu begründenden Beschlusses gebührenfrei. Rechtsmittelbelehrung ist hier, wie stets vor den ordentlichen Gerichten, im Gegensatz zu den Verfahren vor den Gerichten der Sozialgerichtsbarkeit (vgl. hier §66 SGG), nicht erforderlich (a. A. Mellwitz, SGG Anm. B zu § 198). Vorherige Anhörung des Gerichtsvollziehers, der am Verfahren selbst nicht beteiligt ist, ist nobile officium. **Gegen die Entscheidung des Vollstreckungsgerichts gibt es** seitens des durch sie Beschwerten (das ist bei Gebührenverkürzung der Vollstreckungsgläubiger, sonst der Vollstreckungsschuldner) gemäß § 793 ZPO die **binnen einer Frist von einem Monat** (nicht zwei Wochen) seit Beschlußzustellung (vgl. § 198 Abs. 3, § 173 SGG) einzulegende und **an eine Mindestbeschwer von 50,01 DM gebundene** (§ 567 Abs. 2 ZPO) **Vollstreckungskostenbeschwerde an das** übergeordnete **Landgericht** (einzulegen bei diesem oder beim Vollstreckungsgericht schriftlich oder zu Protokoll des Urkundsbeamten, d. h. ohne Anwaltszwang). Das Vollstreckungsgericht ist hier zur Abhilfe berechtigt (vgl. § 198 Abs. 3, § 174 SGG) und bei Nichtabhilfe befugt, die angefochtene und dadurch nicht aufgeschobene Zwangsvollstreckung bis zu seiner Entscheidung gegen oder ohne Sicherheitsleistung einzustellen oder nur noch gegen Sicherheitsleistung zu gestatten (§ 198 Abs. 3, § 175 letzter Satz SGG, § 766 Abs. 1 und § 732 Abs. 2 ZPO). Die entsprechende Befugnis hat bei Einlegung der Beschwerde gegen die Erinnerungsentscheidung gemäß § 572 Abs. 3 ZPO das Beschwerdegericht (vgl. dazu auch den § 572 Abs. 2 ZPO bezüglich der gleichen Befugnis des Erinnerungsgerichts im Falle der Beschwerdeeinlegung).

Die Gerichtsvollziehergebühren fließen, wie ausgeführt, nicht mehr dem Gerichtsvollzieher zu, sondern der Staatskasse. Aber auch diese ist an dem hier behandelten Festsetzungsverfahren, welches das (Erstattungs-)Verhältnis des Vollstreckungsgläubigers zum Vollstreckungsschuldner betrifft, nicht beteiligt. Der Ausgang des Verfahrens bindet daher auch sie nicht (umgekehrt besteht eine solche Bindung ebenfalls nicht). Allerdings können die Kosten gegenüber dem Erstattungspflichtigen niemals höher festgesetzt werden als sie als solche überhaupt verlangt werden.

Die Beschwerdeentscheidung des Landgerichts ist bei negativem Ausgang (Verwerfung, Zurückweisung, vgl. § 97 ZPO und § 46 Abs. 2 GKG) kostenpflichtig, sonst gebührenfrei. Die Entscheidungen ergehen hier ebenfalls stets im Rahmen des Verlangten; eine Schlechterstellung des Erinnerungs- oder Beschwerdeführers ist nicht möglich.

Gegen die Entscheidung (Beschluß mit Begründung) des Landgerichts, die grundsätzlich ohne mündliche Verhandlung ergeht, gibt es keine weitere Beschwerde (§ 568 Abs. 3 ZPO).

Erwähnt sei, daß Erfüllungseinwendungen im Wege der Vollstreckungsgegenklage (s. u. b) geltend gemacht werden müssen; die Einschränkung des § 767 Abs. 2 ZPO, die für das Festsetzungsverfahren nicht paßt, gilt nicht.

b) **Gegen die** mit Rechtsbehelfsbelehrung zu versehende (vgl. § 66 SGG) **förmliche Festsetzung der** Vollstreckungskosten (einschließlich der **Gerichtsvollziehergebühren** und -auslagen) **durch den Urkundsbeamten der Geschäftsstelle der ersten Instanz** (siehe hier oben 1b) **kann** gemäß § 197 Abs. 2 SGG von dem beschwerten

Beteiligten (das ist bei Ansatz der Schuldner, bei Absetzung der Gläubiger) sowohl den Grund wie die Höhe betreffend — Erfüllungseinwendungen können aber, wie stets im Festsetzungsverfahren, nicht gebracht werden — grundsätzlich **binnen eines Monats** nach Bekanntgabe (d. h. Zustellung, vgl. § 63 Abs. 1 SGG) **das Gericht** (das befaßte Sozialgericht als Prozeßgericht erster Instanz) **angerufen werden** (schriftlich oder zu Protokoll des Urkundsbeamten, vgl. § 173 SGG), **das** bei Nichtabhilfe durch den jeweiligen Urkundsbeamten (§ 174 SGG) auf Grund eigenen Sachermessens (§ 128 Abs. 1, § 142 Abs. 1 SGG) ohne mündliche Verhandlung (§ 124 Abs. 3 SGG) durch zu begründenden Beschluß (§ 142 Abs. 2 SGG) kostenfrei (§ 183 SGG) **endgültig entscheidet** (§ 197 Abs. 2, auch § 178 SGG). Die Entscheidung erfolgt im Rahmen des Verlangten; eine Schlechterstellung des das Gericht Anrufenden ist nicht möglich. Der Gerichtsvollzieher ist ebenso wie der Staat an diesem Festsetzungsverfahren nicht beteiligt; die Festsetzung bindet sie daher auch nicht. Umgekehrt ist der gemäß § 197 Abs. 1 SGG festsetzende Urkundsbeamte nicht an die Entscheidung gebunden, die in dem Festsetzungsverfahren (gegen Gläubiger oder Schuldner) ergeht, an dem die Staatskasse beteiligt ist; er darf aber natürlich nicht mehr zur Erstattung festsetzen als die Staatskasse bzw. der Gerichtsvollzieher verlangt.

Erwähnt sei noch, daß Erfüllungseinwendungen im Wege der Vollstreckungsgegenklage (zu erheben regelmäßig beim befaßt gewesenen Sozialgericht, vgl. LSG Bayern in Breith. 1955, 1018) geltend gemacht werden müssen. Die Einschränkung des § 767 Abs. 2 ZPO, die für das ohne mündliche Verhandlung stattfindende Festsetzungsverfahren nicht paßt, gilt hier richtigerweise nicht.

Wegen der Einzelheiten des Anrufungsverfahrens vgl. die Ausführungen im 6. Kap. 28.

c) **Gegen den Ansatz von Gerichtsvollziehergebühren und -auslagen durch den Gerichtsvollzieher ihnen gegenüber** (vgl. hier oben 1c) **haben jeweils der Vollstreckungsgläubiger oder der Vollstreckungsschuldner als Kostenschuldner** der Staatskasse (sie haften nach § 3 Abs. 2 GVKostG als Gesamtschuldner) **und die** durch den Bezirksrevisor o. ä. vertretene **Staatskasse als Kostengläubigerin** (diese bei zu niedriger Ansetzung) wegen Grund und Höhe (ganze oder teilweise Erfüllungseinwände können, da es sich um ein Festsetzungsverfahren handelt, aber nicht gebracht werden) außerhalb der Zwangsvollstreckung (d. h. regelmäßig nach Beendigung derselben, vor allem wegen eingetretener Erfolglosigkeit) gemäß § 9 GVKostG und § 178 SGG, der als verfahrensrechtliche Spezialbestimmung an die Stelle des § 4 GKG tritt, **das Recht zur** — schriftlichen oder zu Protokoll zu erklärenden — Einlegung der gemäß § 178 SGG **fristgebundenen Gerichtsanrufung** (Erinnerung). Die Einlegungsfrist beträgt grundsätzlich einen Monat seit Zustellung (vgl. § 173 SGG). Der „seine" Kosten berechnende Gerichtsvollzieher steht hier dem kostenansetzenden Urkundsbeamten gleich; daher muß er auch Rechtsbehelfsbelehrung vornehmen, vgl. §§ 66, 173 Satz 2 in Verb. mit § 178 SGG). Zwar ist im § 9 GVKostG, der auf den § 4 GKG als Grundlage verweist, eine fristlose „Erinnerung" (Gerichtsanrufung) vorgesehen. Eine solche ist im ganzen Verfahren der Sozialgerichtsbarkeit aber unbekannt. In diesem sind alle Rechtsbehelfe und Rechtsmittel — das entspricht moderner Rechtspraxis, weil es der beschleunigten Abwicklung dient — fristgebunden. Durch das Gerichtsvollzieherkostengesetz kann das Sozialgerichtsgesetz als Verfahrensgrundgesetz nicht ohne ausdrückliche einschränkende Einbeziehung, sei es auch nur für einen Teilbezirk, eine Abänderung erfahren. Zwar gehört die Zwangsvollstreckung an sich nicht zum Verfahren der Sozialgerichtsbarkeit. Die Erinnerung, die der § 9 GVKostG gewährt, richtet sich aber an das Prozeßgericht (vgl. Tschischgale, KostR in ArbSach. S. 32, Baumbach-Lauterbach, KostG 13. Aufl. Anm. 2 zu § 25 GVGebO, der dem jetzigen § 9 GVKostG entspricht). Sie steht im bewußten Gegensatz zu der Erinnerung aus § 766 Abs. 2 ZPO, die sich an das Vollstreckungsgericht wendet. Dieses ist zur Nachprüfung nur dahin geeignet und berufen, ob die konkrete Zwangsvollstreckung vom Gerichtsvollzieher in jeder Hinsicht ordnungsgemäß durchgeführt wird; es entscheidet daher über Anträge und Einwendungen, welche die Art und Weise der Zwangsvollstreckung und ihre — grundsätzlich entgeltliche — Durchführung betreffen. Die sich aus der jeweiligen speziellen Verfahrensordnung ergebende Beantwortung der Frage, nach welchem Gesetz überhaupt zu vollstrecken ist und vollstreckt werden darf — im Sozialgerichtsverfahren kommt eine verschiedene Vollstreckung vor allem je nach dem Gläubiger in Betracht —, die für Erinnerungen aus § 9 GVKostG von grundlegender Bedeutung ist, ist jeweils von dem verfahrensvertrauten Prozeßgericht zu entscheiden. **Nun ist zwar im § 9 Satz 2 GVKostG das Amtsgericht, in dessen Bezirk der Gerichtsvollzieher seinen Amtssitz hat** — es ist vom Vollstreckungsgericht zu unterscheiden, auch wenn, wie regelmäßig, in seinem Bezirk die Vollstreckung stattfindet —, **als das „Prozeßgericht" bestimmt,** das über die Erinnerung (Gerichtsanrufung) aus § 9 GVKostG zu entscheiden hat. Der Gesetzgeber hat hier aber lediglich eine langjährige Zweifelsfrage behoben und beheben wollen, die in der Richtung bestand, ob für die Erinnerung aus dem bisherigen § 25 GVGebO in der ordentlichen Gerichtsbarkeit nur die Zuständigkeit des Amtsgerichts als Prozeßgericht gegeben ist oder ob das jeweilige Gericht erster Instanz, unter Umständen also das Landgericht, zuständig ist. Im modernen Staat bestehen mehrere ausdrücklich geschaffene und verfassungsrechtlich vorgesehene Gerichtsbarkeiten zur Entscheidung jeweils spezieller Streitverhältnisse zwischen den Beteiligten gleichwertig und gleichberechtigt nebeneinander, wobei insbesondere die Vollstreckung der ergehenden Entscheidungen weitgehend mit der Eigenart des Prozeßverfahrens und der in ihm ihr Recht suchenden Beteiligten verknüpft ist. Das hat der Gesetzgeber bei der Schaffung des § 9 Satz 2 GVKostG nicht beachtet. Hier ist ersichtlich nicht berücksichtigt worden, daß als Prozeßgericht unabdingbar auch die Gerichte anderer Gerichtszweige in Frage kommen (vgl. hierzu vor allem die grundlegenden Ausführungen von Hastler, WzS 1955, 109 [112]). Die hier verfassungsrechtlich bestehende und garantierte Abgrenzung der Gerichtsbarkeiten kann nicht durch eine nach Lage der Dinge unvollständige Bestimmung eines Kostengesetzes für Gerichtsvollzieher beseitigt werden. **Als zuständig zur Entscheidung über die Erinnerung gemäß § 9 GVKostG, wenn** die **Vollstreckung auf Grund sozialgerichtlicher Titel vorgenommen wird, ist daher** nach alledem richtigerweise **das** mit der Sache **befaßt gewesene Sozialgericht anzusehen.**

Das Sozialgericht entscheidet bei Nichtabhilfe durch den zuständigen Gerichtsvollzieher (vgl. § 173 SGG) durch zu begründenden Beschluß (§ 142 Abs. 2 SGG) auf Grund eigenen Sachermessens (§ 128 Abs. 1, § 142 Abs. 1 SGG) ohne mündliche Verhandlung (§ 124 Abs. 3 SGG) kostenfrei (§ 183 SGG), und zwar **endgültig** (§ 178 SGG). Die in § 9 GVKostG, § 4 Abs. 2 GKG vorgesehene Beschwerde ist durch die spezielle Verfahrensbestimmung des § 178 SGG ausgeschlossen. Eine fristlose Beschwerde, wie sie der im § 9 GVKostG in Bezug genommene § 4 Abs. 2 GKG vorsieht, gibt es überdies im Sozialgerichtsgesetz gar nicht, wie es hier auch keine Beschwerde gibt, die (vgl. § 4 Abs. 2 GKG und den darin erwähnten § 567 Abs. 2 ZPO) an eine Mindestbeschwer von 50,01 DM gebunden ist. Zudem entscheidet im Verfahren der Sozialgerichtsbarkeit das in Frage kommende Gericht der Instanz über Gebührenfragen immer endgültig, vgl. § 189 Abs. 2, §§ 191, 197 Abs. 2 SGG (allgemeiner Grundsatz).

Die Anrufungsentscheidung ergeht stets nur im Rahmen des Verlangten; eine Schlechterstellung des Anrufenden ist nicht zulässig. Vorherige Anhörung des Gerichtsvollziehers, der am Verfahren selbst nicht beteiligt ist, ist nobile officium. Die Möglichkeit der einstweiligen Einstellung bis zur Entscheidung ergibt sich aus § 175 SGG. Wegen Einzelheiten des Anrufungsverfahrens vgl. das 4. Kap. 3 l γ.

Das Gericht kann bei ersichtlicher Unrichtigkeit seine Entscheidung von sich aus — nach allen Richtungen — ändern (vgl. § 9 Satz 1 GVKostG, § 4 Abs. 1 Satz 2 GKG), nicht aber kann das Landessozialgericht, das ja oberinstanzmäßig nicht tätig wird, hier eingreifen; der Kostenansatz kann auch im Verwaltungswege berichtigt werden, solange nicht eine gerichtliche Entscheidung getroffen ist (vgl. § 9 Satz 1 GVKostG und § 4 Abs. 4 GKG). Dem Vorstehenden steht der § 178 SGG seinem Wortlaute und Sinne nach nicht entgegen.

Erfolgt endgültige Gebühren- oder Auslagenverkürzung, so müssen in allen derartigen Fällen gezahlte Überbeträge von der Staatskasse an den Zahlenden zurückgewährt werden. Diesem steht gegebenenfalls insoweit das Recht zur Klage gegen den Justizfiskus vor den ordentlichen Gerichten zu.

Erwähnt sei noch, daß Erfüllungseinwendungen hier nur mit den Behelfen im Beitreibungsverfahren nach den Bestimmungen der Justizbeitreibungsordnung (vgl. den § 8 daselbst) geltend gemacht werden können.

IV. Die Beitreibung nach dem Verwaltungs-Vollstreckungsgesetz und ihre Kosten

Übersicht

1. **Abgesehen von der im Verzugsfalle** vom Vollstreckungsschuldner **zu zahlenden Mahngebühr** (vgl. § 3 Abs. 3 VwVG und § 2 der dazugehörigen KostO; die Mahngebühr gilt die Mahnauslagen mit ab, § 5 Abs. 2 VwVKostO, auch § 9 AKostVO) in Höhe von 1. v. H. des Mahnbetrages (neben dem Hauptbetrag ohne Zinsen und Kosten, vgl. § 7 Abs. 1 Nr. 1 AKostVO) bis zu 100 DM einschließlich und ½ v. H. vom Mehrbetrage (aufgerundet auf volle 0,10 DM, Mindestbetrag 0,50 DM) **wird für**

die auf Antrag erteilte Abschrift eines Schriftstückes eine Schreibgebühr erhoben, die für die erste Seite und für jede angefangene weitere Seite gegebenenfalls 0,50 DM beträgt (§ 4 VwVKostO unter Berücksichtigung von § 10 Abs. 2 Nr. 2 AKostVO). Sie wird nicht erhoben, wenn der Antrag zurückgenommen wird, bevor mit der Anfertigung der Abschrift begonnen worden ist. Fälligkeit der Gebühr tritt mit der Erstellung der Abschrift ein. Der Vergütungsanspruch als solcher entsteht bereits mit dem Zugang des Antrages (§ 4 Abs. 3 Satz 1 VwVKostO). Erhoben wird auch der Ersatzbetrag entstehender Auslagen (insbesondere eventuelle Schreib- sowie Post-, Telegramm- und Fernsprechgebühren sowie Zustellungskosten), vgl. § 5 VwVKostO. (Hinsichtlich der — kurzen — Verjährung gelten die allgemeinen Bestimmungen, was die Kosten der Gerichtsverwaltung [Staatskasse] anbetrifft vgl. insoweit das 4. Kap. 1 zu a bis c.)

2. **Für Pfändungen wegen Geldforderungen und die anschließende Verwertung der gepfändeten beweglichen Sachen,** die von der im § 4 VwVG vorgesehenen Vollstreckungsbehörde vorgenommen wird, **werden** gemäß § 6 VwVKostO **Gebühren und Auslagen nach § 342 der Abgabenordnung** (AO) **in Verbindung mit der** Verordnung über die Kosten des Mahn- und Zwangsverfahrens nach der Abgabenordnung **(AKostVO)** vom 21. 4. 1923 (RGBl. I 259) in der geltenden Fassung **erhoben.** Diese Kostenverordnung ist, wie folgt, geändert worden:

durch Art. XVI § 2 der 2. Steuernotverordnung vom 19. 12. 1923 (RGBl. I 1205),
durch die 2. VO über die Kosten des Mahn- und Zwangsverfahrens nach der Reichsabgabenordnung vom 22. 11. 1924 (RGBl. I 755),
durch die 3. VO über die Kosten des Mahn- und Zwangsverfahrens nach der Reichsabgabenordnung vom 5. 11. 1925 (RGBl. I 387),
durch die 4. VO über die Kosten des Mahn- und Zwangsverfahrens nach der Reichsabgabenordnung vom 12. 7. 1941 (RGBl. I 385, RStBl. 497, RZBl. 161).

Als Regelgebühren kommen danach in Betracht:

die Pfändungsgebühr (§ 2 Nr. 1 AKostVO),
die Versteigerungsgebühr (§ 2 Nr. 2 AKostVO), die auch den freihändigen Verkauf gepfändeter Sachen abgilt (aaO).

a) Die **Pfändungsgebühr** beträgt von dem zu vollstreckenden Betrag bis zu 100 DM einschließlich $1\frac{1}{2}$ v. H., von dem Mehrbetrag $^{3}/_{4}$ v. H., mindestens jedoch 1 DM für jede Pfändung (§ 3 Abs. 1 AKostVO).

Bei Feststellung des Betrages, von dem die Gebühren berechnet werden, werden Zinsen und Kosten nicht berücksichtigt, wenn sie als Nebenschulden zusammen mit einer Hauptschuld geltend gemacht werden (§ 7 Abs. 1 Nr. 1 Satz 2 AKostVO).

Der sich ergebende Grundlagebetrag wird auf den nächsten durch 10 teilbaren DM-Betrag (nach unten) abgerundet (§ 7 Abs. 2 AKostVO).

Die Pfändungsgebühr wird nicht erhoben, wenn der Vollstreckungsauftrag zurückgenommen wird, bevor der Vollziehungsbeamte Schritte zur Ausführung des Auftrags unternommen hat (§ 3 Abs. 3 Nr. 1 AKostVO).

Die Gebühr wird mit der Ausführung der Pfändung fällig; sie entsteht bereits mit dem Zugang des Pfändungsauftrages (vgl. § 3 Abs. 2 Nr. 1 AKostVO).

Wird die Pfändung abgewendet (vor allem durch Zahlung, vgl. § 345 AO), so ist

α) die volle Pfändungsgebühr zu entrichten, wenn an den Vollziehungsbeamten gezahlt wird, nachdem er sich zur Vornahme der Pfändung an Ort und Stelle begeben hat;

β) die halbe Pfändungsgebühr, mindestens aber 0,30 DM, zu entrichten, wenn an den Vollziehungsbeamten gezahlt wird, bevor er sich an Ort und Stelle begeben hat, oder wenn die Pfändung in anderer Weise (z. B. durch Nachweis der Stundung, vgl. § 345 Abs. 1 AO) abgewendet wird, nachdem der Vollziehungsbeamte an Ort und Stelle erschienen ist;

γ) keine Pfändungsgebühr zu entrichten, wenn die Pfändung in anderer Weise als durch Zahlung (s. o.) abgewendet wird, bevor sich der Vollziehungsbeamte an Ort und Stelle begeben hat (§ 3 Abs. 4 Nr. 1 bis 3 AKostVO).

Wird die Pfändung als Anschlußpfändung (vgl. § 359 AO) ausgeführt, so wird dadurch die Gebührenschuld nicht berührt, d. h. die Pfändungsgebühr wird wie für eine Erstpfändung erhoben. Das gleiche gilt, wenn ein Pfändungsversuch erfolglos bleibt, weil pfändbare Sachen nicht vorgefunden werden oder weil die Voraussetzungen des § 343 Satz 3 AO (Vorfinden nur von Sachen, deren Pfändung sich nicht lohnt) vorliegen (§ 3 Abs. 5 AKostVO). Die Gebührenschuld kann jedenfalls in den zuletzt genannten Fällen zwar nicht beigetrieben werden, sie bleibt aber bis zu einer etwaigen Niederschlagung als solche bestehen.

Die Pfändungsgebühr, die in ungeraden Pfennigbeträgen auslaufen kann, ist nach § 1 der AbrundungsVO vom 31. 10. 1923 (RGBl. I 1049) auf volle 0,05 DM nach unten abzurunden (vgl. Schoop-Geiling, Beitreibungsrecht der Abgabenverwaltung S. 293). Wegen Wertpapieren s. u. zu a und b.

b) Die **Versteigerungsgebühr** beträgt von dem Erlös bis zu 100 DM einschließlich 2 v. H., von dem Mehrbetrag 1 v. H., mindestens jedoch 1 DM (§ 4 Abs. 1 AKostVO). Die Versteigerungsgebühr wird von dem Erlös der Pfandstücke nur berechnet, soweit er nicht die Summe der beizutreibenden Beträge übersteigt; ist der Erlös größer als die genannte Summe, so ist diese maßgebend (vgl. § 7 Abs. 1 Nr. 1 Satz 3 AKostVO).

Der sich ergebende Grundlagebetrag wird auf den nächsten durch 10 teilbaren DM-Betrag (nach unten) abgerundet (§ 7 Abs. 2 AKostVO).

Die Versteigerungsgebühr wird nicht erhoben, wenn der Auftrag zur Versteigerung oder zum freihändigen Verkauf zurückgenommen wird, bevor der beauftragte Beamte Schritte zur Ausführung des Auftrages unternommen hat (§ 4 Abs. 3 AKostVO).

Die Gebühr wird mit der Verwertung fällig; sie entsteht als solche bereits mit dem Zugang des Verwertungsauftrages (§ 4 Abs. 2 AKostVO).

Wird die Versteigerung oder der freihändige Verkauf abgewendet (vgl. § 351 Satz 1 Halbsatz 2, § 345 AO), so finden die Bestimmungen des § 3 Abs. 4 AKostVO betreffend die Pfändungsgebühr mit der Maßgabe entsprechende Anwendung, daß auch im Falle des § 3 Abs. 4 Nr. 1 AKostVO (s. o. 2 a α) nur die halbe Versteigerungsgebühr, mindestens aber 0,30 DM, zu entrichten ist (§ 4 Abs. 4 AKostVO).

Zu a und b: Die Bestimmungen über die Pfändung, die Versteigerung und den freihändigen Verkauf von Sachen gelten entsprechend für Wertpapiere (§ 12 Abs. 2 AKostVO).

Wird gegen Eheleute wegen eines Anspruchs vollstreckt, für den die Eheleute als Gesamtschuldner haften, so werden die Pfändungs- und die Versteigerungsgebühr nur einmal erhoben. Für die Gebühren haften die Eheleute als Gesamtschuldner (§ 8 Abs. 1 AKostVO).

Wird in anderen Fällen gegen mehrere Schuldner vollstreckt, so sind die Gebühren, auch wenn der Vollziehungsbeamte mehrere Vollstreckungsmaßnahmen bei derselben Gelegenheit vornimmt, von jedem Vollstreckungsschuldner besonders zu entrichten (§ 8 Abs. 2 AKostVO).

c) Bezüglich der **Auslagen** gilt das Folgende:

Im Vollstreckungsverfahren sind die Reise- und Zehrkosten des Vollziehungsbeamten von dem Vollstreckungsschuldner nicht zu ersetzen (§ 10 Abs. 1 AKostVO).

Die übrigen baren Auslagen, die im Vollstreckungsverfahren entstehen, hat der Vollstreckungsschuldner zu ersetzen (§ 10 Abs. 2 Satz 1 AKostVO, vgl. auch § 5 VwVKostO).

Zu diesen baren Auslagen gehören insbesondere (vgl. § 10 Abs. 2 Satz 2 AKostVO):

α) die **Post-, Fernsprech- und Telegrammgebühren;**

β) **Bekanntmachungskosten,** die insbesondere durch Einrücken in öffentliche Blätter entstehen, hierzu gehören gegebenenfalls auch die nach den Vorschriften des Gerichtskostengesetzes zu berechnenden Schreibgebühren (grundsätzlich 0,50 DM je Seite) für Schriftstücke, die zum Aushang bestimmt sind;

γ) **Dienstleistungsentschädigungen** für Personen, die zum Öffnen von Türen und Behältnissen zugezogen worden sind, ferner **Transport- und Verwahrungsauslagen** für die Beförderung, Aufbewahrung und Beaufsichtigung gepfändeter Sachen, die Aberntung und Unterbringung gepfändeter Früchte und die Erhaltung gepfändeter Tiere;

δ) **Auskunftsgebühren, Sachverständigenkosten und Treuhändervergütung** (§ 368 AO).

Die auf Antrag zu gewährende Entschädigung der Auskunftspersonen und Sachverständigen darf die Gebühr einschließlich des Teuerungszuschlages nicht übersteigen, die in bürgerlichen Rechtsstreitigkeiten auf Grund des Gesetzes über die Entschädigung von Zeugen und Sachverständigen (in der jeweils geltenden Fassung) gewährt werden kann (§ 11 Abs. 1 und 2 AKostVO). Die Entschädigung der Treuhänder darf die Vergütung nicht übersteigen, die die Justizverwaltungen auf Grund des § 14 des Einführungsgesetzes zu dem Reichsgesetz über die Zwangsversteigerung und Zwangsverwaltung vom 24. 3. 1897 in der Fassung der Bekanntmachung vom 20. 5. 1898 (RGBl. 750) für Verwalter festgesetzt haben (§ 11 Abs. 1 und 3 AKostVO);

ε) die eventuellen **Gerichtskosten** und in den Fällen des § 360 AO (mehrfache Pfändung durch Vollziehungsbeamte und Gerichtsvollzieher) etwaige **Gerichtsvollzieherkosten.**

Zu α bis ε. Die Fälligkeit des Auslagenersatzanspruchs tritt in der üblichen Weise mit der Verauslagung ein. Die Pflicht zur Erstattung der Auslagen, die bei Ausführung einer Vollstreckungsmaßnahme erwachsen, entsteht, sobald der Auftrag zu der Vollstreckungsmaßnahme dem Vollziehungsbeamten zugeht (§ 10 Abs. 3 AKostVO).

Findet zur Versteigerung oder zum freihändigen Verkauf von Sachen, die bei mehreren Vollstreckungsschuldnern gepfändet worden sind, ein einheitliches Verfahren statt, so werden die Auslagen, die in diesem Verfahren entstehen, auf die beteiligten Vollstreckungsschuldner verteilt. Dabei ist auf die besonderen Umstände des einzelnen Falles, insbesondere auf Wert, Umfang und Gewicht der Gegenstände, billige Rücksicht zu nehmen (§ 10 Abs. 4 AKostVO).

Zu a bis c. **Die Kostenforderungen unterliegen der Verjährung** (§ 143 AO). Und zwar verjähren sie (als sogen. übrige Ansprüche) **in einem Jahr** (§ 144 Satz 2 AO), beginnend grundsätzlich mit dem Ablauf des Jahres, in dem der Anspruch entstanden ist (§ 145 Abs. 1 AO).

3. Die Kosten der Zwangsvollstreckung fallen dem Schuldner zur Last (vgl. § 342 AO). Ein besonderes Leistungsgebot (Kostenbescheid) ist bezüglich ihrer nicht erforderlich, § 11 Abs. 3 Abgabenbeitreibungsordnung (ABeitrO) vom 23. 6. 1923 — RMinBl. 595 — i. d. F. der VO vom 19. 1. 1927 — RMinBl. 23). **Die Pfändungsgebühr mit** anhängenden **Auslagen wird** nämlich grundsätzlich **zugleich mit der Hauptforderung** (bestehend aus der eigentlichen Hauptforderung und eventuellen Mahn- und Schreibkosten einschließlich Auslagen nach der Kostenordnung zum Verwaltungs-Vollstreckungsgesetz, vgl. §§ 2, 4 und 3, 5 daselbst) geltend gemacht und **beigetrieben.** Der Vollziehungsbeamte hat zu diesem Zweck die entstehenden Kosten zu berechnen, §§ 16, 17 der Geschäftsanweisung für die Vollziehungsbeamten der Reichsfinanzverwaltung (AOGeschAnw) vom 31. 10. 1932 (RMinBl. 696). Die Kostenberechnung ist auf den Vollstreckungsauftrag zu setzen (§ 65 Abs. 2 Nr. 1c ABeitrO). **Die Versteigerungsgebühr mit** den dazugehörigen **Auslagen wird** in aller Regel **vom erzielten Erlös in Abzug gebracht.** (Nötigenfalls erfolgt besondere Beitreibung, und zwar, wie bezüglich aller öffentlich-rechtlichen Forderungen, regelmäßig im Wege des Verwaltungsvollstreckungsverfahrens nach §§ 1 bis 5 VwVG.)

4. **Gegen die** wiedergegebene **Anforderung von Kosten der Zwangsbeitreibung ist das Rechtsmittel der Beschwerde** (§§ 237, 303, 304 AO) **gegeben,** § 59 Abs. 2 Ziff. 6 ABeitrO. (Gegen eine als Hauptsache beigetriebene Kostenforderung selbst kann hinsichtlich der Anforderung nur mit dem gegen den zugrunde liegenden Kostenbescheid gegebenen Rechtsbehelf beim Gericht vorgegangen werden, vgl. § 178 SGG und das 4. Kap. 1 und 2 je zu a bis c sowie das 6. Kap. 28.) Beschwerdeberechtigt ist der beschwerte Vollstreckungsschuldner. Der Beschwerdeangriff kann sich sowohl gegen den Grund (die Zahlungsverpflichtung) wie gegen die Höhe der Kostenberechnung richten. (Ganze oder teilweise Zahlungs- oder sonstige Erlöschungseinwendungen können aber nur außerhalb des Vollstreckungsverfahrens durch Erhebung des Rückerstattungs- bzw. Rückgängigmachungsanspruchs nach §§ 152, 157 AO geltend gemacht werden, § 59 ABeitrO.)

Durch die Einlegung der Beschwerde wird die Fortsetzung der Zwangsvollstreckung nicht gehindert (§ 59 Abs. 3 ABeitrO). Die Vollstreckungsbehörde kann der Beschwerde abhelfen (§ 304 Abs. 1 AO, § 59 Abs. 3 Nr. 1 ABeitrO). Sie hat auf jeden Fall zu prüfen, ob die Zwangsvollstreckung nicht einstweilen einzustellen oder zu beschränken ist (§ 59 Abs. 3 Nr. 2 ABeitrO).

Soweit der Beschwerde nicht abgeholfen wird, muß eine Entscheidung der Beschwerdeinstanz ergehen. Im allgemeinen entscheidet über die Beschwerde die Oberfinanzdirektion. Grundsätzlich besteht hier bei negativem Verfahrensausgang Kostenpflicht des Rechtsmittels (vgl. §§ 307, 311 und 322 AO).

Gegen die ablehnende Entscheidung der Beschwerdestelle ist die Einleitung des Berufungsverfahrens (§§ 228ff. AO) **möglich, d. h. es ist die Anrufung des Finanzgerichts und** darüber hinaus **gegebenenfalls** — grundsätzlich bei Vorliegen eines Wertes des Streitgegenstandes von wenigstens 200,01 DM — **des Bundesfinanzhofs** (hier im Wege der Rechtsbeschwerde) **zulässig.** Dieser Rechtsmittelzug ergibt sich notwendig auf der Grundlage des Art. 19 Abs. 4 Satz 1 des Grundgesetzes, der gegenüber allen belastend eingreifenden Verwaltungsanordnungen und -bescheiden gerichtlichen Rechtsschutz zwingend vorschreibt (vgl. hierzu Schoop-Geiling, aaO. S. 213 und das Gutachten des BFH vom 17. 4. 1951, BStBl. III 107). Der § 304

Abs. 4 AO, der die — verwaltungsmäßige — Beschwerdeentscheidung grundsätzlich für endgültig erklärt, ist insoweit durch das Grundgesetz überholt und gegenstandslos geworden.

5. **Ist ein Leistungsbescheid hinsichtlich der zu ersetzenden Mahn- und Schreibkosten** sowie etwaiger sonstiger Kosten (Auslagen), vgl. §§ 2, 4 und 5 VwVKostO, **seitens der Anordnungsbehörde** (der Gläubigerin selbst, einschlägigenfalls der Gerichtsverwaltung) **gegen den Schuldner ergangen, so kann er von diesem** auf dem Grundgebiet der Sozialgerichtsbarkeit **durch Widerspruchseinlegung** (vgl. § 327 AO, §§ 78, 79 Nr. 1, §§ 83, 84 und 85 SGG) **angefochten werden.** Der Widerspruch kann Grund (Zahlungspflicht) und Höhe der Kostenforderung betreffen. (Erfüllungseinwendungen sind jedoch im Wege der Vollstreckungsgegenklage nach § 767 ZPO vor dem Sozialgericht geltend zu machen; diese Klage ist nicht — vgl. § 89 SGG — an eine Frist gebunden, Hastler, WzS 1955, 109.) Der Widerspruch ist binnen eines Monats nach Bekanntgabe des Kostenleistungsbescheides (die durch Zustellung zu erfolgen hat, vgl. § 63 Abs. 1 SGG) schriftlich oder zur Niederschrift der Anordnungsbehörde einzulegen. Er hat grundsätzlich keine aufschiebende Wirkung (vgl. § 86 Abs. 2 SGG).

Gegen den kostenfrei **ergehenden verwaltungsmäßigen Widerspruchsbescheid gibt es,** wenn er negativ ausfällt, **die Anfechtungsklage beim** zuständigen **Sozialgericht** (§ 87 Abs. 1, § 90 SGG). Sie ist innerhalb eines Monats nach Bekanntgabe (Zustellung) des Widerspruchsbescheides zu erheben (§ 87 Abs. 1 und 2 SGG). Die — kostenfreie — Klage hat grundsätzlich ebenfalls keine aufschiebende Wirkung (vgl. § 97 SGG). Wegen der Möglichkeit einstweiliger Einstellung vgl. den § 199 Abs. 2 SGG in entsprechender Anwendung. **Das Sozialgericht entscheidet durch Urteil** (§ 125 SGG). **Berufung** gegen dieses Urteil **ist** nach § 144 Abs. 2 SGG **ausgeschlossen.** Dem Artikel 19 Abs. 4 Satz 1 Grundgesetz ist mit der wiedergegebenen Anfechtungsmöglichkeit Genüge getan. (Hinsichtlich der hauptsächlichen Punkte im Ergebnis ebenso Hastler, WzS 1955, 109 [113] und v. Rosen-v. Hoewel, VwVG Vorbem. III vor § 19 und Erl. III 1a zu § 3, vgl. ferner Sebode, DGVZ 1954, 2, auch Weber, ArbA 1954, 303.)

Zehntes Kapitel

Die Entschädigung der Sozial-, Landessozial- und Bundessozialrichter und ihre Festsetzung

SGG: §§ 19, 35, 47

Gesetz über die Entschädigung der ehrenamtlichen Beisitzer bei den Gerichten (BeisEG): §§ 1, 2, 3, 4, 5, 6, 7, 8, 9, 10, 11, 12

§ 19 SGG

Sozialrichter

(1) Der Sozialrichter übt sein Amt als Ehrenamt mit gleichen Rechten wie der Berufsrichter aus.

(2) Die Sozialrichter erhalten eine Entschädigung nach dem Gesetz über die Entschädigung der ehrenamtlichen Beisitzer bei den Gerichten.

§ 35 SGG

Landessozialrichter

(1) Die Landessozialrichter müssen das dreißigste Lebensjahr vollendet haben; sie sollen mindestens vier Jahre Sozialrichter gewesen sein. Im übrigen gelten §§ 13 bis 23.

(2) In den Fällen des § 18 Abs. 4, der §§ 21 und 22 Abs. 2 entscheidet der vom Präsidium (§ 36) für jedes Geschäftsjahr im voraus bestimmte Senat.

§ 47 SGG

Bundessozialrichter

Die Bundessozialrichter müssen das fünfunddreißigste Lebensjahr vollendet haben; sie sollen mindestens vier Jahre Sozialrichter oder Landessozialrichter gewesen sein. Im übrigen gelten §§ 15 bis 23 entsprechend mit der Maßgabe, daß in den Fällen des § 18 Abs. 4, der §§ 21 und 22 Abs. 2 der vom Präsidium (§ 48) für jedes Geschäftsjahr im voraus bestimmte Senat des Bundessozialgerichts entscheidet.

Gesetz über die Entschädigung der ehrenamtlichen Beisitzer bei den Gerichten

§ 1

Geltungsbereich und Grundsatz der Entschädigung

Die ehrenamtlichen Beisitzer bei den ordentlichen Gerichten und den Gerichten für Arbeitssachen sowie bei den Gerichten der Verwaltungs-, der Finanz- und der Sozialgerichtsbarkeit erhalten eine Entschädigung für

1. Zeitversäumnis (§ 2),
2. Fahrtkosten und Fußwegstrecken (§ 3),
3. Aufwand (§§ 4 bis 6).

§ 2

Entschädigung für Zeitversäumnis

(1) Die ehrenamtlichen Beisitzer werden für ihre Zeitversäumnis entschädigt.

(2) Entsteht dem ehrenamtlichen Beisitzer ein Verdienstausfall, so beträgt die Entschädigung für jede Stunde der versäumten Arbeitszeit wenigstens zwei Deutsche Mark und höchstens vier Deutsche Mark. Dabei ist auch die Zeit zu berücksichtigen, in der er seine gewöhnliche Beschäftigung nicht wieder aufnehmen kann. Die letzte, bereits begonnene Stunde wird voll gerechnet. Die Entschädigung richtet sich nach dem regelmäßigen Bruttoverdienst.

(3) Soweit ein Verdienstausfall nicht nachweisbar oder nicht eingetreten ist, erhalten die ehrenamtlichen Beisitzer die nach dem geringsten Satz bemessene Entschädigung.

(4) Die Entschädigung wird für höchstens zehn Stunden je Tag gewährt.

§ 3

Fahrtkosten, Wegegeld

(1) Den ehrenamtlichen Beisitzern werden die notwendigen Fahrtkosten ersetzt.

(2) Bei Benutzung von öffentlichen, regelmäßig verkehrenden Beförderungsmitteln werden die wirklichen Auslagen einschließlich der Kosten für die Beförderung des notwendigen Gepäcks bis zur Höhe der Tarife, bei Benutzung der Eisenbahn oder von Schiffen bis zum Fahrpreis der ersten Wagen- oder Schiffsklasse, ersetzt. Die Mehrkosten für zuschlagpflichtige Züge werden erstattet.

(3) Für Fußwege und bei Benutzung von anderen als öffentlichen, regelmäßig verkehrenden Beförderungsmitteln werden bei Entfernungen von mehr als zwei Kilometern für jedes angefangene Kilometer des Hin- und Rückweges 0,25 Deutsche Mark gewährt. Kann ein Hin- und Rückweg von zusammen mehr als zweihundert Kilometern mit öffentlichen, regelmäßig verkehrenden Beförderungsmitteln zurückgelegt werden, so gilt Satz 1 nur insoweit, als die Mehrkosten gegenüber der Benutzung von öffentlichen, regelmäßig verkehrenden Beförderungsmitteln durch eine Minderausgabe an Entschädigung ausgeglichen werden. Kann der ehrenamtliche Beisitzer wegen besonderer Umstände ein öffentliches, regelmäßig verkehrendes Beförderungsmittel nicht benutzen, so werden die nachgewiesenen Mehrauslagen ersetzt, soweit sie angemessen sind.

(4) Für Reisen während der Tagung werden Fahrtkosten nur insoweit ersetzt, als Mehrbeträge an Entschädigung erspart werden, die beim Verbleiben am Sitzungsort gewährt werden müßten.

(5) Tritt der ehrenamtliche Beisitzer die Reise zum Sitzungsort von einem anderen als seinem Wohnort an oder fährt er nach der Sitzung zu einem anderen Ort als seinem Wohnort, so werden die Fahrtkosten bis zur Höhe der bei der Fahrt von und zum Wohnort zu erstattenden Kosten ersetzt. Mehrkosten werden nach billigem Ermessen ersetzt, wenn der ehrenamtliche Beisitzer zu diesen Fahrten durch besondere Umstände genötigt war.

§ 4

Entschädigung für Aufwand

(1) Die ehrenamtlichen Beisitzer erhalten eine Entschädigung für den mit ihrer Dienstleistung verbundenen Aufwand.

(2) Ehrenamtliche Beisitzer, die innerhalb der Gemeinde, in der die Sitzung stattfindet, weder wohnen noch berufstätig sind, erhalten ein Tagegeld

von fünf Deutsche Mark für jeden Tag, an dem sie aus Anlaß der Dienstleistung mehr als fünf bis acht Stunden, von acht Deutsche Mark für jeden Tag, an dem sie aus Anlaß der Dienstleistung mehr als acht bis zwölf Stunden,

von zwölf Deutsche Mark für jeden Tag, an dem sie aus Anlaß der Dienstleistung mehr als zwölf Stunden

von ihrem Wohnort abwesend sein müssen.

Bei Abwesenheit bis zu fünf Stunden werden die nachgewiesenen notwendigen Auslagen bis zu vier Deutsche Mark erstattet.

(3) Ehrenamtliche Beisitzer, die innerhalb der Gemeinde, in der die Sitzung stattfindet, wohnen oder berufstätig sind, erhalten ein Tagegeld

von vier Deutsche Mark, wenn sie an einer Sitzung mehr als fünf Stunden teilnehmen.

Übersteigen ihre Auslagen diesen Betrag, so werden die nachgewiesenen notwendigen Auslagen bis zur Höhe der in Absatz 2 vorgesehenen Sätze erstattet. Bei einer Sitzungsdauer bis zu fünf Stunden werden die nachgewiesenen notwendigen Auslagen bis zu vier Deutsche Mark ersetzt.

(4) Ist eine auswärtige Übernachtung notwendig, so wird ein Übernachtungsgeld in Höhe des Satzes für Bundesbeamte der Reisekostenstufe II gewährt.

§ 5

Ersatz sonstiger Aufwendungen

Notwendige bare Auslagen, die nicht den durch den Aufenthalt außerhalb der Wohnung verursachten Aufwand betreffen, sind dem ehrenamtlichen Beisitzer zu ersetzen. Dies gilt besonders von den Kosten einer notwendigen Vertretung.

§ 6

Entschädigung des Begleiters

Bedarf der ehrenamtliche Beisitzer wegen Gebrechens eines Begleiters, so sind die Entschädigungen für beide zu gewähren.

§ 7

Ehrenamtliche Beisitzer bei den oberen Bundesgerichten

Die Aufwandsentschädigung der ehrenamtlichen Beisitzer bei den oberen Bundesgerichten erhöht sich im Falle des § 4 Abs. 2 Satz 1 auf das Eineinhalbfache der dort festgelegten Sätze. Im Falle des § 4 Abs. 4 erhalten sie ein Übernachtungsgeld in Höhe des Satzes für Bundesbeamte der Reisekostenstufe I b.

§ 8

Entschädigung in besonderen Fällen des Arbeits- und des Sozialgerichtsgesetzes

Die Entschädigung nach §§ 1 bis 7 wird auch gewährt, wenn die ehrenamtlichen Beisitzer bei den Gerichten für Arbeitssachen und den Gerichten der Sozialgerichtsbarkeit in dieser Eigenschaft an der Wahl von gesetzlich für sie vorgesehenen Ausschüssen oder an den Sitzungen solcher Ausschüsse teilnehmen (§§ 29, 38 des Arbeitsgerichtsgesetzes, §§ 23, 35 Abs. 1, § 47 des Sozialgerichtsgesetzes).

§ 9

Aufrundung

Die dem ehrenamtlichen Beisitzer zu zahlende Gesamtentschädigung wird auf zehn Deutsche Pfennig aufgerundet.

§ 10

Vorschuß

Den ehrenamtlichen Beisitzern ist auf Antrag ein angemessener Vorschuß zu bewilligen.

§ 11

Erlöschen des Anspruchs

Der Anspruch auf Entschädigung erlischt, wenn er nicht binnen eines Jahres nach Beendigung der Dienstleistung bei der Stelle geltend gemacht wird, welche die Entschädigung anzuweisen hat.

§ 12

Gerichtliche Festsetzung

(1) Die dem ehrenamtlichen Beisitzer zu gewährende Entschädigung wird durch gerichtlichen Beschluß festgesetzt, wenn der ehrenamtliche Beisitzer oder die Staatskasse die richterliche Festsetzung beantragen. Zuständig ist das Gericht, bei dem der ehrenamtliche Beisitzer mitgewirkt hat. Das Gericht kann seine Festsetzung von Amts wegen ändern.

(2) Gegen die richterliche Festsetzung ist die Beschwerde zulässig, wenn der Wert des Beschwerdegegenstandes fünfzig Deutsche Mark übersteigt. Beschwerdeberechtigt sind nur der ehrenamtliche Beisitzer und die Staatskasse. Eine Beschwerde an ein oberes Bundesgericht ist nicht zulässig. Die Beschwerde wird bei dem Gericht eingelegt, das die angefochtene Entscheidung erlassen hat. Das Gericht kann der Beschwerde abhelfen.

(3) Die Entscheidung trifft das Gericht ohne die Hinzuziehung der ehrenamtlichen Beisitzer.

(4) Anträge, Erklärungen und Beschwerden können zu Protokoll der Geschäftsstelle gegeben oder schriftlich ohne Mitwirkung eines Rechtsanwalts eingereicht werden.

Übersicht

Spezialabhandlung des Verfassers: Die Entschädigung der ehrenamtlichen Beisitzer bei den Gerichten, JVBl. 1958, 113.

1. **Die** sogenannten **Laienbeisitzer** an den Gerichten der Sozialgerichtsbarkeit **üben ihr Amt als Ehrenamt** mit gleichen Rechten wie die Berufsrichter **aus** (§ 19 Abs. 1, § 35 Abs. 1, § 47 Satz 2 SGG).

2. **Die Laienbeisitzer erhalten eine Entschädigung** nach dem Gesetz über die Entschädigung der ehrenamtlichen Beisitzer bei den Gerichten vom 26. 7. 1957 – BGBl. I 900 – (§ 19 Abs. 2, § 35 Abs. 1 Satz 2, § 47 Satz 2 SGG). Diese Entschädigung gilt ab:

die Zeitversäumnis,
die Fahrtkosten,
den Aufwand (für den Tag und zusätzlich gegebenenfalls für die Nacht) vgl. § 1 BeisEG.

a) **Die Entschädigung für die Zeitversäumnis**

Der ehrenamtliche Beisitzer wird für die erlittene Zeitversäumnis entschädigt (§ 2 Abs. 1 BeisEG). Die Zeitversäumnis umfaßt den Zeitraum, in dem der Beisitzer wegen der Erfüllung seines Ehrenamts zwangsläufig nicht in der Lage ist, seiner Berufs- oder Erwerbstätigkeit nachzugehen. Dieser Zeitraum beginnt in aller Regel mit dem Verlassen der Wohnung zum Zwecke der Sitzungswahrnehmung und endet im Zeitpunkt der Rückkehr. Darüber hinaus ist gegebenenfalls auch die Zeit zu berücksichtigen, in der der Beisitzer seine gewöhnliche Beschäftigung nicht wieder aufzunehmen in der Lage ist (§ 2 Abs. 2 Satz 2 BeisEG), z. B. weil eine ganze Tagesschicht (so von einem Bergmanne) nicht wahrgenommen werden kann. Liegt in der zu entschädigenden Zeit ein tarifmäßig an sich zu bezahlender Ruhetag, so ist er mit zu entschädigen, wenn, wie üblich, die Bezahlung nach dem Tarif auf Grund der Richterdienstleistung entfällt, vgl. Gölkel, SGb (Beil.) 1958, 18 [20] und 24. (Hinsichtlich der Fortzahlung von Dienstbezügen an Arbeitnehmer, die Sozialrichter sind, vgl. den Erl. d. BMF vom 7. 10. 1955.)

Die Entschädigung beträgt für jede Stunde der versäumten Arbeitszeit wenigstens 2 DM und höchstens 4 DM (§ 2 Abs. 2 Satz 1 BeisEG). Die letzte, bereits begonnene Stunde wird voll gerechnet (§ 2 Abs. 2 Satz 3 BeisEG). Die Entschädigung richtet sich im einzelnen nach dem nachzuweisenden regelmäßigen (evtl. durchschnittlichen) Bruttoverdienst einschließlich tariflicher Sozialzuschläge (§ 2 Abs. 2 Satz 4 BeisEG). Die Arbeitgeberanteile der Sozialversicherung bleiben außer Betracht. (Sie sind auch nicht besonders zu ersetzen, a. A. LG Hagen, JVBl. 1958, 247.) Wohl aber ist zu berücksichtigen der am Sitzungs- bzw. Reisetag entgangene Lohnausgleich für den nächsten arbeitsfreien Tag; jedoch darf das Höchstentgelt für die eigentliche Versäumung insgesamt nicht überschritten werden. Die Entschädigung wird nämlich stets nur für höchstens 10 Stunden (einschließlich evtl. Überstunden) des jeweils beanspruchten Tages gewährt (§ 2 Abs. 4 BeisEG); erstreckt sich die Zeitversäumnis — z. B. bei Schichtversäumung — auf einen weiteren Tag, so wird er bis zur Erreichung des höchstens zu zahlenden Entgelts der eigentlichen Versäumnis mit berücksichtigt (vgl. 5. Kap. I 2a).

Soweit ein Verdienstausfall nicht nachweisbar oder nicht eingetreten ist, erhalten die Beisitzer die nach dem geringsten Satz bemessene Entschädigung (§ 2 Abs. 3 BeisEG).

b) **Die Ersetzung der Fahrtkosten**

Den ehrenamtlichen Beisitzern werden die notwendigen Fahrtkosten ersetzt (§ 3 Abs. 1 BeisEG).

Werden öffentliche, regelmäßig verkehrende Beförderungsmittel benutzt, so werden die wirklichen Auslagen einschließlich der Kosten für die Beförderung des notwendigen Gepäcks bis zur Höhe der bestehenden Tarife, bei Benutzung der Eisenbahn oder von Schiffen bis zum Fahrpreis der — grundsätzlich in zulässiger Weise — gelösten ersten Wagen- oder Schiffsklasse ersetzt (§ 3 Abs. 2 Satz 1 BeisEG). Die Mehrkosten für erforderlich werdende zuschlagpflichtige Züge werden ebenfalls ersetzt (§ 3 Abs. 2 Satz 2 BeisEG).

Bei Benutzung von anderen als öffentlichen, regelmäßig verkehrenden Beförderungsmitteln — auch eigenen — und für Fußwege werden bei Entfernungen von mehr als 2 km für jedes angefangene Kilometer des Hin- und Rückweges 0,25 DM gewährt (§ 3 Abs. 3 Satz 1 BeisEG). Kann aber ein Hin- und Rückweg von zusammen mehr als 200 km mit öffentlichen, regelmäßig verkehrenden Beförderungsmitteln zurückgelegt werden, so gilt das Vorstehende nur insoweit, als die Mehrkosten gegenüber der Benutzung von öffentlichen, regelmäßig verkehrenden Beförderungsmitteln durch eine Minderausgabe an Entschädigung ausgeglichen werden (§ 3 Abs. 3 Satz 2 BeisEG). Kann der Beisitzer wegen besonderer Umstände (persönlicher oder sachlicher) ein öffentliches, regelmäßig verkehrendes Beförderungsmittel nicht benutzen, so werden die nachgewiesenen Mehrauslagen ersetzt soweit sie angemessen (sachlich billig) sind (§ 3 Abs. 3 Satz 3 BeisEG).

Für Reisen während der Tagung (so nach Hause zur Übernachtung) werden Fahrtkosten nur insoweit ersetzt, als Mehrbeträge an Entschädigung erspart werden, die beim Verbleiben am Sitzungsort gewährt werden müßten (§ 3 Abs. 4 BeisEG).

Tritt der Beisitzer die Reise zum Sitzungsort von einem anderen als seinem Wohnort an oder fährt er nach der Sitzung zu einem anderen Ort als seinem Wohnort, so werden die Fahrtkosten bis zur Höhe der bei der Fahrt von und zum Wohnort zu erstattenden Kosten ersetzt; Mehrkosten (auch für Reisen von und zu einem entfernter liegenden Urlaubsort) werden nach billigem Ermessen ersetzt, wenn der Beisitzer zu diesen Fahrten durch besondere Umstände (sachliche, z. B. Zugausfall, oder persönliche, z. B. Unpäßlichkeit, oder auch sonstige, so Nichtabbestellung trotz rechtzeitig mitgeteilter Reise) genötigt war (§ 3 Abs. 5 BeisEG).

c) **Die Entschädigung für den Aufwand**

α) Die ehrenamtlichen Beisitzer erhalten eine Entschädigung für den mit ihrer Dienstleistung verbundenen Aufwand (§ 4 Abs. 1 BeisEG). Sie bekommen ein **Tagegeld.** Dieses beträgt für Beisitzer, die innerhalb der politischen Gemeinde, in der die Sitzung stattfindet, wohnen oder berufstätig sind, 4 DM, wenn sie an einer Sitzung mehr als 5 Stunden teilnehmen (§ 4 Abs. 3 Satz 1 BeisEG). Bei einer Sitzungsdauer bis zu 5 Stunden werden die nachgewiesenen notwendigen Auslagen bis zu 4 DM ersetzt (§ 4 Abs. 3 Satz 3 BeisEG). Übersteigen die Auslagen der mehr als 5 Stunden teilnehmenden Beisitzer den Betrag von 4 DM, so werden die nachgewiesenen notwendigen Auslagen bis zur Höhe der Sätze für auswärtige Beisitzer erstattet (§ 4 Abs. 3 Satz 2 BeisEG).

Beisitzer, die innerhalb der Gemeinde, in der die Sitzung stattfindet, weder wohnen noch berufstätig sind, erhalten ein Tagegeld von

5 DM für jeden Tag, an dem sie aus Anlaß der Dienstleistung mehr als 5 bis 8 Stunden,

8 DM für jeden Tag, an dem sie aus Anlaß der Dienstleistung mehr als 8 bis 12 Stunden,

12 DM für jeden Tag, an dem sie aus Anlaß der Dienstleistung mehr als 12 Stunden

von ihrem Wohnort abwesend sein müssen (§ 4 Abs. 2 Satz 1 BeisEG). Bei Abwesenheit bis zu 5 Stunden werden die nachgewiesenen notwendigen Auslagen bis zur Höhe von 4 DM erstattet (§ 4 Abs. 2 Satz 2 BeisEG).

β) Ist eine auswärtige Übernachtung notwendig, so wird ein **Übernachtungsgeld** in Höhe von 11 DM (Höhe des Satzes für Bundesbeamte der Reisekostenstufe II) gewährt (§ 4 Abs. 4 BeisEG). Schlafwagenvergütung ist gegebenenfalls auf diesen Betrag anzurechnen.

γ) Notwendige bare Auslagen, die nicht den durch den Aufenthalt außerhalb der Wohnung verursachten Aufwand betreffen, sind dem ehrenamtlichen Beisitzer zu ersetzen (§ 5 Satz 1 BeisEG). Hierher gehören etwa verauslagte Porti und Telefon- und Telegrammgebühren. Vor allem sind auch die **Kosten einer notwendigen Vertretung** zu ersetzen (§ 5 Satz 2 BeisEG). Selbst wenn die bestellte Vertretung die Erwerbsquelle des Beisitzers fortführt, ist hier auch die Versäumnisentschädigung an den Beisitzer zu zahlen, allerdings nur in Höhe des Mindestsatzes (vgl. § 2 Abs. 3 BeisEG). Der Vertreter selbst hat keinen Anspruch an die Staatskasse.

δ) Bedarf der ehrenamtliche Beisitzer wegen Gebrechens eines **Begleiters**, so sind die **Entschädigungen** nach den Vorschriften des Gesetzes für beide — in individueller Höhe — zu gewähren (§ 6 BeisEG). Auf die von dem Beisitzer dem Begleiter zugesagte Vergütung kommt es dabei grundsätzlich nicht an. Einen eigenen Anspruch gegen die Staatskasse hat der Begleiter nicht.

3. **Für die ehrenamtlichen Beisitzer** (nicht auch für ihre etwaigen Begleiter) **beim Bundessozialgericht erhöht sich die Aufwandsentschädigung** (das Tagegeld), **falls sie auswärts wohnen** oder berufstätig sind, **auf das Eineinhalbfache** der festgelegten Sätze. Bei Abwesenheit bis zu 5 Stunden werden die nachgewiesenen notwendigen Auslagen dementsprechend bis zu 6 DM erstattet. Das Übernachtungsgeld dieser Beisitzer beträgt statt 11 DM 14 DM (Höhe des Satzes für Bundesbeamte der Reisekostenstufe Ib), vgl. § 7 BeisEG.

4. **Die Entschädigung** nach den §§ 1 bis 7 BeisEG **wird** nach § 8 BeisEG **auch gewährt, wenn die ehrenamtlichen Beisitzer** bei den Gerichten der Sozialgerichtsbarkeit in dieser Eigenschaft **an der Wahl von** gesetzlich für sie vorgesehenen **Ausschüssen oder an** den **Sitzungen solcher Ausschüsse teilnehmen** (§§ 23, 35 Abs. 1, § 47 SGG), vgl. dazu Gölkel, SGb (Beil.) 1958, 3, ebenda auch 1957, 33.

5. **Die** dem ehrenamtlichen Beisitzer zu zahlende **Gesamtvergütung wird auf 10 DPf. aufgerundet** (§ 9 BeisEG).

6. **Die Entschädigung wird nur auf** — formlosen — **Antrag gewährt** (vgl. § 11 BeisEG). Mit der Antragstellung wird der Anspruch auf Entschädigung, der als solcher mit der Dienstableistung entsteht, fällig. Die Antragstellung ist erst nach der Beendigung der Dienstleistung zulässig bzw. wirksam.

Auf Antrag ist dem ehrenamtlichen Beisitzer in jedem Fall **ein** angemessener **Vorschuß zu gewähren** (§ 10 BeisEG). Dabei müssen vor allem die entstehenden Auslagen berücksichtigt werden. Die Bewilligung erteilt der berechnende Urkundsbeamte. Bei Ablehnung durch den Urkundsbeamten ist das Gericht, bei dem der Beisitzer mitgewirkt hat, anzurufen (entsprechend dem Grundgedanken des § 178 SGG). Gegen dessen ablehnende Entscheidung kann, falls es sich um ein Sozialgericht handelt, gegebenenfalls Beschwerde eingelegt werden, vgl. § 12 BeisEG (ebenso Brocke-Reese, Entsch. BeisZuS Anm. 2 zu § 10 BeisEG).

7. **Der Anspruch** auf Entschädigung **erlischt, wenn er nicht binnen eines Jahres nach Beendigung der Dienstleistung** — mündlich oder schriftlich — bei dem Gericht, bei dem der ehrenamtliche Beisitzer mitgewirkt hat (Anweisungsstelle daselbst), **geltend gemacht wird** (§ 11 BeisEG). Die Frist kann als gesetzliche Ausschlußfrist nicht verlängert werden; auch kann bei Verstreichenlassen derselben nicht die Wiedereinsetzung in den vorigen Stand gewährt werden. Zur Fristwahrung genügt die Geltendmachung ohne Bezifferung.

Die Verjährungsfrist beginnt mit dem Schlusse des Jahres zu laufen, in dem die wirksame rechtzeitige Geltendmachung liegt; sie **beträgt 2 Jahre** (vgl. § 196 Abs. 1 Nr. 15, §§ 199, 201 BGB. Die Beisitzer sind richtigerweise als Personen anzusehen, die ,,zur Besorgung gewisser Geschäfte öffentlich bestellt sind").

8. **Auf die Entschädigung kann** auch — „ausdrücklich" — **verzichtet werden,** vgl. Wudtke, SGb (Beil.) 1957, 6.

9. **Der entstandene Anspruch** auf Entschädigung **ist abtretbar, pfänd- und verpfändbar.**

10. **Die Festsetzung der Entschädigung vollzieht sich wie folgt:**

a) **Die** geltend gemachte **Entschädigung wird von dem** für kostenmäßige Berechnungen grundsätzlich zuständigen **Urkundsbeamten des betreffenden Gerichts berechnet und festgestellt,** anschließend sodann von der zugehörigen Gerichtskasse oder Gerichtszahlstelle ausgezahlt. Das hat das Gesetz, da es sich von selbst versteht, nicht zu bestimmen brauchen, vgl. Gölkel, SGb (Beil.) 1957, 33 [35]. Und zwar wird hier der Urkundsbeamte als reiner Verwaltungsbeamter tätig. Die Rechtslage ist nämlich anders als bei der Festsetzung der Entschädigung für Zeugen und Sachverständige. Die Entschädigung dieser Personen ist prozessual verankert und mit dem jeweiligen Rechtsstreit verknüpft (vgl. für das Sozialgerichtsverfahren § 118 Abs. 1 SGG, §§ 401, 413 ZPO, §§ 1ff. ZuSEG). Der Urkundsbeamte ist daher dort kostenberechnender und feststellender Sachbeauftragter des entscheidenden Gerichts, nicht wie hier Hilfsorgan der allgemeinen Gerichtsverwaltung. Vorliegend ist daher die Anwendung des § 178 SGG als solchem nicht möglich (vgl. dazu Brocke-Reese, Entsch. BeisZuS Anm. 2 zu § 12 BeisEG).

Trotz des Vorstehenden hat die Gerichtsverwaltung auch hier kein Recht, den Kostenbeamten ,,anzuweisen". Ihr ist nämlich hinsichtlich der zu zahlenden Entschädigung im § 12 BeisEG das Antragsrecht gegenüber dem Gericht selbst gegeben.

Eigenabänderungsbefugnis von Amts wegen wird dem Urkundsbeamten nur zur Berichtigung offensichtlicher Unrichtigkeiten zuzugestehen sein.

b) **Gerichtliche Festsetzung** (durch zu begründenden Beschluß) **erfolgt** nur **auf ausdrücklichen Antrag,** aus dem sich ergeben muß, daß die Tätigkeit des Gerichts selbst — von vornherein oder gewissermaßen als Station „über" dem Urkundsbeamten — gewünscht wird. Der Antrag ist nicht an besondere Voraussetzungen geknüpft, insbesondere ist er nicht fristgebunden. Allerdings wird auch hier die Frage der Verwirkung des Antragstellungsrechts zu prüfen sein, wenn der Antrag erst 10 bis 12 Monate nach Beendigung der fraglichen Dienstableistung gestellt wird. (Nach Verstreichenlassen eines Jahres seit diesem Zeitpunkt erlischt der Entschädigungsanspruch ohnehin.) Einer besonderen Form bedarf der Antrag nicht.

Antragsberechtigt ist — nur — der ehrenamtliche Beisitzer oder die ihm gegenüberstehende Staatskasse (§ 12 Abs. 1 Satz 1 BeisEG). Beanstandende Rechnungsprüfungshöfe müssen gegebenenfalls die Staatskasse um Eingreifen bitten. An die Stelle des Beisitzers kann der universelle oder singulare Rechtsnachfolger desselben treten.

Zuständig zur Entscheidung ist das Gericht, bei dem der ehrenamtliche Beisitzer mitgewirkt hat (§ 12 Abs. 1 Satz 2 BeisEG). Unter „Gericht" sind hier die Kammern oder die Senate zu verstehen, bei denen jeweils die Dienstleistung erbracht wurde. Diese Stellen können die vorliegenden Verhältnisse am besten beurteilen. Geschäftsplanmäßig kann daher hier eine besondere Kammer oder ein spezieller Senat nicht bestimmt werden (ebenso Brocke-Reese, aaO Anm. 4 zu § 12 BeisEG). Mehr als insgesamt verlangt, kann niemals bewilligt werden.

Das Gericht entscheidet ohne die Hinzuziehung der ehrenamtlichen Beisitzer (§ 12 Abs. 3 BeisEG). Vorherige Anhörung des Festsetzungsgegners ist in der Regel nicht erforderlich. Auf etwa eingetretene Verjährung muß sich aber die Staatskasse, die in diesen Fällen zu hören ist, stets ausdrücklich berufen. (Das Erlöschen des Entschädigungsanspruchs ist demgegenüber stets von Amts wegen zu berücksichtigen; der Antrag ist dann ohne weiteres abzulehnen.)

Das Gericht in der jeweiligen Besetzung (ebenfalls ohne ehrenamtliche Beisitzer) kann bei Unrichtigkeit seine Festsetzung vom Ants wegen — nach oben oder unten — ändern (vgl. § 12 Abs. 1 Satz 3 BeisEG), allerdings nur innerhalb einer sich von selbst verstehenden angemessenen Frist von 10 bis 12 Monaten. Vorherige Anhörung des Betroffenen ist hier nobile officium. Mündliche Verhandlung ist auch in diesem Falle nicht erforderlich.

Bei allen Festsetzungen ist Rechtsmittelbelehrung notwendig.

Eine Umwandlung der kurzen Verjährung in eine 30jährige (vgl. § 218 BGB) tritt selbst durch die gerichtliche Festsetzung nicht ein, weil diese keinen Vollstreckungstitel abgibt. (Aus diesem Grunde kommt auch keine einstweilige Einstellung bei Rechtsmitteleinlegung in Frage.)

c) **Gegen die richterliche Festsetzung** bzw. ihre Abänderung von Amts wegen **ist, wenn der Beschluß eines Sozialgerichts vorliegt, die Beschwerde gegeben,** die im Gegensatz zu den §§ 172, 173 SGG nicht fristgebunden, aber an die Mindestbeschwer von 50,01 DM geknüpft ist (§ 12 Abs. 2 Satz 1 BeisEG). Das ist hier in verfahrensrechtlicher Hinsicht unbedenklich, weil der § 19 Abs. 2 SGG uneingeschränkt in direkter Weise auf das Gesetz über die Entschädigung der ehrenamtlichen Beisitzer bei den Gerichten verweist und es sich um Vorgänge außerhalb des Rechtsstreits handelt. Beschwerdegegenstand ist der abgesetzte oder zuviel bewilligte Betrag. Eine Erhöhung der Entschädigung gegenüber dem ursprünglich Verlangten kann in der Beschwerdeinstanz, die Nachprüfungsrechtszug ist, nicht erfolgen; es muß insoweit wieder „von vorn" angefangen werden. Eine Anschlußbeschwerde gibt es nicht.

Beschwerdeberechtigt sind nur der Beisitzer (gegebenenfalls sein Rechtsnachfolger) und die Staatskasse (§ 12 Abs. 2 Satz 2 BeisEG). Mit Rücksicht auf das Beschwerderecht hat die Staatskasse auch gegenüber dem Gericht — das versteht sich bereits von selbst — kein Recht zur Anweisung.

Die Beschwerde kann (ebenso wie der Antrag oder eine sonstige Erklärung) zu Protokoll der Geschäftsstelle — des Sozialgerichts oder des Landessozialgerichts — gegeben oder schriftlich ohne Mitwirkung eines Rechtsanwalts eingereicht werden (§ 12 Abs. 4 BeisEG).

Die Beschwerde ist wegen der Abhilfemöglichkeit bei dem Gericht einzulegen, das die angefochtene Entscheidung erlassen hat (§ 12 Abs. 2 Satz 4 BeisEG). Dieses Gericht (in der jeweiligen Besetzung ohne ehrenamtliche Beisitzer) kann — es muß dies bei entsprechender Einsicht tun — der Beschwerde abhelfen (§ 12 Abs. 2 Satz 5 und Abs. 3 BeisEG). Eine gegebenenfalls beim Landessozialgericht unmittelbar eingelegte Beschwerde ist zunächst an das befaßt gewesene Sozialgericht zur entsprechenden Stellungnahme zu senden.

Die Beschwerde kann bis zur Beschwerdeentscheidung jederzeit zurückgenommen werden (im Zweifel mit der Wirkung des Rechtsmittelverlustes ein für allemal).

Das Beschwerdegericht entscheidet ohne Hinzuziehung der ehrenamtlichen Beisitzer auf Grund eigenen Ermessens durch zu begründenden Beschluß grundsätzlich kostenfrei (vgl. § 12 Abs. 3 BeisEG). Mündliche Verhandlung ist nicht erforderlich. Bei Abänderung der Vorentscheidung ist vorherige Anhörung des Gegners geboten. Zurückverweisung zur anderweitigen Festsetzung ist an sich möglich, wegen der eintretenden Verzögerung aber in aller Regel nicht angebracht. Zustellung erfolgt formfrei.

Als Beschwerdegericht kann geschäftsplanmäßig hier ohne weiteres ein bestimmter Senat bestellt werden.

Ein Abänderungsrecht von Amts wegen hat das Beschwerdegericht weder in bezug auf seine eigene noch auf die erste Entscheidung (vgl. Bauer, EntschG Anm. 1 zu § 12 BeisEG). Offensichtliche Unrichtigkeiten können, wie stets, von Amts wegen in der jeweiligen Besetzung (ohne ehrenamtliche Beisitzer) im Beschlußwege berichtigt werden.

Bei nach unten abgeänderter Festsetzung muß Rückzahlung des zuviel erhaltenen Entschädigungsbetrages vorgenommen werden. Nötigenfalls erfolgt Beitreibung im Verwaltungszwangsverfahren (nach dem Verwaltungs-Vollstreckungsgesetz). Der Rückzahlungsanspruch verjährt gemäß § 195 BGB — er ist hier reiner Bereicherungsanspruch — erst in 30 Jahren (vgl. RGZ 86, 96). Der Einwand des Wegfalls der Bereicherung ist zulässig.

d) **Ein Recht zur weiteren Beschwerde besteht** nach dem Gesetz **nicht.** Andere Rechtsbehelfe als die im Gesetz aufgeführten (Inanspruchnahme des Gerichts, Beschwerde) sind nicht gegeben. Nichtigkeits- oder Restitutionsklage kann gegenüber dem endgültigen Festsetzungsbeschluß nicht erhoben werden.

Auch der endgültige gerichtliche Festsetzungsbeschluß stellt keinen Vollstreckungstitel dar. Nötigenfalls muß der Beisitzer unter Vorlegung des Festsetzungsbeschlusses die Entschädigung vor den ordentlichen Gerichten (vgl. § 9 GVG) einklagen (sogen. Judikatsklage).

Elftes Kapitel

Der Übergang zum neuen Kostenrecht

Art. XI § 3 Abs. 4 und 5 KostÄndG

Anwendung des bisherigen Rechts

(4) Für die Gebühren der Rechtsanwälte gilt das bisherige Recht, wenn vor dem Inkrafttreten dieses Gesetzes der Auftrag erteilt oder der Rechtsanwalt als Armenanwalt oder nach § 11a des Arbeitsgerichtsgesetzes beigeordnet oder in einer Strafsache gerichtlich bestellt oder beigeordnet worden ist. Dies gilt nicht im Verfahren über eine Berufung, eine Revision oder über eine Beschwerde gegen eine den Rechtszug beendigende Entscheidung, wenn das Rechtsmittel nach dem Inkrafttreten dieses Gesetzes eingelegt worden ist. Für die vor dem Inkrafttreten dieses Gesetzes entstandenen Auslagen des Rechtsanwalts gilt das bisherige Recht.

(5) Im übrigen gilt das bisherige Recht für Gebühren und Auslagen, die vor dem Inkrafttreten dieses Gesetzes fällig geworden sind.

Übersicht

Spezialabhandlungen des Verfassers: Der Übergang zum neuen Kostenrecht im Verfahren der Sozialgerichtsbarkeit, SGb 1958, 107 und Die Übergangsregelung im Kostenänderungsgesetz, NJW 1958, 365.

Vorab muß bemerkt werden, daß die Überleitungsbestimmungen zum neuen Kostenrecht angesichts ihres Inhalts insgesamt eine geraume Zeit von Bedeutung sein werden.

1. a) Im Zuge der Kostenrechtsreform ist **an die Stelle der Gebührenordnung für Zeugen und Sachverständige mit** grundsätzlicher **Wirkung vom 1. 10. 1957 ab das Gesetz über die Entschädigung von Zeugen und Sachverständigen getreten** (vgl. Art. VII und Art. XI § 4 Nr. 3 und § 10 des Kostenänderungsgesetzes vom 26. 7. 1957, BGBl. I 861).

Für den Übergang hat Art. XI § 3 Abs. 5 KostÄndG eine Regelung getroffen. (Dies zu leugnen, vgl. Sußbauer, JVBl. 1958, 41 [45], auch Bauer, EntschG Einl. 14 zum ZuSEG, weil die einschlägigen Bezüge der Zeugen und Sachverständigen keine Gebühren darstellten, ist fehlsam; an dem Gebührencharakter der Sachverständigenvergütung kann mit Rücksicht auf die staatliche Honorierung einer in öffentlichrechtlicher Pflichterfüllung erbrachten Leistung kein Zweifel bestehen, ähnliches gilt insbesondere heute, nachdem im § 2 Abs. 3 ZuSEG weitgehend von einem echten

Verdienstausfallersatz abgerückt ist, auch von der Zeugenvergütung.) Nach dem einschlägigen Art. XI § 3 Abs. 5 KostÄndG **ist für die Anwendung alten oder neuen Rechts auf die Fälligkeit** der Zeugen- und Sachverständigengebühren und -auslagen **vor oder am bzw. nach dem 1. 10. 1957 abgestellt.** Streitig ist hier, wann die Fälligkeit eintritt. Brocke-Reese (Entsch. BeisZuS Vorbem. VI vor § 1 ZuSEG) stehen auf dem Standpunkt, daß dies mit der Beendigung der Zeugenvernehmung bzw. der Gutachtenerstattung der Fall ist. Das ist jedoch nicht zutreffend. Im Hinblick auf § 14 Abs. 1 ZuSEG wird nämlich die Zahlungspflicht der Staatskasse und damit die Entschädigungsfälligkeit erst ausgelöst, wenn der Zeuge oder Sachverständige die Entschädigung verlangt (vgl. Tschischgale, NJW 1958, 365 [368] und JR 1957, 369 [371]).

Zu bemerken ist, daß das Vorstehende Bedeutung auch für die Entschädigung der Beteiligten gemäß § 191 SGG hat.

b) Durch Art. X § 11 Nr. 6 KostÄndG **ist der § 196 SGG außer Kraft gesetzt worden, der die Vergütung des Rechtsanwalts** im Verfahren der Sozialgerichtsbarkeit **regelte. An seine Stelle sind vom 1. 10. 1957 ab die einschlägigen Bestimmungen der Bundesrechtsanwaltsgebührenordnung** (insbes. der **§ 116**) **getreten** (Art. VIII und Art. XI § 10 KostÄndG).

Für den Übergang hat Art. XI § 3 Abs. 4 eine Regelung getroffen. Danach **wird für die Gebühren des Wahlanwalts hinsichtlich der ersten Instanz auf die Auftragserteilung vor oder am bzw. nach dem 1. 10. 1957 abgestellt** (Art. XI § 3 Abs. 4 Satz 1 KostÄndG). **In den höheren Rechtszügen ist** nach Art. XI § 3 Abs. 4 Satz 2 KostÄndG **entscheidend, ob das Rechtsmittel vor oder am bzw. nach dem 1. 10. 1957 eingelegt worden ist.** (Für die Beschwerdeinstanz gilt dies aber nur dann, wenn es sich — wie bei dem Vorgehen gegen eine Kostenentscheidung nach Erledigung der Hauptsache im weiteren Sinne — um eine Beschwerde gegen eine den Rechtszug beendigende Entscheidung handelt, sonst gilt die Regelung des Satz 1 aaO.) Zwar ist im Gesetz ausdrücklich nur ausgesprochen, daß bei Rechtsmitteleinlegung am bzw. nach dem 1. 10. 1957 neues Recht gilt. Auf Grund einer Art Umkehrschlusses ist aber bei einer vorherigen Rechtsmitteleinlegung anzunehmen, daß dann uneingeschränkt altes Recht, nicht etwa die Regelung des Satz 1 aaO gilt (Sußbauer, JVBl. 1958,41 [43], Tschischgale, NJW 1958, 365 und KG, Rpfleger 1958, 130; a. A. OLG Köln, Rpfleger 1958, 131).

Was die jeweiligen Auslagen des Anwalts anbetrifft, so **gilt für die vor dem 1. 10. 1957 entstandenen Auslagen bisheriges Recht, für die am bzw. nach diesem Tage erwachsenen Auslagen neues Recht** (Art. XI § 3 Abs. 4 Satz 3 KostÄndG). Es kommt hier also auf den Zeitpunkt der Entstehung an.

Das vorstehend bezüglich der Anwaltsgebühren und -auslagen Dargelegte hat Bedeutung auch für Verwaltungsrechtsräte und die ihnen Gleichgestellten (§ 217 Abs. 1 und 2 SGG), ferner für die Rechtsbeistände (vgl. Art. IX, inbes. § 2 in Verb. mit Art. XI § 10 KostÄndG).

c) Durch Art. XI § 4 Abs. 5 Nr. 3 KostÄndG **ist das Gesetz betreffend die Erstattung von Rechtsanwaltsgebühren in Armensachen mit Wirkung vom 1. 10. 1957 ab aufgehoben worden. An seine Stelle sind die** einschlägigen **§§ 121 bis 130 BRAGebO getreten.**

Für den Übergang kommt es nach Art. XI § 3 Abs. 4 Satz 1 KostÄndG **hinsichtlich der Armenanwaltsgebühren im ersten Rechtszug darauf an, ob die Beiordnung** des Armenanwalts **vor dem 1. 10. 1957 oder an diesem Tag bzw. danach erfolgt ist.** Wenn hier zum Teil (vor allem von der nicht bindenden Amtlichen Begründung, BT-Drucks. 2545 2. Wahlperiode S. 285) alternativ auch auf die Auftragserteilung abgestellt wird, falls diese früher liegt, so findet das im Gesetz keine hinreichende Stütze, zumal Übergangsbestimmungen aus Gründen der Eindeutigkeit grundsätzlich nur an einen einzigen Rechtsakt zeitlich anzuknüpfen haben (vgl. Schumann, MDR 1958, 10 und Tschischgale, NJW 1958, 365 [366], ferner KG, Rpfleger 1958, 129; a. A. OLG Hamm, Rpfleger 1958, 96). **In den höheren Instanzen kommt es auf den Zeitpunkt der Einlegung des Rechtsmittels an** (siehe hierzu oben b).

Für die Auslagen des Armenanwalts gilt das gleiche wie für die **Auslagen des Wahlanwalts** (s. o. b).

Das Vorstehende hat Bedeutung auch für beigeordnete Verwaltungsrechtsräte und die ihnen Gleichgestellten (§ 217 Abs. 1 und 2 SGG), gegebenenfalls auch für Rechtsbeistände, die in dritter Instanz allerdings in keinem Falle beigeordnet werden können.

d) **An die Stelle der Gebührenordnung für Gerichtsvollzieher ist mit Wirkung vom 1. 10. 1957 an das Gesetz über die Kosten der Gerichtsvollzieher getreten** (vgl. Art. III und Art. XI § 4 Abs. 3 Nr. 1 und § 10 KostÄndG).

Nach Art. XI § 3 Abs. 5 KostÄndG **ist für die Anwendung alten oder neuen Rechts auf die Fälligkeit der Gerichtsvollzieherkosten vor oder am bzw. nach dem 1. 10. 1957 abgestellt** (vgl. Tschischgale, DGVZ 1957, 145 [154]). Nach § 4 GVKostG werden die Kosten (Gebühren und Auslagen des Gerichtsvollziehers) mit der Beendigung der gebührenpflichtigen Amtshandlung fällig.

e) Durch Art. XI § 4 Abs. 4 Nr. 5 KostÄndG **ist mit Wirkung vom 1. 10. 1957 an** neben den anderen Entschädigungsbestimmungen für ehrenamtliche Beisitzer auch **die Verordnung über die Entschädigung der Sozialrichter, Landessozialrichter und Bundessozialrichter** vom 4. 11. 1954 (BGBl. I 328) **aufgehoben worden. An die Stelle** der aufgehobenen Bestimmungen **ist** einheitlich **das Gesetz über die Entschädigung der ehrenamtlichen Beisitzer bei den Gerichten getreten** (vgl. Art. VI und Art. XI § 10 KostÄndG).

Was den Übergang vom alten zum neuen Entschädigungsrecht für ehrenamtliche Beisitzer **anbetrifft,** so **enthält das Kostenänderungsgesetz,** das nur die zu zahlenden Gebühren und Auslagen übergangsrechtlich regelt, **keine Vorschriften.** (Bei der Vergütung der ehrenamtlichen Beisitzer handelt es sich um eine echte Entschädigung.) Eine besondere Übergangsregelung war hier auch nicht erforderlich, **da es sich** ohne weiteres **von selbst versteht, daß es für** die Entschädigung der Beisitzer, insbesondere was die Höhe anbetrifft, **auf den Tag der Dienstleistung** (vor dem 1. 10. 1957 oder an bzw. nach diesem Stichtag) **ankommt** (ebenso Bauer, EntschG Einl. 7 zum BeisEG).

2. Erwähnt sei, **daß das Kostenänderungsgesetz** (vgl. Art. XI § 8 und § 9 des Gesetzes) zwar **in (West-)Berlin** (GVBl. 1957, 900), **nicht dagegen im Saarland gilt,** das sich erst nach und nach dem bundesdeutschen Rechtszustand voll angleicht. Was das Sozialgerichtsgesetz vom 3.9.1953 (BGBl. I 1239, 1326) in der Fassung des Gesetzes zur Änderung des Sozialgerichtsgesetzes vom 10.8.1954 (BGBl. I 239), des Gesetzes über Änderungen von Vorschriften des Zweiten Buches der Reichsversicherungsordnung und zur Ergänzung des Sozialgerichtsgesetzes vom 17.8.1955 (BGBl. I 513), des Gesetzes zur Änderung und Ergänzung des Gesetzes über Arbeitsvermittlung und Arbeitslosenversicherung vom 23. 12. 1956 (BGBl. I 1018, 1056), des Gesetzes zur Änderung und Ergänzung kostenrechtlicher Vorschriften vom 26. 7. 1957 (BGBl. I 861, 933) und des zweiten Gesetzes zur Änderung des Sozialgerichtsgesetzes vom 25. 6. 1958 (BGBl. I 409) — Neubekanntmachung vom 23. 8. 1958 (BGBl. I 613) —

selbst anbetrifft, so gilt es sowohl in(West-)Berlin (vgl. GVBl. 1958, 883) wie nunmehr (vom 1. 1. 1959 ab) auf Grund des am 18. 6. 1958 in dritter Lesung im saarländischen Landtag beschlossenen Ein- und Ausführungsgesetzes über die Sozialgerichtsbarkeit (Amtsbl. 1224, 1225) auch im Saarland, vgl. dazu das Gesetz über die Eingliederung des Saarlandes vom 23. 12. 1956 (BGBl. I 1011), insbes. §§ 6 und 16. Und zwar bestimmen sich auf Grund ausdrücklicher Vorschrift (§ 4 des EinfGes) die Gebühren für die Berufstätigkeit der Rechtsanwälte vor den saarländischen Sozialgerichten ebenfalls nach der Bundesgebührenordnung für Rechtsanwälte. (Die Gebühren der Rechtsbeistände betragen die Hälfte.) Bis zum Übergang der Währung auf DM erfolgt jeweils kursmäßige Umrechnung.

3. **Was Darstellungen des bisherigen Gesetzeszustandes anbetrifft, vergleiche:** hinsichtlich der früheren **Gebühren für Zeugen und Sachverständige,** Tschischgale, Die Vergütung der Sachverständigen im Sozialgerichtsverfahren, SGb 1957, 6;

hinsichtlich der früheren **Gebühren der Rechtsanwälte im Sozialgerichtsverfahren,** Tschischgale, Die Gebührenfestsetzung nach § 196 Abs. 4 SGG, SGb 1957, 34, Zur Frage der Erstattungsfähigkeit der Umsatzsteuer für Anwaltsgebühren nach dem SGG, JurBüro 1956, 416, Das Verhältnis des § 196 Abs. 4 zum § 197 Abs. 1 SGG, SGb 1956, 251;

hinsichtlich der früheren **Gebühren der Armenanwälte im Sozialgerichtsverfahren,** Tschischgale, Das Armenrecht im Verfahren der Sozialgerichtsbarkeit, NJW 1957, 164, Das Beitreibungsrecht des Armenanwalts gegenüber dem unterlegenen Gegner im Verfahren der Sozialgerichtsbarkeit, JurBüro 1957, 89 und Das Rückgriffsrecht der Staatskasse im Armenrechtsverfahren der Zivil-, Arbeits- und Sozialgerichtsbarkeit, JVBl. 1957, 4;

hinsichtlich der früheren **Gebühren der Gerichtsvollzieher,** Tschischgale, Die Vollstreckung der sozialgerichtlichen Entscheidungen und ihre Kosten, DGVZ 1957, 145;

hinsichtlich der früheren **Entschädigung der ehrenamtlichen Beisitzer,** Tschischgale, JVBl. 1958, 113 (Einl.).

Tabellen

Tabelle der von den Körperschaften und Anstalten des öffentlichen Rechts zu entrichtenden Gebühr je Streitsache

Bei Werten einer einmaligen Leistung bis DM	SG				LSG				BSG	
	ohne Gutachtenkosten		mit Gutachtenkosten		ohne Gutachtenkosten		mit Gutachtenkosten			
	1/1	1/2	1/1	1/2	1/1	1/2	1/1	1/2	1/1	1/2
4,00	2,00	2,00	60,00	30,00	2,00	2,00	90,00	45,00	120,00	60,00
4,20	2,10	2,00	60,00	30,00	2,10	2,00	90,00	45,00	120,00	60,00
4,40	2,20	2,00	60,00	30,00	2,20	2,00	90,00	45,00	120,00	60,00
4,60	2,30	2,00	60,00	30,00	2,30	2,00	90,00	45,00	120,00	60,00
4,80	2,40	2,00	60,00	30,00	2,40	2,00	90,00	45,00	120,00	60,00
5,00	2,50	2,00	60,00	30,00	2,50	2,00	90,00	45,00	120,00	60,00
5,20	2,60	2,00	60,00	30,00	2,60	2,00	90,00	45,00	120,00	60,00
5,40	2,70	2,00	60,00	30,00	2,70	2,00	90,00	45,00	120,00	60,00
5,60	2,80	2,00	60,00	30,00	2,80	2,00	90,00	45,00	120,00	60,00
5,80	2,90	2,00	60,00	30,00	2,90	2,00	90,00	45,00	120,00	60,00
6,00	3,00	2,00	60,00	30,00	3,00	2,00	90,00	45,00	120,00	60,00
6,20	3,10	2,00	60,00	30,00	3,10	2,00	90,00	45,00	120,00	60,00
6,40	3,20	2,00	60,00	30,00	3,20	2,00	90,00	45,00	120,00	60,00
6,60	3,30	2,00	60,00	30,00	3,30	2,00	90,00	45,00	120,00	60,00
6,80	3,40	2,00	60,00	30,00	3,40	2,00	90,00	45,00	120,00	60,00
7,00	3,50	2,00	60,00	30,00	3,50	2,00	90,00	45,00	120,00	60,00
7,20	3,60	2,00	60,00	30,00	3,60	2,00	90,00	45,00	120,00	60,00
7,40	3,70	2,00	60,00	30,00	3,70	2,00	90,00	45,00	120,00	60,00
7,60	3,80	2,00	60,00	30,00	3,80	2,00	90,00	45,00	120,00	60,00
7,80	3,90	2,00	60,00	30,00	3,90	2,00	90,00	45,00	120,00	60,00
8,00	4,00	2,00	60,00	30,00	4,00	2,00	90,00	45,00	120,00	60,00
8,20	4,10	2,10*)	60,00	30,00	4,10	2,10*)	90,00	45,00	120,00	60,00
8,40	4,20	2,10	60,00	30,00	4,20	2,10	90,00	45,00	120,00	60,00
8,60	4,30	2,20	60,00	30,00	4,30	2,20	90,00	45,00	120,00	60,00
8,80	4,40	2,20	60,00	30,00	4,40	2,20	90,00	45,00	120,00	60,00
9,00	4,50	2,30	60,00	30,00	4,50	2,30	90,00	45,00	120,00	60,00
9,20	4,60	2,30	60,00	30,00	4,60	2,30	90,00	45,00	120,00	60,00
9,40	4,70	2,40	60,00	30,00	4,70	2,40	90,00	45,00	120,00	60,00
9,60	4,80	2,40	60,00	30,00	4,80	2,40	90,00	45,00	120,00	60,00
9,80	4,90	2,50	60,00	30,00	4,90	2,50	90,00	45,00	120,00	60,00
10,00	5,00	2,50	60,00	30,00	5,00	2,50	90,00	45,00	120,00	60,00
10,20	5,10	2,60	60,00	30,00	5,10	2,60	90,00	45,00	120,00	60,00
10,40	5,20	2,60	60,00	30,00	5,20	2,60	90,00	45,00	120,00	60,00
10,60	5,30	2,70	60,00	30,00	5,30	2,70	90,00	45,00	120,00	60,00
10,80	5,40	2,70	60,00	30,00	5,40	2,70	90,00	45,00	120,00	60,00

*) Vgl. den aus § 9 Abs. 2 GKG sich ergebenden allgemeinen Aufrundungsgrundsatz.

Bei Werten einer einmaligen Leistung bis DM	SG				LSG				BSG	
	ohne Gutachtenkosten		mit Gutachtenkosten		ohne Gutachtenkosten		mit Gutachtenkosten			
	1/1	1/2	1/1	1/2	1/1	1/2	1/1	1/2	1/1	1/2
11,00	5,50	2,80	60,00	30,00	5,50	2,80	90,00	45,00	120,00	60,00
11,20	5,60	2,80	60,00	30,00	5,60	2,80	90,00	45,00	120,00	60,00
11,40	5,70	2,90	60,00	30,00	5,70	2,90	90,00	45,00	120,00	60,00
11,60	5,80	2,90	60,00	30,00	5,80	2,90	90,00	45,00	120,00	60,00
11,80	5,90	3,00	60,00	30,00	5,90	3,00	90,00	45,00	120,00	60,00
12,00	6,00	3,00	60,00	30,00	6,00	3,00	90,00	45,00	120,00	60,00
12,20	6,10	3,10	60,00	30,00	6,10	3,10	90,00	45,00	120,00	60,00
12,40	6,20	3,10	60,00	30,00	6,20	3,10	90,00	45,00	120,00	60,00
12,60	6,30	3,20	60,00	30,00	6,30	3,20	90,00	45,00	120,00	60,00
12,80	6,40	3,20	60,00	30,00	6,40	3,20	90,00	45,00	120,00	60,00
13,00	6,50	3,30	60,00	30,00	6,50	3,30	90,00	45,00	120,00	60,00
13,20	6,60	3,30	60,00	30,00	6,60	3,30	90,00	45,00	120,00	60,00
13,40	6,70	3,40	60,00	30,00	6,70	3,40	90,00	45,00	120,00	60,00
13,60	6,80	3,40	60,00	30,00	6,80	3,40	90,00	45,00	120,00	60,00
13,80	6,90	3,50	60,00	30,00	6,90	3,50	90,00	45,00	120,00	60,00
14,00	7,00	3,50	60,00	30,00	7,00	3,50	90,00	45,00	120,00	60,00
14,20	7,10	3,60	60,00	30,00	7,10	3,60	90,00	45,00	120,00	60,00
14,40	7,20	3,60	60,00	30,00	7,20	3,60	90,00	45,00	120,00	60,00
14,60	7,30	3,70	60,00	30,00	7,30	3,70	90,00	45,00	120,00	60,00
14,80	7,40	3,70	60,00	30,00	7,40	3,70	90,00	45,00	120,00	60,00
15,00	7,50	3,80	60,00	30,00	7,50	3,80	90,00	45,00	120,00	60,00
15,20	7,60	3,80	60,00	30,00	7,60	3,80	90,00	45,00	120,00	60,00
15,40	7,70	3,90	60,00	30,00	7,70	3,90	90,00	45,00	120,00	60,00
15,60	7,80	3,90	60,00	30,00	7,80	3,90	90,00	45,00	120,00	60,00
15,80	7,90	4,00	60,00	30,00	7,90	4,00	90,00	45,00	120,00	60,00
16,00	8,00	4,00	60,00	30,00	8,00	4,00	90,00	45,00	120,00	60,00
16,20	8,10	4,10	60,00	30,00	8,10	4,10	90,00	45,00	120,00	60,00
16,40	8,20	4,10	60,00	30,00	8,20	4,10	90,00	45,00	120,00	60,00
16,60	8,30	4,20	60,00	30,00	8,30	4,20	90,00	45,00	120,00	60,00
16,80	8,40	4,20	60,00	30,00	8,40	4,20	90,00	45,00	120,00	60,00
17,00	8,50	4,30	60,00	30,00	8,50	4,30	90,00	45,00	120,00	60,00
17,20	8,60	4,30	60,00	30,00	8,60	4,30	90,00	45,00	120,00	60,00
17,40	8,70	4,40	60,00	30,00	8,70	4,40	90,00	45,00	120,00	60,00
17,60	8,80	4,40	60,00	30,00	8,80	4,40	90,00	45,00	120,00	60,00
17,80	8,90	4,50	60,00	30,00	8,90	4,50	90,00	45,00	120,00	60,00
18,00	9,00	4,50	60,00	30,00	9,00	4,50	90,00	45,00	120,00	60,00
18,20	9,10	4,60	60,00	30,00	9,10	4,60	90,00	45,00	120,00	60,00
18,40	9,20	4,60	60,00	30,00	9,20	4,60	90,00	45,00	120,00	60,00
18,60	9,30	4,70	60,00	30,00	9,30	4,70	90,00	45,00	120,00	60,00
18,80	9,40	4,70	60,00	30,00	9,40	4,70	90,00	45,00	120,00	60,00

Bei Werten einer einmaligen Leistung bis DM	SG ohne Gutachtenkosten 1/1	SG ohne Gutachtenkosten 1/2	SG mit Gutachtenkosten 1/1	SG mit Gutachtenkosten 1/2	LSG ohne Gutachtenkosten 1/1	LSG ohne Gutachtenkosten 1/2	LSG mit Gutachtenkosten 1/1	LSG mit Gutachtenkosten 1/2	BSG 1/1	BSG 1/2
19,00	9,50	4,80	60,00	30,00	9,50	4,80	90,00	45,00	120,00	60,00
19,20	9,60	4,80	60,00	30,00	9,60	4,80	90,00	45,00	120,00	60,00
19,40	9,70	4,90	60,00	30,00	9,70	4,90	90,00	45,00	120,00	60,00
19,60	9,80	4,90	60,00	30,00	9,80	4,90	90,00	45,00	120,00	60,00
19,80	9,90	5,00	60,00	30,00	9,90	5,00	90,00	45,00	120,00	60,00
20,00	10,00	5,00	60,00	30,00	10,00	5,00	90,00	45,00	120,00	60,00
20,20	10,10	5,10	60,00	30,00	10,10	5,10	90,00	45,00	120,00	60,00
20,40	10,20	5,10	60,00	30,00	10,20	5,10	90,00	45,00	120,00	60,00
20,60	10,30	5,20	60,00	30,00	10,30	5,20	90,00	45,00	120,00	60,00
20,80	10,40	5,20	60,00	30,00	10,40	5,20	90,00	45,00	120,00	60,00
21,00	10,50	5,30	60,00	30,00	10,50	5,30	90,00	45,00	120,00	60,00
21,20	10,60	5,30	60,00	30,00	10,60	5,30	90,00	45,00	120,00	60,00
21,40	10,70	5,40	60,00	30,00	10,70	5,40	90,00	45,00	120,00	60,00
21,60	10,80	5,40	60,00	30,00	10,80	5,40	90,00	45,00	120,00	60,00
21,80	10,90	5,50	60,00	30,00	10,90	5,50	90,00	45,00	120,00	60,00
22,00	11,00	5,50	60,00	30,00	11,00	5,50	90,00	45,00	120,00	60,00
22,20	11,10	5,60	60,00	30,00	11,10	5,60	90,00	45,00	120,00	60,00
22,40	11,20	5,60	60,00	30,00	11,20	5,60	90,00	45,00	120,00	60,00
22,60	11,30	5,70	60,00	30,00	11,30	5,70	90,00	45,00	120,00	60,00
22,80	11,40	5,70	60,00	30,00	11,40	5,70	90,00	45,00	120,00	60,00
23,00	11,50	5,80	60,00	30,00	11,50	5,80	90,00	45,00	120,00	60,00
23,20	11,60	5,80	60,00	30,00	11,60	5,80	90,00	45,00	120,00	60,00
23,40	11,70	5,90	60,00	30,00	11,70	5,90	90,00	45,00	120,00	60,00
23,60	11,80	5,90	60,00	30,00	11,80	5,90	90,00	45,00	120,00	60,00
23,80	11,90	6,00	60,00	30,00	11,90	6,00	90,00	45,00	120,00	60,00
24,00	12,00	6,00	60,00	30,00	12,00	6,00	90,00	45,00	120,00	60,00
24,20	12,10	6,10	60,00	30,00	12,10	6,10	90,00	45,00	120,00	60,00
24,40	12,20	6,10	60,00	30,00	12,20	6,10	90,00	45,00	120,00	60,00
24,60	12,30	6,20	60,00	30,00	12,30	6,20	90,00	45,00	120,00	60,00
24,80	12,40	6,20	60,00	30,00	12,40	6,20	90,00	45,00	120,00	60,00
25,00	12,50	6,30	60,00	30,00	12,50	6,30	90,00	45,00	120,00	60,00
bis										
299,99	15,00	7,50	60,00	30,00	15,00	7,50	90,00	45,00	120,00	60,00
alle übrigen Leistungen	30,00	15,00	60,00	30,00	40,00	20,00	90,00	45,00	120,00	60,00

Tabelle der von der Staatskasse zu zahlenden Entschädigung für die Zeitversäumnis eines Beteiligten (je Tag)

Brutto-Verdienst je Std. bis DM	1 Std. DM	2 Std. DM	3 Std. DM	4 Std. DM	5 Std. DM	6 Std. DM	7 Std. DM	8 Std. DM	9 Std. DM	10 Std. u.mehr DM
0,50	0,50	1,00	1,50	2,00	2,50	3,00	3,50	4,00	4,50	5,00
0,60	0,60	1,20	1,80	2,40	3,00	3,60	4,20	4,80	5,40	6,00
0,70	0,70	1,40	2,10	2,80	3,50	4,20	4,90	5,60	6,30	7,00
0,80	0,80	1,60	2,40	3,20	4,00	4,80	5,60	6,40	7,20	8,00
0,90	0,90	1,80	2,70	3,60	4,50	5,40	6,30	7,20	8,10	9,00
1,00	1,00	2,00	3,00	4,00	5,00	6,00	7,00	8,00	9,00	10,00
1,10	1,10	2,20	3,30	4,40	5,50	6,60	7,70	8,80	9,90	11,00
1,20	1,20	2,40	3,60	4,80	6,00	7,20	8,40	9,60	10,80	12,00
1,30	1,30	2,60	3,90	5,20	6,50	7,80	9,10	10,40	11,70	13,00
1,40	1,40	2,80	4,20	5,60	7,00	8,40	9,80	11,20	12,60	14,00
1,50	1,50	3,00	4,50	6,00	7,50	9,00	10,50	12,00	13,50	15,00
1,60	1,60	3,20	4,80	6,40	8,00	9,60	11,20	12,80	14,40	16,00
1,70	1,70	3,40	5,10	6,80	8,50	10,20	11,90	13,60	15,30	17,00
1,80	1,80	3,60	5,40	7,20	9,00	10,80	12,60	14,40	16,20	18,00
1,90	1,90	3,80	5,70	7,60	9,50	11,40	13,30	15,20	17,10	19,00
2,00	2,00	4,00	6,00	8,00	10,00	12,00	14,00	16,00	18,00	20,00
2,10	2,10	4,20	6,30	8,40	10,50	12,60	14,70	16,80	18,90	21,00
2,20	2,20	4,40	6,60	8,80	11,00	13,20	15,40	17,60	19,80	22,00
2,30	2,30	4,60	6,90	9,20	11,50	13,80	16,10	18,40	20,70	23,00
2,40	2,40	4,80	7,20	9,60	12,00	14,40	16,80	19,20	21,60	24,00
2,50	2,50	5,00	7,50	10,00	12,50	15,00	17,50	20,00	22,50	25,00
2,60	2,60	5,20	7,80	10,40	13,00	15,60	18,20	20,80	23,40	26,00
2,70	2,70	5,40	8,10	10,80	13,50	16,20	18,90	21,60	24,30	27,00
2,80	2,80	5,60	8,40	11,20	14,00	16,80	19,60	22,40	25,20	28,00
2,90	2,90	5,80	8,70	11,60	14,50	17,40	20,30	23,20	26,10	29,00
3,00 u. mehr	3,00	6,00	9,00	12,00	15,00	18,00	21,00	24,00	27,00	30,00

Tabelle der von der Staatskasse zu zahlenden Entschädigung für die Zeitversäumnis eines Zeugen (je Tag)

Brutto-verdienst je Std. bis DM	1 Std. DM	2 Std. DM	3 Std. DM	4 Std. DM	5 Std. DM	6 Std. DM	7 Std. DM	8 Std. DM	9 Std. DM	10 Std. u. mehr DM
0,50	0,50	1,00	1,50	2,00	2,50	3,00	3,50	4,00	4,50	5,00
0,60	0,60	1,20	1,80	2,40	3,00	3,60	4,20	4,80	5,40	6,00
0,70	0,70	1,40	2,10	2,80	3,50	4,20	4,90	5,60	6,30	7,00
0,80	0,80	1,60	2,40	3,20	4,00	4,80	5,60	6,40	7,20	8,00
0,90	0,90	1,80	2,70	3,60	4,50	5,40	6,30	7,20	8,10	9,00
1,00	1,00	2,00	3,00	4,00	5,00	6,00	7,00	8,00	9,00	10,00
1,10	1,10	2,20	3,30	4,40	5,50	6,60	7,70	8,80	9,90	11,00
1,20	1,20	2,40	3,60	4,80	6,00	7,20	8,40	9,60	10,80	12,00
1,30	1,30	2,60	3,90	5,20	6,50	7,80	9,10	10,40	11,70	13,00
1,40	1,40	2,80	4,20	5,60	7,00	8,40	9,80	11,20	12,60	14,00
1,50	1,50	3,00	4,50	6,00	7,50	9,00	10,50	12,00	13,50	15,00
1,60	1,60	3,20	4,80	6,40	8,00	9,60	11,20	12,80	14,40	16,00
1,70	1,70	3,40	5,10	6,80	8,50	10,20	11,90	13,60	15,30	17,00
1,80	1,80	3,60	5,40	7,20	9,00	10,80	12,60	14,40	16,20	18,00
1,90	1,90	3,80	5,70	7,60	9,50	11,40	13,30	15,20	17,10	19,00
2,00	2,00	4,00	6,00	8,00	10,00	12,00	14,00	16,00	18,00	20,00
2,10	2,10	4,20	6,30	8,40	10,50	12,60	14,70	16,80	18,90	21,00
2,20	2,20	4,40	6,60	8,80	11,00	13,20	15,40	17,60	19,80	22,00
2,30	2,30	4,60	6,90	9,20	11,50	13,80	16,10	18,40	20,70	23,00
2,40	2,40	4,80	7,20	9,60	12,00	14,40	16,80	19,20	21,60	24,00
2,50	2,50	5,00	7,50	10,00	12,50	15,00	17,50	20,00	22,50	25,00
2,60	2,60	5,20	7,80	10,40	13,00	15,60	18,20	20,80	23,40	26,00
2,70	2,70	5,40	8,10	10,80	13,50	16,20	18,90	21,60	24,30	27,00
2,80	2,80	5,60	8,40	11,20	14,00	16,80	19,60	22,40	25,20	28,00
2,90	2,90	5,80	8,70	11,60	14,50	17,40	20,30	23,20	26,10	29,00
3,00 u. mehr	3,00	6,00	9,00	12,00	15,00	18,00	21,00	24,00	27,00	30,00

Tabelle der von der Staatskasse zu zahlenden Entschädigung

Satz DM	1 Std. DM	2 Std. DM	3 Std. DM	4 Std. DM	5 Std. DM	6 Std. DM	7 Std. DM	8 Std. DM	9 Std. DM
a) Regelentschädigung (§ 3 Abs. 2 ZuSEG)									
3,00	3,00	6,00	9,00	12,00	15,00	18,00	21,00	24,00	27,00
3,50	3,50	7,00	10,50	14,00	17,50	21,00	24,50	28,00	31,50
4,00	4,00	8,00	12,00	16,00	20,00	24,00	28,00	32,00	36,00
4,50	4,50	9,00	13,50	18,00	22,50	27,00	31,50	36,00	40,50
5,00	5,00	10,00	15,00	20,00	25,00	30,00	35,00	40,00	45,00
5,50	5,50	11,00	16,50	22,00	27,50	33,00	38,50	44,00	49,50
6,00	6,00	12,00	18,00	24,00	30,00	36,00	42,00	48,00	54,00
6,50	6,50	13,00	19,50	26,00	32,50	39,00	45,50	52,00	58,50
7,00	7,00	14,00	21,00	28,00	35,00	42,00	49,00	56,00	63,00
7,50	7,50	15,00	22,50	30,00	37,50	45,00	52,50	60,00	67,50
8,00	8,00	16,00	24,00	32,00	40,00	48,00	56,00	64,00	72,00
8,50	8,50	17,00	25,50	34,00	42,50	51,00	59,50	68,00	76,50
9,00	9,00	18,00	27,00	36,00	45,00	54,00	63,00	72,00	81,00
9,50	9,50	19,00	28,50	38,00	47,50	57,00	66,50	76,00	85,50
10,00	10,00	20,00	30,00	40,00	50,00	60,00	70,00	80,00	90,00
b) Sonderentschädigung (§ 3 Abs. 3 ZuSEG)									
8,25 (5,50 + 2,75)	8,25	16,50	24,75	33,00	41,25	49,50	57,75	66,00	74,25
9,00 (6,00 + 3,00)	9,00	18,00	27,00	36,00	45,00	54,00	63,00	72,00	81,00
9,75 (6,50 + 3,25)	9,75	19,50	29,25	39,00	48,75	58,50	68,25	78,00	87,75
10,50 (7,00 + 3,50)	10,50	21,00	31,50	42,00	52,50	63,00	73,50	84,00	94,50
11,25 (7,50 + 3,75)	11,25	22,50	33,75	45,00	56,25	67,50	78,75	90,00	101,25
12,00 (8,00 + 4,00)	12,00	24,00	36,00	48,00	60,00	72,00	84,00	96,00	108,00
12,75 (8,50 + 4,25)	12,75	25,50	38,25	51,00	63,75	76,50	89,25	102,00	114,75
13,50 (9,00 + 4,50)	13,50	27,00	40,50	54,00	67,50	81,00	94,50	108,00	121,50
14,25 (9,50 + 4,75)	14,25	28,50	42,75	57,00	71,25	85,50	99,75	114,00	128,25
15,00 (10,00 + 5,00)	15,00	30,00	45,00	60,00	75,00	90,00	105,00	120,00	135,00

Tabellen

für die Leistung eines Sachverständigen je Gutachten

10 Std. DM	20 Std. DM	30 Std. DM	40 Std. DM	50 Std. DM	60 Std. DM	70 Std. DM	80 Std. DM	90 Std. DM	100 Std. DM
30,00	60,00	90,00	120,00	150,00	180,00	210,00	240,00	270,00	300,00
35,00	70,00	105,00	140,00	175,00	210,00	245,00	280,00	315,00	350,00
40,00	80,00	120,00	160,00	200,00	240,00	280,00	320,00	360,00	400,00
45,00	90,00	135,00	180,00	225,00	270,00	315,00	360,00	405,00	450,00
50,00	100,00	150,00	200,00	250,00	300,00	350,00	400,00	450,00	500,00
55,00	110,00	165,00	220,00	275,00	330,00	385,00	440,00	495,00	550,00
60,00	120,00	180,00	240,00	300,00	360,00	420,00	480,00	540,00	600,00
65,00	130,00	195,00	260,00	325,00	390,00	455,00	520,00	585,00	650,00
70,00	140,00	210,00	280,00	350,00	420,00	490,00	560,00	630,00	700,00
75,00	150,00	225,00	300,00	375,00	450,00	525,00	600,00	675,00	750,00
80,00	160,00	240,00	320,00	400,00	480,00	560,00	640,00	720,00	800,00
85,00	170,00	255,00	340,00	425,00	510,00	595,00	680,00	765,00	850,00
90,00	180,00	270,00	360,00	450,00	540,00	630,00	720,00	810,00	900,00
95,00	190,00	285,00	380,00	475,00	570,00	665,00	760,00	855,00	950,00
100,00	200,00	300,00	400,00	500,00	600,00	700,00	800,00	900,00	1000,00
82,50	165,00	247,50	330,00	412,50	495,00	577,50	660,00	742,50	825,00
90,00	180,00	270,00	360,00	450,00	540,00	630,00	720,00	810,00	900,00
97,50	195,00	292,50	390,00	487,50	585,00	682,50	780,00	877,50	975,00
105,00	210,00	315,00	420,00	525,00	630,00	735,00	840,00	945,00	1050,00
112,50	225,00	337,50	450,00	562,50	675,00	787,50	900,00	1012,50	1125,00
120,00	240,00	360,00	480,00	600,00	720,00	840,00	960,00	1080,00	1200,00
127,50	255,00	382,50	510,00	637,50	765,00	892,50	1020,00	1147,50	1275,00
135,00	270,00	405,00	540,00	675,00	810,00	945,00	1080,00	1215,00	1350,00
142,50	285,00	427,50	570,00	712,50	855,00	997,50	1140,00	1284,50	1425,00
150,00	300,00	450,00	600,00	750,00	900,00	1050,00	1200,00	1350,00	1500,00

Tabelle der vom Auftraggeber zu zahlenden Vergütung für die Tätigkeit eines Rechtsanwalts je Streitsache

	Mindestgebühr DM	Höchstgebühr DM	Durchschnittsgebühr DM
Vor dem Sozialgericht	40	120	80
Vor dem Landessozialgericht . . .	60	180	120
Vor dem Bundessozialgericht . . .	100	300	200

Tabelle der vom Auftraggeber zu zahlenden Vergütung für die Tätigkeit eines Rechtsbeistandes je Streitsache

	Mindestgebühr DM	Höchstgebühr DM	Durchschnittsgebühr DM
Vor dem Sozialgericht	20	60	40
Vor dem Landessozialgericht . . .	30	90	60

Tabelle der von der Staatskasse zu zahlenden Vergütung für die Tätigkeit eines Armenanwalts je Streitsache

	Mindest-gebühr DM	Höchst-gebühr DM	Durch-schnitts-gebühr DM
Vor dem Sozialgericht	40	120	80
Vor dem Landessozialgericht . . .	60	180	120
Vor dem Bundessozialgericht . . .	100	300	200

Tabelle der von der Staatskasse zu zahlenden Vergütung für die Tätigkeit eines Armenrechtsbeistandes je Streitsache

	Mindest-gebühr DM	Höchst-gebühr DM	Durch-schnitts-gebühr DM
Vor dem Sozialgericht	20	60	40
Vor dem Landessozialgericht . . .	30	90	60

Tabelle der vom Kostenschuldner zu zahlenden Vergütung für die Tätigkeit eines Gerichtsvollziehers nach § 17 GVKostG (je Pfändung; volle Gebühr) und nach § 21 GVKostG (je Versteigerung; 2½fache Gebühr)

Wertstufe bis einschl. DM	Pfändungsgebühr DM	Versteigerungsgebühr DM
50	1,00	2,50
100	2,00	5,00
150	3,00	7,50
200	4,00	10,00
300	5,00	12,50
400	6,00	15,00
500	7,00	17,50
600	8,00	20,00
900	10,00	25,00
1 200	12,00	30,00
1 500	14,00	35,00
2 000	17,00	42,50
2 500	20,00	50,00
3 000	23,00	57,50
3 500	26,00	65,00
4 000	29,00	72,50
4 500	32,00	80,00
5 000	35,00	87,50
6 000	40,00	100,00
7 000	45,00	112,50
8 000	50,00	125,00
9 000	55,00	137,50
10 000	60,00	150,00
11 000	65,00	162,50
12 000	70,00	175,00
13 000	75,00	187,50
14 000	80,00	200,00
15 000	85,00	212,50
16 000	90,00	225,00
17 000	95,00	237,50
18 000	100,00	250,00
19 000	105,00	262,50
20 000	110,00	275,00

Von dem Mehrbetrag für je 1000 DM steigt die volle Gebühr um 5,00 DM. Werte über 20 000 DM sind auf volle 1000 DM aufzurunden.

Tabelle der vom Kostenschuldner zu zahlenden Vergütung für die Tätigkeit eines Vollziehungsbeamten nach § 3 AKostVO (je Pfändung; 1½% der Vollstreckungssumme, vom Mehrbetrag über 100 DM ¾%) und § 4 AKostVO (je Versteigerung; 2% vom Erlös, von dem Mehrbetrag über 100 DM 1%).

Betrag DM	Pfändungsgebühr DM	Versteigerungsgebühr DM	Betrag DM	Pfändungsgebühr DM	Versteigerungsgebühr DM
10	1,00	1,00	400	3,75	5,00
20	1,00	1,00	410	3,80	5,10
30	1,00	1,00	420	3,90	5,20
40	1,00	1,00	430	3,95	5,30
50	1,00	1,00	440	4,05	5,40
60	1,00	1,20	450	4,10	5,50
70	1,05	1,40	460	4,20	5,60
80	1,20	1,60	470	4,25	5,70
90	1,35	1,80	480	4,35	5,80
100	1,50	2,00	490	4,40	5,90
110	1,55	2,10	500	4,50	6,00
120	1,65	2,20	510	4,55	6,10
130	1,70	2,30	520	4,65	6,20
140	1,80	2,40	530	4,70	6,30
150	1,85	2,50	540	4,80	6,40
160	1,95	2,60	550	4,85	6,50
170	2,00	2,70	560	4,95	6,60
180	2,10	2,80	570	5,00	6,70
190	2,15	2,90	580	5,10	6,80
200	2,25	3,00	590	5,15	6,90
210	2,30	3,10	600	5,25	7,00
220	2,40	3,20	610	5,30	7,10
230	2,45	3,30	620	5,40	7,20
240	2,55	3,40	630	5,45	7,30
250	2,60	3,50	640	5,55	7,40
260	2,70	3,60	650	5,60	7,50
270	2,75	3,70	660	5,70	7,60
280	2,85	3,80	670	5,75	7,70
290	2,90	3,90	680	5,85	7,80
300	3,00	4,00	690	5,90	7,90
310	3,05	4,10	700	6,00	8,00
320	3,15	4,20	710	6,05	8,10
330	3,20	4,30	720	6,15	8,20
340	3,30	4,40	730	6,20	8,30
350	3,35	4,50	740	6,30	8,40
360	3,45	4,60	750	6,35	8,50
370	3,50	4,70	760	6,45	8,60
380	3,60	4,80	770	6,50	8,70
390	3,65	3,90	780	6,60	8,80
			790	6,65	8,90

Betrag DM	Pfändungsgebühr DM	Versteigerungsgebühr DM	Betrag DM	Pfändungsgebühr DM	Versteigerungsgebühr DM
800	6,75	9,00	1220	9,90	13,20
810	6,80	9,10	1230	9,95	13,30
820	6,90	9,20	1240	10,05	13,40
830	6,95	9,30			
840	7,05	9,40	1250	10,10	13,50
			1260	10,20	13,60
850	7,10	9,50	1270	10,25	13,70
860	7,20	9,60	1280	10,35	13,80
870	7,25	9,70	1290	10,40	13,90
880	7,35	9,80			
890	7,40	9,90	1300	10,50	14,00
			1310	10,55	14,10
900	7,50	10,00	1320	10,65	14,20
910	7,55	10,10	1330	10,70	14,30
920	7,65	10,20	1340	10,80	14,40
930	7,70	10,30			
940	7,80	10,40	1350	10,85	14,50
			1360	10,95	14,60
950	7,85	10,50	1370	11,00	14,70
960	7,95	10,60	1380	11,10	14,80
970	8,00	10,70	1390	11,15	14,90
980	8,10	10,80			
990	8,15	10,90	1400	11,25	15,00
			1410	11,30	15,10
1000	8,25	11,00	1420	11,40	15,20
1010	8,30	11,10	1430	11,45	15,30
1020	8,40	11,20	1440	11,55	15,40
1030	8,45	11,30			
1040	8,55	11,40	1450	11,60	15,50
			1460	11,70	15,60
1050	8,60	11,50	1470	11,75	15,70
1060	8,70	11,60	1480	11,85	15,80
1070	8,75	11,70	1490	11,90	15,90
1080	8,85	11,80			
1090	8,90	11,90	1500	12,00	16,00
			1510	12,05	16,10
1100	9,00	12,00	1520	12,15	16,20
1110	9,05	12,10	1530	12,20	16,30
1120	9,15	12,20	1540	12,30	16,40
1130	9,20	12,30			
1140	9,30	12,40	1550	12,35	16,50
			1560	12,45	16,60
			1570	12,50	16,70
1150	9,35	12,50	1580	12,60	16,80
1160	9,45	12,60	1590	12,65	16,90
1170	9,50	12,70			
1180	9,60	12,80	1600	12,75	17,00
1190	9,65	12,90	1610	12,80	17,10
			1620	12,90	17,20
1200	9,75	13,00	1630	12,95	17,30
1210	9,80	13,10	1640	13,05	17,40

Betrag DM	Pfändungsgebühr DM	Versteigerungsgebühr DM
1650	13,10	17,50
1660	13,20	17,60
1670	13,25	17,70
1680	13,35	17,80
1690	13,40	17,90
1700	13,50	18,00
1710	13,55	18,10
1720	13,65	18,20
1730	13,70	18,30
1740	13,80	18,40
1750	13,85	18,50
1760	13,95	18,60
1770	14,00	18,70
1780	14,10	18,80
1790	14,15	18,90
1800	14,25	19,00
1810	14,30	19,10
1820	14,40	19,20
1830	14,45	19,30
1840	14,55	19,40
1850	14,60	19,50
1860	14,70	19,60
1870	14,75	19,70
1880	14,85	19,80
1890	14,90	19,90
1900	15,00	20,00
1910	15,05	20,10
1920	15,15	20,20
1930	15,20	20,30
1940	15,30	20,40
1950	15,35	20,50
1960	15,45	20,60
1970	15,50	20,70
1980	15,60	20,80
1990	15,65	20,90
2000	15,75	21,00
2010	15,80	21,10
2020	15,90	21,20
2030	15,95	21,30
2040	16,05	21,40
2050	16,10	21,50
2060	16,20	21,60
2070	16,25	21,70
2080	16,35	21,80
2090	16,45	21,90
2100	16,50	22,00
2110	16,55	22,10
2120	16,65	22,20
2130	16,70	22,30
2140	16,80	22,40
2150	16,85	22,50
2160	16,95	22,60
2170	17,00	22,70
2180	17,10	22,80
2190	17,15	22,90
2200	17,25	23,00
2210	17,30	23,10
2220	17,40	23,20
2230	17,45	23,30
2240	17,55	23,40
2250	17,60	23,50
2260	17,70	23,60
2270	17,75	23,70
2280	17,85	23,80
2290	17,90	23,90
2300	18,00	24,00
2310	18,05	24,10
2320	18,15	24,20
2330	18,20	24,30
2340	18,30	24,40
2350	18,35	24,50
2360	18,45	24,60
2370	18,50	24,70
2380	18,60	24,80
2390	18,65	24,90
2400	18,75	25,00
2410	18,80	25,10
2420	18,90	25,20
2430	18,95	25,30
2440	19,05	25,40
2450	19,10	25,50
2460	29,20	25,60
2470	19,25	25,70
2480	19,35	25,80
2490	19,40	25,90

Betrag DM	Pfändungsgebühr DM	Versteigerungsgebühr DM
2500	19,50	26,00
2510	19,55	26,10
2520	19,65	26,20
2530	19,70	26,30
2540	19,80	26,40
2550	19,85	26,50
2560	19,95	26,60
2570	20,00	26,70
2580	20,10	26,80
2590	20,15	26,90
2600	20,25	27,00
2610	20,30	27,10
2620	20,40	27,20
2630	20,45	27,30
2640	20,55	27,40
2650	20,60	27,50
2660	20,70	27,60
2670	20,75	27,70
2680	20,85	27,80
2690	20,90	27,90
2700	21,00	28,00
2710	21,05	28,10
2720	21,15	28,20
2730	21,20	28,30
2740	21,30	28,40
2750	21,35	28,50
2760	21,45	28,60
2770	21,50	28,70
2780	21,60	28,80
2790	21,65	28,90
2800	21,75	29,00
2810	21,80	29,10
2820	21,90	29,20
2830	21,95	29,30
2840	22,05	29,40
2850	22,10	29,50
2860	22,20	29,60
2870	22,25	29,70
2880	22,35	29,80
2890	22,40	29,90
2900	22,50	30,00
2910	22,55	30,10
2920	22,65	30,20
2930	22,70	30,30
2940	22,80	30,40
2950	22,85	30,50
2960	22,95	30,60
2970	23,00	30,70
2980	23,10	30,80
2990	23,15	30,90
3000	23,25	31,00
3010	23,30	31,10
3020	23,40	31,20
3030	23,45	31,30
3040	23,55	31,40
3050	23,60	31,50
3060	23,70	31,60
3070	23,75	31,70
3080	23,85	31,80
3090	23,90	31,90
3100	24,00	32,00
3110	24,05	32,10
3120	24,15	32,20
3130	24,20	32,30
3140	24,30	32,40
3150	24,35	32,50
3160	24,45	32,60
3170	24,50	32,70
3180	24,60	32,80
3190	24,65	32,90
3200	24,75	33,00
3210	24,80	33,10
3220	24,90	33,20
3230	24,95	33,30
3240	25,05	33,40
3250	25,10	33,50
3260	25,20	33,60
3270	25,25	33,70
3280	25,35	33,80
3290	25,40	33,90
3300	25,50	34,00
3310	25,55	34,10
3320	25,65	34,20
3330	25,70	34,30
3340	25,80	34,40

Betrag DM	Pfändungsgebühr DM	Versteigerungsgebühr DM
3350	25,85	34,50
3360	25,95	34,60
3370	26,00	34,70
3380	26,10	34,80
3390	26,15	34,90
3400	26,25	35,00
3410	26,30	35,10
3420	26,40	35,20
3430	26,45	35,30
3440	26,55	35,40
3450	26,60	35,50
3460	26,70	35,60
3470	26,75	35,70
3480	26,85	35,80
3490	26,90	35,90
3500	27,00	36,00
3510	27,05	36,10
3520	27,15	36,20
3530	27,20	36,30
3540	27,30	36,40
3550	27,35	36,50
3560	27,45	36,60
3570	27,50	36,70
3580	27,60	36,80
3590	27,65	36,90
3600	27,75	37,00
3610	27,80	37,10
3620	27,90	37,20
3630	27,95	37,30
3640	28,05	37,40
3650	28,10	37,50
3660	28,20	37,60
3670	28,25	37,70
3680	28,35	37,80
3690	28,40	37,90
3700	28,50	38,00
3710	28,55	38,10
3720	28,65	38,20
3730	28,70	38,30
3740	28,80	38,40
3750	28,85	38,50
3760	28,95	38,60
3770	29,00	38,70
3780	29,10	38,80
3790	29,15	38,90
3800	29,25	39,00
3810	29,30	39,10
3820	29,40	39,20
3830	29,45	39,30
3840	29,55	39,40
3850	29,60	39,50
3860	29,70	39,60
3870	29,75	39,70
3880	29,85	39,80
3890	29,90	39,90
3900	30,00	40,00
3910	30,05	40,10
3920	30,15	40,20
3930	30,20	40,30
3940	30,30	40,40
3950	30,35	40,50
3960	30,45	40,60
3970	30,50	40,70
3980	30,60	40,80
3990	30,65	40,90
4000	30,75	41,00
4010	30,80	41,10
4020	30,90	41,20
4030	30,95	41,30
4040	31,05	41,40
4050	31,10	41,50
4060	31,20	41,60
4070	31,25	41,70
4080	31,35	41,80
4090	31,40	41,90
4100	31,50	42,00
4110	31,55	42,10
4120	31,65	42,20
4130	31,70	42,30
4140	31,80	42,40
4150	31,85	42,50
4160	31,95	42,60
4170	32,00	42,70
4180	32,10	42,80
4190	32,15	42,90

Betrag DM	Pfändungsgebühr DM	Versteigerungsgebühr DM	Betrag DM	Pfändungsgebühr DM	Versteigerungsgebühr DM
4200	32,25	43,00	4600	35,25	47,00
4210	32,30	43,10	4610	35,30	47,10
4220	32,40	43,20	4620	35,40	47,20
4230	32,45	43,30	4630	35,45	47,30
4240	32,55	43,40	4640	35,55	47,40
4250	32,60	43,50	4650	35,60	47,50
4260	32,70	43,60	4660	35,70	47,60
4270	32,75	43,70	4670	35,75	47,70
4280	32,85	43,80	4680	35,85	47,80
4290	32,90	43,90	4690	35,90	47,90
4300	33,00	44,00	4700	36,00	48,00
4310	33,05	44,10	4710	36,05	48,10
4320	33,15	44,20	4720	36,15	48,20
4330	33,20	44,30	4730	36,20	48,30
4340	33,30	44,40	4740	36,30	48,40
4350	33,35	44,50	4750	36,35	48,50
4360	33,45	44,60	4760	36,45	48,60
4370	33,50	44,70	4770	36,50	48,70
4380	33,60	44,80	4780	36,60	48,80
4390	33,65	44,90	4790	36,65	48,90
4400	33,75	45,00	4800	36,75	49,00
4410	33,80	45,10	4810	36,80	49,10
4420	33,90	45,20	4820	36,90	49,20
4430	33,95	45,30	4830	36,95	49,30
4440	34,05	45,40	4840	37,05	49,40
4450	34,10	45,50	4850	37,10	49,50
4460	34,20	45,60	4860	37,20	49,60
4470	34,25	45,70	4870	37,25	49,70
4480	34,35	45,80	4880	37,35	49,80
4490	34,40	45,90	4890	37,40	49,90
4500	34,50	46,00	4900	37,50	50,00
4510	34,55	46,10	4910	37,55	50,10
4520	34,65	46,20	4920	37,65	50,20
4530	34,70	46,30	4930	37,70	50,30
4540	34,80	46,40	4940	37,80	50,40
4550	34,85	46,50	4950	37,85	50,50
4560	34,95	46,60	4960	37,95	50,60
4570	35,00	46,70	4970	38,00	50,70
4580	35,10	46,80	4980	38,10	50,80
4590	35,15	46,90	4990	38,15	50,90
			5000	38,25	51,00

Tabelle der von der Staatskasse zu zahlenden Entschädigung für die Zeitversäumnis eines Beisitzers (je Tag)

Brutto-verdienst je Std. bis DM	1 Std. DM	2 Std. DM	3 Std. DM	4 Std. DM	5 Std. DM	6 Std. DM	7 Std. DM	8 Std. DM	9 Std. DM	10 Std. u.mehr DM
2,00	2,00	4,00	6,00	8,00	10,00	12,00	14,00	16,00	18,00	20,00
2,10	2,10	4,20	6,30	8,40	10,50	12,60	14,70	16,80	18,90	21,00
2,20	2,20	4,40	6,60	8,80	11,00	13,20	15,40	17,60	19,80	22,00
2,30	2,30	4,60	6,90	9,20	11,50	13,80	16,10	18,40	20,70	23,00
2,40	2,40	4,80	7,20	9,60	12,00	14,40	16,80	19,20	21,60	24,00
2,50	2,50	5,00	7,50	10,00	12,50	15,00	17,50	20,00	22,50	25,00
2,60	2,60	5,20	7,80	10,40	13,00	15,60	18,20	20,80	23,40	26,00
2,70	2,70	5,40	8,10	10,80	13,50	16,20	18,90	21,60	24,30	27,00
2,80	2,80	5,60	8,40	11,20	14,00	16,80	19,60	22,40	25,20	28,00
2,90	2,90	5,80	8,70	11,60	14,50	17,40	20,30	23,20	26,10	29,00
3,00	3,00	6,00	9,00	12,00	15,00	18,00	21,00	24,00	27,00	30,00
3,10	3,10	6,20	9,30	12,40	15,50	18,60	21,70	24,80	27,90	31,00
3,20	3,20	6,40	9,60	12,80	16,00	19,20	22,40	25,60	28,80	32,00
3,30	3,30	6,60	9,90	13,20	16,50	19,80	23,10	26,40	29,70	33,00
3,40	3,40	6,80	10,20	13,60	17,00	20,40	23,80	27,20	30,60	34,00
3,50	3,50	7,00	10,50	14,00	17,50	21,00	24,50	28,00	31,50	35,00
3,60	3,60	7,20	10,80	14,40	18,00	21,60	25,20	28,80	32,40	36,00
3,70	3,70	7,40	11,10	14,80	18,50	22,20	25,90	29,60	33,30	37,00
3,80	3,80	7,60	11,40	15,20	19,00	22,80	26,60	30,40	34,20	38,00
3,90	3,90	7,80	11,70	15,60	19,50	23,40	27,30	31,20	35,10	39,00
4,00 u. mehr	4,00	8,00	12,00	16,00	20,00	24,00	28,00	32,00	36,00	40,00

Tabelle der vom Auftraggeber zu zahlenden Vergütung für die Tätigkeit eines Rechtsanwalts je Streitsache in der DDR

Mindest-gebühr DM-Ost	Höchst-gebühr DM-Ost	Durch-schnitts-gebühr DM-Ost
10,00	100,00	55,00

Die Instanzenzüge in den sozialgerichtlichen Kostenverfahren

1. Kostenverfahren mit Beschwerderecht

Auferlegung von Kosten durch das Gericht der Instanz (Kostengrundentscheidung)	Auferlegung von Strafen evtl. mit Kosten durch das Gericht der Instanz (Strafbeschluß)	Festsetzung der Entschädigung der ehrenamtlichen Beisitzer durch das Gericht der Instanz (falls ausdrücklich beantragt)
Dagegen grundsätzlich Beschwerde an das übergeordnete LSG, falls es sich um eine isolierte Kostenentscheidung des SG handelt	Dagegen grundsätzlich Beschwerde an das übergeordnete LSG, falls es sich um einen Beschluß des SG handelt	Dagegen Beschwerde an das LSG, falls es sich um einen Festsetzungsbeschluß des SG handelt
Kein Anwaltszwang	Kein Anwaltszwang	Kein Anwaltszwang
Frist: ein Monat	Frist: ein Monat	Keine Frist
Keine bestimmte Beschwer	Keine bestimmte Beschwer	Mindestbeschwer von 50,01 DM

2. Gebührenverfahren mit Anrufungsrecht

Streitwertfestsetzung	Gerichtskostenfestsetzung	Beteiligten-, Zeugen- und Sachverständigenkostenfestsetzung
Annahme durch den Urkundsbeamten der Instanz	Ansatz durch den Urkundsbeamten der Instanz	Feststellung durch den Urkundsbeamten der Instanz
Anrufung des Gerichts der Instanz	Anrufung des Gerichts der Instanz	Anrufung des Gerichts der Instanz
Kein Anwaltszwang	Kein Anwaltszwang	Kein Anwaltszwang
Frist: ein Monat	Frist: ein Monat	Frist: ein Monat
Keine bestimmte Beschwer	Keine bestimmte Beschwer	Keine bestimmte Beschwer

Parteikosten-festsetzung	Anwaltskosten-festsetzung	Armenanwalts-kostenfestsetzung	Gerichtsvollzieher-kostenfestsetzung
Festsetzung durch den Urkundsbeamten des SG	Festsetzung durch den Urkundsbeamten des SG (bei Fest- und Mindestgebühren)	Festsetzung durch den Urkundsbeamten der Instanz	Ansetzung durch den Gerichtsvollzieher
Anrufung des SG	Anrufung des SG	Anrufung des Gerichts der Instanz	Anrufung des SG, sofern keine Vollstreckungsrechtsbehelfe vorliegen
Kein Anwaltszwang	Kein Anwaltszwang	Kein Anwaltszwang	Kein Anwaltszwang
Frist: ein Monat	Frist: ein Monat	Frist: ein Monat	Frist: ein Monat
Keine bestimmte Beschwer	Keine bestimmte Beschwer	Keine bestimmte Beschwer	Keine bestimmte Beschwer

Anhang

Das Sozialgerichtsverfahren in der DDR*)

Verfahrensordnung für die Sozialversicherung vom 11. 5. 1953 (GBl. 698) i. d. F. der Anordnung zur Änderung der Verfahrensordnung für die Sozialversicherung vom 22. 5. 1956 (GBl. I 522) und der Anordnung Nr. 2 zur Änderung der Verfahrensordnung für die Sozialversicherung vom 3. 9. 1957 (GBl. I 488): §§ 1 bis 39

Anordnung über das Verfahren für die Sozialversicherung bei der Deutschen Versicherungs-Anstalt. — Verfahrensordnung — vom 9. 5. 1958 (GBl. I 398): §§ 1 bis 19.

Verfahrensordnung für die Sozialversicherung

Auf Grund des § 5 der Verordnung vom 26. April 1951 über die Sozialversicherung (GBl. S. 325) wird im Einvernehmen mit dem Bundesvorstand des Freien Deutschen Gewerkschaftsbundes und nach Anhören der Ministerien, der Staatssekretariate und der Landeshandwerkskammern hiermit zur Erledigung von Anträgen auf Leistungen und zur Regelung von Streitfällen aus der Sozialversicherung folgende Verfahrensordnung erlassen:

Anträge auf Leistungen

§ 1

(1) Die Leistungen der Sozialversicherung werden nur auf Antrag gewährt. Bei der Stellung von Anträgen auf Leistungen ist der Versicherungsausweis der Sozialversicherung vorzulegen.

(2) Anträge auf kurzfristige Barleistungen, wie Krankengeld, Hausgeld, Heil- und Genesungskuren, Schwangerschafts- und Wochenhilfe, einmalige Beihilfe an kinderreiche Mütter, Beihilfe für Entbindungskosten, Sterbegeld sind

a) im Betrieb zu stellen, wenn der Betrieb Barleistungen auszahlt,

b) bei der für die Versicherten zuständigen Außenstelle der Verwaltung der Sozialversicherung bei den Bezirksvorständen des Freien Deutschen Gewerkschaftsbundes einzureichen, wenn der Betrieb keine Barleistungen auszahlt oder der Versicherte in keinem Arbeitsvertragsverhältnis steht.

---

*) In Ostberlin gilt Entsprechendes (vgl. die VO vom 19. 9. 1953 — VOBl. 323 — mit Durchf.Best. vom gleichen Tage — VOBl. 325 — und dazu Tschischgale, KostR in ArbSach. S. 34ff., insbes. 4a, b und 5, ferner Anm. 2 sowie Hoffmann, Die Neuordnung des Gerichtswesens des sowjetisch besetzten Gebietes, JR 1954, 93. Das aufgelöste Kammergericht [Berlin Ost] ist als besonderes Kassationsgericht in Wegfall gekommen).

(3) Anträge auf Erholungskuren sind beim Rat oder bei der Kommission für Sozialversicherung des Betriebes zu stellen.

(4) Die Gewährung von Renten, Pflegegeld und laufenden staatlichen Unterstützungen ist bei der Außenstelle der Verwaltung der Sozialversicherung bei den Bezirksvorständen des Freien Deutschen Gewerkschaftsbundes des Wohnsitzes des Berechtigten schriftlich zu beantragen.

§ 2

Ist der Versicherungsfall für die Zahlung der Alters- oder Hinterbliebenenrente eingetreten, so unterliegt der Rentenanspruch keiner Verjährung oder Verwirkung. § 1 Abs. 1 wird durch diese Bestimmung nicht berührt.

Entscheidung über Anträge auf Leistungen

§ 3

(1) Über Anträge auf kurzfristige Leistungen und Sachleistungen entscheidet

a) der Rat für Sozialversicherung oder die Kommission für Sozialversicherung im Betriebe, soweit die Auszahlung der Barleistungen im Betrieb erfolgt,
b) in allen anderen Fällen die Außenstelle der Verwaltung der Sozialversicherung bei den Bezirksvorständen des Freien Deutschen Gewerkschaftsbundes.

(2) Über Anträge auf Renten, Pflegegeld und laufende staatliche Unterstützungen entscheidet die Außenstelle der Verwaltung der Sozialversicherung bei den Bezirksvorständen des Freien Deutschen Gewerkschaftsbundes. Über diese Anträge ist ein schriftlicher Bescheid zu erteilen. Der Bescheid muß enthalten

a) bei stattgegebenen Anträgen die Art und Weise der Berechnung,
b) bei abgelehnten Anträgen eine genaue und allgemeinverständliche Begründung der Ablehnung,
c) in jedem Falle die Rechtsmittelbelehrung.

(3) Die Bescheide über Rentenansprüche sind den Versicherten gegen Empfangsbestätigung zu übermitteln.

(4) Der Bescheid wird mit dem Ersten des Monats, in dem der Antrag gestellt wird, wirksam, sofern nicht die Voraussetzungen für den Bezug von Rente, Pflegegeld oder die laufende staatliche Unterstützung erst nach Antragstellung eingetreten sind. In letzterem Falle wird der Bescheid mit dem Ersten des Monats wirksam, in dem diese Voraussetzungen vorliegen.

§ 3a

(1) Wird Altersrente, Ehegatten- und Kinderzuschlag bis zum Ablauf des auf den Versicherungsfall folgenden Kalendermonats beantragt, so wird der Bescheid mit dem 1. des Monats wirksam, in dem der Versicherungsfall eingetreten ist.

(2) Der Bescheid über die Zahlung einer Invalidenrente (§ 54 der Verordnung vom 28. Januar 1947 über die Sozialpflichtversicherung) wird mit dem Tage wirksam, der auf den Wegfall der kurzfristigen Barleistungen folgt. Voraussetzung ist, daß bei Wegfall der kurzfristigen Barleistungen Invalidität bestand und vom Tage des Wegfalls an der Antrag innerhalb eines Monats gestellt wurde. Wird

der Antrag später gestellt oder bestand kein Anspruch auf kurzfristige Barleistungen, so beginnt die Zahlung der Invalidenrente mit dem 1. des Monats, in dem der Antrag gestellt wurde.

(3) Die Hinterbliebenenrente wird von dem auf den Todestag folgenden Tag an gewährt, wenn der Antrag vor Ablauf des auf den Todestag folgenden Monats gestellt wurde. Von dieser Bestimmung bleibt unberührt die Bestimmung des § 56 Abs. 2 der Verordnung vom 28. Januar 1947 über die Sozialpflichtversicherung. War der Verstorbene Vollrentner, so beginnt die Zahlung der Hinterbliebenenrente frühestens mit dem 1. des Monats, der dem Todestag folgt.

(4) Wenn Arbeitsunfähigkeit als Folge eines Betriebsunfalles oder einer anerkannten Berufskrankheit vor Ablauf von 26 Wochen nach diesem Betriebsunfall oder der anerkannten Berufskrankheit endet, so wird Unfallrente vom Tage des Beginns der Arbeitsfähigkeit an gezahlt, wenn spätestens innerhalb eines Monats von diesem Zeitpunkt an der Antrag gestellt wird. Wird der Antrag später gestellt, so beginnt die Zahlung der Unfallrente mit dem 1. des Monats, in dem der Antrag gestellt wurde.

(5) Wird bei Arbeitsunfähigkeit infolge eines Betriebsunfalles oder einer anerkannten Berufskrankheit festgestellt, daß innerhalb von 52 Wochen nach Eintritt des Versicherungsfalles mit der Wiederherstellung der Arbeitsfähigkeit nicht zu rechnen ist, so beginnt die Zahlung der Unfallrente mit Beginn der 27. Woche nach Eintritt des Versicherungsfalles.

§ 4

(1) Tritt in den Verhältnissen, die für die Zahlung von Rente oder Pflegegeld maßgebend waren, eine Änderung ein, so kann jederzeit eine neue Entscheidung getroffen werden.

(2) Wird die Leistung erhöht, so wird der Bescheid mit dem 1. des Monats, in dem der Antrag auf Erhöhung gestellt wurde, wirksam.

(3) Wird die Leistung gemindert oder entzogen, so wird die Entscheidung mit dem Ablauf des auf den Zugang des Bescheides folgenden Monats wirksam.

(4) Stellt die Sozialversicherung ungesetzliche Leistungen fest, so muß der Bescheid über die Gewährung dieser Leistung aufgehoben und durch einen neuen ersetzt werden. Gegen den neuen Bescheid können alle in dieser Verfahrensordnung vorgesehenen Rechtsmittel eingelegt werden.

(5) Ist durch den rechtskräftig gewordenen Beschluß einer Beschwerdekommission oder durch Gerichtsurteil eine Rentensache entschieden worden, so können die im § 3 genannten Organe einen neuen Rentenbescheid in dieser Sache nur erlassen, wenn die Beschlußfassung oder die Urteilsfindung durch wissentlich falsche Angaben des Versicherten beeinflußt worden ist.

(6) Schreib- und Rechenfehler können jederzeit berichtigt werden.

Beschwerden

§ 5

(1) Gegen eine Entscheidung einer Betriebsgewerkschaftsleitung, eines Rates oder einer Kommission für Sozialversicherung eines Betriebes oder einer Außenstelle der Verwaltung der Sozialversicherung des Bezirksvorstandes des Freien Deutschen Gewerkschaftsbundes ist die Beschwerde an die Kreisbeschwerdekommission zulässig.

(2) Die Beschwerde ist schriftlich oder zu Protokoll bei der Beschwerdekommission des Kreises einzulegen, in dem der Anspruch auf Leistungen entstanden ist.

§ 6

(1) Die Beschwerdefrist beträgt einen Monat nach Zugang des Bescheides.

(2) Die Beschwerdefrist ist auch dann gewahrt, wenn die Beschwerde fristgemäß bei einer anderen staatlichen Verwaltung oder bei einem Organ des Freien Deutschen Gewerkschaftsbundes eingeht, oder wenn sie innerhalb der Beschwerdefrist nachweislich der Post zur Beförderung übergeben worden ist.

(3) Bei Versäumung der Beschwerdefrist finden die Vorschriften der Zivilprozeßordnung über die Wiedereinsetzung in den vorigen Stand (§§ 233ff.) entsprechende Anwendung.

Errichtung von Beschwerdekommissionen

§ 7

(1) Bei den Bezirksvorständen des Freien Deutschen Gewerkschaftsbundes bestehen für die Bereiche der Außenstellen der Verwaltung der Sozialversicherung Kreisbeschwerdekommissionen und für die Bereiche der Bezirke Bezirksbeschwerdekommissionen.

(2) Beim Bundesvorstand des Freien Deutschen Gewerkschaftsbundes — Verwaltung der Sozialversicherung — besteht eine Zentrale Beschwerdekommission.

§ 8

Die Beschwerdekommissionen sind zur strengen Einhaltung der demokratischen Gesetzlichkeit verpflichtet.

Zusammensetzung der Beschwerdekommissionen

§ 9

(1) Die Kreisbeschwerdekommission besteht aus drei, die Bezirksbeschwerdekommission aus fünf und die Zentrale Beschwerdekommission aus sieben Mitgliedern.

(2) Den Vorsitzenden und die Mitglieder berufen

a) für die Kreisbeschwerdekommission — das Kreisaktiv des FDGB
b) für die Bezirksbeschwerdekommission — der Bezirksvorstand des FDGB
c) für die Zentrale Beschwerdekommission — der Bundesvorstand des FDGB.

§ 10

An den Beratungen der Beschwerdekommissionen können auf Antrag des Versicherten mit beratender Stimme

a) ein Vertreter der zuständigen Industriegewerkschaft oder Gewerkschaft
b) bei einem anerkannten Verfolgten des Naziregimes (VdN) ein Vertreter der VdN-Sozialkommission beim Sachgebiet Sozialfürsorge des Rates des Kreises oder ein Vertreter des Prüfungsausschusses beim Referat Sozialfürsorge des Rates des Bezirkes

teilnehmen.

Anhang

Ablehnung von Mitgliedern der Beschwerdekommissionen

§ 11

Von der Mitwirkung an einer Entscheidung sind Personen ausgeschlossen, die mit dem Antragsteller verheiratet, verschwägert oder in gerader Linie verwandt sind, sowie seine Geschwister. Im übrigen sind die Bestimmungen der §§ 41 und 42 der Zivilprozeßordnung entsprechend anzuwenden.

Durchführung des Verfahrens

§ 12

(1) Der Vorsitzende bereitet die mündliche Verhandlung des Streitfalles vor. Er kann vor der Verhandlung Beweis erheben, Gutachten von Ärzten und amtliche Auskünfte jeder Art einholen. Auf Antrag eines der Beteiligten ist die Beweisaufnahme bei der mündlichen Verhandlung zu wiederholen.

(2) Die Beschwerdekommission ist zur Entgegennahme eidesstattlicher Versicherungen berechtigt. Durch Beschluß der Beschwerdekommission ist die eidliche Vernehmung von Zeugen und Sachverständigen im Wege der Rechtshilfe von dem örtlich zuständigen Kreisarbeits- oder Kreisgericht vorzunehmen.

(3) Der Vorsitzende bestimmt die Verhandlungszeit. Er kann für die mündliche Verhandlung Zeugen und Sachverständige laden und auch das persönliche Erscheinen des Beschwerdeführers und eines Vertreters der Sozialversicherung verlangen.

§ 13

Der Antragsteller und ein Vertreter der Sozialversicherung können zur mündlichen Verhandlung vor der Beschwerdekommission erscheinen. Sie können sich vertreten lassen, sofern nicht ihr persönliches Erscheinen nach § 12 Abs. 3 Satz 2 angeordnet ist. Die Erschienenen sind zu hören. Eine Vertretung durch Rechtsanwälte ist nicht zulässig.

§ 14

Die Beschwerdekommission entscheidet mit Stimmenmehrheit. Hält die Beschwerdekommission den Anspruch für begründet, so ist sie verpflichtet, die Höhe und den Beginn der Leistung festzustellen.

§ 15

Die Beschwerdekommission bestimmt, ob und in welcher Höhe dem Beschwerdeführer die zur Wahrung seiner Rechte entstandenen notwendigen Kosten zu erstatten sind.

§ 16

Der Beschluß der Beschwerdekommission wird in der Verhandlung schriftlich festgelegt und verkündet. Er wird mit Gründen und der Rechtsmittelbelehrung versehen, von dem Vorsitzenden der Beschwerdekommission unterzeichnet und dem Beschwerdeführer gegen Empfangsbestätigung sowie der Sozialversicherung zugestellt.

§ 17

Das Verfahren vor der Beschwerdekommission ist kostenfrei.

Anhang

Weitere Beschwerde und Anfechtungsklage

§ 18

(1) Gegen den Beschluß der Kreisbeschwerdekommission sind folgende Rechtsmittel zulässig:

a) die weitere Beschwerde an die Bezirksbeschwerdekommission oder
b) die Anfechtungsklage bei dem Bezirksarbeitsgericht.

(2) Werden von beiden Parteien eines Streites verschiedene Rechtsmittel eingelegt, so ist die Anfechtungsklage bei dem Bezirksarbeitsgericht durchzuführen. Der Rechtsstreit ist in diesem Falle von der Bezirksbeschwerdekommission auf Antrag an das Bezirksarbeitsgericht zu verweisen. Der Antrag kann bis zum Schluß der ersten mündlichen Verhandlung gestellt werden.

Die weitere Beschwerde

§ 19

(1) Die weitere Beschwerde ist bei der Bezirksbeschwerdekommission einzureichen, in deren Gebiet die Kreisbeschwerdekommission ihren Sitz hat.

(2) Die Beschwerdefrist beträgt einen Monat nach Zugang des Beschlusses der Kreisbeschwerdekommission.

(3) Die Beschwerdefrist ist auch dann gewahrt, wenn die weitere Beschwerde fristgemäß bei der Kreisbeschwerdekommission, deren Beschluß angefochten wird, eingeht oder innerhalb der Beschwerdefrist nachweislich der Post zur Beförderung übergeben worden ist.

(4) Bei Versäumung der Beschwerdefrist finden die Vorschriften der Zivilprozeßordnung über die Wiedereinsetzung in den vorigen Stand (§§ 233ff.) entsprechende Anwendung.

(5) Für die Ablehnung von Mitgliedern der Bezirksbeschwerdekommission und die Kosten des Verfahrens gelten die §§ 11, 15 und 17 dieser Verfahrensordnung entsprechend.

§ 20

(1) Der Vorsitzende bereitet die mündliche Verhandlung des Streitfalles vor. Er kann vor der Verhandlung Beweis erheben, Gutachten von Ärzten und amtliche Auskünfte jeder Art einholen. Auf Antrag eines der Beteiligten ist die Beweisaufnahme bei der mündlichen Verhandlung zu wiederholen.

(2) Der Versicherte oder die Sozialversicherung kann beantragen, daß ein bestimmter Arzt gutachtlich gehört wird. Die Bezirksbeschwerdekommission kann dessen Anhörung davon abhängig machen, daß der Antragsteller die Kosten vorschießt, und beschließen, daß er sie endgültig trägt.

(3) Die Bezirksbeschwerdekommission ist zur Entgegennahme eidesstattlicher Versicherungen berechtigt. Durch Beschluß der Bezirksbeschwerdekommission ist die eidliche Vernehmung von Zeugen und Sachverständigen im Wege der Rechtshilfe von dem örtlich zuständigen Kreisarbeits- oder Kreisgericht vorzunehmen.

(4) Der Vorsitzende bestimmt die Verhandlungszeit. Er kann für die mündliche Verhandlung Zeugen und Sachverständige laden und das persönliche Erscheinen des Beschwerdeführers und eines Vertreters der Sozialversicherung verlangen.

(5) Die Vorschrift des § 28 dieser Verfahrensordnung gilt entsprechend.

Anhang

§ 21

(1) Der Beschluß der Bezirksbeschwerdekommission ist endgültig.

(2) Hat das Verfahren zu keinem anderen als dem von der Kreisbeschwerdekommission festgestellten Ergebnis geführt, so kann auf den Tatbestand und die Gründe des Beschlusses der Kreisbeschwerdekommission verwiesen werden.

Aufhebung von Fehlentscheidungen der Bezirksbeschwerdekommission

§ 22

Die Zentrale Beschwerdekommission ist berechtigt, auf Antrag des Bundesvorstandes des Freien Deutschen Gewerkschaftsbundes Fehlentscheidungen der Bezirksbeschwerdekommission aufzuheben. Das Verfahren zur Aufhebung muß innerhalb von sechs Monaten nach Eintritt der Rechtskraft der Entscheidung der Bezirksbeschwerdekommission eingeleitet werden.

Die Anfechtungsklage

§ 23

Die Anfechtungsklage ist bei dem Bezirksarbeitsgericht des Bezirkes einzureichen, in dem die Kreisbeschwerdekommission ihren Sitz hat.

§ 24

(1) Die Anfechtungsfrist beträgt einen Monat nach Zugang des Beschlusses der Kreisbeschwerdekommission. Bei einer Versäumung dieser Frist finden die Vorschriften der Zivilprozeßordnung über die Wiedereinsetzung in den vorigen Stand (§§ 233ff.) entsprechende Anwendung. Liegen die Voraussetzungen für eine Wiedereinsetzung offensichtlich vor, so kann das Gericht diese von Amts wegen bewilligen.

(2) Die Frist gilt auch dann als gewahrt, wenn die Klage spätestens bis zum Ablauf der Frist nachweislich der Post zur Beförderung an das Bezirksarbeitsgericht übergeben wurde.

§ 25

Für Rentenstreitfälle findet das Urteilsverfahren nach §§ 46ff. Arbeitsgerichtsgesetz, für alle sonstigen sozialversicherungsrechtlichen Streitfälle das Beschlußverfahren nach §§ 80ff. Arbeitsgerichtsgesetz Anwendung, sofern nicht in dieser Verfahrensordnung etwas anderes bestimmt wird. Maßgebend ist der Text des Arbeitsgerichtsgesetzes vom 23. Dezember 1926.

§ 26

(1) Es besteht kein Anwaltszwang. Rechtsanwälte, die bei einem Gericht der Deutschen Demokratischen Republik zugelassen sind, können vor dem Bezirksarbeitsgericht als Prozeßbevollmächtigte auftreten.

(2) Ihre Vergütung beträgt für jeden Streitfall mindestens 10,— DM, höchstens jedoch 100,— DM ausschließlich der baren Auslagen. Innerhalb dieser Grenzen wird die Vergütung entweder vom Gericht im Urteil oder vom Vorsitzenden durch Beschluß festgesetzt.

§ 27

Die Beiordnung eines Rechtsanwaltes oder eines Angestellten des Bezirksarbeitsgerichts steht im Ermessen des Vorsitzenden.

§ 28

Das schriftliche Verfahren ist zulässig, wenn beide Parteien dies beantragen. Die erklärte Zustimmung gilt für das gesamte Verfahren. Das Gericht kann die mündliche Verhandlung wieder aufnehmen, wenn es dies für erforderlich hält.

§ 29

(1) Eine Güteverhandlung findet nicht statt.

(2) Die Vorschriften über das Versäumnisverfahren sind nicht anzuwenden.

§ 30

(1) Zur Aufklärung des Sachverhalts kann der Vorsitzende des Gerichts zur Vorbereitung der mündlichen Verhandlung Beweis erheben und nach seinem Ermessen Urkunden einsehen. Er kann Gutachten von Ärzten und amtliche Auskünfte jeder Art einholen. Hierbei ist er an Beweisanträge der Parteien nicht gebunden.

(2) Das Gericht kann beschließen, inwieweit es von den vorbereitenden Maßnahmen des Vorsitzenden Gebrauch machen oder diese wiederholen will.

§ 31

Der Versicherte oder die Sozialversicherung kann beantragen, daß ein bestimmter Arzt gutachtlich gehört wird. Das Gericht kann dessen Anhörung davon abhängig machen, daß der Antragsteller die Kosten vorschießt, und beschließen, daß er sie endgültig trägt.

§ 32

(1) Das Urteil ist zu verkünden. Ist das Urteil verkündet worden, genügt formlose Übersendung der Urteilsausfertigung an die Parteien.

(2) Das Gericht kann in Ausnahmefällen auf Grund der mündlichen Verhandlung beschließen, daß das Urteil auf schriftlichem Wege ergeht. In diesem Fall ist die schriftliche Ausfertigung innerhalb von 14 Tagen nach der letzten mündlichen Verhandlung den Parteien zuzustellen.

§ 33

Hat das Verfahren zu keinem anderen als dem von der Kreisbeschwerdekommission festgestellten Ergebnis geführt, so kann auf den Tatbestand und die Gründe des Beschlusses der Kreisbeschwerdekommission verwiesen werden.

§ 34

(1) Gerichtskosten werden bei Streitfällen zwischen der Sozialversicherung und den Versicherten über kurzfristige Barleistungen und Renten nicht erhoben.

Eine Festsetzung des Streitwertes findet in diesen Fällen nicht statt. Die Bestimmungen der §§ 91ff. der Zivilprozeßordnung sind insoweit nicht anzuwenden.

(2) Ob und in welcher Höhe außergerichtliche Kosten zu erstatten sind, bestimmt das Gericht.

§ 35

Gebührenfrei sind alle Verhandlungen und Urkunden, die zur Begründung oder zur Klärung der Rechtsverhältnisse zwischen der Sozialversicherung einerseits und den Versicherten oder ihren Hinterbliebenen andererseits erforderlich sind und von den Organen der Rechtspflege oder anderen staatlichen Organen geführt bzw. ausgestellt werden.

§ 36

Nach Einreichung der Anfechtungsklage bei dem Bezirksarbeitsgericht ist von Amts wegen unverzüglich festzustellen, ob von dem Kläger in dem gleichen Rechtsstreit bei der zuständigen Bezirksbeschwerdekommission Beschwerde eingelegt wurde. Ist dies der Fall, so entscheidet die Bezirksbeschwerdekommission.

Bestimmungen über Schadensersatzansprüche

§ 37

gestrichen

§ 38

(1) Über Ersatzansprüche der Sozialversicherung gegen die im § 2 der Verordnung zum Schutze der Arbeitskraft vom 25. Oktober 1951 (GBl. S. 957) genannten Personen und Betriebe aus Verletzung der Arbeitsschutzbestimmungen entscheiden die Arbeitsgerichte.

(2) Diese Streitigkeiten werden im Urteilsverfahren nach den Bestimmungen des Arbeitsgerichtsgesetzes (Text vom 23. Dezember 1926) entschieden.

§ 39

Die in dieser Verfahrensordnung vorgesehenen Rechtsmittel können auch gegen Bescheide über Leistungen der Sozialversicherung, die aus Haushaltsmitteln gewährt werden, eingelegt werden.

Anordnung über das Verfahren für die Sozialversicherung bei der Deutschen Versicherungs-Anstalt. — Verfahrensordnung —

Im Einvernehmen mit dem Minister der Justiz und dem Minister der Finanzen wird über das Verfahren für die Sozialversicherung bei der Deutschen Versicherungs-Anstalt für Bauern, Handwerker, selbständig Erwerbstätige und Unternehmer sowie freiberuflich Tätige folgendes angeordnet:

Anträge auf Leistungen

§ 1

(1) Die Leistungen der Sozialversicherung bei der Deutschen Versicherungs-Anstalt werden nur auf Antrag gewährt. Bei der Stellung von Anträgen auf Leistungen ist der Versicherungsausweis vorzulegen.

(2) Anträge auf kurzfristige Leistungen sind bei der für den Versicherten zuständigen Dienststelle der Sozialversicherung bei der Deutschen Versicherungs-Anstalt einzureichen.

(3) Die Gewährung von Renten, Pflegegeld und laufenden staatlichen Unterstützungen ist bei der für den Wohnsitz des Berechtigten zuständigen Dienststelle der Sozialversicherung bei der Deutschen Versicherungs-Anstalt schriftlich zu beantragen.

Entscheidung über Anträge auf Leistungen

§ 2

(1) Über Anträge auf kurzfristige Leistungen entscheidet die Dienststelle der Sozialversicherung bei der Deutschen Versicherungs-Anstalt im Kreis oder die für diesen Kreis für bestimmte Leistungsarten zuständige zentrale Bearbeitungsstelle der Sozialversicherung bei der Deutschen Versicherungs-Anstalt.

(2) Über Anträge auf Rente und Pflegegeld aus der Sozialversicherung bei der Deutschen Versicherungs-Anstalt entscheidet die zuständige Dienststelle der Sozialversicherung bei der Deutschen Versicherungs-Anstalt im Bezirk. Über diese Anträge ist ein schriftlicher Bescheid zu erteilen. Der Bescheid muß enthalten:

a) bei stattgegebenen Anträgen die Art und Weise der Berechnung;
b) bei abgelehnten Anträgen eine genaue und allgemeinverständliche Begründung der Ablehnung;
c) in jedem Fall die Rechtsmittelbelehrung.

(3) Anträge auf Haushaltsrenten und laufende staatliche Unterstützungen werden an die Außenstellen der Bezirksvorstände des Freien Deutschen Gewerkschaftsbundes in den Kreisen, Verwaltungen der Sozialversicherung, zur Bearbeitung und Entscheidung abgegeben.

(4) Die Bescheide über Renten- und Pflegegeldansprüche sind den Versicherten gegen Empfangsbescheinigung zu übermitteln.

§ 3

Der Bescheid wird wirksam:

a) bei Unfallrente mit dem ersten Tage des Monats, in dem der Antrag auf Unfallrente gestellt wird, frühestens mit dem auf den Wegfall des Unfallkrankengeldes folgenden Tag. Versicherte ohne Barleistungsanspruch erhalten Unfallrente nach Ablauf von 26 Wochen Arbeitsunfähigkeit. Tritt die Arbeitsfähigkeit vor Ablauf der 26. Woche ein, so beginnt die Rentenzahlung mit dem Tage des Eintritts der Arbeitsfähigkeit, wenn der Antrag auf Unfallrente bis zum Ablauf des auf den Eintritt der Arbeitsfähigkeit folgenden Monats gestellt wird. Bei späterer Antragstellung beginnt die Unfallrentenzahlung mit dem ersten Tage des Monats, in dem der Antrag auf Unfallrente gestellt wird;
b) bei Invalidenrente mit dem ersten Tage des Monats, in dem der Antrag gestellt wird, sofern ein Anspruch auf Krankengeld besteht, frühestens an dem auf den Wegfall des Krankengeldes folgenden Tag;
c) bei Altersrente mit dem ersten Tage des Monats, in dem Frauen das 60. bzw. Männer das 65. Lebensjahr vollenden, wenn der Antrag bis zum Ablauf des folgenden Monats gestellt wird. Bei späterer Antrag-

stellung beginnt die Rentenzahlung mit dem ersten Tage des Monats, in dem der Antrag gestellt wird;

d) bei Witwen- und Halbwaisenrente mit dem auf den Todestag folgenden Tag, wenn der Antrag bis zum Ablauf des auf den Todestag folgenden Monats gestellt wird. War der Verstorbene bereits Vollrentner, beginnt die Rentenzahlung mit dem ersten Tage des auf den Todestag folgenden Monats, wenn der Antrag bis zum Ablauf des auf den Todestag folgenden Monats gestellt wird. Werden die Voraussetzungen zum Rentenbezug erst später erfüllt, wird der Bescheid mit dem ersten Tage des Monats wirksam, in dem die Voraussetzungen zum Rentenbezug erfüllt sind, wenn der Antrag bis zum Ablauf des folgenden Monats gestellt wird. Bei späterer Antragstellung in den genannten Fällen beginnt die Zahlung der Witwen- und Halbwaisenrente mit dem ersten Tage des Monats, in dem der Antrag gestellt wird;

e) bei Vollwaisenrente mit dem auf den Todestag folgenden Tag, wenn der Antrag bis zum Ablauf des auf die Ausstellung der Bestallungsurkunde des Vormundes folgenden Monats gestellt wird. Bei späterer Antragstellung beginnt die Rentenzahlung mit dem ersten Tage des Monats, in dem der Antrag auf Vollwaisenrente gestellt wird;

f) bei Kinderzuschlag und Ehegattenzuschlag mit dem ersten Tage des Monats, in dem die Voraussetzungen für die Zahlung des Zuschlages erfüllt sind, wenn der Antrag bis zum Ablauf des folgenden Monats gestellt wird. Bei späterer Antragstellung beginnt die Zahlung des Zuschlages mit dem ersten Tage des Monats, in dem der Antrag gestellt wird;

g) bei Pflegegeld mit dem ersten Tage des Monats, in dem der Antrag auf Pflegegeld gestellt wird.

§ 4

(1) Tritt in den Verhältnissen, die für die Zahlung von Rente oder Pflegegeld maßgebend waren, eine Änderung ein, so kann jederzeit eine neue Entscheidung getroffen werden.

(2) Wird die Leistung erhöht, so wird der Bescheid mit dem ersten Tage des Monats, in dem der Antrag auf Erhöhung gestellt wurde, wirksam.

(3) Wird die Leistung gemindert oder entzogen, so wird die Entscheidung mit dem Ablauf des auf den Zugang des Bescheides folgenden Monats wirksam.

(4) Schreib- und Rechenfehler können jederzeit berichtigt werden.

(5) Stellt die Sozialversicherung bei der Deutschen Versicherungs-Anstalt ungesetzliche Leistungen fest, so muß der Bescheid über die Gewährung der Leistungen aufgehoben und durch einen neuen ersetzt werden. Gegen den neuen Bescheid können alle in dieser Verfahrensordnung vorgesehenen Rechtsmittel eingelegt werden.

(6) Ist durch rechtskräftig gewordenen Beschluß einer Beschwerdekommission entschieden worden, so können die Dienststellen der Sozialversicherung bei der Deutschen Versicherungs-Anstalt einen neuen Bescheid in dieser Sache nur erlassen, wenn die Beschlußfassung durch wissentlich falsche Angaben des Versicherten beeinflußt worden ist.

(7) Ein auf wissentlich falschen Angaben des Versicherten beruhendes rechtskräftiges Gerichtsurteil kann durch Wiederaufnahme des Verfahrens nach den Bestimmungen der §§ 578 bis 598 der Zivilprozeßordnung angefochten werden.

Beschwerden

§ 5

(1) Gegen die Entscheidung einer Dienststelle der Sozialversicherung bei der Deutschen Versicherungs-Anstalt ist die Beschwerde an die zuständige Beschwerdekommission bei der Dienststelle der Sozialversicherung bei der Deutschen Versicherungs-Anstalt im Kreis (Kreisbeschwerdekommission) zulässig.

(2) Die Beschwerde ist schriftlich oder zu Protokoll bei der für den Wohnort des Beschwerdeführers zuständigen Dienststelle der Sozialversicherung bei der Deutschen Versicherungs-Anstalt einzulegen.

§ 6

(1) Die Beschwerdefrist beträgt einen Monat und beginnt mit dem Zugang des Bescheides.

(2) Die Beschwerdefrist ist auch gewahrt, wenn die Beschwerde innerhalb dieser Frist bei einer staatlichen Dienststelle, der Vereinigung der gegenseitigen Bauernhilfe, einer Handwerkskammer oder einer Industrie- und Handelskammer eingereicht oder innerhalb dieser Frist nachweislich der Post zur Beförderung übergeben wurde.

(3) Wird die Beschwerdefrist versäumt, so finden die Bestimmungen der Zivilprozeßordnung über die Wiedereinsetzung in den vorigen Stand (§§ 233 ff.) entsprechende Anwendung.

Errichtung der Beschwerdekommissionen

§ 7

(1) Bei den Dienststellen der Sozialversicherung bei der Deutschen Versicherungs-Anstalt in den Kreisen sind Beschwerdekommissionen zu bilden.

(2) Die Beschwerdekommissionen in den Kreisen bestehen aus je drei Mitgliedern.

(3) Die Mitglieder der Beschwerdekommission müssen gleichzeitig Mitglieder der Beiräte im Kreis sein.

(4) Je ein Mitglied der Beschwerdekommission wird berufen

a) durch den Beirat der Bauern im Kreis;

b) durch den Beirat der Handwerker im Kreis;

c) durch den Beirat der selbständig Erwerbstätigen im Kreis.

(5) Die Beschwerdekommissionen wählen aus ihrer Mitte selbst ihren ständigen Vorsitzenden.

§ 8

(1) Die Tätigkeit in den Beschwerdekommissionen ist ehrenamtlich.

(2) Die Erstattung von Reisekosten sowie die Zahlung einer Entschädigung für versäumte Arbeitszeit erfolgt entsprechend dem jeweiligen Statut des Beirates.

Anhang

§ 9

Von der Mitwirkung an einer Entscheidung sind Personen ausgeschlossen, die mit dem Beschwerdeführer verheiratet, verschwägert oder in gerader Linie verwandt sind, sowie seine Geschwister. Die Bestimmungen der §§ 41 bis 48 der Zivilprozeßordnung finden entsprechende Anwendung.

Durchführung des Verfahrens

§ 10

(1) Der Vorsitzende bereitet die mündliche Verhandlung des Streitfalles vor. Er kann vor der Verhandlung Beweis erheben, Gutachten von Ärzten und amtliche Auskünfte jederzeit einholen. Auf Antrag eines der Beteiligten ist die Beweisaufnahme bei der mündlichen Verhandlung zu wiederholen.

(2) Der Vorsitzende bestimmt die Verhandlungszeit. Er kann für die mündliche Verhandlung Zeugen und Sachverständige laden und auch das persönliche Erscheinen des Versicherten und eines Vertreters der Sozialversicherung bei der Deutschen Versicherungs-Anstalt verlangen.

§ 11

Der Versicherte und ein Vertreter der Sozialversicherung bei der Deutschen Versicherungs-Anstalt können zur mündlichen Verhandlung vor der Beschwerdekommission erscheinen. Der Versicherte kann sich vertreten lassen, sofern nicht sein persönliches Erscheinen nach § 10 Abs. 2 angeordnet ist. Die Erschienenen sind zu hören.

§ 12

Die Beschwerdekommission entscheidet mit Stimmenmehrheit. Hält die Beschwerdekommission die Beschwerde für begründet, so ist sie verpflichtet, über den Beginn und die Höhe der Leistungen zu entscheiden.

§ 13

Die Beschwerdekommission bestimmt, ob dem Versicherten die zur Wahrung seiner Rechte entstandenen notwendigen Kosten zu erstatten sind. Die Höhe der Kosten ist durch die Beschwerdekommission festzusetzen.

§ 14

Der Beschluß der Beschwerdekommission wird am Ende der Verhandlung schriftlich festgelegt und verkündet. Er ist zu begründen, mit der Rechtsmittelbelehrung zu versehen und vom Vorsitzenden der Beschwerdekommission zu unterzeichnen. Der Beschluß ist den am Streit Beteiligten gegen Empfangsbestätigung auszuhändigen bzw. zuzustellen.

§ 15

Das Verfahren vor der Beschwerdekommission ist kostenfrei.

Anfechtungsklage

§ 16

(1) Der Beschluß der Beschwerdekommission kann innerhalb eines Monats nach Aushändigung bzw. Zustellung durch Klage beim zuständigen Arbeitsgericht angefochten werden.

(2) Zuständig für die Anfechtungsklage ist das Bezirksarbeitsgericht des Bezirkes, in dem die Beschwerdekommission ihren Sitz hat.

§ 17

Auf das Verfahren vor dem Bezirksarbeitsgericht finden die §§ 24 bis 35 der Verfahrensordnung vom 11. Mai 1953 für die Sozialversicherung (GBl. S. 698) in der Fassung der Anordnung vom 22. Mai 1956 zur Änderung der Verfahrensordnung für die Sozialversicherung (GBl. I S. 522) entsprechende Anwendung.

Bestimmungen über Schadensersatzansprüche

§ 18

Über Schadensersatzansprüche der Sozialversicherung bei der Deutschen Versicherungs-Anstalt gegen Dritte entscheiden die Zivilgerichte.

Haushaltsleistungen

§ 19

Die in dieser Verfahrensordnung vorgesehenen Rechtsmittel können auch gegen Bescheide über Leistungen aus Haushaltsmitteln eingelegt werden, die von der Sozialversicherung bei der Deutschen Versicherungs-Anstalt gewährt werden.

Übersicht

Spezialabhandlung des Verfassers: Das Kostenrecht in Arbeitssachen, VIII S. 34ff.

I. In der DDR gilt zur Regelung von Streitfällen aus der Sozialversicherung die Verfahrensordnung für die Sozialversicherung vom 11. 5. 1953 (GBl. 698, geändert durch Anordnnung vom 22. 5. 1956, GBl. 522 und durch Anordnung vom 3. 9. 1957, GBl. I 488). Danach entscheidet über Anträge auf sog. kurzfristige Barleistungen (wie Krankengeld, Hausgeld, Heil- und Genesungskurvergütung, Schwangerschafts- und Wochenhilfsunterstützung, einmalige Beihilfe an kinderreiche Mütter, Beihilfe für Entbindungskosten, Sterbegeld, vgl.

§ 1 Abs. 2) der Rat für Sozialversicherung oder die Kommission für Sozialversicherung (bzw. die Gewerkschaftsleitung) im Betrieb, soweit die Auszahlung in diesem erfolgt, in allen anderen Fällen die Kreisgeschäftsstelle der Sozialversicherung (§ 3 Abs. 1; jetzt „Außenstelle der Verwaltung der Sozialversicherung bei den Bezirksvorständen des Freien Deutschen Gewerkschaftsbundes" genannt, vgl. §§ 1 und 4 der 2. Anordnung zur Änderung der Verfahrensordnung für die Sozialversicherung). Die zuletzt genannte Stelle entscheidet ferner über Anträge auf Renten, Pflegegeld und laufende staatliche Unterstützungen (§ 3 Abs. 2). Gegen die Entscheidung des Rates oder einer Kommission für Sozialversicherung bzw. einer Betriebsgewerkschaftsleitung oder der „Kreisgeschäftsstelle der Sozialversicherung" (siehe dazu oben) ist die schriftlich oder zu Protokoll der Beschwerdekommission innerhalb eines Monats seit Zugang des Antragsbescheides einzulegende Beschwerde an die Kreisbeschwerdekommission (bestehend aus drei Mitgliedern, vgl. § 9) bei dem Rat für Sozialversicherung des Kreises, in welchem der Anspruch auf Leistungen entstanden ist, gegeben (§§ 5, 6 Abs. 1 und 2). Gegen die Versäumung der Beschwerdefrist ist bei Verhinderung durch Naturereignisse oder andere unabwendbare Zufälle auf Antrag die Wiedereinsetzung in den vorigen Stand zulässig (§ 6 Abs. 3). Die Beschwerdekommission entscheidet, gegebenenfalls auf Grund Beweisaufnahme, nach mündlicher Verhandlung, in der die Vertretung durch Anwälte nicht zugelassen ist (§§ 12ff. i. d. F. der Änderungsanordnung). Das Verfahren vor der Beschwerdekommission ist kostenfrei (§ 17). Die Kommission bestimmt, ob und in welcher Höhe dem Beschwerdeführer die zur Wahrung seiner Rechte entstandenen notwendigen Kosten zu erstatten sind (§ 15).

Gegen den Beschluß der Kreisbeschwerdekommission sind folgende Rechtsmittel gegeben:

die weitere Beschwerde an die Bezirksbeschwerdekommission (bestehend aus fünf Mitgliedern, § 9) oder

die Anfechtungsklage bei dem Bezirksarbeitsgericht (§ 18 Abs. 1).

Werden vom Beschwerten (dem Versicherten oder der Sozialversicherung) beide Rechtsmittel eingelegt, so entscheidet die Bezirksbeschwerdekommission (§ 36).

Die weitere Beschwerde ist schriftlich binnen eines Monats nach Zugang der Beschwerdeentscheidung bei der Bezirksbeschwerdekommission einzureichen, in deren Gebiet die Kreisbeschwerdekommission ihren Sitz hat (§ 19 Abs. 1, 2 und 3). Gegen die Versäumung der Frist ist bei Verhinderung durch höhere Gewalt (s. o.) auf Antrag die Wiedereinsetzung in den vorigen Stand zulässig (§ 19 Abs. 4). Die Bezirksbeschwerdekommission entscheidet, gegebenenfalls auf Grund Beweisaufnahme, regelmäßig nach mündlicher Verhandlung (§ 20). Der Versicherte oder die Sozialversicherung kann hier beantragen, daß ein bestimmter Arzt gutachtlich gehört wird (§ 20 Abs. 2 Satz 1). Die Bezirksbeschwerdekommission kann dessen Anhörung davon abhängig machen, daß der Antragsteller die Kosten vorschießt, und beschließen, daß er sie endgültig trägt (§ 20 Abs. 2 Satz 2). Im übrigen ist das Verfahren auch vor der Bezirksbeschwerdekommission kostenfrei (§ 19 Abs. 5, § 17). Die Kommission bestimmt, ob und in welcher Höhe dem Führer der weiteren Beschwerde die zur Wahrnehmung seiner Rechte erwachsenen notwendigen Kosten zu erstatten sind (§ 19 Abs. 5, § 15). Der Beschluß der Bezirksbeschwerdekommission ist an sich endgültig (§ 21 Abs. 1). Doch ist die Zentrale Beschwerdekommission (bestehend aus sieben Mitgliedern, § 9) berechtigt, auf Antrag des Bundesvorstandes des Freien Deutschen Gewerkschaftsbundes Fehlentscheidungen der Bezirksbeschwerdekommission aufzuheben. Das Verfahren zur Aufhebung muß innerhalb von 6 Monaten nach Eintritt der Rechtskraft der Entscheidung der Bezirksbeschwerdekommission eingeleitet werden (§ 22 i. d. F. der 1. Änderungsanordnung).

Werden von beiden Parteien eines Streites verschiedene Rechtsmittel eingelegt, so ist die Anfechtungsklage bei dem Bezirksarbeitsgericht durchzuführen. Der Rechtsstreit ist in diesem Falle von der Bezirksbeschwerdekommission auf Antrag an das Bezirksarbeitsgericht zu verweisen. Der Verweisungsantrag kann bis zum Schlusse der ersten mündlichen Verhandlung gestellt werden (§ 18 Abs. 2).

II. 1. Die Anfechtungsklage ist bei dem Bezirksarbeitsgericht des Bezirkes (schriftlich oder zu Protokoll der Geschäftsstelle) einzureichen, in welchem die Kreisbeschwerdekommission, die entschieden hat, ihren Sitz inne hat (§ 23, vgl. auch § 9 der VO vom 30. 4. 1953 über die Neugliederung und die Aufgaben der Arbeitsgerichte, GBl. 693).

Die Anfechtungsfrist beträgt einen Monat seit Zugang des Beschlusses der Kreisbeschwerdekommission (§ 24 Abs. 1 Satz 1). Die Frist gilt auch dann als gewahrt, wenn die Klage spätestens bis zum Ablauf der Frist nachweislich der Post zur Beförderung an das Bezirksarbeitsgericht übergeben wurde (§ 24 Abs. 2). Bei einer Versäumung dieser Frist findet, wenn Hinderung durch höhere Gewalt vorliegt, auf Antrag Wiedereinsetzung in den vorigen Stand statt (§ 24 Abs. 1 Satz 2). Liegen die Voraussetzungen für eine Wiedereinsetzung offensichtlich vor, so kann das Gericht diese von Amts wegen bewilligen (§ 24 Abs. 1 Satz 3).

Für Rentenstreitfälle kommt grundsätzlich das Urteilsverfahren nach §§ 46ff. AGG, für alle sonstigen sozialversicherungsrechtlichen Fälle das sog. Beschlußverfahren nach §§ 80ff. AGG zur Anwendung. (Maßgebend ist dabei der Text des Arbeitsgerichtsgesetzes vom 23. 12. 1926 — RGBl. I 507, vgl. § 25). Mündliche Verhandlung ist im Beschlußverfahren nur fakultativ (vgl. § 83 Abs. 1 AGG).

Es besteht in diesen Verfahren kein Anwaltszwang. Rechtsanwälte, die bei einem Gericht der DDR zugelassen sind, können aber als Prozeßbevollmächtigte auftreten (§ 26 Abs. 1).

Die Beiordnung eines Rechtsanwalts aus dem sog. Rechtsanwaltskollegium (oder von Angestellten des Bezirksarbeitsgerichts) bei Bewilligung einstweiliger Kostenbefreiung (d. h. des Armenrechts) steht im Ermessen des Vorsitzenden (§ 27).

Im Urteilsverfahren findet grundsätzlich mündliche Verhandlung statt. Schriftliches Verfahren ist nur zulässig, wenn beide Parteien es beantragen. Die erklärte Zustimmung gilt für das gesamte Verfahren. Das Gericht kann die mündliche Verhandlung wieder aufnehmen, wenn es dies für erforderlich hält (§ 28).

Eine Güteverhandlung findet nicht statt (§ 29 Abs. 1).

Die Vorschriften über das Versäumnisverfahren finden keine Anwendung (§ 29 Abs. 2). Gegebenenfalls ist nach Lage der Akten zu entscheiden (vgl. Kunz-Paul, Das arbeitsgerichtliche Verfahren S. 268).

Zur Aufklärung des Sachverhalts kann der Vorsitzende des Gerichts in Vorbereitung der mündlichen Verhandlung Beweis erheben und nach seinem Ermessen Urkunden einsehen. Er kann Gutachten von Ärzten und amtliche Auskünfte jeder Art einholen. Hierbei ist er an Beweisanträge der Parteien nicht gebunden

(§ 30 Abs. 1). Das Gericht kann beschließen, inwieweit es von den vorbereitenden Maßnahmen des Vorsitzenden Gebrauch machen oder diese wiederholen will (§ 30 Abs. 2).

Der Versicherte oder die Sozialversicherung kann beantragen, daß ein bestimmter Arzt gutachtlich gehört wird (§ 31 Satz 1; wegen der entstehenden Kosten s. u. 2).

Das ergehende Urteil bzw. der erlassene Beschluß ist nach der Verhandlung zu verkünden. Ist die Entscheidung verkündet worden, genügt formlose Übersendung der Ausfertigung an die Parteien (§ 32 Abs. 1 i. d. F. der 1. Änderungsanordnung).

Das Gericht kann trotz erfolgter mündlicher Verhandlung beschließen, daß das Urteil (der Beschluß) auf schriftlichem Wege ergeht. In diesem Fall ist die Ausfertigung innerhalb von 14 Tagen nach der letzten mündlichen Verhandlung den Parteien zuzustellen (§ 32 Abs. 2 i. d. F. der 1. Änderungsanordnung).

Hat das Verfahren zu keinem anderen als dem von der Kreisbeschwerdekommission festgestellten Ergebnis geführt, so kann auf den Tatbestand und die Gründe des Beschlusses der Kreisbeschwerdekommission verwiesen werden (§ 33).

Von der Vollstreckbarkeit der zuerkennenden Entscheidungen gegen die — öffentlich-rechtliche — Sozialversicherung (vgl. § 39) ist in der Verfahrensordnung vom 11. 5. 1953 nichts gesagt. Sie ist ersichtlich nicht vorgesehen, zumal der jetzige § 85 ArbGG, der die Vollstreckbarkeit von Entscheidungen regelt, die in dem sozialrechtlich so wichtigen Beschlußverfahren (s. o.) ergangen sind, im Arbeitsgerichtsgesetz vom 23. 12. 1926 — auch in ähnlicher Form — nicht enthalten ist (vgl. Dietz-Nikisch, ArbGG Anm. 1 zu § 85).

2. Im einzelnen ist in kosten- und gebührenrechtlicher Hinsicht das Folgende zu bemerken:

a) Eine Kostenauferlegung kommt nur in den äußerst seltenen Fällen der Geltendmachung von nicht kurzfristigen Barleistungen (vgl. § 1 Abs. 2) in Betracht (§ 34 Abs. 1 Satz 3). Im übrigen, d. h. grundsätzlich kommen die Bestimmungen der §§ 91ff. ZPO nicht zur Anwendung. Ob und in welcher Höhe außergerichtliche Kosten (insbesondere Anwaltskosten) zu erstatten sind, bestimmt das Gericht (§ 34 Abs. 2). Im allgemeinen wird aus sozialen bzw. gesellschaftlichen Gründen von der Anordnung der Erstattungspflicht abgesehen.

b) Im Hinblick auf das weitestgehende Entfallen der Anordnung einer — die Gerichtskosten betreffenden — Kostentragungspflicht und der — die außergerichtlichen Kosten betreffenden — Kostenerstattungsverpflichtung (vgl. a) findet eine Festsetzung des Streitwerts grundsätzlich nicht statt (§ 34 Abs. 1 Satz 2).

c) Gerichtskosten werden bei Streitfällen zwischen der Sozialversicherung und den Versicherten über kurzfristige Barleistungen (s. o. I) und Renten nicht erhoben, d. h. das Verfahren ist grundsätzlich gebühren- und auslagenersatzfrei (§ 34 Abs. 1 Satz 1).

Gebührenfrei sind in diesem Zusammenhang auch alle Verhandlungen und Aufnahmen von Urkunden, die zur Begründung oder zur Klärung der Rechtsverhältnisse zwischen der Sozialversicherung einerseits und den Versicherten oder ihren Hinterbliebenen andererseits erforderlich sind und von den Organen der Rechtspflege oder anderen staatlichen Sachbeauftragten geführt bzw. vorgenommen werden.

d) Hat der Versicherte oder die Sozialversicherung beantragt, daß ein bestimmter Arzt gutachtlich gehört wird, so kann das Gericht dessen Anhörung davon abhängig machen, daß der Antragsteller die Kosten (vgl. hierzu die VO vom 20. 3. 1956 über die Entschädigung von Zeugen, Sachverständigen und Dolmetschern, GBl. 298) vorschießt, und beschließen, daß er sie endgültig trägt (§ 31 Satz 2; Auferlegung regelmäßig bei von vornherein ersichtlich gewesenem negativen Ausgang der Anhörung).

e) Eine Parteikostenfestsetzung entfällt grundsätzlich, wie sich aus a ergibt (vgl. § 34 Abs. 2, von dem nur in Ausnahmefällen — dann grundsätzlich zu Lasten der Versicherung — Gebrauch gemacht wird).

f) Tritt in den behandelten Fällen ein Rechtsanwalt vor dem Bezirksarbeitsgericht auf, so beträgt seine Vergütung für jeden Streitfall mindestens 10 DM (Ost), höchstens jedoch 100 DM (Ost) ausschließlich der zu ersetzenden baren Auslagen (§ 26 Abs. 2 Satz 1). Innerhalb dieser Grenzen wird die Vergütung entweder vom Gericht im Urteil oder vom Vorsitzenden durch Beschluß festgesetzt (§ 26 Abs. 2 Satz 2).

g) Die Vergütung des beigeordneten (Armen-)Anwalts erfolgt richtigerweise in Höhe des Mindestbetrages — 10 DM (Ost), vgl. § 65 RAGebO, zumal der vollen Gebühr von 10 DM eine Armenanwaltsgebühr in annähernd gleicher Höhe entspricht (siehe § 1 Abs. 1 Nr. 1 ArmAnwG).

h) Eine zu vergütende Gerichtsvollziehertätigkeit kommt wegen der Nichtvollstreckbarkeit der Hauptsache (s. o. 1) und wegen der grundsätzlichen Nichtanordnung der Erstattungsverpflichtung (s. a und e) in aller Regel nicht in Frage.

3. Gegen die an sich rechtskräftige Entscheidung des Bezirksarbeitsgerichts ist in den Fällen des Vorliegens einer normalerweise revisiblen Gesetzesverletzung oder bei gröblichem Verstoß gegen die Gerechtigkeit auf Antrag des Generalstaatsanwaltes oder des Präsidenten des Obersten Gerichtshofes der DDR binnen eines Jahres seit Rechtskraft die Einleitung des Kassationsverfahrens zulässig (§ 11 Abs. 2, §§ 12, 13 und 14 des Gesetzes über die Errichtung des Obersten Gerichtshofes und der Obersten Staatsanwaltschaft der DDR vom 8. 12. 1949, GBl. 111 und § 23 des Gesetzes vom 23. 5. 1952 über die Staatsanwaltschaft der DDR, GBl. 408 sowie § 55 Abs. 1 Nr. 3 des Gesetzes vom 2. 10. 1952 über die Verfassung der Gerichte der DDR, GBl. 983, vgl. dazu die Entscheidung des Obersten Gerichtshofes in OGZ 3, 49ff.). Über die Kassation entscheidet nach mündlicher Verhandlung der bei dem Obersten Gerichtshof gebildete Senat für Arbeitsgerichtssachen (§ 1 Abs. 1 der Ersten Verordnung vom 20. 12. 1951 zur Durchführung des Gesetzes über die Errichtung des Obersten Gerichtshofes und der Obersten Staatsanwaltschaft der Deutschen Demokratischen Republik, GBl. 1179). Das Kassationsverfahren ist kostenfrei (§ 1 Abs. 1 der Ersten Durchführungsbestimmung vom 31. 8. 1953 zum Gerichtsverfassungsgesetz, GBl. 959). Die Kostenentscheidung des unteren Gerichts hat die Kassationsentscheidung so zu ändern, daß sie dem Inhalt der erlassenen Sachentscheidung entspricht (§ 1 Abs. 3 aaO). Eine Erstattung außergerichtlicher Kosten erfolgt nicht. Bei Zurückverweisung der Kassationssache zur erneuten Verhandlung und Entscheidung an das Gericht der unteren Instanz bildet das weitere Verfahren mit dem früheren Verfahren vor diesem Gericht kostenrechtlich einen Rechtszug (§ 1 Abs. 2 aaO).

III. Die Arbeitsgerichte entscheiden (im Urteilsverfahren) nach § 38 i. d. F. der 1. Änderungsanordnung auch über Ersatzansprüche der Sozialversicherung gegen die im § 2 der Verordnung zum Schutze der Arbeitskraft vom 25. 10. 1951 (GBl. 957) genannten Personen (nämlich die Betriebsleiter) und die Betriebsinhaber aus Verletzung der Arbeitsschutzbestimmungen. Ebenso entscheiden die Arbeitsgerichte über Entschädigungsklagen der Betriebsunfallverletzten und Berufskrankheitsgeschädigten bzw. ihrer Hinterbliebenen, soweit es sich hierbei um Ansprüche handelt, die über die Entschädigung durch die Sozialversicherung hinausgehen (§ 40 der VO vom 28. 1. 1947 über die Sozialpflichtversicherung, abgedruckt in „Arbeit und Sozialfürsorge", Heft 5 S. 92; vgl. hierzu Stelter, Die Zuständigkeit der Arbeitsgerichte, NJ 1956, 526). Der § 37, der das Arbeitsgericht bei der diesbezüglichen Entscheidung hinsichtlich des Grundes an den Ausgang des durchzuführenden Strafverfahrens band, ist durch § 6 der 1. Änderungsanordnung aufgehoben worden.

IV. Für die Geltendmachung von Ansprüchen aus der Sozialversicherung — bei der Deutschen Versicherungs-Anstalt — für Bauern, Handwerker, selbständig Erwerbstätige und Unternehmer sowie freiberuflich Tätige gilt in der DDR eine besondere Verfahrensordnung vom 9. 5. 1958 (GBl. I 398). Nach ihren Bestimmungen entscheidet über Anträge auf kurzfristige Leistungen die Dienststelle der Sozialversicherung bei der Deutschen Versicherungs-Anstalt im Kreis oder die für diesen Kreis für bestimmte Leistungsarten zuständige Zentrale Bearbeitungsstelle der Sozialversicherung bei der Deutschen Versicherungs-Anstalt. Über Anträge auf Renten und Pflegegeld aus der Sozialversicherung bei der Deutschen Versicherungs-Anstalt entscheidet die zuständige Dienststelle der Sozialversicherung bei der Deutschen Versicherungs-Anstalt im Bezirk (vgl. § 2 Abs. 1 und 2 VerfO). Anträge auf Haushaltsrenten und laufende staatliche Unterstützungen werden an die Außenstellen der Bezirksvorstände des Freien Deutschen Gewerkschaftsbundes in den Kreisen, Verwaltungen der Sozialversicherung, zur Bearbeitung und Entscheidung abgegeben (§ 2 Abs. 3 VerfO).

Gegen die Entscheidung einer Dienststelle der Sozialversicherung bei der Deutschen Versicherungs-Anstalt ist die Beschwerde an die zuständige dreiköpfige Beschwerdekommission bei der Dienststelle der Sozialversicherung bei der Deutschen Versicherungs-Anstalt im Kreis (Kreisbeschwerdekommission) zulässig (§ 5 Abs. 1 VerfO). Die Beschwerde ist schriftlich oder zu Protokoll bei der für den Wohnort des Beschwerdeführers zuständigen Dienststelle der Sozialversicherung bei der Deutschen Versicherungs-Anstalt einzulegen (§ 5 Abs. 2 VerfO). Die Beschwerdefrist beträgt einen Monat und beginnt mit dem Zugang des Bescheides (§ 6 Abs. 1 VerfO). Wird die Beschwerdefrist versäumt, so finden die Bestimmungen der Zivilprozeßordnung über die Wiedereinsetzung in den vorigen Stand (§§ 233ff.) entsprechende Anwendung (§ 6 Abs. 3 VerfO). Das Verfahren vor der Beschwerdekommission ist kostenfrei (§ 15 VerfO). Der Beschluß der Beschwerdekommission wird am Ende der obligatorischen mündlichen Verhandlung, gegebenenfalls nach Beweisaufnahme, schriftlich festgelegt und verkündet. Er ist zu begründen, mit Rechtsmittelbelehrung zu versehen und vom Vorsitzenden der Beschwerdekommission zu unterzeichnen. Der Beschluß ist den am Streit Beteiligten gegen Empfangsbestätigung auszuhändigen bzw. zuzustellen (vgl. §§ 10 und 14 VerfO). Die Beschwerdekommission bestimmt, ob dem Versicherten die zur Wahrung seiner Rechte entstandenen notwendigen Kosten zu erstatten sind. Die Höhe der Kosten ist durch die Beschwerdekommission festzusetzen (§ 13 VerfO).

Der Beschluß der Beschwerdekommission kann innerhalb eines Monats nach Aushändigung bzw. Zustellung durch Klage beim zuständigen Arbeitsgericht angefochten werden (§ 16 Abs. 1 VerfO). Zuständig für die Anfechtungsklage ist das Bezirksarbeitsgericht des Bezirkes, in dem die Beschwerdekommission ihren Sitz hat (§ 16 Abs. 2 VerfO). Auf das Verfahren vor dem Bezirksarbeitsgericht finden die §§ 24 bis 35 der Verfahrensordnung vom 11. 5. 1953 für die Sozialversicherung — der Arbeiter und Angestellten — (GBl. 698) in der geltenden Fassung entsprechende Anwendung (§ 17 VerfO).

Die in der Verfahrensordnung für die Sozialversicherung der Bauern, Handwerker, selbständig Erwerbstätigen, Unternehmer und freiberuflich Tätigen vorgesehenen Rechtsmittel können auch gegen Bescheide über Leistungen aus Haushaltsmitteln eingelegt werden, die von der Sozialversicherung bei der Deutschen Versicherungs-Anstalt gewährt werden (§ 19 VerfO).

Über Schadensersatzansprüche der Sozialversicherung bei der Deutschen Versicherungs-Anstalt gegen Dritte entscheiden die Zivilgerichte (§ 18 VerfO).

V. Abschließend sei erwähnt, daß es im Hinblick auf die auch den letztmöglichen Fall regelnde Zuständigkeitsbestimmung des § 57 Abs. 3 SGG sog. Ostsachen im Verfahren der Westberliner Sozialgerichtsbarkeit nicht gibt. Nach dieser Bestimmung ist jedenfalls das Sozialgericht örtlich zuständig, in dessen Bezirk der Beklagte (der Versicherungsträger Westberlins) seinen Sitz hat, wenn der sonst maßgebende Kläger außerhalb des Geltungsbereiches dieses Gesetzes wohnt oder sich aufhält (d. h. im Auslande oder in der DDR bzw. Ostberlin, vgl. hierzu Tschischgale, KostR in ArbSach. S. 37 und KostR in ZivSach. S. 113ff.).

Sachregister

(Die Zahlen bedeuten die Seiten)

B

D

E

F

G

L

R

Sch

W

Bei Fragen zur Produktsicherheit wenden Sie sich bitte an:
If you have any questions regarding product safety,
please contact:

Walter de Gruyter GmbH
Genthiner Straße 13
10785 Berlin
productsafety@degruyterbrill.com